THE OXFORD HANDBOOK OF

EARLY MODERN ENGLISH ENGLISH LITERATURE AND RELIGION

THE OXFORD HANDBOOK OF

EARLY MODERN ENGLISH LITERATURE AND RELIGION

Edited by

ANDREW HISCOCK

and

HELEN WILCOX

OXFORD
UNIVERSITY PRESS

OXFORD

UNIVERSITY PRESS

Great Clarendon Street, Oxford, OX2 6DP,
United Kingdom

Oxford University Press is a department of the University of Oxford.
It furthers the University's objective of excellence in research, scholarship,
and education by publishing worldwide. Oxford is a registered trade mark of
Oxford University Press in the UK and in certain other countries

Published in the United States of America by Oxford University Press
198 Madison Avenue, New York, NY 10016, United States of America

British Library Cataloguing in Publication Data
Data available

Library of Congress Control Number: 2016961459

ISBN 978-0-19-967280-6

Printed and bound by
CPI Group (UK) Ltd, Croydon, CR0 4YY

For our parents
James and Margaret Boulton
Eric and Gladys Hiscock

ACKNOWLEDGEMENTS

WE would express our sincere gratitude to Jacqueline Baker at OUP for proposing this volume to us and for supporting us attentively through the genesis and evolution of this *magnum opus*. Rachel Platt, Eleanor Collins, Megan Wakely, Susan Frampton, and Aimee Wright at OUP have all at different times guided us expertly through the preparation of this collection with unstinting courtesy and advice. To each of them, our thanks.

Naturally, a very significant debt of thanks in the preparation of this volume is owed to the contributors, who undertook original research for the benefit of the project and showed great scholarship, dedication, and patience in the several years between commissioning and publication. We express our warmest thanks to them all and trust that they, as well as the wider readership, will find the finished product informative, stimulating, and inspiring.

During much of the gestation period of this handbook, we were immensely supported by our colleague Linda Jones, whose calm professionalism and efficient copyediting skills were of enormous benefit to contributors and editors alike. We are most grateful for her excellent work, and only regret that retirement prevented her from being able to help us to the very end of the project. We hope that she will be proud of the book and recognize in it the many improvements which she introduced.

We should like to thank our colleagues at Bangor University, especially those in the School of English Literature and the Library, for their support and encouragement to us during the preparation of this volume. In particular, we would mention our late colleague, Stephen Colclough, who was a willing adviser and a fund of invaluable information when asked to field questions on book history. In addition, we acknowledge the permission to reproduce images granted to us by libraries and other institutions, as listed on p. xiii and detailed in the relevant chapters.

Finally, it gives us great pleasure to express our heartfelt thanks to our families for their continued tolerance, generous flexibility, and enthusiastic helpfulness, without which a project such as this would simply be impossible. To our dear and ever-cheerful spouses, Siân and Allan: thank you.

AH & HW

CONTENTS

PART II LITERARY GENRES FOR THE EXPRESSION OF FAITH

PART III RELIGION AND THE EARLY MODERN WRITER

PART IV INTERPRETATIVE COMMUNITIES

PART V EARLY MODERN RELIGIOUS LIFE: DEBATES AND ISSUES

LIST OF ILLUSTRATIONS

LIST OF ABBREVIATIONS

BCP	*The Book of Common Prayer: The Texts of 1549, 1559, and 1662,* edited by B. Cummings. Oxford: Oxford University Press, 2011.
BL	British Library
CJ	Commons Journals
CL	Congregational Library
CMRS	Center for Medieval and Renaissance Studies, Arizona
CSP	Calendar of State Papers
DNB	*Dictionary of National Biography*, edited by L. Stephen and S. Lee. 63 vols. London: Smith, Elder & Co. 1885–1901.
ed.	editor
edn	edition
ELH	*English Literary History*
ELR	*English Literary Renaissance*
HMSO	Her/His Majesty's Stationery Office
KJV	*The Bible: Authorized King James Version*, edited by R. Carroll and S. Prickett. Oxford and New York: Oxford University Press, 1997.
LCSH	Library of Congress Subject Headings
LJ	*Lords Journals*
Lewis and Short	C. Lewis and C. Short, *A Latin Dictionary*. Oxford: Clarendon Press, 1969.
MRTS	Medieval and Renaissance Texts and Studies
MS	manuscript
n.d.	date unspecified
n.p.	no pagination
n. pl.	no place of publication given
n. pub.	no printer's or publisher's name given
n.s.	new series
NA	National Archives
NLS	National Library of Scotland

NLW	National Library of Wales
ODNB	*Oxford Dictionary of National Biography*, edited by H. C. G. Matthew et al. Oxford: Oxford University Press. Online edition, 2004, 2008, and 2010.
PRO	Public Record Office (London)
repr.	reprinted
RETS	Renaissance English Text Society
SP	State Papers
STC	A. W. Pollard, G. R. Redgrave, W. A. Jackson, F. S. Ferguson, and Katharine F. Pantzer, *A Short-Title Catalogue of Books Printed in England, Scotland, & Ireland, and of English Books Printed Abroad, 1475–1640*. 2nd edn, rev. and enlarged, 3 vols. London: Bibliographical Society, 1976–91.
TRHS	*Transactions of the Royal Historical Society*
trans.	translator

NOTES ON CONTRIBUTORS

Hugh Adlington is senior lecturer in English literature at the University of Birmingham. He is editor (with Peter McCullough and Emma Rhatigan) of *The Oxford Handbook of the Early Modern Sermon* (Oxford University Press, 2011) and editor (with Tom Lockwood and Gillian Wright) of *Chaplains in Early Modern England: Literature, Patronage and Religion* (Manchester University Press, 2013). He is editing volume 2 of the *Oxford Edition of the Sermons of John Donne*, and is writing a monograph, *John Donne's Books: Reading, Writing, and the Uses of Knowledge*.

Bernadette Andrea is the Celia Jacobs Endowed Professor in British Literature, University of Texas, San Antonio. She is the author of *The Lives of Girls and Women from the Islamic World in Early Modern British Literature and Culture* (University of Toronto Press, 2017) and *Women and Islam in Early Modern English Literature* (Cambridge University Press, 2007); editor of *English Women Staging Islam, 1696–1707: Delarivier Manley and Mary Pix* (ITER and Centre for Reformation and Renaissance Studies, University of Toronto, 2012); and co-editor of *Early Modern England and Islamic Worlds* (Palgrave Macmillan, 2011). Her co-edited collection, *Traveling/Travailing Women: Early Modern England and the Wider World*, is forthcoming from the University of Nebraska Press.

David Bagchi is senior lecturer in ecclesiastical history at the University of Hull. He specializes in the history and theology of the Reformation, and has a particular interest in the theology of Martin Luther, early modern religious polemic, and the use of the printing press for disseminating theological ideas (in which context he has written about the Tudor formularies). His major publications include *The Cambridge Companion to Reformation Theology* (Cambridge University Press, 2004), co-edited with David Steinmetz, and *Luther's Earliest Opponents: Catholic Controversialists, 1518–25* (Fortress Press, 2nd edn, 2009).

Jan Bloemendal was awarded his PhD in 1997 in neo-Latin literature, Utrecht University, and is a senior researcher at the Huygens Institute of the Royal Netherlands Academy of Arts and Sciences. From 2006 to 2012 he was a professor by special appointment of neo-Latin studies at the University of Amsterdam. He is editor or co-editor of: *Joost van den Vondel (1587–1679): Dutch Playwright in the Golden Age* (Brill, 2012); *Neo-Latin Drama and Theatre in Early Modern Europe* (Brill, 2013); *Bilingual Europe: Bilingualism and Multilingualism. Brill's Encyclopaedia of the Neo-Latin World* (Brill, 2014). He also edited *G. J. Vossius: Poeticae institutiones* (Brill, 2010).

Peter Carlson is assistant professor of religion at California Lutheran University. His research focuses on late medieval and early modern religion in England. He studies monasticism broadly, and libraries, learning, and the relationships between texts and religious practice specifically. He has lately started researching constructions of gender and male intimacy in the late medieval period. He is completing his monograph on the learning community of the *Boni Homines*, or 'Good Men' of the monastic college at Ashridge, England.

Elizabeth Clarke is professor of English literature at Warwick University. She specializes in seventeenth-century religious poetry, spirituality, and religious writing, particularly by nonconformists and women. She leads the Perdita Project for early modern women's manuscript compilations and also led The John Nichols Project at Warwick University, whose five-volume *Progresses of Queen Elizabeth I* (Oxford University Press) was published in 2014. Her publications include *Politics, Religion and the Song of Songs in Seventeenth-Century England* (Palgrave Macmillan, 2011) and *The Double Voice: Gendered Writing in Early Modern England*, with Danielle Clarke (Palgrave Macmillan, 2000). At present, she is working on the OUP edition of *The Complete Works of Lucy Hutchinson*, vol. 2.

Jacqueline Eales is professor of early modern history at Canterbury Christ Church University, where she is the director of research for the Faculty of Arts and Humanities. She is a former convenor of History UK (2008–11) and was president of the Historical Association from 2011 to 2014. Her research specialisms include women in early modern England, the English civil wars, and the puritan clergy. She is currently writing a book on The Campden Wonder, a notorious seventeenth-century miscarriage of justice.

Margaret J. M. Ezell is a Distinguished Professor of English and the John and Sara Lindsey Chair of Liberal Arts at Texas A&M University.

Catie Gill is a lecturer in early modern writing at Loughborough University. Her research has appeared in a number of books and collections, including *Women in the Seventeenth-Century Quaker Community* (Ashgate, 2005), *Theatre and Culture* (editor, Ashgate, 2010), *Expanding the Canon of Early Modern Women's Writing* (Cambridge Scholars, 2010), and *Radical Voices* (Manchester University Press, 2016). *New Critical Studies on Early Quaker Women, 1650–1800* (co-edited with Michele Lise Tarter) is forthcoming from Oxford University Press.

Jaime Goodrich is an associate professor of English at Wayne State University in Detroit, Michigan. Her work on early modern Englishwomen's writings has appeared in *ANQ, British Catholic History, English Literary Renaissance, Huntington Library Quarterly, Renaissance and Reformation, Sixteenth Century Journal*, and several edited collections. She has also published a monograph on the social and political functions of early modern Englishwomen's devotional translations (*Faithful Translators: Authorship, Gender, and Religion in Early Modern England*, Northwestern University Press, 2014). Her current research examines textual production within English Benedictine convents on the Continent between 1600 and 1800.

Nicky Hallett retired as a reader from the School of English at the University of Sheffield. She has published articles and books on early modern nuns' writing, including *The Senses in Religious Communities, 1600–1800: Early Modern 'Convents of Pleasure'* (Ashgate, 2013); *English Convents in Exile, 1600–1800: Life Writing* (Pickering & Chatto, 2012); *Lives of Spirit: English Carmelite Self-Writing of the Early Modern Period* (Ashgate, 2007); *Witchcraft, Exorcism and the Politics of Possession in a Seventeenth-Century Convent: 'How Sister Ursula was once bewiched and Sister Margaret twice'* (Ashgate, 2007).

Hannibal Hamlin is professor of English at The Ohio State University. He is the author of *The Bible in Shakespeare* (Oxford University Press, 2013) and *Psalm Culture and Early Modern English Literature* (Cambridge University Press, 2004), and co-editor of *The Sidney Psalter: Psalms of Philip and Mary Sidney* (Oxford University Press, 2009) and *The King James Bible after Four Hundred Years: Literary, Linguistic, and Cultural Influences* (Cambridge University Press, 2010). He is currently editing two books: *The Psalms in English, 1530–1633* for the MHRA New Tudor & Stuart Translations and *The Cambridge Companion to Shakespeare and Religion*.

Johanna Harris is senior lecturer in English literature at the University of Exeter. She is the author of articles and chapters on early modern letter writing, English Puritanism, Lady Brilliana Harley, Andrew Marvell, and a forthcoming monograph on English puritan epistolary culture. With Elizabeth Scott-Baumann she co-edited *The Intellectual Culture of Puritan Women, 1558–1680* (Palgrave Macmillan, 2011). She also works on editing early modern texts, as co-general editor (with Alison Searle) of the OUP *Correspondence of Richard Baxter* (projected for 2020–2), and The Oxford Traherne (Vol. 3).

Elizabeth Heale taught for many years in the English Department of the University of Reading, and is now retired. Publications include *The Faerie Queene: A Reader's Guide* (rev. edn 1999), *Wyatt, Surrey and Early Tudor Poetry* (Longman, 1998), and *Autobiography and Authorship in Renaissance Verse* (Palgrave Macmillan, 2003). She has also published an edition of *The Devonshire Manuscript: A Women's Book of Courtly Poetry*, for The Other Voice in Early Modern Europe series (University of Chicago Press, 2013). She now lives in Scotland and has begun an education in Scottish history and poetry.

Andrew Hiscock is professor of English literature at Bangor University, Wales and Marie Skłodowska-Curie Research Fellow at the *Institut de Recherche sur la Renaissance, l'Âge Classique et les Lumières* (Université Paul-Valéry, Montpellier III). A fellow of the English Association and a trustee of the Modern Humanities Research Association, he has published widely on English and French early modern literature. He is English literature editor of the academic journal *MLR* and series editor for *The Yearbook of English Studies*. In addition, he is series co-editor of the *Arden Early Modern Drama Guides*. His most recent monograph is *Reading Memory in Early Modern Literature* (Cambridge

University Press, 2011) and he is at present co-editing a critical collection *Shakespeare and Memory* and preparing a critical study of Shakespeare's history plays.

Katharine Hodgkin is professor of cultural history at the University of East London. She has published on various aspects of early modern culture and subjectivity, including madness, melancholy, dreams, and witchcraft, and has edited an early seventeenth-century autobiographical manuscript, *Women, Madness and Sin: The Autobiographical Writings of Dionys Fitzherbert* (Ashgate, 2010). Her current research focuses on cultures of memory in early modern England, and she will be co-editing a special issue of the journal *Memory Studies*, 'Memory and the Early Modern', forthcoming in 2018.

Christopher Hodgkins is professor of Renaissance literature and Atlantic World studies at the University of North Carolina-Greensboro. The author of *Authority, Church, and Society in George Herbert: Return to the Middle Way* (University of Missouri Press, 1993), he has edited four essay collections and many articles on George Herbert and on seventeenth-century literature. With Robert Whalen, he co-edits *The Digital Temple* (University of Virginia Press, 2012), and *The Complete Digital Works of George Herbert*, which have been supported by two multi-year NEH grants. He also has published *Reforming Empire: Protestant Colonialism and Conscience in British Literature* (University of Missouri Press, 2002), and numerous articles on the British imperial imagination.

Lisa Hopkins is professor of English and head of Graduate School at Sheffield Hallam University. She is co-editor of *Shakespeare*, the journal of the British Shakespeare Assocation, and of the *Arden Early Modern Drama Guides*. Her publications include *Christopher Marlowe, Dramatist* (Edinburgh University Press, 2008), *A Christopher Marlowe Chronology* (Palgrave Macmillan, 2005), *Christopher Marlowe: A Literary Life* (London: Palgrave Macmillan, 2000), and most recently *Shakespearean Allusion in Crime Fiction: DCI Shakespeare* (Palgrave Macmillan, 2016). She is currently completing a book on *From the Romans to the Normans on the English Renaissance Stage*.

Simon Jackson is a Leverhulme Early Career Fellow at the University of Warwick. His research explores the relationship between poetry and music in the sixteenth and seventeenth centuries. He won the George Herbert Society *Chauncey Wood Dissertation Award* (2011–13), and has published a number of articles on literary and musical topics; he is currently working on a book on George Herbert and his musical activities. In addition to his academic research, he is organist and director of music at Little St Mary's Church, Cambridge.

Stephen Kelly is head of English at the School of Arts, English and Languages at Queen's University Belfast. He is co-editor, with Ryan Perry, of *Devotional Culture in Late Medieval England and Europe: Diverse Imaginations of Christ's Life* (Brepols, 2014) and his monograph *Imagining History in Medieval Britain* is forthcoming with Bloomsbury in 2018.

John N. King is Distinguished University Professor Emeritus and Arts & Humanities Distinguished Professor Emeritus of English and of Religious Studies at Ohio

State University. His books include *English Reformation Literature: The Tudor Origins of the Protestant Tradition* (Princeton University Press, 1982); *Tudor Royal Iconography: Literature and Art in an Age of Religious Crisis* (Princeton University Press, 1989); *Spenser's Poetry and the Reformation Tradition* (Princeton University Press, 1990); *Milton and Religious Controversy: Satire and Polemic in* Paradise Lost (Cambridge University Press, 2000); *Voices of the English Reformation: A Sourcebook* (University of Pennsylvania Press, 2004); *Foxe's Book of Martyrs and Early Modern English Print Culture* (Cambridge University Press, 2006); and *Tudor Books and Readers* (Cambridge University Press, 2010).

Torrance Kirby is professor of ecclesiastical history at McGill University, Montreal. He received a DPhil in Modern History from Oxford University in 1988. He is a life member of Corpus Christi College, Cambridge and the Princeton Center of Theological Inquiry. Recent books include *Persuasion and Conversion: Religion, Politics and the Public Sphere in Early Modern England* (Brill, 2013), *The Zurich Connection and Tudor Political Theology* (Brill, 2007), and *Richard Hooker, Reformer and Platonist* (Ashgate, 2005). He is also editor of *A Companion to Richard Hooker* (Brill, 2008), and co-editor of *Paul's Cross and the Culture of Persuasion* (Brill, 2014). He is general editor of *Sermons at Paul's Cross, 1521–1642* (Oxford University Press, 2017).

Erica Longfellow is Dean of Divinity of New College, Oxford. She is the author of *Women and Religious Writing in Early Modern England* (Cambridge University Press, 2004), as well as several articles on post-Reformation religious writing and culture. She is currently editing vol. VII, *Sermons Preached at Marriages, Churchings and Christenings*, of the *Oxford Edition of the Sermons of John Donne*.

Catherine Gimelli Martin, a Dunavant Professor at the University of Memphis in 2005–8, and Fulbright Scholar, 2014, has published numerous articles on early modern literature and the history of science. Her many publications include: *The Ruins of Allegory: "Paradise Lost" and the Metamorphosis of Epic Convention* (Duke, 1998, James Holly Hanford Award, 1999); *Milton and Gender* (Cambridge, 2004); *Francis Bacon and the Refiguring of Modern Thought* (co-edited with Julie R. Solomon, Ashgate, 2005); *Milton among the Puritans* (Ashgate, 2010); and *French Connections in the English Renaissance* (co-edited with Hassan Melehy, Ashgate, 2013). Her most recent monograph, *Milton's Italy*, was published by Routledge in 2017.

Nandra Perry is an associate professor of English at Texas A&M University. Her book, *Imitatio Christi: The Poetics of Piety in Early Modern England* (Notre Dame University Press, 2014), explores the relationship of the traditional devotional paradigm of 'the imitation of Christ' to the theory and practice of literary imitation as practiced by Philip Sidney and his many literary admirers and imitators. She is currently working on a book about the relationship of religious ritual to early modern habits of reading.

Mike Pincombe teaches at Newcastle University. He is the co-editor (with Cathy Shrank) of *The Oxford Handbook of Tudor Literature* (Oxford University Press, 2009). He has edited several other collections, and has also written books and articles on a wide range of Tudor and Elizabethan texts and authors from a more or less historicist perspective (though more recent research has led towards an anarcho-structuralist approach to these same topics).

Anne Lake Prescott is the Helen Goodhart Altschul Professor Emeritus of English at Barnard College. She has been president of the Sixteenth Century Society and the Donne Society, and the Spenser Society. Author of *French Poets and the English Renaissance* (Yale University Press, 1978) and *Imagining Rabelais in Renaissance England* (Yale University Press, 1998), she is, with Andrew Hadfield, co-editor of the Norton edition of Spenser and, until recently, of *Spenser Studies*. She has published essays on *Utopia*, David in the Renaissance, psalm translation, Spenser, Drayton's *Poly-Olbion*, Gargantua in English polemic, Donne as a Menippean satirist, Marguerite de Navarre, English verse satire, and (with Ian Munro) English jestbooks.

Bronwen Price is a principal lecturer in English literature at the University of Portsmouth, where she teaches on early modern literature. She has particular research interests in seventeenth-century women's writing, literature of the Civil War and Republican periods, and early modern ideas about natural philosophy, retreat, friendship, and community. She is editor of *Francis Bacon's New Atlantis* (Manchester University Press, 2002) and is currently writing a book on Mary Chudleigh for Manchester.

Charles W. A. Prior is senior lecturer in early modern history at the University of Hull. His book *A Confusion of Tongues* (Oxford University Press, 2012) is a study of church and state in the British civil wars.

Timothy Rosendale is an associate professor of English literature at Southern Methodist University in Dallas, where he teaches in the undergraduate, graduate, and honours programmes. He is the author of *Liturgy and Literature in the Making of Protestant England* (Cambridge University Press, 2007) and various essays and articles on early modern literature, history, and theology, as well as pedagogy. His second book project (*Unperfect Actors: Theological Problems of Agency in Early Modern Literature*) rereads centrally canonical literary texts by situating them in contemporary and perennial, but now often overlooked or misunderstood, debates over human will and action.

Gavin Schwartz-Leeper is teaching fellow and director of student experience for liberal arts at the University of Warwick. He is the author of *From Princes to Pages: The Literary Lives of Cardinal Wolsey, Tudor England's 'Other King'* (Brill, 2016), and he has published on John Foxe, John Skelton, and William Shakespeare's history plays. His current projects include work on narrative and perception in liberal arts pedagogy and a new monograph on Richard Grafton, royal printer to Edward VI (Brill, forthcoming).

Alison Searle is a university academic fellow in textual studies and digital editing at the University of Leeds. She is co-general editor of *The Complete Correspondence of Richard Baxter* (forthcoming in nine volumes with Oxford University Press) and editor of *The Sisters* (1642) by James Shirley (also for Oxford University Press). Alongside these editing projects, she is researching the performance of religious Nonconformity in early modern Britain.

Jeanne Shami is professor emerita at the University of Regina where she taught for thirty-five years. Her interest in sermons, particularly those of John Donne, spans four decades. In 1992, she identified a manuscript of Donne's 1622 Gunpowder sermon, corrected in his hand, at the British Library. She has also written on women as preachers, consumers, and patrons of sermons. She is currently serving as contributing editor to the Oxford Donne *Letters*, and as executive editor of the Donne Variorum *Verse Letters* volume. Her most recent SSHRC-funded project, with colleague Anne James, is GEMMS (Gateway to Early Modern Manuscript Sermons), a database of English manuscript sermons (1530–1715) launched in 2017 (www.gemms.itercommunities.org).

Jesse David Sharpe is an assistant professor of English and the director of the Writing Center at LeTourneau University. He studied library science at Drexel University and received a PhD in English from the University of St Andrews. Formerly a librarian, his research looks to combine his interests in library science and early modern literature. His current projects focus on seventeenth-century devotional poetry, book history, and information ethics. He is interested in the process of information creation, dissemination, and consumption, and is researching how information was understood and legislated in early modern England and Scotland.

Jeffrey Shoulson is the Doris and Simon Konover Chair in Judaic Studies and professor of literatures, cultures, and languages and professor of English at the University of Connecticut. He writes on early modern literary, cultural, and religious studies with a particular focus on Jewish–Christian interactions. His books include *Milton and the Rabbis: Hebraism, Hellenism, and Christianity* (Columbia University Press, 2001), *Hebraica Veritas: Christian Hebraism and the Study of Judaism in Early Modern Europe* (University of Pennsylvania Press, 2004), and *Fictions of Conversion: Jews, Christians, and Cultures of Change in Early Modern England* (University of Pennsylvania Press, 2013).

P. G. Stanwood is professor emeritus of English at the University of British Columbia. He has published extensively on Renaissance and seventeenth-century English literature, especially John Donne and John Milton. His editions include the posthumous books of Richard Hooker's *Of the Lawes of Ecclesiastical Polity* (Belknap Harvard, 1981); Jeremy Taylor, *Holy Living* and *Holy Dying* (2 vols. Oxford University Press, 1989). He recently co-edited *Paul's Cross and the Culture of Persuasion in England, 1520–1640* (Brill, 2014).

Robert E. Stillman is the Kenneth C. Curry Professor of English at the University of Tennessee, Knoxville. His most recent book is entitled *Philip Sidney and the Poetics of Renaissance Cosmopolitanism* (Ashgate, 2008). He has published several recent articles about Sidney's fiction-making and religion, in *ELR, The Sidney Journal, The Ashgate Research Companion to the Sidneys*, and *Modern Philology*. At present, he is finishing a book manuscript about the piety, politics, and poetry of early moderns seeking to move beyond confessional Christianity.

Adrian Streete is senior lecturer in English literature 1500–1780, at the University of Glasgow. He is the author of *Protestantism and Drama in Early Modern England* (Cambridge University Press, 2009), editor of *Early Modern Drama and the Bible: Contexts and Readings, 1570–1625* (Palgrave Macmillan, 2012), and co-editor of *Filming and Performing Renaissance History* (Palgrave Macmillan, 2011), and *The Edinburgh Companion to Shakespeare and the Arts* (Edinburgh University Press, 2011). He has published widely on early modern literature and his book *Apocalypse and Anti-Catholicism in Seventeenth-Century English Drama* is forthcoming with Cambridge University Press.

Grant Tapsell is fellow and tutor in history at Lady Margaret Hall, Oxford. He is the author of *The Personal Rule of Charles II, 1681–85* (Boydell Press, 2007), the co-author of *Restoration Politics, Religion and Culture: Britain and Ireland, 1660–1714* (Palgrave Macmillan, 2010—with George Southcombe), the editor of *The Later Stuart Church, 1660–1714* (Manchester University Press, 2012), a contributor to OUP's forthcoming *Oxford History of Anglicanism*, and is currently working on a biography of Archbishop William Sancroft.

Suzanne Trill is senior lecturer in English literature at the University of Edinburgh. Her research focuses on women's writing in England and Scotland (*c.*1550–1700), especially devotional literature. Her publications include *Lady Anne Halkett: Selected Self-Writings* (Ashgate, 2008).

Robert Wilcher graduated from Exeter College, Oxford, in 1963 and was awarded an MA and PhD by the University of Birmingham. He retired as Reader in Early Modern Studies at the University of Birmingham in 2007 and is an honorary fellow of the Shakespeare Institute. His publications include *Andrew Marvell* (Cambridge University Press, 1985), an edition of selected poetry and prose by Andrew Marvell (Methuen, 1986), *Understanding Arnold Wesker* (University of South Carolina Press, 1991), *The Writing of Royalism 1628–1660* (Cambridge University Press, 2001), *The Discontented Cavalier: The Work of Sir John Suckling in its Social, Religious, Political, and Literary Contexts* (University of Delaware Press, 2007), and *Henry Vaughan and the Usk Valley*, co-edited with Elizabeth Siberry (Logaston Press, 2016). He has also published articles and chapters on Shakespeare, Milton, Quarles, Marvell, Vaughan, *Eikon Basilike*, Lucy Hutchinson, Beckett, Stoppard, Rudkin, and other modern playwrights. He is co-editor of a forthcoming edition of the *Works of Henry Vaughan* for Oxford University Press.

Helen Wilcox is professor of English literature at Bangor University, Wales. She teaches and publishes widely on Renaissance devotional poetry and prose, Shakespearean tragicomedy, early modern women's writing, autobiography, and the relationship between literature and music. She is the editor of the acclaimed Cambridge annotated edition of *The English Poems of George Herbert* (2007/2011), and her most recent book is *1611: Authority, Gender and the Word in Early Modern England* (Wiley-Blackwell, 2014).

Rachel Willie is senior lecturer in English at Liverpool John Moores University and honorary research associate at the Bangor-Aberystwyth Institute for Medieval and Early Modern Studies. She is author of *Staging the Revolution: Drama, Reinvention and History, 1647–72* (Manchester University Press, 2015) and co-editor with Kevin Killeen and Helen Smith of *The Oxford Handbook of the Bible in Early Modern England, c.1530–1700* (Oxford University Press, 2015).

INTRODUCTION

Early Modern English Literature and Religion

HELEN WILCOX AND ANDREW HISCOCK

ONE would be hard pressed to imagine a time in the history of the British nations when questions of religion were more central to the development of society and culture than the early modern period. Religious belief and practice were already at the heart of daily lives, both public and private, but the consequences of the Reformation in the mid-sixteenth century had such an enormous and direct impact that very few people on those islands would remain unaffected by it. Temporal and spiritual allegiances shifted; churches and liturgies were re-ordered. English replaced Latin as the language of prayer and Scripture, and reforms challenged long-established ways of understanding the bases of faith and the consequences of sin and spiritual failure. This was a turbulent era, full of debate, dissent, and contention on fundamental issues not only of life, but also of death and eternity. From the opening of Henry VII's reign to the death of Queen Anne, the realm witnessed a sequence of momentous religious and political events: the decisive break between the monarchy and the papacy; a succession of arresting changes to the religious regime; the proliferation of spy networks, plots of infiltration, and an unending process of international factionalizing; the establishment of a Protestant national Church; the formation of sectarian groups; civil wars and insurrections, and the great religio-political debates that followed in their wake. It was a time of danger and exile, of conspiracy and planned invasion, of war and bloodshed (both on the battlefield and the scaffold), but also of impassioned argument, of the genesis of faith communities, and of a multiplicity of visions testing key tenets of belief.

The relationship between these religious developments and the literature produced in English from the first Tudor sovereign to the last of the later Stuarts is profound and fascinating, and continues to constitute one of the most dynamic areas of early modern scholarship. Moreover, just as the era was one of the liveliest in Britain's religious and political history, so, too, it stands as one of the greatest periods of writing in English—a strikingly fertile age of literary innovation and creativity. As each chapter of this collection indicates, to a very great extent this literary output was deeply exercised by religious issues, not only because spiritual questions were central to the early modern sense of the world and the self, but also because theology and rhetoric, the very ability to give expression to thought, went hand in hand. The key controversies of the Reformation were focused on the power of the word, the agency of intercession, and the efficacy of the sacraments: should the Bible be given pride of place above tradition and priestly authority, and what did it mean to repeat Christ's words 'This is my body' over the bread of the Eucharist? These two central questions so often went straight to the heart of the undertaking of writing in the period: the power of language, and the function of the metaphorical imagination. Prose, drama, and poetry were deeply affected by the theological debates which engaged tightly with the fundamental undertakings of writing itself from a host of differing perspectives. Furthermore, the interaction between literature and religion irrevocably shaped modes of textual production, circulation, and consumption throughout the period covered in this collection in constantly changing ways. The doctrinal disputes and intellectual energies of the era were given vent through the power of oral rhetoric in sermons, dramas, demagogy, and polemical debate, and through the circulation of myriad written texts in manuscript and, primarily, print. Spirituality and textuality were intimately aligned.

In order to offer a firm historical basis for the subsequent discussions of literature and theology, this handbook begins with a section in which the hotly debated religious history of early modern Britain is set out in a clear and informative manner. The individual chapters in the section, proceeding in chronological sequence, analyse the events, doctrines, forms, and practices pertaining to each distinctive stage of the two hundred and fifty years under consideration. Nonetheless, at no point in the handbook's preparation has there been any wish to neglect, or deflect attention from, the critical controversies of interpretation which surround the subject of early modern English literature and religion. Contributors were given full rein to speak to and, where the need arose, to speak at variance with each other, giving telling insights into aspects of early modern culture and belief which continue to challenge scrutiny and analysis.

In all of the five sections which structure this collection, each chapter presents original research bringing together history, theology, and literary texts in innovative and thought-provoking ways. In the first section, the rapid changes in religious allegiances and practices during the early modern period are consistently nuanced by an awareness of the continuities underlying even the most disputed points of doctrine and faith. The second section lays the literary foundations for the discussion of religion and literature by studying the basic materials available to writers in this era—that is, the literary genres in and through which faith was most often expressed and defined. Some of these may not surprise a modern reader (lyric poetry, plays, polemics, and autobiographies, for example) but other, less familiar kinds of texts perhaps (such as translations, prophecies, newsbooks, sermons, and neo-Latin writings) were equally important literary modes at the time. Each chapter in this second section discusses the nature of the genre, its appropriateness to the exploration of religion, and the ways in which it developed during the period, using a wide variety of textual examples to bring the genre vividly to life on the page.

Mid-way through the collection, the third section focuses on a number (rather than an exhaustive listing) of representative individual writers who made significant contributions to the early modern literature of religion. Any selection of this kind is bound to displease some readers, but we have chosen authors to reflect a range of historical moments, literary genres, and religious perspectives. Beginning with the early sixteenth-century humanists and ending with Milton, the chapters in this section address the work of writers of theology, philosophy, martyrology, drama, lyric, epic, translation, sermons, and polemics. However, no author writes in isolation, and at least two of the chapters in this third section acknowledge this by looking at the work of a circle of writers (Erasmus, More, Colet, and friends) and a brother and sister literary partnership (Philip and Mary Sidney). This theme of collaboration is developed further in the fourth section, which recognizes the importance of communities both in terms of religious experience and literary production. Ranging from Catholic women in continental convents to groups of Quakers meeting nearer home, and from supranational communities of Jews or Muslims to puritan settlers in the new world, these interpretative groups formed a vital part of the creative interplay of early modern literature and religion. The handbook concludes with a fifth section that addresses some of the recurring themes debated in early modern religious life, from the nature and function of the Bible to the much disputed relationships of *la vita activa* and *la vita contemplativa*, religion and science, the parameters of the godly and the ungodly life, body and soul, death and judgement. Having begun with the specific details of historical contexts, the volume ends, appropriately, with the vastness of eternity.

As the sections unfold, it soon becomes evident that the hallmarks of this handbook are: the breadth and range of approaches to literature and religion; the chronological span of its interests; the spectrum of religious faiths, denominations, and allegiances; the variety of literary genres and authors; the multiplicity of interpretative communities and their locations; and the spread of creative and spiritual issues addressed. We also considered it vital to attend to early modern religion not simply as a matter of written doctrine or private spirituality—important though these are—but also as an experience processed through liturgical, cultural, and theatrical performance and polemic, and as understood within households, faith communities, and like-minded groups. Across the chapters and sections of this book, significant attention is devoted to some categories of writers whose role may have been underplayed in earlier studies. These include the sectarian groups for whom preaching and printed conversion narratives became a central aspect of their identity, and early modern women writers, whose work was both challenged and facilitated by religious experience and spiritual reflection. The handbook also demonstrates a pioneering approach to the study of English literature and religion by its attention to groups based outside Britain, including exile and settler groups abroad and the non-Christian faith communities of Judaism and Islam.

We do not anticipate (or advise) that users of this handbook will read it from cover to cover. It is obviously a book to be used selectively and not necessarily sequentially, and we trust that the various supporting features surrounding the main body of the book will assist readers in making the most of what it has to offer. The chronology preceding the first section gives a detailed factual overview of religiously significant events and texts in parallel, and, as a reference guide, it is designed to enhance the reading of any of the chapters. It highlights the interaction of state decisions, Church authority, authors, texts, readers, and audiences, indicating just how closely religious change and literary intervention dovetailed during this period of relentless flux. The handbook sets out to welcome the broadest readership, and the research guide following the final chapter should assist those who are new to working in this period or on a given topic. Equally importantly, we believe that the extensive bibliography will be an invaluable resource to all readers, giving both a range of primary texts and an overview of secondary reading on all aspects of our subject. Finally, the comprehensive index will enable readers to make cross-references and discern otherwise hidden continuities across the period. A reader interested in one author, theme, denomination, or doctrine, for instance, may not find a chapter devoted to that particular topic, but is advised to make use of the index to discover the variety of contexts in which it nevertheless features.

No single book can hope to deal comprehensively with such a wide-ranging and complex topic as the interaction of religion and literature across several countries over a period of nearly two hundred and fifty years. However, it is our hope that the five sections of this handbook, supported by the chronology and bibliography, will open up a sufficiently wide range of topics and approaches to enable newly enlightened readings and inspire further research into this fascinating era of literary and religious experience.

CHRONOLOGY

Year	Historical and Cultural	Textual History [Publication date unless indicated otherwise]
1485	Battle of Bosworth. Death of Richard III. Accession of Henry Tudor to English throne as Henry VII.	
1492	Arrival of Columbus in the Caribbean. Jews expelled from Spain.	
1493		Anon. *The chastysing of goddes chyldern*.
1494		Walter Hilton, *Scala perfeccionis*.
1496		John Alcock, *Mons perfeccionis*. Denis the Carthusian (1402–71), *The foure last thynges* (English translation).
1502	Chairs of Divinity founded at Oxford and Cambridge by Lady Margaret Beaufort, mother of Henry VII.	
1506		Richard Rolle (*d.* 1349), *Contemplacyons of the drede and loue of god with other dyuerse tytles*. Jacobus de Gruytrode (*d.* 1472), *The mirroure of golde for the synfull soule*, trans. Margaret Beaufort.
1508		William Dunbar, *The Flyting of Dunbar and Kennedy*. Richard Rolle, *The remedy against the troubles of temptations*.
1509	Henry VII dies and is succeeded by his second son, Henry VIII (his first son, Arthur, having died in 1502).	Two versions of *The Shyppe of Fooles* published (translated from Sebastian Brandt's German original).
1510		Andrew Chertsey, *Ihesus. The floure of the commaundementes of God with many examples and auctorytees extracte and drawen as well of holy scryptures as of other doctours and good auncient faders*. Richard Rolle, *Speculum spiritualium*.

(continued)

Year	Historical and Cultural	Textual History [Publication date unless indicated otherwise]
1511	Erasmus appointed Greek Reader at Cambridge.	Desiderius Erasmus, *In Praise of Folly* (published in Latin).
1514		Simon (the Anchorite), *The fruyte of redemcyon.*
1515	Thomas Wolsey made a Cardinal and subsequently Lord Chancellor.	
1516		Thomas More, *Utopia* (published in Latin). Lodovico Ariosto, *Orlando Furioso.*
1517	Martin Luther nails his ninety-five theses to the door of Wittenburg church.	
1518	Cardinal Wolsey appointed as Papal Legate.	
1519	Luther declared a heretic; Henry VIII meets King François I of France at the Field of the Cloth of Gold.	Erasmus, *Colloquies.*
1520		Sir Thomas Wyatt's poems known to be circulating in manuscript.
1521	Luther excommunicated by the Pope. Henry awarded the title 'Defender of the Faith' by the Pope in response to the publication of *Assertio Septem Sacramentorum* (written with the assistance of Sir Thomas More).	John Fisher, *The Sermon of John the Bysshop of Rochester.* St. Edmund of Abingdon (c.1170–1240), *The myrrour of the chyrche.*
1526		William Tyndale, *The New Testament* (complete English translation) published in Worms, Germany. Margaret More Roper, *A Devout Treatise upon the Pater Noster* (translation of Erasmus's *Precatio Dominica*, 1525).
1528		William Tyndale, *The Obedience of a Christen Man* (published anonymously).
1529	Wolsey is replaced as Lord Chancellor by Thomas More.	Sir Thomas More, *A Dialogue Conernynge Heresyes & Matters of Religion.*
1530		William Tyndale, *The Pentateuch* (English translation of the first five books of the Old Testament).
1531	Henry VIII declares himself Supreme Head of the Church in England and Wales.	Sir Thomas Elyot, *The Governor.* William Tyndale, *An Answer unto Sir Thomas Mores Dialogue.*
1532	More resigns as Lord Chancellor. Henry excommunicated by the Pope.	Sir Thomas More, *The Confutacyon of Tyndales Answere.*

Year	Historical and Cultural	Textual History [Publication date unless indicated otherwise]
1533	Thomas Cranmer becomes Archbishop of Canterbury and within two months annuls Henry's first marriage to Catherine of Aragon. Henry's second wife, Anne Boleyn, gives birth to a daughter, the future Elizabeth I.	Denis the Carthusian (1402–71), *The lyfe of prestes*. William Tyndale, *An exposicion vppon the v. vi. vii. chapters of Mathew which thre chaptres are the keye and the dore of the scripture*. Erasmus, *A booke called in latyn Enchiridion militis christiani, and in englysshe the manuell of the christen knight*.
1534	Act of Supremacy enshrines in law Henry's role as Supreme Head of the Church.	John Colet, *The Ordre of a Good Chrysten Mannes Lyfe*.
1535	Jean Calvin arrives in Geneva to establish his Protestant community there. Thomas More and John Fisher executed in London for their opposition to the King's break with Rome.	Miles Coverdale, complete translation of *The Bible* in English, and *Ghostly Psalmes and Spirituall Songes* (published with music).
1536	Dissolution of the Monasteries begins under the direction of Thomas Cromwell. Anne Boleyn executed. Act of Union brings Wales directly under English control. The Pilgrimage of Grace, a popular northern uprising against Henry's religious reforms, begins in the autumn. William Tyndale charged with heresy and put to death in Brabant.	Jean Calvin, *The Institutes of the Christian Religion* (Eng. trans. 1561). Death of Erasmus.
1537	Henry VIII's third wife, Jane Seymour, dies after giving birth to a son, the future Edward VI.	*The Matthew Bible* (based on the translations of Tyndale and Coverdale).
1539		*The Great Bible* (commissioned by Thomas Cromwell, based on the Coverdale Bible and intended to be made available in every parish in the country).
1543		Copernicus, *On the Revolutions of the Heavenly Spheres*.
1545	Council of Trent (Roman Catholic Counter-Reformation council), continuing in Trento and Bologna until 1563.	Katherine Parr, *Prayers Stirrying the Mynd unto Heavenlye Medytacions*.
1546	Protestant Anne Askew burned at the stake in Smithfield.	Anne Askew, *The First Examination*.
1547	Henry VIII dies and is succeeded by his nine-year-old son, Edward VI. The country is governed by a Regency Council favouring further Protestant reformation in England and Wales.	Katherine Parr, *The Lamentation of a Sinner*.

(*continued*)

Year	Historical and Cultural	Textual History [Publication date unless indicated otherwise]
1548		Elizabeth I (at this point still Princess Elizabeth), *A Godly Medytacyon of the Christen Sowle* (translation of *Le Miroir de l'âme pécheresse* by Marguerite de Navarre). Hugh Latimer, *A Notable Sermon of Maister Hughe Latemer.*
1549		The Book of Common Prayer. *Certayne Sermons … appointed by the Kinges Majestie.* Thomas Wyatt, *Certayne Psalmes Chosen Out of the Psalter of David.*
1552	First Jesuit College opens in Rome.	Heinrich Bullinger, *The Christen state of matrymonye.* John Hooper, *A godly confession and protestacion of the christian faith.*
1553	Edward VI dies (aged 15) and is succeeded by his Catholic half-sister, Mary I (Mary Tudor).	Richard Beard, *A godly psalme of Marye Queene which brought vs comfort al, through God, whom wee of dewtye prayse, that giues her foes a fal.* Stephen Gardiner, *De vera obedientia.*
1554	The marriage of Mary to Philip of Spain in Winchester. Execution of Lady Jane Grey. English Church returns to Rome with Mary retaining title of Supreme Head.	Thomas Becon, *An humble supplicacion vnto God for the restoring of hys holye woorde, vnto the churche of Englande, mooste mete to be sayde in these oure dayes, euen with teares of euery true and faythfull English harte* (pub. in Strasbourg). John Knox, *An admonition or warning that the faithful Christians in London, Newcastle Barwycke and others, may auoide Gods vengeaunce bothe in thys life and in the life to come.* John Ponet, *The humble and vnfained confession of the belefe of certain poore banished men.* John Standish, *A discourse wherin is debated whether it be expedient that the scripture should be in English for al men to reade.*
1555-6	A growing number of English Protestant martyrs burned or executed, including Hugh Latimer, Nicholas Ridley, and Thomas Cranmer.	Edmund Bonner, *Homelies.*
1557		*Tottel's Miscellany.* Martin Bucer, *A treatise, how by the Worde of God, Christian mens almose ought to be distributed.*

Year	Historical and Cultural	Textual History [Publication date unless indicated otherwise]
1558	Mary I dies and is succeeded by her Protestant half-sister, Elizabeth I.	Cuthbert Tunstall, *Certaine godly and deuout prayers*. Thomas Watson, *Holsome and catholyke doctryne concerninge the seuen Sacramentes of Chrystes Church expedient to be knowen of all men*.
1559	Act of Uniformity establishes the Church of England. Second Act of Supremacy reasserts that the monarch is head of the Church.	William Baldwin and George Ferrers, *A Myrroure for Magistrates*. Nicholas Ridley, *A Friendly Farewell ... unto all his true lovers and frendes in God, a litl before that he suffred* (posthumous, edited by John Foxe). First edition in Latin of John Foxe, *Acts and Monuments of the Christian Church*.
1560		The Calvinist *Geneva Bible* (otherwise known as the 'Breeches Bible' because of its translation of the garments made from fig leaves by Adam and Eve). Anne Vaughan Lok, *Meditation of a Penitent Sinner* (appended to *Sermons of John Calvin*).
1562	Slaving operations to Africa begun by John Hawkins. First 'War of Religion' in France.	*The Whole Book of Psalms*, metrical Psalm translations into English verse by Thomas Sternhold and John Hopkins to be sung in churches.
1563	Thirty-Nine Articles of Anglican Church.	John Foxe's *Actes and Monuments*, otherwise known as the *Book of Martyrs*, published in English and placed in many parish churches alongside the Bible.
1565	Turkish siege of Malta.	*The Gude and Godlie Balattis*.
1566		Thomas Churchyard, *Churchyardes Lamentacion of Freyndshyp*.
1567	Dutch revolt against Spanish (Catholic) rule, leading to involvement of English Protestant troops in the Low Countries throughout the reign of Elizabeth and beyond. Construction of the Red Lion Theatre in London.	
1568		The *Bishops' Bible*.
1570	Elizabeth excommunicated by the Pope.	
1571		*Certain Sermons or Homilies Appointed to be Read in Churches*, the second 'Book of Homilies' (an expansion and revision of the first book of 1549). Sir Arthur Golding, *The Psalms of David and Others* (Calvin's Latin text 'Rendered into English').

(*continued*)

Year	Historical and Cultural	Textual History [Publication date unless indicated otherwise]
1572	St Bartholomew's Day massacre of French Protestants (Huguenots) in Paris.	
1576	The first Catholic priests are sent back into England from Douai. Construction of the playhouse, The Theatre, in London.	
1577		First edition of Raphael Holinshed, *The Chronicles of England, and Ireland* (1577–8)
1582		The Catholic translation of the New Testament into English, known as the *Douay-Rheims Bible*.
1586	Philip Sidney dies as a result of a wound sustained at the Battle of Zutphen during the military campaign against the Spanish in the Low Countries.	
1587	Mary Queen of Scots, Catholic cousin of Elizabeth, executed.	
1588	Defeat of the Spanish Armada.	*Y Beibl Cymraeg* [The Welsh Bible], translated by William Morgan. William Byrd, *Psalms, Sonnets and Songs.*
1589		Christopher Marlowe, *The Jew of Malta.* Richard Hackluyt, *Principal Navigations, Voyages, Traffiques and Discoveries of the English Nation.* *Marre Mar-Martin or Marre-Martins medling, in a manner misliked* (anonymous verse satire).
1590		Edmund Spenser, *The Faerie Queene* Books 1–3.
1591		Philip Sidney, *Astrophil and Stella* (posthumously published).
1593	Murder of Christopher Marlowe at a tavern in Deptford, London.	Richard Hooker, *Of The Lawes of Ecclesiasticall Politie.*
1594		William Shakespeare, *The Rape of Lucrece.*
1595	Robert Southwell, poet and Jesuit priest, hanged, drawn, and quartered at Tyburn.	Robert Southwell, *Saint Peters Complaint, with Other Poems* (anonymous posthumous publication).
1596		Sir Walter Ralegh, *The discovery of the large, rich, and beautiful Empire of Guiana.*
1597		James VI of Scotland, *Daemonologie.*
1599	Opening of the Globe Theatre. Bishops' ban on satires.	James VI of Scotland, *Basilikon Doron* (1st edition, seven copies published).

Year	Historical and Cultural	Textual History [Publication date unless indicated otherwise]
1600		Mary Sidney completes her verse translation of the Psalms (begun by her brother Philip), dedicating the manuscript to Elizabeth I. William Perkins, *A Golden Chaine*.
1601	Rebellion against Elizabeth, led by the earl of Essex, quickly fails, leading to the earl's execution.	
1603	Elizabeth I dies and is succeeded by her Stuart cousin, James VI of Scotland, who becomes James I of England, Wales, and Ireland.	Shakespeare, *Hamlet* first Quarto.
1604	Hampton Court Conference on the future of the Church of England.	Thomas Wright, *The Passions of the Minde in Generall*.
1605	Gunpowder Plot fails in its attempt to blow up King and Parliament.	Francis Bacon, *The Advancement of Learning, Divine and Humane*.
1606	Virginia Company founded.	Thomas Middleton, *The Puritan Widow*.
1608		Thomas Bell, *The tryall of the new religion*. George Downame, *A Sermon defending the office of Bishops*.
1609		Thomas Middleton, *The Two Gates of Salvation*.
1610	Assassination of Henri IV, King of France, a Huguenot who had converted to Catholicism but strove for religious liberty.	*A briefe and plaine narration of proceedings at an assemsemblie* [sic] *in Glasco, 8. Iun. 1610. anent the innovation of the Kirk-governement*.
1611		Authorized King James Version of the Bible. Aemilia Lanyer, *Salve Deus Rex Judaeorum*. Shakespeare, *The Tempest,* first performance.
1612	Death of Henry, prince of Wales, champion of European Protestantism.	Second edition of Lewis Bayly, *The Practise of Piety* (date of the first edition unknown, as no copies survive). Thomas Wilson, *A Christian Dictionarie*. John Webster, *The White Devil*.
1614	James issues a proclamation ordering Roman Catholic priests to leave Ireland (not rigorously enforced).	Sir Walter Ralegh, *The History of the World*.
1616		Ben Jonson, *Works*. François de Sales, *An Introduction to a Deuout Life* (first English translation).
1617	Scottish Church assembly refuses to implement James's five Perth articles, which include the enforcement of kneeling at Communion.	

(*continued*)

Year	Historical and Cultural	Textual History [Publication date unless indicated otherwise]
1618	James issues his controversial proclamation known as the *Book of Sports*, encouraging the playing of sports and games on Sundays.	
1618-19	Synod of Dort (Protestant assembly to deal with Arminianism) in the town of Dordrecht in the Low Countries, including representatives of the English Church.	
1620	Frederick, the Protestant Elector Palatine, and his wife Elizabeth (daughter of James I), who had been declared King and Queen of Bohemia in 1619, lose their territory to Catholic forces and live the rest of their lives in exile.	David Calderwood, *A defence of our arguments against kneeling in the act of receiving*.
1621		Robert Burton, *The Anatomy of Melancholy*. Mary Wroth, *The Countess of Montgomeries Urania*.
1622		James I, *Directions Concerning Preachers*. William Gouge, *Of Domesticall Duties*.
1623		Shakespeare (d. 1616), *First Folio*.
1624		John Donne, *Devotions upon Emergent Occasions*. Thomas Bedford, *Luthers Predecessours*. Thomas Middleton, *A Game at Chess*. George Webbe, *Catalogus Protestantium: or, the Protestants kalender*.
1625	James I dies and is succeeded by his second son, Charles I (his first son, Henry, having died in 1612). Charles marries Henrietta Maria of France.	
1627		Sir Francis Bacon, *The New Atlantis*. John Donne, *A Sermon of Commemoration of the Lady Danvers* (preached at the funeral of George Herbert's mother). Daniel Featley, *Ancilla pietatis: or, the hand-maid to priuate deuotion*.
1628	Assassination of the royal favourite, the duke of Buckingham.	Joseph Hall, *The Olde Religion: Wherin is laid downe the difference betwixt the reformed, and Romane church*. William Harvey, *Exercitatio Anatomica de Motu Cordis* (on the circulation of the blood).
1629	Charles suspends Parliament.	Lancelot Andrewes, *XCVI Sermons* (posthumous publication).

Year	Historical and Cultural	Textual History [Publication date unless indicated otherwise]
1632		George Wither, *The Psalmes of David Translated into Lyrick Verse.*
1633	William Laud becomes Archbishop of Canterbury. Witch trials are conducted in Lancashire. Charles reissues the anti-sabbatarian *Book of Sports* (first published by his father in 1618).	John Donne, *Poems* and George Herbert, *The Temple* (both books posthumously published). William Prynne, *Histrio-Mastix: The Players Scourge, or, Actors Tragaedie.*
1635		Francis Quarles, *Emblemes.*
1637	Charles imposes *The Book of Common Prayer* on the Scottish Church.	
1638		Inigo Jones and William Davenant, *Britannia Triumphans: A Masque.*
1639	First Bishops' War against Scotland.	
1640	Parliament recalled after eleven years of Charles's 'Personal Rule'.	*Bay Psalm Book*, for the use of the New England colony in Massachusetts.
1641		*The Arminian Nunnery, or a Brief Description and Relation of ... Little Gidding.*
1642	Charles raises the royal standard at Nottingham Castle and the Civil War begins. Public theatres closed by the parliamentarian authorities.	Sir Thomas Browne, *Religio Medici.* *The Flaming Hart or the Life of the Glorious S. Teresa* (first English translation).
1644	Queen Henrietta Maria seeks safety in France from the ongoing Civil War in England.	John Milton, *Areopagitica.*
1645	Archbishop Laud executed.	
1646	Presbyterian Church system established by Parliament. Charles surrenders to the Scots.	Thomas Edwards, *Gangraena: or a Catalogue and Discovery of many of the Errours, Heresies, Blasphemies and pernicious Practices of the Sectaries of this time.* Richard Crashaw, *Steps to the Temple.* John Milton, *Poems.*
1647		Christopher Harvey, *The School of the Heart ... in 47 Emblems* (anonymous publication adapted from Benedict van Haeften's 1629 *Schola Cordis*).
1648	Society of Friends (Quakers) founded by George Fox.	*A Manual of the Private Devotions of the Right Reverend Father in God, Lancelot Andrewes* (d. 1626). Gerrard Winstanley, *The Breaking of the Day of God.* Robert Herrick, *Hesperides.*

(*continued*)

Year	Historical and Cultural	Textual History [Publication date unless indicated otherwise]
1649	Charles I executed at Whitehall after being found guilty of treason against his own people. Commonwealth declared.	*Eikon Basilike: The poutraicture of His Sacred Majestie, in his solitudes and sufferings* (anonymous publication, known as 'The King's Book'). John Milton, *Eikonoklastes: In answer to a book intitl'd Eikon Basilike.*
1650	Book of Common Prayer abolished by Parliament.	Richard Baxter, *The Saints Everlasting Rest.* Jacob Bauthumley, *The Light and Dark Sides of God.* Anne Bradstreet, *The Tenth Muse Lately Sprung Up in America.* Jeremy Taylor, *The Rule and Exercises of Holy Living* and *The Rule and Exercises of Holy Dying* (1650–1).
1651	Charles II crowned King in Scotland, but later in the year defeated by Cromwell and flees to France.	Thomas Hobbes, *Leviathan: Or, The Matter, Forme, & Power of a Common-Wealth Eccelsiasticall and Civill.*
1652	First Anglo-Dutch War (subsequent wars take place in 1665–7 and 1672–4).	*Eliza's Babes: or The Virgins-Offering* (anonymous female-authored devotional lyrics). Richard Crashaw, *Carmen Deo Nostro: Sacred Poems.* Gerrard Winstanley, *The Law of Freedom.*
1653	Rump Parliament dissolved. Oliver Cromwell becomes Lord Protector.	Margaret Cavendish, Duchess of Newcastle, *Poems, and Fancies.* An Collins, *Divine Songs and Meditacions.* Thomas Middleton (*d.* 1627) and William Rowley (*d.* c.1642), *The Changeling.* Henry More, *An Antidote against Atheisme.*
1654		Anna Trapnel, *The Cry of a Stone.*
1655	Whitehall Conference on the readmission of the Jews to England.	Andrew Marvell, *The First Anniversary of the Government Under His Highness the Lord Protector* (published anonymously). Henry Vaughan, *Silex Scintillans* (parts I and II).
1656	Quaker James Naylor rides into Bristol in a re-enactment of Christ's entry into Jerusalem on the first Palm Sunday; Naylor subsequently branded and imprisoned for blasphemy.	John Bunyan, *Some Gospel-Truths Opened.* Sir William Davenant, *The Siege of Rhodes.* James Harrington, *The Commonwealth of Oceana.* Abraham Cowley, *Poems.*
1657	Cromwell refuses the title of King.	Henry King, *Poems, Elegies, Paradoxes and Sonnets.*

Year	Historical and Cultural	Textual History [Publication date unless indicated otherwise]
1658	Oliver Cromwell dies and is succeeded as Lord Protector by his son Richard.	Sir Thomas Browne, *Hydriotaphia, or Urne Buriall* and *The Garden of Cyrus*. Anna Trapnel, *Voice for the King of Saints and Nations*. Gertrude More, *The Spiritval Exercises of the Most Vertuous and Religious D.Gertrude More of the holy order of S. Bennet* (published in Paris).
1659	Richard Cromwell resigns as Protector.	John Bunyan, *The Doctrine of the Law and Grace Unfolded*.
1660	Restoration of the monarchy with the return of Charles II from exile on the continent (May). The king's Declaration of Breda promises religious toleration in Britain. The London theatres re-open.	Abraham Cowley, *Ode, Upon the Blessed Restoration and Returne of His Sacred Majestie*. John Dryden, *Astraea Redux*. Milton, *The Readie and Easie Way to Establish a Free Commonwealth*. Richard Baxter, *Catholick Unity: or the Only Way to Bring Us All To Be of One Religion*.
1661	The Savoy Conference on the future of the Church under Charles II.	George Fox et al., *A Declaration from the Harmles & Innocent People of God, called Quakers*.
1662	Act of Uniformity restores the Church of England. The newly founded Royal Society gains its charter from the king.	The *Book of Common Prayer* reissued and reinstated.
1664	Conventicles Act passed, forbidding religious gatherings of more than five people (except in the Church of England).	
1665-6	Major outbreak of plague in London. Second Anglo-Dutch War, 1665–7.	
1666	Great Fire of London.	John Bunyan, *Grace Abounding to the Chief of Sinners*. Margaret Fell, *Women's Speaking Justified*.
1667		John Dryden, *Annus Mirabilis: The Year of Wonders, 1666*. Milton, *Paradise Lost*. Katherine Philips, *Poems by the most deservedly admir'd ... the Matchless Orinda*.
1668	John Dryden becomes Poet Laureate.	William Penn, *Truth Exalted*.
1670		Izaak Walton, *The Lives of Dr John Donne, Sir Henry Wooton, Mr Richard Hooker, Mr George Herbert*.

(continued)

Year	Historical and Cultural	Textual History [Publication date unless indicated otherwise]
1672	Royal 'Declaration of Indulgence' towards Roman Catholics and Nonconformists (withdrawn after a year). Third Anglo-Dutch War, 1672–4.	(1671–3) Julia Palmer, two 'Centuries' of Presbyterian devotional verse (preserved in manuscript, unpublished until 2001).
1673	The Test Act excludes Roman Catholics from holding public office.	
1677		Andrew Marvell, *An Account of the Growth of Popery and Arbitrary Government* (published in Amsterdam). Anne Wentworth, *The Vindication of Anne Wentworth*.
1678–81	The Popish Plot, fabricated by Titus Oates, stirs up anti-Catholic sentiment.	John Bunyan, *The Pilgrim's Progress*.
1679		Richard Baxter, *The Nonconformists Plea for Peace*. Lucy Hutchinson, *Order and Disorder* Books 1–5. John Wilmot, earl of Rochester, *Upon Nothing*.
1679-81	The Exclusion Crisis (relating to the desire of leading Protestants in Parliament to exclude Charles's brother James from the succession to the throne on account of his Roman Catholicism).	Richard Baxter, *A Breviate* (on the life of Margaret Baxter) and *Poetical Fragments* (1681). John Dryden, *Absalom and Achitophel* (1681–2).
1682	Moroccan ambassador visits the court of Charles II, as well as Oxford, Cambridge, and the Royal Society.	
1683	The Rye House Plot (to assassinate Charles and James) discovered. Vienna besieged by the Turks.	Peter Sterry, *The Rise, Race and Royalty of the Kingdom of God*. Hannah Allen, *A Narrative of God's Gracious Dealings with that Choice Christian Mrs Hannah Allen*.
1685	Charles II dies and is succeeded by his Roman Catholic brother, James II. Monmouth's rebellion against the succession is defeated and the duke of Monmouth (Charles II's illegitimate Protestant heir) is beheaded for treason.	
1687	'Declaration of Indulgence' issued by James, relaxing the prohibition on Nonconformist religious preaching and worship.	Dryden, *The Hind and the Panther*. William Penn, *Good Advice to the Church of England*.

Year	Historical and Cultural	Textual History [Publication date unless indicated otherwise]
1688-9	As a result of the so-called 'Glorious Revolution', James II is ousted from the throne, declared to have abdicated, and replaced by the Protestant monarchs William (of the Dutch House of Orange) and Mary (daughter of James II).	Richard Baxter, *The Saints Everlasting Rest.*
1689		Aphra Behn, *The History of the Nun; or, The Fair Vow-Breaker.*
1690	English and Dutch fleets lose to the French at Beachy Head. James II defeated at the Battle of the Boyne.	Aphra Behn, *The Widow Ranter.* Robert Boyle, *The Christian Virtuoso.* George Keith, *The pretended antidote proved poyson: or, The true principles of the Christian & Protestant religion defended.* John Locke, *A letter concerning toleration* and *A second letter concerning toleration.*
1691		Joan Vokins, *God's Mighty Power Magnified: as manifested and revealed in his faithful handmaid Joan Vokins.*
1692	Massacre of Glencoe. Witch hunts begin in Salem, Massachusetts.	Anne, Viscountess Conway, *The Principles of the Most Ancient and Modern Philosophy concerning God, Christ and the Creatures* (posthumous publication). Richard Bentley, *A confutation of atheism.* Henry Compton, *The Bishop of London's eighth letter to his clergy upon a conference how they ought to behave themselves under the Toleration.* John Winthrop, *A short story of the rise, reign, and ruin of the Antinomians, Familists, and libertines that infected the churches of New-England.*
1693		John Norris, *Practical Discourses upon Several Divine Subjects.* Robert Fleming, *The confirming work of religion.*
1694	Death of Mary II, after which William reigns alone.	Sir Robert Howard, *The history of religion written by a person of quality.* John Locke, *Reason and religion in some useful reflections on the most eminent hypotheses concerning the first principles, and nature of things: with advice suitable to the subject, and seasonable for these times.* William Wilson, *A discourse of religion shewing its truth and reality, or, The suitableness of religion to humane nature.*

(continued)

Year	Historical and Cultural	Textual History [Publication date unless indicated otherwise]
1695		John Locke, *The reasonableness of Christianity as delivered in the Scriptures.*
		William Turner, *The history of all religions in the world, from the creation down to this present time in two parts: the first containing their theory, and the other relating to their practices ... to which is added, a table of heresies.*
1696		Damaris Masham, *A Discourse Concerning the Love of God.*
		Richard Baxter, *Reliquiae Baxterianae* (posthumous collection of autobiographical writings).
		Alexander Ross, *Pansebeia, or, A view of all religions in the world with the several church-governments, from the creation till these times: also a discovery of all known heresies in all ages and places.*
1697	Treaty of Ryswick ends the War of the Grand Alliance, in which England fought alongside Spain, the Holy Roman Empire, and the Dutch Republic against France.	William Sherlock, *The danger of corrupting the faith by philosophy.*
		Edward Synge, *A peaceable and friendly address to the non-conformists.*
1698	Society for Promoting Christian Knowledge (S.P.C.K.) founded.	George Fox, *A Collection of Many Select and Christian Epistles* (posthumous publication).
		John Goodman, *The old religion demonstrated in its principles and described in the life and practices thereof by John Goodman.*
1699		earl of Shaftesbury, *An inquiry concerning virtue in two discourses.*
		Edward Ward, *Modern religion and ancient loyalty a dialogue.*
1700		Richard Claridge, *Mercy covering the Judgement-seat.*
		Benjamin Coole, *Religion and reason united.*
		Hugo Grotius, *The truth of Christian religion in six books, written in Latin by Hugo Grotius; and now translated into English, with the edition of a seventh book against the present Roman church, by Simon Patrick.*
		Cotton Mather, *A letter of advice to the churches of the non-conformists in the English nation.*
1702	William III dies, and is succeeded by his sister-in-law Anne, second daughter of James II.	
1705		Edward Synge, *A Gentleman's Religion.*

Year	Historical and Cultural	Textual History [Publication date unless indicated otherwise]
1707	Bishoprics Crisis (highlighting ongoing struggles between royal and political patronage of the ecclesiastical hierarchy in England).	Daniel Defoe, *The Dissenters Vindicated*. Thomas Emes, *The atheist turn'd deist and the deist turn'd Christian, or, The reasonableness and union of natural and the true Christian religion*. Matthew Henry publishes the first volume of what becomes his *Exposition of the Old and New Testament*.
1708	Failed invasion of Scotland by the Jacobite 'Pretender', James Stuart (son of James II), from exile in France.	
1709		Richard Steele, *The Christian Hero*. Edward Stillingfleet, *Origines Sacrae*. Jonathan Swift, *A project for the advancement of religion, and the reformation of manners*.
1713	Treaty of Utrecht agreed between England, France, Spain, and the Dutch Republic, to end prolonged political and religious wars on the European mainland.	Cotton Mather, *Reasonable Religion*.
1714	Anne I dies, and is succeeded by George I, Protestant Elector of Hanover.	Henry Matthew, *A Church in the House. A Sermon concerning Family-Religion*.

PART I

THE RELIGIOUS HISTORY OF EARLY MODERN BRITAIN

Forms, Practices, Beliefs

CHAPTER 1

···

THE PRE-REFORMATION LANDSCAPE

···

STEPHEN KELLY

ONE of the most seductive representations of late medieval religious landscape is not English, but Burgundian. Rogier van der Weyden's *Seven Sacraments Altarpiece*, completed around 1450, models the social world as imagined by the late medieval clergy (see Figure 1.1). The image, which is also reproduced on the jacket of this volume, was produced in the southern Flemish city of Tournai, at the behest of Jean Chevrot, the city's bishop between 1436 and 1460. Chevrot was one of the key advisers of Duke Philip the Good, under whom Burgundy achieved its greatest cultural and economic prosperity.[1] The *Seven Sacraments Altarpiece* was executed by Rogier and his studio for Chevrot's episcopal chapel.[2] We can guess that when the bishop regarded the image, he enjoyed the pleasing surety of orthodox liturgical and devotional praxis given visual manifestation and material confirmation. The painting's aim is, after all, to embody Catholic orthodoxy: to celebrate the mediating role between heaven and earth of the bishop himself and the clergy of whom he is the foremost local representative.

On the left panel, we are shown baptism, confirmation (administered by Chevrot himself), and confession, conducted in public, as was the custom in the medieval Church; on the right panel, marriage, holy orders (again administered by Chevrot), and last rights; and, pre-eminently, in the central panel, the consecration of the Eucharist, the social contract between man and God—captured in the priest's gesture of *elevatio*, bringing the lower and upper worlds into union. And lest we forget what that contract

---

[1] On Philip the Good, see Vaughn 2010. On the cultural significance of Chevrot, see Nash 2008.

[2] Van der Weyden, or Rogier de la Pasture to give him his familial name, was himself born in Tournai, now a city in the French-speaking region of Belgium, probably in 1400, and in the *Seven Sacraments Altarpiece* there is a kind of homecoming, because the artist had spent most of his career as the official civic painter of the city of Brussels. He returned to Tournai perhaps as the most famous and most copied artist in Europe. See Kemperdick and Sander 2009: 75–94.

FIGURE 1.1 Rogier van der Weyden and studio, *Seven Sacraments Altarpiece*, 1445–50. Oil on oak panel, 200 × 97 cm (central panel), 119 × 63 cm (side panel, each). Reproduced by kind permission of the Koninklijk Museum voor Schone Kunsten, Antwerp.

means, we are presented in the foreground with a crucifixion scene which could have been meditated into being by any pious reader of the myriad narrative lives of Christ which circulated in Europe from the thirteenth century. The anachronistic costuming reminds us that the Eucharist is not, or is not only, an act of commemoration, but is, rather, an act of instantiation: Christ redeems us; here, now.

However, we forget at our peril that the *Seven Sacraments* triptych is also an argument. It is an argument for the salvific centrality of the sacraments themselves, and therefore of the pastoral and ecclesiastical structures which support their distribution to the laity. It is less the embodiment of orthodoxy than its articulation or assertion. Members of the laity, of a particularly bourgeois character, are represented in the painting as passive recipients or as pious consumers of devotional verities: an earnest contemplative, crossing between mundane and visionary realities, clasps the Virgin's hand; a huddled penitent awaits her turn to confess; a maid weeps into a handkerchief. This is what orthodoxy brings into being: *I, we, make society possible*, thinks the spectating Bishop Chevrot.

Neverthless, the vision of his pastoral role before which Chevrot genuflected in his private chapel is an institutional one, and as with any institutional vision, its relation to social realities is tenuous. And yet, historiography of the late medieval Church is too often seduced by narratives of hegemonic dominance or crisis. 'In the late quarter of the fourteenth century', argues Gerald Harriss, 'the English Church faced a multiple crisis of authority' (Harriss 2005: 352). Narratives of crisis can be disarmingly seductive. Historical crises necessitate explanation, and historians offer a service of thicket-clearing, clarifying, and explaining (away?) their complex causes and effects. As Harriss says of the Church:

> Schism in the papacy, talk in parliament of disendowment, and the emergence of heresy at both learned and popular levels threatened its structure and faith, so firmly established in the preceding century. Traditionally the Church had identified with the priesthood, as the essential mediators of divine grace through the sacraments, with the laity in a subordinate and passive role. The thirteenth century had seen this consolidated and extended. The formulation of the doctrine of transubstantiation, the obligation of annual confession and communion for the laity, and the drive to enforce clerical celibacy reinforced the status of the clergy as a sacred and separate order. They were set new standards of morals and learning through the surveillance of archdeacons, visitations, and church courts, while the friars began the evangelization of the urban laity. The apparatus of centralization extended hierarchical control from the papacy down through the dioceses, and in the universities scholastic theology provided greater intellectual coherence in the synthesis of faith and reason propounded by Thomism.

However, Harriss concludes, 'the integrated character thus given to Western Catholicism began to dissolve in the fourteenth century' (2005: 352).

The issue here is not with the substance of Harriss's description of late medieval religious culture, with which few medievalists would disagree, but with its *emplotment*. As in Van der Weyden's image, its main witness is the Church itself: it takes for granted the Church's own view of the verticality of its relationship with lay culture. Here, in sophisticated form, is the hegemonic Church: a monolithic transnational corporation driven to 'consolidate' and 'extend' its 'surveillance' (notably, of its own clergy, as well as the laity). Nonetheless, as with Van der Weyden's triptych, we forget that the Church's image of itself is precisely that, an image; the map is not the territory, in other words. As Harriss points out, from the later half of the fourteenth century 'the Church could no longer be equated with the priesthood and an exclusively Latinized culture. It had to accommodate the laity and the vernacular, but to what extent it could do so while preserving its control of the faith was problematic' (Harriss 2005: 353).

THE REFRAIN OF REFORM

In England, as in much of Europe, it is tempting to suggest that the greatest challenge posed to the Church prior to the Reformation was probably the Black Death. Reaching England in 1348, it devastated the clergy as much as the general population. What are crises if not the suspension of normative frameworks of meaning: events defy interpretation, producing 'morbid symptoms' (as Antonio Gramsci might put it), which trouble culture until they can be neutralized hermeneutically, incorporated once again into the narratives with which ruling polities maintain their authority. With a devastated clergy at the parochial level, the English Church had to contend with a potentially catastrophic challenge to the integrity of its institutions.

However, it is precisely because the medieval Church was in fact a highly diffuse and localized institution, in which doctrinal coherence and administrative stability could only ever be an aspiration, that events of the fourteenth century should be understood only as the latest 'crisis' to face the clergy. The refrain of 'reform' had arguably accompanied the Church since its incorporation of Roman political culture and it is *the* leitmotif of late medieval Christianity. Devotion and institutional 'traditions', which were perceived as faithful to the exemplarity of Christ's life and the lives of the early martyrs, were consolidated—if not fetishized—as *orthodox*, ahead of any kind of liturgical or theological novelty. Reformism effected an historical swerve: it worked to protect the present and future of ecclesiastical authority by idealizing a supposedly stable past of doctrinal and liturgical continuity. However, reformism was arguably also a response to a collapse of confidence among aristocratic and lay communities in sacerdotal authority: the corruption or indifferent performances of priests and prelates at the local level allowed secular authority to assert itself with a confidence that threatened the political claims of the Church. Hence, the widespread anti-clerical backlash, often among clerics themselves (from Robert Mannyng and William Langland in the fourteenth century to John Skelton a hundred years later), but it is less pointedly suggested in ecclesiastical anxiety about the definition of doctrinal 'orthodoxy', which in many respects becomes a fixation for the Church's sense of its own institutional and bureaucratic disarray.

Such anxiety underpinned the Fourth Lateran Council of 1215, which has traditionally been historicized as a watershed in the pastoral care of lay Christians. Described by Eamon Duffy as 'the highpoint of the medieval papacy's involvement with and promotion of the best reforming energies in the Church at large', Lateran IV encapsulated the reformist vigour and political ambition of its pope, Innocent III (Duffy 2006: 148). 'In so many ways', writes Dairmuid MacCulloch, 'Innocent represents the culmination of the age of reform which [began] in Cluny' (2009: 404). For Duffy, 'orthodoxy was one of Innocent's major preoccupations'. If one might question Duffy's characterization of the impetus for Lateran IV's reformism—'the wealth and worldliness of many Churchmen and the embedding of the Church in the heart of the European establishment produced waves of revulsion in the devout, which often spun off into heresy' (Duffy 2006: 149)[3]— it cannot be doubted that the articulation of orthodoxy was seen by Innocent as extending both the pastoral and political authority of the Church. For MacCulloch, Lateran IV 'embodied the Gregorian aim of imposing regulated holiness on the laity and ensuring uniformity in both belief and devotional practice' (2009: 405). The Council gave legislative imprimatur to the pastoral activities of the new mendicant orders, the Dominicans and Franciscans, and established an instrument of orthodoxy in which the Dominicans, in particular, would play a critical role, as MacCulloch points out: 'in order to ensure uniformity of belief among the faithful, the Lateran Council created procedures for inquisitions to try heretics' (2009: 409).

One of the consequences of Lateran IV has been supposed to concern the liberalization, if not democratization, of piety. The Council legislated into being a profusion of new devotional and liturgical practices, such as the localized propagation, for example, of saints' cults (Vauchez 1997); it tolerated, and in places promoted, women as religious *auctors* (Newman 1985 and 1995; Elliot 2004); and the Church became more willing to license new forms of mendicant evangelism or, indeed, lay collectivity, as represented in the fifteenth and sixteenth centuries by the Devotio Moderna (Van Engen 2008). The vernacular was to be used to propagate religious ideas; visual art was to be used to instruct lay people, and drama assumed a new para-liturgical role. Rather than initiating a period of democratization, it might be better to describe the Council as trying to articulate, as Berndt Hamm puts it, 'a standardizing, authoritative, regulating and legitimizing focal point' in the concept of orthodoxy itself—and in this the figure of the heretic would play a critical role (2004: 3). The later medieval Church needed to respond with energy and creativity to the challenges of maintaining its prestige and political significance in a context where its *auctoritas* was increasingly undermined. However, the Church's institutional and catechetical 'creativity' arose particularly in response to the recognition that the Cathar heresy—which had emerged in the south of France in the twelfth century and rejected the sacerdotal authority of the Church—was as much the product of doctrinal confusion, pastoral indifference, and ecclesiastical fragmentation.

The period from Lateran IV onwards represents the Church's attempt to define 'orthodoxy', in what Hamm has characterized as a process of 'normative centering' (Hamm 2004: 1–49). As much a bureaucratic exercise as anything else—precisely because it issues in legislative discourses which presume their own efficacy regardless of their actual impact—the elaboration of orthodox doctrine became a barometer of the success or otherwise of institutional reform. The reformist mentality was expressed in the

[3] In this context, see also Diarmaid MacCulloch: ' "A more complex and positive response to dynamic popular movements"—those groups described by Duffy as having "spun off into heresy"—"emerged at the end of the twelfth century, although in the end it allied itself and indeed helped to structure [the] "formation of a persecuting society" ' (2009: 401).

elaborate array of liturgical and devotional practices, which assumed ever greater complexity after Lateran IV. Such practices gave structure to everyday life. In England, where there were around nine thousand parishes at the turn of the fifteenth century, a variation on the Roman Rite of the Church had been in use since the eleventh century, although the origins and general coherence of what became known as the Sarum rite (after the diocese of Salisbury in which it was assumed to have originated) is questionable before the fourteenth century (Pfaff 2009). However, by the fifteenth century, many parishes in England had implemented the Sarum rite, which had become an extraordinarily elaborate, 'multimedia' expression of the liturgy. The Mass grew to incorporate highly ritualistic and musical elements and many pastoral manuals were produced, such as *The Lay Folks' Mass Book*, to help lay people understand the ceremonies of the liturgy. As Robert Swanson has suggested, the *Mass Book* provided 'a lay liturgy in counterpoint with, and directed by, that of the celebrant' (1999: 184). Time, too, was legislated by the Church, which had long ago mapped its liturgical celebrations onto the sequence of the seasons, and in doing so had absorbed pre-Christian religious rituals into its own normative practices (Duffy 2005: 37–52).

The liturgical year began with the feast of Advent, four weeks before Christmas, followed by Epiphany (January), the Purification of the Virgin (February), and the Annunciation (March). These fixed feasts made of the year a theatre of Christ's incarnation. They were accompanied by saints' feasts throughout the year (which further proliferated after Lateran IV). However, the central ritual portion of the year surrounded the moveable feast of Easter, which marked the death and resurrection of Christ. In the temporal logic of the liturgical year, cosmic time, which stretched from the sin of Adam to the birth of Christ, was concentrated in the historical life of Christ, which in turn completed and fulfilled time itself in the singular event of Christ's death. In atoning for Adam's sin, Christ abolished death and redeemed history. In order to mark the significance of Easter, Christians too were encouraged to atone: Ash Wednesday, the Wednesday before the Sunday which was itself forty days before Easter, reminded Christians of their mortality, and their culpability in Christ's death. Lent, a period of abstinence and penance, stretched from Ash Wednesday until Easter Sunday. Easter Sunday was preceded by the most ritually intense period of the Christian calendar, Holy Week, beginning on Palm Sunday, which marked Christ's entry into Jerusalem and the beginning of the sequence of events that would culminate in his Passion. The provisions of Lateran IV dictated that, in order to save their souls, Christians must confess and receive Communion once a year, and it is likely, thanks to its highly public, collaborative, and performative nature, that most did so at Easter time. Easter Sunday was succeeded by the feast of the Ascension, forty days later, marking Christ's bodily ascent into heaven. The week leading up to the Ascension had its own accompanying rituals, the minor Rogation Days, in which fields, livestock, streets, and towns were blessed and ritual processions professing the litany of the saints were performed. 'Blessings', as Derek Rivard reminds us, 'represent the active negotiation' of the relationship between penitent, the priest, and the divine, 'mingling speech, song, gesture, and motion to affirm a contractual relationship that provided divine protection and sacred power in exchange for human worship, veneration, and moral probity' (Rivard 2009: 292).

Such practices may have married the clergy to the community, but we must not assume that the marriage was a happy one, and vernacular literature, from anti-clerical doggerel to Langland's *Piers Plowman*, rehearses resentments toward parish priests. Ten days after the Ascension, Christians marked Pentecost, which commemorated the descent of the Holy Spirit into Christ's Apostles and the beginning of their evangelical mission. In 1264, again as a consequence of the provisions of Lateran IV, another feast was inaugurated eleven days after Pentecost. Corpus Christi, inspired by the visions of Juliana of Liege, celebrated the Eucharist as the body of Christ, and hence was a very public articulation of the recently formalized doctrine of transubstantiation. Given that the 'sacring' of the host was generally hidden from the congregation's view behind the church's Rood Screen, Corpus Christi enabled the public adoration of the Eucharist, typically in an elaborate procession. However, it was also an assertion of ideology: of the Church's singular authority over the *cura animarum*, or care of souls.[4] By the fifteenth century, in towns and cities such as York and Chester, the feast of Corpus Christi was accompanied by extraordinarily complex sequences of biblical Cycle or Mystery Plays, which dramatized Christian history, from Creation to Last Judgement. The logistics of the Cycle Plays are staggering, with sometimes over a dozen plays performed repeatedly on pageant wagons by members of the community on a route, in the case of York, that began outside the city and traversed most of its major public spaces. Audiences were free to move between performances at will, and the performance of particular plays at specific sites heightened their symbolic intensity (for example, the Entry into Jerusalem at the gates of the city, or the Crucifixion or Last Judgement at the Shambles or Pavement). While the plays served as dramatic representations of biblical narratives, as their textual and performative complexity increased, they provided opportunities for the expression of any range of civic and political concerns, made all the more dynamic because these plays spoke directly to urban experience (Beckwith 2003; King 2006). Business, again in cities such as York, boomed when the plays were performed, with all sectors of the economy, from hostels and taverns to prostitutes, benefiting from the influx of 'pious' spectators.

If the requirement to undertake confession and receive the Eucharist once a year pales by comparison with the more stringent penitential demands of nineteenth-century Catholicism, the centrality of the Church to the lives of medieval communities should not be underestimated. As a site, a community's church fulfilled a range of functions, facilitating market days, acting as a court, or supporting the development of guilds and religious fraternities. Such organizations, typically aligned with a particular profession and dedicated to a local saint or the Virgin, played an important role after the Black Death, given the scarcity of trained priests (Duffy 2005: 141–53); indeed, by end of the fifteenth century there may have been around thirty thousand of them in England.

---

[4] The landmark study of Corpus Christi is Rubin 1991.

This posed a challenge to the independence from lay influence of the parish, as the economic benefits which accrued from association with fraternities allowed for the upkeep, renovation, and extension of churches. Indeed, in larger conurbations, parishes were regularly in competition with one another for lay and fraternity attention, attracting parishioners with more potent tokens of holiness, such as relics, or by accommodating, as in Bishop's Lynn, Norwich, and myriad other cities, anchorholds, where enclosed holy men and women enhanced the sanctity of the parish church by offering spiritual advice to lay people. As an expression of the success of the 'affective piety' promoted by the Church, which will be discussed below, a number of cults sponsored by lay organizations emerged in the fifteenth century, dedicated variously to the Five Wounds of Christ, or to the Holy Name.

Monasteries and friaries too competed for lay investment. Monastic houses served as hospitals and fulfilled various other charitable functions. As with the parish church, donations to such houses helped donors accrue spiritual 'capital'. However, monasteries, with their control over land, their legal muscle, and economic power, bred resentment in many English communities. The Benedictines aroused particular suspicion, with their alleged corruption and deviation from their rule such that Henry V instigated an investigation of their houses. The tensions between the regular clergy and their king which boiled over into the Henrician Reformation were not new; indeed, the Dissolution could likely not have taken place without some ambivalence or passivity regarding the fate of religious houses within lay communities. The anti-clericalism of Chaucer and Langland, or of poems such as 'Of Thes Frer Mynours' or 'Thou That Sellest the Worde of God' (Dean 1996) captures resentment, but it also expresses the confidence of lay culture in contesting the religious authority of the Church:

> Men may se by thair contynaunce
> That thai are men of grete penaunce,
> And also that thair sustynaunce
>   Simple is and wayke.
> I have lyved now fourty yers,
> And fatter men about the neres
> Yit sawe I never than are these frers,
> In contreys ther thai rayke.
> Meteles so megre are thai made,
> And penaunce so puttes ham doun,
> That ichone is an hors-lade
> When he shall trusse of toun. (Dean 1996)

The poet of 'Preste, Ne Monke, Ne Yit Chanoun' expresses the material resentments of lay people who struggled to sustain themselves while the clergy, and the friars in particular, grew fat on their piety.

Resentment could be expressed in other ways too. Robert Swanson highlights that the 'failure to bow at certain points in the mass, or to honor a consecrated Host in procession, were not merely signs of disrespect; they were considered signs of unortho-doxy, hinting at Lollardy' (1999: 179). Duffy adds that:

> holding up of the hands and the more or less audible recitation of elevation prayers at the sacring was a gesture expected of everyone: refusal or omission was a frequent cause of the detection of Lollards. And the refusal of such gestures might be held to exclude one from the human community, since they excluded one from the church, as when Thomas Halfaker denounced a group of his Buckinghamshire neighbours because 'coming to church, and especially at the elevation time, [they] would say no prayers, but did sit mum (as he termed it) like beasts'. (Duffy 2005: 119)

While regularly perceived, both by contemporaries and historians, as evidence of her-esy, the refusal to participate in the liturgy should act as a corrective to any notion of the medieval laity as passively devout. From dissatisfaction with individual priests, to questions of the credibility or otherwise of the claims of the Church, the temptation to imagine an 'Age of Faith' must be resisted at all costs.[5] As well as providing an explan-ation of individuals' place in the cosmos and in history, Christianity provided a vocabu-lary for everyday experience which did not necessitate reflection on the credibility or otherwise of doctrinal or liturgical ideas: participation in religious practices need not, for many lay people, have meant acceptance. As the late anthropologist Roy Rappaport underlined:

> liturgical orders are public, and participation in them constitutes a public acceptance of a public order, regardless of the private state of belief. Acceptance is, thus, a fun-damental social act, and forms the basis of public social orders. But acceptance is not belief, nor does it even imply belief. Whereas acceptance is an outward act, belief is an inward state, knowable subjectively, if at all. (Rappaport 1999: 396)

In many respects, Lateran IV and succeeding pastoral initiatives had as their goal not the suppression of heresy, but of apathy. The license to teach in the vernacular, to develop forms of dramatic exposition of religious ideas and narrative, and to involve lay people in the liturgical performance of faith was designed precisely to *re-engage* ordinary people in the life of the Church. However, by the fourteenth century, the com-plexity of medieval theology rivalled the abstractions of modern physics, and liturgy, while pragmatic, was undergirded by religious ideas to which the laity were given lit-tle access. Hence, the development of theologies that sponsored devotional practices rooted in the humanity of Christ. Lay Christians were encouraged to meditate on the physical suffering of Christ, and the *compassio* of his mother, family, and followers. Such theologies encouraged 'affective piety': they sought to evince, on the part of viewers,

---

[5] 'Naturalizing or demystifying accounts of belief not only are available to medieval sources, but are internal to their acts of belief' (Justice 2008: 18). Scholarship, including work by Reynolds 1991, Flanagan 2009, Arnold 2005, and Kim 2013, is challenging the long-held view of the medieval world as a credulous 'Age of Faith', which has complex implications for the ways in which the European reformations are historicized.

readers, or listeners—whether enclosed or secular religious, professional theologians, or lay people—*emotive identification* with Christ, his mother, or other holy surrogate. Contemplative religious practices, formerly the privilege of the regular clergy, were increasingly appropriated outside the cloister and an array of literatures emerged to cultivate lay practices of meditation.

Pre-eminent in England in the fourteenth century were the writings of the Yorkshire hermit Richard Rolle (*d.* 1349). Around four hundred manuscripts of Rolle's writings survive and the authorship of *The Prick of Conscience* was long attributed to him. Rolle's writings range from commentaries on the Psalms, letters to nuns and fellow recluses, to accounts of his mystical experiences. His *Meditation on the Passion* captures precisely the emotionalism and vivid pictorialism of affective devotion:

> A, Lord, þi sorwe, why were it not my deth? Now þei lede the forþe nakyd os a worm, the turmentoures abowtyn þe, and armede kny3ts; þe prees of þe peple was wonderly strong, þei hurled þe and haryed þe so schamefully, þei spurned þe with here feet, os thou hadde been a dogge. I se in my soule how reufully þou gost: þi body is so blody, so rowed and so bledderyd; þi crowne is so kene, þat sytteth on þi hed; þi heere mevyth with þe wynde, clemyd with þe blood; þi lovely face so wan and so bolnyd with bofetynge and with betynge, with spyttynge, with spowtynge; the blood ran þerewith, þat grysyth in my sy3t; so lothly and so wlatsome þe Jues han þe mad, þat a mysel art thou lyckere þan a clene man. Þe cros is so hevy, so hye and so stark, that þei hangyd on þi bare bac trossyd so harde. (Allen 1931: 21)

Rolle's extraordinary prose prioritizes imagination as a tool of prayerful contemplation, thus internalizing the narrative and ritual elements of the liturgy in a reconstruction of the Passion. Rolle's most important successors were the Carthusian Nicholas Love (*d.* 1423/4) and the Augustinian Walter Hilton (*d.* 1396). The writings of Love and Hilton capture the devotional trends of the century preceding the English reformations. Like Rolle, their fixation with the psychology of religious experience prefigures the highly individuated spirituality that would be a mark of Protestantism.

Love was the Prior of Mount Grace Charterhouse in the early decades of the fifteenth century and his is the most important English adaptation of the pseudo-Bonaventuran *Meditationes vitae Christi* (composed by the fourteenth-century radical Franciscan Jacobus de Sancto Geminiano).[6] Initially a translation for use by Carthusian novices and lay-brothers, the text was quickly found in noble and gentry reading circles with connections to the Carthusian and Brigittine houses of Mount Grace and Syon (Falls 2013; Perry 2013). The text was printed, in a variety of folio, recto, and sextodecimo editions, by Caxton in 1484 (*STC* 3259) and 1490 (*STC* 3260), and was reprinted by Wynkyn de Worde (*STC* 3261) and Richard Pynson (*STC*

---

[6] Tóth and Falvay (2014) overturn definitively its traditional attribution to Johannes de Caulibus. On the pseudo-Bonaventuran tradition in English, see the AHRC-funded Geographies of Orthodoxy project: http://www.qub.ac.uk/geographies-of-orthodoxy.

3262) in 1494, by Pynson in 1506 (*STC* 3263), and again by de Worde in 1507, 1517, 1525, and 1530 (*STC* 3263.5, 3264, 3266, 3267). Interestingly, the text was not reprinted again in England after 1530, although the pseudo-Bonaventure *vita* provides the template for Carthusian John Fewterer's *Myrrour of Glasse* (1533). The folio editions of Love's *Mirror* contain twenty-five illustrations of the life and Passion of Christ; as Lotte Hellinga has commented, 'the illustrated version in print offered an advantage over most of the manuscripts of Nicholas Love's translation, and also over the Latin original text, both in manuscript and print' (Hellinga 1997: 146). The affective immediacy that Love's text was designed to stimulate is thus not just characteristic of fifteenth-century devotionalism, but is at a material high point in its early sixteenth-century circulation.

Hilton was initially a canon lawyer, before joining the Augustinian house at Thurgarton. His two most renowned texts *The Scale of Perfection* and *Of Mixed Life*, frame and respond to the dominant trajectories of later medieval spirituality. The *Scale* is a contemplative manual, designed to assist enclosed, intellectual religious in the development of their meditative regimes (the text is dedicated to a female solitary). The book was inevitably attractive to Carthusian readers. The Carthusians saw themselves as the spiritual elite of the monastic orders and lived a frugal and solitary life dedicated to contemplation of God. They had a particular interest in texts describing or atomizing mystical experience. Just under half of the manuscripts of *The Scale*'s first book derive from the second half of the fifteenth century and two manuscripts post-date 1500 (Sargent 2005: 77). Again, there are a significant number of prints from the late fifteenth and early sixteenth centuries.[7] If the *Scale* is a work for use by the spiritually elite, then *Of Mixed Life* pre-empts the devotional appetites of the fifteenth-century laity. In it, Hilton instructs his noble addressee, 'þou ȝernist gretli to serue oure lord bi goostl occupacioun al holli, wiþoute lettynge or trobolynge of worldeli busynesse' (Ogilvie-Thompson 1986: 7), but advises instead that he emulate the biblical examples of Mary and Martha, adumbrating both the contemplative and active lives in a third form of pious practice appropriate to lay people, the mixed life. Hilton admits in the *Mixed Life* a concern for a burgeoning appetite not just for religious literature but for the imitation of clerical practices amongst the laity: this was an abiding preoccupation of devotional culture in the century after Hilton's death and a plethora of religious texts were produced to answer to it. Texts written with the laity in mind, such as *The Lay Folks' Catechism*, *The Pore Caitif*, *A Myrour to Lewde Men and Wymmen*, *Jacob's Well*, *Dives and Pauper*, or *Eight Ghostly Dwelling Places*, produced, it is assumed, an appetite among lay people for religious speculation. In turn, texts written for the consumption

---

[7] The *Scale* is printed by de Worde in 1494 (*STC* 14042), 1519 (*STC* 14043.5), 1525 (*STC* 14044), and 1533 (*STC* 14045); and by one 'Iulyan Notary' in 1507 (*STC* 14043). *STC* 14042–5 interpolate *Of Mixed Life* (*Vita Mixta*) as the assumed third book of the *Scale*. The *Mixed Life* also appears in a 1494 printing of *Kalendre of the newe legende of Englande* (*STC* 4602). See Powell 2011. Manuscript copies of *Mixed Life* are found in the possession of enclosed women during the early decades of the sixteenth century. See Hutchinson 1995.

of enclosed religious, priests, or for instruction of the professional clergy began to 'leak' out of their institutional reading communities from the late fourteenth century onwards. The mechanics of this process are understood poorly: it is likely that noble and gentry sponsors of religious institutions received in exchange for their patronage religious texts in the vernacular, which they in turn circulated, copied, and recompiled within their own affinities (in urban centres, this process was led by pious mercantile elites). Gestures designed to demonstrate the piety of a given patron had as an interesting side-effect the development of canons of literary taste, with particular texts, such as *The Pricke of Conscience*, various writings by or attributed to Rolle or Hilton, and myriad pastoral texts clustering in their production and distribution around lay reading communities. The possession of books, particularly religious books, quickly became a marker of social status. Often, such texts would be read with the assistance of a spiritual advisor, or the text would incorporate, as a meta-literary device (typically in the form of an address from a mentor to a young devotee, a contrivance initially of use in communication between religious houses), a 'textual advisor', whose role was to structure and frame the reading process. A range of penitential and devotional works are printed by de Worde: in 1492–3, *The Chastising of God's Children* and in 1497 *The Abbey of the Holy Ghost*, in addition to Love's *Mirror* and Hilton's *Scale* (*STC* 5056 and *STC* 13609 respectively). Caxton and Pynson print texts that address practical devotional matters, such as *The Art and Craft of Dying*, the *Ars Moriendi*, and *The Dyetary of Gostly Helthe*, as well as more christological materials, such as the enormously popular *The Fifteen Oes* (in 1491), and *The Seven Sheddings of the Blood of Jesus Christ* (in 1500, discussed in Powell 2011: 527–9). 'The overwhelmingly traditional and orthodox character of the religious literature printed before 1530 did not mean it was of one sort', stresses Eamon Duffy, and printers dictated and responded to readerly demand by covering the gamut of fifteenth-century tastes (2005: 78). Mirk's *Festial*, a collection of sermons from the 1380s, was printed by Caxton in 1483, who 'made it a best-seller' according to Susan Powell (2011: 533). The *Festial* was often accompanied by Pecham's syllabus (an influential set of thirteenth-century prescriptions dedicated to the pastoral education both of the laity and a dysfunctional clergy) in the form of the *Quattuor sermones*. Pecham's influence echoes across the Reformation, underpinning pro-Reformation texts such as *The Ten Articles* (1536), the *Institution of a Christen Man* (1537), and *The Necessary Doctrine* (1543). Susan Wabuda underlines that 'Thomas Cromwell's reliance upon Peckham's [*sic*] standards is particularly remarkable in the First Royal Injunctions of 1536, and his Second Royal Injunctions of 1538' (2002: 37). The circulation, recombination, and appropriation of explicitly orthodox Catholic texts amongst proto- and fully fledged Protestant readers should chastise any acceptance of the notion that late fifteenth- and early sixteenth-century literature represents a culture in decline. Rather, the fifteenth century is marked, says Vincent Gillespie, by the 'multiple vernacular theologies' that 'were emerging to cater for the needs and abilities of an increasingly diverse range of religious competencies' (2012: 176). As in the past, central to these theologies was the refrain of reform itself, whether of the Church or the individual Christian.

From Vernacular Theologies to the 'English Heresy'

The pastoral innovations that followed Lateran IV may have sponsored an explosion in liturgy, drama, and vernacular religious writing (from pastoralia, guides to contemplation, religious poetry, and manuals for mystical ascent), but they also inspired academic theologians to re-assess the bases of doctrine. The efforts of reformers to put their own house in order were arguably jeopardized by the liberties the Church had allowed historically to the universities (Leff 1968; Kerby-Fulton 2006: 1–11). It is no accident in an atmosphere of reformist 'centering' that academic theology and philosophy, at first in Paris, but then later in Oxford, should come under ecclesiastical scrutiny. One wonders what the history of later medieval English Christianity, and the English Reformation itself, would look like had the ideas of theologian John Wyclif (*d.* 1384) not escaped the cloisters of Oxford University. That Wyclif and his followers came to perceive in his theology pragmatic ethical and political implications, albeit with no little help from aristocratic patrons who sought to curtail the political and economic reach of the English Church, is expressive of the larger reformist impulse that had been legislated into existence by the Church itself (Bose 2010: 276–82; Walsham 2014: 244–6).

If the Lambeth Constitutions of Archbishop Pecham issued in 1281 opened the English chapter of ecclesiastical and pastoral reform, then by the beginning of the fifteenth century, the anxiety sown by Wycliffite thought and propagated by his ecclesiastically defined 'successors', the Lollards, caused the English Church, in one influential narrative, to bring its reformist project to a close (Watson 1995). Archbishop Arundel's Constitutions, applied to the University of Oxford in 1407 and extended to every diocese in the land in 1409, curtailed speculative theology in Oxford (university provosts were to monitor carefully the orthodoxy of the curriculum) and required that preachers were licensed and regulated by bishops. The Constitutions prevented priests from criticizing the ecclesiastical hierarchy in sermons to the laity; and, of especial significance, they banned the propagation of pastoral literature in English without permission; likewise, translations of the Bible, which had begun to circulate in high-status manuscripts among high-status readers—including, ironically, Archbishop Arundel himself—were prohibited. However, it has been hard for scholars to assess the significance of the Constitutions without succumbing to the vertiginous influence of the Reformation-to-come. In his account of the Oxford Translation Debate of 1401 and after, in which many of the issues later addressed by the Constitutions are discussed, Nicholas Watson characterizes the academic Richard Ullerston's defence of vernacular translation in the following manner:

> Ullerston's defense helps us see the Constitutions as they must have been seen by numbers of moderates, who did not accept that the fight against heresy justi-
> fied reversing the great program of education whose foundations had been laid at

> Lateran IV two centuries earlier and built on by Pecham and others ever since. From the viewpoint of this (ill-defined and little-studied) group, the Constitutions must have seemed a huge mistake, a setting back of the clock two hundred years: *a premature Counter-Reformation*. (Watson 1995: 846; emphasis mine)

Here, the Constitutions are understood as both the annulment of the pastoral initiatives of Pecham and Lateran IV and somehow prefigurative of the Council of Trent (which itself is implicitly caricatured in terms of retrenchment). According to Michael Sargent, such an account promotes an 'Hegelian epistemology, treating historical periods, religious movements, and national identities as if they were ideal essences' (Sargent 2011: 56). Rather, argues Sargent, 'it is the very idea that there is an impersonal, external, objective history, according to which things may be said to be "premature"—before (or after) their time' (61) that must be contested. Thanks to the periodizing temptations to which Watson's discussion succumbs, the Constitutions are allowed to inaugurate a cultural and literary 'year zero':

> It was evidently an inadvertent side effect of the Constitutions to help precipitate this creation of a canon of theological writing by simply sealing it up, making it so hard for later writers to contribute further to this literature that it is fair to say that original theological writing in English was, for a century, almost extinct. (Watson 1995: 835)

For all the brilliance and influence of Watson's argument, its conclusions have been vigorously contested—see essays in Gillespie and Ghosh 2011; Johnson and Westphall 2013; and Corbellini 2013, as well as Kerby-Fulton 2006. Indeed, the material evidence of the circulation of religious writing among lay readers in the fifteenth century stands as the most compelling indictment of the narrative of decay he presents (Sargent 2005: 74–8 and 2008). It is significant, for example, that the texts Watson collates as representative of the boom in fourteenth-century pastoral and catechetical writing circulate for the most part in fifteenth-century manuscripts and printed books. Indeed, Pecham's Lambeth Constitutions find themselves repackaged throughout the fifteenth century, issuing in the compendia *Disce Mori* and the *Ignorancia Sacerdotum* (I have already noted their importance for Cromwellian reform). If Watson's account of the fifteenth century necessitates an explicit model of cultural decline, advocates of more 'positive' histories of medieval religion demonstrate their own susceptibility to periodizing models which serve to marginalize the Middle Ages when they characterize pastoral reform as the 'democratization' of later medieval religious culture (Duffy 2005). Rather than democratization, we might be better to call this process, in an admittedly clumsy term, 'lay clericalization', as lay people—often women (Erler 2002)—sought to emulate the devotional practices of enclosed religious. The explosive popularity of *Horae*, Books of Hours, from the end of the fifteenth century testifies to the collision of popular taste and technologies capable of satisfying demand (Duffy 2006).

Nonetheless, not all texts participated passively in the devotionalism promoted by the pastoralia. A number of key works emerge both to challenge and push beyond the theological goals of orthodox catechesis, among them *Dives and Pauper* and the *Lanterne of*

Liȝht. William Langland's *Piers Plowman* (1360s–1390s) is the most important literary response to pastoral initiatives of the later medieval English Church and illustrates, to devastating effect, the continuing inadequacy of ecclesiastical provision for lay people. A hortatory dream-vision and personification allegory, *Piers Plowman* is exasperated by the Church's abdication of its responsibility to the 'lewd' laity. Satirical and apocalyptical in equal measure and committed to narrative failure at every turn (the poem's various episodes, such as the marriage of Conscience to Lady Mede, the Pilgrimage to Truth or the Ploughing of the Half-Acre are never completed), *Piers Plowman* generates a loose confederacy of imitations in the fifteenth century, before its extraordinarily challenging allegorical poetics lose their transmissibility in the mid-fifteenth century (Simpson 2002: 328–33). That said, the figure of the ploughman is deployed in Lollard tracts, including *Jack Upland,* the *Omnis plantacio,* the *Epistola Santanae ad Cleros, The Praier and Complaynte of the Ploweman,* and orthodox texts, such as *A Lytte Geste how the plowman lerned his Paternoster,* which was printed by de Worde in 1510 (Hudson 1988: 452; Rodman Jones 2011, 85–101). It is significant, for example, that *Piers* was not printed until after the Reformation, when its rhetoric was revivified by Robert Crowley (in 1550; see Simpson 2002: 368–70; Rodman Jones 2011: 116–32). Crowley, like John Bale before him and his contemporary John Foxe, recruited Langland as a Protestant *avant la lettre.*

THE SEDUCTIONS OF HETERODOXY

However, Langland was not a Protestant, and neither was he a Wycliffite. For a brief period, from the 1370s until the 1420s, Wycliffism articulated a coherent and robust assault on formulations of orthodox authority. There is good reason to suspect, with Paul Strohm, that 'Lollardy', the term applied to the popular off-shoots of Wycliffism, was as much a bogey-man invented by the Lancastrian regime as a coherent movement with long-lasting influence: Strohm asks, 'was the Lollard a genuine threat or a political pawn, agent of destabilising challenge, or a hapless threat of self-legitimizing Lancastrian discourse?' (1998: 33). Not mumblers, as traditionally assumed, but botherers, gabblers, criers, whose 'obstreperous vocality', argues Andrew Cole (2008: 160–1), could never, according to their opponents, issue in coherence: the Lollards were placed 'at a discursive disadvantage at the outset' (36), serving as stooges who legitimated the usurpation of the effete Richard II by his cousin Henry Bolingbroke in 1399.[8] Under Bolingbroke, now Henry IV, the legislation *De heretico comburendo* (1401) aligned heresy with sedition and authorized the immolation of those who refused to recant (among the first on the pyre was Norfolk visionary Margery Kempe's parish priest, William

---

[8] 'What remains in question … is whether the term lollard has ever had sufficiently stable and objective content to warrant its use as a neutral, descriptive term in modern historiography' (Bose and Hornbeck 2011: 3).

Sawtre). The legislation would be cited approvingly by Sir Thomas More over a century later. Indeed, it might be said that under Henry IV, and particularly his son Henry V, the legislative lineaments of the Act of Supremacy were being drawn: in arguing for heresy not as a defect of belief, but as an act of ideological enunciation that threatened the body politic, the Lancastrians set the stage for Henry Tudor's appropriation of ecclesiastical authority to himself. 'In all but name', remarks Jeremy Catto, 'more than a century before the title could be used, Henry V had begun to act as the supreme governor of the Church of England' (1985: 115; see also Gillespie 2012: 163–5). If irony can be prospective, then in this instance it is particularly appropriate to Henry V, whose ambition was to be paragon and protector of Catholic *orthodoxy*.[9] Here, he perhaps emulated Sigismund, Holy Roman Emperor and host of the Council of Constance (1414–18), the most important ecclesiastical gathering of the fifteenth century:

> The Council of Constance described its mission as the reform of the church 'in head and members' and recommended a return to the apostolic simplicity and missionary zeal of the early church. It also addressed the problem of burgeoning heresy, retrospectively condemning Wyclif, and trying and executing the Bohemian Jan Hus as an alleged disciple of the arch-heresiarch. Although many of the reforms agreed at these councils were either ignored or watered down in Europe as a whole, the intellectual and cultural impact on the English church should not be underestimated. Henry V became the figurehead and the inspiration for an English church that speedily acquired new confidence and a new sense of direction and purpose. (Gillespie 2012: 165; see also Gillespie 2011)

That sense of direction and purpose, led by Arundel's successor Henry Chicele and propagated by a number of 'ecclesiastical humanist' bishops from the 1420s onwards, seems to have side-stepped the Arundelian prohibitions regarding devotional writing in the vernacular.[10] 'Far from eschewing vernacular theology', argues Vincent Gillespie, 'writers of Chicele's generation created for it a whole new high-style register, seeking to reclaim the vernacular for orthodoxy, and to make it fit for precise and nuanced theological thought, just as Ullerston has said they should do in his defence of translation at the Oxford debate' (2011: 35–6). These included John Audelay (*d.* 1426) and Reginald Pecock (*d. c.*1459). Pecock was an energetic reformist, but his career is a story of hermeneutic tragedy. His writings, tempered by a humanistic commitment to 'resoun', sought to undercut the theological bases of Wycliffite theology but, as a consequence of political manoeuvres against Pecock and what was claimed to be his denial of key tenets of orthodox doctrine, he was charged with heresy and was forced to abjure his writings and indeed burn his books at St Paul's Cross (Gillespie 2012: 176; see also Scase 1995 and Campbell 2010).

---

[9] Henry established the Carthusian house of Sheen and the Brigittine house of Syon in 1414–15.

[10] On ecclesiastical humanism see Cole 2007 and essays by Wakelin and Cole in Gillespie and Ghosh 2011.

'Is Wycliffism better understood as a dialect of reformist thought that was eventually hereticated?' (that is, criminalized) ask Mistooni Bose and Patrick Hornbeck (Bose and Hornbeck 2011: 3). The answer must be yes. While Wycliffite and Lollard dissenters of the fifteenth century were doctrinally at odds with ecclesiastical orthodoxy, especially on issues of sacramentality and ecclesiastical hierarchy, they were a product of the centuries of pastoral and theological reform we have already discussed. The effect of back-projecting the sectarianism of post-Reformation religious strife has been to divide sharply Wycliffite dissent from a broad, vital, and heterogeneous culture of later medieval religious speculation (Marshall 2011). Certainly, Lollard anti-sacerdotalism must have appealed to pious individuals and groups tired of the socially divisive materialism of the performance of piety in later medieval English communities (Marks 2004). Similarly, the dubious capabilities of their parish priests, widespread corruption of mendicants, or the bullying of the monasteries or the ecclesiastical courts, among other offices of the clergy, must have fuelled Christians' search for alternative forms of religious practice (Lutton 2006). However, Lollard books for Lollard readers are an exception when examined in relation to a majority of 'grey area' (Hudson 1988: 390–445) fifteenth-century codices that promiscuously commingle 'orthodox' and 'heterodox' texts. Indeed, many avowedly Wycliffite codices were owned by assiduously orthodox readers, such the Carthusians and Brigittines (Catto 1999). Furthermore, there are hardly any Lollard or Wycliffite texts which postdate 1440 (Hudson 1988: 451). The argument for the tacit 'secularization' of Wycliffite devotion—that it withdraws from the marketplace into the 'privy' and 'secret' places of the home, and thus disappears from the documentary record (Jurkowski 2011: 275)—draws its legitimacy from inquisitorial records that deride 'scoles of heresie' led, most threateningly, by women (see, for example, the 'Confession of Hawisia Moone of Loddon, 1430' in Hudson 1997). It also ignores the extent to which orthodox devotional texts recommended the same practices. Hence, it 'it is hard to construct a coherent picture of late fifteenth-century Lollardy', according to the leading scholar of the movement, Anne Hudson (1998: 459). The persistence of Lollards in Kent, where there are identifiable communities from the late fifteenth century until they are suppressed in 1511–12, is arguably an exception that proves the rule (Lutton 2006: 152–71).

Nevertheless, the resurgence in the prosecution of heresy in the 1490s demands explanation. It is tempting to suggest that Henry VII simply appropriated the strategies of his royal namesakes and predecessors and used the rooting out of heresy as a means of tightening his authority on both ecclesiastical and civil society after the Wars of the Roses. The persecutions continued under Henry VIII. Particularly active was John Longland, bishop of Lincoln, who acted against Lollard clergy and their followers in Amersham, Buckingham, Newbury, Berkshire, and Burford (Hudson 1988: 464–72).[11] There were trials in London, Coventry, Hereford, and throughout Kent. Burnings of those branded Lollards followed, but most of those accused of heresy recanted. Is it

---

[11] Bernard (2012: 209–11, 220–1) reminds us that Longland's activities are conveyed to us by the not-disinterested John Foxe.

clear, as Anne Hudson claims, 'that there were a substantial number of Lollards, or at least of men and women who at some stage had shown sympathy with Lollard causes and teachings' (Hudson 1988: 466) in late fifteenth-century England? There is throughout the closing chapter of Hudson's magisterial *The Premature Reformation: Wycliffite Texts and Lollard History* on late fifteenth- and early sixteenth-century religious dissent a wilful, if not wishful, yearning to compensate imaginatively for the gaps in surviving evidence: to conjure from the exceedingly small (but individually significant) groups of surviving Lollards a tradition of religious Nonconformism that irrigates the flowering of Protestantism. In the scholarship that has followed Hudson's groundbreaking work, texts have been obliged to play a critical role: indeed, if rejection of the doctrine of transubstantiation was the 'litmus-test' in trials of heretics, possession of books, and in particular, *the* Book, the Bible in English, has long been held to demonstrate the survival of Lollardy. The famous case of London merchant Richard Hunne, who died in 1514 under mysterious circumstances in the Lollards' Tower of St Paul's, exemplifies the susceptibility both of contemporary polemicists and historians to this narrative. It seems that Hunne was an agitator who took umbrage, in particular, at the Church's claims upon his purse. He was posthumously declared a heretic on the basis of books he was said to possess:

> Most damningly, he possessed a Wycliffite Bible. But did he realise its heretical nature? Was possession of a Wycliffite Bible necessarily evidence that its owners believed in heresies: were Henry VI and Richard III therefore heretics? Was the Bible's previous owner, Thomas Downes, an heretic? Yet in his will he left money for torches to burn in honour of the blessed sacrament and for 100 pounds of wax to burn before the crucifix, asking to be buried before the image of the Virgin in his parish church. (Bernard 2012: 219)

It is evident that what we should now probably call the Middle English Bible—rather than, as it is traditionally labelled, the *Wycliffite* Bible—was in fact categorically orthodox (Poleg 2013). Possession of the Bible speaks to the broad appetite among lay readers for ownership of religious texts. The pre-Reformation English Church may have prohibited the ownership of the Middle English Bible by certain estates, but it also acknowledged that readers might and did have access to it. Contrary to Nicholas Watson's claim, for example, that Nicholas Love's *Mirror of the Blessed Life of Jesus Christ* was written 'to provide the substitute of devout meditation for the increasingly widespread (and by now suspect) lay practice of Bible study' (Watson 1995: 853), the *Mirror* in fact readily admits that readers might consult the scriptures. 'We passen ouer at þis tyme', says Love of his account of the woman Samaritan from John 4, 'for als miche as it is opun & pleynly writen in þe gospel of Jon' (Sargent 2005: 94). Rather, the *Mirror* is representative of the fifteenth-century view that vernacular religious writing should supplement and expand on biblical materials, itself an assertion of confidence in the theoretical and theological capabilities of the vernacular. As Love puts it, in Caxton's version of his Proheme:

> Wherfore we mowen to styrynge of deuocyo[n] ymagyne and thynke dyuerse wordes and dedes of hym and other that we finde not wreton to that so that it be

not ageynst the byleue as Saynte Gregore and other doctours sayen | that holy wryte maye be expowned and understonde in dyuerse maners and to dyuerse purposes | Soo that it be not ageynst the byleue or good maners. And so what tyme or in what place that in thys book is wreton that thus dyde or thus spake our lord Jesus or other that ben spoken of and it maye not be preued by holy wryte or gronded in expresse sayenges of hooly doctours hyt shalle be taken none otherwyse than as a deuoute medytacyon that hyt myght so be spoken or done. (*STC* 3260, 5)

Love legitimizes the fictional expansion on Christ's life as it is presented in the Gospels precisely in terms of the accumulative, accretive traditions of orthodox commentary and exegesis. As Kantik Ghosh puts it, 'the biblical text is used as the occasion for an affective and theoretical literary creativity which implicitly denies the Wycliffite disjunction of divine text and human hermeneutics. Instead the *Mirror* in effect insists on the univocity, the continuity of the Divine Word and the human through a constant violation of what Vincent Gillespie calls "the decorum of textual boundaries"' (Ghosh 1991: 153). For Love, and later for Sir Thomas More, the Wycliffite (or Lutheran) addiction to the literal word represents a diminishment of human capacity. It declares a desultory preference for the theology—thoroughly Augustinian, of course—of the Fall as opposed to that of the Redemption, as represented by the exemplarity of Christ's life. The 'resurgence' of heresy was, for More, simply a case of history repeating itself. After all, as Richard Rex comments, 'Thomas More never encountered "the Reformation": history had not yet bestowed that appellation on the crisis in which he lived' (2011: 97). Heresy, says More in *A Confutation to Tyndale's Answer* (1532), is a 'poysoned adder ... lyeng and lurkynge amonge the drye fruteless fagottes [that] catcheth good folke by the fyngers, and so hangeth on theyr handes wyth the poyson styng'. A key word here is 'fruteless': heresy's commitment is to the sterile literal word, from which the participation of human imagination has been banned. Wycliffite or Lutheran hermeneutics were perceived by More, as they had been by Nicholas Love, as no kind of hermeneutics at all; they represented, fundamentally, the repudiation of the role of human perception in understanding the plenitude of God's creation (Simpson 2007). By contrast, we might assume that More has in mind an antonym, 'fructuose', used in myriad devotional tracts across the fourteenth and fifteenth centuries, but especially central to Nicholas Love's *Mirror*, which since the 1450s had been considered the 'official' textual response of Lollardy (Sargent 2005). Indeed, More proceeds to outline a canon of fifteenth-century devotional reading that speaks to the continuing 'fructuoseness' of such writing: he counsels that 'the people vnlerned', in addition to 'prayour' and 'good medytacyon', should read:

suche englysshe bookes as most may norysshe and encrease deuocyon. Of whyche kynde is Bonaunture of the lyfe of Cryste, Gerson of the folowynge of Cryste, and the deuote contemplatyue booke of Scala perfectionis wyth such other lyke | then in the lernynge what may well be answered vnto heretykes. (More 1977: 37)

Here are invoked those two most significant figures in fifteenth-century English religious writing: Love ('Bonaunture of the lyfe of Cryste') and Hilton ('Scala perfectionis'), scrupulous moderator of contemplative theology; as well as one of the century's most important texts, the *Imitatio Christi*, attributed to Jean Gerson, chancellor of the University of Paris and guardian of visionary *discretio*, but now thought to have been authored by Thomas à Kempis. More's evocation of these writers should problematize any account of sixteenth-century writing in terms of naive periodizing schemes of representing the past in terms of continuity or change, because neither 'past', 'present', nor 'future' can be so simplistically conceived (Summit 2000: 121–2). Periodization may divide, but tragically for Thomas More, the past also does not simply 'continue' unproblematically, as twentieth-century theologian and bishop Charles Gore would have it: 'there is, after all, a faith which has been held *semper, ubique, ab omnibus* in such sense that what fragments of the Christian body have not held it hardly count in the total effect' (Gore 1907: 213; discussed in Kelly and Perry 2014). Such an attitude is precisely the basis of More's dismissive circumscription of religious dissent, and the reason why he fatally misread the political circumstances within which attitudes to religious orthodoxy were changing (in this context, see chapter 16).

The purpose of the devout imagining espoused by Love and commended by More is careful, penitential self-examination. Love asserts that it is only with 'clennesse of conscience' that his readers might begin to achieve, through 'deuoute imaginacioun', the affective identification with Christ's sufferings which will enable their own awakening from sin. His text's overriding objective is the recognition of culpability on the reader's part: the reader should feel and recognize her sinful complicity in Christ's death. From 'inwarde affeccione' will 'come many deuout felynges & stirynges ... neuer supposede before' (Sargent 2005: 160).

The systematic inquisition of the self permeates devotional and contemplative texts prior to the Reformation (Bryan 2008). 'And therfore whoso wil travayle in this werk', says the author of *The Cloud of Unknowing*, 'lat him first clense his concience; and sithen, when he hath done that in him is lawefuly, lat him dispose him booldly bot meekly therto. And lat him think that he hath ful longe ben holden therfro; for this is that werk in the whiche a soule schuld travaile alle his liiftyme, thof he had never sinnid deedly' (Gallacher 1997: 58). In language which pre-empts Love's Proheme, in which Christ's life is offered to his readers as a mirror, the *Cloud*-Author asserts:

> Goddes worde, outher wretyn or spokyn, is licnid to a mirour. Goostly, the ighe of thi soule is thi reson; thi conscience is thi visage goostly. And right as thou seest that yif a foule spot be in thi bodily visage, the ighe of the same visage may not see that spotte, ne wite wher it is, withoutyen a myrour or a teching of another than itself: right so it is goostly. Withouten redyng or heryng of Godes worde, it is inpossible to mans understondyng that a soule is bleendid in custom of synne schuld see the foule spot in his concyence. (64)

Elsewhere, in a characteristically arresting image, Walter Hilton admonishes his reader to 'ransake' her conscience:

> Yif thou wolt witen thanne yif thi soule be reformed to the image of God or noo, bi that that I have seid thou maist have an entré. Ransake thyn owen conscience and loke what thi wille is, for thereinne stondeth al. Yif it be turned from al deedli synne, that thou woldest for nothynge wityngeli and wilfulli breke the comaundement of God, and for that thou hast mysdoon here bifore agens his biddynge, thou haste beschreven mekeli, with ful herte to leve it and with sorwe that thou dedest it, I seie thanne sikirli that thi soule is reformed in feith to the likenesse of God. (Bestul 2000: 39)

Here, again, is the refrain of reform, now applied to the individual soul. The structured scrutiny of the self accompanies contemplative and pastoral writing alike, and speaks not to 'democratization' but perhaps to the privatization of piety in the fifteenth and sixteenth centuries, in which religious books played a key role. This is witnessed to in wills, such as that of Cecily Neville, Duchess of York, who died in 1495:

> I geve to my dovghter Brigitte the boke of the Legenda avrea in velem a boke | of the life of Kateryn of Sene a boke of saint Matilde … Also, I geve to my | dovghter Anne Priores of Sion a boke of Bonaventvre and Hilton in the same in Englishe | and a boke of the Revelacions of Saint Bvrgitte … Also I geve to Sir John | Blotte a gospell boke a pistill covered with ledder. (Spedding 2010)

Neville's will lists the late fifteenth-century best-sellers: Love, Hilton, but also the *Legende Aurea*, printed in an English translation by Caxton in 1483 (*STC* 24873). Most significantly, Cecily reveals her penchant for exemplars of female piety: Catherine of Siena, whose *Dialogo* was translated into Middle English at Syon in the first half of the fifteenth century as *The Orcherd of Syon* and printed by Wynkyn de Worde in 1519 (*STC* 4815); the *Revelations* of St Bridget, who was the patron of the Brigittine Order at Syon; and a life of Mechtild of Hackeborn (presumably the *Book of Ghostly Grace*; Armstrong 1983).

Neville seemed to lack the evangelizing zeal of her cousin, Lady Margaret Beaufort, Countess of Richmond and Derby, and mother to Henry VII. Beaufort confounds historians' efforts to divide piety from humanism in later medieval England: in many respects, she is a recipient and proponent of the 'ecclesiastical humanism' which coalesced in the middle decades of the fifteenth century. In addition to establishing the Cambridge colleges of St John's and Christ's, Beaufort translated *The Mirror of Gold for the Sinful Soul* and, most significantly, the fourth book of the *Imitatio Christi*, of Thomas à Kempis (completed with William Atkinson) (her translation is assessed by Dremmer 2012). Both texts were printed for Beaufort by Pynson in 1506 (*STC* 6894.5) and 1504 (*STC* 23955) respectively, the last printer whose work she sponsored. Her commitment to the most austere orders of English monasticism—she visited Sheen and Syon in 1504 by papal license—fed her patronage of Caxton and Wynkyn de Worde; both printed

The Fifteen Oes, attributed to Bridget of Sweden, and de Worde was commissioned to produce a print of Hilton's *Scale* in 1494.[12] The texts Beaufort used to inform her piety stressed both the accessibility and the mundanity of the lives of the saints and Christ. The *Imitatio Christi*, in particular, was the product of the devotional pragmatism associated with the Devotia Moderna, but again it 'was primarily concerned with interior reform' (Von Habsburg 2011: 25).

'STRYF AMONG CRISTIS DISCIPLIS': PERIODIZING RELIGIOUS CHANGE

When, months before her death, Lady Margaret attended the coronation of her grandson, Henry VIII, she must have felt assured that the project to which she and the ecclesiastical establishment had been dedicated in the fifteenth century, the elaboration of lay and clerical reform, had all but been completed, making England the apotheosis of Catholic orthodoxy. That Henry would initiate the process by which the material and theological fabric of her religious world would be undone must have been unthinkable. However, she could not, of course, think the future into being. Neither can we. And yet, the historiography of the English Reformation has consistently sought to historicize medieval English religion in relation to the Reformation-to-come. This has too often involved scholars in powerful gestures of retroactive identification, as sectarian apologists of various persuasions have found in the period what Michael Sargent has recently termed 'harbingers of their own post-medieval mentalities'. As John van Engen has underlined, 'we maintain discrete epochs by wearing interpretive blinkers':

> Few eras have suffered from this as much as fifteenth-century Europe, caught in the Catholic/Protestant polemic from the sixteenth to the early twentieth centuries no less than in the medieval/modern, scholastic/humanist disputes. The fifteenth century as a distinct epoch, a Europe with multiple and sometimes contradictory options, not merely autumnal or traditional or devotional or indeed humanist or pre-reforming (whatever truths those rubrics may also capture), steeped in inheritances yet productive of innovations—this historians are only beginning to imagine. (Van Engen 2008: 260)

Our problem has its roots in the simultaneous ripeness and rhetorical consistency of the language deployed by orthodox and heterodox writers alike. For example, the

---

[12]   On Beaufort's patronage of the book trade see Jones and Underwood 1992: 180–7. On the impact of *The Fifteen Oes* see Summit 2000: 111–38.

description of the Church by one group of fifteenth-century Wycliffites chimes seductively with later Protestant attacks, from Bale to Foxe. The *Twelve Conclusions of the Lollards*, as the text has come to be known, sought to persuade parliamentarians to challenge the authority of the Church in language that seems to prefigure that of Protestant reformers:

> Qwan þe chirche of Yngelond began to dote in temperalte aftir hir stepmodir þe grete chirche of Rome, and chirchis were slayne be appropriacion to diuerse placys, feyth, hope and charite begunne for to fle out of our chirche. (Hudson 1997: 24)

How prescient, for an earlier generation of historians, that this text should be pinned to Westminster Hall,[13] the first public salvo in an attack on the Church that would culminate in the nailing of Luther's *Ninety-Five Theses* to the doors of Wittenberg cathedral (the historiographical logic is that repetition legitimates).[14] It is precisely as a consequence of the muddied terrain of reformist rhetoric that it is so difficult to disentangle the specificities of Reformation 'innovation' from a fifteenth-century appetite for novel and diverse modes of religious literature and practice. Consequently, it has proven too easy for historians to absorb and reproduce the rhetoric of reform, whether in its mild, anticlerical or anti-papal registers. 'I have become painfully aware', Alexandra Walsham has submitted, 'of the extent to which I am both a product and a prisoner of the historiographical and epistemological trends I ... describe' (2014: 241–2).

How, as Walsham asks, are we to 'conceptualize and explain religious change in medieval and early modern Europe without perpetuating distorting paradigms inherited from the very era of the past that is the subject of our study?' (2014: 241). We must admit that change is identified only in retrospect and only because recognizing it does cultural work for us, now. Kathleen Davis has recently argued, 'Periodization ... does not refer to a mere back-description that divides history into segments, but to a fundamental political technique—a way to moderate, divide, and regulate—always rendering its services *now*' (2008: 5).[15] Indeed, in his magisterial and controversial *Reform and Cultural Revolution*, James Simpson (2002: 558–9) has stressed equally compellingly the retrenchment of the reformist strategies of fifteenth-century writing under the Henrician Reformation:

> the main features of 'medieval' cultural practice turn out to be as follows: a sense of long and continuous histories; and accretive reception of texts, where the historicity of the reader receiving the old text is not at all suppressed; clearly demarcated and unresolved generic, stylistic, and/or discursive divisions within texts; and, above all, an affirmation of human initiative, whether in politics or theology.

---

[13] The nailing of the *Twelve Conclusions* to the doors of Westminster Hall in 1395 is reported in Roger Dymmok's *Liber contra duodecim errores et hereses Lollardum*. See Hudson 1997: 150–1.

[14] The historicity of this event remains in question.

[15] See also Marshall 2012: 1–3.

By contrast, Simpson characterizes the sixteenth century as a 'cultural revolution', which demanded 'both repudiation of the old order and a vigorous affirmation of novelty', all in the service of a 'newly conceived transcendence of power' (2002: 558–9). Subsequent discussions in this volume will affirm, contest, and problematize such views. It is worth noting, with Thomas Betteridge, that books published after the death of Henry VIII 'can be seen as returning to the norms of Simpson's fourteenth- and fifteenth-century reformist literature' (Betteridge 2005: 92–3). Might it be that, even as he seeks to turn the tables on traditional scholarly accounts of the fate of medieval culture, Simpson succumbs to the continuing dominance of Reformation conceptions of history? As Brian Cummings has noted, 'since the primal act of Reformation historiography, John Foxe's *Acts and Monuments* of 1563, the Reformation has acted as an icon of historical change, subjecting circumstance to an overriding narrative of inevitable and salutary revolution' (Cummings 1999: 822).

Thus, we might be wise to resist tropes of continuity, rupture, or revolution, which do little but serve historiographies of triumph, for one or another religious constituency. Perhaps we would be better to attend precisely to 'circumstance': to those moments when fifteenth- and sixteenth-century writers reflected on the religious tensions of their own times without capitulating to narratives of supersession. Among the twenty-seven items in Oxford, Bodleian Library, MS Laud Misc. 23, a devotional compilation made in London in the first half of the fifteenth century, there is a unique sermon, named in a rubricated title 'Vos estis ciues sanctorum'. An allegorical sermon describing the fractious state of the contemporary English Church in terms of a besieged city, the sermon envisages the resolution of sectarian dissent as follows:

> Now moste we lerne to belde aȝen þis cite. And among þese cetesynis to make a fynial vnite. In Cristis tyme þer was a stryf among cristis disciplis, but crist pesid hem. And tawȝt a lessoun how his chirche shulde be reconsilid w[i]t[h]outen ende.[16]

Division between 'orthodox' and dissenting religious positions is compared to 'stryf among cristis disciplis'. However, in order for the city to be rebuilt, there must be a 'fynial vnite', in which religious difference will 'be reconsilid wtouten ende'. The sermon's ethics may be rooted in the scriptural past, but its assessment of the present depends on a conceptualization of the future patterned on *hope*. That such hope was not fulfilled in the period under discussion should not be a concern for literary historians. Rather, it is our task to scrutinize such moments of enunciation and to note, not mourn or celebrate, their consequences and implications.

---

[16] The sermon appears fols 61ʳ–70ʳ, with this passage appearing on fol. 68ʳ. The sermon is edited in a modern English translation by Lahey et al. 2013: 285–300. The sermon is discussed in Kelly and Perry 2011: 362–80 and 2013: 215–38. A detailed codicological account of the manuscript can be accessed on the Geographies of Orthodoxy website: http://www.qub.ac.uk/geographies-of-orthodoxy/resources/?section=manuscript&id=73.

CHAPTER 2

THE HENRICIAN REFORM

DAVID BAGCHI

By 1509, when the young Henry VIII acceded to the throne of England, propaganda had already become an important tool of government. His father, for instance, had used it to bolster the Tudor claim to legitimacy. However, the pen and the press differed from other instruments of policy (such as statute law and the headsman's axe) in that they were also available to the regime's opponents, and could therefore be used to challenge policy as much as to support it. The story of the Henrician reform is in part the story of the publications it provoked, both for and against, at home and abroad.

I have deliberately used the rather neutral word 'reform' to describe the religious policy of Henry's reign. It was too ideologically inconsistent to be called a 'Reformation' (though this term describes perfectly the respective Protestant and Catholic programmes pursued by his children Edward and Mary). And it was too unsettled to be called a 'Settlement', the term often applied to his daughter Elizabeth's reign. A good example of its turbulence and inconsistency can be seen in the most significant publishing event associated with Henry, the official English translation of the Bible in 1539, and the associated injunction that every parish in the land should equip itself with a copy. This reversed more than a century of official hostility towards popular access to the vernacular Scriptures, and was carried out in the face of opposition from conservative bishops (Daniell 2003: 166). To those outside the court, or outside the country, it might have seemed that England was now firmly in the Protestant camp. In fact, the reforming tide was already beginning to ebb, and in 1543 access to the English Bible was once again restricted.

The apparently violent changes of religious policy direction in Henry's reign are notoriously hard to explain. Should they be attributed to the king's own mercurial temperament? Do they instead reflect the success or failure of competing court factions—one reforming, one conservative—as they fought for control of the ship of state? Or was Henry at the helm throughout, cleverly playing off the rival factions against each other in order to achieve his own ends while denying direct responsibility? And how is the resultant Henrician reform to be characterized? As 'Catholicism without the Pope' or as 'Lutheranism without justification by faith' (Marshall 2005: 22–48; Ryrie 2002: 67)? Was

Henry himself just a wayward Catholic, or a principled Erasmian reformer (Scarisbrick 1968: ch. 12; McConica 1965; Bernard 2005)? Or was his theology simply 'a ragbag of emotional preferences' (MacCulloch 1998: 178)?

However historians might characterize the religious policy of Henry's reign, they are mostly agreed on its broad outline. From his accession until the late 1520s, young King Henry was a model of orthodox piety. There are strong suggestions that he read some theology in his youth; he certainly took a strong if fitful interest in it thereafter. When he took up the sword, in the war with France in 1513, it was at least ostensibly in defence of the Pope. And when he took up the pen in 1521, it was to champion the Church's sacramental system against Martin Luther. That he expected to be rewarded for such displays of filial devotion (the Pope's bestowal of the title *Defensor fidei* for his book against Luther finally gave Henry a place on the world stage alongside France's *rex christianissimus* or Spain's *rex catholicissimus*—the sixteenth-century equivalent of a seat on the UN Security Council), does not count decisively against his sincerity.

Pope Clement VII's refusal in 1529 to annul Henry's marriage to Catherine of Aragon (despite having annulled his sister's marriage on weaker grounds) marked the beginning of a second phase, characterized by anti-papalism and a degree of openness to reformist ideas. This phase, which lasted until 1539, saw the break with Rome, which was followed by a moderate evangelical reformation which included the Dissolution of the Monasteries (1536 and 1539), the promulgation of evangelical formularies such as the Ten Articles (1536), and the publication of the Great Bible (1539).

The third phase, which lasted from the passing of the Six Articles Act in 1539 until the last few months of Henry's reign, represents a distinct lurch in a conservative direction. The Six Articles themselves reasserted such unequivocally Catholic doctrines as transubstantiation, and effectively ended the regime's brief flirtation with Protestantism. Even the flagship of moderate reformism, the English Bible, was put into dry dock with the Act for the Advancement of True Religion in 1543. In principle, this restricted the reading of the vernacular scriptures to males above the rank of yeomen and to noble and gentry women, and was a complete reversal of Cromwell's and Cranmer's great vision. However, the clock was not put all the way back to the 1520s, and in some respects Henry VIII's phase of Catholic reformism ran ahead of what even some moderate English evangelicals would have wished. This can be seen most clearly in the campaign against idolatry, which resulted in the destruction of many shrines and a severe curtailment of the cult of the saints (Marshall 1995). In addition, although prayer for the dead was still permitted and even encouraged, the later Henrician regime refused to endorse any speculation as to 'the place where the souls remain, the name thereof, and the state and condition which they be in', leaving such matters to God's merciful ordering of all things (*The King's Book*, 1543: Tvij^v). In effect, the regime abolished Purgatory in 1543, dismissing it as a scam invented by the papacy to increase revenue.

In the brief survey which follows of the literature engendered by Henry's religious policy, it is important to bear in mind this broad scheme of periodization.

HENRICIAN PROPAGANDA, 1520–47

Religious publishing in Henry VIII's reign was strongly and effectively policed, a situation assisted by the fact that, in contrast with more developed European countries, printing presses in England were still largely confined to the metropolis (Pettegree 2002). These presses issued both official and semi-official publications, while any material likely to fall foul of censorship had to be printed abroad and smuggled in.

The printing press was used as a means of propaganda throughout Henry's reign. This was not a new thing in England. His father, the first Henry Tudor, had resorted to the press regularly, for example to assert the legitimacy of his marriage to Elizabeth of York and thus his claim to the throne, or to win financial and military support for his invasion of France (Innocent VIII 1486; Pisan 1489). When he died, he bequeathed to his son both an official 'king's printer' in Richard Pynson and a first-rate minister of propaganda in Thomas Wolsey. Henry VIII's use of the press at first echoed his father's, and included the publication of volumes, in both Latin and English, justifying war with France and celebrating the victory at Flodden over the Scots (Neville-Sington 1999: 582). However, the Wolsey-Pynson propaganda machine stepped up a gear in response to Henry's personal crusade for religious orthodoxy against Martin Luther, and ironically provided a model for a later propaganda campaign with entirely different aims.

Given the enthusiasm with which he engaged in theological disputes, there is no reason to doubt that Henry's *Defence of the Seven Sacraments against Martin Luther* of 1521 was very largely his own work, though the assistance of others was openly acknowledged at the time (Henry VIII 1992). It was clearly intended to be the publishing event of the decade, if not of the century: apart from the formal presentation of a fair copy in manuscript into the Pope's hands by Wolsey's agent in Rome, printed copies of the book (some extravagantly printed on vellum) were sent to the other crowned heads of Europe. Henry's objective, and that of his chief minister, was to secure his reputation as the foremost royal defender of the Christian faith, as much by the pen as by the sword, and of course to have that reputation officially endorsed by the Pope. Henry's book against Luther in effect put his name on the map. Over the next two years, further anti-Lutheran works followed the *Assertio* from Pynson's press: Alfonso de Villa Sancta, a Franciscan and one of Queen Catherine's confessors, defended indulgences from Luther's critique and also attacked Luther's lieutenant Melanchthon on the questions of sin, grace, and free will; Edward Powell provided a further defence of the seven sacraments and of the priesthood; and Thomas More, writing as 'William Ross', answered Luther's rude riposte to the king's book with his equally rude *Responsio* (Villa Sancta 1523a and 1523b; Powell 1523; More 1523). Alongside the positive promotion of the official voice went the violent suppression of dissentient ones: 'Lutheran' books and writers were burned in spectacular *autos da fé*, and concerted efforts were made to prevent the printing, import, and distribution of books deemed heretical (in this context, see chapter 16).

Wolsey's and Pynson's campaign belonged to what we described above as the first phase of Henry's reign, and indeed to some extent defines it. The perceived success of that campaign would have confirmed for Henry the usefulness of the press as an arm of policy, and guaranteed that he would call upon it again whenever he needed to undermine his opponents, defend his actions, or otherwise manage his reputation at home or abroad. Open resistance to his efforts to annul the Aragon marriage, and at least muted opposition to his claim to ecclesiastical supremacy, occasioned such a need. Given the success of the earlier Wolsey-Pynson campaign, it is entirely just to criticize Geoffrey Elton for having claimed too much originality for Thomas Cromwell's exploitation of the press in the 1530s (Neville-Sington 1999: 589). One should however recognize that Elton had in his turn criticized earlier scholars who had exaggerated Cromwell's agency by including within his 'propaganda campaign' much literary activity that did not in fact fall under his direct control. According to Elton's stricter definition, Christopher St German's works, for example, must be excluded from the campaign because they were not published by the king's printer and because their author was not known to have been paid by the government for his services (Elton 1972: 171–6; cf. Baker 2004).

Cromwell's propaganda, according to Elton's definition, was restricted to four topics, which succeeded each other in rapid succession. The first was the 'divorce', which occasioned two pamphlets, a dialogue between a lawyer and a divine entitled *A glasse of the truth* (1532), which may have been partly written by the king himself, and a significant set of nine *Articles* (1533), which not only denies 'the bishop of Rome' any primacy over other provinces, but also declares the current holder of the office a heretic (*Articles*, 1533: 10^v). The second topic was the Royal Supremacy. The campaign to support the legislation of 1534 opened with apologies by Edward Foxe (*De vera differentia regiae potestatis et ecclesiasticae*) and Richard Sampson (*Oratio*). Both were in Latin, and therefore presumably intended for an international market, though in this aim they would be supplanted by Stephen Gardiner's superior *De vera obedientia* of 1535. At home, overt opposition to the Act of Supremacy was rare; but muted, or rather muttered, opposition was feared to be widespread, prompting the *Litel treatise ageynste the mutterynge of some papistis in corners* (1534). The third topic, the regime's battle for hearts and minds in the English north during the Pilgrimage of Grace, produced another work at least attributed to Henry's own pen, the *Answere to the petitions of the traytours and rebelles in Lyncolnshyre* (1536), Thomas Starkey's *An Exhortation to the people instructynge theym to Unitie and Obedience* (1536), and Richard Morison's *A lamentation in whiche is shewed what ruyne and destruction cometh of seditious rebellion* and *A remedy for sedition wherin are conteyned many thynges, concerning the true and loyall obeisance, that commens owe unto their prince and soueraygne lorde the Kynge* (both 1536) (Mayer 1989; Sowerby 2010). Elton's final topic was that perennial favourite of the early Tudors, the justification of war with France. The dependable Morison again obliged, with an *Exhortation to styrre all Englyshe men to the defence of theyr countreye*, and a translation of the Roman author Frontinus entitled *The stratagems, sleyghtes, and policies of warre* (both 1539).

Elton's strict criteria are undoubtedly helpful in bringing into sharper focus Cromwell's core propaganda activities. However, they are arguably too restrictive, and ignore the important penumbra of semi-official publications which is as much part of the story: by John Foxe's time, it was understood that the chief minister had 'retained unto him … helpers and furtherers' who produced anti-papal ballads as well as books, and we know that Cromwell also provided John Bale with a theatrical troupe to perform his plays (King 1982: 48–9). A case in point is the freelancer William Marshall. Neither of his two most important translations, Marsiglio of Padua's *Defensor pacis* (which excluded the Pope from any consideration of the body politic) and Lorenzo Valla's *De donatione Constantini* (which exposed as a forgery the document on which the papacy's claims to temporal power were based), was published by Berthelet, the king's printer, and so fall foul of one of Elton's conditions for seeing them as part of the official campaign (Marsiglio 1535; Valla 1534; see also Watt 1534; Bucer 1535). Moreover, although we know that Cromwell gave Marshall the considerable sum of £20 towards the publication of the Marsiglio (there is no indication that Marshall's other ventures were similarly supported), it was a loan rather than a subsidy and suggests that Cromwell may have been lukewarm about the project (Ryrie 2004; cf. Underwood 2004). Yet Elton himself includes these two translations by Marshall as central to Cromwell's propaganda campaign (Elton 1972: 186).

In addition to Marshall, the penumbra must also be considered to include an author like St German. His *Treatise concernynge the diuision between the spiritualtie and temporalitie* (1532) went through at least two editions, and was printed by Robert Redman as well as by Thomas Berthelet. Attacked by Thomas More, St German defended his position with *Salem and Bizance* (1533), and finally *The addicions of Salem and Byzance* (1534). Throughout the exchanges, his defence of royal ecclesiastical supremacy holds firm, and although his arguments are legal more than theological, they would have been no less welcome to the regime because of that. It could also include shadowy figures such as Clement Armstrong, whose function may have been to circulate radical ideas in manuscript and to influence the opinion-formers (Shagan 2002). Torrance Kirby makes a good case for regarding these more marginal authors as constituting the 'Tudor evangelical *avant-garde*, whose main object was to prod the government to move in an increasingly radical break with the Roman hierarchy and with the old religion' (Kirby 2013a: 31). However, it was not restricted to evangelicals. Just as the Eltonian canon of Cromwellian propagandists included conservatives like Stephen Gardiner, so the semi-official penumbra included Cuthbert Tunstall, who as bishop of Durham preached a stirring call to arms at a time of national crisis and had it published by Berthelet the same year (Tunstall 1539).

Henrician propaganda did not end with the fall of Cromwell, but it did become much more piecemeal and conventional. In effect, it reverted to the type of royal propaganda seen in the previous reign, for instance in the publication, in 1542, of a justification of war with Scotland, or in 1545 of Queen Catherine's prayer book, which included prayers for those going into battle (Parr 1545). Government exploitation of the press would accelerate once again after Henry's death, and would indeed become a notable feature of all his children's reigns.

OFFICIAL RELIGION: FORMULARIES
AND INJUNCTIONS

The new supreme head of the English Church had transferred from the papacy the right to determine its faith and its order, and there was clearly a need to formulate and to promulgate both. Unlike his daughter Elizabeth, who established a religious 'settlement' (though not, as events would prove, a religious consensus) within a few years of her accession and never departed from it significantly thereafter, Henry oversaw a series of official formularies and injunctions, supplemented by localized versions of the latter at diocesan level, which over the years reflected the vicissitudes of the reign's religious policy. The formularies were broadly concerned with matters of belief, and were largely the product of theological horse-trading involving Archbishop Cranmer, committees of bishops, and the king himself (MacCulloch 1996). The injunctions were broadly concerned with matters of order (though there was of course a good deal of overlap between the two categories), and were more directly an expression of the mind of Cromwell, as Henry's vicegerent in ecclesiastical affairs.

The first published formulary of the independent English Church were the so-called Ten Articles of 1536 (Henry VIII 1536). The document, which had its origin partly in a doctrinal statement agreed with Lutheran divines, sets out the essentials of Christian faith, but does so in a recognizably evangelical, and indeed Cranmerian, fashion. It makes a clear distinction between articles relating to faith, which are necessary for salvation, and those relating to ceremonies, which are not, and names the sacraments of baptism, of the altar, and of penance, while leaving unmentioned the other four traditional sacraments: confirmation, matrimony, ordination, and extreme unction. (If the inclusion of penance as a sacrament seems distinctly unevangelical, it should be remembered that Luther himself vacillated over the question of its sacramentality throughout his life [Bagchi 2004].) Henry, who a decade and a half earlier had won his theological spurs by so vigorously defending the sevenfold nature of the sacraments, seems not to have noticed the silent emendation. Instead, he lent his name to the preface, a direct and surprisingly winsome appeal to his own subjects to adopt the articles supposedly devised by him.

The Ten Articles were followed immediately by an instrument setting out their detailed implementation, Cromwell's *Injunctions* of 1536. These required the removal of some holy days and saints' days from the Church calendar, a coordinated attempt by parents and priests to catechize the young in the Ten Commandments, the Apostles' Creed, and the Lord's Prayer, and also the provision, by the following year, of both a Latin and an English Bible in every parish. The last was a wildly unrealistic demand, not least because no complete English Bible had yet been published with official permission, and it was soon dropped (Bray 1994: 175–8).

The Ten Articles were also followed a year later by the Bishops' Book (*Institution*, 1537). This was an attempt to provide the course of vernacular catechetical instruction alluded to in the injunctions, and it is significant in that respect that the king's printer brought it out in two formats, a more formal quarto and a cheaper octavo, presumably designed for widespread popular consumption. However, it also illustrates how inter-dependent the official and semi-official arms of the regime's publishing programme were. The Bishops' Book borrowed extensively from the primer composed by the William Marshall previously mentioned, who in turn had borrowed heavily from a selection of Luther's writings.

A second set of Cromwellian *Injunctions* followed in 1538. These consolidated the changes made so far and went further in forbidding completely the veneration of images. They also repeated the requirement that each parish should provide itself with a copy of the English Bible—the equal requirement for a Bible in Latin was dropped. The 1538 injunctions, and the authorization of the Great Bible of the following year, marked the high water mark of evangelical influence, and already the tide was beginning to turn. 1539 saw the passing of the Act of Six Articles.

Article 1 affirmed the real, physical presence of Christ in the bread and wine of the Eucharist. This article clearly disenfranchised those who understood Christ's words at the Last Supper, 'This is my body/blood', as purely symbolical. It also excluded belief in a real, spiritual presence (the bread and wine, by grace, become Christ's flesh and blood to believers, while to non-believers they remain bread and wine). But most mainstream evangelicals of a Lutheran persuasion could happily have accepted the article, were it not for the addition of a fateful clause: 'that after the consecration there remaineth no substance of bread and wine, nor any other substance, but the substance of Christ, God and man' (Bray 1994: 224). The effect of this clause was to commit the English people, on pain of death by burning, to a particular, scientific understanding of Christ's phys-ical presence, known as transubstantiation: only the 'accidents', i.e. the outward appear-ance of the consecrated elements remain, while its 'substance', i.e. its underlying reality, becomes that of flesh or blood (Brooks 1992). Lutherans could accept the simultan-eous coexistence of the earthly and the spiritual as a matter of faith, but baulked at any explanation which relied on Aristotelian physics. It is difficult to avoid the inference that the transubstantiation clause was a deliberate shibboleth designed by conservatives such as Gardiner and Audley to undermine the dominance of moderate, i.e. Lutheran, Protestantism in England, and in this it achieved some success.

The same tactic can be seen in relation to Article 2: Lutherans could happily accept its proposition that reception of Communion in both kinds is not necessary for salva-tion, but the article goes on to enjoin belief in the doctrine of concomitance (that the blood is included under the species of the bread, and the flesh is included under the spe-cies of the wine) which Luther and his followers rejected as unscriptural and pointless speculation (Bagchi 1996). For an excellent discussion of the process by which moder-ate Protestantism lost ground during the latter part of Henry's reign, see Ryrie (2002). Ryrie, however, dates the decline from 1543, and does not explicitly consider the role of the Six Articles in the process.

After the fall of Cromwell, Cranmer became isolated and exposed. A measure of his weakness, and that of the evangelical cause in England, was the promulgation of *The*

King's Book in 1543. This reaffirmation of Catholic principles crushed any hopes that justification by faith alone fell within the range of permissible belief in England. At the same time, it combined in a somewhat inconsistent way, as we have seen, a trenchant justification of prayer for the souls of the departed with an equally trenchant rejection of Purgatory. In its puzzling inconsistency, *The King's Book* reflected the king's mind better than any other formulary published during his reign.

THE BIBLE

It would be difficult to overstate the impact of the Bible on early modern English literature, or on early modern England generally. Given that, it seems extraordinary, especially when compared with the flourishing of printed vernacular Bibles on the continent, that the first English Bible was printed only as late as 1525. The reason is simple: the so-called *Constitutions* of Archbishop Arundel of 1409, which codified the anti-Lollard measures agreed by the provincial synod of Oxford of the previous year, had prohibited unauthorized Bible translations (in this context, see chapter 1). The measure had of course been directed at manuscript Bibles, but continued to be observed after the advent of the hand press. Even Latin Bibles for the English market were printed abroad, especially at Lyons, though this was possibly due more to the tendency of the book trade to specialize along regional lines rather than to any inhibiting effect of the legislation. Somewhat ironically, the first complete Latin Bible was not printed in England until well into the reign of the Protestant Queen Elizabeth.

Arundel's *Constitutions* had never, of course, been observed by the underground Lollard communities who continued to create and to circulate illicit vernacular religious literature in manuscript. Some 250 copies of Wycliffite Bibles still survive, making them the most well-represented medieval English texts we have. We can assume that these survivors represent only the tip of an iceberg, given that many more would have been destroyed by the authorities or by the ravages of time (Hudson 1988; Dove 2007: 281–306). What this body of literature, which should be held to include the other surviving Lollard works of devotion and propaganda, can tell us about the strength of the Lollard community in the 1520s is debated (Marshall 2011). Equally debatable is the extent to which the Wycliffite Bibles influenced the early Tudor Bible translators. William Tyndale and Miles Coverdale would have been foolish to associate their versions openly with the products of a movement so long synonymous with civil rebellion, even if there were such an association.

There was in any case a more important difference between the earlier and the Tudor translations which effectively sweeps the path clear of any telltale trail of breadcrumbs. The Wycliffite Bibles, for all their perceived heterodoxy, were translations from the Vulgate. This was the most commonly used Latin version of the Bible in the medieval West (hence the name *Biblia vulgata*, or 'common Bible') which was largely the work of Jerome (*d.* 420). The Vulgate would remain the touchstone of Catholic orthodoxy to the

Council of Trent and beyond. By contrast, Tyndale and Coverdale both departed from the Vulgate. Tyndale went 'back to the sources', in good humanist fashion, using the Hebrew text and Erasmus's fresh edition of the Greek New Testament. Coverdale, who seems to have lacked Greek and Hebrew, englished his Bible out of a range of German and Latin translations by Luther and other continental reformers.

By the early 1520s, there seems to have been a sense abroad in England that the tide was about to turn against the Arundel ban. This may indeed have been because, as some have suggested, the threat and perhaps the existence of Lollardy was now only a memory. Nonetheless, a more likely reason is the immense enthusiasm in England for humanism in general, and for the biblical humanism of its star proponent, Desiderius Erasmus (c.1466–1536) in particular. In the *Paraclesis* (or 'encouragement'), the preface to his 1516 edition of the New Testament in Greek, Erasmus appealed in ringing tones for the translation of the Christian Scriptures 'into all languages, so that they could be read and understood not only by Scots and Irish but also by Turks and Saracens.... Would that, as a result, the farmer sing some portion of them at the plough, the weaver hum some parts of them to the movement of the shuttle, the traveller lighten the weariness of his journey with stories of this kind. Let all the conversations of every Christian be drawn from this source' (Erasmus 1987b: 101; in this context, see also chapter 16). This appeal must have seemed pious and reasonable to many of his supporters, and would be echoed by them.

Publishers certainly seemed to sense a change of mood, and began to push at the limits of what was possible. In violation of the strict sense of the Arundel *Constitutions*, English translations of French devotional literature began to include translated biblical quotations as well. These could be extensive, so that in 1521, Wynkyn de Worde included English versions of the Ten Commandments, the Lord's Prayer, and the Beatitudes in *The myrrour of the chyrche*. Others followed his lead (Darlow, Moule, and Herbert 1968: xxxi). Certainly, when in 1523 Tyndale went to the distinguished humanist, Cuthbert Tunstall (then bishop of London), to pitch his idea for the first English translation of the Bible from the original languages, he presumably did so in the expectation of a favourable hearing from a fellow Erasmian. Instead, he was forced to leave England to continue his translation work abroad, largely clandestinely. Harried from Cologne to Worms and arriving in Antwerp around 1528, he managed to translate and publish the complete New Testament and the first half of the Old before finally meeting his end as an impenitent heretic against a stake outside Brussels (Daniell 1994).

It has been calculated that, between them, Tyndale and Coverdale were responsible for publishing fifty thousand Bibles in English by 1539 (Daniell 2003: 135). Not all of these would have reached England, and many of those that did would have been confiscated and burned. However, it must still mean that, in the decade and a half before the publication of the Great Bible, many more printed English Bibles were in circulation than there had been manuscript Wycliffite Bibles in the preceding century and a half. This was partly the triumph of technology, but it was as much a triumph of scholarship and better translation. There is a famous anecdote, found by Strype amongst Foxe's papers, about two villagers of Steeple Bumpstead in Essex who visited the reformer Robert Barnes at

Austin Friars in London, and showed him what remained of their battered Wycliffite Gospels. Barnes, sensing the opportunity of a sale, lost no time in promoting the superiority of the new translation over their old gospels. 'A point for them,' he told his visitors, 'for that they be not to be regarded toward the new printed Testament in English, for it is of more cleaner English' (Dickens and Carr 1967: 35–6). Even if this scene does not signal the moment when indigenous English Lollardy was joined by the relieving forces of pan-European Protestantism, it does illustrate how printed Bibles superseded their manuscript equivalents.

The first official initiative to translate the Bible into English was agreed by the Convocation of the Canterbury province in 1534. However, nothing had come of this by August 1537, when Cranmer, in a letter to Cromwell, despaired of seeing an English Bible from this quarter 'till a day after doomsday' (MacCulloch 1996: 196). He evidently decided to take matters into his own hands. Accompanying his letter was a forwarded copy of an English Bible translation by Thomas Matthew, which Cranmer commended to Cromwell as the best English translation available. Matthew was in fact the pseudonym of John Rogers, and the Bible was Rogers's completion of Tyndale's version. Cranmer was knocking at an open door. Cromwell authorized Matthew's Bible for a short print run before adopting it as the basis, with revisions by Miles Coverdale, of a new, official version in 1537. After an abortive attempt to print the work in Paris, the publishers, Grafton and Whitchurch, set up shop in London, and by April 1539 the first edition had been printed.

Known as the 'Great Bible' principally because of its size (fulfilling the requirement of the 1538 *Injunctions* for 'a whole Bible of the largest volume'), it has perhaps ironically attracted more attention in recent years for the iconography of its elaborate Holbeinesque title page than for 'the Word of God' which that woodcut proclaims is contained within. This depicts Henry VIII graciously distributing copies of the Bible to Cranmer and Cromwell, who in turn pass it down to the lower clerical and lay officials depicted beneath them, to a grateful populace along the bottom who respond with a 'God save the King!' or, more usually, 'Vivat Rex!'. God himself is depicted at the top border, but is nearly squeezed out of the picture by a much larger Henry VIII. It can certainly be seen as a piece of xylographic theatre, designed to impress upon the reading public the immense favour they were having done to them in being given the Scriptures in their own language. But it is perhaps more realistic to read it as an exercise in flattering the royal ego, without which the whole project of the vernacular Bible might easily have foundered. The imagery implies that what the king has given he can also take away. Even the 1538 *Injunctions* had contained a warning that access to the Bible was not to be an excuse for contentiousness, or even for individual interpretation, and 'for the next five years the regime continued to warn that royal permission to read the Bible was conditional on its being used rightly' (Bray 1994: 180; Ryrie 2002: 185). This woodcut was to an extent prophetic of developments in 1543, when that permission would be severely curtailed.

The woodcut was however more than flattery. It was also an idealized representation of Cromwellian polity in action, specifically his doctrine of royal supremacy over both church and state and his belief that through each the king exercises a distinct but related God-given ministry. This achieved early and definitive expression in the pre-amble to the Act in Restraint of Appeals of 1533: 'this realm of England is an empire … governed by one supreme head and king … unto whom a body politic, compact of all sorts and degrees of people divided in terms and by names of spiritualty and tempo-ralty, be bounden and ought to bear, next to God, a natural and humble obedience' (Bray 1994: 78). So Henry sits directly under God, whose Word he entrusts equally to the spir-itualty, in the person of the Archbishop of Canterbury, on his right hand, and to the temporalty, in the person of his chief minister, on his left. The banderoles which issue from Henry's mouth illustrate the division of labour through biblical verses: ministers of religion are to teach the Word of God ('These things command and teach', I Tim. 4:11), ministers of state are to maintain the impartial administration of justice on the basis of it ('Judge what is just…. You shall hear the small as well as the great', Deut. 1:16, 17). In the middle panels, Cranmer is shown handing the Bible to his clergy, charging them to feed their flocks (I Peter 5:2), while Cromwell gives his to men of quality (justices of the peace?), instructing them to avoid evil, do good, and pursue peace (Psalm 34:14). It is of course ironic that the biblical verses quoted on the title page of the first official English Bible are all in Latin! The bottom panel, which constitutes a continuous scene though the separation of ministries is maintained by the presence of a supporting column in the centre of the panel, envisages the dissemination of the Bible's message to the peo-ple: the pulpit on the left symbolizes the agency of the church, the prison on the right the agency of the state.[1] Read in this way, the Bible's title page can be seen as a vindication of Cromwell as much as a mollification of Henry.[2]

CRITICISM OF HENRICIAN REFORM

So far we have seen how the Henrician regime exploited the printing press as a means of promoting its message. Nonetheless, the press could equally be used as a platform for dissent, and dissent came from two directions, those who believed that the king-dom had travelled too far from Rome, and those who believed that there was still a long way to go. The doyen of the conservative literary opposition was Reginald Pole, who

[1] Many scholars read the depiction of Newgate gaol as principally a spur to obedience. See for example David Daniell's lucid exposition of this woodcut in *The Bible in English*, pp. 205–7. That is, I believe, to miss its wider meaning.

[2] The temporalty–spiritualty duality of this woodcut is an interesting, peculiarly Henrician, variation on the traditional (Lutheran) law–gospel contrast evident for instance on the title page of Coverdale's 1535 Bible, published as *Biblia. The Bible, that is, the holy Scripture of the Olde and New Testament, faithfully and truly translated out of Douche and Latyn in to Englishe* ([Cologne: E. Cervicornus & J. Soter?], 1535). Matthew's Bible, printed in Antwerp, also bore a law–gospel image on its title page. See Andrew Pettegree, 'The law and the gospel: the evolution of an evangelical pictorial theme in the Bibles of the Reformation', in Orlaith O'Sullivan (ed.), *The Bible as Book: The Reformation* (London, 2000), 123–36.

became the regime's public enemy number one. The fact that he was mostly in Italy and safe from retaliation was almost as galling as the fact that, through his Plantagenet descent, he was thought by many conservatives to have a realistic claim to the throne in the event of Henry's deposition by insurgency or invasion. Criticism from the second direction, from those frustrated that the early promise of radical reformation after Henry's heroic break with Rome had not remotely been fulfilled, had several spokesmen, especially after Cromwell's execution. One influential strand—that of the social gospel or 'commonwealth' tendency—was represented by the pseudonymous writer known as 'Roderyck Mors'. We shall consider these two authors in turn.

Pole was an unusual controversialist in that, while he wrote a very great deal, he committed very little of it to print. His reluctance was due partly to aristocratic disdain for the press, partly to a fear of having his words used against him later (Mayer 2000). His works were able to spread nonetheless in the form of manuscript letters. His most famous work, usually abbreviated to *De unitate*, was intended as a long letter addressed to King Henry himself (Pole 1538). Much of the text was a refutation of Richard Sampson's defence of the Royal Supremacy mentioned above, drawn from biblical and historical examples. However, this was no dispassionate theological treatise. Its pages are peppered with vitriolic abuse of the king, accusing him of being driven by lust in his pursuit of Anne Boleyn, and by Satan himself in his persecution of Thomas More, accusations which would frame the Catholic view of Henry for centuries (Pole 1538: 72^r–80^v, 89^r). Did Pole really mean to recall his notoriously touchy monarch to Roman obedience with such blandishments as these? It was more likely that the treatise was intended to comfort and strengthen the sinews of conservative loyalists: in 1537 Pole was appointed cardinal-legate to support the Pilgrimage of Grace, and was granted unlimited papal credit to raise as much funding as he needed (Mayer 2004). *De unitate* should perhaps be read in such a context, though there is no evidence that the manuscript was sent to any but a few Catholic nobles. Cromwell was fully aware of the threat *De unitate* constituted, and in September 1537 tried to get Pole to surrender the original manuscript of 'his frantic book' before it could do further harm.[3] Unable to persuade Pole to return from the continent, and all his assassination attempts having failed, King Henry took grim revenge upon his family in England.

If Pole exemplified how powerful an individual critic of the regime could be, 'Roderyck Mors' was an instance of a literary figure who claimed to speak for a sizeable movement. It was John Bale who revealed in the 1550s that Mors was the pseudonym of Henry Brinklow, a respectable and wealthy London cloth-merchant who created the persona of a former Franciscan now exiled abroad. Given Bale's own credentials, the identification seems reliable. Brinklow's critique of Henry's England ranges widely, from laments over rack-renting and enclosures and delays in the law courts to demands for the provision of church services in the vernacular. However, two principal complaints

---

[3] James Gairdner (ed.), *Letters and Papers, Foreign and Domestic, Henry VIII*, vol. 12, part 2, no. 620, *British History Online*.

emerge (Brinklow 1542a, 1542b). First, that the English seek their private wealth and ignore the commonwealth, specifically the needs of the poor. Secondly, that the English Reformation is incomplete: the pope's name might have been banished from England, but what use is that when his body (conservative bishops and other higher clergy) and tail (canon law and other repressive legislation) remain? Brinklow prophesies God-sent plagues if England does not repent and reform.

It is significant that Brinklow seems to have begun writing only in 1542, when Cromwell had gone and the conservative phase of Henry's reign was well under way (Ryrie 2003). Casting Henry in the role of a benevolent monarch misguided by unscrupulous traditionalist bishops 'and other the pope's shavelings', he chronicled year-by-year what he saw as a reformation in reverse. 'How shamefully haue thei and their membres in many placys of England dreuyn men from readyng the byble?' he asked. First they tried to stop the publication of the Great Bible, and to have the 'byble of Thomas mathy' (i.e. the Matthew Bible) called in. In 1540, Bishop Bonner thought fit to imprison people for reading the Bible, and in 1541 the conservatives railed against the imperfections of the official translation but did nothing to supply a better one. If such actions as these 'be not heresy to god, than what is heresy? And if it be not treason to the kyng to deface his iniunccyons, than what is treason? And agayne, if it be not theft to the comon welth, to steale from them their spirytual fode, than what is robry and theft?' Their evident intent, he alleged, was to vacillate and block until the day when the king, and with him his reform, lay safely in his grave (Brinklow 1542a: F5^v–F6^r). In the event, of course, it was Brinklow himself, and the others who longed for the establishment of a godly commonwealth, who would have to look for the death of one king and the accession of another.

CONCLUSION

The modern student of the Henrician reform is, frustratingly, in an analogous position to Henry Brinklow. Like him, we are familiar enough with the incidents and injunctions of the reign; but like him, we also stand, as it were, outside the court and are able only to guess at the mind of the regime—assuming that it had a common mind. Brinklow's own explanation, that after 1540 a reforming prince was being thwarted by traditionalists, does not convince. More likely is a scenario in which the evangelical horizon of expectations had progressively advanced, while Henry's own, more limited and idiosyncratic, vision of reform had long since been realized. However, the forces unleashed and fed by Cromwell's propaganda campaign of the 1530s did not go away. And there were many who would hail the accession of the Protestant boy king Edward as an opportunity to turn reform into reformation.

CHAPTER 3

....

RELIGIOUS CHANGE IN
THE MID-TUDOR PERIOD

....

JOHN N. KING

THE reigns of Edward VI and Mary I (1547–58) witnessed unprecedented religio-political turmoil. Not only was this brief interval unsettled by a royal minority, a disputed line of royal succession, unprecedented government by a woman, and repeated crop failures, but it witnessed violent controversy triggered by radical shifts in ecclesiastical policy that incited multiple insurrections. Radical swings in official religion were accompanied by concomitant changes in censorship, dissemination of devotional books, and attitudes concerning the validity of venerating religious images. Furthermore, the two reigns exemplify sharply contrasting responses to the use and control of the book trade as an ideological instrument and vehicle for disseminating religious propaganda.

At the death of Henry VIII (28 January 1547), Edward VI succeeded to the throne as a nine-year-old boy incapable of governing in his own right. The Protestant lords who governed England during the royal minority—first Edward Seymour, duke of Somerset and Protector of the Realm, who was the young king's eldest uncle, and second John Dudley, earl of Warwick and later duke of Northumberland—fostered a controversial programme of sweeping Protestant reform of theological doctrine, ecclesiastical practice, and worship. It veered away from the largely political Reformation countenanced by Henry VIII. Seymour and Dudley were military leaders and men of affairs who delegated religious leadership to Thomas Cranmer, archbishop of Canterbury.

Cranmer presided over the abolition of the Latin rite and promulgation of a vernacular church service in the first Book of Common Prayer, which came into use on 9 June 1549. A single slender volume in the English language thus replaced a profusion of Latin service books. Although the new prayer book rejected transubstantiation, it adhered largely to the Latin use of Sarum and retained the Mass and wearing of clerical vestments (see also chapter 1). Despite the Prayer Book Rebellion (June–August 1549), which arose in Cornwell and Devon in protest against the new English liturgy, the second Book of Common Prayer (published after 27 October 1552) responded to criticism lodged by theologians such as Martin Bucer and Peter Martyr (Pietro Martire Vermigli). This revised liturgy disestablished the Mass, forbade the wearing of chasubles, and ordered the replacement of high altars with a table placed in the naves of churches for the celebration of Holy Communion in the form of a communal meal. In order to placate militant divines associated with John Hooper, bishop of Gloucester and Worcester, the Privy Council ordered the insertion into the 1552 prayer book of the 'Black Rubric', which denied that kneeling at Communion implied transubstantiation, the Real Presence of Christ, or any form of adoration. The second prayer book was published not long after the government issued the definitive formulation of the Edwardian religious settlement, the Forty-two Articles, which deny purgatory, insist on justification by faith alone, and define the Eucharist as a commemoration of the Passion rather than a repeated sacrifice.

Everything changed with the death of Edward VI on 6 July 1553. After the failure of the duke of Northumberland's effort to engineer the succession to the throne of his daughter-in-law, Lady Jane Dudley (the 'nine-day queen'), Mary I succeeded to the throne on 19 July and thereupon undertook a thoroughgoing reversal of changes in religion introduced under her late father and brother in an attempt to restore the *status quo ante* (with the exception of the dissolution of monastic houses) as it existed before Henry VIII divorced her mother, Catherine of Aragon (see Haigh 1993: 14, *et seq.*). Queen Mary's profound Roman Catholic convictions and planned marriage to her cousin, Philip of Spain, triggered the insurrection led by Sir Thomas Wyatt the Younger (January–February 1554). During the aftermath of this rising, Lady Jane Grey and her young husband, Guildford Dudley, were decapitated, and Lady Elizabeth, heir to the throne and apparent beneficiary of this plot, was imprisoned, initially at the Tower of London and then under house arrest at Woodstock. Reformers such as Edmund Grindal (later archbishop of Canterbury) began to flee abroad by the end of 1554, although a number of prominent clerics refused to go into exile. Cardinal Reginald Pole, an heir of the Plantagenet dynasty, returned from Rome as papal legate in November 1554, prior to his replacement of Cranmer as archbishop of Canterbury. During the same month, Parliament passed a second Act of Repeal, which undid Henry VIII's schism from the Church of Rome. Further legislation restored the primacy of the Pope as the bishop of Rome. Early in 1555, reinstitution of heresy laws initiated more than three hundred burnings of Protestant martyrs, who included prominent leaders such as John Hooper, Hugh Latimer, and Thomas Cranmer, in addition to scores of humble men and women. Following the cessation of burnings at the accession of Mary's half-sister, Elizabeth, on 17 November 1558, another swing of the pendulum led to the restoration of changes in religion introduced under Henry VIII and Edward VI. Although the Edwardian religious settlement had undergone reversal under Mary I, it provided the foundation for the settlement of religion at the outset of the reign of Elizabeth I (1559) (see MacCulloch 1996: 351–3; and Loades 1979).

PROTESTANT ASCENDANCY

As Henry VIII's life drew to a close, members of the Catholic faction at court had fallen into disfavour following the disgrace of Catherine Howard, the king's fifth wife. Thomas Howard, 3rd duke of Norfolk, and his son, Henry Howard, earl of Surrey, were condemned to death. On the ground that the younger Howard had treasonously claimed that he, rather than Prince Edward, was the true heir to the throne, the Earl was decapitated little more than one week before Henry VIII died on 28 January 1547. His father survived the late king, but he was imprisoned in the Tower of London throughout the reign of Edward VI. Gardiner had recently led the Privy Council's examination of Anne Askew, a young gentlewoman on the fringes of the royal court who was burnt alive at Smithfield (16 July 1546) for her heretical denial of transubstantiation and the Mass and insistence upon expounding the Bible. This investigation constituted a thinly veiled effort to engineer the downfall of Catherine Parr, the sixth wife of Henry VIII, whose evangelical convictions were akin to those of Anne Askew. Her poignant memorial account of interrogation and torture, which stirred up a *cause célèbre*, is notable for plain-spoken eloquence and biblical language as when she inscribes her confession concerning her religious beliefs, while at Newgate: 'Written by me, Anne Askew, that neither wish death nor yet fear his [God's] might, and as merry as one that is bound towards heaven. Truth is laid in prison, Luke 21; the law is turned to wormwood, Amos 6' (King 2004: 235–6).

The publication of the two parts of the *Examinations of Anne Askew* (November 1546 and 16 January 1547) throws into sharp relief the dramatic shift in censorship soon to take place under King Edward. Although Askew's manuscripts are no longer extant, they were evidently spirited abroad into the hands of John Bale, a former Carmelite prior who had converted to Protestantism soon after England's schism from the Church of Rome. He was an extraordinarily forceful and prolific propagandist who composed evangelical plays performed by an itinerant troupe patronized of Thomas Cromwell, chief minister to Henry VIII. Bale was also a preacher, an editor and translator of religious books, and the compiler of the earliest bibliographies of books written by English writers. He fled to continental Europe after Cromwell's downfall and execution, which terminated the first, cautious phase of the English Reformation. Evangelical books were proscribed England, but Bale arranged for publication of Askew's *Examinations* in Wesel in the County of Cleves, a Rhineland port from which books could readily be smuggled across the English Channel. In order further to confuse authorities, he pays homage to William Tyndale, translator of the first printed edition of the New Testament, by designating the Hessian city of Marburg as the place of publication in a false imprint previously used to conceal the origins of tracts by Tyndale, who had been burnt alive in 1536. Bale amplified Askew's *Examinations* with a pugnacious commentary that bluntly blames her martyrdom on Bishop Gardiner and other members of the conservative faction at court.

When the regency council selected Edward Seymour to govern England as Lord Protector, he was in a position to implement a reformist programme undertaken under the leadership of Archbishop Cranmer, the leading ecclesiastic on the Privy Council. With Seymour in power as *de facto* ruler of England, royal edicts and Parliamentary legislation promoted far-reaching alteration of official religion and replacement of the Roman-rite Mass with a Protestant worship service in the vernacular. Royal Injunctions published on 31 July 1547 (*STC* 10087.5–93.7) went beyond the attack against pilgrimages and veneration of relics and religious images in the Royal Injunctions of 1536 by ordering clergy to preach officially authorized sermons from the Book of Homilies—*Certain sermons, or homilies* (1547) (*STC* 13638.5–13643)—newly issued under Cranmer's supervision. Designed for delivery week in and week out by clerics, many of them unlearned, who were not licensed to compose sermons on their own, this collection of sermons expounded the Protestant doctrines of justification by faith (*sola fide*) and Scripture alone (*sola scriptura*) and undermined the traditional doctrine of justification by good works (e.g., alms giving). In tandem with these changes in state religion, the outset of King Edward's reign was notable for spontaneous outbursts of popular iconoclasm marked by the smashing of saints' images, shattering of stained glass windows, and despoliation of shrines.

Reversing the 1543 Act for the Advancement of True Religion, which prohibited Bible reading by low-ranking individuals and women (Anne Askew had run afoul of this edict), the Edwardian Injunctions of 1547 encouraged Bible reading on the part of the laity by ordering parishes to provide copies for unrestricted reading by parishioners of the Great Bible (containing Tyndale's New Testament and translation of other parts of the Bible) and the new English translation of Erasmus's *Paraphrases of the New Testament* (2 vols, 1548–9). Henry VIII's widow, Catherine Parr, patronized the first volume. Parliament went on to abolish the chantries (endowments for celebration of perpetual Masses for the souls of the dead); to drop insistence on clerical celibacy; and to abrogate heresy statutes repugnant to Protestants, including the Act of Six Articles (1539), which imposed the death penalty on those who denied transubstantiation, clerical celibacy, and other traditional theological doctrines. These laws included notorious *De heretico comburendo* (1401), which ordered the burning of heretics. Most recently, Anne Askew had been ensnared by this legislation, which dated back to Archbishop Thomas Arundel's attack against Lollardry during the reign of Henry IV. Only a few years after priests apprehended Askew for expounding the Bible at Lincoln Minster, performance of *Lusty Juventus* (*c*.1550), a moral interlude by Richard Weaver, dramatizes a radically different time when youths and apprentices flocked to sermons and bibliocentric plays. Good Counsel confers a New Testament on Juventus (Youth) as a mark of religious conversion, but this elder soon censures him as a 'great gospeller in the mouth' (l. 1002) after Juventus is drawn into backsliding by traditional pleasures of youth (gambling and fornication), as were many of the 'gospellers' who made a hypocritical show of Bible reading under Edward VI. This play dramatizes an appeal for 'true' conversion and sincere reading and application of the scriptures (King 2004: 109–38).

Further changes under Edward VI included the renunciation of prior censorship and licensing regulations that had been imposed during the reign of Henry VIII. The removal of restraints enabled Protestant propaganda to flood London bookstalls and provincial markets. English printers produced books at a higher rate than at any point since William Caxton founded his press at Westminster (1476). Previously banned books by reformers such as Tyndale and Bale appeared in great numbers. Publication rates would fall after the Privy Council reinstituted prior censorship following the deposition of Edward Seymour as Lord Protector.[1] He was imprisoned at the Tower of London from late 1549 until early 1550. After his second downfall, he would be imprisoned from late 1551 until his execution on 22 January 1552.

By the time that copies of Askew's *Examinations* were on sale in England, they had metamorphosed from prohibited documents into books that could circulate with impunity. Alteration of copies to eradicate an attack on William Paget, Secretary of State, who remained in office after Henry VIII's death, deftly converted a piece of antiestablishmentarian propaganda into what had taken on the appearance of a pro-government book. Returning from exile not long afterward, John Bale published a number of books in response to popular resistance to recent changes in religion. They include *The apology of Johan Bale agaynste a ranke papyst* (Stephen Mierdman for John Day, 1550?), which inveighs against the survival of Roman Catholic beliefs and practices, and *An Expostulation or complaynte agaynste the blasphemyes of a franticke papyst of Hamshyre* (1552?), a vehement personal narrative concerning time that Bale spent as a rural vicar. His colorful prose recounts his effort to track down recusants who concealed forbidden religious images 'in hope of a change' in regime (that King Edward would die) (C2ʳ) and who opposed Bale's production of his own evangelical play, *A Comedy concerning Three Laws*. In the latter case, an old believer rather wittily convinced an actor in Bale's play to insert a speech insulting to the author, 'whych was to call the compiler of that Comedie, both heretike and knave, concludyng that it was a boke of most perniciouse heresie' (*Expostulation*, C3ʳ).

In contrast to Parliament's relaxation of prior restraints upon publication and extension of relative freedom of discussion to the Protestant reformers at the outset of King Edward's reign, his government effectively silenced the opposition. Catholic printers such as Robert Caly went into exile in France at roughly the same time that Protestant exiles such as Bale returned to their homeland. The new government muzzled old believers such as Richard Smith, Regius Professor of Divinity at Oxford University, who had published treatises in support of traditional Catholic doctrine including transubstantiation not long before Henry VIII's death (*STC* 22815 and 22820). Although the orthodoxy of these books was indisputable while the old king remained alive, the Privy Council ordered Smith to bring his views in line with the forthcoming publication of the Royal Injunctions by delivering a formal recantation at Paul's Cross (15 May 1547), an out-of-doors wooden pulpit where licensed preachers delivered sermons that

---

[1] Concerning mid-Tudor printing, publication, and censorship, see King 1999: 164–78. On mid-Tudor literature, see King 1982: *passim*; and Betteridge 2004: 87–173.

disseminated official doctrine to throngs that gathered in the churchyard of St Paul's Cathedral. He was ordered to repeat this sermon at Oxford on 24 July. The London and Oxford deliveries of Smith's recantation were accompanied by the burning of his newly forbidden books. Following Smith's removal from the Regius Professorship, he was made to attend lectures on 1 Corinthians delivered by his successor, Peter Martyr, who joined the cadre of foreign theologians newly invited into residence at English universities. Smith soon went into exile at the University of Louvain.

The delivery of sermons constituted spectacular occasions at Paul's Cross, the royal court, and other pulpits throughout the land. In a memorable instance, Stephen Gardiner preached before Edward VI at the Chapel Royal at Whitehall Palace on the feast of Sts Peter and Paul (29 June 1548). In defiance of the Privy Council order that Gardiner affirm the validity of religious reforms undertaken during the royal minority, the bishop took issue with preaching by royal license, public attack on the Mass, and relaxation of the vow of clerical celibacy. This dramatic confrontation resulted in Gardiner's imprisonment in the Tower of London, which brought to an end open defense of Catholic doctrine. Covert resistance continued, of course, as noted in Bale's *Expostulation* and William Baldwin's *Beware the Cat* (below).

In contrast to Gardiner's audacity, Hugh Latimer, the spiritual leader of the first generation of English evangelicals, had resigned from the pulpit because of his opposition to the Act of Six Articles. At the time of Henry VIII's death, Latimer was in prison in the Tower of London during the aftermath of the Anne Askew affair. Restored to favour, he broke eight years of silence when he preached his memorable *Sermon on the Plowers* (18 January 1548), which expounds the Parable of the Sower (Luke 8:4–15) as a figurative appeal for a humble preaching ministry. He spoke in a crypt beneath St. Paul's Cathedral where preachers delivered sermons when rainfall disrupted preaching at Paul's Cross. Latimer's delivery was notable for colloquial plainness, homely diction and figures of speech, and an anecdotal style for which he gained renown. Insistent alliteration and consonance rendered his words memorable to a socially stratified audience heavily reliant on oral instruction. These devices could confer a satirical edge on his preaching, as in his emphatic linkage of indolent loitering (wasting of time) with the lordliness of transgressive prelates who have grown rich through holding multiple benefices and farming out their pastoral duties to ill-trained clerics at the parish level: 'Therfore preache and teache, and let your ploughe be doyng, ye lordes I saye that lyve lyke loyterers, loke well to your office.... If you live idle and loyter, you do not your duetye, you folowe not youre vocacion' (108).[2]

Individual sermons and collections of sermons represented an important and profitable component of the flood of print under Edward VI. For example, Reginald Wolfe published the London and Oxford versions of Richard Smith's recantation in the form of affordable octavo copies that placed these books within the reach of ordinary citizens. In partnership with William Seres, John Day published the *Sermon on the Plowers* not long after Hugh Latimer delivered it. During their active partnership (1548–50), Day and Seres published

---

[2] 'Sermon on the Plowers', edited by J. N. King in T. Kirby et al. (eds) (2017). See also King 2014: 141–59.

treatises opposed to the doctrine of transubstantiation and Roman-rite Mass and in favour of Cranmer's step-by-step introduction of a new English service. They went on to publish successive editions of Lenten sermons that Latimer preached at the royal court in 1549. Day operated under the patronage of Catherine Brandon (née Willoughby), Dowager Duchess of Suffolk, as did Latimer, who continued to preach at her home in Lincolnshire after the preacher withdrew from court in 1550. It is worthy of note that Anne Askew acknowledged familiarity with Latimer at a time when interrogators at the Tower of London unsuccessfully pressed the prisoner to acknowledge receiving financial support from members of the circle of Catherine Parr, including Catherine Brandon and Anne Stanhope (wife of Edward Seymour) (Beilin 1996: 102, 122, 125–6). Day went on to produce multiple editions of Latimer's sermons, as gathered by the preacher's amanuensis, Augustine Bernher.

Epitomizing the role of the printing press in the defence of the government's effort to implement religious change, John Day published English Bibles (partial and complete) and books written by leading reformers at home (William Tyndale, John Frith, and Hugh Latimer) and abroad (translations of Continental theologians including John Calvin). Circumstantial evidence links him to the highest circles in the land. After all, he published books and tracts by Thomas Becon and John Hooper, who served as chaplains in the household of Protector Somerset, in addition to an influential herbal by William Turner, who served as Seymour's household physician. (All three of these Protestant ideologues had withdrawn from the book world of London following promulgation of the Act of Six Articles, Becon into concealment in the English countryside and Hooper and Turner to safe havens overseas.) Perhaps more suggestive is Day's publication of *A godly meditacion upon .20. select psalms of David* (1547) written by Anthony Cope. Its dedication as a New Year gift to Catherine Parr was clearly carried over from a presentation manuscript. Knighted under Edward VI, Cope served as the principal chamberlain in the household of the dowager queen and stepmother of the boy king.

Day's publications included books attributed to Luke Shepherd, a shadowy figure who wrote a spate of anti-Catholic satires circa 1548. They included scurrilous allegorical attacks on the Mass personified as a harlot, Mistress Missa, which overflow with obscene invective against the Church of Rome as the Whore of Babylon. When Shepherd and Day were jailed at Fleet Prison following the publication of *John Bon and Mast Person*, a satire against transubstantiation and the Mass, they obtained release on the ground that this satire had a great following at the royal court. A courtier shielded Day by presenting the Lord Mayor of London with a copy and informing him that 'there is many off them at courte'. After reading 'a little off it', the Mayor indicated that 'it was bothe pythye and mery' (Nichols 1859: 171–2). It was reported that this 'book took much at the court, and the courtiers wore it in their pockets' (Strype 1721: II, 116). The feigned naiveté and humility of a plowman named John Bon, who speaks an invented rural dialect, enforce the views of an agrarian radical who plows his field at the time of the festival of Corpus Christi, which commemorated the Last Supper and doctrine of transubstantiation. This rustic mocks this feast day (knowingly or unknowingly) by misconstruing it as a saint known as 'Copsi Cursty'. His skepticism concerning the transubstantiation of the elements of bread and wine into the body and blood of Christ is akin to his rational perception that his ox is black rather than white, when he rebuts the unlearned cleric:

> Yea but, Mast Parson, think ye it were right
> That if I desired you to make my black ox white
> And you say it is dun, and still is black in sight,
> Ye might me deem a fool for to believe so light. (King 2004: 184, lines 128–31)

Day and Seres may have timed publication of this chapbook to coincide with the 1548 ban on the festival of Corpus Christi.

Robert Crowley was another Protestant controversialist whose books had been published by John Day (1547–8). Unlike Day, who functioned as both printer and publisher, Crowley appears to have functioned solely as a publisher of books produced by other printers, including Day. Crowley's publications included his own treatises, which are notable for densely scriptural language and apocalyptic attacks on religious and social abuses, as well as writings by others. Crowley also contributed a polemical preface to editions of Tyndale's *Supper of the Lord* (1547?), probably printed by Day (*STC* 24470–1); they constitute an opening salvo in the pamphlet attack on the Roman Catholic Mass that would proliferate during 1548–9. *The confutation of the mishapen answer to the ballade, called the Abuse of yᵉ blessed sacrament of the aultare* (*STC* 6082; 1548) contains an anonymous anti-Mass ballad in addition to a versified response to a defence of the Mass by Miles Hogarde, along with Crowley's confutation in prose. Day also published Crowley's *An informacion and peticion agaynst the oppressours of the pore commons of this realme* (1548), an appeal to Parliament for reform of the commonwealth through prohibition of abuses such as hoarding, exaction of undue price increases, and rack-renting (*STC* 6086).

Crowley is best remembered for editing *The vision of Pierce Plowman* (3 edns, 1550). Although this medieval visionary allegory was theologically orthodox, the editor's commentary associates it with Lollardry and interprets it as a proto-Protestant attack on clerical corruption and monasticism that anticipated the Dissolution of the Monasteries. Informed by a gospel ethic favourable to social reform, Crowley's books attack the corruption of clerics, whose holding of multiple benefices deprived parishes of pastoral care, and landlords and merchants, whose enclosure of land, rack-renting, and hoarding of goods worsened the impoverishment of the poor. He targeted these vices in a sequence of versified estates satires: *The voyce of the last Trumpet blowen bi the seventh angel wherein are contayned 12. lessons to twelve several estates of menne* (1549), *One and thyrtye epigrams, wherein are bryefly touched so many abuses, that ought to be put away* (1550), *The way to wealth, wherein is taught a remedy for sedicion* (1550), and *Pleasure and payne, heaven and hell: remember these foure, and all shall be well* (1551). Crowley follows Tyndale and social reformers such as Simon Fish and Henry Brinkelow in claiming that Henry VIII should have distributed the property of dissolved monasteries to the poor rather than to himself and the aristocracy. Perhaps his most interesting satire is *Philargyrie of Great Britain* (1551) (King 2004: 139–51), which personifies Avarice in the form of a despotic giant, Philargyry ('lover of silver'), whose insatiable appetite for wealth is fed by Hypocrisy and Philaute ('self-love'), who serve in sequence as his chief minister. Their respective personification of Roman Catholic and Protestant doctrine mirrors Henry VIII's ecclesiastical policy. In acquiring vast wealth and property, however, Hypocrisy is indistinguishable from Philaute, who represents the Protestant elite as a successor to Roman Catholic clergy in oppressing the commonwealth.

William Baldwin is another book man whose publications typify the evangelical heyday under Edward VI. His chief claim to our attention is based upon a fanciful satire on the concealed survival of Roman Catholic ritual practices, compiled c.1553 and published in 1570 and 1584: *A marvellous hystory intitulede Beware the Cat* (King 2004: 152–65; see Ringler and Flachmann 1988). We know that Baldwin had an intimate acquaintance with John Day's printing house at Aldersgate, because he purports to retell an intricately layered set of narratives recounted by Gabriel Streamer, an apparently fictional figure, when they lodged at Day's premises. Baldwin's commentary mocks Streamer's ludicrous retelling of testimony delivered by a cat named Mouse-slayer when she defends herself before a feline tribunal against a charge of violating the feline law of promiscuity. Her picaresque wanderings enable her to provide a cat's-eye account of covert resistance to recent changes in religion on the part of her owners, who variously participate in secret celebration of the Roman Catholic Mass and other forbidden practices. In one case she recounts how she exacted excruciating revenge upon a man who succeeded in seducing a married wife through the intervention of an old woman who worships a statue of the Virgin Mary that she conceals in a closet. When the husband returns unannounced, Mouse-slayer learns that scratching the legs and buttocks of the unclothed adulterer, who has taken shelter behind a tapestry, are insufficient to expose this illicit liaison:

> But I … seeing that scratching could not move him, suddenly I leaped up and caught him by the genitals with my teeth, and bote [bit] so hard that, when he had restrained more than I thought any man could, at last he cried out, and caught me by the neck thinking to strangle me. My master, not smelling but hearing such a rat as was not wont to be about such walls, came to the cloth and lift it up, and there found this bare-arsed gentleman strangling me who had his stones in my mouth. (160, 164)

Marginal glosses supply tongue-in-check moralizations: 'All are not mice that are behind painted cloths' and 'It is justice to punish those parts that offend.' In the context of the bibliocentric reign of Edward VI, this tableau brings to life attacks on idolatry as 'spiritual adultery' found in Hosea and other prophetic books of the Old Testament (see Hos. 4:10–14).

ROMAN CATHOLIC REACTION

In the face of Queen Mary's return to the Church of Rome, William Baldwin prudently held back the manuscript of *Beware the Cat* following the death of Edward VI. His response could not have been more unlike that of John Bale, who was ever ready to take flight when the winds shifted. Yet again, Bale captured the moment of transition to a new regime. Indeed, *The vocacyon of Johan Bale* exemplifies the opposition that the Marian authorities faced from dissidents who fled abroad. This book is a vivid personal narrative concerning Bale's experience as bishop of Ossory in Ireland from the time that he was appointed by Edward VI on 16 August 1552 until his flight into exile at the king's death. Bale's chief goal as an uncompromising missionary bishop had been to replace the Roman-rite Mass with a Protestant Communion service, to stamp out the worldliness and sexual transgressions of the clergy, and to educate the laity. In addition to reporting the poisoning of the archbishop of Armagh and murder of Bale's servants for mowing hay on a Catholic feast day, his uncommonly brisk prose recounts ludicrous anecdotes about disorderly clerics who boast about being sired by an abbot, who father bastards in order to increase church offerings, and who employ Eucharistic bread as fish bait. Yet another 'had pissed in ... [a congregant's] mouth, being gaping asleep in the church after evensong'. After news of King Edward's death had belatedly reached Ireland, Bale took flight from murderous priests who were 'still conspiring my death.... I shook the dust off my feet ... according to Christ's commandment (Matthew 10), that it might stand against them as a witness at the day of judgment'. He then fell into the hands of a pirate who handed him over to his Flemish shipowners, one of whom locked him up until the payment of ransom. Attributing his deliverance to divine providence, Bale frames his narrative as a consolatory address to beleaguered Protestants in England (King 2004: 250, 252). A spurious colophon dated December 1553 mocks the papacy by assigning publication to 'Rome, before the castle of Sant' Angelo at the sign of Saint Peter'. This device conceals the identity of the printer, possibly Joos Lambrecht in Wesel, but the book boldly proclaims Bale's identity.

As typified by Bishop Bale's flight from Ireland, the death of Edward VI triggered a sea change throughout the Tudor church and state. Parliament acted swiftly to reverse changes in religion since Henry VIII's breach from the Church of Rome. A sequence of Marian proclamations, injunctions, and other measures forbade the printing and sale of works of religious controversy. Public burnings consumed Protestant heretics and the books that they wrote and read. The government succeeded at shutting down open domestic production of Protestant propaganda, indeed its chartering of the Stationer's Company in 1557 encouraged self-monitoring on the part of members of the book trade.

Book publication underwent a general contraction under Mary I, and the number of active stationers decreased dramatically. Nonetheless, it is inappropriate to conclude that the new regime ignored the printing press and its potential for generating effective propaganda. It addressed propaganda to a foreign audience, rather than domestic readers. At home Church authorities stressed the production of traditional primers, catechisms, and sermons. Although the new regime was not technically hostile to Bible translation, the total absence of vernacular Bibles printed in England indicates that the cautious views of Stephen Gardiner held sway until the Queen's death. In contrast, dozens of editions of the Bible or parts of the Bible flowed from London printing presses under Edward VI (see Loach 1986: 138–42).

It may be an overstatement to say that literary creativity dried up, but Marian publication did lack the inventiveness and stridency of the flood of satires and polemics under Edward VI. Literary publication took on a retrospective character as publishers turned to highly stylized courtly poetry and noncontroversial medieval classics, even though they avoided works by Chaucer and Langland, who were commonly misinterpreted as proto-Protestant Lollards. Dream visions and personification allegories replaced gospelling paraphrases. For example, republication of Stephen Hawes's *Pastime of Pleasure* (2 edns, 1554–5), originally published in 1509, revived the courtly taste for allegorical romance in the Burgundian manner. As groom of the chamber under Henry VII and relative by marriage to the family of Thomas More, Hawes had dedicated this work in manuscript to his master in 1506. John Heywood (another relative of the More family) brought forth *The Spider and the Flie* (1556), a prolix and all but impenetrable allegory whose composition stretched back over two decades during which he was involved in entertainment at the royal court. Personified in the unlikely guise of a maid who wields a new broom, as it were, Mary I receives praise for sweeping cobwebs and debris out of the household of England, thus rescuing the Catholic fly from predatory Protestant spiders.

A retrospective medieval flavour also pervades controversial writings by Miles Hogarde (or Huggarde), whom John Bale mocked as *Milo Porcarius*, that is, as Miles Swineherd (Bale 1557–9: II, 111). This tradesman poet (he received appointment as hosier to the Mary I) had been effectively silenced during the reign of Edward VI. The text of one of his tracts survives only because Robert Crowley quotes it in its entirety in the course of attacking Hogarde (see above). Newly returned from exile in France, Robert Caly printed Hogarde's anti-Protestant polemics including *The Assault of the Sacrament of the Altar* (King 2004: 166–78; see Martin 1981: 359–83, *passim*). Composed in 1549, it remained in manuscript until after the death of Edward VI. In dedicating this work to 'the Quenes moste excellent majestie, beyng then ladie Marie: in whiche tyme (heresie then raigning)', Hogarde reflects that its publication was forbidden until the change in regime. The allegorical meaning of this dream vision resists interpretation until an aged man symbolic of the old religion provides keys to understanding how Lady Faith is defended by the Four Gospels and St Paul, who protect the Roman-rite Mass against Protestantism personified in the form of Reason (infidelity). Recounting attacks on the doctrine of transubstantiation that date back as far as the twelfth century, this historical allegory attacks Bale, Crowley, Hooper, Rogers, and Becon for treating veneration of the elements of bread and wine as idolatry. Other books by Hogarde include *A treatise declaring howe Christ by perverse preachyng was banished out of this realme* (1554) and *The displaying of the protestantes, with a description of divers their abuses* (1556), a satire that advocates the burning of Protestants for heresy.

Unlike Baldwin and Hogarde, who held back manuscripts when they were at variance with official policy, Protestant dissidents employed different strategies in order to circumvent censorship. For example, Bale, John Day, and others resorted to false imprints in countering official resistance to the dissemination of newly heterodox books. Day assumed the pseudonym of Michael Wood of Rouen when he operated a secret printing press at Stamford in Lincolnshire under the patronage of Sir William Cooke. He was the brother-in-law of William Cecil, a protégé of Protector Somerset who had served as Secretary of State under Edward VI (Evenden 2008: 29–37). In this way Day received support from an individual linked to the highest circles of the Edwardian establishment.

Day's attribution of easily concealed octavo editions to the pseudonymous printing press of Michael Wood did not keep him out of prison, because he was confined in the Tower of London late in 1554 for having printed 'noythy' [naughty] books (Machyn 1848: 72). During the following year he was in Newgate Prison in the company of John Rogers (Foxe 1583: 1492), whose burning at Smithfield (4 February) marked the beginning of the persecution of Protestants for which Mary I's reign is notorious. The anonymous Michael Wood pamphlets include *A sovereign cordial for a christian conscience* (1554), possibly written by John Hooper or John Bale; John Hooper's *Whether christian faith maye be kepte secret in the heart, without confession therof openly* (1553, printed by Day?); *A letter sent from a banished minister unto the christian flocke in England* (1554); *A dialogue or familiar talke betwene two neighbours, concernyng the chyefest ceremonyes, suppressed in Englande, and nowe set up agayne* (1554, written by Bale?). These books offer advice and consolation to beleaguered Protestant believers who are unwilling or unable to join co-religionists who fled into exile. Of particular interest are anonymous tracts that are designed to attack or embarrass Bishop Stephen Gardiner, who served as Lord Chancellor after the accession of Mary I: *De vera obedientia* (1553), possibly translated by Bale; *An admonishion to the bishoppes of Winchester, London, and others* (1553); *An excellent and a right learned meditacion, compiled in two prayers, to be used in these daungerous daies of affliction* (1554).[3]

Unlike many evangelicals who fled abroad, William Baldwin remained in his homeland. Despite his prudence, he ran afoul of Marian authorities when he undertook a commission from John Wayland, in whose printing house Baldwin worked, to compile *A Mirror for Magistrates*. Modelled on Lydgate's *Fall of Princes*, which in turn is modelled on Boccaccio's *Falls of Illustrious Men*, the *Mirror* consists of a series of *de casibus* tragedies about past statesmen who met disastrous deaths. In revision after revision, this collection attained great popularity and exerted a powerful influence on Shakespeare's history plays and other works. Although publication of this book was completed under Elizabeth I, we must remember that it is a product of the Marian moment.

As Lord Chancellor, Stephen Gardiner suppressed publication when Wayland initially attempted to produce this book under the title of *A memorial of suche princes, as since the tyme of king Richard the seconde, have been unfortunate in the realme of England* (c.1554).[4] The tragedies in the many editions that follow Baldwin's first surviving edition, published in 1559, enable us to understand why Gardiner took this action. Other than Baldwin, only the identities of Sir Thomas Chaloner and George Ferrers are known with certainty among the multiple contributors to this book. All three authors supported religious changes introduced under Edward VI, and their sympathies are evident

---

[3] *STC* 5157, 5160.3. 10016, 10383, 11585–6, 11593, 17773.
[4] It survives only in the form of a single leaf preserved in duplicate at the British Library (*STC* 2146) and scattered title pages bound into another book printed by Wayland (*STC* 3178).

in topical allusions that they wove into some of the tragedies. One set of topical poems addresses 'admonitory exampla' to Marian authorities in an attempt to 'dissuade them from … political action to which the *Memorial* authors were opposed'. These poems reflect apprehension concerning persecution of Protestants at the outset of Mary's reign, at a time when Sir Thomas Wyatt the younger attempted to overthrow the new regime. *Memorial* authors addressed a second set of political poems to sympathizers of Protector Somerset, who regarded his downfall and execution as a catastrophic event. This is the case in Ferrers' 'Humfrey Duke of Gloucester', which provides a thinly veiled 'mirror' of the predicament of Protector Somerset, whose death is blamed on 'a conspiratorial cabal of envious opponents'. Its admonitions to magistrates to disobey regal injustice 'made the *Mirror* one of the chief repositories for elements of Edwardian commonwealth thought and Marian resistance theory in the Elizabethan and Jacobean periods' (Lucas 2009: 364–6). The ticklishness of this subject matter is apparent in the holding back of the tragedies of Duke Humphrey and his wife, Eleanor Cobham until the 1578 edition.

At about the time that Lord Chancellor Gardiner suppressed Baldwin's *Memorial*, John Foxe published the first Latin instalment of his martyrological history (Strasbourg, 1554). Like his associate, Robert Crowley, and many like-minded Protestants, he had gone into exile on the Continent, where he eventually joined John Bale in Basel. Continuing to labor on this project throughout the reign of Mary I, Foxe received many manuscript transcriptions of interrogations and dying testimonials of martyrs who had been burnt alive in England. After producing a greatly expanded Latin text in 1559, he returned to England during the same year and continued to amass material that contributed to the great bulk of the largely vernacular text of the *Book of Martyrs*,[5] first published in 1563 by John Day under the patronage of Sir William Cecil, who functioned as chief minister from the outset of the reign of Elizabeth I. During the next two decades, Foxe oversaw expansion of the text from about 1,800,000 to 3,800,000 words. The fourth and final edition published during the lifetime of Day and Foxe (1583) was the most physically imposing and complex English book to date.

The best-remembered parts the *Book of Martyrs* consist of detailed narratives concerning the lives of 'true' Christian believers who were condemned to death because of their religious convictions. These martyrologies include moving accounts of William Tyndale's career from his university days until his execution in the Low Countries and Anne Askew's refusal to remain silent concerning biblical interpretation (King 2004: 268–78; Beilin 1996). Day published this book under Queen Elizabeth, but we must recall that the narratives for which it is famous had been written for the most part during the previous reign. Foxe memorializes the Marian martyrs in a collection packed with moving accounts of the death of John Rogers, the proto-martyr who stands at the head of the list of victims of Marian heresy inquisitions; Thomas Cranmer, the all-too-human prelate who wavered in his beliefs only to reaffirm his faith, as he was consumed with flames, by first plunging into flames the hand with which he had signed his

---

[5] The popular title of Foxe 1583, et seq.

recantation; and Nicholas Ridley and aged Hugh Latimer, who were burnt alive in the same pyre in Broad Street at the University of Oxford; and many more. Having returned from Louvain, Dr Richard Smith preached from a portable pulpit before Latimer and Ridley died.

It should come as no surprise that heresy was on the mind of William Rastell as he compiled the collected English works of his uncle, Thomas More. After all More had written most of them in opposition to the spread of Protestant ideas while he served as Lord Chancellor (1529–32). Rastell had printed most of More's controversial books, but he withdrew from the book trade career following his uncle's arrest in 1534. During exile in Louvain, Rastell laid plans for the massive folio edition of *The workes of Sir Thomas More Knyght* (April 1557), to which he added a considerable amount of manuscript material. (This book is a precursor of More 1963–85.) In dedicating this book to Mary I, Rastell explains that he is motivated to enable English readers to imbibe not only More's eloquence, but also his 'confutacion of detestable heresyes', and to preserve writings that 'should in time percase [perchance] perish and utterly vanish away ... unlesse they were gathered together and printed in one whole volume'. Rastell's dedication to Mary I articulates the pious hope that this volume 'shall much helpe forwarde youre Majesties most godly purpose, in purging this youre realme of all wicked heresies . . . .' (¶ 2^{r-v}). Richard Tottel printed virtually the whole of this massive folio for a partnership that included himself, John Walley, and the Queen's Printer, John Cawood. Other than Rastell's edition of a devotional work that More wrote during imprisonment at the Tower of London, *A dialoge of comfort against tribulacion* (published by Tottel published on 18 November 1553), Raphe Robynson's translation of *Utopia* was the sole work by More printed in England since his death. Its publication in 1551, during the reign of Edward VI, is no doubt due to the absence of religious controversy in a work published during the year before Luther is said to have tacked his Ninety-Five Theses to the door of Castle Church in Wittenberg.

More's *Workes* represented a departure from the staple output of Tottel's printing press, namely law books on which students at the nearby Inns of the Court based their studies. Also in 1557, the printer again departed from his stock-in-trade in publishing *Songes and sonettes, written by the ryght honorable Lorde Henry Haward late Earle of Surrey, and other*, a collection of Tudor poetry generally known as *Tottel's Miscellany*. It is a momentous book because it introduced Italianate poetic forms such as the sonnet, terza rima, ottava rima, and so forth into the mainstream of English versification previously dominated by the blunt and irregular forms of native English poetry. The title is significant because it pays homage to the most high-ranking contributor to this collection, whose untimely death at the executioner's block had ushered in the accession of Edward VI. In actual fact, his contribution to this anthology consists of forty poems, whereas Sir Thomas Wyatt contributed more than one-third of its 271 poems, as did 'Uncertain Authors'.

William Rastell makes clear the relevance of More's *Workes* to a time when hundreds of victims were burnt alive for heresy, but what about *Tottel's Miscellany*? Its multitude of love poems has no apparent link to the anthology's contemporary historical moment.

Nonetheless, more than one scholar has commented on the remarkable correspondence between the production of this anthology in the printing quarter of London and the burning of martyrs only a short walk away. Poems in this collection are notable for their non-controversial character. Having been published initially under Mary I, no obstacle blocked their continued publication in this book after a return to Protestantism under Elizabeth I. If Tottel's collaborators were, as seems likely, students at the Inns of the Court, who constituted the book-buying clientele of Tottel's establishment, they are notable both for their overt disinterest in the burning of martyrs and their apparent disinclination to espouse heretical ideas that might lead to an untimely death at Smithfield. Only in the verbal texture of the collection do we encounter concern with martyrdom, but it is transferred figuratively to the suffering of lovers whose hearts are inflamed with passion: 'Critically, to be a martyr to love ... means not to be tortured and burned as a religious martyr' (Warner 2013: 1–2, 160–1, 183–5). Such martyrdom constituted an antidote to the suffering of those whose bodies were consumed by flames.

English Protestants regarded the death of Mary I and accession of Elizabeth I as a providential deliverance. As evangelical exiles returned from continental Europe, the new queen's government restored changes in religion instituted during the minority of Edward VI. The presence of Sir William Cecil close to the centre of power under both Edward and Elizabeth typifies this continuity. The religious settlement of 1559 structured public worship upon readings from the Elizabethan Book of Common Prayer (based on the 1552 prayer book), Book of Homilies, and Great Bible. The Thirty-Nine Articles of Religion effectively restored the Forty-two Articles implemented under Edward VI. Edwardian publications that fell under ban during the reign of Queen Mary came back into print. Previously illicit writings, including William Baldwin's *Beware the Cat* and the *Mirror for Magistrates*, were published for the first time. Although John Day's business had fallen into ruin during the Marian regime, it attained great prosperity due to patronage from William Cecil that enabled Day to re-establish his printing establishment and publish lucrative books, such as his two-volume edition of the sermons of Hugh Latimer and the *Book of Martyrs*, which emerged largely from manuscripts written under Mary I and the Latin martyrology that John Foxe had published during his continental exile. Developments of this kind enable us to recognize that the Elizabethan age, at least at its outset, entailed a return to what had gone before, namely the religious settlement under Edward VI, as much as it functioned as a new beginning (see King 1982: 425–43).

CHAPTER 4

THE ELIZABETHAN CHURCH OF ENGLAND AND THE ORIGINS OF ANGLICANISM

TORRANCE KIRBY

THE identity of '*ecclesia anglicana*' has, broadly speaking, three major phases of meaning. The first phase, traceable back to the earliest years of Christianity in Britain, employs the term in a neutral geographical sense; at the time of the Reformation a second phase emerges with the sense of provincial autonomy; a third phase associated with the mid-nineteenth-century expansion of the global Anglican communion identifies the term 'Anglican' with a distinctive ecclesiology.

Ecclesia Anglicana—the 'English Church'—designates in the first instance a geographically specific area, namely two provinces of the Western Church with their two respective sees of Canterbury and York, located in 'Anglia'. In his correspondence early in the seventh century with the missionary bishop Augustine of Canterbury, first metropolitan of the former see, Pope Gregory the Great refers to the Church of the Angles, *Ecclesia Anglorum*. During this early phase of the expansion of Latin Christendom, as with the term *Ecclesia Gallicana*, there are no specific or distinctive ecclesiological associations attending this designation. Anselm of Laon, Archbishop of Canterbury at the end of the eleventh century, speaks similarly of '*Ecclesia Angliæ*', while the precise term '*Ecclesia Anglicana*' as a geographical division of the Western Church is common usage from the middle of the twelfth century onward. The *Magna Carta* (1215) commences with the affirmation '*quod Anglicana Ecclesia libera sit*' (Davis 1989; *Magna Carta Libertatum* [the 'great charter of freedoms'], article 1). Like his father Henry II before him, who had clashed with Thomas à Becket on the matter of royal governance of the Church, King John saw the appointment of the Archbishop of Canterbury as his prerogative. Following Innocent III's Interdict forbidding public worship in 1208 and his excommunication of John in 1209, the king eventually backed down and accepted the Pope's nominee to Canterbury, Stephen Langton, who had been 'freely elected' by English monks in exile. The independence of the Church from royal control is strongly affirmed in the opening article of *Magna Carta*.[1] The 'Anglican Church' of the thirteenth century looked to the papacy as the ultimate source of ecclesiastical jurisdiction and as the guarantor of her corporate liberty and independence of royal interference.

By the middle of the fourteenth century, however, the English Parliament moved to impose limits on papal jurisdiction with the passage of the Statutes of Provisors (1350) and Praemunire (1393). The former refers to 'the holy Church of England' (*'la seinte eglise d'Engleterre'*) as having been founded 'by the sovereigns and the nobles to inform them and the people of the law of God and also to make hospitalities, alms, and other works of charity'. In this statutory account, an ecclesiological distinctiveness and national particularity of the English Church begins to acquire some purchase. Yet in the context of the Great Schism and with the Conciliar movement making headway, the assertion of the regional autonomy of churches against a centralized papal monarchy was not a stance which in any way set England outside the mainstream of the Western Church.

The Act of Supremacy of 1534, reaffirmed by statute under Edward VI and Elizabeth I, brought about a truly decisive ecclesiological shift in meaning. The Henrician legislation marks the legal and constitutional commencement of the Reformation in England with its declaration that Henry VIII as sovereign was 'the only supreme head on earth of the Church of England called *Anglicana Ecclesia*' (26 Henry VIII, cap. 1, *Statutes of the Realm*, III.492).[2] This was a decisive watershed in the history of the English Church, and marks a radically new phase by attaching a significance of provincial autonomy to the term: the Catholic Church in England no longer recognized the ecclesiastical jurisdiction of the papacy. In the previous year, 1533, Henry had been excommunicated by Pope Clement VII for his divorce of Katherine of Aragon and his marriage to Anne Boleyn. Papal exercise of spiritual jurisdiction in such circumstances presupposed the concept of the so-called 'plenitude of power' (*plenitudo potestatis*), whereby spiritual and temporal authority were bound together *dispositively*, that is, in a hierarchical relation. Clement's excommunication of Henry cut the thread of hierarchy which linked the king—and through him, his entire realm—to the sacramentally interconnected framework that was Christendom. Conversely, by virtue of his adamant defiance of papal jurisdiction,

---

[1] *Magna Carta*, article 1 (Davis 1989): 'In the first place [I, John] have granted to God, and by this our present charter confirmed for us and our heirs for ever that the English church (*ecclesia anglicana*) shall be free, and shall have its rights undiminished and its liberties unimpaired; and it is our will that it be thus observed; which is evident from the fact that, before the quarrel between us and our barons began, we willingly and spontaneously granted and by our charter confirmed the freedom of elections which is reckoned most important and very essential to the English church (*ecclesia anglicana*), and obtained confirmation of it from the lord Pope Innocent III; the which we will observe and we wish our heirs to observe it in good faith forever.'

[2] 'Albeit, the King's Majesty justly and rightfully is and oweth to be the supreme head of the Church of England, and so is recognised by the clergy of this realm in their Convocations; yet nevertheless for corroboration and confirmation thereof, and for increase of virtue in Christ's religion within this realm of England, and to repress and extirp all errors, heresies and other enormities and abuses heretofore used in the same, Be it enacted by authority of this present Parliament that the King our sovereign lord, his heirs and successors kings of this realm, shall be taken, accepted and reputed the only supreme head in earth of the Church of England called *Anglicana Ecclesia*.'

Henry confirmed this momentous breaking of the bond between the temporal and spiritual orders. The excommunication of Henry may be viewed as an archetypical instance of the dissolution of the received medieval sense of the cosmos as a coherent, unified, and continuous order of spiritual/eternal and external/temporal realms and powers—a process Max Weber defined as the 'disenchantment of the world' (1946: 139, 155; see Thomas 1997). It may also be viewed as signalling what could be described as an ecclesiological revolution—the meaning of the term 'Anglicana Ecclesia' would never be quite the same again.

Through their respective actions, Clement and Henry together shattered the deepest assumptions—the ontological horizon of Christendom, so to speak—which had defined the way in which Catholic Christians in England had, until then, lived out their religious lives. Through a simple sacramental act and through a determined assertion of political will to ignore that act, Clement and Henry together launched a sequence of events—the English Reformation—which would result in the eventual annulment of 'the sacramental' itself as the governing hermeneutical framework of the English nation's religious identity and hence of the very definition of the nature of the Church which had been assumed for almost a millennium. *Ecclesia anglicana* was now autocephalous—an autonomous province—with the prince as head. By the end of the sixteenth century, the full hermeneutical, ecclesiological, and sacramental significance of this newfound political independence of the English Church would be worked out theologically by Thomas Cranmer, Martin Bucer, Peter Martyr Vermigli, John Jewel, John Whitgift, and Richard Hooker. The English Reformation thus defines the 'second' principal meaning of 'Anglicana ecclesia', the sense of the national Church as an autonomous, autocephalous province of the Western Church. At the same time, this ecclesiology of national autonomy was shared by the other Protestant Churches of northern Europe—by the Lutherans in various principalities of the Empire and in Denmark, and by the Calvinists in Geneva, Heidelberg, and the Netherlands—and was not thought to be in any exclusive way a peculiar characteristic of the English Church more than any other.

A third use of the term 'Anglican' refers to a theological, or more precisely to an *ecclesiological* distinctiveness. The first usage of the term in this substantive theological sense does not occur until well into the seventeenth century. The term 'l'Anglicanisme' is employed pejoratively in a Catholic pamphlet of 1616, but this is more a reflection of our second sense of the term, referring to provincial autonomy (see A. Milton 1995: 379). It is not until the nineteenth century, however, that Anglicanism comes to be identified explicitly with a distinctive theological position, a confessional identity neither completely Catholic nor Protestant, although whether the Church of England actually has any truly 'distinctive' teachings continues to be a matter of heated dispute. On the one hand, Henry McAdoo, Stephen Neil, and Michael Ramsey have argued that the Church of England is 'catholic' and consequently has no properly 'distinctive' or confessional doctrine (Neill 1958; Ramsey 1945; and McAdoo 1965: 1, cited by Avis 2007: 39). On the other side, Rowan Williams (2004: 1), Stephen Sykes (1995: ch. 6), and Paul Avis (2007: 39–55) argue the contrary, that there are indeed distinctively 'Anglican' positions on doctrine, order, and worship. This question of doctrinal and institutional distinctiveness marks the third principal usage of the term *Ecclesia Anglicana*, namely as a label of distinctive confessional identity (or not, as the case may be!). It is chiefly the second and third senses that we propose to address in the following discussion.

DOCTRINE, ORDER, AND WORSHIP IN THE REIGN OF ELIZABETH

The principal formularies of the doctrine, order, and worship of the Church of England all attained their mature form during the early years of the reign of Elizabeth: the *Articles of Religion* (1563/71) commonly called the 'Thirty-Nine Articles' (Kirby 2009), the Book of Common Prayer (1549, revised 1552, 1559, and 1662),[3] and the *Ordinal* (1549, revised 1552, 1662)—that is, the 'Form and Manner of making, ordaining, and consecrating Bishops, Priests, and Deacons'.[4] In their respective fashion all three formularies emphasize the commitment of the English Church to the ecclesiology confessed in the three ancient creeds of Christendom—viz. the Apostle's, Constantinopolitan-Nicene, and Athanasian creeds. According to the ancient ecclesiology, the Church is 'one, holy, catholic, and apostolic'. Precisely how the ecclesiology of the creeds is to be interpreted is of great moment to Anglican identity.

While confessing one and the same doctrinal matter with the Roman Catholic and Orthodox Churches, since the Reformation the Church of England has parted company in its basic interpretation of what the unity, sanctity, catholicity, and apostolicity of the visible church actually consist in. The Canons claim that the Church of England '*belongs* to the true and apostolic Church of Christ' but they do not insist on equating *ecclesia anglicana* with the Christ's universal 'church militant here in earth'.[5] From the early Middle Ages, the Roman Church on the other hand had tended to identify communion with the bishop of Rome as one and the same as membership of the universal church confessed in the creeds. Since the Second Vatican Council such absolute claims have been tempered to a degree, although the recent doctrinal statement *Dominus Jesus* (2000) authorized by John Paul II denies other communions the status of full membership in the 'church catholic'. Anglicans since Richard Hooker (1554–1600) have maintained that the Church of England 'participates' in the universal church of

---

[3] Thomas Cranmer's Book of Common Prayer was first put into general liturgical use on Whitsunday, 1549 and subsequently went through three important later revisions in 1552, 1559, and 1662. The version of 1662 continues to have statutory authority under the Act of Uniformity as definitive of the faith and order of the Church of England.

[4] The first version of the Ordinal composed by Thomas Cranmer and published in 1549 under the title *The forme and maner of makyng and consecratyng of archebishoppes, bishoppes, priestes and deacons* ([London]: Richardus Grafton, 1549). The ordinal was revised in 1552 and again in 1662. It was customarily published as an addendum to the Prayerbook.

[5] This expression leads off the Prayer of Intercession in the 1662 Order of the Holy Communion.

Christ as do others including the Reformed and Lutheran Churches, the Methodists, Congregationalists, and the Old Catholics of the Union of Utrecht. According to Robert Runcie, former Archbishop of Canterbury, speaking at the Lambeth Conference of 1988 (13), 'Anglicanism has a radically provisional character' (Anglican Consultative Council 1988: 13). What is the ecclesiological source of this provisionality? What is that renders the Church partial, provisional, and incomplete but, at the same time, allows it to claim that it is 'one, holy, catholic, and apostolic'? In Anglican ecclesiology (as compared with both the Roman and the Orthodox Churches) there is a radically different account of the relation between the empirical church and the universal church, a difference owing entirely to the emergence of a new hermeneutics (in actuality, as we shall see, the restoration of an ancient patristic hermeneutics) together with the rise of a radically altered 'moral ontology', what might be called the ontology of modernity. The English reformers of the sixteenth century achieved an ecclesiological revolution based upon this new hermeneutics. In order to appreciate fully the manner in which the empirical or phenomenal church (the visible church militant) came to be understood as both standing apart from and united with the eschatologically perfect or mystical church of the creed (the invisible church triumphant), it is necessary to explore the hermeneutics which made this revolution in ecclesiological thinking possible.

JOHN JEWEL AND THE HERMENEUTICS OF THE ELIZABETHAN CHURCH

The first systematic theological exposition of the new ecclesiology of the reformed Church of England was undertaken by John Jewel in his famous 'Challenge Sermon' of 1559 preached at Paul's Cross shortly after the accession of Elizabeth I and later published in expanded form under the title *Apologia ecclesiæ anglicanæ* (Jewel 1562). [An English translation by Lady Anne Bacon, wife of Privy Councillor Sir Nicholas Bacon, appeared not long afterwards: see Bacon 1564.] Jewel called into question the doctrine and order of the Church of Rome and issued the challenge whether 'any learned man of our adversaries be able to bring any one sufficient sentence out of any old doctor or father, or out of any general council, or out of the holy Scripture, or any one example out of the primitive Church for the space of six hundred years after Christ' in their support. Jewel identifies the authority of the early Church Fathers and of Augustine in particular as the touchstone of doctrinal and ecclesiological orthodoxy. In subsequent polemical exchanges with Thomas Harding, a leader among the community of English Catholic exiles in Douai, and in the elaboration of his challenge both in the *Apology* and in his later massive *Defence of the Apology* (1567), Jewel set out a detailed and systematic theological exposition of the principles underpinning the 'reformed' Church of England—the autonomous *ecclesia anglicana*. Jewel accounts for the faith of the English Church in accordance with the principles of a distinctly Augustinian hermeneutics. The identity of the newly 'reformed' English Church is essentially established on the foundation of this self-conscious return to patristic hermeneutics.

For Jewel, the key difference between the ecclesiologies of the Church of England and the Church of Rome was one of hermeneutical method. Drawing upon Augustine's *De doctrina Christiana*, Jewel succinctly summarizes the key principle which would be definitive of Anglican hermeneutics, ecclesiology, and sacramental teaching for centuries to come: 'we put a difference between the sign and the thing itself that is signified.'[6] Augustinian clarity of distinction between the visible sign and the mystical reality signified constitutes the hallmark of Jewel's reformed hermeneutics and is of altogether pivotal significance for the Anglican reformers' thinking on the Eucharist as well as on a multitude of other questions concerning the faith, order, and worship of the Church (see Augustine, *de bono Perseverantiae*, 2.13). In the Eucharist the preparation of the mind for the reception of Communion is all important, for the 'figure' (*signum*) of the thing is not to be confused with that which it represents, the referent or the 'thing itself' (*res significata*). ' "How shall I hold him," saith Augustine, "which is absent? How shall I reach my hand up to heaven, to lay hold upon him that sitteth there?" He answereth, "Reach thither thy faith, and then thou hast laid hold on him. Faith had in the sacraments," saith Augustine, "doth justify, and not the sacraments" ' (Jewel 1562: 64). Augustine's dictum '*In sacramentis videndum est, non quid sint, sed quid significent*' is quoted by Jewel on numerous occasions (1845: I, 453, 759; II, 1122, qtd. Augustine, *Contra Maximinum*, III.22). Jewel summarizes the Augustinian foundation of his reformed account of sacramental Communion: 'That we be thus in Christ, and Christ in us, requireth not any corporal or local being, as in things natural. We are in Christ sitting in heaven, and Christ sitting in heaven is here in us, not by a natural, but by a spiritual mean of being. St. Augustine saith: "*postquam ex mortuis resurrexit, et ascendit ad Patrem, est in nobis per Spiritum*" ' (1845: I, 477; Augustine, *De Trinitate*, Bk IV).

The hermeneutics of the distinction between sign and thing takes on a deeper Christological significance for Jewel when he cautions against so maintaining the divine nature of Christ as to take away the truth of his bodily human nature. He quotes Augustine's proto-Chalcedonian formulation: 'We confess there are in Christ two substances or natures; the one of the godhead, the other of the manhood; the one of the creator, the other of the creature; which substances notwithstanding are not confused, but united, and in one selfsame person inseparable, and remaining evermore in their own properties' (Jewel 1845: I, 482; Augustine, *De Verb. Dom. in Evang sec. Johan.*, lviii). To confuse sign and thing is tantamount to overthrowing this most crucial formula of patristic orthodoxy. Jewel's Augustinian hermeneutic of 'sign and thing', and the classically 'reformed' account of sacramental presence built upon that hermeneutic,

---

[6] Jewel quotes *De doctrina Christiana* 2.1.1: 'A sign is a thing that, besides the sight itself which it offereth unto the senses, causeth of itself some other certain thing to come into knowledge.' In applying this hermeneutic to the interpretation of sacramental presence, Jewel invokes Augustine's treatment of the '*sursum corda*' ('Lift up your hearts') as the archetype of the distinction between signs and things.

reverberate throughout his critique of private masses, the adoration of images, and prayers in a strange tongue, as well as in his affirmation of Communion under both kinds, his definition of the jurisdiction of bishops, and finally in his defence of the ecclesiastical supremacy of princes.

It is no exaggeration to state that Jewel launched the hermeneutics—and thus by consequence also the ecclesiology of the English Church—on a revolutionary new course. The great achievement of his *Apologia ecclesiæ anglicanæ* is to link together all of the distinctive characteristics of the faith, order, and worship of the reformed Church of England as they had emerged piece by piece during the previous three decades under Henry VIII, Edward VI, and most recently under Elizabeth, and to show their coherence in terms of a fully self-conscious restoration of an Augustinian hermeneutic of *'signum et res'*. The ecclesiological coherence of the reformed and autonomous *ecclesia anglicana* under Elizabeth was, in effect, largely the achievement of scriptural and sacramental hermeneutics—a conservative achievement in one important respect, namely that Jewel's new approach was a 'return' to the authority of the Fathers of the early Church.

The differing logics of Tridentine and Jewel's reformed ecclesiology are perhaps most plainly evident in their distinct accounts of sacramental theology. Whereas the traditional doctrine of the Mass and transubstantiation tended to collapse the distinction between signifier and signified in their assertion of an *objectified* 'real presence', the liturgy of the Book of Common Prayer reasserts (in tune with an Augustinian hermeneutic) a much sharper distinction between the two. According to Jewel's critique of transubstantiation in his *Apologia*, this traditional hermeneutic of sacramental presence fails to distinguish sufficiently between *signum* and *res*. This distinction between a literal and figurative interpretation of sacramental 'presence' is of crucial ontological significance for the emergence of a distinctively reformed Anglican ecclesiology, foremost that is for the reinterpretation of the relation between the empirical, phenomenal reality of the visible church and the church universal. The new hermeneutics, in short, gives rise to a redefinition of catholicity (as well as of the unity, sanctity, and apostolicity) of the universal church. The hermeneutic of 'presence' associated with the doctrine of transubstantiation, on the other hand, requires as its ecclesiological corollary a close identification of the phenomenal church with the church universal. Like the consecrated host, the visible, empirical, incarnational aspect of the church is the outward showing in the world of the universal, divine reality of the supernatural community.

The liturgy of the thoroughly reformed revision of the Book of Common Prayer of 1552 shifts the focus of 'presence' very decisively away from the elements of the sacrament in the words of distribution. Whereas the formula of the old Roman rite (retained in the vernacular in Cranmer's first version of the Prayerbook of 1549) asserts an externalized real presence—'*Accipite et comedite, Hoc est corpus meum*' (Take, eat; this is my body)—the revised words of 1552 transfer the *locus* of presence to the inner, subjective experience of the worshipper—'Take and eat this in remembrance that Christ died for thee, and feed on him in thy heart by faith, with thanksgiving' (for a full and most interesting discussion of Cranmer's doctrine of presence, see Rosendale 2007). Consequently, 'presence' is interpreted in the Anglican liturgy as a 'figural' or 'conceptual' synthesis of word and elements performed in the subjective forum of the minds of worshippers, and thus inseparable from reception of the host.

It is interesting in this connection to note that in the Book of Common Prayer of 1552, as well as in the subsequent revisions of 1559 and 1662, the administration of the Communion occurs at precisely the stage in the liturgy at which the elevation of the host had occurred in the old Mass—i.e. the moment of transubstantiation— thus serving to underline most vividly the difference between the two divergent liturgical accounts of presence. The chasm between sign and signified is thus bridged not through the external theurgical action of the priest, but rather in an inner, subjective act of remembrance on the part of the worshippers (priest, of course, included). As Timothy Rosendale points out, 'the internalization of this figural sacrament is thus a necessarily interpretative act; though it takes place in a communal context, it ultimately requires a highly individual mode of understanding the elements as metaphors whose effectuality is dependent on faithful personal reading' (2007: 96). The Elizabethan revision of the Book of Common Prayer in 1559 altered the strictly memorialist (i.e. sacramentarian) words of administration of the 1552 liturgy by combining the words 'This is my body...' with 'Do this in remembrance of me.' While it is certainly the case that assertion of the 'figural sense' of the Eucharist, and hence of the distinction between signifier and signified, is a key concern of the Protestant reformers, in his distinctive and highly original reading, Rosendale argues that the Elizabethan liturgy of 1559 emphasizes even more strongly the importance of the role of the individual subject in interpreting the meaning of the sacrament. One might well be tempted to regard the strict memorialism of 1552 as setting the benchmark of the high reformed position. Nonetheless, by defusing the clarity of 1552, the Elizabethan compromise of combining realist and memorialist words of administration serves, in effect, to extend even further the latitude of the worshipper's hermeneutical responsibility. Since this liturgical revision becomes the hermeneutical touchstone of the entire subsequent history of *anglicana ecclesia*, its significance can hardly be overestimated. For Rosendale:

> the *Book of Common Prayer* in both form and content holds in tension two radically different discourses, out of which it endeavours to construct a productive textual synthesis. It discursively constructs the Christian nation characterized centrally by order even as it elevates individual discretion over that order. Its theology simultaneously legitimates and undermines its political discourse of autonomous hierarchical authority ... The BCP officially instituted the individual as a primary component of religion, without abrogating the normative claims of the hierarchical socio-politico-ecclesiastical order that had traditionally been the sole determinant of religious affairs. (2007: 111)

Thus, in a nutshell, Rosendale draws out the link between worship and ecclesiology.

The *Articles of Religion* (1571)

The faith of the Church of England and of the Anglican Communion as defined in the initial five titles of the *Articles of Religion* (1571) is grounded on the affirmation of traditional Trinitarian and Christological orthodoxy established by the first four General Councils of the early Church—Nicaea (325), Constantinople (381), Ephesus (431), and Chalcedon (451). Belonging to the one true universal Church of Christ is thus a matter of doctrinal commitment to these essentials of patristic orthodoxy: adherence to unity of the Godhead in three persons, the true divinity and complete humanity joined together in the one person of Christ, and the procession of the Holy Ghost from both the Father and the Son. Jewel's definition of catholicity as a 'return' to patristic orthodoxy is shared by John Calvin who sought in his *Institutio christianæ religionis* (1559) to 'restore the face of the ancient catholic church'. There is not much disagreement, if any at all, between the magisterial reformers and the Council of Trent on the substantive doctrines of the Trinity and Chalcedonian Christology. However, the sixth article 'Of the sufficiency of the Holy Scriptures for salvation', marks out a distinctive departure for the reformed Church of England from the medieval and Tridentine positions. The orthodox faith is said to be 'uniquely revealed' in Scripture which effectively establishes Scripture alone (*sola scriptura*) as the *regula fidei*—or, as the *Lambeth Quadrilateral* of 1888 states the matter, 'Holy Scripture is the rule and ultimate standard of the faith' (Wright 1988). Thus, the authority of the Church's traditional doctrinal formulæ is clearly subordinated to the ultimate authority of Scripture alone such that 'whatsoever is not read therein, nor may be proved thereby, is not to be required of any man, that it should be believed as an article of the Faith, or be thought requisite or necessary to salvation' (*Articles of Religion*, article VI).

Moreover, according to the *Articles of Religion*, the three ancient creeds derive their magisterial authority from being demonstrably consistent with Scripture. The Nicene, the Athanasian, and the Apostles' Creeds 'ought thoroughly to be received and believed: for they may be proved by most certain warrants of holy Scripture' (*Articles of Religion*, article VIII). The persuasion that saving doctrine is 'uniquely revealed' in the Holy Scriptures clearly distinguishes Scripture and tradition from each other, and subordinates the authority of the latter with respect to the former in a manner closely analogous to the clarity of the distinction and subordination of *signum* to *res*, and of the distinction and subordination of the empirical and phenomenal church to the mystical and universal church to which it points. In its formulation of the relation between Scripture and tradition the *Articles of Religion* set out to distinguish between human and divine authority. Just as *signum* must be neither confused with *res* nor separated from that to which it points, so also tradition and Scripture must be kept distinct and yet united. 'Holy Scripture containeth all things necessary to salvation.' At the same time, the *Articles* do not allow that Scripture alone, independently of tradition, is the source of binding rules and precedents which should determine the shape of Church polity and worship, a position urged by the more radical, biblicizing Protestants for whom the assertion of the sole authority of Scripture led to the annulment of tradition. At the end of the sixteenth century Richard Hooker states this fundamental principle with utmost clarity:

> Two opinions therefore there are concerning sufficiencie of holy scripture, each extreamly opposite vnto the other, & bothe repugnant vnto truth. The schooles of Rome teach scripture to be so vnsufficient, as if, except traditions were added, it did not conteine all reuealed and supernaturall truth, which absolutely is necessary for the children of men in this life to know that they may in the next be saued. Others iustly condemning this opinion, growe likewise vnto a dangerous extremitie, as if scripture did not only containe all thinges in that kinde necessary, but all thinges simply, and in such sorte that to doe any thing according to any other lawe, were not onely vnnecessary, but euen opposite vnto saluation, vnlawfull and sinfull. (Hooker 1593: III.8)

The question of the relative authority of Scripture and tradition hinges on the 'hypostatic' logic of the hermeneutical model, viz. to clearly distinguish (but not to separate) the natural, the human, and merely practical from the supernatural, mystical, and the revealed. Articles IX through XIX address the critical matter of sixteenth-century soteriological debate: original sin, the freedom of the will, grace, faith and justification, works, and predestination. Articles XX to XXV treat ecclesiology, XXVI to XXX the sacraments, XXXI to XXXVI discipline, worship, and ceremonies, and XXXVII through the final article address the office of civil magistracy and the political duty of Christians.

Unlike the essential doctrines of the Trinity and the Incarnation, matters of Church order come closest to expressing a distinctively Anglican confessional identity. The Ordinal of 1549 (revised in 1552) prescribes '*The forme and maner of makyng and consecratyng of bishoppes, priestes and deacons*' and thus affirms the ancient structure of a 'three-fold' ministry. Other continental Churches of the Reformed and Lutheran traditions saw fit to abolish such distinctions of order. Anglicans have traditionally regarded the three-fold ministry as a sign of catholicity and apostolicity. The Preface to the *Ordinal* begins with the assertion that 'it is evident unto all men diligently reading holy Scripture and ancient Authors, that from the Apostles' time there have been these Orders of Ministers in Christ's Church; Bishops, Priests, and Deacons'. By retaining these orders of ministry shared with the Roman Catholic, Orthodox, and some of the Lutheran and Reformed Churches—for example, the Lutheran Church of Sweden and the Reformed Church of Hungary—the Elizabethan Church of England maintained an outward institutional continuity at the time of the Reformation with the ancient Church. At the same time, however, in its ecclesiological teaching it refused to insist that such a form of ministerial polity belonged to the 'esse' of the Church. Article XIX defines the essential marks of the visible church—the so-called '*notæ ecclesiæ*'—as follows:

> The visible Church of Christ is a congregation of faithful men, in the which the pure Word of God is preached, and the Sacraments be duly ministered according to Christ's ordinance in all those things that of necessity are requisite to the same.

The three-fold ministry was later urged by some to be a third 'essential' mark of cathol-icity, apostolicity, and therefore of unity with the Catholic Church, but Anglican theory has never been quite willing to pass critical judgement on the validity of the ministries of non-episcopally ordained clergy. The three-fold ministry belongs to ecclesiastical tradition and as such is affirmed as 'not repugnant to the Word of God'. Yet traditions 'may be changed according to the diversity of countries, times, and men's manners, so that nothing be ordained against God's Word' (article XXXIV). The three-fold orders of ministry are conducive to the well-being (*bene esse*) of the Church, but are intrinsically *adiaphora* and therefore not definitive of the Church's essence. Once again we can recog-nize in this traditional account of order the hermeneutical paradigm. What is definitive of the polity of the Church of England belongs to the Church in its external or phenom-enal aspect, and therefore is not to be taken as an intrinsic mark of either catholicity or apostolicity which expresses its doctrinal commitments. In the nineteenth century, romantic Tractarians of the Oxford Movement preferred to portray Anglican polity as having more in common with Roman Catholicism and the Orthodox, and were apt to 'unchurch' the non-episcopal Protestant Churches.

Another key defining characteristic of the order of the Elizabethan Church of England is the principle of provincial autonomy which derives in large part from the Royal Supremacy. While the three-fold hierarchy of ministers was retained at the Reformation, these were nonetheless detached from their subordination to the papacy from the time of Henry VIII's appropriation of the title 'Supreme Head of the Church' in the Act of Supremacy of 1534, reaffirmed by Parliament in 1559 (1 Elizabeth I, cap. 1). According to the statute, the supreme hierarch so far as external political jurisdiction over the Church is concerned is none other than the civil sovereign. This doctrine con-tinues to hold immense ecclesiological significance for Anglicanism. Article XXXVII attributes to the king:

> the chief power in this Realm of England, and other his dominions, unto whom the chief Government of all Estates of this Realm, whether they be Ecclesiastical or Civil, in all causes doth appertain, and is not, nor ought to be, subject to any foreign juris-diction … we give not to our Princes the ministering either of god's Word, or of the Sacraments … but that only prerogative, which we see to have been given always to all godly Princes in holy Scriptures by God himself; that is, that they should rule all estates and degrees committed to their charge.

This is without doubt one of the more distinctive features of the reformed Church of England, although shared in varying forms by quite a number of the other Churches of the Reformation. When Anglicans insisted historically that they were not innovating in faith or order, they did not mean that the English Church altogether lacked distinguish-ing features vis-à-vis either Rome or the continental reformed Churches. Certainly they did not they mean that Anglicanism was indistinguishable from the unreformed Church of Rome or from the Anabaptists or other radical Protestants. As far as having the sovereign as head of the Church is concerned, plainly there is a major distinctive mark vis-à-vis other ecclesial bodies. The forty-odd Churches of the contemporary Anglican Communion share a mutual recognition of provincial autonomy, the inheritance of the ecclesiology of the autocephalous national Church. In this respect, the Church of England can be said to have produced offspring in her own image. What, then, is the ecclesiological significance of royal headship? Returning to the hermeneutical framework, it is precisely owing to the Augustinian hypostatic model that a sharp distinction is made between the Church as a mystical, supernatural, divine body, on the one hand, and the Church as a phenomenal, historical, and human-political body on the other. Over against this hypostatic ecclesiological model of Protestant reform can be placed the alternative model of the *lex divinitatis* which arranges the spiritual and temporal powers in hierarchical relation. The hierarchical premise of medieval ecclesiology was famously formulated in the bull *Unam Sanctam* promulgated by Pope Boniface VIII at the Roman Council of October 1302 during his dispute with Philip the Fair, King of France:

> One sword ought to be subordinated to the other and temporal authority subjected to spiritual power. For, since the Apostle said: 'There is no power except from God and those that are, are ordained of God' [Rom 13:1–2], they would not be ordained if one sword were not subordinated to the other and if the inferior one, as it were, were not led upwards by the other. For according to the Blessed Dionysius, it is the law of divinity (*lex divinitatis*) that the lowest things are led to the highest by intermediaries. Then, according to the order of the universe, all things are not led back equally and immediately, but the lowest by the intermediary, and the inferior by the superior … Therefore if the terrestrial power err, it will be judged by the spiritual power. (*Reg. Vatic.*, L, fol. 387)[7]

According to the logic of the *lex divinitatis*—traced back to the mystical theology of Pseudo-Dionyius the Areopagite—there is commensurability between spiritual and temporal power which allows for hierarchical mediation between them. The Augustinian logic of the Protestant reformers, on the other, radically hypostasizes spiritual and temporal powers in such a manner as to render hierarchical mediation between them impossible. Just as the *signum* and *res* are to be kept clearly distinct in the theology of sacramental presence, so in the sphere of political theology the Augustinian hermeneutic requires that power be immediately derived from the divine source without the mediation of a hierarch in the invisible realm of the *civitas Dei*. In the external and phenomenal realm of the *civitas terrena*, on the other hand, the Church is an empirical and therefore human political society such that jurisdiction over both it and the commonwealth can be united in the person of the prince or civil magistrate. Closely following Augustine's hermeneutic, the ecclesiology of Royal Supremacy acknowledges

---

[7] The Bull was formally issued on 18 November of the same year. See also *Extravagantes Decretales Communes*, I.8.1, 'De Maioritate et Obedientia', *Corpus Iuris Canonici*, edited by Emil Friedberg (Leipzig: Bernhard Tauchnitz, 1879; repr. Graz: Akademische Druk-u. Verlagsanstalt, 1955, 1959) vol. 2, col. 1245–6. An English translation of the Bull is available in Tierney 1988: 188–9.

Christocentric *immediacy* in the relation between soul and God in the internal spiritual sphere, while in the external political sphere, the logic of hierarchical subordination lends stability to the visible Church through the three-fold ministry as well as to the institutions of the Christian commonwealth, both in subordination to the godly Prince. The ecclesiology of the Church of England's institution of Royal Supremacy is a significant species of political Augustinianism.

Provincial autonomy of the Churches in the modern Anglican Communion is an extension of this Elizabethan ecclesiology, even though none of the provinces other than the Church of England is formally established. The chief point is that each embodies the principle of autocephalous autonomy. There is no universal or monarchical Primate, and the relation among member Churches of the Communion is essentially conciliar. Some historians have noted that the Anglican Communion exemplifies the ecclesiology of the fourteenth and fifteenth centuries. This model of conciliarity is also reflected in the internal constitutions of the ecclesiastical provinces where governance is vested jointly in bishop and representatives of both the lower clergy and the laity. All three 'estates' of the Church have constitutional voices while the bishops remain guardians of doctrine and worship. Another corollary of provincial autonomy is that the Archbishop of Canterbury has no authority whatever to govern the Anglican Communion—indeed the 'Communion' properly speaking is not a Church, but rather a conciliar fellowship of Churches. The bonds connecting one to another are not those of jurisdiction. Councils, moreover, do not claim infallibility: 'as the Church of Jerusalem, Alexandria, and Antioch, have erred; so also the Church of Rome hath erred, not only in their living and manner of Ceremonies, but also in matters of faith' (article XIX). The phenomenal Church (the *signum*) is not to be conflated with the true Church universal (the *res*), but nonetheless through preaching the Word and administering the Sacraments of the Eucharist and Baptism the former enables the worshipper's 'participation' of the latter.

CATHOLIC AND REFORMED

From the time of the Reformation of the sixteenth century, *ecclesia anglicana* has understood herself to be both 'Catholic and Reformed', although the actual interpretation of this identity has undergone diverse and not always mutually consistent formulations. In the sixteenth century, catholicity was associated foremost with the Church's embrace of the key tenets of Patristic Christological and Trinitarian orthodoxy. On this substance of primary doctrine, as observed already, Hooker, Calvin, and the Council of Trent could all agree. As we have also seen, the definition of ecclesiological catholicity was, however, quite another matter. Catholicity according to the moral ontology embodied in the *lex divinitatis* was not at all the same thing as catholicity according the reformed hermeneutic of *signum* and *res* nor, for that matter, were the sanctity, apostolicity, and unity of the Church. In effect, the reformed Church of England, in company with other magisterial Protestant Churches, redefined the creedal 'marks' along distinctly Augustinian lines. The continuation of adherence to the three ancient creeds, acceptance of the *consensus patrum* within the limits set by the primacy of Scripture, the ancient three-fold ministry, the cathedral foundations, the outward splendour of worship—all are taken to be marks of catholicity, but a catholicity radically redefined in terms of this underlying hermeneutical presupposition. The hermeneutic itself, as we have attempted to show, was thoroughly reformed in scope. Thus, the retention of hierarchical orders of ministry is framed *within* the Protestant assumption of a universal priesthood. Ministry of word and sacraments in a congregation required 'lawful calling' by 'publick authority' (article XXIII). Moreover, it was not the function of the priesthood to offer sacrifice—Christ himself who suffered death upon the cross 'made there (by his one oblation of himself once offered) a full, perfect, sufficient sacrifice, oblation, and satisfaction, for the sins of the whole world'.[8] Until the mid-nineteenth century there was broad consensus that the Church of England was a reformed Church with her acknowledgement of the Scripture as *regula fidei* (article VI), the doctrine of justification by faith alone (article XI), and affirmation of the role of the laity in the governance of the Church, namely both sovereign as Head and Parliament, by whose authority the *Articles of Religion*, the *Ordinal*, and the Book of Common Prayer were (and still are) promulgated. Lay participation in church governance was also affirmed locally at the parish level in the canonically defined office of the church wardens (see *Reformatio legum ecclesiasticarum* 1571: Title XX).

The Elizabethan period was profoundly influential in defining the identity of the reformed Church of England. With the revision of the Book of Common Prayer in 1559 the liturgy acquired the shape it would retain for the next four hundred years, with some minor adjustments in 1662. The *Thirty-Nine Articles of Religion* agreed by the Convocation of Canterbury in 1563 and subsequently approved by Parliament and ratified by Queen Elizabeth I in 1571 established the parameters of doctrine. Although attempts to bring about a reform of the Canon Law eventually foundered, the institutional customs and practices of the later sixteenth century became normative for centuries to come (see Kirby 2007). In the learned scholarship of such Elizabethan divines as John Jewel, John Whitgift, Richard Bancroft, and Richard Hooker the theological character of the modern English Church was set on course. Sermon culture, as evidenced by the institution of the outdoor pulpit at Paul's Cross, contributed greatly to the shaping of England's early modern religious and political identity. In all of these respects the later sixteenth century proved an altogether decisive period in the confessional and constitutional formation of the Church of England.

---

[8] See the 'Prayer of Consecration' in the Order of the Holy Communion in the Book of Common Prayer (1662).

CHAPTER 5

EARLY STUART CONTROVERSY

Church, State, and the Sacred

CHARLES W. A. PRIOR

BETWEEN 1603 and 1642, England declined from a period of relative peace to a condition of civil war. Or so runs the standard historical account. According to this story, James VI and I lived up to his reputation as peacemaker: the Somerset House conference ended the Nine Years' War; the Hampton Court Conference settled the Church of England; and the Union of the Crowns brought the often restive northern kingdom of Scotland into the moderate fold of England. This all ended in 1625, when Charles I came to power. Where the father favoured peace, the son prosecuted reckless military campaigns against Spain; the moderate harmony of the Jacobean Church was shattered by the ceremonialism and rough discipline of the Laudians; and the British peace of 1603 unravelled in St Giles Cathedral, where the Bishops' Wars began in 1638. When Parliament returned in 1640, Charles found himself branded as the Arminian architect of a conspiracy against the 'ameliorating bond' of Jacobean Calvinism (Russell 1990).

The role of religion in this version of events has been the subject of sustained scholarly attention and debate (Prior 2013b). However, the overwhelming focus has been on theology. As Patrick Collinson (1982) and Nicholas Tyacke (1987a) argued, the majority of English Protestants identified themselves with a Calvinist theology, rooted in predestinarian piety. It was this feature of English doctrinal thinking that helped to accommodate a range of Protestant groups within an idea of the Church, if not always the Church itself. Under Charles I, this compromise was briskly undermined by a vogue for the ideas of Arminius, a Dutch theologian who challenged aspects of Calvin's theology of grace; it so happened that the main exponents of Arminianism were also prominent figures in the Caroline ecclesiastical hierarchy (Russell 1991). This interpretation of religious conflict coincided with a wider historiographical reconsideration of the causes, nature, and course of the English Civil War. The so-called 'revisionists' were united in their belief that Whig and Marxist accounts that described the conflict as a 'puritan revolution' could not be squared with powerful evidence of ideological disputes, and so they sought to place religion closer to the centre of political conflict (Prior and Burgess 2011: 1–25).

While there were debates within revisionism concerning the exact nature of the ideological tensions within early Stuart politics, there was broad agreement that religion featured prominently among them (Burgess 1992; Sommerville 1999). One seminal interpretation described the English civil wars as the last of Europe's 'wars of religion' (Morrill 1984). This suggestion served as the point of departure for a number of studies of the politics of religion in the early Stuart period, many of which have moved beyond a narrowly theological approach to religion and toward an examination of the manner in which the Church was bound up with law, politics, and the state (Prior 2005a, 2013b: 27–8; Collins 2005). This approach, in turn, has been shaped by two broader developments. First, scholars have returned to the Reformation as a *process* that transformed the structures of politics within the realm and, second, they have begun to trace the effects of this process as it was captured in the literature of religious controversy (Rose 2011; Shagan 2011; Prior 2012).

This chapter seeks to provide an overview of these two related developments, and argues that religious controversy should be seen as an important conduit for the discussion of complex matters of politics, law, and the nature of the state. This does not mean that religion is drained of its spiritual content and transformed into the servant of politics, but rather that debate over ecclesiology cut across a range of topics that reveal the fluidity of the boundary between church and state. In fact, it was the precise location of that boundary—and whether it existed at all—that is perhaps the foundational issue in early Stuart religious controversy. Not only did this question exert a powerful influence on internal debates on religion and politics, but it also shaped similar (and often interlinked) arguments about the politics of religion within the British kingdoms and the wider colonial Atlantic world, a world whose origins were shaped by a backdrop of confessional conflict in Britain and Europe (Prior 2013a).

THE POLITICS OF REFORMATION CONTROVERSY

According to a classic study of the English Reformation, the 'one definite thing' that could be said about it was that it 'was an act of state' (Powicke 1941: 1). The Reformation was an act of state in the sense that it was effected not by a groundswell of Protestant fervour, but by the key instrument of political authority in England, the common law. The foundational document in this sense is the Henrician Act in Restraint of Appeals (24 Hen. VIII, *c.*12, 1533), which negated the legal jurisdiction of the Church of Rome within England by pointing to a historically rooted concept of royal supremacy:

> Where by divers sundry old authentic histories and chronicles it is manifestly declared and expressed that this realm of England is an empire, and so hath been

accepted in the world, governed by one supreme head and king having the dignity and royal estate of the imperial crown of the same, unto whom a body politic, compact of all sorts and degrees of people divided in terms and by names of spirituality and temporality, be bounden and owe to bear to God a natural and humble obedience. (Elton 1982: 353)

Here, the ecclesiastical power of the Crown is portrayed as grounded in the history of the realm, therefore forming part of the body of custom on which rested the authority of the common law (Pocock 1987: ch. 2). Second, the realm is defined as an 'empire', by which is meant an independently sovereign state, recognized as such by other such states. However, matters grow more complex when this state is described as a 'body politic' (suggesting unity) that is nevertheless 'divided' into apparently distinct spiritual and temporal spheres. Theoretically, this meant that both spheres operated under the unified sovereignty of the Crown, but the practical question of how this relationship would work was something that framed religious controversy for the next 150 years.

In fact, a number of historians see the Act of the Appeals as a vital clue to understanding the problem of church and state in post-Reformation England. One influential view is that the Act created 'enduring problems' that shaped political thought for the remainder of the early modern period (Pocock 1983: 381). More recently, Ethan Shagan has argued that reformation in England produced a 'fundamental restructuring of power within the realm' while Jacqueline Rose has demonstrated how tensions within the Tudor formulation of church and state exerted a profound influence on ecclesiological debate up to the Revolution of 1688 (Shagan 2003: 29; Rose 2011: ch. 2). These wider perspectives have provided a means to situate the early Stuart period within a longer process of Reformation, rather than acting as a mere staging ground for civil war. Moreover, there is now an identifiable set of interpretations that approach the conflict of the 1640s from the point of view of a fundamental debate about the place of the Church in the realm (Pocock 1985a: 287; Russell 2000; Orr 2002; Prior 2012). The phrase 'Reformation politics' is now used to describe the more or less unbroken line of argument about church and state that furnishes one of the major continuities in early modern British history.

The texture of Reformation politics in the early Stuart period was directly influenced by the statutes that framed the religious settlement in the reigns of Henry VIII and Elizabeth I (see also chapters 2 and 4). In particular, the Act of Appeals focused attention on a number of key issues, namely, how the royal ecclesiastical supremacy could be reconciled with the laws of the realm, and how the body politic of spiritual and temporal people was to be defined and related to existing notions of the realm as a legal commonwealth.

In the first instance, the Act grounded the ecclesiastical power of the Crown within the depths of English history, and subsequent talk of the supremacy cited the examples of 'Godly' kings both real and imagined (Heal 2005). Henry himself was fond of making parallels between himself and Old Testament kings, and later sovereigns would continue this evocation of their historic predecessors (Nicholson 1988). Indeed, the Bible contained both precedent and precept: in the book of Isaiah, kings (and queens) are described as 'nursing fathers' of the Church, ensuring the proper pursuit of worship, and correcting heresy where they find it. This power of discipline was codified in subsequent statutes. The Henrician Act of Supremacy (1534) declared the king's power to 'reform, order, correct' heresies and abuses, while its Elizabethan successor noted that the power of 'reformation, order and correction' was 'annexed to the imperial crown of this realm' (Elton 1982: 365, 374). The important point here is that the power of kings was legitimized by both Scripture and statute; the divinely instituted status of 'nursing father' was made an explicitly *legal* power by virtue of being declared by statute.

This raised the complex question of the jurisdictional relationship between civil and ecclesiastical law. A major impetus of the Act of Appeals was to ensure that English subjects were not compelled to appeal to a foreign court for decisions in 'causes testamentary', that is, in legal cases concerning the disposition of property. Instead, cases of property fell within the jurisdiction of the common law, and thus a major premise of the argument against papal power in England derived from the view that the laws and customs of the realm were free from foreign interference. Hence the Act decried the fact that English subjects (and the king himself) suffered delays of justice because they were obliged to appeal to courts 'so far out of this realm' (Elton 1982: 354). From the point of view of law, therefore, the Act of Appeals put an end to a theory of dualism, whereby the powers of kings and priests ran in separate channels (Collins 2005: 15–18; Watt 1988).

Yet it is nevertheless the case that the English Reformation created a dualism of another kind. For while the statutes declared the Crown to be the principal agent of religious discipline, the mechanisms by which this discipline was enforced remained firmly in the hands of churchmen. The most notorious of these was the Court of High Commission, established by letters patent under Elizabeth I (Elton 1982: 222). This meant that the Commission derived its power exclusively from the Royal Supremacy, which raised the question of where it sat in relation to the other courts of the realm. This question was most keenly explored when the powers of the Commission were exercised in ways that seemed to trespass on the legal rights of subjects under the common law. A frequently discussed example of this occurred in 1583, and led lawyers and clerics into a debate about the relationship of church and civil courts (Shagan 2004). The official line was that both fell under the ambit of the Royal Supremacy. As Richard Cosin put it:

> Now seeing all jurisdiction and authoritie in this Realme, as well *ecclesiasticall* as *temporall* was ever in *right*, but now is also (justly) acknowledged, and is *in fact* united and incorporated unto the *crowne* of this Realme: therefore inquire, whether upon the premises it may not be probably said (albeit not according to the usual speech) that a judgement duely given by the *jurisdiction ecclesiasticall* is given *by the law of the land.* (Cosin 1591: Pt 1, 103–4)

In Cosin's view, the Royal Supremacy was a *de facto* power that united spiritual and civil law within a single sovereignty. Yet the fact that he had to devote several hundred pages to arguing this point reveals that, for some, the Royal Supremacy as defined by the Reformation settlement created legal powers that actually threatened the liberties of subjects (Brooks 2008: 97–101; Prior 2012: 26).

The antidote to the revival of a medieval condition of dualism was to suggest that the church and state overlapped, and did so in a complementary fashion. This was accomplished by framing the concept of the Royal Supremacy in terms of *imperium* and *dominium*—that is, the right to rule, and the place where that rule was exercised (MacMillan 2006). It is important to note that this was explicitly imperial language, which helps to explain why the Act of Appeals referred to the realm as an 'empire' (Pocock 2005: 136–8). Moreover, the Acts of Supremacy (1534, 1559) forged explicit links between Church, realm, and sovereignty; the first defined the Church in national terms, as an '*Anglicana Ecclesia*', while the second declared that the sovereignty of the 'imperial crown' applied equally throughout 'all dominions' (Elton 1982: 364, 372).

This elision was in place at an early point in the Reformation process, and forms a vital component of contemporary understandings of the relationship of church and state. Writing in the mid-1530s, Stephen Gardiner noted that 'I see no cause why any man should be offended that the kinge is called the headde of churche of England [*sic*] rather than the headde of the realme of Englande'. He continued by noting that the word 'Realme ... comprehendeth all subjectes of the kings dominions', and that the 'churche of Englande' comprised the 'same sortes of people at this daye that are comprised in this word realme' (Gardiner 1968: 93). The link between church and realm was initially forged as a foil to papal claims to legal jurisdiction within England, but it gradually became a central part of the logic of the Royal Supremacy (Rose 2011: 27–60). Notwithstanding, historians of religion have expressed severe reservations about any attempt to trace the roots of a 'bland and consensual' Anglicanism in this period (Lake 2006a: 9–10). However, such warnings go too far in the opposite direction: the identity of the Church 'of the realm' was a key component of a wider cluster of concepts that formed the basis of how the Church 'by law established' was understood (Prior 2012: ch. 2).

Indeed, it is vital to grasp the complexities of contemporary opinion on this issue, since the Reformation took place within a culture that understood its internal politics in legal and customary terms (Cromartie 2006). The pressing political question was how the historic understanding of the realm as a legal commonwealth was affected by a doctrine of royal supremacy over a newly constituted 'ecclesiastical politie' (Prior 2015). There were two broad positions on this topic. The first emphasized the legalistic character of reformation, from which it followed that the 'state' was supreme over the church; this view was rooted in theories of medieval constitutionalism, and has informed influential discussions of historical and conceptual foundations of the 'modern' state (Brooks 2008: 97–8; Harding 1994; Skinner 1978). A second strand of argument approached the doctrine of ecclesiastical supremacy as fluid and contestable: was supremacy held by the king alone, king in Parliament, or by the clergy sitting in consistories and convocation? Instead of a positive legal power, rule over and within the Church was approached from the perspectives furnished by a range of historical precedents, ranging from the ancient practices of the Hebrews, to the Apostolic Church, the Christianized Roman Empire, and finally to the various 'national' Churches established during the transmission of

Christianity throughout the post-Roman world, including England (Goffart 1988; Kidd 1999: ch. 4).

These larger themes of politics, history, and sovereignty fed into a process of state-formation, a process that affected not only the internal politics of England, but also relations between the 'British' kingdoms and colonies that constituted the anglophone Protestant world of the early seventeenth century (Pocock 2005: chs 4–6). It is also the case that these themes underpin a wide range of controversies over religion, the majority of which are concerned with the nature and extent of human authority over the Church. The remainder of this chapter takes up this question by drawing out some of the prominent political themes that emerged in a succession of controversies between 1603 and 1642. The focus is on debates within English Protestantism, which is necessary given the limits of space. Catholics represented a lingering state within the state, and their challenges to the legitimacy of the Royal Supremacy forms another facet of the broader problem of church and state (Questier 1996; Tutino 2007). The outbreak of the Civil War was defined by a crisis in church *and* state, and to fully appreciate this we need to recapture the texture of contemporary understandings of how these two bodies related to one another as elements of post-Reformation Protestant thought.

A CHURCH OF THE REALMS?
JACOBEAN CONTROVERSIES

When James VI of Scotland assumed the throne of England in 1603, the 'union' of the kingdoms was presented as 'the basis of the preservation of all spiritual and temporal felicity' (Gordon 1604: 1). The king had long and often bitter experience of religious dispute in his native kingdom, where Presbyterians advocated a 'two kingdoms' theory of ecclesiastical governance. Power over the Kirk was held by the General Assembly, whereas the king sought to tame the Kirk by placing it under the rule of bishops, who he regarded as natural allies of monarchy (Lee 1974; Mullan 1986). English bishops and spokesmen of the established Church were keenly aware of this, and offered support to the king by waging a polemical assault on Presbyterian discipline. Preaching a sermon at Paul's Cross in February 1588, Richard Bancroft branded the Presbyterians as monarchomachs, who 'under the pretence of their presbyteries, they trod upon his sceptre, and labored to establish an ecclesiastical tyranny of an infinite jurisdiction, such as neither the law of God or man could tollerate' (Bancroft 1588–9: 74).

The point is that James's own ecclesiological views complemented those of the Church hierarchy in England. One key fissure in Elizabethan Protestantism concerned the liturgy and ceremonies of the Church, along with the related issue of strict clerical discipline overseen by bishops who seemed to have assumed to themselves the royal power to 'reform, order and correct' (Milward 1977: 25–33, 35–8). The Thirty-Nine Articles stipulated that worship was to be conducted 'according to Christ's ordinance', but they also stated that worship would be conducted only by men who were 'lawfully called' by others who possessed 'public authoritie' (Church of England 1581: sig. B2^r, B3^r). This suggested that there were orders of the clergy, some of whom held power to depose 'evil ministers' (Article 26). However, the most serious ecclesiological issue concerned the tension between the 'ordinances' of God and the 'traditions of the Church'. As Article 34 expressed it:

> Every particular or national Church, hath authoritie to ordeine, change, and abolish ceremonies or rites of the Church ordained only by mans authoritie, so that all things be done to edifying. (Church of England 1581: C1^v)

The term of art for this position is 'adiaphora', or 'things indifferent': this referred to rites and ceremonies introduced into daily worship merely for the purposes of encouraging reverence in the congregation. It would become a mainstay of English ecclesiology in the early Stuart period, and was the means by which the clerical hierarchy claimed power over the Church and its often disaffected population of ministers.

On his arrival in England, the new king was presented with a petition signed by a thousand ministers, requesting 'reformation of certain ceremonies and abuses in the church'. The authors of the petition were careful to state that they sought neither a 'popular parity' in the Church, nor did they aim 'at the dissolution of the state ecclesiastical'— both charges frequently levelled at the Presbyterians of Scotland. Instead, they appealed to the king to redress 'abuses' in the Church, and chiefly 'the common burden of human rites and ceremonies' (Kenyon 1986: 177). The principal targets were a set of rites—the signing of the cross in baptism, the use of rings in marriage, the wearing of cap and surplice, bowing at the name of Jesus—that were quotidian, and which would be obvious to all members of the congregation. The main target of this criticism was the Prayer Book that mandated these rituals, along with the measures by which conformity to them was policed and enforced: discipline and the disparity of the clerical hierarchy were criticized at length, as was the practice whereby non-conforming ministers were 'suspended, silenced, disgraced, imprisoned, for men's traditions' (Kenyon 1986: 118, 119).

True to his reputation as a seeker of conciliation, James ordered that the matter of the Church be discussed at an ecclesiastical conference at Hampton Court Palace in January of 1604 (Patterson 1997: ch. 2). In the meantime, a sharp reply to the 'humble petition' of the ministers came from the clerics of the two universities of Oxford and Cambridge, who declared that the English Church reflected 'the Purity of Religion, perpetually supported by one Uniform most ancient kind of commendable Church government; and the plenty of al manner of good learning, abundantly derived from the Wel-springs thereof, into all the parts, both of the Church and Commonwealth' (University of Oxford 1603: ¶2). Here, a Church defined by 'purity' of worship, and overseen by a learned body of clerics trained at the universities is presented as a support to the 'supreme civil state' (University of Oxford 1603: 30). This was music to the king's ears, and the Hampton Court conference was less an open exchange of views than it was a demonstration that the Church 'by law established' would remain as it stood.

Following a Convocation of the Church in May 1604, a new set of Canons was published and these provided a lengthy and explicit defence of the Church of England. They reiterated the controversial practices of the ring in marriage and the signing of the cross in baptism. An accompanying royal proclamation warned that anyone claiming that 'the form of God's worship in the Church of England, established by law, and contained in the Book of Common Prayer and Administration of Sacraments' was in any way corrupt or 'unlawful' was liable to immediate excommunication (Larkin and Hughes 1973: I, 249–50). All ministers were further required to swear an oath attached to three specific articles, affirming the Royal Supremacy, episcopal government, and the soundness of the disputed Prayer Book and Thirty-Nine Articles. The newly appointed Archbishop of Canterbury, Richard Bancroft, confessed in a letter that he had not previously desired 'any severe course' but concluded that such a course was now vital to preserve the stability and unity of the Church (Prior 2005a: 87–8).

The ensuing debate on the Canons raised important issues of legal and scriptural principle. The court of High Commission was charged with the administration of clerical discipline, which took the form of permanent suspension from office, or 'deprivation'. The court of Star Chamber lodged an opinion which held that the Commission was not exercising any 'new power', but rather discharging the 'Ancient power' (Carte fol. 59 n. 427). However, a group of ministers disagreed, and put the case clearly in a pamphlet—printed abroad—that offered a systematic refutation of the Canons of 1604. On deprivation, they argued when any subject sought to 'deliver justice in any cause to any of the King's subjects ... within the King's dominions' then by implication they denied the Parliament 'to have full power to allow and disallow lawes in all causes' (Babington 1605: 30–1). Another pamphlet argued that 'canon law' was 'contrary to Magna Carta' and the 'law of nations', noting that benefices were 'free holds' and thus a kind of property that was guaranteed by the common law (Anon. 1606a: 6–7). These examples can be multiplied, but what is clear is that the Canons of 1604 provoked a debate on the relationship between the Church and the common law (Prior 2005a: 89–112).

For many writers, the root of the problem lay in clerical power. This was a complaint of long standing in the English Church, where the episcopal order was condemned as a popish remnant, a threat to the liberties of subjects, and as a usurpation of the Royal Supremacy. What tied this all together was law, as was made clear by an anonymous attack on the powers of convocation:

> I know but two sorts of law in this kingdom, the one customary or common law as we call it, the other the statute or parliament law. But the canons and constitutions of the convocation house are neither common nor statute law, therefore no laws of England, nor of the kingdom. (Bray 1998: lvii)

Nicholas Fuller, a lawyer who defended Nonconformists before the High Commission, argued that the means to 'continue a perfect agreement' between church and commonwealth lay in the 'right distribution' of jurisdiction between church and state (Fuller 1607: 2). Where Fuller argued that the common law was always supreme, others maintained that the close relationship of church and state necessitated 'proceedings … which are merely civil, or mixt sometimes of both' (Tichborne 1609: 8). That is to say, given that the church was itself so intimately tied to the state, then it followed that proceedings of the law would reflect a similar intermingling of spiritual and civil elements.

Conscious of the fact that the common law relied on notions of custom and precedent, defenders of episcopacy adopted similar tactics to defend the order of bishops. For example, George Downame appealed to the 'monuments of Antiquitie' in order to demonstrate that, in the earliest years of the Church, the Apostles themselves acted in an episcopal capacity, 'All which while, bishops were not so needful; the Apostles providing for the necessity of those Churches'. The continuity of this ministry was provided by 'successors' to whom the Apostles 'committed the government of the Churches' (Downame 1608: 69–70). If the function of bishops was established by the Apostles, the argument ran, then surely it was a divine ordinance carried out by the first true Christians, 'of God's ordinance, and as it were from the Lord's hands' (Downame 1608: 93). In a much larger book, written to address a number of criticisms of his original defence of episcopacy, Downame expanded on this point:

> Though in respect of the first institution, there is a small difference between an Apostolical and Divine ordinance, because what was ordained by the Apostles proceeded from God (in which sense and no other, I doe hold the Episcopal function to be a divine Ordinance, I meane in respect of the first institution), yet in respect of perpetuitie, difference by some is made between those things which be *Divini*, and those which be *Apostolicii jurii*: the former, in their understanding being generally, perpetually and immutably necessary, the latter not so. (Downame 1611: bk 4, ch. 6, 139)

Here, Downame circumvented arguments that held that bishops were merely an example of human ordinance imposed upon the Church, by noting that while the Church was not bound to follow *everything* done by the Apostles, in this one respect it must, given that episcopacy was of the 'first institution'.

Further sources of controversy were the ceremonies stipulated by the Canons of 1604, and once again arguments turned on the permissibility of 'devices' imposed by governors of the Church. This practice was flatly condemned by a group of ministers who had refused to 'subscribe' the oath attached to the Canons. Scripture, they argued:

> delivered an exact Platforme of policie for the House of God which is the Church, and yet the same be alterable according to the will of Princes, and the forms of civill government there where Religion is established, we hold it as a wrong done to the Magestie of God, that his councils should … give place to Men's devices and that order should be forced to yield to Humane Ordinance. (Anon. 1606b: 39)

The broader implication here was that the creation of a Church 'by law established' represented a similar intrusion of civil government on the Church, which opponents of the Canons regarded as a spiritual, as opposed to political, association. The response to this was to suggest that some measure of order and government was necessary, lest the Church be toppled by 'papists' or undermined by sectaries and internal disputes.

Thomas Sparke, a chaplain to the bishop of Lincoln, would have known the virulent debates over the Canons which took place in that diocese; ministers there had argued that while the king was 'supreme governor', he 'may not appoynt to the Church, what rites and orders he thinks good' (Anon. 1605: 44). By contrast, Sparke argued that the king was a 'nurse father' to the Church, and thus had a duty to ensure its 'orderly government' and to this end 'prescribe ordinances' that were 'consonant to the general rules' found in the scriptures (Sparke 1607: 8). In this formulation, the governor of the Church had a 'libertie' to establish 'accidental and changeable' rites and ceremonies, that is, in the realm of 'things indifferent' (Sparke 1607: 11).

As it evolved, the debate on the ceremonial practice stipulated by the Canons turned to increasingly fine-grained discussions of the Scripture as an historical text. For example, the issue of kneeling at Communion was approached from the point of view of custom. Jesus and his Apostles reclined in the Roman fashion at the last supper, and in so doing simply adopted the customs of the country and the time (Gordon 1612: F2^r). However, this did not amount to a divine ordinance, for if it did then Christians themselves would recline at Communion. Rather, the gestural aspects of rites and ceremonies were matters of custom, and all the better if they were aids to reverence and edification. Stephen Denison, writing in 1621, took this argument to great lengths, noting that at the Last Supper, Christ washed the feet of His companions, and that the meal itself took place in an upper chamber, around a single table, at which the participants either sat or reclined. The present Church, he concluded 'observeth no such ceremonies', and this revealed that if Christ had ordained anything, it was the use of custom (Denison 1621: 72).

The final arena of controversy in the Jacobean period concerned relations between the Churches drawn together by the Union of the Crowns in 1603. Here the issues were concerned with both ecclesiology and constitutionalism, for the Kirk was itself the product of a Parliamentary reformation at a time when that Parliament was wholly sovereign over Scottish affairs (Lyall 1980). After 1603, the Kirk found itself under direct pressure to align itself with English ecclesiological practice, and there is little doubt that James's previous experience with Presbyterian spokesmen like Andrew Melville served as a motivation to more firmly settle religion in the northern kingdom (King 2000). At a General Assembly held in Glasgow in the summer of 1610 the Kirk was placed under the jurisdiction of arch-episcopal sees at Glasgow and St Andrews; as in England, conformity was enforced via subscription, and deprivations were carried out according to the directions of High Commission (Anon. 1610a: A8^r). General Assemblies themselves would be moderated by a bishop, and a new group of bishops was consecrated in London in December 1610. One contemporary writer noted that these policies constituted a significant departure from the reformed posture of the Kirk, 'expressed in the confession of our Faith, established and publicly confirmed by sundrie Acts of Parliament' (Anon. 1610: 4). The Kirk was itself 'by law established', and its worship was shaped by the Book of Discipline, yet the English clerisy regarded this as an 'arbitrarie' form or 'corner divinitie' (Hampton 1611: 17; MacDonald 1998: ch. 6).

In 1617 the king and English bishops took a decisive step in harmonizing the Churches of the realm, through the imposition of the Articles of Perth (Prior 2005a: 220–1; Ford

1995). Of the five, two were particularly controversial: that the sacrament should be received in a kneeling posture, and that children of eight years of age should be catechized by a bishop, a provision which indicated the prominence of the episcopal order as direct agents of discipline. Two General Assemblies were held in rapid succession, and David Calderwood, who would emerge as the principal defender of the Presbyterian order, condemned 'the insolent domination of the Prelates' who 'by unlawful means' denied the 'libertie granted to our Church' to determine its own pattern of worship (Calderwood 1619: 'To the Reader'). A flurry of texts followed, and the debate turned, as it had in England, on whether there was sound scriptural evidence for kneeling at Communion (Prior 2005a: 222–35). Scots writers pressed the argument that the English not only robbed the Kirk of its native liberty, but imposed false modes of worship upon it. This led Calderwood to argue that the Royal Supremacy mattered little if what it enforced was demonstrably false: 'The commandment of the Magistrate cannot make a thing, which of itself is scandalous, and hurtful, not to be hurtful, but rather by the strength of his authoritie maketh it more scandalous and hurtful' (Calderwood 1620: 57).

In response, defenders of the English policy argued for the supremacy of law, and emphasized the notion of a 'British' Church. In a sharp reply to Calderwood, David Lindsay claimed that 'it is ever more expedient to obey a Law, and keepe a lawfull custom, then to doe a thing thought more expedient' (Lindsay 1621: C3^r). Episcopacy was just such a custom, traceable to the Apostolic Church and now a form of government suited to a 'National Church'; Lindsay noted that 'antiquity in such things' was to be preferred above the 'customs of private persons, and Churches' (Lindsay 1621: 6–7). Rather than attempt to win a theological argument with the Scots, promoters of ecclesiastical union adopted the notion of a unity of church and state, where the state was a composite of two kingdoms. Writing in response to Calderwood, Patrick Scot argued that a 'Church of Great Britain' was the best solution to 'disorder and scandal' (Scot 1622: 2). Three years later the argument in defence of an imperial Church was made even more explicit: Scot argued that there was one Church of 'Great Brittaine' and that it was a support of 'the heavy frame of Empire'. He warned against those who sought to 'touch the string of Sovereignty with too rough a hand' merely to enlarge 'popular libertie'; without due order, 'the great frame of sovereign Empire' is fundamentally weakened (Scot 1625: 38, 53). Clearly, the political logic of the Act of Appeals still informed understandings of the relationship of church and state, both in England and between the British kingdoms.

BODIES, SOULS, AND ESTATES: WARS OF REFORMATION

Religious debate during the reign of Charles I continued in much the same way as it had during that of his father. Perhaps the main difference lay in the ecclesiology that Charles embraced. His vision of the Church emphasized its baroque elements: the centrality of ritual, the arrangement of sacred space, the visual and aural elements of worship, and the alignment of the Church with a particular strand of sacred history, notably the Hebrew temple. The main driver of this vision was William Laud, Archbishop of Canterbury, a much maligned and greatly misunderstood figure in this story, whose ideas of the Church are only now receiving the attention they merit (Cromartie 2011). Laud was a firm believer in the unity of church and state, a point which he made explicitly in a sermon of 1621, and which he reiterated in another sermon that marked the opening of Parliament in the spring of 1625:

> And one thing more I'le be bold to speake out of a like duetie to the *Church* of *England* and the *House* of *David*. They, whoever they bee, that would overthrow *Sedes Ecclesiae*, the *Seates* of Ecclesiastical Government, will not spare (if they ever get power) to have a plucke at the *Throne* of *David*. And there is not a man that is for *Paritie*, all Fellowes in the *Church*, but hee is not for *Monarchie* in the *State*. (Laud 1625: 40)

Rather than heading in a radical new direction, Laud was simply giving voice to the political logic of the Tudor supremacy over the co-extensive church and state. His politicization of the costs of dissent is aimed directly at Presbyterian critics of the supremacy as it had been applied in Scotland, as well as a growing Protestant diaspora in the Low Countries and in the rapidly forming British Atlantic world.

In England itself, the opening years of the reign of Charles I were defined by sharp conflict, and by 1629 he opted to rule without Parliament. While the business of the state was carried out by the traditional organs of local and county government, the king sought a centralized reform of the Church (Sharpe 1992: ch. 6). Briefly, this centred around the renewed emphasis on conformity to the official (and still disputed) liturgy, and an emphasis on ritual such as kneeling at Communion and, most controversially, the replacement of Communion tables with altars (Fincham and Tyacke 2007). As it had in the previous reign, this debate proceeded by way of complex arguments about the rituals that defined the worship of Christians from the earlier point in their history. Peter Heylyn argued that the Communion table was merely an '*accessorie*, and a point of Circumstance', and reprising the argument that the Last Supper itself was replete with customs and aspects of ritual that no Church had replicated (Heylyn 1636: 44).

This opened up a fundamental question: if the ritual practice of the Church was customary, then what customs would be used to shape the form it took? This debate was influenced by an important intellectual development of the late sixteenth and early seventeenth century: the Hebrew revival. Informed by a humanist desire to recover the classical past and apply its political maxims to the present, Hebraists sought to revive elements of the ancient worship, customs, and law of the people of the original Covenant (Nelson 2010: 1–22; Guibbory 2010). Applied to the debate on altars, the model for Hebraists was the Jewish Temple, where the precedent of combining commemoration of sacrifice and altars was firmly evident. Not only this, but the Jewish example also elevated the clergy to a position of power and esteem, in a manner exemplified by the council of the Sanhedrin (Prior 2012: 39–40).

An alternate view rejected this 'Judaizing', and argued that the use of Communion tables was not a matter of historical custom, but rather a question of law. In a series of substantial texts on the issue, the lawyer and MP William Prynne argued that the Act of Supremacy remained in force, as did the articles that stipulated a 'fair joyned table', neither fixed nor railed off like the Laudian altar. What is notable is how Prynne tied an element of worship to the liberties of subjects:

> [A]*ll of them* direct Innouations, *not used nor heard of from the beginning of Queen Elizabeth raigne till of late*, they are contrary to the Purity of that Doctrine & Discipline established in the time of Queen Elizabeth, where by the Church of England hath stood and flourished euer since … *They are contrary to* the ancient and just Rights & Liberties of the Subjects, who ought not to have any such Nouelties thrust vpon them, much lesse to be excommunicated fined, suspended, imprisoned, & thrust from their freeholds, Lectures & Cures but by the Law of the Land, & some speciall Act of parleament as the Statute of Magna Charta. (Prynne 1637: 189)

Prynne's position embodies a constitutional approach to the Church that emphasized its origins in statute and employed common law arguments against the jurisdiction of ecclesiastical courts. It was this view that informed so much of the criticism of the ecclesiastical policies of Charles I and Laud—howsoever they might be presented as reifications of the most sacred customs of the Jews and Apostles, they were nevertheless illegal (Prior 2012: 73–9).

This emphasis on law also dominated the question of the relationship between the British Churches. Charles and Laud pursued a policy of 'ecclesial acculturation' by imposing the English Prayer Book and a new set of Canons on the Kirk in 1636 (Morrill 1994). This prompted a coherent resistance among the Presbyterians, whose leadership drafted a document known in its time as the 'Confession of Faith' and known now as the National Covenant. This defended the Kirk on the grounds that its liturgy and governance were established by a process of legal reformation, and thus any attempt to alter it was an assault on the 'Religion, Lawes, and Liberties of this Kingdome' (Henderson and Johnston 1638: 11). The appearance of the 'Confession' generated a widespread controversy over the location of sovereignty over the Kirk: Charles's defenders claimed that the Act of Supremacy was not altered by the Union of the Crowns, and that the Crown was therefore sovereign over the Kirk; this view was strenuously opposed by the General Assembly of the Kirk and its many defenders, who argued that, in seeking to suspend the powers of the Assembly, the king was guilty of neglect, leaving the Kirk 'at liberty' to make laws for itself (Prior 2012: 83–105). The force of Scots opposition was large enough to lead Charles I to assemble an army in order to bring the northern kingdom into a posture of obedience; however, the military campaign was a disaster and the 'Bishops' Wars' served only to bring the Protestant opponents of the king together as a single bloc, pledging their 'Soules, Bodies, and Estates' in defence of 'true Religion and just liberty' (Scotland 1640: 8).

A similar conflation of religion and liberty is a dominant feature of ideas of church and state that underpin the foundation of colonial societies in the British Atlantic world. This is a vital, but largely neglected, part of the story of early Stuart religion and politics, but it bears directly on events in England in the 1640s (Prior 2013b: 31–2; Donoghue 2013). Those who risked the journey across the Atlantic identified themselves as exiles from a commonwealth whose religion had fallen under the sway of 'popery'—an epithet that contemporaries used to describe the clericalism and ceremonialism that defined the early Stuart religious settlements (Winship 2009). Therefore, the foundation of colonial society was guided by an ethos that blended ideas of republican government with a vision of the Church as a kind of civil society, small in scale and where magistrates were constrained in their power over religion (Winship 2012). As John Cotton wrote to Lord Saye and Sele, the Scripture contained a 'platform, not only of theology, but also of other sacred sciences', among which he included the 'right ordering of a man's family, yea, of the commonwealth too'. He continued by noting that 'Gods institutions (such as the government of church and commonwealth be) may be close and compact, and coordinate one to the another, and yet not be confounded' (Hutchinson 1765: 497; Kupperman 1989). The irony here is that advocates of a theocratic basis of society were also able to suggest that such a constitutional order *preserved* the separation of church and state. However, in spite of this ambition, colonial societies would struggle with issues of persecution and religious toleration during the 1640s, and their struggles with church and state directly influenced key debates on ecclesiology in Civil War England (Murphy 2001).

Back in England, contemporaries were obliged to work within existing understandings of church and state, and these were confounded in the extreme. Having failed in his first attempt to compel the Scots by force, the king recalled Parliament in the spring of 1640, where the issue of religion took its place among a range of constitutional grievances. Parliament denied the king funds unless specific grievances were addressed, namely the liberty of Parliament, 'innovations in matters of religion', and 'propriety of goods'. In a wide-ranging speech, John Pym listed altars, the decline of the 'constitution of the reformed religion', rough discipline, and the High Commission as the chief issues (Kenyon 1986: 184–6). Denied support for the Scots campaign, the king prorogued Parliament, allowing (illegally) the Convocation of the Church to remain in session; loyal churchmen not only granted the funds necessary to resume the fight with the Covenanters, but they seized the opportunity to introduce new Canons for the Church (Sharpe 1992: 872–3, 877–84). The Canons of 1640 contained a sweeping new defence of the regal supremacy, and prohibited any innovation (or reformation) of the doctrine and episcopal governance of the Church. When the Long Parliament met in the autumn of 1640, its members began a protracted attack on the Church, an effort that was guided by the desire to drastically curb the Royal Supremacy, and to abolish episcopacy and the illegal mechanisms of conformity (Morrill 1993: ch. 4; Prior 2012: 110–39, 143–71).

Between 1640 and 1642, debate in press and Parliament was dominated by the problem of church and state—in fact, about 75 per cent of the prodigious output of the presses dealt with religious issues (Morrill 1990: 105). The dominant issues were episcopacy and the link between religion and liberty. Historically, bishops sat in the House of Lords by virtue of their offices, and thus exerted an influence on the civil affairs of the realm. One writer argued that their political function took them 'out of their owne Sphere and calling', and insisted that Parliament should be composed of those with knowledge of the law; an alternate view derived examples from Jewish history, and maintained that bishops in Parliament merely continued the custom of the 'Priests and Levites' as members of the 'civil courts of Justice, and Assemblies of the State' (Burges 1641: 2; Langbaine 1641: 30). The rift between these positions concerned the nature of Parliament itself, as either a wholly legal body or one composed of a mixture of civil and ecclesiastical laws, traditions, and officers. In the spring of 1641, the Commons issued a 'Protestation' whose aim was to force direct and explicit links between the 'reformed religion' and the 'power and privilege of parliament' and the 'lawful rights and liberties of the subjects' (Kenyon 1986: 200–1; Cressy 2002; Prior 2012: 158–71). As one writer remarked, religion and the law were the two 'generall public foundations' which the Protestation 'fenced and fortified' (Bond 1641: 10, 100). The war that broke out between the three kingdoms was driven, in large part, by a debate on the relationship of religion and law, church and state, conscience and liberty.

The rich literature of early Stuart controversy was a vital conduit for the discussion of church and state. The Henrician Reformation was predicated on a mingling of civil and sacred power, and it took place within a deeply legalistic culture; the relationship between church and state was therefore a pressing legal and theological question, and writers sought to shed light upon it by appealing to precedent and history, both of the realm and its laws and of the Church and its sacred foundations and legacies. In short, while it is evident that the Reformation was 'an act of state', what this meant in practice was far from being definitive, and the notion of what constituted the Church 'by law established' was the major theme in early Stuart religious controversy (Burgess 2000: 200). Not only did it drive the process of state-formation in the reformed polity of England, the united polity of Britain, and in the 'Godly republics' of the new world, but it was also a source of conflict and disruption, and a driver of key debates on liberty, toleration, and freedom of conscience.

CHAPTER 6

....

RELIGION IN TIMES OF WAR AND REPUBLIC, 1642–60

....

JACQUELINE EALES

Religion was not the thing at first contested for, but God brought it to that issue at last; and gave it unto us by way of redundancy; and at last it proved to be that which was most dear to us.

(Oliver Cromwell, *Speech to Parliament*, 22 January 1655)

CROMWELL'S address to his first Protectorate Parliament is often cited to suggest that religion was not the prime cause of the English Civil Wars (Foxley 2011). It is, however, worth quoting his words at greater length, for he continued: 'And wherein consisted this more than in obtaining that liberty from the tyranny of the bishops to all species of Protestants to worship God according to their own light and consciences? For want of which, many of our brethren forsook their native countries to seek their bread from strangers' (Abbott 1937: 586). In harking back to the puritan exodus to the Netherlands and the New World in the years before the outbreak of civil war, Cromwell was emphasizing the centrality of the overthrow of the bishops to the Parliamentarian cause. In these passages he was also specifically talking about the desire of his fellow Independents for a congregational system of worship outside a national Church, but the assault on episcopal power had been driven by those of a Presbyterian persuasion as well.

The importance of religion as a motivating force for both groups has long been reflected in the historiography of the civil wars. The great Victorian historian of the early Stuarts, S. R. Gardiner, characterized the civil wars as the 'puritan revolution' and in modern times John Morrill has defined them as the last of the European 'Wars of Religion'. Responses to Morrill have addressed the religious and constitutional causes of the civil wars in a series of nuanced readings, which recognize that the modern distinction between the sacred and the secular should not be mapped back onto the past (Gardiner 1889; Morrill 1984; Prior and Burgess 2011; and chapter 5). One of the key areas of contention between king and parliament in the 1640s was undoubtedly the nature and structure of the national Church and its leadership by bishops. The extent to which political and religious power were entwined in this issue is reflected in the fact that the argument for the divine institution of monarchy was mirrored by a parallel theory of episcopal divine right. James I's dictum 'No Bishop! No King!' was based on the contemporary understanding of this relationship, and the fates of episcopacy and the crown were thus intimately linked in the revolutionary years of 1642–60. As the controls operated by these institutions collapsed, previously outlawed and novel ideas about religion were able to flourish.

From the start of the Long Parliament in November 1640 the religious debates at Westminster drew their urgency from the petitions, counter-petitions, letters, and complaints received by MPs from their constituents and other contacts in the provinces (Fletcher 1981). Amongst the issues under dispute were whether bishops should be retained, the legality of the religious changes introduced during the Personal Rule of Charles I, and the suitability of the national liturgy contained in the Book of Common Prayer issued in 1559 by Elizabeth I (Durston and Eales 1996b: 17–20; Maltby 1998). Puritans in particular objected to the set forms of prayer in the *Book* and the fact that its use implied acceptance of the hierarchy of bishops, deans, chapters, and other ecclesiastical officers. The majority of moderate puritan gentlemen in the House of Commons would have been content with a restricted episcopacy or modified form of Presbyterianism in 1640–1, because it was unclear how far their plans for reform could be pushed. There were, however, demands from outside Parliament for more drastic religious reforms, as those who favoured Independent or 'gathered' Churches began to make their voices heard through the pulpit and the press. Moreover, the disparity in the religious make-up of Charles I's three kingdoms served to create further religious divisions within the British Isles. In Ireland Roman Catholics were in the majority, in Scotland Calvinist Presbyterians held sway, while in England uniformity to the episcopal Church was a legal requirement, despite the existence of a variety of Nonconformist, separatist, or semi-separatist congregations.

Archbishop William Laud's promotion of the rituals and church decorations introduced during the 1630s also gave rise to fears that the king would impose this 'Laudian' style of religious conformity across his three kingdoms, and even force a return to Roman Catholicism. In Scotland this led to the Bishops' Wars of 1639–40, amidst demands for the abolition of the Scottish bishops and a limitation on royal power. In consequence the Scots abolished bishops in 1641 a full five years before the English Parliament took the same action. In Ireland a nationalist, Catholic rebellion had broken out in late 1641 while in England and Wales a civil war, fuelled significantly by religious issues, would follow in August 1642 (Russell 1991). *The Nineteen Propositions* presented by the Long Parliament to Charles I on 1 June 1642 called for the reformation of the government and liturgy of the English Church, financial support for a preaching ministry in England and Wales, and the passage of laws against clerics who held more than one living or who were otherwise scandalous in the performance of their duties or personal life. Laws against the Laudian innovations of the 1630s, particularly the railed altar, were also included in these demands (Coward and Gaunt 2010: 686–90; Fincham and Tyacke 2007). Eventually all these reforms would be achieved through unilateral parliamentary legislation and without the royal assent. During the years of the first English Civil War (1642–6), the impetus towards reform crystallized into demands for the abolition of bishops and (spurred on by the Scottish example) the experimental introduction of a Presbyterian Church in England and Wales.

The Church courts, the key arenas for enforcing religious conformity and meting out moral discipline, stopped functioning in 1641–2, as the royalist bishops and cathedral clergy withdrew from their public roles. The cathedrals were powerful centres of royalist preaching and, in response, in the mid-1640s the Long Parliament replaced the cathedral clergy with preachers who were 'well affected' to the 'common cause' against the king (CJ III: 299, 359; LJ VII: 10). Sermons were prominent vehicles for the discussion of a range of political issues including, on the royalist side, the sacrality of kingship and the sin of rebellion and, on the parliamentarian side, the legality of resistance to the crown and the vindication of a defensive or even an offensive war (Eales 2002; Asch 2011; Burgess 2011; Mortimer 2011). The clergy were therefore regarded as active participants in the politics of civil war. Fourteen bishops were sequestered for supporting the king's war effort in March 1643 and many of them later sought refuge in royalist regions in the West Country and Wales. The most militant were Archbishop John Williams of York, who helped in the defence of Conway, and Bishop Walter Curll of Winchester, who raised a troop of royalist horse and later encouraged the city to hold out against Cromwell in 1645. In the same year, Archbishop Laud was executed as a traitor for having promoted the religious policies of the 1630s, while Bishop Wren of Norwich was kept a prisoner in the Tower of London for eighteen years without trial until his release in 1660. Only nine bishops would live to see the Restoration (Firth and Rait 1911: I, 106–17, 254–60; King 1968; Hardacre 1956: 44).

As bishops 'went down', the time seemed ripe to the godly for the introduction of a 'new Jerusalem'. However, after his defeat in 1646, Charles I's refusal to come to terms with the English Parliament, the New Model Army, and the Scots prevented any clear-cut religious change from taking place. Instead, piecemeal measures were introduced, including the abolition of episcopacy, which created considerable leeway for individuals to follow their own consciences and spiritual inclinations (Morrill 1982). The Presbyterian agenda, which was supported by some puritan MPs and clerics, was thus overtaken by the proliferation of Independent churches and religious sects in the late 1640s. One of the king's last bargaining chips after 1646 was his offer to both the Long Parliament and to the Scots that he would introduce a Presbyterian system into England as an experiment. His execution in January 1649 meant that this plan became irrelevant to the settlements of the 1650s.

The religious uncertainties of the civil war and republican eras concerned not only ecclesiastical hierarchies and structures, but also theologies. Anti-Catholicism and fear of a rapprochement with Rome were powerful motives for the king's opponents throughout the British Isles. These impulses harked back to the days of the Reformation and the Marian burnings, but were also based on a number of current factors, including

Charles's marriage to the French Catholic princess, Henrietta Maria (White 2006). The king's favour towards anti-Calvinist or Arminian clerics, his support for the so-called Church 'innovations' of the 1630s, and his ill-considered imposition of the English prayer book in Scotland in 1637–8 all reinforced suspicions about his religious policies. The Arminians were associated with the rejection of predestination in favour of salvation or grace freely available to all. Concomitant with this was a belief in free will and the ability of the individual to turn from sin to a state of grace at any time, which to staunch Calvinists smacked too much of Roman Catholicism. Belief in universal grace was not restricted to the Arminians, but also fertilized the beliefs of many of the Independent churches. In particular the Baptists, who rejected infant baptism in favour of adult baptism, had already developed two strands of thought by the late 1630s. The General Baptists adhered to a belief in free grace while the particular Baptists were committed to the doctrine of predestination. As Stephen Wright has demonstrated, the differences between the two groups were not as rigid as this suggests and there was a good deal of co-operation and fluidity between these stances (Wright 2006). Moderate Calvinism, or a belief in predestination, has been seen as a unifying theology in England before Charles I's accession (Tyacke 1987a). Yet this was a question of degree, and for the most self-consciously godly and Calvinist Puritans, predestination was a central organizing tenet of belief. It could be exalted to the extent that some puritan clergy and laity claimed to recognize the signs of election, or predestination to heaven in other people and even resorted to a constant scrutiny of their own daily lives, in order to detect these signs in themselves (Eales 1990: 50–2). In contrast, for the more moderate Calvinists and the Arminians alike, any claim to know the mind of God was an attempt to delve too far into the mysteries of religion and the divine will.

In the early 1640s the relative freedom of religious debate about these issues served to generate a heightened fear of the contamination of heresy. Rightly or wrongly, accusations of socinianism (or anti-trinitarianism), and libertinism linked to antinomianism (which exalted the power of free grace over the workings of the Moral Law of the Old Testament), were thus regularly used to discredit the more radical religious sects. At the same time the breakdown of print censorship from 1641 meant that these previously outlawed ideas could indeed circulate more freely and were openly espoused in the pulpit and by the laity, having previously been part of a clandestine and underground movement (Como 2004).

The king's loss of control over the London printers, after his flight from the capital in January 1642, also contributed to a dramatic increase in the publication of political and religious polemic (Raymond 2003; Peacey 2004, 2013) (see chapter 14). One of the most contested topics was what constituted right religious belief at a time when the concept of a national Church was under attack. The growth of the religious sects prompted the Presbyterians and conformists to level the charge of heterodoxy against a range of groups. Amongst the most active and popular 'heresy hunters' were the London Presbyterian clerics, Ephraim Pagett and Thomas Edwards. Pagett published a review of what he regarded as current heresies culled largely from contemporary publications in *Heresiography, or, A Description of the Heretickes and Sectaries of these Latter Times*

(1645), which ran into six more, increasingly enlarged, editions between 1645 and 1661. In contrast, Edwards relied on correspondents, who were ear- and eye-witnesses to what they regarded as scandalous beliefs and practices, which they reported to him. These were published in three volumes in 1646 under the provocative title of *Gangraena: or a Catalogue and Discovery of Many of the Errours, Heresies, Blasphemies and Pernicious Practices of the Sectaries of this Time*. In this book, Edwards excoriated the growth of lay preaching, Anabaptism, and atheism, which he saw as the inevitable outcome of religious toleration. Instead he urged his readers to support the order and orthodoxy of Presbyterianism as the antidote to the terrible gangrene of heresy. Historians have rightly been wary of relying on *Gangraena*, a work of obvious propaganda, to trace the spread of religious heterodoxy. Edwards's tales, for example, of the intellectual errors of women preachers and of the sexual involvement of female acolytes with male sectaries, made titillating reading but are impossible to substantiate. Nevertheless, as Ann Hughes's sophisticated analysis has demonstrated, *Gangraena* stands as the 'most debated, most notorious text in a revolution to which print was crucial' and it played a key role in the complex interplay between the print culture and religious divisions of the time (Hughes 2004: 440).

The works of the heresiographers can be supplemented, of course, by more personal accounts, which reveal that the beliefs and membership of the many different churches and religious groups of the period could be highly fluid. Some individuals were self-identified seekers, moving between religious brands in the search for religious truth. Others did not fit comfortably with any particular grouping; for example Thomas Coleman, the rector of St Peter Cornhill in London, described himself in 1645 as totally disliking the gathered churches of the Independents 'as not consistible with this Kingdome', while also being 'no rigid Presbyterian' (Wildridge 1886: 103). Coleman has been described as 'the most prominent Erastian pamphleteer' of the period, who argued for the sovereignty of the state over the Church and looked to Parliament to establish and control Church government (*ODNB* entry for Coleman).

The creation of Parliament's New Model Army in 1645 brought a new political force into play. As the beliefs of the Independents and the Levellers spread within the soldiery, demands for religious toleration became part of the army agenda. During 1647 and 1648 the attempt of the Presbyterian majority in the House of Commons to maintain their political control was undermined by the spectre of a military coup, which culminated in the purge of Presbyterian MPs by the army in December 1648, leaving just a rump to press ahead with the trial of Charles I (Underdown 1971). The subsequent regicide and the retreat of some Presbyterians from both local and national politics laid the emphasis of the apparent triumph on the Independents. In 1650 the Rump of the Long Parliament repealed the penalties for not attending church, although the act stipulated that religious observance was still required in some public or other place. As Lord Protector, Oliver Cromwell and the Council of State issued a series of Ordinances in 1654 designed to revive a national Church, which included provision for increased stipends for the less well paid parish clergy (Hughes 2006a). Two further measures set up teams of local commissioners or triers to approve public preachers, and ejectors to remove 'scandalous, ignorant and insufficient' ministers and schoolmasters (Coward and Gaunt 2010: 1028–42). The latter ordinance was part of a wider purge in the 1640s and 1650s of the parish clergy of England and Wales, as royalist and otherwise inadequate clerics were replaced by the godly supporters of the various *de facto* regimes in London (McCall 2013). The restoration of the Anglican Church after 1660, however, caused a mass crisis of conscience amongst the puritan clergy, who could not accept a national Church with bishops and who were consequently ejected from their livings. Between 1660 and 1662 as many as a fifth of the parish clergy were forced out of their parishes in what would prove to be a futile attempt to restore uniformity of worship across England and Wales (Appleby 2007).

THE DEBATES OVER A NATIONAL CHURCH IN THE 1640S

By the time that *The Nineteen Propositions* were being formulated, the Long Parliament had already signalled its support for Church reform. Draft legislation for the 'root and branch' abolition of episcopacy and of diocesan deans and chapters had been drawn up by a committee of the House of Commons in the previous year. Accordingly, the fate of the Church hierarchy became a litmus test of political loyalty, with increasing numbers of MPs and gentry rejecting the militant stance of Parliament in favour of support for the royalist cause. Abolition was so clearly a sensitive subject that the king's opponents allowed the bill to sleep rather than to pursue such a divisive measure. So it was not until 1646 that episcopacy was formally abolished by a parliamentary ordinance (Firth and Rait 1911: I, 879–83). The majority of MPs, who remained at Westminster in 1642 rather than joining the king at his headquarters in Oxford, favoured a Presbyterian Church settlement, but their motives for doing so have been interpreted as a political manoeuvre to gain the support of the Presbyterian Scots. It is clear, however, that some MPs such as the Herefordshire gentleman, Sir Robert Harley, supported the bill out of conviction rather than solely for reasons of state (Eales 1990: 111–13).

The members of the Long Parliament were also convinced that religious reform could not take place without the advice of the clergy. The Grand Remonstrance of December 1641 setting out the failings of Charles I had called for a general synod of 'pious' and 'learned' divines to settle religious issues. This demand also surfaced in petitions from the counties, but it was not until July 1643 that Parliament summoned 121 clergy, representing the universities and the counties and thirty lay members from the two houses of Parliament, to constitute the Westminster Assembly. William Twisse, the respected controversialist, presided over the members of the Assembly, who were predominantly Presbyterians, but who also included a small group of committed Independent divines including William Carter, Philip Nye, and Sidrach Simpson. Some bishops were also invited to attend, but most of them did not appear, apart from Archbishop James

Ussher of Armagh, who was regarded as a moderate influence and untainted by Laudian influences. The Assembly's initial task was to review the Thirty-Nine Articles and their debates covered a range of theological issues including the divinity of Christ, justification by faith, and the role of good works. Parliament also consulted the Assembly on a variety of topics including translations and heresy (Van Dixhoorn et al. 2012: I).

Following the agreement of the Solemn League and Covenant between the Long Parliament and the Scottish Covenanters in August 1643, a group of lay and clerical Scots commissioners joined the Assembly. Most prominent amongst them were the Presbyterian clerics Robert Baillie, George Gillespie, Alexander Henderson, and Samuel Rutherford, who were actively involved in the Assembly's deliberations. The Solemn League and Covenant bound those who took it to support the abolition of episcopacy and the introduction of religious uniformity in the three kingdoms in the form of a common confession of faith, Church government, and directions for worship and catechizing (Coward and Gaunt 2010: 582–4). While the Scots hoped that this would lead to the export of Presbyterianism into England, the oath was so vaguely worded that it could be taken with a clear conscience or 'mental reservation' even by Cromwell and the English Independents.

Between 1643 and 1648 the Assembly's work was geared to providing the confessional doctrines and documents which would underpin this union. A *Directory of Public Worship* was produced by the Assembly and approved by the Parliaments of England and Scotland in 1645. It was intended to replace the Book of Common Prayer in England, which was now outlawed, although it continued to be used by traditionalists throughout the late 1640s and 1650s. In 1646, for example, Bishop Morton of Durham was imprisoned by the Commons for 'christening a child in the old way' (King 1968: 527). John Evelyn, the diarist, continued to use the prayer book for christenings and in the 1650s attended church services at Christmas, although its celebration had been banned in 1647 by Parliament as part of the puritan attack on unscriptural religious observances, including Easter and Whitsun (Firth and Rait 1911: I, 954). In 1647 the ban provoked a series of Christmas riots in London, Ipswich, Oxford, and most notably in Canterbury. This was the prelude to the outbreak of the Second Civil War of 1648, in which royalist hopes for a reinstatement of the king were finally crushed (Ashton 1994: 96–7, 238–41).

The *Directory* avoided set forms of liturgy and instead provided guidance on religious worship. The Assembly also presented a draft Confession of Faith to the Long Parliament late in 1646 and this was subjected to a number of revisions. The Edinburgh general assembly of the Scottish kirk approved the Confession in 1647, whilst highlighting its failure to address Church government. In England a slightly modified version was approved by Parliament in 1648 under the title *Articles of Christian Religion*, which was intended to replace the Thirty-Nine Articles. The Confession also formed the basis of the Assembly's Shorter and Longer Catechisms published in London and Edinburgh in 1647 and approved by the English and Scottish parliaments in the following year. Together these three documents emphasized the Calvinist doctrine of election, the covenant of works made by God with Adam and his posterity, and the covenant of grace made through Christ with believers. The Confession rapidly became the defining doctrinal statement of Presbyterian belief in both Britain and North America (Van Dixhoorn et al. 2012: I).

In tandem with the work of the Assembly, the Long Parliament also attempted to negotiate religious reform with Charles I. The peace propositions offered to the king at Oxford in early 1643 called for his assent to a bill abolishing the Church hierarchy and to the passage of other 'good bills for settling of church government'. The Uxbridge Propositions of November 1644 and the Newcastle Propositions of July 1646 similarly demanded the passage of a bill for the abolition of episcopacy and the removal of the cathedral clergy and their officers in England and Ireland. In his third answer to the Newcastle Propositions in July 1647 Charles offered to accept a Presbyterian Church in England for three years while the Westminster Assembly deliberated on the settlement of an ecclesiastical government. The half-hearted nature of this suggestion was underlined by the king's demand that he and the royal household should be allowed to continue to use the Book of Common Prayer. Towards the end of the year, Charles also made the same offer to the Scots in a separate negotiation, known as the Engagement, in the hope of playing his opponents against each other (Coward and Gaunt 2010: 690–723).

The king's refusal to accept Church reform without endless negotiation was countered by a series of isolated measures by the Long Parliament. In 1645 a parliamentary ordinance was passed setting out a Presbyterian Church structure. This was followed the next year by two further ordinances, one concerning the introduction of a Presbyterian Church government, and another which abolished episcopacy and allowed for the sale of Church lands. Adherence to the instructions set out in these ordinances for the election of parish elders, the grouping of parishes into classes and the meeting of provincial and national assemblies was minimal. A Presbyterian system of sorts operated in London and in counties such as Shropshire and Lancashire, but elsewhere, for example in Kent, there is little evidence that a unified Presbyterian system made much impact on parish life. Furthermore, the Presbyterian project was being overtaken by the growing numbers following 'the congregational way'. The Independent churches were based on a covenant between the members of each congregation and while some of them accepted the need for a loose national Church structure, most did not. The Presbyterian push for a new religious conformity was opposed by the Independent churches and the radical sects, who argued for a degree of toleration, which crucially did not extend to Catholics or other faiths. The issue was heavily debated in print between 1644 and 1647 by the Independents such as Jeremiah Burroughs, and John and Thomas Goodwin, who were in favour of religious freedom for the godly, but they were fiercely challenged by Presbyterian writers, including Samuel Rutherford, Thomas Edwards, and the MP William Prynne (Coffey 2006c).

However, in practice, the Independent churches were free to worship both within the traditional structure of the parishes and outside it. Religious freedom for the Independents also flourished in Parliament's New Model Army. *De facto* toleration for the new sects was secured by the legislation of the 1650s and, as Lord Protector from 1653 until his death in 1658, Cromwell's Independent leanings led him to favour puritan diversity, but Anglicans and Catholics were outlawed and harassed, while the newly formed Quakers fared no better.

The Origins of Religious Dissent

Historians of the period have debated at length whether the religious fissures of the 1640s and 1650s were primarily a reaction to the policies pursued by Charles I in the first fifteen years of his reign or whether they were more deeply rooted. While the king's support for his Arminian clergy and for the religious changes of the Laudian era gave an undeniable impetus to the demands for ecclesiastical reform of the early 1640s, it is also clearly the case that such demands had a long-established history. Moreover, many of those advocating reforms to the Long Parliament had been influenced by earlier networks of separatist or semi-separatist congregations operating in England, the Netherlands, and New England during the reigns of Elizabeth I and James I. Those who wished to separate in some degree from a national inclusive Church and its ungodly members were emboldened by two distinct traditions which had emerged in the sixteenth century. On the one hand, secret religious gatherings had been developed as a necessity to preserve Protestantism against Roman Catholic persecution during the Reformation. On the other hand, the Protestant 'stranger' churches, established by religious exiles and foreign traders, were allowed to operate openly outside the confines of national Church structures both in Britain and on the continent. A third strand would develop in the 1620s and 1630s as English Nonconformists settled in New England and founded covenanted churches free from the supervision of a national Church.

Despite the establishment of Protestantism under Elizabeth, small separatist congregations operated in London and the provinces during the early years of her reign (see chapter 4). Robert Browne also led a separatist group in Norwich in the early 1580s and briefly went into exile in the Netherlands with some of his followers before recanting his views. The publication in 1582 of his influential tract *A Treatise of Reformation Without Tarrying for Any* gave rise to the word 'Brownists', as a loose term of abuse for Puritans. In tandem with these developments, Presbyterian ideas were gaining influence amongst English clerical and lay circles. In 1570 the Lady Margaret Professor of Divinity at Cambridge University, Thomas Cartwright, was dismissed for advocating Presbyterian principles in his lectures. The following year he travelled with his Cambridge colleague, Walter Travers, to Geneva where both men defended their positions in print and both later acted as ministers to the English merchants in Antwerp, before returning to England. Cartwright in particular argued against religious separation and subsequently challenged the legitimacy of Robert Brown's exiled congregation. Travers took a leading role in writing the Presbyterian book of discipline entitled *A Directory of Church Government*, which was to become the central evidence of their Nonconformity in the 1591 trial of Cartwright and eight other Presbyterian ministers. Two years later, the infamous execution of the London separatist leaders John Greenwood and Henry

Barrow and the Welshman John Penry seemed, both to contemporaries and to later historians alike, to mark an abrupt end to Elizabethan puritan demands for Church reforms.

The scholarship of the past two decades has demonstrated, however, the strong continuities between religious dissent in Elizabeth's reign and in the early Stuart period (see chapter 5). We can take as an example the will of the Presbyterian minister Humphrey Fenn, which was published in 1641 and which contained an astonishing preamble arguing that in England the maintenance of bishops represented a 'shameful schism' from the reformed churches, yet nevertheless, separation from the Church of England was not lawful. As the date of publication indicates, this was indeed part and parcel of the debate about the abolition of episcopacy in the Long Parliament, but Fenn had also been an associate of Thomas Cartwright and had been one of the ministers arrested and tried with Cartwright in 1590. Fenn had died in 1534 and the bishop of Lichfield and Coventry, in whose diocese the will had been proved, instantly informed Archbishop Laud about its explosive contents. The preamble to the will circulated in an underground manuscript form in puritan circles before its appearance in print (Fenn 1641; NA SP16/260/83; Eales 1996: 194–5).

Fenn's example demonstrates that the religious preferences of some individuals could provide living links between the Elizabethan puritan movement and the civil war years. Moreover, aristocratic, gentry, and merchant patrons were well placed to offer protection to the many puritan clerics, who kept alive the ambitions for reform held by their Elizabethan predecessors. Debates about the merits and demerits of conformity, models of Church government, issues of separation, and adherence to the moral law were thus continued in print, in the circulation of manuscripts, and in person during the fifty years after the apparent demise of the Presbyterian and Congregationalist movements in the early 1590s.

It has also become increasingly apparent that, during the early Stuart period, the advocates of Nonconformity did not simply develop their ideas in opposition to the established, orthodox Church, but also in tension with other dissenting groups. Polly Ha has thus demonstrated that during the course of setting up what has been seen as the first English congregational church in Southwark in 1616, the semi-separatist Henry Jacob was involved in a vigorous debate with Walter Travers and other Presbyterian clerics about the legitimacy of his position. Similarly, David Como has shown that London was the site of an acrimonious clash between puritan clerics and a burgeoning group of antinomian opponents in the 1620s and 1630s, which led to heightened fears about heresy amongst both the authorities and their mainstream puritan critics (Ha 2011; Como 2004).

In terms of continuity it is also striking that the early 1640s witnessed the revival of the political tactics used by the Presbyterians to lobby the Elizabethan Parliaments of the late 1580s, which had then included clerical meetings, local petitioning campaigns, and surveys of the sufficiency of the clergy undertaken on a county basis. Similarly, in the summer of 1640 the puritan clergy organized meetings in London and the provinces to consider a response to the 'etc oath' promoted by the Church canons of 1640, which bound all who took it to the support of the doctrine and discipline of the Church of England. Their meetings soon turned into a wide-ranging debate about the justification for episcopacy and the nature of Church government. As a result of these meetings, in January 1641 a national petition and remonstrance attacking the divine right argument for episcopacy and carrying 'near upon a thousand ministers names' was presented to the House of Commons on 23 January 1641. This description was a deliberate reference to the 1603 Millenary petition to James I from a thousand puritan clerics demanding Church reform, which had called for the removal of non-godly clergy from their parishes. In December 1640 the House of Commons had already revived the idea of surveying the state of the ministry in the provinces by asking all MPs to return information about the clergy in their counties within six weeks. A committee for scandalous ministers was set up to receive the information and this set in motion a rolling purge of royalist, Arminian, or lax clergy, which continued throughout the next two decades (Eales 1990: 113, 109).

The surveys of the ministry led to the first ever outbreak of political correctness in the British Isles, as clerical complaints about the Scots were seen as evidence of ultra royalism. In Kent in early 1641 three disapproving parishioners from Capel complained about their minister Edward Wallis, for his neglect and 'popish practices'. They charged that 'he doth rail against the Scots in his pulpit and out of his pulpit, calling them dogs and devils, and saying he knows not how to call them bad enough'. Allegedly Wallis also said 'that if ever Scot go to Heaven, the Devill will go too' (Larking 1862: 149). In 1643 the chairman of the committee and London lawyer, John White, published the splendidly entitled *The First Century of Scandalous, Malignant Priests* chronicling the first 100 clerical ejections made by his committee. Amongst White's century of 'naughty vicars' were not only those who had criticized Parliament's Scottish allies from their pulpits, but also clerics who had shown excessive signs of drunkenness, lewd behaviour, or zeal for the king's cause.

Like *Gangraena*, *The First Century* raises questions about how such texts can be used to analyse the past. At one level, we are faced with smear tactics, designed to create a moral or political panic, but we can learn much from the nature of those smears and how they mapped onto other contemporary concerns. Complaints about drunkenness, for example, had been raised in the church courts both by parishioners and the ecclesiastical authorities in earlier decades and by the Laudian Church authorities immediately before the civil wars. Even Archbishop Laud had been minutely concerned about the excessive drinking of some ministers in the parishes near to his episcopal seat at Canterbury in the late 1630s (NA SP16\330\16, 17). We can conclude that in 1643 clerical alcohol abuse was clearly perceived as an ongoing problem and not simply as a fabricated way of castigating unwary royalists.

Until the mid-1640s, only counties controlled by Parliament such as Essex, Kent, Middlesex, and Suffolk were affected by this clerical purge, but after Parliament's victory in 1646, clergy in former royalist strongholds also came under scrutiny. By 1660, as many as a quarter of the parishes of England and Wales had been subjected to sequestrations by the Long Parliament and its county committees. This work was officially taken over by the local committees of ejectors in the 1650s. The men who replaced ejected ministers had a mix of Presbyterian, Independent, and even conformist opinions, and as we have seen, many would themselves face eviction from their livings at the Restoration (Green 1979).

BAPTISTS, RANTERS, AND MUGGLETONIANS

Many of the religious groups which emerged during the civil war period were so loosely organized that they did not long survive the Restoration. In contrast, the Baptists were sufficiently coherent in their structures and beliefs that they were able to survive, spread, and flourish throughout the English-speaking world to become a major Christian denomination. One of their defining beliefs was in adult or 'believer's' baptism, which meant that they were frequently associated by their detractors with the Anabaptist movement emanating from central Germany during the Reformation. Edwards certainly made the link between the Baptists and social disorder in *Gangraena* as did other commentators. In 1534 Anabaptists had taken over government in Münster, where they introduced common ownership and executed their opponents. The local authorities had only regained control of the town through the use of ferocious bloodshed and retribution. Some surviving Anabaptists fled to the Netherlands and to England, where their ideas survived long enough to influence the emergence of the first identifiable English Baptist congregation, which left for Holland in 1608 under the leadership of John Smyth. Here the group split and those who believed in general salvation returned to England led by the Nottinghamshire gentleman, Thomas Helwys, to set up the first English Baptist church in Spitalfields in London in 1612. The first Particular Baptist congregation in England was formed by the remnants of Henry Jacob's followers in 1638, when they joined the leadership of a London button-maker, Jonathan Spilsbury. The divisions between the two branches of the Baptists were not always clear-cut, however, as some individuals modified their stance and moved between congregations both within and outside the movement. Moreover, it was not only Presbyterians like Thomas Edwards who claimed that the Baptists were the heirs of Münster. Royalist critics also used this emotive claim to discredit the movement; thus Henry Rogers, a prebend in Hereford Cathedral, preached in April 1642 that London had become a centre of religious sects, of Anabaptists, separatists, and others, where the 'base, rabble rout' dictated government to the parliament and made 'laws of their owne' (British Library Add. MS. 70003 fols 237^r–238^r).

Like other groups, the Baptists relied on missionary work to gain new recruits. In 1643–4 William Kiffin, the pastor of a Particular Baptist congregation in London, visited East Kent and rebaptized groups of adults in Canterbury and elsewhere (Acheson 1983). In 1644 Kiffin also joined with fourteen other representatives of the seven Particular Baptist congregations in London to publish the first Baptist *Confession of Faith of those Churches which are commonly (though falsely) called Anabaptists*. In contrast with the

Westminster Confession, this was not the product of university-educated clerics, but the work of men with no formal theological training. It was a Calvinistic document, which made it clear that Baptist congregations were distinct bodies, but yet they were to follow 'one and the same rule'. In their introduction, Kiffin and his fellow subscribers refuted the accusations made in print and from the pulpit that the Baptists believed in free will and falling from grace, that they denied original sin and rejected the lawful commands of magistracy, and even that they had performed unseemly acts in dispensing baptism, 'not to be named amongst Christians'. They disclaimed these charges as 'notoriously' untrue, but because of these calumnies many 'that know not God' gathered at their meetings to stone them. The *Confession* was thus published to clear Baptist beliefs from these slurs (Kiffin et al. 1644).

In common with many other Independent churches, the Baptists wanted to maintain a clear division between church and state and they rejected the payment of tithes, the central licensing of preachers, and the power of the state to regulate church discipline. They also called for religious toleration for the Independents, which they hoped to achieve in alliance with the Leveller leaders Richard Overton, William Walwyn, and John Lilburne, the last of whom had been a fellow apprentice with Kiffin. The Levellers were largely focused on constitutional and parliamentary reforms, which would have widened the franchise and made Parliaments more accountable to the people, but between 1645 and 1648 they benefited from Baptist support and organization. The tensions between the secular programme of the Levellers and the Baptist desire to limit state interference in religion meant that their alliance could not survive indefinitely. The split came after the regicide, when the Levellers wanted to press for further constitutional reform, while the Baptists accepted the *de facto* regime. The abrupt severing of these ties by the Baptists in 1649 left their former allies with a strong sense of betrayal, but the influence of the Leveller movement itself was soon to lose its momentum.

In contrast, the Baptists regarded the regicide as a turning point in their favour. In May 1648 the Presbyterian majority in Parliament had passed an ordinance against blasphemy, which had included adult baptism in a list of outlawed practices punishable by imprisonment. It was passed as the outbreak of the second civil war had become a certainty, but the measure, which called for the death penalty for some second offences of blasphemy, was to become a dead letter under the republican regimes of the 1650s (Wright 2006; Firth and Rait 1911: I, 133–6). By the late 1650s, Baptist churches had been formed in Wales, Ireland, the Midlands, and the North, as well as in southern England, and it has been estimated that the Baptists numbered 25,000 by 1660.

The 1650 Act against blasphemy was aimed more specifically against the activities of the Ranters, whose ideas had emerged in the aftermath of the regicide in a series of intriguing pamphlets, which signalled disillusion with the religious policies of the Rump of the Long Parliament. In June a parliamentary committee was set up to report on the 'abominable practices of a sect called Ranters', who were believed to represent the extreme manifestations of antinomianism. Amongst their apologists were the army chaplains, Joseph Salmon, Abiezer Coppe, and Lawrence Clarkson, all of whom had flirted with a variety of religious affiliations including Baptist worship (First and Rait 1911: II, 409–12).

J. C. Davis has argued that as a movement the Ranters were largely a construct of the popular press, which characterized their beliefs in the abnegation of the moral law as leading to drunkenness, swearing, and unbridled carnal lust. It is clear enough that there was no formal Ranter organization and that their writings contained no practical campaign for reform. The most notorious Ranter publications appeared for a brief period between 1649 and 1651 and were characterized by forms of charismatic and prophetic writing (Davis 1986). In response the blasphemy act was aimed at anyone who maintained or believed that God dwelt within the 'Creature' or human body, or claimed that human perfection was to be found in the men and women who committed the greatest sins with the least remorse. One key question is how far the activities of the Ranter leaders helped to create a following in London and the provinces? A. L. Morton has argued that evidence of Ranterism can be found in Norfolk, Surrey, Warwickshire, Yorkshire, and other counties (Morton 1970). In 1655 Richard Coppin, a suspected Ranter preacher at Rochester Cathedral, was challenged to a four-day debate by a group of local Presbyterian clerics and then arrested under the terms of the 1650 blasphemy act. He was probably the only person to be apprehended under the terms of this legislation in Kent, as its provisions were rarely invoked. Coppin was accused of stating that heaven and hell were located in men's consciences and of denying the resurrection of the body. Major General Thomas Kelsey informed Cromwell, as Lord Protector, that he was worried that some of the soldiers at the garrison in Rochester had been infected with Coppin's heresies and asked that they should be replaced (Clement 2013).

Coppin continued to deny that he was a Ranter, although he had links with Coppe, who had provided a preface to one of Coppin's books in 1649. Both men were associates of John Pordage, a Berkshire minister, whose preaching and later publications display the influence of the German visionary Jakob Boehme. The thinking of Pordage and later English Behmenists involved a feminized manifestation of the deity called Sophia or wisdom (Gibbons 1996). While most of the key Ranters had faded from the public eye by the second half of the 1650s, Laurence Clarkson made an unsuccessful bid to take over the leadership of the Muggletonians in Kent. Their founder, Lodowicke Muggleton, and his cousin John Reeve, had experienced religious conversions in 1652, which led them to believe that they were the two witnesses prophesied in the Book of Revelations and chosen by God to proclaim the second coming of Christ. Clarkson was excommunicated from this sect in 1660, the year in which he also published his sensational spiritual autobiography *A Lost Sheep Found* (1660), in which his revelations of his life as a Ranter and libertine added weight to the earlier accusations that the Ranters were a dangerously debauched and heretical group.

Clarkson was, however, soon reconciled with Muggleton, whose followers were concentrated in a small area around Maidstone and Ashford in mid-Kent. In 1676 it was reported that there were thirty Muggletonians in the Ashford area, but nevertheless, they survived as a small sect into the twentieth century. Their archive of eighty-eight volumes of papers was discovered in 1974 in the possession of a Kent farmer, who gave them to the British Library (*ODNB* entry for Lodowicke Muggleton).

The Quakers and
the Fifth Monarchists

Like the Baptists, the Quakers were another of the religious groups to survive the Restoration and to flourish in the present day as the Society of Friends. Unlike the Baptists, they did not trace their origins into the pre-civil war period, but looked to a group of founders and missionaries, who were active in the 1650s, including George Fox and his wife Margaret Fell. In 1652 Fox had become convinced that he should found a new church after several years of religious meetings with 'friends'. He was one of a number of itinerant preachers, who starting out from Lancashire and the North of England 'convinced' thousands of people in Scotland, Ireland, Wales, England, and eventually the Americas, to join them. Margaret Fell was one of Fox's early converts and her home at Swarthmore Hall in Lancashire became a notable hub of Quaker organization (Kunze 1993).

The Quakers rejected the need for an ordained ministry and believed that anyone, man or woman, could be moved by the inward spirit of God to minister His word. Without the reliance on a university-educated clergy or on an especially ordained group of leaders, the Quakers were especially welcoming to the activities of women 'friends'. Patricia Crawford has demonstrated that in the 1650s half of all the books published by female authors in England were written by Quaker women. Even so, publications by women accounted for less than 1 per cent of the total in the period. Nevertheless, the writing of Quaker women and others such as the Fifth Monarchist, Anna Trapnel, illustrate the leading role that women could take in these religious groupings (Crawford 1985; Peters 2005). George and Margaret Fox insisted on the spiritual and social equality of men and women and this was manifested in the refusal of men Quakers to perform 'hat honour' by removing their hats in the presence of their putative social superiors and in the preaching of women Quakers. In 1666 Margaret published a tract defending the right of women to speak in public—*Women's Speaking Justified*—although by the time of the Restoration there had been a clampdown on lay preaching in general. Their refusal to pay tithes to the national Church, along with the Quakers' belief in an inner guiding 'light', their emphasis on lay missionary work, and refusal to take religious or civil oaths, all help to explain why Quakerism was seen as such a dangerous phenomenon. Male and female Quakers played into this role by actively challenging parish clergy in their pulpits and by noisily disrupting church services. A typical example is provided by the arrest in 1655 of Richard Clayton and Elizabeth Court, who had 'exhorted the People in the Steeple-House' at Wymondham in Norfolk after the church service. Approximately three hundred Quakers, a third of whom were women, were similarly imprisoned for their interventions during or after church services or in market and other public places in the 1650s (Besse 1753: I, 487; Reay 1985).

The Quakers kept very careful records of their missionary journeys, their sufferings at the hands of the republican and later authorities, and of their letters both to fellow friends and to the communities, which they hoped to 'convince'. An overview of the early history of the Quakers based on such records was published by Jospeh Besse in 1753 under the title *A Collection of the Sufferings of the People called Quakers, Taken from Original Records and Authentick Accounts*. Here Besse recorded that the earliest suffering of the Quakers in Cambridgeshire was the public whipping in 1653 of Elizabeth Williams and Mary Fisher, who had journeyed to Cambridge from the North. After engaging some 'scholars' of Sidney Sussex College in debate about religion, the two women denounced their adversaries as 'Antichrists' and their college as 'a Cage of unclean Birds, and the Synagogue of Satan'. Their punishment was dispensed in an unusually severe manner so that their flesh was torn, but according to Besse the women endured this torture with religious singing and rejoicing. Women were also in the forefront of the public suffering and witnessing of the Quakers in other counties including the City of London, where Anne Downer was arrested for ten weeks in 1655 for 'some Expressions against the Preacher' at Stepney (Besse 1753: I, 84–5, 361).

The most notorious public display made by Quakers took place in 1656 when James Nayler, an influential rival to George Fox's leadership of the movement, entered Bristol on horseback accompanied by female followers crying 'holy, holy, holy' in imitation of Christ's entry into Jerusalem. Nayler was arrested and charged under the 1650 blasphemy legislation: his case occupied parliamentary debate for several weeks with some MPs, including the Major Generals Whalley, Goffe, and Boteler arguing for the death penalty. Nayler was subjected instead to a series of testing physical punishments including a severe whipping, pillorying, tongue boring, and branding with a 'B' for blasphemer on his forehead, before being imprisoned (*ODNB* entry under Nayler).

THE RESTORATION

At the Restoration the Quakers were at pains to repudiate their reputation as disrupters of the religious, social, and gender hierarchies. In particular, the role of female Quakers as preachers and missionaries was constrained by the development of separate women's meetings, which were dedicated to fundraising and offering support to the families of imprisoned friends. The Quakers were also keen to distance themselves from groups such as the Fifth Monarchists, who were extreme millenarianists with a conviction in the imminent second coming of Christ. The Fifth Monarchists were seen as particularly dangerous to civil society because of their belief that secular government would have to be overthrown by force, if necessary, before the rule of Christ could begin. Some Fifth Monarchists had great influence in republican circles in the 1650s, including Thomas Harrison, one of Cromwell's major generals, who had signed the death warrant of Charles I. Harrison was one of the first of the regicides to be tried and suffer a traitor's death under the restored monarchy. Three months later, a failed uprising in January 1661 resulted in the execution of Thomas Venner, one of the Fifth Monarchists' most militant leaders and the head of the Fifth Monarchist congregation in London's Coleman Street. Despite these deaths, Fifth Monarchists were reputedly active in London and the South into the 1680s (Capp 1972).

In contrast, the Quakers began to distance themselves from the violence of the revolutionary period and espoused pacifism, which became one of their defining characteristics. In response to a royal proclamation, sixteen Quakers, including George Fox, Richard Hubbethorne, and Samuel Fisher, addressed Charles II in November 1660 with an assurance of Quaker loyalty and a repudiation of all 'outward Wars, and Strife, and Fightings with outward Weapons, for any end, under any pretence whatsoever, and this is our Testimony to the whole World' (Fox et al. 1661: 2).

The terms of Charles II's return from exile was based on his undertakings in the Declaration of Breda, in which amongst other things he had agreed to 'a Liberty to Tender Consciences, and that no man shall be disquieted or called in question for differences of opinion in matters of Religion, which do not disturb the Peace of the Kingdom'. He went on to indicate a willingness to consent to an Act 'for the full granting of [religious] indulgence' (Declaration of Breda 1660). The suspicion that an Act of toleration would open the way to freedoms for Catholic worship delayed the passage of this measure until the accession of the staunchly Protestant monarchs, William III and Mary II, who specifically excluded Roman Catholics from the provisions of the Toleration Act of 1689. The Cavalier Parliament of 1661–79 was dominated by royalists and Charles II also bowed to their pressure in passing a series of laws against the puritan dissenters to protect the resurgent Church of England. These included the Act of Uniformity of 1662 and an Act against Conventicles passed in 1664.

The royalists and conformists, who had kept prayer-book worship alive during the civil wars and Interregnum certainly welcomed the restoration of traditional worship. When Charles II returned to England in May 1660 as king, he heard a Sunday service in Canterbury Cathedral, a building described by the earl of Clarendon as 'very much dilapidated and out of repair; yet the people seemed glad to hear the Common Prayer again'. Nevertheless, the tumultuous decades of the 1640s and 1650s, when religious freedom had been debated and seized by an array of different sects and congregations, had created a legacy of dissent which could not easily be eradicated. A new generation of worshippers had grown up since the powers of the episcopal Church had waned in the early 1640s. In October 1660 the famous diarist Samuel Pepys recorded seeing the translation of Dr Accepted Frewen to the archbishopric of York. Also present were the bishops of Winchester, Bangor, Rochester, Bath and Wells, and Salisbury, 'but Lord, at their going out, how people did most of them look upon them as strange Creatures, and few with any kind of love or Respect' (Clarendon 1888: 233; Latham and Matthews 1970: I, 259). Fourteen years after the abolition of episcopacy, people would indeed have found the bishops 'all in their habitts' a strange sight, but the feelings of those who had sided with Parliament and the Republic against the king ran deeper. Despite the general acceptance of the return of the monarchy, for the religious dissenters Cromwell's contest against 'the tyranny of the bishops' was to remain a live issue in the decades to come.

CHAPTER 7

....

RELIGION AND THE GOVERNMENT OF THE LATER STUARTS

....

GRANT TAPSELL

WHEN Charles II set foot within his kingdoms on 25 May 1660 as he returned from continental exile, the mayor of Dover's chaplain presented him with a 'very rich Bible'. Another copy would be pressed into the king's hands four days later as he entered London on his thirtieth birthday. Having told the assembled dignitaries of Dover that the Bible was 'the thing that he loved above all things in the world', Charles warmed to his theme when speaking to the ministers of London: 'he would make that book the rule of his life and government' (Pepys 2000: I, 158 and n. 2). Although his new subjects would soon have good reason to doubt the nature and depth of the king's religious sensibilities, the fact that Charles's carefully choreographed return to England featured such prominent set-piece engagements with Scripture is richly significant. Religious issues were at the heart of the problematic Restoration process, just as they had been twenty years earlier when civil war had engulfed England (Morrill 1984; Prior and Burgess 2011). Indeed, they would prove to be the biggest persistent problem for the government of the later Stuarts. That this was so reflected both a difficult religious inheritance, and the enduring capacity of religious divisions to complicate public affairs. The interaction of the past and the present would result in chronic instability in public affairs right through to the end of the seventeenth century. In order to explain why neither the 1660 Restoration nor the 1688 Revolution 'settlements' resulted in religious and political harmony, this chapter will examine in turn the conflict between ideas of toleration and uniformity; the interactions between church and state; and the prominence of religion in the information culture of later seventeenth-century England. However, first, it is necessary to set the scene by examining shifting scholarly attitudes towards the period.

HISTORIOGRAPHY

Historians have developed varying labels and conceptual frameworks to make sense of the later Stuart era. Many of these have their roots in rival contemporary perspectives on events that were powerfully conditioned by religious belief. Christopher Hill memorably examined 'the experience of defeat' for radicals who felt that successive conservative reactions from the late 1640s through into the 1660s represented dire apostasy from God's cause and left them wandering in the wilderness (Hill 1984: 297–303 and *passim*). This obviously reflected Hill's unrivalled sensitivity towards radicals' hopes and fears as expressed in printed literature. He thus echoed the perception of Puritans that the Restoration had been hijacked by their enemies—though Hill's presentation of events arguably failed to capture the range of continued efforts by many different kinds of Protestant Nonconformists to engage creatively with public life (Southcombe and Tapsell 2010: 32–6). At the other end of the historiographical spectrum, J. C. D. Clark has powerfully framed the whole 1660–1832 period as an English *ancien régime*, one in which religious identity was a crucial determinant of political respectability (Clark 2000). In describing a 'confessional state' Clark drew inspiration from figures as far removed from Hill's chosen people as it is possible to imagine. In 1702, for instance, the High Church preacher Dr Henry Sacheverell proclaimed that 'The *Civil* and *Ecclesiastical* State are the Two Parts and Divisions, that Both United make up One entire compounded Constitution, and Body Politick, sharing the same Fate and Circumstances, Twisted and Interwoven into the very Being and Principles of each Other' (Clark 2000: 28). Ventriloquizing reactionary thinkers has not attracted universal approbation for Clark's thesis: Sacheverell was making a shrill polemical point in the face of what he believed to be a rising tide of popular irreligion and neglect of the state church by leading politicians (Sirota 2014b: 89–90; Knights 2012; Champion 1992).

From their very different perspectives, both Hill and Clark engaged with an overall question of meta-narrative: how did the Restoration era fit into longer-term trends in English history? Older accounts tended to present 1660 as the starting point for a more 'enlightened', secular age in which religious issues gradually lost their potency in public affairs (Jones 1979: 7–8). Such a view was vigorously undermined from the late 1980s by a wave of scholarship that focused on 'the politics of religion' after 1660 (Harris, Seaward, and Goldie 1990). Far from representing the dawn of a new age, the Restoration could more plausibly be understood as witnessing a continuation of seventeenth-century issues and problems, in particular fears of 'popery and arbitrary government' (Scott 2000). Recently there have been renewed efforts to reshape older ideas that stressed change rather than continuity in later Stuart society. It has been argued that 'the English demonstrated increasing skill at separating religious belief and action from other spheres of life', part of a wider series of changes indicative of 'modernity' (Houston and Pincus 2001: 14). Some of this reflects the powerful—or baleful—influence of sociological theory, notably Jürgen Habermas's conception of a 'public sphere' that allegedly emerged in England as a result of events and processes during the 1690s. Such a sphere was described as 'rational-critical' in character, which perforce bleached (irrational) religious belief out of the fabric of public discussion (Habermas 1989; Raymond 1999). Particular attention has been given to a developing language of political economy, rather than older religious concerns, as a prime driver of public affairs, especially foreign policy (Pincus 2007, 2009: 366–99, 2012). However forcefully such views have been expressed, it remains more convincing to see religion permeating the most important events that gave shape and meaning to later seventeenth-century affairs (De Krey 2008: 748–53; Claydon 2000). Although the contemporary politician John Hay, earl of Tweeddale, was wearily referring to Restoration Scotland, his words could almost as readily have been applied to England: 'more than two parts in three of the whole business of the government related to the church' (Burnet 1897–1900: I, 443).

IDEAS: TOLERATION VERSUS UNIFORMITY

At a conceptual level, the connections between religious uniformity and civil peace were axiomatic: a house divided against itself would fall. The justices of the peace who met at the quarter sessions in Exeter in January 1682 ordered the prosecution of 'papists and sectaries' explicitly because 'Religion is the foundation of Civil Governement and whilst faction and Schisme are allowed & permitted in the Church, wee can never expect peace and quiet in the state' (Tapsell 2007: 83). English religious intolerance was, however, much more than a product of age-old political theology. It was also the result of recent experience. The later Stuart age was deeply in the shadow of the puritan revolution that had preceded it: as a preacher noted in April 1663, 'it was not above a few years since … the world turned upside down' (Neufeld 2013; Gregory 1995: 205 n. 1). Contemporaries believed that religious tensions had been of pivotal importance in the collapse of Caroline government, armed rebellion against the king, and the public execution of Charles I on 30 January 1649. The cult of the royal martyr was a powerful presence within the Restoration Church and provided a clinching English proof of a broader European phenomenon: appeals to conscience could destabilize any polity to the point of disaster (Lacey 2006). As the young John Locke noted, with a bitter swipe at radical clerics, in 1660:

> All those flames that have made such havoc and desolation in Europe, and have not been quenched but with the blood of so many millions, have been at first kindled with coals from the altar, and too much blown with the breath of those that attend the altar, who forgetting their calling, which is to promote peace and meekness, have proved the trumpeters of strife. (Locke 1997: 41)

Not all problems were reducible to religious fault lines, but by the last decades of the seventeenth century it was understandable that political elites should have seen secular disobedience lurking behind pious scruples.

There were, however, two very different possible responses to the commonly held view that the English had suffered deeply in the early modern period as a result of religious divisions. One policy, toleration, was pursued by successive monarchs, albeit primarily for pragmatic rather than principled reasons. It presupposed that accommodating, rather than persecuting, a variety of religious positions was the surest way to avoid discontent and upheaval. A vital precursor to the parliamentary invitation that brought Charles back to England was the declaration he issued from the Dutch town of Breda on 4/14 April 1660. In this Charles promised a 'liberty to tender consciences': this was crucial at a time when a puritan governing establishment, notably including the armed forces, was fearful of losing hard-won religious liberties as part of a return to monarchy (Kenyon 1986: 332). Charles's promise could not, however, be honoured, as it was contingent on him being presented with an act of parliament that would never arrive, leaving the Presbyterians who had been critical brokers of the Restoration to experience the next quarter of a century as one 'long betrayal' (Morrice 2007–9: I, 160). Nevertheless, Charles twice attempted, in 1662 and 1672, to use the royal prerogative to dispense those outside the Church of England, as re-established by law, from the penalties prescribed for Nonconformity. Both efforts were in part based on the king's erroneous belief that the Nonconformists were far more numerous than in reality was the case, and therefore more of a potential threat to state stability if unduly antagonized (Whiteman 1986: xxiv). They also reflected Charles's desire to improve the lot of England's Catholic community, with whose beliefs he was well known to be in sympathy long before his death-bed conversion to Roman Catholicism in 1685 (Hutton 1996). His openly Catholic brother, James II, would also issue declarations of indulgence, in 1687 and 1688, albeit in even more controversial circumstances. Viewed in the context of strident efforts to re-Catholicize his kingdoms, James's very wide-ranging indulgences were viewed primarily as means to undermine the long-term existence of the Church of England (Southcombe and Tapsell 2010: 77–87). (Some recent historians, it should be said, have offered more principled, or complex, perspectives on James's policies [Knights 2001; Sowerby 2013].) Toleration was even more strongly espoused by the man who militarily ousted him, William of Orange, ironically even to the extent of trying to rein in the persecution of Catholics. Privately scornful of the pretensions of the Church of England, long-schooled in the tolerationist policies of the Dutch Republic, and necessarily *politique* in order to maintain his multi-confessional European military alliances, William III's reign was marked by the passage of the Toleration Act (1689) (Israel 1991). This cemented in law a long-pursued policy that removed legal penalties for differing styles of religious worship, even if it did not open public office to those not in communion with the Church of England (Williams 1960: 42–6; Spurr 1989). Licensed meeting houses for Protestant Nonconformists duly mushroomed in the 1690s, much to the chagrin of hard-line churchmen.

Such men were not in short supply in the Restoration era. Indeed, in the immediate aftermath of Charles II's return, they had set about frustrating the royal will for toleration with great success. For politicians of this stamp, rallied by figures as prominent as the Archbishop of Canterbury, Gilbert Sheldon, the primary lesson to be drawn from experience of the previous twenty years was the need to enforce a policy of uniformity in religion (Jones 1993). Puritans were perceived to be at heart king-killing republicans, and needed to be kept under by harsh legislation, vigorously enforced locally by watchful justices of the peace. The fact that the king so evidently disagreed with them, and that many justices chose not to prosecute their Nonconformist neighbours, only stimulated this sectional impulse to persecute all the more (Fletcher 1984). Such views would prove very durable. This was partly because they had such a long pedigree: tolerationist views were pushing against a millennium of intolerance, with exclusivist claims to a single religious truth having been defended by the greatest Fathers of the Church, notably Augustine, against those championing rival points of view (Goldie 1991). But it was also the result of continued plots and revolts organized by a small fringe of militant Nonconformists whose only success was to tar wider, pacific, and politically loyal groups with the brush of rebellion (Greaves 1986, 1990, 1992).

Long-standing fears of religious heterodoxy, and ongoing suspicions that contemporary religious dissidents were disloyal subjects, combined in an immensely powerful way in the later Stuart era. This was especially because they provided a language or discourse that readily unitied contemporaries across social groups, both elite clerics and politicians and a wide swathe of the populace. Religious persecution was not an impulse confined either to theologians or uneducated bigots. Until the passage of the Toleration Act, intolerance was legitimized in law: both in the foundational Act of Uniformity (1662), and in the raft of penal legislation, the so-called 'Clarendon Code', that accompanied it, notably the Corporation Act (1661), the Quaker Act (1662), the First Conventicles Act (1664), and the Five Mile Act (1665) (Holmes 1993: 454–5). This represented either a grim panoply of repressive measures, or a series of vital bulwarks for the Church of England, depending on different contemporaries' perspectives. The opening words of one of these acts, the second Conventicles Act (1670), indicates the potent mix of historical memory and anti-puritan allegations of deceit and hypocrisy that marked the whole mindset of intolerance:

> For providing further and more speedy remedies against the growing and dangerous practices of seditious sectaries and other disloyal persons, who under pretence of tender consciences have or may at their meetings contrive insurrections (as late experience hath shown). (Kenyon 1986: 356)

Small wonder that by 1688 the Presbyterian clergyman and intelligencer Roger Morrice could look back bitterly on almost three decades of legally sanctioned oppression, and inveigh against 'the 13 or 14 Oathes Declarations and Subscriptions' that had been used to keep Nonconformists out of public life (Morrice 2007–9: IV, 381). Even after the passage of the Toleration Act, it was not unusual for rioters to express bitterly negative religious slogans, notably during the era of frequent elections that lay between the passage of the Triennial Act in 1694 and the Septennial Act in 1716. During the parliamentary elections held in Suffolk in 1705, for instance, a Tory mob shouted 'no '48, no Presbyterian rebellion, save the Queen's white neck' (Cruickshanks, Handley, and Hayton 2002: II, 544). (Since the contemporary English calendar took the year to begin on 25 March, the execution of Charles on 30 January had by this reckoning taken place in 1648.) As this suggests, the 1690s would witness escalating attempts to peg back, or wholly overturn, toleration, and to return to what some would see as the golden age of monopolistic rights for a narrowly defined Church of England in the early 1680s (Bennett 1975).

STRUCTURES: CHURCH AND STATE

The clash between ideas of toleration and older beliefs in the vital importance of religious uniformity was played out in a world in which church and state were powerfully intermingled. Secular authority received legitimation and support from the preaching and writing of the clergy; the ecclesiastical hierarchy looked to ministers of state and local lay magistrates to protect the interests of the Church. All this was straightforward in theory, but complex and unstable in practice. At the pinnacle of government the later Stuart kings inherited from their forbears the position of supreme governor of the Church of England, nominally making them all 'nursing fathers' to the state church. The reality would prove very different. Charles II was very likely a crypto-Catholic prior to his death-bed conversion; James II's whole reign was defined by his open and passionate Catholicism; William III's Dutch background and acquiescence in a resurgent Presbyterian church settlement in Scotland made him deeply suspect in the eyes of many English churchmen. The later Stuarts' powers in ecclesiastical affairs were nevertheless extensive. Most notoriously, James II created a commission of ecclesiastical causes in order to discipline the Church of England, both in terms of individual clerics and academic colleges, and to advertise more broadly his hostility to anti-Catholic activity of all kinds (Rose 2011: 251–67). But Charles and William would also utilize the Royal Supremacy to create ecclesiastical commissions in 1681 and 1695 that would influence the Church via clerical preferments (Beddard 1967; Tapsell 2015; Bennett 1966: 124). William's distaste for religious intolerance led him to appoint a raft of moderate clerics to the episcopal bench, who were then, as Daniel Defoe would note, attacked as 'Dutch Churchmen ... complying too far with the Dissenters and ... giving up the decent ceremonyes and settled discipline, in exchange for a slovenly rude way of worship' (Israel 1991: 164).

Yet if the Church of England was powerfully influenced by its supreme governors, it was also shaped and reshaped by parliament. Groups of MPs and peers destroyed hopes for a broad church settlement between 1660 and 1662, as well as scotching plans for comprehension during the Exclusion Crisis (1679–81) and again in 1689. In so doing, they triumphed over a significant number of parliamentarians who were either puritan-minded, or else sympathetic to the idea of a broad Protestant interest opposed to 'popery' (Lacey 1969; Swatland 1996: 145–99). Clerics possessed of a high opinion of the significance and powers of the ecclesiastical estate were revealingly sensitive to accusations that theirs was a mere 'parliamentary' religion. They worked hard to resurrect the Church's corollary to parliament, convocation, in the 1690s after decades of lifelessness

(Sykes 1959: 41–4; Sirota 2014a: 187–222). Such activity was, in the final analysis, hypocritical, and smacked of sour grapes: the same figures had not objected to the important parliamentary activity of the bishops, sitting in the House of Lords, before 1688, notably when their votes had been so important in the fight against Whig bills of exclusion to prevent James's succession to the throne. Nor were vocal groups of 'High Church' partisans reticent about seeking to use parliament to further their campaign to save what they alleged was a 'Church in Danger' from dissenters and their 'Low Church' establishment sympathizers during the 1690s and 1700s. In particular, stringent efforts were made to enact legislation to make illegal the practice of 'occasional conformity', whereby dissenters could qualify themselves for public office by paying lip service to communion within the Church of England (Bennett 1975).

As such activity suggests, if the Church was buffeted by broader political trends, religious leaders also influenced the government's actions. Senior bishops and archbishops might become members of the privy council. Some would serve as royal propagandists and vocal public supporters of individual kings, often courting considerable unpopularity in the process, notably in the cases of Thomas Cartwright's activity on behalf of James II, or Gilbert Burnet's preaching and writing in favour of William III (Cartwright 1843; Claydon 1996). Others would make significant stands in opposition to royal policy. Henry Compton, Bishop of London, would be suspended by James's ecclesiastical commission for refusing to stop his clergy preaching anti-Catholic sermons (Carpenter 1956: 78–103). Even more prominently, seven bishops—including William Sancroft, Archbishop of Canterbury—found themselves on trial in June 1688 for allegedly publishing their refusal to read the king's second declaration of indulgence (Sowerby 2013: 153–92; Gibson 2009). In William III's reign, clerics continued to play a highly significant role in opposition to the government. Six bishops and around four hundred lower clergy refused to take the new oath of loyalty to William and Mary, and became nonjurors condemned to life outside the Church of England (Rose 1999: 152–60). Even amongst those clergy who did, often grudgingly, take the oath, voluble groups, notably those rooted in the redoubts of Oxford colleges' common rooms, would criticize the new regime's religious latitude (Bennett 1986).

Bearing in mind the extent to which church and state interpenetrated in this period, it was only natural that whole ministries, and crucial areas of policy, should be viewed through primarily religious lenses. After the fall of Charles II's first chief minister, the earl of Clarendon, in 1667, for instance, the emergence of a 'Cabal' ministry excited the hopes of some and the fears of others in large part because of its leading ministers' striking lack of Anglican credentials. When that in turn collapsed, Charles II found it expedient to raise up a new chief minister, Thomas Osborne, created earl of Danby, who would set out to bolster the established Church, and who would receive much political support from the bishops in the House of Lords (Goldie 1990). Most tellingly of all, the different phases of James II's brief reign were 'sign-posted' by the changing confessional character of his leading office-holders. Initially he sought to reassure the Protestant majority by entrusting government to men like the Hyde brothers, Laurence, earl of Rochester, as Lord Treasurer, and Henry, second earl of Clarendon, as Lord Privy Seal, who were both pillars of the established Church interest. James's shift to more overtly Catholicizing policies would be made manifest to all when the Hydes were dismissed in the winter of 1686/7, and more confessionally malleable figures like Robert Spencer, earl of Sunderland, took their place (Tapsell 2010: 1430–8; Kenyon 1958: 145–223). All of these ministries were significant not just for their domestic political activity, but very importantly also for their execution of successive kings' foreign policies. During the 'Cabal' era, Charles's decision to fight in alliance with Catholic France during the Third Anglo-Dutch War (1672–4) was viewed with horror by many of his subjects, especially when the Dutch Republic came perilously close to being completely overrun in 1672. Lurking behind the fog of war was the Treaty of Dover (1670), whose public terms cemented the Anglo-French alliance, but whose secret terms were even more far-reaching, including as they did a promise that Charles would publicly convert to Catholicism, and enforce that faith on his kingdoms with the aid of France (Hutton 1986; Glickman 2013).

Charles's francophilia would continue to unsettle his rule thereafter. The resurgent power of Louis XIV's France in European terms went alongside increasingly intolerant confessional policies, notably persecution of French Huguenots that was closely followed by anxious English spectators. Revelations that Charles received a pension from Louis were sufficient to bring down Danby's ministry in 1678/9 (Knights, *ODNB*). The French king's decision in 1685 to revoke the Edict of Nantes (1598), the royal grant of limited rights to French Protestants, was a terrible backdrop to James II's efforts to persuade his own subjects that a Catholic ruler of England would not necessarily prove to be a persecutor on the model of Mary Tudor. By deliberate contrast, James's dynastic enemies took care to define themselves as strident Protestants. Charles II's eldest natural son, James Scott, duke of Monmouth, projected himself in the latter part of his father's reign as 'the Protestant Duke', and would attract considerable support from Nonconformists when he invaded southwest England in 1685 to contest the throne (Harris 2004–14; Clifton 1984; Earle 1977). William of Orange's propagandists presented him as a Protestant deliverer, guided by Providence to intervene in English affairs to thwart the advance of Catholicism (Claydon 1996). His reign would be characterized in domestic terms by vocal movements for a 'reformation of manner', an agenda whose puritan roots left it deeply suspect in the eyes of High Churchmen (Sirota 2014a).

DISCUSSION: RELIGION, GOVERNMENT, AND THE PRESS

The fact that religious issues were at the heart of public affairs under the later Stuarts was not due simply to the intrinsic power of competing religious ideals, nor even to the close interactions between church and state. It was also a product of the central position that religion occupied within the information culture of seventeenth-century England. This may be discussed in terms of three key themes: the production of literature designed to instruct the populace in the tenets of the Church of England and to indoctrinate them against Roman Catholicism; the rancorous consequences of Protestant schism after 1662; and the ways in which different religious perspectives powerfully inflected discussions of good government. None of these themes was restricted to printed literature, indeed historians have been at pains to emphasize that even in the later seventeenth century manuscript and oral transmission of ideas remained significant parts of information culture (Atherton 1999; Fox 2001). Nevertheless, in keeping with the broad concerns of this book, the focus will hereafter remain on printed materials. Before turning to detailed discussion of the three themes, it is important first to outline issues of press production and governmental control.

The later Stuart political world operated in a state of profound interaction with the press. Graphs plotting the number of titles printed in every year of the early modern period in England display notable spikes of activity at times of political crisis, prompting intractable 'chicken and egg' style questions: did political events prompt print 'bubbles', or did a sudden efflorescence of printed material prompt deeper public engagement with political affairs (Raymond 2003: 164, fig. 1)? The year of Restoration was evidently 'a boom year' for the press, perhaps even to the extent that it was 'instrumental in bringing a new government into being by helping establish terms and conditions that would make that government broadly acceptable' (MacLean 2011: 620–1). Another great peak of press activity would attend the Exclusion Crisis (1679–81), the parliamentary contest over removing James from the line of succession on the grounds of his Catholicism, and the Popish Plot scare that immediately preceded it. It has been estimated that between five and ten million pamphlets flooded the country in 1679–81 (Knights 1994: 168). Even allowing for the fact that not all of these were directly related to political events, and that their regional distribution beyond the metropolis of London was uneven, this was a matter of huge importance. William of Orange would recognize the significance of the press when he brought a printing press with him during the invasion of England in the winter of 1688/9 (Claydon 1996: 24). Even as king, though, he would not be able to control the output of the presses, with his succession, and the new oath of allegiance, triggering a vehement printed controversy (Goldie 1980).

It is, of course, less difficult to chart the volume of printed material produced in the later seventeenth century than it is to analyse its impact and significance. Successive later Stuart governments certainly thought that the press mattered in the sense of attempting to control its output. Pre-publication supervision was a key facet of government until the Licensing Act (1662) lapsed in 1679, only to be renewed in 1685. It was not until 1695 that this would again lapse, and even then twelve more parliamentary bills would be proposed over the next fifteen years that were designed to regulate the press (Kemp 2012: 47–68). Assessing the extent to which licensing inhibited open discussion is far from straightforward. The limited resources of early modern government could not achieve complete surveillance of all the presses operating in the vast metropolis of London. Much depended on the zeal of key individuals, notably the indefatigable Surveyor of the Press for much of the period, Roger L'Estrange (Love 2004–14; Kemp and McElligott 2009: III, 21–58). Various cultures of evasion were practised, and, as the figures already quoted demonstrate, vast quantities of printed material undoubtedly irrigated English political discourse: closely supervising all of it would have been impossible. Nevertheless, even very small numbers of grisly examples could have proved intimidating for contemporary printers and publishers. The printers John Twyn and William Anderton would be executed in 1664 and 1693 respectively for producing treasonable literature, whilst the satirical ballad *A Ra-Ree Show* (1681) would be used against the Nonconformist poet Stephen College in a successful treason trial that marked the government's vigorous efforts to restrict the press after the Exclusion Crisis (Southcombe and Tapsell 2010: 130–1; De Krey 2004–14; Kemp and McElligott 2009: III, xiii). Most notoriously of all, the republican thinker Algernon Sidney would be put to death in 1683 as a result of a trial that utilized a political tract as the vital second required witness to treasonable activity, Judge Jeffreys controversially ruling that 'scribere est agere': to write treason was to engage in an 'overt' treasonable act (Scott 1991: 329). Sidney's tract was a manuscript that would not be published until 1698, but the broader lessons for authors of all printed materials of all kinds were, and were meant to be, intimidating.

The range of material that emerged from the presses was at least as striking as the volume, and religious forms and themes were consistently to the fore, providing handsome profits for printers as authors sought to instruct and indoctrinate their readers. Works falling within the general category of 'divinity' together constituted an estimated average of 41.8 per cent of all new printed titles across the period 1668–1709, many times greater than the next biggest group ('history', at 7.6 per cent). Nor did the volume of printed religious materials decline over the later Stuart period. Just over 140,000 catechisms and primers, psalters and psalms were produced in 1663. By 1699 the figure had risen to in excess of 180,000 (Barnard and Bell 2002: 788, table 4; Raven 2007: 93, fig. 4.1). Sermons were a particular mainstay of the publishing industry. To take some especially striking examples, William Beveridge's *A Sermon Concerning the Excellency and Usefulness of the Common Prayer* went through twenty-two editions between 1681 and 1714; 200 of Archbishop John Tillotson's sermons were edited for publication after his death, appearing in fourteen volumes between 1695 and 1704; and around a hundred thousand copies of Henry Sacheverell's notorious 1709 sermon attacking Nonconformists, *The Perils of False Brethren*, were sold (Rivers 2009: 593; Holmes 1973: 75). Huge efforts were clearly being made to impress religious messages onto the minds of the later Stuarts' subjects— sometimes from a very young age. *The Protestant Tutor* (1679), for instance, was produced by Benjamin Harris with the goal of 'instructing children to spel and read English, and Grounding them in the True Protestant Religion and Discovering the Errors and Deceits of the Papists'. This was to be achieved by a charming combination of terrifying visual images of 'popish tyranny and cruelty'; guides on how to pronounce words like 'Inquisition', 'superstition', and 'transubstantiation'; potted histories and martyrologies; catechistical exercises asking questions like 'Is the Church of Rome Mother and Mistriss of all Churches?' (correct answer: 'no'); and useful bedtime prayers, in which the suitably traumatized children would be encouraged to pray that God would inspire their parents 'that they may instruct me in thy True Religion that I may not be insnared with

Idolatry and false Doctrines' (Harris 1679: frontispiece, 52, 62, 72, 82, 105, 110, 111, 117, 144). The book was dedicated to James, duke of Monmouth, as a highly polemical exercise during the Exclusion Crisis: a Protestant successor was urgently needed to avoid the likely Catholic tyranny of James, duke of York. Although James II's regime would ultimately make substantial use of the press to transmit positive messages about the Catholic faith, this was pushing against an ocean of pre-existing anti-Catholic literature (Southcombe and Tapsell 2010: 88).

Literature, religion, and politics were inextricably intertwined from the earliest years of the Restoration in large part because of the unparalleled Protestant schism of 1662. Despite lengthy negotiations, and several major conferences, the terms of the Act of Uniformity of that year were intolerable to a significant section of the old puritan wing of the Church. Between the return of the king and the final date for compliance with the terms of the act, 24 August 1662, 'Black Bartholomew's Day', more than two thousand clerics had left or been ejected from their livings in England and Wales (Southcombe and Tapsell 2010: 25–6). The Licensing Act (1662) was the necessary corollary of the Act of Uniformity, prohibiting the publication of anything 'contrary to … the doctrine or discipline of the Church of England' (Love 2004–14). This was intended to prevent a torrent of literature from the ejected puritan ministers, though this proved to be a forlorn hope since large numbers of farewell sermons were published regardless (Appleby 2007). In the years that followed, those now rendered by law 'Nonconformists' with the state Church proved deeply committed to emphasizing in print both their political respectability and the grasping nature of their opponents. The Presbyterian cleric and poet Robert Wild, for instance, penned *The Loyal Nonconformist* in 1666, outraged at the terms of the Five Mile Act (1665) that sought to exile from towns any previously resident ejected ministers who refused an oath not to 'endeavour any Alteration of Government either in Church or State'. As he carefully wrote: 'The Civil-Government I will obey; | But for Church-Policy I swear I doubt it' (Southcombe 2012: I, 221–5). Wild would later savagely contrast the purity of principle of the Nonconformists with the greed of the conformist clergy in his 1672 poem *Dr Wild's Humble Thanks … for Liberty of Conscience*:

> We'l preach in Sackcloth, they shall read in Silk,
> We'l feed the Flock, and let them take the Milk …
> The Tythe-pigg shall be theirs; we'l turn the spit,
> We'l bear the *Cross*, they only *sign* with it. (Southcombe 2012: I, 257)

Such hostility towards the consequences of the narrow Church settlement of 1662 did not, however, mean that there was a united Nonconformist front against it. Indeed literature acted as an outlet for intra-dissenting divisions and mutual suspicion. This was of the first political importance during James's reign, when the majority of the most populous Nonconformist group, the Presbyterians, proved wary of the king's offer of toleration, fearing his ulterior motives, whilst Baptists proved amongst his most zealous supporters (Thomas 1962: 234–8; Morrice 2007–9: IV, xxiv; Sowerby 2013). No less importantly for the more radical groups, there would be an enduring rivalry between Baptists and Quakers, fought out not least in bitter polemical publishing (Underwood: 2001). However variegated its character, though, the 'literary culture of nonconformity' in the later Stuart era would serve as a crucial means of maintaining a sense of identity in the face of persecution (Keeble 1987).

The oxygen of publicity was undoubtedly important for politically marginalized groups. But printed literature was not necessarily an oppositional force: it was powerfully deployed by those seeking to defend the Church of England and the necessity of intolerance towards Nonconformists. In part this would be expressed through ridiculing Nonconformists' claims of persecution as self-interested hypberbole, and emphasizing instead that the restoration of the Church of England had brought peace and order after a period of religious anarchy. According to the anonymous author of a pugnacious printed 'answer' to one of Wild's poems in 1663:

> Is *Preaching down*, and silenced because
> The *Presbyters* may'nt bawl against the Laws?
> Not rail at *Church* and *State*, nor bait the *King*
> With *Pulpit-bulls*, like *Dogs* a *Bear-baiting*.
> So *Wranglers*, *Cheats*, and *Cozeners* may say,
> 'Cause they shut out, *fair Gamesters* do not play:
> So *Quacksalvers* and *Mountebanks* proclaim,
> No Physick's like to theirs, though of the same.
> Once come to hear and they shall understand,
> There ne'r was better *Preaching* in the Land,
> Nor *Prayers* so well compos'd with *words* & matter,
> (Not like unto the *Puritanick chatter*)
> Where *Hum*, *ha*, and *Oh* bear all the *sway*,
> And true *Devotion* is a *Cast-away*. (Anon. *An Answer to Wild* 1663: 1)[1]

Compared to the extempore prayers, and supposedly over-heated preaching of the Nonconformists, conformist authors thus pointed to the restored Church's orderly worship.

Hard-line apologists for the restored Church of England would focus on the alleged dissimulation and hypocrisy of dissenters, re-deploying a long-term anti-puritan discourse in which greed and ambition lurked always behind expressions of pious sentiment (Harris 2009). In particular, it would persistently be argued that whatever Nonconformists might claim in public, in reality they sought to reverse the Restoration and to re-establish the political supremacy that they had enjoyed during the Interregnum. Here, a useful example of hostile reading habits may be found in the diary of Edmund Bohun, a Suffolk justice of the peace from 1675, occasional author, and licenser of the press for a brief and unhappy period in 1692/3 (Kemp 2004–14; Goldie 1977). In March 1677, for instance, Bohun was outraged when he read *A Pacquet of Advices*

---

[1] I owe this reference to the kindness of George Southcombe.

and Animadversions sent from London to the Men of Shaftsbury since it 'exposes the fatal artifices and tumults designed by the presbyterian party, in some recent sessions of parliament, to renew the rebellion' (Bohun 1853: 3). He was particularly agitated by what became a broader leitmotif of a particular kind of conformist writing: that the blandishments of Nonconformists seeking a broad Protestant alliance to defend the country against the threat of Roman Catholicism were merely a disguise for their own insidious purposes. When Bohun read Marvell's anonymously published *Account of the Growth of Popery and Arbitrary Government* in May 1678, he sarcastically noted that at least it was written by 'an honest puritane' who wished to teach another rebellion: 'they who keepe up the schisme and endeavour to introduce toleration, comprehension, and all manner of disorder, are the best factors for popery'. Such people 'must bee crushed before it can bee prevented' (Bohun 1853: 40–1). On this basis, Nonconformists could actually be polemically equated with 'papists' as a threat to the English Protestant body politic, however different their apparent confessional positions might be.

As these comments make clear, religious differences could be a significant factor in presentations of what constituted good and bad government. In the spring of 1660, John Milton unsuccessfully attempted to rally his countrymen against a monarchical restoration, pointing towards 'the antipathie which is in all kings against Presbyterian and Independent discipline ... for they hear the gospel speaking much of libertie; a word which monarchie and her bishops both fear and hate, but a free Commonwealth both favours and promotes' (Milton 1980: 458). In stark contrast, John Dryden would repeatedly emphasize the evils unleashed by the close union of religious 'zeal' and republican spirit. The point was driven home through frequent comparisons between the mid-seventeenth-century upheavals visited upon England as a result of confessional disputes, and the horrors of the French Wars of Religion in the late sixteenth century. The happy linguistic coincidence of the French Catholic League (or Guisards) and the puritan English Solemn League and Covenant allowed Dryden to associate religious dissidence and governmental chaos, whether in his 1660 poem *Astraea Redux* welcoming back Charles II, or in his co-authored play, *The Duke of Guise* (pr. 1683), whose prologue made the connection between French rebels and English opposition politicians clear: 'Our play's a parallel: the Holy League/Begot our cov'nant: Guisards got the Whigg' (Dryden 1987: 11; Salmon 1959: 140; Owen 1996: 147–8).

Efforts to reconstitute monarchy after the Interregnum years as both inherently good and necessary for religious and political peace would run into significant problems both before and after the Glorious Revolution. Before 1688 the very evident immorality of the restored royal court excited opprobrium. Charles II's sexual appetite resulted in fourteen acknowledged (and therefore expensively maintained) bastard children, notably by a series of Catholic mistresses, which renewed an older discourse of popish plots and conspiracies that had proved deeply damaging to the early Stuarts (Harris 2007; Spurr 2000: 204; Hibbard 1983). It also stimulated a new and highly sexualized language of politics that reflected the horror felt by moralizing contemporaries like the diarist John Evelyn: Charles's court more resembled 'a luxurious and abandoned rout than a Christian court' (Spurr 2000: 201). After James's conversion to Catholicism became public knowledge in 1673, politically powerful fears for the future would deepen to crisis point during the 1680s. A crucial literary amplifier for such concerns was Marvell's *Account of the Growth of Popery and Arbitrary Government* (1677/8), which we have already seen infuriating Edmund Bohun. This began with the stark claim that 'There has now for diverse Years, a design been carried on, to change the Lawfull Government of *England* into an absolute Tyranny, and to convert the established Protestant Religion into down-right Popery', and went on to present Charles II's 1672 Declaration of Indulgence not as a measure to heal Protestant wounds but as (in Nigel Smith's words) 'an introduction of popery by royal dictate' (Marvell 1677/8: 3; Smith 2010: 322).

The efflorescence of oppositional pamphlet material during the era of the Popish Plot and Exclusion Crisis conjured up in turn a vehement loyalist response, most famously involving John Dryden, but most prolifically championed by Roger L'Estrange (Harth 1993; Goldie 2008). The latter's *An Account of the Growth of Knavery, under the Pretended Fears of Arbitrary Government and Popery* (1677; 2nd edn 1681) drew a damning parallel between 'the reformers of 1677 and those of 1641' (L'Estrange 1681). For L'Estrange, all allegations of government conspiracies and popish plots were merely cheats or 'juggles' designed to deceive the credulous, and advance the interests of genuinely subversive Nonconformists. This message was remorselessly hammered home in his periodical, *The Observator* (1681–7); 931 issues constituting two million words of 'libel and abuse, tempered by seriocomic moralizing, and philosophy and political theory reduced to epithets and exclamations' that earned him numerous pejorative titles of which the least offensive was probably 'scribbler-general of Tory-land' (Kemp and McElligott 2009: III, 233; Goldie 2008: 67). Such abuse was indicative of the cumulative impact of his writing, which reached a vitriolic crescendo after the revelations of a scheme to assassinate the royal brothers in 1683, the Rye House Plot, involving radical Protestant Nonconformists. L'Estrange's savage irony would then become part of a broader cacophony of loyalist voices, with government supporters publishing tracts like *The Last and Truest Discovery of the Popish Plot* and *No Protestant Plot; or, The Whigs Loyalty* (Harth 1993: 213). As these titles suggest, religious belief was at the heart of nascent partisan political identities, notably the deepening rift of the political nation into rival 'Whig' and 'Tory' political camps from the latter part of the Exclusion Crisis onwards. Support for James's succession, and hostility towards Nonconformists, left Tories vulnerable to the charge of crypto-Catholicism: 'Romish Tory's' were the ultimate offspring of 'the spiteful Copulation of a hot Monk with some distemper'd Protestant Dame, just on the dawn of our *English* Reformation' (Tapsell 2007: 128–9). Far from being 'true' or 'loyal' Protestants as they claimed, Whigs were savaged in turn by Tories for being 'of the *Geneva*-Stamp', each one 'moulded a strong *Presbyterian in the very Womb*' (Owen 1996: 54–5; Tapsell 2007: 138). Religious claims and counter-claims ensured, more than anything else, that partisan passions would be maintained well into the eighteenth century (Holmes 1975).

After the Glorious Revolution the religious character of monarchy would remain a vigorously contested theme since William's successful military intervention naturally lent itself to highly polarized interpretations. As one passionately partisan Williamite cleric preached in 1690, the king was 'our Illustrious Deliverer ... conducted by a special

Providence, which loudly proclaim'd all along, that it was God who had raised him up, to restore our Israel, to deliver our Bodies from the Tyranny of Men, and our Souls from the doctrines of Devils' (Rose 1999: 20). Alternatively he could be presented as a Dutch usurper likely to undermine the Church of England and enslave the English in pursuit of his military goals on the continent. In the latter line of thought, comparisons were frequently made to Oliver Cromwell, another ruler prone to emphasize liberty of conscience whilst relying on military forces of unorthodox religious views (Rose 1999: 33, 259–62). (This line of attack was clearly persuasive: even William's supporters needed to reconcile his military heroism and power on the continent 'with an emphasis on the circumscription of his authority in domestic affairs' (Williams 2005: 108).) Jacobite authors would dwell on William's unprepossessing looks and alleged homosexual tendencies, whilst emphasizing that a ruler who had had 'the misfortune ... to be educated under the Geneva model' was undermining the Church of England through his appointment of bishops 'of notorious presbyterian, or, which is worse, of Erastian principles' (Rose 1999: 32, 34). Although William's queen, Mary II, was an avowed member of the Church of England, her death in 1694 tore away a layer of religious legitimation from the regime that would only be replaced with the accession to the throne of Anne in 1702.

Between Mary's death and Anne's accession a deepening conflict in the Church may be seen to epitomize the core concerns of this chapter, notably the inter-relationship between religious belief and political activity, the often fraught connection between church and state, and the extent to which printed religious literature continued to excite major tensions in English life. In 1696 the London minister Francis Atterbury anonymously published *A Letter to a Convocation Man*. This pursued a rather abstruse theme— the need to recall convocation to safeguard a 'Church in Danger'—but in a deliberately brief, blunt, and aggressive style that helped to make it an immediate publishing 'sensation' that was reprinted multiple times and prompted numerous replies (Bennett 1975: 48–51; Hayton 2004–14). Atterbury's forceful use of the press succeeded in galvanizing significant sections of a lower clergy anxious about William's support for toleration at home and his choice of episcopal appointments. It also gave heart to lay Tory politicians resentful of what they saw as a Whig-supported war on the continent that was beggaring the nation. Even though William was profoundly opposed to the return of convocation, and accurately anticipated how bitterly divisive it would prove, he was ultimately forced to accede to the calls to which Atterbury had given focus, and agree to the calling of convocation, in order to secure in 1700 the ministerial services of Tory grandees like Laurence Hyde, earl of Rochester (Rose 1999: 192–4; Tapsell 2010: 1444). As William's successors would discover to their cost, 'coals from the altar' would continue to inflame popular politics, and complicate the task of government for decades to come.

PART II

LITERARY GENRES FOR THE EXPRESSION OF FAITH

CHAPTER 8

··

TRANSLATION

··

RACHEL WILLIE

In the opening scene to Christopher Marlowe's *Doctor Faustus* (*c*.1588–9), we witness the eponymous anti-hero seated in his study and pondering the various branches of knowledge. After dismissing philosophy, medicine, and law, Faustus then turns to divinity, which he assumes to be the best of all disciplines. However, reading the Bible soon tests his assumptions:

> Jerome's Bible, Faustus view it well.
> [He reads] '*Stipendium peccati mors est.*' Ha!
> '*Stipendium*', etc.
> The reward of sin is death. That's hard.
> [He reads] '*Si peccasse negamus, fallimur*
> *Et nulla est in nobis veritas.*'
> If we say we have no sin,
> We deceive ourselves, and there's no truth in us.
> Why then belike we must die
> Ay, we must die an everlasting death.
> What doctrine call you this? *Che sera, sera,*
> What will be shall be? Divinity, adieu!
>
> (Marlowe 1995; *Dr Faustus* The A Text, I.i.38–50)

Beginning from a position of assumed knowledge, Faustus quickly moves to one of doubt. I do not wish to dwell upon the much-rehearsed arguments relating to Faustus's mis-reading of the Scriptures, or how this connects to soteriological discussions, or even more recent debates that intriguingly point to the interpretive frameworks that have been adopted by contemporary readers leading us to assume that Faustus is engaged in an act of wilful misunderstanding.[1] Instead, I want to focus upon what Faustus is doing

---

[1] For further discussion of the possible interpretations of this speech, see chapter 11 of this volume, as well as Parker 2013.

here in relation to biblical translations. The Vulgate (Jerome's) Bible had been used by the Catholic Church for a thousand years, but the location of Faustus's study is Wittenberg.

The play is loosely based upon the allegedly true story of a learned German doctor who sells his soul to the devil in a reckless attempt to be given ultimate knowledge, but much of its plot is concerned with the Reformation—something which is brought sharply into focus by the markedly anti-Catholic satirical scenes in the B Text of the play. Faustus resides in Lutheran Wittenberg, which makes his engagement with the Vulgate Bible of note—not just in terms of the ecclesiastical politics of place, but also in terms of what this implies about the status of the Vulgate Bible to a late sixteenth-century play-going public. Faustus moves from a position of certainty to one of doubt with regards to salvation as a direct result of his reading Jerome's translation of the Bible: rather than offering guidance into religious matters, the lack of interpretative lens has led Faustus onto the path of damnation.

Whether Faustus wilfully skips over the verses of the Bible that deal with salvation, or is a poor reader of Scripture, or is demonstrating a different mode of textual engagement is open to debate. However, what I am interested in here is precisely what is being presented to the play-going public who are witnessing Faustus in his study. Earlier in the soliloquy, we observe Faustus engaging with other modes of learning:

> …live and die in Aristotle's works,
> Sweet *Analytics*, 'tis thou has ravisht me!
> [He reads] '*Bene dissere est finis logices*'.
> Is to dispute well logic's chiefest end?
> Afford this art no greater miracle?
> …
> Be a physician, Faustus, heap up gold,
> And be eternized for some wondrous cure.
> [He reads] '*Summum bonum medicinae sanitas*':
> The end of physic is our body's health.
> Why Faustus, hast thou not attained that end?
>
> (I.i.5–9 and 14–18)

Here, Faustus is engaging with branches of learning through the mode of translation. In abjuring philosophy, Faustus is quoting and translating Ramus, not the Aristotlean original, and this draws attention to the fact that Jerome's Bible too was a translation. While translating the Bible was not necessarily viewed as heretical by the Catholic Church, the suppression of translations of the Bible into English after Wycliffe's translations (*c*.1382–95) and the controversies that the Lollards elicited meant that, with regards to the English Bible, Reformation and biblical translation were closely aligned (Killeen and Smith 2015).

As has been noted frequently, English biblical translation influenced the development of the English language and introduced many Hebraisms and common phrases into the English language (David Norton 2000; Crystal 2010; Hamlin and Jones 2010). C. S. Lewis queried the literariness of the King James Bible (1611), but the committees who were involved in its translation were intensely concerned with language and drew from previous Protestant and Catholic English Bible translations in an attempt to create a stable and accurate text. But what does 'stable' and 'accurate' mean when it comes to translation? Between 1529 and 1532, Thomas More and William Tyndale entered into a lengthy and at times bilious refutation of each other's stance on biblical translation. More's friend and correspondent Desiderius Erasmus may have pre-empted Miles Coverdale in expressing a wish for the word of God to be made available to every ploughman, but More observes what he perceives to be the dangers of translation:

> But now I pray you let me kno your mynd concernyng ye burning of ye new testament in english which Tindal lately translated & (as men say) right wel whiche makethe men mich meruayl of ye burning.
>   It is q[uoth] I to me gret meruayl that eny good cristen man hauing eny drop of wyt in hys hed wold eny thing meruell or complayn of ye burning of ye boke if he knowe ye mater. which who so callith ye new testament calleth it by a wrong name except they wyl call yt Tyndals testament or Luthers testament. For so had tyndall after Luthers counsayle corrupted & chaunged yt from the good & holsom doctryne of Criste to the deuylysh heresyes of theyr own that it was clene a contrary thing. (More 1529: D3ᵛ)

More argues that, far from disseminating the word of God to a wider audience, biblical translation has become a means by which Tyndale and Martin Luther disseminated Reformist principles to the masses. This is emphasized further in More's *Confutation of Tyndale's Answer* (1532), where he takes Tyndale's *An Answer to More's Dialogue* (1531) chapter by chapter and unrelentingly refutes every statement that Tyndale makes. Taking issue with Tyndale's decision to translate *ekklēsia* as 'congregation' rather than 'Church', More defends Erasmus from similar condemnations of his choice of words:

> Then [Tyndale] asketh me why I haue not contended with Erasmus whom he calleth my derlynge, of all thys longe whyle for translatynge of thys worde *ecclesia* in to thys worde *congregatio*. And then he cometh forth wyth hys fete proper taunte, that I auour hym of lykelyhed for makynge of hys boks of Maris in my howse. There had he hyt melo saue for lakke of a lytell salte. I haue not contended wyth Erasmus my derlynge, bycause I found no suche malycyouse entent wyth Erasmus my derlynge, as I fynde wyth Tyndale. For had I fownde wyth Erasmus my derlyng the shrewde entent and purpose that I fynde in Tindale: Erasmus my derlynge sholde be no more my derlynge.
>
> (More 1532: q4ʳ⁻ᵛ)

The repetition of the words 'my derlyng' is not only rhetorically effective in establishing a binary between the 'heretical' views of Tyndale as opposed to the 'right-minded' beliefs of More and Erasmus, but also points to a larger, European, humanist discourse. A coterie of some of the most learned thinkers of the day corresponded with each other (usually in Latin) across Europe. In order to understand how translation relates to religion and literature, it is vital to understand that translation was integral to a human-ist education: Faustus at his study is not only demonstrating knowledge of the disci-plines he is scrutinizing, he is also exhibiting an understanding of language.

In the sixteenth and seventeenth centuries, very few people spoke English in contin-ental Europe at a time when a knowledge of several languages was common amongst the educated elites and the literate middling sort. At the same time, however, Reformists criticized the lack of understanding—not just amongst the laity, but also by the clergy—of Latin. For Reformists, translating the word of God into vernacular tongues allowed the priest (as much as the ploughman) to understand the Gospels.

Of course, there were Old English precedents for translating elements of the Bible and, in *The Obedience of the Christian Man* (1529), Tyndale asserts that King Æthelstan (*c*.893/4–939), often regarded as the first monarch to rule over a united England, com-missioned a vernacular Bible (B7^v). There is no evidence to support this claim, though there are Old English translations of parts of the Bible, especially the psalms, and Reformists such as John Bayle in his *Actes of the English Votaries* (1560) looked to tales of British Christians battling against marauding Saxons who came to settle on the British Isles as a way to assert that there was a pre-existing Church in the British Isles before St Augustine arrived in England to convert the Anglo Saxons. Reformists could, and did, appropriate a rich literary inheritance and the past to their cause.

Despite these claims of literary precedence when it came to translating the Bible, those in England who continued to support the Church in Rome declared vernacular translation to be heretical and expressed fear that it encouraged readers into misunder-standing the Scriptures. However, as we saw in the way in which Marlowe opens *Doctor Faustus*, knowledge of Latin does not necessarily lead to comprehension. Theorists such as Jacques Derrida made much of the inherent instability of language, but poststruc-turalists were certainly not the first people to recognize the ways in which language obfuscates meaning. This was something that has occupied thinkers since classical times and informed early modern anxieties regarding understanding. In *Bailikon Doron* (printed in Scotland, 1599; England in 1603 and a bilingual Welsh-English text in 1604), King James VI of Scotland (later James I of England) cautioned against the discrepancy between intention and interpretation:

> It is true olde saying, That a King is as one set on a scaffold, whose smallest actions & gestures al the people gazingly do behold: and therefore although a King be neuer so precise in the dischargeing of his office, the people who seeth but the outward parte, will euer judge of the substance by the circumstances, & according to the out warde appearance (if his behauiour be light or dissolute) will conceiue preoc-cupied conceit of the Kings inward intention, which although with time (the tryer of al tru-eth) it wil vanish, by the euidence of the contrarie euents, yet *interim partitur iustus*: and prejudged conceites will (in the meane time) breed Contempt, the Mother of Rebellion and disorder: And besides that it is certain, that all the indifferente actiones and behauiour of a man, haue a certaine holding & dependence, either upon uertue or vice, according as they are used or rules: for there is not a middes betuixt them, no more nor betuixte their rewardes, Heauen and Hell. (James VI 1599: sig. R^r–R^v)

While James believes that time will reveal all, Niccolò Machiavelli presents an alternative view over how the differences between intent and the interpretation of intent can be manipulated in order to successfully govern a territory:

> To those seeing and hearing him, [a prince] should appear a man of compassion, a man of good faith, a man of integrity, a kind and religious man. And there is nothing so important as *to seem* to have this last quality. Men in general judge by their eyes rather than their hands; because everyone is in a position to watch, few are in a position to come in close touch with you. Everyone sees what you appear to be, few experience what you really are. (Machiavelli 1999: 57–8)

The distinction between what one is, what one appears to be, and how a monarch navigates the interpretative lenses of his or her subjects may appear to be a markedly different issue to early modern translation, but at the heart of each is an anxiety with regards to the inherent instability of interpretation. Biblical translation was deliberately archaic as a means to stabilize language, but as Lucy Munro has recently shown, these archaisms took two distinct forms. One type of archaism looked to outmoded words as a means of anchoring the (new) national Church within a literary and linguistic tradition and the other, perhaps paradoxically, took the form of neologisms that swiftly became old-fashioned. Catholic translators, in particular, adopted Latinate neologisms as a means of asserting the linguistic differences between faiths. Past and present becomes combined as archaic style lends text a sense of linguistic simplicity and establishes intimacy between reader, text, and timeless utterances (Munro 2013: ch. 3). Archaism in religious translation becomes a way to authorize the text while allowing writers and readers to inhabit the same religious and literary community and to articulate religious identity.

The use of archaism in religious translation would seem to imply that deliberate interpretive strategies were employed as a means to navigate what translation theorists refer to as the 'source text' and the 'target language' into which the text is translated. Sixteenth- and seventeenth-century writers on translation, however, exercised considerable care in understanding the relationship between source text and translation and what this might imply about the literary and ecclesiastical status of the translation. In Francis Marbury's letter to the Reader that prefaces Henry Holland's translation, *A Treatise of God's Effectual Calling* (1603), Marbury distinguishes between translation and paraphrase and advises that we remain sensitive to the idioms of the target language:

> For a good translator is neither a *paraphrast* nor a *periphrast*, which is committed by needless changing or adding words. He so behaveth himself that the comparing of the original will compare his fidelity, and that they which know of no original would take the translator for the author himself. He must naturalise his translation for the reader without injuring the gift of the author in the native work. (Rhodes, Kendal, and Wilson 2013: 172–3)

Marbury attacks the fallacy of paraphrase, and also convoluted translations that say more of the translator's whims than express fidelity to the source text. In doing so,

Marbury observes that the translator is writing for two distinct audiences: a reading public conversant in the language of the source text and who can therefore judge the quality of the translation, and the monoglots who can assess the merits of the translator's abilities to naturalize the narrative under translation and render it understandable and pleasing to a new audience. Indeed, when reading a translation of French romance in 1653, Dorothy Osborne complained that the quality of the translation was poor due to it being so markedly francophone 'that 'twas impossible for one who understood not French to make any thing of them' (Moore-Smith 1928: 91). For the early modern reader, a good translation ought not to reveal its status as a translation and it ought to be naturalized into the target language.

These discussions would seem to imply that the principles of early modern translation have an affinity with contemporary translation theory, where the translator is an almost anonymous force within the text; he or she is a person who silently and faithfully translates and edits the text into its target language. However, the humanist education presented the methods of translation in a very different way. Writing in 1559, Laurence Humphrey presents his reading public with the literary and the godly qualities of the translated text:

> It is God who enables us to express ourselves through language; hence doing this intelligently, in ways suited and familiar to people's hearing and perception, will bring benefit not just privately to the proprietor of the material, but also in general to everyone who hears him. And when an accurate translation is provided something more than just useful is going on, something wonderfully godlike, whether through the live voice in public assemblies, or through pen and writings for the sake of posterity. This is how—by practicing the good office of translation—we can incite some people to virtue and urge them into the fellowship of the Christian religion, and call others back out of vice and superstition; and (in brief) be of mutual help and benefit to one another on any matter whatever. (Rhodes, Kendal, and Wilson 2013: 264–5)

For Humphrey, translating is a communal and sensory act that is facilitated by God. The act of translating is emotional and spiritual, affecting auditors as well as the translator. Since God is the enabler of verbal utterances and expression, all forms of speech and translation have the potential to become religious or devotional undertakings: Basil, whose *An Exhortation … to the study of humaine learnyne* was translated into English by William Baker in 1557, explicated how the 'good' could be distilled from the 'bad' elements of pagan texts as a way of advocating their being read and translated by Christians. Whereas More and others heavily censured the translating of Bibles as those who undertook the translations were believed by them to be advancing heresies in the vernacular, others perceived the very act of translating as being a spiritual undertaking. While God may facilitate verbal expression, Humphrey still maintained that there was an appropriate method to good translation (Norton 1984: 11–14).

Humphrey observes that there are three modes of translation: the 'overscrupulous or unduly restrained' kind, which translates word for word and in doing so fails to be sympathetic to the target language; the variety that 'is freer and looser and allows itself too much licence', which comprises too many neologisms and embellishments to do justice to the target language or the source text; 'the third method, the "middle way" … is straight-forward but learned, elegant but faithful' (Rhodes, Kendal, and Wilson 2013: 266–8). For Humphrey, translation is like the porridge that Goldilocks steals from the three bears: the perfect translation mediates the perils of remaining too faithful to the source text and the translators allowing themselves too much literary licence. A good translation is sympathetic to both the original text and the language into which it is being translated.

In making these assertions, Humphrey is not presenting a radical view of translation, but merely echoing the practice of the humanist schoolroom. Translation was an integral part of education, where scholars learned the art of composition, rhetoric, and executing a translation creatively. Fidelity to the original text—except where the Scriptures were concerned—was of less importance to the schoolroom translator than producing a stylish text. Whereas Marbury may note a distinction between paraphrase and translation and Humphrey advocates a compromise between fidelity and creativity, in the humanist schoolroom the distinctions between paraphrase and translation, creative writing and rhetorical exercise, break down. Yet the choices made in terms of what is translated shed light on early modern culture: they show us how individuals engaged with past utterances and to what end; how texts circulated across Europe; the status of vernacular languages in relation to the *lingua franca*, Latin, and classical languages; they also reveal the politics of translation in terms of who these texts are being translated for and how the reading public consumed these texts. Despite the printing press being an 'agent of change' (Elizabeth Eisenstein), in the sixteenth and seventeenth centuries, many texts—perhaps especially translations and women's writing—continued to circulate in manuscript form. Scholars are only beginning to unearth the vastness of manuscript circulation, but manuscript texts could—and did—move beyond small coteries who knew the author; they were copied by a wider reading public, sometimes making their way into print. When texts were printed, the material object can enlighten us with regards to how readers engaged with the text.

Eamon Duffy has described Protestant books of hours as 'Trojan Horses': by adopting the appearance and paraphernalia of Catholic texts, printers were making Protestant devotional writing more palatable to a sceptical reading public; they 'smuggled' in new religious and devotional practices as a way of converting an orthodox reading public (Duffy 2006: 171). Elizabeth Salter has modified this argument, offering a fluid representation of popular reading and devotional practices in the Tudor period (Salter 2009: 106–20). However, what these 'Trojan Horses' are also doing is translating Catholic ways of reading into Protestant modes. Far from shielding the text from censure through donning the weeds of Catholicism and transforming it into a text that presents Protestant teachings, these texts blur the distinctions between Catholic and Protestant devotion. Translation, therefore, functions on a variety of levels that may not necessarily be rooted in recreating or adapting the source text to the target language.

So far, I have provided a brief and general overview of early modern translation theory and practice and emphasized how translation was integral to humanist ways of learning as well as outlining some of the issues that arise when translating Scripture. I will now briefly survey some of the types of translation and how they connect to early modern religion and literature. Inevitably such an overview is not exhaustive, but it gives a sense of the diversity of engagement with literary and religious discourses in early modern England. These discussions will focus upon Erasmus, the Sidney Psalter, and Anthony Munday's translations of Iberian prose romances. In so doing, I will give a flavour of the types of translations that are being undertaken within the circles of Northern Renaissance humanist learning, amongst those who had connections at court and in popular culture. As a coda, I will briefly return to drama as a way of seeing how translation operates across all the major literary genres. Of course, this leads to glaring omissions—the translation strategies employed by women and how this feeds into women's devotional writing being one, and the penitential psalm translations of Thomas Wyatt, Henry Howard, and others being another. In order to understand the relationship between religion and literary texts, we must first take into account the divergence of thought between medieval and early modern learning.

More may have defended Erasmus when William Tyndale detected a degree of hypocrisy in More's stance on biblical translation, but Erasmus courted controversy in his use of the Scripture. More and Erasmus were two of the key thinkers of Northern Renaissance humanism and Erasmus was quite scathing of the philosophies that underpinned teaching in the medieval universities. The dominant mode of thought within the medieval universities was scholasticism, which sought to reconcile Christian doctrine with the Aristotelean teachings that had been rediscovered in Western Europe and first translated into Latin in the twelfth and thirteenth centuries. Scholasticism endeavoured to reconcile faith and reason. Quotations from authorities such as Boethius, Aristotle, St Augustine of Hippo, and the Bible would be synthesized in accordance with how the disputer drew distinctions from the meaning of words. In the literary form of the *quæstio*, opposing views would be presented and reconciled: one question leads to another and each question is systematically addressed to give the appearance of a unified whole. Such unity can lead to contradiction; this is seen in Thomas Aquinas's teachings where early criticisms are present within his own work. The scholastics were influential in the development of some branches of linguistics, logic, philosophy, metaphysics, epistemology, ethics, law, and political theory. Although the Scottish scholastic John Duno Scotus (*c.*1265–1308) was admired by modern philosophers such as Heidegger, the Renaissance humanists were critical of their scholastic forefathers. The humanists perceived scholasticism as generating inelegant texts that were too abstract, which defied logic and had too heavy a reliance upon (and deference to) authority.

Despite these criticisms of the scholastics, the humanists still looked to the authority of antiquity. In addition to this, rhetoric and skills in debating were important features of the early modern classroom as were the reading, interpreting, and translating of classical Greek and Latin texts. In this respect, although Renaissance humanists defined the learning that took place in the classroom as different to its precursors, it grew out of medieval scholasticism. Humanists understood the education system and the study and translation of literature as being a way to 'train' a citizen to assume their role in civil society.

Humanists copied, edited, translated, and disseminated classical texts, perhaps most notably the works of Virgil and Cicero. This presents some challenges with regards to how to present pagan authors in a Christian context. These fed into issues regarding original sin, free will, and grace and whether writers who did not have access to Christian teachings could offer anything of moral or spiritual value to a Christian civil society. The problem of will was central to Reformation debates regarding soteriology—the branch of theology concerned with salvation. Aristotelean intellectualism and Arabic Neoplatonism presented a universe governed by necessary connections. These necessary connections allowed little room for human autonomy. In the fourteenth century, the problem of free will led to discussions regarding the absolute power of God (*potentia absoluta dei*) and the ordained power of God (*potentia ordinate dei*). In the fifth century, St Augustine had helped to have Pelagianism—the belief that original sin did not exist and an individual could live sinless and gain salvation without the intervention of the grace of God—declared a heresy, but the difficulties in reconciling predestination and free will continued. In some respects, the Reformation emerged as much as a consequence of debates and doctrinal disputes expressed in the universities as it was a reaction to the perceived iniquities of the papacy, and the most celebrated humanist of his day, Erasmus, found his writings were both praised and censured. Although he saw much to approve in Luther's critiques of the Church, the two men could not be reconciled on the matter of free will: Luther perceived Erasmus's stance to be Pelagian heresy and Erasmus favoured reform of the Church rather than following Luther in rejecting the medieval sacraments and advocating a form of predestination that seemed to deny free will.

Despite their similar disillusionment with, and shared criticism of, the Catholic Church, the two men ended up on different sides of the confessional divide, with Luther sparking a break from the Catholic Church and Erasmus (eventually) publishing critiques of Luther's stance. These debates may seem to have little to do with translation, but both men advocated the translation of religious texts into vernacular languages, though perhaps Luther approached translation from a theological perspective and Erasmus from a rhetorical one that was rooted in the humanist classroom. As the early modern period progressed, Pelagian and Augustinian notions of free will versus predestination would be superseded by Calvinist and Arminian doctrines of salvation, but the unsettled status of the body, soul, grace, and salvation would sow the seeds of a new form of devotional writing, perhaps especially amongst women. Medieval pieties were abandoned, to be replaced with other notions of selfhood, which would culminate in René Descartes's *Meditations* (published 1641).

On the eve of Reformation, however, Erasmus's most famous work, *Moriae ecomium seu laus* (*The Praise of Folly*, 1511) appeared. Here, Erasmus draws upon Lucian's satires to produce an ironic encomium. Folly (Moira—also a pun on the name of his friend, the wise fool, Thomas More), in the garb of a jester, praises herself and her followers. The text is divided into three sections: initially, Folly lampoons her followers, and both celebrates and mocks earthly pleasures before moving on to attack the nobility, the Church, and academia as well as the pretences, hypocrisies, and delusions that govern individuals within their various professions. The nobility come under attack for their love of empty titles and lack of regard for the common good. The Church and the universities are especially rebuked: Folly condemns the Pope's love of worldly pleasures and desire for war, the way the Church profited from the superstitions of the laity, and more generally, she lambasts the corrupt and envious priesthood and orders of monks. Human pretensions and scholarly wrongheadedness come under fire in Folly's criticism of the universities: scholastic theology, in particular, is criticized, but the conceited pride in their learning mean that scholars, rhetoricians, and poets are all seen as abandoning Christian principles. These criticisms have a destabilizing effect upon the text as the rhetoric that Erasmus employs runs parallel to the kinds of arguments that come under fire within the text. There is a degree of playfulness in how Erasmus presents his arguments while at the same time exposing the foibles of human learning.

The final section draws from St Paul's assertion that 'We are all fools for Christ's sake, but ye are wise in Christ; we are weak, but ye are strong; ye are honourable, but we are despised' (I Corinthians 4:10). The 'folly' of Christian piety is here celebrated. Viewing Neoplatonic notions of the relationship between the soul and matter as a way to comprehend Christian revelation, Folly asserts that by abjuring worldly affairs, Christians can set their sights on higher things: Christian piety is a form of madness through which an individual can achieve perfect happiness.

The Praise of Folly is a *tour de force* in rhetoric, the appropriation of classical and humanist learning, and of Christian piety. It was translated into all the major Western European languages and Thomas Chaloner's English translation appeared in 1549. These translations meant Erasmus's text continued to be read by those not versed in Latin throughout the early modern period. Its focus upon the relationship between body and soul and the foibles of the material world rejected medieval scholasticism and the perceived corruptions of the Church. In some respects, Erasmus's *The Praise of Folly* offers a prolonged exegesis on Pauline teachings through synthesizing Christian doctrine with Platonic philosophies. It is a sophisticated text, imbued with wit, wordplay, and the rhetorical flourishes that it lampoons. The allegory becomes as self-critical as it is critical of all human frailty. *The Praise of Folly* is one of the major texts of Northern Renaissance humanism and, although Erasmus remained within the Catholic commune, pre-empted Reformist critiques of the Catholic Church. It was a hugely successful text; it was also controversial, especially after Luther nailed his ninety-five theses to the door of All Saints Church in Wittenberg in 1517.

Erasmus may have been critical of the Catholic Church, but he sought reform of the Church rather than schism and the Reformation. However, his writings appear to have remained popular with Protestants. In 1543, Nicholas Udall was commissioned by Katherine Parr to oversee the translation of Erasmus's Latin *Paraphrases on the New Testament* into English. The project appears to have crossed confessional divides, with translations by the orthodox Princess Mary appearing alongside those by strongly Protestant figures such as Katherine Parr and Miles Coverdale. As noted earlier, Francis Marbury observed a distinction between paraphrase and translation and the two undertakings suggest different relationships between source text and target language. However, these paraphrases formed a part of early modern popular piety, as did the translation of psalms.

Perhaps the most popular form of religious translation in the early modern period was psalm translation. While translating the Bible into English was controversial, psalm translation was not. Translating the psalms was undertaken partly as an act of devotion and partly as a literary exercise. By far the most widely used psalm translation in the early modern period was Sternhold and Hopkins, which are set in common metre. Widely critiqued for their inelegancy, they remained popular in Church worship until the late seventeenth century (Quitslund 2008).

At the other end of the spectrum, amongst the psalms celebrated for their literary merit is the Sidney Psalter. Begun by Philip Sidney, his sister Mary translated the remaining 107 psalms and revised some of Philip's forty-three translations after his death in 1586. The Sidney Psalter would not appear in print until 1823. Despite this, the text circulated widely and the complete psalter and individual psalms were copied by the reading public. The influence that they had on seventeenth-century lyric poetry attests to their popularity. For example, Psalm 88 is riven with a sense of agony, alienation, and supplication that chimes with the tone of John Donne's *Holy Sonnets*. At the same time, its verse form prefigures George Herbert's poetry.

The Sidney Psalter is a dexterous piece of devotional writing: its complex use of varying verse forms suggest that they were not intended for public Church worship, but instead are a feat of private devotional practice. They are also a literary achievement: the Sidney Psalter is not just an exercise in devotional writing, but aligns the psalms with a newfound sense of confidence in vernacular poetry and in the English Church. Philip Sidney's militant Protestant chivalric principles were to cost him his life during the Dutch revolt in the Spanish Netherlands. In this context, verse translation not only becomes a means of asserting the linguistic and literary qualities of the English language, but also reaffirms English Protestant poetics. By completing the psalter, Mary Sidney continues to weave religious devotion with political and social commentary.

Writing of English metrical psalms, Hannibal Hamlin observes that it is not how accurately they are translated that makes them interesting, 'but the imaginative boldness of their error' (Hamlin 2004: 11). It is not so much imaginatively bold inaccuracies in translation that the Sidney Psalter evinces, but rather an audacious refashioning of their form. Donne, in his poem, 'Upon the Translation of the Psalms by Sir Philip Sidney and the Countess of Pembroke his Sister', described the psalms as 'The Highest Matter in the noblest form' (l. 11). For Donne, the Sidney Psalter is not only a work of sophisticated lyric poetry, but also a well-crafted work of devotion. Echoing Humphrey's assertion that good translations are elegant, faithful, and learned, Donne praises the Sidneys' 'sweet learned labours' (l. 54).

Despite (or, perhaps, because of) these claims of poetic value, Donne locates the psalms within a framework that focuses upon national identity:

> A brother and a sister, made by thee
> The organ, where thou art the harmony.
> Two that make one John Baptist's holy voice,
> And who that Psalm 'Now let the Isles rejoice'
> Have both translated, and applied it too,
> Both told us what, and taught us how to do.
> They show us islanders our joy, our King,
> They tell us *why* and teach us *how* to sing. (ll. 15–22)

Taking Psalm 97 as a starting point ('The Lord reigneth; let the earth rejoice; let the multitude of isles be glad *thereof* Psalm 97:1), Donne retranslates the call to rejoice in the Lord to a celebration of translation. The Sidney Psalter takes on a didactic quality, instructing English speakers on how to engage with the Psalms and with God.

Throughout the rest of the poem, Donne makes use of an extended metaphor that connects the harmony of the spheres, God, and David to the Sidneys' lyrical translations. The voices merge into one, implying a cohesive unity between God, the cosmos, David as originator, and the Sidneys as translators. The Psalms become not just a triumph of scholarship and translation, but also one of devotion.

Psalm translation was the most common form of religious translation in the early modern period and practised by men and women, but biblical translation was by no means the only form of religious translation that was undertaken at this time. As we have seen, Erasmus's *The Praise of Folly* was not only a triumph of humanist exposition on Christian teaching, it was also a widely read text that was translated into many languages and crossed national borders and confessional divides. So too were romances.

Vernacular prose romance has long been accused of being the reading matter of the idle and fanciful. While texts such as Spenser's *The Faerie Queene* have been extensively examined—perhaps especially in relation to Ireland and its militant Protestant agenda—the translations into English prose of Iberian romances by Anthony Munday have, until recently, been largely overlooked. As one study observes, Munday was a prolific author who produced more texts and was writing for a longer period of time than almost all of his contemporaries. Yet, Munday is often considered to be a minor literary figure (Hamilton 2005: xv). Perhaps part of the reason for this is that his writing is nebulous and difficult to categorize.

A playwright who wrote an anti-theatrical tract and went on to be one of the dominant pageant-writers for the City of London, Munday has been described as both a rabid Protestant and a converted or lapsed Catholic (C. Turner 1928; McCoog 1993). Donna B. Hamilton makes the case for Munday's denunciations of the Pope and expressions of loyalty to the crown with his apparent lack of Protestant spirituality by proposing that Munday may have been sympathetic to Catholic loyalism. For Catholic loyalists, fidelity to the old faith and to the crown was not incompatible: English Catholics could have the appearance of conformity in the late sixteenth century simply because they did not object to Elizabeth's reign and assumed an appearance of outward conformity by participating in Church of England worship at least once a month. While some chose recusancy and fines, imprisonment and the possible torture that may ensue, or went into exile, or became martyrs for their faith, many Catholics maintained political loyalty to England and either converted to Protestantism or assumed an outward appearance of conformity while continuing to subscribe to Catholic doctrines.

Discussions with regards to Munday's religious beliefs are likely to continue due to what Hamilton identifies throughout her study as the Janus-like stance adopted by the writer. Munday is often regarded as a 'hack' writer and as a purveyor of cheap print and popular culture. While he certainly was no a courtier poet, his varied career included roles such as Messenger of Her Majesty's Chamber, and he was commissioned to write plays by Philip Henslow, to write Lord Mayor shows and to revise John Stow's *The Survey of London*. Such roles place him at the centre of court intrigue and municipal authority and Hamilton argues that Munday used this status to rally against the emerging English Protestant identity presented by contemporaries such as Spenser and Philip Sidney:

> Munday's success ... depended in part on his deflecting attention from any notion of himself as possessing authority or acting autonomously, as is suggested by his work as a gatherer, translator, reporter, government mouthpiece, collaborator and reviser. However, the accumulated effect of tracking his work across decades erases the impression that Munday exercised little agency, leaving instead a sense of Munday as an engaged writer who ... wanted to make an impact upon what would come to be known as English identity. In gathering, translating, reporting, collaborating, and revising, Munday repeatedly put back into print materials that Protestant versions of English or British identity had eliminated and were continuing to invalidate. Cultural work of the first order, these acts involved feeding, even aggressively contaminating, English ideological and historiographical discourses with materials from Catholic, European and pre-Henrician traditions. (Hamilton 2005: xviii–xix)

In Hamilton's reading of Munday's writing, Duffy's 'Trojan Horses' have been inverted: whereas Duffy argued that in the early years of the Reformation in England, Protestants made the new religion palatable to an orthodox public by appropriating the textual apparatus of the Catholic Book of Hours, Hamilton suggests that Munday covertly and subtly maintains the vitality of Catholicism within a country that has become increasingly accustomed to Protestant doctrines and poetics.

Hamilton's discussions are intriguing and make for detailed and startling reappraisals of Munday's work. However, as she acknowledges in her concluding remarks and throughout her discussions, the argument she presents requires some qualification due to the equivocation that is present within Munday's writing and the reading strategies that need to be employed (2005: 197). Furthermore, Munday was known to have informed on priests and other Catholics and worked for Elizabeth's notorious torturer of Catholics, Richard Topcliffe (Hill 2004: 36). At the same time, his translations of Iberian romances and their being dedicated to Catholics or people close to Catholics as well as his collaborations on the controversial play, *Sir Thomas More* (1592–4), would seem to contradict the notion that Munday was a zealous persecutor of Catholics.

Munday's personal beliefs may never be uncovered, nor will we know if early modern readers engaged with his translations as acts of covert religious defiance. However, what this emphasizes is the pliability of religion. Since the 'religious turn' within early modern studies, scholars have come to realize that the weight and volume of religious texts printed in the period vastly outnumbers secular texts. They have also come to understand that the simple binary of 'Catholic' and 'Protestant' underestimates the complexities of faith and religious devotion as an individual experience and part of everyday life and we need to recognize that faith is unique to each individual (Jackson and Marotti 2004). Munday's writing intersects with religious and political discourses in a variety of ways that are often opaque and this is especially true of his romance translations.

These texts were originally written in the early sixteenth century and offer Spanish (Catholic) commentary upon the English conquest of Ireland. Their translation into French and Munday's working from the French translations arrive at key points in relation to European religion and politics. Munday's translations were printed and reprinted between 1588 and 1639—a period that includes the aftermath of the defeat of the Spanish Armada, continued tensions with Spain until the signing of the peace treaty that ended the Anglo–Spanish war in 1604, the disastrously miscalculated Spanish Match, the personal rule of Charles I and reforms in Church worship that led to the Bishops' Wars in the years leading up to Civil War. Given the unpopularity of Spain with the English, the appearance and popularity of outmoded Iberian romances in English seems remarkable.

Whereas the allegory of *The Faerie Queene* presents to a reading public the triumph of Protestantism and endorses a Protestant agenda in Ireland, Munday's romances appear to retain the residues of criticism of English policy. Munday removed much of the Catholic oaths and rituals in the Palmerin and Amadis chivalric cycles, but for Hamilton they still retain the residues of a Catholic agenda, which make them thorny texts in Protestant England (Hamilton 2005: ch. 3). To an extent, this claim could be made of any allegorical texts that transcend national and confessional borders, and Munday's 'unabashedly pragmatic' (Hill 2004: 70) approach to his writing career means it is difficult to decipher the meaning of any political-religious impulses, implicit or explicit. However, Hamilton's discussions do shed light on the complexities of early modern translation and religion. Whereas scriptural translation drew attention to the need to translate word for word to maintain accuracy in the presentation of biblical exegesis, translation of prose romances required modification to make them 'fit' for a Protestant reading public. Such amendments extend to stylistics. As Helen Moore notes, in comparison to French translations, Munday's English translations are heavily inflected and bear the characteristics of Euphuism (Moore 2000: 340).

Regardless of the extent to which Munday removed or sanitized Catholic practices in his translations, the status of the romance genre in relation to religion is of note. The numerous translations across Europe of the Iberian romances attests to their success with the reading public, but, as Louise Wilson observes, 'In the course of the sixteenth century, the terms "Amadis" and "Palmerin" … came to stand metonymically for the kinds of frivolous or harmful text which humanist and religious writers counselled against' (Wilson 2011: 121). Translations of romances, therefore, are not of note so much for their religious content as for the objections raised about the effect that the reading of them would have on the reader. Women, in particular, were believed to be at risk due to their alleged prolific reading of romances. Reading, Helen Smith tells us, was understood in this period as an embodied act and the psychological and physical effects of reading 'dangerous' texts and virtuous texts was therefore a matter of concern to moralists (Smith 2010).

Despite these controversies, Munday's romances were clearly popular as they went into several editions during his lifetime and after his death in 1633. The same cannot be said of John Webster's *The White Devil* (1612), whose lack of box office success Webster blames upon its performance in an 'open and black theatre' in 'so dull a time of winter' to 'ignorant asses' (Webster 2008: 5). In this play, Vittoria is implicated in the murder of her husband and of her lover's wife and is put on trial. This scene has been of interest to critics because of its treatment of women in contrast to men, but what I am interested in here is its attitude to language:

> VITTORIA: Pray my lord, let him speak his usual tongue.
>   I'll make no answer else.
> FRANCISCO: Why you understand Latin.
> VITTORIA: I do sir, but amongst this auditory
>   Which come to hear my cause, the half or more
>   May be ignorant in't. (III.ii.13–17)

This exchange establishes a metadramatic connection with the play-going public, but it also satirizes the judicial process: upon being ordered to speak 'his usual tongue', the lawyer finds it impossible to refrain from interjecting malapropisms and incomprehensible neologisms, so much so that Vittoria remarks, 'Why this is Welsh to Latin' (III.ii.39). The lawyer is unable to move between languages; this draws to attention the absurdity of the trial, which is overseen by a biased Cardinal. In the lack of impartiality displayed by the Cardinal, we see that the play also focuses upon matters of faith. Crucifixes are retranslated into symbols of the family and its disintegration, and the adoption of Priestly robes as disguises by the revengers mirrors the duplicity that Protestants believed laid at the heart of the Catholic faith (Williamson 2007). The play inverts rites of marriage, confession, and extreme unction to present a Catholic society imbued with moral ambiguity, and questions whether faith is compatible with revenge. Here, translation and religion become fragmented, but other dramatic works were translated to voice displeasure at monarchical antics.

Early Tudor interludes such as John Heywood's translation of Lucian, *The Play of the Weather*, which was printed in 1533, have been linked to the king's Great Matter and the religious political concerns that underpinned Henry's decision to break with Katherine of Aragon and with Rome (Walker 2005: ch. 6). A century later, biblical narratives were used to condemn monarchical antics in the early years of the Civil War: a translation of George Buchanan's tragedy, *Baptistes sive Calumnia* (*c*.1542), which tells the death of John the Baptist, entitled *Tyrannicall-Government Anatomised*, was sponsored by Parliament in 1643 (Willie 2013: 66). Latin comedies and tragedies that drew from biblical sources flourished in the sixteenth and seventeenth centuries and were translated from, and to, vernacular languages (Leo 2015).

This chapter has surveyed some of the concepts relating to translation, religion, and literature in the early modern period. Given the weight and volume of translations undertaken at this time, it is not meant to be exhaustive or come to any neat (or reductive) conclusions with regards to the complexities of engaging with early modern translation theory and religion. Rather, it has offered a snapshot of some of the issues that are at stake across a range of religious genres. Translation crossed national and confessional divides and consequently, when considering English literature, we must also consider European perspectives, changing cultural conditions, and how translators recreated a narrative in a new language.

CHAPTER 9

....

PRAYER AND PROPHECY

....

ERICA LONGFELLOW

> Prayer the Churches banquet, Angels age,
>   Gods breath in man returning to his birth,
>   The soul in paraphrase, heart in pilgrimage,
> The Christian plummet sounding heav'n and earth.
>
> (2007: 178; ll. 1–4)

GEORGE Herbert's exquisite sonnet 'Prayer (I)' imparts the sense of mystical delight in prayer that many early modern people experienced. But, in its climaxing litany of impossible things ('Reversed thunder', 'Heaven in ordinarie'; ll. 6, 11), the poem also enacts the immense difficulty of saying what prayer is. In the end, in those famous last words, the poet settles for the seemingly mundane: prayer is 'something understood' (l. 14).

Christian prayer has always been fundamentally ineffable, but for Herbert and his post-Reformation contemporaries, what had always been difficult to describe was now thoroughly re-imagined, in ways that fostered creative anxiety as well as creative opportunity. The early reformers had to invent new systems of prayer to replace the public services of the Mass and the liturgy of the hours, and had to choose what to preserve and adapt from among the many forms of late medieval personal piety, including Books of Hours and structured models of meditation. If it was agreed that prayer in its very nature could not be confined in flawed human language, many other questions remained open: what words and gestures should be used; when, where, and how often the devout should pray; how personal prayer related to public worship in church; whether and in what form the inspiration gained through prayer should be conveyed back to God's people in the form of prophecy. These issues were the subject of intense and fruitful debate in the middle of the sixteenth century, and the inspiration for inventive responses in literature and new styles of prayer and meditation in the late sixteenth and early seventeenth centuries, until they were once more hotly contested in the build-up to the civil wars and the Interregnum. This chapter first discusses Protestant definitions of prayer, and then outlines, in brief, the changing modes of public worship, personal prayer, and prophecy in the sixteenth and seventeenth centuries, focusing on how these dramatic changes spurred poets, prophets, and ordinary people at prayer to invent new forms of religious writing.

DEFINING PRAYER

Although the early reformers understood as well as Herbert that prayer could not be confined in human words, they nevertheless attempted a straightforward definition. For Calvin, prayer was 'a certayne communicatyng of men with God, whereby they entryng into sanctuarie of heauen do in his owne presence cal to him touchyng his promises' (1561: 214ʳ). There are two key elements to this influential description. First, and more simply, prayer is a 'familiar speach with God', as William Perkins put it, through which fallen humanity encounters divine perfection (1591: C3ʳ; see also 1608: 230). More complexly, prayer reshapes and conforms human desires to the divine will. From the first chapter of the *Institutes* Calvin emphasizes the utter dependence of the fallen soul on God: when we first begin to seek knowledge of ourselves and God, then 'by our own nedines' we can glimpse the 'infinite ple[n]ty of good thynges that abydeth in god' (1561: 1ʳ). Faith teaches us that 'whatsoeuer wa[n]teth in vs the same is in God and in our Lord Iesus Christ'. We should therefore, Calvin reasons, 'seke in him, and with praiers craue of him that which we haue learned to be in him', that is, everything we need (1561: 214ʳ). In this sense, prayer is not best understood as the devout individual telling God what she needs, but rather as the devout individual acknowledging that God already knows what she needs, and will supply it.

The fact that God can supply a believer's every need, and wants to do so, of course did not mean that God would grant everything exactly as requested. It was possible to ask for something that was wrong or that was simply not the will of God, such as healing for a loved one. One of the goals of prayer, and one of its chief benefits, was that human need and desire be conformed to God's will, so that the soul would not only receive all that it asked for, but would be converted to godliness. This ideal of prayer as godly desire (and desire for God), drawn ultimately from Calvin's *Institutes*, influenced Protestants for much of the early modern period; late in the seventeenth century Richard Baxter defined '*True Christian Prayer*' as '*The believing and serious expressing or acting of our lawful desires before God*' (1673: 587). Baxter's addition of 'acting' of desires as well as 'expressing' them was a logical extension of the complex interplay between faith, desire, and prayer. Prayer was the expression of the most intimate human needs, and so ready was God to listen that simply desiring something in faith was to pray. Faith itself was 'A perswasion, that these things which we truly desire, God will grant them for Christs sake' (Perkins 1591: C3ᵛ). Desire, faith, and prayer existed in a continuous circle, feeding one another, and in this way one could pray by 'acting' as well as 'expressing'. To put in more modern terms, prayer was not merely words, but a way of being.

This understanding of prayer as desire was not so very different from the prevailing Roman Catholic model of prayer as desire for God, seeking 'the feruentnes of charitie' by which 'our myndes be highly lyfted vp vnto the beholding of god' (Fisher 1560: H2^r). Calvin and his followers also felt that prayer would lead to greater awareness and love of God as the giver of all good things. But reformed prayer achieved this goal by a subtle shift in focus from the goodness of God to the utter dependence of the person praying, and this distinction underpinned several characteristic elements of Protestant spirituality. The emphasis on human need meant that prayer, although generally acknowledged as 'The whole seruice of God, and euery part of it' (Wilson 1612: 369) was usually specifically understood as petition, in which 'we craue things needfull', and its product, thanksgiving 'for things receiued' (Perkins 1591: C3^r) (Ryrie 2013: 108). Contemplation or 'beholding of god' was, strictly speaking, a separate category known as meditation, very loosely understood in the sixteenth century, and more precisely from the beginning of the seventeenth century when Joseph Hall popularized a much simplified and adapted form of late medieval meditation for Protestant use (Ryrie 2013: 113–15). For many individuals prayer and meditation blurred in practice, but they were often treated as distinct activities in didactic literature throughout our period.

In addition to separating prayer and meditation, the need to discern their true desires—what they needed in the eyes of God—also led Protestants to underline the importance of self-awareness in prayer. Calvin urged as the first rule of prayer that the mind be 'free from fleshely cares and thoughtes' that might draw it away from God. But although the mind should be 'lifted vp & caried aboue it self' to speak directly with God, it ought not to be 'so at libertie, that it be pricked & nipped w^t no care', and forgets the need that brought it there in the first place (1561: 215^r). 'In prayeng', Calvin asserts, 'we alway fele our owne wante' (1561: 216^r). What humans most wanted (even if they did not know it) was repentance (Calvin 1561: 1^r). Praying for one's needs was closely intertwined with confession, since the greatest human need was for the grace that would reunite a sinner with God. Protestants were encouraged to pray for their earthly needs as well, but even such ordinary petition was ultimately connected with repentance and salvation, as God gave or withheld earthly goods according to his providential care for the soul, training it to true repentance and utter dependance on God.

The need to know one's own deficits ('ignoraunce, vanitie, beggery, weakenesse, peruersenesse, and corruption', as Calvin put it [1561: 1^r]), and to discern the workings of providence in what God gave or took away, led to the development of ever more complex regimes of self-examination in the seventeenth century. The believer's state of mind in prayer was more important than anything he or she might say or do. 'Prayer it self is properly an affectio[n] of ye inward hart', Calvin explained, 'which is poured fourth and layed ope[n] before God ye searcher of harts' (1561: 228^r). This broad understanding applied to both personal and public prayer.

This definition of prayer as heartfelt desire, expressed in faith, guided believers to a greater understanding of why they prayed, and for what end, but said little about how they should go about it. How did a Christian achieve the appropriate inner sincerity? What words should they use, and where should they pray, with whom, and with what sort of tone or gesture? To answer these questions theologians turned to Jesus's instructions in the sermon on the mount:

And when thou prayest, thou shalt not be as the hypocrites are. For they love to stand and pray in the synagogues, and in the corners of the streets, because they would be seen of men. Verily I say unto you, they have their reward. But when thou prayest, enter into thy chamber, and shut thy door to thee, and pray to thy father which is in secrete: and thy father which seeth in secret, shall reward thee openly. (Tyndale 1989: Matthew 6:5–6)

The first of these verses presented some problems: did it mean that Christians should only pray on their own, in their own chambers? Neither Catholics nor reformed writers were willing to discard all public worship. Catholic writers tended to spiritualize this verse, concluding that 'the secrete chambre, standeth not in the thynges, but in the affeccions and desyres of the har[t]e' (Erasmus 1548: xlvᵛ). Reformed writers wanted to take Jesus at his word as much as possible, so they tended to advise readers to 'be as though thou diddest pray in thy closet, intending onely to approoue thy selfe, and thine heart vnto the Lord', and to seek physical solitude where possible (Perkins 1608: 236; see also Becon 1542: Bvi ʳ⁻ᵛ). In crowded early modern households only a privileged few could be alone at will, so there is a simple practicality in this advice (Ryrie 2013: 154–70).

Believers were encouraged to seek solitude not only to avoid distraction but because an audience might tempt them to show off their piety, to 'be seen of men' like the hypocrites Jesus denounced. The reformers took this temptation very seriously. Whether alone, with their families, or in public worship, believers were to 'obserue such circumstances as may conceale their praiers from others; for all occasions of ostentation must be auoided, that so the heart may apply it selfe wholly towards the Lord' (Perkins 1608: 339). But although the reformers warned against seeking an audience, they also feared the hypocrisy that might arise when prayer was secret, a concern that was particularly acute when the early Protestants faced persecution if they worshipped openly. The early English reformer George Joye insisted, for example, that 'externe gestures' of worship must reveal the believer's inward desire; anything else was 'colourable dissembling' (1545: 84ᵛ). Calvin reasoned that believers should not neglect or change any aspect of their outward duty of prayer lest they appeared to neglect service to God, even if they continued to pray inwardly. 'Yet', he continued, 'do I not say yᵗ we ought to publish euery where whatsoeuer we thinke, so that we should straightwayes be caryed vnto death by the enemies of God and of the Gospell' (1570: 98ʳ⁻ᵛ, 99ʳ).

The reformers devoted as much effort to interpreting the next two verses of the sermon on the mount:

And when ye pray, babble not much, as the heathen do: for they thinke that they shall be heard, for their much babbling's sake. Be ye not like them therefore. For your father knoweth whereof ye have need, before ye ask of him. (Tyndale 1989: Matthew 6:7–8)

William Tyndale's emotive and polemical choice of English vocabulary in translating this passage ('babble much' for βατταλογήσητε (speak stammeringly) and 'much babbling' for πολυλογία (many words)) exerted a wide influence on Protestant criticism of Catholic practice.[1] Catholic writers had themselves used this verse to rebuke their co-religionists who thought 'moche bablyng to be the strength and vertue of prayer' (Erasmus 1533: Bii^v–Biii^r), and Thomas More was fond of mocking Luther and Tyndale for the 'folysh blasphemouse bablynge' of their critiques of the church (1532: xlviii). But 'bablynge' came to refer especially to repetitive forms of Catholic prayer and the canon of the Mass, spoken in Latin and sotto voce so that it was unintelligible to most listeners (Becon 1542: D^v–Dii^r; Calvin 1561: 228^r). For the reformers, prayer had to be clear, intelligible and in the vernacular, so that the thoughts of the heart were revealed in the words of the mouth.

The desire to match outward gesture to inward sincerity governed much of the reformed attitude to prayer, including the rejection of 'superstitious' forms of prayer, such as appealing to the saints as intermediaries, 'vaine repetition' of the Ave Maria and the Lord's Prayer 'vpon your beades' (Willet 1592: 405), venerating the host (the consecrated Communion bread) or the rood (see below), and ritual postures such as prostrating oneself and using the sign of the cross. From the reformed perspective, these practices added to Jesus's simple and clear definition of prayer, and led weak believers to attribute power to the ritual or object itself (the outward), rather than to God, who could only be known inwardly. Yet although they disapproved of these ritual trappings of prayer, the reformers were surprisingly open in their response to many other questions, such as whether prayer should be spoken aloud or quietly, whether the believer should kneel or stand, look up or down, shed tears or seem unmoved. So long as their prayers were orderly, humble, sincere, and directed to God and no one else, believers could follow their hearts in these matters, although in practice social pressure helped to define what was orderly or humble in public prayer (Ryrie 2013: 170–87; Craig 2013: 184–90).

EXPERIENCING PUBLIC PRAYER

The reformed theology of prayer departed from the Catholic tradition in emphasis rather than fundamentals: everyone would have agreed that a greater awareness of God was the goal of prayer, and that a sincere heart was necessary to achieve it. When that theology was put into practice, however, the changes were dramatic and wide-reaching, especially in public worship. Most late medieval English men and women would have experienced the Mass as a sensory ritual that stimulated personal devotion. Lay

---

[1] This is the only instance of both βατταλογήσητε and πολυλογία in the New Testament. In the Geneva Bible this verse reads: 'vse no vaine repetitions such as the Heathen: for they thinke to be heard for their muche babling'. A note offers Tyndale's alternative 'babble not much' for 'use no vain repetitions'. The King James Bible reads 'use not vain repetitions, as the heathen do: for they think that they shall be heard for their much speaking'; the Roman Catholic Douai Rheims translation is even more (and somewhat inaccurately) moderate: 'speake not much, as the heathen. For they thinke that in their much speaking they may be heard.'

worshippers watched the main action of the Mass through the choir screen: the preparation of the bread and wine and the prayer of consecration that culminated in the elevation of the host, when they would kneel, remove their hats, and raise their faces and hands in adoration (Craig 2013: 185; Duffy 1992: 117). Colourful, often expensive vestments and church furnishings would have added to the drama. Hanging from the roof above the screen was the rood, a representation of Christ on the cross, which also acted as a focus for devotion, a reminder that the bread and wine were the very body and blood of Christ. Lay people were not allowed beyond the screen, and usually would not have been able to hear the main prayer of consecration, spoken quietly in Latin. The devout could consult a Mass book or primer that provided personal prayers in Latin, and sometimes in English, to be repeated silently or sotto voce as the Mass progressed (Spinks 2013: 73–5). Clergy and lay people were both intent on the moment of consecration and the adoration it provoked, but there was no expectation that worshippers recited prayers in unison (Duffy 1992: 95–101).

At the Reformation the experience of public worship changed dramatically. Colourful vestments, the rood, and statues of the saints disappeared, as did most stained-glass windows and wall paintings. These imaginative teaching tools were usually replaced by more straightforwardly didactic wooden pulpits and painted tablets containing the three texts an adult Christian was expected to memorize: the creed, the Lord's prayer, and the ten commandments. The minister wore a black cassock and white surplice (although more radical reformers objected to the surplice). On a normal Sunday in most parishes the worship service was not a Mass, but the Book of Common Prayer service of morning prayer, the litany, and the first part of the Communion service, which broke off before the offertory and prayer of consecration (Ryrie 2013: 317). The service gave the laity an opportunity to hear large amounts of Scripture read or recited in English, both as 'lessons' and as set liturgy, and to be instructed in the basics of the faith through the exhortation to confession, the collects (set prayers), and the petitions of the litany, the creed, the Lord's prayer (used four times), and the ten commandments. They were expected to attend to God's word, to join in the unison parts of the service, and to assent silently to the prayers spoken by the minister. In contrast to the way medieval worshippers were moved to personal devotion by the action of the Mass, the reformers emphasized the greater efficacy of communal prayer, spoken and intended in unison. Common prayer was 'most forcible' because it combined 'the prayers of many together with one co[n]sent' (Burton 1594: 58; Ryrie 2013: 324–6).

This new worship experience was one that lay people could understand and learn from, and many strongly resisted when the service was threatened or neglected (Maltby 1998). But although its didactic form stimulated the ears (and through them, the mind), worship according to the Book of Common Prayer provided less for the other four senses, and could be dull and uninspiring when led by an unskilled minister (Ryrie 2013: 320). For lay people it was also a less physical experience than the medieval Mass. The reformed fear of hypocrisy and ostentation meant that believers were encouraged not to let their minds wonder from the text of the service to their own devotional concerns, and not to show by their posture or gesture that they were engaged in personal prayer (Craig 2013: 188). If a person was unable to prepare for worship by praying at home, he 'must conceale all outward signes of praier, & only lift vp his heart vnto God' (Perkins 1608: 339). Gestures such as 'capping' (removing the hat men were expected to wear in worship) and kneeling, which were familiar from heirarchical secular society, were still encouraged, but other physical expressions of devotion were frowned upon (Craig 2013: 188–92).

For some even these dramatic changes were not sufficiently radical. Throughout the sixteenth century those desiring more reform protested in print and in kind against what they considered the more 'popish' aspects of the Book of Common Prayer such as the sign of the cross in baptism and kneeling at Communion. The most extreme opposed any set texts beyond the Lord's Prayer, the ten commandments, and the creed. At the same time, those who missed some of the more ceremonial elements of the Mass longed for more ritual and drama; Elizabeth I famously kept a crucifix and silver candlesticks in the Chapel Royal. 'In practice,' a recent editor laments, 'the Book of Common Prayer at times seemed to please almost no one' (Cummings 2011: xxxvii). King James attempted, unsuccessfully, to resolve these disagreements at the Hampton Court Conference in 1604. They came to a height in the 1620s and 1630s with the reintroduction, under Archbishop Laud, of the more ceremonial elements of worship, including altars, altar rails, more elaborate gestures, and increased observance of feast days (Fincham and Tyacke 2007: 176–273). These changes in turn intensified the puritan demand that the task of reforming worship be completed, and in 1645 Parliament replaced the Book of Common Prayer with the *Directory of Public Worship*, which rather than prescribing what the minister should say, outlined topics for prayer in public worship services such as Holy Communion, 'like a set of stage directions without the speaking parts' (Maltby 2013: 225). From the 1640s worship practices began to vary widely; the disruptions of the civil wars enabled churches to develop around different forms of church government, but these groups also developed different worship customs. The most radical Protestants, including Milton and the Quakers, argued that worship should be entirely spirit-led, with no set form at all.

The extensive changes in worship at the Reformation, and the ongoing debate about the degree of change, affected literature as much as other aspects of English culture. The changes to public worship that were most significant for literary culture were the growth in congregational Psalm singing and in the popularity of sermons. Singing simple metrical English translations of the Psalms began among exiled Protestants in Geneva during the reign of Mary, and became increasingly a part of worship in England during Elizabeth's reign, either before, after, or between the sections of the service described above (Ryrie 2013: 317–18). The most popular metrical translation of the Psalms, by Thomas Sternhold and John Hopkins, was printed more frequently than the Bible in the seventeenth century (Quitslund 2012: 241–3). The Psalms exercised a pervasive influence on early modern English literature, inspiring some of the best English poets to imaginative translations, and influencing the popular sonnet sequences as well as the lyrics of poets such as George Herbert (Hamlin 2004).

Sunday worship in most parishes was also increasingly enlivened by a sermon as more university-educated clergy became available, and if the surviving comments in letters, notebooks, and diaries provide an accurate picture of lay people's experience of worship, it was sermons, not prayerbook worship, that proved the most engaging for ordinary Christians (Hunt 2010). In urban areas Puritans founded mid-week lectureships, free-standing sermon series that drew attendees from far and wide. Sermons were also popular in print, and, since the clergy had some licence to offer counsel to those in authority, they proved to be one of the more politically charged forms of literature. In the pens of Lancelot Andrewes, John Donne, and others, the sermon fostered the development of a sophisticated English prose style.[2]

Personal Prayer

The changes to personal prayer in Protestant England were not as visible or as dramatic as those to public worship, but they were nevertheless profound. For their devotion at home, literate lay people before the Reformation would have used a printed primer or, for the wealthy, a manuscript Book of Hours. These would have included many prayers and scripture texts but were centred on a simplified form of the monastic hours of prayer, focused on the Virgin Mary (Duffy 1992: 210–11). For many devout lay Christians, used to guided contemplation and repeatedly recited prayers, primarily in Latin, the Protestant way of addressing God from the heart in English must have seemed alien. At the same time, the important devotional experience of the Mass also disappeared, and the new public worship services according to the Book of Common Prayer encouraged communal rather than personal devotion. Protestants needed new forms of prayer for the home as much as they needed new public services for the church.

What they achieved, however, was not the unity of the *Book of Common Prayer*, but a proliferation of different forms and styles of prayer. Officially, each of the Tudor monarchs authorized a revision of the primer. The first, in 1545 near the end of Henry VIII's reign, kept the core of the late medieval primer, in the English and Latin parallel texts that had become popular from the 1520s, but reduced the references to the Virgin and the saints. Under Edward a new primer appeared in 1553 that incorporated the new public worship services from the *Book of Common Prayer*. Mary returned to late medieval Catholic forms in Latin and English, and Elizabeth reissued her father's primer in 1560, but also allowed several editions of her brother's more reformed version (Felch 2008: 29). Alongside these official forms, unofficial prayerbooks began to appear. Some of these were based on the traditional form of the primer, with a daily office that mirrored public worship, but some were simply compilations of prayers for use on different occasions, such as rising from sleep, going to sea, or preparing for childbirth. Queen Katherine Parr's

---

[2] See chapter 12 of this volume.

Prayers and Meditations (1545), for example, included five original prayers by the queen alongside her partial paraphrase of Thomas à Kempis's *The Imitation of Christ* (2011: 369–421). In the Elizabethan period these occasional prayerbooks flourished, including large composite volumes such as *Christian prayers and meditations* (1569, reprinted and augmented several times) and the *The monument of matrones* (1582). The proliferation of these books helped to encourage vernacular literacy, and opened up opportunities for lay people, and particularly women of high social status whose pious writing was valued as a form of Protestant proganda. Elizabeth Tyrwhit, a close associate of Katherine Parr, produced her own *Morning and Evening Prayers* in 1574; Mary Sidney completed the translation of the Psalms begun by her brother (Felch 2011; Coles 2008). The sheer variety of prayerbooks also helped to move Protestant personal devotion away from public forms of worship: simplified forms of morning and evening prayer from the Book of Common Prayer were now only one of many ways to pray at home (Felch 2008: 19–32).

Modern scholarship often refers to the new forms as 'private' prayerbooks but most of the Tudor prayerbooks were 'private' not in the modern sense of 'individual', but in the early modern sense, designed for use in the private household rather than the public space of the church. Reformed writers expected householders to lead morning and evening prayer for their family, including servants, although surviving evidence suggests that few households managed to meet this requirement (Ryrie 2013: 368). Individual prayer was also encouraged by the early reformers, but was not regarded as an obligation until the late sixteenth century. Throughout this period many individuals would have found it difficult to find time and space to pray alone in crowded early modern households, and in a culture where solitude was often viewed with suspicion. In that environment, what mattered was the inward disposition of the believer, free from the distractions of the world. Gervase Babington interpreted Jesus's command to his disciples to enter into their chambers as approving 'al priuat places whatsoeuer, which the godly drawe themselues into: to make their priuat prayer', including 'at home or abroad, in the Citie or in the Countrey, in our shops working, or in our beds lying, whither we bee sitting, standing walking', in other words, almost anywhere that was not a church building, regardless of how many people were around (1588: 69–[70]). Many early modern men and women took this advice to heart, finding quiet space for prayer in attics, woods, gardens, and on the open road (Ryrie 2013: 154–70).

For late sixteenth-century writers like Babington, individual devotion was necessary as a preparation for public worship, which was seen as the culmination of religious experience. The poet George Herbert clearly agreed; in his long poem 'The Church Porch', on the Christian life, he advises:

> Though private prayer be a brave designe,
>> Yet publick hath more promises, more love:
>> And love's a weight to hearts, to eies a signe.
> We all are but cold suitours; let us move
>> Where it is warmest. Leave thy six and seven;
>> Pray with the most: for where most pray, is heaven. (2007: 61: 397–402)

Although the poem by no means discounts personal prayer, it implies that, if the Christian has a choice, she should always opt for public prayer, rather than the uncertain 'six and seven'—a gambling term—of solitude (Herbert 2007: 81 n. 401). As well as prescribing it in this didactic poem, Herbert seems to have lived the principle that the Christian's chief duty was to 'Pray with the most'. Nicholas Ferrar noted that Herbert 'abounded in private devotions' but still took himself and his family to the church twice daily for the offices, and persuaded many of his parishioners to join them (42). A similar preference for public prayer is also apparent in *A priest to the temple*. Chapter VI, 'The Parson praying' (1941: 231–2) makes no mention of solitary devotions, but instead concerns the parson's duty in public worship. Other chapters seem to imply that an individual's basic duty was prayer twice daily with his or her household, ideally in the church, and the repetition of brief, memorized prayers before and after sleep (1941: 240–1). In addition, Herbert notes, 'the Godly have ever added some hours of prayer, as at nine, or at three, or at midnight, or as they think fit, & see cause, or rather as Gods spirit leads them. But these prayers are not necessary, but additionary'. If the lay Christian is interrupted in them, or even sleeps through his time of prayer, the parson was to remind him that he shouldn't be troubled by his neglect of such 'additionary' duties (1941: 272–3).

Herbert's fairly gentle approach to the duties of prayer probably reflected the reality of his country parishioners' lives, but in some ways, he was behind the times when he was writing in the 1620s and 1630s. By this time, the accessible form of meditation introduced by Joseph Hall in the early seventeenth century had become an important part of Protestant devotional life, and it was much more common for writers to take for granted that the duty of prayer was threefold—public worship in the church, family worship in the household, and secret or private individual prayers and meditation (Ryrie 2013: 113–15). In this climate Herbert's marked preference for public prayer in 'The Church Porch' looks rather anachronistic. But his desire to integrate his readers' personal devotional lives with the worship of the church was part of a growing trend, not only among the ceremonialists, but also among more Calvinist writers such as Daniel Featley. Featley's popular manual *Ancilla Pietatis* (1626) was, in its way, a return to the reformed primer, re-introducing a form of personal devotion that incorporated the rhythms of public worship, not only in daily and weekly form but in marking the feasts and fasts of the Christian year (Longfellow 2012: 63). *Ancilla Pietatis* is a good example of how forms of prayer in this period can defy simple categorization; not only were there many different forms, but individuals and even prescriptive writers often did not confine themselves to a particular style or party. The autobiographer Elizabeth Isham, for example, valued the feasts and ceremonies of her parish church but used an extensive library of puritan texts in her personal devotion (Stephens 2011).

One notable aspect of all of these different forms of prayer and meditation is that they are set texts meant to be read by the person praying, or sometimes merely as a model to inspire prayer. The public liturgy of the *Book of Common Prayer*, which set out nearly every prayer the minister was to say, verbatim, sparked debates about whether worship should use only set texts or be more (or mostly) extemporaneous. All but the most radical writers, however, acknowledged that vernacular set forms were useful and acceptable for personal prayer. Even if puritan writers tended to view extemporaneous prayer as more likely to be sincere, they recognized that deficiencies in prayer—babbling, dissembling, or self-conscious rhetoric—had more to do with the character of the individual praying than with set or extemporaneous prayer (Ryrie 2013: 215–20). From 1640, however, as the demand for further reform of the Book of Common Prayer intensified, radicals increasingly denounced the use of set forms in personal prayer. Most prominent among them was John Milton, who ridiculed set forms not only for limiting the ability of the individual at prayer to speak from the heart, but also for commoditizing piety; he mocked the production of prayerbooks, and the popular *Ancilla Pietatis* in particular, as 'any ord'nary and salable peece of English Divinity, that the Shops value' (Milton 1962a: 360). Selling any book of prayers, even generic models, was for Milton fundamentally hypocritical, because the writer might be distracted from the holy task of prayer by the fickle desires of a buying public.

Milton, and later the Quakers, were at the far extremes of this debate. The more moderate of the new sects allowed for some set forms or set structure of worship and prayer. The influence of these groups on the changing landscape of Protestant devotion lay more in their embrace of an affective piety that insisted that a ravishing emotional experience of prayer was not merely desirable, but vital for salvation. To be assured of their salvation, the faithful needed to experience a transporting delight in Christ's love, frequently allegorized in the language of mystical marriage. 'There is a chamber within us,' wrote Francis Rous in one such tract, 'and a bed of love in that chamber, wherein Christ meets and rests with the soule' (1635: A3ʳ; see Clarke 2011). Even for the learned John Owen union with Christ consisted of the emotional states of sweetness, delight, safety, and comfort. A believer who wanted to be sure of his election was advised to first judge the place of Christ in his emotions: 'consider a little with your selves: hath Christ his *due place* in your hearts? is he *your all*? does he dwell *in your* thoughts? do you know him in his *excellency* and desireablenesse?' (1657: 43–8, 57). All Christian writers taught that a sincere engagement in prayer was important, but this new style of piety insisted that a passionate experience of Christ was necessary for salvation, in an extension of the relationship between prayer, faith, and desire that was prominent in early English Calvinism. This emotional turn would open a divide between 'rational' conformist religion and 'enthusiastic' nonconformity that dominated the remainder of the century.

PRAYER AND LITERARY INSPIRATION

The new Protestant devotional forms had an even more widespread effect on the development of English literature than the Book of Common Prayer. There was need for more than didactic descriptions of how to pray and collections of prose prayers, and skilled writers produced new types of prayer in prose and poetry as well as increasingly sophisticated records of their own devotional lives. One relatively early Protestant text, Anne Vaughan Locke's *A meditation of a penitent sinner*, aptly illustrates how the characteristics of Protestant prayer discussed at the start of this essay influenced English literature. Locke was a Protestant activist who housed the Scottish reformer John Knox in London in 1552–3 and, at his behest, took her small children to Geneva in 1557, leaving her husband behind. She returned to London in 1559 to act as the exiled Knox's agent (Collinson 2004). *A meditation*, a contemplative paraphrase of the penitential Psalm 51, is appended to her translation of Calvin's sermons on the song of Hezekiah in Isaiah 38, and the whole volume, published in 1560, shortly after her return, is integral to her Protestant activism (Locke 1999; Coles 2008: 113–48). *A meditation* is also the first sonnet sequence in English, borrowing a form that had been primarily used to express intense erotic desire. Locke's sequence draws on the heightened emotional tension of the form, as the speaker, like an anxious lover, pleads with God not to drive her away, but to take pity on her sighs and tears. Locke's sonnets convey the complex relationship between prayer and desire for a Calvinist Christian, as conscious of her unworthiness before God as the lover is unworthy of the beloved.

In addition to the connection between prayer and desire that made the love lyric such a useful form for Protestant poets, Locke's sequence also illustrates the prominence of the Psalms in English literature. The Psalms were, as we have seen, a significant part of public worship in England from the 1560s onwards, in simple metrical translations that could be easily recited or sung by a congregation. But the Psalms were also increasingly important as models for how one should approach God in personal devotion, and Locke's *Meditation* on Psalm 51 crafts a devotional posture in imitation of the Psalmist's heartfelt penitence. Similarly, the most influential English literary translation, begun by Sir Philip Sidney but largely completed by his sister Mary, employs a wide variety of poetic forms, and uses tightly wrought images to convey the emotions of the psalmist. Locke's sequence and the Sidney psalms are particularly sophisticated examples of devotional psalms, but many other less skilled writers used the form of psalm collage and psalm paraphrase to enhance and express their own devotional experience (Felch 2011; Hamlin 2012). The ubiquity of the psalms provided a recognizable and easily imitated poetic form for prayer, but they also encouraged pious Protestants to express their devotion in poetic form.

Locke's sonnet sequence also illustrates the growth in self-expression that was characteristic of English Protestant literature. Although it was not until the early seventeenth century that Protestant devotional manuals actively encouraged writing as part of a devotional regime, the emphasis on self-examination in Calvinist spirituality often naturally led to self-writing. Locke's sonnets are in many ways typical in that, like the Psalms, they express emotions that are both personal and universal; the speaker expresses her sorrow, doubt, and fear but does not give any details of her particular sins. Fitting one's own experience into a salvation narrative was one of the key goals of Protestant self-examination; believers were meant to ask themselves how God was using their sins and afflictions to teach them to repent. The need for self-examination inspired diaries, journals, commonplace books, and other forms of life writing as early as the mid-sixteenth century, although these did not begin to mature until the mid-seventeenth century. The Northamptonshire gentlewoman Elizabeth Isham, inspired by a new Protestant English translation of Augustine's *Confessions* and Calvinist forms of self-examination, became the first person to write her own life story in English from birth to the present day (Isham 2008). The growth in affective forms of piety in the same period helped to enrich and validate the emotional vocabulary of life writing.

In addition to fostering new forms of self-writing, the need for self-examination also shaped the tone of English Protestant literature and the limits of what it could express. The need for a Calvinist writer such as Locke to acknowledge her wretched state opened up literary tensions as the poet 'can not pray without thy movyng ayde, | Ne can I ryse, ne can I stande alone'. She can, in effect, do nothing for herself, and even her words of penitence are the product of grace (1999: 70). This paradox both challenged and inspired poets such as George Herbert and John Donne, who were by turns fascinated, stymied, and inspired by what might be called the paradox of prayer: its ability to transmute human language, through grace, into something that was ultimately unsayable (Cummings 2002). An ageing Herbert, fearing the loss of his 'beauteous words', boldly tells them to take their way, 'For, *Thou art still my God*, is all that ye | Perhaps with more embellishment can say' (2007: 612: 30, 32–3). In the end, the most lyrical poem can say no more than the simplest expression of sincere faith. For all that the images of Herbert's sonnet 'Prayer (I)' reach beyond the stars, prayer, and human efforts to convey it, can in this life never be more than 'something understood'.

Prophecy

If prayer is speaking to God, prophecy is speaking God's word, gained in prayer, back to God's people. In his *Christian Dictionarie* Thomas Wilson summarized the two most common understandings of prophecy: 1. 'To fore-shew something that afterward should be fulfild' and 2. 'To expound and apply the scriptures to the edification of the Church' (1612: 378–9). It was in this second sense that the word was most commonly used in the period, and especially as it applied to preaching, 'Prophecying in the name and roome of Christ,' as William Perkins put it in his influential manual on preaching, *The Arte of Prophecying* (1607: 3). A prefatory letter to Wilson's *Christian Dictionarie* describes its interpretations of scripture as '*A light for Ministers, whereat they may borrow light; A Lanthorne for the people, to direct them in the Light*: And to bee short, the way to make all the Lords people to prophesie, as *Moses* wished' (1612: ¶4ᵛ). As this comment suggests, even in this more general form prophecy had a potentially radical edge, if even ordinary lay people could be empowered to proclaim their interpretations of Scripture. The clergy themselves, educated and licenced to preach, were nevertheless not immune from suspicion. Preachers frequently exploited their role as interpreters of Scripture to apply the moral warnings of the ancient prophets to current situations, and the line between prophetic counsel and sedition was very fine. Elizabeth I was particularly concerned about the growth of 'prophesyings', gatherings of ministers and lay people to hear three or four sermons on the same text, so that preachers could better their technique. The queen's letter of 1577 ordering the suppression of prophesyings demonstrates her fear of uncontrolled interpretation of Scripture. Lay people, she wrote, were drawn from far and wide to hear 'new devised opinions, upon points of divinity, far and unmeet of unlearned people', and thus 'brought to idleness, and seduced; and in manner schismatically divided among themselves into variety of dangerous opinions' (qtd. in McCullough et al. 2011: 553).

Even more dangerous was prophecy in the Old Testament sense, not just interpreting Scripture, but speaking the word of God directly. In spite of Wilson's first definition, in the sixteenth and seventeenth centuries this kind of prophecy did not always predict specific future events, but, like biblical prophecy, admonished God's people, and especially those in power, warning them of punishments to come. The clergy generally agreed that God had ceased to ordain such divine messengers once the church was established; some allowed that in exceptional circumstances or religious turmoil, including the wholesale reformation of the church, such prophets might arise again (Walsham 2001: 205–6). In general, however, ecstatic prophets were treated with great suspicion by both religious and secular authorities until the 1640s. Lord Burghley kept a dossier of letters from such fanatics, who thought themselves the offspring of God the Father or the new incarnation of biblical prophets such as John the Baptist (Walsham 2001: 204). Most found themselves facing severe punishment; even the noble Lady Eleanor Davies was imprisoned several times and committed to Bedlam. Not surprisingly, political prophets tended to appear more commonly, and come to prominence, in times of turmoil; statutes against prophecy were enacted in 1541–2, 1549–50, 1552–3, 1562–3, and 1580–1. In the 1640s as new religious sects proliferated, and people revisited the questions of religious authority that had shaped the Reformation, more prophets began to appear, and prominent figures were more prepared to accept that prophetic inspiration could exist in such a troubled time (Gillespie 2012: 2–3). As press censorship laxed in the Civil War years political prophecies in prose and verse flew off the press in such great numbers that the sheer volume of predictions and dire warnings may have done more to undermine the genre than censorship had ever achieved (Walsham 2001: 221).

Because prophets purported to speak not their own words but those of God, ecstatic prophecy was a genre often favoured by the unlearned, especially the poor, children, and women, who could claim that their simplicity made them ideal vessels for God (Walsham 2001: 208–13). Medieval visionaries such as Bridget of Sweden, Catherine of Sienna, and Joan of Arc provided a model for a number of women visionaries who appeared in the sixteenth and seventeenth centuries. They tended to speak in verse, often from a trance, refused or went without food, and relied on followers to write down their prophecies (Watt 1997: 144). Many of these women, such as a Jane Hawkins who began to prophecy in 1629, were quickly denounced by the ecclesiastical and secular authorities, and the only record of their prophecy is in official documents condemning them (Longfellow 2004b: 155–7). But others attracted more attention and were not so easily quelled. Elizabeth Barton, the 'Holy Maid of Kent', is one of the most famous. Barton began to prophesy during an illness when she was still a servant, in 1525. Repeatedly she fell into a trancelike state yet was miraculously able to speak clearly, and to predict events that she could not see. She was examined and declared orthodox, and entered a convent after her illness was miraculously cured. At first, a number of prominent religious houses, and even authorities such as Thomas More, Cardinal Wolsey, and the king himself granted her audience. A pamphlet of her writings (no longer extant) was printed in 1527. Soon, however, her prophecies began to be openly political; she wrote to the Pope to urge him to reject Henry VIII's petition for divorce, and prophesied the fall of Wolsey and others (Watt 1997: 140–3, 150–1). She was considered especially dangerous because she had the sympathy of many important figures at court who also opposed the royal divorce. In an orchestrated campaign, Barton and her followers were arrested, and she was forced to recant and do public penance and then hanged on 20 April 1634 (Watt 1997: 155, 157–9).

Although Elizabeth Barton was eventually silenced by the regime, the elaborate response of the state to her prophecy demonstrates how effectively she and her followers were able to manipulate the role of the simple female visionary. More than a century later Anna Trapnel, a shipwright's daughter, also crafted a platform for herself as a political prophet. Trapnel experienced her first vision in 1642, but her visionary career reached its height in December 1653, just after Cromwell declared himself Protector. Accompanying the Welsh Independent minister Vavasour Powell during his trial for treason at Whitehall, Trapnel fell into a trance and had to be carried off to an inn. She remained in the trance for eleven days and twelve nights, eating almost nothing and uttering prophecies sotto voce in her trance. Radical Protestants flocked to her bedside, and a scribe wrote down her prophecies, which were quickly printed as *A cry of a stone* (1654). Within weeks she embarked on a missionary trip to Cornwall, where she was arrested and appeared at the Assizes, accused of witchcraft and vagrancy. Trapnel skilfully exploited the indeterminate position of the woman prophet, defending herself as a single woman of means (and thus no vagrant) and insisting that she acted modestly by praying and speaking of God in the privacy of her chamber; the faithful and curious who flocked to hear her in her trance were, she implied, not her responsibility. The journalist Marchamont Needham, who had gone incognito to her congregation of All Hallows the Great, advised the Protector that she and her followers were 'silly wretches'; it was perhaps on this advice that Trapnel was sent from Cornwall back to London for a spell in Bridewell, the prison of debtors and prostitutes. Although she continued to prophesy until the late 1650s, Trapnel never faced the more serious and fatal charges that brought down Elizabeth Barton. The Cromwellian regime had perhaps learned that it was more effective to ridicule prophets like Trapnel than to treat their proclamations as serious threats (Longfellow 2004b: 149–79; Gillespie 2012).[3]

Like prayer, prophecy's influence on English literature is best understood as a diffuse phenomenon, a style and mode of address that went far beyond the narrowly understood genre. Sermons, lyric poetry, life writing, and other forms of devotional writing took on a prophetic tone when they proclaimed the word of God as received or interpreted

---

[3] See chapter 27 for further discussion of Quakers, prophecy, and print.

by the writer. The ballad attributed to the early Protestant martyr Anne Askew is one example of many texts that acquired the aura of prophecy although they were not prophetic in the narrower sense. Askew was twice interrogated for heresy, illegally tortured, and finally burned at the stake on 16 July 1646. Accounts of Askew's interrogation and torture were edited and published by the militant Protestant John Bale, and John Foxe included her own account in his highly influential *Acts and Monuments*, ensuring her importance as a Protestant martyr. 'The Balade whych Anne Askewe made and sange whan she was in Newgate' appears at the end of the account of her second interrogation. It is a simple metrical assertion of Askew's faith and ends with a Christ-like plea for mercy for the 'modye cruell wytt' (Henry VIII) that had usurped the place of Justice on the royal throne (Askew 1996: 150). The ballad, whether it is authentic or not, takes its power from the context of Askew's imprisonment and torture, which implicitly aligns her with the persecuted prophets of old, and, like the illness and inedia of Barton, Trapnel, and other women prophets, gives her a weakness that makes her the perfect vessel for God's word. This association with prophecy enables these writers, and others marginalized by gender, education, or status, to speak boldly in times of turmoil and to critique the highest authorities. But Askew and Barton's fates indicate why prophetic discourse remained a niche genre: in the early modern period prophecy belonged to the brave, or the mad.

CHAPTER 10

....

LYRIC POETRY

....

ELIZABETH CLARKE AND SIMON JACKSON

THE blossoming of the English devotional lyrics is undoubtedly one of the most significant consequences of the close relationship between literature and religion in the early
modern period. Cutting across denominational divides from Jesuit to nonconformists,
the lyric poem enabled the expression of spiritual experience by men and women in
manuscript and print collections, employing traditional and newly invented stanzaic
forms, and writing for a range of purposes from personal devotion to communal, pastoral, and liturgical usefulness. Since the lyric is such a dynamic phenomenon at the
heart of the early modern period covered in this book, many of these lyrics, inevitably,
are also to be found in discussions in other sections of the volume.[1] The particular focus
of this chapter is on selected key aspects of early modern devotional lyrics: their origins
in the Bible (both the Psalms and the Song of Songs), their relationship with music, and
their strong links with the contemporary contexts of political and social interaction.

BIBLICAL POETICS: PSALMODY

....

Early modern devotional poets seeking legitimacy for their literary work needed to look
no further than that 'book of starres', the Bible (Herbert 2007: 210). As George Herbert's
conceit suggests, the books contained in Scripture not only shed illumination on a dark-
ened world, but also—as these stars combine to create patterns and constellations in
the night sky—their words offer readers a navigational aid, simultaneously helping us
to make sense of this world and helping us to see beyond it, 'light[ing] to eternall blisse'
(l. 14). Elsewhere, it is for Herbert a book of 'Infinite sweetnesse' (208) and for Henry
Vaughan (in a poetic tribute to Herbert's 'H. Scripture' sonnets) 'soul's joy, and food!

---

[1] See, for example, chapters 20 (Philip Sidney and Mary Sidney Herbert), 21 (John Donne), 36 (Body
and Soul), and 37 (Sacred and Secular Love).

The feast | Of spirits' (Vaughan 1976: 197). As food nourishes the body, the Word of God nourishes and enriches the soul. In words that resonate with the language they use to describe the 'sweet, and sacred feast' of Holy Communion (Vaughan 1976: 216), both poets imagine the act of reading as a salvific gustatory act, tasting the Word and finding pleasure in its sweetness; discovering in this act a true, God-given sustenance: 'In thee ... the *manna* lies' (Vaughan 1976: 198). It is, in these models, the Book that builds and sustains, lights and guides all its readers.

For the devotional poet, to be led and fed by reading God's Word is to be confronted by a literary model that inevitably precedes, excels, and overwhelms his or her own creative acts; but it is also to find authority and legitimacy for one's own literary discipline. The Psalms are, in John Donne's formulation, 'The highest matter in the noblest forme' (Donne 1985: 468); and when Sir Philip Sidney came to write *The Defence of Poesy*, he offered 'the holy David's Psalms' as the very model of a divine poetic:

> For what else is the awaking his musical instruments, the often and free changing of persons, his notable *prosopopoeias* when he maketh you, as it were, see God coming in His majesty, his telling of the beasts' joyfulness and hills' leaping, but a heavenly poesy, wherein almost he showeth himself a passionate lover of that unspeakable and everlasting beauty, to be seen by the eyes of the mind, only cleared by faith? (Sidney 2004: 7)

Sidney maps on to the Book of Psalms the features of a contemporary, apparently secular poetic to display the ancient and distinguished heritage of contemporary verse. There he finds the dramatic qualities of the contemporary courtly love lyric: its rhetorical figures, its song-like construction, the platonic ideal of an 'unspeakable and everlasting beauty', and even the intimacy of the 'passionate lover' which makes the King David's verse sound closely allied to the sensuous poetic of King Solomon's Song of Songs. Problematically, as Sidney goes on to acknowledge, by employing such an argument, 'I fear me I seem to profane that holy name, applying it to poetry, which is among us thrown down to so ridiculous an estimation': by linking poetry and Psalmody so closely, Sidney risks denigrating the latter rather than promoting the former. But the relationship he establishes so clearly here between the Psalter and the contemporary lyric offered a valuable template for thinking about devotional poetics in the early modern period. John Donne's words, writing in tribute of Sir Philip and Mary Sidney's achievement in translating the Psalter into virtuosic English verse, might be extended to the Psalms of David as a whole: 'They tell us *why*, and teach us *how* to sing' (Donne 1985: 468).

The Psalms represented, for early modern society, arguably some of the most familiar passages of the entire Bible. Taking a prominent place in both the public formal liturgy of the Church and in private domestic devotions of the household, the saying and singing of these Old Testament lyrics formed an integral part of the texture and rhythm of early modern religious worship. Records survive to suggest that both the Herbert family and the Ferrar family each gathered regularly to sing Psalms, either as part of their weekly devotions or (in the more extreme case of the Ferrar community at Little Gidding) on an hourly schedule.[2] Much of this familiarity with Psalmody in the period was due in no small part to the vogue for the singing of metricalized translations of the Psalms. The translation of Psalms into simple, common metres, allied with the setting of these texts to familiar ballad-like melodies, created a corpus of singable and memorable biblical lyric verse. The mnemonic properties of this body of verse were particularly important in establishing the popularity of metrical Psalmody, enabling it to become a touchstone for the prayers and devotions of members of all levels of society. Nicholas Ferrar used it as an educational tool, inviting children from neighbouring villages to his community at Little Gidding each Sunday, where he would provide them with dinner and pay them a penny for each Psalm memorized. Local ministers applauded the initiative:

> for now their ears heard the houses and doors and streets sound out the sweet music of David's harp in all places and at all times of the day, the women hearing and the children repeating and conning the Psalms without book as they sat a-spinning and knitting. (Ferrar 1996: 71)

As Christopher Marsh has noted, metrical Psalmody could be heard across early modern society: 'the feature of Psalmody that most impressed itself upon [the Elizabethan chronicler] Henry Machyn was its unprecedented inclusiveness: "men and women all do syng, and boys" … Back at home, the Psalms were said to be on the lips of "the soldier … in war, the artisans at their work, wenches spinning and sewing, apprentices in their shops, and wayfaring men on their travels"' (Marsh 2010: 435–6).

Despite its popularity, the vogue for metrical Psalmody was born not in the streets and parishes of England, but in the fashionable environs of the court, and throughout the sixteenth and early seventeenth centuries the list of poets who wrote their own paraphrases and translations of the Psalms reads like a roll call of some of the most fashionable poets of the period, including Sir Thomas Wyatt, Sir Philip and Mary Sidney, and Sir Francis Bacon (Zim 1987; Freer 1972; Watson 1997; Hamlin 2004). As George Puttenham reminds us, even the most populist of the singing psalters, Sternhold and Hopkins, had its origins in the Royal court: 'king *Henry* the 8. her *Maiesties* father for a few Psalms of *Dauid* turned into English meetre by Sternhold made him groome of his priuy chamber, & gave him many other good gifts' (Puttenham 1936: 16–17). The Book of Psalms contains lyrics that articulate a huge range of religious experience, capturing the full gamut of human emotions from glorious, ecstatic poems of praise such as Psalm 150, through comforting Psalms acknowledging God's protective presence even in 'the valley, | Where triumphant darknesse hovers | With a sable wing' (Psalm 23, Crashaw 1957: 103), to the depths of despair characterized by Psalm 130 (*De profundis*)

---

[2] In his funeral sermon for his friend Magdalen Herbert Danvers (George Herbert's mother), John Donne records how she would gather the household each Sunday: 'So her selfe, with her whole family … did, euery Sabbath, shut vp the day, at night, with a general, with a cheerfull *singing of Psalmes*; This Act of *cheerfullnesse*, was still the last Act of that family, vnited in it selfe, and with God' (Donne 1627: G1ʳ). The daily routine of the Ferrar community is recorded in detail in Ferrar 1996: 69–76.

and the seven penitential Psalms. Throughout the doctrinal and theological reforms and counter-reforms of the sixteenth and seventeenth centuries, poets of all confessional and political backgrounds could find in the Psalms a model for their celebrations and laments. Protestant Reformers could gather behind a tradition of vernacular Psalm- and hymn-singing modelled by Luther and Calvin on the Continent, while Surrey could write metrical versions of the Psalms during his imprisonment in the Tower of London (Zim 1987: 80–111), and recusant Catholics and exiled Protestants alike could find an expressive model for their situation and their complaints in the song of David by the waters of Babylon, singing the Lord's song in a strange land (Ps. 137, *Super flumina*).[3]

The variety of subject matter found in the Psalms was matched, in the early modern period, by an astonishing variety of literary approaches to this material—from the prosodic simplicity (and, admittedly, frequent poetic infelicities) of the Sternhold and Hopkins ballad-like 'Old' Version of the Psalms, to the metrical sophistication of the Sidney Psalter, described by one critic as 'a School of English Versification' (Hallett Smith 1946: 269). Started by Sir Philip Sidney (who translated the first forty-three Psalms before his untimely death in 1586), it was completed by his sister Mary Sidney Herbert, countess of Pembroke, as a tribute to her brother's memory.

Even a volume of such prosodic virtuosity seems—at least in part—not to have forgotten the musical, song-imbued origins of the Psalms, and where metrical models have been found for Sir Philip and Mary Sidney's Psalms it is not unusual for that model to be a musical one, as at least one early reader of the Sidney Psalter recognized.[4] Sir Philip Sidney's Psalm 38, for example, borrows the prosodic framework of its continental counterpart:

> Ie n'ay sur moy chair ne veine
> Qui soit saine,
> Par l'ire en quoy ie t'ay mis:
> Mes os n'ont de repos ferme
> Iour ne terme,
> Par les maux que I'ay commis.[5]

---

[3] For a case study of the use of Psalm 137 during the early modern period by poets from a range of confessional standpoints, see Hamlin 2004: 218–52.

[4] In 1632, John Standish included adaptations of three of Philip's Psalms (40–2) and drew heavily on Mary Sidney's Psalm 97 in his anonymous singing psalter *All the French Psalm Tunes with English Words* (Standish 1632). Ringler notes where Philip's metrics coincide with the metrics of the French Marot-Bèze Psalter, but suggests—counter to our argument here—that he 'appears to have regarded only the words, and not the music of the French psalter' (Sidney 1962: 508).

[5] Ps. 38:2, in the Coverdale translation: 'There is no whole part in my body, because of thy displeasure: there is no rest in my bones by reason of my sins.' From Clement Marot and Théodore de Bèze, *Les Pseaumes en Vers Français avec leurs melodies*, the Genevan Psalter published by Michel Blanchier, 1562, cited here from a facsimile introduced by Pierre Pidoux (Marot and Bèze 1986: 121). The French Psalm has one extra syllable at the end of ll. 1, 2, 4, and 5 (the terminal 'e' is pronounced, producing feminine rhymes); Sidney's translation nevertheless fits easily to the Genevan melody.

By appropriating the metrical framework of the continental Marot-Bèze psalter, the Sidneys did much more than simply borrow patterns that would enable them and their readers to sing English words to a pre-existing melody: they could set up echoes and resonances, finding a shared, common voice that seems to bring the private, personal Psalmic devotions of the Sidneys into harmony with their fellow Christians singing these Psalms on the continent. 'No sound part ... My flesh hath', Sidney complains (Ps. 38, ll. 7–8); but as he sounds out his sin, his translation sounds out the French version of the Psalm in a very literal way:

> My wounds putrify and stink
>   In the sinck
> Of my filthy folly lai'd:
> Earthly I do bow and crooke,
>   With a look
> Still in mourning chear arayd.
>
> In my reines hot torment raignes,
>   There remains
> Nothing in my body sound. (Sidney 1962: 328)

As his empty body becomes a sounding board, a hollow acoustic space like the body of the lute that may accompany his singing, it begins to echo the words of the French translator. His words are informed and inflected by the French translation—the French 'chair' ('flesh') becomes 'chear', and the rhyme 'veine/saine' finds an aural equivalent in Sidney's 'reines/raignes/remains' to create an aurally allusive texture. The original Psalm complains (in Coverdale's translation) that 'There is no whole parte in my body'; here, it is as if Sidney is trying to use sound to reunite this sinfully broken, fragmented, fractured body.

The process is taken further still in Herbert's two Eucharistic poems, 'The Invitation' and 'The Banquet'. Although neither poem is a direct metrical Psalm translation, both are constructed on the prosodic model of the Marot-Sidney Psalm 38 and resonate with the aural soundworld of their Psalmic antecedents:

> Come ye hither all, whom pain
>   Doth arraigne,
> Bringing all your sinnes to sight:
> Taste and fear not: God is here
>   In this cheer,
> And on sinne doth cast the fright. (Herbert 2007: 624)

As Herbert further transforms the Psalm, he combines it with words from Psalm 34: 'O taste and see how gracious the Lord is'. Sidney's 'arayd' and 'raignes' become united into a single word, 'arrainge', as if the disjointed is now rebonded; and this new word continues to participate in the rhyming established Marot and Sidney. The host of the Eucharist becomes 'cheer' in Herbert's poem: his term for the consecrated bread ringing with Marot's 'chaire' and the 'mourning chear' of Sidney's Psalm, lest we forget the suffering that accompanies God's gracious gift of his flesh as food; but, in the context of an invitation to 'The Banquet', it now also suggests the convivial joy of the shared Eucharistic feast. The Old Testament promise of the Psalms is transformed into the New Testament promise of the Last Supper; the broken body is healed through the ministrations of another broken body; and—through the allusively echoing verbal texture and prosodic structure of these poems—the broken body of the Church is bound together in the singing of one shared, common song. Through the lens of psalmody, we can encounter the early modern religious lyric as a form of devotional song. To perform these works to a musical setting was to be one voice among many, to contribute a single voice to a universal song of praise. It enacts a process of reuniting the Church that brings to mind the etymological roots of the word 'religion': *re-ligio*, literally a re-binding. 'The Church with Psalms must shout | No door can keep them out,' wrote Herbert in his poem 'Antiphon (I)', acknowledging not only that this music may at times be coarse, but also that this is a fully social form of music-making, engaging all voices and permeating the artificial boundaries that humanity insistently constructs to separate or parcel itself out in the world: *'Let all the world in ev'ry corner sing'* (Herbert 2007: 187).

The Bible offered female poets a lyric mode with which to express their religious faith. In completing Philip's project to translate the Psalter, Mary Sidney not only found a means to pay tribute to her lost brother but also found in the poems of an ancient Hebrew king a voice that could express and articulate her religious faith and something of her experiences of female life in early modern society:

> Thou, how my back was beam-wise laid,
>   and raft'ring of my ribbs dost know:
>   know'st every point
>   of bone and joynt,
>   how to this whole these parts did grow,
> in brave embrodry faire araid,
>   though wrought in shopp both dark and low.
>
>   (Sidney Herbert 1998: 235)

As the recent editors of the Sidney Psalter have noted, in Mary's version of Psalm 139 God's creative powers become interwoven with ideas of feminine handicraft; the womb, by contrast, becomes a 'shopp both dark and low', resonating with the visceral and painful 'pangs of childbed' which we encounter in her translations of Psalms 48 and 58.[6]

---

[6] The recent editors of the *Sidney Psalter* explore at greater length than possible here the ways in which Mary's Psalm translations are inflected with her female perspective (Sidney 2009: xix–xxiii).

BIBLICAL POETICS: THE SONG OF SONGS

Like the Psalter, the Song of Songs also offered a model of divinely inspired religious verse that shaped the development of the lyrical voice of female poets during the early modern period. The reading of the Song of Songs by women had a substantial impact on female authorship in the seventeenth century (Clarke 2011: 134–73). Women used the text not only as subject matter, as a way of describing a relationship with Christ about which they were encouraged to write, but as encouragement for their wider activity as authors of poetry and prophecy. They responded to and identified with the female figure of the Bride; and while such a reading weakens the allegorical status of the text, in the love story of the Song of Songs women inevitably found a model for their relationship with Christ. This in turn leads to questions about the explicit eroticism of the text: perhaps it might, as Sharon Achinstein has suggested, affirm women's sexuality and help to voice female sexual desire in a period when such articulations are rare (Achinstein 2002: 417).

As one might expect, it was women poets rather than male ministers who responded most expressively to the feminine voice of the Bride. Aemilia Lanyer's women-oriented *Salve Deus Rex Judaeorum* (1611) is a poem dedicated to various élite women, expressly articulated by a female voice (Longfellow 2004b: 59–91). It contains some women-centred interpretations of the Bible such as '*Eve's Apologie*' (ll. 761–832), which is followed by a vindication of Pilate's wife. It also includes a sympathetic address to the women at the foot of the cross entitled '*The teares of the daughters of Jerusalem*' (ll. 969–1000), in which female compassionate behaviour is explicitly contrasted with male cruelty. Lanyer's evocation of the Resurrection is accompanied by two stanzas labelled in the margin '*A brief description of his beautie upon the Canticles*' (ll. 1305–20). Appropriately enough, this extract is for the most part a version of the woman's description of her lover in chapter 5 of The Song of Songs, although an extra metaphor for the lips, 'like scarlet threeds', is imported from the blazon of the woman in chapter 4. The first sight of the risen Christ is offered in the context of the love affair with the Church:

> This is that Bridegroome that appeares so faire,
> So sweet, so lovely in his Spouses sight. (Lanyer 1993: 107)

Anne Lady Southwell, writing in manuscript in the 1620s, uses biblical women—Debora, Abigail, Jael, and Judith—to boost her confidence as a 'weake female' who dares to write poetry.[7] Two manuscripts survive of Southwell's long poem on the Decalogue, and the second, British Library MS Lansdowne 740, meditates more intensively on the position of the woman writer, and takes comfort in the figure of the biblical Bride. In

---

[7] For Anne Southwell, see Burke 2002: 94–120; Longfellow 2004b: 92–121; Longfellow 2004a; Clarke 2001: 10–11.

the face of the scorn heaped by men on the early seventeenth-century woman writer, and especially the prophetess, she asserts the appropriateness of expressing her love for Christ in the terms of the Song of Songs:

> Away, base world, hence shadows, hence away.
> You shalbee noe corriualls to my loue
> for hee is fresh as is the flourye may
> & truly constant as the turtle doue
>   his breth like beddes of roses cheere the morne,
>   his hayres reflex the sunne beames doth adorne.

She also has to confront a puritan disapproval of poetry, and although she very strongly disapproves of printed publication, she nevertheless asserts her right to use verse, as the divine Lover did:

> & though some amorous Idiotts doe disgrace it
> in making verse the packhorse of theyr passion
> such cloudes may dimme the sunne but not deface it
> nor marvell I that love doth love this fashion
>   To speak in verse, yf sweet & smoothly carryed
>   to true proportions love is ever maryed. (Klene 1996: 152)

Anne Southwell insists here that poetry is the correct medium for divine Love, as the Bible demonstrates in books of poetry like the Song of Songs and the Psalms. This similarity invites parody of the love poetry of the early modern period, which Jamie Reid Baxter has found in extensive manuscript poetry by Elizabeth Melville, known until now only as the author of the 1606 'Ane godlie Dreame'. Sarah Ross identifies many Petrarchan strategies in Melville's divine verse, which draws on the Scottish *Gude and Godlie Ballatis*, first published in 1565 and reprinted in 1567, 1578, 1600, and 1621, which includes numerous adaptations of secular songs and ballads for spiritual uses. Perhaps Melville's most spectacular parody is found in her rewriting of Christopher Marlowe's 'A Passionate Shepherd to His Love', transforming this secular love lyric into a sacred song. As Sarah Ross demonstrates, in Melville's adaptations of Sir Philip Sidney's Petrarchan verse the lyrics tend to reach a surer resolution than the original poems on which they are based, finding an answer to desire in the unfailing passion of a divine Lover (Ross 2010: 96–107).

Perhaps the most exquisite use of the Song of Songs in a Scottish context is a verse paraphrase in manuscript dedicated to the countess of Caithness by Barbara Mackay.[8] Mary Sinclair, countess of Caithness, was the sister of the duke of Argyll. Barbara Mackay was from a devout Presbyterian family, whose allegiances were complex: her brother, Hugh Mackay, was a major general with James II's army, but landed with

---

[8] National Library of Scotland MS.Wod.Qu.XXVII, fols 9–28, mentioned in Trill 2004: 223.

William in 1688 and became his commander-in-chief in Scotland (*ODNB*). The Song represents the most important truths that Mackay has learned. The introductory verse gives the framework within which the Song should be interpreted:

> This sweet dealogue that point out the Love
> Betwixt the creature and his Lord Above. (fol. 10ʳ)

In the paraphrase, however, as in the biblical Song of Songs, there is no explicit mention of Christ at all. Just occasionally there is a touch of theological interpretation, when the wall or lattice behind which the lover is obscured is described as being the result of sin (fol. 11ʳ). In true Presbyterian fashion, there is a reference to predestination as God's decree inserted in 5:12, where the lover's eyes are described as washed so that 'he can always see | What e'res the lot off all he did decree' (fol. 14v). The focus of Mackay's paraphrase is not doctrine, however. The introduction to the Song of Songs explains why it is more important than any other song, 'most pretious rare' as Mackay puts it. It is a poem of overwhelming emotion, even eroticism, yet it remains absolutely chaste and legitimate:

> For puritie it is the truth most pure.
> It ravisheth, it captivates, it charmes
> All sound affections in the beloveds armes. (fol. 10ʳ)

Verse paraphrases of the Song of Songs tend to preserve the eroticism of the text simply because there are so many sense impressions that are part of the imagery, and the two lovers' bodily presence is so strongly realized. Mackay's verse is even more sensual than that of most paraphrasers of the Song of Songs, as her brief expansions of the text can emphasize the physicality of the love affair. What Barbara Mackay has learnt in her life, the thing that is most precious, is that for her Christ is a real and sensuous presence. Because the Song of Songs is holy, she can use its extravagant language, and even elaborate on it, without the fear, particularly strong for women, that she will be carried away in excessive and illegitimate emotion. It is possible that Sharon Achinstein is right in positing the origins of this imagined experience in the romance genre, rather than in the spiritual 'ungendered quest' that Sarah Ross, following seventeenth-century religious orthodoxy, finds in it. For nonconformists, however, this type of writing was deeply transgressive, and certainly not on their reading lists. The Song of Songs becomes the true romance of which romantic fiction is a Satanic copy.

When male poets turned to the Song of Songs, the results could be startling. Donne's Sonnet 14, 'Batter my heart, three person'd God', figures the poet as the Bride who needs to 'rise, and stand'; the Divine Lover from the Song of Songs 5:2 is standing at the door, knocking and asking to be let in. Like most interpretations of the Song of Songs, the sonnet reaches out from what is figured as a state of spiritual adultery towards a chaste devotion to a heavenly Bridegroom. Donne stresses the gentleness of the action that

Christ takes, having been rejected; the speaker would prefer the door of his heart to be battered down:

> Batter my heart, three person'd God; for, you
> As yet but knocke, breathe, shine, and seeke to mend.
>
> (Donne 1985: 443)

Donne is looking for something much more violent to get him on his feet, although he acknowledges that a kind of death must precede this resurrection: 'That I may rise and stand, o'erthrow me'. He is voicing a classic Reformed paradox here, which only the Holy Spirit can deal with. The Spirit has the power to mortify sinful human nature and resurrect the individual in the power of God. It is this divine intervention that Donne is seeking. The word he uses here is 'ravish', as he expresses the need for some powerful force to be exerted on him. Explicitly taking the subject position of the loving but wayward Bride of Christ, he knows he needs to be 'chaste', but unless something violent occurs, that is not going to happen:

> Yet dearely' I love you,' and would be loved faine,
> But am betroth'd unto your enemie:
> Divorce mee,' untie or breake that knot againe,
> Take mee to you, imprison mee, for I,
> Except you'enthrall mee, never shall be free,
> Nor ever chast, except you ravish mee.

Donne, of course, is aware of the full spectrum of meaning of the word 'ravish'. The context of sexual politics that he has carefully set up entails that the immediate effect of the word is one of brute sexual violence, a deliberately shocking end to the poem. The whole poem is an illustration of Romans 7:19, 'the good that I would, I do not; but the evil which I would not, that I do', a dilemma expressed in the first part of that chapter in the same terms as this poem, that the victim is married to the wrong partner. At the end of Romans 7, the power of God to free the soul is celebrated: by 'dying' to the power of the sinful human flesh, the soul is free to be married to Christ.

Donne's poem ends with a wish for a fate worse than death: the end of the false marriage for him is envisaged as a rape. Donne's sonnet is probably an explicit comment on Calvinist interpretation of the Song of Songs, and the implication of its gender politics. All Calvinist commentary represents the Bride of the Song of Songs as passive, a role conducive not only to early modern patriarchy but to the inculcation of Calvinist doctrine, in which Christ does all the work of election, justification, and sanctification. Donne's Bride is just not passive enough: whilst the Bride of the Song of Songs is too laid back to open the door to Christ, Donne 'labour[s] to admit' the divine Lover. Within Calvinist theology the subject's plight is hopeless unless Christ is prepared to use a shocking amount of force to counteract the sinful activity of his errant Bride. Perhaps Donne is drawing attention to the huge imbalance envisaged by Calvinism in the power relationship between the partners in the marriage with which the bond between God and the believer is figured. In the poem, the discomfort caused by use of the word 'ravish' is strengthened, not weakened, by knowledge of its current value in puritan spirituality. Donne's sonnet is surely stressing the inappropriateness of this vocabulary in spiritual discourse—can it be healthy to induce this kind of masochistic need in an individual? There are also some alarming questions raised in this lyric poem, about the implications of puritan use of the allegory of marriage: human sexuality is too easily perverted to serve as a stable vehicle with which to convey a relationship with God.

POLITICAL, SOCIAL, AND OCCASIONAL RELIGIOUS LYRIC

For all its ostensibly private nature, it is difficult and problematic to extract the early modern religious lyric from its wider public context (in both social and political terms). As Michael McKeon, charting the development of our modern sense of privacy from the end of the medieval period, has recently argued, 'In "traditional" culture, the differential relationship between public and private modes of experience is conceived as a *distinction* that does not admit of *separation*. In "modernity" the public and private are separated out from each other' (McKeon 2005: xix). These lyrics were written during this period of transition, as a clear sense of the separation between the public and private realms was developing and emerging. Arthur Marotti's pioneering study of the socio-cultural setting of John Donne's verse argued that 'the context of Donne's religious verse was not only that of Donne's personal desires and private relationships with friends, patrons, and patronesses; it was also the more general one of Jacobean culture'. Marotti comments:

> In both Tudor and early Stuart times religious poetry served as a way for courtier-careerists to express slight or serious political disappointment … [whereas] the very act of composing sacred verse in the reign of a monarch who had himself written religious poetry and especially favored pious and polemical writing was a political gesture. (Marotti 1986: 245–6)

As Marotti makes clear, the religious lyric must be considered in religio-political terms, sitting uneasily—like Donne's 'Litanie'—on the cusp of the public and the private.

Donne's poem opens with the scrutiny of the repentant sinner, intensely self-critical:

> … come
> And re-create mee, now growne ruinous:
> My heart is by dejection clay,
> And by self-murder, red.
> From this red-earth, O Father, purge away

> All vicious tinctures, that new fashioned
> I may rise up from death, before I'am dead. (Donne 1985: 456)

This first person singular soon becomes subsumed into collective first person pronouns, as Donne's poem engages more directly with the public liturgy of the Church,
explicitly echoing the refrain of the 'Litany' in the Book of Common Prayer ('Good
Lorde delyver us').[9] At the same time, Donne's language registers personal dissatisfaction and disappointment, characterizing 'his own behavior and interests as those
of a witty, depressed, ambitious but frustrated careerist seeking preferment at the
Jacobean court' (Marotti 1986: 249):

> From being anxious, or secure,
> Dead clods of sadnesse, or light squibs of mirth,
> From thinking, that great courts immure
> All, or no happinesse, or that this earth
> Is only for our prison fram'd
> …Good Lord deliver us. (Donne 1985: 462)

Even at his most intimate and personal, Donne's religious lyrics rarely escape the public sphere completely: Donne's 'A Hymne to God the Father', with its self-indulgence of
the repeated pun on done/Donne, was set to music as Izaac Walton records; the poet,
'caused [it] … often to be sung to the *Organ* by the Choristers of St *Paul's* Church, in
his own hearing; and especially at the Evening Service' (Walton 1927: 62). The personal-
ized, self-inscribed devotion of the poet becomes—through the voices of the choristers,
raised in common prayer—the voice of public worship, ringing around the building of
one of the capital's great churches.

In recent years, scholars have drawn attention to the ways in which the early modern lyric circulated within coteries and in manuscripts and enriching our readings of
this verse with a vibrant and vivid sense of the occasional nature of much of this verse
(Marotti 1995; Woudhuysen 1996). Cristina Malcolmson has offered a portrait of George
Herbert that is similarly alert to the way in which his devotional lyrics are embedded in
a social coterie culture (Malcolmson 1994, 2004; Rienstra 2010–11). Both Donne's and
Herbert's verse need to be considered in the light of a wider literary (and, it might be
added, musical) coterie that extended (as we have seen) back to Philip and Mary Sidney,
and included William Herbert, third earl of Pembroke, George's brother Edward, First
Lord Herbert of Cherbury, and Lady Mary Wroth. Beyond these limits, the social and
sociable activities of these poets inspired numerous followers and imitators throughout the seventeenth century: Gavin Alexander has drawn attention to the rich literary
legacy of Sir Philip Sidney's writings in the aftermath of his death and the ensuing publication of his works (Alexander 2006). Herbert's devotional verse—which, as we have
seen in our discussion of Psalm 38 above, participates in this process of posthumous

---

[9] BCP 117. On the relationship of this poem to the public prayer of the Church, see Targoff 2001: 92–4.

celebration and memorialization of the dead Sidney—itself prompted a rich corpus of literary responses that we might think of as a network or coterie of poets, writing lyrics that respond and answer to the words and works of their poetic forebear.[10]

In 'The Authors Preface' to the second edition of *Silex Scintillans* (1655), Henry Vaughan explicitly acknowledged his debt to 'the blessed man, Mr. *George Herbert*, whose holy *life* and *verse* gained many pious *Converts*, (of whom I am the least) and gave the first check to a most flourishing and admired *wit* of his time' (Vaughan 1957a: 220). When Richard Crashaw's devotional verse appeared in print, his editors made explicit the author's poetic ancestry: its title, *Steps to the Temple* (London, 1646) acknowledged the poet's indebtedness to Herbert. However, the volume also claims to travel further than this, offering, in the 'Preface to the Reader' (probably written by Crashaw's friend and colleague Joseph Beaumont) 'Stepps for happy soules to climbe to heaven by'. This preface hails Crashaw as 'Herbert's second, but equall'—an ascription that neatly captures the courteously competitive strain that the coterie fostered, some sense of the instinct for deference, and the claim to social equivalence that coteries might inspire among their members.[11]

In Crashaw's hands, we see Herbert's verse continue to play a literal role in the continued social circulation of poetry, since Crashaw himself writes a poem to accompany the gift of a copy of *The Temple* 'sent to a Gentlewoman', in a complicated, socially imbued gesture that appropriates Herbert's religious meditations, praises them, and gives them away:

> And though *Herberts* name doe owe
> These devotions, fairest; know
> That while I lay them on the shrine
> Of your white hand, they are mine. (Crashaw 1927: 130–1)

In this social, sociable approach to lyric, Herbert's verse seems to take on a life of its own. The open leaves of the book become an angel's wings, 'flutter[ing] in the balmy aire, | Of your well perfumed prayer' (ll. 9–10): Herbert's inspired devotional meditations are moved once again by the breath of his readers, who are themselves in turn moved to prayer. 'Looke on the following leaves, and see him breath', Crashaw encourages us at the end of his poem 'Vpon Bishop Andrewes his Picture' (Crashaw 1927: 163–4), advice repeated verbatim by Crashaw's friend Beaumont at the conclusion of his Preface to *Steps to the Temple*: to read a text is bring it into the present moment, to fill it with one's own breath, and to make it live.

Musical performance offers a particularly vivid model for thinking about the way in which the early modern religious lyric 'breathes' in this way, and how we might

---

[10] See, for example, Ray 1986 and Wilcox 2009.
[11] Crashaw 1957: 75. Such 'double motions' of submission as assertion are common in the early modern lyric as established by Herbert; for the fullest treatment of this topic, see Schoenfeldt 1991.

understand its 'occasional' nature.[12] Because musical performance exists and unfolds in time, the singing of a lyric lifts the poem off the silent page, and allows us to think about the way in which it may be located in a specific historical context, in a specific time and place. But it may also, simultaneously and counterintuitively, allow us to think about the ways in which the lyric—and particularly the religious lyric— attempts to exist outside the moment. When Sir Philip Sidney famously describes how the poet 'cometh to you with words set in delightful proportion, either accompanied with or prepared for the well-enchanting skill of music' (Sidney 2004: 23), he is thinking of the possibilities of musical performance ('either accompanied with or prepared for...'). He is also gesturing towards classical musical theory, with its understanding of the mathematical ratios and proportions that underlie the harmonic and rhythmic language of music. 'The World is made by Simmetry and proportion,' wrote the poet-composer Thomas Campion, 'and is in that respect compared to Musick, and Musick to Poetry' (Campion 1967: 293). Building on classical theories about music, Campion sees music and poetry in terms of a mathematical model: recognizing the mathematical proportions that underlie the harmonies and rhythms of music and poetry, Campion argues that these art forms make audible and perceptible the mathematical coherence of nature. From a Christian perspective, when words and music are brought into harmony with each other in devotional song, they can offer one of the most expressive modes for articulating a divinely constructed, coherent creation.[13]

Campion takes this musico-poetic model to its logical extremes in the final song of his *Booke of Ayres* (London, 1601). Coming at the end of a collection that mixes secular and sacred lute-song, the volume concludes by dedicating its final song to God:

> Come, let us sound with melody the praises
> Of the kings king, th'omnipotent creator,
> Author of number, that hath all the world in
> Harmonie framed.
>
> (Campion 1967: 48–9)

God's status as 'Author of number' is expressed in a number of interlocking ways: as we sing, 'sound[ing] with melody' our praise of God, we physically realize the mathematical harmony of the created world. Campion's prosody also works hard to articulate the proportions immanent in God's Creation. The lyric is constructed according to classical quantitative theories: rather than being patterned by accentual stress, Campion

---

[12] For recent studies of musico-poetic relations in the early modern period, see Jorgens 1982, McColley 1997, Schleiner 1984, Winn 1981, and Jackson 2011. For full surveys of modern criticism on the topic, see Schleiner 1986 and Dunn 2008.

[13] For good introductions to classical ideas of speculative musical theory, with its emphasis on proportion and ratio as the building block of harmonic and musical theory, and the implications of such models on early modern English verse, see Hollander 1961, particularly pp. 20–51, and Lindley 2006: 13– 49. For the fullest account of such theories, see Spitzer 1963.

here understands metre in terms of long and short syllables (in which a 'long' syllable lasts twice as long as a 'short' syllable), and Campion reproduces this prosodic rhythm precisely in the pattern of minims and crotchets of his musical setting. It is an unusual experiment—and one that Campion never repeated—but one that captures some of the richly inventive and expressive ways in which early modern poets could use the lyric form to gesture beyond the limitations of the mundane world, to engage with religion and ideas of divinity, 'And record,' as Campion's song concludes, 'with more than an earthly voice, [God's] | Infinite honours' (ll. 23–4).

CHAPTER 11

··

DRAMA

··

ADRIAN STREETE

DURING the years with which this chapter is mainly concerned, 1558 to 1642, playwrights of various political persuasions demonstrate a recurrent interest in religious matters when writing for the public stage.[1] Certainly the influence of medieval liturgical drama continued to be felt well into what is conventionally designated the 'early modern' period (Whitfield White 2008). Moreover, as scholars have shown, there is no shortage of religious interest in civil war, republic, and post-Restoration drama (Wiseman 1998; Owen 1996; Kewes 1998). However, for the purposes of this chapter, I will focus largely on the middle section of the period dealt with in this handbook, whilst also glancing forwards and backwards when appropriate to the start and end of our period. Accordingly, the first section will offer a necessarily selective overview of dramatic interest in religio-political matters.[2] Unsurprisingly, the contours of this engagement change in tandem with shifting ideological realities over the period. But there can be little doubt that the early modern stage is an important civic site for religious debate. It is often noted that a significant number of the books written, printed, and sold in early modern England were on religious topics (Shuger 1998: 1–10). It would doubtless be going too far to classify the drama of the period as 'religious literature'. Yet in a period where doctrinal debate was at the forefront of intellectual and political life, the interrogation of religious ideology on stage often provoked controversy and reaction. I will argue that periodic attempts by the authorities to 'reform' the stage were only partially successful. Paradoxically, however, the incompletion of these efforts were deeply generative for dramatists, opening up a wide range of aesthetic possibilities that were exploited throughout the period (Diehl

[1] I am grateful to the editors for their helpful comments on this chapter.
[2] For reasons of space, this chapter is largely confined to drama produced for the public stage or public theatres between 1558 and 1642. Of course, drama was also played in a wide variety of other locations, including at court, at the universities, at the Inns of Court (in all three of these locations, religious drama was played regularly), on the street, at fairs, during processions, in taverns and pubs, and in private houses. For a good collection of essays on varieties of early modern performance spaces, see Dutton 2009, and see too Findlay 2009.

1997; Streete 2009a; Shell 2010). The second part of this chapter examines some of these possibilities in more detail, and in light of the 'turn to religion' in recent scholarship, looking in particular at drama and the Bible, and the exploration of various religious passions on stage (see Jackson and Marotti 2011: 1–21).

'REFOURMING' THE STAGE

In May 1559, the newly crowned Elizabeth I issued a proclamation that addressed the relationship between drama and religion. The document states that in order for the 'good orderd [*sic*] Christian Common weale' to prevail, it is necessary that all 'common Interludes in the Englishe tongue' are first licensed by authority. Specifically, magistrates and other officials must 'permyt none to be played wherein either matters of religion or of the gouernance of the estate of the common weale shalbe handled or treated' (Chambers 1965: IV, 263). The proclamation makes an important connection between the treatment of religious doctrine and the government of the commonwealth: it assumes that discussion of one implies discussion of the other. It is also a document that reflects the realities of the new Reformed political dispensation. Any attempt to separate *res publica* and *res ecclesiae* was likely to fail. After all, religion and politics had been linked in statute during the Henrician Reformation (Walker 2007). The English monarch's new role as head of state and Church meant that politics and religion were now intertwined in ways that were politically necessary, if hardly straightforward. Despite the religious polarities experienced by the populace during the reigns of her half-siblings Edward and Mary, Elizabeth's Acts of Supremacy and Uniformity, also published in 1559, are an attempt by the new regime to find a moderate Protestant mean in matters of divinity and state alike (Shagan 2011: 111–30). The fact that the proclamation on drama was published in the same year as these major constitutional Acts shows that the theatrical discussion of religion and governance was considered to be a matter of some political import.

As David Womersley has argued: 'What disturbed Elizabethan magistrates when they reflected on the stage was the power of drama to fuse heresy and sedition (that is to say, religious and political error, respectively), and to embody that complicated error in vivid, memorable images unfit, so they thought, to be placed before a general audience' (Womersley 2010: 3–4). Throughout the period, the authorities wanted to ensure that, to adopt early modern religious terminology, the stage conformed. As modern scholarship has shown, by any objective measure Elizabeth's 1559 proclamation can only be considered as a partial success. Certainly the gradual emergence of various state and civic mechanisms for the regulation and censorship of drama is an important feature of the second half of the sixteenth century, especially in the metropolis of London. The theatres were regularly identified as sites of civic disorder and incubators of disease by the city authorities and moralists alike, even though the city authorities did harness the political power of pageants and drama at various points. Anti-theatricalists and preachers of the 'hotter' type criticized drama and the playhouses on explicitly theological grounds

(Barish 1981; Crockett 1995; Waldron 2013). For example, in 1577 John Northbrooke criticized the playing of 'histories out of the scriptures', stating that the people claim 'that playes are as good as sermons, and that they learne as much or more at a playe, than they do at God's worde preached' (Chambers 1965: IV, 198). Dramatic interest in religion continued to be viewed with intermittent suspicion by the authorities throughout the period. Legislation was passed in 1606 prohibiting the name of God from being spoken on stage (Chambers 1965: IV, 338–9). Moreover, censorship of politically and religiously sensitive matters did occur (Dutton 2000). Dramatists had to approach divine matters with a degree of care.

Nevertheless, the regulatory mechanisms set in place by the 1559 proclamation, and the various attempts made to reform the stage thereafter, were not consistently effective. Writers found ways of negotiating state regulation (Patterson 1984; Clare 1990; Dutton 1991; Clegg 1997). As the commercial theatres burgeoned from the 1570s onwards, official proclamations alternate between reforming and facilitating drama. There is no straightforward narrative of how the authorities tried to control theatrical discussions of divinity: most of the surviving evidence arises in response to contingent political events, to localized moral purges, or to recurrent social and economic concerns. To take another example, in February 1592, Sir William Rowe, the Lord Mayor of London, wrote to John Whitgift, the Archbishop of Canterbury, to complain that theatre-going is keeping the 'prentizes & seruants' from their work, and that 'light & lewd dispersed persons' congregate in the playhouses to consort and engage in 'confederacies, & conspiracies'. The Lord Mayor asks Whitgift that he enact 'the refourming of so great abuses tending to the offence of almightie god, the prophenation & sclaunder of his true religion, & the corrupting of our youth, which are the seed of the Church of god & the common wealth'. Again, we see the close connection between divinity and state and the desire to bring the two into conformity ('refourming') in the theatre. Rowe also refers to the queen's 'lettres Pattents' awarded to 'Mr Tilney Master of hir Revells' and asks Whitgift to ensure that he 'refourm' the stage too (Chambers 1965: IV, 307–8). This is a significant request. If there *is* a larger narrative at work here then it is probably related to the ongoing tussle between the court, the Church, and the city concerning the ultimate jurisdiction over what was staged in the commercial theatres. The growing authority of the Master of the Revels from the early 1580s over theatrical production had to be balanced against the desire of the city fathers to maintain orderly economic activity (Dutton 1997: 294–7). Though this was often an uneasy relationship, reform rather than repression of the theatres was usually the aim of both parties.

Another important factor is aristocratic patronage. Nobles like Thomas Cromwell and, later, the earl of Leicester used the theatre as a means of supporting Reformist ideals, as well as their own political agendas. Companies patronized by aristocrats vied for performances at court, and the patron could also be appealed to when the city authorities or, later, the Master of the Revels, sought to limit their activities (see Chambers 1965: IV, 276). The various adult companies that were formed throughout the period all perform plays that use religious language and address religious topics, although certain theatres like the Red Bull were particularly known for staging plays with a strongly

Protestant flavour (Bayer 2009: 232). The boys companies did not shy away from religion either. The plays of John Marston, such as *Antonio and Mellida* (*c*.1599–1600), *Antonio's Revenge* (*c*.1600–1), *The Malcontent* (*c*.1603), and *The Dutch Courtesan* (*c*.1604–5) are a good case in point.[3] Biblical and liturgically based medieval drama did not, despite legislation designed to curb its popularity, die out completely in early modern England. Away from the metropolis of London, as the REED project has shown, explicitly religious drama continued to be performed throughout England (Whitfield White 1993 and 2008; O'Connell 2000; Groves 2007). As we have seen from the complaints of the anti-theatricalists, biblical drama is an important feature of the early modern commercial stage. George Peele's *David and Bethsabe* (*c*.1581–94), Thomas Lodge and Robert Greene's *A Looking Glass for London and England* (*c*.1586–91) and Greene's play (now lost) of *Job* (*c*.1586) demonstrate the prevalence of the genre (Roston 1968; Groves 2007; Streete 2012). Less directly, it is not hard to find biblical allusions and references throughout the corpus of early modern drama. In a culture dominated by the Bible, plays draw regularly on biblical idioms—more on this later. More prosaically, but no less importantly, dramatists continued to address religious matters because it was commercially lucrative to do so. One of the most regularly performed plays of the period, Christopher Marlowe's *Doctor Faustus*, is steeped in biblical and theological language. As Leah Marcus has suggested, the various textual differences between the A (1604) and B (1616) texts of the play may well reflect important shifts in religious ideology: 'from a *Faustus* associated with religio-political autonomy and radical Protestantism to a *Faustus* associated with greater religious conservatism and complicity with empire' (Marcus 1996: 38–67). Marlowe's 'mighty line', the play's demonic theme, and its spectacular theatricality were all key factors in keeping the play on stage. But we should not discount the religious aspects of *Faustus*—especially the play's reworking of older religious forms associated with 'morality' drama—as a major factor in its continuing popularity at the box office. Faustus debates divinity in a way that was of enduring appeal to early modern audiences.[4]

Although not invariably politically conservative, the function of much medieval drama is to underwrite doctrinal orthodoxy and ecclesiastical authority. In the early years of the Reformation in England, drama continues to be used as a means to proselytize the public (King 1982; Whitfield White 1993 and 2008). Indeed, one of the earliest surviving Protestant English plays, John Bale's *King Johan* (*c*.1537–40), is a fascinating amalgam of late medieval dramaturgy and Reformed theology and historiography. It explores the relationship between monarchical and papal authority through the lens of history, a model that would be adopted and adapted by playwrights throughout the sixteenth and seventeenth centuries (Kamps 1996: 51–66; Cavanagh 2003: 16–35). The later Henrician, Edwardian, and early Elizabethan periods all see a range of interludes, morals, and plays that promulgate Protestant doctrine, often with a distinctly anti-Catholic

---

[3] A comprehensive study of Marston and religion still needs to be undertaken.

[4] See chapter 19 of this volume for further discussion of Marlowe and religion.

tinge, for example, Thomas Kirchmeyer's anti-papal and apocalyptic Latin academic drama *Pammachius* (1536–8), John Foxe's similarly polemical *Christus Triumphans* (1556), the plays of Lewis Wager, such as *The Life and Repentance of Mary Magdalene* (*c*.1550–66), *The Longer Thou Livest The More Fool Thou Art* (*c*.1559–68), and *Enough is as Good as a Feast* (*c*.1559–70), and Nathaniel Woodes's *The Conflict of Conscience* (*c*.1570–81). Although each of these plays can be understood in their specific historical and political contexts, it is fair to say that this early phase of Reformist drama is more concerned with the didactic and often allegorical reinforcement of Protestantism at a doctrinal level, underpinning the religious values of the state. The last scene of *The Longer Thou Livest* stages a discussion between Discipline, Piety, and Exercitation that references Ezekiel, Solomon, Plato, Aristotle, Cicero, Valerius, Augustine, and Theophylactus, and concludes with a prayer that 'the Queen's most honourable Council' and her 'Magistrates' will 'agree to maintain God's Gospell' and to 'root out Antichrist' (Wager 1968: 1975–9). But whereas this kind of learned religious didacticism was broadly acceptable to many Protestants, theatrical innovation was pushing theatre in new, and often more secularly oriented directions. As McMillin and MacLean have shown, the 1570s and 1580s saw a radical puritan backlash against this particular kind of secular theatre; this is the period in which Stephen Gosson, Philip Stubbes, and John Northbrooke wrote their antitheatrical tracts (McMillin and MacLean 1998: 30–2). It is also the period in which various puritan and nonconformist identities come to the forefront of public debate, agitating for further reform of the Church of England. The establishment of the Queen's Men in 1583 can thus be seen as an effort to counter radical Puritanism and to form 'an acting company bearing the queen's name and performing plays of such English and Protestant moderation as could displease only those reformers opposed to playing itself' (McMillin and MacLean 1998: 32).

In practice, this moderate, reforming theatre took other roads, some of which could not have been anticipated. Politically, the early 1580s sees England becoming more closely engaged with conflict on the European continent, especially in the Low Countries. As the public theatres become more established as a social phenomenon supported by the state, theatrical engagement with religious matters becomes more politically animated and interventionist. During the later 1580s and 1590s, theatrical experimentation goes hand in hand with a bolder exploration of religious ideology, often tied to an interest in political and military matters (Taunton 2001; Barker 2007). For instance, in addition to Marlowe's *Faustus*, all his other plays show a keen interest in religion, but perhaps the most notably political are *The Jew of Malta* (*c*.1590), which examines the intersection between the Christian, Jewish, and Islamic religions, and *The Massacre at Paris* (*c*.1592), which deals with the slaughter of the French Huguenots in 1572. Another popular late Elizabethan play, Thomas Kyd's Senecan revenge tragedy *The Spanish Tragedy* (*c*.1587–92) offers, amongst other things, a religio-political critique of Spanish imperialism at a time when militant Protestantism was being more forcefully articulated in the public sphere, as does George Peele's *The Battle of Alcazar* (see Ardolino 1995: 12; Griffin 2009: 67–96). Less demotically, John Lyly's court play *Midas* (1589) clearly has the Spanish in its allegorical sights. In *Selimus, Emperor of the Turks*

(1594) Robert Greene addresses fears of the expanding Ottoman Empire, and his *Friar Bacon and Friar Bungay* (c.1589–92) capitalizes on the interest sparked by *Faustus* in demonism and magical esoterica. Greene's play is an early example of dramatists exploring the Islamic religion, and later plays like Robert Daborne's *A Christian Turned Turk* (1612) and Philip Massinger's *The Renegado* (c.1623–4) follow in this line. Given the pejorative rhetoric that generally accompanies discussion of Islam in these plays, it would be going too far to call them an early example of comparative religious study. Nevertheless, these English constructions of Islam do reflect a series of anxieties about Christian hegemony and masculinity in the face of Ottoman power (Vitkus 2003; Dimmock 2013b).

Though it is unlikely that Shakespeare knew Bale's *King Johan* directly, his history plays of the late 1580s and 1590s show him responding to the religio-political challenges posed by the Reformation. In particular, he is well aware that the medieval English landscape that he explores is, historically speaking, peopled by Roman Catholics (see Morse, Cooper, and Holland 2013; Woods 2013). This is important because the Reformed historiography practised by writers like Bale and Foxe looked to reclaim some of the medieval past as anticipatory of the Reformation, drawing on the biblical book of Revelation in order to distinguish between the 'true', godly Protestant Church and the 'false', anti-Christian Roman Catholic Church (Hamilton 1992: 137–49). This Reformed model of historiography was popular and well known, and Shakespeare engages with it at various points throughout his dramatic career, most notably in the early histories (Womersley 2010: 237–60). The original model for Falstaff in the *Henry IV* plays was the Lollard radical Sir John Oldcastle, executed in 1417 for his unorthodox beliefs, and lionized by Foxe in his *Acts and Monuments*. Shakespeare's use of these sources is typically careful, but it seems likely that surviving members of the Oldcastle family took offence at early depictions of their ancestor and that Falstaff was born in order to forestall further offence (Poole 2000: 16–44).

Moreover, while Shakespeare generally steers clear of the polemical tone of other contemporaries, he does deploy the rhetoric of anti-Catholicism at points in his history plays. The depiction of the bishop of Winchester in 1 and 2 *Henry VI* is clearly inflected with this language—Gloucester warns him: 'Under my feet I'll stamp thy bishop's mitre. | In spite of Pope, or dignities of church, | Here by the cheeks I'll drag thee up and down' (Shakespeare 1997a: 1.4.48–50). These words and threatened actions may well draw on popular Protestant polemical iconography showing the trampling of the false Roman Catholic church by the English monarch. Figure 11.1 is an example from John Foxe's popular *Acts And Monuments*, showing Henry VIII trampling on Pope Clement VII.

In *King John* (1596), the king defends his 'great supremacy' and rails against the papal legate Pandolf with the words: 'no Italian priest | Shall tithe or toll in our dominions' (Shakespeare 1997a: III.i.79–82). Such language could have evoked a range of responses. Historically, the Henrician Reformation ended the paying of tithes ('Peter's Pence') to Rome. To invoke and reject this possibility could have been seen as an assertion of English freedom from Rome, an expression of nationalistic self-determination that is

FIGURE 11.1 'Henry VIII and Pope Clement VII'. Woodcut from John Foxe, *Actes and Monuments…*, vol. 2 (London: John Daye, 1583), Sp Coll, f291–293, Vol. 2, p. 799. Image courtesy of University of Glasgow Library, Special Collections.

typical of much drama in the 1590s. Conversely, it can also be read as a reminder of the fragility of England's Reformation, especially in a European context (Scott 2000: 29–30). By the mid-1590s, the Elizabethan 'supremacy' had witnessed a number of challenges. Internally, it struggled to contain the more radical puritan wing who agitated for greater reformation of the Church against the moderate Elizabethan settlement. Externally, the Spanish threat remained. Indeed in 1595, Hugh O'Neill, the earl of Tyrone had raised a rebellion against the English and in 1596 another Spanish Armada set sail for England with the intention of using Ireland as a staging post for its invasion. Although the venture failed, the spectre of the Roman Catholic international determining religious and political doctrine in England underpins this scene in *King John*: it is a less assertive moment than a first reading might suggest.

Despite inevitable tensions, the peaceful accession of James VI and I in 1603 was taken by many as a providential sign that the English were secure in their Reformation. The discovery of the Gunpowder Plot in 1605 both affirmed and also undermined that belief. Dramatists responded in a variety of ways to the event, from the polemically anti-Catholic (Thomas Dekker's *The Whore of Babylon* (1605) and Barnabe Barnes's *The Devil's Charter* (1607)) to the subtly analogical (Ben Jonson's *Volpone* (1606)), to the obliquely inferential (William Shakespeare's *Macbeth* (c.1606–7) (see Gasper 1990; Wills 1995; Dutton 2008). Indeed, the proclamation of 1606 prohibiting the name of God being spoken on stage may well reflect anxieties about the boldness with which playwrights were now addressing the religio-political sphere. The major tragedies of John Webster, *The White Devil* (1612) and *The Duchess of Malfi* (1613–14), depict a shadowy world of Roman Catholic court life, where Italian *politiques* flash dangerously across the firmament. Webster's use of the rhetorical tropes of anti-Catholicism has been well documented (Shell 1999: 23–55; Marcus 2009: 23–32). By contrast, his subtle use of biblical idioms is only beginning to receive the attention that it deserves (Rhatigan 2012: 176–94). Atheism and freethinking of various kinds, often associated with classical philosophies of Stoicism and Epicureanism, are explored in plays like Tourneur's *The Atheist's Tragedy* (1609–10), George Chapman's Bussy D'Ambois plays (1604; 1609), and John Ford's *'Tis Pity She's a Whore* (c.1629–33) (Hamlin 2005). And, of course, the discussion of religion is not only confined to tragedy and history: the lampooning of Puritans for dramatic effect can be seen in a range of comedies, from Chapman's Florilla in *An Humorous Day's Mirth* (c.1599), to Shakespeare's Malvolio in *Twelfth Night* (1601), to Jonson's Ananias and Tribulation Wholesome in *The Alchemist* (1610) and Zeal-of-the-Land Busy in *Bartholomew Fair* (1614), to the Maid in Brome's *The Antipodes* (1640). Clearly early modern audiences could see a wide variety of religious identities explored on the stage.

In the case of Thomas Middleton, he is one of the few early modern dramatists, like Bale and Foxe, who we can confidently also identify as a writer of theological and exegetical works (Middleton 2007: 679–720). Scholars are perhaps less inclined now to be as definitive as Margot Heinemann in her seminal 1980 study that Middleton was a Calvinist with puritan sympathies, (Heinemann 1980; Archer 2011: 135–44). Despite the historically oriented scholarship that predominates in the study of early modern drama and religion today, one lasting legacy of post-modernism is a reluctance to see plays as reflecting a dramatist's particular religious faith. Shakespeare is one exception, but usually only when it is being argued that he was a Roman Catholic (Wilson 2004). Generally, literary historians now prefer to describe this period as one of religious flux or fluidity, extending that understanding to their consideration of authorship and religious identity (Streete 2009a: 6–11). This may say more about current preoccupations in the modern academy than it does about religion in the early modern period. Nevertheless, there is little doubt that Middleton had a keen interest in the doctrinal and political ramifications of theology. *The Revenger's Tragedy* (1606) casts an eye that is both sardonic and wary on predestinarian ideology. *The Second Maiden's Tragedy* (1611) can be read as a Protestant 'saint's play' that offers a critique of Roman Catholic political power in the aftermath of Henri IV's assassination. And in an extraordinary run of plays written between 1619 and 1624, including *Women Beware Women*, *The Changeling*, and, arguably the most politically controversial of all early modern plays, *A Game at Chess*, Middleton's religio-political critique of the late Jacobean regime becomes even more pointed (Limon 1986; Bromham and Bruzzi 1990). Indeed, this last play, like Dekker's earlier *The Whore of Babylon*, deploys an allegorical idiom that draws on the Spenserian and polemical traditions. The period between 1618 and 1624 is one of the highpoints of religio-political critique on the early modern stage, perhaps matched only by the plays produced between 1679 and 1682 during the Popish Plot. Both these periods see playwrights adopting drama as a polemical vehicle, and while both periods have received detailed attention from scholars, a definitive study of early modern drama as polemic still remains to be undertaken, especially in relation to the European vernacular and Latin traditions of controversial literature (see Lander 2006).

Other major dramatists ran up against the censor for dealing too directly with religio-political matters: the example of Philip Massinger is instructive here. His co-written 1619 play *Sir John van Olden Barnavelt* was censored for staging a contemporary Dutch political conflict and for suggesting that the controversial theology of Arminianism was politically seditious. *The Virgin Martyr* (1620), co-written with Thomas Dekker, was marked by the censor for 'reforming', probably because it was too 'hotly' Protestant. Julia Gasper has called it a Foxean *tragoedia apocalyptica*, 'an example of how militant Protestants of the Jacobean era engaged in a process of self-mythologizing' (Gasper 1990: 143, 164). The fact that this play was written for the Red Bull Theatre gives credence to this argument. Massinger's 1631 drama *Believe as You List* was censored because its historical source material was seen as offering too close a contemporary critique of the Caroline regime (Massinger 1976: III, 293). And his 1638 play *The King and the Subject* (now lost) was censored on the orders of the king himself, Charles I, and the play was only allowed to be performed with 'the reformations most strictly observed, and not otherwise' (Howard 2008: 118). As has long been observed, there is an aesthetic shift in Caroline drama towards the pastoral, the bucolic, and the fantastical. But such plays also exist alongside texts like Thomas May's republican-inflected dramas *Cleopatra* (1626) and *Julia Agrippina* (1628), Robert Gomersall's revenge tragedy *Lodovick Sforza* (1628), Robert Davenport's history play *King John and Matilda* (*c.*1628–32), Henry Glapthorne's topical history *Albertus Wallenstein* (*c.*1634–9), Nathaniel Richard's satiric classical tragedy *Messalina* (*c.*1635), and Francis Quarles's allegorical play *The Virgin Widow* (*c.*1640), all of which use religious language and imagery to a variety of political ends. The old assumption that much Caroline drama and court masque promulgates an overwhelmingly 'Cavalier' ideology that uses Neoplatonism as a way of bypassing religious or political critique no longer pertains (Butler 1984 and 2009; Britland 2006; Zucker and Farmer 2006; Dyson 2013). As Butler has demonstrated, the later dramas of Richard Brome are keenly engaged with religious controversy, for instance his 1640 play *The Court Beggar* (Butler 1984: 228–50). And James Shirley's 1641 play *The Cardinal* offers a fascinatingly conflicted response to the fall of the Laudian regime. Moreover, as studies of civil war and Restoration drama have shown, the interface between religion and politics continues to spark controversy (Potter 1989; Maguire 1992; Randall 1995; Wiseman 1998; Clare 2002). A good later example is provided by anti-Catholic plays like Nathaniel Lee's *The Massacre at Paris* (1679) and *Caesar Borgia* (1679), Thomas Jordan's *London in Luster* (1679), Elkanah Settle's *The Female Prelate* (1680), and Thomas Shadwell's *The Lancashire Witches, and Tegue O' Divelly The Irish Priest* (1681). All of these plays were written during the Popish Plot. A group led by the renegade Titus Oates managed to persuade the political nation that Charles II's life was in imminent danger from Roman Catholic assassins, and that his brother, the duke of York (later James II) should be excluded from the throne by an act of Parliament (Owen 1996; Kewes 1998). A number of people who were falsely accused or else implicated by Oates and his associates were executed, and although Oates was later discredited, the febrile atmosphere of this period is reflected in these plays. Many of these late seventeenth-century plays are also in dialogue with their pre-Restoration dramatic precursors. Religious matters continue to be keenly debated on the post-Restoration stage. It is precisely because the 'reformation' of early modern drama is only partially successful that it is able to be so aesthetically generative and commercially viable well into the late seventeenth century.

BIBLICAL GRAMMAR ON STAGE

Drawing upon the seminal work of Debora Kuller Shuger and Brian Cummings, recent work on the religious grammar of early modern drama has considered further what Cummings calls 'the literary culture of the Reformation' (Cummings 2002: 20; Shuger 1998). He suggests that in early modern religious writing, doctrine does not precede its grammatical or textual iteration; rather, it emerges in the act of writing and disputation (Cummings 2002: 51). This approach has borne fruit in fine studies by Sarah Beckwith and Heather Hirschfeld, which have drawn attention respectively to the uses of the terms 'penance' and 'satisfaction' in early modern drama (Beckwith 2011; Hirschfeld 2014). This grammatical turn has also informed recent reconsiderations of the place and use of the Bible in early modern drama (DeCook and Galey 2012; Streete 2012). For while not all uses of Scriptural language on stage will be religiously or politically significant, drama is an inherently dialogic form, meaning that, even in soliloquy, a speaker who invokes the Bible does so in conversation with his audience. To invoke and discuss Scripture on the public stage is, by implication, to assume that the public has a right to hear and even participate in that debate: this is one of the keenest political legacies of the Reformation. One of the most interesting examples of this phenomenon is found in the use of biblical texts within soliloquies and theatrical dialogue. Here drama and exegesis are brought into conversation in a way that is both generative and contentious. Probably the most famous instance is Antonio's superior Christian incredulity when Shylock uses a story from the Pentateuch/Old Testament in debate on the Rialto: 'The devil can cite Scripture for his purpose' (Shakespeare 1997: I.iii.94). But there are many other examples of the dramatic use of Scripture.

We might begin with Faustus's well-known dismissal of conventional academic knowledge at the start of Marlowe's play:

> When all is done, divinity is best.
> Jerome's Bible, Faustus, view it well.
> [*He reads.*] *Stipendium peccati mors est.* Ha!
> *Stipendium*, etc.
> The reward of sin is death. That's hard.
> [*He reads.*] *Si peccasse negamus, fallimur*
> *Et nulla est in nobis veritas.*
> If we say that we have no sin,
> We deceive ourselves, and there's no truth in us.
> Why then belike we must sin,
> And so consequently die.
> Ay, we must die an everlasting death.
> What doctrine call you this, *Che serà, sera,*
> What will be, shall be? Divinity, adieu! (Marlowe 1993: I.i.37–50)

Is this brusque dismissal of divinity daring, foolhardy, both, or neither? The most common critical argument is that Faustus deliberately neglects to quote the New Testament verses in full, thus choosing to bypass a more capacious understanding of salvation that would be implied had he done so. This also allows him to criticize the theological doctrine of salvation associated with predestinarian Calvinism as a kind of unpleasant determinism ('What will be, shall be?'). Alternatively, of course, Faustus may be a fool, a charlatan whose shallow academic knowledge is shown up through his misunderstanding of Scripture. As Calvin often pointed out, ignorance will not save anyone from damnation. Perhaps Marlowe raises both readings of the magician's actions, allowing the audience to decide which is the more plausible? A fourth possibility, recently advanced by John Parker, is that Faustus's so-called biblical 'omissions' are not as significant as modern critics commonly assume, especially when understood in relation to 'the highly flexible hermeneutic tradition' that Marlowe was trained in (Parker 2013: 39). The act of quoting biblical verses in different contexts in order to create new interpretative possibilities is a feature of the New Testament itself, especially the writings of Paul:

> whose knack for 'selective quotation' has inspired the most formidable Christian exegetes. Duelling textual fragments do not merely constitute biblical criticism; they constitute the Bible as such, above all its Christian appendix, whose entire legitimacy rests on quotations, paraphrases, and (mis)translations of earlier scriptures that Jesus is supposed to fulfil, despite his having had what many consider an alien agenda.... Faustus's fixation on a small increment of text to sanction a tendentious revelation does not depart from the norm: his approach is the norm. (Parker 2013: 34–5)

While I would not want to dismiss out of hand traditional readings of this scene—exegetes like Luther and Calvin *were* concerned by the partial interpretation of biblical verses—Parker does enable us to see that scholars of early modern drama need to do more to integrate an understanding of contemporary exegetical practice with the dramatic quotation of Scripture on stage. In particular, the typological relationship between Old and New Testament which is at the heart of Protestant hermeneutics implies a model of promise and fulfilment, one that is theologically flexible, textually complex, and dramatically productive. Scholars have long been interested in the literary uses of typology (see the seminal article by Lewalski 1962). But in the light of recent work in the field (Luxon 1995; Lupton 1996; Freinkel 2002; Streete 2009b), there is more to be done on the intersection between early modern biblical hermeneutics and theatre, especially in non-Shakespearean drama.[5]

An example of what I mean can be found in John Ford's tragedy *'Tis Pity She's a Whore*. In the first scene, Friar Bonaventura tries to dissuade the freethinking Giovanni from pursuing his incestuous relationship with his sister any further:

> O, Giovannni, hast thou left the schools
> Of knowledge to converse with lust and death?
> For death waits on thy lust. Look through the world,
> And thou shalt see a thousand faces shine
> More glorious than this idol thou ador'st (Ford 2000: I.i.57–61)

The language of idolatrous love, which permeates this play, can be related to the steady debasement of Petrarchan language that runs in parallel to the lovers' fall. The Friar's words may also have reminded an audience of various Old Testament prohibitions against idolatry in the Ten Commandments, or in verses like Leviticus 19:4: 'Ye shall not turne unto idoles, nor make you molten gods: I am the Lord your God.'[6] At least in the

---

[5] For a discussion of the relationship between Faustus's speech and issues of early modern biblical translation, see the opening of chapter 8.

[6] All references are to the Geneva Bible: *The Bible, That Is, The Holy Scriptures* (London: Christopher Barker, 1599). Giovanni's wish, 'O that it were not in religion sin | To make our love a God, and worship it' (I.ii.145–6), reinforces this perception of his transgressive desire.

opening scene, the Friar represents religious authority. However, his speech also draws on New Testament idioms in order to reform Giovanni: an example of the textual 'duelling' that Parker refers to above. The shift from knowledge to lust and death may recall James 1:15: 'Then when lust hath conceiued, it bringeth forth a sinne, and sinne when it is finished, bringeth forth death.' This passage is interpreted in markedly different ways by Protestant and Roman Catholic exegetes of the period. As Calvin notes: 'Papists show their ignorance in seizing on this text, in a wish to prove from it that vicious, yes, filthy, criminal and unspeakable desires are not sins, so long as one does not fall in with them' (Calvin 1995: 269). Given ongoing scholarly debate about whether or not Ford had Roman Catholic sympathies, as well as the sensitive presentation of the incestuous lovers in the play, this passage throws interesting light on the contested moral terrain that the paywright is exploring in the opening scene (Hopkins 1994).

Perhaps most intriguingly, the Friar's assertion that, should Giovanni look more widely, he would see others who would 'shine more glorious' than Annabella may well draw upon the third chapter of 2 Corinthians. Here, Paul writes of the typological shift from Old Law and Testament to New Law and Gospel, from the 'ministration of death *written* with letters and ingrauen in stones' associated with the Ten Commandments, to the 'ministration of the Sprit' promised in Christ (2 Corinthians 3:7–8). Paul uses the words 'glory', 'glorified', or 'glorious' some nine times in the Geneva translation in order to describe this movement. Read in this context, the Friar's invocation of this passage could cast Giovanni as one whose actions disable the 'glorious' typological fulfilment described by Paul, impelling the hero into a new and contested ethical space. Paul describes his epistle as being written on and for the 'fleshly tables of the heart' (2 Corinthians 3:3), a metaphor that Giovanni takes literally. In the final act, he says: 'let not the curse | Of old prescription rend from me the gall | Of courage, which enrols a glorious death' (V.iv.74–6). The anti-hero refuses to acknowledge the prohibition against incest laid out in Old Testament texts like Leviticus 20:17, preferring instead a 'glorious' and literal death, one that he associates with 'the gall | Of courage'. This is an unusual sentiment. For one thing, the word 'gall' is always placed within a negative semantic field in the Bible: there is no place in Scripture where the term is used positively. An EEBO search of sermons printed between 1558 and 1642 confirms the overwhelmingly negative semantic associations of the term. And as the subject matter of much of this sermon literature also demonstrates, daringly, Giovanni's use of the word could well have brought to mind Christ on the cross ('They gaue him vinegar to drinke, mingled with gall: and when hee tasted thereof, hee would not drinke', Matthew 27:34). Is the biblical inflection of Giovanni's 'courage' affirmed here, writing him as a *miles Christi*? Or is it undermined by the anti-hero's self-aggrandizing attempt to align himself with Christ's sacrifice?

The play's shocking *denouement*, with Giovanni presenting his sister's heart on a dagger to the assembled company, is commonly read as the final subversion and literalization of the Petrarchan conceits that the play trades in (Bolam 2003: 278–81). We can also argue that the end of the play confirms a failure of Pauline typology. Yet its failure is double-edged. Giovanni calls the murder something 'Which I most glory in' (V.v.91). This is not the figurative, spiritual glory promised in 2 Corinthians. Indeed, his final use of the term—'The glory of my deed | Darkened the midday sun, made noon as night' (V.vi.22–3)—again sees a potential alignment of his actions with Christ's sacrifice. In the Gospels, the period before Christ's death is marked by 'darknesse ouer all the land' (Matthew 27:45). Perhaps some in the audience might have thrilled to this freethinking attempt to justify the taboo of incest in such daring terms. Others would no doubt have seen Giovanni's (mis)appropriation of Scriptural idioms as confirmation of his damnation: fleshly glory is no glory at all. The key point is that the play raises both possibilities. This is in keeping with Ford's extremely subtle deployment of biblical language throughout the play. He uses Scripture to actively create space for dramatic debate, enabling various interpretative frameworks to be formulated, and inviting his audience to pass moral judgement.

Religious Passions on Stage

Giovanni's insistence in the final act that his behaviour is something that he glories 'in' emphasizes the affective nature of his actions. Recent scholarship has examined the affective turn in relation to early modern literature, looking at how the passions are explored onstage (Paster et al. 2004a, 2004b; Craik 2007; Craik and Pollard 2013). Some of the most exciting work in this field looks at the intersection between the passions, religious language, and early modern drama (see Tillmouth 2010; Cummings and Sierhuis 2013; Waldron 2013). Writing of Protestantism and affectivity, Jennifer Waldron has observed that:

> Instead of ceding the body to the domain of the secular or the profane, many Protestants competed for it as fiercely as they competed with 'idolatrous' regimes for control of the visible church or the English nation. And rather than presenting their embrace of the body as a compromise with Catholic doctrine or practice, a broad range of writers set out to reform the bodily experience of the worshipper and to reorient his or her sensory apparatus towards the "plain marks" that God had left for his believers in the world. (Waldron 2013: 8)

The desire to 'reform' the senses towards the plain truth, as well as the failure to properly enact that change, helps us to understand Giovanni's tragic trajectory in 'Tis Pity She's a Whore. More generally throughout the period, dramatists use the language of religious passions to explore the various ways in which affect might alter identity. Although a comprehensive study of the relationship between religious identity and the language of affect in early modern drama is beyond the scope of this chapter, and indeed remains to be written, I want to explore this topic further in the final part of my discussion, beginning with some broad questions. Do dramatic characters associated with the major religions explored on stage during this period—Protestantism, Roman Catholicism, Judaism, and Islam—have different languages of affect? What about subgroups within broader religious confessions, such as the Puritan, the Jesuit, the Freethinker, or the temporizer? And how do playwrights use the language of religious affect to explore identity?

In the case of the Puritan, we might consider John Marston's depiction of Malhereux in *The Dutch Courtesan*. At the start of the play, we find him trying to control his passions, especially his sexual desires: 'lust is a most deadly sin' (I.i.72). While some may have associated this sentiment with Puritanism, there is a long philosophical tradition which holds that the attainment of reason is predicated upon the successful tempering of the passions (Tillmouth 2010: 15–36). So when Malhereux finds himself attracted to the eponymous prostitute Franceschina, whom he has previously dismissed as 'an immodest, vulgar woman' (I.i.155–6), his struggle to retain control over his passions is expressed in religious and philosophical terms:

> Is she unchaste? Can such a one be damned?
> O love and beauty, ye two eldest seeds
> Of the vast chaos, what strong right you have
> Even in things divine, our very souls! (Marston 1997: I.ii.129–32)

This speech brings Puritanical fastidiousness into conversation with neo-Stoic control. Both of these philosophies seek to order the passions, but to different moral ends. Audiences at Blackfriars might well have paused at a Calvinist predestinarian also holding to the view that there is a 'vast chaos' preceding creation whose 'eldest seeds' are 'love and beauty'. As such, the attempt to find an affective language that would reconcile these competing philosophical positions becomes the stuff of dramatic debate.

Later, Malhereux reflects bitterly, and in a similar vein to Angelo in *Measure for Measure*, on the religious prohibitions attendant upon the passions:

> O you happy beasts,
> In whom an inborn heat is not held a sin,
> How far transcend you wretched, wretched man,
> Whom national custom, tyrannous respects
> Of slavish order, fetters, lames his power,
> Calling that sin in us which in all things else
> Is nature's highest virtue! (Marston 1997: II.i.72–8)

Strikingly, Malhereux re-imagines the heat of sexual passion as original sin, claiming that animals who are able to act on will are more fortunate than men who have to order their affect according to various religious and social proscriptions. The fact that Malhereux sees this ordering in political terms, using words such as 'tyrannous' and 'slavish', pits the ideological precepts of religion against nature. Is Marston suggesting that Puritanism and neo-Stoicism alike lead to unhealthy repression of the passions?

Of course, as with Angelo, Malhereux soon finds that the ability to act uninhibitedly according to one's passions puts oneself in conflict with 'nature' in other ways. He threatens Franceschina with sexual violence ('O, my impatient heat endures no resistance, no protraction! There is no being for me but your sudden enjoying'; II.ii.162–4) and briefly finds himself embroiled in a plot to kill his friend Freevill: 'To gain a woman, to lose a virtuous self | For appetite and sensual end' (II.ii.211–12). Malhereux's decision not to follow this course of action is the turning point in the plot. He calls friendship 'spiritual' (II.ii.216) and concludes as follows:

> 'Tis sin of cold blood, mischief with waked eyes,
> That is the damned and the truly vice,
> Not he that's passionless, but he 'bove passion's wise.
> My friend shall know it all. (II.ii.225–8)

Reconciling the language of puritan restraint and neo-Stoic self-control in this way allows Marston to re-assert the centrality of male homosocial friendship, an ideology that undergirds this play. Certainly, this does not preclude Malhereux continuing to express his desire to 'enjoy Franceschina' (IV.ii.17). But the exposure and humiliation of the prostitute is only achieved by turning conventional religious and humoral language against her: 'O thou comely damnation! | ... what is woman merely made of blood!' (V.iii.48–50). Malhereux now declares himself deserving of Freevill's friendship with these words: 'I am now worthy yours, when, before, | The beast of man, loose blood, distempered us. | He that lust rules cannot be virtuous' (V.iii.65–7). The play concludes that sexual and religious passions do need to be controlled, but for a purpose that goes beyond the subjective. Only by subordinating individual passions to the ordered bonds of homosociality underwriting the patriarchal order can political stability, which necessarily involves the regulation and chastisement of female sexuality, be maintained.

The language of neo-Stoic affective control could also be deployed to explore other religious identities. Philip Massinger's *The Renegado* contains one of the few sympathetic depictions of a Jesuit on the early modern stage. As the play's most recent editor Michael Neill has suggested, this may be the result of the very specific historical context of the play's production in late 1623/early 1624 when a political *rapprochement* between Protestant, Roman Catholic, and Arminian positions was being sought (Neill 2010: 38–41). To this end, the Jesuit in question, Francisco, enters with a speech that could have been culled from Seneca's *Epistles*:

> You give too much to Fortune and your passions—
> O'er which a wise man, if religious, triumphs.
> That name fools worship; and those tyrants which
> We arm against our better part, our reason,
> May add but never take from our afflictions. (Massinger 2010: I.i.70–4)

The effort to recast a Jesuit as the spokesperson for rational affective control is a daring one indeed, even if the better educated amongst the audience would have understood the close affinity between Jesuit theology and neo-Stoicism (see Miller 2000: 115). It is also a speech that counterpoises the temporizing attitude of Vitelli: 'I would not be confined in my belief ... | Live I in England, Spain, France, Rome, Geneva, | I am of that country's faith' (I.i.32–7). The audience are asked to weigh Francisco's attractive expression of rational self-control against Vitteli's Laodicean cynicism, bearing in mind that Francisco is also a Jesuit, traditional enemy of English Protestantism. To decide on this matter is also to make a religious and a political judgement. By contrast, August 1624 saw nine performances of Thomas Middleton's controversial *A Game at Chess* at the Globe before it was banned. Here, the perceived threat of Jesuit infiltration is dealt with in a much less tempered fashion in the figures of Loyola and Error. The former is a dramatic and political grand master, determining the game from behind the scenes on behalf of the Roman Catholic international: 'My wrath's up, and methinks | I could with the first syllable of my name | Blow up their colleges' (Middleton 2007: Induction, 33–5). Political control and mastery is contrasted here with the ever-present threat, as decades of anti-Catholic polemic had taught, of Jesuit combustibility. As these very different examples show, the political inflection of religious affect on the early modern stage is a recurrent and rich topic.

That said, the discussion of religious affect is not always connected to religio-political controversy. Although it has been read in these terms, Thomas Middleton and William Rowley's *The Changeling* also offers an acute exploration of murderous complicity, sexual obsession, and affective identity in the figures of DeFlores and Beatrice Joanna. The former has murdered a suitor of the latter, but when Beatrice Joanna treats DeFlores with disdain, he turns the screw. Beatrice Joanna tries to assert her social superiority: 'Think but upon the distance that creation | Set 'twixt thy blood and mine, and keep thee there' (Middleton and Rowley 2006: III.iii.130–1). She cleaves to the idea of 'blood' as a social marker; but of course DeFlores reads the words in more humoral (and Epicurean) terms as the incipient manifestation of 'pleasure' (III.iii.160). He also evokes the religious implications of the term in this chilling speech:

> Look but into your conscience, read me there—
> 'Tis but a true book, you'll find me there your equal.
> In what the act has made you, you're no more now;
> You must forget your parentage to me—
> You're the deed's creature: by that name
> You lost your first condition; and I challenge you,
> As peace and innocency has turned you out
> And made you one with me. (III.iii.132–40)

DeFlores reimagines the Protestant idea of the moral conscience, making himself the internal marker encountered by Beatrice Joanne's moral gaze. When she looks inwardly, she finds DeFlores staring back at her, their complicity in murder levelling all social distinctions between them. DeFlores then goes on to imagine that this act enables a figurative rebirthing, with the crime standing as a synecdoche for Beatrice Joanna's sexual fall from grace. She is birthed by DeFlores, a fallen Eve to his Adam, but her crime also binds her to him in perpetuity, a striking reworking of the doctrine of original sin.

Beatrice Joanna tries to buy her tormentor off and weeps at his feet. DeFlores's responds with one of the most terrifying lines in early modern drama: 'Can you weep Fate from its determined purpose? | So soon may you weep me' (III.iii.161–2). Bound together by their crimes, Beatrice Joanna's tears, which may otherwise be seen as a marker of her individuated passions, metamorphose into DeFlores himself. Her tears are him. The most horrible aspect of all this, as DeFlores notes, is that this bargain is predicated upon mutual silence and affective control, something that he gets a sexual thrill from acknowledging: 'Come, rise, and shroud your blushes in my bosom. | Silence is one of pleasure's best receipts: | Thy peace is wrought for ever in this yielding' (III.iii.166–8). Affective self-control masks sexual violence, social transgression, and murder. If there is 'pleasure' to be had in this bargain, then it is the pleasure of the sociopath.

Conclusion

As this chapter has argued, the political effort to 'reform' the stage is a crucial aesthetic impetus for early modern drama. The Elizabethan state's desire to establish and define the Church of England as a reformed church was supported on the public stage in interludes and plays that combined religious didacticism and political self-assertion against the Roman Catholic Church. This polemical aspect of early modern drama is never far from the surface throughout the period explored in this chapter. As the public theatres were established and became more popular, religious discussion was pushed in new directions by dramatists for various ends that could encompass the theological, the political, the aesthetic, and the commercial. The efforts of the state and the city fathers to regulate the theatres were not always consistent and had to be balanced with more practical considerations. The mid-Elizabethan anti-theatrical backlash against the stage was part of the broader godly argument that the reformation had not gone far enough (Lake and Questier 2002: 425–79). Attempts at 'reformation' continued intermittently under James. However, by the Jacobean and Caroline periods, the civic right of the dramatist to explore religious topics was broadly accepted, even if, as the cases of Middleton and Massinger show, there were limits and they were enforced. This is an exploration that continues well into the Restoration.

The sheer ubiquity of biblical language and idioms in use throughout the corpus of early modern drama is one of the most enduring legacies of the Reformation. While I have outlined some of the ways in which these Scriptural presences can be read and understood, this is a subject worthy of further study, especially in relation to exegetical and sermon culture, and to biblical literature written in other genres. Drama is part of the 'literary culture of the Reformation'. Playwrights like Marlowe, Jonson, and Middleton were as well-versed in the grammar of theology as they were the rhetoric of humanism, and more work needs to be done to bring these two intellectual strands into conversation with each other. Such a conversation would also help us to understand better the religious language of affect in drama. Shylock's passions are explored differently to Antonio's; Titania's humoral language works in marked contrast to that of the Empress of Bablylon; the Duchess of Malfi experiences affect in other ways to Bosola. As these last two examples suggest, the gendered aspect of religious affect in drama also needs further exploration. Indeed, a more finely calibrated critical account of religious affect would throw new and important light on how identities were formed and reformed on the early modern stage.

CHAPTER 12

....

THE SERMON

....

JEANNE SHAMI

THE sermon was the dominant cultural form of post-Reformation English literature. Defined by contemporary John Deios as 'the expounding of scripture and applying of it to the present state, by the working of Gods spirit in the mouth of a man called for that purpose' (Deios 1590: 139; Morrissey 2011: 50), it functioned as an instrument of God, conveying saving grace to instruct, move, and convert. It also functioned as an instrument of the state through its controversial, polemical, and political modes. As a genre it transcended boundaries of class, geography, gender, and doctrinal difference, and expressed the official as well as the lived religious experiences of the vast majority of people who attended sermons regularly. This chapter examines how sermons framed, restrained, and enabled the writing of early modern religion. Peter McCullough has noted that early modern preachers attended 'not only to the formal, literary aspects of the genre itself, but also to the Bible, to patristic, classical, and other sources, as well as to the arts of delivery'. By doing so too, this chapter aims to illuminate sermons as 'radically occasional pieces of performed writing, contingent upon the contexts [including place and auditory] in and for which they were delivered' (McCullough 2011: 213).

Several factors explain the genre's dominance: vernacular biblical translations (necessitating priestly guidance), episcopal efforts to support conformable preaching (through licensing, education, visitations, and the example of their own assiduous preaching), increased lay patronage, emphasis on sermons as conduits of grace, and the proliferation of religious controversy. Their sheer quantity—regulated by statutory minimums, diocesan and local requirements—was overwhelming. Moreover, the common post-Reformation expectation that every pulpit would acquire a preaching minister fostered preachers who encompassed every doctrinal position (from the most biblicist Puritans and Calvinists to the most ceremonially inclined conformists and anti-Calvinists) and an increasing number of preaching occasions (well above the statutory requirements). Add to this the increase in preaching opportunities—regular weekday lectures or combination lectures across the kingdom, reinforced by the requirement to read the *Homilies* where sermons were unavailable—and it is apparent that exposure to sermons reached its zenith during our period. At the height of the sermon's prestige and popularity during the 1620s, a group of clerics led by Archbishop Laud and Lancelot Andrewes complained that decades of overemphasis on preaching in the English Church to the detriment of prayer and sacraments had actually 'devalued preaching' by emphasizing 'externals of style, elocution, and rhetoric' at the expense of the fundamentals of faith (Hunt 2010: 165–6), but their efforts to curb preaching proved temporary and counter-productive.

Despite its dominance, the sermon is also a frustratingly elusive genre. Only a fraction of sermons prepared or delivered survive, ranging from anecdotal accounts or fragmentary sermon notes to fully fledged orations and treatises, amplified and revised into print. Moreover, scholars treating sermons as literary rather than theological or historical artefacts have been drawn to sermons by celebrated preachers such as Donne or Andrewes, while the sermons that comprised the common majority have been neglected. And, frustratingly, while the *content* of some sermons has survived, we can only glimpse their original immediacy and performative impact.

Earlier twentieth-century literary scholarship placed sermons within the history of English prose style, leading to outmoded taxonomies that obscured the genre's complexity and bequeathed inaccurate labels (such as the anachronistic 'Anglo-Catholic') to cover widely divergent sermon practitioners (Ferrell and McCullough 2000: 4; Blench 1964; Mitchell 1962; Davies 1986). Revisionist historiography has also challenged simplistic labels and distinctions (between Anglican and puritan preachers, for example) by proposing a more nuanced spectrum of mainstream Protestant positions (Puritans, conformist Calvinists, anti-Calvinists, Laudians) and sensitivity to nonconforming sects, including Quakers, Nonconformists, Independents, Baptists, and Dissenters later in the century (Lake 1987, 1988; Milton 2005; Tyacke 1987, 2001; Spurr 1991; Green 1978, 2009; Haigh 1995). Labelling these remains contentious, and threatens to derail discussion of the genre—the sermon—that they shared (Ferrell and McCullough 2000). That preaching spectrum also needs to be enlarged to include Catholic preachers whose influence among important Catholic families over our period, as Questier highlights, proved 'quite out of proportion to their numbers and even to the material resources of their patrons' (Questier 2006: 289). For all involved, the sermon remained the pre-eminent genre of religious instruction, edification, and conversion, and commitment to preaching was common to believers of all stripes.

Traditions and Continuities

Sermons did not appear suddenly in England following Henry VIII's separation from Rome. In fact, reformers grafted their discourses onto a robust medieval tradition of Catholic preaching and sermon attendance that included homilies delivered at Sunday Mass, quarterly sermons required by canon law, and outdoor sermons at pulpit crosses delivered to crowds larger than medieval churches could accommodate (Wabuda 2002: 26–7; Wooding 2011: 330, 332). As Eric Carlson concludes: 'The English

Reformation cannot, therefore, be credited with introducing occasions for preaching, official commitment to regular preaching (however unevenly enforced) or even orthodox statements on the centrality of preaching' (Carlson 2003: 254). The Reformation, however, encouraged the proliferation and development of sermons—the most prominent of the preacher's ministerial duties—as part of the liturgy and as free-standing events.

Reformed preachers also inherited the preaching arts and the canons of classical rhetoric filtered through Jewish and Christian exegetes, including the Christian humanists of the late medieval and early modern periods. Over the course of our period, these traditions had metamorphosed into four principal sermon forms, which Greg Kneidel identifies as 'the homily, the thematic sermon, the classical oration, and the doctrine-use scheme' (Kneidel 2011a: 3).

The first of these forms—the patristic *homily*—was 'a word-by-word or phrase-by-phrase explanation of the meanings (or levels of meaning) of a lengthy scriptural passage' structured according to the 'written sequence of the scriptural text' (Kneidel 2011a: 6). Derived from this patristic pattern, pre-Reformation homilies were commentaries read during Mass as part of a Eucharistic celebration, based upon the day's Epistle or Gospel verses (Wabuda 2002: 27–8). At the outset of the Reformation, before a preaching ministry had been established and its duties clarified, the government relied on printed *Homilies* to announce and enforce official doctrines. Unlike their patristic namesakes, these homilies used the Bible and simple language to cover basic doctrines (faith, good works, sacraments) and major festivals (Christmas, Easter), were divided into parts (each of which took no more than ten minutes to read), and aimed to reach the simplest parishioners, even where the ministers themselves were unlearned or unpractised in the preaching arts (Green 2011: 139). Parishes were required to own and read the *Homilies* in their printed order on Sundays where no sermon was offered. That both Reformed and Catholic versions of the *Homilies* were produced under the Tudor monarchs (over 60,000 copies were published, 'more than enough for the needs of both parishes and clergy' (Green 2011: 139)) attests to their perceived utility as 'a manifesto of the regime's theological agenda and the means of its revolutionary implementation' (Null 2011: 348). The substitution of official homilies for sermons, while promoting shared religious values, however, also de-emphasized the sermons' affective elements by separating instruction from exhortation and application. They succeeded, nonetheless, as doctrinal guides and exercises promoting religious piety and behaviour deemed desirable by authorities.

The *thematic sermon* was associated with the universities, where it thrived in both Latin and vernacular forms. Typically, it addressed a short scriptural passage, announced by an antitheme, and followed by a *divisio* that split the theme into parts. This form was further subdivided to provide a skeletal structure, subsequently dilated by various Scriptural and 'non-scriptural proofs' (patristic authorities, elaborate allegories, moral exempla, popular fables). The form was criticized as both too scholastic (with its divisions and subdivisions) and too vulgar (with its legends, fables, and lore), although some of its features survived (Kneidel 2011a: 10–11).

The third form, the *oration*, was mediated through medieval *artes praedicandi*. It adapted the traditional structure from classical rhetoric to a specifically Christian purpose: to convey transforming grace through Scriptural exegesis. The five canons of classical rhetoric were foundational to the sermon genre: *inventio* (finding the most useful arguments), *dispositio* (the most useful means to arrange these arguments), *elocutio* (ways of describing the verbal and cognitive patterns of the text, often determined by whether the purpose of the sermon was to teach, delight, or move), *memoria* (methods for mental storage and retrieval), and *actio* (presentation by voice and gesture) (Kneidel 2011a: 3). Preaching manuals adopted Erasmus's suggestion to structure sermons as classical orations—a branch of epideictic rhetoric—so that they used these canons to move through exordium, narration, division, confirmation, refutation, and conclusion, although other, simpler, arrangements were also possible (McCullough 2006: 169). The process of researching and selecting evidence to support arguments derived from the scriptural text, arranging them in a rhetorically effective structure, and selecting diction, syntax, and rhetorical devices to enhance the preacher's message was crucial to the sermon's success, as were the final elements—*memoria, pronunciatio*, and *actio*—focusing on the sermons' aural delivery. McCullough's explication of John Donne's funeral sermon for William Cokayne (2011: 213–64) offers a paradigmatic and exemplary elucidation of this material.

Manuals outlining the theory and practice of preaching and hearing sermons, editions of medieval sermon collections, and volumes of patristic commentary supported a robust sermon culture, mediated through new editions of the Fathers, theological tracts, vernacular translations, Bible commentaries, handbooks of patristic theology, and excerpt collections (Ettenhuber 2011: 39ff). Paradoxically, vernacular Scriptures necessitated more preaching to curb heterodox, private, or singular readings. Equally, competing Biblical translations, especially the portable Geneva Bible with its radicalized marginal glosses, challenged those charged with maintaining orthodoxy.

The fourth form, the 'doctrine-use' scheme favoured by Puritans, grafted on to these traditions a Ramist exegetical 'method' authorizing the preacher to cut the scriptural text into pieces, first to uncover the doctrines opened by that scriptural place, then the uses to which they could be put, ending with application to the audience's lives. Perhaps to compensate for the schematic complexity of this sermon structure, writers of preaching manuals such as William Perkins in *The Arte of Prophecying* (1607) advocated plain and simple speech as the best rhetorical register for making Scripture 'operative' for the hearers (Morrissey 2002: 690).

The forms so carefully defined and circumscribed in the age's major preaching manuals were, in practice, often blurred and do not characterize most extant sermons, which effectively recombined or refined the structural elements of the homilies, orations, and doctrine-use schemes (Kneidel 2011a: 6). Mary Morrissey delineates what she calls the *English Reformed* generic sermon prototype (Morrissey 2011: 58–9). This form took from the homily the idea of explicating and applying a single scriptural text, from the thematic sermon the idea of dividing and subdividing according to logical or grammatical categories, and from the classical humanist traditions respect for biblical languages

(Greek and Hebrew), patristic commentary, and classical rhetoric, philosophy, and literature.[1] Using this method, 'the preacher studied his text, derived doctrines from his explication of it, and decided on the uses to be made of the doctrines. He divided his text, arriving at a structure built around the biblical "core" of his oration. Finally he provided himself with scriptural proof-texts and quotations from the Fathers and modern commentators to support each of the doctrines he presented' (Morrissey 2011: 57). These constituted his authorities, and doctrinal rivals used them polemically to establish the priority of their positions. The division was especially crucial to the auditors' ability to absorb the sermon's message, and to remember it for repetition and reflection. The 'uses' to which biblical texts could be put were classified by categories drawn from 1 Timothy 3:16 and Romans 15:4 to produce sermon genres: *confutation* (opposing error and heresy), *instruction* (explaining faith and morals), *correction* (exposing and criticizing sin), and *consolation* (assisting those with wounded consciences or grieving either for personal or national losses or calamities). At its core, however, the post-Reformation sermon, despite generic variations, was essentially the explication and application of a scriptural quotation (Morrissey 2011: 57–8). A new method of sermon composition— moving away from dividing, explicating, and applying biblical texts—did not emerge until the Restoration (Morrissey 2002: 700–2), when a theory of direct inspiration by the Spirit led to complaints of stylistic excess that undermined the Word's perspicuity and emphasized instead the preacher's passionate vehemence.

Preachers used the Bible and the rhetorical tools of their classical humanist training in grammar schools and universities to different ends. The universities' emphasis on languages, rhetoric and style, and immersion in Greek and rabbinic exegetical traditions, combined with access to the translations and compendia of commentary noted above, provided moral and linguistic training for preaching ministers, but also sowed the seeds of controversy and conversion for at least a century (Wooding 2011: 334). University graduates could receive additional instruction within 'household seminaries' (Webster 1997: 25–35), usually under the tutor-mentorship of a minister offering on-the-job training in the practices of sermon composition, repetition, and delivery required for godly preaching. This context also provided exposure to sermons and lectures in a supportive environment that fostered community among like-minded clerics. Style became controversial when larger issues of doctrine, politics or communal values were at stake, or as part of the search for what best moved audiences, what was truest to Scripture, and what particular congregations demanded. Stricter stylists rejected ornaments of eloquence and citations from non-Biblical sources (the Fathers, pagan authorities, Greek, and Hebrew) as elegant distractions from the influence of the Spirit rather than integral features of rhetorical persuasion, offensive primarily in their excess.

The sermon as an instrument of controversy built on these traditions, bolstered throughout our period by theorists such as Hyperius, Neils Hemmingsen, Richard Barnard, and Richard Baxter who characterized controversial preaching as 'skilled

---

[1] See Kneidel 2011a: 18; on the homiletic use of prophane learning, see Reisner 2011.

knightly combat' against dangerous opponents (Lares 2001: 98) and mandated strict rules of engagement. Using political sermons to legitimate regime change was a controversial function first wielded to promote and defend Henry VIII's break with Rome in 1534. From the moment of this breach, preachers were enlisted by the state to preach nation-wide against the bishop of Rome's usurpations of power (Null 2011: 349), to defend the Royal Supremacy and the Boleyn marriage, and to introduce hearers to the new doctrines necessary for salvation. Under Edward, with the imposition of a Protestant liturgy, a preaching campaign to bring the Gospel to the villages advanced the Reforming project. Subsequent books of *Homilies* (Edwardian, Elizabethan) reinforced the anti-Roman nature of the new Reformed religion (Null 2011: 363–4) and were disseminated in parishes across the country to soften opposition to religious change. They complemented an official Elizabethan programme of 'preaching, printing, and prosecution' (Haigh 1995: 22) aimed at breaking popular Catholic resistance to Protestantism.

Again at crucial moments of religious and political tension associated with changes in monarchy (and feared changes in religion), pulpits promoted order and obedience to official religious policies. Mary's state Catholicism necessitated a vital preaching programme to undo the 'evil' preaching by her father's and her half-brother's clergy establishing Protestantism.[2] Elizabeth used her pulpits to re-establish Protestantism. Preachers in these battles adopted an 'aggressive, confrontational strategy' against their opponents, especially at Paul's Cross, a theatre of state in the heart of London where political force was not unidirectional—from the authorities, through the preacher, to the people (Hunt 2011: 367). William Barlow preached on the execution of Robert Devereux, second earl of Essex, and the discovery of the Gunpowder Plot, for example, offering his political masters valuable rhetorical strategies shaping later interpretations of these events (James 2014) and demonstrating that sermons could both shape and reflect official interpretations of controversial public events.

Preaching campaigns justified every crucial political and religious transition. Sermons marked James I's attempts to curb criticism of a proposed Spanish Match for his son Charles (1622); Parliamentary Fast Sermons promoted an anti-Laudian reforming agenda; sermons forged the post-Restoration settlement (1660); Restoration court sermons, 'enjoyed, endured, or slept through' (Jenkinson 2011: 455) by Charles II, concealed his openly Catholic royal family, mistresses, and courtiers; and sermons constituted the 'elaborate tuning of the pulpit' (Claydon 2011: 481) to legitimate the rule of William and Mary, prince and princess of Orange and silence the deposed James II's supporters.

The sermon genre also includes *lectures,* a mainly puritan institution for expanding a vital preaching ministry dedicated to further Church reformation, reaching its apogee during the civil war. John Donne offers this contemporary generic analysis: 'a Sermon intends *Exhortation* principally, and *Edification,* and a holy stirring of religious affections, and then *matters of Doctrine,* and points of *Divinity,* occasionally, secondarily, as

---

[2] BL Harleian MS. 444: f. 27; see Loades 2014.

the words of the text may invite them; But *Lectures* intend principally *Doctrinall points*, and matter of *Divinity*, and matter of *Exhortation* but *occasionally*, and as in a second place' (Donne 1953–62: VIII, 95). This difference in emphasis, however, should not preclude recognizing the lecture as a species of sermon.

Lectures took many forms, all with antecedents in the medieval Catholic church: cathedral lectureships, addressed to clergy; parish lectureships, the most common variety; or lectureships sponsored by the city corporation, intended for 'edification of the whole urban population' (Seaver 1970: 84). For mainstream puritan clergy, a lectureship was a customary part of a clerical career, supported by lay patrons but often challenged by ecclesiastical authorities who believed it eroded parish life by encouraging gadding to hear celebrity preachers or those who preached more sympathetic doctrine. These expository lectures were delivered by both stipendiary preachers and beneficed clergy, under the supervision of lay magistrates who frequently selected, and paid the salaries of, their lecturers. The diversity of lectureships allowed local preaching cultures quite distinct from one another to thrive. Of course, not all lecturers were Puritan (witness, for example, Richard Montagu's brief appointment at Windsor or Bishop Williams's sermon at the market town of Kettering). Especially in London, the priority in appointing lecturers was extending the preaching ministry more than adopting specific doctrines. While Laudians attempted to enforce ceremonial and disciplinary conformity and reduced the numbers licensed to preach (by requiring lecturers to be beneficed), they were unsuccessful, finally, in destroying lectureships or regulating them to conformity because the institution, rooted in community life, resisted the hierarchical authority of the Church by satisfying local sensitivities.

Sermons and lectures were part of the rhythm of Sunday worship, consisting normally of a morning sermon and an afternoon catechetical sermon, with intervals filled with repetition, conference, prayer, and psalms. Weekday sermons were part of this world where there was a preaching minister, a salaried lecturer, or a domestic chaplain; where there were none of these, parishioners sought out sermons in neighbouring area(s). Some communities instituted regular conference days (a kind of professional development exercise), where preaching ministers met to support lectures by combination—a descendant, especially in market towns, of Elizabethan 'prophesyings' (Collinson 1983: 472–5). In addition to these sermons and exercises, communities also gathered to hear sermons on days of fasting, solemn humiliation, celebration, and funerals, establishing their own unique worship rhythms. Julia Merritt's treatment of the diverse preaching cultures of Westminster parishes, 1580–1640, illustrates the complex role sermons played in one community's religious life (Merritt 2002).

RESTRAINTS ON PREACHING

Sermons were molded by pressures exerted by the contexts in which they were preached. Some of these historical contexts have already been mentioned: paucity of preaching ministers, levels of education and ability, access to preaching aids, official church and state controls, demands of particular congregations, parish and community politics, doctrinal and disciplinary controversies, the economics of maintaining a preaching ministry, the substitution of state-prepared homilies for local sermons, and the impact of the reigning monarch. To these can be added far-reaching conditions that permeated the social fabric: the limitations of gender (women's roles in sermon culture (Shami 2011b)), and the effects of censorship, licensing, and regulatory practices.

Women's roles within an emerging sermon culture were limited by Pauline scriptural injunctions (1 Corinthians 14:34, 35, and 1 Timothy 2:11, 12) against women's public speaking and teaching. However, Thomas Becon's stipulation that women (especially 'old and ancient matrons') were 'straitly commanded' to assume their role as 'bishops in their own house' (Ayre 1844: 376) suggests that women preached within a *domestic* context by hearing, copying, memorizing, and repeating sermons for the instruction of children and servants, and reading them privately to foster personal religious devotion. The influence that these activities exerted should not be underestimated (Shami 2011b: 166–72).

While women preachers were not part of *mainstream* religious culture, however, they flourished briefly (despite vociferous opposition) among radical, nonconforming, and marginal groups during the 1640s and 1650s in England, and as missionaries to Ireland, Barbados, Massachusetts, and (in the case of Mary Fisher) to the sultan of Turkey himself. Although scattered reports exist, from the Lollards onwards, of women preaching (such as 'Mrs Slowe' in Salisbury in the 1620s and 1630s (Spurr 2014: 316)), Quakers were the most advanced supporters of women preachers. A theoretical defence of women's public utterance, Margaret Fell Fox's *Women's Speaking Justified* (1646), tackled the question head on, although her own sermons are not extant. However, by the end of the seventeenth century, even Quakerism was less open to female religious leadership; the women's meetings declined, 'women preachers seemed unnatural even to women' (Crawford 1993: 207), and those who persisted as preachers suffered verbal and physical retaliation. Despite a period of intense experimentation among nonconformists in the 1640s and 1650s, women's preaching, therefore, remained largely in the domestic sphere.

Several funeral sermons for women, however, reveal a religious culture in which women not only heard sermons, but also wrote down their biblical interpretations, often in consultation with their chaplains, and even prepared sermons, some of which are quoted for the first time in these sermons (Shami 2013: 288, 301–2; Houlbrooke 1998: 295–330; O'Hara 2006). Margaret Corbet's life narrative (appended to her funeral sermon) reports that 'She wrote the Sermons she heard … and she hath left many volumes of Sermons of her own handwriting.' Although Mrs Corbet could apparently discourse on all material points of religion, and 'search't Expositors, and Practicall Divines' to assist her interpretations, the notes are likely to be those 'Sermon notes … which she took at Church' and read to her servants rather than her own scriptural interpretations (Wilkinson 1657: 64). Similarly, Stephen Denison published the writings of Elizabeth Juxon, who heard 'nine or ten Sermons euery weeke' (Denison 1620: 85). Not only did Mrs Juxon select the text for her funeral sermon (Job 7:3, 4), the first task of sermon composition, but Denison records Mrs Juxon's twenty marks of election, accompanied by commentary, analysis, and application of these marks to the sermon's larger audience. Nehemiah Wallington's annotated copy of it indicates that Christians applied these marks to their own spiritual lives, confirming that the women's lives commemorated in sermons were exemplary to both men and women (Seaver 1985: 37–8).

A sermon by Anna Walker, a literate, witty court lady, was composed for her mistress Queen Anne of Denmark in c.1606, in a bid for patronage that arguably served self-expressive needs. It follows many of the sermon's generic codes, including self-conscious choice of text (in Walker's case, introducing a pun on her surname interwoven throughout the manuscript), division and application of that text, and a dedication to the Queen. Our knowledge of women's practices of writing out scriptural interpretations makes this sermon (if it is one) appear less anomalous than it might at first glance outside an active domestic sermon culture (Trill 2002). Such practices also predate the apparently sudden flourishing of female preaching and prophecy in the 1640s and 1650s among radical sects, especially the Quakers.

The sermon's ability to frame religious expression was also influenced by regulations governing preaching and printing sermons, and the stresses they placed on preachers to modify, restrain, or otherwise censor their words. Such considerations seem far removed from formal and structural features, until we understand these laws as the political filter through which to view all sermons—including those that appear politically innocent. Even to approach a pulpit, a preacher required a license, creating an administrative nightmare immediately after the break with Rome. Replacing itinerant preaching friars required negotiating a 'confusing welter of practice, heavily individualized by place and patron', in which each diocesan jurisdiction was 'a rule unto itself, inside the general frame created by the crown' (Wabuda 2002: 139). Morrissey (2011: 26–8) and McCullough (1998: 73–6, 105–7, 185–7) have described appointment procedures for Paul's Cross and court preachers, respectively, indicating how ecclesiastical authorities and patrons exercised control over the content and quality of sermons, while divergent voices jockeyed for interpretative authority. The multitude of authorities (the Privy Council, the bishops, and the Corporation of London) exerting a claim on the Paul's Cross pulpit 'did not always share the same policies and objectives. Nor were they unwilling to use the public forum provided by the Paul's Cross sermons to forward their aims to the detriment of their fellow governors' (Morrissey 2011: 69). What is true of this pulpit is replicated in different ways and on different scales throughout the kingdom across the entire period.

Although licensing regulations, laws against seditious speech (including print and pulpit utterances), and pre-publication (or even pre-preaching) censorship were difficult to enforce under the pressures of circumstance, the power of sermons to shape and respond to public opinion resulted in an array of state instruments (McCullough, Adlington, and Rhatigan 2011: 546–69) to control preaching. These included statutes, royal proclamations, injunctions, ordinances, Star Chamber decrees, and royal grants of letters patent. The Stationers' Company assisted the Crown in enforcing bookselling and printing regulations, and royal grants of monopolies for certain kinds of religious works made identifying offenders easier.

Nonetheless, 'incessant tampering with the formula for approving materials before publication betrays the frustrations which the crown experienced in its attempts to control the religious press' (Towers 2003: 32). Clearly, laws controlling seditious or heterodox pulpit speech remained practically ineffectual, exacerbated by unpredictable law enforcement, uncertainty about what a preacher would say in the moment or how his message would be heard (even when an advance copy of his sermon had been procured), and uncertainty about what would attract official attention or how severely punishment would be meted out. Authorities seemed willing to allow all but the most egregious criticisms and blunders if they were subordinated to a larger message of conformity, uttered in passion rather than premeditated, not directed personally against the king or court members, or not intended by the preacher (or if such a claim could be plausibly made). John Stoughton's sermon ostensibly supporting treaties for a French marriage for Prince Charles (a Catholic marriage only slightly more acceptable than the hated Spanish Match that had provoked James's *Directions for Preachers*) illustrates these principles. In that sermon, Stoughton preached his core message—the importance of true religion in marriage and the duty to pray and even intervene militarily to support continental Protestants—within a gilded frame of flattery that softened its oppositional message and provided a face-saving way to celebrate this match and demonstrate the conformity of even James's most oppositional clergy (Shami 2014: 407). So, while it would be naive to claim that early modern authorities could not exert control, it would equally naive 'to say that they could exercise a high level of control consistently, week in, week out; or that they behaved with unanimity of purpose' (Morrissey 2011: 78).

Restraint of Catholic preaching constitutes a special case. Except for a resurgence during the Catholic reign of Queen Mary, public sermons by Catholic priests ended with the Reformation. Mary's state Catholicism died with her, but that is not to say that Catholic preaching had no impact on subsequent English religious culture. Michael Questier has demonstrated that chaplains in lay households acted as 'sounding-boards' for their patrons and within groups debating key points of Catholic religious and political theory (Questier 2006: 289). Seminary clergy used ties to gentry families to survive, as did Jesuits who established domestic family 'churches' where they maintained, and sometimes even promoted, Catholicism in a rabidly anti-Catholic culture.

Although preaching was the first ministry of the Word listed in the Jesuit *Formula* (O'Malley 1993: 92), we have little evidence of Jesuit sermons, with the exception of one spectacular incident at the French ambassador's residence in London, Sunday 26 October 1623, where three hundred people had gathered to hear celebrated Jesuit, Robert Drury. The residence collapsed suddenly in mid-sermon, plummeting the preacher, a fellow priest, and over ninety auditors to their deaths (Walsham 1994: 36; Shami 2003: 194–8). The incident added fuel to the anti-popery unleashed by the Spanish Match, specifically the failure of the marriage negotiations, and not only bolstered Catholicism's reputation for superstition and idolatry, but prompted William Gouge's sermon at Blackfriars church on 5 November, the Gunpowder Plot anniversary. That sermon frames this incident providentially, as God's finger in action (Gouge 1631: 401).

Despite persecution, Catholic laypeople, especially women, supported Catholic preaching in parts of England. Lady Montague's house at Battle Abbey included a chapel complete with pulpit where 'almost every week was a sermon made' during Elizabeth's reign (Hanlon 1966: 382). In 1624, the Jesuit, John Layton, held Masses and preached in an enlarged barn, apparently attracting recusants, nominal members of the English Church and occasional conformists in numbers highlighting the near-desertion of the nearby parish church (Haigh 1987: 184). Evidently, preaching was deployed not only between Protestants, but on a much wider—indeed, illegal—scale between recusants and the established church as a key polemical and persuasive instrument in that conflict.

THE EXPERIENCE OF SERMONS

A sermon—delivered or heard—was a living, dramatic experience. These experiential features mark another continuity with medieval preaching traditions that imparted 'a sense of the sermon as performance; a belief that preaching could transform the lives of those who stood before them; and a belief that the spirit of God was embodied in the preacher, and that the preacher's rhetorical skill worked with divine grace' (Pettegree 2005: 17). This three-way interaction between preacher, auditors, and Holy Spirit informs early modern theory on how sermons acted on their audiences (Morrissey 2002: 689–93; Adlington 2003: 213–28).

While sermons could convey grace, preachers sometimes found their audiences unruly, disengaged, and difficult receptacles. Many preachers perceived a lack of connection between what John Craig describes as 'the profusion of preaching' and the 'paucity of individual and social transformation'; in some cases they took responsibility for their failures to adjust to the capacities of their hearers, but in some cases they blamed the hearers (Craig 2011: 180). Sermons—attendance at which was mandatory on the Sabbath—commonly castigated auditors' frailties, including their wandering thoughts, sloth, sleepiness, preference for alehouses or adulterous assignations, indifference, and bad manners (Craig 2011: 181). Donne, for one, expected congregations to fulfil their vocation as 'hearers' and thereby doers of the Word, chastising mere passive spectators (Donne 1953–62: I, 207). Other preachers confronted the problem by publishing simple instructional treatises for hearing sermons, in which they outlined who was responsible for household attendance, where to look during the sermon, how to screen out the rest of the congregation, and whether to bring Bibles or take notes, a practice which could distract from 'sustained self-application' to the preacher's words (Hunt 2010: 68).

Most English Protestants saw preaching as both necessary and good, and treated non-preaching ministers contemptuously. John Rogers famously attacked those who 'either cannot or will not Preach the Word; such are no feeders but starvers, blinde leaders of the blinde, Soul slayers, blood suckers, yea, worse than Cannibals, as living of the blood of souls, whereas these live on men's flesh' (Rogers 1650: 619). In 1578, a preacher in Barton, Bedfordshire, who never read the *Homilies* but only preached sermons he himself had prepared, provoked complaints (Maltby 1998: 66). More typically, however, congregations demanded sermons by educated men who could preach according to their auditors' capacities, display sufficient learning without deploying it ostentatiously, and move their hearers. Preachers were expected to be 'painful'—to have prepared through study and meditation to preach plainly and clearly, to know their auditors, and to rebuke the particular sins of the congregation without alienating them, a challenging rhetorical tightrope.[3]

Audience demographics remain elusive, even when sermons purport to tell us about their hearers. We therefore need to consider patterns of sermon attendance, proximity of local parishes to 'common' pulpits, acknowledged motives of sermon-gadders, scheduling of sermons and lectures, and population pressures within parishes. Preaching ministers encountered resistance to sermons that challenged orthodox and obedient parishioners to become committed Protestants. Audiences generally seemed to prefer learned sermons, delivered from memory or spoken from notes rather than read, on the Gospel message of love and promise rather than on Old Testament texts with their threatening emphasis on law, sin, and repentance. The rebuke of sinfulness certainly promoted disaffection, especially in small, close-knit parishes where individuals remained vulnerable to exposure of their particular sins and where a 'community of neighbours and the fellowship of the elect' were ideally identical (Carlson 2003: 264, 290). Rebuke of elite auditories was no easier. John Donne calls effective reproof the 'fishing of whales', a witty take on the preacher as a fisher of men and a reminder that while 'the Marke is great enough; one can scarce misse hitting it', the preacher needs 'sea room and line enough, and dexterity in letting out that line' (rhetorical skill and a keen sense of the appropriate distance to allow between preacher and sinner) that will allow him to reel in his catch without endangering himself or his 'boate' (Donne 1953–62: V, 199). Simon Hacksuppe's assault on local sinfulness almost ruined him, partly because he did not confine his criticisms to generalities, or even to the pulpit, but pursued 'sinners' in the church courts and brawled with the locals. At least he avoided the fate of William Storr in Lincolnshire who was murdered in 1602 for a sermon comparing Market Rasen in Lincolnshire to Sodom and Gomorrah (Carlson 2003: 259).

Auditors responded in wildly different ways to the immediate moment of delivery; some shouted 'Amen' (Craig 2011: 189), while others threw stones or rotten eggs, and still others disputed vigorously the doctrines preached. Responses could be extreme and unpredictable. Elizabeth I's interjection during a sermon by Alexander Nowell, then Dean of St. Paul's, commanding him to leave the 'threadbare' topic of religious images and saints, discomfited the preacher enough that he ended his sermon abruptly (McCullough 1998a: 47). At the opposite extreme, John Donne's recognized professional gifts were so eminent that he was fast-tracked as a royal chaplain to James I, compared to 'golden Chrysostom' the great preaching Church Father, and applauded for his moving

---

[3] See Merritt 2002 on the career of Robert Hill.

voice, gestures, and the arrows of his insight. Dutch statesman Constantijn Huygens accorded him 'the speech of Gods' (Shami 2011a: 319).

Despite the popularity of sermons, and the feats of endurance reported (Nehemiah Wallington recorded nineteen sermons in seven days!), auditors criticized excessively lengthy sermons even if preached by a celebrated cleric, but almost certainly if preached by 'strange prattling preachers of no good report' (Haigh 1987: 74). Frequent self-conscious references to hourglasses in sermons express clerical anxiety on this issue. Standards of audience discrimination were as varied as there were auditors. As John Dyos complained:

> Some would have long texts: some short textes. Some would have Doctours, Fathers and Councels: some call yt mans doctrine. Some would have it ordered by Logicke: some terme that mans wisdom. Some would have it polished by Rhetoricke: some call yt persuasibleness of wordes. And agayne in Rhetoricke some would have it holy eloquence, liable to the Ebrue & Greeke phrase: Some would have it proper and fitting to the English capacitie. Some love study and learning in Sermons: Some allow only a sudaine motion of the spirite. Some would have all said by heart: some would have oft recourse made to the booke. Some love gestures: some no gestures. Some love long Sermons: some short Sermons. Some are coy, and can broke no Sermons at all. (Dyos 1579: F3)

Samuel Pepys judged the preaching of eleven ministers on an 'elaborate matrix' of factors ranging from biography to learning, style, and voice. Such connoisseurs felt free to 'commend or criticize' anything: the preacher's doctrines, political partisanship, flattery of the congregation, pride, or rhetorical abilities (Spurr 2013: 4–6).

Audibility was a major obstacle to hearing the word preached. Some parishes initiated measures, including higher pulpits, to project the preacher's voice, and built galleries to accommodate larger congregations. Since salvation was effected by hearing, controlling noise was paramount. The minor office of dog-whipper, initially created to cast dogs from churches, gradually extended to keeping children quiet, waking sleepy hearers, and ensuring attentiveness. Not all noise signified inattention. Against a background of cacophonous ambient noise, 'the hum or buzz of whispers, groans, sighs, exclamations, murmurs, page-turning and other engaged forms of interaction' clearly signified audience engagement, as did behaviour common to theatres, including applause, vocal acclamations, interjections, and critique, even from those too far away to hear the preacher properly (Craig 2011: 188).

Despite these circumstances, the 'converting power of the spoken voice' of a sermon was a powerful instrument, rendered even more so by biblical authority (Romans 10:14–17) exalting hearing above seeing as the pathway to salvation. Most Protestants associated 'eye' worship with Roman Catholic idolatry, and emphasized the spoken word's superiority, although Puritans, in particular, popularized this view. Sadly, for parishes without preaching, or where sermons were inaudible (not to mention for the deaf), the apparently theological pre-eminence of hearing posed challenges. Although the competition between preaching and reading declined over time as printed sermons flourished and the debarring of the deaf from salvation disappeared when it was learned that they could be taught lip-reading (Hunt 2010: 55), the debate had considerable polemical power. In dispute with conformists, Puritans argued that reading and preaching were different in kind; in dispute with papists and separatists they argued that they were essentially the same (Hunt 2010: 41), the targeted audience dictating the polemical strategy. Certainly by the end of our period and its transition into print culture, maintaining this distinction, or thinking of preaching as purely a speech act, was increasingly difficult.

Clearly, a sermon was a dynamic experience where hearers expected to be 'stirred' or 'melted' by doctrines effectively performed, resulting in an almost theatrical catharsis (Spurr 2013: 8; Hunt 2010: 81). In the words of John Rogers, preachers had to manifest the spirit of God in them by 'Preach[ing] Christ Crucified in a Crucified Phrase' (Rogers 1650: 236), inducing in their listeners, as Martin Ingram puts it, 'conversion by shock' (Ingram 1996: 78). Quaker practices such as preaching naked were only extreme versions of the same technique. Emotional preaching, though an important aspect of early modern sermon culture, generally declined in favour by the end of the seventeenth century, maligned as hypocritical and insincere, and associated with too public a display of private religious experience. However, the period witnessed continuing debates about the relative merits of memorized, well-structured discourses as opposed to more dramatic performances as conduits of grace.[4]

The theatrical appeal of sermons reminds us that audiences for plays and sermons overlapped (Lake with Questier 2002a: 429; Crockett 1995: 64) and that contemporaries underscored the generic parallels (Fetzer 2010: 49). Even before the break with Rome, Henry VIII was apparently pleased with a learned sermon wherein the preacher demonstrated 'in his pronunciation very good eloquence, with gesture apt and convenient' (cited by Wooding 2011: 337). If the relatively limited theatricality of the court sermon could elicit such commentary, the outdoor pulpit at Paul's Cross could meaningfully be described as 'an open theatre of the streets in a way which makes the Globe Theatre seem like a private club by comparison' (Cummings 2002: 366). At these theatres, listeners were invited not only to hear, but to apply the sermon's discourse and examples to themselves 'in order to stage and perform the conversion to and reconciliation with God that is at issue on the level of the Biblical text' (Fetzer 2010: 51). The corrupt and sinful world castigated by prophetic preachers at the Cross and redeemed through the alliance of magistrate and minister was the inverted world that the same auditors saw depicted in murder pamphlets and contemporary plays (Lake with Questier 2002a: 337). The common concerns dramatized in these contested discursive spaces suggests that the rhetorical features of Jonson's stereotypical puritan preachers, for example, are strongly reminiscent of actual preachers and bring us 'as close as we ever can to the rhythm and

---

[4] See also Poole 2000: 112–13 on the conservative resistance to 'tub preachers' in the mid-seventeenth century.

timbre, the feel, of London preachers as they extemporized and improvised on the scriptural or moral themes of their sermons' (Lake with Questier 2002a: 604).

While contemporaries compared theatres and pulpits, the analogy was seldom positive: Donne complained of interruptions and even applause at sermons. But sermons reveal a complex and fruitful commerce between pulpit and theatre even at the level of borrowed speech. Hunt describes a sermon passage that prints as prose Portia's famous 'mercy' speech from *The Merchant of Venice*: 'Here we have a passage written for oral delivery in the theatre, later published in a printed playbook, borrowed by Andrewes [the preacher] and perhaps repeated by him in a sermon to his Wiltshire parishioners, and then produced in a printed sermon, which may in turn have been read aloud by its earliest readers' (Hunt 2010: 172). A sermon by Robert Harris, vicar of Hanwell, re-issued in 1624, refers throughout to 'a game at Chesse' including the way in which kings and bishops tumble into the chess bag, a moral concept figuring a hell-mouth in Thomas Middleton's notoriously political play, *A Game at Chesse*, performed for nine days before it was shut down in August 1624 (Shami 1995).

Listeners were expected to combine their real-life personalities with the sermon's examples targeted by the preacher's 'nearnesse': 'as if,' to quote John Donne, 'he had been behind the arras when I sinned' (Donne 1953–62: III, 142). The best preachers achieved this effect by combining intimate moments generating self-reflection, with words reinforcing communal values, using shifting personal pronouns, appeals to particular audience members, including the monarch, and split-second timing of text and examples in the sermon's application to engage listeners as active participants. With the aid of the Holy Spirit—the third actor in the sermon experience—preacher and auditor joined together to trouble the conscience and to move it to recognition, catharsis, and conformity with Christ. Despite the virtual impossibility of recreating the circumstances and affect of a sermon's delivery, we know that the preacher was judged according to the effectiveness of his *pronunciatio* and *actio*, including bodily carriage, facial expression, intonation, and gesture (Armstrong 2011: 121–3). No doubt the 'violence of delivery' that resulted in one preacher, William Hubberdine, landing among his auditors and breaking his leg was deemed excessive, but preachers had to 'now and then play the fools in the pulpit' to avoid preaching 'to bare walls' (Heal 2003: 289).

Our knowledge of sermon audiences is obscured by our inability to recreate the experience of the sermon's delivery, and by the practice of sermon-gadding: 'crossing parish boundaries to attend sermons in other churches' (Hunt 2010: 289). Debates about the propriety (and even the legality) of the practice do not divide along doctrinal or sectarian lines, and despite their commitment to hearing a multitude of sermons, puritan clergy were 'deeply ambivalent' (196) about the practice. Some considered it a form of spiritual adultery, a view supported by analogies between a minister and his flock as husband and wife. Some saw opposition to the practice as largely self-serving on the part of offended preachers. Especially in London where sermons were widely available, the practice of hearing sermons in multiple locations was common. In fact, strong commitment to a local parish was entirely consonant with sermon-gadding. The times at which sermons were offered would have made them available to women, servants, and apprentices outside normal work hours, and Sunday afternoon and weekday lectures would have attracted large numbers of outsiders. Gadders might also cross parish boundaries to accommodate the overflow of parishioners who could not find room in their own local church, usually an influx from the suburbs. So, while many factors restrained sermon-gadding (Hunt 2010: 228), a free market for sermons developed over our period.

SETTINGS FOR PREACHING

The theatrical underpinnings of sermons as performances are reinforced by preachers' efforts 'to shape their oratory to a particular congregation and to exploit the architectural and spatial dynamic of their performance space in order to enhance the rhetorical potential of their sermons' (Rhatigan 2011: 87–8). This essay provides only the briefest of surveys, focusing primarily on the generic implications of the preaching situations described.

Most sermons were delivered in a parish context wherein competition between architectural features—the sermon and its pulpit, the Eucharist and its Communion tables—marked the relative importance of sermons and the sacrament and the accommodations required to support preaching within this liturgical 'theatre'. The nave and pulpit emerged in the Tudor period as the focus of Reformed worship, with the pulpit variously positioned to increase the acoustic quality and symbolic importance of the sermon; the altar—the centerpiece of medieval Catholic liturgy—was replaced with a Communion table (Rhatigan 2011: 90–1). In the 1630s the Laudians reversed this change, restoring altars to redress the perceived overemphasis on preaching at the expense of prayer and sacraments. These changes proved transitory, and by the 1640s the Reformation innovations were reinstated until, following the Restoration, especially in London, Christopher Wren designed 'auditories', single-room churches dominated by elaborate pulpits, designed to facilitate the audience in hearing and seeing the preacher (Rhatigan 2011: 99).

The most prominent preaching setting was the parish church, although first-hand evidence of the content, style, delivery, and reception of parish sermons is fragmentary and idiosyncratic. From the 1540s to the 1580s, a 'transitional phase' in which licensed preachers, both settled and itinerant, attempted to preach even in the 'dark corners' of the pro-Catholic north and west, the great majority of clerics probably did little more than read the official homilies. From the 1590s to the 1630s, the 1604 Canons required sermons once a month rather than four times yearly, the number of educated clerics increased, and sermons attempted to settle Protestantism rather than simply to purge auditors of Catholicism. Sermons became more diverse (not just routine Sunday sermons), and pulpit rhetoric developed in two directions: plain divinity more suitable to the uneducated, being instructional rather than controversial, and courtly rhetoric more suitable to elite, sophisticated auditories. Over this period, sermon sequences preached consecutively to specific congregations flourished, as did short series or single sermons linked to the liturgical calendar and Eucharistic celebrations (Green 2009b, 2011). Preachers selected biblical texts for their difficulty, significance, exegetical history, and place in the official liturgy, and could count on audiences to bring interpretative expectations to the sermon. Texts were also chosen for political valences, building on typological readings of Old Testament figures familiar to auditors to offer thinly veiled political criticism of current magistrates and governors, including monarchs (Killeen 2011). It is no wonder that the sermon form itself, as much as any particular example of it, was deemed more dangerous than silence, and why prayer was thought by most authorities to be a safer form of speech.

During the 1640s and 1650s, the 'continuities of parish life were badly disrupted'. Many Episcopalians were ejected and Presbyterians and moderate Independents appointed, while sectaries (Baptists and Quakers) gathered congregations from different parishes and set up rival meeting places to the 'steeple-houses' (Green 2011: 150). The sermon became a 'dynamic instrument for criticism or defence of the status quo' (Green 2011: 150), but what parishioners heard depended on the pre-war history of the parish and its preacher's background and views, as case studies by, among others, Jacqueline Eales (2002) and William Sheils (1994, 2006) attest. Eales, for example, provides a snapshot of rival preaching campaigns during the First English Civil War (1640–6) demonstrating that many provincial pulpits became battlegrounds involving violent and emotional confrontations pitting Presbyterian supporters of Parliament against royalists as well as Independents and lay preachers. Parliament ejected scandalous, non-preaching, royalist, and ceremonious clergy, prompting sermons in the capital and in provincial pulpits handling the touchy issue of resistance to authority. Both sides claimed God's providential support. Successive purges of the ministry initiated by Parliament underscored political correctness in preaching, creating 'high levels of religious and political tension in both urban and rural communities' (Eales 2002: 207). Sheils (1994) examines West Riding fast sermons on the eve of civil war in the early 1640s, and uses the careers of two friends, John Shawes and Edward Bowles, to examine the shifting priorities of preachers and their auditors as godly rule was implemented in the mid-century in Yorkshire, away from Parliament and the centres of government.

Abundant evidence establishes the character of post-Restoration preaching, with its emphasis on obedience and conformity, and its rejection of both the 'highly decorated sermons given by some preachers favoured by the educated elite, and the "crumbling" of scripture texts into scores of doctrines and uses by some "godly" clergy' (Green 2011: 151). Many preachers advocated a plain style, avoidance of enthusiasm, and adherence to basics of faith and works that aligns them more clearly with the homilies and 'country divinity' traditions of early modern preaching than with the more ornate, classically inflected sermons preached to earlier court and cathedral audiences. Moreover, we see an enhanced sphere of influence for these sermons, when expanded audiences were again required by statute to attend church services, and when readily accessible, cheaply produced printed formats ensured the social penetration of sermons (Claydon 2011: 213). Unbound copies of printed sermons made them even more inexpensive and collectable, while their political nature and denominational variety enhanced their marketability (Claydon 2011: 219)

Outdoor pulpits filled a need for more preaching theatres, and over the course of our period facilitated sermons for unauthorized sects, from the Family of Love, Anabaptists, Barrowists, and Brownists of the Elizabethan period to Quakers, Dissenters, and other nonconformists before they established meeting houses. Outdoor pulpits, however, with their medieval roots, also served more orthodox needs. The most famous of these were in London: Paul's Cross (Morrissey 2011), St. Mary's Spital, and the Preaching Place at Whitehall (McCullough 1998a: 42–9). At the former, a rota of preachers gave lengthy sermons each week, attracting large heterogeneous crowds (including Privy Councillors, Inns of Court members, Parliamentarians, the Lord Mayor and aldermen of London, and humbler citizens, merchants, and tradespeople). Audiences as large as six thousand persons on Sundays heard statements of government policy and doctrine (especially at times of crisis or celebration) and witnessed public recantations, book burnings, and other performances in the theatre of religious experience.

Other outdoor pulpits continued to flourish, particularly among Protestant dissenters and their Lollard precursors hoping to reject ungodly multitudes, seek instruction, escape persecution, find solitude for reflection, or to worship collectively (Walsham 2011: 235–52). Along with abandoned buildings, public taverns, and private homes, these open-air pulpits offered preaching opportunities to evangelical laymen and supported a spiritual life partially separate from what some saw as an inadequately reformed institution. Sermon-gadding was part of this phenomenon, undertaken in the same spirit as medieval pilgrimages and involving large crowds covering considerable distances in the rural landscape to attend these festal worship services while reclaiming nature's least habitable spaces for God's purposes. Often these occasions were both social and edifying, mingling long perambulations with psalm-singing and discussion of sermons. An air of contingency and danger marked these services: preachers on horseback ready to make a quick escape, spies reporting on what was heard and said. Religious minorities followed these open-air practices—long, exhausting days of preaching and listening, fasting, walking long distances, singing, simple communal meals—throughout our period, until later in the seventeenth century when these enthusiastic 'holy fairs' were deemed subversive (Walsham 2011: 242).

Elite sermons at court, the Inns, and in university settings contributed to the range and variety of preaching occasions and auditories, their status as preaching theatres thoroughly treated by McCullough (1998) and Rhatigan (2011). These occasions along with others not examined here—Restoration sermons celebrating the cult of St Charles the Martyr; the great liturgical feasts of Easter, Christmas, and Whitsunday; weddings; funerals; providential deliveries such as the Gunpowder and Gowrie conspiracies, or the defeat of the Spanish Armada; or marking Parliamentary fasts, episcopal visitations, and assizes—tailored their messages and linguistic strategies to their auditors' expectations and to the demands (formal, thematic, social, and political) of the occasion. On this view, each sermon, despite its family resemblance to other sermons, despite its rehearsal of traditional themes, texts, and practical morality, was always a multilayered discourse unique to the urgencies of the moment, spiritually transcendent in its articulation of core Christian beliefs, but inextricably earthbound in its material contexts and details.

THE SERMON AND OTHER LITERARY GENRES

Early modern sermons connected most directly with other genres of scriptural exegesis (the homily and the lecture), and most dynamically with theatrical works and performances. In this section, it remains to link sermons to cathechisms, conduct books, newsbooks, and satiric pamphlets. Here we are mindful that over our period boundaries between sermons and other forms of instruction and exhortation blurred, to produce many sermon-like discourses—sometimes termed exercises, discourses, lectures, or exhortations—as supplements to the sermon. Not all of these were delivered orally, or from a pulpit, as we see in cases where material originally preached was simplified for catechetical purposes, and restructured into the question-and-answer form typical of that genre (Green 2011: 145). These works confirm the content, if not the form, of 'catechetical' sermons, which were frequently the staple of Sunday afternoon preaching, particularly after the 1622 *Directions to Preachers*, and were considered preparatory to the effectual hearing of sermons.

Domestic conduct books published by puritan preachers between the Elizabethan Settlement and the Civil War originated as sermons and delineated how the male head's absolute authority, women's subordination, and the disciplined upbringing of children should organize puritan households to become little commonwealths (Fletcher 2006: 162–3). They were 'the bedrock of evangelisation', derived from marriage sermons, and often they went through numerous editions (164), attesting to the strong public demand for this kind of edifying and/or prescriptive literature (Fletcher 2006: 163, 164). The sermon that spawned William Gouge's treatise *Of Domesticall Duties* apparently infuriated its female auditors when it was preached, although the printed book set the duties of husbands and wives parallel to one another, offering a humane, sensitive approach to the work that underpins a good marriage. Most conduct books, while they offer practical advice for reaching day-to-day harmony and accommodation on issues (including explicit discussions of sexual relations), are vitiated by repeated, unimaginative calls to obedience, as well as suggestions for husbands about how best to reprove their wives. Too often, the books resort to idealized, outdated views of marriage even for this period, untroubled by questions about gender roles. They were probably read more often by men as manuals of domestic governance than by women as pious exhortations to idealized wifely behaviour.

Sermons, of course, were an important conduit for news (Pettegree 2014: 135). The pulpit was the first place where most congregations, educated or illiterate, would hear of impending religious or political change, and it retained its power 'to shape and disturb local opinion' by channelling interpretation of important 'changes of government and worship practices, declarations of war and peace, natural disaster and catastrophe' (Pettegree 2014: 137). But as the mid-seventeenth-century theologian Thomas Lushington observed, with some insight, news 'goes not as things are in themselves, but as men's fancies are fashioned … and as they stand diverse in religion, and fain affect different news, by their news you may know their religion, and by their religion you may know their news' (Chandos 1971: 256). Towards the end of our period, this public, instructive function of the sermon was radically reshaped, as 'other channels—the newspaper, the journal, the novel, the public lecture, the coffee house, the debating club, and the learned society—rapidly appropriated its educational and moralizing functions' (Rigney 2011: 208).

Arnold Hunt has connected the 'dramatic, performative' features of Paul's Cross sermons, how 'they play to their audience by shifting abruptly from theological controversy to personal mockery', to the Marprelate tracts (1588–9), noting that the attacks against these tracts for adopting strategies of the popular stage could be levelled at the sermons twenty years earlier preached to consolidate the Elizabethan Settlement (Hunt 2011: 383). The 'contest for popular allegiance' waged from this outdoor pulpit overlaps with the impact of the murder pamphlets and popular plays that have been read as distorted reflections of these sermons (Lake with Questier 2002a). The Paul's Cross sermons employed smear campaigns, *ad hominem* attacks, and weapons of scorn and ridicule, persuading their audiences not in a high moral or intellectual way, but in a vulgar, popular manner, though one that was undoubtedly memorable and engaging. Not surprisingly, Donne locates the satiric impulse in both the preacher (who can turn an epigram into a satire or an invective) and the malicious auditor who can turn a sermon into a satire by hearing according to his humour, indicating the mutual responsibilities of both players in this theatrical dynamic (Donne 1953–62: III, 56; IV, 91).

Afterlife

Despite their initial immediacy, sermons preached enjoyed an afterlife in clerical preaching diaries, auditors' compiled commonplace books, and other records of sermons composed, heard, and read. Many families, churches, colleges, libraries, and record offices have maintained manuscript archives of such records that are now being explored for evidence of early modern sermon experiences.[5] More easily observed are the printed sermons that take the words as delivered from the local to the public stage, often changing and re-purposing the sermon to such a degree that its constitutes a new life rather than an afterlife. These 'domestick, present, judicious, pertinent, yea and powerful Sermons' (Baxter 1673: I3ᵛ) published posthumously could make dead men

---

[5] An example of such activity is the *Gateway to Early Modern Manuscript Sermons* project (GEMMS) run by Anne James and Jeanne Shami, comprising a bibliographic database of manuscript sermons from 1530 to 1715. The work is funded by the Social Sciences and Humanities Research Council of Canada, and can be viewed at [database to be launched in May 2017—author will supply details at that point].

speak (McCullough 1998b), and could appeal both to the eye and the ear, through practices of repetition and communal reading. Printed sermons also enabled 'exchange of
views', not only extending the preacher's reach but making space for 'alternative voices
and for the intrusive annotations of readers' (Rigney 2011: 202). They permitted 'effective
and efficient transmission of ideas, along with a range of additional resources for elabo-
rating, refining, expressing, and enclosing meaning—through layout, typographical
design, and textual *apparata*' (Rigney 2011: 202). Prefatory epistles to readers and other
paratextual materials (marginalia, revisions, dedications, title pages) added a theoretical
dimension to their discourse, and 'function[ed] as a place to guide the reader towards
right reading, to warn and exhort, and, more broadly, to develop theories about the process of religious reading, and the complexity of its perceived effects' (Lund 2010: 158). In
thus expanding the sermon's persuasive reach, they allowed preachers to battle repeatedly against heretical, heterodox, and extreme positions.

Printed sermons became consumer commodities, collected by clerics for reference
and by families to facilitate pious devotion. The formats ranged widely, from expensive
folios such as the sermons of Lancelot Andrewes (1629), a textual event dubbed 'the creation of a Church Father for the new age' (Ettenhuber 2011: 50; McCullough 1998b), to
less expensive quarto, octavo, duodecimo, and even broadsheet formats ('penny god-
lies') accessed by a broader range of still-literate readers. Certainly by the end of our
period, Edmund Hickeringill could lament the weight of sermons under which the
bookstalls were groaning, 'as common (and as commonly cryed about the Streets) as
Ballads' (Dixon 2011: 460). Sermons ranging from chapbooks hawked on the street to
printed sermons preached to court and Parliament represented authors from lowly
parish clergy to the Archbishop of Canterbury, across confessional positions, including nonconformists and dissenters. Sermons preached by leading Church of England
clergymen on important occasions dominated publishing, arguably shaping public
response to national events. Usually printed by demand of their auditors, including
monarchs, these sermons were distanced from their original occasion, thereby general-
izing their political and moral application.

Nonconformist preachers ejected after 1662 and denied pulpit access used print to
instruct their flocks, although access to publication was severely limited by legal restrictions. Some nonconformists, especially Quakers, eschewed printed sermons as anathema to the Word's living spirit.[6] Religious chapbook publication expanded considerably,
along with romances and ballads, 'loosely based on the sermon form', consisting of 'the
explanation and application of a scriptural text' (Dixon 2011: 475). These cheap formats were collected and annotated by serious readers, including Frances Wolfreston,
whose library also included formal printed sermons (Morgan 1989). By this point, the
generic conventions of the sermon were so well established—broadly, the explication
and application of a specific biblical text—that mock sermons satirizing the form were

---

[6] For a discussion of the relationship between the Quakers and print, see Peters 2005 and chapter 27 of
this volume.

also printed (although not preached, as far as we know). Some early eighteenth-century printed examples are extant (Dixon 2011: 461), but a seventeenth-century Oxford manuscript indicates that the form developed much earlier. Entitled *A newe sermon of the newest fashion*, the parodic sermon is said to have been '*cutt out and made up by Ananias Snip a new inspired Taylor*'. Based on the text '*Wee are fooles*', it sets forth the '*superstition of the Byshops, the abhomination of the Surplice, and unlawfulnesse of the Lyturgie*', and is said to have been printed by '*Ignoramus Prick-eares, Preacher to the famous Ninni-versity of Round-heads*'.

This account of the early modern sermon can hardly do justice to the subject's vast reach in permeating literary, religious, and political culture in our period. Nonetheless, we can draw certain conclusions. Sermons flourished both as popular public theatrical occasions and as instruments for private reflection and devotion, and they were appropriated as polemical instruments of church and state to advance particular religio-political agendas. The evidentiary archive of manuscript and print materials has expanded our resources for this study immeasurably over the last few decades. As we advance this study, however, it seems clear that broad preaching surveys that supplement, correct, and reshape our thinking on the nature and impact of sermons acquire nuance from local studies that enable more detailed and complex understanding of its form, function, and impact.

....

CHAPTER 13

AUTOBIOGRAPHICAL WRITINGS

....

KATHARINE HODGKIN

WHEN the musician Thomas Whythorne's autobiographical manuscript, written in the 1560s, first appeared in print in 1962, it was published in two separate editions. One was aimed at a scholarly readership, reproducing his original text exactly (including his challenging revisionist orthography). The second, for the general reader, modernized the spelling and also cut 'some repetitive or otherwise tedious passages' from the original (Whythorne 1962: vi)—primarily Whythorne's religious reflections. 'Here Whythorne presents a long discourse on Divine punishments', notes the editor, James Osborn, while omitting it; 'Here Whythorne distinguishes between worldly sorrow and Godly sorrow' (Whythorne 1962: 124, 126). Self-evidently, such material was uninteresting—generic and predictable, adding little to our understanding of Whythorne the man.

The transformation in scholarly views of such writing over the last half-century has been dramatic. Narratives of religious experience, once regarded as dull pieties, or as records of misrecognized mental illness, have moved to the centre of debates about the early modern self. Spiritual autobiography illuminates early modern inner worlds. It grapples with the problems of self-knowledge, self-assertion and self-denial, and the relation between self and others (including the divine); it shows how religious convictions and commitments frame and direct individual lives, highlighting the shaping force of religious language in early modern understandings of the self. The urge to tell the story of one's own spiritual quest became increasingly pressing during the sixteenth and seventeenth centuries. It spread across confessional boundaries; Anglicans, Catholics, Baptists, Fifth Monarchists, perhaps especially Quakers, were caught up in the desire to understand and explain God's workings in their hearts and lives. It drew in men and women whose lives were marginal and insignificant, from artisans and shepherds to the disregarded single daughters of the gentry. Participating in the great project of spiritual renewal, above all during the years of the English Revolution and afterwards, many found new meaning in their own experiences, and no less importantly the possibility of access to an audience.

The rich mix of modes in which they wrote, along with the centrality of autobiography to the history of the self in this period more generally, has in turn generated extensive debate about how this material is to be defined and understood. Autobiography, once limited to an extended and generally chronological first-person life story, has fractured and fragmented into new modes and terminologies. Early modern autobiographical narratives took many forms. Recent work has interrogated recipe collections, parish registers, and account books for traces of the autobiographical voice; terms such as life writing and ego-documents have gathered together a fluid mix of genres and styles, complicating the boundaries we set today between private and public, between letter, diary, memoir, and autobiography.[1] Religious discourse, however, remains strikingly at the centre of many of these forms of self-expression. Writing the self, for many early modern people, *was* writing about religion.

Religion was also very commonly the context in which stories about lives were summoned up. The century after the Reformation in England saw a rapid expansion of devotional writing across a range of areas. Rising levels of literacy, among women as well as men (though women's literacy remained significantly lower), opened new possibilities for the dedicated Christian. The Bible was, of course, the central pillar of Protestant reading and writing, but it was supplemented by a steady stream of print: sermons, homilies, guides to practical divinity, religious poetry, meditations, mother's legacies. Exemplary lives of the godly were widely circulated; Foxe's *Book of Martyrs* was succeeded by many accounts of the spiritual struggles of ordinary people, men and women. Even writing that was not explicitly an account of a life often implied some element of spiritual narrative: what sufferings and trials did this person undergo (inward or outward), what were their experiences and what did they learn from them? Alongside printed works, too, letters, journals, meditations, and prayers circulated in manuscript within communities of the godly, part of an extensive devotional culture in which people shared thoughts and experiences, encouraging those in despair and recounting doubts and triumphs. The question of what it meant to lead a godly life and to be among the elect was posed repeatedly; and the idea that it could be answered through a retrospective narrative of personal experience became increasingly familiar.

Spiritual autobiography thus emerges as part of the wider culture of devotional writing, both print and manuscript, that permeated early modern England. The incorporation of these dispersed fragments of individual lives into a narrative offering the reader a story of the self, however, does not happen immediately or consistently; and in many ways it seems to have been almost a process of spontaneous generation. Journals, surviving from the sixteenth century in increasing numbers, are often held to have been encouraged as part of the Protestant project of self-examination, though texts recommending the practice only appear in the mid-seventeenth century. Retrospective narratives emerge slightly later, but very few early autobiographers mention influences or

---

[1] See, for example, Graham 1996; Mascuch 1997; Shuger 2000; Dragstra, Otway, and Wilcox 2000a; Dekker 2002; Hinds 2002; Bedford, Davis, and Kelly 2006, 2007; Dowd and Eckerle 2007; Hindmarsh 2007; Cambers 2007, 2011; Hodgkin 2007, 2012; Clarke and Longfellow 2008; Smyth 2010; Lynch 2012.

models for their enterprise; Elizabeth Isham, writing in the 1630s, explicitly models her account on Augustine, but she is surprisingly unusual in doing so. But even without direct precursors, a life plan was laid down within the framework of Calvinist theology which shaped the narrative of the self. Early autobiographers interpreted their stories through the categories of election and reprobation, following the phases of the regenerate soul's life, and interrogated their experiences for signs of grace; their accounts thus have generic elements even before there is a genre. Dionys Fitzherbert, writing around 1608, uses this framework to explain her experience as one of spiritual crisis rather than mental disorder, and other early manuscripts, such as Richard Norwood's, use the same model. These works seldom made it into print, although some circulated in manuscript (as Fitzherbert's did), but their reliance on the same spiritual structure underlines the importance of the common culture in which they were embedded. It is a culture and a framework that retains its force throughout the seventeenth century.

Until the mid-seventeenth century, most surviving autobiographical narratives are manuscripts, often lengthy, and intended for a restricted audience; their authors were of relatively elite background. The spiritual energy and upheaval that was part of the mid-century revolution in England transformed and radicalized the writing of spiritual autobiography, along with much else. The rise of dissenting religious groups was accompanied by an explosion of publications. The gathered churches were engines of literary production; books and pamphlets streamed off the presses, to be sold by small booksellers up and down the country. Censorship was suspended for much of the 1640s, and even once it had been restored, the publication of spiritual and devotional literature continued at a high rate. And from the early 1650s on, much of this literature was autobiographical, bringing new voices—small artisans and traders, women and men—into the public domain. As with earlier traditions of devotional literature, generic boundaries are blurred. A spiritual autobiography may consist of three pages on the writer's spiritual experiences as a brief digression in a long polemic; it may be two hundred pages of close analysis and reflection on the inner life; it may be an account of spiritual activities—preaching, prophecy, travel, prison. These later narratives, many published under the controlling influence of the group and with more or less explicitly missionary aims, are often very short and formulaic, though this is not necessarily to say that there is (as the writers may claim) 'no self in this'. But the printed writings of the later period also include long and intensely self-analytical accounts, even if what they analyse is the movements of the soul rather than the emotions; and longer manuscript narratives continue throughout the century, often with spiritual and secular concerns inseparably intertwined.

The theological centrality of personal experience is central to the expansion of spiritual autobiography. To speak or write of one's own experience, important from the Reformation onwards in devotional circles, increasingly becomes a spiritual communication in itself, supported by Calvinist experimental theology. This emerges especially forcefully in the gathered churches of the revolutionary period. In the new world God's spirit would pour out, and the obscurantist priests of the old churches, with their learned languages and their supposed expertise in matters of religion, would be cast down by those they had despised, who would emerge as God's true voices. The poor and lowly could bear witness to the workings of God's grace in their own hearts, and this would be more valuable than learned commentaries on texts. Many radical churches required aspirant members to declare their spiritual experiences in public before accepting them into the congregation, and a few collections of these were published (Rogers 1653; Powell 1653). These fragmentary autobiographical narratives, with their debatable authorship and scanty detail, nonetheless reinforce the idea that faith and election can be demonstrated in narrative, as the story of what brought you to the place where you stand.

The textual as well as the generic status of these accounts, as this suggests, is complicated. Oral and written accounts intersect; prominent figures like George Fox and Anna Trapnel left multiple versions of the same event, sometimes taken down by an amanuensis. First- and third-person narratives may co-exist in the same text, with testimonies, commentaries, and letters added in. For published texts, above all those supervised by church authorities, there are undoubtedly other mediations; occasionally, as for Fitzherbert, both original and public versions of a text survive, but in most cases it is impossible to know the level of editorial intervention between the original narrative (spoken or written) and the eventual publication. The genre is thus more diverse and problematic than can fully be explored in this discussion. Drawing mainly on the printed texts of the later seventeenth century, and working with a narrow definition of spiritual autobiography as a retrospective prose first-person account of a life that is centred on religious experience, with the relationship to God as the organizing principle, I have flattened out many distinctions between different sects, as well as change over time. However, it should be emphasized that authorship and authority here are textually and conceptually complex.

Both 'autobiography' and 'self', in fact, can be challenged as terms with which to approach these writings. The genre of autobiography is only problematically present at the time; the self, too, is differently understood and experienced. Early modern spiritual autobiography implies assumptions about the self which trouble the very idea of autobiographical writing. Subjectivity is complicated by a spiritual discourse that sees selfhood as a problem rather than something to be celebrated; the goal of the spiritual journey is self-transcendence rather than the self-assertion conventionally associated with autobiography. Since the project of spiritual autobiography is authorized by God, the place of the self as author is always only provisional. The focus on inner rather than outer life disrupts temporality and leads to wildly varying levels of detail in relation to the defining elements of modern selfhood. The trajectory of the conversion narrative, in which the self is made new, is in these accounts often ambiguous and uncertain, characterized by recurrent doubts and anxieties. And while autobiography has been commonly defined in relation to an autonomous individualist subject, spiritual autobiography is often more concerned to demonstrate what is shared with others; it frequently traces a journey from isolation and doubt into a collective voice and identity, offering a life as exemplification of a pattern. Spiritual autobiography throws up tensions: between private and public, individual and collective, self-assertion and self-annihilation, divine and personal agency.

At the same time none of these oppositions is simple. Early modern spiritual autobiography is marked by a series of negotiations between autonomy and self-abnegation, between inner and outer worlds. It aims to describe and enact a journey of self-transcendence rather than self-discovery; but the formal paradox implicit here makes that annihilation more ambiguous than it would perhaps like to acknowledge. 'Oh! let me be unto thee, O God, what I am', writes Elizabeth Stirredge, 'and not unto man'; but the implicitly asserted 'I am' remains to disrupt its own denial (Stirredge 1711: 17). The self in spiritual self-narrative remains present even if problematically, and in unfamiliar ways. Gender and class also inflect our understanding of voice and selfhood in these texts. For women and non-elite men, spiritual auto-biography offered an unprecedented public voice. The value that could be claimed by marginal selves in the experiential theology of radical Protestantism, even if claimed under the sign of disavowal, complicates any reading of these accounts as merely formulaic, and reminds us that it is problematic to define authentic self-hood in terms that have historically belonged to the privileged. These texts invite us to reflect on the contingency and historical specificity of concepts of self, but not necessarily to suppose that early modern selves are without interiority, or that genre and subjectivity are in fact identical.

AUTOBIOGRAPHICAL SELVES: ANNIHILATION, AFFLICTION, COLLECTIVITY

The self is a problematic presence in early modern spiritual autobiography. The aim of the narrative is not to say 'this is how I became the person I am', so much as 'this is how the person I was managed to transcend the bonds of self'; the ideal is to reach a point where self is nothing. The very word 'self' is commonly used to identify all that is worldly and must be done away with. 'Let none conclude that the Self is here set up;' writes Dorothea Gotherson, 'for by denying the earthly, the sensual, and the devilish part, is this so come to pass' (Gotherson 1661: 30); Alice Hayes declares, 'let nothing be attributed to that Monster Self, which too often appears both in Preachers and Writers' (Hayes 1723: 65). Yet these and many other writers published narratives that placed the self—or some version of it—as the subject. The validation of spiritual experiences, and their value in supporting and encouraging others, outweighed anxieties about self-aggrandizement.

However, the self is defined in relation to very different priorities and interests. In a theology that privileges the inner over the outer as source of meaning and truth, what matters is above all the relation to God. Time spent on matters not spiritual is time wasted; anything perishing, as Jane Turner remarks, is 'too low for them [Saints] to spend much of their precious time or thoughts about' (Turner 1653: 194). For the sectarian writers in particular, this is often taken to an extreme point, as details of what now seem the central elements of a life—childhood, love, family, work—are relegated to the domain of the worldly. Childhood, now generally seen as key to an understanding of the adult self, is often passed over in a couple of sentences. Human relationships are important to the extent that they affect the relationship to God; so a minister or a neighbour who spoke to one's condition may be far more significant in the life story than husband, wife, or parents. Work in the sense of earning a living is often disregarded; the true work is happening internally. The movements of the soul, by contrast, may be debated at great length. Dreams, visions, temptations, reflections, doubts, and fears, all call for extensive exploration and interpretation.

The analysis of the self is directed at interpretation of divine intent, and the examination of a life—one's own or that of others—is in such retrospective narratives less a balance sheet, measuring sins against evidences of grace, than a hermeneutical inquiry into the meaning of signs, and how to determine election. But while this attention to the inward implies rigorous self-examination, the self is examined for conformity to a pattern rather than uniqueness. Exemplarity suggests a very different set of priorities for the autobiographer: not exceptionality and autonomy, but typicality and dependence (on the divine and on other believers), define the contours of the self. Thus many spiritual autobiographies present a conventionally structured and described set of experiences, characterized by a common purpose, especially as the dissemination of autobiographical narratives becomes increasingly conditional on conformity to the expectations of religious authorities.

However, the project of self-examination could not always be contained in the structures offered by theology or by the expectations of the group; the practices of self-interrogation and self-narrative in themselves encouraged a degree of overspill. The consequences of the inquiry are intensely emotional; not just self-knowledge but eternity depends on successful reading of the signs, and for many writers the experience of self-examination seems to have been a challenging one. Writers such as Bunyan or Turner record a sense of self-exposure, of stepping out in an unknown direction and baring one's innermost self; even seemingly conventional and generic accounts often suggest the struggle of going through the process of self-analysis and self-representation, understanding and capturing the nature of spiritual experience. The language of interiority at this period remains relatively restricted; complex emotions were organized by the imperatives of election and the need to fit oneself to the divine model. But the language of spiritual experience, embedded in biblical stories and enriching its vocabulary as the sharing of life stories developed across the century, offered an increasingly flexible and expressive framework for the articulation of emotion, as introspection became embedded in spiritual practice.

The journey of the early modern spiritual self is defined by its encounter with peril. Spiritual autobiographers locate their authority to write in their experiential knowledge of religious doubt and terror; the extremity of their condition, so long as it can be assimilated into the frame of spiritual affliction, strengthens their claim to special knowledge. Where the self becomes interesting, for spiritual autobiography, is where it struggles and suffers. And a primary site of anguish is the encounter with one's own sinfulness. Searching the self to the depths revealed iniquity—and if it did not, you needed to look harder. 'I am thronged with unruly passions, madd, if let loose to wickednesse', writes Richard Carpenter, '…I am the void, and empty Cave of ignorance, the muddy fountaine of evill concupiscence; dark in my understanding, weake in my will, and very forgetfull of good things … left to my selfe, I am not my selfe, but a devill in my shape' (Carpenter 1642: 34). This vileness need never issue in behaviour; sin is an inward condition. When Hannah Allen announces that she is a monster of sin, her family protest, 'We see no such a thing in you'; 'But you will', she responds (Allen 1683: 23). Anna Trapnel struggles to understand that she is as sinful as the worst murderer or adulterer in the world, despite outward appearances; but she does eventually accept it. A virtuous exterior may signal no more than hypocrisy, and in the Calvinist sense one may be a hypocrite without knowing it; hence Jane Turner's advice, that 'self-examination, self-watching, self-judging, self-humbling', are duties 'no hypocrite can truly do' (Turner 1653: 185). It is only by knowing the self to the worst depths that one can find at least a provisional assurance.

The fragility of faith, how to sustain it, how to live in accordance with it, how to be sure one has it—these are constant anxieties. The soul is imperilled by sin and weakness, but also by the cost of struggling with these. Faced with the apparent impossibility of being certain of salvation, believers are assailed by temptations to doubt, anger, and blasphemy; misery engulfs them, and they become convinced of their own damnation. The recurrence of melancholy and mental disorder in these narratives also registers the suffering of the self as a mode of spiritual experience, in which the foundations of the self are shaken. Early modern autobiographers repeatedly describe a struggle back from the brink of breakdown, if not a complete collapse. The boundaries between affliction for sin, melancholy, and outright madness were unstable and constantly renegotiated; devotional writers dedicated many pages to elucidating the differences, while the language of distraction is commonly invoked to describe periods of intense distress. Thus Crook 'thought I should have been Distracted, because of God's Terrors that were upon my Soul' (Crook 1706: 32); John Rogers behaved so wildly that, he says, few who saw him thought him 'fit for any place but *Bedlam*' (Rogers 1653: 429). Suicide is a recurrent theme. Trapnel was 'forced by *Sathan* to walk up and down the field, attempting to throw my self into a Well … I took Knives to bed with me, to destroy my self' (1654b: 8). Rivers and rafters beckon Fitzherbert, who is tempted 'by some menes to make away myself … to unburdon my mind of thes unsoportable thoughts & sting of concenc wherwith I was continually aflicted' (Fitzherbert c.1608: 212). The assumption that a period of deep affliction is inevitable for the regenerate soul places spiritual anguish at the heart of the Christian experience.

Suffering and weakness overcome, however, illuminate God's power more wonderfully. Especially for women, the weakness of the self and the rejection of the flesh are often literalized in bodily weakness. Fasting, trance, and prophecy were visible signs of grace, though they could also be temptations; the suffering of Christ was imitated in the bodies of the faithful. Bodily collapse, in these narratives, is tied to spiritual authority. The Quaker Joan Vokins, confronting the dark powers tormenting Friends in Long Island, struggled also with sickness: 'the night before the General Meeting I was near unto death, and many *Friends* were with me, who did not expect my life, and I was so weak when I came there, that two *women-friends* led me into the meeting'; but God 'filled me with the word of his power, and I stood up in the strength thereof' (Vokins 1691: 34). The language of spirituality, indeed, is intensely embodied and fleshly; spiritual experiences are articulated through the body, the bowels, the heart, the eyes. 'Vision! the body crumbles before it, and becomes weak', exclaims Trapnel, and describes in detail the corruption of her flesh during a dramatic period of prophesy and sickness, before God raises her up again (Trapnel 1654b: 74).

This focus on physical collapse is part of a wider insistence on human helplessness before God. The gathered churches were strongly attracted by the Christian tradition that saw wealth, power, and wisdom as hindrances in pursuit of truth:

> He is a God of wisdom unto the foolish, and strength unto the weak, and honours his power in contemptible vessels ... but those that are in the wisdom of the world, which comes from beneath, and have many arts and parts ... that provokes him to wrath. Vokins (1691: 30)

Better to be a contemptible vessel and cast yourself abjectly on the mercy of the Lord, than to take any pride in your own position, qualities, or capacities. For many this was a rhetoric that could legitimize apparent immodesty in putting forward their own views, or indeed their own lives: God speaks through them. 'And this I must say, and that in the Bowedness of my Spirit,' writes Alice Hayes, 'that I have no Might of my own, nor Power, nor Ability, but what he shall be pleased to give me' (Hayes 1723: 65). For the powerful the evacuation of agency is more challenging. John Crook struggles with himself to relinquish his worldly authority, but the moment when he finally lets go is one of release; God 'subjected the Spirit of my Mind unto himself, that I was made through its Prevalency to yield, and be still, that so he might do with me what himself pleased' (Crook 1706: 32–3). When the self acknowledges its own incapacities and is abandoned to God it can cease to struggle. Henceforth it will be at God's command that the writers act, and their choices are described in a new language.

Perhaps not surprisingly, this self-relinquishment also opens new possibilities; alongside suffering and weakness, for some, are power and agency. Quakers in particular were repeatedly moved by the spirit to confront and defy ministers, judges, and even (like Elizabeth Stirredge) the king. Stirredge argues with other Quakers about women preaching, with constables who come to distrain her possessions, with justices of the peace. 'I will not wrong my Conscience for the King, nor no man else;' she tells a justice trying her for speaking at a burial, 'and I do not know whether ever the Lord may open my Mouth again; but if he do, and unloose my Tongue to speak, I shall not keep silent' (Stirredge 1711: 117–19). (He calls her an 'Old Prophetess' and a 'subtil Woman', not as a compliment.) Agnes Beaumont similarly appeals to higher authority to reject her father's order that she should give up Baptist meetings: 'My soul is of more worth then so ... if yow could stand in my steed before god to give an Account for me at the great day, then I would obay yow in this as well as other things' (1998: 201). And for the intrepid few who travel as missionaries to America, or to the Ottoman empire like Katharine

Evans and Sarah Cheevers, relinquishing self-will to divine authority opened up the possibility of extraordinary adventure and activity. Refusal of God's command is not an option. 'I hid the Word of the Lord in my Heart until it was as a Fire in me till I had declared it', writes Alice Curwen, under orders to go to the 'Bloody Town of Boston'; and although it is painful to her to leave her husband and children, 'the Lord made me willing to leave all' and head for persecution (Curwen 1680: 2). This is a rhetoric that is perhaps especially potent for women; but in the hierarchical family and social structures of early modern England, self-abnegation paradoxically legitimized a degree of autonomy for men and women alike, under obedience to God's law.

The new version of the self towards which these narratives reach is positioned in relation not only to God, but to other people. The boundaries of subjectivity are fluid and open; the self whose life is being told seldom appears as a contained and neatly delimited entity. Subjectivity is permeable, constituted by other people's stories, and the story of the person at the centre of the narrative is understood in relation to a network of others. The Bible offers countless analogues; the sufferings of David, the weakness and betrayal of Peter, are cited repeatedly by spiritual writers. Similarly, stories of friends and relatives, of fellow believers or of those who proved weak, of good and bad deaths, are part of the currency of spiritual discourse. To write one's own story adds it in to the circulation of these significant lives, and makes the writer an instance who may later console others in the same case, as well as one whose example can reinforce and confirm a collective truth—an impulse that supports all the many proximate genres through which spiritual experiences are communicated.

The reiterated motive of helping others who are suffering highlights the importance of shared experience, whether on the title page (from Fitzherbert's 1608 dedication to 'the poore in spirritt', through to Susannah Blandford's *Small Account* in 1698, subtitled 'Incouragement to the Weary to go forward') or directly stated. Alice Hayes, recollecting 'the Struglings that I felt in those Times', hopes 'that these *Lines of Experience* may … be of Service to some poor, distressed Traveller, that may have these Steps to trace through' (Hayes 1723: 29). It also reminds us again of the psychic stress inflicted by much early modern religion. Vast quantities of spiritual writing were dedicated to the encouragement of the afflicted (much of it not very likely to encourage), and testimonies of personal experience are especially likely to focus on this. Many describe a conviction that their suffering was unique, that nobody else had been through such an experience (despite the increasing number of published accounts). 'Truly I have thought', wrote Hayes, 'that if I had met with the like Account of any that had gone through such Exercise, it would have been some help to me. I searched the Scriptures from one End to the other, and read several Books, but I thought none reached my State to the full' (Hayes 1723: 29). To discover that one was wrong in thinking one's anguish unique is a consolation; likeness, rather than uniqueness, affirms the truth of experience. By sharing suffering writers claim both membership of and contribution to a wider spiritual community, and celebrate the mercy that has brought the suffering to an end.

The spiritual community is in many cases physical as well as literary. The wish to find like-minded believers is a powerful impulse in these narratives, and the move from isolation and unhappiness to collectivity and content is retold again and again. For the radical sectarian writers, of course, this is a driving force that shapes both the writing and the publication of their accounts, often with clear missionary aims; the joy of finding a church in which one feels at home is presented as a finding of one's true self in a collective enterprise, to be shared with and extended to others. The identification with the stories of others is perhaps most powerfully visible in the group autobiographies that emerge from the gathered churches. As the minister Vavasor Powell, introducing his collection, explains, 'that which cometh from one spiritual heart reacheth another spiritual heart ... herein you may see not only your own hearts, but many hearts' (Powell 1653: 3); John Rogers similarly introduces his collection with the observation that, '*Spiritual Experiences* declared out of the heart, *Mat.* 12.35 are like a *store-house* opened, whence a man fetcheth forth *things*, for use and need' (Rogers 1653: 386). Testimonies collected from the gathered churches work formulaically through a series of points which serve to confirm the truth of all other stories through their mutual resemblance. Publication, whether oral or written, is an opening out, a move away from the hidden and private self to a shared and public one.

In this move towards collectivity and typicality, the self dissolves into a community rather than representing a fixed core of individual difference: the part is subsumed into the whole, and the boundaries of subjectivity are experienced as permeable. Instead of laying claim to a unique inner self, the speakers put their lives at the service of common experience, in which similarity to others is what allows them to believe that they too can be saved. But the importance of this shared identity is founded on a previous experience of difference; the spiritual autobiographer is driven by an initial sense of being out of step with others, not satisfied with the forms of religion as they have been experienced in the past. Dissatisfaction propels the self from one collective to another, through a constant assertion that this is not one's place. Arguments about the autonomy or individuality of the subject of spiritual autobiography are thus complicated by shifting positions. Spiritual affiliations are the product of an assertion of difference; and such affiliations sustain the self at the same time as absorbing it.

CONVERSION NARRATIVES: REMEMBERING THE PAST, REMAKING THE SELF

For writers of autobiography the past is both the subject matter and the problem. The founding paradox of autobiography, notoriously, is the relation between the I who writes, in the present, and the I who is written, in the past, somebody who was me but now is not. In spiritual autobiography, as in other narratives pivoting on a transformative moment, the paradox is especially sharp: the self 'before' is by definition someone who is different to the self now—worldly, unhappy, mistaken. St Augustine's declaration, 'I am not what I was', could be seen as the foundational model for conversion narrative, widening the gap between the I who writes and the I who is written to a chasm, and retrospectively changing the meaning of all past events. The writers of spiritual auto-biography are thus engaged in complex negotiations around the relation of past and present, the place of memory, and the nature of the self whose progress is recounted in the narrative.

If the theological framework for early modern spiritual autobiographies is over-whelmingly Calvinist, tracing the journey of the soul to regeneration, the generic frame-work is that of the conversion narrative, founded on a transformation of the self. The old sinful self, in this model, is radically different. Thus Richard Norwood at twenty-five was 'wholy taken up with the lusts of the flesh with pride and self conceiptednes and with vanity and lying imaginations' (Norwood c.1639: 144), and confesses that 'for many years … I so greivously stayned my life, and lived so dissolutely, that I even abhor the remem-brance of those times'; grace has since shown him the error of his ways (125–6). Mary Rich describes herself at the time of her marriage as 'as vain, as idle and as inconsiderate a person as was possible, minding nothing but fine and rich clothes, and spending my precious time in nothing else but reading romances and in reading and seeing plays, and in going to court and Hide Park and Spring Garden', but (after a period of sanctified affliction in marriage) she is brought to a new understanding: 'I was so much changed to my self that I hardly knew my self, and could say with that converted person, "I am not I"' (Rich 1672: 21). However this model of conversion, sharply contrasting sinful youth with the reborn new self, is surprisingly rare, especially among published accounts (both Rich and Norwood left manuscript lives). For most the story told is one of a continuing journey, in which it is hard to be sure when the destination has been reached—a quest as much as a conversion narrative.

Thus what we see in many narratives is not a clear and positive transformation, but rather something muted and oblique. Many writers represent themselves as hav-ing been lost and unhappy, longing for religion but unable to find it. 'When I came to eleven years of age', recalls George Fox, 'I knew pureness and righteousness; for while I was a child I was taught how to walk to be kept pure' (Fox c.1675: 1). Elizabeth Stirredge was similarly sober and serious, rather than wild: 'In my tender years I was one of a sad heart, and much concerned and surprized with inward fear what would become of me when I should die'. Even her godly parents, indeed, thought she carried things a bit far: 'my Mother feared I was going into a Consumption … and would say unto me, *Canst thou take delight in nothing? I would have thee walk forth into the Fields with the young People, for Recreation, and delight thy self in something.* And to please her I have sometimes … gone forth with sober young People, but I found no comfort in that' (Stirredge 1711: 7). John Crook before the age of ten or eleven 'often mourned and went heavily, not taking that delight in Play and Pastime which I saw other Children took'; this made him conclude they were saved and he was not, and he spent much of his time praying in by-corners (Crook 1706: 6). The pre-converted self is preoccupied with secrecy: in one account after another the suffering seeker prays in secret, goes away into hidden places, feels secluded or excluded from the common play and pas-time of their contemporaries.

With such starting points, it is hardly surprising that the sins of which they accuse themselves are generally mild and minor—at least to the view of the outside world. Confessing to past misdeeds, of course, is complicated; some sins, even firmly located in the past, would count as unspeakable, especially for women. Both the writers and the churches under whose auspices many of them were published had reputations to protect. Thus women reproach themselves for 'foolish mirth, carding, dancing, singing, and frequenting of music meetings' (Penington c.1680: 17), or 'Dancing, Singing, telling idle Stories' (Hayes 1723: 14). Fine clothes are a source of temptation and sin in both sexes. John Crook, as an apprentice admired for his godliness and ability in extemporary prayer, reproaches himself for youthful vanities: 'never much to outward Prophaneness, but only to idle Talk, and vain Company … minding Pride too much in my Apparel … wearing long Hair, and spending my Money in vain' when he might have bought good books and given charity (Crook 1706: 9–10). Some men (not women) also accuse themselves of too much love of sport, or drunkenness, and very occasionally confess to 'pollutions' or sexual indiscretion. Norwood hints at masturbation—'my master sin' (Norwood c.1639: 145). George Trosse has an entanglement with a pious young woman who 'pretended to more *Religion*' than her family, but although the two of them behaved 'foolishly and wantonly together' in private, he claims that God restrained them 'from grosser Enormities'; unsurprisingly, no pious young woman records herself behaving like this (Trosse 1714: 58, 59). Bunyan, on the other hand, insists that he always disliked women. Even when the writers accuse themselves of worldly pleasures, too, they emphasize how deeply unpleasurable they really are. 'But in the midst of all this' says Mary Penington 'my heart was constantly sad, and pained beyond expression' (Penington c.1680: 17). Joan Vokins declares, 'if I had at any time, through persuasion of others, gone to that they called recreation, I should be so condemned for passing away my precious time, that … I could take no delight in their pastime' (Vokins 1691: 15); Hayes was so consumed with guilt at her idleness that she 'would seek some secret Place, and there I would fall upon my Knees' (Hayes 1723: 16). Many stress their misery and dissatisfaction with the forms of religion, and the emptiness of their lives and pleasures.

Similarly, while conversion itself may be experienced as a moment of dramatic transformation, it is seldom conclusive: the narrator continues to be assailed by temptations, fails to live up fully to the new commitment, and struggles with the demand that everything worldly be relinquished. This is particularly the case for those committed to constant self-monitoring for election, like John Bunyan, whose conversion—recorded in *Grace Abounding to the Chief of Sinners* (1666)—is famously provisional. Repeatedly interrupted by doubts, temptations, and struggles with Satan, it needs constant renewal—'suddenly there fell upon me a great cloud of darkness, which did so hide from me the things of God and Christ, that I was as if I had never seen or known them in my life', he writes, on one of many such occasions; 'I could not feel my Soul to move or stir after grace' (Bunyan 1998: 74). Norwood reflects on his similarly insecure experience of conversion, 'It may seem strange that a man should be so suddainly changed from so much peace and comfort to such perturbations and terrours, and it seemed strange to me even at those times' (Norwood c.1639: 151); but it is an experience recorded by many.

Others struggle with the outward transformation required by their new convictions. Alice Hayes cries to God, *'spare me a little longer, and I will become a New Creature'*; she 'found a very strange Alteration and Opperation in me … the Foundation of the Earth began to be shaken in me, and strange and wonderful it was'; but for years she continues to go to the 'Steeple-house'—'sorrowful went I in, and so I came out'—before eventually finding her way to the Quakers, to her husband's outrage (Hayes 1723: 22, 32). Crook experiences spiritual renewal when he encounters the Quakers: 'my Eyes were opened, and my Strength was renewed, and Victory I obtained … over those Lusts and corrupt Desires which rose against those little Stirrings and Movings after the living God, which I had felt working at times in my Heart' (Crook 1706: 24). But the rigorous demands of living as a Quaker, for one who had been a justice of the peace with 'great Acquaintance' and 'publick Employment', result in a lengthy battle with 'the Reasoning-Part' before he can subdue worldly pride (74). The consequences for many were serious: family conflict, financial penalties, whippings, and gaol might follow conversion to a new church, and while these could become the evidence of suffering for God and of divine favour and rewards (as in the Quaker books of suffering) they were not easy to undertake.

A further structural complication for the conversion narrative is that writers not only have inconclusive or delayed conversions; they also realize with hindsight that they have previously been mistaken about their spiritual condition—whether through a wrong choice of church, or through an apparent state of grace which turns out to have been error. Confessional choice is seldom a prominent issue in the earlier decades of the seventeenth century. Occasionally Catholics and Anglicans may cross boundaries, like Carpenter and Norwood, who both temporarily became Catholics; or in the opposite direction, like Catherine Holland, whose account for her confessor describes how she defied her father to become a Catholic. Carpenter, a Catholic convert who returned to the Church of England, describes rather defensively how he was seduced by Rome: 'What mervaile now, if greene in Age, and shallow in experience, I gave up my soule, into the black hands of errour?' (1643: 20). As the radical congregations of the revolutionary years proliferated, however, the question of how to be certain that the search was over and that finally one had arrived at a state of grace was complex, and involved constant reinterpretation, of inward as well as of outward conditions.

The first step on the path for many was a state of being under the law, as they would subsequently call it: attending church, studying Scripture intensively, and worrying about the state of their souls, but still (they later realize) in darkness, even if they appeared godly and regenerate to others. The stories repeatedly proceed from this apparent state of election to a realization that it is all outward; the inward person is still in bondage, and the quest must continue. Anna Trapnel describes repeatedly being convinced of her election, only to discover that she was mistaken. John Crook as a young man spent some years as a member of an Independent congregation, where the spiritual tone was elevated and the emphasis was on collective self-examination:

> we were kept watchful and tender, with our Minds inwardly retired, and our Words few and savoury; which frame of Spirit we were preserved in, by communicating our

Experiences each to other ... with an Account of most Days Passages between God and our own Souls.

But after a while 'it grew formal; and then we began to consider ... whether we were in the right Order of the Gospel ... we began to be divided and shattered in our Minds and Judgments about it', and the congregation fell apart (Crook 1706: 19). Laurence Clarkson goes from the Church of England to Presbyterianism, and on through Independents, Baptists ('I was satisfied we onely were the Church of Christ in this world'), and Seekers, preaching as he goes; he concludes as a rare self-professed Ranter, declaring, 'of all my formal righteousness, and professed wickedness, I am stripped naked, and in room thereof clothed with innocency of life, perfect assurance, and seed of discerning with the spirit of revelation' (Claxton [pseudonym of Clarkson] 1660: 12, 34). Such accounts suggest the disconcerting possibility that the same person writing a few years earlier would have told a different story—and indeed that they might revise their views again in the future.

Jane Turner's reflective and analytical account of her own spiritual path in *Choice Experiences* (1654) highlights the difficulty of understanding one's own experience, at the time or subsequently. Her narrative is organized into 'Notes of Experience', in which she describes a set of events, followed in each case by 'brief observations from this note of experience', where she draws the appropriate lesson; the whole is concluded by 'a few lines as to Experience it self, what it is, how, and by what means it is attained' (Turner 1653: 193). But this apparent privileging of experience as the means to know truth is increasingly problematized. Her narrative is framed according to the usual pattern. After an irreligious childhood ('It pleased the Lord I was civilly brought up from a child, and kept from such gross evils as persons meerly civil do not allow, but otherwaies very vain'), she went through a period of faith in 'Kings and Bishops': 'I grew very superstitiously zealous in all things suitable to the service Book, or a Cathedrall kind of Worship, and I thought the more I abounded in fasting, book prayer, and observation of daies and times, mourning and afflicting my self for sin, the better it was' (10, 11). In the second phase she had 'affectionate heart-workings towards God and godliness', but was still under the law: 'the more strict I was ... the more my bondage was increased' (26). Emerging from a period of spiritual anguish into a state of contentment, she spends some years believing herself to be regenerate; but although change had taken place, it was not yet '*life by believing*' (41).

After a further period of heart-searching, reading, and discussion, Turner arrives at sanctification by faith rather than law, and along with her husband becomes a Baptist, 'being sweetly satisfied and comforted therein' (Turner 1653: 88); but then she lapses into Quakerism. This experience requires careful handling in order to preserve her own condition as elect; she needs to explain how persuasive the Quakers were, though wrong. Thus she observes 'under how many veils Satan comes ... beguiling and deceiving with the most plausible spiritual, Angel-like glorious appearances' (142); she reflects on the state of confusion and uncertainty in those days, which left many people unsettled and lacking in judgement. And she notes the particular attraction of the Quakers to people like her, who tended to:

> an extreme in minding truth as it relates to the inward man in point of experience, and inward workings; which is in it self very good; but being in an extreme on that hand, Satan took advantage by it. (Turner 1653: 151)

These repeated and contradictory conversion experiences leave her with a strong sense of the insufficiency of experience on its own to bring the believer into the true path. The problem of how we remember and understand our own experiences, at the time and with hindsight, is thus at the heart of her text, and her focus is above all on the difficulty of knowing what is actually happening. As she observes, 'there is much corrupt experience in the world, and persons have been much mistaken in their experience' (201). She thus distinguishes between 'things merely historical or traditional'—the 'simple facts' of one's life—and 'Experience from a true sanctified knowledge'—experience guided by Scripture (196). What her memory tells her is problematic; what she remembers has changed its meaning since she lived through it, and accordingly it must be re-explained.

Memory as the guarantee of autobiographical truth is a problem in these accounts. Spiritual autobiographers, urgently required to know and to speak the truth, are constantly reminded by memory of the fallibility of human judgement, and the inconsistency of self-knowledge; the spiritual journey is one of disruption and discontinuity, destabilizing knowledge of the self. At the same time they are peculiarly reliant on memory, since what they describe is above all inward states of mind and soul. The pressing question of the security of memory is resolved primarily by appeal to God as the ultimate author of the narrative. When Jane Turner expresses anxiety about the reach of her memory—'it would be very hard, if not impossible, for me to remember that which has been so long since', as well as 'fearing lest through forgetfulness as I knew I should leave out something which was, so I might possibly write something which was not'—she is reassured by God's promise that she would write 'as in his presence', and this would guarantee her truth (1653: 4). But records help too. Alice Curwen 'questioned in my Mind, Why I should write, fearing the Subtility of the Enemy, and also not minding to keep Copies of several Papers that had been written; yet as I waited patiently to see my Clearness, it was said in the secret of my Heart, *What thou hast kept, write*'; a very Quaker formulation, in its reliance simultaneously on waiting for the secret voice in the heart, and on keeping documentary records (Curwen 1680: 2). Memory is also a matter of rehearsal, as the practice of learning and repeating Biblical passages or sermons in godly households underlines; such skills can be translated into the repetition of one's own experiences. But these are still under God's eye. Anna Trapnel's complex reflections on memory suggest it is supported by repetition:

> Though I fail in an orderly penning down these things, yet not in a true Relation, of as much as I remember, and what is expedient to be written; I could not have related so much from the shallow memory I have naturally, but through often relating these

things, they become as a written book, spread open before me, and after which
I write. (Trapnel 1654a: 34)

But at the same time, in distinguishing between 'an orderly penning down' and 'a true
Relation', and implying that she copies truth from a pre-written book, Trapnel locates
truth as separate from the normal processes of memory, with sources beyond the self.

In principle memory asserts the continuity of the self: where the self and the world
have been turned upside down, memory holds old and new selves together in narrative,
giving the past a shape that conforms to the requirements of the present, and autobiography articulates that continuity. But the past is uncertain territory for these writers, as
they reflect back on the 'merely historical' and 'true sanctified knowledge': whether to
know it, how to know it, how to understand it. And so of course is the self: the establishment of the self as secure and autonomous is what must be done away with, rather than
what the autobiographical narrative is seeking to constitute. The aim of self-examination
is not, ultimately, that the past should enable you to understand and explain, but that it
should enable you to understand only so as to move rapidly on, to transcend.

Looking to the past, indeed, for many, marks an attachment to the old world, and a
refusal to allow the self to be remade. Dorothea Gotherson urges her readers to let go
of the past: 'do not longer backward turn, | But if it burn, why let it burn'; and she sum-
mons up the figure of Lot's wife who turned back to look at Sodom as they fled, and was
turned into a pillar of salt. 'And all you that are travelling out of Sodom with your faces
towards Sion,' she reminds her readers, 'look not back; remember Lot's wife' (Gotherson
1661: a3^v, 94). Gotherson's insistence on regeneration as a move from death to new life
sits uneasily with the project of looking back over her own story. Self-examination is in
tension with self-abandonment, and this tension underlies her injunction to know one's
own past, and the contrary injunction to look forward, not back. The journey desired
and described ultimately is unspeakable and incomprehensible, the stopping point of
narrative and communication: as she describes it, 'too hard to be uttered, or by you to be
borne' (93). Sion is a place without memory or narrative, so as to be, implicitly, a place
without self. It is a curious paradox that autobiography surges into popularity in order to
describe these absences.

CHAPTER 14

··

SATIRE AND POLEMIC

··

ANNE LAKE PRESCOTT

IN 1656 John Collop, a fairly tolerant royalist writing under Cromwell, lamented the proliferation of religious polemic:

> Their pens have swords bin which the Church did wound,
> Whence all these scars are on her body found.
> Polemicks of Religion sure have writ,
> Not for the truth, but exercise of wit:
> While Scriptures, Fathers, Councells, they do wrest.
> As I name them, they use their names in jest. (Collop 1962: 59)

On the facing page, however, Jesuits resemble 'empty purses open wide; | Yet nought within them, doth but air abide', and Collop had earlier lamented that the 'Itch of Dispute, the Scab of th'Church doth breed' while irritably listing '*Wickliffe, Husse*, and Malecontents of *Prague*' and '*Waldo's* Disciples, *Albigenses*'. It is easier to denounce the denunciatory than to avoid denouncing.

A discussion fully tracing 'Polemicks of Religion' in this period would be impossible. Verse satire is easily recognized, but prose debate can unexpectedly swerve into rhetorical aggression, and then there are the many verse libels, some obscene, that remained in manuscript if sometimes circulating (the Elizabethan ones now published and annotated online by Steven May and Alan Bryson).[1] What follow, then, are mere samplings of polemical writing on matters religious, from the 1520s to 1660. This exploration barely takes in drama, although Shakespeare imagines the 'puritan' spoilsport Malvolio for *Twelfth Night*, Barnabe Barnes features Pope Alexander VI in *The Divils charter*, and in *Bartholomew Fair* Ben Jonson's Zeal-of-the-Land Busy scorns pleasure until he smells roast pig. Satire was amongst the Restoration's glories, but for reasons of space this survey stops before that richly polemical (and more widely discussed) period begins.

---

[1] May and Bryson have provided a massive, edited, online collection of *Elizabethan Verse Libel*, with full introduction and notes by the editors.

Those of us writing on the Reformation must also decide on vocabulary. Are those who wanted purification 'Puritans'? The word began as an insult. The 'godly' might seem a safer term, but Jesuits, too, can be godly. What of 'Catholic'? The Church of England's creed acknowledges 'one Catholike [universal] and Apostolike Churche' (BCP 22). For convenience, I often use 'Puritan' and 'Catholic' or 'papist'; 'Anglican' is probably anachronistic. I regret the paucity of female voices in the following sample of texts, but few women joined printed religious debate with rhetorical guns blazing. As for the locations from which printed polemics emerge, some remain unknown but the books cited here were all printed in London unless otherwise indicated.

This survey will begin by examining the genres of satire and epigram and then consider two recurring targets of early modern polemics: rank and the monstrous. The chapter will end with case studies of two much-discussed polemical exchanges: Thomas More's defence of Catholicism and the satirical pamphlets known as the Marprelate tracts.

SATIRES

After Luther's storm broke, but before Henry VIII's separation from Rome, English poets gleefully deployed satires against easily parodied ecclesiastical targets. As its modern editor says, in *Rede Me and Be Nott Wrothe* by Jerome Barlowe and William Roy (Strasbourg, 1528), anti-Catholic invective, hyperbole, diatribe, and burlesque 'tumble about playfully' in this extended satirical poem (Barlowe and Roy 1992). The style may seem to be a kind of playfulness, but the teeth are bared. Sex and money figure, of course: oh the poor Mass—how will we maintain 'our whores and harlotes' in 'rhyche felicite'? Our brothels go unfunded and 'Our bastardes' must 'go astraye'. No more 'mery jestes', 'greate lordshippes', or 'rhyche juelles and sompous plate' (61–3). True, we English still keep the French pox. And that priest—is he a Lutheran? No, he has no wife, just 'whoares' (88). As polemicists of all sorts would claim about their own 'others', papists are said to prefer the many to the one: witness their profusion of saints and fictions, and their setting 'tales of Robyn hode' over Scripture (95). They turn 'olde wyves tales' into 'holy narracions' (104), using the verbal alchemy that anticipates Ananias's assurance in Jonson's *Alchemist* (1610) that although 'Bells are profane; a tune may be religious' (3.2.61) or that illegally 'coining' money might be just 'casting' metal (3.2.153). Catholics counterattacked. The prolific Miles Huggarde marshals the alphabet against heretics, for example, giving each letter a quatrain. Thus 'F: gets 'Fained falshode with flatery | Faithles folke have founde, | Faininge a face fraudelently | Frendship for to counfounde' (Huggarde 1557: A3). But Puritans knew the alphabet, too, so years later the anonymous prose *Romes ABC* (1641) would say of the 'Towred up' Archbishop Laud that he is 'A Bishop, Climbing' (A2).

One major verse satirist in the 1540s was the learned doctor Luke Shepherd. The author of polemical dialogues, he also versified in jouncing scoffs that mix Latin and

English. Thus *Phylogamus* (1548) addresses Sir John Mason: 'O Poete rare and Recent | Dedocorate | and endecent | Insolent and insensate | Contendyng and condensate | Obtused and obturate | Obumbylate, obdurate' (Shepherd 2001: xxiv, 255–60). Likewise macaronic, perhaps suggesting that priests babble in semi-Latin, are lines in *The Upcheringe of the Messe* (1548): 'Wherfore nowe totus mundus | That round is and rotundus | Be mery and Jocundus' (21). Shepherd even feigns urinary problems when pseudo-lamenting the Mass's departure: 'A good mestres missa | Shal ye go from us thissa | Wel yet I muste ye kyssa | Alacke for payne I pyssa' (24). In *Doctour doubble ale* (1548) a lascivious priest waits for a husband to go out 'aboute his busines' and then 'Before the woman he sayd Messe | And shewed his prety popishnes' (93). As for clerics' arrogant ignorance, in Shepherd's *John Bon and Mast Person [Parson]* (1548), a puzzled John, hearing of 'corpus christi', asks, 'What saynt is copsi cursty a man or a woman?' A man, says the priest: 'Christe his owne selfe', whom we carry in the procession. But can a whole man fit in that little glass? The parson sneers that he would rather not reason with 'a stubble cur that eateth beanes and peason' (50). There were other pre-Elizabethan satires, of course, such as William Kethe's *Ballet declaringe the fal of the whore of babylone* (1548), which tells Rome that her rites are mere cheating and rejoices at her exile.[2] The title page of the more socially radical Robert Crowley's 1551 satire *Philargyrie of greate Britayne* (Crowley 1980) shows a well-dressed figure grabbing coins. As Crowley explains, ancient papal greed has passed to England's new secular giant, silver-lover Philargyrie, who cries: 'Brynge, bryng bryng, bryng | Alwaye somethynge'.[3]

This link between religious reform and social justice never disappeared, but formal verse satire in the 1590s usually has a different tone. Nor would it surprise Augustan satirists (Roman or British) that this satire is conservative, directed at the *ec-centric* and *de-viant*. Some, for example, parodies puritan speech. Such jargon is meant to sound godly, but it constructs verbal barriers between its self-important users and ordinary subjects. Although less given to specialized vocabulary, Catholics are likewise portrayed as eccentric and deviant, loyal to distant Rome. Formal satire glistening with real or assumed cultural confidence, and whatever its mockery of sin and crime, would long remain more implicitly defensive than Huggarde or Shepherd would have liked. One example is John Marston's 1596 *Satyres*. 'Satyre 2' singles out 'yonder sober man, | That same devout meale-mouth'd Precisean ['precisians' exaggerate doctrinal distinctions and minor misbehaviors] | That cries *good brother, kind sister,* makes a duck [bow] | After the Antique grace, can alwayes pluck | A sacred booke, out of his civill hose' [his costume implying the London citizenship associated with puritan merchants] (Marston 1961: ll. 72–6). He then cries 'O manners! Ô times of impurity', imagining 'a church reformed state, | The which the female tongues magnificate' and admiring Plato's communism (ll. 55–68); yet in fact

---

[2] King 1982 describes other satires not included here.
[3] Crowley 1980: 46–75; see also Jones 2011.

he's a 'vile, sober, damn'd, Politician' and usurer (ll. 70, 74–5). Satyre 4 notes the 'Heretick' who thinks one church unholy because once 'defil'd with Popish showes. | The Bells profane and not to be endur'd' (ll. 65–7). Two years later, 'Satyre 8' in *The Scourge of Villanie* (1598) offers a Puritan in love—while laughing at papist idolatry, he worships his mistress with the 'oyle of Sonnets', exorcisms, charms, even thinking the pin with which she scratches herself a 'sacred relique' (90, 101). In *Satyre IX* Curus 'babbles' of 'deepe Divinitie' but lives 'like a Bacchanall', a 'ranke Puritan' dropping such phrases as '*Good brother, sister deere*' but loving 'belly cheere' (106–14). The issue is less belief than the distance between conviction (if any) and action, between word and thing.

Another satirist in the Roman style was the future bishop, Joseph Hall. Hall rejects moderation: in *Virgidemiarum* (1598), Hall asserts that, to be helpfully medicinal, instructive, or punitive, satire must 'be like the Porcupine, | That shoots sharpe quils out in each angry line, | And wounds the blushing cheeke, and fiery eye' of the guilty (Hall 1969: V, 3). Some 'quils' target Catholics, such as one title's punning jeer: *PΩMH PYMH* ['Rome/Rheum'] (IV.7). Rome has melted into Papacy, and 'When once I thinke if carping *Aquines* [Juvenal's] spright | To see now Rome, were licenc'd to the light; | How his enraged Ghost would stampe and stare | That *Caesars* throne is turn'd to *Peters* chayre'. Juvenal, Hall asserts, would be astounded by:

> th'horned Miter, and the bloudy hat,
> The crooked staffe, their coules [cowls'] strang forme and store,
> Saue that he saw the same in hell before,
> To see their broken Nuns with new-shorne heads,
> In a blind Cloyster tosse their idle Beades. (9–12; 21–6)

The satire is a lament, but without the ambivalence that could show grief for ruins yet find room/Rome for later poets. Hall's Rome is fallen in another sense: decadent, being unnaturally celibate yet oversexed, its variety proudly costumed and its leisure mere lazy ignorance.

Hall's taste for puns also informs his 1603 epigram on the Jesuit Robert Bellarmine, playing with 'BELLA sonat, sonat ARMA', and that same year saw a welcome to James I glancing at that 'stale strumpet of imperious *Rome*, | Hie mounted on her seuen-headed beast, | Quaffing the bloud of Saints in boules of gold' (*The Kings Prophecie*, st. 11). The next stanza turns to 'those swarmes of Locusts sent, | Hell's cursed off-spring, hyred slaues of Spaine', whom the margin identifies as Jesuits. What locusts do by slithering in half-hidden masses along branches and the ground, Jesuits do with their tongues: equivocate. No wonder that 1641 saw a pseudo-genealogy for the Pope, *The lineage of Locusts*, or that Phineas Fletcher had called his mini-epic on Jesuits *Locustae* (printed with a translation in 1627). Fletcher describes in proto-Miltonic terms a great consult in Hell that inspires Satan to send Ignatius to destroy England and Fawkes to explode Parliament. Again, papists are depicted as multiple, and sneaky. Here is the Whore of Babylon, cousin of *The Faerie Queene*'s witchy Duessa, with Duessa's pseudo-clerical friend Archimago reborn as 'Equivocus' (F3^v), whom the margin names 'Ignatius':

> To every shape his changing shape is drest,
> Oft seemes a Lambe and bleates, a Wolfe and houles:
> Now like a Dove appeares with candide brest,
> Then like a Falcon, preyes on weaker soules:
> A Badger neat, that flies his 'filed nest:
> But most a Fox, with stinke his cabin foules:
>   A Courtier, Priest, transform'd to thousand fashions,
>   His matter fram'd of slight equivocations,
> His very forme was form'd of mentall reservations. (Fletcher 1627: F4)

As the narrator asks, 'But who can summe this holy rablement?' (Fletcher 1627: J4^v).

In fact, some did indeed try to 'summe' up the opposition. 1641 saw *A Discovery of 29. Sects here in London* that listed 'Protestants', who are 'good', and twenty-eight other 'Divelish' sects from 'Puritans' to 'The Brotherhood', while 1645 brought *XXXVI Several Religions Held And maintained by the Cavaliers*, with a list from 'Cardinals' to 'Shee-Cavaliers'. More conventional is Everard Guilpin's *Skialetheia or A Shadowe of Truth* (1598). With less extreme polemic than Hall or Marston on religious dissent, Guilpin still worries about an acquaintance who seems 'outlandish', turning Dutch or maybe Spanish: now spitting 'controuersies' and now 'prates of *Bellarmine*' (Guilpin 1974). The danger here is that it is impossible to know what such a person really thinks.

The greatest satirist of the 1590s is John Donne, later Dean of St. Paul's, a convert from the Catholicism for which his brother had been martyred. His beliefs and satires have been subjected to extensive debate.[4] If some critics find in him a persisting sympathy for Rome, the satirical *Ignatius His Conclave* (1611) with Loyola as an 'innovator' fit to preside in Hell with Satan and Copernicus suggests little nostalgia. His sermons gesture at toleration, however, and it seems unlikely that he welcomed the fires or ropes that some recusants faced. His satires may register the pain of one who has left the faith of his birth but will not damn those making other choices, and who understands the terror of living under a regime sharp-eyed for signs of sedition, fearing that one of the 'Giant Statutes' might 'ope his jaw | To sucke me in' (Donne 2001: 'Satire IV', 132–3).

In Donne's first satire, based on Horace's Satire I.9 and his effort to shake off a tiresome companion, the speaker and this 'motley humorist' go out into London; among other sights is a 'monstrous, superstitious puritan, | Of refin'd manners, yet ceremonial man', in truth more interested in wealth (Donne 2001: 'Satire I', 27–8). The second satire notes ironically that poets are 'poore, disarm'd, like Papists, not worth hate' (9–10) and mentions 'ruin'd Abbeyes' (60), relics (84), and Luther on the Lord's prayer (92–6). As for himself, 'meanes [moderation] blesse', although ostensibly he has left religious

---

[4] See, in particular, Papazian 2003 and Kneidel 2011b. For a full discussion of Donne's religious writings, see chapter 21 of this volume.

disputes and 'my words none drawes | Within the vast reach of th'huge statute lawes' (111–12). The celebrated third satire considers the search for one truth in a world of multiplicity (with a comparison, perhaps taken from Rabelais, to finding a faithful wife). Thus Mirreus thinks Truth lives in Rome, Crantz looks to Geneva, and Graius finds her in the English church. Because some women are *whores*, Phrygius ab*hors* all, but Graccus loves all: churches resemble women—different costumes, same bodies. Truth herself stands atop a hill, and to win her we 'about must and about must go' (81). Donne has no satisfying advice on the climb, for the exhortation to ask one's father to ask his and so on assumes maternal fidelity. Nor do his fourth and fifth satires offer answers. The fourth returns to Horace and the 'monster' pest. Some allusions are weighted: the speaker has been in 'A Purgatorie', for instance (1. 3), and mentions 'Ten Cardinalls' (l. 214), the Inquisition, Jesuits, and the Calvinist Beza. The discussion of who is the 'best linguist' (l. 53) recalls Reformers' insistence on knowing not just Latin but Hebrew and Greek for biblical scholarship. Donne has also been reading Menippean satires; scholars usually identify the one who 'dreamt he saw hell' in a 'trance' (ll. 157–8) as Dante, but Donne may remember Caelius Curio's anti-Jesuit satire *Pasquin in a Traunce* (1566). The final hope that 'some wise man' shall 'esteeme my writs Canonicall' (l. 244) furthermore again evokes debates, this time over the biblical canon itself. The fifth satire is less risky, but we still hear of a 'Pursivant' (l. 65), doubtless on the alert for subversion.

Verse satire continued, needless to say, if often in manuscript. The online *Early Stuart Libels*, edited by Alastair Bellany and Andrew McRae, includes a vast range of polemical satires, epigrams, and even epitaphs such as that on Archbishop Bancroft's hypocrisy in keeping 'open a Back dore | To let in the Strumpet of Rome' (Bellany and McRae B20).

EPIGRAMS

Thanks in part to the 1599 ban issued by church authorities, the fashion for printed satire would fade for a time, but satire's baby brother the epigram flourished, often indebted to the Roman poet Martial, for whom scorn compressed was scorn intensified. Some epigrams are polemical by nature. Even for a radical like Crowley, the objects of contempt can be those unwilling to conform, who have become ridiculous by being marginal. Few epigrams achieve profundity, although most are deeper than Henry Hutton's punning suggestion in *Follie's Anatomie* that 'Purus doth sermons write, & scripture quote; | And therefore may be tearm'd a man of Note' (Hutton 1619: C4). The number of packed scoffs is beyond huge, and I cite only a few. Some themes recur: Catholic disloyalty and ecclesiastical corruption, but also puritan pride, stinginess, or loquacity. Sex and scatology figure, as do greed and the diversity of what fools and villains affirm or produce.

The most impressive early Tudor epigrams are in the Latin of Thomas More, but soon came more polemical ones. Thus the authors of *Rede me and be nott Wrothe* imagine a coat of arms for 'the prowde Cardinall' Wolsey: borne by two devils, it shows 'sixe blouddy axes in a bare felde', representing the infertile cruelty of this 'red man', 'red', presumably, because blood-stained as well as wearing the Cardinal's scarlet (Barlowe and Roy 1528: ai[v]). Soon such poems could be printed in England. Crowley's *One and thyrtye epigramms* (1550) condemns 'Obstinate Papistes' who sneak to the Continent, but also highlights a corrupt multiplicity best punished by multiplicity: a cleric with many livings should be chopped up and each piece sent to one benefice (Crowley 1550: Dviii[v]–Ei[v]). After Elizabeth's accession, anti-papist rhetoric spread. Claiming to be 'juvenilia', for example, are Latin epigrams in Bishop John Parkhurst's *Ludicra* (1573). 'Alexander [VI] was no eunuch: Lucretia you see | was his wife, daughter, and daughter-in-law', says one (Parkhurst 1573: N2). As for papist Mr Knotts ('Nodosium'): 'On the appointed days, Knotts abstains from flesh. | On no day does Knotts abstain from flesh. | How do you figure that, you ask? | He shrinks back from dead flesh, | But embraces the living' (Parkhurst 1573: O1).

Timothy Kendall's *Flowers of Epigrammes* (1577), which translates many Latin epigrams, some Catholic and some by such Reformation stars as Theodore Beza, likewise imagines Catholicism as corrupt and over-sexed. If the Pope, for example will not save his flock 'from wolves devouring throate', at least 'be not a wolfe thy selfe, | clad in a sheepskin coate' (Kendall 1577: F3). The epigram 'To certaine proude Papisticall persones' concedes that we may call priests 'Fathers' because, after all, 'brats you get amaine' (N5[v]). As for (the mythical) Pope Joan, Rome's 'Carnals' (or he should say 'Cardinalls') now prove their masculinity by filling Rome with bastards and whores (N6). Another epigram, on black-hooded Benedictines, plays on 'Cullus' (hood) and 'Culus' (ass). Kendall notes the supposed incest of Alexander VI (O5[v]), which was also the butt of jokes by Barnes and Parkhurst, above. A fine chronogram gives the date of the Pope's failed effort to kill Elizabeth, and the same volume offers, among many other gems, a comparison of papists and poets and a lively story about popes and peacocks (Kendall 1577: R1[v], R5, R3[v]). The finery of church leaders invited scatology and their stress on chastity invited sexual innuendo, of course, yet at the other extreme the 'Rump Parliament' of the Civil Wars inevitably elicited many jokes. The rudest—aside from *A new Sect of Religion Descryed, called Adamites* (1641) with a title page showing one naked Adamite poking another's erection and saying 'Downe Proud Flesh Downe'—may be a 1661 image in which a Puritan bends over with a rod up his rump so he can serve as a sundial.[5] True, William Winstanley's *Protestant Almanack* (Cambridge, 1669), calculated 'for the Meridian of Babylon, where the Pope is Elevated Ninety Degrees above all Reason, Right, and Religion, above Kings, Canons, Councils, Conscience, and Every Thing that is called God', shows how to mark time by the (Spanish?) nose of a hanging Jesuit (Winstanley 1669: B4).

If much satire was aimed at Puritans' hypocritical rejection of pleasure, the Pope could be similarly scorned. One epigram in Thomas Bastard's *Chrestoleros* (1598) notes that, since the Pope could kill a French king (Henri III) who supported him, it follows

---

[5] See Jenner 2002 for more images, and Greenblatt (1982).

that Elizabeth is safe (D6^v). Another of his epigrams claims that in springtime, when 'sappy Nature' makes roots bloom, the Pope forbids such innocent 'meates' as 'Egs, cheese, butter and milke, and all save hey'; not content to kill the soul, the Pope 'would kill the body to[o]' (Bastard 1598: L2). Thomas Freeman's *Rubbe and A great Cast* (1614) derides both religious extremes. One puritan preacher never cites the Fathers, calling Scripture 'all-sufficient'. Why? 'He ner'e learn'd *Latine*, never read a *Father*' (B3). As for Catholics, one papist courtesan calls herself just that and is regarded as a rarity for her honesty: 'A thing in these our daies to wonder at, | A *Catholicke* not know t'quivocat' (Freeman 1614: C2^v). Other epigrams make the common assumption about priestly sex. In Richard Brathwaite's *Strappado for the Divell* (1615), a priest comes in the dark to absolve a virgin—months later, the result is born (I6). Perhaps Brathwaite's cleverest epigram, though not the sexiest, explores the varied meanings of 'Rome'. A gentleman has 'entreated the Author to distinguish twixt Rome and roome' (then pronounced alike). Rome, he replies, is 'as farre from roome, as Peter [from the] Pope'. He needs room, but not Rome, and although the Pope claims Peter's chair, that's not truly 'his roome'. The epigram/sonnet concludes with distinction between Peter and Pope: '*Peter Romes piller, Cater piller he*' (Brathwaite 1615: 66). Such anti-papist epigrams proliferated, as witness one in John Owen's *Epigrams*, translated from the Latin by John Vicars (1619), which tells a lady that 'With *Papists*, *Gellia*, thou didst e're take part' but she is now worse. Why? '*Catholike* thou art' (E5). Owen puns on 'catholic' as 'universal', but again we hear unease over what is multiple, profligate. Whores, after all, service varied customers: '*Catholike* Love, (I thinke) to *All* thou'lt show' (D4^v). But Owen also argues that the Catholics' frequent fasting from meat, permitting only the eating of fish instead, is a negative phenomenon, merely a way to '*declare*, that *Peters Chaire* | They rightly doe retayne'. For Peter, explains a note, '*was a Fisher*' (Owen 1619: E6^v). Edward May's *Epigrams Divine and Morall* (1633) plays, rather, on the Latin for wolf: 'Papists say' that Franciscan garments will scare away the devil, but Satan can still recognize the monk Lupus as 'a knave' (D1). Other lines note papal corruption and sexual cynicism (May 1633: E3, D3^v).

One would expect writers to distinguish between papist and Puritan, one corruptly rich and the other vaingloriously virtuous, but the concerns overlap: hypocrisy, lust, and (despite reformers' desire for plainness) variability. Like papists, the zealous are refusers, *recusants*. That may be why Owen can address both 'The *Romish Masse-Priest*, and *Genevian Minister*' (Owen 1619: D3). Puritans can slither, too—for, as Henry Parrot says in *Cures for the Itch* (1626), one '*Promus* the Puritaine no longer feares' losing his 'Asses eares': in 'spite of threats or epigram', he says, he can move 'hence to *Amsterdam*', a place which offered safety for Protestants (Parrot 1626: E4^v). To a large extent, epigrammatists can find both papist and Puritan corrupt, oversexed, unpatriotic, and betraying the One. Puritans may advocate simplicity, but they know that reform itself can generate sections/sects. Anti-papist and anti-puritan were not always opposites.

Brathwaite's *Strappado* thus both laughs at the man who slew his cat for killing mice on the Sabbath, and tells of 'Sir *Sensuall* (a wanton Priest)' who shrives a kneeling girl and drops his breeches, 'blowing' her down [seducing her] and claiming a right to 'all *wind-falls*' (Brathwaite 1615: I4ᵛ). For Joseph Martyn, author of *New epigrams* (1621), it is godly hypocrisy that irritates: the name 'Puritan', Martyn writes, 'doth shew his [the Puritan's] nature to be pure', as demonstrated by his swearing only when the '*Spirit*' moves and his loving not only 'his neighbour' but also 'his neighbours wife' (Martyn 1621: B4). No wonder that such men's loquacity seemed vexing, as did their preference for sermons over ritual; puritan sermonizers are mocked for simply not stopping, whatever their hourglass might say, or for not even speaking normally. In his *Two bookes of epigrammes* (1639), Thomas Bancroft mocks the 'iron *Lungs*' and '*throat* of brass' of Vicar Blunder (I, 99), a 'deepe mouth'd' pulpit '*Thumper*' who lets Love go cold but wears garments himself 'because' tis hottest so' (Bancroft 1639: C8ᵛ). This pulpit-thumper is male, but in 1651 John Taylor, writing after the 'turbulent' churchmen had taken over, addresses '*Devout* Margery': she can 'spin a Lecture' and 'stand and preach as long as she can stir. | It is not standing long can trouble her', with a play on 'standing'—Puritans are so stiff (Taylor 1651: A3). Sir John Harington, Elizabeth's godson, translator of Ariosto and celebrator of the flush toilet, also liked writing epigrams. In the collection of his epigrams published posthumously in 1615, one poem laughs at a cleric whose sermons outlast his hourglass (IV, 90). Another clergyman, singing Genevan psalms as he rides along, refuses to give a blind man a coin but says he will bless him instead. Oh, retorts the beggar, 'Priests have learnd, to bless without a cross', mocking Puritan objections to making the sign of the cross and alluding to the English coin with an engraved one (Harington 2009: I, 30).

Harington, though, was not always comfortable with such wit. As I have noted, some satirists and epigram writers longed for a sweeter atmosphere even while souring it, and I offer two more epigrams as examples of ambivalence. The first, worth setting next to Donne's 'Satire III', is Harington's complaint against 'Pure Lynus', who accuses him of 'papistry'. No, says Harington, he is a 'christian Catholicque' (recalling the official creed's commitment to 'one Catholike' church): the names 'Baptist, and Hugonot, | Brownist and Zuinglian' merely 'factions feede' (Harington 2009: III, 45). This was no doubt true, although Harington, if not using such names, had not always been as irenic as this epigram suggests. Years later, when Britain was tormented by worse divisions, Samuel Sheppard in 1651 would address 'pamphleters' with greater vexation:

> Forbeare fond *Pamphleters*, forbeare to vex,
> The giddy world, as with an *Apoplex*,
> Cease rayling *Rabsocka's* cease to disclose,
> And vent such poyson in prophaner Prose,
> Whose *Basilisk*-like Vapors seeme t'impaire
> The squeasie temper of the troubled Ayre. (Sheppard 1651: M1ᵛ)

Venting 'poyson', however, did not cease—and because some of that 'rayling' was directed downwards, a discussion of the importance of social rank in early modern satirical religious writing seems relevant at this point.

SATIRE AND RANK

Climbing from the shop, farm, or stable to the pulpit or its godly equivalent worried many; had not some pre-Lutheran rebels asked, 'When Adam delved and Eve span | Who was then the gentleman?' Yes, David's sheephook became a sceptre, but God propelled that ascent. Ordinary shepherds must stay with their flocks. For some, though, the Reformation brought hope for change, and the late medieval *Piers Ploughman* saw new life as a proto-Protestant satire in which virtues denied the clergy were given to shepherds (Jones 2011: 4; King 1982; Prescott 2000). Eventually not only artisans and farmers but also women would presume to preach. What would they demand next? This nervousness was a departure from early satire, which together with cheerful vulgarity like that in Shepherd's *Upchereinge* or *Pierce the Ploughmans Crede* (*c*.1553) often allowed religious insight to those uncorrupted by money, power, or place. Thus Crowley's *One and thyrtye Epigrammes* can both urge 'Obstinate Papistes' to obey 'their naturall prynce' and blast 'rente raysers' who hurt their tenants (Crowley 1550: E1–E2). In 1589, when such a tone was for the moment diminished, William Roy's *O Read me for I am of great Antiquitie* was published more than fifty years after his death and claimed to be by 'plaine Piers', the grandsire of Martin Marprelate (see section below). Importantly, the text can still say 'But comfort yee yee plough man, Fishers, Tylers, and cobblers' (Roy 1589: C2)—for Christ was poor, and remember Lazarus and Dives.

That Peter was a fisherman and Joseph a carpenter did not stop satirists sympathetic to bishops and ritual from scoffing at radicals in terms affirming social hierarchy: render unto the bishops that which is the bishops'. John Taylor was no gentleman, but his *Swarme of Sectaries, and Schismatiques* (1641), according to its subtitle, attacks 'the strange preaching (or prating) of such as are by their trades Coblers, Tinkers, Pedlers, Weavers, Sow-gelders, and Chymney-Sweepers' (Taylor 1641: title page). A woodcut shows such a preacher exhorting his listeners from a tub. 'Unseemly 'tis a Judge should milke a Cowe', says a prefatory poem; 'A Cobler to a Pulpit should not mount, | Nor can an Asse cast up a true account. | A Clowne to sway a Scepter is too base, | And Princes to turn Pedlers were disgrace' (Taylor 1641: 2–3). These nonconformist 'Vermin', complains an epigram, 'swarm like Caterpillars', holding 'Conventicles in Barnes and Sellars' (7). Taylor's most intense satire is of a 'famous preaching Cobler', a 'holy Brother of the Separation' and his 'postures and impostures' (8–9). Preaching 'like a man inspir'd from Amsterdam', he 'clouted' his text and 'welted' his sermon: 'Gainst Schooles, and learning he exclaim'd amain, | Tongues, Science, Logick, Rhetorick, all are vain' (9). Were the Apostles scholarly? No, says Taylor, but after they died we needed those who could translate the Word into various languages in these later days. Let dolts who claim to be inspired by the Spirit show their credentials by preaching to Moors, Indians, and 'Man-eating Canniballs' (Taylor 1641: 12).

The same impatience, if not as much snobbery, appears in John Earle's witty *Microcosmographie* (1628), a collection of 'characters' that includes both 'A Church-Papist' (no. 11) who conforms outwardly but prefers 'hatching plots against the State', and a 'A Shee-precise Hypocrite' (no. 45) who wears a Geneva ruff, likes two-hour sermons, is vexed that women cannot preach, is 'fiery against the May-pole', and names her daughter 'Hannah' instead of 'Anne' (Earle 1628: C7, C8; H6ᵛ, H9ᵛ, H8). It was Thomas Bancroft, though, who perfected the lofty sneer, imagining in his *Two bookes of epigrammes* a pulpit that complains punningly about a liar who misquotes the fathers and distorts his text; let him imitate the beggar who 'on a Sunny day | Does by his Lice, throw baser lies away' (Bancroft 1639: E1). In *Time's out of Tune* (1658), Bancroft is yet clearer. The title page flashes lines from Juvenal and the dedication to Charles Cotton recycles the porcupine quill pun while anticipating bolts from 'squint ey'd Malevolo's' (Bancroft 1658: A3). 'Satyre II', entitled 'Against Sectaries' (8), offers a parody of nonconformist sermonizing. He once attended a radical service, the narrator reports, hiding behind a screen to muffle his laughter. 'Up stands a fellow with a face of brass, | And a great wood-land beard'. Clearly a hedger, he stretches out his 'pawes, | As Sun-burnt as they had been Cancers [i.e. crab's] clawes' and preaches (8). The preacher reports that he had himself once heard a sermon by someone with 'learned gear' who talked of Jerome and Augustine, of 'Figures, Dialects, Concordances' and such 'rough gibberish', yet, he adds, 'I and my neighbour *Twizzel* can out-preach | Twenty such Doctours' (8). Why learn 'Outlandish Tongues'? '*Latine* is *Babylonish*, fit for Stews | The *Greek* for Heathens, *Hebrew* for the Jews' (8). The narrator leaves, furious to hear 'Rusticks' and 'Goat-herds' play the pastor (11). Alas for learning, its bays blasted by 'the contemptuous and contentious breath | Of Schismaticks'; may 'fair Science' recover and 'more bright appear' (Bancroft 1658: 13, 15).

Bancroft's wishes would be granted, at least officially, but the relation of class and education to the re-established church remained complex. So, too, did another matter that requires a brief detour here: whose church is closest to apostolic belief and organization? Which is the original, legitimate, apostolic church, built, as Jesus foretold, on the rock of Peter? For Christians, both Testaments are inspired; the new law does not abolish the old but fulfils it. Yet the stress on Christ and the injunction to put on the 'new man' privileges a *new* birth, a *new* Adam—Jacob, not Esau—so Reformation leaders claimed to be restoring an ancient truth long obscured by greed, confusion, innovation, and pride (Barnett 1999). Evidence and logic helped them to demonstrate this. In his *Tryall of the new* [i.e., Catholic] *religion* (1608), Thomas Bell worked through thirty topics, from the name 'Pope' to 'generall Councell', ending most sections with 'Ergo' or 'I must conclude that' the belief or practice in question 'is a rotten ragge of the New Religion' (Bell 1608: D3ᵛ). Similarly, Samson Lennard's translation of a tract by J.-P. Perrin calls itself *Luthers Fore-runners: or a Cloud of Witnesses* (1624), and George Webbe's *Catalogus Protestantium: or, the Protestants kalender* tracks martyrdoms backward through the centuries to show that Reformers are not '*Novelists*'. So much for 'Our Priests and Jesuites', whose 'unpleasant clamorous, and obstriperous sound' resembles that of 'Frogs and Locusts' that have 'beene croaking and throtling out his harsh note and noyse to every Protestant passenger, *Where was your Church before LVTHER?*' (Webbe 1624: ¶1–1ᵛ). Thomas Bedford uses this same image from Revelation, noting in *Luthers Predecessours* that 'Amongst all those Creatures that yeeld an unpleasant sound', none 'are so clamorous and obstreperous, as Frogs, and Locusts; these by land, the other by water, saluting each passenger' with '*Where was your Church before Luther?*' (Bedford 1624: A3).

Others have similar arguments, with a vigour suggesting unease. Richard Bernard's *Looke beyond Luther* (1623) denies that England's church is an 'upstart Religion, a patcherie of Judaisme, Paganisme and Heresie' (A3ᵛ). No—the English church does not stand through 'humane devices, faire shewes to the eyes, delights to the eare', nor by 'Satanicall delusions, fabulous narrations, feigned miracles, deceitfull jugglings; nor by pretended apparitions of Angels, or of soules departed; nor by the bare authoritie of mens sayings, Decrees of corrupt Councels, Popes sentences, … idle customes, examples of ignorant forefathers' nor 'by furious and forcible meanes; as by fire and fagot, massacres, treasons, poysons, and stabbing of Kings, and Gun-powder-plots' (Bernard 1623: C2). William Guild's *Popish Glorying in Antiquity* (1627) tosses related insults: '*Romanists*', he says, have in 'sundry wayes' spoiled the 'famous works of the Lords Worthies' by 'intermingling their language of *Babel*, with the language of *Bethel*; and so making their Books lyke a Lincie-woolsie Garment' (Guild 1627: A6).

Monsters

Such reckless ecclesiastical 'intermingling', such mixing, can remind us of those other mixtures that are called monsters, for they often star in satire and polemic. As etymology suggests, 'monsters' show, de*monstra*te. Some are giants, whose huge mouths can, for example, suggest supposed Catholic delusions about the Eucharist, about eating God (Prescott 1999). Other monsters indicate God's anger or portend the Apocalypse, but some, real or fantasized, warn us against papists or Puritans. They can lurk in satirical texts, such as the baby in I.L.'s *A true and perfecte description* (1590), begotten on Pope Sixtus V by Satan and born with Spain's king as his right arm, a Jesuit as his left, a many-headed tail, a cardinal as one leg, a bishop as the other, and a wine barrel for a belly. Verses on Catholic sodomy, murders, and ambition follow. This book contains no illustrations, but *images* of monsters were common and texts on such creatures can deduce warning or punishment (Crawford 2005; Spinks 2009). A monster emerging from the Tiber in late 1495 fascinated Luther and many others; Philip Melanchthon's 1523 allegorization appeared in John Barthlett's *Pedegrewe of Heretiques* (1566), and John Brooke printed a translation in 1579, together with an image of a more northern 'mooncalf'.[6] The monster had an ass's head, breasts, scales, one cloven foot and one with talons, and two heads on its backside that some said spewed evil texts (like the book-vomiting Error in Spenser's *Faerie Queene* I.i.20). Huggarde's *Displaying of the Protestants* (1556), on the

---

[6] Melanchthon 1579. For a full discussion of this 'icon of the Papal Antichrist in Reformation Polemics', see Buck 2014. For our most famous 'mooncalf' (however he was costumed), see Stephano's insult to Caliban in Shakespeare's *The Tempest* III.ii.

other hand, exploits the mooncalf to demonstrate heresy's 'innumerable opinions, and one so contrary to another, that they agre[e] like germaines lippes' (A6ᵛ).

The assumptions generating monsters are intriguing: truth is simple, symmetrical, clear, whereas heresy is misshapen, manifold, outsized, and generative. Understandably, some who illustrated falsity liked trees. Thomas Stapleton's 1565 translation of Fridericus Staphylus' *Apologie* (1558), for example, shows a married arboreal Luther, mooncalf at his root, branching into Zwingli and Melanchthon, who sprout twigs with crowds of labelled leaves (Staphylus 1565: f. 118). Also impressive is the tree illustrating Stanislaus Hozjusz's *Most Excellent Treatise of the begynnyng of heresyes in oure tyme* (translated by Richard Shacklock and, like Stapleton's Staphylus, published in Antwerp in 1565). From 'Rebellion', rooted in 'Rayling', comes foliage of 'atheisme' and 'lyes'. The author stands by with a hatchet while 'Sathan', grinning, holds a whip. Power feared rebellion— but also the profusion of what Satan, says the accompanying poem, begets of 'synfull doctrine' (Hozjusz 1565: aii, aiᵛ). No wonder that, soon after James's accession in 1603, Gabriel Powel's *Refutation of an epistle apologeticall written by a puritan-papist* aims at both locust-like papists and those tolerating 'diversitie of Opinions' (Powel 1605: B1). No monster is pictured, but two years later, on the title page of Robert Pricket's *The Jesuits Miracles*, we find an image of a monstrous head of wheat containing a 'Wondrous Child'—a warning against Jesuits, say the accompanying verses (Pricket 1607). Not all printed monsters were illustrated, but they could be imagined. Lawrence Humphrey's *View of the Romish hydra and monster* (1588) has no pictures but defends its title: 'To passe ouer the corruptions of doctrine, This second Monster of *Rome*, this *Hydra* is of many heades: These Actions of *Popes* are diuerse, both here seen and felt, and vnderstood abroad, and euery where practised' (Humphrey 1588: *2ᵛ).

A monster sent by Pius V figures in Thomas Norton's 1570 *Disclosing of the great [papal] Bull*. Father of 'the famous Monecalfe', the papal monster makes 'calues' only after its crown is shaven (A2ᵛ)—like a monk's, presumably with an implied pun on *calvus*, Latin for 'bald'. May some 'valiant *Theseus*' guide us from this sinfully begotten Minotaur, pleads the author (Norton 1570: A4ᵛ). Two generations later, an anonymous petition to Charles I, published in Amsterdam in 1628, pictures the Dutch 'heretic' Arminius (Protestant but preaching tolerance) with a windmill on his head and a monk blowing in his ear while he himself is holding hands with a female Pope seated on her many-headed Beast (see Figure 14.1).[7] The civil wars brought more monsters. Two headless babies, for example, were born to papist mothers: Mistress Haughton, who laughingly cut off her cat's ears to make it a 'roundhead' (*A declaration* 1646: A3), and Mary Adams, who called herself the Virgin Mary and 'cursed the Independents' (*The Ranters Monster* 1652: title page, A5). The almost identical illustrations show infants with faces in their chests, like members of a traditional monster race. More impressive is *The Kingdomes Monster Uncloaked* (1643), a broadside showing a four-armed Cavalier who

---

[7] The petition is untitled but the opening lines of the verse printed beneath it are: 'Great king protect us with thy gratious hand | Or else Armenius will o're spred this land.' See Figure 14.1.

Veritas

Heresia

Hendrick Laurentz excud. Amstelrodam. 1628

GReat King protect vs with thy gratious hand,
Or elfe *Arminius* will o're fpred this Land:
For if in *England* th'enemy doth appeare,
This is the fhape of him we need to feare.
He raifeth Factions, and that brings in iarres,
Which broacheth Errors, and vpholds the wars:
The *Netherlands* ruine, he fought to bring.
In *England* now he doth the felfe fame thing.
To rayle, to write, to publifh bitter gall,
To change Religion, and fubuert vs all.
His Squint-ey'd lookes & *Lupa-Wolfa* gowne,
Shewes how Religion he wil foone throw down.
His grynding pate with weather-Cocks turn'd
Seeketh the *Churches* tenets for to ftaine: (braine,
The Chriftal ftreams of truth he ftuns moft pure,
The tryall of *Gods* word he'le not endure:
But vnto *Error* caft his blinking eye,
Prefuming *Truth* doth not the fame efpie.
Herefie vpon a ftately *Beaft* doth ftand,
Arminius bids him welcome, holds his hand.

Truth by her brightneffe, and her fincere heart,
Shewes that with *Herefie* fhee takes no part.
Treades on their *Mountebanke* & *Cozning* tricks,
Blowne in his eares, by *Pelagius* and *Iefuites*.
Which makes his *Wind-mil* for promotions grate
Publifh his Bookes abroad in euery place:
And begs protection for his workes of wonder.
Which againft *Truth* he bellowes forth likethun—
Thus doth *Arminius* to preferment rife,   (der.
By Equiuocating and his *Cheuerill* lyes:
And *Truth* to all appeales to open view,
Bidding all Herefies for ere adew   (heart
Defiring our great C H A R L E S to take to
And by the Parlament make *Arminius* fmart.
Which being done *England* fhall euer bleffe
The *King*, the *State*, the *Churches* happineffe,
And if for telling truth, I burne or frye;
What then deferues he that tels a lye?

FINIS.   1628.

FIGURE 14.1 'Great king protect us', an anonymous petition presented to Charles I (Amsterdam, 1628); shelfmark 4° C 80 (1*) Th. Reproduced by kind permission of The Bodleian Libraries, The University of Oxford.

carries Parliament and a firebrand, wears one leg booted and spurred and another foppish, with three heads indicating 'PaPist' [punning on 'pissed'] conspirators', 'Mallignant plotters', and 'Bloudy Irishe'. The chief figure's 'Spanish Ruffe' shows it 'halfe a Papist, and halfe Cavalier' (*Kingdomes Monster* 1643: n.p.). That same year came another broadside polemic: a seven-headed figure with clerical headgear has the Pope astride its barrel-body as well as skeleton archers, scorpion tail, and monks extending chalices to catch skulls from the creature's anus. Lines by John Vicars explain the image, with alliteration ('Romes Rabble rankly rife', '*Romes* all-rotten Reliques'), puns ('hollow-Holinesse'), and rhyme ('So fill'd, are swill'd'). Behold fallen Babylon and its 'Babylonish Blasphemies', the poem urges (Vicars 1643: n.p.), but we also behold filth and obscenity: error is excremental and lawless.

A whore and hence female, the Pope is polemically portrayed as inherently monstrous. S/he appears most colourfully in *Wonderfull Newes of the Death of Paule the III* (1552), translated by William Baldwin from an original probably by Pier Paolo Vergerio (Baldwin 1552).[8] Marke Forius (the Roman statue Marforius on whom one could post libels) writes a warning letter to his friend Publius Esquillus (the statue Pasquil) relating how Pope Paul III enters Hell with an admiring devil escort; dressed as a woman, he has fiery snakes around his hem and images of his sins. He is attended by Egyptians, Pharisees, Essenes, Ebonites, Manicheans, Arians, Muslims, Pelagians, and others invented by Rome. 'Catamites' surround him, naked 'save only theyr arses', and priests ride on human-faced scorpion-tailed locusts as an arch proclaims him and his sons 'Advoutrers, Incestuous, Buggers, defilers, Abusers, and of all Ruffians the chiefest'. Arrived at 'Plutonium', Paul holds a golden chalice into which s/he 'shead fyrst the filth of her menstrue' and then devils add 'theyr engendryng seede'. After the 'kinges of the yearth' kiss her feet, drink the menstrual blood and mate with her, Pluto takes her to a table where in another parody of the Mass they eat her flesh, but then vomit it up to reconstitute Paul (Baldwin 1552: A8, B4, C1^{r-v}). Blood, parodic Mass, gender shifts, and sex: as Michael Pincombe says, 'One almost hears two voices here: the pious and the prurient' (Pincombe 2010: 12).

THOMAS MORE'S DEFENCE OF CATHOLICISM

Notwithstanding his seismic decision to split from Rome, Henry VIII was never Protestant; he despised Luther and persecuted Tyndale. How better to answer them, aside from the king's own efforts, than to ask the author of *Utopia* to pen retorts? More's replies to Luther and Tyndale make crucial points, but just as striking is the intensity of the aggressive imagination that Peter Matheson calls More's 'theological road-rage' (Matheson 2001: 81). I shall concentrate here on More's responses to Luther and

---

[8] See discussions of this propaganda piece in Overell and Lucas 2012, and Pincombe 2010.

Tyndale, but also notable were his attacks on Robert Barnes, Simon Fish, John Frith, and Christopher Saint-German (Pineas 1968; King 2009).

In the *Responsio ad Lutherum* [Response to Luther], printed in 1523 under the pseudo-nym 'William Ross', More sets up his main speaker as a loyal subject who disdains 'Luder'—'Luther' as ludic, a 'clown'. The speaker is witty and indecent, something the prefatory material defends: Luther, as a fool, deserves it, and it seems that Henry himself had burst out laughing at More's 'foolish and scurrilous abuse' of the man (More 1969: I, 29).[9] This drunken Cerberus (75), living in 'the arse-hole of the devil' (77), cannot even argue well (and note the sounds): 'Quid respondet frater, pater, potator, ad haec? ebrius dormit; sepultus est in scypho: non audit' ['What does the friar, father, toper answer? The sot sleeps; buried in his cups, he does not hear'] (More 1969: I, 108). Luther cannot keep his prior and posterior logic straight; so, 'Since he has written that he already has a prior right to bespatter and besmirch the royal crown with shit, will we not have the pos-terior right to proclaim the beshitted tongue of this practioner of posterioristics most fit to lick with his anterior the very posterior of a pissing she-mule?' (181). Elsewhere are mini-dramas, dialogues, ironic marginalia—'The most mild father swells with bom-bast' (313)—and queries: 'Or is not this scripture sufficiently clear, Luther?' (409). We get vivid images: Luther dances naked in a net (439), or brays and bellows after entering a herd of pigs, the same semi-rhetorician drunkards who write his books (497).

More had no more use for Tyndale and his biblical translations. The linguistic issues were crucial, for as Protestants came to stress *sola scriptura* [by Scripture alone] and, up to a point, biblical literalism, the question of how to wrestle the Word into any human tongue became unavoidable (Waswo 1987; Betteridge 2013). Influenced by late Scholasticism, More thought that words signify only what we collectively make them signify—the English word 'congregation' means only what 'the comen custume of us englyshe peple' makes it mean (More 1973: II, 167). Because verbal signs are arbitrary, then, scholarship alone cannot claim a final equivalent for a given Scriptural passage. Revelation has not ceased, though, and with God's guidance the Church can determine significance. More's polemics, however, press beyond logic and linguistics, deploying jibes, mini-dramas, mini-dialogues and, more than ever, jokes.

The Confutation of Tyndale's Answer, which also takes on Robert Barnes, was writ-ten when More was Lord Chancellor (1532–3).[10] Again, what can seem a minor issue in biblical translation, such as word order or the definite article (I, 235–7), matters if God's is the originating voice. Of greater relevance to this chapter are More's sarcasms and invective, hyperboles, alliteration ('But thys drowsy drudge hath dronken so depe in the devyls dregges' (II, 713), and the jests for which he was known. Cicero and Quintilian, after all, had made humour part of an orator's repertoire: the ability to jest demonstrates

---

[9] See also Prescott 2003, and More 1973.

[10] The *Confutation*, originally published in two parts in 1532 and 1533, was reprinted in 1557; the modern edition (More 1973) is in three volumes, the third of which traces More's 'Polemical Career'. For a discussion of More's writings in relation to other humanists dealing with early modern religious issues, see chapter 16 of this Handbook.

the speaker's mental health and balance (Prescott 2003). Laughter itself is medicinal, attracting air to the blood and thereby increasing the sanguine humour and dissolving choler and madness-producing melancholy. More may have wanted to suggest both that he and his Church had a serenity derived from such balance and that what Europe, including its crazed religious 'reformers', needed was a way to relieve hurt and calm wrath—to become more sanguine but less bloody. The jokes touch on crucial issues. Monks wanting to gorge on forbidden pork during Lent, for example, simply dip a pig in water, saying, 'go in pygge and come out pyke' (I, 122); this seems surprising, in the context of arguments over changing bread to flesh, but More may want to demonstrate balance. More's Tyndale thinks he can arbitrarily change 'idole in to ymage' in his rage— change the word and thus change the thing. But no; according to More, Tyndale is like the priest who, aware that Christ is good and the devil bad, went through the Gospels and 'scraped out *diabolus* & wrote *Iesus Cristus*, bycause he thought ye devyls name was not mete to stande in so good a place' (I, 175). As for heretics' logic, More remembers the 'sophyster' who proved to a 'symple soule' that two eggs are three: here's one egg, you see, but since there are two eggs, that makes three (I, 287).

MARTIN MARPRELATE

Even more inventive than More's mockery of the heretics' logic is the series of pamphlets by 'Martin Marprelate' or his relatives and the replies they elicited. Starting in 1588, shortly after the Armada, Martin began his assault on ecclesiastical hierarchy and ritual. Marprelate's belligerent surname is self-explanatory [he sets out to 'mar' the priest or 'prelate'] and 'Martin' recalls Luther, as well as being a common name for a monkey, bird, ass, and fool. The actual author was probably Job Throkmorton, working with confederates and using a secret printing press; seven tracts remain extant (Black 2008).[11] The prose is a triumph of show-off rhetoric, offering alliteration, lists, jests, puns, elbow-grabbing chat with readers, demands of conservative prelates, and directives to the author. As Joseph L. Black says, 'shockingly new' was Martin's 'wittily irreverent and conversational prose', his 'swashbuckling persona, playful experiments with the conventions of print controversy, and willingness to name names and to tell unflattering stories about his opponents' (Black 2008: xvi). Martin can even laugh in print, chortling 'py hy hy hy. I cannot but laugh, py hy hy hy'; as Black points out, print and voice 'blur' (xxvi).

The Epistle (October 1588) offers off-colour puns aplenty: the title page has 'Fyckers ['vicars'] and Currats' (edging toward 'fuck' and suggesting 'cur' and 'rats'), while the epistle is dedicated to the 'Confocation House'. Or take, for 'ilsample', 'his grace of Cant[erbury]' and 'Mass[ter] Dean' (Black 2008: 9, 7). Inevitably we have

---

[11] For critical and historical discussion of the *Tracts*, see King 1982, Griffin 1997, Lander 2006, and Navitsky 2008.

alliteration: 'our bishops and proud, popish, presumptuous, profane, paltry, pestilent and pernicious prelates' (11). We hear a voice: 'do you say so? Do ye? You are a knave I tell you!' or 'Wohoho, brother London' (32). There are jokes: a priest, asked if 'he should be bishop of Ely', replied that he had little hope, and then remarked that 'I may say well enough, *Eli, Eli, lamma sabachthani*, Eli, Eli, why has thou forsaken me', blasphemously alluding to Christ's words upon the cross (Black 2008: 42). In *Epitome* (November 1588), with parodic page titles and errata, Martin is plainspoken, having to 'call a spade a spade, a pope a pope'—indeed, 'the pope of Lambeth' (the palace of the Church of England's own Archbishop of Canterbury). Martin claims to see us, and asks permission, for example, before posing us a question. Such techniques align him with the Menippean satire familiar from Rabelais, the *Satyre Ménippée*, or Philip Marnix's *Beehive of the Romish Church* (trans. 1636). Martin had Continental cousins.

Early in 1589, a year after the Martin Marprelate tracts had begun to emerge, *Certain Mineral and Metaphysical Schoolpoints* came off Martin's press, containing a list of parodic scholastic topics. In March 1589 the more complex *Hay* [Have ye] *any Work for Cooper* was published, aimed at Bishop Thomas Cooper, the author of the 1589 anti-Martinist *Admonition to the People of England*. With a straightforward middle section, *Hay any Work* is playfully polemical with its offering of lists and pseudo-logic: if 'John of Cant.' believes that Jesus when physically dead descended into Hell before the Resurrection, would he think it 'unlawful for a man to pray unto Christ' during that time (Black 2008: 137)? In July came Martin Jr's *Theses Martinianae*, with 110 propositions, and then *The Just Censure and Reproof of Martin Junior* by Martin Senior. There is the inevitable alliteration, such as 'the Canterbury Caiaphas' (Black 2008: 171), but there are also arguments related to class and money: clerical Esau robs Jacob, sucking his blood and sporting gold chains (175). Then the rhetoric moves into verse: 'From Sarum came a goose's egg, | with specks and spots bepatched, | A priest of Lambeth couched thereon: | thus was Mar-Martin hatched' (186). September 1589 brought *The Protestation of Martin Marprelate* with such vivid touches as the 'rage and barking of the Lambethetical whelps', or 'John a Cant' always 'shaking his shins about a May-pole', a pagan blasphemy to Puritans (Black 2008: 201, 204). Martin knew what the authorities feared. In *Hay any Work* he notes that some say (he might have specified Cooper's *Admonition*), 'Why, you enemies to the state, you traitors to God and his word, you Mar-prince, Mar-law, Mar-magistrate, Mar-church, and Mar-commonwealth' (121). Cooper himself had added that Martin hoped for an 'Anabaptisticall eqalitie and communitie', a vision of church and society that anticipates James I's later warning, 'No bishop, no king' (Black 2008: lix–lx).

Cleverly, the authorities sponsored replies to the Marprelate tracts with similar rhetorical swagger. John Bridges' *Defence* (1587) had supported the official church, at such length that it elicited mocks from Martin, but nevertheless with its own rhetorical energy (Vivier 2014). Now to support episcopacy came the talented pamphleteer Thomas Nashe, and John Lyly, author of *Euphues*. Nashe hit back with *A Countercuffe by ... Pasquill of England, Cavaliero* (1589): Pasquil/Pasquin is now English, if a 'cavaliero'. Martin, this giant's 'whelpe', has 'broken into heaven with his blasphemies', jeers Pasquil with an insult recalling that earthy race's rebellion against Olympus (Nashe 1904: I, 59). Martin is also sexually base: 'your faction is suddainlie growne stale like an Oyster, and gapes so wide that every Fishwife at Billings-gate sees into you' (63). 'Stale' had sexual overtones, and bivalves (the hinged shells of an oyster) mean vulvas in Latin slang.[12] Then, in *The Returne of … Pasquill* (1589), the famed statue Pasquil meets his friend Marforius at London's Royal Exchange. The ensuing dialogue takes up 'new points of doctrine' and slings puns: the name 'Puritan' is '*a pruritu*' (73). 'True Religion', moreover, is the 'proppe of all Princes' and the 'Morter that buildeth up all estates', and the 'simpler sort' are inclined 'to rowtes, ryots, commotions, insurrections, and plaine rebellions' when 'any new toy taketh them in the head' (Nashe 1904: I, 77, 81). There is alliteration: Marforius sneers, with implied scatology, that he finds the Puritans 'fitte to preach upon Bellowes, and Bagpipes, and blowne Bladders; they are so full of ventositie that I cannot come at their matter for winde and words' (90). In 1590 Pasquil (Nashe) was still at it: the title page of his *First Parte of Pasquils Apologie* refers to 'the May-games of Martinisme', a nice insult in the light of puritan condemnation of 'pagan' entertainment. And, Pasquil asks, may only experts interpret Scripture? (Nashe 1904: I, 111).

Other anti-Martinist tracts are of doubtful authorship, although Nashe probably wrote *An Almond for a Parrat*, published in 1590 (Black 2008: lxiii; Lyly 1902: III). The title of the tract wittily exploits the parrot's reputation for jabbering (Boehrer 2008). This reviver of Martin's 'traytourshippe' is a mere 'cobbler', and Martin himself has 'blotted' reams of paper with 'huperbolical blasphemies' and 'scurrility'. His allegations will 'bepistle thee so pevishly [bepiss/epistle you with pee]—and do we want '*Cli.*, the Cobler, and *New.*, the souter, jerking out theyr elbowes in everie Pulpit' (Nashe 1904: 344–51)? True, such 'elders' as 'Hicke, Hob, and John, Cutbert C., the Cobler' and 'the broom-seller' are silent, 'having worn out three or four pulpits' with the 'bounsing of his fistes' (363). The attack returns to the issue of the Scriptures: 'Admit they go to the originall (which but few of them understand), they wil have every man his sundry interpretation' (371). Lyly's *Pappe with an hatchet* (1589) uses such techniques: 'Good morrow, good-man *Martin*, good morrow' loosens print's borders while demoting this 'goodman' from gentleman status (Lyly 1598: B1). Lyly may be rude but, as he asks logically, 'Who would currie an Asse' with 'an Ivorie combe?' (A3). Inevitably there are semi-obscene jests: 'But softe Martins, did your Father die at the *Groyne* [the recent battle at the 'Groyne', Coruña in Spain]? It was well groapt at, for I knewe him sicke of a paine in the groyne. A pockes of that religion' when 'al his haires fell off' (B2ᵛ). Martin's father's religion is thus allied with groping in the groin and symptoms of syphilis. Martin's own learning is deficient, moreover: 'They studie to pull downe Bishopps, and to set up Superintendents, which is nothing else, but to raze out good *Greeke*, & enterline bad *Latine*', 'bishop' being from Greek, and 'superintendent' from Latin (Lyly 1589: C2).

Similar insults are versified in *A Whip for an Ape* (1589), perhaps by Lyly and also printed that year as *Rythmes against Martin Marre-Prelate*. A 'Dizard late skipt out upon

---

[12] See, for example, 'concha' in Lewis and Short, definition 2, citing Plautus.

our Stage', we read, who 'mocketh Prince and peasants all alike'. The language itself jigs: 'Such fleering, leering, jarring fooles bopeepe: | Such hahaes, teehees, weehees, wild colts play'. Like an ape, Martin would 'clime aloft and cast downe every where'. He is divisive, hating clerical dress as well as 'Communion bookes, and Homelies', and so 'teares withall the Church of Christ in two'. Someday he will knock down the rooster from the steeple and then ask 'Why Kings? The Saincts [i.e. Presbyterians] are free' (*Whip* 1589: A2–A3). How like those rebellious German peasants! The implication is that Martin loves equality, not England. That same year saw a verse collection, *Mar-Martine* (perhaps by Nashe), with a poem to Parliament fearing that the 'precise' attract women and youths (*Mar* 1589: A1ᵛ). The ancient English church must endure, so 'blessed Prince', please 'looke wel to this' (A2). Then this text returns to the familiar fears: 'Mar-prelat' is 'Mar-Queene, Mar-potentat' (A3), while 'Dickin, Jackin, Tom & Hob, now sit in Rabbies chaire' (A3ᵛ); presumably 'Rabbies' are gentile scholars. These are not 'Reformers' but 'Deformers' (*Marre* 1589: A4). The poor misled commons!

The last word should go to *Marre Mar-Martin or Marre-Martins medling, in a manner misliked* (1589) with a title page denouncing a Protestant 'selfe hate' that might 'pull Religion downe' and leave England defenceless. So:

> While *England* falles a Martining and a marring,
> Religion feares, an utter overthrowe.
> Whil'st we at home among our selves are jarring,
> These seedes take roote which forraign seedes men sow.
> If this be true, as true it is for certen,
> Wo worth *Martin Mar-prelate* and *Marmarten*. (A3)

The author remembers Jesus's words:

> What, Christ at oddes? what Serpents nere a dove?
> Alas our rage, alas our inhumilitie. (*Marre Mar* 1589: A4)

Doves would not soon dominate religious exchanges, but the venom described in this chapter was less often felt as the early modern period came to an end; wise serpents, if they must hiss, also know how to coo a little.

CHAPTER 15

NEO-LATIN WRITINGS AND RELIGION

JAN BLOEMENDAL

WHEN writing about neo-Latin writings and religion, it is essential to define what is meant by 'religion', a multifarious concept encompassing both beliefs and practices. People's beliefs comprise their convictions and their feelings about religious matters: who is God, what is the relationship between God and humankind, what is the place of human life in the universe, and what role should religion play in one's life? An individual's answers to these and related questions do not necessarily coincide with the doctrines of the Church. For example, there is no church dogma to match the vague, often unspecified contemporary belief that there must be 'something' transcendental over and above us—a phenomenon for which the Dutch derogatory term 'ietsisme' ('somethingism') was coined. Nor did the medieval Church look kindly on the lay beliefs of the period, which were denounced as superstitions. On the other hand, 'religion' also denotes people's practices—the everyday acts to which they ascribe religious associations. Nowadays we may think of football players crossing themselves before a match, but also of people attending church services, praying, and reading the Bible. In the medieval period, such practices included pilgrimages and Marian devotion, both going beyond the tenets of the official Church. This observation implies that religion and faith are not synonymous, and that major change in one—for example, from Catholicism to Protestantism in sixteenth-century Britain—need not imply change in the other.

It is also important to define what is meant by 'theology', a concept both attached to and distinct from religion. Theology is a rational, analytical, and detached way of looking at religion. David Ford elaborates on this definition: 'Theology deals with questions of meaning, truth, beauty, and practice raised in relation to religions and pursued through a range of academic disciplines' (Ford 1999: 16). Even when limited to Christianity, theology is a diverse discipline. It includes, for instance, biblical theology—trying to distinguish the beliefs and practices recorded in the Bible—and exegesis, the method of understanding the narratives of the Bible from their own context. Theology also includes hermeneutics—trying to apply one's understanding of a biblical story or fragment to daily life—as well as dogmatics, which deals with the theoretical truths of faith concerning God and creation that can be distilled from the Bible. A further aspect of theology is ethics, the study of those rules for everyday life that can be culled from the books of Holy Writ. Anyone who wants to say something about religion inevitably has a theological standpoint, consciously or not. So if we want to make observations on the relationship between religion and neo-Latin writings in the early modern period, we must make clear exactly what aspect of religion or writing is involved.

Neo-Latin was developed by the scholars whom we call 'humanists', starting in fourteenth-century Italy. There, people teaching the *trivium*—grammar, dialectic, and rhetoric, the three linguistically based disciplines of the seven medieval 'liberal arts'— rediscovered classical languages, literatures, and their values. They adapted them to the Christian world view that dominated culture and society. The concept of *humanitas* (humanity, civility, civilization) that had been developed by, above all, the Roman philosopher, orator, and statesman, Cicero, was linked by the humanists to *charitas*, Christian charity and love of one's neighbour. Gradually, the movement spread to the northern parts of Europe, where Erasmus became the great advocate of humanism and new Latinity. He was deeply influenced by the English humanists Thomas More and John Colet. Erasmus's religious and theological 'programme', as laid down in his *Enchiridion militis Christiani* (Manual/Dagger of the Christian Soldier 1501, reissued 1518), aims at teaching the classical languages in order to facilitate a better understanding of the Bible and the Fathers of the Church, and a return to a kind of pristine state of the Church and to a deeply felt faith practised with as few rules, dogmas, and 'empty' rituals as possible. This programme would deeply influence Northern European Christian humanism. The humanists expressed their views in a kind of Latin which also recalled the classical use of the language, as distinct from medieval Latin practices. Therefore, we tend to label their language 'neo-Latin'.

Since neo-Latin is the language used by scholars and clergymen rather than by the common people, it is likely to be more concerned with theology than directly with religion, although in several literary genres such as poetry, religion may prevail over theology or over what the poet knows about theological issues related to the subject treated. Thus, in Latin writings, too, an individual's beliefs and practices may be present. Since neo-Latin language and literature form an integral part of culture in the early modern period, they are also essential to the study of theology and, as a consequence, of religion. Theological works were written in Latin not only by Roman Catholic authors but also by Protestants, since theologians often exploited this language for their scholarship, lectures, and correspondence. The Roman Catholic theologian and humanist Erasmus wrote all of his works (including those on theology and religion) in Latin, as did the Reformation theologian Martin Luther. The latter, however, like many of his reformist colleagues, increasingly chose his language—Latin or German—according to the audience he wanted to address: Latin for the cultural elite, the vernacular for others. In addition, at the Protestant gymnasia (grammar schools) in the German-speaking countries, Latin was an integral part of education, as it was in schools and universities in Britain.

To summarize the distinguishing features of neo-Latin writing in the early modern period, we may say that neo-Latin theological writings are generally written in a Ciceronian or at least a classical style, with balanced sentences and rhythmic conclusions. By writing in this manner, Renaissance humanists were themselves reacting against medieval writers, especially scholastic theologians (Rummel 1995). On the other hand, those theologians who continued to work in the scholastic tradition were puzzled by the innovative, at times unorthodox language and views of the humanists (Balserak 2014: 723). Another feature of humanist theology, also written down in Latin, was that the authors were more responsive to the Fathers of the Church than their medieval colleagues (Backus 2014). Equally importantly, the humanists tended to blend Christian and pagan ideas. For instance, John Calvin in his *Institutions* (II, 2, 23) quoted Ovid's 'video meliora proboque, deteriora sequor' ('I see what is better, and approve it, I follow what is worse') where he might have referred to Paul's letter to the Romans 7:19 ('For the good which I would I do not, but the evil which I would not, that I practise') (Balserak 2014: 722–4). Finally, the humanists developed an historical consciousness that was not known previously.

In neo-Latin literature in the broadest sense, every genre could be used for religious writings: prayers and prophecies, lyric and epic poetry, drama, sermons, autobiographical writings, as well as satire and polemic, religious treatises and Biblical commentaries. In direct comparison with writings in the vernacular, in Latin, too, texts about religion included more than strictly theological works. In the discussion that follows, the role of religion in a range of genres will be explored, starting with theological works but by no means limited to them. Above all, Latin functioned as a means of contact in the international community; contact between the British Isles and the Continent through neo-Latin writings will be discussed in a separate section. Finally, the interplay between Latin and the vernaculars will be examined in the concluding phase of this chapter.

THEOLOGICAL WRITINGS

As stated above, theology constitutes intellectual engagement with religion. Therefore, theological writings do consider religion, though in an indirect way. Early modern British theologians wrote their works either in English or in Latin. Their choices were related to their intended audiences: Latin for the international world of learning and humanists, English for the 'market' of British readers. The beginnings of 'neo-Latin' as a whole, and those relating to theology, are difficult to trace. However, the age of Erasmus and Thomas More is conventionally taken as their starting-point.

Desiderius Erasmus (1466?–1536) has often been named the 'father of northern humanism'. He was in contact with many theologians and humanists, across Europe as well as in the British Isles. He paid his first visit to England in 1499 when travelling with his pupil William Blount, Lord Mountjoy. There he met Thomas More (1478–1535) who would become a close friend, and the pedagogue and theologian John Colet (1467–1519) who played an important role in Erasmus's formation as a humanist.[1] In due course, Erasmus became a 'biblical humanist', whose main venture was an ambitious scholarly project devoted to the New Testament, offering a new translation, a new edition, a commentary, and a paraphrase. His British contacts also included Cardinal John Fisher (1469–1535), who was executed by Henry VIII for his refusal to acknowledge the king as head of the Church of England (Bietenholz and Deutscher 1985–7; s.vv. More, Colet, and Fisher). Among Fisher's Latin writings is *De veritate corporis et sanguinis Christi in Eucharistia adversus Ioannem Oecolampadium* (On the Reality of Christ's Body and Blood in the Eucharist, Against Johannes Oecolampadius), published in Cologne, 1527. Cuthbert Tunstall (1474–1559)—another correspondent of Erasmus—contributed to this controversy with his *De veritate corporis et sanguinis Domini nostri Jesu Christi in Eucharistia* (On the Reality of Our Lord Jesus Christ's Body and Blood in the Eucharist), published in Paris, 1551 (Davies 1970: 85–7, 88–90). John Colet delivered important Oxford lectures on St Paul's letter to the Romans, given in Latin in 1496 (Springer 2014: 753).

As the titles of the writings cited above clearly indicate, British neo-Latin theology in the early modern period is characterized by strife and conflicts between Catholics and Protestants—and, in later decades, between Anglicans and Puritans. One of the chief issues being contested in such literature was the use of Latin or the vernacular language during worship (Davies 1970). These struggles over matters of belief—such as the character of the Eucharist—and over practices such as the choice of language were fought both in the vernacular and in Latin. Even King Henry VIII had broached such matters in his *Assertio septem sacramentorum adversus Martin Lutherum* (Defence of the Seven Sacraments against Martin Luther, 1521). Since this treatise was in Latin, it could be read by Luther and his allies as well as the leaders of the Catholic Church. The publication earned the king the honorary title from Rome, 'Fidei defensor' (defender of the faith). Luther, against whom the treatise was written, had wished to retain only three sacraments: baptism, absolution, and the Eucharist.

Thomas More's *Utopia*, in full *De optimo reipublicae statu deque nova insula Utopia* (On the Best State of a Republic and on the New Island Utopia, 1516), is no theological tractate or philosophical work, but a fictional dialogue. Nevertheless, in Utopia (coined from the Greek words 'ou-topia', no-place, and 'eu-topia', good-place) there is space for religion. The work is written in two books, the first criticizing English contemporary society, the second offering an outline of an ideal state with communist features such as renunciation of private property. In this second book, More sketches the religious state of the island. Although there are several religions coexisting in peace and tolerance, they

---

[1] For a discussion of the work of Erasmus, Colet, More and their circle, see chapter 16 of this volume.

have common principles or beliefs, as may be witnessed in Book II, Ch. 8 (De educatione et artibus; On Education and the Arts):

> Ea principia sunt huiusmodi. Animam esse immortalem, ac dei beneficentia ad felicitatem natam, uirtutibus ac bene factis nostris praemia post hanc uitam, flagitijs destinata supplicia. Haec tametsi religionis sint, ratione tamen censent ad ea credenda, et concedenda perduci, quibus e medio sublatis, sine ulla cunctatione pronunciant neminem esse tam stupidum, qui non sentiat petendam sibi per fas ac nefas uoluptatem. hoc tantum caueret ne minor uoluptas obstet maiori, aut eam persequatur quam inuicem retaliet dolor.

> These are their religious principles: That the soul of man is immortal, and that God of His goodness has designed that it should be happy; and that He has, therefore, appointed rewards for good and virtuous actions, and punishments for vice, to be distributed after this life. Though these principles of religion are conveyed down among them by tradition, they think that even reason itself determines a man to believe and acknowledge them; and freely confess that if these were taken away, no man would be so insensible as not to seek after pleasure by all possible means, lawful or unlawful, using only this caution—that a lesser pleasure might not stand in the way of a greater, and that no pleasure ought to be pursued that should draw a great deal of pain after it.[2]

Indeed, More devotes a whole chapter (II, 12 De religionibus Utopiensium) to the religious beliefs and practices of the Utopians. In spite of the existence of several religions, the island inhabitants believe in One Supreme Being, although practitioners of each religion revere a particular aspect of that god. After the Utopians were told of Christ, many converted to Christianity. Their different religions meet in the same churches in which the services are led by the same priests, men of the highest moral stature—and consequently few in number. As indicated above, *Utopia* is a work of fiction aimed at an international audience of humanists but at the same time engaging in its own way in religious debates concerning the tenets of faith in the Christian God, the relationships between belief and tolerance, and the multi-functionality of churches. It is striking that the same Thomas More who sketched this ideal of tolerance and peace would play such a prominent role in the persecution of Protestants.

Despite his not being a native Englishman, Erasmus had an impact on British religion with publications such as his *Moriae encomium, Stultitiae laus* or *Praise of Folly* (1511). In this lively and paradoxical Latin declamation, beneficial folly is celebrated as the wisdom of God (I Cor. 3:18) while deluded wisdom is shown to be the true folly (McConica 1997). The *encomium* ends with praise of the ecstasy of the Christian who is enthusiastic for Christ (Screech 1988). The title of this famous satire is a punning reference to the name of Erasmus's friend, Thomas More. Though written at first in Latin, the work was introduced to a wider English readership through several translations (Devereux

---

[2] The translation is taken from http://theopenutopia.org.

1983: 134–9). Erasmus's Latin *Paraphrases* of the New Testament were known in England through the edition by Nicholas Udall, *The First tome or volume of the Paraphrase of Erasmus vpon the newe testamente* (1548, second volume 1549), in which the English translation of the New Testament was interleaved with a translation of the famous paraphrases. A royal *Injunction* of 1547 ordered that a copy should be kept in every parish church in England (Dodds 2009).

However, translations were not needed for everyone. Many of the authors who were widely known for their English works also read Latin and wrote in that language. The most famous one was John Milton (1608–74), who being a Latin secretary to Oliver Cromwell, was fluent in Latin. He is most widely known for his magisterial epic *Paradise Lost* (published 1667; 2nd rev. edn 1674). Milton made an inventory of Christian instruction in his posthumously published *De doctrina Christiana* (On Christian Doctrine), a title borrowed from the Church Father St Augustine. Through this work and through Latin translations of his *Paradise Lost* he was read on the Continent too. In 1676 Robert Barclay published a survey of Quaker theology, *Theologicae vere christianae apologia* (Defence of Truly Christian Theology), in Latin (Springer 2014: 752), indicating the importance of the language for nonconformist groups as well as for established churches.

Many of the debates on faith and religion were fought in Latin, and many of those Latin theological writings are polemical in nature. This may well have to do with the fact that theologians were often prelates anxious to keep controversy away from the laity, as well as desiring to engage in European disputes in a widely read language. With the passage of time, the vernacular gradually gained dominance over Latin. This started with popular instructional and liturgical writings such as catechisms and Thomas Cranmer's Book of Common Prayer (1549). However, throughout the period under consideration many theologians who did not write in Latin nevertheless had the ability to read the language, and thus to appreciate the scholarly precision and sophisticated theological vocabulary developed within neo-Latin texts.

LATIN DRAMA

Latin drama of the early modern period was primarily related to the schools and universities, both on the Continent and in the British Isles. The plays were written for and staged by students. Through the reading and staging of plays, students might improve their Latin skills, as well as learning the arts of conversation, acting, and performing in public. Such dramas were particularly popular at Oxford and Cambridge; the comedies were mainly inspired by the Roman authors Plautus and Terence, and the tragedies were largely modelled on those of Seneca. Many of these plays take as their subjects academic life and pedantry. These include Edward Forsett's *Pedantius* (1581), written for Trinity College, Cambridge, and George Ruggle's *Ignoramus* (1615), first performed at Clare College, Cambridge (Norland 2013b: 486–7, 510–14).

However, playwrights were also drawn towards dramatizing religious subjects. A famous example is the Oxford-trained historian and 'martyrologist' John Foxe (1516/17–87), the author of the popular *Book of Martyrs*, first published in Latin (1559) and issued four years later in English. Foxe's dramatic text, *Christus triumphans* (Christ Triumphant, London 1551; Basle 1556), was composed during his residence in Basle (Norland 2013a; 2013b: 478–9) where he had been forced to flee after the restoration of Roman Catholicism in England by Mary Tudor. *Christus triumphans* is a play about the Second Coming of Christ, echoing the biblical texts of Daniel, Isaiah, and Revelation as well as the Latin play *Pammachius* (The Struggle of All, 1536) by the German playwright Thomas Kirchmeyer (or Naogeorgus). The apocalypse must have seemed an appropriate subject on which to focus at a time when the Turks were threatening Europe, Rome had been sacked (1527), and the Protestant Reformation challenged the unity of the Church. However, Foxe deals with the same subject from a reformist point of view, identifying the evil forces with Mary's persecution of British Protestants. It comes as no surprise, therefore, that among the 'dramatis personae' in Foxe's play are the Antichrist and the Whore of Babylon, conventionally associated with the Pope and the Roman Catholic Church in the popular Protestant imagination. By such means, religious beliefs—in this case concerning the Eschaton, the end of the world—could be brought alive on stage and related to contemporary society.

Many more dramas could be mentioned in this discussion, such as Thomas Watson's *Absolom* (1535–44) on David's rebellious son, William Goldingham's *Herodes* (1567–79), and Nicholas Grimald's two plays, *Archipropheta* (1548) about John the Baptist, and *Christus redivivus* (1540) on Christ's resurrection. In all of these plays, biblical subjects were selected for their moral potential and their ability to offer representations and interpretations demonstrating right—or wrong—behaviour. In a typological manner, these texts often examined the ways in which Old Testament characters prefigured Christ or other leading characters from the New Testament. Some plays also approached the scriptural text in an anagogical mode, revealing how biblical stories could highlight the spiritual mission of the Church or point to signs of the approaching End of Time.

The most famous neo-Latin drama written by an author from Britain was the tragedy *Iephthes sive votum* (Jephthah, or The Vow, 1553), inspired by the biblical story of Jephthah (Judges 11). In a poignant example of tragic irony, Jephthah made a vow that, if granted victory, he would sacrifice the first living thing that he met on his journey home—only to be greeted by his own daughter. The same author also wrote the successful gospel-based *Baptistes sive calumnia* (The Baptist, or Calumny, 1576) on the beheading of John the Baptist (Buchanan 1983; McFarlane 1981). These dramas were written in France by the Scottish humanist George Buchanan (1506–82). They dealt with religious beliefs—for instance, about the status of vows or about the relation between God and Evil (Shuger 1994: 128–66)—but also with practices of worship. Buchanan's Jephthah, for example, says a prayer to God in which perceptions of

God, expressed in a sequence of divine titles and roles, are merged with the practice of prayer itself:

> Regnator orbis, unus et verus Deus,
> Solumque numen propitium pollens potens,
> Idem severus ultor et clemens pater,
> Tuis tremendus et severus hostibus,
> Tuis amicis lenis et salutifer,
> Irae timendae sed tamen placabilis,
> Amore fervens idem et inritabilis. (Buchanan, *Iephthes*, 431–6) (Buchanan 1983: 38)

> Ruler of the world, one true God, unique deity of mercy, power and strength, harsh avenger but kindly father, fearsome to your own and harsh to your foes, gentle bearer of salvation to your friends, figure of dreadful anger yet willing to be appeased, warm in love yet goaded to wrath.
>
> (Buchanan 1983: 72)

Interestingly, Buchanan was not only inspired by the Bible (Ferradou and Green 2009a) but also by antiquity: he recalls the story of Iphigeneia in Euripides's tragedies, for example, by giving Jephthah's daughter the name Iphis. However, it should be stressed that the humanist Buchanan did not write his plays in Scotland but in France, where he taught at the Collège de Guyenne.

There were other British playwrights working on the Continent, in particular Jesuits teaching at colleges there, mainly in the region which is now the west of Belgium (Norland 2013b: 523–33). These colleges offered a welcome haven for British Catholics when Protestantism held sway in Britain. Their curricula included the staging of Latin dramas. Edmund Campion wrote three Latin plays in the years 1574–80 when he taught in Prague at the Jesuit Academy: *The Sacrifice of Abraham*, *King Saul*, and *Ambrosia*. The latter is a play based on a saint's life, a theme typical of Jesuit drama. At the (Jesuit) English College in Rome, for example, two Latin plays were produced in 1612 and 1613: the anonymous *Thomas Morus* and *Thomas Cantuariensis*. Both plays address the contemporary seventeenth-century conflict between church and state by staging earlier events, the martyrdom of St Thomas More and the assassination of Thomas Becket respectively. The best known author of Latin plays depicting saints' lives was the Jesuit father Joseph Simons or Emmanuel Lobb (1594–1671) who worked at the College at St Omer. Among his five tragedies is a *Vitus sive Christiana fortitudo* (Vitus or Christian Courage, 1627) on the martyrdom of St Vitus, who (like Iphigenia) is ultimately saved by an angel and taken to heaven. His neo-Latin plays offered appropriate examples of Christian repentance, conversion, and endurance to pupils who were being trained for the dangerous life of a Jesuit missionary.

PSALM PARAPHRASES

In direct comparison with the drama, the genre of the Psalm paraphrase was related to the schools (Green 2014). Students practised their skills in Latin poetry through the versification of songs from the Psalter paraphrased into classical or medieval Latin metres. When these paraphrases were made by mature poets rather than schoolboys, the texts could display a high level of poetic craftsmanship. Thus, this form of poetry became an opportunity to demonstrate a mixture of devotional, poetical, and intellectual skills, and was a vehicle for the expression of all kinds of (Christian) religious beliefs and practices. In some instances, such paraphrases were used as choral songs in dramas or as *carmina scholastica*, at least on the Continent. They could be found both in Latin and in the vernacular languages. In the Low Countries, for example, the Amsterdam poet and playwright Joost van den Vondel (1589–1679) and the Delft jurist Hugo Grotius (1583–1645) composed beautiful paraphrases of the Psalms in Dutch.

However, the most accomplished and famous paraphrases were made by the Scotsman George Buchanan, who rendered the whole Psalter into Latin poetry of some thirty metrical forms: *Psalmorum Davidis paraphrasis poetica* (Green 2014: 466–8; http://www.philological.bham.ac.uk/buchpsalms/). He started working on the project in France in the 1530s, and finished the paraphrases in the 1560s while he was at the University of Coimbra in Portugal. They were first published by the Estienne printing house in Paris, but Buchanan continued to amend them and the 'final' version was printed by Plantin in Antwerp in 1571. His Latin resembles that of the ancient writers and contains allusions to Virgil and Horace as well as to, among others, Juvenal and Lucretius. In the event, the classical tone of his verse proved no impediment to the expression of devotional and religious feelings. The Psalms were set to music by the French composer Jean Servin in 1579 and by the Cantor of the Rostock Gymnasium, Statius Olthof, in 1585 (Ford and Green 2009a: 73–160).[3]

The following reworking of Psalm 150 will serve as an illuminating example of Buchanan's *Paraphrase*:

> CL.
> Laudate Dominum in sanctis eius
>
> Laudate Dominum, lucidum
> Templum colentem siderum,
> Qui vi suae potentiae
> Firmavit orbis cardines.

---

[3] Interestingly, a Latin *prose* paraphrase of Buchanan's Latin *poetic* Psalm paraphrases by Alexander Yule or Julius (*d.* 1624), entitled *Ecphrasis Paraphraseos Georgii Buchanani in Psalmos Davidis* (1620), has recently been made available on the Internet by Dana Sutton (http://www.philological.bham.ac.uk/ecphrasis/).

Laudate Dominum fortiter   5
Ubique gestis inclytum,
Laudate magnitudinem
Captum supra mortalium.

Laudate Dominum bellicae
Claris tubae clangoribus,   10
Laudate Dominum nabliis,
Lyrisque blande garrulis.

Laudate Dominum tympanis,
Chorique festi cantibus,
Laudate Dominum fidibus, et   15
Sonore dulci tibiae.

Laudate eum tinnitibus
Laetis canori cymbali.
Hunc cuncta laudent, quae trahunt
Vitalis aurae spiritum.   20

Praise ye the Lord, Who inhabiteth the bright temple of the heaven, Who established the foundations of the world by the might of His power. Praise ye the Lord, who is everywhere renowned for His acts of valour. Praise ye His greatness, which is above the conception of mortals. Praise the Lord with the shrill sound of the warlike trumpet. Praise ye the Lord with psalteries and sweetly-warbling harps. Praise ye the Lord with timbrels and the songs of the festive choir. Praise ye the lord with stringed instruments and the sweet sound of the organ. Praise Him with the pleasant notes of the melodious cymbal. Let all who breathe the breath of life praise Him.[4]

The language of this poetic paraphrase in strophic iambic dimeters is quite lucid. It combines a fully classical form in wording and word order with the poetics of Hebrew poetry and its repetitions and anaphors. McFarlane concludes: 'Buchanan's paraphrases ... are the product of a humanist mind deeply penetrated with classical poetry, but also imbued with the attitudes we associate more or less with Erasmian evangelism, and who published them at a time when the genre was still highly relevant to the spirit of the age' (McFarlane 1981: 286).

Neo-Latin Religious Poetry

Verse Psalm paraphrases formed part of the wide and flourishing 'field', to use Bourdieu's term, of neo-Latin religious poetry in Great Britain during the early modern period (Binns 1974; Bradner 1940; Houghton and Manuwald 2012). The practice of neo-Latin religious poetry demanded a fascinating mixture of the cerebral activity required for the writing of classically inspired poems and the expression of spiritual feeling required for

---

[4]   Text and translation: http://www.philological.bham.ac.uk/buchpsalms/.

religious works. Regardless of whether these emotions were experienced at first hand, they were integral to the rhetoric of the genre. In this respect such 'intellectual' poems resemble the metaphysical poetry of, for instance, John Donne, as David Allan points out (2009: 65). English poets turned to Latin in order to engage with an international audience at a time when English was often barely known on the Continent. Milton's *Paradise Lost*, for instance, was mainly read in Latin translations outside Britain (Binns 1974: viii).

Three major English religious poets of the seventeenth century chose to write religious poetry in Latin: George Herbert (1593–1633), John Milton (1608–74), and Richard Crashaw (1612–49). All three composed Latin verse at school, and though they later turned to English, it is clear that they retained and continued to use their prowess in Latin versification. Milton's Latin poetry section in his *Poems ... Both English and Latin* (1645) is divided into 'Elegiae' (Elegies) and 'Sylvae' (Miscellaneous), and ends with the 'Epitaphium Damonis' bemoaning the death of his best friend Charles Diodati. The 'Sylvae' comprised, among other poems, a rendering of Psalm 114 into Greek verse. However, most of his Latin poetry, a product of his youth, is of a secular kind (Condee 1974).

George Herbert's Latin poetry contains more religious poems. Touching are the Greek and Latin poems he wrote for his mother, Lady Danvers in *Memoriae matris sacrum* (To the Memory of my Mother: A Consecrated Gift, 1627). The poems deserve notice for their emotional concentration, poetic range, and versatile imagery (Freis, Freis, and Miller 2012). Unsurprisingly, Herbert's Latin verse on the one hand gives evidence of his submersion in classical Latin poetry, whereas on the other it parallels his English poems, such as those contained in the famous collection, *The Temple*. His *Musae responsoriae* (1662) are responses to Andrew Melville's *Anti-Tami-Cami-Categoria* which in itself was written as an answer 'to the hostile reaction awakened at Oxford and Cambridge by the Puritan Millenary Petition of April 1603' (Kelliher 1974: 27; Doelman 1992; on Melville, see below).

In this context, a particularly appropriate genre was the epigram, of which brevity and pointedness were the main characteristics. In the course of the seventeenth century, the sacred epigram developed and became popular among neo-Latin poets. These epigrams were based on biblical texts or related spiritual topics, and Jesuit Latin poets on the Continent contributed much to the genre (Bradner 1940: 76, 91). Their purpose was to create a counterpart to the frivolous love poetry of antiquity—and of other neo-Latin secular poems. A subgenre of the epigram was the emblem, which also had its religious examples. The first collection to be published in this area was Andrew Willett's *Sacrorum emblematum centuria una* (One Hundred Sacred Emblems, 1596). The year 1634 saw the appearance of the *Epigrammata sacra* (Sacred Epigrams) of Richard Crashaw, whom Leicester Bradner called 'by far the greatest writer of the conventional sacred epigram' (Bradner 1940: 91–6, 92; Larsen 1974; Martin 1957). According to Bradner, Crashaw's ambition was to 'translate the Bible into Ovid', using literary features of Jesuit poets on the Continent and expressions known from phrase books such as Joannes Buchler's widely used *Thesaurus phrasium poeticarum* (Treasure of Poetic Phrases, 1612). Let us quote one example of Crashaw's epigrams, taken from Bradner's *Musae Anglicanae* (Bradner 1940: 92; also Martin 1957: 44). It is based on the fundamental Christian paradox that God allowed his Son to suffer in order to redeem mankind from suffering:

> Joann. 16. 33
> Ego vici mundum
>
> Tu contra mundum dux es meus, optime Iesu?
>   At tu (me miserum!) dux meus ipse iaces.
> Si tu, dux meus, ipse iaces, spes ulla salutis?
>   Immo, ni iaceas tu, mihi nulla salus!
>
> I conquered the world
>
> Are you my guide against the world, divine Jesus?
>   But you (woe to me!), my guide, lie on the ground yourself.
> If you, my leader, lie on the ground yourself, is there any hope for salvation?
>   On the contrary, if you do not lie on the ground, I would have no
>   salvation at all! [translation mine]

Other British neo-Latin sacred epigrammatists from the period included John Saltmarsh (*c.*1619–47), who published his *Poemata sacra* in 1636, and James Duport (1606–79), whose *Epigrammata sacra* saw the light of day in 1662 in the same volume as George Herbert's (1593–1633) *Musae responsoria* and Johannes Vivianus's paraphrase of *Ecclesiastes*. The Anglican Peter Du Moulin (1601–84) attacked the puritan regime and its leaders in his verse collection *Ecclesiae gemitus* (The Sighs of the Church, 1649) (Bradner 1940: 96–9). Polemical religious poetry was also composed by the Scottish poet Andrew Melville (1545–1622), a theologian and reformer, and the philosopher Patrick Adamson (1537–92). Melville, as a leader of the Presbyterian party, opposed Adamson, who supported the court. Adamson's *Poemata sacra* were published in 1618; Melville wrote biblical paraphrases and saw his *Musae*, satires and epigrams against episcopacy, published in 1620, and other poems collected in the *Delitiae poetarum Scotorum* (Delights of Scottish Poets) in 1637 (Bradner 1940: 151–7).

The writing of Latin religious poetry in the British Isles lasted until at least the eighteenth century, when Isaac Hawkins Browne (1705–60) published his *De animi immortalitate* (On the Immortality of the Soul, 1754) and John Burton (1696–1771) composed religious odes (Bradner 1940: 249 and 277–80). The fact that Browne's *De animi*, a defence of the belief in the immortality of the soul against the challenges of deism and atheism, was immediately translated into English is indicative of the shift away from Latin as the language of religious disputation in the eighteenth century

LETTERS

The importance of letter writing in the sixteenth and seventeenth centuries can hardly be overestimated. Letters were personal documents for exchange of information, from gossip to intellectual news. However, they were often intended for publication, either in their original form or in an edited version. Many of these letters were composed in Latin, the *lingua franca* of the international Republic of Letters (De Landtsheer-Nellen 2011; De Landtsheer 2014). Among the topics frequently discussed were religious and theological issues. One of the most important epistolary collections from the early modern period is the correspondence of Erasmus. This humanist and theologian left a vast correspondence of over three thousand letters written by or to him, all in Latin (Allen 2009). As already indicated, some of his leading correspondents lived in the British Isles or were born there. He exchanged letters with, among others, Thomas More, Richard Charnock (*d.* 1505), John Fisher, Cuthbert Tunstall, Bishop Richard Foxe, Archdeacon William Burbank of Carlisle, and the Frisian Johannes Sixtinus (*d.* 1519), who had made an ecclesiastical career for himself in Britain. For Erasmus, as for many others, a letter was a conversation between distant friends, offering an opportunity to exchange news, support each other and maintain 'friendship' which often had a utilitarian character. Such written conversation was especially valuable to Jesuit missionaries abroad, who exchanged letters with their superiors at home. Many more contacts between theologians and humanists in Britain and on the Continent, were maintained through Latin letters. For example, the jurist and theologian Hugo Grotius went with an embassy to England where he spoke with James I about the religious quarrels in Holland between Remonstrants and Counter-Remonstrants on the controversial matter of Predestination. Grotius subsequently exchanged letters with, among others, the scholar, translator and preacher Lancelot Andrewes (1555–1625), Bishop of Ely and Winchester (Davies 1973: 144–8).

Contacts between Great Britain and the Continent, especially the Netherlands

There were many contacts between British and Continental theologians and authors. In particular, the exchange of ideas between British Puritans and Dutch orthodox Calvinists may be mentioned, our knowledge of which has been much enhanced by the work of Willem Jan op't Hof. Many early English Calvinist publications were translated into Dutch, including William Perkins's *Armilla aurea* (The Golden Chain, 1590) on predestination, and *Prophetica* (Prophesies, 1592), and Thomas Brightman's *Apocalypsis apocalypseos* (The Unfolding of the Apocalypse, 1609), a commentary on the Book of Revelation (Op 't Hof 1987: 305–8, 183–7). More generally, the influence of English and Scottish Puritans on the Continent as a whole, as well as in the British colonies across the Atlantic, continued to be pervasive (Spijker et al. 2001).

At the other end of the seventeenth-century British religious spectrum, Charles I was represented in Dutch writings and engravings of the 1650s as a political and religious martyr. This portrayal of Charles started immediately after his execution on 30 January 1649 through Richard Royston's *Eikon basilike* (The Portrait of the King), which soon became known as the 'King's Book' (Helmers 2011: 119–47). Remarkably, as Helmers shows, this cult of the martyr king persisted in the Netherlands even though the country was by then a republic. This trend did not conflict with Dutch republicanism since the Dutch regents were not averse to absolutism and since Charles, by his piety on the scaffold, became a moral example for private meditation. Such writings indicate that beliefs concerning Christian kingship on the one hand, and practices of private meditation on the other, might easily be combined in this period without apparent contradiction. As such examples indicate, inter-cultural translations are always processes of adaptation— and perhaps even of transformation.

LATIN AND THE VERNACULARS

It may seem that neo-Latin literature and theological writings gave their authors scope for separate identities, and that some authors debated in Latin and others in English (or other vernaculars). In fact, the languages met and mingled. Some authors were fully bilingual, as we witnessed with 'the Latin poetry of English poets' such as Herbert and Milton (Binns 1974). The same is also true of theological writings: John Fisher, for instance, not only wrote Latin texts but was also the author of *Treatise concernynge ... the seven penytencyall Psalms* (1508), *The Wayes to Perfect Religion* (1535), and other writings in English.

In polemics, both Latin and vernacular works could participate equally in the discussion. In the Eucharistic controversy, for example, Henry VIII wrote his *Assertio* in Latin in 1521, with Fisher and Tunstall joining in with Latin works in 1527 and 1551, whereas Bishop Stephen Gardiner intervened in the discussion with his English *Explication and Assertion of the true Catholic Faith, touching the most blessed Sacrament of the Altar with confutation of a booke written agaynst the same* (1551). Whereas Gardiner used English to oppose Cranmer's Prayer Book, Richard Hooker also used the vernacular in his *Treatise of the Laws of Ecclesiastical Polity* (1597) to defend the Elizabethan Church settlement. Earlier in the same debate, John Calvin's *De coena Domini* (1540) had been translated into English by Bishop Miles Coverdale as *A faythful and most godly treatise concernynye* [sic] *the sacrament* (1549) (Davies 1970: 76–123).

As has also been witnessed in the course of this discussion, cultural exchange between Latin and vernacular poetry could take place through translations in the other direction, from English to Latin, as in the case of Milton's *Paradise Lost*, translated by William Dobson (*b.* 1714/15) as *Paradisus amissus: Poema Ioannis Miltoni* in 2 volumes (1750–3). More often, however, the focus was prose and the exchange took the form of translations from Latin to English, as the numerous English versions of Erasmus's Latin writings show, including his theological and religious works (Devereux 1983). We have already considered the example of his *Praise of Folly*, but the first of his works to be translated was the *Enchiridion militis christiani*, the anonymous *A booke called in latyn Enchirdion militis christiani and in englyssche the manuell of the christen knyght*, printed in 1533 and probably the same as the translation made by William Tyndale in 1522/3. Parts of Erasmus's Bible project were also translated, including the preliminary texts *Ratio verae theologiae* and *Paraclesis*, and the *Annotationes* and *Paraphrases*, as well as some sermons and the *Institutio principis christiani*. However, texts were also translated into other languages and thus further transmitted, as demonstrated above in the case of English pietistic texts rendered into Dutch. In the case of these writings, the situation is even more interesting. Both Latin and English texts originating in Britain were translated into Dutch. In this way, works from the Latin and vernacular spheres, the one more learned, the other more widely accessible, entered into one literary and theological field.

Concluding Remarks

Latin was widely used as a means of expressing early modern ideas on religion. Neo-Latin writings could be used to reach one's own peers in one's own country, but the use of Latin elevated the audience to an international scale, especially since in the early modern period English was poorly known on the Continent, while Latin was the language of the *respublica literaria*, the international community of the literate. This 'republic of letters' also comprised theologians, who could write for and against each other in this *lingua franca*. However, the lines between Latin and the vernacular were often transgressed. People could react in Latin to writings in the vernacular, or vice versa, and writings were translated into other languages. Latin thus remained an integral part of society. Classical Latin was valued much more highly by early modern scholars and writers than it had been by medieval Latin writers—hence the widely used adjective 'neo-Latin' for the Latin literature of the sixteenth and seventeenth centuries. These writings developed a clear and precise vocabulary, particularly in the area of theology, making neo-Latin an apt vehicle for the expression of religious beliefs, practices, and debates in the early modern period.[5]

[5] I would like to thank Gerard Huijing (†) for correcting my English and for his comments on an earlier draft of this essay.

PART III

RELIGION AND THE EARLY MODERN WRITER

CHAPTER 16

'WHAT ENGLAND HAS
TO OFFER'

Erasmus, Colet, More and their Circle

ANDREW HISCOCK

Tu Virgo illa, aurei seculi renovatrix. Tu vera illa Diana, perpetuae virgin-
itatis, tum auctor, tum exemplum. Tu triforme Numen, quae tergeminum
nobis Gigantem edidisti, quam ter potentem, formidant inferi, venerantur
superi, medius hic adorat orbis.

(Alonso 1979: 87)

You are the virgin who has restored the golden age. You are the true Diana,
both origin and model of perpetual virginity. You are the deity of triple
form who gave birth to the threefold giant, thrice-powerful, whom the
rulers of the underworld dread, the heavenly powers revere, and this middle earth adores.

(Erasmus 1999: 25)

IN this early *Paean Virgini Matri dicendus* (1499) it might be thought that Erasmus
(1466–1536) gives expression to a key commitment of the wider community of humanist scholars across Europe as the fifteenth century gave way to the sixteenth—to engage
expansively (as far as Christian doctrine would allow) with the dual textual legacies of
Scripture and pagan antiquity. Like so many intellectuals who forged a career within
the Church or had close ties within its fold, Erasmus is often viewed as representative
in his desire to combine the scholarly commitment to Christian piety with an enduring appreciation of the ethical undertakings evidenced in writings surviving from the
Greco-Roman world. The humanist project, originating in the labours of distinguished
scholars from the fourteenth-century Italian states, frequently concentrated upon a critical desire to return *ad fontes* in order to complete the thorough scrutiny, commentary,
stylistic analysis, and translation of texts from antiquity with a view to enriching the
cultural, moral, and religious life of the wider society. Erasmus himself unveiled the full

remit of his intellectual undertaking in the essay 'Paraclesis' appended to his 1516 Latin translation of the New Testament in which he declared (here, in its sixteenth-century English publication), 'I wold desire that all women shuld reade the gospell and Paules epistles ... I wold to god ye plowman wold singe a texte of the scripture at his plowbeme and that the wever at his lowme with this wold drive away the tediousnes of tyme' (Erasmus 1534: B1^v–B2^r; see also chapter 1). In the event, such aspirations would seem to take little account of the meagre resources of Latinity in evidence among this larger, multifarious mass of the early modern population.

Nevertheless, at the turn of the sixteenth century, the Netherlander was clearly exploring the ways in which Christian devotional writing and scholarship might acknowledge explicitly the pervasive influences of the diction and epistemology inherited from the ancient world. In these years, amongst other productions, he would not only pen a liturgy for Our Lady of Loreto, an *Obsecratio ad Virginem Matrem Mariam in rebus adversis* (1st pub. 1503) invoking 'illa Diana, triplici Numine pollens' ('our Diana, powerful in triple majesty'. See Alonso 1979: 102; Erasmus 1999: 45), but also a *Precatio ad Virginis filium Iesum* (1499) in which 'most sweet Jesus' is hailed as 'the kindly enchanter and magician: you refashion not only the body but also the soul, not by means of magical charms from Thessaly or Colchis but through your all-powerful mercy' (Erasmus 1999: 10). Indeed, much later, in his 'Convivium religiosum' (The Godly Feast, 1522) from the *Colloquies*, Erasmus not only probed thorny questions of spiritual liberty, he gave a persuasive indication of his own intellectual sympathies on the lips of one Eusebius:

> Sacred Scripture is of course the basic authority in everything; yet I sometimes run across ancient sayings or pagan writings—even the poets—so purely and reverently and admirably expressed that I can't help believing their authors' hearts were moved by some divine power. And perhaps the spirit of Christ is more widespread than we understand, and the company of saints includes many not in our calendar.... So that I would much rather let all of Scotus and others of his sort perish than the books of a single Cicero or Plutarch. (Erasmus 1997a: 192)

Amongst the Church Fathers, Augustine had affirmed in *De Civitate Dei* that 'The gods who presided over the Roman empire were like theatrical spectators' who remained 'quite unmoved' by the tribulations of mortals (Augustine 1998: 112); and increasingly mindful of the denigration of the Greco-Roman pantheon by succeeding generations of Christian thinkers, Erasmus would ultimately regret the figuration of the pagan gods in his early prayers and liturgies. More generally, while he never forsook his intellectual investment in the writings of ancient authors, in direct comparison with many of his fellow humanists he came increasingly to assert that the textual legacies of pagan antiquity could never eclipse or even rival the scriptural riches of the Church. Indeed, his later *Ciceronianus* (1528) would lament, 'The fact is we're Christians only in name. Our bodies may have been dipped in the holy water, but our minds are unbaptized. The sign of the cross may have been put on our brows, but the cross itself is repudiated by the mind within. We have Jesus on our lips, but it's Jupiter Optimus Maximus and Romulus that we have in our hearts' (Erasmus 1986: 394).

ERASMUS AND THE HUMANIST PROJECT

Quite apart from the ongoing commitment to Christian devotion and to ethical instruction, the many and diverse interests of humanists across Europe in pedagogy, public service, and ambitious intellectual endeavour were deeply anchored in the study of *literae humaniores* as they had been set down by ancient pens. These investments were in large measure a vigorous response to the legal, clerical, and political necessities of increasingly sophisticated administrations growing up across the continent in the late medieval and early modern periods. In particular, in their promotion of the *studia humanitatis* (influenced by writers such as Seneca, Pliny, and Plutarch but, above all, Cicero) Erasmus and his fellow scholars remained at pains throughout their careers to stress the life- and spirit-enhancing potential of the study of eloquence, of the renewal of ancient wisdom through translation and commentary, and of intellectual debate and exchange in the Christian pursuit of true piety and moral perfectibility.

Apart from assisting the learning of Latin, Erasmus's *Colloquies* (pub. 1518–33) were explicitly designed to address lively debates surrounding social mores, political misgovernment, and spiritual failings. Unsurprisingly, given the nature of this remit, on a number of occasions the collection incurred condemnation from Catholic authorities (and, indeed, some fellow scholars), unresponsive to the ways in which the Netherlander tested alternating appreciations of orthodox doctrine in dialogue form. In the company of the eminent English theologian John Colet (1467–1519), for example, Erasmus visited the shrines of Walsingham in 1512 and of Canterbury in 1512 and 1514, and yet in his colloquy *Peregrinatio religionis ergo* (A Pilgrimage for Religion's Sake, 1526), the credulous pilgrim Ogygius attests that there was nothing that he would not be 'very eager to do for the sake of the Most Holy Virgin, even if she bade me carry a letter from there to Jerusalem'. Assuming a wonted Erasmian mode of *ironia*, his auditor in this dialogue, Menedemus, retorts, 'Why would she need you as postman when she has so many angels to wait on her hand and foot?' (Erasmus 1997b: 637). The provocative nature of such exchanges would not pass unobserved. The collection was repeatedly banned by the theology faculty at Paris in 1544, 1547, 1551, and 1556, would temporarily find itself on Rome's ('many fish with a golden hook there'—*De captandis sacerdotis* ('In Pursuit of Benefices', 1522) (Erasmus 1997a: 47)) indexes of forbidden works in 1554 and 1559, and be outlawed in an index issued by the Council of Trent and confirmed by Pius IV. However, already by 1526 in the wake of condemnation from theologians at Paris and Louvain, the celebrated Italian scholar naturalized in England, Polydore Vergil (1470–1555) was alerting his friend the author, 'Your opponents have spread a rumour throughout England that you and your writings have recently been condemned in Paris. It is so persistent that everywhere people have been approaching our friend More and [a fellow Netherlander] and myself, along with other friends of yours, to ask if there was any truth in this distressing tale' (Erasmus 2003: 35). Another leading scholar, diplomat, and cleric in Henry VIII's realm, Cuthbert Tunstall (1474–1559), pleaded with his old friend a few years later in 1529, 'I have already warned you about cleansing the *Colloquies* of impurities, since there are things in them that offend many persons who are well informed—things on fasts, rites, decrees of the church ... pilgrimages, invocation of saints in emergencies—which accuse you of scornful disparagement' (Erasmus 1997a: xxxvii). Clearly sensitive to the growing tide of scrutiny (and, at points, censure) which his writings were incurring, Erasmus was called upon on a number of occasions in the later decades of his life to review his intellectual undertaking. In a letter of 1527, for example, he submitted, 'I gave my support to the pursuit of humane letters for no other reason than that they would be the handmaid of higher disciplines, in particular theology ... I also made it my purpose that the study of literature, which among the Italians and especially the Romans smacked of pure paganism, might begin openly to celebrate the name of Christ' (Erasmus 2010: 31).

This determination to privilege what he termed the *philosophia Christi* in his intellectual endeavours would be widely articulated by his fellow scholars across Europe. The Spanish humanist Juan Luis Vives (1493–1540), for example, travelled to England so often in the years 1526–7 that Erasmus styled him 'an amphibious animal' (Erasmus 2010: 151). In *De tradendis disciplinis* (1531) Vives echoed Erasmus's sentiments, arguing that 'Erudition involves four factors: natural capacity, judgement, memory, application. Pray tell me, whence the first three of these come: whence except from God? If praise is to be given to a learned man, it must be sought in the last-named element' (Vives 1913: 275). As will become evident in the course of this discussion, Erasmus was far from being a solitary voice among the humanists remaining within the fold of the Church in shining a light on the shortcomings of late medieval Catholicism. Figures such as Colet, More, and Tunstall remained alert to failings in the cultures of worship about them and showed themselves impatient with the intellectual legacies of scholastic theology, poor textual mediation, and pedagogical practices which their age had inherited—and thus one of the liveliest centres of such learned debate proved to be early Tudor England.

COLET AND CHRISTIAN HUMANISM

In 1499 Erasmus wrote to his continental correspondent, Fausto Andrelini, 'if you were fully aware of what England has to offer, you would rush hither, I tell you, on winged feet' (Erasmus 1974: 193). Moreover, the Netherlander proved himself equally exuberant when communicating with intellectuals native to the island: in the same year Thomas More (1478–1535) was informed, 'Your England is beginning to charm me inexpressibly, partly from acquaintance, which softens all harsh experiences, and partly because of the kindness shown to me by Colet and Prior Charnock' (Erasmus 1974: 228); and to Colet himself he effused, 'one of the many reasons why I find your England most agreeable is this in particular, that it is well supplied with that without which life itself is disagreeable to me: I mean men who are well versed in good literature' (Erasmus 1974: 199).

Given that so little of Colet's teaching and scholarship has survived, Erasmus's account of Colet in a letter to the German cleric (later a notable Reformist), Justus Jonas, dating from June 1521 remains an invaluable, if abbreviated account of the Englishman's life. Here, Erasmus underlines that Colet's early life of ease in London 'could [not] turn him from his passion for the life of the Gospel', and that later as Dean of St Paul's he pursued an ideal of Christian humanism, taking 'the greatest delight in conversation with his friends, which he would often carry on until far into the night; but all his talk was either of books or of Christ' (Erasmus 1988a: 233, 235). Like Erasmus himself, Colet appears to have been frequently unimpressed by the examples of monastic piety he witnessed about him ('It was not that [Colet] disapproved of the orders, but that their members did not live up to their profession') and was much more responsive to the piety he found amongst the laity: 'He used to say that he never found more uncorrupted characters than among married couples; for their natural affection, the care of their children, and the business of a household seemed to fence them in, as it were, so that they could not lapse indiscriminately into sin' (Erasmus 1988a: 239). In addition, like Erasmus, it appears that Colet (as presented in this narrative) was unafraid of incurring the wrath of his superiors: 'there was no class of men to whom [Colet] was more hostile than bishops who behaved like wolves instead of shepherds ... because they appealed to the people with liturgy and ceremonies and solemn benedictions and indulgences while serving the world' (Erasmus 1988a: 239).

The educational world which both men inherited in the closing decades of the fifteenth century was profoundly shaped by the theological meditations and reasonings of medieval thinkers such as Ockham, Scotus, Albertus, and Aquinas (and, where they existed, their exegeses of the ancient authors, notably Aristotle). Erasmus railed that 'Nothing was taught in the schools of Cambridge, except *Alexander*, the *Parva Logicalia* (as they call them), with the old-established readings of *Aristotle*, and the *Questions* of Scotus' (Colet 1965a: xv). For his own part, Colet poured scorn on the manner of Thomist reasoning which, he felt, took too little account of Scripture and pondered questions beyond the remit of mortals. The intellectual range of the medieval theologians might be vast indeed in their surviving writings, but generations of humanist scholars took exception most often to what they perceived as the philosophical *impasses* of their forebears. In his quodlibetal questions (imitating the mode of unrehearsed debate), for example, Aquinas had enquired 'Whether an angel can move from one place to another without passing through an intermediate place?' and volunteered, 'I answer: it must be stated that an angel can if it wants move from one place to another without passing through an intermediate place, and if it wants it can pass through an intermediate place' (Aquinas 1983: 38). Despite Erasmus's claims that the Englishman harboured some sympathy for the arguments of Scotus, more generally Colet found himself uninspired by (if well-versed in) the theology of the Scholastics which, he felt, deflected attention away from questions of ethics and piety towards technical over-distinction and aporetic cogitation. Erasmus assured the Dean publicly in a prefatory address, 'When you tell me that you dislike the modern class of theologians, who spend their lives in sheer hair-splitting and sophistical quibbling, you have my emphatic agreement, dear Colet' (Erasmus 1998: 9). Such impatience would become increasingly evident in Erasmus's writings in the later 1520s and 1530s when he was repeatedly drawn to the defence of

Catholic doctrine against Lutheran theories of salvation. In *Hyperaspistes liber secundus* (1527), for example, he would argue in exasperated fashion, 'In brief, we should devote our efforts to obtaining God's grace rather than to indulging in fine-spun disputations about how grace works in us' (Erasmus 2000: 747).

Erasmus journeyed to early Tudor England six times between 1499 and 1516 and met Colet for the first time in Oxford in October 1499. Colet spent some unknown period in France and Italy in the 1490s, but by 1496 he was beginning his public lectures to Oxford audiences upon all of Paul's epistles. His sermon on 1 Corinthians strikes notes which are widely in evidence throughout the account of his ministry. Assuming an authoritative voice of spiritual counsel, Colet reminded his congregation of the very omnipotence and inexhaustible beneficence of the Creator ('God himself united with human nature (a *Theanthropos*, as the Greeks say), lived here on earth, and mingled with men for men's salvation, that he might recall and reconcile them to God his Father'), and stressed to his flock their own 'dark prison-house of weak human flesh' (Colet 1965b: 20, 17). Moreover, like so many Christian humanists, Colet remained unwavering in his moral outrage when the Church became sullied as it turned its attentions to the 'things of this world':

> all that is temporal and secular, should be despised by the Church, not desired, or sought, or appropriated ... [and clerics] By this looking back from the plough, this turning again, *like dogs to their vomit, and like sows to their wallowing in the mire,* they have weakened themselves ... we are devoid of all merits, and scarce differ from the laity in anything, but our shaven crowns, and hoods, and cassocks. (Colet 1965b: 38, 40–1)

In his preaching upon Paul's Epistle to the Romans, Colet concentrated more squarely upon 'how great is the sublimity and loftiness of the divine majesty', and upon the spiritual emergency of penance ('each one should acknowledge his own sin, and hasten to repent of his own wickedness, and not abuse the forbearance of God') for a fallen race in which no nationality (including the Jewish race who claims precedence 'on account of the Law given specially to them') is more pleasing before divine judgement than any other: 'Whoever owns and believes and observes the mystery of salvation, no matter of what race of men he be, St Paul pronounces that he will be saved' (Colet 1965a: 4, 7). Acknowledging both Judaic and Greek anxieties concerning the human vicissitudes of self-government, Colet insisted that man's 'soul is placed in miserable subjection to folly and lust, and dealt with everything after the judgement of the senses' (Colet 1965a: 22). However, given the ongoing debate detailed above regarding the larger place of scholarly endeavour in the pursuit of piety, Colet in this sermon arrestingly reflects upon the competing identities of the intellectual and the worshipper within the mind of the faithful Christian:

> For while the forces of knowledge consist rather in separation, that of love consists in union. Hence of necessity love is the more impetuous and efficacious, and swifter in attaining what is good, than knowledge is in detecting what is true. Furthermore, it is beyond doubt more pleasing to God himself to be loved by men than to be surveyed;

and to be worshipped, than to be understood. For we bestow nothing upon God by contemplating him; but by loving him we give him all our being, powers, and possessions. (Colet 1965a: 30)

Nonetheless, if Colet is at pains here to emphasize the ways in which worshippers must formulate their ideals of Christian service and piety, his congregation was never in any doubt of the scholarly concerns which must frame our encounters with Scripture—that we must engage with the Bible *historically* in order to apprehend its meanings fully: 'This Epistle to the Romans was written during the reign of Claudius, at the close of his reign, about the twentieth year of St Paul's ministry ... not long before St Paul's last journey to Jerusalem' (Colet 1965a: 94).

The one work which had entered the print market by the time of Colet's death was his Convocation Sermon (1510/1511?). This sermon, a key insight into his soteriological thinking, the human race's yearning for divine grace and its temporal state of abasement, took as its text that of Romans 12:2—'Be you nat conformed to this worlde, but be you reformed in the newnes of your understandynge, that ye may proue what is the good wyll of God, well pleasing and perfecte'. In direct comparison with theologians later in the century, Colet here found himself drawn to consider the status and function of good works as a mark of spiritual devotion. This was a question which not only exercised the late medieval Church and, indeed, later the Reformists, but had also given the Church Fathers and medieval divines pause for thought. Aquinas, for example, had specifically pondered 'Whether a man without grace can prepare himself for grace?' and, taking his lead from a proof lifted from Proverbs, asserted that 'to be able to prepare himself for grace was assigned to the power of man'—though cautioned that 'we must guard against the error of Pelagius who maintained that through free choice a man could fulfill the law and merit eternal life nor needed divine aid except in order to know what to do' (Aquinas 1983: 44). Like other Christian humanists discussed in this chapter, Colet maintained the orthodox position that good works might be indications of piety, but that mortals were wholly dependent upon the redemptive intervention of divine grace for their spiritual journey from this lower world of sin and temptation.

More generally, in the meditations shared with his peers or 'reuerent fathers' in the Convocation Sermon, Colet appealed for all churchmen present to commit themselves 'to the endeuour of reformation of the churches estate', targeting in particular 'carnall concupiscence' ('they drowne them selfe in the delytes of this worlde'), covetousness and the clergy's complicity in warmongering: 'our warrynge is to pray, to rede and study scriptures, to preache the worde of God, to ministre the sacramentes of helth, to do sacrifice for the people, and to offre hostis for this sinnes. For we are mediatours and meanes vnto God for men' (Colet 1909: 294–7). Indeed, in keeping with a pacifist commitment widely in evidence amongst this generation of European humanists, Erasmus records that Colet's Good Friday sermon (1513) *ostensibly* supported Henry VIII's bellicose ambitions in France, and yet in distinct opposition to his sovereign's pleasure and, indeed, the pervasive influence of the chivalric literatures of earlier centuries, 'at the same time he showed how hard it is to die a Christian death, how few enter upon a war without being poisoned by hatred or by greed, how difficult it was for one man at the same time to love his brother—and without that no man will see God—and to plunge a weapon into his brother's entrails. He added that they ought to imitate Christ their King rather than characters like Julius and Alexander' (Erasmus 1988a: 242).

As Dean of St Paul's, Colet reinstituted divinity lectures and was key in the re-establishment of St Paul's school in 1510 in a new location. Colet's works would not be extensively published until the nineteenth century when he was more often revered as an educationalist than a theologian. With the care of a new school, Colet inevitably turned his attentions (like so many of his fellow scholars) to questions of pedagogy, notably the status and function of classical learning in the classroom. In his 'Proheme' (1527) to William Lily's Latin grammar book, for example, he addressed the young readers:

> Wherfore I praye you, al lytel babys, al lytel chyldren, lerne gladly this lytel treatyse, and commende it dylygently vnto your memoryes. Trustynge of this begynnynge that ye shal procede and growe to parfyt lyterature, and come at the last to be gret clarkes. And lyfte vp your lytel whyte handes for me, whiche prayeth for you to god. To whome be al honour and imperyal maieste and glory. Amen. (Colet 1527: A6ᵛ)

As we have seen, the humanist project was in a host of different ways constantly called upon to negotiate the continuities and, indeed, discontinuities in the spiritual and ethical emphases between scriptural and Greco-Roman textual legacies. Richly sensitive to the intellectual riches of the latter and the devotional imperatives of the former, scholars might move on occasions from wonted positions of privileging the Word above all other sources of knowledge to a vigorous desire to unite the sapiential treasures of both traditions. We have already witnessed the depth of veneration which Erasmus might articulate when considering the intellectual achievements of antiquity and, in his own *De initiis, sectis et laudibus philosophiae* (On the Origins, Schools and Merits of Philosophy, 1518), for example, Vives celebrated the classical luminaries Thales, Phocus, Pythagoras, and Cleostratus, declaring, 'What words can do justice to the delight that lay in the discoveries or to the greatness of these illustrious men, whom we might more correctly call immortal gods? For these individuals lifted themselves not only above our level but even beyond the limitations of their own corporeal nature' (Vives 1987: 15).

In *De Civitate Dei*, Augustine had been constantly called upon to review both the travails and achievements of the Roman Empire, but remained convinced that 'It was not God's purpose then to give to [the Romans] eternal life with the angels in His Heavenly City. For only true godliness leads to that fellowship: the godliness which offers to the one true God alone that service of religion which the Greeks call *latreia*' (Augustine 1998: 215). Unpersuaded by such assertions that pagans were necessarily deprived of the salvation to which all Christian souls aspired, humanist scholars turned to the ancient authors not only to establish a *norma loquendi* for intellectual discourse (see, for example, Erasmus's *De ratione studii* [1511]), but also to access the riches of ethical wisdom so widely appreciated across early modern Christendom. Indeed, it should be noted that Augustine himself had been unable to suppress a profound respect for Plato and Platonic writers such as Plotinus and Porphyry whose writings, he acknowledged, foreshadowed Holy Writ: in *De Civitate Dei*, he submitted, 'Certain of our brethren in Christ's grace are amazed when they hear or read that Plato had an understanding of God which, as they see, is in many respects consistent with the truth of our religion' (Augustine 1998: 327).

Aristotle had underlined in the *Nichomachean Ethics* that, 'The perfect form of friend-ship is that between the good, and those who resemble each other in virtue' (Aristotle 1962: 461). Mindful of such sentiments, reiterated in Cicero's widely studied dialogue *De Amicitia*, Colet wrote in 1495 to the most eminent Platonist of the age, Marsilio Ficino, 'While I am reading your books I seem to live, just as I should be more alive if I could see you in person, Marsilio, whom I long to see and pay homage to.' Moreover, for his own part, Ficino paid ample tribute to the Englishman, referring to Colet's writings regularly in his own works and corresponded with *amantissime pariter et amatissime, mi Colete* (my loving and beloved Colet) (Jayne 1963: 82, 81). Like Augustine, Colet maintained a profound interest in Platonic philosophy, alert to its potential synergies with Christian teaching. Its influence is particularly in evidence in the figurative language he employs in his preaching: 'the uniting and all-powerful rays of Christ. For these, streaming as it were from the Sun of Truth, gather and draw together towards themselves and towards unity, those who are in a state of multiplicity; that they may first have light, and then warmth as its consequence' (Colet 1965b: 57). Erasmus wrote grandiloquently in 1499, 'When I listen to Colet it seems to me that I am listening to Plato himself' (Erasmus 1974: 235), but in spite of his extensive knowledge of such classical authors, the dean remained adamant throughout his career that Christians should devote all their ener-gies to the demands of *scriptural* study:

> Therefore we ought to banquet with Christ alone, at the choice table of the Scriptures; and to feast most plentifully with him in the New Testament, wherein the water of Moses has been turned into wine by Christ himself.... Now if any should say, as is often said, that to read heathen authors is of assistance for the right understanding of Holy Writ, let them reflect whether the very fact of such reliance being placed upon them, does not make them a chief obstacle to such understanding. For, in so acting, you distrust your power of understanding the Scriptures by grace alone, and prayer, and by the help of Christ, and of faith; but think you can do so through the means and assistance of heathens.... Those books in which Christ is not found, are but a table of devils. Do not become readers of philosophers, companions of devils. (Colet 1965b: 109–10)

LUTHERANA TRAGŒDIA

Colet died in October 1519 and would find his way in due course into John Bale's *Illustrium maiorum Britanniae* (1548). Erasmus wrote to Richard Pace, Henry VIII's Latin Secretary who would succeed Colet as Dean of St Paul's, 'I feel only half a man,

with myself alive and Colet dead!' (Erasmus 1987a: 97). In the event, the surviving generation of scholars would have no choice but to negotiate the trials and tribulations which
the Reformation posed for their intellectual and spiritual commitments—what Erasmus
would come to term, on occasions, the *Lutherana tragœdia*. He wrote plaintively in 1521,
'If only this tragedy which Luther has begun with such bad omens for us might be given
a happy ending by some god from the machine' (Erasmus 1988a: 258). In this instance,
Erasmus's hopes were in vain. Some scholars would be persuaded by Luther's attacks
on a corrupt Catholic Church and forsake their profession of the *old faith*. Indeed, the
Netherlander acknowledged to the archbishop of Palermo, Jean de Carondelet, in 1527:

> 'But Philippus Melanchthon', they say, 'and several others who know Greek and
> Hebrew have rallied to the side of the condemned faction'. That is not the fault of
> learning but of men; besides, Luther counts more supporters by far amongst those
> who know neither Greek nor Latin. And the great majority of those trained in these
> studies are opposed to Luther. (Erasmus 2010: 50)

With an equal measure of *hauteur*, he would inform a correspondent in 1528 that
'Oecolampadius has recently taken a wife, a quite attractive young woman. He wishes
to mortify the flesh, I imagine. Some call the Lutheran business a tragedy; to me it
seems more of a comedy, for all the commotions end in marriage' (Erasmus 2011: 135).
Interestingly, in these same years, Thomas More would prove himself equally scathing in his assaults upon the ideas *and also the mores* of the Lutheran community. One
of his favoured lines of attack upon his adversaries was Luther's foreswearing of his
vows of celibacy, urging his reader in *The confutacyon of Tyndale's answere* (1532), for
example, to 'loke vppon frere Luther the very father of theyr hole secte, and se hym
ronne out of relygyon, & fallen to flesshe' (More 1990b: 41).

More generally, during the 1520s Erasmus found himself sorely tested as he repeatedly
pointed out in his correspondence from the period:

> Luther is piling on both liberal studies and myself a massive load of unpopularity.
> Everyone knew that the church was burdened with tyranny and ceremonies and laws
> invented by men for their own profit. Many were already hoping for some remedy
> and even planning something; but often remedies unskilfully applied make matters
> worse … Oh, if that man had either left things alone, or made his attempt more cau-
> tiously and in moderation! (Erasmus 1988a: 155)

In the event, Erasmus found himself beleaguered on all sides by: Catholic critics who
condemned him for initiating ecclesiastical critiques which, they believed, had given
added impetus to Reformist fervour; by Catholic scholars who urged him to become
a defender of the Church; and by Lutherans themselves. The latter variously enjoined
him to forsake a corrupt Church, denigrated him for what they perceived as his weak-
kneed eirenicism, or condemned him for his attempts to undermine Lutheran doctrine
(notably, his writings on the spiritual significance of free will—*De libero arbitrio* [1524])

by reaffirming orthodox Catholic doctrine. Luther would make a swift response to Erasmus's arguments in *De servo arbitrio* (1525).

As has been observed, Colet would not live to witness the great turmoils of the Reformation in Europe and remained committed to the orthodox teachings of the Church, to Papal authority, to the seven sacraments, and to the doctrine of transubstantiation: 'In the blessed cup and the broken bread there is a saving communication of the very body and blood of Jesus Christ itself, which is received in common by many, that they may be one in it' (Colet 1965b: 107). The English cleric also deeply invested in the very *inclusivity* of the Church's soteriology, emphasizing that Christ 'was merciful, and rejected no one, but *would have all men to be saved*.... *Abraham* was justified, not only because he believed, but also because he was prepared in very deed to offer up and sacrifice his son Isaac to God. When it follows that *by works a man is justified, and not by faith only*' (Colet 1965b: 51, 56). For the next generations of intellectuals and public servants rising in the administration of Henry VIII, like More and Tunstall, it would prove impossible to be shielded from the turmoils surrounding the divorce from Katherine of Aragon and the break with Rome which racked early Tudor England. From a position of safety across the Channel in 1528, Erasmus would submit in a letter to Vives, 'God forbid that I meddle in the affair of Jupiter and Juno, especially since I am not well informed about it. I would more readily award two Junos to one man than take one away' (Erasmus 2011: 308–9).

THOMAS MORE—'A MAN FOR ALL SEASONS'

More had much in common with Colet in theological matters and clearly looked to the older man as a mentor and spiritual counsellor as he grew to maturity in early Tudor England. Erasmus wrote to More in 1511 commending him as one 'both able and pleased to play with everyone the part of a man for all seasons'—one who might divide his energies between the *vita activa* and that of Christian devotion (Erasmus 1975: 163). Erasmus had entered an Augustinian monastery in 1487 and was ordained in 1492, but would later receive a dispensation, confirmed by Leo X, releasing him from his religious vows to pursue his studies. By the early years of the sixteeth century, Thomas More had become attached to a Carthusian monastic community outside the walls of the City of London and followed its curricula of spiritual devotions without formally taking any vows. However, by 1505 he had turned his attentions to a legal career and married for the first time—he would remarry one month after his first wife died in 1511. Erasmus, who had known the Englishman since 1499, would quip much later in 1519 to a German correspondent that '[More] chose to be a god-fearing husband rather than an immoral priest' (Erasmus 1987a: 21).

It has often been asserted that More's career may be seen to divide broadly into two periods: that of the humanist scholar (until *c.*1520) who engaged enthusiastically with genres inherited from antiquity (such as the dialogue, the exemplary history, the

contemplative essay, political theorizing, satire, as well as medieval writings investing in the *de contemptu mundi* tradition); and that extending beyond 1520 when More
found himself all too frequently called upon to be a state advocate and representative
as well as a religious polemicist. However, on closer inspection, continuities of thought
and diction may be traced across the breadth of his career. Amongst his early writings, the aspiring English scholar wrote a *Life of Pico* (*c.*1510—the Italian humanist Pico
della Mirandola was also much admired by Colet) and, in direct comparison with later
productions by Erasmus (*De praeparatione ad mortem* [1533]), Thomas Lupset (*Waye
of Dyenge Well* [1534]) and Thomas Elyot (*A Preseruative agaynste Deth* [1545]), More
acknowledged the profound influence of the medieval *ars moriendi* tradition upon his
thinking with his unfinished meditative work, *The Last Things* (*c.*1522). Interestingly,
here once again, we discover a humanist scholar pondering sensitively the dual legacies
of Christian and antique writings: 'What profite and commoditye commeth vnto mans
soule by the meditacion of death, is not onelye marked of the chosen people of god, but
also of such as wer the best sorte among gentiles & painims' (More 1997: 139).

From this early period also dates his celebrated *Utopia* (1516) and in that society overseen by tranibors and phylarchs, the islanders are clearly shown to value highly the commitment to intellectual study and spiritual devotion. Those individuals who display
early on 'an outstanding personality, a first-rate intelligence, and an inclination of mind
toward learning' are introduced to the literatures of antiquity: such persons 'discuss virtue and pleasure, but their principal and chief debate is in what thing or things, one or
more, they are to hold that happiness consists' (More 1965a: 159, 161). Hythloday, who
we learn in Book One is 'no bad Latin scholar', shadows More's own passions in the early
years of the century for Greek studies, concluding that 'there is nothing valuable in Latin
except certain treatises of Seneca and Cicero' (More 1965a: 49, 51). Throughout his career, More remained powerfully influenced by medieval thinking concerning the moral
and spiritual integrity of collective experience focused upon *one* culture of worship, and
this would go a long way to feeding his passionate rejection of the heresiarch Luther in
the latter's attacks upon the unity of the Church, its practices and doctrines. Tenaciously,
More would argue in *A Dialogue Concerning Heresies* (1530) that 'his chyrche is a congregacyon of people gathered in to his fayth'; and in *The second parte of the confutacion
of Tyndals answere* (1533) acknowledged (like Colet) the morally chequered nature of
this 'congregacyon' which might nevertheless yearn collectively for divine grace: 'the
company of good and badde togyther is Chrystes church' (More 1981a: 118; More 1973:
1019). In addition, the English humanist could find ideas sympathetic to this belief in
the pagan writings of the ancients: Seneca, for example, had stressed in his *Epistulae
morales* that 'The first thing which philosophy undertakes to give is fellow-feeling with
all men; in other words, sympathy and sociability. We part company with our promise
if we are unlike other men' (Seneca 1925: 21). Unsurprisingly, therefore, it soon becomes
apparent that the religious complexion of Utopia would have been easily identifiable to
sixteenth-century eyes: 'There are different kinds of religion not only on the island as a
whole but also in each city. Some worship as god the sun, others the moon, others one
of the planets.... But by far the majority, and those by far the wiser, believe in nothing

of the kind but in a certain single being, unknown, eternal, immense, inexplicable, far above the reach of the human mind, diffused throughout the universe not in mass but in power' (More 1965a: 217).

In these years, Erasmus could be found lamenting that More, having been tempted into the *vita activa* (namely, of service in Henry VIII's administration), was 'lost to letters' (More 1965a: xxxv). However, if the ambitious English lawyer had a growing family which necessitated an enlarged and regular income, in the early years of the century it is known that he lectured on Augustine's *De Civitate Dei* at the London church of St Lawrence Jewry—and thus he may also have been mindful of the Augustinian tenet that 'The pursuit of wisdom ... consists in both action and contemplation' (Augustine 1998: 316). Later in 1527, Henry VIII himself would write to Erasmus, trying to lure one of the Church's most notable *pugnatores Dei* against Luther across the Channel to join the ranks of his own court: 'In your wisdom you will perceive immediately how we must counter these evils. In our opinion there seems to be no better method and solution than that you abandon Italy and your beloved Germany altogether and agree to take up residence here in our kingdom' (Erasmus 2010: 341). Erasmus resisted vehemently being drawn too closely into the service of monarchs, but More's involvement in Tudor government evolved from the roles of Justice of the Peace, under-sheriff of London, member of Parliament, trade negotiator, diplomat, and counsellor to his appointment to the king's council in 1518, as Chancellor of the Duchy of Lancaster in 1525, as Lord Chancellor in 1529—and, indeed, his role as religious polemicist from the 1520s onward as he sought repeatedly to challenge the Reformist threat from the continent.

The first edition of Luther's *opera omnia* was rolling from Froben's press in Basle in the autumn of 1518, a month before the second edition of *Utopia* issued from the very same source. Soon Luther's ideas were circulating widely across Europe. By June 1520 the papal bull *Exsurge Domine* was promulgated, calling for the burning of the heretic's works. In 1521 the theology faculty of the Sorbonne condemned them and in the same year Cardinal Wolsey presided over a burning of Luther's books in the presence a crowd of some thirty thousand onlookers at St Paul's Cross with John Fisher, bishop of Rochester, delivering the sermon. By 1524 Tunstall, as bishop of London, had summoned the city's booksellers, warning them not to traffic in outlawed publications; two years later, More was involved in a raid by the authorities upon the houses of the Hanseatic merchants and the confiscation of banned Lutheran works, leading to yet another public burning of books in the capital in February 1526. Nonetheless, in spite of all these endeavours, Lutheran sympathizers continued to meet (notably, at the White Horse Tavern in Cambridge), and in early 1526 the first copies of Tyndale's English translation of the New Testament were being introduced surreptiously into the Tudor realm.

Seeking above all to preserve what might be left of a *concordia ecclesiae*, Erasmus urged European potentates (and those in their service) to return erring souls to the fold rather than persecuting them: 'I do not deny that heretical intransigence must be abhorred, if incurable. But meanwhile because of our hatred of one error we must beware of falling into another. Let us preserve that self-control, to prevent controversy from convincing us that the straight is crooked and the bitter sweet and vice versa' (Erasmus 1988b: 260). More would be at the very centre of Catholic resistance to the spread of Lutheranism in the Tudor kingdom in the 1520s and early years of the 1530s, but believed, unlike Erasmus, that recourse to force was warranted in the struggle against unbelievers. In 1521, in response to the assault upon sanctity of the Church's seven sacraments in Luther's *De captivitate Babylonica* (which had argued that only three—baptism, the Eucharist, and penance—might be retained with scriptural authority), Henry VIII wrote (in collaboration with others) the *Assertio septem sacramentorum adversus M. Lutherum* and earned the title of 'Defensor Fidei' as a mark of papal gratitude. Luther's subsequent *Contra Henricum regem Angliæ* (1522) was then countered by More's own *Responsio ad Lutherum* (1523–4). The argumentation of this extensive tract, aimed primarily at a continental audience, deployed short quotation followed by long (often testy) explication and was voiced initially in the guise of one Ferdinandus Baravellus who was then replaced by one William Ross in a second version. One of More's abiding contentions was that the community of the Church and the legitimacy of its practices were established well in advance of the writing of the gospels—and so any affirmation of a *sola scriptura* position remained wholly inadequate as a theological response to the Christian tradition, as he would underline again later in *The confutacyon of Tyndale's answere* (1532): 'the fayth was taught and men were baptysed, and masses sayd and the other sacramentes mynystred amonge crysten people, before any parte of the newe testament was put in wrytynge and that this was done by the word of god vnwryten' (More 1990b: 225). More remained unwavering in his belief that the customs and rituals of the community of the Church derived legitimacy from practices sanctioned by Christ himself.

In the *Responsio* More determines to do battle at length with the *vili et sordido fraterculo* from Wittenberg: 'For when one book after another appeared uninterruptedly, each one worse than the last, there finally appeared the *Babylon*, truly that tower of Babel which was built up against heaven, from which the impious fellow undertook to destroy the heavenly sacraments of Christ' (More 1969: 7). Indeed, the Englishman does not refrain from sullying his pen in the vigorous invectives being then exchanged between the rival faith communities of Europe: 'It would require, not an eyeless Cyclops, but some many-eyed Argos and Lynceus to trace Luther's paths. It would perhaps be a difficult matter to trace the path of a snake over the ground, except that by its offensive odour breaking out wherever it turns and creeps along and by its loathsome corruption infecting the earth it betrays itself only too well' (More 1969: 51). Meanwhile, More's reader was assured that the followers of this *pediculosus fraterculus*: 'After hunting for several months ... had collected from any place whatever, railings, brawlings, scurrilous scoffs, wantonness, obscenities, dirt, filth, muck, shit, all this [sewage] they stuff into the most foul sewer of Luther's breast. All this he vomited up through that foul mouth into that railers' book of his, like devoured dung. From there, reader, you receive that accumulated mass of indecent brawlings, with which alone the utterly foolish books is filled' (More 1969: 61).

As his textual assaults upon the 'lewd sect' of Lutherans became more frequent during the course of the 1520s and early 1530s, More would underline again and again for his *optime lector* a series of deeply held beliefs in defence of the doctrine and practices of the Catholic Church: a passionate resistance to indiscriminate condemnation ('the reverend father, Friar Martin Luther, argues ... some popes have been wicked; therefore, the papacy is wicked ... some Augustinian friars are heretical, seditious, schismatic; therefore, the whole Augustinian brotherhood is heretical, seditious, schismatic' [More 1969: 83]); a belief that the inherited practices of the Church derived a legitimacy quite independent of written record ('If none of the gospels had ever been written, there would still remain written in the hearts of the faithful the gospel which is more ancient than the books of all the evangelists; there would remain the sacraments' [More 1969: 89]); the significance of papal authority ('Surely, as regards the pope, God who put him in charge of His church knew what an evil it would have been to have lacked a pope' [More 1969: 141]); the doctrines of purgatory and transubstantiation ('But I saye that purgatory is ordeyned for the punyshement of suche synnys ... purgatory, & that the very blessed body and blood of Christ is in the sacrament of the aulter, and that therfore it is ther to be honoured' [More 1990b: 289]); the status and function of good works ('For he that hopeth that by fayth alone he shall be saued wythout eny good workys as Lutheranis do byleue in dede he hath an euyll hope & a dampnable' [More 1981a: 383]); and the inexhaustible nature of God's grace open to everyone ('But his assystence is alway at hande y^f we be wyllynge to worke therewith as the lyght is present with the sonne y^f we lyst not wylfully to shyt oure eyen and wynke' [More 1981a: 404]).

More resolved to cross swords again, for example, with the *reuerendus frater, pater potator* in Wittenberg in *A Dialogue Concerning Heresies* (1529). Here, the textual speaker or 'Master Chauncellour' disputes in his house with a visitor or 'messenger' of dissenting sympathies. The 'Chauncellor' takes the 'messenger' into his study and carefully seeks to unpick 'the sowynge and settynge forth of Luthers pestylent heresyes in thys realme' (More 1981a: 22). Resisting the Lutheran suspicion of church ornament and ritual, the host appears thoroughly conversant with the medieval investment in the *devotio moderna* (see Chapter 1) and insists to his *froward* auditor that the 'two wordes *Christus crucifixus* do not so lyuely represent vs the remembraunce of his bytter passyon as doth a blessyd ymage of the crucyfyx neyther to lay man nor vnto a lerned ... yet is there no man I wene so good nor so well lerned nor in medytacyon so well accustomyd but that he fyndeyth hymselfe more mouyd to pyte and compassyon vpon the beholdynge of the holy crucyfyxe than whan he lackyth it' (More 1981a: 47, 56). Elsewhere, the 'messenger' pours scorn upon the ecclesiastical riches lavished on the adoration of relics, but such submissions are dismissed by the 'host', who argues 'Take all the gold that is spent about all the pecys of crystys crosse thorowe crystendome ... yet y^f all y^t golde were gathered togyder it wolde appere a pore porcyon in comparyson of the golde that is bestowed vpon cuppes' (More 1981a: 50). Nor will the host admit of any wrongdoing in 'the offrynge of brede & ale' to saints: 'I haue my selfe sene y^t often tymes and yet am I not remembred that euer I saw preste or clerke fare the better therfore or ones drynke thereof but it is gyuen to chyldren or pore folke to praye for the syke chylde' (More 1981a: 234).

However, perhaps most strikingly, the 'host' (or More) recalls that at Barking Abbey in Essex, 'about .xxx. yeares past', 'an olde ymage' was being set 'in a newe tabernacle' and quite by chance 'out there fell … many relyques that had lyen vnknowen in that ymage go wote howe longe':

> The byshop of London cam then thyder to se there were no deceyte therin. And I amonge other was present there whyle he loked theron and examyned the matter of it.… I remember a lytell pece of wood there was rudely shapen in crosse with threde wrapped about it … among other were there certayne small kercheors which were named there our ladyes and of here owne workynge.… And howe longe that ymage had stande in that olde tabernacle y^t coulde no man tell … they gessyd y^t .iiii. or .v. C. yere ago that ymage was hyden whan the abbey was burned by infydels and those relyques hyden therin.… And so the relyques remayned vnknowen therein tyll nowe y^t god gaue that chaunce that opened it.… but as for pygges bones for holy relyques or dampned wretches to be worshypped for sayntes all be it y^t y^f it happened yet it nothyng hurted the soules of them that mysse take it no more than y^f we worshyp an hoste in the masse whiche percase the neglygence or malyce of some lewde preste hathe lefte vnconsecrate yet is it neuer to be thought thoughe suche a thynge myghte happen sodeynly that euer god wyll suffre suche a thynge to laste and endure in his chyrche. (More 1981a: 222–3)

A Dialogue Concerning Heresies remains distinctive amongst More's anti-Reformist productions for the often genial manner in which Church doctrine is disputed with a resisting auditor. Rather than immediately attacking the beliefs of the 'messenger', the host allows time for them both to collect their thoughts and welcomes his guest back into his house for the debate to unfold in a deliberately composed manner. Again and again, More insists that the Church contains 'the company of good and badde togyther' and that practices which mystify (or even alienate) those such as the 'messenger' might all have their contribution to make to a divine purpose *which passeth all understanding*. As opposed to the fury often expressed in works such as the *Responsio*, the eirenic notes struck in this dialogue and elsewhere in a work such as the *Letter against Frith*, for example, supporting the doctrine of transubstantiation (*c*.1532—'So I decided to reply to your letter and make it clear to everyone that no matter how ignorant I am of theology I am still too loyal a Christian ever to be a Lutheran' [More 1990a: 15]) indicate the breadth of the emotional range upon which More was able to draw in challenging the adversaries of the Catholic Church.

CONCLUDING THOUGHTS—*A TYME OF SOWYNG & A TYME OF REPYNG TO*

Published in 1542, some seven years after More's death, and translated into English in 1595 by 'William Jones Gent.', Giovanni Battista Nenna's popular tract *Nennio, or A Treatise of*

Nobility recalled for its sixteenth-century reader in a timely manner that, 'the ancient noble men of Rome did weare vppon their shooes little Moones, that they might alwaies beare in minde, the instabilitie of the honour of this world, which changeth like vnto the Moone' (Nenna 1595: A3^v). Better than most, More might have had cause to take this lesson to heart. Erasmus remained ever more nimble than the Chancellor in refusing to nail his colours to the mast of any particular ship of state or to become fenced in by pro-liferating articles of faith: he wrote in 1523 to the archbishop of Palermo, 'The sum and substance of our religion is peace and concord. This can hardly remain the case unless we define as few matters as possible and leave each individual's judgement free on many questions' (Erasmus 1988b: 252). Doing battle with *Lutherus scelerum caput, malorum machinator & artifex* (Luther, captain of evildoing, architect and artificer of evil) year on year, More had always been more inclined than some of his fellow scholars to *define matters*—and this would leave him increasingly vulnerable amidst the radically chan-ging allegiances in evidence at the very heart of the Tudor regime which he served. More resigned as Lord Chancellor in May 1532. However, this signalled no retreat on his part from the fray with the Reformists. He continued to write and to attract the attentions of hostile eyes both at home and abroad with works such as *The Confutation of Tyndale's Answer* (1532), the *Apology* (1533), *The Debellation of Salem and Bizance* (1533), and *The Answer to a Poisoned Book* (1533). Moreover, his refusal to attend Anne Boleyn's coron-ation in 1533 or to accept the break with Rome in the 1534 Act of Succession inevitably did little to endear him to his increasingly irascible sovereign.

After being committed to the Tower in 1534, More spent the last fifteen months of his life devoting himself to a range of textual productions which included *A Dialogue of Comfort Against Tribulation, A Treatise to receive the Blessed Body of our Lord, A Treatise upon the Passion, De Tristitia Christi*, as well as various reflections, prayers, and instruc-tions on piety. Investing deeply at this time in the generic expectations of *consolatio* writ-ing influenced by his longstanding knowledge of authors such as Augustine, Boethius, Julian of Norwich, Hilton, and Kempis amongst others, More returned repeatedly to the question of the defence of the Church and its doctrines and how the circumstances of *otium*, of physical and inward withdrawal from the public world, might enable the Christian to assume a greater self-government and to contemplate scriptural promises of spiritual fulfilment in the world to come. In this most ascetic period of his life, the prisoner in the Tower was clearly responsive to the teachings of Ecclesiastes and con-cluded affectingly in the *Dialogue of Comfort* (pub. 1553) that, 'There is also a tyme of sowyng & a tyme of repyng to. Now must we in this world sow, that we may in the tother world repe and in this short sowyng tyme of this wepyng world, must we water our sede with the showers of our teares and than shall we haue in hevyn a mery laughing hervest for euer' (More 1976: 42). Understandably, however, there was little time to be spent in contemplating this 'mery laughing hervest' in the so-called 'Tower works'. When the requisites for writing were withdrawn from him in June 1535, the fruits of his labours in captivity appear to have been smuggled out of the stronghold before he was called upon to face his final ordeals. The disgraced statesman was put on trial on 1 July 1535 and beheaded six days later.

As we have seen, Erasmus, Colet, and More all met with Henry VIII's displeasure, admittedly to quite different degrees, in their refusal to enter fully into the service of his changeful political project. All of them felt compelled through scholarly endeavour and various conceptions of ministry to focus their energies upon safeguarding the spiritual integrity of a Church beleaguered by critics and self-serving individuals, both within and without. And, in the process, they are often discovered drawing deeply, whether they admitted it or not, from the textual riches of pagan antiquity and medieval writing in addition to those of Scripture. We began this discussion contemplating some of Erasmus's early writings and how their undertakings were revisited in complex ways in the later collection of the *Colloquies*, and it seems timely, by way of conclusion, to return to their concerns. Stung by the censure that the dialogues were incurring, the Netherlander wrote to an English correspondent in 1528, insisting that he was not 'the only one to condemn the excessive number of feast days ... [and] The Christian religion today does not depend on miracles, and it is no secret how many false beliefs have been brought into the world through men who are clever in procuring their own gain with the aid of fabricated miracles. We will believe much more firmly in what we read in the Scriptures if we do not believe in any old tales invented by men' (Erasmus 2011: 292–3).

Much of the present discussion has focused upon the selected scholars' responses to the spiritual failings and heresies which they identified in the world about them. It is equally true, however, that More, Colet, and Erasmus remained painfully aware throughout their lives of the flaws in many of the cultures of worship deeply embedded within their revered, late medieval Church:

> In another place a certain pastor, just before the sabbath, secretly put live crabs in a cemetery and placed burning candles on their shells. As they crept among the tombs a frightening spectacles was seen in the night and no one dared to draw near. Terrible rumours resulted. With everyone in a state of shock the pastor taught the people from the pulpit that these were the souls of the dead who demanded to be liberated from their torment by masses and almsgiving. The trick was discovered when a few crabs were found among the rubble, carrying the extinguished candles, which the pastor had failed to collect. (Erasmus 2011: 293)

....

CHAPTER 17

JOHN FOXE'S *BOOK OF MARTYRS*

Tragedies of Tyrants

....

MIKE PINCOMBE
AND GAVIN SCHWARTZ-LEEPER

Book of Martyrs or *Acts and Monuments*? The debate over the title of John Foxe's landmark ecclesiastical history and martyrology has persisted in various forms since the text's initial publication in 1563. (Subsequent editions produced by Foxe appeared in 1570, 1576, and 1583, with numerous editions, additions, and abridgements appearing throughout the centuries following his death.) Modern scholarship generally tends to refer to a text called *Acts and Monuments of These Latter and Perilous Days Touching Matters of the Church*, as Foxe himself designated the work, since this description more closely reflects Foxe's purpose in writing it. The text is an account of the development of the Christian Church, with a teleological focus on the establishment of English Protestantism. Foxe's history is polemical: it attempts to recount the *acts* of the true Church's champions and its enemies, and to relate those acts as *monuments*, or enduring witnesses, of godliness and sacrifice. When this same work, however, is conceived as *The Book of Martyrs*, as it always has been in the popular tradition, it becomes a monument in particular to the Protestant martyrs of the reign of Mary I, some of whom Foxe knew personally. Foxe provides exceptionally vivid anecdotes of the persecutions and deaths of these martyrs, compiled from previous chronicles, episcopal registers, letters, and personal interviews. These he coupled with editorial material designed to guide the reader towards an associative connection between the early Church martyrs and these contemporary sufferers.

The popular title *Book of Martyrs* has been chosen in this case, however, because it points more directly to the tragic structure of Foxe's *magnum opus*. Martyrs belong to tragedy, true, but only if they are persecuted by tyrants; or, at least, that is the schema proposed here as the basis of Foxean tragedy. However, note that the sub-title to this chapter has both its keywords in the plural. This is because it is taken from the title of a work very similar to the *Book of Martyrs*, published in 1575. Thomas Twyne used the words *Tragedies of Tyrants* as an indication of the contents of his translation of a work originally written in German, by the Protestant writer Heinrich Bullinger, as *Von der schweren, langwierigen Verfolgung der heiligen Christlichen Kirchen* [On the Long and Harsh Persecution of the Holy Christian Church] (1573). Twyne englishes the title in this way because he has been influenced by the content of Foxe's work, seeing tragedy and tyranny where Bullinger only alludes to persecution. For Foxe understands tragedy 'in the plural': the godly community of martyrs is constructed through the typologically similar 'tragedies' of persecution, torture, and death that they all undergo. We might deduce, retrospectively, some theoretical type of 'tyrant-tragedy' from all the myriad instances of persecution in Foxe's book, but the point to make is that Foxe was not interested in 'tragedy' as a *literary genre*, but in 'tragedies' as an *historical fact*. Or better still: as an *apocalyptic fact*.

The first part of this discussion offers an outline of 'apocalyptic tragedy', taking as its point of departure Foxe's own 'apocalyptic comedy', *Christus triumphans* (published in Basel in 1556). There follows a more detailed explanation of the structural importance of the tyrants in the *Book of Martyrs*. This theoretical introduction is then followed by a more detailed examination of Foxe's text by way of a discussion of two exemplary tyrants, Edmund Bonner and Stephen Gardiner, in the company of two exemplary martyrs, Hugh Latimer and Nicholas Ridley. A final section deals with the powerfully enigmatic figure of Thomas Wolsey, where it is shown that Foxe was alert not only to the traditional tyrannical vices of cruelty and fury, but also to the more ambivalent quality of the grotesque.

The main aim of this chapter is to point out what seems to be a puzzling omission in the critical discussion of Foxe's *Book of Martyrs*. Why is its tragic element so little studied? A search of the MLA bibliography using the terms 'john foxe' and 'tragedy OR tragic' turned up only three items, none of them really pertinent. Nevertheless, Foxe had a clear and compelling view of tragedy, even if it is not what modern readers might expect, and it informs the meaning of his great work in almost every one of its hundreds of pages.

Tragoedia et Comoedia

Foxe's *Christus triumphans* is not a 'comedy' of the kind that modern readers—or even Elizabethan readers—might easily recognize by that generic label. Here is Foxe's own description of the play in its dedication to certain Englishmen in exile in Frankfurt: 'Chiefly the matter of our comedy turns on descriptions of the persecutions of Ecclesia [i.e. the Church], with which that unhappy old devil, from the time he was driven from heaven by Christ, never stopped harassing the bride of Christ' (1973a: 213). The diabolical persecution of the Church seems hardly a fit theme for comedy, but Foxe would no doubt have argued that his play was a comedy because it ended happily. The play closes with the imminent appearance of Christ as the bridegroom of Ecclesia, still in the wings but hymned in a final epithalamium, which exhorts the characters on stage— and also the audience—to rejoice in the apocalyptic vision of a complete and final reversal of all earthly history: 'Now the sad will be made happy, and the last first; the exalted shall fall, and those who fell before shall stand. You whom the flesh and the world and the madnesses of Satan torment, be happy and applaud with me: the bridegroom is near' (Foxe 1973a: 371).

The emphasis on the word 'happy' (in the Latin: *laetus* and *felix*) gives great spiritual force to a concept—the 'happy ending'—which can seem trivial and banal to modern sensibilities. Nonetheless, it did very well for sixteenth-century scholars, as we can tell from the theoretical discussions of the new genre of 'tragicomedy' which was developing in all parts of Renaissance Europe (Herrick 1955: 16–62). One English example will suffice: Nicholas Grimald's 'new sacred tragi-comedy [*comoedia tragica*]', *Christus redivivus* (1543). We may note in passing that Foxe and Grimald were contemporaries, and that both were students of Brasenose College, Oxford, in 1540, when Grimald wrote his play. Grimald (1925: 109) explains that 'just as the first act yields to tragic sorrow, in order that the subject-matter may keep its title, so the fifth and last adapts itself to delight and joy'. And the play does indeed end happily, with the reappearance of Christ to the Chorus of Disciples, whose final speech ends: 'Now filled with these great joys, and singing the glory of God, let us return to Jerusalem' (Grimald 1925: 215). It is the emphasis on eventual joy and happiness at the comic ending of history that permits—indeed: *requires*—the rehearsal of so many acts of tragic persecution that lead up to it.

In the 'argument' to *Christus triumphans*, we hear how Christ sentences Satan to a thousand years of bondage, after which, however, he escapes: 'Freed at last, Satan incites wondrous tragedies through Pseudamnus, the Antichrist, enemy of the lamb and of Ecclesia' (Foxe 1973a: 233). And Foxe himself believed that Satan had been set loose around the turn of the first millennium, as he states in his five-part synopsis of Christian history in the second edition of the *Book of Martyrs* (1570: 26). It is tempting to see a connection between this five-part structure and the five-act theory of neo-classical drama. However, Foxe originally conceived a four-part history, then added a fifth age (Firth 1979: 69–110). The fourth age (from roughly 900 to 1300) is 'the time of Antichrist, or the desolation of the Churche' (Foxe 1570: 26). The fifth age, however, which is the time of writing, marks a final change for the better:

> the reformation and purging of the Churche of God, wherein Antichrist beginneth to be reveled, and to appear in his coulours, and his antichristian doctrine to be detected, & the number of his church decreaseth, and the number of the true Church increaseth. The durance of which time hath continued from. 260. yeares hetherto, and how long it shal continue more, the Lord & governour of all times only knoweth. (Foxe 1570: 26)

Foxe is not so jubilant here as he is in *Christus triumphans*, but the point is that what the Aristotelian theory of tragedy calls the *metabasis*, or 'turning-point', in the history of the Church, and, thus, the history of humanity, has already been reached and passed. From now on, it is all downhill to a comic rather than a tragic ending.

Within this broadly apocalyptic framework, *tragoediae*, in the plural, are part of the providential narrative which leads to the *comoedia*, in the singular, which is the reunion of the Church with Christ promised in the last moments of *Christus triumphans*. This event is figured in many places of the Bible. For example, a marginal note in one of the manuscript copies of the play tells us words from the Apocalypse are transformed into a joyful anticipation of Christ the bridegroom in the epithalamium. More significant, however, is a passage from the dedication, where Foxe reports that, in the second letter to the Thessalonians, 'who were awaiting the arrival of the bridegroom so many ages ago', Paul warned them that 'he would not come before that hellish Antichrist should appear' (Foxe 1973a: 207). In the words of the Geneva Bible (1560), Paul says: 'Let no man deceive you by any meanes: for that day shall not come, except there come a departing first, and that that man of sinne be disclosed, even the sonne of perdition' (2 Thes. 2:3). A marginal note explains that by 'parting' is meant: 'A wonderful departing of the moste parte from the faith'. This is the third age in Foxe's five-part history of the Church: 'the declining or backeslyding time of the Churche, which comprehendeth other 300. yeares, until the loosing out of Sathan, which was about the thousand yeare after Christ' (Foxe 1570: 26). Moreover, the 'man of sinne' is none other than 'Antichrist', and 'comprehendeth the whole succession of the persecutors of the Church'; and here we are back in Foxe's fourth and fifth ages. However, these things must happen *before* the bridegroom finally makes his appearance; there must be *tragoedia* before the history of the world—and the course of *Christus triumphans*—can at last realize their joyful destiny as *comoedia*.

Foxe also makes the comparison between the final two acts of *Christus triumphans* and the recent past of his own country as part of this much larger history of humanity. In the dedication of his play, he says: 'Long ago, [Satan] delivered his main blows through the Pharisees, then through the tyrant Caesars and Proconsuls; now he shakes up the world with unspeakable tragedies through the bishops and the priests. Today our own England especially could testify to that' (Foxe 1973a: 213). The last two acts of *Christus triumphans* are thus to some extent to be dated to the time of writing in early 1556. Indeed, the off-stage characters Dynastes and Dynamicus, to whom Pseudamnus sends a rose and a sheathed sword in Act V, are unmistakable allusions to Mary and Philip (the gifts were sent by Pope Julius III in January 1555). Furthermore, it seems highly likely that the characters Hierologus and Theosebes are allegorical representations of two men who would become icons of English Protestant martyrology thanks to Foxe's book: Hugh Latimer and Nicholas Ridley (Foxe 1973b: 31–3).

Nevertheless, for all these detailed and explicit connections between *Christus triumphans*, *The Book of Martyrs*, and the eschatological tradition of the Antichrist as Satan's minion, we need to emphasize that Foxe is only following in the footsteps of hundreds of other writers of sixteenth-century religious polemic. There is insufficient space here to show how widely this idea of 'tragedies'—typically in the plural—permeated English writing of the period; but let us note that this idea should not be confined to the Reformers, as may be seen from comparing two passages written from very different confessional positions. The first is taken from the Reformist Thomas Becon's dialogue *The Fortress of the Faithful Against the Cruel Assaults of Poverty and Hunger* (1550). At one point, the collocutors have paused to remind each other of the exemplary accounts of the way in which God has always punished those who incite sedition and stir up commotions in the commonweal. One says of these troublemakers: 'If they had ben as wel trayned up in learning suche godly histories, as thei were nouseled [*nursed*] in hearing popishe masses, & such other trifeling trumpery, thei had raised up no such tragedies' (Becon 1550, image 25). Thus, popery leads to tragedy for Becon. However, a year earlier, the conservative writer John Proctor (1549, image 6) had turned the tables on the Reformers in the preface of his *Fall of the Late Arrian* (1549): 'in this present tyme, what daungerous tragedyes hathe Satan styrred up: what straunge & perilous heresyes hath he reysed among the people of God?' Like Foxe, Proctor could apply the term *tragedy* to current affairs in his own country, as when he describes his *History of Wyatt's Rebellion* (1554) as a 'tragicall treatise' (Proctor 1554, image 85). The point to make is that 'tragedies' were the work of Satan or his agents—whether heretic or popeling.

However, it is safe to say by the time Foxe was writing, the word *tragoedia* had taken on a special resonance for Reformists across Europe, as had the word *tragedy* in England, by virtue of its association with the Pope and his agents (see chapter 16). One example from the wider European context must suffice, a work which has been chosen because it appeared in the same year that Foxe wrote his *comoedia*: John Old's translation of Rudolph Gwalther's Latin *Antichrist* (1556). Gwalther (1546, image 137; 1556, image 140) recounts how the archbishop of Mainz was deposed by the Pope for complaining about extortion:

> That mater was the occasion of wonderful sore dissensiones, and warres, that many princes of Germanie (yea and that the greatest princes) were combred with al. But the ende of that tragedie was a most bloody piece of worke [*Finis uero Tragoediae funestissimus extitit*]. For at leing[the] the citie of Mence (after grevous and bloody fieldes foughten) was betraied and taken, euery strete ranne streames of the slayne citezines blood, and all maner of wickednesse done in it (that the insolencie of a prowde conquerour lusteth to doo) and so the citie was miserably spoiled of her libertie: that wher it hade ben afore an emperial citie, it is in subjection (perforce) to abominable bawdie bishops, & lecherous polleshorne [*shaven-headed*] masse-monging priestes, even unto this daye.

Gwalther's *Antichristus* (1546) is a particularly relevant point of comparison with Foxe's *Christus*, not only because of their theological material, but also because of Gwalther's close connections with the English Reformers, to many of whom he gave shelter at his house in Zürich during the reign of Queen Mary (*ODNB*). However, as we have said, in his presentation of the Pope and his agents as *agents provocateurs* forever sowing the seed of civil dissension and violent tumult, and his description of these activities as 'anti-Christian' *tragoediae*, he is quite in line with legions of other Reformist writers across Europe.

Apocalyptic Tragedy

This tradition of 'apocalyptic tragedy' may not be so familiar to most students of English literature, because it does not present itself as a literary *genre*, unlike the tradition of *de casibus* tragedy which is well known and understood as the hegemonic form of tragedy before the 1580s (Farnham 1963). Here, the emphasis falls squarely on the fall (*casus*) of a great man or woman from power and prosperity to a wretched or otherwise remarkable death, expressed in the form of a first-person monologue or 'complaint'. Nevertheless, the non-generic kind of tragedy explored above is in some respects quite similar to the *de casibus* genre represented primarily by Lydgate's *Fall of Princes* and the various versions of *A Mirror for Magistrates*. Most importantly, both kinds of tragedy come in multitudes; and this is what makes them so different from the vast array of tragic plays from Sophocles to Shakespeare to Voltaire to Ibsen, where a single character, often named in the title of the play, takes centre stage. As with Lydgate and the *Mirror*, Foxe's *Book of Martyrs* contains so many tragedies within its pages that each one cancels out the claim to uniqueness that might be made by any other. Whatever truth apocalyptic and *de casibus* tragedies may have to tell is based not in the individual but in the collective experience expressed in an endless repetition of the same tragic narrative.

However, apocalyptic tragedy differs from its *de casibus* contemporary in its attitude towards causality. Lydgate does not seem to be too much concerned with the reasons *why* his princes fell, and there is frank confusion on this matter amongst the various authors of the *Mirror*. However, in apocalyptic tragedy, at least of the mainstream Reformist variety, the blame always falls squarely on the shoulders of Satan, Antichrist, the Pope, or others of their crew. There is never any questioning of causality here because the whole concept of apocalyptic tragedy as it is sketched here is polemical, so that the origin of these *tragoediae* is *de facto* 'evil', and thus one or all of the above. This structural clarity gives rise to a basic scenario which is repeated again and again and again: the *agon* between the 'martyr' and the 'tyrant'. This simple schema underlies Foxe's basic idea of tragedy.

Let us note first of all, however, that Foxe uses the word *tragedy* in a variety of different senses in the *Book of Martyrs*, as examples from the 1563 edition will indicate (and the same range of senses can be found in the later editions as well). It can refer, for example, to an interlude (500); an excessively forceful interrogation (588); a violent exchange of opinions (657); a 'tragicall history' in the manner of the *Mirror* (936); and an examination divided into parts (1474). Nonetheless, with the exception of the first, all these instances are based squarely on the idea of 'persecution'. For Foxe (1232), trials in which innocent men and women are arraigned as heretics are examples of blatant injustice, and the 'Consistorye at Paules', where many such trials took place, can be described as 'the common stage for these tragedies'. The point seems to be that these particular events all ended in the death-sentence for the accused, so that it is but a difference of degree between these trials and the actual execution, such as that of Anthony Person, Robert Testwood, and John Marbeck, at Windsor, where Foxe (1563: 682) reports: 'The chiefe autors of this cruel and bloudye tragedy was doctor London and William Simons'.

The way Foxe uses the word *tragedies* elsewhere in the 1563 *Book of Martyrs* returns us to the world-historical arena of apocalyptic tragedy. We read of the opposition to Wycliff: 'Then began the Pharisies again to swarm and gather together with marvelous tragedies, striving against the light of the gospell, which began to shine abrode' (Foxe 1563: 142). A marginal note tells us that the 'Pharises' are the 'Catholic clergy'. Or again: 'let us see what manner of thinges they are, where about these gready Papistes make so much a do, wyth so many tragedies and fires' (184). Halfway through his book, Foxe (677) refreshes his reader with a comic anecdote, since 'we have remembred a great nomber of lamentable and bloudy tragedies of suche as have been slayne through extreme crueltie'. All of these instances are broadly in line with the emphasis not only on violence but also on the alleged historical continuity between the Pharisees and the Catholic clergy as the adversaries of the True Church.

However, violence—by deed or by word—is still very important to Foxe's idea of tragedy; and it is here that we turn to the idea of the persecutor as a 'tyrant'. We have already mentioned Thomas Twyne's *The Tragedies of Tyrants*. This is in fact a translation not from the German original, but *via* the Latin translation of Rudolph Gwalther's father-in-law, Josias Simmler, as *De persecutionibus ecclesiae Christianae* [On the Persecutions of the Christian Church] (1573); but it is typical of the interest in 'tragedy' excited by Lydgate, the *Mirror*, and, more recently, the *Book of Martyrs*—that Twyne should add the word—in the plural—to his title.

The phrase *tragedies of tyrants* is also productively ambiguous. On the one hand, it might refer to the tragedies that 'happen' to tyrants, which is very much the line taken in the English *de casibus* tradition from Lydgate to the *Mirror* and beyond. There are very few 'innocent victims' in these works, whereas, of course, the *Book of Martyrs* is crowded with them. However, the phrase might also refer to tragedies which are caused by tyrants; and that must be what Twyne intended, for Bullinger's tyrants do not come to grief. It is in this second sense that the phrase will be applied to Foxe's *Book of Martyrs*.

FOXE'S TYRANT-TRAGEDIES

Foxe's tyrants are generally marked by spectacular displays of cruelty towards Christians, as in his 'Chapter or treatyse of tyrants and persecutors' (Foxe 1563: 1784). Note the synonymity of the words *tyrant* and *persecutor* here, which is exactly in line with Twyne's translation of Simmler's *persecutiones* as 'tragedies of tyrants'. Foxe's list is headed by two clear front runners: 'no man is ignorant, but that of al Byshop Boner was the chiefest instrument of this persecution, Steven Gardiner ever excepted'.

Foxe continually compares historical events and people to Gardiner and Bonner throughout the many pages of *The Book of Matryrs*, reminding his readers that the persecutions enacted by these men reflect the persecutions of the early Church Fathers in order to legitimize a general connection made between the early Church and the Edwardian Reformist movement. It is in the death-accounts of these men that we can see Foxe's manipulation of the idea of apocalyptic tragedy to condemn persons particularly hated by the Reformers.

The negative characterizations of Gardiner and Bonner tend to come in two varieties: violence—including violence of passion and language—and hypocrisy. In the 1563 preface, Foxe says that God will sometimes allow 'the Tyraunt to rage, and the hypocrite to reigne for the iniquitie of the people' (6); and Gardiner and Bonner, and many others, bear witness to God's discipline. For example, Foxe recounts how Henry VIII was manipulated into making a scapegoat of Reformist John Lambert by 'one Steven Gardener bishop of Winchester, who as in those daies he was moost cruell, so was he also of a mooste subtile and craftye witte, gapynge rounde aboute to get occasion to let and hynder the Gospell' (1563: 585). In a characteristic move, Foxe juxtaposes Gardiner's wickedness with Lambert's godliness, as when Lambert is described as 'a lambe to fight with many lions' (586). Indeed, Lambert's disputation before Henry and his bishops reveals this binary clearly. Foxe repeatedly calls attention to moments where the meek Lambert is confronted by the fury of his nominal superiors: 'Then againe the kinge and the Byshoppes raged againste Lambert, in so much, that he was not onlye forced to silence, but also myghte have beene driven into a rage, if his eares had not bene used to such tauntes afore' (588). Foxe calls Lambert's disputation with the king and his councillors 'a tragedy'; but note how Lambert is *not* driven into the rage that possessed his tormentors.

Gardiner could be cruel, but he was more often seen as 'wily' or 'cunning' (Riordan and Ryrie 2003). However, our second villain, Edmund Bonner, was a monster of fury. A typical anecdote relates how a certain Thomas Tomkins was arrested for his alleged refusal to accept that the body of Christ was physically present at the sacrament of the altar, together with other heresies. The religious authorities in London examined him rigorously for a period of about six months, confessing his heretical views in an examination by Bonner and repeatedly thereafter. He was eventually burned to death in Smithfield on 16 March 16, 'to the glorye of Gods holye name, and confirmacion of the weake' (Foxe 1563: 1172).

Fury defines the actions of Bonner throughout the anecdote about Tomkins. One of the first events related about Tomkins is that his examinations were so 'rigorous' that Bonner 'beat him bitterly about the face, wherby his face was swelled' (Foxe 1570: 1749). Through Bonner's rage, even Tomkins's beard fell victim. When the bishop came across Tomkins labouring in a field (as part of his imprisonment at Fulham), the two debated the link between a beard and a good Christian. Bonner, feeling that Tomkins's answer lacked respect, caused a barber to shave him forcibly. These events are related to convey a sense that Bonner was moved to violence and anger through frustration, as he is unable to convince Tomkins to recant. In one of the more sensational examinations in the *Book of Martyrs*, Bonner, frustrated with Tomkins's stubborn refusals to recant, called for a candle to be brought, saying that 'if thou [Tomkins] lykest the torment of the fire so well, I wyll make thee feele in this flame, what it is to be burned' (Foxe 1563: 1171). Bonner himself holds Tomkins's hand into the flame, and Foxe recounts how Tomkins responds with prayer and patience, with the martyr stating later that 'his spirit was so rapt up, that he felt no payne' despite Bonner holding his hand into the flames until 'the vaines shronke and the synewes brast, and the water did spyrt into M[aster] Harpesfieldes face' (Foxe 1570: 1749–50). Foxe compares Tomkins's fortitude to that of Scaevola, the legendary Roman youth who burned his own left hand in a brazier in front of the Clusian king Porsena. Foxe casts Bonner as exceeding Porsena: whereas the Clusian king was so struck by Scaevola's commitment that he set the young man free, Bonner, being 'more cruell' than the tyrant, condemned Tomkins to the fire. Bonner's rage thus is built up through the course of this anecdote—just one of many—to demonstrate his ineradicable sinfulness, the erroneous beliefs of his Church, and the fundamentally evil nature of both man and Church when confronted with a member of the 'true' Church.

Foxe juxtaposes the tyranny of Bonner and Gardiner with the meek suffering of Hugh Latimer and Nicholas Ridley. Both bishops (of Worcester and London respectively), Latimer and Ridley—along with Thomas Cranmer—were leading Reformers during Edward VI's reign, and, after Mary I's accession and abolishment of the Act of Supremacy, were considered the chief heretics in England. Imprisoned in Oxford, Latimer and Ridley were examined at length by panels of theologians; subsequently, they were found guilty of heresy and burned in Oxford on 16 October 1555. The account of their martyrdom is long, covering some twenty folio pages in the 1570 edition. This includes the lengthy disputations between the two men and their interlocutors as well as the vivid account of their deaths. In addition, Foxe and Day included a woodcut of the event.

It was essential for Foxe to include the woodcut as well as the detailed accounts of the disputations and martyrdom in as full a form as possible: they allow Foxe to channel the conversionary power of the dialogue as a genre, to which can be added the contemporary fame and erudition of Latimer and Ridley themselves. Perhaps the most memorable quotation from the entirety of the *Acts and Monuments* is taken from this account:

> Then brought they a fagot kindled with fyre, and layd the same downe at D. Ridleyes feete. To whom M. Latymer spake in this maner: Be of good comfort M. Ridley, and play the man: we shall this day lyght such a candle by Gods grace in England, as (I trust) shall never be put out. (Foxe 1570: 1976)

Foxe's readers may have been put in mind of the martyrdom of Polycarp, an early bishop of Smyrna, who heard a voice exhorting him to 'play the man' at his own burning. The particular phrasing of 'play the man' is itself a performative metaphor, and its inclusion in the *Book of Martyrs* is therefore particularly apt. It manages to link Latimer and Ridley to the martyrs of the early Church as well as acknowledging the power of the public performance inherent in the Marian martyrdoms that Foxe consistently draws out.

And, of course, it places us squarely back in the more usual understanding of *tragedy* as a stage-play.

The account of the martyrdom itself is similar to the others we have examined in that it is strongly visual and provides editorial interpretation of the events for the reader. One of the most illuminating moments demonstrates exactly the Christian paradox of strength coming through meekness:

> M. Latymer gave nothyng, but very quietly suffered hys keeper to pull of hys hose, and his other aray, which to looke unto was very simple: & beyng stripped into his shrowde, he seemed as comely a person to them that were there present, as one should lightly see: and whereas in hys clothes, he appeared a withered and crooked sely [harmless] old man, he now stode bolt vpryght, as comely a father as one might lightly behold. (Foxe 1570: 1976)

We can juxtapose Latimer's quiet attitude, whereby he visibly gains strength and stature, with Wolsey's shock and sudden illness at receiving the news of his own arrest. The stark contrast between these two depictions—the bent old man receiving strength from his shroud, and the bloated prelate stricken with panic—demonstrates exactly the Christian paradox that runs throughout the accounts of the martyrs in the *Book of Martyrs*. And it is to this episode that we next turn.

Construction and Destruction
of a Tyrant

This final section complicates the relatively simple portrait of Tyrant and Martyr presented in the sketch of Gardiner and Bonner *versus* Latimer and Ridley. Thomas Wolsey, chancellor and cardinal, is not noted by Foxe as a tyrannical persecutor of Christians, like Gardiner and Bonner. But Wolsey exercised great fascination for his contemporaries, as for later Tudor writers, and Foxe seems unable to let him slip by without somehow condemning him as a minion of Antichrist. His attitude towards Wolsey, however, is a mixture of the ridiculous and the portentous which never quite takes on the solidity of his less complex portraits of the other figures we have discussed.

Wolsey is first introduced as a ridiculous marginal figure in the anecdote of the cardinal's hat, which Foxe presents as a humorous but instructive interlude, 'although it be not greatly pertinent unto thys our historye, nor greatly requisite in these so waightie matters', but rather 'to refreshe the reader with some varietie of matter' (1570: 1159). The absurd dignity with which Wolsey expected his *galero*, or cardinal's hat, to be revered is to be taken as an exemplary tale demonstrating the difference between the simplicity of the 'true humble Martyrs and servantes of God' and the 'pompe & pride' of the Roman Church, for whom Wolsey stands as a metonym 'in whom alone, the image and life of all other such like followers and professors of the same church, may be seene and observed'.

Thus, on the one hand, Wosley is a trivial diversion from the main narrative; on the other, he is the very epitome of the Church of Rome. Something seems amiss here.

It is not that Wolsey falls beyond the bound of tragedy. In his conclusion to the hat story, Foxe notes: 'Thys glorious Cardinall in hys tragicall doinges, dyd exceede so farre all measure of a good subjecte, that he became more like a prince then a priest' (1570: 1160). Thus, Wolsey's ambition is 'tragicall' and Foxe goes on to explain how it led to the usual political disorder: 'his restles head was so busie, ruffling in publicke matters, that he never ceassed, before he had set both England, Fraunce, Flaunders, Spayne, and Italye, together by the eares'. Yet, given that the illustration of this tragical vice are given in the tale of his cap, also ridiculous, and thus, to our sensibilities, also 'comical'.

Foxe's ridicule of Wolsey leads us to reflect on a final reconciliation between apocalyptic tragedy and the more familiar kind of *de casibus* tragedy to which it might otherwise be opposed. The English *de casibus* tradition presents a variety of explanations for the falls of its princes and magistrates; but all of them fall in a remarkable way which calls forth immediate comment in the text, either from the compiler (in Lydgate) or the faller (in the *Mirror*). Internal judgement of this kind is also found in mid-Tudor drama. For example, in Thomas Preston's tragedy *Cambyses* (performed in 1561), the play ends with the tyrant staggering on-stage, dying from a wound inflicted by his own sword, which flew from its scabbard and into his side: 'A just reward for my misdeeds, my death dooth plain declare' (Preston 1561, image 23). The moral is pressed home moments later by the First Lord: 'A just rewarde for his misdeeds, the God above hath wrought'; and it is there in the play's notorious title:

> A lamentable tragedy mixed ful of pleasant mirth, conteyning the life of Cambises king of Percia from the beginning of his kingdome unto his death, his one good deed of execution, after that many wicked deeds and tirannous murders, committed by and through him, and last of all, his odious death by Gods justice appointed. (Preston 1570, image 1)

There is surely no doubt as to how we are meant to view Cambyses's death here.

However, there is evidence from George Puttenham's *Art of English Poetry* (1589) that mid-Tudor audiences may also have mocked at the dying tyrant. Puttenham says that tragedy developed only when monarchical regimes emerged from more democratic social formations, when some men lorded it over all the rest and indulged in 'all manner of lusts and licentious of life' (2007: 123). When they died, however:

> their infamous life and tyrannies were laid open to all the world, their wickedness reproached, *their follies and extreme insolencies derided,* and their miserable ends painted out in plays and pageants to show the mutability of fortune and the just punishment of God in revenge of a vicious and evil life [*emphasis added*].

These old sinners were ridiculed, says Puttenham; and Foxe treats Wolsey with the same kind of 'tragic derision' as the death of Preston's Cambyses may have excited.

Even Foxe's portentously grisly account of Wolsey's death and burial is not without a touch of grotesquerie:

> It is testified by one, yet beyng a lyve, in whose armes the sayd Cardinall dyed, that his body beyng dead, was blacke as pitch, also was so heavy, that vi. could scarse beare it. Futhermore, it did so stinke above the ground, that they were constreyned to hasten the buriall therof in the night season, before it was day. At the which buriall, such a tempest, with such a stinche there arose, that all the torches went out, and so he was throwen into the tombe, and there was layd. (1570: 1172)

In his last moments, then, Wolsey's diabolical inner nature, signified by the blackness and stench of the infernal element of pitch, erupts from his body, in such quantity that it even extinguishes the light of the torches, just as he attempted in his life to put out the light of Christianity. His death and burial constitute a *monstrum*: a 'portentous demonstration' of what Puttenham calls 'just punishment of God in revenge of a vicious and evil life'.

Foxe also notes that this black effluvium was observed even before Wolsey died, when he took large doses of purgatives and emetics: 'the matter that came from hym was so blacke, that the steining therof, could not be gotten out of hys blanckets by any meanes'. And Wolsey was not the first to have vomited black matter at his death. The same was reported of Pope Alexander VI (*d.* 1503) by Jacopo Sannazaro in an epigram cited and translated in 1600 by a later English anti-papist, Francis Hastings (1600, image 98), in his *Apology of the Watchword*:

> Mirum cur vomuit nigrum post fata cruorem
> Borgia? quem biberat, concoquere haud poterat.
>
> *Borgia* dead much bloud did vomit from his brest,
> What marvaile that? the store he dranke, could not digest.

Lemeke Avale had also read the epigram and applied it to another corpulent upstart prelate from England's recent history in his *Commemoration of Bastard Edmund Bonner* (1569). Where were the papists, he asks, when Bonner was buried secretly at night: 'Qui vomuit nigrum, post fata cruorem' (Avale, 1569, image 12). Thomas Broke (1569a, image 1) also notes the peculiar circumstances of Bonner's death in his 1569 *Epitaph Declaring the Life and End of Doctor Edmund Bonner*:

> Even so his ende was dolefull to, wherin did well appeare:
> On him the judgement just of God, right wonderfull to heare.
>
> For dead his face as blacke as coale, and monstruous withall:
> His grisly looke so terrible, as might a man appall.

Here is the official Reformist line on Bonner, but Broke was swiftly answered by a Roman Catholic opponent:

> Thou absent at his death reportest,
> his face both blacke and blew:
> But all which saw it witnesse can,
> how that is most untrue. (Knell, 1569b, image 10)

And Broke can only lamely retort that 'his keper Waye did it declare, | with other that beheld his ende' (image 11).

This little squabble over the authority of rival death-bed witnesses is typical of the uneasy relation between 'fact' and 'fiction' in Tudor historiography, a topic which has attracted sustained interest from critics of the *Book of Martyrs* (Collinson 1997; King 1997). Not surprisingly, there was a more sympathetic account of Wolsey's decease as well, this time from the pen of his former gentleman-usher, George Cavendish, in his *Life and Death of Cardinal Wolsey* (written between 1554 and 1558). The text provides a wealth of details about the death of the cardinal, but confirms almost none of the elements Foxe mentions. Cavendish, who claims to have been present when Wolsey died, relates how the cardinal was taken ill while travelling to London to be interviewed by the king. Wolsey had to go to the toilet continually, and 'the matter that he avoided was wonderous blake | the whiche phisicions call Colour Adustum' (Cavendish 1959: 173). Here, it seems, is the medical condition which gave rise to the rumour of the black matter which issued from his body; but it is treated without the sensational speculation in Foxe. Reading the sober account in Cavendish's *Life* against the lurid description in the *Book of Martyrs*, one wonders how much Foxe must have counted on the superstitious credulity of his Protestant readership. And it is worth noting that later Elizabethan writers do not make anything of Foxe when they write of Wolsey's death (Schwartz-Leeper 2016). In 1587, when Thomas Churchyard contributed a tragedy on Wolsey to the latest edition of *A Mirror for Magistrates*, the cardinal does not specify the nature of his illness; though a marginal note refers the reader to the historian John Stowe, who says he died of a 'contynuall flyxe [flux]' (Churchyard 1938: 510). Ten years later, the metaphysical poet Thomas Storer (1599, image 36), in his *Life and Death of Thomas Wolsey*, has 'Wolseius moriens' ('the dying Wolsey') say that he was finally seized by illness: 'Some thought it was a wind, and sooth they say, | It blew my breath, my life, and all away'. Here Wolsey's mortal illness is reduced to the pretext for a quip.

However, Cavendish goes into such meticulous detail that one also wonders what he is trying to say in his account of his master's death. He tells us—what we surely do not need to know—that Wolsey was so troubled with the flux that night that 'he had above [fifty] stoolles' (Cavendish 1959: 173). Cavendish is not trying to be funny or disrespectful; rather, he seems to be trying to produce an almost documentary narrative of the cardinal's last moments in order to refute 'sondry surmysis & Imagyned tales made of his procedynges & doynges' (Cavendish 1959: 4). And we might read his detailed description of the mundane physicality of Wolsey's final illness as a critique of the kind of absurdly 'tragical' distortions of the life and death of his master that Reformists were keen to disseminate.

CONCLUSION

In the introduction to this discussion, attention was drawn to the absence of critical interest in the tragical element of Foxe's *Book of Martyrs*; and now it may be time for a tentative explanation. The obvious answer is that we tend to associate tragedy with the drama in this period; and, though Foxe is clearly aware of the dramatic potential of some of the scenes he describes, much of what might be considered dialogue is in the interminable to-and-fro of the inquisitions that bulk out his narrative. Because he wishes to present these documents as true witnesses to history, he generally does not attempt to work them up into a courtroom drama, but lets them speak for themselves. This does not mean to say that the *Book of Martyrs* was ignored as a source of material for stage-plays by later Elizabethan writers, as several recent studies have demonstrated (Gurnis-Farrell 2005; Höfele 2005; Anderson 2014). However, this material remains nevertheless a very minor strand in the weave of English Renaissance tragedy.

One reason for this is that the vast majority of the latter-day martyrs were of low social status, and that it was still generally believed that stage-tragedy should concern itself only with persons of high rank. The emphasis here, too, has been on martyrs of high rank in church and state, with the single exception of Thomas Tomkins. Nonetheless, the point has been to show how persons of traditionally 'tragic status'—kings, generals, and cardinals—can wreak havoc on the people over whom they bear sway, a people which might remain anonymous were it not for the painstaking testimony of books like Foxe's, or the versified memorial lists of Thomas Brice's *Compendious Register in Metre* (1559), which contains 'the names and patient sufferings of the members of Jesus Christ, and the tormented and cruelly burned within England' in the reign of Queen Mary (Brice, 1559, image 1). Brice's register begins in June 1555, and the first entry (for June 10 and 11) reads:

> when worthy Wattes, w^t constant crie
> Continued in, the flamyng fier
> when Simson, Hawkes, and Jhon Ardlie
> Did tast the tyrantes, raging yre
> when Chamberlaine, was put to death
> we wisht for our, Elizabeth. (Brice 1559: 16)

The very format of Brice's *Register*, with its ruled compartments, each headed by a month and year, and in the left margin the day on which the martyrdoms took place, looks very much like a ledger, a proleptic symbol of the book in which God keeps account of these 'tragedies of tyrants' in preparation for the day of reckoning.

Foxe's *Book of Martyrs* is more expansive, but it has the same function: it is a memorial of all those who suffered persecution, high and low, but particularly men and women of the humbler sort, since there were so many. There is room, of course, for the 'popular voice' in the stage-tragedies of Shakespeare and his contemporaries (Patterson 1989); but an epoch such as ours which prides itself upon its commitment to democracy might well want to look to writers like Brice and Foxe for a more truly 'democratic' kind of tragedy.

CHAPTER 18

EDMUND SPENSER

ELIZABETH HEALE

RELIGION mattered in England in the sixteenth century; for some, indeed, it was literally a life-and-death issue. Individuals' doctrinal beliefs and their attitudes to ecclesiastical governance and rituals could determine their personal and political allegiances, their career prospects, and their views on art and writing. For Edmund Spenser the secretary, who sought advancement in the thick of ecclesiastical debate in London and Cambridge in the late 1570s, and then built a successful career as an agent for Protestant colonial rule in Roman Catholic Ireland in the 1580s and 1590s, religious choices and allegiances were crucial considerations. For Edmund Spenser the poet, religion provided, more often than not, his subject: its contemporaneous debates; its shaping force within individuals and the Tudor State; its complex implications for his art. Matters of faith were integral to his verse from his youthful translations in *A Theatre For Worldlings* (1569), through *The Shepheardes Calender* (1579), to his role as the epic poet of a Protestant nation in *The Faerie Queene* (1590 and 1596), and the quasi-vatic voice of many of his last works.

Protestantism was restored to England in 1558 on Elizabeth's accession, but debate about its nature and form continued throughout the reign (see chapter 4).[1] Doctrinally, there was large agreement: the Elizabethan Church of England was fundamentally a Protestant, and indeed a Calvinist Church. Its core beliefs, as expressed in such key texts as the 'Thirty-Nine Articles' (1562) and the two 'Books of Homilies' (1547 and 1563), designed to be read out in churches, were: faith in the unearned, saving grace of God; predestination; good works as a sign rather than a cause of grace; and the education of the laity through preaching and reading the Bible in English. Nevertheless, controversy persisted in such matters as the authority of the queen and her bishops over the spiritual guidance and temporal governance of the Church, and ceremonies and rituals ordained by the 1559 Prayer Book. Marian exiles returning from years in Calvinist Geneva or other continental centres of Reformed religion often saw in the

---

[1] For information in this paragraph, see Collinson 1967 (particularly Part 1), Haigh 1993, and Lake 1982.

hybrid hierarchy and ceremonies of the English Church deplorable remnants of the Roman Catholic past. Increasingly, by the 1570s, division was growing between those willing to conform to the established Church, and those who were increasingly impatient for further reform—more evangelical preaching and teaching in the parishes, plainer forms of worship, less authority and wealth invested in the episcopacy. Such views, through the 1570s and 1580s, became identified with a reformist 'puritan' faction within the Church. A problem for bishops as well as purist reformers was the serious shortage of trained and learned clergy for the parishes, and, due to the alienation of church lands by the laity, the lack of sufficient funds adequately to support them. At the same time, the threat of Roman Catholicism to the established Protestant English state loomed ever greater. In the 1570s dedicated missionary priests started arriving from the continent. There were a number of plots centring on the Roman Catholic Mary Queen of Scots, in captivity in England; and, in 1588, the anticipated Spanish invasion became a reality. Peter Lake has suggested that while the Roman Catholic threats from abroad tended to unite those conforming to the English Church, a distinguishing feature of the most radical reformists was that 'while they undoubtedly hated Rome ... in practice [they] concentrated on a precision critique of the Antichristian remnants in the English church' (Lake 1982: 56).

Although many of the controversies and concerns that exercised Protestants in England while Spenser was writing figure prominently in his work, his specific confessional allegiances are not always clear. While Spenser seems to articulate with particular clarity reformist points of view in the 'Maye', 'Julye', and 'September' eclogues of *The Shepheardes Calender*, he also gives us highly unsympathetic, and thus 'unpuritan', accounts of iconoclasm in the Kirkrapine and Blatant Beast episodes in *The Faerie Queene* (1.iii.17 and 6.xii.25), suggesting an attitude apparently confirmed by the 'high altar' and organ music, both anathema to purist reformers, that figure in the description of his own wedding in *Epithalamion* (ll. 215–18). Unsurprisingly, there have been many attempts to identify the religious sympathies and affiliations of a poet so actively foregrounding religious matters at a time of passionate and divisive debate. Conclusions have differed radically. A consensus earlier in the twentieth century identified Spenser as a 'Puritan' whose views may have mellowed and become more conservative as he grew older. This view was challenged in 1950 by Virgil K. Whitaker who found Spenser's religious views to be conservative and even 'anti-Puritan' (5–7, 64–5 reviews the controversy prior to his book). Anthea Hume rebutted Whitaker in 1984, arguing, with a nuanced awareness of the range of positions within the Church of England, that Spenser, in the 1570s and 1580s, at least, had 'moderate puritan' views (see also Norbrook 1984: esp. ch. 3). In turn, Hume's views were challenged by John King, who argued that Spenser was a Protestant at ease with the practices and teachings of the established Church of England (1990: 18–20, 36). More recently, in his biography of Spenser, Andrew Hadfield (2012), while outlining in helpful detail the Reformist circles in which Spenser was educated in the 1560s and 1570s, suggested Spenser may have been sympathetic to the Family of Love, a group advocating toleration of Catholicism, and even that he may have become a Catholic sympathizer (e.g. 49–50, 118, 222–5, 403). Claire McEachern (2010) argues that while clearly anti-Catholic, Spenser was not committed to militant reform within the Church.

Discussion of Spenser's personal religious allegiances has to depend largely on his published works which allude to the issues of his day in oblique and complex fictions. They also keep us at a distance from any clear, unmediated access to an authorial voice. In *The Shepheardes Calender*, the 'new Poete', named only 'Immerito', is presented to us refracted through the lens of an editor and commentator E.K., through the dialogue form of eclogues in which opposing points of view are often presented, and through the ambiguous figure of Colin Clout, by whom, E.K. tells us, 'is euer meante the Authour selfe'.[2] Colin Clout reappears in *Colin Clovts Come Home Againe* (1595), and again in a particularly enigmatic episode in the final book of *The Faerie Queene* (1596), presenting in both a highly fictionalized and opaque version of the poet's voice (see especially McCabe's discussion in Spenser 1999: xiv–xvii). Even in the explicitly autobiographical *Amoretti and Epithalamion* (1596), the poet/lover presents himself, his courtship, and marriage within a complex and artful fiction which renders problematic any direct access to Spenser's personal views. The 'Letter to Raleigh', added at the end of the first edition of *The Faerie Queene* (1590) 'for the better vnderstanding' of the reader, is notoriously misleading in its details, and announces the indirection of the poem's methods. While his didactic aim is 'to fashion a gentleman or noble person in vertuous and gentle discipline', this is to be achieved not by delivering 'good discipline deliuered plainly in way of precepts, or sermoned at large', but 'clowdily enwrapped in Allegorical deuises'.[3] The fashioning of the reader as a 'noble person', it seems, must depend more on developing interpretative skills than on explicit authorial guidance.

Spenser's choice of allegory is central to his didactic methods in *The Faerie Queene*, in so doing acknowledging the fundamentally figurative nature of poetry in a period when the image-making faculty of the imagination was subject to some suspicion. His rebuttal of plain precepts in the 'Letter to Raleigh' may glance provocatively at those Protestants who, like the reformist divine Edward Dering in 1572, advocated a plain and simple teaching of God's word and lamented 'the vaine and synfull imaginations of our owne vnbridled wits, which haue now filled so many volumes' (Dering 1572: A.iii.v). Nevertheless, allegory was used by Protestants for the interpretation of such biblical books as the Song of Songs and Revelation, and the technique was admired and even revered in Chaucer's *Parliament of Fowls*, the apocryphal *Plowman's Tale*, or in Langland's *Piers Plowman*, the last two seen as proto-Protestant texts (King 1990: 20–31). Allegory had already been used for an English Protestant poem of chivalric pilgrimage in Steven Bateman's *Travayled Pilgrime* (1569) (King 1990: 186; Borris 2010: 454). What is remarkable about Spenser's use of allegory, however, is its complexity and 'clowdiness'. He offers us not a golden world of poetry to correct the brazen world of history, as envisaged by Sir Philip Sidney, but one in which

---

² *The Shepheardes Calender*, 'September', gloss 176, in Spenser 1999: 126. References to this edition of Spenser's shorter poems will be given after quotations in my text.

³ Spenser 1977. All quotations from the 'Letter' and from *The Faerie Queene* are from Spenser 1977 and references will be given after quotations in my text.

both knights and readers are entangled unawares by appearances and narratives that often prove deceptive and misleading; one in which error is avoided, if at all, by the constant vigilance of interpretation, reassessment, and reinterpretation (Sidney 1965: 100).

Spenser may claim his allegories promote 'good discipline', but their figurative mode aroused anxieties in Elizabethan England. Allegory, like all poetry, embodies ideas in images or icons (Grk *Eikon*, image or picture). Elizabethan Protestantism, however, treated images with great caution. An Injunction of 1559 ordered clergy to 'take away, utterly extinct and destroy all ... pictures, paintings, and all other monuments of feigned miracles, pilgrimages, idolatry and superstition, so that there remain no memory of the same in walls, glasses windows, or elsewhere ... And they shall exhort all their parishioners to do the like within their several houses' (Aston 1996: 94). To many Elizabethan Protestants, such images, associated with Roman Catholicism, were dangerous, making an easy appeal to the fallen senses, telling false stories, and corrupting the spiritual understanding. Spenser, as we have seen, presents such iconoclasm as church robbery and vandalism through the figures of Kirkrapine and the Blatant Beast. Nevertheless, he shared his culture's anxiety about the potentially seductive and dangerous power of images and the image-making faculty of the human mind. In *The Faerie Queene* book II, the imagination is figured as a mad man, Phantastes, whose chamber is full of:

> idle thoughts and fantasies,
> Deuices, dreames, opinions vnsound,
> Shewes, visions, sooth-sayes, and prophesies;
> And all that fained is, as leasings, tales, and lies. (2.ix.51)

As Calvin warned, 'the human mind' is 'so to speak, a perpetual forge of idols' (Calvin 1975: 1.xi.8; this passage is quoted by Gilman 1986: 42).

In *The Faerie Queene*, Spenser repeatedly presents us with dangerous image-makers and false images. Archimago, with his lying shows and tales, is a demonic artist, perhaps a sinister 'dark double' for the poet of *The Faerie Queene* himself (for Spenser's doubling images see King 1990: 68–75, 115, and Kaske 1999: 66–70 and *passim*). Duessa, Acrasia, and Busirane, among many others, are false artificers, creating images and narratives designed to entrap the unwary. Spenser's narratives expose the lies of such figures, stripping and defacing their artefacts with iconoclastic zeal. Thus Acrasia's dangerous bower is destroyed by Guyon:

> But all those pleasant bowres and Pallace braue,
> *Guyon* broke downe, with rigour pittilesse;
> Ne ought their goodly workmanship might saue
> Them from the tempest of his wrathfulnesse. (2.xii.83)

In Spenser's imaginative world of images, some are devilish and corrupting, and some (the poet's own) potentially instructive and illuminating. As Stephen Greenblatt and others have argued, the crucial difference is between art that is potentially idolatrous because it deludes, and, on the contrary, that of the poet which foregrounds its own 'createdness', making its artifice explicit through such devices as archaic language, narrational intrusions, mixing of genres, and forms of allegory (Greenblatt 1984: 188–90; Gilman 1986: 71; Gregerson 1995: esp. 64, 119–20, and 146). The onus of discrimination, understanding, and interpretation is vested in the reader who is repeatedly challenged by the text to read warily and thoughtfully. The Blatant Beast figures for Spenser, not only the indiscriminate iconoclast, but the ignorant and censorious reader who turns, after destroying the images in churches, to misinterpret and savage the poet's own work (6.xii.40–1). In so doing he is like that statesman whom Spenser describes in the Proem to Book 4 of *The Faerie Queene*, who blamed the poet's 'looser rimes' for alluring 'fraile youth … | That better were in vertues discipled'. Beastly readers, it seems, are sometimes inclined to impose idols forged in their own imaginations on the complex, educative fictions of Spenser's work.

In what follows, I shall pay attention to Spenser's sophisticated use of his art, while examining some of the debates about religion in *The Shepheardes Calender* and its role in *The Faerie Queene*. In a final section, I will suggest ways in which Spenser's depiction of religion in relation to poetry and the state changed in the work of the 1590s.

THE SHEPHEARDES CALENDER (1579)

The Shepheardes Calender consists of twelve eclogues in which, following a long literary tradition, shepherds debate, in apparently rustic terms, matters that may touch on sensitive political or religious matters (Cullen 1970: 1–26 usefully reviews the Classical and Renaissance traditions). In those eclogues which particularly deal with religion, 'Maye', 'Julye', and 'September', Spenser also draws on an English tradition in which rustic plain-speakers expose the abuses of the Church in their own time (King 1990: 14–46 discusses the *Calender* in the context of native traditions). By using the name Colin Clout in the *Calender* as a figure for the poet himself, Spenser is, in particular, harking back to a savage satire by John Skelton, *Collyn Clout* (*c*.1522), which attacked the corruptions of the Henrician Church under Cardinal Wolsey. The figure of the shepherd as pastor or clergyman, responsible for the spiritual welfare of their flocks, or parishioners, goes back, of course, to the gospels themselves where the good shepherd is Christ himself.

It is in keeping with the genre as Spenser inherited it that the ecclesiastical eclogues deal with issues of contemporaneous concern. As Hume has shown, the criticisms voiced by Piers in 'Maye', Thomalin in 'Julye', and Diggon Davie in 'September', were frequently made by those impatient for further reform within the Elizabethan Church: ignorant and inactive pastors who failed to protect their flocks from proto-Catholic practices within the church or Roman evangelism from without; prelates interested only in accumulating wealth for themselves and their families; and the impropriation of church livings by greedy secular patrons, leaving little left to pay properly qualified incumbents (1984: 14–40). Spenser also airs a number of these concerns in his satire, *Mother Hubberds Tale*, printed in 1591, but possibly partly written at the same time as the *Calender*. There, a fox and an ape, on the look-out for an easy way to make a living, meet a 'formall Priest' (l. 361), a lazy, ignorant man whose notion of life as a pastor is that it entails few duties and many freedoms. He offers shrewd advice on how to 'obtaine a Beneficiall [parish]' (line 486), that is, through hypocrisy, sycophancy, and/or bribery of powerful secular patrons who have such livings in their gift:

> The Courtier needes must recompenced bee
> With a Beneuolence, or haue in gage
> The *Primitias* of your Parsonage. (ll. 516–18) [first year's income]

Spenser, it seems clear, felt that there was plenty to satirize in the current state of the Church and its clergy, but his personal position in relation to the debates of the *Calender* remains disputed. Paul E. McLane thought that the ecclesiastical eclogues showed that Spenser was 'anti-Puritan' (1961: 95–234), while Hume (1984: 13–40) and Norbrook (1984: ch. 3) argued that the eclogues support 'moderately puritan' views; Norbrook provides evidence that the *Calender* was read as a puritan text by contemporaries (1984: 89–90). More recent readings have taken the view that the eclogues are genuinely dialogic (an approach pioneered by Cullen 1970: 29–68; see also King 1990: 41; Shore 1985: e.g. 34; Kinney 2010). In what follows, I suggest that the eclogues, like *The Faerie Queene*, call on readers actively to discriminate and judge by offering us multiple perspectives, none of them unambiguously that of the author. Levels of fiction mediate the voices of the *Calender*: the editor E.K.'s annotations are not always reliable; the dialogue form pits speakers of different views against each other; and the moral fables and final mottos are not always easy to interpret or apply.

In all three ecclesiastical eclogues, zealous reformers seem at first sight to have the strongest and most consistent voices. This is a view encouraged by E.K. who takes clear sides. Piers and Palinode in 'Maye' are identified as, respectively, Protestant and Catholic ministers ('Argvment'). E.K.'s designation of Palinode is, however implausible: an openly Catholic minister would not be openly tending a flock in England in the 1570s. Palinode seems, rather, to represent an ignorant and negligent pastor, like the 'formall Priest' of *Mother Hubberds Tale*. From a Reformist viewpoint, such a man would be likely to lead his flock into error, but he is not the kind of covert Catholic fox described in Pier's fable, who deliberately deceives and entraps the foolish innocent.

The dispute between Piers and Palinode concerns both their response to the May-games and their views about a pastor's life. The easy-going self-indulgence of Palinode, who hankers to help the ladies bear their Maybushes and follows a *carpe diem* philosophy, is clearly inappropriate in a pastor. Piers's views, on the contrary, are idealistic and uncompromising. He considers the May-games defile like 'Pitch' (l. 74), and looks back to the early Church as a model for pastors:

> The time was once …
> When shepeheardes had none inheritaunce,
> Ne of land, nor fee in sufferaunce:
> But what might arise of the bare sheepe. (ll. 103–7)

Times have, however, changed. Prosperity and security have corrupted the clergy who 'leaue to liue hard, and learne to ligge soft', letting in wolves to ravish the flock (ll. 125–31). E.K. identifies the wolves with the Roman Church, but accusations of venal self-enrichment were also levelled at prelates of the English Church. In 'September', Diggon Davie recounts the corruptions of a Church that similarly seems to be located both abroad and within England. Like Piers, Diggon complains of the self-enrichment of corrupt clergy, more interested in enriching their own families and heirs, than in ministering to their flock, but he also blames the greed of powerful secular patrons: 'bigge Bulles *of Basan*' who 'with theyr hornes butten the more stoute: | But the leane soules treaden vnder foote' (ll. 124–6). While Diggon's experience confirms Piers's criticisms of self-enriching clergy, his account of the corruptions of patronage, drawing, as does *Mother Hubberds Tale*, on a widely recognized grievance, renders problematic Piers's idealist vision of virtuous pastors who, 'nought hauing', might live sufficiently off their flocks. Such idealism seems unrealistic in the realm described by Diggon. Palinode's response to Piers may well have struck a chord in some of the *Calender's* clerical readers: 'How shoulden shepheardes liue … | What? should they pynen in payne and woe?' (ll. 148–9). Piers's reformist zeal may be more admirable than Palinode's self-serving ignorance, but it must also have seemed unrealistically idealistic in the conditions pertaining in the Elizabethan Church.

Both Thomalin in 'Julye' and Diggon Davie in 'September' share Piers's purist vision of what a good pastor should be, combined with a sharply critical view of the Elizabethan Church. In each case, however, the eclogues provide alternative perspectives, though not necessarily through their interlocutors. Thomalin argues that truly virtuous pastors live 'in lowlye leas' ('Julye', l. 122) unlike Morrell who prefers to live on a hill, a sign, according to E.K., of his pride and ambition, although Morrell seems affable enough. Certainly, Morell's classical and superstitious examples, which he uses to defend hill-dwellers, however eloquently expressed, seem less appropriate to the debate than the biblical valley-dwelling shepherds cited by Thomalin, learned from his admired teacher Algrind: 'Sike one (sayd *Algrin*) Moses was, | that sawe hys makers face … and spake to him in place' (ll. 157–60). However, both Moses and Algrind are troubling models for Thomalin. Moses's face shone after he saw his 'maker's face' on Mount Sinai when he climbed up to receive the Ten Commandments to pass on to his flock (Exodus 34.29–35). Algrind, it transpires, has also ascended a hill where one day a soaring eagle drops a shellfish on his head, bruising his brain (ll. 217–28). The story alludes to Grindal, a reforming Archbishop of Canterbury in the 1570s, who dared to challenge the queen's conservative interference in Church matters, and was suspended from his archbishopric as a result (see Collinson 1967: 191–8; McLane 1961: 140–57). May Thomalin's love of valleys be due to a failure of courage—'But I am taught by *Algrins* ill, | to loue the lowe degree' (ll. 219–20)? The concluding mottos of this eclogue, '*In medio virtus*' and '*In summo foelicitas*', are not at all easy to apply.

'September's' Diggon Davie is another purist, outspoken in his horror at the corruptions and depredations that he has witnessed 'in forrein costes' (l. 28), a place that clearly denotes the Church within England rather than, as E.K. indicates, that of Rome.

However, as was the case in 'Maye' and 'Julye', his idealist voice seems subtly undercut. Diggon went abroad out of 'vayne desire, and hope to be enricht' (l. 75), and having led his flock to starve 'with pyne and penuree', he abandons them (ll. 65–7). He has certainly been no Roffyn whose watchful protection of his flock against a wolf he approvingly recounts. In contrast to Diggon's idealism are the cautious views of Hobbinoll who warns Diggon not to be so outspoken. Like Palinode in 'Maye', Hobinoll is disinclined to martyr himself by watching all night: 'We bene of fleshe, men as other bee. | Why should we be bound to such miseree?'(ll. 238–9). Hobbinoll and Palinode may be venial and self-serving, falling far short of the ideal pastors envisaged by their interlocutors, but they provide a stubbornly realist perspective, that, in Hobbinoll's case, accompanies a practical, kindly neighbourliness. Imperfect as this accommodating realism might be, it nevertheless offers a sceptical perspective on the inflexible and impractical idealism of the purists.

Hobbinoll cautions Diggon 'a little to feyne' ('September', l. 137). The ambiguous perspectives of these eclogues may similarly be designed to accommodate different factions of the powerful. E.K.'s misleading references to Roman abuses when English ones are meant may be politic in the face of potential ecclesiastical censorship, while the airing of reformist criticisms, artfully disassociated from the voice of the poet himself, may have been designed to please Spenser's patron, the earl of Leicester, leader of religious reformists at court. However self-serving its strategies, we find in the *Calender* just such a complex interaction between text and reader as we also find in *The Faerie Queene*.

THE FAERIE QUEENE

The first book of *The Faerie Queene* leaves us in no doubt about its distinctively Protestant agenda. Redcrosse, the knight of Holiness, appears in the first stanzas of canto i dressed in 'the armour of a Christian man specified by Saint Paul v. Ephes' ('Letter to Raleigh'; Spenser 1977: 738). The reference is to Ephesians 6:11–17 (on the armour and Christian knighthood, see King 1990: 194–5). Redcrosse's distinctively Protestant narrative unfolds gradually as he discovers that his 'fleshly might' and fallen judgement lead him repeatedly into error, illustrating the narrator's orthodox Calvinist warning; 'if any strength we haue, it is to ill' (1.x.1).[4] Brought to despair by his guilt, Redcrosse is saved by Una's timely reminder of freely given grace and salvation:

> In heauenly mercies has thou not a part?
> Why shouldst thou then despeire, that chosen art?
> Where iustice growes, there grows eke greater grace. (1.ix.53)

---

[4] For a detailed account of the theology of this stanza and Book 1 generally, see Gless 1994: chs 2–6, esp. 148–9.

Una (a figure for truth and the true Church) voices the 'sweete, pleasaunt, and vnspeakable comforte' of core Protestant beliefs: the elect 'be called accordyng to Gods purpose by his spirite working in due season: they through grace obey the calling: they be iustified freelye: they be made sonnes of God by adoption ... they walke religiously in good workes: and at length, by Gods mercy, they attayne to euerlastyng felicitie'.[5] From the den of Despair, Redcrosse is led through the House of Holiness to repentance and an understanding of his faith and of its fruits in good works. Finally he is shown a vision of the Heavenly Jerusalem and we learn that he figures not only the individual elect Christian, but also his elect Protestant nation whose role is to overcome the rule of Antichrist in the world:

> For thou emongst those Saints, whom thou doest see,
> Shalt be a Saint, and thine owne nations frend
> And Patrone: thou Saint *George* shalt called bee,
> Saint *George* of mery England, the signe of victoree. (1.x.61)

The explicitly Protestant and, to a lesser extent, the nationalist agendas of Book 1 recur in Books 2 and 3 (the 1590 edition of the poem).[6] Book 2 explores the limitations of man's powers of reason and will, unaided by grace, to resist the taint of original sin, while Book 3 focuses on the Protestant ideal of marriage. The English monarchy and its potentially providential role in establishing godly rule on earth feature in both Books, but the fallen imperfections of its history, and, more obliquely, its problematic future in the hands of an unmarried queen, Elizabeth, temper any triumphalism. None of the first three Books of *The Faerie Queene* offer an entirely optimistic vision of an earthly, let alone English resolution of the problems of a fallen world, but in Books 4–6, published in 1596, this pessimism seems more pronounced. Book 5, the Book of Justice, imagines a world in which Astrea, the goddess of Justice, has departed, leaving the imperfect knight of Justice, Arthegall, and his iron man, Talus, to administer the rule of law in a fallen world. In the final cantos, Arthegall and the British Prince Arthur, knights of the Fairy Queen, combat proliferating manifestations of Roman Catholicism both within and from without the realm, clearly allegorizing those threatening late sixteenth-century Protestant England and its allies. In Ireland, in particular, the grim efforts of Arthegall and Talus are left incomplete and conspicuously unrewarded.

While it is clear that a number of Books deal with theological, moral, and political issues of crucial importance in Elizabethan England, the experience of reading and interpreting Spenser's narratives is not at all straightforward, 'clowdily enwrapped' as they are 'in Allegoricall deuises' ('Letter to Raleigh'). To those who find such methods 'displeasaunt', Spenser replies that they are appropriate for the times, 'seeing all things

---

[5] From Article XVII, 'Of predestination and election' from *Articles whereupon it was agreed by the Archbyshoppes and Byshoppes ... in the yere of our Lorde God, 1562* (John Cawood, 1571), [the Thirty-Nine Articles] (http://eebo.chadwyck.com, accessed January 2014).

[6] On Protestant and theological themes in Books 2–6, see Hume 1984: ch. 6, and Gless 1994: ch. 7.

accounted by their showes, and nothing esteemed of, that is not delightfull and pleasing to commune sence.' The dangers of shows and the human senses are fundamental concerns in *The Faerie Queene*. In its fallen world, appearances and false assumptions all too easily lead the unwary, both knights and readers, astray, and Spenser's educative programme, his fashioning of a noble person, depends on the reader's constantly vigilant scrutiny and discrimination (see Gregerson 1995: 64; also McEachern 2010: 41–3).

The need for caution when confronted with false shows and deceiving appearances was of particular concern for Protestants in the sixteenth century. Catholic priests were regularly figured, as we saw in the *Calendar*, as disguised wolves and foxes eager to gobble up gullible souls, or they were mountebank necromancers, fooling the simple with painted images and superstitious rituals (King 1990: 47). As dangerous was the susceptibility of fallen human senses and understanding to specious tales and pleasing images. The productions of Phantastes—'all that fained is, as leasings, tales, and lies' (2.ix.51)—could also exert a disturbingly powerful hold on the fantasies and passions of others. The glamorous but dangerous Duessas, Acrasias, False Florimells, and Radigunds that beguile the characters in the poem abundantly show the ease with which fallen humanity is corrupted. It is not only the knights who err through the narratives of the poem; the reader must also beware. Archimago appears at first 'sober and sagely sad' (1.i.29) to the reader as well as to Redcrosse and Una. It is only as his hidden nature is revealed that the reader is led to realize how dangerous this archmaker of false images and stories is, and how vulnerable the human judgement of Redcrosse, led astray by his senses and his desires. The reader is perhaps more easily trapped by the plausible narratives of the poem rather than by its gorgeous shows. Redcrosse's narrative seems to follow the familiar conventions of chivalric romance, with the knight seeking to demonstrate his prowess by defeating aggressors and rescuing ladies. It is only when we find the Knight of Holiness claiming the shield of faithlessness and false Duessa as his prizes in the House of Pride that we realize the values of knight errantry have led Redcrosse far astray and are not those to be followed by a Christian knight.

Redcrosse is not the only knight whose adventures seem designed to test the reader's interpretative powers. What are we to make of Guyon's attempts to wash the stain of original sin from the hands of Ruddymane (2.ii 3)? Or his confident prescriptions of human reason and temperance as a sufficient cure for the excesses of man's fallen nature when such remedies have failed so dramatically in Amavia's attempts to cure Mortdant (2.i.54 and 57–8; see Gless 1994: 181–3 for a very useful discussion)? Why does an angel still have to rescue Guyon after he succeeds in resisting the temptations of Mammon? How should we interpret the spectacular House of Busirane in 3.xi–xii, unaided as we are by a puzzled Britomart and an enigmatic narrator, and how does this episode relate to Scudamour's claiming of Amoret as his bride in The Temple of Venus in 4.x? How should we judge Calidore's stay among the shepherds in 6.ix.26–34? *The Faerie Queene*, through its complex images and narratives requires of its readers a constant process of interpretation, comparison, and reflection that tests and often challenges our theological, moral, and political judgements. It is through its opaque fictions, the 'continued

Allegory, or darke conceit' of its methods, that the poem fashions its ideal reader as a wary moral actor in a fallen world.

While the fallen mind may be a 'forge of idols', images can be used for good and ill in *The Faerie Queene*. The poem gives us 'dark doubles' of the image-making powers of the poet: the arch image-maker, Archimago, who conjures up dreams and false stories, Acrasia whose spider bower is a miracle of artifice, or Busyrane, that master of erotic genres (see King 1990: 75–6, and, for the phrase 'dark double', 114). The productions of such artificers, in David Norbrook's words, deceive and seduce by encouraging 'readers to take sign for reality, representation for thing represented'. Spenser, on the contrary, 'problematises the act of reading, discouraging his audience from taking the interpretations they are offered immediately on trust' (Norbrook 1984: 111; see also King 1990: 68; Gregerson 1995: 5; and Gross 1985: 15). Spenser's artful allegorical poem encourages us to recognize its images as images, its fictions as man-made representations of an imperfect fallen world in which, at best, we perceive the truth darkly.

'LOVE IS THE LESSON WHICH THE LORD US TAUGHT' (*AMORETTI* 68)

Few experiences more severely test Spenser's characters' abilities to discriminate between true and false, the godly and the unregenerate, than those of love and desire. In Book 3, the narrator hails love as emanating from God:

> Most sacred fire, that burnest mightily
> In liuing brests, ykindled first aboue,
> Emongst th'eternall spheres and lamping sky,
> And thence pourd into men, which men call Loue. (3.iii.1)

However, such love, an eros that inspires heroes (stz. 2), is quite different from 'that same, which doth base affections moue | In brutish minds, and filthy lust inflame' (stz. 1). From *The Shepheardes Calender* on, the power of love, its significance, and the importance, but also the difficulty, of distinguishing between love as a 'sacred fire' and love as a 'base affection', are central themes in Spenser's work.

Love and its effects, particularly on the poet, appear as a troubling theme in the *Calender* (Pugh 2005: 36; Heale 2010: 591–600). There, the shepherd-poet Colin Clout has had his poetic gifts blighted by his unrequited love for Rosalind ('Aprill', ll. 9–28). He can no longer play 'his wonted songs' ('Aprill', l. 16) and at the end of a final December lament hangs up his pipe ('December', l. 141). Colin's experience of the pains of love, like Thomalin's at the end of the March eclogue, to some extent fit into an expected reformist pattern. Barnabe Googe, one of Spenser's predecessors as a writer of eclogues, repeatedly insists on the vanity of love and its harmful effects: 'The fickle fading form and face | that once so much I sought, | Hath made me lose the skies above, | and me to hell hath brought' (1989: eclogue 4, ll. 77–80). Protestant suspicion of the disruptive powers of erotic love extended to the songs and sonnets that took love as their theme. Attacks on such profane writings were gathering to a head in 1579 (Herman 1996: esp. ch. 1; see also Collinson 1986: esp. 11–12, 18–19). Godly revisions of erotic verse had appeared, for example, in John Hall's *The Courte of Vertue* (1565), and Spenser would certainly have known of George Gascoigne's *A Hundreth Sundrie Flowres* (1573) which was censored by the 'reverende Divines' of the Court of High Commission which 'thought requysite that all ydle Bookes or wanton Pamphlettes shoulde bee forbidden' (2000: 360). Erotic love and its place in the work of the ambitious Protestant poet of the *Calender* was thus a problematic matter in 1579, especially as the poet twice identifies himself with the love-sick poet Colin Clout (in the 'Epistle' and in 'September' note 176).

In 'October', Cuddie and Piers explicitly debate love as a fitting theme for verse. For the first time we glimpse what will become an increasingly important topic in Spenser's work: the elevated and elevating potential of erotic love. Cuddie is described by E.K. as 'the perfecte paterne of a Poete' ('Argvment'), but it is Piers who is given the higher, less mercenary, view of poetry: its fittest subject, he tells us, is heaven from whence it comes (ll. 79–84). Only Colin Clout has such genius, Cuddie replies, were it not for love: 'He, were he not with loue so ill bedight, | Would mount as high, and sing as soote as Swanne' (ll. 89–90). Piers, however, takes a different view of love as the subject of verse:

> for loue does teach him climbe so hie,
> And lyftes him vp out of the loathsome myre:
> Such immortall mirrhor, as he doth admire,
> Would rayse ones mynd aboue the starry skie. (ll. 91–4)

Cuddie dismisses Piers's enthusiasm, 'lordly loue is such a Tyranne fell: | That where he rules, all power he doth expell' (ll. 98–9). At the end of the *Calender*, Colin's broken bag-pipes seem to confirm this view. From the perspective of Spenser's later works, we can, however, see Piers's assertion that love can inspire the highest poetry as the first sign of Spenser's commitment to a new reformed poetry of love, a 'revision of Petrarchan and Ovidian love, which will ultimately place a reformed eros at the centre of Spenser's moral, political and religious teachings' (Pugh 2005: 36).

In Book 3 of *The Faerie Queene*, the narrator's paean to erotic love (quoted above) intertwines the personal and the political. Love spurs Britomart on to seek a husband, but that alliance, Merlin assures her, will found a race culminating in the Tudor Protestant monarchy. Through Books 3 and 4, into Book 5, Britomart's erotic love for Arthegall is a force for goodness and order in a fallen world in which lust, and the less heroic subjects of desire, cause error and disorder. Book 6, however, gives us a less positive view of love as a force for public good and order. The knight of Courtesy, Calidore, loves Pastorella, but his pursuit of her leads him to play the part of a shepherd, rather than a hero. He abandons his quest for the Blatant Beast who continues unchecked to ravish the inhabitants and institutions of Faeryland. It is Colin Clout, the shepherd poet of the *Calendar*, who gives us a more inspiring image of love in Book 6, but his vision is set apart from the public world of Gloriana and her knights. Coming across Colin on a hill sacred to Venus, Calidore glimpses for a moment a vision that is both erotic and sublime, a perfect circle of 'an hundred naked maidens lilly white', dancing to Colin's music (6.x.6–28). In their midst, the three Graces, linked as a garland, dance round 'another Grace' (x.27), Colin's own love, 'to whom that shepheard pypt alone, | That made him pipe so merrily, as neuer none' (x.15). Colin's vision is a gift, bestowed upon him from above, though it responds to his piping. It cannot be summoned at will: 'none can them bring in place, | But whom they of them selues list so to grace' (x.20). Even 'Great *Gloriana*' (x.28) has to take second place for a while to this song that Colin plays for his own private pleasure. When Calidore intrudes on Colin's vision, causing it to disappear, the shepherd/poet, in despair, 'broke his bag-pipe quight' (x.18). The gesture recalls the broken and hung-up pipe of the *Calender*, but its significance has changed. It is no longer a sign of Colin's failure in love, but an acknowledgment of the divine source of such poetry, of its rarity, and of its vulnerability in the public world of men.

Colin also reappears as an inspired poet of love in *Colin Clovts Come Home Againe* (1595). As in Book 6, his vision of love is given expression far from the court. Returning 'home' to Ireland, Colin describes his horror at the degenerate kind of love he found versified and practiced at the royal court in London: 'For all the walls and windows there are writ, | All full of loue, and loue, and loue my deare' (ll. 776–7). Love's:

> mightie mysteries they do prophane,
> And vse his ydle name to other needs,
> But as a complement for courting vaine. (ll. 788–90)

Colin is no more the friend of 'wanton Pamphlettes' than were the divines who censored Gascoigne's verse, but that does not mean erotic love should be banished from the highest poetry. In a 'celestiall rage', Colin tells the shepherds what love is, rightly understood: a force that at the Creation bound the elements together in an orderly and fruitful harmony that produced all living things including mankind:

> For beautie is the bayt which with delight
> Doth man allure, for to enlarge his kynd,
> Beautie the burning lamp of heauens light,
> Darting her beames into each feeble mynd:
> Against whose powre, nor God nor man can fynd
> Defence. (ll. 871–6)

Colin sets his vision of love's power in a cosmology of pagan gods, Venus and Cupid, but the terms he uses suggest a pastoral version of a Reformed theology of election and grace: 'and when he list shew grace, | Does graunt them grace that otherwise would die. | So loue is Lord of all the world by right' (ll. 881–3). Human love, in this perspective, is an agent and reflection of the divine love of God.

In *Amoretti and Epithalamion* (1596), Spenser abandons the persona of Colin for another quasi-autobiographical voice, that of the lover and bridegroom whose story is told in the poems. Through the sonnet sequence of the *Amoretti*, the lover is gradually drawn away from the conventional Petrarchan discourse typical of contemporary sonnet sequences, with their narratives of unchaste desire, disdainful ladies, and erotic frustration, to a new Protestant understanding of mutual, chaste, erotic love. Love proves to be a discipline that reforms the lover's importunity as admiration, humility, and patience, and transforms the lady's virginal pride to mercy and a chaste readiness to accept the lover's embrace in marriage. As Carole Kaske has noted, 'the entire *Amoretti* glows with sacred analogies' (2004: 39). In particular, the Church calendar for Lent structures the crucial sequence of sonnets from the lover's idolatrous worship of his beloved on Ash Wednesday (22) to the triumphant Easter sonnet (68) in which mutual erotic love is placed in an emphatically Christian context: 'So let vs loue, deare loue, lyke as we ought, | loue is the lesson which the Lord vs taught' (Dunlop 1970). This sonnet sequence culminates, uniquely, in a marriage hymn, the *Epithalamion*, in which the marriage is sanctified in a decidedly unpuritanical church complete with high altar and organ music. While endorsing the central Protestant affirmation of marriage, *Epithalamion* seems to indicate that Spenser, at least by the 1590s, shared the queen's conservative views on church architecture and fine music (on Elizabeth's personal views, see Collinson 1986: 29 and 35, and on music, Davies 1996: 396–8). The volume, however, conspicuously marginalizes Elizabeth herself. Twice begging pardon for setting aside his epic poem (*Amoretti* 33 and 80), Spenser instead represents his own marriage as the source of civil order, an exemplum of the disciplining and harmonious power of a love whose influence spreads out from the private couple to the wider community, in this poem a community in Ireland; one in particular need of such discipline and harmony (Heale 2003: 115–19).

The semi-autobiographical personae of Colin Clout and the lover/bridegroom of *Amoretti and Epithalamion*, lend particular authority to these poems' visions of virtuous, erotic love as a divine, ordering, disciplining, and inspiring force in the fallen world. As in the *Calender*, however, hints of less idealized perspectives provide more sceptical perspectives. Might Thestylis be right in claiming that Colin's attack on the court stems from spite and envy because he has not been fortunate there (*CCCHA*, ll. 676–9)? Is the court and its practices marginal to Colin's vision of the transforming power of love, or is Colin's distance from the court a sign of his own marginality? Even in *Epithalamion*, which imagines a harmonious community centred on mutual love, the menacing Irish world of 'wylde wolues' (l. 69), 'false treason', and 'dread disquiet' (ll. 323–4) reminds the reader that such poetic visions are not enough, any more than were the songs of the bridegroom/poet's model, Orpheus (l. 16), to keep death and disorder at bay.

Spenser's final two works, *The Fowre Hymnes* (1596) and the *Cantos of Mutabilitie* (published posthumously in 1609) open yet another perspective on the transforming power of love. The first two 'Hymnes in Honour of Love' and 'Beautie' (*HL* and *HB*), celebrate erotic love in terms very similar to those used in *The Faerie Queene* 3, *CCCHA*, and *Amoretti*: love, through beauty, inspires men and women in the sublunary world to lift themselves 'out of the lowly dust, | On golden plumes vp to the purest skie' (*HL*, ll. 177–8), aspiring to act nobly to win the beloved in whose beauty they see a spark of the divine. In the 'Hymnes of Heavenly Love' and 'Beautie' (*HHL* and *HHB*), even this aspiring human love is eclipsed by visions of the divine love of the crucified Christ, while sublunary beauty is replaced by an ecstatic vision of the eternal beauty of Heaven. From such perspectives, 'all other sights but fayned shadowes bee' (*HHB* l. 273). In these poems, McCabe has argued, Spenser presents poets as 'conduits of vision', speaking Divine, not Tudor, truths (2009: 446). At the end of the *Mutabilitie Cantos*, in his last published stanzas, Spenser turns from the competing temporal perspectives of Jove, Mutability, and Nature, and the pageant of the fallen world's changing spectacle, with a prayer that he might see and adore a truth beyond human representation, face to face:

> thence-forth all shall rest eternally
> With Him that is the God of Sabbaoth hight:
> O that great Sabbaoth God, graunt me that Sabaoths sight. (7.viii.2)

CHAPTER 19

CHRISTOPHER MARLOWE AND RELIGION

LISA HOPKINS

CHRISTOPHER Marlowe was born into circumstances which promised firmly for religious orthodoxy. The marriage of his parents and the baptisms and burials of their children are recorded in due form, and John Marlowe, unlike the father of Marlowe's exact contemporary Shakespeare, is not to be found being fined for non-attendance at church. The young Marlowe attended the King's School, Canterbury, in the very shadow of Canterbury Cathedral, where the Primate of England had his seat; later, he attended Cambridge on the strength of a scholarship established by a former Archbishop of Canterbury, Matthew Parker, which was expressly intended to be held by those proceeding to holy orders. Yet despite such auspicious-seeming beginnings, my very title of 'Christopher Marlowe and Religion' might well seem to be virtually an oxymoron, coupling two things which have nothing in common with each other, for to many of his contemporaries Marlowe was associated not with religion but, publicly and repeatedly, with irreligion. In this discussion, I shall first suggest a possible reason why a man apparently initially destined for the Church ended his life as a playwright and poet, then examine some of the various representations of religion in his works, and finally attempt to trace some of the effect these had on his contemporaries.

THE NEW GEOGRAPHY CALLS ALL IN DOUBT

During Marlowe's lifetime, the first English ship sailed for Virginia, where colonizers were left in Roanoke, and Thomas Hariot, whom Marlowe may well have known, began the first recorded attempt to learn some of the language of the Native Americans and enter into their ways of thinking. All Marlowe's major works can be seen as responding in one way or another to this dramatic moment of change, because all are in effect first contact narratives. His two great poems, *Hero and Leander* and 'The Passionate Shepherd to his Love', both focus on love, capturing the moment when one person first fully registers and reaches out for the elusive subjectivity of another. His plays are certainly more various, and yet they can, I think, be seen as united by this common element. In what may have been the earliest of them, *Dido, Queen of Carthage*, we see the first encounter between the dying civilization of Troy and the still-thriving one of Libya, and Marlowe's audience knew well that it would be from this fateful meeting, which furnishes Aeneas with ships and wherewithal to renew his voyage, that the Roman and ultimately, according to legend, the British empires would eventually be born. In *Tamburlaine the Great*, successive groups of people with conventional abilities and aspirations find themselves initially baffled and ultimately destroyed by a species of superman, who thinks and acts on an entirely different scale and is subject to few, if any, of the doubts and emotions that we generally consider as human. In *Doctor Faustus*, man meets devil; in *The Jew of Malta*, Christians, Jews, and Muslims are forced by the confines of a tiny Mediterranean island into closer contact than any of them wishes; in *The Massacre at Paris*, Catholics and Huguenots encounter each other at increasingly close quarters in the charged context of a marriage between members of the two different persuasions; and in *Edward II* men who define themselves as normal, in both sexual and political terms, face men whom they define as absolutely and abhorrently abnormal.

In all these cases, the audience watches, wonders, and will almost invariably find something to respond to in both of the opposing parties. The barons may be right that Edward is politically irresponsible, but it is surely impossible to ignore the passion of his relationship with Gaveston, or to watch unmoved his suffering at the end. The prince of darkness is a gentleman; the demonized Muslim keeps his word and the despised Jewess is guided wholly by love; Tamburlaine is at least briefly humanized by his love for Zenocrate, and even the Guise may claim our understanding when he is shown as a cuckold. Though it might be a stretch to call Marlowe a balanced writer, he is at least one who knows how to create and use a certain distance of viewpoint, and this is a point to which I shall return when considering the extent to which his work intervened in debates about religion.

First, however, what of my initial claim that all or any of this should be seen as in some sense conditioned by Virginia, Roanoke, or Hariot? Here, external rather than internal evidence is needed, and it must be conceded at the beginning that it is external evidence of a not wholly reliable kind. Either very shortly before or very shortly after Marlowe's death, an erstwhile acquaintance of his named Richard Baines submitted a 'Note' to the authorities on 'the opinion of one Christopher Marly Concerning his Damnable Judgment of Religion, and scorn of gods word' in which he detailed several of Marlowe's supposedly heretical opinions. The first and second of these were 'That the Indians, and many authors of antiquity, have assuredly written of above 16 thousand years agone, wheras Adam is proved to have lived within six thousand years' and 'He affirmeth that Moses was but a juggler, and that one Heriots being Sir Walter Raleigh's man can do more than he'. This is a very suggestive collocation. For some, the discovery of America had in itself been enough to shake their faith, since it clearly revealed the existence of things not mentioned in the Bible; for Marlowe, the mechanism is more specific. Marlowe, according to Baines, knows Hariot, and he also has access to information about the beliefs of Indians which directly challenges Christian Scripture; between them, Hariot's skills and the Indians' and ancients' traditions have fatally undermined whatever belief Marlowe may once have had in the teachings of the established Church, so that 'one Richard Cholmley hath confessed that he was persuaded by Marlowe's reasons to become an atheist' (see Hopkins 2005: 135–6).

There are, of course, reasons why we might want to be sceptical about what Baines says, in that there was a history of bad blood between him and Marlowe and that Roy Kendall has suggested that the 'Marlowe' whom Baines constructs is in fact a mirror-image of Baines himself rather than a testimony to independent and unbiased observation (see Kendall 2003). Nevertheless, it is worth noting that we do have independent evidence of the existence of actual Indians whom Marlowe could in fact have spoken to, for Hariot brought two, whom he named Manteo and Wanchese, back with him from Roanoke (see for instance Milton 2000: 66–77). For Donne, 'the new philosophy' produced by geographical and scientific discourse 'calls all in doubt': in Marlowe's apparent response to the very different perspectives of 'Indians', we seem almost to catch a glimpse of that in process.

ALTERNATIVES TO CHRISTIANITY

In a sense, it does not even matter whether Baines's account is true or not, for what was unquestionably the case is that Marlowe's contemporaries found it credible. With the possible exception of Machiavelli, no other sixteenth-century figure had so securely established a reputation for atheism as Marlowe had in Tudor England. Although atheism itself could be a slightly nebulous concept, being sometimes used as little better than a catch-all insult and one which many Protestants were, however perversely, particularly fond of applying to Catholics, the one thing that was certain was that Marlowe was its public face. It was the general impression that he did not believe, or at least that he did not believe as other men did. In this respect there is a certain appropriateness to the otherwise lamentable textual state of so many of his works: *Doctor Faustus* exists in two different versions; *The Massacre at Paris* and *The Jew of Malta* both show signs of having been garbled or damaged in transmission; *Hero and Leander* is probably unfinished; *Tamburlaine the Great* apparently had scenes removed by the printer; our understanding of *Dido, Queen of Carthage* is troubled by the difficult question of whether and, if so, what Thomas Nashe contributed to it; and even *Edward II*, which we can be reasonably confident exists in the form in which Marlowe wrote it, may have been inflected by the non-availability of Edward Alleyn, who had played the lead in Marlowe's previous plays and whose absence may have led him to rethink his usual preference for a massively dominant central character. The fact that we cannot in any of these cases feel fully confident about Marlowe's original design can paradoxically be seen as having in some sense acted as a liberating factor in the cases of at least some of these works: thus Leah Marcus has argued that *Doctor Faustus* in particular owes at least some of its textual instability to the fact that successive productions of the play experimented with and updated it in ways which directly reflected on very specific religious controversies and on changes to the dominant theology of the Church of England (Marcus 1996). The combination of the literal death of the author and of the innate power of the play seems in this respect to have proved a particularly enabling one, making the drama malleable and allowing it to continue to generate maximum charge. The negative concomitant of this is that it is never easy to be sure what exactly Marlowe is saying about religion, because his work may have been changed after his death and because his meanings may in any case have been so dangerous that they had to be mediated and disguised even in their original forms. Nevertheless, there can be little doubt that all of his works in one form or other spoke to their original audiences about religion, and that they spoke loudly, powerfully, and potentially dangerously about it.

In both what may have been his first work, *Dido, Queen of Carthage*, and what was probably his last, *Hero and Leander*, the focus is on classical mythology. Although this was no longer an active belief system, it was one which the Elizabethan education system made extremely familiar and one too whose image benefited from the prestige which accrued to virtually all aspects of classical civilization. It is a recurrent presence in all Marlowe's works, but it is in *Dido, Queen of Carthage* and *Hero and Leander* that it is put under the closest scrutiny and pressure, and this is done in ways which make it possible to read implied strictures on classical religion as potentially applicable to Christian religion too, for the aspects on which Marlowe homes in most closely are the idea of a father god and the relationship between religious belief and personal morality. *Dido, Queen of Carthage* opens with a very striking image of a god, Jupiter, who is defined primarily by his interactions with both an actual though unrelated child and his adult daughter. In the first part of the scene, we see Jupiter ruthlessly exploiting his position to buy the sexual favours of a young boy; in the second, we see him having to be nagged and badgered into taking an interest in the affairs of his daughter and her son, who is in distress and danger. Both spectacles are wholly unedifying and collectively present a picture of a deity governed solely by self-interest and consulting only his own inclinations and convenience. In the case of *Hero and Leander*, a crystal floor holds up the actions of the gods as in a mirror, and what it shows is them 'Committing heady riots, incests, rapes' (Marlowe 2006: l. 144). These speak less of any concept of man made in the image of god and far more of one of gods made in the image of man, with all the inherent flaws and limitations implicit in the human condition, and the effect of the behaviour of these deities on their followers is predictably debilitating: belief in such beings has nothing ennobling or inspiring about it.

PEOPLE OF THE BOOK

In these two cases, the subversive force of such representations is muted by the fact that no one among Marlowe's audience or readership was required to believe in the deities presented and referred to. The picture is very different when it comes to the play which probably followed *Dido, Tamburlaine the Great*. Here, we meet representations of two religions, Islam and Christianity, the latter being imported into the plot through a bit of chronological sleight-of-hand on Marlowe's part when he borrows material from a sequence of events which in fact took place well after the lifetime of the historical Tamburlaine. Marlowe's treatment of both is characteristically irreverent and provocative. The Christian king breaks the oath he swears by Christ and is killed as a result. The Muslim Tamburlaine, by contrast, goes from strength to strength until he burns a copy of the Qu'ran, and dies. The text does not articulate a connection between these two events, but it is clearly possible for the audience to infer one, and to speculate on what it might mean. Perhaps the Church was right after all and there is indeed an omnipotent, all-seeing God, only it is Allah? The suggestion that Islam, a religion feared and hated in Elizabethan England, might be the one true faith would have been virtually unthinkable to an Englishman of the late 1580s, and yet Marlowe might just have been the one man able and willing to think it. Perhaps, though, there is another possibility. In a production of the play at the Barbican Centre, London, in 2005, David Farr attracted considerable press attention when he changed the text so that Tamburlaine no longer burnt the Qu'ran but some unspecified holy books. In the face of media accusations that he was kow-towing to a misplaced notion of political correctness, Farr replied that actually he felt that Marlowe would have chosen to burn the Bible if he had thought that he could have got away with it, and that the Qu'ran had been chosen as a convenient substitute rather than as a way of making any kind of point about Islam (Farr 2005). The idea is an interesting one in its own right, and also entails the possibility that if the Qu'ran might just as well be the Bible, then the god who seems to avenge its burning might just as well be the Christian one. But then it is also possible that Tamburlaine's death is not directly attributable to the book-burning at all: his sudden illness might be food poisoning, or illness of some other sort, as the attendant physician suggests when he attributes it to a humoral imbalance. As so often in Marlowe, we do not know what to think, but then we had already been forewarned by the Prologue, which exhorts the audience to 'judge [Tamburlaine's] fortunes as you please' (*Tamburlaine the Great*, Part One, in Marlowe 1999, Prologue, 8), that we should be ready to expect more questions than answers.

We are given even less guidance in *Doctor Faustus*, the play which probably followed immediately after *Tamburlaine the Great*, because there we cannot even be sure which text we ought to read. In this respect, what is generally recognized as Marlowe's greatest play is also his most baffling. However, Goethe's view of it was 'How greatly is it all planned!' and that is absolutely right: however imprecise the detail, the overall shape of the story is clear, and what it shows us is a man who turns from God to the devil and finds that once he has stepped off the path of righteousness there is no way of getting back onto it and he is consequently condemned to eternal damnation. Once this overall architecture comes into focus, something unexpected and serendipitous happens, because the existence of the two different texts can in fact become a powerful metaphor for the existence of the two different confessions (and indeed of subdivisions within those confessions) which made it difficult, if not impossible, for serious thinkers of the late sixteenth century to be sure of where the path of righteousness actually lay. A particularly powerful example of this is a small but hugely significant difference between the A and B texts of the play. In the 1616 B text, the Good Angel tells Faustus that it is 'Never too late, if Faustus will repent' (II.ii.82). This would be the standard Lutheran position: repentance is possible if the person chooses it. In the 1604 A text, however, the Good Angel's words are 'Never too late, if Faustus can repent' (II.ii.84), suggesting the Calvinist position that it may be impossible to repent because God may have chosen to withhold from the individual the grace that would enable him or her to do so (*Doctor Faustus*, in Marlowe 1999). Our perplexity when forced to choose between these two texts mirrors that of Marlowe's contemporaries when forced to choose between at least two competing theologies. Moreover, the reference at the beginning of the play to 'Jerome's Bible' (A, I.i.38), present in both texts, reminds us that while the Bible may claim to be the work of God, it has been mediated and translated by man, and that it too may say different things in different versions. For all the deceptive simplicity of its architecture, this play too asks some very probing and, from a sixteenth-century point of view, some potentially very subversive questions about religion.

In my discussion of *Tamburlaine the Great*, I suggested that it might be possible to see the Bible and the Qu'ran as being in some sense interchangeable for Marlowe's purposes. Whether it is present in *Tamburlaine* or not, such a correspondence certainly seems to underlie *The Jew of Malta*, the play which seems most likely to have been written immediately after *Doctor Faustus*, for this offers what amounts to a systematic exploration of the three religions of the book, Christianity, Judaism, and Islam, in ways which constantly stress the affinities between them, so that we may well be tempted to attach an ironic double meaning to the Christian Mathias's assurance to his mother that during his conversation with the Jewish Barabas 'my talk with him was | About the borrowing of a book or two' (*The Jew of Malta*, in Marlowe 1999, II.iii.159–60), given that Christianity shares the five books of the Pentateuch with Judaism. One might also note a suggestive possible interface between Richard Baines's observation that Marlowe's table talk included the observation that 'All the New Testament is filthily written' and T. S. Eliot's famous observation on *The Jew of Malta* that 'it has always been said that the end, even the last two acts, are unworthy of the first three' (1920: 92). I concur with Eliot's assessment, except to my mind the change begins rather earlier, at III.i, and I want to suggest that this shift in *The Jew of Malta* might actually be designed to deliberately mirror that between the Old and New Testaments. The change in tone and texture between the two halves, assuming it is admitted to exist, can be seen as marked to a certain extent by an explicit reference to the New Testament when Jacomo says '—*Virgo, salve*' ('Hail, virgin) (*The Jew of Malta*, in Marlowe 1999, III.iii.56; all further quotations from the play will be taken from this edition and reference will be given in the text), while the first half of the play is rich in allusions to the collective history of the Jewish people as told in the Old Testament: Barabas's exile from his house and his loss of wealth parallel the Jews' exile in Egypt, while a key figure from the Old Testament is recalled when Barabas twice refers to Abraham (I.i.105, II.i.14–15). Another Old Testament figure is evoked when the First

Jew says 'Yet, brother Barabas, remember Job' (I.ii.183), and the long history of conflict between Jews and Philistines is glanced at when Barabas says to Abigail of Lodowick:

> Provided that you keep your maidenhead,
> Use him as if he were a [*Aside*] Philistine.
> Dissemble, swear, protest, vow love to him;
> He is not of the seed of Abraham. (II.iii.232–5)

There are, though, also plenty of foreshadowings of worse times to come for the Jews. The First Knight says scornfully to Barabas, 'If your first curse fall heavy on thy head' (I.ii.110), where the change from plural 'your' to singular 'thou' makes it clear that, though on this occasion its force will be specially felt by Barabas, the curse in question is the collective one supposedly incurred by the Jews, and the Officer reminds us of the fate that befell many European Jews in the Middle Ages and Renaissance when he says 'he that denies to pay shall straight become a Christian' (I.ii.74–5). Indeed Barabas directly alludes to the disaster which befell Jerusalem when he speaks of the time when 'Titus and Vespasian conquered us' (II.iii.10). In the second half, by contrast, we see a 'resurrection' and the unchallenged triumph of Christianity, while Barabas could well be seen as inverting the iconography of St John the Evangelist, who was supposed to have survived both being placed in a cauldron of boiling oil and drinking poisoned wine (hence his two symbols of a cauldron and of a dragon or snake emerging from a chalice) when he dispenses poison which does kill and himself dies in a cauldron. We might also note that the names of Mathias and Lodovico look uncannily like the evangelists Matthew and Luke, and that Barabas compares Abigail to a light shining in the East, like the light which guided the Magi to the infant Jesus, as if we were watching the emergence of a Christianity in a previously Jewish world. This all makes for a complex effect in which the future is in some sense already in the past, while the present is richly evocative of the past. The play develops this sense of blurred temporalities by slyly and repeatedly insisting that the divide between Jews and Christians is far narrower and more permeable than either of the two sides in the play would wish to think; indeed the full name of the Order to which the Knights of the play belong was 'Knights Hospitaller of the Order of St John of Jerusalem', and arguably the most famous person ever to have landed on their island, St Paul, was in his own person an epitome of the continuity between Judaism and Christianity.

It is also notable that representatives of all three faiths in *Jew* are mutually intelligible and that each understands only too well the thought processes and motivations of the other two, so that the conflicts between them come across almost as sibling rivalry. It might be a fundamental tenet of domestic and foreign policy in virtually every European nation that Christianity was infinitely superior to Judaism or Islam, but Marlowe's play might well leave us wondering what there is to choose between them. Ironically, there is a far greater sense of difference between the opposing sides in *A Massacre at Paris*, though they represent different confessions rather than different faiths. Jews, Turks, and knights of Malta may possess the basic common understanding of one another necessary to reach a *modus vivendi*, but Catholics and Huguenots seem locked in a conflict fuelled by genuine hate and doomed to end in annihilation for one side or the other. Something of the same animus also enters the language of *Edward II*, where Edward parrots virtually identical anti-Catholic rhetoric to that of Henry III in *Massacre* (*Edward II*, I.iv.100–1 and *The Massacre at Paris*, Scene 24, 62–4, both in Marlowe 1999), and treats the bishop of Coventry with open contempt, though his motive on that occasion is personal rather than ideological. Here, too, we might well wonder whether there is a not a truer kind of piety to be found outside the Church than in it, since there is real unselfishness in Edward's love for his son, and it might even be possible to see something Christ-like in his suffering during the final scenes of the play.

The Face of Atheism

Thus, Marlowe thinks the unthinkable right across his *oeuvre*, entering into the arena of religious debate in literature with trumpets blaring and asking louder and more dangerous questions than any writer before him. When it comes to the response he elicited, the picture is more complex. In personal terms, it is probably safe to say that, however unsure we may be about the precise mechanism at work, his stridency led more or less directly to his death. There is also a sense in which it is difficult to separate his literary effect from his personal effect. In 1641 the Canterbury writer Henry Oxinden noted that Simon Aldrich, a local clergyman who had studied at Cambridge rather later than Marlowe, had told him that:

> Marlo who wrot Hero & Leander was an Atheist: & had writ a booke against the Scripture; how that it was al one man's making, & would haue printed it but could not be suffered. He was the son of a shomaker in Cant. He said hee was an excellent scoller & made excellent verses in Lattin & died aged about 30; he was stabd in the head with a dagger & dyed swearing.

Here, we catch the same implicit scepticism which I have suggested underlies Faustus's reference to 'Jerome's Bible'—Scripture is not a document given by God but is 'al one man's making'—but it has obviously also caught Aldrich's attention that Marlowe 'was the son of a shomaker in Cant', and whether the point is Marlowe's relatively lowly origins or his status as a local boy, his personal circumstances as well as his works are clearly of interest to Aldrich and to Oxinden too, not least because Aldrich clearly believes that because of censorship, not all of Marlowe's thought is to be found in his writings. Nor did Oxinden stop there; he further reported that:

> Mr Ald. sayd that mr Fineux of Douer was an Atheist & that hee would go out at midnight into a wood, & fall down uppon his knees & pray heartily that that Deuil would come, that he might see him (for hee did not beleiue that there was a Deuil) Mr Ald: sayd that hee was a verie good scholler, but would neuer haue aboue one booke at a time, & when hee was perfect in it, he would sell it away & buy another: he learnd all *Marlo* by heart & diuers other bookes: *Marlo* made him an *Atheist*. This

Fineaux was faine to make a speech uppon *The foole hath said in his heart there is no God*, to get his degree. Fineaux would say as Galen sayd that man was of a more excellent composition then a beast, & thereby could speake; but affirmed that his soule dyed with his body, & as we remember nothing before wee were borne, so we shall remember nothing after wee are dead. (qtd. in Eccles 1935: 40–1)

'Mr Fineux of Dover' must be either Thomas Fineux, who had studied at Corpus Christi some time after Marlowe, or his brother John, and the presence of a personal connection in the shape of a shared college (not to mention the fact that Marlowe's mother came from Dover) means that once again it is impossible to distinguish between the man and his works: 'he learnd all *Marlo* by heart & diuers other bookes: *Marlo* made him an *Atheist*'—'*Marlo*' here refers equally to a set of books, which can be compared with 'other bookes', and to an (implicitly personal) entity with agency, as implied by the verb 'made'.

Intriguingly, both the last part of Fineux's credo, that 'as we remember nothing before wee were borne, so we shall remember nothing after wee are dead', and also the text assigned for his punishment, '*The foole hath said in his heart there is no God*', are echoed in a text which seems also to remember Marlowe, John Ford's '*Tis Pity She's a Whore*. Here the hero Giovanni, who has been compared to both Faustus and Tamburlaine (Hoy 1960: 145–54), is warned by his mentor the Friar that:

> wits that presumed
> On wit too much, by striving how to prove
> There was no God, with foolish grounds of art,
> Discovered first the nearest way to hell,
> And filled the world with devilish atheism. (Ford 1997: I.i.4–8)

This could have provided a useful source for Fineux for his prescribed disquisition on '*The foole hath said in his heart there is no God*', spelling out as it does the consequences of that position. Later, Giovanni assures his sister Annabella that if he could credit what theologians teach about the eventual destruction of the earth:

> I could believe as well
> There might be hell or heaven.
> *Annabella.*   That's most certain.
> *Giovanni.*   A dream, a dream; else in this other world
> We should know one another.
> *Annabella.*   So we shall.
> *Giovanni.*   Have you heard so?
> *Annabella.*   For certain.
> *Giovanni.*   But d'ee think
> That I shall see you there, you look on me;
> May we kiss one another, prate or laugh,
> As we do here?
> *Annabella.*   I know not that. (V.v.34–41)

Ford, who was only seven when Marlowe died, could not have known him personally; thus, this must be one playwright's informed and considered response to the works of another, in much the same way as so many of Ford's plays rework and revisit *Othello* in ways which collectively offer what is in effect a critical reading of it. However, Ford too remembers not only the work but the man.

LITERARY INFLUENCES

A more purely literary response to Marlowe's plays can be identified in two very specific uses of him. First, as Dominic Green notes, 'On 1 February 1594, three days after Doctor Lopez was transferred to the Tower, *The Jew of Malta* was revived at the recently reopened Rose Theatre' (2003: 244): the alleged crimes of one Jew, accused of attempting to poison the queen, have clearly prompted recollection of the crimes of another, without any apparent need for the mediating figure of Marlowe himself. The second comes in a document which was found affixed to the wall of the Dutch Church in Broad Street on Saturday 5 May 1593, and which consequently became known as 'The Dutch Church Libel'. This too is a document that has some bearing on Marlowe's personal life, since it is a central component of the complex series of events which led up to his death, but its own interest is very much in his works, which it draws on repeatedly in stark warning to 'Ye strangers yt doe inhabite in this lande' of dire consequences if they do not return to their countries of origin. Among the accusations against the 'strangers' are that 'Your Machiavellian Marchant spoyles the state ... | And like the Jewes, you eate us vp as bread', evoking *The Jew of Malta*, in which Machiavelli appears as a character; therefore, the doggerel goes on to insist,

> Weele cutte your throtes, in your temples praying
> Not paris massacre so much blood did spill
> As we will doe iust vengeance on you all
> In counterfeitinge religion for your flight.

There is an obvious allusion to *The Massacre at Paris* here, and *The Jew of Malta* too may once again be evoked in the reference to counterfeiting, since Barabas's advice to Abigail is that 'A counterfeit profession is better | Than unseen hypocrisy' (I.ii.294–5). Finally the whole document is signed 'per. Tamberlaine'. In both these cases, Marlowe's own sophisticated understanding of the intersections between religious and national identities has been reduced to crude parody, but the fact that it has been so is not entirely without its uses, for it does serve to underline the extent to which early modern fear of cultural and religious difference was driven not simply by xenophobia but by fears about national security and prosperity.

The adopting of the persona of Tamburlaine at the end of the Dutch Church Libel is characteristic of the widespread interest in Marlowe's barnstorming hero. In the 1590s in particular, a number of dramatists offered varyingly pale imitations of the defiant rhetoric and exotic syllables so characteristic of the Tamburlaine plays (see Berek 1982), and as late as 1629 R. M.'s *Micrologia* attested to the continuing popularity of the play by observing that when Bridewell inmates are made to clean the streets, 'as they passe, the people scoffing say, | "Holla, ye pampered jades of Asia!" '. Perhaps most intriguingly, Tamburlaine even entered the repertoire of names by which boys might be christened (Bowers 1998: 362). Although it was the style of Tamburlaine that was most frequently imitated, however, in many ways it was *Dido, Queen of Carthage* which had the most profound intellectual influence on other playwrights, often in unexpected and richly suggestive ways. Shakespeare's *The Tempest* is a text which is clearly, as Marlowe himself seems to have been, fascinated by America, since it so obviously borrows from the account of the wreck of the *Sea Venture* off the coast of Bermuda while on its way to the fledgling English colony at Jamestown. It also revisits exactly the same territory as Marlowe had in *Dido, Queen of Carthage*, for it too is steeped in memories of Virgil: Ferdinand's 'Most sure the goddess | On whom these airs attend!' directly echoes Aeneas's 'O dea certe' (Shakespeare 1999, *The Tempest*, I.2.423–4, and see Tudeau-Clayton 1998), and again a storm has blown some would-be colonizers off course (as Shakespeare's original audience would have been well aware, most of the Neapolitan characters in the play are of Spanish origin and are effectively colonizing southern Italy, and the choice of the king of Tunis as Claribel's husband is no casual one but directly evokes Charles V's conquest of that city). Of particular interest is Caliban's reference to 'My dam's god Setebos' (I.2.374), for this has something of the same sense of god as constructed by man rather than man as constructed by god as animates both Faustus's reference to Jerome's Bible and *Dido, Queen of Carthage*'s sustained insistence on the flaws and frailties of the deities it presents.

The second play in which I would like to propose an influence from *Dido* is *The Duchess of Malfi*, in which, as in *Dido*, a young widow seeks a second husband, and in which the story of the Trojan war is indeed directly recalled when Antonio says of French horsemen, 'As out of the Grecian horse issued many famous princes, so, out of brave horsemanship arise the first sparks of growing resolution, that raise the mind to noble action' (I.i.142–3). At a number of points in *The Duchess of Malfi*, the language of *The Tempest* is found. The character names Ferdinand and Antonio are found in both plays, and the word 'tempest' itself recurs obsessively in the play. *The Tempest* is also echoed in the fact that it, like *The Duchess of Malfi*, focuses on the situation and legacy of the Aragonese in Italy, and the genesis of the Shakespeare play, in the shipwreck of *The Sea Venture* off the coast of Bermuda, is clearly gestured at in the Webster one when Bosola says, 'I would sooner swim to the Bermudas on | Two politicians' rotten bladders' (III.ii.266–7; see Hopkins 2011a). (It is perhaps suggestive that the two plays of Shakespeare's in which the influence of *Dido* is most strongly and directly visible are *Midsummer Night's Dream* and *Tempest*, in both of which there are definite supernatural powers at work; on the presence of *Dido* in *Dream*, see Connolly 2007a.) Looking at *The Duchess of Malfi* and *The Tempest* through the lens of Marlowe brings into close focus the extent to which all three of these texts address issues which proved problematic for Renaissance believers. All involve or evoke the discovery of new lands. All highlight the capriciousness of divine power—'We are merely the stars' tennis balls, struck and banded | Which way please them' (V.iv.54–5) says Bosola in *The Duchess of Malfi*—and all invite us to be aware of the proliferation of competing and mutually incompatible belief systems: what place has Prospero's apparent ability to raise the dead in a Christian universe, and what is the status of the Echo or of the apparent power of the stars in *The Duchess of Malfi*? All too invite or come close to inviting us to see the apparently divine as in fact man-made—Ariel's casual 'When I presented Ceres' (4.1.167) lays bare the device and shows us the machine behind the god, while the Cardinal in *The Duchess of Malfi* blatantly suborns the authority of the sacred for his own crudely secular purposes.

AMBIGUITY AND
THE DEATH OF THE AUTHOR

If the debt in these two plays is specifically to *Dido*, there is a more general aspect of Marlowe's dramaturgy which proved, I think, even more influential. One of the most intriguing aspects of Marlowe's treatment of religion is the extent to which he can say the right thing but nevertheless be generally received as meaning the wrong thing. On the face of it, the plays are choked with unimpeachably sound anti-Catholic rhetoric. The passage shared between *Massacre at Paris* and *Edward II*, to which I have already referred, is tub-thumping enough not to have been out of place in a play by the rabidly patriotic Queen's Men:

> I'll fire thy crazed buildings and enforce
> The papal towers to kiss the lowly ground,
> With slaughtered priests make Tiber's channel swell
>
> (*Edward II*, I.iv.100–3)

Equally, Barbara L. Parker has recently argued that 'anti-Catholic satire is the ... governing concept' of *Doctor Faustus* (2011: 60). However, Marlowe could never have written for the Queen's Men, and both he and his characters were persistently presented as irreligious. This suggests that there is an additional layer of complexity and irony at work, a veil which shimmers over the text and refracts and distorts its apparent meaning. Has Marlowe discovered the subtext, or is the phenomenon an effect of an ambiguity of the same sort as underlies the refusal to commit of 'Applaud his fortunes as you please'? In fact I want to suggest that, counter-intuitive as this may seem in the case of so risk-taking a dramatist, it is the result of caution. What Marlowe was most powerfully aware of was religion's ability to stir up political trouble, and I suggest that in his own drama, iconoclast though he was, he did not in fact want to stir up trouble. In this respect if in no other the Baines Note is, I think, an unreliable guide. Baines implies that Marlowe incited young men such as Cholmley to atheism, but his plays conspicuously shy away from obvious opportunities to do just that. Paradoxically, the inclusion of loud anti-Catholicism is in fact tantamount to putting a silencer on a more dangerous and provocative strain which might otherwise have made itself audible, which is a doubt of the value of any religion at all. Marlowe's cultivation of ambiguity can thus be seen as akin to, and indeed perhaps a direct forerunner of, the quietism which caused Shakespeare to modulate the stridently anti-papal rhetoric of a play like *The Troublesome Reign of King John* into something more measured which is both less angry in itself and less likely to provoke anger in others. Indeed, this is perhaps not the least striking example of Marlowe's influence on the tenor of discussion of religion in drama. The one dramatist of the period who was in his own person strongly identified with atheism does not use his plays to propound an atheist agenda; Greene showed himself an insensitive reader when he thought he detected an authorial voice 'daring God out of heaven with that atheist Tamburlan' (1588, *Perimedes the Blacksmith*, sig. A3ʳ), for if Tamburlaine is an atheist, it cannot be supposed that he gets away with it, any more than Marlowe's pupil Ford can reasonably be supposed to be endorsing incest through the mere fact of representing it. It would be truer to the case to see Marlowe as pioneering a mode of staging events without associating oneself with them, a creation of authorial distance which Shakespeare among others will seize on as a way of making drama an arena for debate rather than a seedbed for propaganda which might spill dangerously out of the fictional world of the stage into the real-life one of the London around it.

In this respect, what is arguably Marlowe's most unsatisfactory play is also perhaps his most instructive and illuminating, for it is here that we catch the method most clearly at work. There is clearly something wrong with the text of *The Massacre at Paris*, and indeed in 1825 John Payne Collier announced that he had discovered a much longer version of a speech from the play. Unfortunately, Collier is known to have forged many of the Elizabethan documents he claimed to have discovered, but *The Massacre at Paris* certainly does read like a garbled and truncated text, and there is nothing inherently implausible in the 'Collier leaf' (for a recent discussion of the authenticity or otherwise of this, see Hailey 2011: 34–6). It is, though, also worth noting that despite the unsatisfactoriness of the text, which has led to its relative neglect, *A Massacre at Paris* is in some sense also one of the most personal of Marlowe's plays. Marlowe never met an Uzbek warlord or a homosexual king of England and probably not a Maltese Jew either, but his childhood in Canterbury inevitably brought him into the proximity of a considerable number of Huguenot refugees who had fled across the channel, including Cardinal Odet de Coligny, the Admiral's brother, who is buried in Canterbury Cathedral. (This too is something Marlowe had in common with Shakespeare, who lodged with Huguenots in Silver Street and may be seen as applying something of Marlowe's method in his own carefully non-committal representations of French politics in *Love's Labour's Lost* and *All's Well that Ends Well*.) There is, however, a surprising lack of heat in the portrait of the Guise: Marlowe may be, as I have argued elsewhere (Hopkins 2011b), fascinated by fire, but he is being unusually careful to douse it here. Unlike Tamburlaine or even Faustus, the Guise unquestionably *is* an atheist: he unashamedly declares:

> My policy hath framed religion.
> Religion: *O Diabole!*
> Fie, I am ashamed, how ever that I seem,
> To think a word of such a simple sound
> Of so great matter should be made the ground. (ii.62–6)

He also cheerfully associates himself with the most notorious of the excesses stereotypically ascribed to Catholicism when he notes that Paris 'in one cloister keeps | Five hundred fat Franciscan friars and priests' (ii.81–2). Nevertheless, the Guise is by no means the most repellent character in the play—Anjou is worse because he is a hypocrite, denying that he has participated in the massacre when the audience have seen him do so, while the queen mother murders her way through most of her immediate family—and the Guise is arguably a little redeemed by the fact that his response to the discovery of his wife's infidelity is not to kill her but to talk of his love for her: 'Is all my love forgot which held thee dear' (xv.27). He does also have pleasures to offer the audience, as is made clear when he speaks of how he contrives 'Matters of import aimed at by many, | Yet understood by none' (ii.51–2), for this knowledge sought by so many in vain is of course being offered freely to us. Finally, Marlowe also takes the sting out of his representation of events by subtle but insistent reminders that this is, after all, happening a long way away: the Guise's dismissive 'There are a hundred Huguenots and more | Which in the woods do hold their synagogue' (xi.20–1) offers a fundamentally estranging perspective which prevents us from equating Huguenots with Protestants and thus implicitly reminds us that the characters are, after all, all French apart from Catherine de' Medici who is Italian (and thus arguably even worse), while the audience are lucky enough to be subjects of 'the Queen of England specially, | Whom God hath blessed for hating papistry' (xxiv.68–9).

In this too Marlowe was influential, for Shakespeare will use the same technique in *Richard III*, and other aspects of *The Massacre at Paris* seem also to have provided him with inspiration: Scene Twenty-One opens with three murderers in a way that perhaps prefigures *Macbeth*, as does the Guise's question to the third of those Murderers, 'Villain, why dost thou look so ghastly? Speak!' (xxi.59). The very short (only seven lines long) Scene Seven in which someone called Loreine is killed by 'Monsieur of Lorraine' may prefigure the Cinna the Poet scene in *Julius Caesar*, a play which certainly remembers the Guise's declaration that 'Yet Caesar shall go forth' (xxi.68), while Catherine's cruel remark to Henry III that 'Thou art a changeling, not my son' (xxi.149) may have been remembered by Shakespeare when he was creating Volumnia. These are all local hints, but their number emphasizes the extent to which Shakespeare has a more general interest in Marlovian dramaturgy and its effects. They thus testify to the way that, moving well away from his safely orthodox background, Marlowe had by the time of his death created a distinctive, challenging dramatic voice, one which both asked questions itself and also prompted others to do so.

In this way, Marlowe exerted a major influence on ways of both thinking about and writing about religion in early modern English culture. He tackled new topics, many of which seem to have been suggested to him by new geographical discoveries and expanding cultural horizons, and he did so in a new way. He represents religions other than Christianity in ways which do not simply demonize them but reveal them as interrogating Christianity's claim to superiority and as constituting major cultural forces in their own right, and he probes the disabling divisions within Christianity itself. Finally, he affords a fascinating case study of the intersection between perceptions of an author's personal religious beliefs and perceptions of his writings, but at the same time he deploys irony and ambiguity in ways which prise apart writer and play, and which lay the foundations for other dramatists to do the same.

CHAPTER 20

PHILIP SIDNEY AND MARY SIDNEY HERBERT

Piety and Poetry

NANDRA PERRY AND ROBERT E. STILLMAN

A sacrifice at the battle of Zutphen in 1586 to the international cause of Reformed Christianity, Philip Sidney's corpse produced early modern England's richest harvest of literature inside any single family. The corpus famously followed the corpse. From the late Elizabethan period onwards, piety and poetry were intimately conjoined in the Sidney family because of how Sir Philip Sidney came to be seen as a martyr. Philip Sidney's corpus inspired writings among authors both allied to and remote from the Sidneys—from Fulke Greville and Ben Jonson to John Donne and George Herbert, from Aemilia Lanyer and Anna Weamys to Elizabeth Cary and Lucy Hutchinson—but the important story to trace here belongs to the siblings Philip and Mary (Alexander 2006; Brennan 2006; Mazzola 2003; Waller 1993).

THE SIDNEY FAMILY DYNASTY

The Sidneys were very much what Philip Sidney claimed they were, a family of 'well esteemed and well matched gentry,' and plainly important enough to have been what Roger Kuin calls 'a family-conscious family' (Kuin in Brennan 2006: 8, 11). Family was the centre of that intricate web of personal and public alliances enabling social advancement in early modern England, and the Sidneys flourished because of their commitment to civic service—military, diplomatic, and administrative—and because of their mastery of the art of marriage-making, connecting their family with other more powerful families. However, the Sidneys were not 'ancient' (Brennan 2006: 8). Comparative newcomers, they rose to prominence as the Tudors rose to power. Philip and Mary Sidney's great-grandfather was Nicholas Sidney (*c.*1451–1512), a landowner in Surrey who married brilliantly. His wife was Anne Brandon, aunt of Charles Brandon (1484–1545), duke of Suffolk, who became Henry VIII's favourite. The Brandons proved vital to the Sidney family's fortunes, and gave them their first opportunity to display their civic skills at the Tudor court. Nicholas Sidney and Anne Brandon were the parents of William Sidney (c.1482–1554), the grandfather of Philip (1554–86) and Mary Sidney (1561–1621). Because of his education in the household of Sir Thomas Brandon (d. 1510), a prominent courtier in the early Tudor court (brother to Anne and uncle to Charles Brandon), William Sidney was schooled in manners, languages, and diplomacy. As Thomas Brandon performed diplomatic duties for Henry, William Sidney travelled with him, and became the first in an extended line of Sidneys to gain an expertise in Continental politics (Kuin 2015). William Sidney was also a soldier: he led the vanguard at the battle of Flodden Field (1513), and fought as a captain in the English campaign against France (1523). By 1538, William had established himself as Chamberlain to Prince Edward, right at the centre of the world of Tudor privilege.

As Prince Edward became the boy-king Edward VI, he chose as his closest companion William's oldest son Henry Sidney (1529–86). Henry became a courtier then a diplomat; he was skilled in foreign languages and dedicated to loyal administrative service. He is best remembered now for his tenure as President of the Council of Wales and for his controversial—both personally and publicly ruinous—administration as Lord Deputy of Ireland under Elizabeth I. Henry Sidney too made a brilliant marriage—his bride was Mary Dudley (1531–86), the daughter of the powerful John Dudley, earl of Warwick and duke of Northumberland (1504–53), and sister to the future favourite among favourites in Elizabeth's court, Robert Dudley, earl of Leicester (1531–88). Henry Sidney and Mary Dudley were Philip and Mary's parents, and while Philip was proud of his good gentry blood from the Sidneys, he always counted it his 'chiefest honor' to be a Dudley (Brennan 2006: 8). Ties to the Dudleys were not, however, unambiguously advantageous. When Henry Sidney's father-in-law Northumberland (John Dudley) installed Lady Jane Grey on the throne after Edward VI's early death, Henry escaped execution for complicity in the plot by some combination of sheer luck and a reputation for skilful service. Thus, Henry Sidney was a survivor. He managed to maintain a place at court through a quick succession of wholescale Reformations that turned England from evangelical Protestant (under Edward VI) to Roman Catholic (under Mary Tudor) and back to Protestant (under Elizabeth I).

Like the Sidneys before him, Philip Sidney (1554–86) was a soldier, courtier, and diplomat (Stewart 2001). He was educated at the Shrewsbury School in the company of his lifelong friend Fulke Greville; he attended Oxford University; and was schooled afterward (1572–5) during a three-year tour of the Continent by Hubert Languet, an internationally regarded humanist, diplomat, and Reformed Christian, the devotee of Philip Melanchthon. From Languet, Sidney received the kind of education suited to a young man of great expectation, Reformed Christianity's best hope to lead the cause against the tyranny of the Catholic League and Spain. Sidney headed a diplomatic mission in 1577 to reconcile opposing factions of Reformed Christians among the German states and to explore the creation of a Protestant league in defense of the cause—among the first in a continuing series of such missions. He advised Elizabeth against her proposed marriage to the French Catholic, Henry, duke of Anjou. Without serious employment at court (or to paraphrase Greville, without any fit stage for his eminence to act upon), Sidney retired for long periods to Mary Sidney's house at Wilton where he engaged in what he called, ironically and truthfully, his 'unelected vocation' as a writer (Greville, *Defence*: 95). Sidney is often remembered because of his early death at the battle of Zutphen while fighting for Dutch independence from Spanish rule. He is importantly remembered because of his literary work—the astonishing productivity of his career as a fiction-maker, who produced during the space of five years (1579–84) a seminal body of texts that transformed the English literary landscape.

That transformation is perhaps equally the brainchild of his grief-stricken younger sister, Mary Sidney Herbert (1561–1621). Her editorial acumen and aristocratic stature brought her dead brother into print and print into prestige as the medium of a new generation. His junior by seven years, Mary was arguably Philip's twin for poetic talent, and as the wife of the wealthy and powerful Henry Herbert, second earl of Pembroke, his unquestioned social superior. Combined with her genius for self-promotion, these two qualifications positioned Mary, if not exactly as the head, then at the hub of the Sidney literary dynasty. Strictly speaking that dynasty was founded by Philip, whose posthumously published *Arcadia* would remain the most popular work of English prose fiction for some two hundred years (Hannay 2009). However, it was Mary's draw as patron and poetic collaborator that shaped the wide and widely influential circle of late Elizabethan writers inspired by Philip's religio-political interests and literary tastes. Celebrated in her lifetime for her poetic gifts, piety, and learning, Sidney Herbert was not herself an author of fictions. Her surviving corpus includes only a handful of original poems, all of them either dedicatory or occasional. However, her public career as a translator, editor, and Sidnean muse-in-chief nurtured a new print culture that legitimated the publication of literary fictions by men like Edmund Spenser, Thomas Lodge, and Samuel Daniel and eventually by women like Aemelia Lanyer and Elizabeth Cary. Indeed, although her legacy as an important patron was carried on by her two sons, William and Philip (the 3rd and 4th earls of Pembroke respectively), her true heirs were her literary daughters. In this sense, Philip's 'phoenix' was both her brother's keeper—for it was her careful fostering of Philip's Arcadian 'child' that likely inspired the trail-blazing career of their brother Robert's firstborn daughter, Mary Sidney Wroth (1587–1651), author of the first English prose romance and the first Petrarchan sonnet sequence to be published by a woman.

The Sidney family's religious history merits a moment's attention. Like all English families, the Sidneys were fashioned by the multiplicity of England's Reformations, and fashioned differently from generation to generation. There is no single story to tell about the various beliefs of the family members, occluded as they often were by pragmatic or principled refusals to make those beliefs explicit. Early in the century, Sir William Sidney embraced the 'new' Protestant faith; he needed to because of his position as Chamberlain to Edward VI, whose reign marked the apex of England's domestication of international evangelical Protestantism by Thomas Cranmer—in concert with religious thinkers like Martin Bucer and Philip Melanchthon. Henry Sidney was raised in Edward's court, educated as a Protestant, but practised a piety sufficiently flexible to negotiate the changing rulers and changing religions of sixteenth-century England. After all, he named his son Philip after the Catholic Philip II of Spain (who became his godfather) and named his first daughter Mary (1556–8) after her mother and the Catholic Mary Tudor. At Elizabeth's accession, Henry resumed his practice of Protestant conformity. Necessarily divorced from the shifting tides of faith that ruled England's churches, Henry's flexible piety—independent from ever-mutable institutional requirements—created both a precedent and a model for the flexible and tolerant Reformed Christianity practised by both of his children, Philip and Mary.

At the heart of this dynasty and of this chapter stand Philip and Mary Sidney. Inside their relationship resides a miniature history of real importance for understanding how religion—and that personal piety linking religion to lived experience—contributed to one of the most significant achievements of early modern English literature. Philip Sidney did not set out to inspire a religious literature in England. Rather, what he imagined and helped substantially to create was a new vernacular literature in celebration of fiction-making, both energized by pious commitments to God and public service to the cause of Reformed Christianity. In time, the Sidney dynasty created a culture in which piety, politics, and poetry could intermingle as intimately as a trinity (Hannay 1990; Norbrook 1984).

LITERARY AND SPIRITUAL UNDERTAKINGS

Three works define Philip Sidney as among the seminal writers of the Elizabethan era. *Astrophil and Stella* initiated the vogue of the Petrarchan sonnet sequence in England as a major literary form. *The Defence of Poesy* provided the critical foundation for his own literary practice and the practice of many of his contemporaries, and argued for the first time in English that fiction-making is a culturally important (even pre-eminently important) activity. *The Countess of Pembroke's Arcadia* established the model for courtly prose fiction. It was written first as a pastoral romance (*The Old Arcadia*), then subsequently revised as a heroic poem in prose (posthumously published as *The New Arcadia*, 1590), and ultimately completed by the addition of the last two books of *The Old* to the first three books of *The New* in what scholars now call the 'composite' *Arcadia* (published 1593). At a time when England's literature seemed negligible by comparison to Italy's or to France's—and when Sidney's generation sought to demonstrate that the English language was, as the *Defence* claimed, 'capable of any excellent exercising of it'—his poetry and poetics appeared to substantiate that claim (*Defence*: 140; Hamilton 1977: 9–10). As is widely appreciated, Philip Sidney published no fictions in his lifetime; however, as few recall, the popularity of his work and the prominence of manuscript circulation made him, most probably, the best published writer of his day. As the editor of his poetry William Ringler highlights: 'Seventeenth-century readers called for three editions of Spenser's collected works and four of Shakespeare's, but for nine of Sidney's

... For more than a century after his death he continued to be the most admired and the most read writer of his generation' (xv). When Sidney turned from fiction-making to religious writing—from poetry to piety—he did so through translations: he began a translation of the Psalms that Mary Sidney Herbert completed after his death. He translated the extended philosophical work of his friend Philippe Duplessis-Mornay, *A Woorke Concerning the Trewnesse of the Christian Religion*, as well as some now lost translations from Guillaume Du Bartas's enormously popular Reformed epic about the creation, *La Semaine ou Création du Monde*.

Aside from her hand in shaping Philip's fictions, Mary's greatest claim to literary fame is as a translator, first and foremost of the Psalms (*c.*1599). It is an achievement not to be underestimated. Recent years have seen increased appreciation for the Psalms as a focal point for poetic imitation and innovation in the early modern period, on par with Petrarch's *Rime Sparse* as a 'master text through which the writers of the age tested their capacities' (Greene, 'Sir Philip': 19). If this is so, then Mary's contribution of Psalms 44–150 to Philip's unfinished manuscript must have more than proved her mettle to her contemporaries as a gifted poet in her own right. Indeed, the Sidney Psalter continues to reveal the depth and breadth of Mary's piety, political acumen, and humanist education. No mere 'Englishing', it reflects extensive consultation with the best available biblical scholarship in English, French, Latin, and possibly Hebrew. It also represents Mary's continued engagement—equal parts tactful and tactical—in her brother's cause of international Protestantism, all but lost in England by 1599. Although not printed in its entirety until 1963, the metrical Sidney Psalter circulated widely in manuscript in Sidney Herbert's lifetime, and its profound influence on seventeenth-century English verse can be discerned in the 'Protestant poetics' of authors such as George Herbert, John Donne, and Aemelia Lanyer (Hannay 2009).

Second to the Psalms in importance are Mary's translations of Robert Garnier's neo-Senecan closet drama, *Marc Antoine* (1578) and Philippe Duplessis-Mornay's Christian stoical meditation *Discours de la vie et de la mort* (1576). Published together as single volume in 1592, they established Sidney Herbert's reputation as an accomplished translator of morally edifying works. Like the Sidney-Herbert Psalms, these translation projects attend to unfinished family business. Mary's *Antonius* reflects Philip's interest in reforming (and reformist) drama, while the *Discourse of Life and Death* indirectly champions the Huguenot cause of his personal friend, Mornay (who Mary probably met on his visit to England in 1578). The shared thematic emphasis of Garnier and Mornay on the transience of earthly life offered Mary matter sufficiently decorous for a woman, while providing all the political subtext a Sidney could want. The *Discourse* diplomatically critiqued the decadence of the Elizabethan Court, while the *Antonius* introduced into England the Continental fashion of using Roman drama as a vehicle for contemporary political commentary. William Shakespeare (who seems to have been aware of the translation for both *Antony and Cleopatra* and *Measure for Measure*) would go on, Margaret Hannay argues, to be her most famous imitator (Hannay 2009).

Not surprisingly, given the anxieties surrounding female authorship and print publication in her era, Sidney Herbert's surviving original work is limited to a smattering of elegiac and occasional verse. The Tixall Psalms MS includes two dedicatory poems, one of which ('To That Angell Spirit of the Most Excellent Sir Philip Sidney') apparently enjoyed limited circulation in Mary's lifetime and was eventually erroneously printed with the poems of Samuel Daniel in 1623 (Hannay 2009). In contrast, her dedicatory poem to Elizabeth ('Even Now that Care') exists only in the single presentation copy intended for the queen's abortive visit to Wilton in 1599 and seems never to have circulated with other copies of the Psalter (Hannay 2009). Her 'A Dialogue between Two Shepherds, *Thenot* and *Piers*, in Praise of *Astraea*,' also written for the queen's visit to Wilton, got a second life in Francis Davidson's 1602 anthology, *A Poetical Rapsodie*. Davidson's anthology was reprinted three times by 1621, making it Mary's most widely circulated poem in print (Hannay 2009). Finally, there may also be good reason to believe that Mary is author of 'The Doleful Lay of Clorinda,' which was published in 1595 in *Astrophel*, an anthology of elegies for Philip (Hannay 2009). If this output of original material seems limited, both in quantity and in scope, it is only because Sidney Herbert's unprecedented public career as a Englishwoman of letters set the stage for a new generation of female authors to create (and publish) golden worlds of their own.

PHILIP SIDNEY AND THE BIRTH OF A LITERARY DYNASTY

When Sidney turns at the beginning of his *Defence of Poesy* to offer his first illustration of poetic mimesis (the definitive activity of imitation by which fiction-makers represent not what is but instead 'what may be and should be'), he celebrates the chaste Roman matron Lucretia. Lucretia is a woman of Roman legend, whose rape by Sextus—the son of Tarquin the Proud—led to her stabbing herself to death. Lucretia's self-inflicted death at once freed her from the tyranny of Tarquin ('when she punished in herself another's fault') and gave life to Rome's republic (*Defence*: 102). The revolt that ensued upon Lucretia's death drove the Tarquins from power. Depicted as a speaking picture of chastity—that universal 'Idea' which her 'outward beauty' embodies—Lucretia triumphs over Tarquin as an emblem of fiction's triumph over history (*Defence*: 102). She is liberated twice by her chastity, once from Tarquin's tyranny and a second time (as fictive image on the painter's canvas) from the tyranny of verisimilitude.

Sidney insisted in a now celebrated manner in *The Defence of Poetry* that 'our erected wit maketh us know what perfection is, and yet our infected will keepeth us from reaching unto it'. History is conceived in unmistakably Christian terms as fallen. In turn, poetry's energizing power over the (infected) will in moving it toward the virtues that the (erected) wit apprehends imparts to fiction-making real agency in remediating (at least in part) the effects of the Fall. Indeed, Philip Sidney's literary undertakings engage tightly with a line of early modern meditations extending from Erasmus to Melanchthon about the causative power of words to imitate the Word. For Sidney (as for these earlier humanists) imitation assumes its ultimate authority (directly or indirectly) from the desire to imitate that which is godly, as an *imitatio Christi*—that ultimate incarnation of truth authorized by the body and the Passion of the crucified Christ (Perry 2014; Warren 2010; Cummings 2002; Waswo 1987). In early modern culture, fiction-making always has reference to the Maker.

Sidney's decision to deploy the body of Lucretia in *The Defence of Poetry* offers at one level an idealized version of poetic meaning (a mimetic power to enable moral and spiritual heroism against political tyranny) while, at another, Lucretia's violated body is filled with potent reminders of the contamination traditionally associated with female sexuality, the stubborn recalcitrance of human sinfulness (Jed 1989). Nothing in Sidney's work is more stubbornly present than sin. When Sidney turned to the paraphrasing of the Psalms, he assumed the voice of David—a figure whose praise and petitions and repentance needed no defense as the chaste work of a divine poet, however much he needed rescuing from his tyrannical lust by Nathan's right poetry. Nathan was a prophet (and poet, Sidney insists) who shamed David into recognizing his sin by arranging the death of Bathsheba's husband, so that he might have her for himself: he did so by telling him a story about a rich man who defrauds a poor man of his favourite lamb. David's psalms are heavenly; Nathan's tale is simple pastoral—and both, Sidney opines in the *Defence*, have a place in 'the church of God' (Hamlin 2004; Prescott 1989; Zim 1987). Moreover, in his sonnet collection *Astrophil and Stella*, Sidney impersonates a reluctant would-be Petrarchan lover whose courtly Stella seems as unfit for spiritual adulation as Astrophil is for spiritual exaltation, a poetically brilliant case study in failed fiction-making wherein erected wit is overmatched by infected will (Kuin 1998a). As these examples illustrate, the same Philip Sidney who celebrates fiction-making as a pious vehicle for chastening private and public bodies into virtue simultaneously enabled the exploration of poetic perils, linguistic failures, and sinful recalcitrance which other members of his family, notably Mary Sidney and Mary Sidney Wroth, would continue to explore in the years after his death (Sanchez 2011).

Despite all of the distinctions made between them, Sidney's poetics persistently associate humane and sacred letters—Aesop's fables and Christ's parables, Plautus's comedies and Buchanan's tragedies. During the same months or years that he wrote *Astrophil and Stella*, Sidney appears to have been translating the first forty-three Psalms of David, or so verbal and formal parallels among the poems suggest (Klein 1998). At the same time that Sidney translated his friend Philippe Duplessis-Mornay's philosophically learned exposition of the universality of Christian truth (*De veritatis*) as well as the first two books of Guillaume Du Bartas's *La semaine* (the enormously popular Reformed celebration of God's creation), he continued to transform his single, sustained, career-long fictional project, the *Arcadia*, from its early romance form into its revised and expanded pastoral-heroic shape (Davis 2011). Sidney did not have a 'secular' literary career followed by a 'sacred' one: the truth is that the humane and the sacred intermingle at every point—among the works and within them—because for Philip as for Mary the human and the divine engage intimately at every turn.

From Sidney's perspective, poetry stimulates self-knowledge, and that knowledge is connected meaningfully to what Sidney names in his *Defence* anthropologically as our 'divine essence' (104). Sidney's literary undertaking throughout his career remains distinctively Christian and purposefully metaphorical. Among Sidney's most frequently deployed poetic resources, for example, is *energeia*—or what Aristotle, Quintilian, and the ancient rhetorical tradition called 'forcibleness' (Rudenstine 1967). Employed 671 times in Aristotle's corpus (from his *Rhetoric* to his *Ethics* to his *Metaphysics*) as a term characterizing change of a purposeful kind, *energeia* enjoyed a long history in theological discussions among the early fathers of the Greek Church, before being reformed for Christian rhetorical and philosophical purposes first by Erasmus and then by Melanchthon (Bradshaw 2004). Energized by the Holy Spirit, the Word has power to effect *metanoia*, the 'purposeful' change of the old man into the new. Imitated by the poet, *energeia* is metamorphically powerful: poetry can change people, mitigating (in some part) the consequences of the Fall. Sidney celebrates the poet's forcibleness in moving readers to virtue (Stillman 2009). Everywhere in Sidney's poetry and poetics, myth and metaphor relate, by comparison and contrast, the potentially restorative world of the Christian's spiritual fulfilment to the brazen world of lived experience.

Sidney's piety, like his extensive learning, was the product of his education abroad and of his Reformed Christian commitment (Stewart 2001; Osborn 1972). At Strasbourg, he began an enduring friendship with Johann Sturm, the ecumenically minded rector of an Academy that educated Reformed and Catholic elites alike. In the year of Sidney's visit, Sturm published his *De imitatione* (1574), whose justification for citizenship in the humanist republic of letters was that knowledge undoes provincialism, or what like-minded humanist scholars called the sovereignty of self-love: 'Imitation leads [the mind] beyond the boundaries of nature: so that [the individual] ceases to love himself: and begins to love better things' (Sturm: n.p.). That love of better things has a special prominence in Sidney's fictions: his revised *Arcadia*, for example, begins with Strephon and Klaius's haunting vision of Urania 'whose beauty taught the beholders chastity' (*Arcadia*: 5). Elsewhere, at the outset of Sidney's *Defence*, two English gentlemen receive a lesson in horsemanship from an Italian riding master at the Viennese court, home to the late Maximilian II, Emperor of the Holy Roman Empire. The setting is courtly and Continental, the characters internationally various, and the style, studiously urbane. The lesson in horsemanship that emerges from its comic cautionary tale about Signor Pugliano—the horseman who nearly induces Sidney to be a horse—is the peril of provincialism, the peril of solipsism in a world where all sins achieve their sovereignty because of that original sin of self-love (Prescott 2005b). (For a *Phil-hippus*, lover of the horse, the lesson hit home personally.) As the vocabulary of self-love indicates, Sidney's text is indebted to his experiences in Sturm's Academy and deeply influenced also by his experiences in Vienna. The latter was his chief place of study during his Continental tour (1572–5) in the company of a community of so-called Philippists—the followers of Philip Melanchthon, the man whom Sturm called 'the father of most educated men' ('To Michael Beuther' in Spitz and Tinsley 1995: 291).

In the same manner as his brother Robert, Philip travelled to the Continent for three formative years of his education under the care of Hubert Languet, himself a sort of Philippist Ulysses: Languet was a seasoned traveller and *factotum* in the service of Philip Melanchthon (Nicollier-de Weck 1995). Tutored by the Burgundian Languet in the company of other notable Philippists (such as the Silesian physician and diplomat, Johannes Crato, and the French botanist, Charles de l'Ecluse), Sidney absorbed a moderate, cosmopolitan version of Reformed Christianity that afforded to his poetics and his poetry its own distinctive vision (Maag 1999). At the core of Melanchthon's thought was his reading of the Fall as a product of self-love, and consequently, at the core of his lifelong rehabilitation of the *studia humanitatis* was the creation of a new Protestant culture—international in scope, ecumenical in design, and fiercely anti-tyrannical in purpose (Gehring 2013; Meerhof 2001). Philip Sidney was only one of two Philips tutored by Languet: the other was Philippe Duplessis-Mornay, philosopher of an inclusive natural theology and a tyrannomachist politics (Kuin 1999).[1] Sidney's godfather, on the other hand, was Philip II of Spain, head of Europe's leading Catholic dynasty. Henry's choice of an anti-confessional mentor for his son was the consequence of his own history spent negotiating confessional change during the course of the Tudor century. Sir Henry Sidney survived wave after wave of religious change from the court of Edward VI to Mary Tudor to Elizabeth I.

The aristocratic Philip Sidney was nothing if not stylish, and the stylishness of his self-presentations is a reminder always that his education was not wholly shaped by the culture of Wittenberg (home of Luther and Lutheranism) among black-cloaked clerics who found their exemplars in the austere St Basils of old, but instead in Vienna, where fashionable religious moderates, like Jacopo Strada, could showcase both their knowledge and taste (Louthan 1997). Titian painted Strada in a richly furred gown, a pint-sized naked Venus in his palms, surrounded by books that advertise both humanist credentials and ecumenical piety—his shelves stocked with volumes, Catholic and Reformed. In many ways, reading Sidney's texts is like repeating his travels. His prose romance *Arcadia* grew by leaps and bounds, old version to new, precisely because of Sidney's commitment to inclusiveness—an inclusiveness that is at once literary and pious. In the wide range of his *Defence*'s illustrations, for example, we alternate to and fro—from Homer to Tasso, from Chaucer to Dante, from the blind ballad-maker to the zodiacal visionary—moving from the past to the present, from England to the Continent, from popular to high culture.

The inclusivity of Sidney's piety, always eager to shun the appearance of partisan confessional politics from his poetics and poetry, is implicit too in the *Defence*'s setting. As Sidney opens his argument evoking the memory of the cosmopolitan Vienna of Maximilian II (the Emperor was famous for calling himself not a Catholic but a

---

[1] Natural theology is a Christian complement of natural law philosophy, with the belief that moral principles are universal to human kind and implanted by God, and that nature is created in order for God to make himself known. Tyrannomachy ('tyrant-slaying') is the philosophical justification of killing tyrannical rulers, ordinarily grounded on a natural right to self-preservation.

Christian), he does so with no little nostalgia for the world lost there. Between the time of Sidney's visit to Vienna and the date of the *Defence's* composition, Maximilian had died and the Imperial capital had shifted to Prague. The relocation was more than geographical in its importance. Vienna's religiously tolerant world was lost, only to be replaced by the fiercely anti-Protestant, pro-Spanish regime of Rudolf II. Rudolf was a proponent of the counter-Reformation, which was a movement on the part of conservative forces to mobilize support for the traditions of the Roman Catholic Church against the innovations of the Reformers. The counter-Reformation's central event was the Council of Trent (concluding in 1563), which asserted, clarified, and defended the orthodoxy of the Church's dogma, liturgy, and ecclesiastical practices. From the vantage of Reformed Christians like Sidney, the Council of Trent was an outrageous arrogation of spiritual authority by an arrogant papacy. In turn, a counter-Reformation Emperor in Prague was a Tridentine tyrant who threatened to undo civil life, civil arts, civil everything (Fictner 2001). Rudolf II's accession to power threatened to make permanently unavailable the religious moderation and comparative tolerance of Maximilian II's Vienna. For this reason, Sidney's setting of the *Defence* is revealing about the character of his piety. Sidney's Philippist-style moderation is evident also in the roll call of worthies that he assembles late in the work to dignify the status of poetry. He summons 'Such cardinals as Bembus and Bibiena' in parallel to the preachers and teachers, Beza and Melanchthon—in this way, Catholics balanced ecumenically with Protestants, Calvinists with Lutherans. When Sidney expands his list, he includes 'learned philosophers', 'great orators', and 'piercing wits', only to conclude his roll call with the celebration of a 'grave' counsellor to be preferred 'before all': 'that Hospital of France, than whom (I think) that realm never brought forth a more accomplished judgment, more firmly builded upon virtue' (*Defence*: 131). Sidney's praise for Michel de L'Hospital is the pointed culmination of this cosmopolitan parade of worthies: as the longtime Chancellor of France, L'Hospital was a champion of toleration, personally important to Languet for his endeavours in securing peace for the Huguenots (Wanegffelen 2002). Thus, interestingly, in contrast to the sometimes splenetic Spenser or militant Milton, Sidney writes fictions almost entirely free of anti-Catholic sentiment.

Freedom matters to Sidney's piety and poetics. Writing in the shadow of the Fall, Sidney states in the *Defence*: 'with no small argument to the incredulous of that first accursed fall of Adam ... our erected wit maketh us know what perfection is, and yet our infected will keepeth us from reaching unto it' (*Defence*: 101). From this perspective, the body is conceived as a dungeon because the will is infected, and the mind as retaining its own 'divine essence' because the wit remains erect. Like Lucretia, the poet strives to procure freedom from the tyranny of original sin, the ordinary 'dungeon' of the human condition. As the wit is informed and the will moved, the chastening work of transformation is enabled—'if' (Sidney conditions his optimism) readers will learn aright how and why the maker makes those fictions (*Defence*: 101). This kind of optimism concerning the effective nature of human and poetic agency could not be learned in the company of Anglo-Calvinists, but it is a distinctive feature of that moderate piety that Sidney absorbed among the Philippists in Vienna.

Both Professor of Greek and theologian, practising humanist and systematic exposi-
tor of Reformed theology, editor of some ninety-three editions of classical texts and
author of the Augsburg Confession, Philip Melanchthon laboured to assert a complex continuity between nature and spirit, the human and the divine, the secular and
the sacred (Scheible 1997). From the 1530s forward, he developed a natural theology
that is remarkably responsive both to the existence of true discernment in the human
mind, and (more quietly) about the power of the human will to cooperate (synergistic-
ally) with God in securing salvation. The assumption that Reformed Christianity can
be understood as dogma proceeding from the writings of a single person, John Calvin,
has obscured the plurality of its origins, the variety of its institutional forms, the eclecticism of its sources, and the diversity of philosophical and theological tenets espoused by
its proponents (Fesko 2012; Muller 2003; Benedict 2002). The Reformed did not speak
with one voice on the ruins of the intellect and depravity of the passions. Sidney, among
others, heard the great variety of those voices, and surely, only an unhistorical reading of
Reformed Christianity would mistake him either as a secular humanist or a Catholic for
so doing (Duncan-Jones in McCoog 1996).

Philip Sidney, Poetics,
and Poetic Ambition

When Sidney attends to the moral commonplaces of Christ's parables, he conjoins
them with Aesop's pretty allegories (both illustrate the virtues of *claritas* for the right
poet). When he offers proofs of the 'strange effects' of poetry in moving both people
and prince, he again balances deliberately secular and sacred texts, moving between
the stories of Agrippa and Nathan (*Defence*: 114). Like a tour guide, Sidney constantly
directs attention to what is 'notable': this may be Plato (with his 'notable fable of the
Atlantic Island' (97)), David (with his 'notable *prosopopeias*' of the divine (99), or speaking pictures of God's majesty), or Plutarch (with his 'notable testimonie of the abominable tyrant … Pheraeus' (118)). Elsewhere, Sidney calls attention to his heart moved by
poetry or 'notable examples' of moral painting, such 'as Abraham sacrificing' his son
Isaac (125). (The word 'notable' occurs eleven times in the *Defence*.) Indeed, in a key
definition of art itself, Sidney refers (as a variation upon a theme) to the poet's making of 'notable images of virtue and vice' (103). These notable images are important
because they impart knowledge. When Sidney agrees with those 'learned men who
have so learnedly thought' that 'in Nature we know it is well to do well, and what is
well and what is evil', he does so by appealing to Philippist belief that there is a natural
law written in the heart of human beings that teaches them truths—truths that extend
from basic tenets of moral philosophy to the recognition of the soul's immortality and
the providence of God (113). Such truths are called by Melanchthon '*notitiae*' (Stillman
2008). These are the truths that Duplessis-Mornay discovers among the writings of the

ancients and the truths that Sidney assigns to the virtuous pagans in his own works—to *The Old Arcadia*'s Pyrocles and Musidorus, for example, as they contemplate immortality the night before their deaths, and to Pamela and Philoclea as they awaken into heroic awareness of God's providence in *The New Arcadia*. Thus, when Sidney concludes his discussion of the golden world by signalling the poet's distinctive power to address the fallen condition, he can do so because he shares Melanchthon's cautious optimism about human agency—the range of the wit, the ameliorative potential of the will. In good Philippist style, no theological arguments are forthcoming to bolster these assumptions. Sidney was too courtly, too urbane, *and* too pious to indulge in wrangling (Friedeburg 2002).

Nonetheless, the question of tyranny in a range of different contexts repeatedly haunts his thinking about poetry—from the early discussion of imitation linked to Lucretia's portrait, to his diverse celebrations of the dramatic talents of George Buchanan, that Scottish tyrannomachist par excellence. In the aftermath of the 1572 Bartholomew's Day Massacre (that targeted Protestants in France)—an event survived by Sidney and his mentor Languet—Sidney would return repeatedly to the question of tyranny in both his political and pious meditations. In his *Arcadia*, for example, we are presented with a golden world free from the contaminations of history—a landscape free from a past that too often records the triumph of vice over virtue, and free from a present that too often divides Christian from Christian in endless confessional warfare. Inside the *Arcadia*'s fictional world, the poet takes aim against the Idea of tyranny in order to exemplify the evils of self-love and injustice in both private and public spheres. There are no Tridentine Catholics in *Arcadia*, and neither are there Calvinists or Lutherans, much less English longbows or Spanish pikes. Rather, in poetry's counterfactual world, removed from the always partisan debates of polemical history, we are asked to attend to 'notable images' of virtue and vice, to learn from and be moved by them, and once moved, to enact justice in the world.

MARY SIDNEY HERBERT AND THE GROWTH OF A LITERARY DYNASTY

Sidney's death at the age of thirty-one from a gangrenous gunshot wound acquired at the battle of Zutphen in 1586 translated him overnight from a promising (but underemployed) courtier into a Protestant martyr. His literary remains were seized upon as would-be relics by unscrupulous printers eager to make a profit from his posthumous reputation (Hannay 2002). As it turns out, Sidney was his own best Lucretia. Mary Sidney Herbert's heroic labours to preserve and present intact her brother's authorial corpus have long been recognized as a small miracle of literary history. Her 1593 folio edition of *The Countess of Pembroke's Arcadia* (a public rebuke to Fulke Greville's more didactic and politically partisan 1590 quarto), together with her 1598 edition, which she expanded to include Sidney's other major works, made Philip Sidney the most celebrated and only collected English poet besides Chaucer in early modern print culture to that date (Davis 2004; Trill 2010; Skretkowicz 1986). Even more significantly, Sidney Herbert's elected vocation as Sidney family editor and the leading Sidney patron lent a considerable aristocratic and religious *cachet* to a new generation of literary 'makers', or poets, working primarily in the still-suspect 'public' medium of print (Davis 2011; Hannay 2009; Wall 1993). So lasting was her legacy in this regard that it is perhaps not too much to say that the countess of Pembroke and her *Arcadia* authorized what we now think of as the English literary Renaissance (Davis 2011; Brennan 1988). However, if *The Countess of Pembroke's Arcadia* helps mark the birth of the early modern English 'author', it also invites us to remember the hard realities of that birth which inspired Mary Sidney Herbert to embark upon publishing her dead brother's body of work.

In 1588, after a lengthy period of mourning for her parents and brother (all of whom had died in 1586, some two years after the devastating loss of her three-year-old daughter, Katherine), the twenty-seven-year-old Mary Sidney Herbert returned to public life in spectacular form. Arriving just in time for the Accession Day celebrations marking the defeat of the Spanish Armada, she entered London in a coach preceded by forty gentlemen on horseback wearing gold chains and followed by a small army of servants dressed in Sidney blue. So began her second life as a religio-poetical icon, the resurrected 'phoenix' of her martyred brother, whose massive funeral cortège (delayed for months owing to its expense) had been the talk of Reformed Europe only the year before. From the late 1580s until her husband's death in 1601, Sidney Herbert devoted herself to securing her brother's literary legacy. She composed elegiac verse in his honour, patronized writers he had supported or who celebrated him posthumously, stabilized his 'secular' canon in print, and published her own translations of works that reflected his Philippist aesthetic. Most importantly, she brought closure to two major poetic projects pending at Sidney's death, his half-revised *Arcadia*, which she edited and published in what was to become its authoritative version, and an incomplete verse metaphrase of the Psalms, which she finished and circulated in manuscript (Hannay 1990).

It would be hard to say which Sidneian artifact—print romance or manuscript psalter—lent most lustre to the 'aura of semi-divinity' subsequently surrounding Mary Sidney Herbert (Brennan 1988: 82) who was acclaimed throughout her lifetime for effecting the literary reincarnation of her brother (Alexander 2006). In any case, her construction of herself through the *imago Philippi* was the enabling fiction which allowed her to accomplish a gender-defying, genre- and media-crossing literary career that explicitly and insistently linked the sacred/secular art of Sidneian literary writings to the public/private rites (and rights) of a grieving woman (Alexander 2006; Kinney 2003; Hannay 2002; Goldberg 1997; Walker 1996; Wall 1993; Lamb 1990). Sidney Herbert's many contemporary admirers collaborated with her in the formation of this complex authorial identity, almost invariably tracing her twin celebrity as patron and poet, Castiglionian mistress and Christian muse, to her 'natural' talent for faithful family resemblance and remembrance (Hannay 2009; Demers 2006; Distiller 1998; Krontiris

1998; Brennan 1988). If she was, as Spenser would have it, England's 'Urania', she was first and foremost 'sister unto Astrofell' ('Colin Clouts Come Home Again', 1595).[2]

The habit of reading Mary Sidney Herbert as the personal and poetic supplement to her brother is understandably resisted by modern-day critics, who have done much in recent years to liberate her corpus from the corpse of Philip Sidney.[3] Reacting against an earlier generation of scholarship, which either ignored or maligned her contributions to the *Arcadia* and the Psalms (not to mention her lyrics and free-standing translations), feminist reappraisals of Sidney Herbert have rightly cautioned against a 'biographical hermeneutic' that would misconstrue her widely published attachments to Philip as straightforward indicators of gendered or generic dependency (Miller 2001; Clarke 1997: 282). These more recent close readings have highlighted how 'grief-work' might offer strategic cover for a woman author's entry into print and manuscript culture. Such cover would be particularly necessary for a woman like Mary Sidney, the female figurehead of a forward Protestant court faction increasingly out of favour with a monarch jealous of her own image as England's phoenix and principal muse (Kinney 2003: 31). Moreover, we would also do well to remember the centrality of such literary activities as imitation, collaboration, and translation to early modern literary and religio-political discourse (Wall 1993; Clarke 1997; Benson 2005; Goldberg 1997; Walker 1996). Only from our own historical distance could such 'obsequies' (Sidney Herbert I—'Angell Spirit': 112) be taken as simply obsequious. However, even with these important revisionist readings in mind, it may well be worth hazarding a return to the poetic *pietà* of Philip and Mary Sidney. If we consider the writings of both figures together, we see how essential Mary's contribution was to one of the founding myths of an early modern English 'public sphere' birthed in religious conflicts and divisions unfolding across Europe and baptized in the blood of latter-day Reformed martyrs brought to life in the pages of texts such as Foxe's *Actes and Monuments* (Lake and Questier 2000b; see also chapter 17).[4]

To read Sidney Herbert as at once Philip's 'author' and imitator in this regard is to contemplate the paradox which lies at the heart of the Sidneian *imitatio*. On the one hand, her extreme identification with both his image and literary commitments may explain the degree to which sacrifice operates as a structuring principle of the Sidneian aesthetic. On the other hand, with death comes the promise of resurrection and the possibilities

---

[2] Spenser 1989: 519–62.

[3] See Hannay 1990, 2002, 2009; Clarke 2001, 2007; Beilin 1987; Demers 2006; Lamb 1990; Raber 2001; Bennett 2004; Fisken 1985, 1990; Krontiris 1998; Miller 2001; Moore 2000; Pearson 1996; Quilligan 2005; Richards 1996; Rienstra and Kinnamon 2002; Skretkowicz 1996, 1999; Wall 1993; Waller 1990; Trill 2010; Wilcox 1997, 2000b.

[4] The 'public sphere' is a term for the social space where private individuals come together to engage in critical debate about public matters. In his groundbreaking book, *The Structural Transformation of the Public Sphere* (1962), Jürgen Habermas links the origin of this liminal zone between the individual and government authority to the dominance of print culture in the eighteenth century. However, recent scholarship has made the case for a nascent early modern 'public sphere', in which print began to emerge as a medium of public or 'political' discourse and debate. See Lake and Questier 2000b.

of a transfigured textual body, capable of bridging (though not entirely erasing) the gap between heaven and earth, 'high' and 'low', male and female. This paradoxical authorial persona is perhaps most fully figured forth in 'To the Angell spirit of the most excellent Sir Philip Sidney', one of two original dedicatory poems included in a 1599 presentation copy of the Sidney Psalms prepared for (but never presented) to Elizabeth (Brennan 2002). Read as a poetic retrospective upon her decade-long effort to complete and properly lay out Philip's 'Immortall Monuments' (Sidney Herbert I: 112), it represents what might be viewed as Sidney Herbert's own *Defence of Poetry* (Kinney 2003). However, as such, it begins rather unpromisingly, with what looks like a full-scale retreat from Philip's spiritual and intellectual vision. Indeed, the first stanza would seem to be a declaration of near-incestuous poetic dependence on his higher flying Muse:

> To thee pure sprite, to thee alone's addres't
> this coupled worke, by double int'rest thine:
> First rais'de by thy blest hand, and what is mine
> inspired by thee, thy secrett power impressed.
> So dar'd my Muse with thine it selfe combine,
> as mortall stuffe with that which is divine,
> Thy light'ning beams give luster to the rest. (Sidney Herbert I: 110)

Recent criticism has done much to help us see this sort of textual posturing on Sidney Herbert's part as a strategy for stage-managing the gender politics of early modern authorship (Hannay 2009; Kinney 2003; Miller 2001). However, there is arguably more at stake here than meets the merely self-authorizing eye/I. Sidney Herbert is not so much playing the lady as presenting the necessary conditions for the good practice of *imitatio*. If she figures forth a martyrdom of sorts, she also proclaims the 'end and working' (*Defence*: 99) of the Sidney/Sidney Herbert corpus in a glorified, golden world where even authors assume new 'forms such as never were in Nature' (*Defence*: 100). This annunciation is Mary's, not Philip's: it takes its inspiration from his initial dedication of the *Arcadia* to her, but finds its fulfilment in her radical reimagining of Philip's earlier resort to the not-so-polite fiction of divine paternity. In this earlier dedication Philip plays the part of Zeus, presumably to Mary's Metis since it is her 'desire' that brings forth (if it does not actually beget) the deformed 'child' in his 'young head'.[5] This decidedly ungolden image of poetic making-as-monstrous-birth is augmented by Philip's comparison of his 'idle work' to a cobweb, the very antithesis of the apian imitative ideal.[6]

---

[5] Metis was the divine personification of thought or wise council in Greek mythology. According to the poet Hesiod, Metis was the first wife of Zeus and the mother of Athena, who was born from Zeus's head because he swallowed his pregnant wife for fear that she would someday give birth to a son who would overthrow him.

[6] The Roman poet, Horace compares the imitative labours of the good poet to the work of the honey bee, who synthesizes something useful, pleasing, and altogether new from many flowers. In contrast, the spider's web is associated with a monstrous originality.

What could be the source of hope in such a situation?—it is the Herbert livery, which keeps all imperfections under respectable courtly cover (*Arcadia*, Appendix III: 506). Philip is only joking in this instance, of course, as he plays seriously with his own fears about conceiving fictions. However, by 1599, Mary had cause to be deadly serious. Her 'Angell Spirit' counts the costs of redeeming Sidneian *imitatio* from the scandal of illicit generativity: a brother transfigured by death; a sister consumed by his 'lightning beames' (Sidney Herbert I: 110).

For the Christian, however, death is not the end. Picking up mid-statement where stanza one leaves off, the second stanza draws Philip's 'lustre' and Mary's 'mortall stuffe' into the divinely sanctioned pattern of Christian imitation, imagined here as an artfully woven heavenly livery:

> That heavens King may daigne his owne transform'd
> in substance no, but superficiall tire
> by thee put on; to praise, not to aspire
> To, those high Tons, so in themselves adorn'd,
> which Angells sing in their cealestiall Quire,
> and all of tongues with soule and voice admire
> Theise sacred Hymmes thy Kinglie Prophet form'd. (Sidney Herbert I: 110)

This process does not end in divine birth but in human metamorphosis—and not just for Philip. In her re-working of the Zeus-Semele myth (in which Zeus sews the unborn Dionysus into his own thigh after his mortal mother Semele's untimely death) Sidney Herbert is transformed from the lightning-struck Semele to a Zeus-like seamstress; Mary's skill safely delivers Philip's 'half-maimed piece' from the 'deep wounds enlarged, long festered in their gall' of her own bleeding heart (Sidney Herbert I: 111).[7] While Mary supplies the matter ('mortall stuffe') for Philip's inseminating spirit (or in the case of the Psalms, the common cloth for his lightning beam 'lustre'), she also bears witness to how profoundly her proper fashioning of matter *matters* to their collective poetic project. She is an inspired vessel and poetic weaver, a triumphantly creative Zeus whose poetry matters in its own right.

The religio-political sensibility underlying Mary's particularly strong emphasis here and throughout her work on what she likely would have called 'decorum' finds fullest expression in Philip's *Defence*, where the stress falls upon the 'right use both of matter and manner' (140). In the *Defence*, the 'honey-flowing matron eloquence' must be properly dressed if she is to avoid unseemly and unsafe associations with 'courtesan-like painted affectation' (*Defence*: 138), not to mention (as Fulke Greville does mention) the dangers of her own inherent 'aptness' to 'allure men to evil, [rather] than to fashion any goodness in them' (*Dedication*: 11). Insofar as such labour is women's work, the Sidney

---

[7] Semele was inadvertently incinerated by lightning after she requested to see her divine lover in all his glory.

siblings's pioneering collaboration suggests how their shared poetics paved the way for definitions of 'author' that could accommodate such Sidneian imitators as Mary Wroth and Aemelia Lanyer. In this sense, it is Pamela in the *Arcadia* rather than Lucretia in the *Defence* who most thoroughly embodies the possibilities of Sidneian *imitatio*. It is perhaps no coincidence that Philip's most iconic speaking picture was an accomplished seamstress much like the real-life Mary, whose needlework was in fact the stuff of print panegyric (Hannay 1990). Clearly, the double of her beautiful and carefully composed person, the purse Pamela embroiders throughout her climactic confrontation with Cecropia epitomizes the decorous interplay of surface and essence, matter and spirit that affords her famous prayer its 'strange working power' (*Arcadia*: 464). More to the point, it suggests how that same power is aligned in the Sidney–Sidney aesthetic with the artful, 'feminine' figuring of surfaces. Mary's appropriately ladylike reworking of Philip's feminized corpus does not entirely liberate her from the gender politics of early modern authorship any more than Pamela's 'majesty of virtue' fully defeats Cecropian-style tyranny (*Arcadia*: 465). Mary never makes an *Arcadia*. She does, however, author the self-authorizing fiction that is Philip and Mary Sidney. In doing so, she opens up a space of decorous free play every bit as metamorphically powerful: a golden room of her own, where it is possible to imagine a Philip turned Lucretia turned Stella; or, with John Donne, the Holy Spirit descended as a cloven tongue upon 'A brother and a sister, made by Thee | The organ, where Thou art the harmony'. From such entirely proper couplings of 'highest matter in the noblest form' all manner of new things might be born, perhaps even the scandalously hermaphroditic art of a Mary Wroth ('Upon the Translation of the Psalms').[8]

Sidney Herbert's decorous interventions in the gender politics of early modern authorship offer a useful heuristic for reconstructing her religio-politics writ large. Mary's Anglo-Calvinist connections have seemed to many readers more clearly defined than Philip's, and perhaps necessarily closer, given her more domestic, less cosmopolitan existence as the mistress of a country estate and wife of a prominent Protestant earl (Hannay 1990). Certainly, there is no denying the Sidney Psalter's proud Genevan pedigree. Two of its primary sources are the Geneva Bible and the Marot-Bèza Psalter, both of which had been sent to Elizabeth in the early years of her reign, when hopes were high in Leicester's circle that she would prove a more militant champion of the Reformed cause than she chose to become (Hannay 1985; Clarke 2001; Brennan 2002). Had Elizabeth actually reached Wilton to be presented with the Tixall manuscript in 1599, its dedication's attention to 'what Europe acts in theise most active times' might have made for an awkward moment, given the long-standing resistance within the Dudley/Sidney alliance to her emphatic political pragmatism both at home and abroad (Sidney Herbert I: 102). However, the politics of Pembroke's circle were anything but straight-forward by the late 1590s when Mary was completing her Psalm translations (Alexander

---

[8] Donne 2007: 150–2.

2006; Prescott 2008), and it may be more than happenstance that her presentation copy (with its dedication) never reached Elizabeth, and noteworthy that she decided not to print it (Davis 2011; Rienstra and Kinnamon 2002).

Sidney Herbert's other translation projects point frequently in the direction of princes. Her manuscript translation of Petrarch's *Triumph of Death* has been read as a critique of Elizabethan politics (Clarke 2007; Benson 2005; Catty 1999), as has her print pairing of the Reformed monarchomach Phillippe Duplessis-Mornay's *Discourse of Life and Death* with that of Catholic Leaguer Robert Garnier's *Antonius*.[9] Clearly, Sidney Herbert shared her brother's eye for tyrannomachist subtexts. As the enigmatic pairing of Garnier and Duplessis-Mornay would suggest, however, she also seems to have shared Philip's taste for inclusivity. Mary turned to the Continent for texts to translate: prose and poetry; secular and religious; Reformed and Catholic writers. Especially in moments of great emotional intensity, as in the *Discourse*, her personal piety is expressed in remarkably non-sectarian terms (Hannay 1990). This should come as no surprise considering the fact that Duplessis-Mornay, her brother, and their mentor, Hubert Languet, derived their piety principally from Melanchthon rather than Calvin, in a tradition that encouraged the faithful to settle their differences in a unified alliance against Spain and the Pope, where the rejection of the post-Tridentine Church coincided with amicable, even affectionate friendship with Catholics. Ben Jonson, openly Catholic, won patronage from the earl of Pembroke, befriended Philip and Mary's brother, Robert, as early as 1603, and later gained employment and hospitality at Penshurst tutoring the difficult young William. The inclusivity that counts most in this particular context, however, is literary. Huguenots wrote prose and poetry in the service of God and the godly cause, but none of them wrote the kind of 'right poetry' to which Philip and Mary Sidney devoted the majority of their creative lives: the making, remaking, and preservation of fictional literature. We have *The Countess of Pembroke's Arcadia* complete—as we have nearly the full canon of Sidney complete—only as a result of Mary Sidney Herbert's editorial labours.

Interestingly, one can most clearly see the outlines of a political poetical space in Mary's Sidney Herbert's oeuvre in the exceptionally 'private' dedication of her Psalms to Elizabeth. Here, Mary and Philip's jointly woven 'webb' is returned to the queen as an English 'liverie robe' for the 'Hebrue borne' David, whose royal status and divinely inspired eloquence establish him as her perfect mate (Sidney Herbert I: 102–3). By offering up their 'rent' to her through poetic productivity rather than political productivity more narrowly defined, Mary and Philip invite Elizabeth into intimate dialogue with the exemplary poet-monarch of exemplary poet-monarchs. Almost as importantly, they inscribe her into a domestic discursive sphere of which she is both literal sovereign and literary subject (Alexander 2006). Ultimately, it is this latter dialogue that will prove

[9] Monarchomachs were sixteenth-century French Huguenot theorists who opposed monarchy to the point of justifying tyrannicide. See Brennan 1988; Clarke 1997; Ferguson 2002; Krontiris 1998; Hannay 1990; Prescott 2008; Catty 1999; Raber 2001.

most transformative. There is more than one way, it would seem, to build a new Israel. If Mary never felt authorized to engage Elizabeth directly in the project, it did not stop her from erecting and perfecting imaginative spaces where prosaic princes and right poets might decorously meet.

Concluding Thoughts

This *architectural* view of Sidney Herbert's religio-political aesthetic takes its cue from her own imagery. In 'Angell Spirit' she compares Philip's works to 'goodly buildings' which she must finish according to his fore-conceit. This metaphor invites attention to the less spectacular properties of Sidneian speaking pictures: the 'harmonious composition of parts' every bit as integral to poetic *energeia* as colourful figures and finely drawn characters (Alexander 2006: 113). The Sidney Psalms in particular repay this sort of attention. Celebrated by both contemporaries and modern critics for its technical virtuosity, Mary's completed psalter provided, as Hannibal Hamlin has highlighted, a 'sourcebook of English poetic form' (Hamlin 2004: 119) for a new generation of literary innovators looking to prove the expressive potential of English verse, sacred and secular alike. Its 167 verse forms (126 of which can be attributed to Mary) not only inspired figures such as Mary Wroth, Aemilia Lanyer, George Herbert, John Donne, Henry Vaughan, and John Milton, they also pushed the boundaries of biblical translation, challenging the aesthetic of what Rienstra and Kinnamon term 'transparent mediation' that dominated the public (print) culture of English psalmody (Rienstra and Kinnamon 2002: 243).

In the 'divine poem' of the Psalms, the Sidneys found matter for the goodliest of buildings, capacious enough to allow for the meeting of prince and poet, the mixing of 'sacred' and 'secular'. In completing the Psalter, Mary Sidney Herbert generates an imaginative space where impediments of gender, status, and creed can be artfully translated, even if they cannot be altogether thrown off. In such a space, one can even hope to commune with the dead. Indeed, the Sidney Psalms are a literal communion of the literary 'saints', putting Mary's David in dialogue not only with Philip, but also with Sir Thomas Wyatt, Petrarch, and Edmund Spenser. Similarly, her translation of Garnier's playtext as *Antonius* brings to life the matter of Rome for a new generation of English playwrights (Shakespeare among them) looking to speak decorously to their own political moment (Hannay 1991).

This affinity for speaking with the dead circles back to the beginning of this discussion: to the disquieting intimacy of corpse and corpus in the collaborative aesthetic of Philip and Mary Sidney. As we have seen, Philip haunts Mary's literary labours. He is her source, her subject, and the shadow interlocutor who defines her conversations with both the Christian and the classical past. However, Mary's inspired and inspiring revisioning of Philip's maimed body (natural and textual) is most fully appreciated as an

expression of the shared Sidney passion for good ends: formal, political, and finally religious. Viewed from this broader perspective, death emerges as what it naturally is, the
ultimate boundary against the twin tyrannies of fallen history and misdirected desire.
For Mary and for us, it is also the paradoxical point of entry to Philip's golden world: the
catalyst for the incarnational miracle of publication and the key to the Sidneys' vision
of its proper end and working in the charitable incorporation of fallen bodies—natural
and politic—into the mystical body of Christ. As the divine poet David puts it in the
final Psalm, fittingly fashioned by Mary into a Sidneian sonnet: 'conclud: by all that aire,
or life enfold, | lett high Jehova highly be extold' (Sidney Herbert II: 253).

....

CHAPTER 21

JOHN DONNE

....

HUGH ADLINGTON

LANGUAGE, in all its variety, lies at the heart of John Donne's experience of religion. Inspired by the metaphorical richness of the Psalms, the Song of Songs, the Old Testament prophets, and the gospels, Donne's own religious writing strove to emulate a scriptural eloquence in which 'there is such a height of *figures* … such *peregrinations* to fetch remote and precious *metaphors* … such *Curtaines of Allegories* … such *sinewes* even in thy *milke*' (Raspa 1975: 99). As the discussions in this volume demonstrate, the distinctiveness of a period's religious culture, in all of its contradictoriness and variety, is revealed as much through the manner or expressive mode of its poems, plays, and other forms of imaginative writing as it is through the matter or doctrinal content of its theological tracts, creeds, canons, and articles. For Donne and his age, the God revealed in the words of Scripture was both a '*literall God*' and a '*figurative, a metaphoricall God* too' (99). Accordingly, 'figures', 'metaphors', 'allegories' are central to this chapter's study of the ways in which Donne's writing, in a process of scriptural emulation, expresses his religious thinking and experience. That process of emulation in Donne's writing takes place in a host of genres: lyric and satirical poetry, exegetical treatises, devotional tracts, prayers, translations, verse and prose letters, neo-Latin verses and inscriptions, and in over a hundred and fifty surviving sermons (out of many more) originally preached to different congregations, from country parishes to London lawyers, courtiers, and the king. However, rather than attempt to do justice to every branch and instance of Donne's religious writing, this study will focus centrally on a single poem, Donne's holy sonnet 'Oh, to vex me'. While no one work could ever be representative of the entire span or variety of Donne's religious thought and writing, the form, style, and content of 'Oh, to vex me' contain much that is characteristic both of Donne's distinctive habits of religious expression and of early modern British religious and literary culture more broadly. *Stilus virum et mundum arguit*; the style betrays the man *and* the world to which he belongs.

Before turning to the poem, a brief review of critical debates about Donne's religious identity and allegiance will be helpful. Born into a Roman Catholic family, Donne famously switched confessional allegiance in adulthood to the Protestant Church of England; in his preface to *Pseudo-Martyr* (1610), Donne himself established the pattern for later explanatory narratives: 'I used no inordinate hast, nor precipitation in binding my conscience to any locall Religion … till I had, to the measure of my poore wit and judgement, survayed and digested the whole body of Divinity, controverted between ours and the Romane Church' (Raspa 1993: 13). Izaak Walton, Donne's first biographer, reiterated and endorsed this account of scholarly, disinterested religious enquiry (1640: A6ʳ), and subsequent biographers followed suit: Thomas Birch (1734), Augustus Jessopp (1888), and Edmund Gosse (1899) all made Donne's switch of 'locall Religion' from Rome to the English Church central to their accounts, taking Donne's estimate of his conscientiousness at face value. In 1970, however, R. C. Bald's portrait of Donne striving to find a place in the world as well as in heaven prompted questions about the sincerity of Donne's conversion and about his apparent willingness to subordinate prin-ciple to ambition. Such questions have been keenly debated ever since.[1] In recent years, however, biographical battle lines have been redrawn as revisionist Reformation histori-ography, through its emphasis on the fluidity of confessional allegiances, has reminded us that the movement from one confession to another, then as now, was never a straight-forward matter of religious conviction on the one hand, or of politics or expedience on the other (Milton 1995; Questier 1996). This critical accent on the flexibility and com-plexity of early modern religious identity is key to understanding the religious culture of Tudor-Stuart England; it is also crucial for understanding the remarkable journey of the poet and preacher John Donne, from rakish poetic scion of a famous Catholic family to Dean of St Paul's, respectable pillar of the Jacobean and Caroline Churches.

Questions about Donne's religious identity typically ask not only *why* he converted, but *what* he believed. For some, the positions Donne adopts in his post-ordination prose on fiercely contested matters of doctrine (e.g. predestination) and worship (e.g. the rela-tive importance of preaching and sacrament) place him at the puritan end of the doctri-nal and ecclesiastical spectrum (Doerksen 1995). Others detect continuities of Catholic thought and practice throughout Donne's writing: for example, in what they see as the debt owed by Donne's holy sonnets to the Ignatian meditative exercises (Gardner 1952; Martz 1954; Carey 1981), or, it is argued, in Donne's increasing affinity in his Caroline sermons with Arminian theology and ceremonialism (Tyacke 1987b; Strier 1996; Guibbory 2001). A third group finds Donne's religious thought and writing occupying the conformist Calvinist middle ground (Scodel 1995; Shami 2003). There is debate too about the representativeness or otherwise of Donne's religious orientation and identity. For some, Donne's writing and religious stance is *sui generis*, demonstrating an 'almost unique *via media* in theology and churchmanship', constituted by the combination of a 'high view of preaching' with a 'universalist doctrine of grace' and a willingness to accept Church enforcement of 'ceremonial conformity' (McCullough 2003: 192–3; see also Lein 2011: 613). Others prefer to emphasize the compatibility of Donne's broad vision of the *ecclesia Christiana*, combined with antagonism towards papal supremacy,

---

[1] See, for example: Carey 1981, 1990; Marotti 1986; Goldberg 1989; Shuger 1990; Flynn 1995; for excellent overviews of Donne's religious identity and personality, see Johnson 1999; Shell and Hunt 2006; Wilcox 2006a; and Guibbory 2011.

superstition, and the Jesuits, 'with a broad swathe of Jacobean churchmanship, embracing avant-garde conformists and Calvinist conformists alike' (Milton 2011: 494; see also Targoff 2008: 22, for the orthodoxy of Donne's conception of the relationship between the soul and body). Critical debate will no doubt continue: the publication of the *Oxford Edition of the Sermons of John Donne* (the first volume of which appeared in 2013), and its guiding editorial principle of arranging sermons by place of preaching, will inevitably lead to reconsideration of the beliefs and churchmanship that comprise Donne's divinity. Nonetheless, however we draw the precise shades of Donne's religious words, thoughts, and actions, it is important to remember that Donne rarely wrote or thought as a systematic theologian or academic disputant. Different works were written with different rhetorical and religious purposes in mind: polemical in controversial works such as *Pseudo-Martyr* (1610), exegetical in *Essayes in Divinity* (*c.*1614; first published in 1651), meditative in *Devotions upon Emergent Occasions* (1624), and largely, though by no means exclusively, pastoral in Donne's sermons. As Donne put it in *Deaths Duell*, his famous last sermon: '*Discourses* of *Religion* should not be *out* of *curiosity*, but to *edification*' (Colclough 2013: 244). The focus in what follows, then, is not so much on what or why Donne believed, but rather on how his writing expresses his religious thinking and experience.

'Oh, to Vex Me': Rhetoric, Prosody, Theology

> 19.
> Oh, to vex me, contraryes meete in one:
>   Inconstancy vnnaturally hath begott
>   A constant habit; that when I would not
> I change in vowes, and in devotione.
> As humorous is my contritione
>   As my prophane love, and as soone forgott:
>   As ridlingly distemperd, cold and hott,
> As praying, as mute; as infinite, as none.
> I durst not view heauen yesterday; and to day
>   In prayers, and flattering Speaches I court God:
>   To morrow I quake with true feare of his rod.
> So my deuout fitts come and go away
>   Like a fantastique Ague: Save that here
>   Those are my best dayes, when I shake with feare. (Stringer 2005: 20)

We are struck here, even at the briefest reading, by the sheer force of poetic personality. The speaker's manner is self-revealing, anguished, and intensely self-dramatizing, referring to 'me', 'my', or 'I' eleven times in fourteen lines. In one sense 'Oh, to vex me' is the recognizable lament of the lover's complaint, familiar from a thousand poetic echoes and reworkings of Petrarch's *Rime sparse*, and in particular his Rima 134, 'Pace non trovo' (I find no peace). Yet Donne's focus on spiritual rather than 'prophane' love increases the philosophical weight of his poem and intensifies its emotional impact. That impact would have been even greater for seventeenth-century readers given that 'to vex' in this period had a meaning close to physically shaking in anguish, far stronger rather than the sense it has today (*OED, v.* 6; Gill 1990: 107) (cf. Milton's use of the word in Sin's description of her offspring gnawing her entrails in *Paradise Lost* 2.795–801: 'These yelling Monsters ... bursting forth | A fresh with conscious terrours vex me round'). Donne's usage here also connotes two other seventeenth-century senses of the word; first, the sense of prolonged academic disputation or cross-examination (*OED, v.* 7) that Donne himself uses in *Biathanatos*: 'the best way to finde the truith in this matter was to debate and vexe it' (Sullivan 1984: 30); and second, appropriately given the sonnet's development of its medical imagery, 'to vex' meaning 'to afflict or distress physically' (*OED, v.* 2), a sense used by Donne in a letter to his friend Sir Henry Goodere, conjecturally dated to 1608 (1651: 71).[2] All three of these overlapping senses—spiritual, disputational, and medical—are key elements in 'Oh, to vex me', the holy sonnets, and Donne's religious writing more widely. They are constitutive of a recognizable mood of spiritual restlessness, questioning and irony, encapsulated in Donne's paraphrase of St Gregory the Great: 'The mind of a curious man delights ... to vexe it selfe with such doubts as it cannot resolve' (Donne 1953–62: II, 84). While these elements and this mood are familiar from other religious sonnets of the period, by poets such as Anne and Henry Lok, Henry Constable and William Alabaster, they are present in a uniquely dramatic and compelling form in Donne, and markedly so, I would argue, in Donne's writing of what might be called his middle years, 1606–14.

This period represents a key phase in Donne's religious career and development. Living with his wife Ann and growing family in Mitcham, some ten miles from court, Donne read and studied intensively yet was without secure employment and was acutely conscious that 'to be no part of any body, is to be nothing' (Donne 1651: 51). In the wake of the accession of James VI and I in 1603 and the beginning of the Oath of Allegiance controversy in 1606, a cluster of Donne's literary works from this period reflects his growing preoccupation with religious matters, controversial and devotional. Some of the prose works in this group can be dated with a degree of certainty: *Biathanatos* (*c.*1607; first published in 1647), *Pseudo-Martyr* (1610), *Ignatius His Conclave* (1611), and *Essayes in Divinity* (1614). The dates of others, however, including some of the letters and poems such as 'Of the Cross' (*c.*1606), 'A Litany' (*c.*1608), and Donne's holy sonnets remain a matter of conjecture. Dating 'Oh, to vex me' is especially challenging, and bibliographical and biographical records are of little help. Only one manuscript witness survives: the Westmoreland manuscript, held in the New York Public Library, in which

---

[2] I follow the conjectural dating of Robin Robbins here (2010: 494). The editors of the *Oxford Edition of the Letters of John Donne* (2017) tentatively date this letter to November 1610 (priv. comm.), though the only certain reference point is the mention of Goodere's father. Given that he died in 1611, the letter must date to before 1611.

the poem is numbered '19', the last in the sequence of Donne's holy sonnets. The poem thus appears outside of the main phases and groups of manuscripts that reflect Donne's composition of this group of poems. Because of this, and because the Westmoreland manuscript also contains 'Since she whom I loved', which was almost certainly written after the death of Ann Donne in 1617, some scholars have argued for a similar date of composition for 'Oh, to vex me', some years after Donne's ordination in 1614. Others argue for an earlier date of *c*.1608, finding thematic and stylistic parallels with other works by Donne in this period.[3] This chapter supports the arguments for a composition date of *c*.1608 by adducing further verbal, rhetorical, and thematic parallels between the poem and Donne's writing of his middle years.

We find one such parallel in the opening paradox in 'Oh, to vex me', where the speaker laments his 'constant habit' of religious inconstancy (ll. 1–3). This witty picking up and turning about of the idea of constancy finds an intriguing verbal echo in the closing words of a self-punishing letter from Donne to Goodere in September 1608: 'Though I be in such a planetary and erratique fortune, that I can do nothing constantly, yet you may finde some constancy in my constant advising you to it' (Donne 1651: 52). The clever-young-man wordplay on constant/constantly/constancy here is characteristic; riddling verbal patterns, variations, and seeming contradictions and paradoxes are pervasive features of Donne's writing. Moments where 'contraryes meete in one' abound in Donne's epigrams ('"I am unable", yonder beggar cries, | "To stand or move!" If he says true, he lies' (Robbins 2010: 10)), his holy sonnets ('for I | Except you inthrall mee, neuer shalbee free' (Stringer 2005: 25)), and even his sermons. At Lincoln's Inn, Donne pairs two apparently contradictory scriptural texts in consecutive sermons: 'The Father judgeth no man, but hath committed all judgement to the Sonne (John 5:22)' and Christ's words in John 8:15, 'I judge no man' (Donne 1953–62: II, 311–24, 325–34). Donne's fascination with such conjunctions of opposites, a palpable and persistent feature of his writing, was a recognizable habit of mind in the period, deriving in part from student training in *rhetorica controversia* and formal logical and legal argumentation at the universities and the Inns of Court. Other poets also thought and expressed themselves in such terms. Contraries meeting in one in 'Oh, to vex me' echo, consciously or otherwise, William Alabaster's sonnet, 'O wretched man, the knot of contraries'.[4] Indeed, the pairing of opposites was a standard literary convention in the period: the catalogue of contraries in the second quatrain of 'Oh, to vex me' is one of the commonest modes of the sixteenth-century lover's complaint (Ferry 1983). Yet even granting the conventional nature of Donne's poetic rhetoric here, the direct verbal and thematic parallels between the opening lines of 'Oh, to vex me' on the one hand, and Donne's letter to Goodere on

---

[3] For detailed accounts of the dating of the poem and its textual history, see Stringer (2005: ci); Robbins (2010: 494); Young (2011: 231–2).

[4] This is not the only echo in Donne's holy sonnets of Alabaster's *Divine Meditations*, unpublished in Alabaster's lifetime (1568–1640). The congruity between Donne's 'I am a little world made cunningly' and Alabaster's 'My soul a world is by contraction' ('Sonnet 15', l. 1) has often been noted.

the other, in their shared fascination with the notion of religious constancy, are suggestive, and may offer further support for a date of 1608 for the poem's composition.

It is a critical commonplace that paradox (such as the one in the first quatrain of 'Oh, to vex me') operates as a rhetorical principle in Donne's writing, pervading his 'mode of argumentation' (Sloane 1985: 292, n. 4). It is less often recognized, however, that Donne uses paradox not only rhetorically, in an effort to persuade (as, most famously, in erotic poems such as 'The Flea' or 'To His Mistress Going to Bed'), but also dialectically, in the scholastic sense of the logical pursuit of a priori truth, as in 'Oh, to vex me'. In this latter kind of usage, a state of mind is evoked in which opposing desires, inclinations, and points of view are pitted against one another in a strenuous attempt to expel falsity, illusion, and self-deception. Donne's distinctive prosody plays a crucial role in this evocation. Donne's friend Ben Jonson remarked 'That Donne, for not keeping of an accent, deserved hanging', yet it is now recognized that what distinguishes Donne's versification is not its harshness or apparent unmetricality per se, which was consistent with Elizabethan and Jacobean poetics (Stein 1944; Hollander 1972), but rather the uses to which it is put. In 'Oh, to vex me' we observe several characteristic features of Donne's handling of rhythm and their contribution to the poem's larger dialectical purpose. A delight in explosive vigour is evident in the resounding trochaic stress on the poem's first syllable; rhythm then swerves sharply from the normal pattern causing the reader to founder on the muddy, indistinct syllables of 'contraryes'; and still in the first line, stress-shift re-establishes a more conventional iambic, rising rhythm, allowing the emphasis to fall resonantly on 'one'. The poem's distinctive pitch—that 'familiar low-flying melody of everyday speech'—is achieved by opposing, on the one hand, 'the peculiar qualities of loose monosyllabic flexibility and strength' to, on the other, 'the tense but delicate flowing of syllables in longer words of Latin and French origin' (e.g. words such as 'Inconstancy' and 'vnnaturally') (Stein 1942: 686–7). In the second quatrain, changes in rhythm go hand in hand with the speaker's rhetorical development and amplification. A series of analogies linked by anaphora mimic the speaker's 'humorous' or vacillating mood of contrition: in rapid succession we oscillate between the feeling of 'prophane love' and forgetting about it, between the 'cold and hott' or ice and fire that are the conventional physical symptoms of Petrarchan passion, and between prayer and silence, infinity and nothing. Donne's associative leaps, from one analogy for contrition to another, help to conjure the 'ridlingly distemperd' mood. Changes in rhythm, effected by stress-shifts in lines 5–7, and the unresolved pairing of contraries conveyed through compressed syntax, heavy pointing, and elision ('As praying, as mute; as infinite, as none') in line 8, similarly evoke the feverish, agitated state of internal restlessness and oscillation, of fluctuating from one emotional state to another, of impassioned reasoning, which runs through all of Donne's poetry, sacred and profane. If it is true that Donne's poems invite us to think at once about the arguments we are hearing, and about the motives which make someone argue that way (Burrow 2006: xxvi), it is also equally true, though less often noticed, that Donne's versification, as much as his subject matter, diction, or point of view, makes us think that way.

While we may be only partially aware of the ways in which Donne's prosody affects our reading of his verse, at least we know it is there and doing *something*. The same cannot always be said of the theological framework of a poem, some of which may be invisible to us at first reading. Take, for example, Donne's allusion to 'contritione' in 'Oh, to vex me'. Contrition, then as now, may indicate a general sense of sorrow for some fault or injury done, but it also has a specific theological sense, meaning penitence for sin (*OED*, *n*. 2). Predictably, early modern theologians struggled to agree on the precise definition and role of contrition in salvation, but for present purposes there was one key doctrinal difference separating the Catholic and English Churches on this issue. After the Council Trent (1545–63), Catholics recognized 'a formal distinction between perfect and imperfect contrition (attrition)' (Peterson 1959: 506); for post-Tridentine Catholics, both perfect contrition ('sorrow motivated by a hatred of sin in itself and a love for God') and imperfect contrition, or attrition ('sorrow motivated by a fear of divine punishment'), were sufficient for salvation. By contrast, the English Church held that only perfect contrition was sufficient for salvation, insisting absolutely 'that sorrow must be motivated by a hatred for sin in itself and that it must be precipitated by love for God' (506). In a sermon preached at Paul's Cross in 1617, Donne underscores this doctrinal distinction: 'a Confession made with this Attrition and no more, is enough for salvation, say they ['our new *Romane Chymists*']; ... To have a purpose to leave a sin ... this is their *Attrition*, and this is their enough for salvation. A sigh of the penitent, a word of the *Priest*, makes all clean, and induces an absolute pureness' (Donne 1953–62: I, 203–4). As an ordained minister in the English Church, Donne unsurprisingly preaches here against the Catholic position. For Douglas Peterson, Donne's 1617 Paul's Cross sermon and 'Oh, to vex me' share the same stance on the conformist Calvinist doctrine of perfect contrition: only sorrow motivated by love of God is sufficient for salvation. According to Peterson, unless fear is transcended by this love, then we miss the terrible irony of the poem's concluding line—'Those are my best dayes, when I shake with feare'—and fail to recognize that the sonnet is an admission of near-despair (517).

To some extent, Peterson's reading of Donne's orthodox theology in 'Oh, to vex me' is vindicated by evidence found elsewhere in Donne's writing. In *Biathanatos*, for example, Donne cites Calvin's commentary on the synoptic gospels in order to mock the Roman Catholic doctrine of repentance. Calvin, Donne observes coolly, went so far as to claim that Judas Iscariot himself possessed all that Catholic doctrine requires for salvation: 'And *Caluin*, (though his purpose be to eneruate and mayme (or at least declare it to be so defectiue) that Repentance, which is admitted for sufficient in the *Roman* Churche) sayes, that *in Iudas there was perfect contrition of hart*' (Sullivan 1984: 140 Pt 3, Dist. 5, Sect. 7). Similarly, in the sermons Donne follows Calvin's discussion in the *Institutes*, where Calvin criticizes the scholastic, Roman Catholic fourfold division of the stages of penance: contrition, confession, satisfaction, and absolution (Colclough 2013: 447). However, in *Essayes in Divinity*, where Donne again espouses a conformist Calvinist definition of contrition and its role in salvation, he nonetheless warns against delving too deeply into the whys and wherefores of God's 'acceptation': 'To enquire further the way and manner by which God makes a few do acceptable works; or, how out of a corrupt lumpe he selects and purifies a few, is but a stumbling block and a tentation: Who asks a charitable man that gives him an almes, where he got it, or why he gave it?' (Raspa 2001: 94–5). Donne frequently sounds a similar note of caution in his religious writing. 'To enquire further the way and manner' of God is both to transgress the acceptable boundary between human and divine knowledge, and to risk straying into areas of doctrinal or confessional controversy. And yet, ironically, such warnings and careful circumspection only serve to remind us of the pressure of contemporary religious disputes and controversies—about matters of doctrine such as the means of salvation, or matters of religious politics such as the Oath of Allegiance—that bear down upon and at least partly inform Donne's religious writing, even apparently personal, introspective lyrics such as 'Oh, to vex me'.

Donne engages with contemporary religious issues to varying degrees in the poetry of his middle years. 'Of the Cross', written in the wake of the Hampton Court Conference (1604), is both an intervention in a fierce public debate about the signing of the cross—Puritans proposed a complete removal of the symbol of the cross, especially of the signing after baptism—and a commentary on the conduct of religious controversies. Donne's poem adopts a moderate position, that signing the cross holds no dangers so long as we value spiritual over material crosses: 'Material crosses then good physic be, | And yet spiritual have chief dignity' (Robbins 2010: 471, ll. 25–6). Yet an undertow of satire is evident throughout, not least in the poem's incessant wordplay ('therefore cross | Your joy in crosses, else 'tis double loss' (ll. 41–2)), breaking out into open irritation and defiance in lines 9–10: 'From me no pulpit, nor misgrounded law, | Nor scandal taken, shall this cross withdraw'. Preachers, lawyers, and those who take religious offence or 'scandal' too easily are all indicted here. By contrast, Donne's 'A Litany' treads far more lightly over equally potentially controversial ground. Thought to have been written in 1608, 'A Litany' is a plea both to God and to a panoply of holy figures, including the Virgin Mary, for delivery from sin. In a 1608 letter to Goodere accompanying the poem, Donne comments wryly that 'neither the Roman Church need call it ['A Litany'] defective, because it abhors not the particular mention of the blessed Triumphers in heaven; nor the Reformed can discreetly accuse it, of attributing more then a rectified devotion ought to doe' (1651: 34). This is a studiedly middle path, quite different in style and approach to the trenchancy of 'Of the Cross'. Just as Donne treats the speaker's contrition (or lack of it) in 'Oh, to vex me' in terms sufficiently broad to avoid controversy, so in 'A Litany' Donne averts potential danger by removing fraught doctrinal concepts such as the Trinity from the realm of rational enquiry: 'O Blessed glorious Trinity, | Bones to philosophy but milk to faith' (Robbins 2010: 500). Thus, it is important to notice that Donne appears to have avoided courting religious controversy when writing poems such as 'A Litany' and 'Oh, to vex me', but equally important to recognize that that decision was consciously and deliberately taken.

The extent to which 'Oh, to vex me' was shaped in response to or avoidance of current religious controversy may perhaps be most clearly gauged in the poem's concluding sestet. In these lines the poem's theological emphasis shifts from the speaker's wavering sense of contrition ('So my deuout fitts come and go away') to a focus on the role of shaking with godly fear in the achievement of salvation. The theological and psychological nature of the speaker's attitude in these lines is pivotal to the meaning of the sonnet. First, we encounter the speaker's disarmingly understated declaration of his spiritual state: 'I durst not view heaven yesterday.' This mitigation of the abstract or profound (viewing, or not viewing, heaven) with the concrete or prosaic ('yesterday') is a staple of Donne's verse—a favourite device by which metaphysical ideas or spiritual states are made vividly and sometimes discomfortingly tangible. There is a generic kinship here with dream vision poetry, in which a sleeper slips unobtrusively between worlds; the same sense of the nearness of the spiritual to the earthly is discernible too in some of the allegorical miniatures of George Herbert ('In heaven at his manour I him sought') and in the visionary poetics of Henry Vaughan ('I saw Eternity the other night'). Daring not to view heaven, or to face God directly, has biblical precedents in Adam and Eve's shame after the Fall, 'the man & his wife hid themselues from the presence of the Lorde God among the trees of the garden' (*Geneva Bible*, Genesis 3:8), and Moses on Mount Sinai, 'Then Moses hid his face: for he was afraid to looke vpon God' (*Geneva Bible*, Exodus 3:6). Concentrating on images of the divine was also an important aspect of devotional and meditative exercises in this period and such images appear frequently in Donne's religious thinking and writing. In another of Donne's holy sonnets, 'This is my Playes last Scene', the speaker imagines the moment after death when his soul shall 'see that face | Whose feare allredy shakes my euery ioynt' (ll. 7–8; 2005: 13), and in two other poems of Donne's middle years, 'What yf this present were the worlds last night?' and 'Good Friday 1613, Riding Westwards', the speaker alludes to the dread associated with looking upon the image of Christ crucified: 'on these things I durst not look' (Robbins 2010: 566, l. 29). Excavating Donne's sources in this way, or tracing his participation in literary and scriptural traditions, in no way diminishes the singular nature of his poetic achievement; rather, it is only by situating Donne's religious writing in these contexts that we are able fully to appreciate the distinctiveness of his creative appropriations, elaborations, and reinventions of existing literary and scriptural models and conventions.

In this vein, two other key contexts for interpreting the concluding lines of 'Oh, to vex me' are the Renaissance psychology and Protestant theology of godly fear. As the poem indicates, fear of God, central to biblical and post-Reformation religious culture in early modern Europe, is a concept containing degrees and gradations: yesterday the speaker was afraid to face God or his conscience directly, a fear expressed through passivity and avoidance, but tomorrow, actively and in anguish, he will 'quake with true feare of his rod' (l. 11). Between these gradations or stages of fear lies the language of the courtship of God, familiar from biblical sources such as the Song of Songs, and an instantly recognizable stamp of Donne's religious writing (e.g. 'Here the admyring her my Mind did whett | To seeke thee God', and 'Show me deare Christ, thy Spouse, so bright and cleare'). Yet the speaker in 'Oh, to vex me' is an impure suitor, a petitioner courting God in 'prayers, and flattering Speaches'. Donne's diction here exploits the connotation of courtship in the seventeenth century not only with wooing but also with attempting to win favour with the powerful (*OED, v.* II.3.a): for Donne's fellow satirist and preacher Joseph Hall, Roman Catholic liturgical courtship connoted fraud, 'Our unlettred Grand-fathers were wont to court God Almighty with false Latin' (Hall 1660: 39), a view expressed in characteristically plain terms by Nonconformist minister Thomas Watson: 'Hypocrites court God, and speak him fair, but refuse to go on his errand; they are not children, but rebels' (Watson 1660: 309). Each of these senses is discernible in 'Oh, to vex me' in the speaker's unsparing self-criticism, helping to distinguish 'true feare' from lesser variants. The Old Testament sources for the abjectness of this 'true feare of his rod' are many, including Psalm 2:11 and 111:10, Job 26:11, and Hebrews 12:21, though the quaking of the speaker in 'Oh, to vex me' accords most directly with the Pauline instruction: 'make an end of your owne saluation with feare and trembling' (*Geneva Bible*, Philippians 2:12). Divine punishment is feared and welcomed in equal measure in Donne's poetry and prose, but the welcoming of it is not, as some have supposed, a reflection of a masochistic personality; rather it is an affirmation of Scripture's designation of divine retribution as an instigator of renewal and recovery. In *Devotions Upon Emergent Occasions* (1624), for example, Donne explicitly links godly fear with deliverance from illness (and ultimately of salvation): 'this sicknesse is thy immediate correction, and not meerely a *naturall accident*'. Lying ill, the sufferer's fear reassures him of God's curative and protective presence: 'and … this feare preserves me from all inordinate feare, arising out of the infirmitie of Nature, because thy hand being upon me, thou wilt never let me fall out of thy hand' (Raspa 1975: 33). In this way, 'True feare' of God is welcomed in 'Oh, to vex me' as a sign of God's presence, which, even when retributive, brings consolation and the promise of spiritual renewal.

The speaker's 'true feare of his rod' in 'Oh, to vex me' not only reflects an aspect of Donne's religious thought, but may also, as both an idea and phrase, help to support the argument for the dating of the poem to 1608. Fear 'of his rod' echoes Donne's translation of *Lamentations of Jeremy, for the most part according to Tremellius*: 'I am the man which hath affliction seen, | Under the rod of God's wrath having been' (Robbins 2010: 598, ch. 3, ll. 177–8). The biblical Lamentations was composed in response to the destruction of Jerusalem in c.586 BCE, and, in the early modern period, frequently served as a biblical analogy or parallel for contemporary catastrophes. Various dates have been proposed for Donne's composition of his translation, but one theory holds that the translation was completed in two versions, first in the 1590s and later in 1608 (Klause 1993: 337–59). A letter from Donne to Goodere in 1608 speaks of an enclosed 'Translation', which Donne hopes that Goodere will read and place among the papers of his patroness, Lucy, countess of Bedford. According to this theory, Donne undertook this later version of his translation in the same period in which he composed the majority of the holy sonnets. The influence exerted by the Book of Lamentations on Donne's holy sonnets has often been noted (Patrides 1985: xlviii), and both Donne's translation and the group of sonnets were evidently used in bids for patronage: Donne sent the holy sonnets to the 'E. of D', thought to be either the third earl of Dorset, or the sixth earl of Derby. Donne's translation of Lamentations, in its overt adoption of Tremellius's Protestant text, also clearly signals his confessional allegiance. If Donne did indeed undertake the revised, Protestant version of his translation in 1608, might it not also be the case that 'Oh, to vex me', in its powerful concluding emphasis on the 'true feare of his rod' and startling final line, shares this confessional sensibility and at the same time makes its stance evident to readers?

To answer this question it is helpful to recall one of the most influential recent readings of the theology of the holy sonnets. Paul Cefalu, in a refinement of the arguments of, respectively, Douglas Peterson (1959), John Stachniewski (1981), and Richard Strier (1989), proposes that Donne follows Calvin in emphasizing a direct causal link between godly fear and sanctification or growth in holiness (2003: 71–87). Cefalu points out the Pauline distinction between justification ('a once-for-all, juridical or forensic act by which the sinner is imputed righteousness by God') and sanctification ('the gratuitous but gradual and continuous operation by which the Holy Ghost renews the nature of the justified sinner'), and reads 'Oh, to vex me' in light of this distinction. He concludes, therefore, *pace* Stachniewski, that the speaker in the poem is not in doubt about his justification, nor, *pace* Strier, about the means of that justification. He also logically rejects readings that see the speaker as insufficiently advanced towards transforming fear into love (Peterson). Instead, in Cefalu's view the speaker of 'Oh, to vex me' suffers anguish because he is in doubt 'about his ability to maintain the status of his sanctification (regeneration) that has followed from his justification' (2003: 72). This 'reverential' or 'filial' fear belongs to the elect, and is to be distinguished from the 'servile' fear of reprobation. Cefalu argues that the speaker in Donne's holy sonnets primarily exhibits a filial fear of backsliding from his election; he represents himself as well advanced in the *ordo salutis*, but unsure of the status of the relationship between his old and new natures.

The distinction drawn here between justification and sanctification is a crucial one for understanding not only 'Oh, to vex me' but also Donne's soteriological thinking throughout his religious writing. Donne writes, in other words, as one of the elect, but one whose sanctification is far from complete or assured. Cefalu's approach, however, while it usefully places the poem in a more finely grained theological context, tends to overlook more immediate resonances in the poem of contemporary religio-political matters, such as the Oath of Allegiance controversy. In chapter 8 of *Pseudo-Martyr*, for example, Donne discusses the concept of 'just fear' ('*Metum iustum*') as a mitigating circumstances enabling Catholics to swear the Oath. Donne explains that the common opinion of casuists and divines is, '*That this iust feare excuses a man from the breaking of any humane law, whether Civill or Ecclesiasticque*' (Raspa 1993: 175). To bolster his argument, Donne shows how Catholic and Jesuit commentators such as Paulus Comitolus, Iacobus Simancha, and Juan Azor themselves argue that in cases of *metum iustum*, such as 'feare of *Torture, Imprisonment, Exile, Bondage, Losse of temporall goods, or the greater part thereof, or infamy, and dishonour*' (175), Catholics may obey heretical commands. On these grounds, Donne argues that English Catholics may swear the Oath of Allegiance with impunity, regarding it as a matter of security and civil obedience rather than one of conscience. *Pseudo-Martyr* was published in 1610 and I would argue that Donne's emphasis on 'true feare' in 'Oh, to vex me' may be understood at least in part in the light of Donne's contribution to the Oath of Allegiance controversy, and in particular of his reading of Italian and Spanish casuists and divines on concepts of practical divinity such as '*metum iustum*'. The 'true feare' with which the speaker shakes on his 'best dayes' is pointedly *not* the same thing as the pragmatic doctrine of 'just fear'. Donne's rhetorical effort in the sestet of 'Oh, to vex me' is precisely to distinguish a 'true feare' of God from more legalistic and expedient categories of religious experience. And yet, in this overt effort to distinguish the mental and spiritual landscape of the holy sonnet from the world around him, Donne can't help but remind his reader of the polemical, compromised, controversial contours of that world.

Rhetoric, Logic, and Falling into Discourse

A number of conclusions follow from this reading of 'Oh, to vex me'. The first is the importance of remembering that the holy sonnets and indeed much of Donne's religious writing is in some way informed by, inflected, or written in response to contemporary religious controversy. This is as true for seemingly personal, meditative works such as 'La Corona' or *Devotions* as it is for obviously satirical works such as 'Of the Cross' or *Ignatius His Conclave*, or works designed for public audiences such as Donne's Paul's Cross sermons. The second connected point is that Donne's active immersion and participation in religious argument and controversy imbues his mode of religious expression, at least in part, with its unique character. William Alabaster's *Divine Meditations* are as conceited as Donne's holy sonnets and George Herbert's inventive lyrics are as questioning and questing, but Donne's thirst for enlightenment, his desire 'to know', dramatized in his use of paradox for dialectical ends, is unmatched among early modern British religious poets. This 'hydroptic' desire for understanding is central to Donne's expression of his religious experience, but takes on a particularly bookish form during his middle years, 1606–14. Donne's letters from this time are full of references to books on religious topics being read, studied, borrowed, and returned. In a postscript to a letter to Goodere, for example, Donne asks his friend to hunt out a copy of *Baldvinus de officio pii hominis in controversiis* (a work by the French jurist François Baudouin, aimed at reconciling the Catholic and Protestant Churches in sixteenth-century France), concluding, as one might of the presence of a lover, 'I long for it' (Donne 1651: 69). Throughout this period surviving manuscript notes and marginalia show Donne reviewing, commenting on, and criticizing newly published works of religious controversy. We find an example of Donne's sharpest criticism in a famous letter to Goodere, written after Donne had read William Barlow's *An Answer to a Catholicke English-man* (1609). Barlow had been commissioned by James VI and I to respond to the Jesuit Robert Persons, but Donne was bitterly disappointed with the result: 'the Divines of these times, are become meer Advocates, as though Religion were a temporall inheritance; they plead for it with all sophistications, and illusions, and forgeries … They write for Religion, without it' (160). In his own works of religious controversy, such as *Pseudo-Martyr* and *Ignatius His Conclave*, Donne deploys many of the legal and rhetorical techniques of 'meer

Advocates', yet a sense of Donne's own personal commitment, both scholarly and spiritual, is always present even in the densest and most allusive passages, just as it lies more openly in view in 'A Litany', 'Oh, to vex me', and the other holy sonnets.

At the heart of this sense of personal commitment, common to all of Donne's religious prose and poetry, we find the same distinctive fusion of rhetoric and logic present in 'Oh to vex me'. First, Donne's dialectical cast of mind (honed through his training as a rhetorician, lawyer, diplomat, casuist, and exegete) finds expression in the pursuit of a priori truth in the argumentativeness of his verse and in the case-putting and syllogistic style of his controversial prose and sermons. Second, Donne's associative manner of thought and expression is evident in the poet's discovery of unsuspected affinities or analogies between one thing and another—lovers and a pair of compasses, most famously. It is in his love of analogy, or what Robert Whalen calls Donne's 'uniquely alchemical intellect, keenly appreciative of the intricate web of correspondences' (2002: 59), that these two ways of thinking and communicating—associative and dialectical—combine and unite in Donne's work. For example, the visionary, Augustinian response to experience, finding expression in rhetoric, in tandem with the traditional scholastic approach to the universe, rooted in logic, can be found in Donne's habitual recourse to typology in his responses to the Bible, in his detection of parallels and likenesses between the physical and the spiritual, between the Church militant and the Church Triumphant, and between the three metaphoric books in his system of theology (the Book of Life (or Register of the Elect), the Book of Nature (or historical world of space and time), the Book of Scriptures/Bible (or saving knowledge)). It has been argued that Donne possessed an instinctively typological way of thinking (Raspa 2001: xlix; Lewalski 1979: 211, 253), that typology allowed the intervention of rational speculation, in partnership with faith, and went some way to slake his intellectual thirst and desire to understand what he believed, even though he knew that this was impossible (Raspa 2001: xxxv). This paradox of wanting to know yet knowing it is impossible is captured in Donne's religious theory of knowledge, expressed in the second part of *Essayes in Divinity*, where Donne asks how we can know God: 'I beleeve he is somewhat which no man can say nor know. For, *si scirem quid Deus esset, Deus essem*. For all acquired knowledge is by degrees, and successive; but God is impartible, and only faith which can receive it all at once, can comprehend him' (Raspa 2001: 24–5).

Thus, everything must be interpreted through analogy or typology, as Donne describes it in the twenty-first expostulation in *Devotions*. Everything in this world is a type or analogy for something in the world of spirit:

> My *God*, my *God*, how large a *glasse* of the next *World* is *this*? As wee have an *Art*, to cast from one *glasse* to another, and so to carry the *Species* a great way off, so hast thou, that way, much more; wee shall have a *Resurrection* in *Heaven*; the knowledge of that thou castest by another *glasse* upon us here. (Raspa 1975: 112)

In this brief extract we see here the characteristic movement of Donne's religious thought and writing. As in 'Oh, to vex me', a series of comparisons and analogies radiates outwards from a central, governing conceit: the idea that this world (earthly) is a mirror for the next (spiritual). Typically, Donne illustrates divine communication by comparing it to the manipulation of images in this world through the placement of mirrors ('to carry the *Species* a great way off'). This extract is just the beginning of a lengthy meditative sequence coloured by Donne's distinctive combination of the ruminative, self-reflexive, deductive, and exploratory. In yet another missive to Goodere, Donne confesses apologetically, 'I mean to write a Letter, and I am fallen into a discourse' (1651: 72), and this dilatory, digressive tendency (what Anthony Raspa calls Donne's 'crab-like' movement in *Pseudo-Martyr*) (1993: xi) finds its ideal literary form in the sermons' rhetorical compound of dialectical reason and scriptural eloquence.

One example will have to suffice. In his Christmas sermon of 1624, preached at St Paul's, Donne is inspired to enact in prose the words of Psalm 101:1, '*I will sing of thy mercy and judgement*, sayes *David*' (1953–62: VI, 170). Having traced the etymological root of the word 'mercy' to the Hebrew term *Racham*, which Donne renders in Latin as *diligere*, 'to love', Donne embarks on a sinuous dilation of the claim that 'as long as there hath been love (and *God is love*) there hath been mercy' (6.170):

> God takes all occasions to exercise that action, and to shed that mercy upon us: for particular mercies are feathers of his wings, and that prayer, *Lord let thy mercy lighten upon us, as our trust is in thee*, is our birdlime; particular mercies are that cloud of Quailes which hovered over the host of Israel, and that prayer, *Lord let thy mercy lighten upon us*, is our net to catch, our Gomer to fill of those Quailes. The aire is not so full of Moats, of Atomes, as the Church is of Mercies; and as we can suck in no part of aire, but we take in those Moats, those Atomes; so here in the Congregation we cannot suck in a word from the preacher, we cannot speak, we cannot sigh a prayer to God, but that that whole breath and aire is made of mercy. (6.170–1)

Just as in 'Oh, to vex me' Donne offers multiple analogies for contrition, here he casts and recasts the images of mercy: as feathers, clouds of quails, atoms of air. Incantatory rhythm springs from the repetition of the *Te Deum*, '*Lord let thy mercy lighten upon us*'; it is enhanced by the remote alliteration of 'Moats' and 'Mercies', and punctuated by shifts in lexical register, from the biblical, 'gomer', to the earthy, 'birdlime'. The propulsive, scene-shifting motion of the passage exemplifies the rhetorical device of *incrementum*, described by the Elizabethan rhetorician Angel Day as the technique 'where by degrees we not onley rise to the summe of eueriething but also sometimes go beyond' (Day 1607: Pt 2, 91). In his exploration of the fullness of 'mercy', the plenitude of the text, Donne emulates medieval Franco-Spanish Jewish exegetes such as Abraham Ibn Ezra, Moses ben Maimon, and Solomon ben Isaac (Rashi), known to him from sixteenth-century Catholic and Protestant biblical commentators such as Cajetan and Tremellius respectively. As A. C. Partridge has remarked, 'The mythopoeic value of words was as essential to Donne as to the fathers of biblical exegesis' (Partridge 1978: 227). In this vein, reasoning by similitude from adjunct (feathers, quails, atoms) to subject (mercy)—as Abraham Fraunce prescribes in *The Lawiers Logicke* (1588: fol. 75ᵛ)—Donne peels back the layers of normal usage, carrying his auditory via a stream of deductions to his audacious final image: 'we cannot speak, we cannot sigh a prayer to God, but that that whole breath and aire is made of mercy' (6.171). It is a rhetorical tour de force, a fusion of sound and sense every bit as exhilarating as the most compelling of Donne's dramatized lyric arguments.

Donne's captivating union here of dialectical reason and associative poesis evokes Izaak Walton's famous description of Donne in the pulpit: 'A Preacher in earnest, weeping sometimes for his Auditory, sometimes with them, always preaching to himselfe, like an Angel from a cloud, though in none' (Walton 1640: B2^r). Such 'holy raptures', though, are balanced in Donne's religious thought and writing by a tough-minded critical faculty, equally sceptical of over-heated religious zeal on the one hand, and over-reliance on human reason on the other. Instances of this scepticism abound in Donne's satirical catalogue of imaginary books, *Catalogus librorum aulicorum* or *The Courtier's Library*, thought to have been composed between 1600 and 1610; typical of them is the following jest at the expense of Matthew Sutcliffe, dean of Exeter, founder of the anti-Catholic Chelsea College and fierce defender of orthodox Calvinist conformity:

32. *What not? or, A Refutation of all the errors, past, present and future, not only in Theology but in the other branches of knowledge, and the technical Arts, of all men dead, living, and as yet unborn*: put together in a single night after supper, by Doctor Sutcliffe. (Simpson 1930: 52)

Notionally, Donne and Sutcliffe shared a conformist outlook: hostile to papacy and wary of ''Those false teachers ... among us that palliate popish-heresies, and under the name of Arminius, seeke to bringe in poperie' (Sutcliffe 1629: fol. 271^r). Yet Sutcliffe's hardline views and unvarnished polemical rhetoric made him an irresistible target for Donne's irony, though in a relatively mild and even affectionately teasing form in this case. Less forgiving is Donne's Lipsian mockery in *Ignatius His Conclave* of what he sees as the theological innovations and self-importance of the Jesuits. A prime example of this more outrageous, polemical wit comes in Donne's rendering of a blasphemous travesty of the Nicene Creed, addressed by Machiavelli to Lucifer: 'out of your aboundant love, you begot this deerely beloved sonne of yours, *Ignatius*, which stands at your right hand. And from both of you proceedes a spirit, whom you have sent into the world, who triumphing both with *Mitre* and *Crowne*, governes your Militant Church there' (Healy 1969: 27). The literary kind or genre here, of course, informs the mood, just as it does in *The Courtier's Library*, the sermons or *Devotions*. But what remains constant throughout all of Donne's religious writing, in poetry and prose, is that familiar glinting amalgam of logic and rhetoric, meditating, expostulating, arguing, and praying in the service of an insatiable appetite for insight and a futile but dazzling attempt to match 'the inexpressible *texture*, and *composition* of thy *word*' (Raspa 1975: 99).

This chapter has attempted to leave to one side a story told often before, of Donne as a 'second S. *Augustine*', of sinner turned saint. In its place, this account of 'Oh, to vex me' has tried to show how Donne's habits of expression, some unique to him and some common to his age, reveal both the individual character of Donne's religious temperament and activity of mind—sceptical, querulous, acerbic, unsettling, and, at the same time, avid, impassioned, compelling, consoling—*and* reflect literary traits and mentalities found in other religious writers of the early modern period, from, in verse, William Alabaster to Henry Vaughan, and, in prose, from Joseph Hall even to Thomas Browne, in Browne and Donne's shared appetite for the '*o altitudo*' of metaphysical enquiry. The date of Donne's composition of 'Oh, to vex me' remains an enigma, though parallels of thought and expression with Donne's letters, poems, and prose works belonging to his middle years may support an argument for an earlier rather than later date. Almost a century and half ago, A. B. Grosart, speaking of Donne's digressive, ratiocinative habit in his verse letters, observed that, 'One characteristic of this thinking is its sudden out-flashing from the common level of the subject in hand—a characteristic common to all Donne's poetry. Shakespeare describes it memorably in the 'dolphin', which 'shows its back *above the element*' in which it moves (Ant. and Cleo. v. 1) [*sic*], all lustrous and iridescent' (Grosart 1872–3: II, xxxv). Donne, as some have argued, left no school, being inimitable, and was only fully rediscovered in the first decades of the twentieth century. This being the case, Grosart's terms, and Shakespeare's, might as well be applied to his verse letters as to the relationship of Donne's religious writing to that of his age: a 'sudden out-flashing from the common level', like the dolphin, showing its back above the element in which it moves.

CHAPTER 22

LUCY HUTCHINSON

ROBERT WILCHER

EARLY YEARS

WHAT little is known of Lucy Hutchinson's childhood and adolescence has been mainly gleaned from her fragment of autobiography and her 'Life' of her husband with its introductory letter 'To My Children' (quotations from these three texts are all from Hutchinson 2000). She was born in the Tower of London on 29 January 1620. The life of her father, Sir Allen Apsley, Lieutenant of the Tower, 'was a continued exercise of faith and charity' which 'concluded with prayers and blessings', and she recalls that he was 'very well pleased' when she 'outstripped' her brothers at Latin (Hutchinson 2000: 12–15). She also remembers being 'carried to sermons' while she was still 'very young' and enjoying the praise lavished upon her ability to 'repeat them' exactly (14). By the time she was four, she was a fluent reader and she soon began to show a preference for reading at the expense of all other accomplishments. Her mother took measures to 'moderate' such an unhealthy addiction, but to no avail: 'Every moment I could steal from my play I would employ in any book I could find, when my own were locked up from me' (14). Her father died in May 1630 and her mother was left to bring up a young family of three sons and two daughters.

Before she became the second wife of Sir Allen Apsley, her mother, Lucy St John, had spent some time in Jersey, where she was instructed in the 'Geneva discipline' by a French minister and his wife and came to dislike what her daughter calls the 'superstitious service' of the Church of England (Hutchinson 2000: 10). The religion she absorbed from these exiled Calvinists was probably of a more Puritan cast than the orthodox piety of her future husband, a loyal servant of the Stuart kings: 'She was a constant frequenter of weekday lectures, and a great lover and encourager of good ministers, and most diligent in her private reading and devotions' (2000: 13). Some of the sermons memorized by the infant Lucy Apsley would have been preached by godly ministers who were at odds with the Laudian faction that had risen to power in the Church of England; and it was under her mother's guidance that she 'learnt [her] catechizes with as much attention as any of [her] age' (Hutchinson 1817: 7) and, as she grew older, became 'convinced that the knowledge of God was the most excellent study' (Hutchinson 2000: 15; see also chapter 5).

Lucy's youthful interests, however, were by no means confined to religion. She confesses that 'on the Lord's day', after she had turned the 'idle discourses' of her mother's maids 'to good subjects' and performed her 'due tasks of reading and praying', she 'thought it no sin to learn or hear witty songs and amorous sonnets or poems, and twenty things of that kind' (Hutchinson 2000: 15). Elizabeth Scott-Baumann has recently suggested that she may be alluding specifically to the 'Songs and Sonnets' of John Donne, first published in the posthumous *Poems* of 1633, and has demonstrated that the elegies she wrote in the 1660s 'echo the poetry of Donne' (2013: 125). There is evidence of a continuing interest in contemporary poetry in her literary commonplace book, which contains material apparently copied in two distinct periods: around 1634–6 and from the late 1640s to about 1655. Along with translations of extracts from Virgil's *Aeneid* by Godolphin and Denham, there are masque choruses and versions of psalms by Carew, a New Year poem and a panegyric on Cromwell by Waller, a song by Jonson, a sonnet by Théophile de Viau, a popular ballad, two satires by Cleveland, and Hutchinson's own translations of a Latin epigram by the Jesuit Mathias Casimire and lines on love by Ovid. From 'the several hands at work', Jerome de Groot concludes that she must have been actively participating in the kind of manuscript transmission associated with domestic and courtly coteries that flourished in the mid-1630s (2008: 152). The earlier section contains several extracts, transcribed by Lucy herself, from a work described by de Groot as 'the textbook of Stuart courtly *preciosité*', which suggests that she may have had social contact at this time with adherents of Charles I's Roman Catholic queen in Richmond, where her mother had taken a house (2008: 150–1).

Richmond attracted 'a great deal of good young company, and many ingenious persons' because the courtiers of the young princes 'entertained themselves' there; and it was in Richmond that John Hutchinson heard a song written by the young Lucy Apsley, which so impressed him with its 'rationality' that it led to courtship and eventually marriage in July 1638 (Hutchinson 2000: 45–52). Looking back from the 1660s, the widow and biographer of Colonel Hutchinson took a severely Calvinist view of the situation that had prevailed in the national church during her adolescence. She descanted upon the abusive term 'Puritan' that was attached to the 'few' who were 'established in faith and holiness' and accused 'the Archbishop and his prelatical crew' of abetting Queen Henrietta Maria 'in the cruel design of rooting out the godly out of the land' (2000: 63–5, 70). That she was also apparently sharing courtly and Catholic texts 'as part of a poetic and intellectual community' in Richmond 'complicates our understanding of her intellectual development' (de Groot 2008: 151).

The 1640s: Civil War and Regicide

The maturing of Lucy Hutchinson's own beliefs and practices owed more to her husband than to the mother who had begun her religious instruction. Indeed, she represents herself as 'a very faithful mirror, reflecting truly, though but dimly, his own glories upon him' and 'a compliant subject to his own wise government'; and, in the prefatory letter to her children, as 'the faithful depository of all his secrets' (Hutchinson 2000: 51–2, 22). This may be her way of acknowledging that she had been his close companion on his intellectual journey towards strict Calvinist doctrines and Independency. The process had begun during the interlude in a house he had rented just outside London. While Lucy was bearing twin sons and 'weaning' herself from familiar 'friends and places' before moving north to Nottinghamshire, her husband was 'making an entrance upon the study of school divinity' (Hutchinson 2000: 53). After two years in the company of 'an excellent scholar in that kind of learning', he became convinced that predestination was a fundamental doctrine and even succeeded in converting his resident scholar from Arminianism; and an examination of the institutional features of religion at this 'time of dawning' led him to 'suspect' the 'whorish dress and behaviour of that which called itself the Church of England' and which he had 'never yet called into question' (Hutchinson 2000: 53–4). His wife would later interpret the two years of leisure at the start of their married life as 'a remarkable providence' that enabled him to 'lay foundation principles of holy faith and practices firmly in his soul, before the noise of war and tumult came upon him' (2000: 56).

Soon after the birth of a third son, the couple finally took up residence on the Owthorpe estate near Nottingham in October 1641. During the year leading up to the first battle of the civil war at Edgehill, John Hutchinson 'read all the public papers that came forth between the King and Parliament, besides many other private treatises' and became 'convinced in conscience' that the cause of Parliament was just 'in point of civil right' (Hutchinson 2000: 75). He was appointed to the Commission of the Peace for Nottinghamshire and oversaw the removal of images and destruction of stained glass windows in a local church in obedience to a resolution of the House of Commons, thereby earning himself 'the name of Puritan' among the 'ill-affected' in a predominantly royalist neighbourhood (Hutchinson 2000: 76). More than a year passed, however, before he found 'a clear call from the Lord' to take up arms; and in the summer of 1643, 'believing that God hereby called him to the defence of his country', he accepted the governorship of Nottingham castle, which he held for Parliament until the end of the civil war (Hutchinson 2000: 89, 110). There can be little doubt that such public decisions, including an invitation to army chaplains to preach in his house when they had been banned from church pulpits by Nottingham's Presbyterian ministers, were discussed with the wife who was privy to all his secrets. In matters relating to the couple's own religious beliefs and practice, she could 'exert considerable influence' (Keeble 1990: 240). For example, she describes how her husband was forced to bow to pressure from the local clergy and imprison a group of cannoniers belonging to the castle garrison. Having perused some notes about paedobaptism taken from the chamber where these separatists had held their conventicle and 'compared them with the Scriptures', she found herself unable to contradict 'the truths they asserted concerning the misapplication of that ordinance to infants' (Hutchinson 2000: 210). Since she was reluctant to challenge 'the judgment and practice of most churches', she 'communicated her doubts to her husband'—all the more urgently because she was pregnant at the time—and after searching the Scriptures and consulting 'all the eminent treatises on both sides', he endorsed the opinion of his wife that there was 'no ground at all for that practice' (210).

As a result, they refused to have their new baby baptized, and although they continued to attend church services, they were 'reviled' and 'called fanatic and Anabaptists'
(Hutchinson 2000: 211). This mutual step forward on the road to Independency, which
had been initiated by Lucy Hutchinson, has been described as 'simultaneously a family decision and a community action undertaken with religio-political intentions and
consequences' (Bennett 2006: 148). Her influence was also exercised in the case of a
Presbyterian minister who had been engaged as the family chaplain. This man's discourse during the Colonel's absence had alerted her to his support for the Scottish
army that invaded England in 1648. When she explained 'that she could not bear with
nor join in his prayers', her husband listened to his sermon on the following day and
promptly dismissed him from the household—an action which served to exacerbate
the couple's reputation as 'violent sectaries' (Hutchinson 2000: 221). In the context of
this growing animosity on the part of the local Presbyterian clergy, the inclusion of
Cleveland's 'The Hue and Cry after Sir John Presbyter' among the later entries in Lucy's
commonplace book may be evidence of more than the compilers' contact with 'the
world of Loyalist textual circulation' that has been deduced from it (de Groot 2008: 152).
Although Cleveland was indeed 'a resolutely Royalist polemical writer', some Royalists
and Independents were making common cause against the Presbyterian majority in the
House of Commons at the end of the 1640s and an interest in Cleveland's satire reflects
the Hutchinsons' gradual separation from a national church that had replaced the Book
of Common Prayer with the Westminster Directory.[1]

The last and most difficult decision required of Colonel Hutchinson as the decade of
civil war drew to a close was made only after 'serious debate' with himself and his God,
'and in conferences with conscientious, upright unbiased persons', prominent among
whom must have been his wife (Hutchinson 2000: 235). At last he was convinced in conscience that it was his duty to sign the king's death warrant at the end of the trial in
January 1649. He accepted a position on the Council of State appointed to govern the
new republic 'much against his own will', but in obedience to a divine call to serve 'in
councils as formerly in arms' (Hutchinson 2000: 236–7). Alienated by the growing personal power of Oliver Cromwell, however, he withdrew in February 1651 and returned to
Nottinghamshire.

The 1650s: Owthorpe and Lucretius

Retirement from the demands of office into the relative peace of the countryside opened
a new phase in the married life of the Hutchinsons: John devoted himself to his library,
the improvement of his estate, and the education of his children; Owthorpe became a

---

[1] Colonel Hutchinson's resistance to the imposition of the Directory soon got him noticed 'for one of
the Independent faction' (Hutchinson 2000: 207).

centre of hospitality and intellectual activity; and Lucy began translating the Latin epic, *De rerum natura*.[2] Her motives for rendering the Epicurean philosophy of Lucretius into English are still 'something of a conundrum', according to Reid Barbour, but recent research into the surge of interest in atomism in England during the Interregnum has led her to conclude that 'Hutchinson's translation was as typical of her social circles and intellectual milieu as it was exceptional for a seventeenth-century woman operating within the culturally bounded masculine jurisdiction of both amateur science and classicism' (Barbour 1997: 122–3). Howard Jones has shown that the medieval perception of Epicurus as the champion of sensual living had already been challenged by a group of scientific theorists, including Thomas Harriot and Francis Bacon, who took up his ideas about the nature of the physical world. It was not until the 1650s, however, that atomist theories began to circulate among a wider English public, made current by returning royalist exiles who had 'found themselves at the centre of lively Epicurean discussions in Paris' (Jones 1989: 196). These discussions were stimulated by the work of Pierre Gassendi, a Catholic priest and professor of mathematics, who had been instrumental in reintegrating the ethics and the scientific thought of Epicurus to create 'a persuasive and radically materialist paradigm applicable to a whole range of religious, political, moral and scientific issues' (Smith 1996: 188). Lucy Hutchinson would later claim that she had translated *De rerum natura* 'out of youthfull curiositie, to vnderstand things I heard so much discourse of at second hand' (2012: 7). It is likely that her interest in the new ideas emanating from Paris was aroused in the course of conversation with returned exiles, since she makes it clear in her account of life at Owthorpe that, 'while the grand quarrel slept' under the tyranny of 'the new usurpers', her husband 'was very much courted and visited by all of all parties' (Hutchinson 2000: 256). The teachings of Gassendi and his followers were also being disseminated in print during the 1650s, most diligently by Walter Charleton, whose *Physiologia Epicuro-Gassendo-Charltoniana or A Fabrick of Science Natural* (1654) gave the English reading public 'its first authoritative and comprehensive account' of 'the essentials of the "new" atomism' (Jones 1989: 201).[3]

Epicureanism appealed to a rising generation of empirical scientists as a viable alternative to an outmoded scholasticism. Gassendi had rendered atomism less offensive to wary Christians by arguing persuasively that the laws of the material world were God's working principles and that careful study of them might lead to a better appreciation of the divine role in physical processes. Furthermore, Lucretius's attacks on religion could be construed as a rejection of superstition, so that Hutchinson was able to begin her translation of one famous passage with the comment, 'Such mischeifes superstition [*relligio*] could perswade' [1:103].[4] Nevertheless, she unflinchingly follows the Lucretian

---

[2] During these years she composed a set of Horatian verses extolling the value of 'contented quietness' (reprinted in Hutchinson 2000: 339–40).

[3] For details of Epicurean works by Charleton and others written or published in the 1650s, including Lucy Hutchinson's manuscript translation of Lucretius, see Jones 1989: 197–205.

[4] Quotations from Hutchinson's translation of *De rerum natura* are from *The Works of Lucy Hutchinson: Volume I, Part 1* (2012), ed. Barbour and Norbook, with book and line numbers given in square brackets in the text.

account of how 'first bodies' or 'principles' [atoms], raised 'in infinite time' and meeting in 'all congressions'—without any intervention from a creating deity—'were at last | After all coniunctions and all motions cast | Into that forme, whence heaven, earth, sea, and all | That liue in them draw their originall' [5:435–47]; and she translates accurately a passage which denies any divine supervision of the universe thus brought about by chance:

> Nature, if this you rightly vnderstand,
> Will thus appeare free from the proud command
> Of soveraigne power, who of her owne accord
> Doth all things act, subiected to no lord. [2:1118–21]

The fact that her translation was 'faithful, responsive, engaged' in this way has led one critic to reject the widespread assumption 'that Hutchinson's religious beliefs and Lucretian philosophy are necessarily antithetical and that for Hutchinson to be drawn to Lucretius must mean some kind of conflict with her Christianity' (Goldberg 2006: 280, 277).

There are a number of plausible answers to the conundrum of why a woman holding Calvinist beliefs should have devoted so much time and care to a task that presented her with such demanding linguistic and doctrinal problems.[5] Perhaps Hugh de Quehen was right in rephrasing her stated desire to investigate what she had heard 'at second hand'—the 'Puritan drive towards truth and the concomitant distrust of intermediaries' (Hutchinson 1996: 1). Perhaps she was confirming the strength of her faith by putting it to the test. Perhaps, as Norbrook speculates, her Calvinism 'may have been slightly different' from that which she defined in later life, especially since we have 'no direct evidence for her views during the 1650s' (Hutchinson 2012: lxxxvi, xxv). Or perhaps, her curiosity having been aroused in a stimulating intellectual atmosphere and at a time when the burdens of military and political service had been lifted temporarily from her husband's back, she was free for the first time since her adolescence to follow the calling of her own nature to be a writer as well as a reader, wife, and mother.

The 1660s: Widowhood, Hagiography, and Christian Principles

The end of the Owthorpe idyll was signalled by the collapse of the Protectorate. John Hutchinson was drawn back into political life and elected to the Convention Parliament that met in April 1660. In June, the Commons discharged him and barred him from holding public office for his part in the trial of Charles I, although he was permitted

---

[5] No one had yet attempted to translate the whole of *De rerum natura* into English and there were far fewer commentaries on it than on the other major Latin epics to provide help with its notoriously difficult Latin and the arcane vocabulary in which its scientific concepts and processes are expressed.

to retain his estates. A few days later his name was removed from the list of regicides excepted from the Bill of Indemnity. As his wife relates these events, 'the integrity of his heart, in all he had done, made him as cheerfully ready to suffer as to triumph in a good cause'; and his freedom was only secured by her soliciting 'all her friends for his safety' and forging his signature on a letter to the Speaker that set out 'what might be in his favour' (Hutchinson 2000: 280–1). It has long been suspected, however, that those well-wishers invented 'a number of good-natured fictions' in his defence and that the 'abject expression of penitence' in the letter was partly of his own contriving (Hutchinson 1906: xv).[6] The couple lived quietly on their country estate until 1663, when the Colonel's name was linked with a plot in Yorkshire and he was confined in the Tower of London. He was later moved to Sandown Castle in Kent, where he contracted a fever and died on 11 September 1664. His widow, the youngest of whose seven surviving children had been born as recently as 1662, was forced to sell family property to pay his debts, and eventually Owthorpe itself in 1672.

Her sense of utter desolation was expressed in a 'Final Meditation' appended to the 'Life of John Hutchinson': 'Yet after all this he is gone hence and I remain, an airy phantasm walking about his sepulchre and waiting for the harbinger of day to summon me out of these midnight shades to my desired rest' (Hutchinson 2000: 337). She found a literary outlet for her grief in a collection of twenty-three elegies and epitaphs. In many of them, her sense of personal loss is uppermost: awake at night, she longs for his hand to dry her tears and his 'kind Encircling arme'; she pores over likenesses of him, but 'painted fire' gives 'no heate'; even her books are no 'Sollace' for her 'Sicke Thoughts'; and as late as 1668, she complains that the return of Spring only adds 'more payne' to her 'bleard Eies' (Norbrook 1997: 502, 504, 510, 513). In some of them, she banishes 'rash Thoughts' by recollecting that 'Firme hope begins where fraile hope ends' and finds Christian consolation in the certainty that her dead saint has soared from mortal sight 'on wings of heauenly Loue' (Norbrook 1997: 511, 503). The tenth poem, which Erica Longfellow describes as 'the centrepiece of her elegies', asserts 'the Hutchinsons' faith in the power of Word-centred piety' and tells how the storm-tossed poet casts anchor on a rock where 'the earthly is mystically changed to the heavenly' (Longfellow, 2004: 193–4). This process is conveyed through a remarkable fusion of images from alchemy and Catholic Eucharistic dogma:

> Here heauens bright glorie to fraile earth descends
> Here earth aduanct to heauen its frailty ends
> For the pure Nature taking in The Crosse
> By its powerfull touch to Gold conuerts ye Drosse
> And as it Through ye fleshly medium shines
> That body transubstantiates and refines. (Norbrook 1997: 505)

---

[6] Derek Hirst (2004) confirms Firth's suspicions by setting Lucy Hutchinson's account of the episode against certain verifiable facts. David Norbrook provides a much fuller political context for her claim that she forged the letter and concludes that the senses in which she actually wrote it 'remain equivocal' (2012: 238).

The plain narrative account of John Hutchinson's last hours in the 'Life'—'he fetched a sigh, and within a little while departed, his countenance settling … amiably and cheerful in death'—gives way in the final meditation to a vision similar to that in the elegy: before his soul 'was translated out of this world into the Father's glory', he had already been 'so immortalized' by 'virtue and grace' that 'death hath very little of him', and the malice of his enemies served only as 'the fire that refined his gold' (Hutchinson 2000: 331, 337).

The prose work that began as a means of moderating the author's grief by preserving her husband's memory became much more than a portrait in words or a record of events and actions. As she presents the unfolding of his life, it becomes an exemplification of what Longfellow calls 'a Puritan element of human perfectibility' (2004: 195). Hutchinson herself, in a treatise she wrote for her daughters towards the end of the 1660s, uses the theological term Sanctification for a process that begins with Justification and culminates in Glorification, when believers are 'taken up into an everlasting communion with God, and participation of his glory' (Hutchinson 1817: 80). This explains why she omits facts 'unfavourable to her husband's character', such as the torturing of royalist spies, and 'conceals much of the truth' relating to his escape from execution as a regicide (Hutchinson 1906: xiv–xv). It also accounts for the emphasis she places on the exercise of conscience at critical moments in his career and leads to the recent judgement that 'the conscience she fashioned for her husband in the *Memoirs* may have been closer to her own conscience rather than his' (Lobo 2012a: 339).

In common with other puritan diaries and 'lives', Hutchinson's narrative 'follows a familiar, even formulaic pattern' and is 'providentially driven' (Sleeper 2000: 6–7). Alexandra Walsham has demonstrated that the belief in a 'deity who constantly intervened in human affairs' ran through the entire spectrum of religious faiths in early modern England, but that it 'played a pivotal role in forging a collective Protestant consciousness' (1999: 2, 5). Other historians have pointed out that Calvin had 'placed the doctrine at the heart of the true believer's interpretation of the world around him' and that his puritan disciples were subject to 'intense psychological experience in which every event was imbued with providential significance for personal salvation' (Worden 1985: 60; Spurr 1990: 32). Lucy Hutchinson herself stresses that, although the Creator's universal care for mankind extends 'to the wicked', his providence works in 'a most especiall manner … for the good of his church, and his elect' (1817: 31). Her fragment of autobiography begins by invoking the 'Almighty Author of all beings', who 'conducts the lives of men from the cradle to the tomb'; and throughout the 'Life' of her husband, she records the particular care taken of him, from 'the good providence of God' that reserved him 'to a more glorious death' when he was thrown to safety as a child from a runaway coach to his preservation by 'daily and hourly providences' during the siege of Nottingham (Hutchinson 2000: 3, 38, 205). The transformation of the mundane reality of a fever contracted in a damp prison into a 'more glorious death' is a direct consequence of the belief that the 'most fundamental of the dispensations which God vouchsafed to the saint was to keep him alive while the process of sanctification was accomplished' (Worden 1985: 71).

Many of the providences she reports, however, relate to national rather than personal history.[7] From the beginnings of the Reformation, when 'it pleased God to cause that light to break forth about Luther's time', England had occupied a special place in the divine plan and the controlling hand of the deity could be seen everywhere in the progress of the civil wars: in 1639, God had 'most miraculously ordered providences' to save 'his servants' from 'prelatical' persecution by raising up the army of Scottish Covenanters; in 1643, 'God by his providence' had brought Waller's plot 'timely to light'; and nearer home, when Prince Rupert had 'advanced within three miles of Nottingham' in 1644, 'it pleased God to divert him from coming against the town' (Hutchinson 2000: 58, 70–1, 105, 159). Like many others in 1660, Colonel Hutchinson had been forced to re-examine 'all his former ways and actions' when 'God turned the great wheel in this nation'; and 'the more he examined the cause from the first, the more he became confirmed in it' (2000: 22, 286). His wife had her own way of coping with political doubt as well as personal grief in the memorial texts that she composed after his death. When Christopher Hill discounted her as a witness to the 'experience of defeat' because 'she is far too concerned to cover up the Colonel's weaknesses to allow her own views to come through', he did not know of the existence of the elegies (Hill 1984: 21). In this more private mode of writing, she chides the 'alseeing Sun' not only for upbraiding her own 'rewin' but also for gilding the 'tyrants bloody Throne' and for coming 'as a gay courtier' to 'deride' the public ruins 'we would in Silent Shadowes hide' (Norbrook 1997: 489, 493). One answer to such political despair is to invoke an eschatological counterpart of the personal desire for the 'quiet of a graue' (Norbrook 1997: 511):

> While y:^{r} polluted spheres about y:^{w} burne
> And ye Elementall heauen like melting lead
> Drops downe Vpon ye impious rebells head
> Then Shall our King his Shining host display
> At whose approach our mists shall fly away. (Norbrook 1997: 493)

Another is to adjure the 'sons of England' to look for divine vengeance within human history upon those who have shed innocent blood in 'This prodigious age' (Norbrook 1997: 519).[8] The elegies, *On the Principles of the Christian Religion, On Theology*, and the two private statements of belief still in manuscript—all written in the wake of her husband's death—are the work of someone who, in Robert Mayer's perceptive analysis, needs to examine and affirm a faith 'under stress' and who 'uses writing to clarify and ground her personal beliefs' (Mayer 2007: 322). These texts, along with the *Memoirs*, deserve to be read 'beside *Samson Agonistes*, Baxter's *Reliquiae*, and the body of

---

[7] She drew upon Thomas May's published histories for the 'digressions' on national events that provided a context for the more local history of her husband's role in defending Nottingham through the war years.

[8] Scott-Baumann (2011: 134) examines the way images derived from Donne are transformed 'from erotic to apocalyptic' in the elegies.

Nonconformist writing, as an attempt to perceive and accept God's purpose in and after the Restoration' (Keeble 1990: 229).

The 1670s: Refuting Lucretius
and Paraphrasing Genesis

In her later years, Lucy Hutchinson was 'falling more and more under the influence of a narrowing creed' (Hutchinson 1906: xix). This process can be traced in material copied from Calvin's *Institutes* into her religious notebook and in the treatise intended to fortify her daughters against false teaching by the sects, in which she set out the Calvinist doctrine of double predestination with uncompromising rigour: 'By the decree of God some men and angells are from eternity predestinated to everlasting life, and others foreordeined to everlasting death; … and their number soe definite and certeine that it can neither be encreased or diminished' (Hutchinson 1817: 20).[9] She was confirmed in her commitment to this doctrine and to other aspects of Calvin's theology by her acquaintance with the Congregationalist minister John Owen, whose sermons she is known to have attended in 1673 and whose publications probably figured among the books from which she assembled her various statements of faith. She certainly knew *Theologoumena pantodoupa* (1661), the partial translation of which as *On Theology* probably dates from the 1670s. From 1673, Owen was serving a congregation in Leadenhall Street, where she may have encountered Robert Ferguson, one of his assistants, whom she engaged as tutor to her son.

Another significant acquaintance was the earl of Anglesey, a devout Presbyterian and member of the Royal Society, to whom Hutchinson dedicated a manuscript of her translation of Lucretius in 1675. Norbrook describes him as 'a mediating figure' in the political, religious, and intellectual circles in which she was moving at this time (Hutchinson 2012: cxiii–cxv). He was opposed to religious intolerance—his wife attended the Nonconformist meetings of Owen, who preached in his house in July 1674—and his library contained five Latin editions of *De rerum natura* and John Evelyn's translation of the first book. Hutchinson completed her own translation to present to Anglesey, but she must have resumed the task in a different spirit from that in which she had first undertaken it.[10] By the 1670s, Epicureanism had become identified with both the libertinism of the court wits and the rise of natural theology, which had been a primary target of Owen's 1661 treatise. She had copied Calvin's assault on 'the sacrilegious discourses of that unclean dog Lucretius' into her religious notebook; Owen had dismissed

---

[9] See also her religious commonplace book, Nottingham Archives, DD/HU3: 62–3.

[10] She had used the 1631 edition of Daniel Pareus for most of her translation, but switched to the 1570 edition of Lambinus for the latter part of Book 6. She also transcribed the last book herself and added the arguments for each book in her own hand. (See Hutchinson 2012: xliii, cxxii.)

'that Epicurean' for making a 'ridiculous mockerie' of 'the doctrine of eternall iudgment'; and she had advised her daughters not to 'amuse' themselves with 'the uncerteineties, that poore dull philosophers have gropd out in the darke' (Hutchinson, DD/HU3: 255; 1817: 255; 1817: 12). It is no surprise, therefore, that in dedicating her 'vnworthy Translation' to Anglesey she insists on her abhorrence of 'all the Atheismes & impieties in it' and denies that she ever intended to 'propagate' any of its 'wicked pernitious doctrines' (Hutchinson 2012: 5, 7). In the text of the poem, she adds marginal glosses that highlight dangerous ideas—that the world was created by 'the casuall congression of attoms' or that 'soules grow & decay with the Bodie'—and on occasion repudiates them directly with horror and scorn as 'impious' or the work of a 'poore deluded bewitcht mad wretch' (2012: 323, 179, 145, 205).

Hutchinson may have begun to paraphrase the first books of Genesis in order to 'redeem poetry as well as her own personal career as a writer' from the taint of Lucretius (Norbrook 2000: 277).[11] A survey of the evidence relating to the only manuscript of the twenty-canto poem, which breaks off in the middle of the quarrel between Jacob and Esau, suggests to Norbrook that the whole work was composed during the 1670s (Norbrook 2000: 275). The preface she wrote when the first five cantos were published anonymously in 1679 under the title *Order and Disorder* reiterates her penitence for being drawn by 'vain curiosity' to 'consider and translate the account some old poets and philosophers give of the original of things' (Hutchinson 2001: 3). More than one commentator has seen her poem as a rebuke to the author of *Paradise Lost*.[12] Her narrative of the Creation and the Fall in the printed cantos—the only section of her paraphrase properly entitled *Order and Disorder: Or, the World Made and Undone*—certainly engages with much of the same material treated by Lucretius and Milton (see chapter 23); and she goes out of her way to refute uncongenial aspects of her puritan predecessor's theology as well as the pagan 'impieties' of the Roman poet in what her editor calls 'this militantly Trinitarian and Calvinistic epic' (Hutchinson 2001: xv). In the opening invocation, she not only attributes the 'universal harmony' of the created universe to 'stupendous Providence' [1:5–8] in contradiction to Lucretius' chance concourse of atoms but also rejects the 'presumptuous folly' of inquiring—as Milton did in his account of the rebellion and war in heaven—into 'what hath been | Before the race of time did first begin' [1:38–41].[13] A passage describing the 'sovereign sacred Unity' of the Three Persons of the Trinity [1:85–124]—a doctrine conspicuously underplayed in *Paradise Lost*—was 'greatly enlarged' in the printed version of Hutchinson's poem in order to 'leave the reader in no doubt as to where she stood' (Norbrook 2003: 50–1). Shannon Miller argues that Hutchinson's response to Milton's epic 'is configured through a sustained

[11] Goldberg finds in reiterated references to the 'boundless' power of the Creator an 'attempt to place God where Lucretian matter prevails' (2006: 293).

[12] See Norbrook 2003; Wilcher 2006; Miller 2008; Norbrook 2010.

[13] Quotations from Hutchinson's biblical epic are from *Order and Disorder* (2001), edited by Norbrook, with book and line numbers given in square brackets in the text. The phrase 'race of time' occurs in *Paradise Lost* 12.554.

meditation on the role of the maternal in the events of Genesis', in which Adam and Eve are jointly 'given dominion' over the inferior creation 'as part of their union in marriage'; Eve rather than Adam names their children; and matriarchal succession is emphasized in expanded histories of Sarah, Rebecca, and Rachel, whose roles as wives and mothers are foregrounded at the expense of 'male-derived lists of "begetting"' (Miller 2008: 108, 117, 125, 129). The implications of beginning the account of humankind with 'an emphasis on the first couple, not the first father' are explored further by Erin Murphy (Murphy 2011: 167). In later books, when romance conventions are harnessed to narrate the courtship, marriages, and domestic lives of Old Testament women, Hutchinson carefully accommodates references to 'Fortune' (often symbolized by the sea) to the belief that God 'orders all our human accidents' [8:404]: 'And to relieve frail man, the Lord besides | Varies his fortunes with alternate tides' [17:295–6]. Reinforcing this providential reading of the narrative are cross-references to other Biblical passages in the margins of the printed text, which puts into practice Hutchinson's puritan conviction that 'Scripture is the best interpreter and reconciler of itselfe' (Hutchinson, DD/HU3: 54). One critic argues that such marginal annotation, derived from the Geneva Bible, effectively denies individualistic 'conjecture' while adding 'layers of interpretation' (Scott-Baumann 2011: 186, 184); another that the 'unarticulated connection between the marginal text and the main text' emphasizes 'the difference between the holy past and the unholy present' (Murphy 2011: 167).

Problems of Authorship

The manuscripts that passed down through Hutchinson's family constitute a literary workshop that reveals how she shaped 'a life as an author, acting in the world by writing, and, indeed, *writing* her life' (Mayer 2007: 308). One striking feature is the number of unfinished projects it contains, reflecting the conditions under which she wrote: the long gap in the literary commonplace book marking the decade of her earliest pregnancies and the civil wars; a record of events in Nottingham compiled between 1642 and 1645 and left untouched for twenty years until it was incorporated into the 'Life' of her husband; the fragment of her own 'Life', ending abruptly with pages torn out; the translation of Lucretius, probably interrupted by the turmoil of the late 1650s and only completed for presentation to Lord Anglesey; the unfulfilled promise of a book about outward worship at the end of the *Principles*; the translation of *On Theology* that goes only as far as the second of Owen's six books, perhaps overtaken by the return to Lucretius and the paraphrase of *Genesis* that she was still working on when she died in 1681. In the dedication to Anglesey, she offers a glimpse of her more practical difficulties, translating 'in a roome where my children practizd the severall quallities they were taught' and numbering the syllables of the verse 'by the threds of the canvas I wrought in' before setting them down 'with a pen & inke that stood by me' (Hutchinson 2012: 7).

Because all her known work remained in manuscript until the nineteenth century, it was widely assumed that she was a 'private' author, who 'did not seek an audience' beyond her family; but recent studies have established the importance of 'manuscript circulation' in the seventeenth century (Looser 2000: 31–2). Margaret Ezell, for example, has argued that manuscript volumes were not 'closet productions' but 'first and foremost presentation pieces', intended to make 'their content available and attractive for future generations of readers', and that the circulation in manuscript—of works by men and women—'did not prevent one from having a reputation as a poet or philosopher' (Ezell 1987: 68, 70). Hutchinson's early verse translations are now considered to have had some currency through the shared commonplace book; and among the reasons she gives for preparing a fair copy of her Lucretius is that a manuscript has gone out of her hands 'by misfortune'. She clearly does not expect the new copy to sit unopened on Anglesey's shelves, since she begs him to include her repudiation of its atheistic contents, 'whereuer your Lordship shall dispose this booke', in the hope of protecting 'any novice who by chance might prie into it' (Hutchinson 2012: 5, 7, 15). The 'Life' of her husband may originally have been written to preserve the memory of their saintly father for her children, but commentators agree that 'her manuscripts continued to enjoy an audience and a reputation' right through the eighteenth century (Looser 2000: 32). Admittedly, she claims to have composed the *Principles* out of a mother's duty to 'exhort and admonish' her daughters and 'not for the presse' (Hutchinson 1817: 90, 91). But the even more 'private' elegies have been lauded as the work of a 'careful and conscious' artist, while one of several epitaphs tried out in the manuscript was displayed to the world on the Colonel's monument in Owthorpe church (Norbrook 1997: 470, 519).

Until recent years, critical interest has focused largely on Hutchinson's predicament as a female author in a patriarchal society. In Keeble's influential view, the 'tension' in the *Memoirs* between the 'dutiful wife' and the 'creatively bold writer' compelled her into a 'narrative deviousness' that reduces her, in the third person, to 'a minor character' in her husband's story but permits her to deploy material 'as best suits the Colonel's biography' in the role of a 'controlling' authorial 'I' (Hutchinson 2000: xxvi; Keeble 1990: 243, 237–8). Susan Cook suggests that it was 'the very act of dealing with these concepts of male and female roles in her writing' that gave her 'an individual voice' and enabled her to develop 'her own narrative style that tells her own story as much as it tells that of her husband' (1993: 271–2). A new perspective on her as a writer has now been opened up by the revelation that she was the author of *Order and Disorder*, the one work printed in her lifetime. She states in the preface that her 'meditations' on Genesis 'were not at first designed for public view' but goes on to defend the decision to publish them on religious rather than feminist grounds. She seeks 'no glory by it but what is rendered to him to whom it is only due' and measures success by the extent to which her work brings others 'to admire the glories and excellencies of our great Creator'. As for 'elevations of style', she would rather 'breath forth grace cordially [from the heart] than words artificially'; and she eschews the play of 'fancy', trembling 'to think of turning Scripture into a romance'. The use of verse is justified, however, by the Scriptures themselves, which command us 'to exercise our spiritual mirth in psalms and hymns and spiritual songs' (Hutchinson 2001: 3–5). In her versified account of the Creation and Fall, she confines herself rigorously to what is 'kept upon record | In the Creator's own revealèd Word' [1:177–8] and 'will not dare t'invent' details 'that we cannot know' about the rebellion in heaven [4:43–5], dismissing with contempt the 'gross poetic fables' [4:49] of the ancients and anxiously avoiding the dubious products of 'men's inventive brains' [3:158]. In the later cantos of what must now be regarded as her crowning achievement, she grows more confident in managing the biblical narrative, drawing out its significance, and supplying words and motives to the patriarchs and their wives (see Wilcher 2010). Robert Walker's painting of Lucy Hutchinson, designed as a companion to his portrait of Colonel Hutchinson in armour, fittingly depicts her with a child at her knee and a poet's laurel wreath in her hands.[14]

[14] The two portraits are reproduced in Sutherland's edition of *Memoirs*, facing pages 66 and 67.

CHAPTER 23

....

JOHN MILTON

....

CATHERINE GIMELLI MARTIN

MILTON has long been considered England's premier religious poet, a reputation he earned soon after the 1667 publication of his biblical epic, *Paradise Lost*. His most sympathetic early critic, John Dennis (1657–1734), located the epic's excellence in its inimitably sublime style, an assessment that endures today. Yet of all Christian poets, Milton is the one for whom the exact nature and provenance of his religious beliefs and commitments have proved most unusually elusive and remain controversial. Although long considered a Puritan poet, Milton never claimed that title or in fact any other than that of a staunch English Protestant. In his youth he trained for the ministry and subscribed to mainstream Church of England beliefs, but even that fact is somewhat unhelpful since the Church was by then increasingly split between reformers and traditionalists, ceremonialists and anti-ceremonialists, and the young Milton gives evidence of having been something of each. In maturity and to the end of his life, his beliefs became more idiosyncratic and he attended no religious services of any kind, simply worshipping at home with music and scriptural study. Evidence of his later, radical beliefs were recorded in his *De doctrina Christiana*, but mislaid in the Record Office of London until almost one hundred and fifty years after his death. The text was discovered in 1823, translated from Latin, and published in English in 1825. Daniel Skinner, Milton's amanuensis, seems to have attempted but failed to publish it in 1675, although the reasons for his failure remain murky. Its long-delayed publication made Milton's rejection of the co-eternal status of the Holy Trinity and the immortality of the soul far more shocking to conventional readers of the time than they would have been to his contemporaries, at least some of whom questioned these same doctrines. William B. Hunter's 1998 *Vision Unimplored* reviewed and rejected Milton's authorship of the treatise, but his objections were never widely accepted and have by now been largely disproved by stylistic analysis, which supports Milton's composition of this late work (Campbell et al. 2008).

Hunter's case was further hampered by the fact that in his own lifetime Milton was rightly considered a heterodox thinker in both religion and politics. Dennis was not alone in suspecting that *Paradise Lost* bore the 'taint' of Socinianism (a form of anti-Trinitarianism), even though he had no outside proof (1939: 345). This heresy is certainly not as marked in the epic as in *De doctrina*, but the poem's holy trinity is not as standard as it at first seems (Dobranski and Rumrich 1998). Yet in many ways, stressing Milton's heterodoxy may be missing the point, since he lived in an era when, as he frequently claims, being a staunch Protestant meant questioning received ideas, not clinging to narrow confessional criteria of faith. For instance, both Socinians and their 'cousins', the Deists, who believed that Christ was fully human, not divine, were commonly denounced for dishonouring him, but they themselves regarded his sacrifice as more superlative for that very reason. Adopting a more neutral and less anachronistic perspective on this and related questions surrounding Milton's Christianity is an important goal of this discussion, as too often his beliefs have been made to fit narrow definitions which he himself rejected. His final decision against taking holy orders was probably made to free himself from the narrow doctrinal commitments that sometimes perplexed the two great poet-priests of his era, John Donne and George Herbert. Whether he arrived at his unorthodoxy independently, as *De doctrina*'s preface claims, or through additional outside influences, is equally questionable, although he certainly did know and license the Socinians' *Racovian Catechism*. Like other decisions in Milton's public life, that led to trouble with the authorities, but he was never fined or incarcerated until 1660, when the Stuart Restoration led to his arrest and the burning of his anti-monarchical tracts.

Emphasizing Milton's life-long independence of mind is another central goal of this chapter, especially since it suggests the inadequacy of his twentieth-century reputation as a strict, dour Puritan. Historically, that reputation rests almost entirely on two political choices, his opposition to episcopacy in the initial phases of the English Civil War, and his support of Oliver Cromwell's regime afterward. Like the Lord Protector himself, that regime was certainly a product of religious Puritanism, yet like those who joined the cause against Archbishop William Laud, its supporters were more united by resistance to the policies and court of Charles I than by any common ideology (Tyacke 2001). Erroneous assumptions about the monolithic role of religion in the 'Puritan Revolution' were popularized in the late-nineteenth century by two prominent historians and a novelist turned historian, Thomas Carlyle.[1] The latter's highly romanticized and popularized edition of Oliver Cromwell's letters and papers inspired Samuel Gardiner and Sir Charles Firth to include his theories in their own empirical studies of the Civil War era (Samuel 1998: 279–89), resulting in a combined 'Puritan Revolution' theory that completely captivated Milton's first great biographer, the Victorian 'inventor' of the great Puritan Poet, David Masson. Few if any serious historians any longer accept their simplistic and ultimately anachronistic account of the Civil Wars, but until very recently, Milton's biographers have followed Masson's lead. Not only did his six volume account of Milton's life and times set a high benchmark for future scholarship, but few new facts about his or his family's religion

---

[1] The main problem lay in Carlyle's romantic belief that Puritans were liberals, whereas subsequent scholarship supports the long-held wisdom that they were conservatives (Tyacke 2001), radicals mainly in their extreme iconoclasm, which Milton never endorsed.

were thereafter discovered. That began to change with Gordon Campbell and Thomas Corns's 2008 biography, although long before, old myths such as Milton's personal closeness to Cromwell had begun to be discarded as pure legend. Ironically, Milton was one of the few poets to serve the Protectorate who produced no elegy or tribute upon its leader's untimely death, and despite his heroic opposition to the coming Stuart Restoration, Milton often blamed the failures of the revolutionary cause on excesses associated with the Puritan majority.[2]

Milton's career as a Puritan still lives on in the scholarship of a number of prominent critics,[3] in part because the romantic legend still appeals to many, and in part because Masson's 'Whig' account was written into the Yale edition of Milton's prose from the mid-1950s onward (Martin 2006). Many prominent reputations were thereafter invested in this account, the most prominent being that of the Marxist historian Christopher Hill, who both in his 1977 biography of Milton and other writings, continued Gardiner and Firth's practice of misidentifying Puritanism with radical social revolution, as numerous 'revisionist' historians have justly complained.[4] Nevertheless, a number of literary historians have begun to reassess Milton as a 'free' or even 'libertine' thinker who pursued unusually progressive causes all his life: freedom of speech; religion; marriage; politics; and greater sexual equality between men and women.[5] These causes repeatedly offended both Puritans and the general English public, for even in a controversial era, his opinions were far ahead of their time. Divorce, he believed, should be granted on grounds of incompatibility, not just adultery (the standard position), and Parliaments should be able to execute kings on grounds of suspected tyranny, not just treason, a far more radical position than the traditional 'divine right' belief that tyrant-kings could only be deposed by God. These were not Milton's only unpopular beliefs: he also opposed pre-publication censorship and a state-maintained, national church, both of which were supported by the vast majority of Englishmen and women; and he eventually rejected any form of monarchy and any suppression of Protestant heterodoxy.

In 1660 Milton's *The Readie and Easie Way to Establish a Free Commonwealth* proposed that England should be reconstituted as a republic ruled by a permanent senate, a most dangerous idea after King Charles II ascended his father's vacant throne that same year. The circumstances surrounding Milton's subsequent arrest and release remain cloudy, but his case was no doubt helped by the fact that he played no actual role in Charles I's execution. He was also aided by yet unknown friends or admirers, perhaps including his politician-friend, Andrew Marvell, the Royalist poet William Davenant, whose life he had reputedly saved, and Lady Katherine Ranelegh,

---

[2] See *Ad Ioannem Rousium* and below, especially on the 'Digression' from Milton's *History of Britain*.

[3] See, for example: Lewalski 2003a, 2003b; Loewenstein 2001; N. Smith 2009a.

[4] Some of the most outspoken include Pocock (1985b: 53), J. Clark (1986: 16, 106), and Morrill (1993: 279, 282).

[5] See, for example: Turner 2007a, 2007b; Martin 2004, 2010; Achinstein and Sauer 2007.

whose son he had tutored. Despite these well-connected allies, there is little doubt that Milton was consistently a rebel in religion, politics, and private life. Those who knew him well noted his highly sceptical, ironic, and at times irreverent wit (Aubrey 1960: 202), and even before he decided against taking holy orders, he turned against the universities and the clergy who ran them. Milton's Latin *Elegia* 1 (1626, at age 17) records his joy at being 'sent down' or suspended by his Cambridge tutor, William Chappell, while a personal letter to his friend Alexander Gil registers his keen disappointment with the conventionality of his fellow divinity students (Milton 1953–8 [hereafter referred to as *CPW*]: I, 314). In general, however, Milton's early poetry is less innovative than his great epic, but like his early masque, it often anticipates that achievement by consistently pushing or even reimagining the normative boundaries of generic convention.

In the early days of the English Civil Wars (1641–2) Milton composed five prose treatises bitterly denouncing prelacy, the episcopal system of church government controlled by the king, his bishops, and upper clergy. Two of these boldly mock his highly respected opponent, Bishop Joseph Hall, but much like Milton's other work, these tracts mainly identify him as an advanced intellectual earnestly struggling against mindless custom and tradition. At home his life seems to have been entirely amicable—he appears sincerely beloved and honoured by his family, his early tutor, Thomas Young, and his own pupils, including the two nephews Milton mostly raised, Edward and John Phillips. Like the rest of his family, Milton was deeply individualistic but rarely doctrinaire in personal matters (Saurat 1944; Zagorin 1992). His father hired the Puritan Young as his tutor, but at the same time sent him to St Paul's School, where both the headmaster Alexander Gil and his son of the same name held quite liberal Protestant views (D. Clark 1948). At Cambridge, Milton became friends with a ministerial candidate, Edward King, the much lamented 'Lycidas' of his famous elegy, who was himself a Laudian or 'high church' conservative. Later, his nephew Edward tells us that he freely reconciled with his estranged wife Mary Powell and her family despite their Royalist politics and his own hope of remarrying a certain 'witty Miss Davis', about whom nothing more is known (Phillips 1957: 1032). After losing Mary and their infant son, Milton remarried and enjoyed a brief but apparently deep happiness with Katharine Woodcock, whom he memorialized in an extremely moving Petrarchan dream vision, numbered Sonnet 23 in most editions. Milton's third and final marriage to Elizabeth Minshul seems to have been successful if also mostly practical, as he was by then completely blind with three difficult daughters to raise. Previously, he seems not to have been the best of parents, probably leaving most child-rearing duties to Mary and his decidedly hostile mother-in-law, but there is little evidence to support Samuel Johnson's charges of misogyny against Milton, which he blatantly used to undermine his politics (Martin 2004).

Milton did, however, enter into an apparently brief family conflict after completing his Cambridge MA degree and deciding to dedicate his life to poetry rather than the ministry. His Latin poem to his father, *Ad Patrem*, expresses his youthful hopes and fears for his future while lamenting his father's disapproval of his decision to abandon his original vocation. His affection and concern for his disappointed parent seem entirely convincing, but his rationale for exclusively pursuing poetry is less so, since Milton did not really face an 'either/or' choice between writing and preaching. Both Donne and Herbert successfully combined clerical with poetic careers, as did other ministers ranging from the pious Puritan Richard Baxter to the jovial cavalier, Robert Herrick (J. Hill 1979). Evasion is not Milton's usual stock-in-trade, so the decision must have been a difficult and, perhaps, guilt-inducing one. His *Reason of Church Government* (1642) compensates for his mixed feelings by claiming the right to 'meddle' with religious reform because he was wrongly 'Church-outed by the Prelats' (*CPW*: I, 823), although at best, this claim is hyperbolic, and at worst, simply wrong: Milton had already taken all necessary oaths for ordination when he left Cambridge to embark on private studies, and the prelates at that time could demand nothing more (Hunter 1989: 181; Fixler 1964: 48).

Milton's early 'Letter to a Friend' seems to come closer to the truth, as does his Sonnet 7, which he originally included in the letter. Both admit to his feeling 'unripe' although already well into his twenties, for despite his early precocity, he has as yet borne little 'fruit' or even decided on what profession to pursue. He denies his friend's charge that he is dreaming his life away, but adds that if ordained, he would likely 'spoyle all the patience of a Parish' (*CPW*: I, 320–1). Evidently his religious interests were too intellectual or idiosyncratic to serve a congregation well, and leaving his solitary pursuits might also 'spoil' his own patience. In addition, Milton may have had strong ethical reservations about leading a congregation since he knew and cited Chaucer's and Spenser's tributes to ideally selfless pastors (*CPW* I, 560, 723). Loving and serving their congregations as a parent loves a child or as Christ loves his 'bride', the church, true pastors must sacrifice their private lives for the greater good of the flock, a sacrifice Milton may have been unable to make. He thus settled on a private teaching career to support himself, his private studies of political and religious history, and his high poetic ambitions, while resolving his perceived conflict between duty and self-fulfilment by using his learning to serve his nation as a public intellectual.

The tracts on church government Milton produced during this period remain of interest because they include overt promises about dedicating his poetic gifts to his God and country. He eventually kept those promises, but both the subject and style of his great poem were as yet undetermined, and they remained so for nearly twenty years (*CPW*: I, 804–23). In part, his efforts were delayed by his later writings in defence of English liberty, which span the years from the first Parliamentary republic through the Protectorate; and in part, they were hindered by disappointments on all sides. Epic poetry had become problematic not just for Milton but for his entire generation (Helgerson 1983): Abraham Cowley abandoned hope and left his biblical epic on King David unfinished, but the blind Milton at last succeeded against all odds in producing not just the greatest of all English epics but also a grand masterpiece of European literature.

Religion and Reform in Milton's Prose Tracts and 'Protest' Sonnets

Milton's rejection of 'implicit faith' both in his anti-episcopal tracts and in *De doctrina Christiana* provides a touchstone for his opposition to most traditional sources of authority, which he frequently identifies with 'tyranny and superstition,' the twin enemies to 'life's well being', as well as to England's intellectual and spiritual reformation (*CPW*: VI, 118). This statement prefaces *De doctrina*, which he probably began at about the time he stopped attending church, since his preface also states that his studies were intensified by the mistakes, spurious linguistic and logical quibbles, and outright 'dishonesty' of most mainstream Protestant theologians (*CPW*: VI, 120). This remark further reflects Milton's lifelong disdain for the logical sophistry of the scholastic divinity he learned at Cambridge, yet that is hardly his only reason for composing his religious treatise (see its chapter 16). Relying on the opinion of others in matters of belief is inherently dangerous, since 'God has revealed the way of eternal salvation only to the individual faith of each man, and demands of us that any man who wishes to be saved should work out his beliefs for himself' (*CPW*: VI, 119). He dates his studies in the original Bible languages to his boyhood, when he began compiling scriptural citations under general headings for reference purposes, just as he does in *De doctrina*. His work was additionally motivated by strong disapproval of complacent Protestants (*CPW*: VI, 119–20), whom *Areopagitica* denounces as 'heretics in the truth' no more faithful to God than the notorious Catholic idolaters of Loretto (*CPW*: II, 543–4).

Similar principles underlie Milton's lifelong objection to Catholicism, which like other Protestants, he elsewhere accuses of neglecting 'the way of eternal salvation' (*CPW*: VI, 119) by not relying on individual faith alone. In practice, however, he seems to have been quite tolerant, openly admiring many Catholic scholars, poets, and Italian patrons of the arts, and also enjoying their company abroad, as both his early poems and private letters reveal (*CPW*: I, 328–36, II, 762–75).[6] Nevertheless, his final prose treatise, *Of True Religion*, again berates Catholics at home for encouraging both 'implicit faith and loyalty to a foreign power', the papacy. Yet it is important to keep in mind that the tract directly responds to the 'No Popery' Parliament of 1673, itself a response to Charles II's Catholic sympathies, which overtly threatened English liberty. It also contains multiple allusions and silent citations of the English Latitudinarians, the most tolerant branch of the established Church (*CPW*: VIII, 408, 413), which similarly supported the inclusion of all Protestants who wished to rejoin its communion. Milton concedes many sects have made pardonable and hence unproblematic 'errors' in theology; and he even admits in *De doctrina* that as Catholics had charged, Calvinists who teach predestination are guilty

---

[6] Milton's *Defensio Secunda* repeats his high respect for a wide variety of Catholic scholars, poets, and personal friends.

of making God responsible for sin (*CPW*: VI, 166). That does not absolve Catholics of 'implicit faith' in their religious authorities, but when Milton began composing *Paradise Lost*, the Calvinist problem was apparently uppermost in his mind: its clearly defined task of justifying 'God's ways to man' depends on proving that sin is the sole invention of Satan, not God (*PL* 1.26 [Milton's longer poems are abbreviated by the first letters in their titles and cited from Milton 2008]). Milton's 'free will' explanation for its existence thus distances him from both traditional Calvinists (Danielson 1982) and their Puritan offshoots (Martin 2010), but his theological independence strengthens both the project and the rhetorical power of *Paradise Lost,* making it a far more universal epic than any doctrinaire Protestant epic could ever be. Although he initially feared that it would be read by only a 'fit, … though few' audience (*PL* 7.31), the epic was destined to appeal to an enormous range of religious readers—Christian, Jewish, Muslim, Hindi—and even many secular doubters of the God who is there in some sense put on trial.

After Milton completed his anti-episcopal tracts, he continued his campaigns for liberty both in his divorce tracts and in *Areopagitica* (1644), where his chief exemplar of the perils of censorship is Galileo, a Catholic victim of the Pope who later reappears in *Paradise Lost* as a great explorer and symbolic cosmic guide. *Areopagitica* also features a stirring millenarian vision of progress wherein Francis Bacon, John Selden, and Lord Brooke (the recently 'martyred' Robert Greville, an early opponent of Charles I) symbolically join Galileo and important earlier English Reformers in leading the way forward. All of these individuals, he states, encourage open debate and innovation that will help shatter the shackles of custom and conformity in both church and state. Like his near-contemporary treatise *Of Education, Areopagitica* portrays a highly idealistic reformer equally steeped in Baconian ideas of progress and in the best traditions of Renaissance humanism. Along with the religious ideals early pioneered in England by John Wyclif and John Huss (*CPW*: II, 553), he hopes that previously suppressed or 'unthinkable' ideas will reinvigorate learning and construct a perpetually unfinished and expanding 'temple' of Truth (*CPW*: II, 540–55). Unfortunately, Milton would never again sound quite so confident about England's future, but strong echoes of *Areopagitica* do reappear in two late tracts on religious liberty and church reform, *Of Civil Power* and *The Likeliest Means to Remove Hirelings Out of the Church* (both 1659). In *The Likeliest Means,* the mature Milton's plans for reforming the clergy have become quite radical: ministers should be educated locally, as his own pupils were, and thereafter serve their home communities. Freed from the burdensome scholastic divinity taught at the universities, they should study the three original languages of the Bible along with ample commentaries and outside sources. These proposals generally support Milton's life-long belief that congregations should learn alongside their ministers and not on their knees before university 'gentlemen'. Following the example of the apostle Paul, ministers should also be self-supporting, ideally serving as physicians like the Waldensian pastors of northern France and Italy whom he so strongly approved. 'On the Late Massacre at Piedmont', his only poem in praise of contemporary Christian martyrs, laments the slaughter that drove these 'saints' from their remote Alpine villages and prays that God will avenge them by spreading true religion across the land.

The Waldensian cause was strongly supported in England by both mainstream Protestants and the reformers of the Samuel Hartlib circle, with which Milton was affiliated and which similarly furthered Bacon's intellectual and scientific proposals for progress (Webster 1970). Bacon's programmes have often been misunderstood by critics as severely utilitarian or even anti-poetic, but more astute commentators like David Faldet (1990) capture the excitement, energy, and challenge also echoed in Milton's *Areopagitica*: 'Anticipating a tremendous growth in [all] areas of learning, Bacon proposes that he is but "stirring the earth a little about the roots of science"' and human knowledge. He 'knows that some of this digging and stirring will seem disturbing' and even disrespectful to traditional humanists, but he feels that their efforts have become stale and static over time and 'sees his age as a kind of springtime of learning which hints at the possibility of a rich harvest'. More radically, he issues a challenge to clear away the 'cobwebs' of the past, the 'misconceptions, false values, bad methods, and burdensome institutional structures' that have produced 'the useless and overly erudite studies of the scholastics' (Faldet 1990: 27, 28).[7] *Areopagitica* uses precisely the same metaphors of springtime and future harvests, and its reformist companion piece, *Of Education*, just as closely echoes Bacon's complaint that 'rhetoric and logic are taught too early in the years of education, dominating the curriculum at a time when students would be better served by instruction which provided them with greater stores of information' (Faldet 1990: 32).

Milton's controversial belief that marriage was not a sacrament but a civil contract ideally free from church jurisdiction is most directly indebted to his early reading of John Selden's Hebrew scholarship on marriage (Rosenblatt), but his own disastrous first marriage also played a part. His nephew and early biographer Phillips relates that Mary Powell—daughter of a fun-loving family whom he wed after an unusually brief courtship—soon proved incompatible with her new husband and his quiet, scholarly lifestyle (Phillips 1957: 1031). When she deserted him and returned home after a few short months of marriage, Milton characteristically responded with his pen, setting to work on divorce arguments probably sketched sometime before, as his first rather lengthy divorce treatise, *The Doctrine and Discipline of Divorce*, appeared less than a year after her departure (August 1643). He was summoned before Parliament for writing it but apparently acquitted. Never one to be discouraged by public defeat, Milton began studying earlier Protestant discussions of marriage and divorce, where he found that the well-respected theologian Martin Bucer had held views very similar to his own. He soon translated and published his discovery as *The Judgement of Martin Bucer concerning Divorce* (1644); when that proved unsuccessful, he wrote two more tracts, the most important of which, *Tetrachordon* (1645), reviews the four biblical 'chords' or chains of marital commentary in Genesis, Deuteronomy, Matthew, and 1 Corinthians, along with opinions based on Roman law and Protestant teaching. His last and least important divorce tract (*Colasterion*, 1645) simply rebuts an anonymous attacker.

---

[7] For a full comparison of these rhetorical congruences, see Fish 1972 and Martin 2010.

The Doctrine and Discipline of Divorce is a first learned consideration of a knotty theological problem: Christ's sudden departure from Jewish marital tradition, which had long permitted both polygamy and divorce on grounds of 'uncleanness'. Milton decides partly on the basis of humanistic considerations and partly on the basis of the Christian 'rule of charity' that Jesus did not literally forbid divorce or remarriage but was instead slyly taunting the Pharisees for their biblical literalism and legalism. These biases led them to disregard God's charitable decrees toward man, as Christians still do in failing to see that God's primary purpose in giving Adam a spouse was to provide a proper helpmate, not simply a vehicle for procreation, as the Church of England traditionally taught. 'Uncleanness' must therefore mean 'unfitness', as no man can be truly 'married' without his wife's 'meet help', which requires not just sexual but emotional, spiritual, and mental compatibility. In arguing this case Milton expresses some personal sentiments about the difficulties inexperienced bachelors find in assessing emotional compatibility in modest maidens, but mutuality remains the basis of true love, not mere physical attraction. His prose *Apology* earlier relates that he learned these romantic ideals from Petrarch and Dante (*CPW*: I, 890), and they later influence his depiction of Adam and Eve's prelapsarian marriage, where sexual satisfaction naturally follows from emotional and intellectual kinship.

Milton's bitterness about his divorce tracts' poor reception surfaces in two powerful poems, Sonnets 11 and 12, 'Upon the Detraction Which Followed upon My Writing Certain Treatises', and 'On the Same' (1646?); both denounce close-minded contemporaries who failed to distinguish between true 'liberty' and 'license'. Another early sonnet is a strongly worded polemic against the Presbyterians, whose system of church government Milton had loosely argued for in both *Of Reformation* (1641) and *The Reason of Church Government* (1642). After prelacy collapsed along with the Laudian regime, the Westminster Assembly led by the Presbyterian faction replaced the bishops, but unfortunately proved, as Milton's 'On the New Forcers of Conscience under the Long Parliament' (1646?) asserts, that they were merely 'Old Priest[s] writ Large' (20). Less than ten years before, Milton's *Lycidas*—long considered the finest, most innovative pastoral elegy in English—just as bitterly condemned the episcopal priests then running the Church. In a famous digression, he imagines St Peter denouncing these hypocrites just as in 'The New Forcers of Conscience' St Paul's example condemns the Presbyterians. Milton never forgave them for his vast disappointment, as his *Tenure of Kings and Magistrates* (1649) makes abundantly clear, but there is no evidence that he thereafter converted to the Independents or Congregationalists, who preached a similar Calvinist theology and were even stricter about church doctrine than the Presbyterians (Martin 2010: 128–43). Yet none of this is really surprising, since the 'Long Digression' initially cut from Milton's *History of Britain* rails against the entire Westminster Assembly of Divines. Milton may, however, have partly forgiven the Church of England since he twice abided by its marriage rites and was buried in it beside his father at St Giles Cripplegate, quite probably in answer to a death bed request made to his brother Christopher.[8]

---

[8] A 'Dissenters' cemetery was actually closer to Milton's home and would have been probably preferred by his third wife, Elizabeth Minshul, a Baptist.

In general, however, Milton's rapid changes of heart are highly principled, reflecting his steadfast commitment to reform amid changing circumstances and frequent disillusionment. Later in life he summarized his prose writings as concerted, progressive efforts to secure religious, domestic, and civil liberty for England, and ideally, the entire Western world (CPW: IV.1, 624, 555–6). Milton never achieved these lofty goals in his lifetime, but he did preserve them for the future, as he himself foresees in Sonnet 22, 'To Mr. Cyriak Skinner on His Blindness'; the poem celebrates both the international success of his *Defensio pro populo Anglicano* [*Defence of the English People*] (1651) and the personal sacrifice of his eyesight in defending Parliament's proceedings against Charles I on charges of treason, along with broader issues of basic human rights.

RELIGION IN MILTON'S EARLY LATIN AND ENGLISH POEMS

Aside from the occasional insights afforded by Milton's prose digressions and protest sonnets, however, significant gaps persist in Milton's biography, since he was often as personally reserved about his domestic and religious affairs as he was publically open when matters of principle were at stake. That reserve extends to his private religious poetry, which is rarely cast in the confessional mode favoured by contemporaries ranging from Donne and Herbert to John Bunyan. Milton's general silence about religious or personal anxieties along with his unflagging commitment to core ideals has led some critics to portray him as incapable of doubt or incertitude (Fallon), although such accusations seem less than just. It is nevertheless true that none of his personal or public disappointments seriously unsettled Milton's faith in God or in his just dispensation toward mankind, much less toward himself, and he never viewed his losses as signs of rejection or desertion by the Holy Spirit. Aside from Edmund Spenser (see chapter 18), near-contemporary religious poets are far less confident, frequently haunted by fears of divine disfavour, but Milton's poetry, letters, and other writings never indicate that he anxiously searched for signs of grace or salvation or ever abjectly pleaded for divine assistance to redeem him from sinful unworthiness. The most probable reason for his deviation from these norms lies in his self-declared reverence for Spenser, whom he considered a better teacher 'than *Aquinas* or *Scotus*' (*CPW*: II, 515–16). What the romance poet Spenser more often 'teaches', however, is the optimistic philosophy of Italian Neoplatonism than the gloomy doctrines of sin and predestination stressed by Calvin and his followers, none of whom Milton cites approvingly.[9]

A secondary reason for Milton's lack of obsession with sin is even better established. Again like Spenser, he seems to have adopted Arminian or 'free will' teachings

---

[9] *De Doctrina*'s stern dismissal of standard teachings on predestination often specifically aim at William Perkins, a seminal English Calvinist theologian, but it generally opposes the doctrine *in toto*.

on salvation *avant la lettre*—that is, probably before he encountered Jacob Arminius's modification of standard Calvinist doctrine, which effectively allows individuals to cooperate in their salvation. When or how seriously he read Arminius is more debatable, but free will theology certainly dominates not only the 'theodicy' of *Paradise Lost* (Danielson 1982) but also very early sonnets like Sonnet 7, Milton's poem on his twenty-third year. During his youth and young manhood his father in fact supported a chapel with pronounced Arminian leanings, although in England that mostly meant that it placed greater emphasis on ceremony and sacraments than on preaching (Corns 2002). As a religious polemicist, Milton later rejected this emphasis in favour of teaching and prayer, but as a poet, his free will teaching is often complemented by traditional symbols, hymns, and ceremonies. In his personal sonnets he is most fearful and vulnerable when he ponders his potential failure to fulfil his poetic vocation or redeem his 'talents', as emphasized in both Sonnet 7 and his more famous Sonnet 19, 'On His Blindness'. In Sonnet 7 he suspects that his late 'flowering' may mean that his early promise was illusory; in Sonnet 19 he worries that loss of sight may leave him permanently unfulfilled, while in many earlier poems he agonizes over premature death. *Lycidas* is usually and rightly read not just as a tribute to Edward King but as an attempt to master fears of dying young, but as usual, here he gains strength by at once acknowledging and overcoming doubt. Not for nothing was his personal motto 'My strength is made perfect in weakness' (2 Cor. 12:9–10), a quotation he often inscribed in autograph albums after he went blind. This Pauline conviction is completely consistent with the religious outlook of his time, as was his devotion to his 'dearest and best possession', the independent scriptural studies that produced *De doctrina* (*CPW*: VI, 121). In all those respects, Milton was by no means exclusively a poet of the future, but a classic Protestant conventionally seeking salvation according to his own lights.

Milton's Latin poetry, including his last and finest effort in this mode—*Epitaphium Damonis*, a pastoral elegy lamenting the premature death of his dear friend Charles Diodati—draws on classical themes and motifs originally derived from pagan ritual and belief but long since Christianized. They include rites of spring, tributes to Orpheus, Apollo, and Cupid (in that order), laments for ideal but fleeting love (also the theme of Milton's Italian sonnets), and holiday meditations set in semi-classical contexts. His Latin Elegia 6 exemplifies the latter approach: at Christmas he meditates upon the stoical and abstemious life demanded by epic verse as opposed to the merrier life permitted by lyric, the mode he jocularly tells Diodati he is best suited to pursue. Yet the poem cannot be taken too literally, since Milton shows himself almost equally divided between the two modes in his Italian theme poems, *L'Allegro* and *Il Penseroso*, which brilliantly contrast poetry's lighter and faster mood ('allegro') with its darker, heavier, and more pensive range ('penseroso'). The debate between these competing 'twins' had been a standard feature of Italian Neoplatonism from Marsilio Ficino onward (Klibansky et al. 1964: 228–31), but even Spenser fails to 'English' this tradition as thoroughly as the young Milton did. The tradition's central aim was to reconcile the 'secret' wisdom of the ancients with Christian revelation, which also meant harmonizing human with physical nature and its various nature spirits or 'genii'. Along with his classical training,

Milton's early interest in this neo-pagan system underlies much of his early Latin poetry and English lyrics as well as the masque popularly known as *Comus*. Here, as in more minor poems, he invokes an inaudible, allegorical 'music of the spheres' and pays homage to divine 'star souls' who have briefly visited the planet but too soon departed. These souls are so pure that their bloom quickly fades when touched by sinful earth, but much as in Spenser's *Four Hymnes*, their virtue shines forth in a physical beauty which at least temporarily illuminates the world.

Whether or not Milton fully credited these Neoplatonic beliefs or was merely indulging in youthful 'dreaming' is difficult to determine, but he artfully employs and refines them throughout his early verse. Some efforts in this vein have gained small critical acclaim or interest, such as the lovely 'On the Death of a Fair Infant Dying of Cough' (an elegy for his infant niece) and his 'Epitaph on the Marchioness of Windsor', while others like *Lycidas* and his masque are considered early masterpieces. Milton's 'On the Morning of Christ's Nativity' is another outstanding success in this mode, showing sinful Nature cleansed with snow and temporarily reborn to receive the infant Jesus. The music of the spheres then becomes newly audible and prophesies an imminent age of gold partly realized by the flight of the pagan gods from their temples. Most of these motifs are traditional features of nativity poems, but Milton's ability to breathe new life into them forecasts his lifelong talent for reconciling pagan myth with Christian revelation. The saviour's eternal rule is naturally postponed, but the pagan gods ironically return as benign nature spirits in 'Arcades', 'At a Solemn Music', and *A Masque Presented at Ludlow Castle*. In the latter, the sinister enchanter Comus, an immortal spirit of immoral mirth, foreshadows the figure of Satan in *Paradise Lost*.

Not all 'star souls' die young in Milton's early poems, most significantly, not if they also happen to be superlative artists like Comus's antithesis, the Lady of the masque, like the Shakespeare of his poetic encomium, or like Leonora Baroni, the famed Italian singer to whom he dedicated three Latin tributes. He accords similar praise to his musical collaborator in *A Masque*, the Royalist musician Henry Lawes, because he, too, successfully united voice with verse. By combining these 'twins' in her rapturous song, Milton's Lady triumphs over temptation, potential rape, and symbolic death, although Comus can and does imprison her in her own mortal body. Yet he can do no more, as her literally 'impenetrable' virtue summons first a Heavenly Attendant and then a mystical water spirit, Sabrina, to rescue her after her brothers forget to reverse Comus's wand. Before that climax, Milton includes a charming debate between the Elder Brother, who believes that voluntary chastity is an invincible force, and his younger, more practical, and less Platonic Brother. Neither 'wins', but the Elder is more right than wrong: Comus is so awe-struck by his victim's self-possessed eloquence and her personal as well as musical purity that his attempt to force her to drink from his enchanted cup is postponed long enough for her rescuers to arrive. In its ending, as always for Milton, music embodies heavenly bliss, which his elegies show both King and Diodati experiencing on high.

Following standard pastoral conventions, both elegies open in the thoroughly pagan world of nymphs and gods derived from the Arcadian landscapes of Theocritus and his

Roman successor, Virgil. Virgil's *Eclogues* set a lasting precedent by at once celebrating the innocence of nature and its loss due to the advent of war and death. Milton's genius for bringing these ancient themes to life significantly contributes to his later success in depicting Eden and its fall from innocence as Satan succeeds in taking revenge for his failed war in heaven. Earlier, *Lycidas* skilfully altered this pattern by showing how his friend's dedication to poetry made him immune to the temptations of the 'nymphs' or country girls but not to an unexpected, unearned death by drowning. Lycidas nevertheless reaps the eternal reward proclaimed by Apollo above, and below, by St Michael, as he becomes the 'genius' or guardian spirit of the English/Welsh shore. Like Milton's *Epitaphium Damonis*, the poem concludes with a heavenly feast, although the Latin poem has a much sadder tone because Diodati's ascent barely compensates for his friend's bitterness that he was absent, enjoying himself in Italy with new poetic brethren, when his boyhood companion died. Sadder still, they all are now absent, incapable of compensating him for a loss expressible only in divine verse.

A predominant theme in Milton's best early work is thus obviously premature death, loss, and partial recovery, either on earth or among the heavenly host. Poems in this mode (where he still evidently believes in the soul's immortality) usually begin with passionate mourning and end with rapturous celebration, but later, as in Sonnet 19 'On his Blindness', both mourning and recovery are increasingly understated. Milton's passionate mode nevertheless returns both in 'On the Late Massacre' and a sonnet sternly warning Cromwell against sanctioning religious intolerance. Otherwise, however, his English sonnets are quietly reserved or 'Horatian' in tone, pointing far ahead to the style of *Paradise Regained*. They alternately praise noble Christian souls like an unnamed 'Lady who in the prime' of life proceeds straight up the narrow path to the pinnacle of truth, or noble 'Romans' like Thomas Fairfax and Henry Vane, and to a lesser extent, Cromwell. Two other important sonnets, 20 and 21, celebrate luscious but tasteful recreations or issue reminders that all work and no play makes Cyriak Skinner a dull boy (Sonnet 21). As a whole, they exhibit dramatic stylistic improvements on the more artificial Petrarchan style of earlier Elizabethan sonnets (Smart). Among these successes, Milton also chalks up two striking failures that testify to his consistent inability to come to terms with Christ's sacrificial suffering on the cross, 'Upon the Circumcision' and 'The Passion', a poem that the poet himself claimed he could not finish because it was 'above his years'.

Milton's mature epics continue this pattern by failing to create a moving portrayal of Christ's crucifixion. *Paradise Lost* barely mentions it, dwelling instead on scenes where the Son of God reigns mercifully beside his heavenly Father, conventionally softening the latter's justice with love. Its 'sequel', *Paradise Regained*, omits the crucifixion altogether, preferring to portray the Son of God's triumph in overcoming Satan's wilderness temptations. Yet, as shown in *Lycidas, Epitaphium Damonis* and his tribute to his 'late espoused saint', Katharine, Milton was not incapable of expressing overwhelming grief or passion. He simply seems far better at imagining dignified godly debate or outrage than abject pain or sorrow; even *Lycidas* psychologically offsets mourning for King with St Peter's thunderous denunciation of the false, 'ear-tickling' clerics corrupting the church. Such diatribes have a long lineage, running from Dante's outrage against corrupt priests through Chaucer's disgust with clerical frauds and hypocrites, and later, from Spenser's satirical invective in *The Shepheardes Calendar* to Milton's own acrimony against the betrayers of religious reform. In much the same spirit, *Paradise Lost* depicts the Father of angels and men angrily denouncing his human children's betrayal, a much criticized choice, but one successfully counterpointed as the Son mounts his Father's chariot and quells the fury raging in heaven much as he later mitigates its damage on earth.

PARADISE LOST

Milton's composition of *Paradise Lost* followed a long dry period in which he produced abundant prose but little poetry aside from the minor verse surveyed above. When he began the epic, his 1638 masque had been his last major work. All his early verse, except his political sonnets, had appeared in a 1645 volume of collected Latin and English poems which was successful—but not exceptionally so. His wife Mary returned that same year, but three years later in 1648 he had still not begun his promised epic, embarking instead on a *History of Britain* finally completed in 1670, three years after *Paradise Lost*. Both works may have been finished much earlier if the political crisis caused by Charles I's execution had not led to Milton's commission to defend Parliament, which he did in *The Tenure of Kings and Magistrates* and *Eikonoklastes* (both 1649), and again in his two Latin defences of the English people (1651, 1654). He was rewarded with an appointment to the Council of State as Secretary for Foreign Tongues, a post which kept him busy until his sight began to fail and he required assistance from his friend Marvell and the young John Dryden. Milton's blindness apparently became total in 1652, but in some ways that was a blessing in disguise. With the help of both paid and volunteer amanuenses, he began the long delayed masterpiece that would at last bring him the 'immortality of fame' he had dreamt of since youth (*CPW*: I, 327). His nephew Edward Phillips relates that he first composed the astonishing speech by Satan that now opens Book 4, a self-reflection soon converted into self-condemnation (Phillips 1957: 1034–45). As the work progressed, the ill effects of the Stuart Restoration further shaped the epic theme Milton announces in the invocation to Book 1, humankind's tragic fall into moral, spiritual, and political sin.

The narrative begins with Satan's awakening in hell after being ejected from heaven, an event loosely derived from Isaiah. Most other details are either Milton's own or loosely derived from Dante, although his daring technique of allowing Satan to tell his own side of the story, then regroup and plot revenge against God by seducing the human race, is almost entirely original. So is Satan's escape from hell with the help of his 'children', Sin and Death, and his subsequent arrival on earth. There he spies on and even pities the first humans, although in their majestic innocence they are anything but pitiable. Their imminent doom has nevertheless already been foreseen (not foreordained) by God, who pardons them in advance, while his Son volunteers to ransom them from eternal death, if not from every enduring ill-effect of sin. God additionally sends the Archangel Raphael to warn and counsel them, which conveniently adds a new account of how Satan began a War in Heaven due to envy at the Son's elevation in rank, and how a new world arose to counterpoise his fall. After this long flashback, Milton focuses on the psychological events leading to Eve's violation of God's sole command, his prohibition of the Tree of the Knowledge of Good and Evil. After Adam voluntarily joins her in eating from it, the dark days recorded in Genesis rapidly unfold, glossed by a lengthy allegorical episode featuring Satan, Sin, and Death, and a moral lecture by a new Archangel, Michael.

Milton's own 'dark days' during the Restoration are recorded in Book 7, at the exact midpoint of the epic. Here he also provides a visually dynamic account of the Genesis story of creation and, in the third of the epic's four invocations, names his epic Muse as 'Urania' (*PL* 7.28–31), not the Greek muse of astronomy but her higher heavenly 'meaning, not the name' (7.5–8). Summoning Urania perfectly complements Milton's second invocation in Book 3, which meditates on how his blindness and exile from the 'book of nature fair' are compensated through inner 'sight' (*PL* 3.45–7). In Book 9 the fourth and final invocation adds more personal revelations, famously claiming that the poet was 'Not sedulous by nature to indite | Wars, hitherto the only argument | Heroic deemed' (*PL* 9.27–9). In fact, however, Milton had long contemplated an epic on an Arthurian theme, but as usual, he is not actually lying: after 'long choosing, and beginning late', he indeed seems to have discovered that his 'unpremeditated verse' flowed most 'easily' after finding an entirely new topic, which he terms 'the better fortitude | Of patience and heroic martyrdom | Unsung' (*PL* 9.31–3). This theme is expansive enough to include a War in Heaven, although Milton's classically armoured good angels cannot achieve the final victory reserved for the Son and his healing 'chariot of paternal deity' (*PL* 6.750). Most likely Milton's new theme especially pleased him because it expresses his disenchantment with futile civil warfare as well as with the Orpheus-destroying, Bacchic 'revelers' who have taken over with the restored Stuart court (*PL* 7.32–7), Orpheus had long been the legendary poet most sacred to Milton, and so he remains here, but he now stands for the 'lower truths' sung by pre-Christian poets. Milton himself sings the higher truths that not just Adam and Eve but all their children need to cope with their fallen condition, which is additionally assisted by divine grace.

In many respects, however, the epic magnificence of the poem only partly derives from this brilliant plot: its setting in a vastly expanded epic universe which retains some familiar, residual elements of earlier cosmic poetry provides the rest. Satan's initial difficulty in locating earth strongly suggests that he is not flying through the old concentric, earth-centred Ptolemaic spheres, but through newly immense, post-Copernican 'multiverses' (Danielson 2010). This cosmic system is implicitly heliocentric since Milton consigns the old Ptolemaic cosmos to his Paradise of Fools, a limbo-like 'nowhere' occupied by idiots blown 'ten thousand leagues' off course before vanishing into the 'devious air' (*PL* 3.481–9). A similar fate will ultimately apply to Satan, but after escaping from Chaos at the boundary of the created world, he significantly discovers 'innumerable stars' which seem to harbour 'other worlds' or 'happy isles' apparently inhabited by unfallen species (*PL* 3.565–8). This discovery provides another clear indicator of the new astronomy, where space is filled with matter, not crystalline spheres or perfect but uninhabited circles (Martin 2001). Satan may seem an unreliable witness, but the expanded material nature of this universe is later confirmed by Raphael, who also informs his pupils that God's creation is an evolving material continuum. That system allows him to descend and 'lunch' with Adam and Eve, and it may also allow them to ascend to heaven as their material bodies become lighter and purer through continued love and obedience (*PL* 5.469–505). This promise is naturally never realized, but the universe's atomistic structure is further confirmed during Satan's voyage through Chaos, a confused void filled with embryonic forms of every atom, gas, and proto-substance discarded from God's co-eternal being, Light, which dwells both around him and under the floor of heaven. Here Satan finds the 'infernal flame' needed to fire his cannons, which appropriately fuel his flaming descent to hell (*PL* 3.1–12, 2.1034–5, 6.474–83).

The three most commonly acknowledged proto-scientific influences on Milton's epic cosmos are Hesiod, Lucretius, and Dante, although the poem as a whole represents a breathtaking synthesis of the mainline classical, Italian, and English epic traditions. Spenser's style of epic allegorizing was out fashion by the time Milton wrote *Paradise Lost*, but he pays partial tribute to it in the Sin and Death episodes of Books 2 and 10, which visually translate the biblical warning that when sin becomes 'fertile' or active, it gives birth to death (James 1:13–15) (Martin 1998). The basic plan of charting a complete voyage through a tripartite universe owes something to Homer, but more to Dante. Satan reverses Dante's ascent, but his expedition seems heroic enough to convince some critics that he is Milton's alter-ego or ideal rebel.[10] By comparison, Dante's hideous Satan frozen to the floor of hell is nobody's candidate for heroism, but Milton's invocations almost certainly recall Dante's device of using himself as a protagonist in the plot. The main contrast is that Satan's inverse voyage contrarily proves that God's free will principles are operative even in hell, where he and his cohort hold debates and councils, hatch plans, play games, sing moving songs, and build themselves gilded palaces symbolizing false or superficial glory. From Hesiod Milton is generally agreed to take the idea that Chaos and Night exist before the 'prime matter' from which everything is made and to which it may again revert (*PL* 2.911). Hesiod is also a main source for the third day of Milton's War in Heaven, a Christianized version of the Greek war of giants, or chthonic rebels against Zeus. Lucretius is present both in Milton's atomistic, evolving notion of creation and in the force that sets it in motion—in Lucretius, love or desire, but in Milton, the divine love visibly enacted by the Son.

Divine love is not entirely absent from the postlapsarian world of Books 10 to 12, but Adam and Eve's new life requires a far grimmer or 'iron age' version of the golden age work ethic governing heaven and Eden. In the heavens, 'saints' like Abdiel and unintentionally erroneous angels, like Uriel, briefly suffer defeat or dishonour, but that only

---

[10] Neil Forsythe is the most recent in a long line beginning with William Blake and other Romantic poets to argue in this vein, but earlier critics saw Satan as Milton's hero only in the sense of 'main protagonist'.

makes their recovery more glorious. In Eden, humans like Eve may experience guilty dreams that leave no 'spot or trace behind' if their 'love and obedience' to God remains intact (*PL* 5.118, 501–2), but once fallen, they must exert great individual effort despite gravely limited knowledge and power. As in heaven, however, God rewards even their most imperfect efforts, as Uriel, his 'eyes' on the sun, especially shows. Uriel is easily deceived into directing Satan to earth since this disguised 'cherub' claims to be seeking greater knowledge, itself a praise-worthy goal. Yet the archangel is undiminished by this error since only God can detect hypocrisy and since further observation allows him to correct his mistake, thus setting a pattern of trial and error for the rest of creation. Observing Satan's rage at the new proof on earth of the Almighty's majesty, benevolence, and power, Uriel warns earth's guardian angels, who then discover but cannot expel him from Eden without God's assistance. This limitation stresses the creatures' universal need for cooperative but not unilateral grace, while the entire episode is crucial to understanding Eve's fall, for while she too is deceived, her reasons for believing Satan's baseless claim that God envies and wrongly inhibits humans signal her rejection of his love, gifts, and offered assistance.

As much earlier in *Areopagitica*, trial and error is thus integral to the providential plan of *Paradise Lost*, where Adam's final re-education by Michael follows much the same pattern. Although at first consumed by guilt, Adam learns that though he and Eve have rejected God's 'meet help', he has not rejected them. He not only offers healing grace but helps them understand that their disobedience has mainly impaired liberty and joy: they have sacrificed harmony between themselves, with the animals, and with their Father through their selfish and ironically 'fruitless' desires. Yet through God's grace, Eve actually gains more freedom to take the lead over her official 'head', who is now less wise, more self-righteous, misogynistic, and in need of her guidance. After she soothes Adam's just but also wholly disproportionate anger by offering to die for him, he begins to grasp that neither one of them can unilaterally compensate for their sins, which they must strenuously resist together. God's Son then descends to seal this understanding by ministering to them in ways that foreshadow his ultimate sacrifice for them and their race in Book 12, while Michael's concluding lesson teaches that through a combination of trial and error, love and fortitude, they can regain a 'paradise within' (*PL* 12.586).

Yet aside from the Son, in this poem no creature has any special access to grace, which even the Son (like later 'heroes' of faith) uniquely earns as God's loving and willing instrument. Milton's opening invocation to the Holy Spirit therefore claims only limited access to heaven. He hopes to succeed in relating Christian truth more successfully than any previous poet and he prays for God's assistance, but in Book 7, he admits he would be doomed to failure without Urania's 'gracious' inspiration. Yet her role like that of the Spirit is strictly instrumental: neither is co-equal to God, and both are lower than the Son, mere links in a 'ladder' joining the lesser creation to its otherwise invisible and transcendent Father. Some readers object to this ladder as undemocratic and therefore un-Miltonic, but like Adam and Eve's postlapsarian marriage, it actually permits individuals to interpret God's will equally but independently, as originally required in Eden, if rightly understood. The fallen world thus mainly differs from unfallen creation in its more malign physical and moral climate, including a host of temptations that demand more 'heroic martyrdom' than Eden ever did, and of course, in its temporary mortality.[11] Through the Son's sacrifice, that too will be reversed upon his final return.

This elegant moral justification of God's ways to man subtly complements Milton's most spectacular achievement, his brilliant characterization of Satan. He doubtless based this persona on his own political experiences, disappointments, and confrontations with power and lies. Yet Satan is no cheap trickster; his speeches are so powerful and often moving that at least one prominent critic (Fish), maintains that Milton planned for his readers to be so convinced by him and that they convict themselves of sin. Yet from the beginning, the poet provides abundant evidence that Satan is a clever con man whose conflicting claims about what he is and why God 'envied' and 'demoted' him easily betray him to careful readers. For instance, Satan illogically insists that the peaceful deity purposefully concealed his true power in order to tempt his revolt, and that by persisting against all odds, he can still punish his Creator, who does not deserve that title since he and the other angels 'arose' from heaven through spontaneous generation. All these lies are shown up as soon as he arrives on earth but, in accordance with Milton's free will principles, Satan is allowed to pursue his fantasies until his inward malice and spite take their toll and he and his cohort are transformed into slithering, hissing snakes craving ashy apples in hell. The reader is nevertheless free to choose between the epic narrator's glosses on Satan's actions and his own, so that more than any previous epic, *Paradise Lost* features open-ended dialogues and soliloquies heard very differently by different readers. This ambiguity is intensified by Milton's polyglot 'grand style', which inflates English into a heroic idiom so amplified with verbal polyvalency that even simple words frequently mean opposite things (Ricks 1963).

THE FINAL POEMS, *PARADISE REGAINED* AND *SAMSON AGONISTES*

Milton's final poems have long been faulted for falling off from the grand style of *Paradise Lost*, a point on which it is difficult entirely to disagree. The calm, self-possessed Son of *Paradise Regained* is never really challenged by his opponent, Satan, whom he simply dismisses with sardonic scorn. This Satan is by general consensus completely changed from the great rebel of the previous epic, while the Son's heroism is strangely limited to wise insights into how weak Satan's stratagems actually are. Dismissing the false heroes of Greek tragedy and philosophy, Milton's Son of God now seems more like a redeemed young Socrates than a young David combating a Goliath or a King Saul, much less like the victor of Milton's War in Heaven. The poet's mastery of dialogic technique is again

---

[11] Milton's late doctrine of mortalism or 'soul-sleeping' means that the soul dies with the body, but both will be resurrected together at the Last Day.

evident, but it is now cast in the understated style of his later sonnets. This brief epic's four relatively short books are carefully structured to complement their lack of action with abrupt and often spectacular scene changes, but their chief interest lies in Milton's thorough, masterful reworking and supplementation of his 'original', the brief biblical account of Christ's largely 'unsung' testing by Satan in the wilderness (Luke 4:1–13; Matt. 4:1–11). This revision expands Satan's temptations from three to at least five and possibly seven, depending how one counts.

Satan's first, unsubtle suggestion to turn stone into bread is easily dismissed since man does not live by bread alone, but the Son is then led to an elaborate banquet scene offering every kind of sensual and prideful pleasure: beautiful young women and men, wine, song, and exotic food. Satan's temptation to rule all the kingdoms of the world is similarly redoubled as he offers the Son both external or military and internal stratagems for deposing the aging, utterly decadent Roman emperor, Tiberius. Since the Son deems gaining Rome intrinsically unworthy and inglorious by any of these means, Satan then offers him an utterly extra-biblical temptation: to master the world through the arts of Greek wisdom and rhetoric. The Son aptly replies that these arts are best summed up in Socrates's belief that he who knows most admits to knowing nothing, while revealed Hebrew wisdom and poetry is all that mankind really needs. Along the way, Plato and his heirs are dismissed as fablers or fakers, as is Satan himself, who next sends an unbiblical storm to frighten the fearless hero before finally tempting him to prove his identity by leaping from the pinnacle of the Jewish temple. The Son instead simply 'stands and waits' God's will until ministering angels escort him to a truly heavenly feast.

Generations of critics believed that *Paradise Regained* bluntly rejects Milton's early humanism, but considered in its own cultural moment, the poem simply reflects a widespread shift away from Greek and Italian Neoplatonist mythologizing and allegorizing, and towards actual history (here ironically more Roman than Hebrew) and 'plain' rather than grandiose language (Martin 2010). Perhaps to counter any potential misunderstanding, Milton added *Samson Agonistes* as a kind of sequel to a sequel, a Greek tragedy featuring a deeply flawed Hebrew hero recovering from the spiritual and physical blindness that prevented him from reviving the cause of Jewish liberty. Although Samson is initially too impaired to believe in his own recovery, it is providentially forced on him by the self-reflections initiated by visits from his father and fellow tribesmen, and then from his wife Dalila and the Philistine champion, Harapha. These friends and foes alike lead him and his chorus to review Hebrew history and the reason why Judges like himself had consistently failed to free their people. As in the biblical account, Samson is then taken to the Philistine temple, where to avenge his disgrace, he brings down the structure on his enemies' heads. Yet since the drama does not end with any actual Hebrew liberation, its conclusion appears somewhat mysterious: is Samson a failed hero (Wittreich), a model for coming liberation (Loewenstein), or a prototype of Christian regeneration (Radzinowicz)? Conflicting answers to these questions prove what may be one of its most important points: since God's ways toward man are ultimately inscrutable, the best anyone can do is what Samson does do. He uses his innate, God-given gifts and 'calling' to testify to the Dalilas and Haraphas of the world that the true God eternally exists and empowers his people. The long-held view that Samson is Milton's self-portrait is no longer credited, but in the end Milton indeed 'quit[s] himself | Like Samson' (*SA* 1709–10), going out with a bang both by reviving the rhetoric of religious passion and yet once again forcing his unwary readers to choose. Just as every Christian must run his own race, each reader must understand and accept the consequences of her own reading. For that reason alone, Milton is rightly understood as the ultimate 'poet of choice' (Brisman 1973), although for him, that right is always God-given, the result *and* the proof of the deity's supreme respect for liberty.

PART IV

INTERPRETATIVE COMMUNITIES

CHAPTER 24

....

LAY HOUSEHOLDS

....

SUZANNE TRILL

> Oh if the head and the seuerall members of a family would be perswaded
> euery one of them to be conscionable in performing their owne par-
> ticular duties, what a sweet society, and happy harmony would there be
> in houses? ... Necessary it is that good order be first set in families: for
> as they were before other polities, so they are somewhat the more neces-
> sary: and good members of a family are like to make good members of
> Church and commonwealth.
>
> (Gouge 1622: ¶2v)

IN early modern Britain, the household was the foundational unit of social organization which, as numerous contemporary commentators and succeeding historians and
critics have noted, was frequently identified as 'a little commonwealth' (Richardson
2004: 165; Todd 1980: 23; Wilcox 2002: 744). Thus, as Susan Amussen has argued, 'we
cannot understand politics (as conventionally defined) without understanding the politics of the family' (1988: 2). Indeed, before John Locke, the household was integral to
contemporary political theory and represented a space in which the public and the private overlapped (and, from the perspective of those in power, ideally reinforced each
other). Crucially, the composition of early modern households suggests that this space
was rather less 'private' than we might be accustomed to considering it today. Even relatively lowly households could extend beyond a husband and wife and their offspring
to at least one servant, as well as other family members (aunts, uncles, or in-laws) and/
or other long-term residents or boarders, and, of course, higher-class households frequently accommodated much larger numbers of people (Banks 1800; Merry 2009: 205–
6; Wilcox 2002: 744).

However, whatever its size, the household required organization, and an incred-
ible array of early modern texts—in both print and manuscript—offered advice on

every conceivable aspect of household management. These ranged from practical texts on maintaining the pantry to precepts outlining the hierarchical relations among household members according to biblical principles, such as *Of Domesticall Duties* (Hunter 2014; Wilcox 2002). While the most important book for Protestants was, of course, the Bible, for adherents of the Church of England a close second was the Book of Common Prayer (BCP). While many Presbyterians and other 'Puritans' might be sceptical about the BCP, it was a culturally well-known text which left traces even upon its opponents (Cummings 2011; Rosendale 2015; Willen 1992: 561–2). Also incredibly popular among divergent Protestant groups were the *Sternhold and Hopkins' Psalter* and Foxe's *Book of Martyrs*. While these might be defined as the central texts for English Protestants, a multitude of others vied for readers' attention, including catechisms, sermons, meditations, exegetical texts on various books of the Bible or biblical figures, exemplary lives and/or funeral sermons, parental advice books, and devotional manuals. It is with how devotional texts were used within lay (that is, non-clerical) households that this chapter is primarily concerned.

In *Being Protestant in Reformation Britain*, Alex Ryrie poses the question which informs this chapter: what did it mean 'to be a Protestant in early modern Britain' (2015: 1)? While other chapters in this volume examine different religions and different Christian sects, this chapter is primarily focused on addressing what Protestant practice meant for the 'everyday', lay household. Importantly, while the ideal household envisaged by Gouge epitomized social order, this precept did not always work out in practice. As James Daybell has observed, in some ways it is surprising that the household was seen as the epitome of order as it could also be the site of internal strife and dissent; indeed, even Christ declares that his presence will create conflict and division specifically within the household (2010: 51; Luke 12:51–3). While a lot of work has recently been done on the intersection between public and private devotions, with a special focus on lay practice, for the most part general studies make 1640 their endpoint; that is, around the start of the English Civil Wars (Cambers 2011; Green 2000; Narveson 2012; Rosendale 2015; Ryrie 2015). There are many good reasons for this, not least the fact that families could be more noticeably divided and the complexity of even an individual's shifting allegiances make generalizations about any single household challenging. Furthermore, as the vicissitudes of state-sanctioned religion continually shifted over the mid- to late seventeenth century, any household which maintained its position could become viewed as a site of dissent. This chapter will focus on three quite distinct seventeenth-century households: the controversial community established at Little Gidding by Nicholas Ferrar; the Presbyterian practice of Nehemiah Wallington's household in Eastcheap; and, finally, the experience of Anne, Lady Halkett (née Murray) who solidly maintained her commitment to the Church of England whatever household she inhabited (whether in England or Scotland). The differences between these households are numerous; looked at side by side, however, they collectively bear witness to the material ways in which early modern household devotions were a political minefield.

LITTLE GIDDING: *THE ARMINIAN NUNNERY?*

The problematic politics of household devotions is epitomized by the admittedly excep-tional example of the Little Gidding community; indeed, its identification is so contested that it could arguably belong more properly to the previous chapter. In 1626, Nicholas Ferrar, disappointed in 'worldly' pursuits (as an MP and a member of the Virginia Company) moved to Little Gidding to pursue a life of contemplation, and his house-hold followed a rigorous devotional practice which by the early 1630s led to their being a 'reputed (at least reported) nunnery' (Mayor 1855: xxvi). This description comes from a letter written by Edward Lenton (*c.*1633/4) which, in an extensively revised format, became the source for an anonymous pamphlet entitled *The Arminian Nunnery or a Brief Description and Relation of the late erected monasticall Place … at Little Gidding in Huntington-shire* (Anon. 1641b). Printed by Thomas Underhill, the text is 'Humbly recom-mended to the wise consideration of this present Parliament' and the title page includes a woodcut of a nun holding a rosary and a book, standing outside a church (see Figure 24.1). The title, printer, image, and specifically designated audience (that is, the Long Parliament which sat from 3 November 1640) leaves no doubt as to the originator's political pur-pose: the Ferrar's household embodies the dangers of Laudianism, which is tanta-mount to 'Popery', and therefore represents an affront to Parliament. As the rumoured Parliamentary sacking of Little Gidding in the 1640s has recently been disputed, and the house inhabited into the 1680s, it is difficult to ascertain how much influence that pamph-let had or how widespread the concerns about the Ferrar household actually were (Carter 1893: 312; West 2015). However, by comparing Lenton's original letter with *The Arminian Nunnery* it is possible to glimpse the different reactions provoked by the same household which chime with issues recently raised primarily by historians about the categories we have used to understand 'Protestantism' in the seventeenth century.[1]

The 'Little Gidding community' comprised: the bachelor deacon, Nicholas Ferrar; his widowed mother Mary; his brother John (and his family); and his sister, Susannah (and her family). Altogether, including servants and children, it is generally agreed that the household consisted of around thirty to forty people (Carter 1893: 108; Cooper 2012: 199). There is also agreement about how 'carefully regulated' their daily devotions were:

> each weekday started at 4 a.m. (5 a.m. in winter) with household prayers, and the children reciting scripture by heart. Three times every day the household walked in formal procession the 50 yards to the small church at the end of their garden, for matins, the litany, and evening prayer, all bowing as they entered through the west door. Through the rest of the day there were regular 15-minute offices, or short ser-vices, held in the house, attended by the family on a rota system. The day ended with further prayers. (Cooper 2012: 200)

---

[1] A copy of Lenton's original letter, along with another disclaiming responsibility for the pamphlet's publication, is reproduced in Mayor 1855: xxiii–xxxvi.

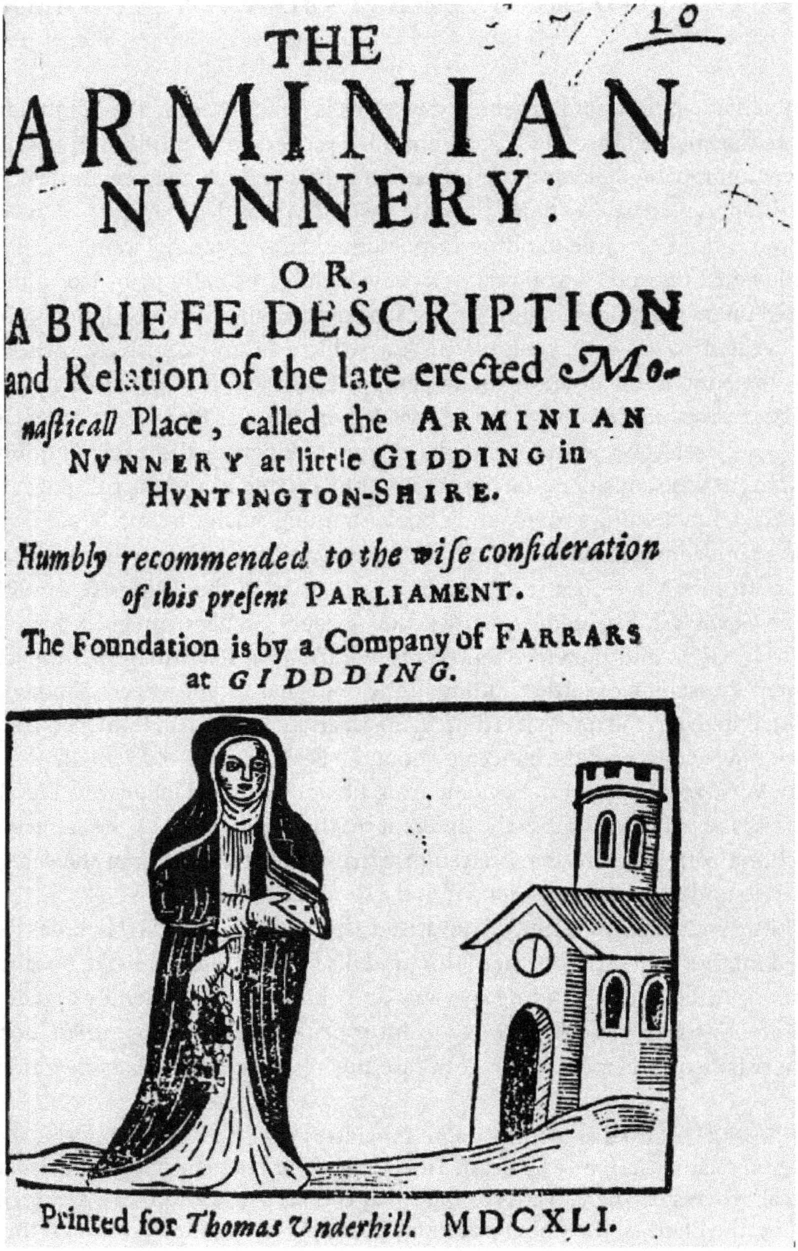

FIGURE 24.1 Title-page of the anonymous work, *The Arminian Nunnery* (London, 1641); shelf-mark oo oo. Reproduced by kind permission of The Bodleian Libraries, The University of Oxford.

It is less clear exactly what religious/political significance should be attributed to their practices. The keeping of set hours, along with regular offices, bowing at the entrance to the church and, latterly, keeping a night-watch, are certainly reminiscent of Catholic practice. However, the regular recitation of matins and evening prayer is perfectly conformable with the BCP. Potentially less conformable was the daily recitation of the Litany; however, the inhabitants had permission from their bishop to do this (Carter 1893: 115). Yet, the contents of their daily offices 'were devised by Nicholas, and consisted of psalms, a reading from their own harmony of the Gospels, and the singing of a hymn' (Cooper 2012: 200); thus, the Little Gidding community was exceptionally saturated with what Narveson identifies as 'Scripture-phrase' (3). Following the BCP alone meant reading the Psalms once a month, most of the Old Testament and the Apocrypha once a year, and the New Testament (apart from *Revelation*) twice a year. However, adding readings from their 'Harmony' (or concordance of the Gospels) suggests they also read through the Gospels once a month. According to John Ferrar, that book 'contained 150 heads of chapters, and there was so allotted to each hour of the days so many heads to be said', so that, like the Psalms, 'all the heads were said over in every month's time, which was twelve times in the year' (Mayor 1855: 36; Ransome 2005: 24–5). Such an amount of bible reading and psalm singing (in English) might more usually be associated with the 'hotter' sort of 'Puritan'.

Nevertheless, Lenton's letter and *The Arminian Nunnery* apparently agree on which aspects of the community's practices 'might savour of Superstition and Popery'; that is, 'what I had heard of the nuns of Gidding; of two, watching and praying all night, of their canonical hours, of their crosses on the outside and inside of their chapel, of an altar there, richly decked with plate, tapestry, and tapers, of their adorations and/geniculations at their entering therein' (Mayor 1855: xxviii; 2). Yet the different ways in which these texts deal with such theological matters is ideologically revealing. For example, when describing the organization and decoration of the chapel, the printed text reads 'upon that half-pace stood the *Altar-like Table*' (7, original emphasis); whereas Lenton wrote 'upon that half-pace, stood the communion-table (*not altar-wise as reported*)' (Mayor 1855: xxxiii, my emphasis). What, to a modern audience, might seem like a small change could make a crucial difference in signification which, especially in the anti-Laudian context of 1641, had very specific political implications.[2] On the issue of their crosses, *The Arminian Nunnery* emphasizes their diversity and reinforces Nicholas Ferrar's position as 'the Prolocuter' (4) or spokesman and thereby stresses Ferrar's 'priest-like' role as intermediary. Furthermore, the printed text inserts a dismissal of Ferrar's answer with a leading appeal to the reader: 'How confused and absurd this Crosse Answere was, let every Christian man judge' (4). Characteristically, *The Arminian Nunnery* inserts weighted adjectives and adverbs (including 'Shrill' (6), 'Speciously' (7), 'pregnant' (2, 3), 'bowings and prostrations' (7, 8)) and numerous brief judgemental asides (such as 'unto which this Priest-like pregnant Prolocutor answered but flubbringly' (3)). Tellingly

---

[2] For a detailed account of the architecture of Little Gidding's church, see Cooper 2012.

omitted are any of Lenton's positive comments on the Little Gidding community, who draws his account to a conclusion by extolling their 'humanity and humility' (Mayor 1855: xxxvi). He carefully represents himself as a non-judgemental, 'devil's advocate' figure: 'My opposing of some of their opinions and practises, as you see in this my relation (wherein I may have varied in some circumstances, but nothing from the substance) was only by way of argument, and for my own better information' (Mayor 1855: xxxvi). By contrast, the printed text concludes with two pages of anti-Arminian vitriol, with the 'fond and fanaticall *Family of Ferrars*, being represented as 'crouching, cringing, and prostrating to the ground to the Altar-like poore Communion-Table' (9). The language here suggests that the Ferrars' were primarily a vehicle for the pamphlet's true focus of attack: Archbishop Laud. With its concluding reference to the 'thick wall of the late Parliamentary national Protestation' (drawn up in May 1641) it would appear that *The Arminian Nunnery* was published while Laud was committed to the Tower of London, perhaps in the hope of expediting his trial (Milton 2009).

Margaret Aston has recently demonstrated that *The Arminian Nunnery*'s suggestion that 'for another shew that they would nott bee accounted Popish, they have gotten the *Booke of Martyrs* in the *Chapell*; but few or none are suffered to read therein' is, in Aston's words, 'about as far from the truth as it was possible to be' (9; 2007: 83). Aston charts the family's fondness for Foxe's volume and traces how some of the images from the *Table of the First Ten Persecutions of the Primitive Church* found their way into the version of the Gospel 'Harmony' the Ferrars presented to Charles I. While Lenton's letter made no reference to the 'Harmonies', their unique combination of text and image (along with the close connections they created between the Little Gidding community, King Charles, and Archbishop Laud) hardly helped to allay suspicions of Arminian leanings (Aston 2007; Ransome 2005). Initially devised as aids to family devotions, the Harmonies evolved into extremely complex texts and might have developed further had it not been for the untimely death of Nicholas Ferrar the younger. While most of the scholarly apparatus was undertaken by the two Nicholas's, the Harmonies' material production was primarily the result of intensive labour on the part of the women, especially Mary and Anna Collett.

It is in part because of the Collett sisters that the printed pamphlet refers to Little Gidding as a nunnery. In Lenton's letter, Nicholas Ferrar pronounced 'that the name of nuns was odious' but surmised that such an 'untrue report might arise' from Mary and Anna's resolution to remain virgins (Mayor 1855: xxviii). Here another small but significant distinction is crucial to the Ferrars' theological positioning: Nicholas admits that his nieces had resolved to remain virgins but is adamant that they have taken no *vows* to do so. Although there are some discrepancies on this point between Hacket's biography of Archbishop Williams and Jebb's 'Life of Nicholas Ferrar', among the surviving Ferrar papers there are letters between Anna and Nicholas in which she is obviously considering devoting herself to God 'without Greater encumbrances of this world, which doe of necessitie accompany a married Estate' (Carter 1893: 139, 144–6). There is also 'a fragment without date, signature, or endorsement' which appears to be in Anna's hand in which the writer records her 'humblest thanks' to her 'honoured Parents and dearest friends' for 'freely' giving their 'love and consents ... that I may end my days in a Virgin Estate' (Carter 1893: 141). The layout of this fragment bears striking similarity to a personal covenant which verifies the voluntary nature of this decision. This fits with their general practice; after all, the members of the Little Gidding community had chosen to be there, and any extra activities, such as an experiment with an 'austere dietary regimen', were explicitly assented to by a formal, familial covenant (Ransome 2009).

This included the 'Little Academy' which, although steered by Nicholas ('The Guardian') and John ('The Visitor'), was centred on the women of the household. The principal participants were identified in allegorical terms: Mrs Ferrar ('The Founder'), Mary Collett ('The Chiefe'), Anna Collett ('The Patient'), and Margaret and Elizabeth Collett ('The Cheerefull' and 'The Affectionate'). The women held frequent discussions, or 'Conversations', about ancient and modern history, saints' lives, and other tales which related to the assigned topic. The practice was initiated on 'The feast of the Purification, 1630' (intended, in part, to enable the 'maiden sisters' to 'bee Imitators of those glorious Saints by whose Names they were Called' (Sharland 1899: xlv)) and primarily took place on major festival days (as identified in the Church of England Calendar). The female-centred nature of this endeavour is attested to not only by the sex of the majority of the participants but in Mary and Anna's choosing to bind a collection of the stories together as a gift for their grandmother which she, in turn, lent to their aunt Susannah (Ransome 2005). A near contemporary, Dr Jebb, commented that 'If ever women merited the title of the devout sex, these gentlewomen won it by their carriage, and deserved to wear it' (Sharland 1899: xlii). Or, as Herbert might have put it, they were 'Ladies' who by their devout life looked into 'the thankfull glasse, | That mends the lookers eyes'; indeed, they may even not only have read, but also copied these words out, while assisting their uncle in preparing *The Temple* for publication.[3] Nevertheless, the women's names, their continued adherence to festivals and, in Mary and Anna's case, the choice to remain chaste, makes Little Gidding's designation as a 'nunnery' comprehensible. While the community was mixed, the gendered demarcations of space within the household and the church provides evidence of some sense of separate male and female spheres. However, in its references to night vigils and its emphasis on taking a 'second kisse' of the 'Virgins lippes', *The Arminian Nunnery* also alludes to the fact that, in seventeenth-century parlance, a 'nunnery' was slang for a brothel (*OED* 1.b).

Arguably, Little Gidding embodied a curious paradox at the heart of seventeenth-century English Protestantism: taken to its logical extremes, continuously reading, speaking, and living in the Word required a 'monastic' lifestyle, so how did one practise one's beliefs without turning into a 'Papist'? Nevertheless, although 'the Little Gidding community's practice of reading Scripture and other improving books at meal-times has been called an echo of monasticism,' as Alex Ryrie points out, 'it was an echo heard more

---

[3] 'The Holy Scriptures. I,' ls. 8–9 in Wilcox 2007: 208. Wilcox notes that 'the later manuscript, B ... is not in Herbert's hand but was copied out at Little Gidding, probably by Nicholas Ferrar's nieces, Anna and Mary Collett' (Wilcox 2004).

widely' (2015: 387). Even those most vehemently opposed to Catholicism recommended daily 'duties' which were difficult to distinguish from their 'Popish' counterparts: in *The Poore Mans Family Book*, Baxter provides directions for daily activities and his suggestions for Sunday family worship in particular almost perfectly accord with what was practised at Little Gidding (326–8).

NEHEMIAH WALLINGTON: A PRESBYTERIAN PATRIARCH?

As he died in 1658, Nehemiah Wallington could not have read Baxter's book; however, his extensive 'Notebooks' (*fl.* 1618–54) demonstrate that he not only owned, borrowed, and read many similar texts but also that he actively sought to emulate their suggested practices. In 1622, Wallington specifically records that:

> My Family incressing and now having a wife a child a mansarvant and a maid-sarvant: and thus having the charge of so many souls I then bought Master Goughes Booke of Domisticall Duties that so every one of us may larne and know our Dutyes and honour God every one in his place where God had sett them, for I was resolved with Joshua that I and my house will sarve the Lord. (Booy 2007: 271)

Wallington was not only quick off the mark in acquiring this book but he was swift to put its precepts into practice, as he used Gouge's book to help 'draw out 31 Artickls for my family for the Reforming of our lives' (Booy 2007: 271), which outlined both required daily devotional duties and prohibited activities (and associates each with a financial punishment for (non)performance). Unsurprisingly, the first undertaking is 'that we pray all together every morning and evening if we can convenient or eles by ourselvs' (Booy 2007: 271) which, if not done, is subject to a fine of a penny (to be put in the poor box); less common is the farthing's fine for quarrelling or the same amount 'if any consele the falts of the ware [shop goods] or use words of decait or take more for the ware then it is worth' (Booy 2007: 272). The list concludes with the statement 'To these laws we all set out hands', and is signed by Nehemiah and his wife, Grace, along with four servants/apprentices. Here, a well-known prescriptive text is adapted to suit specific needs which become the basis for a household covenant.

While it is impossible wholly to reconstruct Wallington's library, his frequent allusions to specific texts, along with the survival of copious notes from various books and pamphlets, offers an unparalleled insight into a lower-class, lay-person's reading habits. Collectively, the books which Wallington mentions by name affirm that his collection contained large numbers of 'puritan bestsellers', including the Geneva Bible and Arthur Dent's *Plaine Mans Pathway to Heaven*, as well as books by John Dod, Edward Elton, and William Perkins.[4] By 1650, Wallington had not only written ' "above forty books and read over the Bible many times" but had also read "above two hundred other books"' (Seaver 1985: 5); he thus epitomizes how 'methods of reading spurred forays into writing and shaped the forms that writing took' (Narveson 2012: 13). Whether he is reading or writing, books are crucial both to Wallington's personal spiritual development and to the creation of his own holy household.

In what he intended to be his final 'Notebook' (*An Extract of the passages of my life* (*fl.* 1654?)), Wallington's account of his own life embodies the inseparability of the reading and writing processes. Not only is this account a condensation of his previous notebooks (derived from conscientiously re-reading them) but it also makes reference to particular texts which clearly have deep significance for him. Touchingly, these also reaffirm familial connections as the first books he mentions are the 'many good Bookes given to me by my Father and my Brother John' (Booy 2007: 267). Among these, the first he recalls by name are his father's gift of a Bible and, from his brother, a copy of 'Master Brinsly Book called the True Watch and Rule of Life' (Booy 2007: 267). A supporter of religious reform, Brinsley was suspended from his Ashby-de-la-Zouch curacy in 1604 and apparently turned his attention to writing mostly classical translations or educational texts; however, his devotional text, *The True Watch,* became something of an early modern bestseller and by 1615 it was in its seventh edition (Green 2000: 602). Typically for the period, Brinsley's book had a protracted subtitle which elaborated on its contents: what began as 'A Direction for The examination of our spiritual estate' concluded with furthering 'our daily growth in Christ'. It is, therefore, perhaps not coincidental that the notebook in which Wallington records 'that Gods holy spirit moves me now to set on holy dutys with holy preparation' is entitled 'The groth of a Christian' (*fl.* 1641). Here, recognizing the benefits he has received from such preparation prompts Wallington: to consider further 'how one duty fets us for an<other> duty' (in which he highlights his habit of praying 'with my wife alone'); to regret his prior 'backward[ness]' (Booy 2007: 159) in such duties; and to recommend this practice to an imaginary reader of his own text.

Only seven of Wallington's fifty 'Notebooks' remain extant; however, he helpfully created a catalogue of their titles, the dates at which they were written, and, in many cases, a brief description of either its contents and/or its material form ('A black cover book', 'a thin paper book with parchment cover' (Seaver 1985: 199–202)). The titles indicate that his main topics were: God's mercies and God's judgements; meditations on these and other subjects; copies of sermons, psalms, and contemporary pamphlets (frequently relating to contemporary political events); as well as extensive accounts of faith and (returns of) prayer. In terms of gender it is intriguing that the first book in his list is entitled 'The Poor Widow's Mite' (*fl.* 1620) which seems to be a scriptural commonplace

---

[4] Cambers 2011: 138; Seaver confirms that Wallington owned books by these authors though the specified texts are not always the same as those mentioned by Cambers (1985: 4–6). Wallington does not record which edition of the Bible his father gave him, although in 1618 he bought himself a Geneva Bible (Booy 2007: 267).

book comprised of 'some places of Scripture I had gathered and written out'. The fact that the seventh book is 'The Marks that I am a Child of God' (*fl.* 1632) offers the tantalizing possibility that Wallington had read Anne Locke Vaughan Prowse's translation *Of the Markes of the Children of God*.[5] While Wallington records that he and his son-in-law (Jonathan Houghton) read over one of his books in 1647, he also wrote some of books specifically for his wife: two of these contained copies of sermons; another was 'A book of some choice Psalms, which my father chose out'; and another which appears to have been an 'original' piece 'called The Mighty Works of the Lord, which is a Prop to Faith'.[6] These gifts of sermons and psalms in particular suggest Wallington's sense of appropriate female reading, which is also evidenced in his book about 'the grace of patience' given to his sister—Patience.[7]

While he is unlikely to have owned a copy of the BCP, Wallington's various comments concerning it illustrate the complexities involved in trying to reconstruct any 'reader's response' to this controversial text. Many a scholar would concur with Wallington's sagacious observation that it 'was not good, for it was the masse Booke translated into English, and although there mite be some good in it, yet it was mingle mangel, linse wolsie together' (Booy 2007: 250). And given his Presbyterian beliefs, it is unsurprising that he approvingly recalls the date on which the Lords 'concurred with the House of Commons in the amendments of the Derectory for worship and Ordinance for the taking away of the Booke of Common Prayer' (Booy 2007: 281). Nevertheless, the language of the BCP is so familiar to him that, when writing to his minister Henry Roborough regarding the sacraments, he echoes its wording ('as you will Answer it at the grate day of accounts' (Booy 2007: 244)) to lend his own argument authority. Significantly, Wallington's main objection is not to 'set forms' of any sort. Indeed, in March 1642, he writes evocatively of the emotional impact and spiritual refreshment he gained from a period of prayer, which consisted simply of reading out Psalm 25, where 'some of those verses I did find them much fellingly and senchably unto my soule' (Booy 2007: 158). However, he is careful to establish that 'my Judgment is (not pleading for the servise Booke) by this my one [own] experiance that some set forme of prayr may be used as find fet for our occasions' (Booy 2007: 158). Ultimately, then, Wallington's objections relate specifically to the changes introduced to the 1637 Prayer Book under the influence of Archbishop Laud: 'Oh how cuningly and craftily hath the enemies of Gods <free> grace brought in superstition and mans inventions and tradicions (and in their sarvis booke) bring in now a little and then ading a little more' (Booy 2007: 116). Indeed, Wallington knows the BCP so well that he chronicles omissions as well as additions,

[5] Prowse's text was first published in 1590 but there are also imprints bearing the dates 1591, 1597, 1608, 1609, 1615, and 1634 (*STC*); as Wallington was composing this notebook in 1632, it is possible that he was instead referring to *Heavens happiness ... With a short discourse of the markes of Gods children*, attributed to the printer John Beale (*STC*: S92897).

[6] No. 11, *fl.* 1639 and No. 34, *fl.* 1647; No. 14, *fl.* 1639; No. 33, *fl.* 1646, see Seaver 1985: 199–202.

[7] This book was added to Wallington's list and is numbered 48, but he notes that he wrote it 'near twenty years ago', which dates its composition at around 1634 (Seaver 1985: 202).

and unambiguously criticizes the 'dashing' out of 'Thou hast delivered us from superstition and Idolatry' (Booy 2007: 116). In a critical letter addressed to 'Master Calfe' (actually Abraham Colfe 'the absentee rector of St Leonards' (Seaver 1985: 106)), it becomes apparent that Wallington's main issue is with Colfe's use of the BCP, especially his practise of 'praying for lordly Bishops'. Utilizing 'scripture-phrase', Wallington argues that the bishops cause a 'stinke in the nostrels of all good men that love God' and that whereas 'in former time of our Ignorance God winked at us but now God would have you and I and all men come to the knowledge of the truth' (Booy 2007: 249; Amos 4:10; Acts 17:30). In the context of the ejection of ministers, Wallington is not too subtly warning Colfe that he could lose his ministry and is attempting to play a part in ensuring the appointment of a more Presbyterian-minded minister to take care of the Parish.

In this Wallington's writings manifest the intersection between the 'personal' and the 'political' insofar as his desire to maintain his own godly life simultaneously entails the regulation of others' activities, both within his immediate household and his local community. Another way in which he demonstrates that connection is in his adherence to the practice of fasting. In 1624 he notes that, being aware of his own 'corruptions' and seeing also 'many things amisse in my family' as well as 'considering of the sinnes of the land', he and his family set the next Sabbath aside for fasting and prayer to 'humbel our soules privately together' (Booy 2007: 55). Their private practice is paralleled by their observance of the copious public fasts sanctioned by the authorities which, from 1642, included weekly fasts on a Wednesday. While Wallington approves of this practice in principle, he also regularly registers his concerns about his own—and others'—lack of preparation for this activity. He particularly worries that that 'slighting and profaining Fast days' by 'our formale and costomerry could prayers' (Booy 2007: 219) might so anger God that he will allow 'the bloodthirsty Enemie to prevaile' (Booy 2007: 220). Crucially, Wallington's writings bear witness to his conviction of the very practical and material impact of such practices upon political proceedings. On the 11th of January 1642, apprehensive of a potential Royalist attack in London, Wallington equates prayer with physical exertion when he resolves 'to put that day apart for to humble our souls in fasting and prayr that as our armies went up to fight at Westminster, we would be at home wraseling with the grat God in prayer' (Booy 2007: 155). As a dedicated Presbyterian Parliamentarian, Wallington is devastated in mid-1643 when it appeared for a time that some accommodation might be made between the king and Parliament. In a rare insight into his emotional life with his wife, Wallington poignantly tells us that 'I never did know my wives heart to break so much for anything as it did at this time in prayr which did my soule good to see her so to lay to heart the dishonours don to our God, and I shall love her for it the better as long as I live' (Booy 2007: 203): companionate prayer creates a spiritual bond between Grace and Nehemiah which binds them together in a time of political crisis. Throughout his writings, Wallington is acutely aware of the power of prayer as a political activity with direct consequences for earthly powers which is epitomized by his extensive list of God's great mercies to him, his family, and the three kingdoms c.1640–1: Wallington's patriarchal holy household was a highly politicized 'little commonwealth' (Booy 2007: 160–2).

Anne, Lady Halkett: Prayer-book Protestantism at Abbot House

Whereas Wallington was born, bred, and buried in St Leonard's in Eastcheap, Anne, Lady Halkett inhabited a number of households over her peripatetic lifetime. Born in London, of Scottish parents, she spent her early life in and around the English capital city. We have only glimpses of her childhood: her earliest years were spent at Berkhamsted in Hertfordshire and, in her youth, she lived with her mother in London (although after her sister Elizabeth's marriage to Henry Newton-Puckering they were also frequently at Charlton House in Greenwich). After her mother's death in 1647, Halkett lived with her eldest brother Henry for a couple of years before heading north to Naworth Castle with her friend Lady Anne Howard to escape probable arrest following her involvement in the duke of York's escape from St James's Palace (Couper 1701a: 15; Trill 2007: 78–9). By 6 June 1650, Halkett was in Edinburgh and, at the invitation of Sir James Douglas (later 11th earl of Morton), made her first visit to Fife nine days later. Inadvertently falling over while Douglas welcomed her there, Halkett recalls having joked that 'I thinke I am going to take posesion of itt'; writing about it twenty-six years later, Halkett remarks '[B]utt what I thought then accidentall[,] I haue Since Looked vpon as a presage of ye future blessings I inioyed in fife for wch I shall for euer blese my God' (Trill, 2007: 100). Indeed, Halkett was to spend almost all of the rest of her life in Fife (specifically in the proximity of Dunfermline);[8] thus, even a joke has the potential to become a sign of God's providence as, with hindsight, she reinterprets her experiences in 'A True Account of my Life'.

Halkett's life-writings, like Wallington's, are extensive and the extant volumes provide far-reaching insights into her personality and piety. Central to Halkett's sense of self is her faith which she traces to her mother: it was her 'greatest Care[,] & for wch I shall euer owne to her memory the highest gratitude ... that euen from our infancy wee were ins[t]ructed neuer to neglect to begin & end the day with prayer[,] and orderly euery morning to read the bible' (Trill 2007: 55). Alongside this personal routine, Halkett was also encouraged 'to keepe the Church as offten as there was occation to meett there, either for prayers or preaching', which, she explains, meant daily attendance at morning 'deuine Seruice' at 5 or 6 a.m. (Trill 2007: 55). Importantly, she emphasizes that her 'puplicke worship' conformed to the requirements of the Church of England and that she carefully emulated her mother in keeping 'Constantt to her owne parish Church' and maintaining respect for the incumbent minister (Trill 2007: 55). Halkett's unwavering commitment to such practices is evidenced in later life by her avowal: 'I esteeme itt the

---

[8]   After two years at Fyvie, Halkett leads an itinerant lifestyle for much of the 1650s; after her marriage to Sir James (at Charlton) in 1656 until his death in 1670, she primarily resided at Pitfirrane Castle; from shortly after his death until her own, April 1699, she lived at Abbot House in Dunfermline.

greatest honour I haue that I haue beene educated in ye Church of England in the time <in> wch itt had greatest incouragements' (8 January 1690/1, Trill 2007: 162). In an entry dated Monday, 9 September 1695, Halkett reveals that she still reads 'the Psalmes and Chapters for euery day of the Month', and successive volumes confirm that she continued to commemorate Church of England festivals and stalwartly refused to abandon her celebration of Christmas.[9] Thus, despite her relocation to predominantly Presbyterian Scotland, Halkett's household devotions demonstrate her persistent adherence to the Church of England's liturgy.

It is perhaps telling that one of the earliest entries explaining the development of her private devotions is found in a volume which culminates in over one hundred and fifty pages dedicated to 'Meditations & Prayers vpon euery <seuerall> day that is ordained to bee kept holy in the Church of England' (Halkett MS 6491: 96–257). In an occasional meditation, 'vpon a dispute with my Selfe', having affirmed her twice-daily practice of private prayer, she explains that 'the first time that I added one prayer more in the day' was after hearing a sermon at St James's (preached by Mr Gail, the countess of Devonshire's chaplain) exhorting those present to pray for 'the breach <& distance> betwixt the king & his people' (Halkett MS 6491: 85–6). Consequently, around 1643/4, she 'dedicated the time imediately affter dinner' to praying for the King's preservation and safety; thus, like Wallington—although to completely different ends—Halkett steadfastly believes that her private devotions have political efficacy. The 1660/1 meditation asserts that, in total, Halkett 'spent 4 halfe howers in the day (att least) one time with another in prayer & reading either the bible or some other pious booke' (Halkett MS 6491: 88). No doubt most modern readers would be inclined to agree with her that this might make one '*thinke* mee very deuoutt' (Halkett MS 6490: 88); yet the biographical *Life of the Lady Halket* (1701) declares that she preserved five full hours of daily devotions: 5–7 a.m.; 1–2 p.m.; 6–7 p.m.; 9–10 p.m. (55). While there may be some exaggeration in what is an intentionally exemplary biography, the apparent discrepancy is perhaps more pragmatically accounted for by the fact that, around 1660, Halkett was probably more preoccupied with pregnancy and childcare.

To date, very little attention has been paid to Halkett as a mother; however, she clearly emulated her own mother in seeking to imbue her children with her own religious principles, as is demonstrated in both her 'occasional Meditations' and the three different 'Mothers' Advice Books' that she authored over her lifetime.[10] The first, 'The Mother's Will to her vnborne child' (Halkett MS 6489: 198–259), was written

---

[9] MS 6500: 240/38; for example, Ash Wednesday, MS 6502: 202; Michaelmas Day, MS 6501: 329; Christmas, New Year, Easter are celebrated annually.

[10] Her children were Elizabeth ('Betty'), Henry ('Hary'), Robert ('Robin'), and Jane (Trill 2007: xxiii); for examples of how she writes about them in her 'Occasional Meditations', see: Elizabeth, MS 6491: 1–18 and Trill 2007: 15–19; Henry, MS 6491: 52–56; Robert (Robin), MS 6490: 297–324; MS 6493: 351–2 and Trill 2007: 171–2; Jane, MS 6491: 64, and Trill 2007: 22; MS 6492: 128 and Trill 2007: 33–4, and MS 6498 and Trill 2007: 152. Halkett also records her miscarriage of twins, MS 6490: 1–9. For studies of other 'Mothers' Advice Books', see Brown 1999, 1998; Dowd 2007; Poole 1995, and on 'Parental Advice', see Richardson 2002 and Wayne 1996.

in 1656 while she was pregnant; the second, 'Instructions for my Son' (Halkett MS 6492: 245–348), was prompted by the death of her husband, Sir James, and composed in 1670; and the third was published by Couper as *Instructions for Youth* ('For the Use of those young Noblemen and Gentlemen, whose Education was committed to her care') in Edinburgh in 1701. Collectively, these texts rehearse many of the same general principles (such as beginning and ending the day in prayer, daily reading of Scripture 'following the method prescribed by the Church of England' (Couper 1701b: 7), working hard, avoiding sin, and keeping the Lord's day holy). All three texts stress the importance of prayer and, in 'The Mother's Will', recognizing that it takes time and knowledge to be able 'to pray without helpe', she recommends three books by 'sound authours': Bayly's *The Practise of Piety*; Scudder's *The Christian's Daily Walk*; and *A Manual of the Private Devotions and Meditations* by Lancelot Andrewes (Halkett MS 6489: 203).[11] Here, as elsewhere, Halkett displays an openness to writers from diverse doctrinal positions, which underscores the need to pay more attention to who is reading what book, at which time, as well as their reason for doing so (Trill 2007: xxvii; Cambers 2011: 87).

Although her 'Advice Books' are stylistically calibrated for their immediate audiences, what is most striking is the consistency of the advice offered regardless of the sex of the anticipated recipient. This is perhaps most obvious in Halkett's self-conscious inclusiveness when writing 'The Mother's Will' in which she either uses the ungendered pronoun 'it/itt' to refer to her child or, where gender is grammatically unavoidable, she deploys 'him (or her)'. For the most part, her advice is concerned with devotional practices and sex remains unspecified; on the few occasions where she does register potential sexual difference, the advice is notably more socially directed (Halkett MS 6489: 221, 223). By the time Halkett concludes this text she has given birth to her first child, Elizabeth (Betty); despite this, the remainder of the text does not become any more sex-specific. Rather it seems Halkett saw the advice she provided as equally applicable to either her daughter(s) or son(s); indeed, she closes her 'Instructions to her Son' by recommending that he read 'the Mothers will to her vnborne child' (Halkett MS 6492: 306). While the title page of *Instructions for Youth* declares that its primary audience is male, the offspring who boarded in Halkett's home in order to attend the local school included both boys and girls. Significantly, of those identified, their families had all been Royalists during the wars of the three kingdoms and, after 1688, had predominantly Jacobite sympathies, a position certainly shared by Halkett herself (Trill 2007: xxv).

---

[11]   Bayly, *The Practise of Pietie*, first known in its 2nd edition, 1612. According to Green, this went through a minimum of fifty-seven editions over the period 1612–1728 (Green 2000: 599); see also J. Gwynfor Jones and Vivienne Larminie 2008. Scudder, *The Christians daily walke*, first published 1627, with at least eleven editions up to 1690 (Green 2000: 655); see also Gibson 2010. Andrewes, *A manual of the private devotions and meditations* (London, WD for Humphrey Moseley, 1648). This text does not make it into Green's list; see also McCullough 2008.

As an inexperienced mistress, Halkett meditated 'Vpon discention among the saruants' and prayed to God that he would enable her to say, 'with Iosuah … Lett others doe what they please as for mee and my howse wee will sarue the Lord, & lett all our actions wittnese the truth of what wee doe profese' (Halkett MS 6490: 131). Like Wallington, Halkett's authorization of her household organization was derived from Joshua 24:15; unlike Wallington, she does not allude directly to Gouge, although, as a widow living in Abbot House, she clearly led her family in regular household devotions (which included daily morning prayers and the whole household attending public worship on a Sunday). Apprehensive of what she would find in Dunfermline, Halkett determined to be an exemplary figure among the community as 'a widow indeed … well reported of for good works' (I Tim. 5:10), which included nourishing children, lodging strangers, assisting those in adversity, and spending as much time as possible in prayer. However, Halkett's activities could be controversial; for example, in 1674, when accused of being uncharitable to 'those who now Separate themselues from the Church', Halkett's attempted self-justification creates further conflict and culminates in her being branded 'a papist' (Halkett MS 6493: 291–2). Those who suspected her of Catholicism were no doubt also troubled by her persistence in kneeling to receive the sacrament (Halkett MS 6497: 286; Trill 2007: xxvi; Ryrie 2015: 172). However, as tensions increased between the Episcopalians and the Presbyterians, Halkett progressively records her, and her household's, absence from public worship. In 1690/1, she refuses to attend the 'weekely sermon' because it related to a fast proclaimed by the General Assembly which was contentious to Episcopalians for a number of reasons.[12] By 1696, Halkett's personal attendance at church is frequently prevented by physical incapacity; however, because 'an intruder preaches in the Church', Halkett stubbornly insists that even 'if I were well I would nott goe my selfe' and further determines that 'none that belongs to mee' should do so either (Halkett MS 6501: 320–2). As external opposition to Episcopalians intensifies, despite her lifelong commitment to the Church, in February 1697/8 Halkett finally decides to circumvent her misgivings and attend the gatherings which have evidently evolved at the home of her favourite (though ejected) minister, Simon Couper. Now a veteran mistress, Halkett leads her 'Seruants through the Greene' to Couper's door; unfortunately, 'it was Loocked And with Loud knocking could nott bee heard', so they 'returned home againe' where Halkett 'read to [her] Seruants the pious instruction of other good Ministers wanting what wee vse to haue from our owne' (Halkett MS 6502: 258–9, 221–2). Although best known as a female activist during the 1640s and 1650s, Halkett's royalism and religion ensured she remained politically engaged throughout her life and, while her later involvements may appear initially more parochial, being a Prayer-Book Protestant in Presbyterian Fife made her household a site of political dissent.

---

[12] Raffe, 2012: 82–3. Halkett's justification suggests that her primary objection was to its denouncement of 'Prelacy', MS 6499: 63–4; Trill 2007: 162–3. The full Act can be accessed at http://www.british-history.ac.uk/church-scotland-records/acts/1638-1842/pp221-235#h2-0015.

CONCLUSION: FROM 'DOMESTICALL DUTIES' TO 'FAMILY RELIGION'

Of course, it was not only in the seventeenth century that households facilitated political dissent, maintained patriarchal authority, or were subject to varying interpretations depending on the vicissitudes of state-sanctioned religious practice. A much earlier example would be Sir Thomas More's household which thrived while England and Henry VIII embraced Catholicism but became excoriated after its master's execution.[13] Additionally numerous families during Elizabeth's reign, among them the Howards of Naworth Castle, constructed priest holes to harbour their own or visiting priests which was a different form of resistance.[14] Nor is it the case that 'domesticall duties' only began to be practised in the seventeenth century: as Duffy (1992; 2006) has demonstrated, previous 'Catholic' practices were adapted for Protestant use, and books to guide householders in daily devotions emerged in the sixteenth century (Green 2000; White 1931, 1951). Among the early adherents of such activities were Lady Margaret Hoby and Lady Grace Sherrington Mildmay, whose self-writings and meditations were produced *c.*1590–1620 and therefore predate Halkett's prolific output by up to a hundred years (Meads 1930; Pollock 1993 and 2010; Slack 2013; Narveson 2012). However, the households discussed above collectively reveal something about the processes by which the Church of England was 'transformed ... from an inclusive national church whose "communities" were territorially defined parishes to which all inhabitants were automatically deemed to belong, to one that ... was compelled to co-exist with "communities" that were voluntary societies brought together by shared convictions and religious experiences that transcended parochial boundaries' (Ransome 2009: 52).

In different ways, the three sample households in this chapter provide insights into the processes by which 'Voluntary Anglicanism' and 'Family Religion' were able to emerge by the late seventeenth and into the early eighteenth centuries (Cambers and Wolfe 2004; Goldie 2003; Ransome 2009). Despite its perceived 'monasticism', Ransome has demonstrated how the example of Little Gidding become a reassuring example of the positive aspects of voluntarism when reinterpreted later in the century (2009: 65). While Wallington and Halkett were divided in doctrine, their devotional practices exhibit a surprising degree of commonality, perhaps because they both undeniably display a deep sense of ' "earnestness" ' (Ryrie 2015: 9). Their reading practices suggest that a closer analysis of who was reading what, when, and where might further complicate

[13] For an insight into the More household, see Margaret More-Roper's account of it (Manning 1852). More's 'household was known for its piety and erudition, "a school for the knowledge and practice of the Christian faith" as Erasmus noted (Stapleton 1984: 91), and More's interest in educating his daughters as well as their brother was as laudable as it was rare' (House 2008).

[14] 'It is not known exactly who built the priest hole at Naworth Castle but according to Lord William's household accounts, Benedictine priests and other recusants from the Catholic community' resided there (http://www.medieval-castle.com/architecture_design/medieval_priest_hole.htm).

our understanding of how Protestant identities were (re)formulated over the course of the seventeenth century. Although it is striking that Halkett recommended the Calvinist Bayly's *The Practise of Piety* for her son, it is perhaps more startling to discover that Wallington 'copied with obvious approval several pious letters of spiritual comfort by ' "Dr Joseph Hall" '(Seaver 1985: 187). Significantly, Wallington refuses to define Hall as a bishop but this still means that the puritan Wallington was reading material by a defender of the Church who was also one of Halkett's favourite authors (Trill 2007: xxxv). As his response to the BCP demonstrates, it is likely that Wallington was reading Hall's text in a very different way; however, this example reinforces the urgent need for 'a series of studies on individual and collective reading practices, and contrast in reading competence, and in attitudes and expectations between different communities of readers' (Green 2000: 190). A more detailed analysis of these households might enable us to discern fluctuations in the association between gender and devotional practice, and perhaps to connect these to political changes. Recently, there has been much emphasis upon the emergence of the public sphere (Raffe 2012: 6–12), yet, the Lockean distinction between 'family' and 'commonwealth' perhaps suggests that what emerged at the end of the seventeenth century was the *private* sphere (Schochet 1975; Longfellow 2006). As an adherent of the Church of England, whose family held various positions of service within King James VI/I and Charles I's households, the young Anne Murray's involvement in the duke of York's escape was a political act motivated as much by interpersonal connection as by principle or ideology. By the end of the century, as an Episcopalian English widow with Jacobite sympathies living in Scotland under the rule of William III, Halkett was physically—and psychically—disconnected from the centre of political power. In this, Halkett's changing devotional practice reflects the seismic shift in the relationship between the 'household' and the 'commonwealth' which occurs over the century.

CHAPTER 25

FEMALE RELIGIOUS HOUSES

NICKY HALLETT

IN May 1616, Anne Clifford (1590–1676) was ensconced reluctantly in her husband's house in Kent while her spouse went 'much abroad to Cocking, to Bowling Alleys, to Plays and Horse Races'. In her isolation, amidst marital and legal strife, 'condemned by most folks', she wrote: 'I may truly say, I am like an owl in the desert' (Clifford 1990: 33). She was echoing Psalm 102 that begins with the plea 'Hear my prayer and let my cry come to you': 'I am like an owl of the desert. I watch, and am as a sparrow alone upon the house top. Mine enemies reproach me all the day...' (Psalm 102:6–7). Clifford certainly felt herself beleaguered for her refusal to relinquish legal claims to her family estate, yet even in despair she appeared confident her petition would be heard and she would be restored to her rightful home.

Clifford's sense of internal estrangement and her frequent use of scriptural texts finds a useful counterpoint in writing by other female readers—those in actual exile from their homeland: communities of English Catholic nuns living on the European continent during periods of persecution. From the later sixteenth century onwards, with the foundation of Benedictine convent in Brussels in 1598, to 1678 with the establishment of a third Carmelite community at Hoogstraeten in the Spanish Netherlands, some twenty-two contemplative convents were created for English women across the northern continent. These were centres of piety and cultural exchange, where books were written, read, and circulated, and in which some four thousand women professed.[1] Their histories have largely been overlooked in our attention to Protestant household reading and male literary circles, and for this reason I wish to focus on these convents, to explore the ways in which habitual use of Scriptures connected and distinguished women in domestic and devotional spheres: Anne Clifford's 'sparrow alone upon the housetop', like the voice crying from the wilderness of exile, is one to which we will return through close analysis of shared yet different literary-biblical preoccupations.

---

[1] On the female foundation movement, see Bowden 2012a: xi–xxxiv; Walker 2003: 1–30. On the male Catholic diaspora in colleges, seminaries, and monasteries from 1568 onwards (with the English College at Douai), see Erler 2012; Guilday 1914: 1–40; Johnston 2000: 462–5.

'Serious Readinge'

In her isolation Clifford heard *Arcadia* read by one of her household (Clifford 1990: 61).[2] Nuns also listened, largely to spiritual material at mealtimes and as part of the liturgy; they also read privately in their cells and sometimes in the sickroom, borrowing books from libraries for which we have detailed contents lists.[3] When we picture a community thus engaged it is tempting to imagine them following instructions for 'spirituall Reading': 'like the drinking of a Hen, which drinkes by little, and little, and so lifteth vp the head agayne' (Rodriguez 1627: 245). Such an image is at once compelling and convincing. It appears in a text that was read by nuns who chart their determination to follow guidance in reading as in other matters. The translation of this particular book, *A Treatise of Mentall Prayer* by the Spanish Jesuit Alfonso Rodriguez (1526–1616), was dedicated to the English Benedictine community in Ghent, one version naming its abbess, Lucy Knatchbull (1584–1629) 'from whome I first receued it' (dedicatory epistle), suggesting the two-way process of literary exchange. Its translator, Tobie Matthew (1577–1655) later compiled a Life of Knatchbull, and produced important spiritual books for several English convents with which he was closely associated.[4] For Rodriguez, reading provided 'spirituall foode', to be well chewed before digestion: 'I may reflect vpon and reuolue it in my mind by Reading it once or twice agayne; and by ruminating and pondering it, and so it will grow to make a great impression in me' (Rodriguez 1627: 250–1).

Another prolific author, Barbara Constable (1617–84), a Benedictine at Cambrai, claimed 'god speakes by no externall meanes more then by readinge'; sermons tend 'to goe in one eare & out at another, but serious reading penetrates to the verie bottome of the hart & works great effects' (Constable 1655: 190–1).[5] It is clear that nuns were well-aware of early modern claims about reading; its capacity to 'inflame the soul' (Rodriguez 1627: 252) and to wreak emotional and devotional havoc if unwisely practised.[6] It is no surprise, therefore, that instructional manuals stressed the need to read the right sorts of books with due diligence, to turn passionate inspiration to devotional ends. It is one of the claims of this chapter that such philosophies shaped the convents as particular kinds of interpretative communities.

In recent years, increasing insight into the reading practices of religious houses and of Catholic women in exile has enabled us to redraw the English literary landscape. We now have a greater sense of convent 'coteries', those groups of discerning women who arrived from domestic circles to embrace a religious life on the European continent,

---

[2] See Crawford 2014: 82–3; and Hallett 2012b on a nun reading *Arcadia*.

[3] On convent book lists, see Bowden 2012b; Wolfe 2004.

[4] For details of nuns mentioned here and histories of individual English convents, see 'Who Were the Nuns? a Prosopographical Study of English Convents in Exile, 1600–1800': http://wwtn.history.qmul. ac.uk.

[5] On Constable's writing, see Lay 2011; Wolfe 2007; Gertz 2013.

[6] On ideas of reading, see Craik 2007; Hallett 2013: 69–79, the basis of some of the claims in this essay.

large numbers of whom continued to be avid consumers of spiritual texts and to document their responses to them, committed as they were to contemplative self-scrutiny. Through such material the women were exposed to a wide range of classical and spiritual sources. Their writing shows knowledge of works by Aristotle, Boethius, and Virgil among many others; as well as predictable traces of religious texts including works by saints such as Augustine, Bernard, Catherine of Siena, Gregory, Thomas à Kempis, and contemporaries like Francois de Sales (1567–1622) and Teresa de Jesus of Ávila (1515–82). Convent constitutions endorsed material by medieval mystics as well as a wide range of instructional books, some of them translated into English at the behest of the nuns themselves. Indeed, convents were homes to some of the most literate women of their successive generations several thousand of whom in the period 1600–1800 are well documented in their own communities, yet they have often been overlooked, in part, as I have suggested, in favour of critical emphasis on Protestant domestic environments, and also because of the alleged privations of post-Tridentine enclosure, and because anonymous or co-operatively composed material runs against the grain of author-led canonicity. Nuns' personal writing is now gradually being made available in scholarly editions. It reveals a range of genres and, perhaps surprisingly, often employs motifs and styles drawn from fashionable secular works, some of them transposed to a devotional focus. On her deathbed, for example, the Louvain Augustinian Margaret Clement (c.1539–1612) poignantly was given permission to perform 'as ye swan dooth': 'and with that she sett out such a voice that all the company was admirered. It was a Dutch ditty, but the matter was the spous, & the bridgroom' (Shirley: 70; Hallett 2012a: 31). Although women religious eschewed 'romance' and other 'idle' texts, they often incorporated Petrarchan potential into their works or structured it with a rhetorically averted eye, fashioning reception around rejection itself and thereby enacting their diversion of response to devotional ends.

There are several ways in which we might appreciate the nuns' interpretative strategies. For example, we can gain great insight into their elucidatory systems by analysing the annotations they made in convent books.[7] Their use of quotation and of open or oblique citation is similarly revealing. It shows the liturgical-like the women took in literarily enabling experience of the holy via their textual interventions. This again distinguishes nuns from other creative circles. They minister to each other by bearing witness to intercession and to the effects of what Matthew refers to in his Life of Knatchbull as the 'immediate way' by which 'Verityes and feelings' are directly 'infused' into the soul (Knatchbull 1642, in Hallett 2012a: 176).[8] By so doing they create the opportunity for

---

[7] See, for example, Jaime Goodrich's forthcoming work on highly revealing annotations in nuns' work.

[8] On 'sacramentalist theology', see Nandra Perry's compelling argument about Teresa de Jesus to which I will return: 'Teresa's words are not merely interpretable signs, but physical manifestations of divine presence and power. They are, in other words, sacramental (or at least quasi-sacramental), and their effects are immediate and material rather than strictly rhetorical. They bypass the interpretive faculties of the reader, piercing and inflaming him or her with the annihilating dart/wound of divine love' (Perry 2006: 14).

repeated mystical encounters not only by instructing their readers but also by effecting changes on them via the process of their texts. I will focus on some of their specific references, often made at key moments in nuns' lives, in order to bear out this claim and to expose the ways in which certain kinds of biblical exegesis informed their collective contemplative impulse.

CITING CHAPTER AND VERSE

As she too approached death, the Cambrai Benedictine Margaret Gascoigne (1608–37) famously asked for a passage from the 'Holie Virgin Julian the ankresse of Norwich, as appeareth by the old manuscript booke of her *Reuelations*' to be written below a crucifix by her bed: 'Intende (or attende) to me: I am inough for thee; rejoice in me thy Sauiour and in thy saluation.'[9] This passage does not quite quote chapter and verse, but combines references to a text the convent was committed to transcribing for a wider audience.[10] The nun's devotional expressiveness thus appears to be framed through a diffusion of Julian's words. Gascoigne's own compositions are similarly accommodating, weaving phrases from Julian's work with biblical quotation and references to a range of patristic writers. As so often in nuns' writing, immediate sources and personal authorship are obscured; indeed, that is their very purpose, to enact 'the permeability of bodies and subjectivities' and of texts as a continuum of both (Warren 2010: 69).[11] This is more than a meditative mode; for contemplatives, it allows revelatory knowledge to be shared by textual transmission and enables readers through the very act of interpretation to participate in spiritual epiphany. So, while writers bear witness and attend to the needs of intensely individual spiritual experience, they often do so by putting their reader in contact with other pious figures to enable a distinctively contemplative 'felt experience' (Robinson 2010: 13).[12] The patterning here is central to a meditative *midrashim*.

---

[9] Augustine Baker, *Life and Death of Dame Margaret Gascoigne*, 46–7 (http://www.umilta.net/gascoign.html), cited Watson and Jenkins 2006: 439. On Cambrai manuscripts of English mystics, see Wolfe 2007: 163–4; on Gascoigne and Julian of Norwich, see Warren 2010: 63–76.

[10] 'With this sight of the blissid passsion, with the Godhede that I saw in myne understonding, I knew wele that it was strength enow to me' (IV, 129–31); ' "God of thy goodnesse, give me Thyselfe, for thu art enow to me" ' (V, 172); 'tenderly our Lord God toucht us, and blissfully clepyth us seyand in our soule: *Lete be al thi love, my dereworthy child. Entend to me. I am enow to the, and enjoye in thi Savior and in thi salvation*' (XXXVI, 1237–9): http://d.lib.rochester.edu/teams/text/the-shewings-of-julian-of-norwich-part-1.

[11] Nancy Warren insightfully argues for a meditative 'intermingling' of Christ, Julian, and the nun herself (2010: 69–71). See also her discussion of the *vitae* which 'seek to insinuate themselves into and to shape other lives, to become … shared experiences in their own day and afterwards' (Warren 2007: 372). A similarly 'incarnational religious aesthetic' is mentioned by Hackett 2012: 1100.

[12] Marilynne Robinson claims that 'the mind as felt experience had been excluded from important fields of modern thought' (2010: 13). She makes distinctions between positivism and philosophies that allow for the possibility of gaining knowledge beyond the self, through 'mystical' or revelatory intervention.

The reader bears witness to intervention which throws human order out of kilter: she communes with the intermediary whose grace is, in the words of the dedicatory letter of a 1670 edition of *Revelations* held in convent libraries, 'by reflection darted into your own Soul' (see Summit 2009; Hallett 2012b). Gascoigne's quotation combines several passages in *Revelations* that underline the precepts of mental prayer. Here, where 'a sily soule come to Him nakidly and pleynly and homely...' (V, 169–70), the text implicitly invites identification not only with Julian but beyond her, with other figures made typologically available through it. Such nakedness is Job-like, the exegetical figure most often called on as a model for purgative devotional routines towards spiritual union.[13]

Typically, such material performs a number of paradoxes which crucially inform the ways that spiritual experience and the texts which describe them are interpreted. Because a nun at advanced meditative stages has divested herself of somatic dependency, she can be sure that her seemingly sensory experience of God is in fact direct; contemplative union is induced via imageless states. Benet of Canfield's *Rule of Perfection*, addressed to a number of English houses,[14] stresses that the desirous body should see 'her selfe behold her God uncloathed; by this Satisfaction shee receives him into her selfe, and by this Rest, shee meetes him naked' (Benet 1646: 47). She is stripped of all images in mental prayer, 'enabling her so naked and simplified to contemplate without helpe of formes' (49). Benet of Canfield develops an extended and deeply poetic meditation on the imaginary 'profundity' of nought; the 'wildernized solitarinesse of this Nothing' (66). Only through arriving at an imageless state—in Gascoigne's case paradoxically aided by an image which is itself exegetically connected with naked form—can contemplatives reach their desired end: 'Annihilation and uncloathing' (53), a pure substance-less spiritual sublimation. Texts enact the process they describe, disturbing both their reader and the visualizations at their own centre. The convent interpretative community thus centralizes feeling, yet aims to be dispassionate, bodiless, and textless.

Meanwhile, of course, it embraces textuality in order to arrive at its destination. Often, as I suggest, it does so with specific reference to other literary material. The Carmelite Paul of St Ubald mentions chapter 15 of Teresa de Jesus's *Vida* in his 1654 book *The Soul's Delight*, directed to those inside and outside the convent who are 'giuen to mentall prayer, and are desirous of spirituall perfection' (Paul of St Ubald 1654: III, 12). Here Teresa's influential work deals with the effects of the prayer of quiet. In the margin next to Paul's citation there is a reference to the Song of Songs 3:4: 'the soul seemeth truly to haue found whom she loued'. The reader is thus given communion with Teresa de Jesus through the operation as well as the meaning of the printed words. Contemplatives, the main text tells us, 'are vnited forcibly, resting sweetly in the bed of delight' (12).

In similar terms, Thomas Hunter (1666–1725), spiritual director to the English Carmelites at Antwerp, specifically referenced John of the Cross (1542–91) in his

---

[13] 'Naked came I out of my mother's womb, and naked shall I return thither: the Lord gave, and the Lord hath taken away' (Job 1:21). All biblical quotations are from the Douay-Rheims Catholic version.

[14] The 1609 edition has dedications to his Wiseman cousins, English Brigittines at Lisbon, Louvain Augustines, and Brussels Benedictines (*STC*, 2nd edn, 10928.3).

introduction to the Life of Mary Xaveria Burton (1668–1714): 'his 2d book of *ye Ascent to Mount Carmel* esp. 11th discoursing of exterior visions & satisfaction a soul feels in them' and 'his 18 chaptre [in which] he blames very much those directors who seem to put too much value on these supernatural operations' (Hunter n.d.: viii, ix). This enables Hunter to stress both his own initial scepticism about the nun's alleged revelations and her exemplary behaviour which secured them.[15]

The compiler of the Antwerp Carmelite annals cites Hunter's Life along with other textual authorities to reveal a convoluted connectedness in her account of Mary Xaveria:

> amongst other things which is very extraordinary of this Rd Mother I cannot omitt this remarkable passage which her Confessor left in his own hand writing which I allso found writen by Rd Mother Delphina her self being commanded to doe so by her Director and likewise incerted by Rd Mother Mary Xaveria of the Angels in her own life which she writ in Obedience to her Confessors out of which I have drawn the following account in the 8 Chapter and 2d part of the said life of Rd Mother Mary Xaveria, her words are these
>
> Allmighty God was pleased to help one of the Religious by my prayers which I think fitt to mention here. ('Short Colections', 595, in Daemen-de Gelder 2013: 276–7)

Significantly, in chapter 8 Mary Xaveria describes how she exchanged her spiritual state with that of a desolate young nun:

> She was like a soul in purgatory in continual anguish and pain ... then on a suddain like one awakeing out of a slumber she found an unusual peace of mind, all her troubles being at once removed ... I thought I saw our Bd Saviour seated in ye middle of my heart speaking most amorously to me, as if he designed me some great favour, but on a suddain he seemed to ask my consent to go and caress this Sister in place of me ... on a suddain [I] wonder'd to see my self in anguish, desolation and dryness. (Hunter n.d.: 237)

Spiritual surrogacy is thus interpretatively replicated by the process of annals which often elide distinctions between various subjects. The nun now reading the text is put in touch with a source of spiritual intercession, witnessing the continued powers of one who 'offer'd my self to change communions' (239).

On the one hand, writers attempt to shore up the body by instructing the devout to deny the truth of seemingly somatic revelation; on the other, they open possibilities of divinely induced alteration, preparing for the advent of unexpected, unwonted spiritual knowledge. When Lucy Knatchbull writes that her 'hart was made tender towards God' she is being literal as well as figurative; 'I did presently Conceave him to be in my

---

[15] Chapter 11 of *The Ascent* discusses the 'hurt and hindrance' caused by 'the instrumentality of the outward senses'. Chapter 18 refers to different kinds of 'interior locations' (John of the Cross 1906: 103–11, 150–5). See also Hallett 2013: 33–6.

hart holding in his left hand a Cross'. 'It Comes to my mind that I may make a comparison between our Lords drawing my affections to him, and & the Sunnes drawing of vapours from the earth' (Knatchbull 1642, in Hallett 2012a: 210, 169). Meditative mystical encounters are by definition inexplicable and personal, yet by describing their experiences the women enable continuous connections to be made between sequential subjects and the holy figures which inspired them. Sometimes they do so by ekphrasis, embedding visionary images in their accounts to enable fresh or re-experience of the revelatory moment. They do so even in texts which stress the need to attain an 'imageless' state in mental prayer.

Religious writers of this kind are faced with (and enjoy) ineffable paradoxes. On the basis that 'the invisible cannot be examined, the incorporeal cannot be weighed, the limitless cannot be compared', 'insistence on the ontological unlikeness of God to the categories to which the human mind has recourse is at the center of theological reflection' (Robinson 2010: 4).[16] Interpretative communities which seek to explain in this way do so by their very acts of failure and by transmitting testimony to the direct experience of others. Whereas inductive methodologies seek to strip down and identify textual authority (and may suspect obfuscation in those who do not), contemplative writers often present accreted layers (via similitude or metaphor or by weaving sources together, sometimes without direct attribution) even when claiming to make themselves naked in the face of divine energies. Such groups of early modern readers are therefore likely to be distinct from others for whom 'reformation' brought about a different relationship with language and symbolic meaning. While nuns express respect for hieratic authority and hedge their accounts in appropriate terms, the ways in which they mediate between texts and other nuns allows them certain latitude, less in what they have to say than in the means by which they make connections.

In editing material, the nuns shape the spiritual direction of their own communities, for example by compiling documents that combine autobiographical extracts with commentary, extracting, as a Ghent Benedictine states, 'anything of noate' for the edification of others (*Obituary Notices* 1917: 1). They often advertise their authority to do so. The writer of the Paris Benedictine book of obituaries, couched in 'Low & plain stile that the Truth & sencerity may more cleerly apeare', opens by citing chapter and verse of the community's foundational documents:

> Our Constutions in the first chapter, and 13 clause, haveing ordained that a Register should be made of al the names of the Religious that are departed this life—with such Remarkable things as hath happened concerning them in Life, Death, & after death—to be sett downe for an example & memory to posterity & kept in Depositum … that the Memory of their vertues should be the more Deeply imprinted in our harts, and make us like good children faithfully walke in the same paths. (*English Benedictines* 1911: 334)[17]

---

[16]   Robinson cites Gregory of Nyssa in the first sentence quoted here.

[17]   On the role of such material, see Bowden, 2010. The Antwerp annals were intended to be 'red over once a year in the Refectory' (*Short Colections*: 576, in Daemen-de Gelder 2013: 268).

Another Paris Benedictine 'writ out the Epistles & Gospels for the principal Feasts of the year, to save us the trouble of having them to seek then we were to read them at the Table … She also writ another Book for the Infermary of the Episles & Gospels for Lent' (381). At Ghent, the Benedictine Mary Roper (1623–72):

> caused a writing to be sett upon every Common passing door in the monastry, containing these words: IN SILENCE AND RECOLLECTION shall be our profit and hope.[18] As also a pious purpose which she Composed in behalf of all, ordaining every one to Coppy it out, and place it upon their oratory which begins as followeth in these words. '…I will this day be very wary to avert my eyes from seeing, my thoughts from Judging, and my mouth from speaking against Charity towards any spouse of my Saviour in this holy house, but will excuse all, And only be my own accuser'. And this she most earnestly Commended to all for a Constant recitall in the mournings. (*Obituary Notices* 1917: 44)

Thresholds were evidently places for directed devotion in this convent. One nun promised that 'Every time I go in or out at any door, I will adore God in my soul and make an act of indifferency' (9); another had as 'one of her practices … kneeling at every one's cell door whilst she exhibited some pious salutation prayr and petition' (20). They were clearly well aware of the symbolic connotations of their actions, drawing on familiar sources in Jeremiah 9:21 and Job 38:17, often cited in books of meditational instruction.[19] Ruperta Browne (1698–1755) 'mortified her sense of seeing, denying all gratification to whatever could be presented by windows & doors which a natural curiosity might make agreeable' (84). The women were rehearsing precepts of patristic patrol while at the same time directing each other by their own commitments and compositions, to inspire spiritual edification in a semi-autonomous manner.

Some nuns mention particular passages to which they were drawn in their own personal devotion. Again, analysis of their choices can give us insight into their understanding and use of religious material. The Paris Benedictine Maria Apleby (*c.*1652–1704) repeatedly 'writ upon several bits of papers and little pictures this following vers of the Royal Prophet Psal: 93. *Secundum multitudinem dolorum meorum in corde meo, cousolationes tua laetificaverunt animam meam*'; that is: 'According to the multitude of my sorrows in my heart, thy comforts have given joy to my soul' (Psalm 93:19). She seems to have selected phrases which offered scriptural succour, apt for one said to suffer inwardly while appearing affable without (*English Benedictines* 1911: 392).

Thomas à Kempis's *The Imitation of Christ* is frequently referred to in convent papers, often at crisis points in particular nuns' lives. Their use suggests that they followed the advice given in treatises on mental prayer, such as the Carmelite example which states: 'You read in a spiritual treatise, as the holy Scripture, Thomas à Kempis, a chapter now

---

[18] Perhaps a reference to Isaiah 30:15: 'in silence and in hope shall your strength be'.

[19] Jeremiah 9:21: 'For death is come up through our windows, it is entered into our houses to destroy the children from without, the young men from the streets'. Job 38:17: 'Have the gates of death been opened to thee, and hast thou seen the darksome doors?'

and then, or some lives in it; you reflect in what you have read, and endeavour to comprehend the sense & to imbibe it' (*Second Treatise*: 25, in Lux-Sterritt 2012: 181–2). Accordingly, during a period of self-doubt, the Antwerp Carmelite Catherine Wakeman (1636–98) 'opend her Thomas à Kempis she resolved to take the advice it should give her, and the first words she cast her Eyes upon were these, *why fearest thou to take up a Cross that leads to a Kingdome*' (*Short Colections*: 517, in Daemen-de Gelder 2013: 235). This quotation, from book 2, chapter 12 of *The Imitation*, itself refers to Matthew 16:24: 'Then Jesus said to his disciples: If any man will come after me, let him deny himself, and take up his cross, and follow me.'[20] Catherine Wakeman clearly came from a bookish family, several sisters from which joined the convents. The life of Teresa Wakeman (1641–1702) was similarly marked by textual encounter. She was initially drawn to religion by François de Sales's 'Book Intituled the love of God': 'before she had finishd it Allmighty God so powerfully touchd her heart, that … [she] resolved to become a lover and Spouse of Jesus Christ'.[21] Just before she died:

> she had that morning desired one of the Infimarians to read her a point out of Thomas à Kempis who opening the Book Severall times allways litte upon the Chapter of judgment an hour before her death, she was seen to imbrace her Crucifix (with great affection) to which she was ever Singularly devoted. (Daemen-de Gelder 2013: 533)[22]

The chapter to which she was drawn *in extremis*—as with her sister's encounter with à Kempis, seemingly coming by chance to a certain passage—relates to the distractions of rash judgement. 'In judging others, we expend our energy to no purpose':

> Were God Himself the sole and constant object of our desire, we should not be so easily distressed when our opinions are contradicted … if you rely on your own reasoning and ability rather than on the virtue of submission to Jesus Christ, you will but seldom and slowly attain wisdom. For God wills that we become perfectly obedient to Himself, and that we transcend mere reason on the wings of a burning love for Him. (Kempis 1952: 42)

Again there is a textual layering here, as Thomas à Kempis is tacitly referring to Paul's Letter to the Philippians 3:21: 'Who will reform the body of our lowness, made like to the body of his glory, according to the operation whereby also he is able to subdue all things unto himself.' The Antwerp author accordingly shapes her readers' interpretation of Teresa Wakeman's life by incorporating textual detail that alerts us to the nun's own qualities: 'how far she was from troubling or distracting her self with any thing that did

---

[20] *Imitation*'s 'On the Royal Road of the Holy Cross' weaves a series of biblical quotations culminating in a call from Luke 9:23 and Acts 20:22: 'take up his cross, and follow me'; 'that through much tribulation we must enter the Kingdom of God' (Kempis 1952: 83–8).

[21] *An Introduction to a Deuout Life* (Sales 1616); *Short Colections*: 532, in Daemen-de Gelder 2013: 242.

[22] *Imitation*, book 1, chapter 14, 'Avoiding Rash Judgment'.

not concern her, all her industery tending to this, how she might most increase in the love of God and the glorifying him in the present moment'. This is a subtle, almost silent manoeuvre (though perhaps more evident and differently pleasurable to ones who know their Scriptures). We are led to infer that the nun's imitative reading has prepared her: 'tho her death was so sudden, we have all reason to confide most happy being of a most innocent life joynd to a constant preparation for that last moment as a Spirituall testiment which she was dayly wont to recite shews' (*Short Colections*: 534, in Daemen-de Gelder 2013: 242–3). Readers of her Life might in turn copy her, a sequential exercise that the annals themselves centralize: 'there is allways something to be remarked of example and edification for others to imitate' (268).

Other material reveals the ways in which nuns built particular texts into their personal routines, including, as we might expect, extracts from the Book of Psalms which so often informed expressions of penitence as well as joy, and which were ritually invoked during moments of important transition in the nuns' professional lives.[23] A Poor Clare novice from Rouen who had 'some little dispute with her companions' was later found 'shutt up in her chamber, prostrate before her altar with the 7 penitential psalms before her' (Rouen Chronicles MS: 59, in Bowden 2012a: 223). An abbess in the same convent maintained her calm demeanour in the face of trouble during her governance: 'She had often in her mouth this verce of the Psalm: *Auxilium meum a Domino qui fecit coelum & terram, & divinum auxilium maneat semper nobiscum*; saying that God did so strangely help her sometimes when she said them' (125).[24] While in the workhouse and at the grate, Lucy Knatchbull repeated Latin verses to herself, her meditative mind continually employed while her body attended to its necessary routines, in line with instruction.[25] Once, at Mass she shaped her reciprocal response around a particular passage:

> for my misery, and great ingratitude made me exceedingly afrayde to appeere in the presence of his all matchless goodness and that verse of the Psalme. Quid retribuam domino[26] came into my mind and I thought what I had that I might present unto our Lord but could thinke of nothinge which was not already his, only sinne excepted and the meserys which it Contracted in me. (Knatchbull 1642, in Hallett 2012a: 209)

---

[23] On psalms in convent ceremonies, see Lux-Sterritt 2012: 3, 11, 17, 19, 21, 25, including less ideal behaviour: 'There is a great fallt in not coming to the devine Office in due time, sometimes a whole psalme is past before everie one is come in … some also doe not their duties there as they should doe, some laugh & whisper one to another, even the officers of the quire for want of preparing their books & looking before hand what Office was to be said' (484).

[24] Psalm 120:2: 'My help is from the Lord, who made heaven and earth', and the liturgy for Lauds: 'Let divine help always remain with us.'

[25] A Cambrai Benedictine-owned treatise stated: 'There remaines a third danger & defense in point of idle thoughts, to which we have opposed continuall Imployement of mind & body. For this reason our holy founders have for every houre of the day prescribed either spirituall exercises, as reading good books, singing psalmes & divout himes, meditation & prather, or corporall, that is manuall employements … that the devil maie never finde you idle' (*A short treatise*, in Lux-Sterritt 2012: 80).

[26] Psalm 115:12: 'What shall I render to the Lord, for all the things he hath rendered unto me?'

Another time, as 'the Prist beginne to bringe the Blessed Sacrament from the Aulter', she 'thought also upon the psalme, of who will give mine eyes fountaines of teares etc' (200).[27] On another occasion, in delight and 'soberly druncke', she 'tooke pleasure to recite that verse, *Quid mihi est in Caelo* &c'.[28]

Our sense, then, is that the women took comfort from particular scriptural references and drew on familiar phrases to shape, explain, or direct their own experiences at important moments. At times scriptural reference indeed appears to inform the speech and rhythms of daily exchange. The dying Margaret Clement (who sang the 'Dutch ditty' swansong) was asked by her Superior: 'I humbly besech you to be mindfull of us your poore children when you shall come into the hevenly wynseller to be in ebreated'. She replied: 'O Mother shall I come to drink of that wyne indeed' (Shirley n.d.: 72, in Hallett 2012a: 32).[29] Immediately afterwards, on receiving her final sacraments, Clement is movingly described 'reading with us so well as she could the vii psalme for then her spech begane to fayle'. In effect, Clement recites her own Office of the Dead which includes this Psalm.[30] Her action shows in startlingly personal terms the general role of such material in effecting an imaginative transposition between spiritual states, from living into dying well.

One of the main purposes of compilers of this life-writing is clearly to attest to examples of blessedness both within the community (thereby providing models for good living) and also beyond (enhancing the convent's reputation, essential for increasing alms and vocations). In both respects, the nuns ministered to their Sisters' needs, and this is the main justification they give for reading and for writing in the convent. In the final stages of this chapter I will turn to the ways in which the nuns' interpretative impulse reflected and shaped their wider evangelism beyond the cloister as well as inside, in preparing themselves and their nation for the return of Catholicism. Again, imitative practice is at the heart of their enterprise. In particular, I will discuss the figure of Mary Magdalene, to reveal how the nuns' treatment of her informed their contemplative fashioning and their wider mission.

'PUTTING ON ST MAGDALEN'

A seventeenth-century Carmelite treatise leads the contemplative via the prayer of silence through stages marked by citations from the Psalms: 'My soul is before you

---

[27] Psalm 119:136: 'My eyes have sent forth springs of water: because they have not kept thy law.'

[28] Psalm 72:25: 'Quid mihi est in caelo et tecum nolui in terra'; 'For what have I in heaven? And besides thee what do I desire upon earth?' On spiritual inebriation see Song of Songs 2:4, 5:1.

[29] Song of Songs 2:4.

[30] Psalm 7:1: 'Dómine, Deus meus, in te sperávi salvum me fac ex ómnibus persequéntibus me, et líbera me': 'Lord, my God, in you have I put my trust; save me from all them that persecute me, and deliver me.'

like the drie earth which expectes the rain'; 'I am like a sparrow solitarie in the house-topp'; then in transport she cries out, 'My heart and soul are ravish'd with joy'.[31] This typical eight-fold path enjoins the devout to 'Enter into your self with deep inspection of your defects', 'Imagin yourself upon the confines of eternity', and to 'Put on St Magdalen's dispositions, or the Cananean woman's, Samaritan's, or Publican's & c and keep thus silently before God' (*Second Treatise*: 188). The contemplative thus imaginatively moves from aridity into the warm embrace of forgiveness. This treatise echoes Teresa of Ávila: 'Neither the Magdalen, nor the woman of Samaria, nor the Canaanitish woman was dead to the world when she found Him' (Teresa of Ávila 1944–6: III, 267).[32] In Teresa's writing, the Magdalene is frequently aligned with ideal contemplative action (in contrast, of course, with Martha's practicality, a common enough distinction) and, more importantly, with affectivity: 'moved with the deepest emotion' and sick with love for her Saviour.[33] In *Way of Perfection*, Teresa 'imagined herself at [Christ's] feet and wept with the Magdalen exactly as if she had seen Him with her bodily eyes in the Pharisee's house' (Teresa of Ávila 1944–6: II, 147). Her text segues between subjects, giving vicarious access to mercy; ambiguously 'as if she'—they both, one physically, one meditatively—had seen Christ; both weep.

Literary critics have noted how English poets draw allegorical parallels between Mary Magdalene's situation and that of Catholic recusants. Writing about Robert Southwell, F. W. Brownlow comments that the Magdalene 'stands for the Christian soul separated by violence from living Christian truth that is her only happiness. More specifically, she is an English Catholic woman' (Brownlow 1996: 43). When devotional writers urge their readers to 'put on St Magdalene', they are inviting considered meditation both on separation and the means to overcome it, just as the nuns do when they instil imitation of her figure. Both draw on an affective aesthetic to offer comfort to those separated, whether by their apparent sinfulness or by the geographies of politics.

The work of Robert Southwell (1561–95) clearly functions in this way. His poems often appear with other instructional material circulated in manuscripts designed to 'inspire English Catholics, a persecuted flock, cut off from pastoral comfort and ecclesiastical organization' (Miola 2012: 412). In the tight Catholic circles at home and overseas, there were inevitably close connections between Southwell and the English convents. He took refuge with the Copley and the Arundell families, for instance, both of which had members who were nuns. For the countess of Arundell he compiled his guide for lay women, *A Shorte Rule of Good Life*, several copies of which were made for other Catholic families (*ODNB*). His *Marie Magdalens Funeral Teares* (1591) was dedicated to 'Mistres D. A.', namely Dorothy Arundell (1560–1613) who in 1600 professed as a Benedictine in

---

[31] Psalms 143:6; 102:7; 84:2 (*Second Treatise*: 47, in Lux-Sterritt 2012: 188, 515).

[32] This appears in Teresa's commentary on John of the Cross. On Mary Magdalene as a figure for the persecuted and those separated from grace, see her *Interior Castle* (Teresa of Ávila 1944–6: II, 328, 349).

[33] *Interior Castle* (Teresa of Ávila 1944–6: II, 129, 304); *Way of Perfection* (Teresa of Ávila 1944–6: II, 173).

Brussels.[34] In it he draws on the figure of the Magdalene 'to fashion a recusant subject who is spiritually noble in the face of spiritual alienation' (Kuchar 2007: 140). *Funeral Tears*, widely translated and republished, with some editions produced for Protestant readers, is an extended prose meditation on the Magdalene's mourning, shaped around John 20:13: 'Woman, why weepest thou?' It also cites Jeremiah 6:26 in its heading: 'Gird thee with sackcloth, O daughter of my people, and sprinkle thee with ashes: make thee mourning as for an only son, a bitter lamentation, because the destroyer shall suddenly come upon us.'

Southwell's technique is strikingly similar to that of devotional manuals read by both nuns and lay Catholics in which emotions are aroused in order to be diverted to religious ends: 'Passions I allow, and loues I approue, onely I would wishe that men would alter their obiect and better their intent', as the dedication states (Southwell 1591: A3ᵛ).[35] He represents each of the bodily senses in turn, to reciprocate with spiritually functioning alternatives: 'Thy eyes haue lost him, thy hands cannot feele him … and if thy eyes were melted, thy soule in languor, and thy senses decayed, how wouldest thou see him, if he did appeare?' (Southwell 1591: 20). He tempers his polemic with insights from John of the Cross: 'It is clear, then, that these sensual apprehensions and visions cannot be a means to union, since they bear no proportion of God; and this was one of the reasons why Christ desired that the Magdalene and S. Thomas should not touch him' (John of the Cross 1943: XI, 12).

Southwell's consolatory piece is very much in the devotional spirit of such writers and pursues the same method as those of English instructional authors like Richard Brathwaite (1587/8–1673), whose dedicatees included Henry Somerset, earl of Worcester, whose daughter entered the Antwerp Carmel in 1643 and with whose family Tobie Matthew took refuge in 1641. Brathwaite's *Essaies Vpon the Fiue Senses* (1620) likewise redirects somatic sensory impulse towards spiritual ends. The finale of Southwell's piece describes the exact endeavour of the contemplative:

> A submitteth soule soonest winneth his returne, and the deeper it sinketh in self contempt, the higher it climbeth in his highest fauours. And if thou perceiuest in the tombe of thy hart, the presence of his two first messengers … entertaine them with sighes, and welcome them with penitent tears. (Southwell 1591: 68)

In Southwell's techniques we can trace predictable continuity of impetus between domestic and devotional environments, as well as crossover of personnel in lay and professed circles. We can thus identify the ways in which a shared devotional aesthetic informed creative and instructional work inside and outside the English convents, and see how this shaped the ideals of overlapping interpretative communities.

---

[34] Arundell was the author of *Life of Father Cornelius the Martyr*. See the work of Elizabeth Patton, who alleges connections between Arundell and Southwell's work (Patton 2011 and 2013).

[35] Molekamp argues: 'If Southwell demonstrates the dangers of unregulated passion, he does not prevent the reader from feeling the depth of Mary's grief' (Molekamp 2010: 65).

As I suggested earlier in this chapter, writers in both spheres employed literary motifs to convey a sense of love-longing and abandonment in their holy pursuit. Again, for the English nuns such expressiveness informed both their contemplative and their apostolic mission in which they often invoke the figure of the Magdalene, as we can see in this excerpt from the poem beginning 'All things, desires, and loves are vaine' by the English Cambrai Benedictine, Gertrude More (1606–33) which appears in Confession VII of her *Spiritual Exercises*:

> No Stagge in chace so thirsty is,
> Or greedy of sweet spring
> As is my soul of *thee* my *God*
> While I heere sighing sing,
> My soul, where is thy *Loue* and *Lord*,
> Since *him* thou canst not find?
> O cheere up hart, be comforted,
> For *he* is in thy mind! (More 1658: 47, ll. 37–44)

This is More's extended meditation on Augustine, for whom psalmic inspiration was central—'I drew in my breath and now pant after you' (Augustine 1992: X, xxx–vii, 38—and an extract from Thomas à Kempis' *Imitation*, book 3, chapter 21 (Kempis 1952: 118) which she quotes in Latin, translates, and then develops in a lengthy poetic exegesis. It fulfils with ecstatic delight his Disciple's plaint ('For my heart cannot rest nor be wholly content until it rests in You') with Christ's promise ('I have come to your cry. Your tears and your soul's longing, your humiliation and contrition of heart have moved Me to come to you'). The poem is an extended paean in the voice of yearning lover: 'ile never cease | to languish for his *Love*, | Breathing, and sighing after *him*' (ll. 10–11), tacitly referencing Mary Magdalene's words in John 20:13: 'Because they have taken away my Lord; and I know not where they have laid him'. Like Augustine, More blends Psalm 41:2 ('As the hart panteth after the fountains of water; so my soul panteth after thee, O God') with the Song of Songs 2:9 ('My beloved is like a roe, or a young hart'). She shares heavily Petrarchan conceits with other similarly nuanced texts, such as the *Spiritual Canticle* of John of the Cross:

> Where have you hidden,
> My love, and left me moaning?
> Like a stag you fled
> having wounded me.[36]

The nun is clearly working within a wide tradition of European mystical writing to offer interpretative commentary on a range of interwoven sources. Her various influences are

[36] Excerpt from a beautiful translation of Canticle 1 by Peter Tyler (Tyler 2010: 40). On More's metaphors of unrequited love, see Wolfe 2004: 143.

apparent, here as elsewhere, not least in her language of ecstatic union at the finale of this poem where the lover is urged 'be absorpt', to 'melt into that *Love*'. The list of books More compiled as to 'helpe, comfort, and increase the Deuotion of contemplative spirits' (More 1657: 34–5) indeed included works by Augustine, John of the Cross, Teresa de Jesus, François de Sales, Benet of Canfield, Walter Hilton, and others already mentioned here who so shaped convent spiritual methods.

In this poem, as elsewhere in More's writing, the figure of Mary Magdalene is central.[37] Like Teresa of Ávila, More was drawn to both the Magdalene and to St Augustine as affective penitents. Around them she shaped her *Spiritual Exercises*, an instructional text for her convent which reached a wider lay audience when it was published in 1658. Here More extrapolates from a series of texts, including Augustine's *Confessions*, to produce a sermon-like commentary, interspersed with prayers and poems, including reference to Mary Magdalene's role in Luke 24:5: 'Why seek you the living with the dead?' which forms a *leitmotif* for the sequence. More follows a liturgical route aligned with gospel readings in the convent. For example, Confession XLVI references John 20: 'Lord it is read today of *thee* that Saint *Mary Magdalene* approaching to kis *thy* feet, it would not be admitted her by *thee*' (More 1658: 196). Her LII Confession relates to the office of St Mary Magdalene and Luke 7:48, 'Thy sins are forgiven thee'.[38] The editorial gloss informs us that More's penultimate Confession took place on St Magdalene's day before she was 'surprised by a bodily indisposition' that led to her death on 17 August 1633 (More 1658: 237). *Spiritual Exercises* was compiled by Augustine Baker (1575–1641), her spiritual advisor. It was not printed until twenty-five years after the nun's death, and although Baker used this as an opportunity to underline his own teachings (by then held to be controversial), as well as to promote More's legacy, we can be confident that More's own interpretative skill is revealed here, and that she was highly adept in making figurative connections in her writing and her ministry.[39]

This is one of several examples of material which was read both inside and outside the convents and which reveal the shared devotional imperatives of professed and lay Catholic writers. The dedicatory poem to *Spiritual Exercises* suggests the two-way focus of much of this work, towards an historical English Catholic heritage (in which the nun is identified as grandchild of Thomas More), and also towards a European literature that is both courtly poetic and Teresian: like the saint, she is 'Wounded with a *Seraphic Dart*' (More 1658: frontispiece). Such imagery was familiar, of course, from Tobie Matthew's 1642 *The Flaming Hart*, his translation of the *vida* of Teresa de Jesus prepared for the Antwerp English Carmelites. This in turn influenced Richard Crashaw (*c*.1613–49), among others, in his Teresian trilogy written between 1646 and 1652: 'The Hymne to St

[37] 'She treats St Mary Magdalen as a model mystic who abandoned the world of the senses to pursue contemplation' (Marotti 2009: xvi). On Augustine and the spiritual senses, see *Confessions* (Augustine 1992: X, vii, 8).

[38] The 1658 version erroneously numbers the Confession XLII and names Luke 9:5 in the margin.

[39] On the role of the book in 'the renewed controversy surrounding Baker's instruction', see Lay 2011: 104; Van Hyning 2013.

Teresa', 'An Apologie for the fore-goinge Hymn', and 'The Flaming Heart upon the Book and Picture of the seraphicall saint Teresa'. Martin Ven den Enden's engraving of the 1576 portrait of Teresa by Juan de la Miseria which was used as the frontispiece of Matthew's *Flaming Hart* was also used by Crashaw with his hymn in Teresa's honour, 'Love thou art absolute sole Lord' (Scott 2013: 201). Matthew sought to bring European devotional texts to an English readership at home and abroad. He translated Augustine's *Confessions* and works by many Spanish and Italian authors, as well as writing Lives of several women religious, among them that of Knatchbull compiled very soon after completing *Flaming Hart*. Indeed, traces of Teresa's Life can be so clearly discerned in Knatchbull's that the two women often appear, as Matthew himself disingenuously observes, 'as even two dropps of water can be' (Knatchbull 1642, in Hallett 2012a: 194).[40] We can see here, and in Matthew's wider endeavours, an aim that is shared by the exiled nuns: to 'English' their Spanish and other pan-European Catholic influences.[41] As Crashaw writes in 'An Apologie':

> What soule soever in any Language can
>   Speake heaven like hers, is my soules country-man.
>   O 'tis not Spanish, but 'tis heav'n she speakes. (Crashaw 1652: 102)

Moreover, as Nandra Perry so insightfully suggests, we can identify in Crashaw's work a similar process of incorporation that so occupied the nuns themselves as writers, to promote personal spiritual union through the process of their texts. Crashaw's:

> goal is not so much to signify as to transfuse the reader with divine love … the real power of Teresa's *vita* lies not in the rhetorical effect of her words … but in the analogy between the *vita*'s effect on the reader and the experience of divine union it purportedly describes. Teresa's words do not so much persuade as pierce, causing a 'death' in their reader that echoes Teresa's own mystical death. (Perry 2006: 12, 13)

There is correlation here with the nuns who, like Knatchbull, wrote not only of their own ecstatic transport ('my Soule seemed to be soe neerly, and soe amorously united with allmighty God, that she as it were forgott her self'), but who also desired to influence reception:

> I sought to cast the harts of all those Creatures, into the fire of his excessive love; that so, as soe many grains of incense, they might all in one instant, breake forth; and as it were Consume, in most amorous and sweet affections of Praise. (Knatchbull 1642, in Hallett 2012a: 166)

---

[40] Jaime Goodrich notes: 'While Matthew's biography might appear to subordinate Knatchbull's voice, this work's plural authorship reflects the joint religious endeavours undertaken in convent life … a reciprocal and co-operative spiritual relationship' (Goodrich 2013: 110).

[41] A claim I explore more fully in Hallett 2013.

Knatchbull expands Teresa de Jesus's image of rapture from *Interior Castle*, when a soul 'decided to offer no more resistance than a straw does when it is lifted up by amber' (Teresa of Ávila 1944–6: II, 293):

> me thoughts my spiritt was, in a moment fastned or rather united with our Lord. I know not how to say this is done; but me thinks it is, as if the power and virtue of God Almightys Spiritt, had in an excelent quicke manner, drawne mine to it; and (still to speake be way of Comparison) it may be a little understood, by the virtue of amber, or Jett, which we see draws straws, or such other like things, to it self, this I say may serve for a Comparison, though it doe not Perfectly express the things. For the straw, or thredd doth only sticke fast to the Jett, but the vertu of the Jett doth not change the nature of the thredd, or straw by touching it, but here by this devine touch; it seemed, that my spiritt was not only fastned to our Lord; but it was, as it were, Converted into the same spiritt; and mad one thinge with him. (Knatchbull 1642, in Hallett 2012a: 197)

The nun's intermediary source (Teresa as author and as conduit) is thus further opened up to those who recognize the reference, a form of secondary reading embedded in the text; Christ through Teresa as 'living book': 'Blessed be such a Book, which leaves impressed upon us what we are to read and do, in a way that is unforgettable!' (Teresa of Ávila 1944–6: I, 168–9). This is more than affective imitation, though it is that too; it enables individual 'souls' to be 'mad one thinge'. As Perry suggests, in Crashaw's words from 'An Apologie' (politicizing I Corinthians 12:12), this process 'makes but one body of all soules' (Crashaw 1652: 102).

In conclusion, I have argued that enclosed contemplatives shape a distinctive kind of interpretative community. They seek to further a transnational Catholic heritage through a literary evangelism based on transubstantiating ideas of language which distinguish them from other confessional groups. Through this, nuns take an intercessional role in their writing; strikingly, their elucidatory acts enable them to intervene in the spiritual lives of their Sister-religious to instil community both by placing them in touch with blessed figures inside their own convents and by the motion of their texts. Theirs is an imperative directed to the ministry of women in which they share poetic processes employed by other Catholic writers in pursuit of a similar aesthetic and apostolic urge.

CHAPTER 26

....

SECTARIAN GROUPS

....

JOHANNA HARRIS

The Church of England hath three maine Divisions; The Conformist, the
Non-Conformist, and the Separatist.... The Separ[at]ist is subdivided too
(as they say) into Separatist and Semi-Seperatist [*sic*].

(Greville 1641: 90)

THE history of English Protestant radicalism and dissent is characterized by disagreements over the interpretation of Scripture and the role of the Holy Spirit in the believer's faith and experience (and, thus, liberty of conscience). Other concerns, such as
the structure of church gatherings, the roles of the magistracy and the laity in church
order and discipline, the theology and administration of the sacraments (baptism and
the Lord's Supper), and the nature of grace and reformed spirituality stem from this
core. Despite moments of severe persecution, this history was a successful one, dating
back at least as far as the Reformation itself. Simply put, dissent was never eradicated.
Separation was an imperative for the true church (Hill 1977b: 201–2; *OED*, 'millenarianism', 'millenarism'), but the precise nature of that separation is not straightforwardly
definable; the *longue durée* of Protestant sectarianism in the early modern period, as this
chapter will show, must be considered as marked by degrees of separation, just as was
suggested by Robert Greville, Lord Brooke's division in 1641, even within the Church of
England, of Non-Conformist and Separatist, and his further subdivision of 'Separatist
and Semi-Seperatist [*sic*]'.

Christopher Hill's influential thesis of English radicalism's tendency to 'turn the world
upside down' (Acts 17:6) has, to a greater or lesser extent, been maintained in subsequent scholarship, and includes the view that the early to mid-seventeenth century
crisis was an 'English Revolution', asserting that it was a radicalized Puritanism, left-
wing in its politics, which drove in England a progressive if, by definition, marginalized
and proletarian social movement. Doctrinal controversies were at the heart of radical

sectarianism, and studies of the legal, political, and social implications can downplay this. The charges by the conservative Presbyterian minister, Thomas Edwards, among others, against sectarianism's 'illiterate mechanick Preachers' drew attention to a perceived illiterate body familiar with manual labours and trades ('mechanick') but who essentially contended for the freedom to interpret Scripture and to preach, without formal training and mediation of an ecclesiastical class (Edwards 1646b: prefatory epistle; *OED*, 'mechanic', I.1–3; Smith 1989: 288–99; McDowell 2003: ch. 2).

The best language to describe those who withheld from fully supporting monarchical and episcopal hegemony does not reside in a simple binary of sectarian (or dissenting) and non-sectarian (or conforming), and taking greater account of the long history of dissent exacerbates this insufficiency. Despite the hope the Elizabethan Settlement brought of a renewed and fuller reformation, an underground Protestantism never disappeared. Small gatherings of believers that had formed during Mary's reign continued to meet, communicating with similarly minded individuals and groups, geographically distanced (for examples, see Collinson 2006). Among them were the 'Brownists' (sometimes, 'Barrowists'), under the influence of Robert Browne, Robert Harrison, and Henry Barrow. Browne's *Reformation without tarrying for anie* (1571) was an influential contribution to this early swell of separatism, arguing for the kind of voluntary covenant between members that rejected the concept of a national church, particularly on the grounds that the unreformed should not be welcomed to the Lord's Supper. The practice of admitting all to the Lord's Supper regardless of personal reformation especially inflamed Brownists (Paget 1618).

Early challengers to Calvinist orthodoxy included Anabaptists, Familists, and Antinomians. Anabaptists rejected infant baptism as unscriptural, requiring believer's baptism, rebaptizing those baptized as infants. They emphasized the freedom of the Spirit in worship, the exercise of spiritual gifts in corporate involvement, and the authority of Scripture (see Horst 1972; Martin 1976).[1] Their controversiality derived largely from the reputation gained by 'the mad men of *Munster*' and the failed radical Anabaptist theocracy established in 1534. This 'madness' and 'tragicall catastrophe' gained notoriety in literary history through Thomas Nashe's *The Unfortunate Traveller* (1594: n.p.).[2] Along with Anabaptists, Nashe, in *Pierce Penilesse*, refers to 'adulterous Familists', the members of the Family of Love, founded by Henry Niclaes, with similarities to Anabaptism, advocating adult baptism and freedom of conscience. Familists did not require separation from the national church, however (Nashe 1592: sig. C4; Marsh 1994).

Antinomian thought championed the idea of 'free grace', emphasizing that as the believer is saved by faith alone and not by works (Ephesians 2:8–9) he is no longer bound by Old Testament moral law; it is through Christ's death and resurrection that salvation is achieved. Antinomianism was a crucial influence on the developing radicalism

---

[1] The London Baptist Confession of Faith (1644), *Of those Churches which are commonly (though falsely) called ANABAPTISTS*, clearly distinguishes between Baptists and Anabaptists.

[2] 'Mad men' is used widely, including by Loe 1621: 2, Torshell 1632: 68, and Burton 1621: 756. On the Münster Rebellion, see von Kerssenbroch (2007).

of the period and, in the 1620s and 1630s, under Archbishop William Laud's programme of liturgical and sacramental worship and enforcement of uniformity it became questionable whether the Calvinist consensus was still dominant or defended by the ecclesiastical hierarchy (Nuttall, intro Lake, 1992: 36). This intensified reflection increasingly stifled puritan expression, channelling it into perceived radical religious subversion (Como 2000; Como 2004: chs 3–4). An example is the censorship of the moderate conformist Puritans Thomas Gataker and Stephen Denison, who were not notorious for their radicalism. The sharp end of the dispute with conservative Protestantism was with the royal endorsement of the Arminian position, isolating moderate Puritans (Tyacke 1987a, 1990b). Arminianism was strengthening at one end of the conformist wing (at variance with its historical Calvinism) but so too was it emerging in radical puritan circles. Proponents included the Independent John Goodwin and the General Baptists (but not Particular Baptists). This antinomian disposition of the radical wing of Protestantism argued that the believer was guided primarily by the wisdom and inspiration of the Holy Spirit (More 1982–3: 50–70).

Defining Puritanism in relation to sectarianism is a problematic dimension of this discussion. Puritanism was not a uniform movement, and we must be wary of adopting the stereotypical perception of Puritans as hardline Calvinists, intensely predestinarian, and functioning within a strictly reformed and uniform orthodoxy. These are popular markers, but Puritans did not have one common theology (Coffey 2006b: 108). A stronger radical fervour emerged when the perimeters of national church polity began to shrink (Coffey 2006a: 22–4). It was this historical moment—centring on Laud's archbishopric—that arguably propelled conservative Puritans, with a zeal for reform, to question their communion with the established church, increasingly reluctant to compromise with ecclesiastical changes. They reacted against Laud's anti-puritan rhetoric and ceremonial, allegedly popish drive which effectively turned mainstream Calvinist Protestantism into the equivalent of a reviled sect. Sectarianism, like heresy, is largely defined by and against the dominant ecclesiastical power.[3]

To generalize, moderate Puritanism had close connections with the established church; the predominant theological position of bishops was still Calvinist, with emphases on the central reformed tenets of preaching and evangelism. To ally Puritanism with heresy in the period, therefore, is unsustainable, given that it was as involved in charging heretics as it was in allegedly forging them, as Lake has argued (Lake 2006b: 83; Collinson 1967, 1988; Lake 1982). Any 'revolutionary' ideal in English Puritanism was primarily focused on continuing the work of reform that Puritans believed lingered unfinished since the Elizabethan Settlement. This conviction had strong connections with the 'Nadere Reformatie' of continental reformed churches and the traditions of international Protestantism.[4]

---

[3] I am grateful to Karen Edwards for discussion on this point.

[4] The Dutch 'Nadere Reformatie' references 'further reformation' and typically refers to the period of the Dutch second reformation of 1600–1750; on international Calvinist Protestantism, see Adams 1973.

Sectarianism in modern religious sociology is a kind of church assembly polity which perceives itself to be distinct from a church organization allied to the state, a separate and small grouping of Christians (Troeltsch 1931; Weber 1930). A pejorative term in origin, the sectarian was 'bigotedly attached' to a schismatic sect (*OED*, 'sectarian', 1). The term was first wielded by the Presbyterians in the Commonwealth period against the Independents, calling them 'that sectarian party', and only subsequently was it used by the national Church to describe Nonconformists (*OED*, 'sectarian', 3). Catholics also labelled Protestants 'sectarian' (A.S. 1663: 3–4).

Early modern usage of sectarian language, however, betrays more complex origins, groupings, and interrelations. For instance, it is impossible to define the host of ministers who were, as non-separatists, ordained in the established church and held livings during the Interregnum, ejected and Nonconformist in 1662, separatist yet without shifting theological position. Shades of Puritanism and sectarianism, as Lake articulates, were 'spiritually nearer to one another than is any of them to the Roman Catholic Church or to the Laudian party within the Church of England' (Nuttall 1992: 9), with inherent intersections and degrees of a common intellectual radical inheritance that emerged from within 'the social matrix of the godly community' (Como 2008: 242–3).

A rhetoric of severance dominates discussions of England's sectarian landscape. Yet in broad terms, what created a body, or community, of dissent was a shared experience of persecution, with a common antagonist. After all, the designation 'dissenter' applies to 'whatever persuasion' of Nonconformist, in the persecutory aftermath of the Act of Uniformity; in Keeble's words, what they 'shared together separated them as a group from the established church far more pressingly than anything which separated them from each other' (1987: 44). It is these degrees of separation that help to contextualize Lord Brooke's suggestion quoted at the beginning of this chapter, that the Church of England divides into three broad groups.

ROBERT GREVILLE, LORD BROOKE, 'GROSS NOTED SECTARY'

The tripartite division of Protestant religious identity in England, of 'Conformist', 'Non-Conformist', and the subdivided 'Separatist and Semi-Separatist' (Greville 1641: 90), by the parliamentarian officer and writer Robert Greville, second Lord Brooke (1607–43), articulates the vagaries of definition regarding those inside and outside the national church, and those perching precariously between. Monarchical or parliamentary acts are usually the markers of clear division (declarations such as the Act of Uniformity or the Act of Toleration being the most obvious examples), setting clergy clear demands of allegiance or dissent. Such markers alone, however, obscure the full story, especially when the activities of the laity are considered. England's Reformation left a legacy of lay participation in theological and church administrative matters (Kaufman 2004).

Prophesyings, especially, when laity and clergy assembled to improve their Scriptural understanding (particularly for sermons), were indicative of the reformed vision of enhancing corporate biblical knowledge and participation in the life of the church. Arming Protestant pew-dwellers with Scriptural confidence was a way of combating backsliding into Catholicism. In 1576 Elizabeth ordered the suppression of prophesyings, viewing them as a threat to church and state stability and as sectarian (even suspending Grindal for refusing to suppress them), but the seeds of lay participation and, most importantly, of individual access to the Word, had been sown (Collinson 1967: 168–239; Collinson 1979: 233–52). Brooke seems to be aware of such a reformed historical tradition, as the categories he delineates together constitute 'The Church of England', suggesting a broader conception of the nature of the 'Church' than most conformists would admit.

Brooke's discussion of sectarianism and schism in *A Discourse Opening the Nature of that Episcopacie which is exercised in England* (1641) adopts an animadversarial style that suits the context of the Smectymnuuan pamphlet controversy, to which it was a less-heralded contribution, rebutting Bishop Joseph Hall, author of *Episcopacie by Divine Right. Asserted* (1640) and *An Humble Remonstrance* (1641). Brooke writes:

> Would it not bee much better to hazzard the comming in of all These, than still to suffer our soules and bodies, to be groun'd to powder by these Tyrannicall, Antichristian Prelates, that under pretence of keeping out *Separatisme*, introduce downe-right *Popery*, and a sinck of almost all Errors and Heresies? (1641: 99)

His concern was the corruption of episcopal rule, with godly governance integral to full reformation. His argument was indebted to Milton's *Of Prelaticall Episcopacy*, published just three months earlier (Whiting 1936: 161–6). Milton's *Areopagitica* (1644) posthumously praised the 'right and pious Lord' Brooke's *Discourse*, in terms counteracting charges of schismatic intent:

> [Lord Brooke] writing of Episcopacy, and by the way treating of sects and schisms, left Ye his vote, or rather now the last words of his dying charge, which I know will ever be of dear and honour'd regard with Ye, so full of meeknes and breathing charity, that ... I cannot call to mind where I have read or heard words more mild and peacefull.

Milton's call, like Brooke's, was 'to tolerat them, though in some disconformity to ourselves', even in the 1640s. He interpreted Brooke's discussion as an exhortation to 'hear with patience and humility' those sectaries, 'however they be miscall'd', since they 'desire to live purely, in such a use of Gods Ordinances, as the best guidance of their conscience gives them' (Milton 1644: 35). The middle-way man of enforced Nonconformity, Richard Baxter, eventually came also to this view, believing it did not fall within the remit of the institutionalized church to divide believers along the lines of orthodox and heretic: 'I have no great zeale to confine the Church to the party that I best like, nor to shut Christ out of all other Societies, and coope him up to the congregations of these few that say to all the rest of the Church, Stand by, wee are more holy then you' (1670: prefatory epistle).

With this disinclination to classify other Christians, why, then, did Baxter forthrightly declare Brooke a 'noted gross Sectary'? (Clarke 1651: epistle dedicatory; Baxter 1696: 1.63; Strider 1958; Hughes 1987). In Samuel Clarke's hagiography, *A General Martyrologie* (1651), Brooke was a godly moderate with an ancient and honourable lineage (A3^{r-v}). Another biographical account described Brooke as 'a dear foster father ... to many Ministers and Schoole-Masters ... Not only those that went his way, but also such as did conform to the church government were his beneficiaries' (Spencer 1977: 173). An anonymous elegy printed on Brooke's death posits the association with radicalism as the result of slander by 'Romes base abettors' who 'wound thy pure Profession with the name | Of schisme, and a new-found Brownistick frame' (Anon. 1643). Ephraim Huit's *The Prophecy of Daniel explained* (1643), dedicated to Brooke's widow, Lady Katherine, alleged that Brooke would have been the dedicatee had he lived, since he had already perused it, encouraged its publication, and 'was so far affected with it'. The work interprets the prophet Daniel's visions, and is vindication 'against dissenting Opinions'. These dissenters, so construed, were 'the Prelaticall party' who condemned this interpretation of 'the glorious calling and conversion of the Jews' (Huit 1643: title page, 'Epistle Dedicatorie'), signalling Brooke probably adhered to a millenarian outlook (Huit 1643: 357).

Brooke was also a close friend and generous patron to Thomas Dugard, headmaster of Warwick School, introduced through Thomas Gataker, the classicist and moderate Puritan and eventual conformer (*ODNB*, 'Gataker, Thomas'; Hughes 1986: 774). Dugard's Latin diary reveals an intriguing network of university, clergy, county, and family connections, centring on Brooke's home, Warwick Castle, where he regularly gathered an eminent group of lay and clerical Puritans (Hughes 1986: 771–93). Among his patronized ministers were Dugard and John Bryan (a close friend of Baxter), and his long-serving chaplain, Simeon Ashe. Influential godly laity included Lord Saye and Sele, John Pym, Oliver St John, Robert Rich, earl of Warwick, Sir Thomas Lucy, and Richard Knightley.[5] These were among the shareholders of the Providence Island Company, but they were also the leading opponents of royal policy (Kupperman 1993). The group was also closely connected to the nearby Warwick lectureships. Lecturers included the radical Independent preacher Peter Sterry (also Brooke's chaplain), the expelled London preacher John Poynter, George Hughes, Thomas Hill, and John Ball (Hughes 1987: 73; on the Warwick lectureship see also Hughes 1986: 775). The Ranter and sensational radical Abiezer Coppe was, in his earlier years, another visitor to Brooke's circle, preaching Sunday sermons and giving lectures in Warwick (McDowell 2003: 90–3).

A long history underpins why sectarianism is better seen by degrees of separation than stark divisions, leading Brooke, in 1641, to observe the 'semi-Separatist' and 'Separatist' as constituting part of the national Church. What emerged in the coming of Civil War,

---

[5] For more detail on those congregating at Warwick Castle, see Hughes 1987: 72–5.

and is seen in Brooke's observation of an underground movement of, cooperatively, lay and clerical sectarianism rising to the surface at the end of his life, was a continuation of what Patrick Collinson has described as 'the *longue durée* of Post-Reformation religious history', a period which witnessed a shift of 'primary, secondary and tertiary processes from Protestantism through Puritanism to Separatism and Sectarianism' (2006: 129).

RADICAL INHERITANCES

On 19 June 1567, about one hundred men and women gathered in Plumbers' Hall, Anchor Lane, London. They claimed they met together for a wedding but in reality they met as a separatist Protestant congregation. Fifteen of the group were arrested. The next day, eight were interrogated by Edmund Grindal, bishop of London, the dean of Westminster, and eight High Commissioners. Following the example of the Marian persecuted and martyrs, the interrogated left a written account of the exchange, articulating their church desires: 'the worde truely preached, the Sacramentes truly ministred, and Discipline according to the worde of God; & these be the notes by which the true church is known'.[6]

Generally tolerant of reformist puritan zeal as bishop and archbishop, Grindal was nevertheless opposed to the separatism and schism of believers. In a letter to Heinrich Bullinger on 11 June 1568, he commented on the nature and activities of the separatist churches:

> Some London citizens of the lowest order, together with four or five ministers, remarkable neither for their judgment nor learning, have openly separated from us; and sometimes in private houses, sometimes in the fields, and occasionally even in ships, they have held their meetings and administered the sacraments. Besides this, they have ordained ministers, elders, and deacons, after their own way, and have even ex-communicated some who had seceded from their church ... The number of this sect is about two hundred, but consisting of more women than men.[7]

Arrests continued to be made in following years, but the memory of the congregations meeting during Mary's reign continued to motivate many ongoing separatist gatherings, some explicitly choosing to meet in 'the very place where the persecuted Church and Martyrs were enforced to use the like exercises', and arrested in such places. (For those arrested, including the many women, see Powicke 1901–4: 141–58; Barrow and

---

[6] The dramatized account of the interrogation, titled 'The true report of our Examination and conference (as neare as wee can call to remembrance) had the 20 day of June 1567', is in *A parte of a register* (1593: 23–37). See also *The seconde part of a register* (1915); Collinson 1990b: 423, 440; Nicholson 1843: 201–16; Collinson 1979: ch. 9. The group arrested is named in Peel 1920: 10–11.

[7] Edmund Grindal to Heinrich Bullinger (Robinson 1842–5: 201–2); Strype 1710: 154–5; see also Jones 2006: 24.

Mickle-bound 1611: D2^v.) Several examples remain of their early covenants and declarations, signed by individual members, and their justifications for separation and manner of organization, in Strype's formulation, in 'clancular [i.e. clandestine] and separate congregations', with their own prayers and sermons, and (illegally) administering the Lord's Supper.[8] In most cases they did not use the Book of Common Prayer, and if a form of worship was used, it was more likely Calvin's *The Form of prayers*, composed for Geneva's reformed church (including English exiles) (Strype 1710: 168–9; Calvin 1542, 1550).

Protestant Nonconformity gained its traction in this period. A long tradition of dissent and separatism fed the halcyon days of religious radicalism—the 1640s and 1650s—with less emphasis on the concerns of class, order, land, and bourgeois ideology that socialist historical interpretations highlight than religious doctrine and expression. Literary scholarship has largely followed the lead of historians on early modern radicalism, reinforcing such ideological readings, especially of dissent read through social inequality and gender. Literary history has also spent an inordinate amount of time categorizing radicals. To some extent, classification is inevitable, but it does risk overplaying the degree to which 'sectarian groups' excluded one another and did not overlap. The series of mid-seventeenth-century case studies examined here show points of overlap, where members transferred, straddled, or shared allegiances, and where labels exacerbate a false sense of separation. What appears to be an issue of division—the very term, 'sect', is by nature isolated, oppositional, accusatory, deviant (*OED*, 'sect' 4. a,b.)—actually constitutes a broader community, founded on a variety of dissenting opinions but, in many cases, united on many fundamental points and with much mutual sympathy.

Presuming stark divisions between those who conformed and those who dissented also undermines the dualism of church and state in England, a more complexly functioning concept than almost anywhere else in the Protestant world (for instance, in Scotland and Calvin's Geneva). England's national Church—its bishops, particularly—imposed discipline, but the authority to excommunicate and exclude from the sacraments or to emphasize an authority of eldership (particularly the godly) remained without force. There is less evidence of stark division in the period than may be expected. Certainly, widespread terms of description such as 'sectarian', 'separatist', 'conformist', 'Nonconformist', and 'dissenter' were in use, but rarely consistently, and this is largely why they found lively appropriation in debates addressing episcopal rule and liberty of conscience. Liberty of conscience was paramount in the debates around sectarianism, and this primary freedom, of conscience and discourse, and of independent enquiry (particularly to read and respond to Scripture), was the territory upon which most other theological skirmishes were fought.

---

[8]   For example, 'The trewe marks of Christes Church, &c.' (*c*.1571), signed 'Richard Fytz, Minister'. SP 15/20 f.256. See also examples excerpted in Burrage 1912: 13–18.

Dorothy Hazzard
and Bristol Sectarianism

Dorothy Hazzard was one of Bristol's leading Baptists, driven by conscience to separate from the Church of England. Since 1604 the congregation of St Philip and St Jacob, under the ministry of William Yeamans, had been encouraged to meet in one another's homes for devotion and fellowship, in addition to their attendance at common prayer. These gatherings were distinctly puritan in nature, meeting together for fast days, prayer, and to repeat sermon-notes. One such group met in the home of the grocer Anthony Kelly, Hazzard's first husband (Underhill 1847: 8, 11).

Edward Terrill's manuscript account, 'Records of a Church of Christ in Broadmead' (c.1672), is compelling evidence for the strengthening of separatist sentiment under approaching Civil War conditions. In Terrill's account, Hazzard long had separatist leanings, being 'very famous for piety and reformation, well known to all, bearing a living testimony against the superstitions and traditions of those days, and she would not observe their invented times and feasts, called holy days'. This included Christmas when she kept her shop open and would sit publicly sewing. Alongside refusing to kneel, she reportedly left midway through a minister's sermon in her local parish when he began to 'bring in another innovation ... to assert that pictures and images might be used' (Terrill in Underhill 1847: 14). In 1639, she and her second husband, Matthew Hazzard, moved to the parish of St Ewins, where he became minister. The house in which they lived became a 'hospital for [God's] people in their peregrination'. They accommodated exiles waiting to sail to America, and took in pregnant women, so that they would be in the St Ewin's parish when they gave birth, safe from the injunctions of Robert Wright, bishop of Bristol, enforcing women 'to come to church after confinement' (Underhill 1847: 15).[9]

Terrill is unreserved about Hazzard's role in Bristol's rising Nonconformity:

> like a Deborah she *arose*, with strength of holy resolution in her soul from God, even *a mother in Israel*, and so she proved: because she was the first woman in this city of Bristol that practised that truth of the Lord, which was then hated and odious, namely, separation. (Terrill in Underhill 1847: 10–11)

She is described as a 'Priscilla', and like 'a he-goat before the flock', metaphorically setting her in a biblical context advocating separation, extolling Israel to come out of Babylon for fear of God's wrath against that land. God's people, his flock ('my sheep'), have been deceived by their shepherds, who 'have caused them to go astray' (Jeremiah 50:6–8). Terrill's inference parallels Milton's contemporary (1645) condemnation in 'Lycidas'

---

[9] *Articles to be ministred, enquired of, and answered: in the fourth visitation of the Right Reverend father in God, Robert, by Gods divine providence, Lord Bishop of Bristol* (1631).

('The hungry sheep look up, and are not fed, | But, swoll'n with wind and the rank mist they draw, | Rot inwardly, and foul contagion spread', ll. 125–7), and alludes especially to practices of the Lord's Supper in the same way as Milton's poem (the 'worthy bidden guest' welcomed to the 'shearers-feast', ll. 117–18).

The move from private house gatherings and conventicles to formal separation in 1640 took about twenty years in Terrill's account. As the church grew, they could not avoid the attention of the bishops who 'endeavoured to suppress them', despite many continuing to attend common worship. Divisions further emerged, however, as Laudian innovation increased. Participation in the sacrament was a crux issue; when orders were given for communicants to kneel at the sacrament, the godly either persisted in standing or simply did not attend, meeting elsewhere. Another concern was the participation of women. Terrill notes that, among other 'odiums' claimed by their opposition, they were accused of having 'women preachers among them, because there were many good women, that frequented their assembling, who … would speak very heavenly' (Underhill 1847: 13, 11).

In 1640 Hazzard and four others began 'to lead the way out of Babylon', advocating separation from the 'corrupt worship' and 'superstitions' and against hearing common prayer. The complexity of this separation is illustrated through Terrill's exploration of Hazzard's 'sore conflict' of conscience. Her husband's ordained duty to read common prayer remained (even though he withheld administering the sacrament to all), so her defiance was not only a matter of Nonconformity in worship but of neglect of a minister's wife's duty to be present, prompting 'ill report'.

Until now, this reasoning compelled her to attend. Terrill does not suggest it was a matter of marital submission or obedience, and neither is Matthew Hazzard portrayed as vexed by his wife's actions. However, one Sunday, 'as she was going, she had some strong doubts that made her turn back'. In her chamber she opened her Bible to read and 'happened upon that place in Rev. xiv.9,10,11' (Underhill 1847: 16). Hazzard reads St John's apocalyptic vision of the worship of 'the beast and his image'—the antichrist— which shall result in 'the wrath of God'. Terrill quotes the passage, concluding:

> they have no rest day nor night, who worship the beast and his image, and whosoever receiveth the mark of his name, or print as [Hazzard] said it was in her old book; and χάραγμα may be so translated, print, or stamp. This struck terror into her soul, that she dreaded to go; and thereupon, presently, without admitting, or hearkening to any more reasoning, she resolved, in the strength of the Lord, never to go more to hear common prayer. (Underhill 1847: 16–17)

Keeble notes that 'only apocalyptic imagery was adequate to express the detestation for the established church', but it is also the revelation's direct invocation of the imprint—the printed stamp—of Satan on the foreheads of false worshippers that transforms Terrill's account of Hazzard's 'sore conflict' into a violently damning vision for her immediate moment (Keeble 1987: 38). Hazzard's torment envisioning the danger of the printed invention of the Book of Common Prayer at the same time partners the account's promotion of Hazzard's ability to read with careful attention her own translation of the Bible, attending to the possibilities of interpretation. The terror of the moment rests not only on the apocalyptic imagery, but upon her broadening of the semantic range of 'χάραγμα' in Revelation 14:11 beyond 'mark' to 'print' or 'stamp'. Terrill's account cites the Authorized Version's translation of the passage, but Hazzard's widening of interpretation to 'print', as in 'her old book', suggests she was not using the *KJV* or the Geneva, as might be expected of a Nonconformist, but rather the sixteenth century's Tyndale, Coverdale, or Parker translations. Each of these refers to the 'the prynt of his name'. Terrill's discussion of these interpretive variants—and their implications for Hazzard's situation—stresses the Nonconformist awareness that the original sense of the Bible was mediated by an imperfect language, and reliant upon Christ's work by his Spirit in the mind and heart of believers for understanding; sectarian epistemologies of the Spirit mediated attitudes towards the original languages of the Bible (see, for instance, Smith 1989: 268–79). The instance described by Terrill confirms that Hazzard saw the Spirit prompted her to open to Revelation 14:11 on that day of soul-conflict, but it was the associated radical concern to be linguistically erudite which guided her reception and response.

Hazzard's isolated situation in the moment of revelation also suggests she shared the circumstances of her new conviction for the edification of her separating brethren. Terrill situates this experience as the awakening of Atkins, Cole, Moone, Bacon, and Hazzard. They proceeded to meet in her house on Broad Street on Sunday afternoons for a purer 'covenanting', and would only enter the church in the morning (led by Hazzard's husband!) after common prayer was over, 'when the psalm was singing', for the sermon. Such carefully choreographed movements appear the norm for many Nonconformists; Matthew Hazzard himself is recorded by Terrill as having left Bristol during Easter because he 'could not in conscience give the sacrament to the people of the parish' (Underhill 1847: 18–19).

Terrill's style is glaringly partisan; he distinguishes Bristol's Baptist separatists as 'the good people' from 'the obstructors' or 'the world and wicked men' (Underhill 1847: 11–12). Yet his account reveals the reality for separating Christians—some, like Hazzard, with intimate connections to the established Church. She exemplifies a natural—albeit complicated—fruition of what was occurring underground amongst Elizabethan and early Stuart laity but gradually emerged publicly, above ground, under conditions of decreased ecclesiastical opposition and Civil War.

HERESY, ORTHODOXY, AND THOMAS EDWARDS'S *GANGRAENA*

Thomas Edwards strove hard to expel sectarianism from England's Protestant landscape. His sensational depiction of sectarian division in the three-volume heresiography, *Gangraena: or a Catalogue and Discovery of many of the Errours, Heresies, and*

Blasphemies and pernicious Practices of the Sectaries of this time (1646a), contained a lengthy catalogue of the activities and abuses of proliferating sectarian groups in London during the 1640s. *Gangraeana* came on the heels of years of exasperated petitioning for Presbyterianism to be supported by Parliament, for church government to be settled, and severe action to be taken against sectarianism in the struggle for control of the 'godly reformation' (particularly between London Presbyterians and the New Model Army, comprised of many radicals). Edwards provoked a ferocious response, failing to silence his heretical opponents and launching among them an aggressive use of cheap and quickly produced publications (Hughes 2004).[10] Milton famously condemned Edwards as 'shallow' in his sonnet 'On the New Forcers of Conscience Under the Long Parliament' (*c.*1646 but unpublished until 1673), accusing the new Presbyterian leadership of being as despotic in its treatment of sectarians as episcopacy had been ('New *Presbyter* is but old *Priest* writ large', l. 20): 'Men, whose life, learning, faith and pure intent | Would have been held in high esteem with Paul | Must now be named and printed heretics | By shallow Edwards and Scotch What-d'ye-call' (ll. 9–12) (Smith 2009a: 156–7).

Edwards's catalogue was a contribution to the literary-historical tradition of truth-telling, defending truth against error, following the heresiographies of early church fathers, and with several contemporary exemplars (Hughes 2006b: 137; Edwards 1646b: Preface; Hughes 2004: 223).[11] Like these, *Gangraeana* aspired to present orthodoxy as uncontested, distinct from blasphemous sectarian heresies, but the reality was different; 'tightly defined' errors, 'attributed to tightly organized sects', were designed to distinguish sectarians from 'the orthodox and conformable'. Yet this casting evades or masks a situation where 'heterodoxy is far from being a distinct "other", but usually develops uneasily close to home' (Hughes 2006b: 140). Adherents to orthodoxy and heresy were not 'utterly separate' in England's struggle over the true expression of the church, fully reformed, in a Civil War and Interregnum context, but a tangled web of associations set on a 'spectrum' of opinion (Nuttall 1992: xx). Edwards admits as much in *Gangraena*'s preface:

> I fear, that too many Brethren, partly through their relations to many Sectaries, and through that lukewarm temper (in reference to errours of minde) that hath long possessed them, who think every one too-hot that appears against the Sects, will not so cordially approve this work. (1646b: Preface)

This was a contemptible but undeniable grey area in Edwards's stark formulation of heresy and schism. He critiques the 'lukewarm temper' (perhaps alluding to Revelation 3:16) that compromises doctrinal orthodoxy, but also the 'too many Brethren' who maintain 'relations' with 'many Sectaries'. The problem was twofold: many conservative Puritans and Presbyterians counted radicals and sectarians as friends and fellow believers; and

---

[10] The most notorious response was John Goodwin's *Cretensis* (1646b).
[11] Contemporary examples include Pagitt 1645, Baillie 1645, and Prynne 1645b.

the fundamentals of Christian belief were debatable, exposing the possibility that where first principles were unclarified doctrinal compromise and error could be argued.

Gangraena was compiled with the help of a network of London Presbyterian contacts, printed books and sermons, manuscripts, letters, legal records, and oral testimony from 'ear-witnesses and eye-witnesses' (Edwards 1646b: 1–7). Edwards listed 180 'Errours, Blasphemies and Practises of the Sectaries of the time', and sixteen kinds of sectarian groups in his 'Discovery of, and Directions against that many headed monstrous *Hydra* of sectarisme sprung up in these times in *England*': '1. Independents. 2. Brownists. 3. Chiliasts, or Millenaries. 4. Antinomians. 5. Anabaptists. 6. Manifestarians or Arminians. 7. Libertines. 8. Familists. 9. Enthusiasts. 10. Seekers and Waiters. 11. Perfectists. 12. Socinians. 13. Arians. 14. Antitrinitarians. 15. Antiscripturists. 16. Scepticks and Questionists' (1646a: 13). His lengthy 'Synopsis of Sectarisme' was rhetorically designed to indicate not only the circumstances of his writing but the nature of his subject:

> The Reader cannot imagine I found [the sources] thus methodized and laid together, but confused and divided, lying far asunder … to have given them the Reader as I found them, would have been to have brought the Reader into a wildernesse, and to have presented to publick view a rude and undigested Chaos, with an heap of Tautologies, all which are carefully declined in this following discourse, by joyning in one things divided and scattered; by relating but once one and the same errour and practice, and by forbearing to lead the Reader thorow woods, and over the mountains; and in stead of that, carrying him directly and presently to the bird in the nest.

In reality, Edwards's declared methodology is a failure. His text is random and meandering, a compilation arranged in order of acquisition rather than an organized or synthesized gathering (for more on Edwards's method see Hughes 2006b: 148–51). Nevertheless, he cannot resist an analogy between this methodology and the division, disorder, and confusion of the array of sects and sectarians that are his subject, setting them apart from orthodox belief. His purpose is simultaneously rhetorical and ideological: to 'decline' (in the sense of ordering but also of rejecting, gradually diminishing or decaying, indicating moral failure) the 'Tautologies' of sectarian belief and behaviour through his account, unifying the communities that are 'divided and scattered' and 'joyning' them 'in one' (*OED*, 'decline', *v.* and *n.*). His purpose is to highlight the moral and spiritual wilderness, the woods and mountains, into which sectaries are led by their errors, as well as to isolate them from one another ('lying far asunder'). Throughout his text he maintains a rhetoric of exposing this information to 'publick view' or, more frequently, to the light: the sectaries are, in his printer James Cranford's words, 'the pretended New Lights', they 'blemish and cast a dark shadow upon all the light part' of 'our Reformation', using the common appellation in rebuttal of sectarians (Edwards 1646b: Imprimatur, epistle dedicatory; see examples by Gataker 1646; Prynne 1645a; Prideaux 1655). Finally, Edwards's allusion to sectarian groups as 'the bird in the nest' partners a tradition of teaching on rebellion through the story of King David's son,

Absalom, his unnatural hatred of his father, Absalom's death, and David's lament, whilst also adopting a conceit that makes them not truly formidable or to be feared, liable to multiply yet vulnerable (L[inch]. S. 1660: 55).

We cannot survey every sectary identified by Edwards, but we can highlight how frequently the stories and networks of sectarians are more connected and overlapping than he elaborates. His prefatory revelation, that too many 'Brethren' were too close to such sectaries, prompts further exploration of the close affiliation of many of these noted figures of 'the plague of Sectarisme' with mainstream Presbyterians and Puritans (1646b: 1).

KATHERINE CHIDLEY, WILLIAM GREENHILL, AND ANNA TRAPNEL

One of Edwards's most outspoken adversaries before *Gangraena* was begun was the Leveller, Katherine Chidley. Chidley's *Justification of the Independent Churches of Christ* (1641) was the only notable rebuttal to Edwards's *Reasons Against the Independent Government*, and her *A New Yeares Gift* (1645) was the most detailed response he received to *Antapologia* (1644). The notoriety of her work garnered from John Goodwin the observation that Edwards's piece 'hath been convicted, and baffled by the pen of a woman, and was never yet reliev'd by him with any REJOYNDER' (Goodwin 1646a: 12).

Mother of eight, Chidley was active in Shrewsbury conventicles in the 1620s and pursued by the consistory courts for non-attendance at church. She moved to London around 1629 and became associated with other separatists, including John Lilburne, and active in radical protest. With others she founded a separatist congregation in London in 1630 (part of a collective of separatist churches in London), and founded separatist churches with her son, Samuel, in Stepney, Bury St Edmunds, and elsewhere (Gillespie 2004: 73–5; *ODNB*, 'Katherine Chidley'). She emerged as a pamphleteering leader of Leveller women in their besiegement of Parliament, helping author a petition of (allegedly) over six thousand women's names, to demand the release of Leveller men (including Lilburne) from prison (Gentles 1978: 281–309).[12]

Chidley was relentless in her pursuit of Edwards. Her style was not one of prophesy, like better known female sectarian voices in the period, but of animadversion, perhaps more suitable to this particular context of religious controversy. Edwards called her 'an old Brownist' and sharply criticized her evangelistic fervour: with her son they 'goe down into the Country to gather people to them'. 'Katherine Chidly and her sons Books', he wrote (dispossessing her of autonomous authorship), 'are highly magnified.' Edwards particularly reacted to Chidley's seeming aggression on the title page of

---

[12] *The humble petition of diverse wel-affected weomen of the cities of London and Westminster, the borough of Southwark, hamblets, and places adjacent. Affecters and approvers of the petition of Sept. 11. 1648* (1649).

Justification where she cites Judges 4:21, the story of Jael the wife of Hebers, who 'took a naile of the tent, and tooke an hammer in her hand, and went softly unto him, and smote the naile into his temples and fastened it into the ground' (Chidley 1641: title page). Jael's act delivered victory to Deborah and the Israelites against their oppressors (Judges 5). John Lanseter defended Chidley-as-Jael, interpreting the act as striking 'the naile of Independency into the head of their Sisera, with the hammer of God's holy word' (1646: 'To the Reader', A2^r), but Edwards focused on the violence of her citation, labelling her 'a brazen-faced audacious old woman resembled unto Jael' (1646c: 170–1), excising Chidley's self-approximation to the biblical heroine through his chiding 'resembled unto', an inappropriate effort at type-casting (on Jael in early modern literature, see Osherow 2009: 78–86).

In her last published pamphlet, *Good counsel* (1645), Chidley invited Presbyterians to debate with her fellow separatists on any matter of church doctrine: 'examine the gifts of such whom these call *illiterate* (that so it may appear how reasonable we are) either by disputation between the Presbyters and them: or by proving them, to give the sence of any Scripture which they shall appoint' (1645: n.p.; on the common accusation of radicals as illiterates, see McDowell 2003: ch. 1). Adding to her disrepute as a female interlocutor, Chidley's encounter with the moderate Independent William Greenhill in Stepney was an apposite example for Edwards of the way separatism gave women a misplaced sense of prophetic and preaching authority: 'she with a great deal of violence and bitterness spake against all Ministers and people that meet in our Churches, and in places where any idolatrous services have been performed'; she is 'talkative and clamourous' while Greenhill is depicted as restrained and calm, reasoning with biblical defenses (he 'answered her by scripture') (Thomas Alle 1646: 4 confirms the encounter). As a female sectary lacking in formal education her public disputation is conveyed as immodest and without solid biblical foundation, given only Greenhill's biblical learning is praised, and it feeds a wider culture of ridicule of sectors of separatism that tolerated women's preaching and ministry (Edwards 1646b: 79–80; Anon. 1641; Anon. 1647; Hughes 1990: 41; Trubowitz 1992: 112–33).

The Greenhill–Chidley encounter elucidates the 'spectrum' of separatism. Bernard Capp examines the culture of confrontation and disputation in England's 'marketplace' of religious ideas in this unique period, when Cromwell's Instrument of government had 'enshrined religious liberty (within limits) as a constitutional right'. Public disputation, with a Protestant history embedded in the growth of the continental Reformation, became an important and surprisingly accessible tool in debates of religious toleration, often instigated from below and wielded as empowering opportunities for laymen and women to challenge ministers and leaders on a range of theological issues. Capp shows this culture ranged well beyond London and involved 'every possible permutation' of participating parties: 'Episcopalians, Presbyterians, Independents, Baptists of all kinds, Fifth Monarchists, Quakers, and even (more privately) Catholics' (Capp 2013: 47, 48–9).

Murray Tolmie's excavation of London separatism highlights St George's, Southwark, the church of Henry Jacob, an early voluntary congregational membership, as an example of the 'ecumenical spirit' shared between orthodox and semi-separatist

Londoners which continued. Jacob's church shared the Lord's Supper with an orthodox puritan parish and tolerated radicals and opponents of infant baptism within the same congregation (Tolmie 1977; Brachlow 1989). This church came under the leadership of the Baptist and eventual Fifth Monarchist, Henry Jessey by 1637, and gave rise to several further separatist congregations, yet it continued to maintain close relationships with more radical splinter groups (Seaver 1979; White 1979: 98–110).[13] Issues that would be thought to bring about fracture—infant baptism, Communion, free grace—did not necessarily preclude a shared ecumenical spirit amongst Nonconformists, whether they were clerically deprived or earlier radical dissenters. Despite *Gangraena*'s stark presentation of factional resentment, Edwards's warning to the 'lukewarm' invites examination of the real nature of sectarianism and the extensive degree not merely of interconnection but of intercommunion and conjointed intellectual examination.

It is in this lively context of disputation that Chidley's encounter with Greenhill must be viewed. As one of London's most respected Independents, it is notable Greenhill did not disdain to dispute publicly with a woman. Around the same time, he had cultivated an acquaintance with the Fifth Monarchist Anna Trapnel which reveals deep sympathy, conviction, and mutual esteem, despite obvious theological divergences. Trapnel was an avowed antinomian, and her ecstatic visions and prophecies are presented as testament to and dependent upon her transformation from Calvinist orthodoxy to the doctrine of free grace (later recounted in *A Legacy for Saints*; 1654c: 1–15). Yet despite the profound chasm between free-willers and predestinarians, 'the major proponents of antinomian or anti-legal religion had been raised in the milieu of (often radical) English puritanism' (Como 2004: 29–30). That is, not only past connections, but enduring social and personal associations sustained a broad community of radical Protestantism that was heterogeneous in its common identity though fraught in its quotidian experience.

In 1646 Trapnel underwent an intense illness at Whitehall and experienced the first of her trances. During this illness Greenhill visited her, and her account suggests an established familiarity and security in his presence: 'On the third day of the week, the Lord sent me Mr. *Greenhil*, Minister of Gods word, who as soon as I beheld, I could not but say, behold the man of God, such joy was in my spirits, which I could not but utter forth' (Trapnel 1654b: 29). Trapnel's visionary state compelled her to seek communion with Greenhill in prayer. His willingness to oblige and with words 'from the Spirit' is Trapnel's confirmation not only of the truth of her prophetic experience but of the shared communion of saints and its capacity to affirm a spiritual commission despite areas of intellectual disagreement:

> to me it appeared such a prayer of faith, that I never heard him pray so, and when the Spirit breathed in him for my recovery, he said Lord strengthen thine hand-maids perswasion; no sooner were these words gone forth, which I am sure was from the Spirit, and it was the purpose of God at that time to seal to that which was before spoken. (1654b: 31)

---

[13] Jessey published the widely read account of Sarah Wight's ecstatic experiences, *The Exceeding Riches of Grace advanced by the spirit of grace, in an empty nothing creature, viz. Mris. Sarah Wight* (1647).

Trapnel indicates she has previously prayed and fellowshipped with Greenhill ('I never heard him pray so') and reveals a conception of this fellow radical as God's vessel in a work that transcends sectarian division and factional exclusivity. Trapnel's communion with Greenhill reflects a vision of a corporate faith, mutually edifying, which affirmed the commissions of its members, men and 'hand-maids' alike. Such a communion of saints did not shy from doctrinal combat (as the disputations demonstrate), and neither did it strip believers of the Reformation gift of individually reading and responding to the Word. In this context, sectarians across the spectrum like the occasional conformist and sometime radical Puritan Brooke, the Baptist Hazzard, the Leveller Chidley, the Fifth Monarchist Trapnel, and the Independent Greenhill participated in the *longue durée* of English Protestant dissent. Once the laity were enabled to read the vernacular Bible for themselves, dissent was inevitable. The crucial difference is that prior to the 1640s, separatism was illegal (enforced by the Act of Uniformity). The Plumber's Hall congregation is an early example of the consequences of testing the waters, forcing dissent underground. Yet it re-emerges, albeit in new forms, when Laud and other anti-Calvinists attempt to reinterpret conformist Puritanism as a form of dissent, punishing it in the 1620s and 1630s. Dorothy Hazzard is a classic example of this evolved sectarianism: a woman participating in underground meetings until Civil War conditions and Cromwell's rule permits its flourishing. From the 1640s onwards we see the coalescing of the underground with the new sectarians, now with the freedom to dispute the issues openly, free of the jurisdiction of the ecclesiastical establishment and church courts and, pre-eminently, the freedom to read and interpret Scripture, like Hazzard, reliant on Christ through the Spirit. This is the heart and soul of English Protestant sectarianism.

CHAPTER 27

....

QUAKERS

....

CATIE GILL

THE middle decades of the seventeenth century witnessed the birth of the Quaker movement and, simultaneously, a relaxing of censorship that led to an increase in published material. As a result of this concurrence, 'Friends' (as they were known) quickly recognized that they could disseminate their message through print. A branch of radical Protestantism that practised impromptu preaching, Quakerism inspired its adherents to declare that 'the truth of the Lord' must be 'spread', and to demonstrate the leading of an inward light: 'the Lord God hath lighted my Candle, and it must not be hid' (Graves 2009; White 1660: 6). Sharing moments of religious insight and religio-political commentary with others was soon widely practised, and Quaker utilization of print for these purposes can be seen in the remaining decades of the century. Friends published nearly a thousand texts during their first decade (the 1650s) alone, even as the 'valiant sixty', who were the stalwarts of the new movement during the early years, grew to sixty thousand converts by the end of the Commonwealth period (Runyan 1973; Vipont 1975; Reay 1985: 9). Inevitably, their published works were influenced by the social and historical conditions that obtained during these years. After the return of the Stuart monarchy in 1660, output continued to be high; yet this declined to an estimated fifty to seventy-five texts per year in the latter decades of the century (Runyan 1973; Green 2002: 70–1).[1] Connecting to the readers of published works was always part of the plan, as Quakers sought to carve their presence in print culture from their movement's inception. Indeed, mapping the changes in emphasis during the first fifty years of Quakerism is one of the themes of this chapter, as the movement went through many radical changes between 1650 and 1700.

It may be thought strange that a general claim can be made for so broad a spectrum of literature, but it is the case that the Quakers' central religious *tenets* are pervasive and relatively consistent. As noted in the only survey, to date, of Quaker writing's first

---

[1] See also Rosemary Moore's online checklists of Quaker publications. http://www.qhpress.org/rmoore/.

seventy-five years, 'practically every [autobiographical] narrative contains a detailed account of the surrender of individual will to the leadings of the inner light' (Wright 1932: 156). Moreover, as William Frost argues, 'the key to Quakerism was the inward light of Christ. Both opponents and Friends recognised this theme' (Frost 1970: 508). In perceiving spiritual insight as personal, as when Sarah Blackborrow declares that 'a resolution [was] begotten in me, to find Christ in me' (Blackborrow 1660: 8), Quakers echo the earlier Protestant reformers who urged believers to look within for signs of God's grace. The Quakers from the first decade established the practices that later writers would either emulate themselves, or drawn back from, even when writing from altered social contexts about the light spoken of in the gospels (John 1:9, 12:46). Since it was so often returned to, no account of Quaker writing can afford to ignore their repeated theological insistence on the divinizing light, or illuminated conscience, that was an extension of Protestant theology.

Nevertheless, literary criticism has in recent years brought a new emphasis on the *modes* of writing adopted by Quakers, as well as attention to matters such as authorial *voice*, since the manipulation of print was the 'means by which Quakers argued for their ideas in a hostile world' (Hughes 1994: 144). The special issue of *Prose Studies*, from which this observation has been taken, provided the first edited collection of essays to explore the 'development of Quaker writing' as its sole focus (Corns 1994: 2). Now, it is generally conceded that the Quakers' deployment of print made them amongst the most effective religio-political pamphleteers of the century (Peters 2005).

In the discussion which follows, I will segment Quaker writing according to the standard temporal division that the historian William Braithwaite introduced. Namely, I will work chronologically from the first phase (1650–60) to the second period of Quakerism (1661–1700) (Braithwaite 1981, 1979), with the second phase itself divided into two politically defined sections, 1660–89 and 1690–1700. Quaker writing resonates with readers today because of the immediacy and urgency of its prose, which often has a reformist, socially egalitarian message (Hobby 1991). Nevertheless, it has often been asserted that the second phase of Quakerism lost its vigour as it moved, in Maurice A. Creasy's memorable phrase, 'from the meeting to the study' (1962: 11). The emphasis in the course of this chapter will be on the importance of collective experiences to religious writers, since 'individual expression was not a paramount aesthetic concern' of the early Quakers (McDowell 1998: 103).[2] I assume, in other words, that pamphleteers wrote *as Quakers*, conveying not only their individual connection to the living God working within the believer but, also, an equally developed understanding of their place within the Quaker corpus when trying to shape the movement's public image.

In the seventeenth century, sympathetic readers pointed out the 'Service to the Truth', while hostile reading communities drew attention to the perceived errors of a Quaker text (Burrough 1672: A3ʳ). As I will show through discussion of representative texts from

---

[2] The extent to which Quakerism's supposed decline was in fact co-determinate with the development of organizational structures that helped the movement to survive, is beyond the scope of this article; see Braithwaite 1979: 215–350.

across the range of the corpus, Quakers exploited print culture to inform, reprehend, and offer inspiration to their readers through highly persuasive writing. Characteristic in their discussion of socio-political themes was the admonition of those persons viewed as impervious to Quaker imperatives for reform of the individual and the state in matters of conscience. Quakers did not only communicate disparagingly, however, as though outsiders were to be repelled. By inflecting the personal and autobiographical into the written accounts of their spiritual leadings, Friends showed others how they, too, could be saved by the light within. The key genres analysed here are not static or fixed in nature; I shall refer to the most significant modes, as well as contending that there is significant generic overlap among them.[3]

THE WORD OF THE LORD:
QUAKER WRITING, 1650–9

Quaker writers during the first decade of the movement's inception developed their eschatology to engage in highly charged modes of address. Writers frequently envisaged that the language of the text would stir readers by working on them to examine the grounds of their faith, and so learn of God's work from the text. They are reader-centred in their approach to reformist work, as can be seen even from their titles. Market-conscious printers may have been more active than the writers of tracts in setting out the title pages, but these are no less useful for what they show about Quaker methods of appealing to readers. For example, William Dewsbury's *The Mighty Day of the Lord, is Coming* uses the main title to declare the eschatological belief in Christ's immanency, while the extended subtitle addresses two camps: those with 'desires to know the onely true God', and those who 'reject his counsel' (1656b). Striking title pages in Dewsbury's other works show the same originating force, just as *The Mighty Day* was said to be 'the word of the Lord' (title page; Wing 1945: 444–5). His *The Discovery of Mans Return to his First Estate* instances that it is 'from the Spirit of the Lord' (1654b), as does his *A True Prophecy of the Mighty Day of the Lord* (1654a). It is small wonder that Quaker writing is perceived critically to be 'often using ecstatic language' (Garman 1996: 31).

According to a contemporary witness, Dewsbury was both a prolific writer and a compelling orator: 'his testimony … was piercing and very powerful, so as the earth shook before him' (Braithwaite 1981 [1912], 74). The fortitude of people that shaped the movement in the early years, and wrote extensively, like Dewsbury, was recognized when their works were '[re]printed for future service' (Dewsbury [1689], title page). In particular,

---

[3] I refer only in passing to a key feature of the Quaker corpus: doctrinal writing and animadversion. However, T. L. Underwood's study of the Baptist/Quaker controversy fills this gap (Underwood 1997). Where I have omitted detailed comment on any other key variety of Quaker writing, I note this in the main text.

prefatory material in the form of testimonies and addresses 'to the Reader' establish the framework through which to interpret the perceived value of Quaker writing to others; hence, utilization of later editions of a writer's works can be key to assessing their reception. In fact, some of the most interesting observations on pamphleteering belong not to the 1650s, but to periods considerably later, including the beginning of the eighteenth century. John Whiting, for instance, remarked on the context behind the production of Dewsbury's 'several books' about persecution (Whiting 1715: 181). In the late seventeenth century, however, those commending Dewsbury's complete works, *The Faithful Testimony*, praised him for the combined 'boldness', 'plainness', and 'simplicity' of his pamphleteering, which brought many to see 'the benefit of his Labours' (Dewsbury 1689: A2^v–A3^r). The same inspired language used on the title pages of his individual pamphlets from the 1650s was repeated in the preface which describes how Dewsbury was 'made an eminent Instrument in his [God's] hand' (Dewsbury 1689: A2^v). As Hilary Hinds has observed, persons willing to be guided by the Holy Spirit were often defined as 'instruments' (1996: 96–100). Hence, the term denotes that through this unity with the godhead the individual is both passive and empowered.

Titles that use the word 'admonition' or 'warning' are just as likely to exhibit that the central message being imparted is 'from the Lord', resulting in a difficulty with establishing with any degree of rigour the generic breakdown of Quaker texts. Although David Runyan's tabular analysis (1973) does at least provide a long view of the century, it lacks precision. Smaller, more qualitative, cross-sections of Quaker literature best confirm what can be seen already in Dewsbury's writing: a preponderance of inspired works. Taking the texts published during the five-year period by Quaker printer Mary Westwood as her sample, Maureen Bell found that prophecies are 'well represented' in her corpus (1988: 39). Bonnylyn Young Kunze categorized Quaker women's writing, and found thirty-one calls to repentance, fifty-four statements of religious doctrine, and eighteen polemical tracts (1994: 132). Any of these varieties of writing might also have a prophetic tenor. For instance, the 'inspiration of the Spirit of Jesus Christ … who is found worthy to open the Seals of the Book, and is *the way, the truth, and the life*', is invoked in a polemical text, here the work of Dewsbury in response to an Anti-Quaker writer (Dewsbury 1656 a: 25, citing Revelation 5 and John 14:6). The admonitory stance adopted with regard to non-Quakers could be bombastic, such as when Dewsbury spoke in the voice of God: 'I will overturn, overturn, overturn' (Dewsbury 1654a: 6). Polemic, doctrine, admonition, warning, and prophecy—these may all be combined in Quaker works.

Dorothy White's short Quaker tracts from 1659 to 1662 (seventeen in total) are all prophetical in nature, even though some are defined as '*Epistles*' and others directly address '*England's Rulers*' or '*The Parliament*' (Foxton 1994: 72–4; White 1661, 1662b, [1662c]). The designation of the term 'prophet' during the seventeenth century was 'frighteningly open-ended' (Gilman Richey 1998: 1), but it usually involved union and, more rapturously, 'an exclusive transcendent intuition of the Godhead' (Hessayon 2007: 91). Maintaining that 'in the Name of the Lord God, and in his Authority I do proclaim', White establishes that she is an emissary since her 'language', as Hilary Hinds contends, shows its 'divine origin'

(White 1662a: 5; Hinds 1996: 138). The key feature in her writing is that she adopts a three-stage process. Firstly, God prepares the ground by bringing out the prophetic spirit in his people. Thereafter, during the second stage, it is characteristic that the relationship with the godhead is shown to be beyond full expression (though represented textually, to the best of the writer's ability). This sort of experience benefits from an associative, allegorical style, such as when White refers to how '[her] soul doth swim within the Sea of love, as fishes in the water move' (1661: 8–9). Once it has been acknowledged that God has a purpose, and that the individual Quaker is attuned to this through a vision, a calling, or else being moved by the inward light, the prophecy can begin.

In *An Epistle of Love and Consolation*, White moves smoothly into the third stage, which is speaking and writing. She declares, 'The Kingdom of Glory is revealed, the Son of Righteousness is risen in his Beauty, in his transparent Brightness, the Glory of all Nations is come; and this is the Day, wherein the Lord God is binding up his Jewels, in the bond of Life, in the tye [*sic*] of his own Spirit; and the Lamb is come to Reign in his Temple' (1661: 1). Phyllis Mack's term for such an occurrence is 'self-transcendence' (1992: 127–64), though where there are direct comments on the authorial role, as in this instance of White's *Epistle*, 'merging' would better describe the process, since the woman inscribes her own physical presence into the account: 'And the Lord God hath spoken, and therefore I will speak, for God hath unloosed my tongue, to speak to the praise of his name' (1661: 2). White concludes: 'the ravishing Glory of God did overshadow me, and the word of Eternal Life run through me, often saying, Publish the day of the Lord God, lift up thy voice like a Trumpet, as a mighty shout; and this is to go through the Nation' (1661: 6). Such works reach out to the reader by asking that the light and word working through the prophet be recognized.

It is more difficult to gauge the responses of readers to Quaker women's writing than it is to the equivalent works of the men, especially those who, like Dewsbury, were honoured with collected editions of their writings. With the exception of Margaret Fell, the eminent Quaker leader (Fell 1710), there are no published collected works for Quaker women. Dorothy White was the second most prolific female writer after Fell, but the neglect of her in a commemorative edition is unsurprising for two reasons (Foxton 1994: 72–4). The first is that her works tended to be short and in total they add up to only 180 printed pages (with an additional three broadsides). The second reason is that a woman with this name was a follower of the disowned Quaker, John Perrot, a situation which may go some way to explaining the apologetic tenor of the works she published in the 1680s, after twenty years of silence (Farnworth 1665: 15).[4] James Nayler, the Quaker who brought shame on the movement when convicted for blasphemy, was able to be rehabilitated and republished (1716); but White was not afforded equal stature or deemed as important as this early Friend.

This absence of collected works is not the only reason why the impact of Quaker women's work on readers cannot easily be measured. Another is the general paucity

---

[4] When I wrote the *ODNB* article on White I could find no solid information about her absence from Quaker records. Michele Lise Tartar (2015) has subsequently substantiated the connection.

of prefaces or comments 'To The Reader' in 1650s Quaker writing. This is significant because prefaces are important for framing the writer, and comparison might therefore be made with a Fifth Monarchist/Baptist writer like Anna Trapnel, for instance, who benefited from positive commentary about the efficacy of her prophecies (Holstun 2000: 257–303; Adcock 2011: 207–51). Republication is another way of measuring the perceived significance of a work. However, women's pamphlets rarely run to second editions, though Fell and Anne Audland are an exception (Foxton 1994: 47–8). Some works by Margaret Fell were also translated into other languages, indicating her value as a spokesperson for the movement (Foxton 1994: 53–6). Although excellent scholarly work offers insights into the relationship between writers of pamphlets and their readership, much remains to be done with regards to the very specific case of Quaker women (Peacey 2013; Raymond 1996).

Though this might seem to suggest that women's contribution to the literary profile of the movement was slight, female Quakers in fact produced a corpus of work that was far larger than contemporary Baptists, Anglicans, and Independents (Bell 1990: 250). Moreover, if the presentation of women's writing tends to be materially different from that of some esteemed male writers' works—for example, lacking prefaces—it nevertheless holds true to some of the key tropes, specifically the idea of writing 'for the Lord', practised in a movement that perceived spiritual equality. Indeed, another way in which Quaker women's writing can be considered significant is that it was used at the time to shape the public image of Quakerism. Evidence of the women's connection to and integration into the wider Quaker movement is one of the vital aspects of their writing (Gill 2005).

The dubious honour of having one's work responded to by a virulently anti-Quaker writer is an important way of judging the impact of Friends' publications. William Dewsbury, for instance, was reviled by John Timson in 1656 for his tract entitled *A True Prophecy* (Timson 1656; Dewsbury 1654a), resulting in an answer from Dewsbury the same year (Dewsbury 1656a). Similarly negative impacts on readers can contextualize the writing of other Quaker leaders of the 1650s, such as the response to George Fox's *Saul's Errand to Damascus* and Edward Burrough's political writings (Weld and others 1654: 5; Leslie 1696: XCVIII, C, CCXCVI–CCXCVIII, CCCIV, 166). James Nayler is the subject of the most concerted anti-Quaker riposte, and many contemporary pamphlets commented on his 'fall' after the ill-fated Christ-like entry into Bristol and his severe public punishment for blasphemy (Damrosch 1996; Moore 2000: 43). It is usual for anti-sectarian writers to draw particular attention to women whom they perceived to be especially transgressive, and the heresiographer Thomas Edwards, writing of 1640s sectarianism, took this approach (Hughes 2004: 113–15). Friends such as 'Williamson's Wife', who was said to have asserted that she was the son of God, also feature in anti-Quaker literature, for the similar reason that they exaggerated the threat of Quakerism to contemporary society (Higginson 1653: 3–4). The women involved in the Nayler affair also drew comment, particularly Martha Simmonds. Being well connected to the London print-market (she was married to a Quaker printer), she wrote and published some short texts (Foxton 1994: 66). In one of the anti-Nayler works, it is Simmonds's publications that are censured, rather than, as was more usual, her actions and character.

Christopher Wade sneers that her 'gross ignorance' was 'published in print' (1657: 35). The reactions of anti-Quaker writers offer only a jaded view of the impact of Quaker writing on their readership, and in Wade we see how a woman's work could be pored over in order to show 'the Devil speaking in thee' (Wade 1657: 36).

Although writers who were critical of Quaker writings shared a general impulse to question the legitimacy of their messages, even these clerics reveal the movement's bibliophilic focus. Metaphors of disease are widely in evidence in the description of the Quaker menace, since the idea that their writing was attacking the body politic was common scare-mongering. However, it does seem from these antagonistic writings that the textual profligacy of the Quaker movement was apparent to all. Its members are depicted as excessively print-centred: '[Quakers] would trouble me with divers of their Books ... twelve of their Books were brought to me' (Firmin 1656: 1). The movement was said to publish works of excessive virulence, taking 'sinful liberty to themselves in their printed books' (Higginson 1653: a1^v). Quaker words were quoted back to 'let all Christian Readers consider' their 'railing', and admonish them for not knowing when to 'bridle their tongues' (Weld et al. 1654: 17; Collier 1657: 1; Miller 1655: 6). Anti-Quaker books, then, claimed to protect their readers against vulnerability to Quakerism: 'I hope where ever this Book shall arrive before them, the people will so well know them, as to abhor any further acquaintance with them' (Underhill 1660: 35). Quakers continued to embrace the public forum of print, even so, and Edward Burrough, one of the Quakers' chief political writers, stipulates that his text should be circulated by readers, 'sent from one to another as they are moved' (1657: [14]). Moreover, he suggested a remedy in cases where the book itself was not sufficient to answer all queries: 'if any be unsatisfied still in the matter, And if any, especially of the Heads and Rulers have Jealousies raised in them, concerning us ... [we] make freely and cheerfully, four, ten, twenty, thirty, or more or fewer of us, [to] give as many of the wisest and ablest Priests and Professors a meeting for dispute' (1672: C4^v). The saturation of the print market with popular print may well have had the effect of gradually educating the readership to sort the truth from the lies, but Burrough, for one, was still willing to enter into further conversation (Peacey 2013: 93–114).

In addition to prophecy, a second major feature of the Quaker output during the 1650s was, as Runyan points out, 'an appeal to the political leaders or parliament' (Runyan 1973: 567). Since the genre of the 'appeal' is also typically written as though it is from God, it further exemplifies this recurrent feature of Friends' works. Named a 'Son of Thunder', Edward Burrough was particularly valued by Quakers who gave him this nomenclature to show his energetic and inspired character (Burrough 1672, title page). As is typical of auto/biographical sketches from the period,[5] *The Memorable Works* show the integration of a believer into the religious community in addition to their personal qualities, and Burrough is praised for his service to the Quaker movement (Gill 2005). Richard Bauman, in *Let your Words be Few*, suggests that Burrough was 'one of the most effective of the early Quaker tract writers at systematizing Quaker doctrine

---

[5] For fuller discussion of early modern religious autobiographical writings, see chapter 13.

for public presentation' (1998: 24). Burrough's orientation in his political pamphlets emerges clearly: a Parliament man with love for the good old cause, and hopeful that the Army could be its agents, he nevertheless instructed the rulers on how they could better serve the people and God. In the 1660s, even such a committed commonwealth man could speak reasonably accommodatingly to the restored monarch (Moore 2000: 177). He wrote texts of the kind John Whiting described as 'Reproof and Warning as a Prophet to the Rulers and People of divers sorts' (1715: 131). Quakers also published their petitions to parliament, but in this discussion I will not examine them as a distinct genre.

Interestingly, Burrough's addresses to rulers do not draw much on the ecstasy of merging with the godhead, nor does he use the word prophecy in the titles of his political tracts, thus distinguishing his mode of writing from that of Dewsbury and White. Yet the absence of these features allows Burrough to develop another mode when speaking 'the word of the Lord'. In *A Message* (November, 1659) he notes: 'this is the very substance of my message to you, that my master hath given me to say unto you' (1659b: 10). He continues: 'I have told you the Lords present message unto you, which I received from him,' and 'I must tell you, as he said unto me so to do' (1659b: 16, 2). He looks for the providential message, with an apocalyptic fervour confirming what Bernard Capp has claimed to be the period's 'widespread apocalyptic and millenarian beliefs' (1972: 35). Burrough, in sadness, comments on the state of the nation: 'there is no establishment in the Earth, but strife and contention, and heart-burnings in the bowels of the Nation, and great want of true love, true unity, and true peace, and all the contrary doth abound among the people, because of which the Nation is subject to present misery ... we have seen the cause of thy distractions to be the sins of thy Rulers and People' (1659a: 2). What to Burrough, and indeed to many Quakers, was so obvious that it hardly needed expressing, was that God was angry at the mistreatment of the people of God. Enthymeme—'a syllogism in which one premiss is suppressed' (*OED* 3)—is a common feature in religious works because this rhetorical mechanism combines two ideas without fully articulating the relationship between proposition 'a' and proposition 'b' (Stark 2008). This gave the reader scope to construct for him/herself the providential message hinted at in the text, recognizing that the people of God are the Quakers.

When exercising choice in his rhetorical tactics, Burrough is like the Quaker women petitioning parliament in that, as Kirilka Stavreva has observed of them, they 'heeded closely the divergent responses of the assembled audience' (2007: 35). Burrough's tone can be more measured, though, unlike some religio-political writers of the period, never neutral or dispassionate (Caldwell 2007). On the issue of toleration, for example, he proposed solutions that could reduce persecution, while on matters of religious conscience he speaks thoughtfully. He expounds that '[God] alone will setle and establish Religion by his own power and by his own Law, and through his own Ministry, as people comes to that of God in them, to feel the Spirit and power of the Lord God to change them; hereby will every one particularly be setled in Religion, and by no other way nor means; and this I know from the Lord' (Burrough 1659e: 5–6). He is, however, more acerbic when defining the Church's role in persecution, since he notes the irony that only when groups are pressing to establish themselves do they preach liberty of conscience. Conveniently ignoring their initial idealism once they have to extend liberty of conscience to others, such groups follow 'the great Whore … the beast … false worships and Churches', as Burrough notes only a few sentences after his calming tone has assured the readership of God's plan (Burrough 1659e: 6). In many of his political tracts, he employs a rhetorical signature that serves to show he is a sincere defender of the people's rights, representing himself as inconsolably honest, virtuously so: 'I do answer on my Lords behalf: and I must tell you plainly…' (Burrough 1659b: 15). He is like the Digger Gerrard Winstanley in knowing that a pamphlet intended for rulers will contain 'some things inserted which you may not like' (Burrough 1652: 11; Winstanley 2009: 288). Burrough also shows God's will is greater, so 'read and consider', and that he is 'a friend to righteous men', a 'lover of Justice', a 'Friend to this Nation' (1659c; 1659e, 12; 1659f; 1659d).

Quakers quoted the Bible often in their speech and writing, but they neverthe-less maintained that the basis of their own faith was spiritual, not scriptural (Fox 1656; Graves 2009: 69–76). The practice of reading was therefore afforded the same status as other sorts of religious activity, as can be seen from the comments of Rebecca Travers. Wholly typical of the Quaker attitude, Travers explains, 'the Scripture … were written by holy men as they were moved by the holy Ghost, and are revealed and interpreted by the same spirit' (Travers 1659: 4–5). Quaker prophets affirm that they write in the spirit, and read the Bible in the same inspired state. Moreover, given the heart-changes that could be affected by connecting to the godhead, it could be argued that they also endeavoured to work on the consciences of the political elite, making them both better readers, and men (Lobo 2012b). Across the period, the prophetical impulse in Quaker writing led them to use print knowingly, and, indeed, inspiringly.

Quakers did not write for writing's sake, but for a purpose: to convey the inner workings of the light as it led them to admonish, guide, or engage the reader. 1650s prophets such as Dewsbury, White, and Burrough sought thorough societal and spiritual reformation, so used their pamphlets to argue for radical change across the nation. In the Restoration, Quakers continued to write 'For the Lord', but also recorded their sufferings under an increasingly partisan legal code that criminalized religious dissenters, in a period when persecution was 'carried on with very great severity and rigour' (Ellwood 1885: 249).

1660–89: 'Divine Providence … sometimes Vouchsafest to Bring Good out of Evil'

Hester Biddle, a vocal Quaker prophet with six publications to her name, observed in the early 1660s: 'I had rather die the cruellest Death that ever was, or can be delivered by man, than to neglect or abstain from meeting together in his Name' (1662: 21). The tenor of most Quaker anti-persecution pamphlets of the Restoration period was as defiant as Biddle's. Margaret Fell wrote retrospectively in a similar vein, of her experiences in

1664: 'I rather choose a prison for obeying of God, than my liberty for obeying of men contrary to my conscience' (Fell 1992: 109). 'Men' stood for persons who were 'unedified' by religion, referring in this context to the adherents of the legal system who upheld the stinging legislation of the 1660s, such as the Quaker Act of February, 1662 (Braithwaite 1979: 23, 21–115). Quakers quite often termed such people 'the generation of Cain', and blemished the reputations of persons who acted as judges against them with charges of corruption (Cotton 1655: 2). In effect, they made liberty to worship as much a moral matter as it was a legal or religio-political one. In contrast to the unregenerate, Quakers insisted that persons that held to their beliefs, though the cost to them was great, were 'of another spirit, of another image, or another make, of another heart' (Barbour 1973: 374; Penington 1661: 8). As Richard C. Allen has explored in the Restoration context, Quakers used forthright language to condemn the wider society for compelling people to worship in the state Church (Allen 2013).

The penal system that prosecuted religious dissenters during the reign of Charles II led not only to the imprisonment of Quakers but also, after repeat offences, to the sentence of transportation and *praemunire*.[6] Though the focus of this chapter is, in the main, English Quakerism, very notable instances of persecution took place in other countries, and it is reductive to limit an account of their 'suffering' (as Quakers called it) merely to the Carolean context (Lise Tarter 1993; Herbert 2011). Indeed, some of the news of Quaker persecution abroad is to be found in texts printed with especial care— either receiving editorial attention from several authors, or being devotedly republished—which signifies that these works were thought to be of quite widespread interest to British readers. Quakers in Boston, New England, for example, were served with the death penalty for failing to recant their faith or adhere by the court's sentence of banishment. As a consequence, several pamphlets from the early 1660s told of the persecution of three Quakers in the colonies: George Bishop's *New England Judged* (1661); [Anon.], *A Call from Death to Life* (1660); and Edward Burrough's *A Declaration of the Sad and Great Persecution and Martyrdom* [1661] (Barbour 1973: 116–40). The last of these is given prestige treatment as the printer used black-letter typeface to add textual enhancement to the account, making it atypical of Quaker texts. The printer's (or Burrough's) use of the word '*martyrdom*' in the title was typical of work that was informed by John Foxe's *Acts and Monuments*. Some Quakers are known to have owned this book, and others make reference to it in their work on persecution (Kunze 1994: 210; *A Narrative of the Cruelties and Abuses*, 1683: 28; Fell 1664: 15). However, these confirming details only add to the picture that, through print, '[Quakers] reinforced their sense of themselves as belonging to the line of martyrs [from the Bible and from Foxe] for God's truth' (Knott 1993: 218). Mary Dyer was one of the Quakers sent to the scaffold in Boston, where she used her protest to affirm: 'I came in Obedience to the Will of God' in order to reverse the '*unrighteous Lawes*' (Burrough and Dyer 1661: 28).

---

[6] The term refers to the loss of goods and property, inflicted as punishment for a breach of the statute of *praemunire*—that is, for disobedience in ecclesiastical matters (*OED* 2b)

As John Knott has persuasively observed, 'no religious community of the late seventeenth century suffered more than the Quakers, or did more to record and publicise their sufferings' (1993: 216). Each different stage of the judicial process received detailed comment, from being taken to a JP, to the trial, to imprisonment. Moreover, differing depictions of selfhood emerge in Quaker publications from this period, depending on the aspect of persecution being described. It is noteworthy that there is as much to contrast as to compare in the two main accounts of George Fox's imprisonment at Lancaster prison. The contemporaneous text of 1664 by Margaret Fell focused on the crucial moment when Fox protested his innocence at trial. Fox's subsequent account of his experience in Lancaster (published in 1694, though probably written before 1679), reaches a climax when describing the privation resulting from his sentence (Fell 1664; Keeble 1987: 50; Fox 1998: 346).

In addition to the different points of emphasis to be found in Quaker narratives, Friends also used varied modes when writing of suffering. In part because the Psalms inspired them, and in part because the early modern prison was a 'muses habitation', Friends also wrote significant amounts of poetry (Murray 2009: 149; Moore 2004). Poetry engenders a different voice as its modes of diction often move from admonition to a feature we have not yet observed in Friend's writing: complaint. Towards the end of the 1650s, two Quaker women, Katharine Evans and Sarah Cheevers, were imprisoned by the Italian inquisition in Malta. As in the case of the sufferings of the New England Quakers, the publication history seems to show that Friends anticipated a general readership for the women's account of their suffering. A Short Relation had a preface, was published twice, and was later updated to take account of Evans and Cheevers's release from prison (Foxton 1994: 52; Fabrizio 2013). Katharine Evans was responsible for much of the verse, and her work expresses the ardent resolve of many Friends when faced with incarceration:

> My Love to *Truth* doth me constrain
> In Prison ever to remain;
> If it in truth be so that even I
> Cannot in truth be set at Liberty. (Evans and Cheevers 1662: 48)

In like manner, Thomas Ellwood's *Journal* (1714) contains both verse and prose accounts of 1660s suffering. His poetry, on occasion, is a cautionary warning to Friends: 'Oh that no unbelieving heart | Among us may be found' (1885: 256–7). Such comments add a different register to the literature of persecution. Rather than a confident or unrepentant strain, Ellwood's verse shows, perhaps, some anxiety that he will not be found worthy:

> 'To the Holy One'
> Surround me, Father, with thy mighty Power
> Support me daily by thine holy arm…
> Preserve me faithful in evil hour,
> Stretch forth thine hand to save me from all harm. (Ellwood 1885: 227)

Quaker writings from the period of the Stuart monarchy, infused as they are with accounts of that 'evil hour' for the Friends, suggest that it was hard for them to discern God's plan for his people (Rose 2011). The Quakers had started to compile records of their sufferings in the late 1650s (Braithwaite 1981: 314). These sources would later provide the material for Joseph Besse's *A Collection of the Sufferings* (1753), a text which situates such hardships providentially. Observing that 'it pleased Almighty God, to whom only the Intentions and Designs of Princes are foreseen and foreknown ... to place upon the Throne King William ... [for] the Glory of establishing to Protestant Dissenters a general Liberty of Conscience in religious Worship,' Besse traced the path to toleration (1753: xlv). Seventeenth-century narratives of Quaker sufferings, lacking the teleological understanding of Besse, nevertheless also tried to reveal God's purpose. A series of pamphlets concerning the persecution of the 1660s declare their perspective in the vocabulary of sorrow and innocence shared by their titles: *The Third Part of the Cry of the Innocent* (1662), *The Cry of the Innocent and Oppressed* (1664), and *Another Out-Cry* (1665). In yet another similarly entitled pamphlet, *Another Cry*, the writers promise their persecutors that 'the hand of the Lord will over take them' (1664: 11). In 'R.C.'s' *God's Holy Name*, suffering was twinned with a Revelation-style prophecy in order to show the disastrous consequences of intolerance (1661). The plague and fire of the mid-1660s gave further cause for reflection (*Another Out-Cry* 1665). Quaker writers could also see God's hand when a judge, jury-member, or prison warder suffered either an unexpected or painful death; details such as these register that Foxe's *Acts and Monuments* was still the literary model to be invoked.[7] As Thomas Ellwood observed, 'Divine Providence ... sometimes vouchsafeth to bring Good out of Evil' (Ellwood 1885: 249).

William Penn sought to influence the toleration debate by his insistence that the Quakers be reprieved in the name of liberty of conscience. The 'bulk' of Penn's writing on religious liberty was produced by the mid-1670s (Morris 2012: 203). Penn saw that the mass imprisonment of worshippers on matters of conscience was a blot on the nation's character. When he wrote a series of pamphlets at the end of the 1680s, he formulated his argument, in part, in language that had been used in earlier works. For instance, he commented on the Foxeian idea that 'the Martyrs Blood won the day' (1687: 11). However, Penn's aim was clearly to look beyond the Foxeian framework that had been so useful to Quakers in the early days, and that remained in evidence in the accounts of the sufferings of Friends in distant locations, such as America. Although Penn left 'no direct testimony to the sources of his intellectual and theological development', it seems that he 'may have made searching use of humanist and philosophical resources' (Morris 2012: 208; Angell 2012: 166). Quakers had not always been so willing to use or embrace non-Quaker writers, though on legal matters an exception was often made in the case of John Selden, who had been so useful to Quakers appealing against having to pay tithes (Nevitt 2006: 145–78). Indeed, John Crook had apologized early in the Restoration for

---

[7] See, for example, the anonymous pamphlet *A Narrative of the Cruelties and Abuses Acted by Isaac Dennis* (1683).

'using the Laws of men' in his argument (Crook 1662: 47). However, Penn had no such compunction and could, indeed, be employing the humanist belief that rhetoric, well-argued and logically set out, could win the day (Remer 1996). He writes with the authority of one that knows the wider discourse: 'Why then may not that be done here that has been so happily acted elsewhere?' (Penn 1688: 9).

Penn wrote of the parlous situation of Quakers: 'If ever it were time to speak, or write, it is now' (1993: 135). Quakers indeed took this literally across the near thirty years between the Restoration and toleration, writing at least 167 sufferings narratives from 1660 to 1688, the most standard being those already discussed in this chapter (Runyan 1973: 569–72). However, Quaker suffering was even more ubiquitous than has been shown; indeed, it is a feature of much more than the collected trials and imprisonments that established the community-wide persecution. The Quaker sense of the importance of print emerges in a narrative that focuses in its early sections on the trial of Edward Burrough, who speaks first:

> Let all take notice, I am *denyed Law and Custome at the bar,* if ye deny me this motion of Arrest of Judgement. Then Alderman *Brown* spoke to him in these words, *This is all ye shall have, and print it (said he) if ye will through the Land*; To which E.B. again replyed, that he was no very great Printer, yet he thought it his duty to publish these things as many as he could, that all the World may know the Proceedings. (*The Third Part of the Cry* 1662: 26)

The trope, here, is one that recurs in much Restoration Quaker suffering writing: that the reading public must be educated as to the proper way to interpret the sufferings of Quakers (as injustice), to see the hardships they bore, and to recognize that liberty of conscience was the only solution. In a similar manner, bold statements were also made at other trials, such as when William Penn and William Mead reminded their reader (in gendered language), 'you are Englishmen, mind your privilege' (1993: 148). But these sufferings narratives could also have power when simply recording, for posterity, the names of those who suffered:

> Here followeth the Names of 32. more Sentenced the 16th of the 11th Moneth (called *January*) 1664. at the *Sessions* held in the *Old Baily*, and also of four Sentenced as a Sessions held at Hicks-Hall on the 12th. of the aforesaid Moneth.
>   Robert Hayes, Robert Pute, John Fox, John Tilby, Edward Walker, John Tisdell, William Garrald, John Grane, Mathias Gardener, George Tayler, Richard Lambert, Evan Jones, William Tilleby, William Tillet, Isaac Mason, Josiah Clare, Christopher Disckinson, Isaac Warner, Edward Brush, Richard Smith, Mary Powell, Ann Dance, Elizabeth Dixson, Katherin Charles, Susanna Horn, Dorothy Hall, Allice Richardson, Margaret Ushor, Thomas Stokes, Thomas Clarke, Thomas Burbuke, Bartholomew Harne. (*Another Cry of the Innocent* 1664: 17)

Such lists were common to a movement that valued the collective protest of all Friends. Moreover, prison writing has an even wider scope, and includes works written from prison, though not necessarily wholly concerned with the theme of persecution. Dorcas Dole, a woman whose life is discussed in John Whiting's *Persecution Expos'd*, wrote three works of admonition and warning while in prison (Whiting 1715: 71, 75, 92; Foxton 1994: 51).

Suffering is also the theme in a number of other texts, and many reach out primarily or solely to Quaker readers. The Quakers in Bristol during the early 1680s suffered intense persecution, since meeting houses were nailed up, there were mass arrests, and law enforcers even incarcerated children. Though a string of texts for public consumption show the Bristol experience,[8] more inward-facing responses survive too. In his 'To Suffering Friends in Prison at Bristol' (1683), for instance, George Fox reminds these Friends that through being stalwart in their sufferings they will be rewarded by God, the true judge. 'He that endures faithful to the End shall be saved', Fox affirms, before concluding 'And so with my *Love* in the *Seed*, in which you and all nations are blest. G. F.' (Fox 1698: 490). Autobiographies and memorials also took up the theme of persecution. Barbara Blaugdone, at end of her autobiography, explains why she puts her life on record: 'I have written these Things that Friends may be encouraged, and go on in the Faith, in the Work of the Lord: For many have been the Tryals, Tribulations and Afflictions that I have passed through, but the Lord hath delivered me out of them all' (Blaugdone 1691: 38). Likewise, accounts of recently deceased Quakers also contain addresses to Friends on the subject of persecution. One writer interjects in John Story's biography that 'we believe those who stand not to their Testimony, but flyes therefrom in the Day of Persecution, may truly be counted, either weak in Faith, or departed from the Faith' (Story 1683: 39). These many and varied textual accounts show that there is leakage of the generic concerns of 'sufferings' writings into other kinds of texts. The mixing of genres means that there is probably even more writing on suffering than statistics (previously referred to) show, the subject being of such import to the Quakers.

1690–1700: 'Why Should I Write of These Things to Thee?'

The central literary event of the 1690s was the publication of the *Journal* of George Fox. He had dictated the main events of his life up to 1675 to Friends, and Thomas Ellwood sketched in the remaining details for the later period, before the posthumous publication in 1694. The *Journal* is a classic spiritual autobiography, moving from accounts of Fox's early religious experiences to his becoming the leader of the new movement, and later showing the endurance that was required in order to maintain his beliefs despite

---

[8] See, for example, the following anonymous pamphlets, all of which were published in 1682: *More Sad and Lamentable News from Bristol*, *The New and Strange Imprisonment of the People Called Quakers* and *The Sad and Lamentable Cry of Oppression*.

widespread opposition. Fox's *Journal* stands alongside other Quaker autobiographies, some preceding him, such as William Caton's (1689) and Margaret Fell's (1992, published in 1690), and some post-dating him, such as John Banks's (1712), and Thomas Ellwood's (1714). Indeed, the confessional autobiography is another major genre of Quaker print culture (Runyan 1973). Many of these journals focus considerable attention on the early years of Quakerism, particularly the person's conversion to the faith (which Friends called 'convincement') and the times when Quakerism was gaining a foothold (Wright 1932: 110–21; Wright 1937). Fox's most recent editor, Nigel Smith, has argued that the *Journal* 'captures the features of the prophetic Quaker tracts' and hence, the movement's early days (Fox 1998: xviii–xix), though the radicalism of the text has, in fact, been much debated (Hinds 2011: 9–11). This ambivalence is caused by how one judges the turning of the Quaker movement into 'a structured institution', as Matthew Horn terms it, such as through the committees that ruled on the value of published works from the mid-1670s onwards (Horn 2013: 297; O'Malley 1982). In the year prior to the publication of the *Journal*, for instance, the annual meeting had called for writers to exercise 'care' in their printed works (*Renewed Advice* 1693: 1). When John Banks posed the question in relation to his own life narrative, 'Why should I write of these things to thee?' his answer was that giving an account of a life could 'edify' the other members of the spiritual community (Banks 1712: 142). This was certainly the ideal underlying the autobiographical imperative.

This ideal did not always work in practice. Woven into Fox's *Journal* as part of its *modus operandi* was the assumption that he understood the light to be working within or through him, guiding his every action. The prophetic elements of Fox's *Journal* were features with which a writer hostile both to Fox and to the Quaker movement could take issue, and this is what Charles Leslie's *The Snake in the Grass* did. Leslie was Anglican, and prior to this attack on Friends he had penned an earlier polemic against his other main target, Socinians (Kolbrener 2003).[9] Writers in the genre of 'controversy' frequently drew on earlier works of denunciation, and, as Braithwaite demonstrated, *The Snake in the Grass* borrowed freely from an ex-Quaker turned controversialist, Francis Bugg (Braithwaite 1979: 489). Quakers who left the movement were particularly useful for antagonists, even though such attacks were answered by Friends as a matter of principle. Leslie insisted that the Quaker movement needed to break its ties with the early days, the 'original Rabbis' and, in particular, Fox (Leslie 1696: 8). The *Journal* was one of his targets; *The Great Mistery* [sic] *of the Great Whore* (1659) was another. He characterizes Fox's immanentist beliefs as delusion, and mocks 'his foolish legend of a Journal' (Leslie 1696: lxix). One of the *Journal's* key accounts of a formative religious experience looked, to Leslie, like the 'mad joy' of a 'despairing soul' (Leslie 1696: lxxxx). He was referring to a moment when Fox described the Flaming Sword leading him 'into the paradise of God' (Fox 1998: 27).

The final text for consideration in this chapter could not be more different from Fox's *Journal*, though it exemplifies another, related aspect of Quaker writing. A more domestic side to Quakerism, as a religion uniting families, emerged in the deathbed testimonies

---

[9] Socinians were a Protestant sect subscribing to a radical anti-trinitarian creed.

that were published as part of the tradition of *ars moriendi* (Gill 2005: 147–82).[10] These gave particular prominence to women, since they were often collaborative ventures between family members remembering the deceased. Elizabeth Moss's testimony to her mother, Mary Moss, is one such text:

> And for my own part, I have been, as it were raised from the very brink of the Grave, and I am as one of the Monuments of the Lords Mercy, desiring that the Day may never be forgot by me. And when I was in my greatest Calamity, the Thoughts of her from whence I came, was as Marrow to my Bones, blessing the Lord on her behalf, That he was pleas'd to suffer me to spring from such a Root ... O the remembrance of this my dear and tender Mother bows my Heart in Humility, and tenders my Soul causing me to say *O! thou God of the Righteous* ... Oh! the loss of so dear and tender a Mother, (which I have with my dear Sisters who beheld her upon her dying Bed) is more than I can sufficiently express; and though we Mourn yet not as without hope. (Watson 1695: 12, 14)

Neither Mary Moss, nor her daughter, Elizabeth, figure in standard histories of the Quakers. The compiler of the volume, Samuel Watson (Mary's stepfather), joined the movement early, and became a writer, a minister and a sufferer, making it likely that his influence led to this work being published (Watson 1712; Feild [*sic*] 1711: 165). Women like Mary Moss and Elizabeth Moss capture a different spirit of Quakerism from that of the visionaries like Fox, certainly, but in this testimony we are reminded that a movement needs mothers and daughters as much as it needs leaders.

As the century drew to a close, the Quaker movement remained true to its roots in that its literature still had the power to generate controversy. In contrast to the hostile reception to Quaker work by writers like Leslie, there is evidence of the perceived benefit to the reader of a Quaker text in John Whiting's comments that he often derived comfort from this work (Whiting 1714: 27, 228, 236). Many other uses for print can be discerned, since Quakers employed print as effectively as any other religious pressure group of the seventeenth century. In the process, Quakerism gave a voice to hundreds of men and women who made the incidents of their life—prophecy, imprisonment, religio-political protest, the domestic ties that bound them, their links to co-religionists—count to the full. It is little wonder that Quakerism continues to generate notable historical interest and, even, fresh critical controversy.[11] My thanks to Claire Bowditch, David Campling, and Helen Wilcox for commenting on the first draft of this essay.

---

[10] For further discussion of death-bed testimonies and the early modern art of dying, see chapter 38.

[11] I have tried as far as possible to include new scholarship in this essay. See also Richard Allen's 'Restoration Quakerism 1660–1691' (2015), and Kristiana Polder's *Courtship and Marriage Approbation in the Seventeenth-Century Quaker Community: George Fox Margaret Fell and Matrimony in the True Church* (Ashgate, 2015).

CHAPTER 28

....

EXILES AT HOME

....

ALISON SEARLE

THERE were numerous groups who found themselves in exile at home in England during the sixteenth and seventeenth centuries. This chapter focuses on the experience of Protestant Nonconformists in the later seventeenth century, the radical and repeated changes in state religion, accompanied by persecution of any who openly dissented from the status quo.[1] The Protestant Reformation created an initial fissure between the state religion and the convictions of individual conscience that radically undermined contemporary assumptions that the two were synonymous. In an early modern state such as seventeenth-century England theologians and philosophers, like Richard Hooker, defined the civic and religious identities of the subject as coterminous: an English citizen and subject of the queen was, by necessity, also a member of the state church.[2] Subsequent changes of religious allegiance on the part of Tudor, then Stuart, monarchs did nothing to mitigate the complexities (Crosignani, McCoog, and Questier 2010: xvi). This was particularly the case for those who maintained their allegiance to Catholicism after Henry VIII's decision to break with Rome and create a national church. His Lord Chancellor, the humanist Sir Thomas More, was just one amongst many Catholics who were executed for their faith and were revered as martyrs for their commitment to traditional religion and resistance to replacing the Pope with an English monarch as head of the church. Though Mary made a determined effort to reverse these changes—and could draw on strong residual support for Catholicism amongst her subjects—the qualified Protestant settlement achieved under Elizabeth I in 1559 proved to be decisive. Michael Questier (1996, 2006) following John Bossy (1975) has argued that the role of the aristocracy was crucial in shaping the identity of recusant Catholic communities in England once Mary's religious reforms, with their associated political, social, and

---

[1] I am grateful to Drs Rebecca McNamara, Ian O'Harae, Penelope Woods, and Helen Young for feedback on earlier versions of this chapter.

[2] 'We hold that seeing there is not any man of the Church of England, but the same man is also a member of the Commonwealth, nor any man a member of the Commonwealth which is not also of the Church of England' (Richard Hooker, cited McGrade 1989: 130).

cultural implications, were overturned. Significant examples include the household of Lady Magdalene Browne (1538–1608) at Battle in East Sussex and the Tresham and Vaux families in Northamptonshire (Murphy 2014: 242, 245–50). Bossy (1975) suggests that this resulted in a transformation of the nature of Catholicism in England and created a structural affinity between the experience of Catholic recusants and Protestant Nonconformist communities in contradistinction to the legally established Church of England.

The call for ongoing reformation in the latter sixteenth century and the civil wars of the mid-seventeenth century created space for the proliferation of diverse Nonconformist Protestant groups. Indeed Hannah Cleugh argues that it also 'highlight[ed] the very real tension between having an established church to which everyone was supposed to conform, and the desire to build a godly community. Predestinarian theology had ecclesiological and ethical implications, and these sat uneasily with the inclusivity of the Elizabethan church whose liturgy implied a pastoral and pragmatic universalism' (2013: 29). The state's consistent emphasis on the need to conform to the church established by law, despite a brief hiatus during the Commonwealth and Protectorate, meant that numerous individuals were positioned as religious and political 'exiles' in the country of their birth. This often entailed persecution by the state for their Nonconformist principles and practice. Religious Nonconformity in early modern England was a capacious term. Other possible synonyms for such individuals in the period are Puritans, separatists, and dissenters. The *OED* (1. a) defines the noun *Nonconformist* as:

> Originally ... a person adhering to the doctrine but not the usages of the Church of England ... Later (esp[ecially] after the Act of Uniformity of 1662 and the consequent ejection from their livings of those ministers who refused to conform): a member of a Church which is separated from the Church of England ... The term has been sometimes applied analogically to the Puritan section of the Church of England in the reigns of Edward VI and Elizabeth I.

Nonconformist, as used here, will incorporate both the historical and analogical meanings of the term.

Recent work (Major 2010; Spohnholz and Waite 2014) has demonstrated the ways in which the fact of exile—as a physical experience of fleeing to another country, or as an existential anxiety as a refugee in the country of one's birth—profoundly influenced religious identities and shaped individual and communal experience in ways that were shared across confessional boundaries. Though it is important not to flatten out the remarkable diversity of exilic experiences across Europe during this turbulent period, a shared exposure to exile could, as Major points out, inextricably bind 'royalist and non-royalist, Anglican and puritan alike', for example, and open up 'new ways of understanding important historical and social issues about mid-seventeenth-century English society, particularly English exile communities under pressure' (2010: 4). The concept of exile is freighted with biblical and historical significance which could give politically disempowered religious Nonconformists the moral high ground, aligning them, for example, with Israel against Egypt and Pharaoh, or with the persecuted apostles and martyrs of the early church against the evil state (often figured as Babylon). The re-establishment of the state church in 1662 following a period where there had been an unprecedented freedom to live, gather, and worship according to the dictates of one's conscience meant that large numbers of people found themselves unable to conform and consequently politically disenfranchised exiles at home. Steed Vernyl Davidson notes that Homi Bhabha defines such people as the '"unhomely". [Bhabha] speaks of the experience of the "unhomely" as those for whom the boundaries between the world and home collapse, where the divisions between the private and the public no longer exist … For him the concern centres not on lack of shelter, but on new positionalities that require new strategies for identity retention and (re)formation, both individual and communal.' Davidson uses 'Bhabha's notions of hybridity and diaspora' as a way of reading Jeremiah's letters to the deported Jewish community in Babylon (see especially Jeremiah 29:1–14) (Davidson 2011: 131–2). The concept of exile, as inflected through biblical typology, is a helpful way of thinking about the experience of Nonconformists in England. However, Erica Longfellow observes that individuals and households in early modern England did not construct their identity around 'the tension between public and private' as 'part of a grand narrative' and it is important to 'isolate the concepts— including self-examination and secrecy—that were part of a significant cultural debate for early modern individuals' (2006: 334).

Interpretive communities of Nonconformists can be traced from the early sixteenth century through to the eventual repeal of the Corporation Act (1661) and the Test Act (1673) in 1828. However, as noted above, I will focus here on the experience of individuals and congregations between the passing of the Act of Uniformity (1662) and the Toleration Act (1689). Many Nonconformists, including prominent leaders such as Richard Baxter and John Howe, desired comprehension within the state church and yet because of scruples of conscience found themselves unable to subscribe and therefore positioned with separatists, like John Bunyan and John Owen, whose ecclesiology enabled them to accept with equanimity or even enthusiasm exclusion from the national body, though not the associated persecution. Such Nonconformists or exiles, like Bhabha's 'unhomely', needed to develop new ways of positioning themselves and formulating their identities as individuals and local communities of believers. Kristen Poole has noted that the 'phenomenon of religious nonconformity' led people 'to contemplate and interrogate the basis of their familial, parochial, and national communities'. The 'organization of church and state' was discussed in 'the alehouse and home'. The stakes of conversations regarding sectarianism and separatism were high and had 'far-reaching implications for the relationship of the individual to the community; the grounds for political authority; the autonomy of the individual conscience; the right to participate in public discourse; and the right to determine one's own religious society' (2000: 13).[3]

---

[3] Poole notes further: 'While *Hudibras* begins with the comic partnership of the antithetical Presbyterian and Independent, by the end of the poem the distinction has nearly vanished. By merging together Presbyterians and Anabaptists, Butler recasts the multi-headed conflict of the civil wars into

This discussion examines the ways in which Nonconformist communities interpreted their experiences, interrogating and recording these in a variety of literary genres. The concept of exile at home is analysed through five discrete and interconnected categories: imprisonment, legal disputation in the courts, corporate worship, itinerant preaching, and letter writing. Each section draws upon a number of case studies that illustrate the wide range of spiritual experiences and theological convictions in Nonconformist communities and how these were encapsulated, transformed, and disputed in journals, letters, sermons, and biographies, amongst other literary genres.

Imprisonment

Imprisonment was probably the most acute form of internal exile that the state could inflict on its subjects. However, as Lake and Questier (1998) have argued, prisons could also act as clerical lodging houses and facilitate the pastoral and propaganda activities of Catholic priests. A similar effect resulted from the concentration of Nonconformists imprisoned following the Restoration. Nonetheless, experiences of imprisonment during this period could vary widely depending on the attitude of the gaoler and the number of prisoners incarcerated at a particular location. Theodosia Alleine records of her husband, Joseph, imprisoned at Ilchester:

> There were also Five more Ministers, with Fifty *Quakers*, which all had their Lodgings in the same Room ... It was not long after before Mr. Coven, and Mr. Powel, with Eight more, were brought into the same place, being taken at Meetings; which made their Rooms very straight, and it was so nigh to the upper part of the Prison, that they could touch the Tiles as they lay in their Beds ... they had very little Air ... and had no place but a small Garden, joyned to the place where all the common Prisoners were, which was no Retirement for them, they having there and in their Chamber, the constant noise of those Wretches, except when they slept ... there was the sight of their Clothes hanging full of Vermin, and themselves in their Rags and Chains. (1671: E5^r)

Elsewhere, Richard Baxter writes of his wife, Margaret:

> When I was carried thence to the common Gaol for teaching them ... I never perceived her troubled at it: she cheerfully went with me into Prison; *she brought her best bed thither*, and did much to remove the removable inconveniences of the Prison. I think she had scarce ever a pleasanter time in her life than while she was with me there. (1681: H2^r)

a polarized comparison: all those opposed to episcopacy are grouped together as dissenters. The saga begins to be told in terms which lend themselves to a labeling of "Puritans" and "Anglicans"' (2000: 185).

Mary Smith married the Nonconformist Presbyterian minister Robert Franklin in 1669. Shortly after Franklin was arrested for preaching and imprisoned in Aylesbury gaol; Mary was heavily pregnant at this time. During Robert's imprisonment they exchanged several letters and Mary's spiritual journal recounting her experience of grace from childhood to marriage and motherhood provides a vivid account both of the impact of Robert's imprisonment (in 1670, 1684, and on at least one other occasion) and of the ways in which principled Nonconformity could disrupt the security of the home and render families intensely vulnerable, resulting in the violent disturbance of activities from attendance at conventicles to breastfeeding and other aspects of daily life. The letters and journal also reveal the crucial importance of fellowship between believers and the local support networks that these provided: facilitating payments ensuring that the prisoner was adequately cared for; maintaining up-to-date communication regarding preaching and the publication of good books, the activity of informers, and the physical health and spiritual condition of members of the congregation; and, more generally, the predicament of other English Nonconformist communities. Mary's journal is strongly inflected and shaped by her Calvinist theology of election and providence and offers a graphic, tactile account of what Nonconformity entailed for one relatively ordinary woman and her family. The desire to preserve an account of God's provision for the edification of her children led to the creation of a manuscript document that selectively shapes and filters her life experience in a reasonably self-conscious literary form.[4]

Mary's first extant letter to her husband imprisoned in Aylesbury (4 July [dated 1667, but actually 1670]) notes that she is 'now more alone' as her mother has left her to care for her brother who was very sick, but concludes: 'I hope the Lord is with me, and so Long I cannot say that I am alone, for he is the best company, as I beleive you do find by Experience'. She has received the book 'a wellcome to the plague' from a friend: it speaks counsel to her condition and she requests her husband to pray to the Lord 'for his blessing in ye reading of it'. With a typical female apology she asks twice that he 'Excuse ye bad writing and spelling for I am in great hast'. A postscript informs Robert that: 'through ye goodness of god wee have injoyed another sabath in peace, though we had. 3 . sermons ... but m^r parthridg was disturbed by ye soulders who were very rude they shots bulets to shut open his door and killd his mayd and caried severall of his people to prison'. Her second letter (dated 6 July 1670) notes the safe receipt of his 'Loveing Letters' rejoicing in their mutual health, but troubled regarding her spiritual condition and asking for his prayers that she might follow his 'good and seasonable advice'. Mary is thankful for the glimpses of God's countenance that she has received despite the bitterness of her present cup, observing 'thy heart cannot be more with

---

[4] CL MS I.h.33. It is interesting to note in this context that her granddaughter used the same manuscript book to record her own experiences in the eighteenth century because she could not afford to purchase new paper. I am grateful to the Trustees of the Congregational Memorial Hall Trust for permission to use and cite from the manuscripts in their keeping.

me then mine is with thee, I never so much Expereincd a longing condition as now by reason of thy absence'. She corrects the information sent in her earlier letter: 'ye news that I sent you about m^r partridge is true only that ye maid was dead is not true she was nigh death but is recovered'. She updates him on the possible amputation of an acquaintance's leg, and another's private marriage, and finishes by observing 'my sister Tanner remembers her Love to you her kindness is very great in bearing me company now my mother is absent' (CL MS I.i.25).

Robert responded gratefully on 9 July 1670 acknowledging her loving letters and willingly excusing her 'bad writing wch I could easily doe were thy defects many more but my Dear: I cannot excuse thy defects in Arithmetick in that thy last by the coach was dated 1667 nigh two years before we could call Husband & Wife this Antedateing is an errata y^t requires amendment'. The close proximity in the date of these letters and the loving, intimate, even humorous tone indicates the companionate nature and strength of the marriage: he provided spiritual counsel and she much needed emotional succour during the period of his imprisonment. Robert notes if Mary did but know 'the content I take to see thy handwriteing now I cannot see thy deare face thou wouldest not let me goe a weeke long wthout a letter'. However, as the time for the delivery of their child draws near, she 'will not be in a condition to give me those paper visits thy excuse will y^n be made the God of Heaven draw nigh vnto thee stand by thee p^{re}serve thee & deliver thee spare no needfull thing for thy good Our God will p[ro] vide his providence is our inheritance My Dear I pray let their be care taken the first coach after thy delivery that I may heare of thee'. The remainder of the letter touches on the health of acquaintances, rejoices in her spiritual mind and warns of the hypocrisy of one who went to a meeting and afterward 'betrayed' them 'to penalty of law'. Robert observes, in contrast, 'My Reverend & Worthy Brother Wells wth his good wife & sonne were in towne last night sent for me to their Inn did condole at my suffering ... & further expressed their kindness' by providing almost enough to cover his prison charges for a week (CL MS I.i.25).

The final extant letter from Robert to Mary (10 August 1670) affirms: 'I am greatly refreshed to see againe thy handwriteing & to heare of thy recovery and at the hopes to see & enjoy thee ye next weeke by Divine permission', when she will travel to visit him with his parents. Robert surmises that he might be released at the next Assizes due to the support of a nobleman who is 'much troubled at my imprisonment intends to be at Assize & to doe his utmost for my release'. He then refers to some family business in horse-trading and actively discourages his wife from offering hospitality to a particular woman concluding: 'Howbeit if my ffather & you judge meete I will not absolutely oppose it' (CL MS I.i.25).

Quite a different perspective is thrown on this two-month period in the first-person narrative account provided by Mary's journal. It complements rather than contradicts the information conveyed in the correspondence discussed above. But the death of her first child, referred to elliptically, I think, in Robert's final letter—'I greatly delight in these seasonable & sutible notes thou didst take as to Divine dealeing wth us ... it is much better to have at the hand of God what is good for us then what we desire our selves Gods dispensations are the results of the highest wisdome'—takes centre stage (CL MS I.i.25). Mary writes as follows:

> The . first year after we were marryed my husband was taken, at Colbrook, for preache-
> ing which was .15. mills from london, and was carryed to Ailsbury Jayl which was 15
> mills further; which was . 30 mils from me, and I was big with Child, it pleased God
> I went out my full time, and after very Sore and hard labour I was delivered of a larg man
> Child, but it was stilleborn which was Judged by most, to be occationed by my greif that
> I had upon me by reason of my husbands being so far from me, in my condition, it being
> new work for me to be Exercised in the School of affliction, it was more difficult for me
> to bear, but the lord was graeciously pleased to suport me both in soul and body, and as
> soon as my month was up, my father and mother \&/ I rode to the prison where my hus-
> band was, it being the Sizes; some friend moved the Judges to consider his condition, he
> being Elegally commited, but they would not medle with it. (CL MS I.h.33: 7)

Here, she does not mention the higher wisdom of divine providence, rather the physical distance and absence of her husband is noted, along with her 'very Sore and hard labour' and, though she abstracts herself from the conclusion that the still birth of her first son was 'Judged by most' to be caused by grief at her husband's imprisonment, it was none-theless a 'School of affliction' that she found 'more difficult … to bear' because she had not experienced it before.

Throughout the journal Mary recounts the inextricable correlation between her own bodily health, that of her children, and her family's vulnerability to informers, impris-onment, expulsion from their home, and the forced removal of their goods. She focuses particularly on pregnancies (ten of which are recorded), disrupted breastfeeding and weaning, still birth and the illnesses of very young infants (such as St Anthony's fire), domestic accidents (including a maid scalding her four-year-old daughter, Mary, with a skillet of milk and bread boiling over the fire, resulting in horrendous disfigurement and death several days later), and melancholy (this could have been postnatal depres-sion). Mary's Nonconformity and gender reconfigure the normative generic structure of the spiritual journal in important ways: the individual's passionate pursuit of God, painstaking self-analysis, and obsessive engagement with the scriptural texts are all there, but the voice is somatic, firmly situated in specific domestic spaces and family and congregational networks that are radically disrupted by Mary and Robert's committed Nonconformity and particularly the imprisonment of the latter.

So, for example, shortly after Robert's release from Aylesbury gaol 'there came forth new warrants, to sease our goods, and the Enformers … Endeavored often to get into our house which occasion much disturbance to us, and at this time I … having a young Child, hanging on my brest, and I was forced to wean the Child my milk being disturbed, it did both me and the child hurt' (CL MS I.h.33: 8–9). Similarly, on opening the window of her home to speak to a friend, an:

> informer being, behind, flew up to the window, and snacht it out of my hand; and
> got up into it presently (he was a Glasser by trade which made him soe Expert at the

work) but my husband being in the room thrust him back again ... at this time I gave suck to my 4 fourth Child Joanna, but these frights did so disturb my milk that I was forced to wean her. (CL MS I.h.33: 12)

They were, however, unsuccessful in preventing the informers from entering one Saturday afternoon in November 1684:

> they got the window of the hinges, and quickly got in there being nobody to resist them, only a poor sickly child in the cradle, the other two children being in a great fright followed me up stairs, and when they were got in, they quickly, came up to us, the informer had his drawn sword in his hand ... and laid hold of my husband, and told him, he was the kings prissoner [and was committed by a Justice to prison for half a year for refusing the corporation oaths] ... they returned to our house ... and Eate up our victualls and drank up our drink ... I refused to pay down any mony [for the household goods they had seized] ... they fell in a great rage, to pulling and nock-ing down the things ... not leaveing . so much as a chair to sit in, or a cup to drinke in ... my Cheife end in declareing these things is to acquaint my freinds, and relations, Especially my Children, and also, that I, may not forget my selfe, how greatly the lord Supportd me in this time of trouble. (CL MS I.h.33: 16–18)

The common puritan impulse to record God's faithfulness for the edification of her children led Mary Franklin to produce a remarkable text that demonstrates the ways in which this particular community of Presbyterian Nonconformists made sense of the persecution they experienced at the hands of the state and its powerful impact on every aspect of their lives. Her spiritual journal both enshrines and enacts that interpretation.

LEGAL DISPUTATION IN THE COURTS

Closely related to imprisonment, and providing an effective stage for the perform-ance of Nonconformity, were the court debates that often led to the internal exile or incarceration of religious dissenters. Amongst the correspondence providing details of John Bunyan's imprisonment following the Restoration is a short account of his second wife, Elizabeth's, encounter with the justices at the Midsummer Assizes in August 1661 (Bunyan 1998: 116–18). Bunyan sets out the exchange in the style of a dramatic dialogue, which, he claims, '*I took from her own Mouth*' (1998: 116). There are thus several layers that separate us from Elizabeth's own narration of her encounter with the authorities: the manuscript correspondence detailing Bunyan's imprisonment was not published until 1765 and the originals are no longer extant.[5] Elizabeth's oral performance is textually

---

[5] *A Relation of the Imprisonment of Mr John Bunyan, Minister of the Gospel at Bedford, in November, 1660* (London, 1765). For further discussion of the textual history of *A Relation*, see Sharrock 1959. See also Lynch 2004: 23–33.

mediated through the authorial persona of her husband and shifts freely from the third to the first person in its transcription of her speech; there is, thus, no direct access to Elizabeth's own record of her dramatic engagement on her husband's behalf.[6] John was imprisoned shortly after marrying Elizabeth in 1659. Elizabeth presented John's plea for him before the justices, including Sir Matthew Hale, Sir Thomas Twisden, and Sir Henry Chester, at the Bedford Midsummer Assizes. She followed up on two further occasions attempting to obtain John's release without acknowledging that he had acted illegally by preaching.

Though the law proscribed the practice of Baptist worship, Elizabeth persistently pursued all legal avenues on behalf of her husband. She had already been to London and consulted with members of the House of Lords as to the best way to obtain her husband's freedom. Their advice had been 'that they could not release him, but had committed his releasement to the Judges, at the next assizes' (Bunyan 1998: 118). John characterizes Elizabeth in biblical terms as the poor widow who repeatedly accosted the unjust judge and succeeded simply because he wished to be rid of her (Luke 18:1–8). The analogy is not entirely apt, as Elizabeth was unsuccessful. She did, however, manage to attract the attention of Sir Matthew Hale, one of the few justices at this time who showed some sympathy to dissenters. He 'mildly received [the petition] at her hand' on the first occasion; he was willing, 'as it seemed', 'to give her audience' on the second occasion, but was intercepted by Sir Henry Chester, who dismissed Bunyan as already 'convicted in the court' and 'a hot spirited fellow'; on the third occasion, having been encouraged by the High Sheriff, Edmund Wylde, Elizabeth again approached the court as it was meeting in the upper room of the Swan Inn, near the bridge over the Ouse, and addressed herself to Hale 'with a bashed face, and a trembling heart' (Bunyan 1998: 117).

The literary representation of this dramatic encounter in dialogue form results in a concrete immediacy that instantly engages the reader's interest and sympathy. Richard Greaves describes it as 'arguably Bunyan's most dramatic prose' (2002: 144). Neil Keeble observes further: 'It is not by direct address to the reader nor by tendentious commentary but by the ironic import of its dramatic presentation of events that the *Relation* comes to bear out Bunyan's contention that "those that are most commonly counted foolish by the world, are the wisest before God"' (1987: 54). Elizabeth is denoted simply by the generic 'woman', which highlights her comparative vulnerability and powerlessness alongside the male justices who are usually identified by their surname and often their title as well. Hale, Elizabeth's best hope, is sympathetic towards her condition as the stepmother of four young children, one blind, whilst only a teenager herself, but is unable to do more than offer procedural advice: 'thou must either apply thyself to the King, or sue out his pardon, or get a writ of error' (Bunyan 1998: 119). Even this mild suggestion arouses the ire of his fellow justice, Chester. Elizabeth, however, desires action and insofar as this particular account can be trusted performs more effectively and intelligently than the males on the bench, despite her relative powerlessness as a member

---

[6]   For Tasmin Spargo's discussion of this issue, see Spargo 1997: 40.

of the lower classes, a woman, and a religious Nonconformist. Chester can do no more than idiotically repeat, 'it is recorded, woman, it is recorded', to which Bunyan adds in an acid aside, 'as if it must be of necessity be true because it was recorded ... having no other argument to convince her...' Elizabeth continues to object that Bunyan 'was not lawfully convicted' (Bunyan 1998: 118). Sir Thomas Twisden, perhaps aware of the weakness of Chester's gambit in the face of Elizabeth's claims, seeks to undermine her petition on the grounds of social class. Bunyan is dismissed as 'a pestilent fellow', 'a breaker of the peace', and Elizabeth is accused of making 'poverty her cloak'. She responds with simple efficacy, 'Yes ... and because he is a Tinker, and a poor man; therefore he is despised, and cannot have justice' (Bunyan 1998: 119). The account of Elizabeth's performance ends with her 'break[ing] forth into tears, not so much because they were so hard-hearted against me, and my husband, but to think what a sad account such poor creatures will have to give at the coming of the Lord' (Bunyan 1998: 120). This eschatological frame of reference, invoking the ultimate divine judgement of God, reduces the patriarchal authority of the bench to a travesty of justice, and leaves Elizabeth on the moral high ground, weeping not for herself, but for the ultimate fate of those that ignored the testimony of God who had 'owned' her husband 'and done much good by him' (Bunyan 1998: 120).

Elizabeth's dramatic intervention on behalf of her husband was one of the first of the courtroom scenes that were to be enacted again and again by Nonconformists following the Restoration. Keeble argues:

> There was something irrepressible to the point of flamboyance about the defiance of these defendants. Court room scenes, with their clearly defined conflict, claustrophobic location and increasing suspense as they move through charge, countercharge and disclosure to the climatic verdict, are intrinsically dramatic. The accused, casting themselves as the protagonists, conducted themselves very much as actors upon a stage. And, by putting these proceedings swiftly into print, they played before a far wider audience than the 12 men of the jury. Such reports, in which the participants are identified, the dialogue carefully attributed, and the exchanges reproduced *verbatim*, are dramatic texts as animated as, and far more searching and serious than, the staple fare of the Restoration stage. (1987: 53)

Bunyan's account of Elizabeth's action, however, was not published until 1765; prior to that it was only available via manuscript circulation—perhaps because of its inflammatory political nature, or possibly because it depicted a woman acting in a way that was inconsistent with Bunyan's own theological convictions.[7] That there was significant disagreement within the Nonconformist community—which embraced a reluctant and ill-assorted spectrum ranging from Quaker to Presbyterian—is evident from the fact that one of the latter, Thomas Manton, could indict the behaviour of the former as

---

[7] For further discussion of this point and debate as to the extent to which Bunyan endorsed his wife's actions on his behalf, see Greaves 2002: 145 and Spargo 1997: 40, 85–7.

ostentatious rather than edifying. Manton's critical theological perspective defines the Quaker performance of Nonconformity as 'culpably histrionic' reducing legal authority to 'melodramatic absurdity' (cited by Keeble 1987: 53). Debates about whether or not such dramatic accounts should be published and what constituted an authentic performance of religious Nonconformity demonstrate the fluidity and political fervour that inflected the self-identification of dissenting communities in the early years of Charles II's reign and the significance of their performance in the public arenas of courtroom and print.

Elizabeth Bunyan negotiated the complex political terrain of the reconstituted House of Lords and the Midsummer Assizes in Bedford in an attempt to obtain justice for her imprisoned husband. Bunyan's account of her dramatic performance demonstrates her astute deployment of legal argument, her careful attempt to target the most sympathetic audience member amongst the justices, and her strategic enactment of both female weakness—as the teenage stepmother of four children, one blind—and evangelical sorrow—grieving over the spiritual blindness and potential damnation of her male interlocutors. Bunyan's apparent endorsement of Elizabeth's actions also demonstrates that women, even within the most restrictive of Nonconformist communities, had a crucial impact on the public performance of Nonconformity through their personal intervention in legal and political processes.

CORPORATE WORSHIP

Their status as exiles at home had a profound impact upon the corporate worship practices of all Nonconformists, just as the protection of priests in noble homes and attempts to preserve some aspects of Catholic ritual and worship were crucial to recusant identity and practice after the Protestant Reformation in England. The ways in which Nonconformist sects defined the physical spaces they worshipped in were complex. The abstract concept of such space was inflected both by varying theologies of what constituted the local church together with the practical logistics of worshipping as a group legally proscribed by the civil authorities. As Cynthia Wall notes, space as a concept, due to its historical appearance in London in the aftermath of the Great Fire, began 'a wider cultural moment of more primitive *human* concern'. Her phenomenological approach attempts 'to recover and understand what it might have meant to a tenant or poet of London to suffer the loss of an experiential *given*, to confront the various abrupt intersections and transformations of physically and socially determined spaces' (1998: xiv–xv). Congregationalists and Baptists, amongst others, raised theological objections to a definition of the local church as synonymous with the geographical boundaries of the parish, its spiritual membership consonant with its civil population. For such, the local church was a gathered community of saints—an elect group called out from amongst the general population who covenanted together to form an ecclesial body. The Spirit of God was present wherever his people gathered: this downgraded the importance of a sanctified physical location, though some kind of meeting-place (whether indoors or outside) was obviously required for corporate worship.

Following the Act of Uniformity (1662) and the Five-Mile Act (1665) it became very difficult for Nonconformists of all persuasions to meet together, whether they were officially separatist in their theology—as were the aforementioned Congregationalists and Baptists—or among those who continued to hope for some kind of comprehension into the state church, like the Presbyterians. The Fire of London further exacerbated the political dimension of these religious tensions. Despite the ambitious rebuilding programme headed by Sir Christopher Wren, Nonconformists had often been more efficient in acquiring or rebuilding spaces for religious worship than their counterparts within the state church. As the *London Gazette* (13–16 June 1670, No. 478) records, Charles II authorized the Church of England to re-appropriate these spaces for the use of legally sanctioned worship. This meant that an already toxic situation was further inflamed as a shared civic disaster was used to justify a partisan undermining of cherished property rights: the state attempted to aggressively write out and physically remove worshipping Nonconformists from the city of London.

One of the properties referred to in this notice belonged to the Presbyterian congregation pastored by Thomas Doolittle: 'in *Mugwell-street, Mr. Doolittle's Meeting house*) built of Brick, with three Galleries, full of large Pews, and thirty eight large Pews below, with Locks and Keys to them, besides Benches and Forms' (*London Gazette*, 13–16 June 1670, No. 478). Doolittle had been converted under the powerful Interregnum preaching of Richard Baxter in Kidderminster and was later ordained as a minister. Following his ejection as rector of St Alphage, London Wall, he moved to Moorfields and 'opened his house for boarders'. He instructed children and young people and held conventicles in a variety of locations during the following decade including a house in Bunhill Fields, in Woodford Bridge during the plague of 1665, then in Romford. This was similar in many ways to the activities of the Jesuit Superior in England, Henry Garnet, who rented houses in London that acted as seminaries and shelters for priests from 1587 until his arrest and execution in 1606.[8] After the Fire Doolittle initially set up a meeting house near his home at Bunhill, but this proved to be too small and so he erected 'a large and commodious place of worship' in Monkwell Street, St Giles, Cripplegate—that referred to in the *Gazette*. On the evidence provided by Doolittle's will, Mark Burden has suggested that this meeting house 'was built as a consequence of 'Two Leases to me granted by Elizabeth Vaughan of the ground and buildings thereon by me erected … in Mugwell Street where I now dwell' (TNA, PRO, PROB 11/495/318). The Lord Mayor tried and failed to persuade Doolittle to stop preaching; soldiers were sent to arrest him, beating down the door, but neither this, nor a second attempt in May 1670 was successful (Burden 2013: 141–2). However, it does provide the background context for the state church's appropriation of the property: violence on the authority of the royal prerogative contravened rights established by law.

---

[8]   See, for example, the record of his activity in 1594 in McCoog 2012: 162–4.

Wall notes that this persecution had important implications for the ways in which Nonconformists experienced the physical and cultural space of London, as well as their meeting houses, arguing that they:

> had to occupy space differently. The legal and social pressures to be quiet, private, and concealed, meant that Dissenting ministers moved their congregations into *other* public and private spaces, but occupied those spaces secretly. Schoolrooms, warehouses, public buildings, and barns supplied continually shifting premises as each new location was betrayed and exposed. Pinners' Hall, for example, in Pinners'-Hall-Court, Old Broad Street, where Samuel Annesley ... later preached, and where Defoe in 1681 transcribed six sermons of John Collins, was variously rented out to several congregations on Saturdays and Sundays, and, when not in use by the Pinners' Company, also during the week. Dissenting spaces belonged to someone else; they were borrowed, contingent, temporary, unreliable. (1998: 187)

This perpetual harassment and deliberate exclusion from politics and religion in the public sphere impacted upon the way in which Nonconformist groups or congregations constructed their corporate identity and enhanced the sense that they were exiles in the wilderness of Restoration England longing for home. The most famous literary expression of this is, of course, Bunyan's *Pilgrim's Progress*, with its solitary opening: 'As I walk'd through the Wilderness of this World' (1678: A7^r). Though the corporate dimension of this exilic pilgrimage is more consistently depicted in Part II, Christian and Faithful's journey through Vanity Fair, and the incomprehension and hostility of its inhabitants, vividly captures aspects of Nonconformist religious experience (whether in London or Bedford): 'And as they wondred at their *Apparel*, so they did likewise at their *Speech*; they naturally spoke the Language of *Canaan*; But they that kept the *Fair*, were the men of this world: So that from one end of the *Fair* to the other, they seemed *Barbarians* each to the other' (Bunyan 1678: G10^r).

ITINERANT PREACHING

As Bunyan's linguistic and cultural metaphor makes clear, the Nonconformist experience of internal exile, or exclusion from officially sanctioned political and religious spheres, paradoxically created its own sense of community. Though there was an increasingly complex diversity of devotional groupings and literary practices amongst Nonconformists after the Restoration, the necessity of itinerant preaching in order to meet the spiritual needs of those who were dissatisfied with their parish church, to try and avoid consistent fines, and to fulfil the evangelical imperative to proclaim the gospel, was shared across groups as diverse as Presbyterians, Particular Baptists, and Quakers. The sermon was a corporate event—it could occur in prisons, where a minister might be incarcerated with a significant proportion of his congregation (as was the case with Joseph Alleine), within a domestic house (as Baxter practised in Acton following the parish church service), or in the streets and fields to try and avoid informers. Such events were memorialized in biographies designed to edify, encourage, and challenge the next generation of Nonconformists. As Baxter writes in his preface to the collaborative biography of Joseph Alleine: 'In the Lives of Holy men we see Gods Image, and the Beauties of Holiness, not only in Precept, but in Reality and Practice; not *Pictured*, but in the *Substance*' (Alleine 1671: B1^v–B2^r). In his preface to his biography of his wife, Baxter is even more explicit about the apologetic, pastoral, and entertainment value of history as a genre: '*finding young people naturally much delighted in History, and that for want of better, abundance are quickly corrupted and ensnared by Tale-books, Romances, Play-books, and false or hurtful History, I have long thought that true and useful History is of great use to prevent such evils, and to many profitable ends*' (Baxter 1681: A2^r–A2^v). It is in this generic context that Theodosia Alleine recounts her husband's 'parting Counsels' given to 'many of his Flock confined to the Prison with him'. She notes, 'I shall Recite in his own Words, as they were taken from his Mouth in Short-hand, by an intimate Friend, and fellow Prisoner' (1671: F1^v–F2^r). Inset into her biographical account is the text of this prison sermon.

If not all Nonconformists who engaged in itinerant preaching ended up in prison, the constant threat posed by informers shaped the ways in which they exercised their ministry. Owen Stockton, a Nonconformist minister in Chattisham, Suffolk, records in his writing-book that he had been asked by 'Mr B' to preach at White Colne on 15 October 1665. However, as he prepared to leave on the Saturday, 'H. P. came in [and] told us that the soldiers had seazed Mr B imprisoned him and it would not be safe for me to go at that season'. His friends advised him not to go, and one of his children held him 'in an unusual manner crying & would by no means be pacifyed, saying the troopers would kill me'. Despite eventually taking their advice, as he had 'been very lately sought after by name by the soldiers in those parts', Stockton 'was under much despondency of spirit for missing such an opportunity of service'. It was not until he read Matthew 16:20 in his devotions that evening that he received some ease, noting 'I observed, that the divulging of the most necessary truths was at some seasons … prohibited by Jesus Christ' (Stockton cited by Schildt 2008: 198). As Jeremy Schildt comments, Stockton's experience of such difficulties in attempting to fulfil his vocation as a minister led him to write and publish. Drawing on the precedent of an Old Testament prophet, Stockton writes: 'I observed that when Jeremiah was shut up & could not come forth to preach he caused Baruck to write the words that he had from the Lord & publish them to the people … I saw from hence when we were hindered from preaching, we might do good by writing' (cited by Schildt 2008: 199). This is a refrain that was echoed by many ejected ministers and parallels the way in which the culture of print acted as an 'imperfect proxy and deputy' in the absence of priests enabling the policies of the Council of Trent to shape the worship of English Catholic laity (Walsham 2000: 121).

Gender also influenced how Nonconformists delivered what they believed was a divinely inspired message following the Restoration. For example, the schismatic Particular Baptist, Anne Wentworth, initially attempted to commit the messages she received from God to writing in her manuscript book. However, her husband, William, was deeply concerned by his wife's prophetic activity: 'in a most cruel manner' he hindered Wentworth 'from performing' the commands of her heavenly bridegroom by 'seizing, and running away with [her] Writings' (Wentworth n.d. *Vindication*: A3ʳ). Her recovery from what appears, in her own account, to be domestic abuse, and rejection by her Baptist congregation in London, radicalized her public stance and led her to write a series of printed pamphlets and manuscript letters to those in authority—including the Lord Mayor of London and Charles II—in order to ensure her apocalyptic message reached its intended audience.

LETTER WRITING

The letters exchanged between Robert and Mary Franklin during the former's imprisonment are discussed in some detail earlier. In many ways letters are the genre that best exemplify the history and development of the Nonconformist community in exile at home. Letters demonstrate Nonconformists' shared identity and vision, as well as the tensions and controversies generated and confronted by community members. Letters could be intercepted, censored, and used as grounds for prosecution.[9] However, writing and receiving them was crucial in creating and maintaining interconnections between exiles at home, enabling congregations to retain a corporate identity through correspondence with their ejected ministers, and virtual communities to be established between Nonconformists throughout the country who embraced the same religious vision but could no longer meet in a shared physical space with ease. Letter writing also enabled the complexities of the Restoration religious settlement and the cases of conscience it created for ministers, as well as lay people, to be worked through as they sought to negotiate how to fulfil the biblical commands to gather together in public worship (Hebrews 10:25), to honour those in authority (Romans 13:1–7), and to seek first the kingdom of God (Matthew 6:33), whilst exiled from the public sphere due to legislation enacted by the Cavalier Parliament.

Mary and Robert Franklin's correspondence demonstrates the importance of letter writing in maintaining a companionate marriage, spiritual resolution, and management of practical affairs between husband and wife when the former was imprisoned for his Nonconformist principles. Similarly, it was an essential literary genre deployed by ministers separated from their congregations, either through ejection, imprisonment, or both. As Theodosia Alleine noted of her husband, Joseph:

> although he had many of his Flock confined to the Prison with him, by which means he had the fairer Opportunity of Instructing, and Watching over them, for their Spiritual good; yet he was not forgetful of the rest that were left behind, but would frequently visit them also, by his Letters, full of serious profitable Matter, from which they might Reap no small benefit, while they were debarred of his Bodily presence. (1671: F1ᵛ)

---

[9] See, for example, the postscript to Baxter's letter to John Humfrey (probably sent early in 1669), where he notes: 'I had many more things to have said, & you may see my folly in putting this much into your hand, when I know not who may see it, or what use may be made of it' (Keeble and Nuttall 1991: II, 68 [Letter 766]).

Like Stockton, when he could not preach or undertake pastoral visits, Alleine sought to do good by writing.

However, the most significant archive of correspondence revealing the critical role that letter writing played in maintaining relationships and setting up a series of interconnected communities of ejected ministers and Nonconformist congregations is that of the eminent dissenter, Richard Baxter. There are approximately thirteen hundred letters exchanged with around three hundred and fifty correspondents; the largest single group are some seventy ministers in his epistolary network that became Nonconformists following the Restoration (Keeble and Nuttall 1991: I, xxv). The letters demonstrate the ways in which Baxter and his clerical colleagues negotiated the ecclesiastical, political, and financial implications of the Act of Uniformity (1662) that effectively rendered them exiles at home. The correspondence also demonstrates how the emerging cultures of Nonconformity were shaped, interrogated, and defined through epistolary exchange. The shared experience of involuntary exile did not entail homogeneity and the diverse nature of religious dissent is represented in the variety of convictions held by Baxter's correspondents. These included, for example, the Presbyterians, William Bates and Thomas Manton, the Independents, Philip Nye and John Owen, the Baptist, John Tombes, and the Quaker, William Penn (Keeble and Nuttall 1991: I, xxvi). The letter was absolutely central, generically, textually, and materially, in fostering an epistolary community that was by turns, spiritually nourishing, intellectually curious, inherently disputatious, persecuted, fissured, but irrevocably and influentially literate.

To take several instances: Thomas Manton invited Baxter to re-engage in discussions as to whether a scheme of comprehension could be established that would allow moderate Nonconformists to rejoin the national church. Baxter, however, refused. On 17 February 1670, he stated that it would require 'going to Acton to search among my confused Scripts' and added—though these words were deleted later—'if I do without the leave of his Ma[jesty]; I must expect to go to prison; And I doubt whether if I stay so long in London as that busynes requireth, without leave, it will not be an offense' (Keeble and Nuttall 1991: II, 84–5). John Tombes, who challenged Baxter's position on infant baptism wrote on 22 August 1670 that 'either hate or some other distemper' must have prompted Baxter's letter to him. 'I know no reason why you should turn me off to them [i.e. William Allen and Thomas Lambe] unless you thought me so below your self as that it would be a disparagement to you to condescend to any motion of mine, or thought your writings so infallible as that they neede not a reexamination.' Tombes observes further that 'there is too much of your sceptical and unbrotherly spirit, which you shewed in the dispute at Bewdley [1 January 1649]' (Keeble and Nuttall 1991: II, 98–9). This demonstrates how the tensions and controversies that divided Protestants during the Commonwealth could continue to shape the epistolary culture and sectarian groupings within Nonconformity decades later. However, letters also enabled the formation of a spiritual community that could transcend the distinction between those who embraced a separatist ecclesiology and others, like Baxter, who favoured comprehension. Baxter's letter to Barbara Lambe (married to Thomas, mentioned above) on 22 August 1658 indicates this. He writes: 'unacquaintedness with the Face is no hindrance to the Communion of the Saints … I have an inward sense in my Soul, that told me so feelingly in the reading of your Lines, that your Husband, and you, and I are one in our dear Lord, that if all the self-conceited Dividers in the World should contradict it on the account of Baptism, I could not believe them' (Keeble and Nuttall 1991: I, 332–3).

CONCLUSION

Bhabha describes the invasion of the personal sphere by the public world as an 'unhomely' moment: the boundaries between home and world become confused. 'Private and public, past and present, the psyche and the social develop an interstitial intimacy' (1994: 19). In many ways, with due recognition to the anachronism inherent in an opposition between public and private in the early modern period, Bhabha's concept of the 'unhomely' captures the identity of Nonconformists who found themselves political and religious exiles in their own country. The case studies examined here indicate that Nonconformists experienced a significant degree of community in exclusion. However, it is important to note too the increasingly complex diversity of devotional groupings and literary practices amongst Nonconformists after the Restoration. Sharing the experience of Nonconformity, or exile at home, could create a sense of spiritual kinship, but this was not necessarily the case, as Baxter's very different relationships with several Baptists (the Lambes, Allen, and Tombes) indicate. Similarly, Mary Franklin's journal documents a less spiritually acquiescent and more somatic literary examination of the stillbirth of her first child during Robert's imprisonment than that created and shared in her correspondence with him.

This chapter has analysed the ways that the various environments within which Nonconformity was practised—gaols, homes, streets, courts, other public buildings, families, and, indeed, the human body—influenced the creation and reception of religious or devotional texts. It has traced the history of the community with its shared identity and vision, as well as the tensions and controversies generated and confronted by various members. The spiritual experiences constructed in and through texts such as letters, sermons, and journals written and shared while in exile at home were a powerful factor in the formation of Nonconformist communities between 1662 and 1689. However, as the different literary responses to death and persecution recorded by husbands and wives who shared the same convictions indicate, the religious fervour that led to exile at home was also an intensely private phenomenon.

CHAPTER 29

EXILES ABROAD

JAIME GOODRICH

IN 1629, the Benedictine Augustine (David) Baker wrote to Robert Cotton, an antiquarian with an extensive library, in order to request medieval manuscripts for English Benedictine nuns living in Cambrai, France:

> Ever since my being with you I have lived in a cittie in thes forein partes called Cambraie, assisting a Convent of certein religious English women of the order of St. Benet newlie erected…. They are inclosed, and never seen by us nor by anie other unlesse it be rarelie uppon an extraordinarie occasion, but uppon no occasion maie they go furth, nor maie any man or woman gette in unto them. Yet I have my diet from them, and uppon occasions conferre with them, but see not one another; and live in a house adjoining to theirs. Their lives being contemplative the comon bookes of the worlde are not for their purpose, and litle or nothing is in thes daies printed in English that is proper for them. There were manie good English bookes in olde time…. thereuppon I am in their behallf become an humble suitor unto you to bestowe on them such bookes as you please, either manuscript or printed. (Baker 1629: 12^r)

Oft-cited by scholars as evidence of the community's exposure to medieval mysticism (Summit 2009: 31), this letter also provides a glimpse into the factors that drove textual consumption within one community of English exiles abroad. Cotton may have been especially intrigued by Baker's description of the nuns' withdrawal from the world into monastic enclosure, which would have been impossible in England. The community never 'go[es] furth' or receives 'any man or woman' into their enclosure, and even Baker, their unofficial spiritual director, does not see his charges when he 'conferre[s] with them'. Baker believes that the nuns should likewise spurn 'the comon bookes of the worlde', instead reading texts suitable to their 'contemplative' lives—especially works from England's Catholic past. In Baker's view, the success of the Cambrai convent depended on its members' access to reading material that could strengthen their religious identity as contemplative nuns in retreat from England and the secular world.[1]

The Cambrai Benedictines were only one of many communities of English exiles that formed in response to the political and religious upheavals their country experienced during the early modern period. From the 1520s onward, Henry VIII's mixture of theological conservatism and anti-papal legislation caused both Lutherans and members of dissolved monasteries to flee England (Ryrie 2003: 93–112; Marshall 2006: 227–61). While reformist exiles returned after the government of Edward VI (1547–58) established Protestantism as England's official religion, Catholics in turn departed for Continental cities where they could attend Mass (McConica 1965: 269–71; Erler 2013: 107–25). When Mary I (1553–8) vigorously implemented a Counter-Reformation designed to crush English Protestantism, Catholic exiles came home as Protestant ministers and laity founded English congregations on the Continent (Garrett 1938; Pettegree 1996; Danner 1999). These abrupt shifts in religious policy ended with the accession of Elizabeth I (1558–1603), whose long reign saw both the permanent establishment of a Protestant national Church as well as the foundation of English Catholic seminaries, colleges, monasteries, and lay communities on the Continent (Guilday 1914; Shell 1999; Walker 2003; Gibbons 2011; Bowden and Kelly 2013). These exiled Catholic communities continued to flourish under the Stuarts (1603–1714), even while the court itself went into exile during the Interregnum (1649–60) and Nonconformists established colonies in North America (Wilcox 2006b; D'Addario 2007; Major 2013). As this summary suggests, three major sorts of exiled communities formed: lay congregations, educational institutions, and monastic houses. Examining texts produced by and for representative examples of each of these three groups (the Marian congregation at Geneva, the English colleges at Rheims and Rome, and the Third Order Franciscan convent in Brussels), this chapter will offer case studies of the way that exiled communities adapted certain forms of writing in order to develop and express a collective religious identity. Explaining literary critics' relative disinterest in religious exile as compared to martyrdom, Christopher Highley has observed that 'Exile ... lacked its own distinctive literary modes' (2008: 24). Even so, Christopher D'Addario has recently reminded us that writing offered exiles a crucial means of public self-fashioning: 'For many exiles the performative, be it the public gesture, the fashionable garment and posture, or the published written text, becomes an essential method through which identity is created and the disruptions of exile are overridden' (2007: 9). Scholars have already acknowledged the historical and literary importance of works by exiled individuals such as John Bale and William Tyndale (Daniell 2001; Minton 2010). With a few exceptions such as the texts of English nuns and the influential biblical translations of Englishmen at Geneva and Rheims (Long 2002; Hallett 2007; Bowden 2012–13), the textual production of exiled communities has largely gone unnoticed. As this chapter will demonstrate, certain kinds of writing

---

[1] For further discussion of English Catholic female religious houses as interpretative communities in this period, see chapter 25.

were especially well suited for the performance of exiled communal identity, allowing members of these groups to negotiate their relationships with one another, the English nation, and the broader Continental religious community.

Liturgical Texts, Congregational Identity, and the Genevan Exiles under Mary

During 1649, a Parisian printer issued a slim pamphlet entitled *A Forme of Prayer Used in the King's Chappel upon Tuesdayes in These Times of Trouble & Distresse*. At first glance, its contents may seem fairly innocuous: a liturgy for morning and evening services that is loosely modelled on the 1559 Book of Common Prayer. Yet any English reader encountering this work would have been acutely aware of its political and religious agendas. Not only had Parliament replaced the Book of Common Prayer with a Presbyterian service in 1645, but more recently the English government had sanctioned the execution of Charles I on the final Tuesday in January 1649. Although the late king's heir would be welcomed back to England as Charles II at the Restoration, now the exiled Charles Stuart merely claimed the throne from the Continent. In this way, the 1649 *Forme of Prayer* self-consciously represented a monarch and an English Church in exile. Each Tuesday, the court gathered to commemorate the death of Charles I and to pray for the restoration of the Stuart line with a carefully chosen sequence of Psalms, collects, prayers, and biblical lessons. 'Psalm III', one of the four custom-written psalms, drew a parallel between the expatriate court, for example, and the persecuted Israelites of the Old Testament by citing the opening of Psalm 60: 'O God, Thou ha'st cast us out, & scattered us abroad; Thou ha'st also been displeased, O turne Thee unto us againe' (*Forme* 1649: 7). The exiled court of Charles II was not the only community of Protestant émigrés to create customized liturgical materials such as psalms, prayers, and hymns. While Catholics abroad followed the liturgy of the Roman Catholic Church, Protestants in exile confronted the challenge of developing their own forms of worship. Indeed, the first English book to be printed in the New World was a metrical Psalter intended for puritan congregations that would appreciate its emphasis on biblical fidelity over lyricism (*The Whole Booke of Psalmes*, 1640; see Morris 2005: 76–104). Taking the liturgy produced by English Protestants in Geneva as a case study, this section will consider how texts written for congregational worship could help exiles enact a shared religious identity.

The Forme of Prayers … Used in the Englishe Congregation at Geneva: and Approved, by the Famous and Godly Learned Man, John Calvyn (1556) resulted from a contentious debate among English exiles over the form of their religious services. A preliminary version of *The Forme of Prayers* had been written for the English congregation at Frankfurt, where some members believed that their church should abandon the 1552 Book of

Common Prayer for a new liturgy following biblical precedents. After the Frankfurt community decisively rejected this view, its supporters formed a congregation in the city of Geneva and, with the support of John Calvin, implemented the liturgy rejected by Frankfurt (*Brieff Discourse* 1574; Vander Molen 1973). The *Forme of Prayers* reflected the Geneva congregation's Calvinism in its title, contents (which included an English translation of Calvin's catechism), and theology. For example, 'The Confession of Our Faithe' endorses the Calvinist doctrine of predestination, which holds that God saves the elect from damnation (*Forme*; Anon. 1556b: 39). 'A Prayer Made at the First Assemble of the Congregation' reveals that the Geneva community used this tenet to understand its own exile as a sign of election: 'thow ... haste called us of thy good pleasure from all Idolatries, into this Citie moste christianlye refourmed, to professe thy name, and to suffer some crosse emongeste thy people for thy trewth and gospells sake' (*Catechisme*; Anon. 1556a: 166). This idea is even more fully developed in the preface to the *Forme of Prayers*, which addresses 'Our Bretherne in Englande, and Els Where' in the communal voice of the congregation: 'we, to whome thogh God hath geven more libertie, yet no lesse lamentinge your bondage, then rejoysinge in our owne deliverance, frome that Babylonicall slavery and Antichristian yooke, have earnestly endevored emongste other thinges which might bringe us to the woorthy consideration of gods woorde, to frame our lyves, and refourme our state of religion' (*Forme*; Anon. 1556b: 9). Distinguishing between England's 'bondage' and their own 'deliverance', the Geneva exiles draw on Protestant views of biblical history in order to conceptualize their providential escape from Marian England. English Protestants had associated Edward VI with Josiah, the biblical boy-king who banned idolatry (Dawson 1994: 84–5; MacCulloch 2002). After Josiah's reign the Israelites returned to idolatry (Jeremiah 2), and Nebuchadnezzar sacked Jerusalem twice, destroying the temple and forcibly sending important Jewish families to Babylon (2 Kings 24–5). The Babylonian captivity therefore provided an apt metaphor for conveying the Geneva community's view that the Marian Counter-Reformation was divine punishment for England's failure to produce a fully reformed Church under Edward, especially since Martin Luther's *On the Babylonian Captivity of the Church* (1520) had influentially used the captivity as an allegory of the Roman Catholic Church's enslavement of Christianity. This biblical framework allowed the congregation to present the *Forme of Prayers* as a necessary continuation of the religious reforms begun under Edward.

The preface to the *Forme of Prayers* may have purported to speak for the entire Geneva congregation, but it was probably written by one of its leaders, William Whittingham. The liturgical materials that follow this preface, however, indicate that shared worship offered the community a chance to self-identify with this narrative of religious exile as a sign of election. After the sermon, the liturgy directed the minister to offer a prayer 'for th'assistance of Gods holy spirite' and offered one possibility entitled 'A Prayer for the Whole Estate of Christes Churche' (*Forme*; Anon. 1556b: 56–7). Written in a communal voice, this text encouraged the congregation to join together in the minister's prayer: 'as we be bownde to love, and honor our parentes, kinsfolkes, friendes, and contrye: so we moste humbly beseche thee, to shewe thy pitie, upon our miserable contrie of England, which once through thy mercie, was called to libertie, and now for their and our synnes, is broght unto most vile slavery, and Babylonicall bondage' (61). As the preface had done, this prayer uses the Babylonian captivity as a metaphor for recent English history, attacking Mary's religious policy as 'most vile slavery, and Babylonicall bondage'. This very phrasing seems designed for verbal emphasis as the alliterative 'b', 'l', 's', and 'v' sounds would certainly be striking when read aloud. The prayer also offered the Geneva congregation an opportunity to view themselves as elect due to their escape from this 'Babylonicall bondage'. While the text states that all English people are responsible for the country's tribulations by referring to 'their and our sinnes', the use of two separate pronouns acknowledges the physical separation between the Geneva exiles and England. The community's flight to Geneva reveals God's grace in action since they enjoy a religious freedom reminiscent of the 'libertie' that God's 'mercie' once allowed England to experience. The prayer encapsulates the preface's interpretation of recent English history, inviting members of the congregation to endorse the religious views of their leaders.

The Genevan liturgy allowed the congregation to voice these sentiments for themselves by singing psalms written in common ballad meter. The *Forme of Prayers* included revised versions of metrical psalm translations by Thomas Sternhold and John Hopkins, augmented by psalms translated especially for the Geneva congregation by Whittingham (Leaver 1991: 226–37; Quitslund 2008: 142–92). While the Psalms' polemical applications would likely have been obvious to the Geneva congregation itself, headnotes and marginalia in the *Forme of Prayers* spell out these readings. For example, Whittingham's headnote to his version of Psalm 115 suggests its relevance to the idea that persecution was evidence of election: 'A prayer of the faithfull oppressed by Idolatrous tyrants, against whom they desyre that god wold succor them for asmuche as ther is no comparison betwixt him and their false gods or idolls' (*Psalmes*; Anon. 1556c: 140). Verse four attacks such idolatry by dismissing 'idolee [*sic*] and gods' as 'silver or gold ... at moste, | the woorke even of mans hande', and a marginal note directly associates these lines with Catholic piety: 'if these be their best gods, of what value are they which are made of stone, woode, and wafer cakes?' (141). Besides condemning Catholic use of religious images made of 'stone' or 'wood', this scornful reference to 'wafer cakes' rejects the Catholic view that the consecrated host literally becomes the body of Christ during Mass. The concluding verses of the Psalm contrast the dumbness of the dead ('they that are dead, | shall never praise the lord') with the voices of the living ('we that do here lyve, | shall thancke the Lord always'; 143). This phrasing may have allowed the verse to represent the congregation's gratitude for their deliverance from idolatry since Whittingham's version evokes a specific religious community with the word 'here', which is not present in the biblical original ('we wyll prayse the Lorde, from thys tyme forthe for evermore'; *Byble* 1540: Cc^v). Another marginal note makes the underlying meaning more explicit by directly referring to God's protection of the elect: 'seinge god had elected this people to be glorified in, if they had perished his glorie shude have diminisshed' (*Psalmes*; Anon. 1556c: 143). Psalm 115 therefore could have reinforced the community's interpretation of their exile as evidence of God's preservation of the true Church.

Whittingham also composed a metrical version of Psalm 137, which is known as the Psalm of Exile because it centres on the Babylonian captivity (Hamlin 2004: 218–52; 2010). His headnote evokes the polemical associations that this psalm may have held for the Geneva congregation: 'The people of god in their banishement seinge gods true religion decaye, lyved in great anguishe and sorrowe of hearte, the which grief the Chaldeans did so litell pitie, that they rather increased the same daily with tauntes, reproches, and blasphemies against god' (*Psalmes*; Anon. 1556c: 153). Besides emphasizing the Babylonians' cruel impiety ('tauntes, reproches, and blasphemies'), Whittingham adds the idea that this psalm expresses the Israelites' sorrow in 'seinge gods true religion decaye'. Psalm 137 could therefore voice the Geneva congregation's similar lamentation over England's plight. For example, Whittingham's version emphasizes the Babylonians' ridicule of the Israelites:

> Then they to whome we prisoners were,
> said to us tauntinglie,
> nowe let us heare your hebrewe songes
> and pleasaunte melodie. (154)

Through modifiers such as 'tauntinglie' and 'pleasaunte', Whittingham emphasizes the ironic mockery already present in the psalm: 'they that led us awaye captyve | requyred of us then a songe and melody in our hevynesse' (*Byble* 1540: Dd^r). His use of the word 'prisoners' may have also brought to mind those English Protestants who were jailed for their faith, especially as the liturgy's 'Prayer for the Whole Estate of Christes Churche' mentions 'our bretherne, which are persecuted, cast in prison' (*Forme*; Anon. 1556b: 61). An accompanying marginal note identifies these tribulations as part of God's plan to test the elect, revealing how the psalm may have reinforced the community's view of recent history: 'God suffreth sometymes the wicked to vexe and torment his children with newe and sondrie afflictions' (154). Verse six in turn could have functioned as a communal petition for God to liberate England from Catholic tyranny:

> And let my tonge within my mouthe,
> be tied for ever faste:
> if that I joy, before I see
> thy full deliverance paste.

The biblical exemplar of this psalm emphasizes that the Israelites must not forget Jerusalem ('If I do not remember the, let my tonge cleve to the rofe of my mouth: yee yf I preferre not Jerusalem in my myrth'; *Byble* 1540: Dd^r), but Whittingham introduces a new idea: that the Israelites will not rejoice until Jerusalem receives 'full deliverance'. A marginal note suggests the political implications of this revision: 'The zeale that gods children have towards their fathers glorie' (*Psalmes*; Anon. 1556c: 155). Within the Geneva exiles' framework, God's 'glorie' would best be shown by a fully reformed Church, so that the psalm expresses a collective wish for the restoration of English Protantism in fulfilment of God's plan for the elect. The tension between the singular

'I' of this verse and the plural 'children' of the marginal note is an important reminder that a congregation is always composed of individual voices. The Genevan *Forme of Prayers* represented the congregation in print, yet it also united the members in song and prayer through weekly worship. Above all, the *Forme of Prayers* is a communal document that seeks to use liturgical texts as a focal point for constructing a collective identity as God's elect, called into exile to reform the Church while England experienced the Babylonian captivity of the Counter-Reformation.

APOLOGETICAL WRITING, NATIONAL IDENTITY, AND THE ENGLISH SEMINARIES ABROAD UNDER ELIZABETH I

Over a dozen English nuns were removed under duress from the Benedictine convent in Brussels in 1632, ending a bitter controversy within the house over spiritual direction. This dispute had scandalized English Catholics abroad and at home, and both of the factions involved sought to salvage their reputation by writing manuscript defences of their conduct. The final volley in this polemical battle was *Innocency Justified and Insolency Repressed; or a Round yet Modest Answere, to an Immodest and Slaunderous Libell Bearing this Title: A Briefe and Sincere Relation … of the Late Controversy betwixt the Lady Mary Percy Abbesse and Her Religious* (1634), in which Abbess Mary Percy's supporters offered a point-by-point rebuttal of a polemic written by her opponents. In explaining their decision to refute the *Briefe … Relation*, Percy and her adherents acknowledged that they had hoped the scandal would die away without further mention: 'The thing it self being such as were better buried under ground like unto rotten carcases, then layd open to the offence of others' (*Innocency* 1634, 1ᵛ). Yet the writers believed that restoration of their honor was worth the risk of exposing these skeletons in the house's closet: 'wee could not without doing so much wrong to our selves as to give away our good names which are worthily dearer then life, lett passe soe false & slaunderous a Libell as it is, without answere'. As the Brussels polemics suggest, the apology (or defence) was a vital literary mode for exiles, allowing them to defend their religious beliefs from abroad (see, e.g. Southern 1950). George Joye, for example, published an apologetical treatise justifying the reformist religious views that had led to his exile (*The Letters Which Johan Ashwel … Sente Secretely to the Bishope of Lyncolne … with the Answer of the Sayed George*, 1531). Within religious communities this genre could also serve as a means of identity formation, as Anders-Christian Jacobsen has already remarked of apologies written by early Christians (2009: 10). Exiled institutions like the Brussels Benedictines consequently used the apology to manage their reputation among fellow believers in England, a crucial task since they relied on their native country for financial support and new members. Focusing on William Allen's defence of English seminaries on the Continent (*An Apologie and True Declaration of the Institution and Endevours of the Two English Colleges*, 1581), this section will examine how apology allowed expatriate communities to negotiate their complicated relationship with England by conveying a collective identity to an English audience back home.

Allen's *Apologie* rejected the claims of two proclamations issued by the Elizabethan government that associated English Catholic exiles—and especially the Catholic seminaries for Englishmen in Rheims and Rome—with sedition (Elizabeth 1580, 1581; Southern 1950: 264–70). Allen had established these colleges in order to train a new generation of priests who could sustain English Catholicism through clandestine ministries in England, an aim that directly challenged official religious policy. A 1581 proclamation consequently responded to the establishment of a Jesuit mission in England during 1580 by recalling all English students from these seminaries:

> certaine Colledges ... have beene of late yeeres erected by the Bishop of Rome, aswel in that citie of Rome, as in the dominions of other Princes, especially for the Subjects of her kingdomes, & dominions, with intent and purpose to traine and nourish them up, in false and erronious doctrine: by which meanes, divers of her good and faithfull Subjects have bene thereby perverted, not onely in matters of Religion, but also drawen from the acknowledgement of their naturall dueties unto her highnes. (Elizabeth 1581: A1^r)

The proclamation takes advantage of the seminaries' physical location 'in the dominions of other Princes' in order to suggest that the exiles' primary allegiance is to local political and religious authorities rather than the English monarch and Church. The double meaning of 'faithfull' reflects these intertwined religious and political loyalties, underscoring the proclamation's contention that contact with 'erronious doctrine' results in political disobedience. In turn, the proclamation represents the Jesuit mission as part of a foreign political agenda to subvert the English government by reintroducing these seditious exiles into England: 'divers of her Subjects that have bene trained up in the said Colledges and Seminaries beyond the Seas ... are lately repaired into this Realme by especial direction from the Pope and his delegates, with intent not onely to corrupt and pervert her good and loving Subjects, in manner of conscience & Religion: but also to draw them from their loyaltie & duetie of obedience' (A1^v). In its attempts to discredit the Jesuit missionaries and seminary students, the Elizabethan government thus framed exile not as a matter of conscience, but as an indicator of treasonous sympathies (see also Highley 2008: 50–1).

Allen's *Apologie* asserted a counter-narrative in which the seminary students patriotically fulfilled their duties as Englishmen by implementing a second conversion of England. Written in a combination of first-person plural voice ('we') and third-person plural voice ('they') but signed by Allen himself on the final page, this text claimed to speak for the two seminaries even as it drew on Allen's authority as their founder. In keeping with the genre of the apology, Allen directly rebuts the major charges of the proclamations. For example, he denies allegations that the seminaries spread 'erronious doctrine' by describing the students' religious training as a means of reinforcing English identity: 'our cheefe endevour is … to breede in our Scholers the feare of God, devotion, and desire of salvation: Which is done by divers spiritual exercises, as, daily examinations of their consciences, often Communicating or Receiving the B. Sacrament, often confessing, much praying, continual hearing and meditation of holy things, deepe conceiving and compassion of their Countries state, and danger of their deerest frendes soules' (Allen 1581: 68ᵛ–69ʳ). The seminarians' devotional lives include Catholic rites such as confession and Mass, but these activities are linked to their national identity as Englishmen who 'conceiv[e]' and experience 'compassion' for 'their Countries state' and the spiritual 'danger of their deerest frendes'. This patriotism is an essential part of Allen's larger goal to train priests who will serve England at any cost:

> The … fruite of the said Colleges is … to breede in them zeale and desire to be Priests, even in these daies specially, when they can looke for no wor[l]dly honour, lucre, preferment or promotion thereby, but manifold dangers, disgraces, persecution, vexations: onely by praiers and Sacrifice … to make intercession for our desolate frendes at home: and to adventure into England, there to serve them, whose hartes God shal touch to admitte spiritual comforts, and to preferre salvation before wor[l]dly commodities: and to minister unto them al Sacraments necessarie for the life and grace of their Soules. (25ᵛ)

Allen downplays the political implications of the mission by foregrounding the priests' religious obligations: 'praiers', 'Sacrifice' (i.e. Mass), and 'Sacraments'. At the same time, he dismisses their interest in any potential 'wor[l]dly honour, lucre, preferment or promotion' by describing their patriotic determination to endure tribulations for England's conversion ('dangers, disgraces, persecution, vexations'). The *Apologie* thus suggests that the educational and devotional regimen of the colleges heightens the students' patriotism rather than obliterating their English identity.

Yet as the proclamation had pointed out, missionary priests did encourage their countrymen to obey the religious authority of the Pope rather than Elizabeth. Allen directly addresses the question of the exiles' loyalty by comparing the Jesuit mission to the conversion of England undertaken by Augustine of Canterbury during the Anglo-Saxon period:

> Our holy Apostle S. Augustine came to our Countrie (then wholy in maner heathen) with the like, and no lesse authoritie, to convert the Prince and people to the faith: with order, there to preach the same doctrine that the Catholike fathers and Priests now do, no whit altered since then, until this day: to minister the Sacraments in the same sort as they do, as by the recorde of S. Bedes historie and other appeareth: Who entered in with Crosse, Christes image, and Litanies, much more openly then ours do now: professed to come from Pope Gregorie the first, to a Pagan people, which is now so heinous a matter for us to do, from gregorie the xiii, to a Christian Countrie: brought giftes from him to our King and Queene, even such like consecrated tokens as now can not be had, or brought in, without death and treason. (78ᵛ–79ʳ)

Employing a series of parallel clauses to create antithesis (Steuart 1944: 274–5), Allen skilfully contrasts the differences between the English Churches past and present in order to emphasize the fundamental continuity of Catholicism. Augustine and the English Jesuits share the same mission ('to convert the Prince and people to the faith') by 'the like, and no lesse authoritie'; furthermore, they preach 'the same doctrine' and 'minister the Sacraments in the same sort'. Indeed, Augustine's mission originated with Pope Gregory I, and Pope Gregory XIII has authorized the Jesuit priests' mission. Allen's emphatic repetition of 'now' underscores how differently these missions have been received. While Augustine 'openly' brought 'Crosse, Christes image, and Litanies' to 'a Pagan people' and gave relics as gifts 'to our King and Queene', contemporary Catholic priests are rewarded with 'death and treason'. The Catholic Church remains unchanged, but contemporary England—'a Christian countrie'—ironically surpasses its medieval ancestors in barbarity. Allen continues by asserting that Catholicism itself is responsible for England's political stability, again using parallel clauses to create an antithesis that emphasizes his claim: 'it was no treason, it was no seditious practise: it had a blessed, honorable, and gratious effect in us: it was the beginning of our Christianitie, even the same Christianitie which is of al Nations, and which hath bredde and brought furth al our Princes, Priests, and people, and al this goodly forme of Commonwealth, which our forefathers left us' (Allen 1581: 79^v–80^r). In Allen's view, Catholicism established the medieval political system, including the three estates (nobility, clergy, and commoners) as well as the nation itself ('this goodly forme of Commonwealth'). The missionary priests' propagation of the Roman Catholic Church is therefore not an imposition of foreign rule, but rather a patriotic attempt to restore the faith of their 'forefathers' and in turn to bring about 'blessed, honorable, and gratious effect[s]' for the entire country.

Besides defending the seminaries, Allen encourages readers to participate in this narrative of conversion by assisting missionary priests. Allen reports that the 1581 proclamation only galvanized the seminarians' desire to join the mission: 'they be not (God be praised) much afraid of death or danger in so happie and honorable a quarel, and many desire Martyrdom, if God shal so dispose: by which we ever gaine more to Gods Church, then by any office of our life: and bloud voluntarily yelded, crieth forcibly for mercie toward our Countrie' (86^r). If current and future priests are determined to sacrifice their 'bloud voluntarily' for the patriotic purpose of crying 'for mercie toward our Countrie', Allen notes that the English laity too can play a part in the conversion of England: 'there wil be left many thousands, whose harts, bowels, and doores shal be open to us in our Lord, notwithstanding what lawes of man so ever' (87^r). A marginal note openly addresses sympathetic readers, encouraging them to break the law by helping priests: 'Marke this al ye blessed folke, that entertaine and releeve Gods Priests'. Besides noting that lay Catholics will offer shelter ('doores') and compassion ('harts'), Allen may subtly pun on 'bowels' ('intestines', 'pity'; *OED* II.2.a and II.3.a) to suggest that laypeople may themselves qualify for martyrdom. A traitor's death traditionally included disembowelling, and Allen later mentions St Alban, the first English martyr, as an example for contemporary Catholics: 'England can not lacke Albans, whose Protomartyr being of that name ... suffered, and offered him self to the persecutors, to save his Christian guest a Clergie man, that lay secrete in his house' (87^v–88^r). These direct appeals to the laity reveal another way in which the apology could create a sense of shared religious identity, as its persuasive elements encourage the reader to identify with the views presented. By speaking on behalf of the seminaries, Allen suggests that the priests and students associated with these institutions single-mindedly pursue one shared goal: the patriotic restoration of England's ancient religion. Yet the *Apologie* also goes beyond merely defending the seminaries or mediating their English reputation; it serves a missionary role in its own right by inviting the laity to become part of the seminaries' project. In doing so, Allen's *Apologie* evokes a broader community that includes both Catholics in exile and Catholics in England, attempting to reconcile the seminaries' oppositional relationship with England by expressing a shared religious identity bridging the physical distance between these two groups.

Translation, International Identities, and the Third Order Franciscans under the Stuarts

An Englishman named John Wale returned from the Continent in 1723 with a memento of his visit to an English Augustinian convent in Louvain: a brief history of the house written by one of the nuns. This account praises Mary (Jane) Wiseman (*d.* 1633), the house's first prioress, for translating patristic texts from Latin to English for the convent: 'She was a good latinist & translated all those Homilies, Sermons & Expositions of Psalms out of the Holy Fathers, which we read in our Refectory' (*Account* 1745–6: 32^r). Still read aloud to the community during meals ('in our Refectory') nearly a hundred years after Wiseman's death, these works clearly played an important role in the house's spiritual identity. Wiseman's translations allowed the Louvain Augustinians to develop a shared familiarity with the Church Fathers and perhaps even to view themselves as part of a Catholic religious tradition stretching back centuries. Because translation generally involves cultural exchange, this activity was an ideal means for exiled religious communities to negotiate their relationship with local and international religious authorities, past and present. As previously noted, the Geneva exiles published a translation of Calvin's catechism for use in their community and beyond, demonstrating their support for Calvinist theology. Translation was arguably even more important for enclosed religious communities, offering them access to recent developments in Continental spirituality that were in line with their house's spiritual identity. Several members of the Cambrai Benedictines translated contemporary mystical works from French into English that supported the house's adoption of Baker's mystic and controversial 'way of love' (Goodrich 2014: 168–9). Meanwhile, Abbess Mary of St Francis Taylor (*d.* 1658) of the Rouen Poor Clares translated into English 'the Triple Crown of the blessed Virgin Mother of God' for her house's use, perhaps a reference to the popular treatise *La triple couronne de la bienheureuse Vierge Mère de Dieu* (1630) by François Poiré SJ (Bowden 2012: i. 60). Examining the published translations produced by and for the English Third Order Franciscan convent in Brussels, this section will discuss how translation may have helped the members of this house develop a communal identity as part of an international religious order.

During its initial years, the members of the Brussels convent faced a conundrum: how could they develop a spiritual identity as Third Order Franciscans when they were the first English house of this kind? This question was so pressing that the house's first novices considered abandoning their project altogether after finding their Flemish abbess unsuitable because of cultural issues. Just before the novices were supposed to make their final profession in August 1622, Pope Urban VIII received a letter written on the convent's behalf that succinctly stated the problem: 'they would have no mother of their order [and] language [who is] suitable and necessary for their condition.... Hitherto they have only had a foreigner, ignorant of the English language, who cannot fulfil the office of mother because of her lack of language' (nullam habeant sui ordinis idiomatis matrem sui [*sic*] statui idoneam ac necessariam.... Huc usque, tantum habuerant unam alienigenam, linguae anglicanae ignaram, quae, propter defectum linguae, non potest satisfacere officio matris; Pasture 1930: 223, my translation). The novices clearly felt a need to balance their national identity as Englishwomen with their religious identity as Third Order Franciscans, hoping for an abbess who was both 'of their order' *and* 'of their language' (sui ordinis idiomatis)—a point emphasized by the letter's use of asyndeton (lack of conjunctions) between 'ordinis' and 'idiomatis'. Somewhat ironically given their own status as exiles, they object to having 'a foreigner' (alienigenam) as abbess on linguistic grounds even though she was no doubt well versed in the order's spirituality. In order to resolve these issues, two Poor Clares from the English convent at Gravelines—Margaret of St Paul Radcliffe and Barbara of St Collett (Elizabeth) Radcliffe—served as abbess and vicaress respectively until 1626, when the Third Order nuns were deemed ready to govern themselves. As members of the Second Order of St Francis, these Poor Clares could certainly help the house develop an English Franciscan spiritual identity. Yet the Poor Clares practiced a more rigorous form of Franciscan poverty than the Third Order, which began as a secular order for married laity of both sexes before developing a regular branch of traditional monastic communities. The house's confessor Francis (Arthur) Bell noted these differences while praising the Radcliffes' self-abnegation in governing a convent with a less demanding rule: 'those whom you were to governe, not being in all particulars of your owne observance, nor of so straite and strict a Rule, hence it followeth, that clothing others with linnen, your selves goe wolle-ward: lodging otheres on beds of wolle, your selves doe lie upon the straw: providing others hose and shoes, your selves goe barefoote: finally, sitting at the selfe same Table, and feeding all your Religious with flesh, your daintiest dishe is but only fishe' (Bell 1625: *2ᵛ). Because the house had no direct prototype for its spiritual identity even among English Franciscans, it urgently needed models of Third Order piety.

While serving as the house's confessor from 1623 to 1630, Bell attempted to meet this demand by printing English translations of texts related to the Third Order. Indeed, A. F.

Allison has suggested that the convent had the potential to become 'a centre of literary activity for the whole [Franciscan] province' (1955: 18). While these works participated in a Franciscan tradition of publishing translations that could influence public views of the order (Goodrich 2011), Bell's paratextual materials suggest that his most immediate audience was the Third Order convent itself. In a postscript dedicating his translation of the Third Order Rule to the convent (*The Rule of ... the Thirde Order of Saint Francis*, 1624), Bell notes that the nuns are 'the first of al English that shold undertake the Religious profession of this third order of our seraphic father S. Francis in such maner as hath been treated in the rule above' (F8ʳ). Bell's translation of the Rule gave the nuns a much-needed framework for their endeavour, and he exhorts them to persevere in this way of life: 'go on: I pray our lorde, your seed and this plantation remaine upon the earth until our savior Jesus Christ do come to Judge the same' (F8ʳ). While dedicating his translation of Antonio Daza's Spanish life of Juana de la Cruz to the Radcliffes (*The Historie, Life, and Miracles ... of the Blessed Virgin, Sister Joane, of the Crosse*, 1625), Bell more directly articulates the way that translation fulfils his obligation to provide the convent with spiritual guidance: 'I finde my selfe bound to promote you in the way of Pietie, all that possibly lyeth in my power. Wherein, the better to discharge my dutie, I have thought good to present you with the life of a Saint of our owne Order, who lived and dyed in the profession of the third Rule of holy S. Francis' (*1ᵛ). Exemplifying both Franciscan 'Pietie' as well as 'profession of the third Rule', de la Cruz's life is appropriate to the Radcliffes' double roles as Poor Clares and superiors of the Brussels house. Finally, Bell published Abbess Catherine Francis Greenbury's translation of Franciscus Paludanus' Dutch life of St Elizabeth of Portugal (*A Short Relation, of the Life, Virtues, and Miracles of S. Elizabeth*, 1628). His preface notes that the translation first circulated within the convent in manuscript, and it may predate Greenbury's abbacy since the source text was published the year before her 1626 election as abbess. Yet in dedicating the published translation to Greenbury herself, Bell connects her knowledge of saints' lives with her exemplary leadership as abbess:

> I dedicate your worck to your owne selfe, willing you to go forward in so good exercise, for nothing moveth more to perfection then the examples of those saintes that were in all respectes of the same profession that our selves are ... Verely, to your serious looking into theyr lives (next unto your dayly, and nightly exercise of quire and meditation) I must attribute that principall spirit of governement, to which in short time you have attained by the assistance of him who needeth no long times in teaching, Almightie God. (A2ᵛ–A3ʳ)

Bell presents pious reading as an important part of attaining monastic 'perfection', subordinate only to the Divine Office ('quire') and contemplative prayer ('meditation'). Moving from novice to abbess in the 'short time' of four years, Greenbury herself demonstrates the benefits derived from reading lives of saints who are of 'the same profession'. As these prefaces suggest, Bell viewed translation as an important way of encouraging the house to develop its spiritual identity during its early years.

Certainly the lives of Juana de la Cruz and St Elizabeth of Portugal provided the Brussels nuns with foreign exemplars of Third Order Franciscanism that may have become models for their own spiritual lives. De la Cruz's patron saint was St Anthony of Padua OFM, and she experienced several visions that supplied a template for a Franciscan-oriented form of meditation: 'the glorious Saint appeared to her, and saide: Daughter, who pleaseth her sweetest espouse so much as thou dost please him, may demand much of him. And the saint contemplating the beauty of that most sweet childe which S. Antonie brought in his hand, beganne to speake to him such loving speaches, and so sweet, that she stood so for a great while' (Bell 1625: 73). Anthony brings the infant Jesus 'in his hand' to de la Cruz, allowing her to contemplate 'that most sweet childe' and to address him with 'loving speaches'; such intercession suggests how devotion to Franciscan saints might facilitate contemplation of God. De la Cruz's frequent visions may have been outside the experience of many nuns, but she also displayed a monastic humility that was immediately applicable to every member of any religious order: 'shee was so well contented in serving of the other religious, in offices of humilitie and obedience, as if therin had been her glory, her blisse, and her heaven. And intruth so it was, for in these offices shee found God, who is the blisse and true heaven of the just, as this virgin found him in the porterie [gatehouse]' (41). Rather than being distracted by administrative roles such as portress (doorkeeper), de la Cruz finds these 'offices of humilitie and obedience' a means of encountering God. Meanwhile, Elizabeth of Portugal was a queen and lived as an unenclosed member of the Third Order, yet she demonstrated a fervent dedication to monastic spirituality. By the age of eight she was already reading the Divine Office—the canonical hours of prayer that structure monastic life—on a daily basis (Greenbury 1628: 3), and after her marriage to Denis of Portugal she continued to observe a quasi-monastic regime that included the Divine Office and set times for meditative prayer and pious reading (9–10). Upon her husband's death, Elizabeth joined the Third Order and established a Poor Clare convent in Coimbra where she could participate in the community's religious life: 'Her recreation was, not in seing playes, nor any other vaine delightes of this world, but her greatest joy was to be with the Clarisses, where she often remained in her littell house she had caused to be builded by the port of the Cloister, that she might live and take her refection with them' (49). Turning away from 'vaine delightes' such as 'playes', Elizabeth models monastic detachment from the secular world. Notably, Elizabeth read the Divine Office 'in a lower [softer] voice with the religious' (48), displaying a praiseworthy humility that undercuts her royal rank. Whether read silently by individuals or aloud to the community, both of these translations offered ample material for the Brussels convent to develop its own monastic identity as an English Third Order community.

At the same time, Bell's and Greenbury's translations provided opportunities for the Brussels convent to consider its relationship to the wider Catholic community. The nuns, of course, would have been well aware of their ties to the international Franciscan order since the house had been established by a license from Andreas de Soto, local Commissary General of the Franciscan order and confessor to the Infanta Isabella (Trappes-Lomax 1922: 4–5). Both translations served as textual witnesses of the house's position within this larger network. Daza's life of de la Cruz had created controversy in Spain by mentioning unauthenticated miracles, and the final third of Bell's translation contains English versions of approbations by Spanish friars and religious authorities attesting the text's orthodoxy (Bell 1625: 217–98). These approbations are followed by the Latin imprimaturs of an English Benedictine monk (Franciscus Crathorne) and two leading English Franciscans who had helped found the Brussels convent: Franciscus à Sancta Clara (Christopher Davenport) and John Gennings (T6^r–T7^r). By printing Spanish and English approbations side by side, Bell's translation supplied tangible evidence of the links between English and Spanish Franciscans. Greenbury's translation participated even more obviously within the international Catholic community. As Bell's preface notes, Paludanus had produced his life of St Elizabeth of Portugal to celebrate her canonization: 'F. Paludanus abbridged [this book], and gave out to all the people in Spanish, French, and Dutch, in the solemnitie made at the publishing of her Canonisation, in Bruxelles' (Greenbury 1628: A2^r). By situating Greenbury's work in relation to versions written in the major languages used in Brussels (Spanish, French, and Dutch), Bell suggests that the translation allows Greenbury and her convent to join in the city's celebrations. The translation's contents may have also encouraged the convent to view itself as part of an international Catholic community with links to the Third Order. Paludanus' preface to the life justifies Catholic dominion in Europe by identifying Elizabeth of Portugal as an ancestor of contemporary rulers such as Holy Roman Emperor Ferdinand II, Philip IV of Spain, and Louis XIII of France (A3^v; Blom and Blom 2006: xiii). As Paludanus summarizes, 'of her are come, 7 Emperours … six Empresses: 36 Kings: and 43 Queenes' (A5^v–A6^r). While the Third Order convent in Brussels did not have blood ties to Elizabeth of Portugal, as members of her order the English nuns too could count themselves part of Elizabeth's illustrious spiritual family. Greenbury's translation may therefore have helped the convent to conceptualize its relationship with local and international Catholicism. In bridging cultural and linguistic differences, translation offered the Brussels Franciscans the chance to develop a spiritual identity that reconciled the multiple points of self-identification available to them: as Englishwomen living in Brussels, as members of the Franciscan Third Order, and as part of the international Catholic community on the Continent.

Conclusions

As this discussion has attempted to show, exiled communities wrote texts that developed, sustained, and publicized their collective identity. While individual émigrés may have also composed liturgical texts, apologies, and translations, these modes of writing proved especially useful for communities because of their generic characteristics. By its very nature, a liturgy provides a rubric for communal worship. Making the most of this fact, the Genevan *Forme of Prayers* both expressed the community's self-identification as God's elect and served as a framework for collective resistance to the Marian

Counter-Reformation. Apology, meanwhile, defends and explains the views of those accused of heterodoxy, simultaneously serving as a vehicle for self-justification and self-definition. William Allen took full advantage of the genre's potential in his *Apologie*, refuting the Elizabethan government's claims that the English seminaries fostered treason by redefining the English mission as a second conversion of England—a patriotic venture in which even the laity could play a part. Finally, translation entails both cultural and linguistic exchanges. The translations of Francis Bell and Catherine Greenbury introduced the Brussels Franciscans to exemplary figures from the Third Order, offering a potential basis for the house to develop its identity as the first English branch of an international religious order. Produced by and for specific religious communities, these texts also bear distinct marks of their communal origins. The Genevan liturgy suppresses individual authorship in favour of anonymity and a collective voice, so that the liturgy could effectively speak for the community. Similarly, Allen's *Apologie* adopts an inconsistent narrative voice that shifts from first-person plural to third-person plural, conveying the collective opinion of the seminarians as well as his own views on the colleges. Bell also situates the translations issuing from the Third Order Franciscans within a communal context by dedicating these publications to the house itself and its leaders: the Radcliffe sisters and Greenbury. This tendency to emphasize the collective over the individual helps to explain why writing was such an essential form of identity formation for exiled communities. Through its evocation of the local, national, and international identities associated with a specific group of exiles, the written text could overcome the physical dislocation of exile by inviting readers to join an imagined religious community unconstrained by place.

CHAPTER 30

THE JEWISH DIASPORA

JEFFREY SHOULSON

To speak of the Jewish Diaspora in early modern English literature and culture is, in certain important respects, to speak of a phantasm, a ghostly, largely disembodied community whose influence was less a function of their physical existence in the British Isles than the product of their persistent presence within the English cultural imaginary. Jews were officially banned from England in 1290, a ban that was not effectively lifted until the second half of the seventeenth century. Before their expulsion, Jews were permitted to live in England under the protection of the Crown, whose interests they were expected to serve, especially by playing the roles of financiers. The special status enjoyed by medieval English Jews made them particularly vulnerable as targets for hatred and violence by the king's political and economic rivals; the medieval Jewish settlement was thus characterized by periods of relative peace punctuated by outbreaks of violence, usually initiated by the burghers and nobility in opposition to royal prerogative and protection. In this respect, as in others, Jewish life in medieval England was not unlike Jewish life in medieval Christian Europe more generally. If Jews found some degree of protection, it was typically under the aegis of the reigning prince, who depended on them for economic purposes; but any financial success Jews enjoyed was precisely the cause of a good deal of the hostility expressed by their rivals.

Under Richard I, in about 1200, a state bureaucracy was established to handle all matters pertaining to the Jews, which included the *Scaccarium Judaeorum*, the Exchequer of the Jews, and the *Presbyter Judaeorum*, a figure who is sometimes referred to as the Chief Rabbi but who probably played more of a political or representative role than a religious one. All legal documents between Jews throughout the medieval period were drawn up in Hebrew and according to Rabbinic formulae. The enforcement of these Hebrew agreements by the civil authority was guaranteed by the threat of forfeit to the king in cases of non-fulfilment. The ultimate sanction wielded by the Jewish community on its own members, however, was *herem*, excommunication, which was also recognized by the Crown. Medieval English Jews thus enjoyed a degree of self-governance (backed, of course, by royal power) that was meant to (re)inforce their social and cultural, not to mention religious, segregation from the surrounding Christian population. Given its relatively small size and isolation from co-religionists on the Continent, from a literary and intellectual standpoint medieval English Jewry was fairly unremarkable, having produced relatively few figures of import. Those who did make names for themselves beyond England were mostly transplants from elsewhere (sojourning in England on a permanent or temporary basis).

In 1232, in response to a new push for Jewish conversion and not unrelated to the Crusades (similar efforts were undertaken throughout Europe), the *Domus Conversorum* was established, just outside London and under royal auspices, for the reception of Jewish converts to Christianity. For the next sixty years proselytization was carried on within the Jewish population more systematically than it had been previously. But when the Jews could no longer serve the king's economic purposes, having been bankrupted by previous exploitations, Edward I succumbed to pressures from his people and expelled them in 1290. Until recently, the number of Jews expelled had been estimated in the range of sixteen thousand. New studies of the poll tax records have suggested that that number ought to be reduced considerably, to the 2,000–2,500 range.[1] The *Domus Conversorum* was never quite empty, but at the time of the expulsion it appears to have housed only about a hundred men and women. Most of the Jews left England for France. Some then moved on to the Iberian peninsula, where they remained until they were banished from Spain and Portugal two centuries later. Some became part of the Jewish communities in Italy, Germany, and eastern Europe. Still others found homes in the relatively more welcoming communities of Muslim Europe, Asia, and northern Africa. A very small number of Jews remained in England secretly, some as converts, but there was no significant, visible Jewish presence in England again until the end of the seventeenth-century, although, as we shall see below, occasional Jewish visitors and some more recently converted New Christians (mostly from Spain and Portugal) came to England.

Recent archival research suggests that a few Jews began to trickle back into England fairly soon after the expulsion. The 1492 expulsion from Spain, followed by the 1497 expulsion from Portugal, prompted the migration into England of a number of Jews and crypto-Jews (converts to Christianity, many of them against their will, who remained committed to some form of Jewish identity and practice in secret). Once in England they took on various roles, including as merchants, teachers, translators, and physicians. The status and security of these *marranos* changed with the shifts in Spanish–English diplomatic and economic relations. While affairs with Spain were still good and there were efforts to establish stronger ties through royal matches, Henry VII sought to assure the Spanish ambassador to England that he would punish any *conversos* found in his realms who were suspected of continuing to practise Judaism.[2] This proved to be a

---

[1] See Shapiro 1996: 43ff. for an extensive discussion of the fraught and indecisive historiography of the 1290 expulsion.

[2] Although one often finds them used interchangeably, I am using the terms *marranos* and *conversos* to name two different categories of Jewish converts of Iberian origins. I use *conversos* to refer to the general group of Jewish converts to Christianity, those who, regardless of their personal beliefs or hidden practices, carried themselves as Christians in the larger world. I use *marranos* to identify those *conversos* who did retain some notion of a Jewish identity through persistent (and typically secret) Jewish practices and customs.

rather empty promise and, especially as Spanish–English relations soured, any English interest in enforcing Spanish policies towards crypto-Jews quickly waned. Nor is it particularly clear how many of these Spanish and Portuguese *conversos* were, in fact, continuing to practise secretly any Jewish rituals or customs. There were, no doubt, some who did, as is attested by English accounts of visits to homes where Jewish prayers and practices were observed. But there were also many *conversos* (probably the majority) who fully embraced their (relatively new) Christian identities even as events occasionally led them to be (re)associated with their former (and even ancestral) religious affiliations against their will.

JEWS AND THE ENGLISH REFORMATION

At key moments in the history of the English Reformation, Jews and Jewish learning served important functions. In 1530–1, Henry VIII consulted with several Jewish authorities and recent converts in his efforts to obtain approval for his divorce from Catherine of Aragon. This weighty matter, with crucial political and theological implications, turned on the relationship—and apparent contradiction—between the biblical prohibition against a man marrying his brother's wife (Leviticus 18:16) and the biblical institution of the levirate marriage (Deuteronomy 25:5–10) which specifically permitted, and could even be read as mandating, the marriage of a man to his brother's childless widow. The weight of Christian exegesis and Canon law on this issue heavily favoured the Pope's position that Henry's marriage to Catherine was permitted by the passage in Deuteronomy; indeed, the institution of the levirate marriage was the basis of the original dispensation that permitted the marriage between Henry and his brother Arthur's widow. Not finding much support from standard Christian interpretations for his argument that his marriage to Catherine should never have been approved by the Pope, Henry turned to Jewish interpreters for help in his case for annulment. Most prominent amongst these Jewish authorities was the Jewish physician, rabbi, and kabbalist, Elijah Menahem Helfan, the scion of a renowned and highly respected family and the author of a number of important rabbinic *responsa* including, long after his interactions with Henry's representatives, a strong statement supporting the teaching of the Hebrew language and rabbinic interpretations to non-Jews.

But Henry's hope that he would find support in the Jewish tradition for his argument failed to account for the complexities of Jewish legal (halakhic) discourse. The biblical institution of the levirate marriage and its continuing post-biblical applicability to contemporary Jewish life was a matter of no small disagreement within the Jewish world. Differences of opinion about the degree to which a levirate marriage was or was not preferable to its refusal through the ritual of *halitzah* (as described in Deuteronomy 25:7–10) date back to some of the earliest rabbinic discussions in the Babylonian and Palestinian Talmuds. By the Middle Ages, the most important difference of opinion on levirate marriage was that between Ashkenazi and Sephardi Jews. Sephardim (Jews of Iberian, Italian, northern African, and Levantine origins) followed the rulings of

their great rabbinic sages, including Maimonides (1135–1204), holding that since polygamy was accepted within the Sephardic world, the levir was permitted—and often
encouraged—to fulfil his duty by marrying his brother's widow. Ashkenazim (Jews of
German or eastern European origin) were bound by the dictum of Rabbeinu Gershom
(c.960–1028) prohibiting polygamy, which they took to indicate that levirate obligations should always be abrogated through the ritual of *halitzah* (since the levir was often
already married). This position was affirmed by the most important Ashkenazic rabbinic authorities of the medieval and early modern periods, including Rashi (1040–
1105) and his grandson, Rabbeinu Tam (1100–71).[3]

That such a dramatic difference of opinion existed within the Jewish community, and
that this difference appeared to map directly onto the opposing sides in the controversy
surrounding Henry's marriage to Catherine, meant that engaging Jewish scholars in
the question led to a much more intensive and extensive encounter with Jewish legal
discourse than might otherwise have been expected.[4] By the time the matter officially
came before the Pope for his consideration, the political pressure from Charles V (Holy
Roman Emperor, Papal ally, and Catherine's nephew) was great enough that there was
little chance the Vatican would be persuaded by Jewish arguments even if they had been
univocal. But the Pope was nevertheless not displeased to have his own Jewish precedents to cite in response to those cited by Henry and his supporters. Most important,
for our purposes, the divorce controversy had the effect of (re)introducing Jewish interpretive approaches to the Bible to English religious and political discourse even in the
absence of a significant Jewish presence in England. What is more, it became one of the
first of many ways in which Jews and Judaism informed the complex theological divisions and polemics that arose during the prolonged disputes between Catholics and
Protestants (and, eventually, among different Protestant denominations). The sixteenth
and seventeenth centuries saw the discovery of a plurality of Judaisms by Christian
Hebraists and humanists. This was the period in which Christians first became aware
not only of the differences between Sephardic and Ashkenazic practice, but of the far
more divergent views and practices of Karaites, Samaritans, and, as we shall see below,
messianic enthusiasts (Sabbatians). By the second half of the seventeenth century these
divisions were even used as a means to characterize confessional and doctrinal splits
within Christianity.

Henry's break with the Roman Church was the context for another—and far more
influential—means through which Jewish approaches to biblical interpretation came to
be injected into English culture. Once Martin Luther made translating the Bible into the

---

[3] See Katz 1994: ch. 1, for a thorough account of the complex negotiations and communications that
characterized this controversy and, particularly, for fuller explanations of the divergent Jewish opinions
that were enlisted by opposing sides of the argument.

[4] Jason Rosenblatt offers a brilliant discussion of how this marriage controversy and its reliance on
Jewish interpretations serve as important contexts for Shakespeare's *Hamlet* and Ben Jonson's *Epicoene*,
noting also how John Selden, the most skilled Hebraist in England in the first half of the seventeenth
century, called attention to Henry's tendentious manipulation of Jewish traditions to support his claims.
See Rosenblatt 2006: ch. 1.

vernacular a central element of the Reformation, it was only a matter of time before his earliest English followers undertook the production of their own English version of the Bible, done directly out of the original languages (the Hebrew Old Testament and Greek New Testament). William Tyndale began the effort even before Henry's marriage problems led to his split with Rome—his efforts were cut short when Henry's agents seized Tyndale in Antwerp and he was tried and burned at the stake for heresy in 1536. But a mere four years after Tyndale's execution, under Henry's auspices and with his encouragement, the Great Bible was published (much of it based on Tyndale's work), the first of no fewer than eight distinct English Bible translations, culminating in the King James (Authorized) version of 1611.[5] Many of the scholars who participated in these translation efforts were—and are—widely acknowledged to have been among the most accomplished linguists of their generation, students of Hebrew and Greek philology, the beneficiaries of the extraordinary achievements of Christian scholars of previous generations, when the combined stimuli of Renaissance humanism and doctrinal disputes between Catholics and Protestants led to significant advances in the study of ancient texts.

Cultural and intellectual historians have documented the progress of Christian Hebraism and the dissemination of Hebrew and Judaic learning amongst Christian scholars. When he wanted to learn Hebrew, having no teachers in England, Tyndale had to travel to Germany, quite possibly to study with Jewish scholars willing to instruct him in the language. By the time most of those who worked on the King James translation had begun to study Hebrew and Aramaic, however, it was possible for many of them to make significant progress in these languages *exclusively* under the tutelage of other Christian scholars, with little or no need to consult the Jewish sages who had served as the primary source of so much of this knowledge in the earliest years of the Christian study of Hebrew texts. Even without a visible Jewish presence in England, therefore, Jewish learning found its way into English discourse, however tendentious and incomplete these Christian mediations of that material might have been. There remains much to be recovered about the influence, direct or indirect, of Jewish learning and Jewish texts on early modern English Bible translations, but there can be no doubt that these significant achievements in scriptural interpretation and Hebraic philology would have been unimaginable without significant access to, and interest in, Hebrew and Jewish writings.[6]

JEWS IN TUDOR AND STUART ENGLAND

Throughout much of the sixteenth century, the Jewish presence in England remained quite small, mostly quiet and unobtrusive. In 1540–1, with the help of several informants,

[5] For further discussion of early modern biblical translation, see chapters 8 and 33 in this volume.
[6] See, among other studies of this phenomenon, Coudert and Shoulson 2004, and Grafton and Weinberg 2011.

Spanish authorities did manage to prevail on the English government to arrest certain persons suspected of being Jews. We have evidence of between fifty and a hundred Jews and *conversos* who spent some significant time living in the British Isles, not just in London, but in Bristol and other towns. These new Christians, some of them secretly practising their Judaism, appear to have presented themselves as Protestant refugees, which meant that with Queen Mary's accession to the throne they had to disperse and be far more circumspect in how they carried on—they were, after all, carrying on a double masquerade, Jews trying to pass as Protestants but also seeking to avoid garnering the attention of Catholic authorities. One noteworthy example of this fraught negotiation of multiple religious identities is that of the important scholar of Hebrew and rabbinic texts, Immanuel Tremellius, a convert from Judaism to Protestantism by way of Catholicism, who sought refuge in England in 1547, assuming Paul Fagius's position as Regius Professor of Hebrew at Cambridge. When Mary came to power, however, he was compelled to flee to the Continent, only returning in 1565 following Elizabeth's accession.

Perhaps the most notorious English example of a *converso* whose Jewish ancestry proved to be his downfall is that of Roderigo Lopez. Born in Portugal to a family of Jewish origin (but which had converted from Judaism prior to his birth), Lopez was part of the small group of Portuguese merchants and physicians who immigrated to London in the late 1550s, immediately in the wake of Elizabeth's accession to the throne. Lopez enjoyed a successful career as a doctor, gaining entry to the College of Physicians and being appointed house physician to St Bartholomew's Hospital. He also provided medical service to a number of influential noblemen, among them Francis Walsingham and Robert Dudley, the earl of Leicester. He reached the pinnacle of his career as a physician when he was appointed doctor to Queen Elizabeth herself in 1586. Soon after this appointment, however, he became involved in the complex court politics surrounding the royal succession in Portugal, backing the interests of King Philip of Spain against the contender whom Queen Elizabeth had been supporting, Don Antonio.[7] Lopez's (apparent) conspiracy with the enemies of the queen was discovered, however, and he was arrested in 1594. Tried before a special commission, Lopez was found guilty and executed that June. The queen's preservation of Lopez's estate for his widow and son seems to suggest some clemency on her part. There is certainly no direct evidence that she held his Jewish ancestry against him. But it *is* clear that in the various accounts of Lopez's conspiracy and trial, his Jewish roots served as a compelling explanation for his treachery; indeed, most accounts imply that despite his claims to the contrary, Lopez retained his Jewish identity even though he had been born into a family that had already converted to Christianity. His infamous last words on the scaffold, as reported some thirty years later by William Camden, leave no doubt for the reader that Lopez's conspiracy against the queen is inextricably linked to his treacherous nature as a Jew, 'Lopez affirming that he loved the Queen as he loved Jesus Christ, which from a man of the Jewish profession was heard not without laughter' (Camden 1630: 59).

---

[7] Lopez's motives for this alliance remain a matter of dispute, and some modern historians have argued that he may have even been trying to uncover Spanish plans against England. See Katz 1994: ch. 2.

Literary historians never tire of reminding students of Marlowe and Shakespeare that the former's *Jew of Malta*, with its treacherous Jew, Barabas, enjoyed a revival in the exact same year as Lopez's trial and execution. It would also not be long after this notorious event that Shakespeare produced his own blood-thirsty Jew for the English theatre in *The Merchant of Venice*. Clearly, the timing of these events is worth further study, but readers would do well to be cautious of drawing too direct a causal relation between Lopez's story and these productions of the Elizabethan stage.[8]

For reasons made manifest by the fortunes of Roderigo Lopez, most *conversos* kept their Jewish ancestry quiet, but at least some of them were open enough about their Jewish practices that Thomas Coryate could attest to their presence and to some of their ritual observances (Coryate 1611). A group of Portuguese crypto-Jews living in London in the very early 1600s numbered at least eighty to ninety, including several very prominent figures in trade and medicine, among them Hector Nuñez, Alvano deLima, Jeronimo Lopez, Gabriel Fernandes, Fernando del Mercado, and Dunstan Ames (Samuel 1958). In 1609 a business quarrel within this Portuguese community ended especially badly when one party denounced another party as Judaizers, which prompted the Lord Chamberlain, the earl of Suffolk, to expel all Portuguese merchants living in London, most of whom had significant Jewish ancestry.

Though they did occasionally face efforts to have them removed (again) from England, as this story of the Portuguese merchants demonstrates, those Jews who took up residence in England in the sixteenth and seventeenth centuries were not subject to the same violent attacks and efforts at forced conversion or required to live in ghettoes as they were elsewhere in Europe (with some notable exceptions). In part, this was because there were so few of them; but their relatively benign treatment may have also been due, on the one hand, to a recognition of the economic benefits these commercially well-connected residents could bring to a country seeking to position itself better in emerging world markets and, on the other hand, to the expectation widely—and increasingly—held of voluntary Jewish conversion on a large scale.[9]

Jews had stubbornly resisted conversion for so long, English Protestants told themselves, because they had been faced with the wrong, corrupted kind of Christianity. Even as the English Reformation gave rise to the providentialist historiography of John Foxe and others, it also precipitated a distinctively English interest in—some might even call it an obsession with—the Jews.[10] English millenarian and eschatological writings inevitably included speculations about the 'Calling of the Jews' or 'the Great Restauration', the anticipated mass conversion of the Jews to (a specifically English version of) Christianity as one of the final steps preceding Christ's Second Coming. Now that England, God's new elect nation, had freed itself from the abuses of the papacy,

---

[8] For lively discussion of this question and its wider consequences for the depiction of Jews in early modern literary texts, see Adelman 2008; Fisch 1964; Gross 1992, 2006; Hirsch 2009; Hirschfeld 2006; Kaplan 2007; Klause 2003; Metzger 1998; Shapiro 1996; and Yaffe 1997.

[9] See Scult 1978 and Shoulson 2013.

[10] See Achinstein 2001; Glaser 2007; Hill 1986: II, 269–300; Matar 1990.

Christianity would re-emerge as it was meant to be, the Jews would (finally) recognize their errors, and would come flocking to Christ's sheep-fold. While Jews continued to be reviled for their congenital stubbornness and treachery, they were also regarded as potential co-religionists whose conversion would confirm the peculiar validity of English Christianity. English millenarians and apocalyptic writers beginning with Andrew Willet, in 1590, and including others such as Thomas Brightman, Hugh Broughton, Henry Finch, Joseph Mede, and more, wrote extensively and enthusiastically about the calling of Jews. But English hopes for Jewish conversion were offset by anxieties about the permanence and reliability of such conversions (as can be seen in the numerous sermons about Jewish conversion or even in the plays in which such conversions were depicted). The Inquisition, whose ostensible targets were not Jews but rather converts, exacerbated a problem that had long existed concerning Jewish conversion to Christianity, raising the spectre of false conversion; with the dispersion of Iberian *conversos* throughout Europe and England, the fear of counterfeit Christianity spread, too. Jews and Judaism became inevitably linked with secrecy, deceit, and corruption.

The late medieval and early modern English stage offered audiences encounters with Jewish moneylenders and merchants, powerbrokers and panderers who were forced or who (seemingly) chose to convert; but also with desirable Jewish women, potential wives and mothers to future Christian children, who converted by marrying Christian husbands. English sermons celebrated the baptisms of individual Jews; but they also inveighed against stubborn Jewish resistance to Christian salvation, often in the same sermon. Jews held out the tantalizing possibility of redemption through conversion, particularly powerful insofar as they had once been God's chosen people and could recover that status again, even as they also manifested the fearful effects of preterition, to use Calvin's term for those *not* elected to salvation. The Jewish trajectory of falling in and out of divine favour was seen as anticipating the more recent trajectory of English providential history in its peripatetic path of reformation. But depending on where that Jewish history resolved itself—with God or as God's enemies—such parallels could bode well or ill for English Christianity. Jewish conversion (collective or individual) offered the most dramatic form of divine reconciliation; but Jews also threatened to undermine the salvific power of conversion whenever they refused, reneged or, worse, revealed themselves to have converted under false pretences.

JEWISH COMMUNITIES
AND CHRISTIAN IDENTITIES

As I have already noted, to speak of Jews in Tudor and Stuart England was, with almost no exception, to speak of Iberian Jews and their descendants, those who had fled the forced conversions, expulsions, and subsequent Inquisition that had obliterated the largest and most prosperous Jewish population of the Middle Ages (Hymanson 1951). The *limpieza di sangre*, or blood purity laws that were the legacy of the forced conversions of fourteenth-century Spain, gave legal justification for Old Christian antipathy toward *conversos*, enforcing a Jewish designation on those who had converted to Christianity in order to avoid expulsion, forfeit of property, or execution. English encounters with Jews—occasionally on English soil, more often in the Levant, and especially in the growing Jewish communities of the Low Countries—were nearly always with descendants of this recent history of forced conversion. English Protestants like Henry Ainsworth spent considerable portions of their lives in close proximity to, and learning from, the Jews of Amsterdam. It is no coincidence that Ainsworth, and other English scholars like Hugh Broughton, Matthew Slade, and John Paget, drew so heavily on Jewish scholarship in their own biblical commentaries. Nor is it surprising that these puritan Hebraists wrote extensively on and worked for the conversion of the Jews to Christianity.[11] The Amsterdam Jewish community, concentrated primarily in the Vloomberg quarter of the city, was composed almost entirely of descendants from the Spanish and Portuguese Sephardic community that had fled either before or after undergoing conversion to Catholicism. Many of those who had converted to Christianity used their migration to Amsterdam as the occasion openly to recover their Jewish identities. Others remained Christians, even as they retained ties with this recently reconstituted Jewish community. The experiences of *conversos* and former *conversos* called particular attention to the persistence of a naturalized notion of Jewishness, one that could be construed positively and not just in the negative light it was cast as a function of the Iberian blood purity laws. *Conversos* who reclaimed their Jewishness often did so explicitly as a recovery of an identity embedded in the body and familial lineage. But even those *conversos* who remained (proudly) Christian made special claims about the value of their Jewish ancestry, asserting the importance of the seed of Israel to the vitality and future of Christianity.

Narratives about Jews and their communities circulated in English laws and chronicles, keeping these figures of otherness and difference alive in public discourse even when they were mostly physically absent. What Jews lacked in a demographic presence in England, they retained in their persistent appearance in the English imaginary, haunting the religious and literary culture of a society that found in the figure of the 'Jew' an extremely powerful and versatile tool for the shaping and re-shaping of English identity.[12] The dominant religious conflict in early modern England, of course, took place not between Jews and Christians, but between Protestants and Catholics. As religious antagonists in the conflicts produced by the Reformation struggled to claim legitimacy for their differing approaches to Christianity, the accusation of 'Jew' or of 'Judaizer' was often used to disparage and encapsulate the shortcomings of the opposing side. English anxieties about the persistence of Jewishness and the possibility of its re-emergence

---

[11] On the history of the English Puritans' relations with the Amsterdam Jewish community, see Sprunger 1982 and 1994, and Katchen 1984.

[12] For discussion of this cultural impact, see, for example, Felsenstein 1995; Glassman 1975; Guibbory 2010; Harris 1998; Kidd 1999; Ragussis 1995; and Roth 1941, 1965.

or resurgence were aggravated by, and became a theme of, the polemics between and among Catholics and Protestants throughout the long English Reformation.

The promulgation of 'philo-semitic' writing in mid-seventeenth-century England reveals the intense ambivalence with which Jews and Jewish conversion were regarded during this time. On the one hand, advocates of Jewish toleration made their case for the legal readmission of Jews on the strength of the millenarian expectation of mass Jewish conversion: Jews should be welcomed to a tolerant, Protestant England because it would accelerate the process of their total elimination through their transformation into Christians. On the other hand, what was more worrying to many English writers than the thought that Jews had not converted, or would not convert, was the possibility that they would indeed convert, for the successful conversion of the Jew would signal the disruption and destabilization of the organizing differences that gave definition to Christianity in opposition to Judaism. And yet, the notoriously embattled nature of *converso* identity—its exemplification of the disputed permanence of conversion— could also contain a potentially advantageous, if also unsettling, property, the quality of changeability. In the figure of the *converso*, early modern Englishmen and women would have recognized an uncannily familiar religious chameleon, someone whose economic, social, and political circumstances required a religious conversion, conformity, or counterfeiting that challenged the consolidation of a coherent identity. The legacy of forced conversions practised in previous centuries in Spain and Portugal found its way into the writings of English Protestants, particularly in their efforts to distinguish their religion from what they regarded as the corrupt and ineffective practices of the Catholic Church. Though English Protestants prided themselves on the self-evident truth of the Christianity they professed, one of the effects of the history of forced conversions they sought to disown and, especially, of the Judaism *marranos* were believed to continue to practise secretly, was to underscore anxieties about permanence and change, authenticity and pretense, in the accounts of Christian conversions that proliferated during the period.

THE WHITEHALL CONFERENCE, 1655

Until the middle of the seventeenth century, most Englishmen and women would have been entirely unaware of the small but active presence of a Jewish and *converso* community in London. And this was entirely to that community's liking, since any exposure would have been regarded as highly problematic and potentially quite dangerous. When the Dutch rabbi Menasseh ben Israel arrived in London in 1655 to make a case for the official readmission of the Jews to England, his exposure of this small Jewish community already present was, in fact, very much against their will. Indeed, as David Katz has demonstrated, the initiative to readmit the Jews came from the English, rather than from the Jews. Economic factors may have been part of the effort to bring Jews into England, though many English merchants feared the increased competition that would accompany a larger and more active Jewish presence. The rapid growth of interest in Hebrew, in Judaism and Jewish practice, and in Jewish mysticism certainly contributed to a cultural and religious atmosphere potentially more hospitable to Jews. These interests could—and sometimes did—cut in the opposite direction as anxieties about religious contamination and the purity of evangelical Christianity led some to become increasingly hostile to anything that smacked of Judaism or Judaizers. As we have already seen, millenarian enthusiasm for the 'great Restauration' and the calling of the Jews prompted some to advocate for Jewish readmission. But again, others were highly sceptical that such a mass conversion would ever occur; William Prynne (1656) wrote at length against readmission, insisting that Jews could never become true Christians (Saltman 1995).

Having published his plea for readmission, *The Hope of Israel* (published first in Hebrew as *Mikveh Yisrael* and in Latin as *Spes Israelis* before appearing in English in 1652), Menasseh ben Israel travelled to London in 1655 and met with several important English officials, including Cromwell himself. He submitted a formal petition in late October 1655. Given the intense ambivalence that characterized all of the possible arguments proposed, it is not surprising that when the question of Jewish readmission was finally addressed in an official capacity at the Whitehall Conference called by Oliver Cromwell in 1655, the final decision was neither a resounding yes nor a resounding no. Acknowledging the general legitimacy of Menasseh's request, the Council of State nevertheless appended a list of numerous restrictions and concerns preventing anything approximating unrestricted Jewish immigration. The conference that met to consider the Council's recommendations captured wide-ranging attention both in England and on the Continent. Opinions differed dramatically amongst the participants; by the time of its conclusion, no decision favouring readmission could be reached. As disappointing as the results were for Menasseh ben Israel's English supporters, the Conference did serve as the impulse for efforts by the (still largely secret) Jewish community in England, led by Antonio Ferdinando Carvajal and Antonio Rodrigues Robles, to petition Cromwell for more tolerant conditions, a petition that does appear to have resulted in a more open Anglo-Jewish community.[13]

JEWS IN THE RESTORATION PERIOD

If the sixteenth and seventeenth centuries were witness to a period of dramatic transformations in England, early modernity was also a period of rapid, often traumatic, change for its Jewish population, which experienced extensive shifts in its make-up, its locations, and its collective identity. Having been expelled from Spain and Portugal in

---

[13] For accounts of the Whitehall Conference and what preceded it, see Katz 1982, and Katz 1994 (particularly chapter 3). See also Guibbory 2010: 220–51; Matar 1987.

the late fifteenth century, by the third quarter of the sixteenth century Jews had also been expelled from much of central and western Europe. These new tribulations, coupled with the political, religious, and cultural upheavals in the Christian world of the early modern period, led to the emergence of a renewed Jewish interest in mysticism, messianism, anti-Christian polemics, and literary arts. These developments did not go unnoticed by contemporary Catholics and Protestants, who saw them alternately (or sometimes simultaneously) as signs of Jewish crisis and decline, but also as signs of an approaching mass conversion to Christianity. The news of a Jewish enthusiast claiming the title of messiah and reports of his massive following throughout Europe, Asia, and North Africa found avid audience in an England that had been pondering the fate of the Jews in relation to its own status as chosen nation for more than half a century. When reports began to circulate in 1665 and 1666 of Sabbatai Sevi and the astonishing numbers of Jews who were greeting his identification as the messiah with excitement and anticipation, many English men and women received the news with more than passing interest. Reports came in a variety of forms, from letters exchanged between mercantile trading partners to extended narratives such as that of Paul Rycaut, who became interested in the Jewish question upon hearing Cromwell raise the matter in 1655 and who initially published his account anonymously, as part of John Evelyn's *The History of the Three Late Imposters* (1669).[14] Rycaut marvelled how 'millions of People were possessed, when *Sabatai Sevi* first appear'd at *Smyrna*, and published himself to the *Jewes* for their *Messiah*, relating the greatness of their approaching Kingdome, the strong hand whereby God was about to deliver them from Bondage, and gather them from all partes of the World' (Evelyn 1669: 42–3).[15]

Throughout the 1660s we find extensive mention of the Sabbatian movement in English letters, sermons, and treatises; the interest was not limited to one political or religious group, either, and included Royalists, supporters of the Good Old Cause, members of the Royal Society, and puritan divines. Michael McKeon has illustrated how widely the news of the Sabbatian movement circulated in late 1665 and 1666, finding its way into official English newspapers, private correspondences, and popular rumours (McKeon 1977). The year 1666 was, of course, the *annus mirabilis* that witnessed so many apparently apocalyptic events, from the London Fire to the reappearance of the plague and the intensities of the second Anglo-Dutch War. In his poem commemorating this year of wonders, even the writer most directly associated with Restoration poetics, John Dryden, could not help making mention of the Jewish enthusiast: 'The wily Dutch, who, like fallen angels, feared | This new Messiah's coming, there did wait, | And round the verge their braving vessels steered, | To tempt his courage with so fair a bait' (Dryden 1987: stanza 114). Petrus Serrarius (1600–69), an Anglo-Dutch theologian, was probably Sabbatai's most enthusiastic Christian follower,

---

[14] For a detailed account of Rycaut's travels and writings see Anderson 1989.
[15] Rycaut would republish his account in 1680 under his own name as part of his *History of the Turkish Empire*.

responsible for disseminating news about the Jewish messiah to Christian correspondents throughout Europe.[16]

The Sabbatian movement became a cipher for different tensions characteristic of the Christian discourses of enthusiasm, messianism, and conversion. On the one hand, we find ongoing and explicit analogies between Sabbatai Sevi and the Quakers. The purpose of the comparison may have been in part to give the reader a better orientation concerning the phenomenon of the Jewish messiah by comparing the exotic to a phenomenon closer to home, namely, the Quakers. Nevertheless, the criticism of the Quakers themselves implied by such a comparison is unmistakeable.[17] On the other hand, there are reports that stress the political and militaristic aspects of Sabbatai's followers, reports that strongly resonate with the memory of Thomas Venner's abortive Fifth Monarchy uprising only five years earlier. One letter describes how the Turkish Bashaw:

> resolved to march on with his Forces [against the Israelites], and coming within sight of the City, discovered an Innumerable multitude of people getting out of their Tent, whereupon the Turks gave Fire and shot against them, but after a little fighting, a pannick fear took them, and terror seized on them and made them cry out, *Who can fight these people, seeing our Arrows return back upon our selves!!*[18]

As seemingly incompatible as these two views are—the Sabbatians as pacifist Quakers and the Sabbatians as advocates of military action like Venner's Fifth Monarchists—they both manifest the anxieties felt by entrenched, normative Christianity in the face of various enthusiastic movements agitating for dramatic change, individually and collectively. These were movements of rapid, often violent, transformation over which their members had little control.

Christian reactions to Sabbatai Sevi were part of a debate that was conducted between established intellectuals and clergymen, on the one hand, and those who challenged their status, on the other. Since many of the enthusiasts of the time, including Sabbatai Sevi, also challenged the secular authorities, this was a confrontation with obvious

---

[16] Ernestine G. E. van der Wall has compiled a remarkable list of Serrarius's correspondents, who included a striking cross-section of English political and religious society: Nathaniel Homes (Menasseh ben Israel's correspondent), Henry Oldenburg (secretary of the Royal Society), Joshua Sprigge (Congregationalist minister), Anthony Grey (friend of Baptist Henry Jessey), the millenarians John Dury and Jan Comenius, and many others. These correspondents, in turn, passed the news of Sabbatai Sevi on to a veritable 'who's who' list of English writers and intellectuals, including the Fifth Monarchist Thomas Chappell, James Fitton (Henry Jessey's successor in his London Baptist congregation), Robert Boyle, Lord Brereton, Secretary of State Joseph Williamson, Oxford Hebraist Edward Pococke, and astrologer Samuel Jeake (van der Wall 1988).

[17] Heyd 2004 offers an extended discussion of this aspect of the reports of Sabbatai Sevi in Christian Europe. See also McKeon 1977.

[18] *The Restauration of the Jews: Or, A true Relation of Their Progress and Proceedings in order to the regaining of their Ancient Kingdom Being of the Substance of several LETTERS Viz. from ANTWERP, LEGORN, FLORENCE, etc.* (London, 1665). This and three other English pamphlets are reprinted with annotations in Wilinsky 1952.

political as well as purely religious implications. The Jewish messiah from Smyrna thereby played a role in both the religious and political discourse in England, offering a discursive site in which the fraught relationship between material/historical reality and religious authenticity could be interrogated. Rycaut positions himself in sympathy with the Jewish intelligentsia, the rabbis and elders in the community, who understand the extent of the threat the Sabbatians pose to the survival of the Jewish community (see, for example, Evelyn 1669: 78–9). Alongside the critique of popular beliefs among both Christians and Jews, there runs throughout Rycaut's text a sense of solidarity between the Christian elite (political, religious, and intellectual) and that part of the Jewish elite that opposed Sabbatai Sevi. The parallels between the Christian and Jewish enthusiastic movements were believed to be so strong that Rycaut even suggests that the Sabbatian movement was itself produced by the proselytizing fervour of Christian millenarianism, though this is still a subject of debate.[19] However it is interpreted, the Sabbatian movement inevitably became enfolded within the extensive English discussions of Jewish restoration and conversion that were such defining elements of the discourse of Jews and Judaism in the seventeenth century.

[19] Gershom Scholem's magisterial account of the Sabbatian movement takes strong issue with this claim (Scholem 1973: esp. ch. 5).

CHAPTER 31

....

ISLAMIC COMMUNITIES

....

BERNADETTE ANDREA

'ISLAMIC communities' in England (and, more broadly speaking, the British Isles) prior to the mid-nineteenth century is arguably a phantom concept, despite Nabil Matar and other critics' findings that during the sixteenth and seventeenth centuries 'thousands of Turks and Moors visited and traded in English and Welsh ports; hundreds were captured on the high seas and brought to stand trial in English courts; scores of ambassadors and emissaries dazzled the London populace with their charm, cuisine and "Araby" horses' (1999: 5–6).[1] On a broader scale, as Michael H. Fisher documents in *Counterflows to Colonialism: Indian Travellers and Settlers in Britain, 1600–1857*, 'far more Muslims than Hindus went to Britain' during the pre- and early-colonial era (2004: 4). Also, 'many more Indian men than women entered Britain,' dozens of whom 'had marriages or liaisons with British women' (2004: 10–11). Crucially, 'in order to marry legally, these men had to be Christians, or convert—at least nominally—to Christianity' (2004: 11), which

---

[1] Matar qualifies this claim when he acknowledges, 'The Muslims who came to England and the British Isles were in the hundreds, and may have reached a few thousand, although during no period were there more than a few score together on British soil' (1999: 39). He speculates about the 'possibility of a community infrastructure' in London when he asks about the ten documented (and possibly thirty other) 'Turkes leaving [living]' and working in London as tailors, shoemakers, menders, button makers, and a solicitor, as recorded in the State Papers Foreign, Barbary States: 'Was there a prayerhouse or mosque where they assembled? Were they able to sustain their daily prayer ritual, their Friday gathering, and their avoidance of pork and wine (or for the English, ale)?' (1999: 30). However, he concedes that the evidence is slim (Matar 1998: 46–7). The tract he cites, *A Discovery of 29. Sects here in London, all of which, except the first, are most Divelish and Damnable*, begins with the initial exception, 'The Protestant' (sig. A^v), and moves through a list that includes 'The Mahometans' (sig. A2^v), but also 'The Panonians', or those who 'worship the Heathen [Greek] God *Pan*'; 'The Saturnians', who 'worship one Saturne'; 'The Iunonians', who '[c]ontrary are these to the opinions of the *Saturnians*, for they say that *Saturne* dyed, and left his Daughter *Iuno* [Juno] Queen of heaven, who married with this *Jupiter*, and made him God, and from their loines have proceeded the rest of the Gods'; and 'The Baccanalians' (sig. A4), among others. The eight-page tract is clearly satirical; it represents neither serious religious polemic nor a sound sociological source. The parallel case of individuals from a Jewish background in London, who could not openly practise their ancestral faith, suggests that a community of practising Muslims would have been unsustainable (Katz 1982; Shapiro 1996; Glaser 2007; Shoulson 2013).

a significant number did. Fisher also records the high percentage of Indian Muslim servants who 'converted to Christianity, either out of conviction or nominally to suit their European employers' (2004: 222). Scholars focusing on immigrants—voluntary and involuntary—to Britain from other regions of the Islamic world—including Islamic West Africa, the peripheries of the Ottoman (Turkish) Empire, and the Safavid (Persian) Empire—document a similar situation (Habib 2008; Andrea 2011a; Dimmock 2013a). The conditions for girls and women who travelled from the Islamic world to Britain prior to the eighteenth century was even more constraining (Andrea 2017). However, 'Islamic communities'—or in the parlance of the era, 'Mahometanism' (Dimmock 2013b)—is also a facilitating concept for the outpouring of histories, travel narratives, plays, poems, and other forms of what Raymond Williams calls ' "serious" writing' that characterized English literary culture from the middle of the sixteenth century until the end of the seventeenth (1983: 186).

England at the beginning of this period was 'marginal' to the established Islamic empires of the era, as well as the global empire centred on Spain (Stallybrass 2006). However, as Lisa Jardine and Jerry Brotton point out, its learned and popular writers concurrently articulated 'imperial aspiration[s]' and 'imperial dream[s]' projected across the Islamicate landscape of Eurasia and the northeastern shores of the American continent (2000: 14, 16; Andrea 2016b). This era consequently has been defined as 'proto-imperial' (Baldwin 1987: 1754), 'para-colonial' (Archer 2001: 16–18), and 'proto-orientalist' (Barbour 2003: 3–5, 17, 46). However, by the end of the seventeenth century England had laid claims, however tentative, to colonies in North America (Virginia and New England), the Caribbean (Barbados and the Bahamas), the Mediterranean (Tangier), and India (Bombay) (Canny 1998). Around the same time, the English crown also claimed the monopoly over the trans-Atlantic trade in Africans, a significant percentage of whom were Muslim (Curtis 2009: 1–22). If 'Queen Elizabeth was not an imperialist', as Kenneth R. Andrews argues, and if 'it was the reign of James [I of England] that saw the effective [if still tentative] beginnings of the British Empire' (1984: 11, 13; see Matar 1998: 11–12; Goffman 1998: 4), by the end of the century England was more securely advancing towards an imperial domain which at its height 'embraced substantially more than half the Muslim peoples of the world' (Robinson 1999: 398).

Although no practising Muslims outside of a few foreign embassies lived in England from 1550 to 1690, then, an 'imagined community' of 'Mohametans' existed in the English literary and cultural imagination. In his influential study, *Imagined Communities: Reflections on the Origin and Spread of Nationalism*, Benedict Anderson asserts: 'In fact, all communities larger than primordial villages of face-to-face contact (and perhaps even these) are imagined. Communities are to be distinguished, not by their falsity/genuineness, but by the style in which they are imagined' (2006: 6; see Helgerson 1992; Grabes 2001). Anderson is theorizing the consolidation of the 'nation' as 'both inherently limited and sovereign' (2006: 6) during the 'early modern/colonial period' (Mignolo 2003: vii): that is, from the rise of print capitalism during the sixteenth and seventeenth centuries to the challenges of anti-colonial movements in the twentieth. However, the concept of an 'imagined community' during the proto-imperial,

-colonial, and -orientalist era defined above functions less to demarcate what Anderson calls 'a deep, horizontal comradeship' of Muslims in the British Isles than to specify Britons', and specifically English, negotiations of their national identity during a time when this identity was unsettled by encounters with contemporaneous Islamic empires (2006: 7; see Schmuck 2012; Britton 2014).

A cognate term comes from Edward Said's *Orientalism*, where he defines 'imaginative geography' as 'entirely arbitrary' because 'it is enough for "us" to set up these boundaries in our own minds; "they" become "they" accordingly, and both their territory and their mentality are designated as different from "ours" ' (1979: 54). While he casts this process of identity formation through the binary opposition of 'us' and 'them' as a 'universal practice', it bears specifically on his discussion of 'Orientalism' as 'a Western style for dominating, restructuring, and having authority over the Orient' whereby 'European culture gained in strength and identity by setting itself off against the Orient as a sur-rogate and even underground self' (1979: 54, 3). Numerous critics have questioned the blanket application of Said's definition of orientalism to the early modern period, with Srinivas Aravamudan providing a nuanced discussion of 'Enlightenment Orientalism' starting in the mid-seventeenth century, along with earlier varieties of 'Renaissance Orientalism' (2012: 10–18). As Aravamudan asks, 'what would we discover if we picked apart the lead-up to a shift of such global magnitude?' such as Said documents for the nineteenth and twentieth centuries; furthermore, 'Did all previous curiosity about the East inevitably lead to negative forms of Orientalism?' (2012: 2). His answer is to stress 'an alternative to the implicit value judgments contained in terms such as *pre-Orientalism, pseudo-Orientalism*, and *protonovel*' (2012: 8), as well as proto-orientalist.

With 'over sixty dramatic works featuring Islamic themes, characters, or settings … produced in England' prior to the closure by ordinance of the English public stage in 1642 (Burton 2005: 11; see Vitkus 2003; Barbour 2003; Dimmock 2005b; McJannet 2006; Degenhardt 2010), and many more after its restoration in 1660 (Orr 2001; Ballaster 2005; Birchwood 2007; Andrea 2012), we might adapt both concepts—Anderson's 'imag-ined communities' and Said's 'imaginative geographies'—to assess the English projec-tion of 'Islamic communities' in the absence of a critical mass of practising Muslims in Britain. This phantom concept functions as a mechanism for consolidating a national identity through what Gerald MacLean calls a 'tradition of bigoted disinformation' epitomized by the clergyman William Biddulph *and* an attitude of respect and admir-ation expressed by the cosmopolitan Sir Henry Blount (MacLean 2004: 86, 167; Suranyi 2008). Accordingly, this chapter will examine four 'time-spaces' (Bakhtin 1981: 253) to situate the lives of individuals from the Islamic world in early modern England and their impact on its literary imagination: (1) the presence of Tartars, Chaldeans, and scattered 'Others' from the Islamic world in England from the 1550s to the 1570s; (2) the letters Queen Elizabeth I issued to various Muslim sovereigns from the 1580s to the 1590s; (3) Moroccan and Persian embassies at the English court through the 1680s; and (4) Muslim converts and captives in England through the 1690s. This history of the mar-ginal presence of individuals from the Islamic world in England prior to the eighteenth century and their disproportionate resonance in the literature of the era becomes one of the facilitating conditions for the emerging Anglocentric discourse of empire on a global scale. By the end of the seventeenth century, it also allows for a radical reconfiguration of English views of Islam as an admirable moral and political system (Garcia 2012; Meggitt 2013; Matar 2014), if not necessarily a religion in its own right, rather than the anti-Islamic bigotry that had dominated for a millennium (Tolan 2002; Akbari 2009).

1550S TO 1570S: TARTARS, CHALDEANS, AND 'OTHERS' FROM THE ISLAMIC WORLD IN EARLY MODERN ENGLAND

Whereas Queen Elizabeth I's engagement with the Ottoman Empire and the 'independent sovereign state' of Morocco from the 1580s onwards resulted in an 'explosion' of literary responses that extended into the seventeenth century (Ungerer 2003: 92; Dimmock 2006: 5), the first English efforts to match the Iberian imperialists' global reach involved the search for a northeast passage to Cathay (roughly speaking, China) via Russia, Central Asia, and Persia that began in the mid-1550s and stalled due to political instability in the region by the 1580s (Andrews 1984: 64–86; Willan 1956: 153). While the next section focuses on Queen Elizabeth's correspondence with various Muslim sovereigns, beginning with the Safavid Persian shah and continuing with her letters to the Ottoman sultan and his mother, the *valide sultan*, this section dwells on a scattered group of individuals from the Islamic world who were associated with these northeast ventures and whose lives resonated in England's literary culture into the seventeenth century. While elsewhere I focus on the 'presences of women' from the Islamic world in British cultural productions and print culture from the turn of the sixteenth century onwards (Andrea 2015; Coldiron 2010), here I attend to an amorphous community of men from the periphery of the Islamic world who resided in England and left their traces on its emerging discourse of empire from the middle of the century.

In his influential *The Principal Navigations, Voyages, Traffiques and Discoveries of the English Nation* (1589; expanded edition 1599–1600), Richard Hakluyt, 'the leading promoter of English commercial and colonial expansion in the late Tudor and early Stuart period' (Carey and Jowitt 2012: 1), offers a tantalizing glimpse into a loose community of men from the Islamic world who arrived in England during its proto-imperial era.[2] On the cusp of the northeast ventures, its aristocratic and merchant backers, who would eventually incorporate as the Russia or Muscovy company, called upon '2. Tartarians, which were then of the Kings [Edward VI's] Stable'—probably stable hands—to act as native informants for a region traditionally populated by Central Asian Muslims but increasingly displaced by the Russian Tsar Ivan IV's expansionist drive eastward.

---

[2] Unless otherwise indicated, I use the title from the second edition of Hakluyt. I retain the original spelling and punctuation in all early modern sources; however, I adjust the i/j and u/v letterforms to accord with modern conventions.

Featured in Hakluyt's first edition, this account continues: 'an interpreter was gotten to be present, by whom they were demanded touching their Countrey and the maners of their nation. But they were able to answere nothing to the purpose: being in deede more acquainted (as one there merily and openly saide) to tosse pottes, then to learne the states and dispositions of people' (1589: 281). This reference confirms that Tartars (properly speaking, Tatars) were not simply remnants from classical and medieval sources, but residents within early modern English society (Andrea 2010: 31–2; Dimmock 2013a: 458n.4, 466). Importantly, it is preceded by a speech (or approximation thereof) by Henry Sidney, who was actively involved with the Muscovy trade. He was also the father of the famous English writer, Philip Sidney, and the grandfather of Mary Wroth, who followed in her uncle's footsteps. His contemporary, William, the first earl of Pembroke, was likewise involved in the merchant companies that financed the early voyages to Russia, Central Asia, and Persia (Willan 1953: 122, 10–11). Wroth's aunt and mentor, Mary Sidney, became countess of Pembroke upon marrying his son, Henry Herbert (Hannay 1990). Influenced by the literary efforts of her illustrious relatives (Lamb, 1990), Wroth, who published the first non-translated romance and non-religious sonnet sequence by an English woman—*The Countesse of Mountgomeries Urania* in 1621 (Hannay 2010)—accordingly had multiple avenues through her family to contemporary reports about Tartars, who figure prominently in her manuscript continuation of the *Urania* (Andrea 2011b; see Cavanagh 2001: 37–52; Bearden 2012: 158–95).

These northeast voyages across Central Asia to Persia—led in their early years by Anthony Jenkinson, the Muscovy company agent who became Queen Elizabeth I's envoy to the Russian and Persian courts, also yielded a 'Tartar girl' whose acquisition for the queen during the mid-sixteenth century was imprinted in the margins of the Muscovy Company records and rehearsed in Shakespeare's plays decades later. This multiply subaltern subject receives a fleeting reference in 'A letter of *Master Anthonie Jenkinson* upon his returne from *Boghar* [Bukhara] to the worshipful *Master Henry Lane*, agent for the *Moscovie* Companie resident in Vologda, written in the *Mosco* the 18. of September 1559', and published in the second edition of Hakluyt's *Principal Navigations* forty years later in 1599 (I, 305). This letter conveys the results, mostly disappointing, of Jenkinson's first attempt to 'voyage toward the lande of *Cathay*' via Central Asia, where 'uncessant and continuall warres' made him turn back once he reached what is now Uzbekistan and was then a contested region between the Russian, Safavid, and Ottoman empires (Hakluyt 1599: I, 305). After this brief report, Jenkinson signs off, 'thus giving you most heartie thanks for my wench Aura Soltana, I commend you to the tuition of God, who send you health with hearts desire', a classic example of the exchange of women between men. However, Hakluyt's marginal note—'This was a yong Tartar girle which he gave to the Queene afterward' (1599: I, 305)—complicates the patriarchal circuit of this exchange by incorporating women privileged by class. This is the only direct evidence we have of this gendered subaltern from the Islamic world. However, by reading these traces contextually and linking them to other traces that have also been dismissed as enigmas, I have determined that this 'Tartar girl' is 'Ipolita the Tartarian', denoted Queen Elizabeth's 'deare and welbeloved woman' in court inventories (qtd. in Arnold 1988: 107; Andrea 2011a). Beyond the scanty documentary record, she resonates in salient literature from the period, including the Gray's Inn Revels (1594–5), in which Shakespeare debuted *The Comedy of Errors*; Shakespeare's *A Midsummer Night's Dream*, which followed shortly thereafter; and Wroth's *Urania*, especially its manuscript continuation (Andrea 2016a). We have no indication that the 'Tartar girl'-cum-'Ipolita the Tartarian', with her intimate connection to the queen, consorted with the 'Tartarians' who worked in the royal stables. However, these scattered references in the English records, and their resonance in its literature, arguably constitute one of the 'imagined communities' that shaped early modern English perceptions of the Islamic world.

Another tantalizing piece of evidence that shows how medieval male authors and contemporary male informants from the Islamic world were incorporated into the emerging Anglocentric discourse of empire comes from John Dee's proto-imperial treatise *Of Famous and Rich Discoveries* (1577). William H. Sherman identifies one of Dee's 'most influential sources for the geography of the Far East' as 'Abdulfeda' (the other being Marco Polo). 'Abdulfeda' or Abul-Fida' al-Ḥamawi was a historian and geographer renowned throughout the medieval era, as well as an Ayyubid governor in early fourteenth-century Syria. The second instance consists of a sixteenth-century traveller from Iraq: as Sherman continues, Dee 'was visited at Mortlake by Mr. Alexander Simon, a "Ninevite" [Chaldean Christian] born in Mosul near the river Tigris…. He gave Dee details of an overland route to Cathay and offered him … "servise into Persia"' (1995: 178).[3] With the first book issued from the printing press of William Caxton, *Dictes or sayengis of the philosophres* [Dicts or Sayings of the Philosophers] (*c*.1477) having established the Arabic treatise *Mukhtar al-hikam wa mahasin al-kalim* [The Choicest Maxims and Best Sayings], via successive Spanish, Latin, and French translations, at the foundation of English print culture (Rosenthal 1960/1), this 'imagined community' of scattered individuals, both virtual and literal, from the peripheries and interstices of the Islamic world likewise shaped early modern England's literature and culture.

1580S TO 1590S: LETTERS FROM THE QUEEN OF ENGLAND TO MUSLIM SOVEREIGNS

Despite the intense interest in the Ottoman Empire and other Muslim polities in the latter part of the sixteenth century, the sultan did not deign to send an official embassy to England. Among more dubious instances, Matar mentions one 'Chinano a Turke' as having converted to Anglicanism in the late sixteenth century, a few ' "Turkish" seaman' as roaming the English countryside during the seventeenth century, and individual 'Chiaus or Messengers' claiming to be emissaries of the Ottoman sultan to the Elizabethan and

---

[3] For a relatively better-known Chaldean Christian, Ilyas Hanna al-Mawsuli from Mosul, who published an account of his travels from Mesopotamia to Mesoamerica, 1668 to 1683, see Matar 2003: 45–111.

Stuart courts (1999: 21, 23, 34; see Matar 1998: 126–9; Bak 2006: 126–8).[4] 'Turk' generally served as the generic term for any Muslim rather than an ethnic or national designation (Schmuck 2006); in any case, as Susan Skilliter documents, such envoys from 'the Great Turk', or Ottoman sultan, were usually Western European converts (1977: 42–4, 51–3, 125, 127–31). Moreover, while much attention has been paid to the Anglo-Ottoman alliance of the 1580s and 1590s along with the related Anglo-Moroccan rapprochement, the first attempts of the English to forge relations with Islamdom were with the Persian shah via the northeast route, as previously noted. Building on this history, this section assesses the phantom 'Islamic communities' constructed via Queen Elizabeth's diplomatic correspondence with several Muslim sovereigns: most notably, the Safavid Persian shah, who was contacted by Jenkinson and other agents of the Muscovy company, and the Ottoman Turkish sultan, who was accessed through England's first ambassador in Constantinople (Istanbul), William Harborne, resident from 1582 to 1588. If this correspondence did not result in an actual community of Ottoman and Safavid subjects in England during the sixteenth century—although embassies from sultanate of Morocco and the Safavid empire arrived throughout the seventeenth century, as detailed below—it did instantiate a cross-cultural, cross-confessional, and gender-inflected network of relations that subtended, however uneasily, English–Ottoman and English–Moroccan alliances against their common Catholic-Christian foes.

Hakluyt's aforementioned *The Principal Navigations, Voyages, Traffiques and Discoveries of the English Nation*, in particular, features Queen Elizabeth's correspondence with several Muslim sovereigns including 'the Great Turk [Sultan Murad III]' (1589: 163–6, 171, 183–4, 199–200; 1599: II, 137–40, 145–6, 158–9, 191–2); 'the king of Cambaia [Alauddin Riayat Shah, Sultan of Aceh]' (1589: 207; 1599: II, 245); 'the Emperour of Marocco [Ahmad I al-Mansur, Sultan of Morocco]' (1589: 239; 1599: II, 119–20); and 'the great Sophie of Persia [Shah Tahmasp I]' (1589: 361–2; 1599: I, 340–1).[5] Because the balance of power favoured

---

[4] For early modern Ottoman diplomatic travellers to France, starting with the embassy of 1553, see McCabe 2008. For an example of captive Ottoman women in France, see Skilliter 1975.

[5] Note that page numbers are not continuous in Hakluyt 1589 or 1599. In the 1589 edition, all but the letter to 'the great Sophie' are grouped under 'The Ambassages, Letters, Privileges, and other necessarie matters of circumstance appertaining to the voyages of the first part ["made to the South and Southeast regions"]', which precedes 'The Ambassages, Treatises, Privileges, Letters, and other observations depending upon the voyages of the second part ["made to the North and Northeast quarters"]'. The latter includes the voyages to Safavid Persia. In the 1599 edition, this order is reversed, with the first volume focusing on 'the worthy Discoveries, &c. of the *English* toward the North and Northeast by Sea' and the second volume focusing on 'the South and South-east parts of the World, as well within as without the Streight of *Gibraltar*'. The third volume focuses on 'the *Newfound* world of *America,* or the *West Indies*' (1600), which also concluded the 1589 edition under the title 'The voyages … made to the West, Southwest, and Northwest regions'. Letters to Muslim sovereigns and related authority figures, including the Ottoman queen mother or *valide sultan*, added in the second edition of the *Principal Navigations* include 'The Queenes Majesties letters to *Shaugh Thamas* the great Sophi of *Persia,* sent by *Arthur Edwards, William Turnbull, Matthew Tailbois,* and *Peter Gerard* appointed Agents for the Moscovie companie, in their sixt voyage to *Persia,* begun in the yeere 1579' (1599: I, 418) and 'A letter written by the most high and mighty Empresse the wife of the Grand Signor *Sultan Murad Can* to the Queenes Majesty of *England,* in the year of our Lord, 1594' (1599: II, 311–12).

Islamic empires such as the Ottomans and the Safavids, Queen Elizabeth did not—and, indeed, could not—take an orientalist stance in her correspondence (Andrea 2011a: 171; see Burton 2005: 57–68; Markley 2006: 37–41; Andrea 2007: 12–29; Allinson 2012: 131–50). Instead, she had to finesse these Muslim sovereigns' perceptions of her as a supplicant and of her kingdom as a potential tributary. Later in the century, this eastern trade became more propitious for several reasons, including England's post-Reformation isolation from Catholic Europe, which led the queen to make strategic alliances with Muslims as like-minded iconoclasts and monotheists. Still, in negotiating this double-edged stance as a defender of the Protestant faith, the queen sought to conceal her efforts from domestic audiences, not only through secret diplomatic negotiations, but also through distancing the crown from this trade by delegating it to joint-stock companies.

Queen Elizabeth's first letter to 'the Great Sophy of *Persia*' (1599: I, 340) which Jenkinson carried on his voyage of 1561, was preceded by one from Edward VI '*to the Kings, Princes, and other Potentates,* inhabiting the Northeast partes of the worlde, toward the mighty Empire of Cathay', which reached the Russian Tsar Ivan IV in the early 1550s (Hakluyt 1599: I, 231). The separate account of 'The newe Navigation and discoverie of the kingdome of *Muscovia by the Northeast, in the yeere 1553: Enterprized by Sir Hugh* Willoughbie knight, and perfourmed by Richard Chancelor Pilot major of the voyage' highlights the power differential between England, which was experiencing the instability of rapidly changing sovereigns with significantly different religious views, and Russia, whose dominions were steadily expanding under Ivan's absolutist reign (Hakluyt 1599: I, 243). Hence, Jenkinson's first voyage northward in 1558 was launched under one set of rulers, the Catholic- and Spanish-oriented Mary and Philip, and returned to another, the Protestant and proudly English Elizabeth. With this shift in sovereigns came a shift in geopolitics, with the English nation increasingly distanced from Catholic Europe, particularly after the excommunica-tion of its queen in 1570 (Dimmock 2005a: 43). As noted above, this isolation led Queen Elizabeth to turn toward unlikely allies, including Muslim ones.

With this context in mind, 'The Queenes Majesties Letters to the Emperour of *Russia,* requesting licence, and safe conduct for M. *Anthony Jenkinson,* to passe thorow [through] his *kingdome of* Russia, *into* Persia, *to the Great Sophie*', dated 1561 (Hakluyt 1599: I, 338), introduces her as 'Queene of England etc', addresses Ivan as 'Emperor of all Russia, etc.'; references her brother, King Edward VI's correspondence as a precedent for Anglo-Russian relations, skipping over the reign of her sister, the Catholic Mary Tudor; and asks for Jenkinson's safe passage, which he received (Hakluyt 1599: I, 339). Ivan did not respect Elizabeth's claims of sovereignty, wrongly considering her an elected rather than a dyn-astic queen (De Madariaga 2005: 168–9). As a ruler of a marginal island kingdom caught between several great powers, she necessarily prevaricated in her response, despite veiled threats and even insults (Willan 1956: 91–4, 97–107, 112–28). Similar tensions inform the companion letter Jenkinson carried, 'The Queenes Majesties letters to the Great Sophy of Persia', also dated 1561 (Hakluyt 1599: I, 340), with the greater gap in religion creating fur-ther difficulties. As previously mentioned, this letter marked Elizabeth's first formal contact with a Muslim sovereign; it consequently became a touchstone for her subsequent corres-pondence with members of the Ottoman dynasty and other polities within Islamdom.

As with her letter to the Russian emperor, Elizabeth begins by denoting herself 'by the grace of God, Queene of England, &c.' and her interlocutor as 'the right mightie, and right victorious Prince, the great Sophie, Emperour of the *Persians, Medes, Parthians, Hircans, Carmanians, Margians*, of the people on this side, and beyond the river of *Tygris*, and of all men, and nations, betweene the *Caspian* sea, and the gulfe of *Persia*, greeting, and most happie increase in all prosperitie' (Hakluyt 1599: I, 341). Relying on classical references, the lens through which Persia was frequently viewed during the Renaissance (Grogan 2014: 32–69), this salutation heightens the extent of the Safavid empire, which under Tahmasp was constantly beleaguered by the Uzbeks on its northeastern and the Ottomans on its western flank. Using a strategy that would inform her correspondence with a range of Muslim sovereigns, Queen Elizabeth's letter 'to the great Sophie' repeatedly evokes 'the Almightie God' as a point of commonality (Hakluyt 1599: I, 341), avoiding the Trinitarian references that characterized her letters to Christian rulers. Yet, as with her first letter to the Russian tsar, she inadvertently undercuts her claims to sovereignty by presenting herself as queen of a realm completely unknown to the shah, despite her signature from 'our famous citie of London' (Hakluyt 1599: I, 341).[6] As Jenkinson records in his narrative of his 'voyage … made from the citie of *Mosco* in *Russia,* to the citie of *Boghar* in *Bactria,* in the yeere 1558' (Hakluyt 1599: I, 324), upon arriving at the court of Shah Tahmasp to deliver the queen's letter, he was degraded for 'being a Christian, and called amongst them *Gower* [Giaour], that is, unbeleever, and uncleane' and for hailing from a marginal and unknown region, with the shah demanding 'of what countrey of Franks' he was and dismissing his identification as 'of the famous Citie of London within the noble Realme of *England*' and as a representative 'sent thither from the most excellent and gracious soveraigne Lady Elizabeth Queene of the saide Realme' (Hakluyt 1599: I, 349). By the time the queen addressed her first letter to Sultan Murad III in 1579, she had expanded her titles and positioned herself prior to the sultan in her salutation, learning from her earlier correspondence with the shah the deleterious effects of the reverse order.

Even with these lessons in mind, Queen Elizabeth's correspondence with powerful members of the Ottoman dynasty, including the sultan and the *valide sultan*, continued to be informed by an acute sense of English 'belatedness': in this case, not in the race for global empire initiated by the Spanish, but to gain access to the lucrative Ottoman trade goods and routes monopolized by the Venetians and French (Wood 1935). In support of this initiative, the queen sent several letters to Sultan Murad III from 1579 to 1581 with the expressed purpose of establishing a trade, and perhaps a political and military, pact with the Ottoman Empire. As supplicant to the sultan, in these letters she stresses the religious connections between English Protestants and Ottoman Muslims even while downplaying the gender difference between herself and her interlocutor. Presenting herself as one iconoclast and sovereign corresponding with another, she

---

[6] By the 'fourth voyage into Persia, begunne in the monthe of Julie 1568', 'Londro, meaning thereby London' and its 'mayden Queene' were better known at the Safavid court (qtd. in Morgan and Coote 1886: II, 415, 454).

hails as, 'Elizabeth by the grace of the most mightie God, and onely Creatour of heaven and earth, of England, France and Ireland Queene, the most invincible and most mighty defender of the Christian faith against all kinde of idolatries, of all that live among the Christians, and falsly professe the Name of Christ' (Hakluyt 1599: II, 139). Subverting crusader rhetoric, she evokes the epithet 'Defender of the Faith' to ally herself with the Ottoman sultan; together they worship 'that God (who onely is above all things, and all men, and is a most severe revenger of all idolatrie, and is jealous of his honour against the false gods of the nations)' (Hakluyt 1599: II, 140). Ottoman officials, for their part, honoured Elizabeth as the 'Lutheran Queen' and welcomed her representative as the 'Lutheran Ambassador.' ('Lutheran' was the blanket term for Protestants in this period.) Strategically, yet possibly ominously for an English audience, the Grand Vizier in the year of the Spanish Armada (1588) boasted 'there was nothing lacking for the English to become Muslims, except for them to raise their forefingers and recite the confession of faith' (qtd. in Skilliter 1977: 37).

In response to this potential for England's incorporation into the Ottoman Empire as a tributary, in subsequent letters Queen Elizabeth limits the sultan's reach to the Orient. Moreover, her subjects offered a range of responses to these initiatives. Some expressed concern that England was allying with 'infidelles' (qtd. in Vella 1972: 18). The queen herself seconded such views in her conversations with the Spanish ambassador, who reported her remark that 'many people think we are Turks or Moors here, whereas we only differ from other Catholics in things of small importance'. As Carole Levin adds, 'In 1565 the queen told de Silva when she heard of Turks defeating Christians that "she was very sorry, and said she wished she was a man to be there in person"' (2013: 35, 138). Others misread the Ottoman sultan's fulsome address to the queen, which was a stand-ard feature of *diwan* rhetoric (Matar 2009: 76; MacLean and Matar 2011: 54), as an indi-cation of what puritan writer Thomas Nelson declares: 'how much the verie heathen do admire at hir proceedings, and therewithall, giving hir such honorable and due titles of commendatio[n]s as never prince nor potentate hath had the like' (1591: sig. A2ᵛ).[7] In advancing his providential history of *The Blessed State of England* (1591), and specific-ally Protestant England, in the wake of the dispersion of the Spanish Armada, Nelson acknowledges the realm's diminutive status compared with the expansionist empires, Catholic and Muslim, of the era. As he elaborates using a distinctly compensatory strat-egy, 'although England be but an Island of small compasse, yet such is the blessing of God upon the same, that happie is that region and commonwealth, that nation, that king, that kingdome, that province or countrie, that is in league, d[ig]nitie, friendship, love and amitie with the queenes majestie of England' (1591: sig. B2). As with Jenkinson's experience of his marginality at the shah's court in the 1570s, Englishmen who travelled to the Levant at the beginning of the seventeenth century, then under Ottoman rule,

---

[7] While Nelson is identified as a 'printer and ballad writer' (Shaw 1894: 213), and not a religious polemicist per se, his stance in *The Blessed State of England* aligns with 'puritan' views. The year before he wrote an epitaph on Francis Walsingham (Nelson 1590), whom Queen Elizabeth described as a 'rank Puritan' (Budiansky 2005: 37); see Dimmock 2006: 5.

were reduced to the generic ranks of '*Frankes*' and had to travel disguised as Eastern Christians or Catholics (Lithgow 1614: sig. N3; Bosworth 2006). Nelson concludes that 'Her Majestie is a stranger and altogether unknown unto the great Turke, & yet fame which telleth truth al[l] the world over, hath made her name, her vertues, her wisedome, her judgement and justice verie sufficientlie knowen unto him'; he adds hopefully, 'it is a rare thing to see a heathen Prince professe and vowe to perfourme matter of so greate a moment unto a Christian Prince ... but that the secrete worke of God by her majestie may been such as may be some occasion heereafter of the Turkes conversion' (1591: sig. B2ᵛ). He therefore mimics the wish-fulfilment characteristic of English Renaissance prose romances that projected a 'universal Christian empire' covering Eurasia (Andrea 2011b: 73; see Headley 1998: 46; Robinson 2007: 14).

A decade after Sultan Murad III granted trading concessions to the English similar to those held by the French, Safiye, the *valide sultan* or 'mother of the sultan', and Queen Elizabeth exchanged a series of gifts and letters confirming Anglo-Ottoman political, economic, and cultural ties. Hakluyt included Italian and English versions of 'A letter written by the most high and mighty Empresse the wife of the Grand Signior *Sultan Murad Can* to the Queenes Majesty of *England*, in the yeere of our Lord, 1594', in the second edition of *The Principal Navigations* (1599: II, 311–12). Yet, he wrongly identifies Safiye Sultan as the wife of Murad: while influential as Murad's *haseki*, a concubine of the sultan who gave birth to a *şehzade* (prince), she became the most powerful woman in the Ottoman Empire as *valide sultan* when her son Mehmet III ascended to the throne. The two regal women also exchanged gifts: Safiye received 'a jewel of her majesties [Elizabeth's] picture, set with some rubies and diamants [diamonds]' along with other luxury items; in return, she sent to Elizabeth 'a sute of princely attire being after the Turkish fashion' (qtd. in Skilliter 1965: 146; Arnold 1988: 108n.37). With Queen Elizabeth accused by the Pope of being in league with 'our pote[n]t and cruell enemy *the Turke*' (Sixtus 1588), her 'textual conversation' (Larson 2011: 3) with Muslim sovereigns—and especially her exchange of gifts and letters with the *valide sultan*—arguably constitutes yet another phantom, albeit significant 'Islamic community' in early modern England.

MOROCCAN AND PERSIAN EMBASSIES TO THE ENGLISH COURT FROM THE LATE SIXTEENTH CENTURY THROUGH THE SEVENTEENTH CENTURY

Despite the paucity of practising Muslims in sixteenth- and seventeenth-century England, Londoners were able to view directly a small community of foreign dignitaries from Morocco and Safavid Persia. As Virginia Mason Vaughan documents, English observers 'frequently noted difference in dietary laws, religious practices, living arrangements, dress, and language' between themselves and these 'others' (2005: 58–9; Stone 2012). 'The first Moroccan ambassador ever to set foot in Elizabethan London', in Gustav Ungerer's words, 'was Marzaq Rais (Mushac Reyz) ... on Sunday night, 12 January 1589' (2003: 102), four years after the Barbary Company was incorporated (Willan 1959). However, the most famous was sent in 1600 by Sultan Mulay Ahmad al-Mansur in response to mutual Anglo-Moroccan efforts to ally against the Spanish Hapsburgs in the Mediterranean (MacLean and Matar 2011: 49–61). As early as the 1570s, as Andrew Vella notes, 'Queen Elizabeth essayed a commercial understanding with Abd el-Malik of Fez.' Vella adds that 'the merchant [Edmund Hogan] employed as her ambassador' was probably supplying 'the Moors (though not on her [the queen's] instructions) with guns and shot' to advance the Moroccan sultan's aim to (re)conquer Spain (1972: 19; Hakluyt 1599: II, 64–7). By the turn of the seventeenth century, this alliance had metamorphosed into what Matar calls a possible 'joint operation to seize the Spanish possessions in America', which the queen deferred as not in her nation's interest. Nevertheless, she was amenable to 'enticing' the sultan's 'elite force of Morisco warriors ... to come to England and serve on her fleet', a plan that was quashed once the sultan learned of it (Matar 2011: 158). The Moroccan embassy, led by 'Abd el-Ouahed ben Messaoud ben Mohammed Anoun ['Abd al-Wahid ibn Masoud], supported by al Hage Messa and al Hage Bahanet, and accompanied by an interpreter Abd el-Dodar, by birth Andalusian', was memorialized by a famous portrait of the ambassador, which 'now hangs in the Shakespeare Institute at Stratford-upon-Avon' (Harris 2000: 27; Vaughan 2005: 57). It also resonated in the dedication 'To the Right Honorable Sir Robert Cecil Knight, Principall Secretarie to her Majestie' from John Pory's translation of *A Geographical Historie of Africa, Written in Arabicke and Italian by John Leo a More, borne in Granada, and brought up in Barbarie,* sponsored by Hakluyt and published in 1600, and in literary productions such as Shakespeare's *The Tragedy of Othello, the Moor of Venice* (c.1603), along with other lesser known plays and pamphlets (Vaughan 2005: 59–73). The embassy to King Charles I was memorialized in the pamphlet *The Arrivall and Intertainments of the Embassador, Alkaid Jaurar ben Abdella,* who was 'by birth a Portugall ... taken Captive in his Child-hood' (Baker 1637: 5). As Matar underscores, this embassy marked 'the first visit of a Muslim given detailed coverage in the London press' (1999: 35). In 1682, another Moroccan ambassador, Muhammad 'Ben Haddu', arrived at the Restoration court of Charles II. He visited the Royal Society, as well as the universities of Cambridge and Oxford, with the seventeenth-century diarist John Evelyn describing him as 'a handsome person, well-featured, of a wise look, subtle, and extremely civil' (1906: III, 74). The urbane Evelyn emphasizes that in all his interactions 'the *Ambassador & Retinue* behaved themselves with extraordinary Moderation & modestie' (1906: III, 77). Other embassies continued into the eighteenth century, attesting to the impact that Muslims from Morocco—including exiles from Islamic Spain—had on the English imagination from the late sixteenth century onwards (MacLean and Matar 2011: 182–8).

A related series of embassies from the Safavid Shah Abbas were launched around the same time as the Anglo-Moroccan entente: however, in this case, an Anglo-Safavid alliance was not sought by Queen Elizabeth, who favoured an alliance with the Safavids' foe, the Ottomans. The instigator, Anthony Sherley, was universally deemed 'a great plotter and projector in matters of State' (Wadsworth 1630: 62; Subrahmanyam 2011: 73–132; Şahin and Schleck 2016). While Anthony never made it past Spain on his first mission for the Persian shah, his brother Robert was sent almost a decade later as the shah's 'Embassador' to the 'Christian Princes' of Europe (Penrose 1938: 170–1; Burton 2009). If Anthony was condemned as 'a man of bad character' (Penrose 1938: 107n.1), Robert was praised by the playwright and pamphleteer Thomas Middleton as 'this famous English Persian' (1609: 13; Limon and Vitkus 2007: 670–2; Schleck 2011: 86–9) and by a member of the subsequent English embassy, Sir Thomas Herbert, as 'the greatest Traveller in his time' (1634: 125; Butler 2012: 474). Both Sherleys were accused of 'turning Turk' by various adversaries; however, while they converted on their travels, it was to Catholicism not Islam. Robert's itinerary on his two embassies took him through Russia, Poland, Germany, Italy, and Spain (where he records a potentially murderous encounter with his impecunious brother, Anthony), and finally to England (Penrose 1938: 173–88, 207–27). His Circassian wife, Teresa Sampsonia, who also converted to Catholicism in Isfahan, accompanied him on these voyages (Andrea 2007: 42–52). While in Rome, Robert insisted on wearing his 'Persian habit', or apparel, topped with a large turban, to which he affixed a cross to accommodate Catholic sensibilities. In Kate Arthur's estimation, Robert fashioned 'a hybrid livery designed to appeal to multiple audiences, but which conversely could easily signify divided loyalty, and open the possibility of duplicity' (2011: 38). While in England during his first embassy of 1611–13, he re-enacted this disorienting masquerade through the diplomatic imbroglio over whether he would remove his turban in front of King James (Penrose 1938: 183–4; Chew 1937: 310–11).

During his second embassy of 1624–7, 'a new ambassador, Naqd Ali Beg', whom Boise Penrose describes as 'a Persian nobleman who had been appointed through the intrigues of the [East India] Company's officials in the East', challenged Robert's legitimacy to the point of open fisticuffs (1938: 214–15). Despite this 'blot' on Robert's reputation, the departure of a *de facto* royal commission of Persian and English representatives (including Thomas Herbert) on East India Company ships to determine the truth of the matter revealed Naqd Ali Beg's duplicity. As Penrose summarizes, 'Ere they reached the anchorage [off Surat] Nadq Ali Beg ended his miserable life by an overdose of opium, fearing lest the Shah sacrifice him on his return, and confessing thereby the justice of Sherley's commission' (1938: 216, 230). Whatever the final truth of the matter, the shah was not able to adjudicate this dispute between the two 'ambassadors' as Robert died on the inland journey; however, his wife, Teresa Sampsonia, lived for many decades afterwards, finally settling in Rome (Andrea 2017). The couple's hybrid identities and adventures inspired a wide array of literary and visual works, including two sets of portraits (one prepared by the famous painter Anthony van Dyck in Italy and another by an anonymous painter in England); a series of pamphlets in several languages; and even a stage play, John Day, William Rowley, and George Wilkins's 1607 production of *The Travailes* [Travels] *of the Three English Brothers* (Parr 1995). As Muhammad Nezam-Mafi establishes in his astute study, 'Persian Recreations: Theatricality in Anglo-Persian

Diplomatic History, 1599–1828', the intense attention to contemporary 'Persians' in English literature and culture dissipated after Robert and Teresa's final departure, with interest renewing in the early nineteenth century (1999: 139). This motley crew of Savafid subjects in England, including Robert Sherley, nevertheless comprised an 'Islamic(ate) community' with a cultural impact disproportionate to its meagre numbers and political influence.

MUSLIM CONVERTS AND CAPTIVES IN SEVENTEENTH-CENTURY AND EARLY EIGHTEENTH-CENTURY ENGLAND

In addition to the individual Muslim ambassadors and their suites who stayed in England for extended periods during the first half of the seventeenth century, by the end of the century a significant number of former converts from Christianity to Islam, or 'renegades', resided in the coastal regions, which is not surprising given most of them were sailors captured by Muslim corsairs or pirates in the Mediterranean. Matar, who has documented their fraught subject position upon their return to the Anglican fold, concludes, 'in English seventeenth-century thought, the renegade shared the infamy of the Machiavellian, Faustian and Moorish villains because he threatened not just the faith but the idea of England' (1998: 71). Their stories—and those of the British Muslims who did not return—were represented with varying degrees of distortion in plays such as Robert Daborne's *A Christian Turned Turk: or, The Tragical Lives and Deaths of the two Famous Pyrates, Ward and Dansiker* (1612) and Philip Massinger's *The Renegado, A Tragæcomedie* (1630) (Vitkus 2000). Numerous pamphlets were also published—especially about John ('Jack') Ward (aka Yusuf Reis), who was alternately represented as 'a renegade, traitor, and thief' and as 'an attractive antihero' (Vitkus 2000: 24; see Bak 2006; Jowitt 2010). Further mentions of British Muslims living in the Ottoman Empire and the Maghreb appear in narratives such as Thomas Dallam's account at the end of the sixteenth century and Joseph Pitts's at the end of the seventeenth. Dallam describes 'a Turke, but a Cornishe man borne' (1893: 79; MacLean 2004: 3–47); Pitts mentions an '*Irish Renegado*' he met in Alexandria (1731: 160; Auchterlonie 2012: 206). Pitts himself lived as a Muslim for over a decade after having been captured by the corsairs of Algiers, and he is credited as the first Englishman to publish an eyewitness account of the Muslim *hajj* to Mecca and Medina, in which he participated. While this body of reclaimed English renegades may not constitute a community per se, since they would have avoided any contact that might jeopardize their reintegration into English society, as another phantom 'Islamic community' they cast a long shadow on English literature and culture throughout the seventeenth century.

Concurrently, several communities of Muslim sailors and corsairs found their way to England: some to be hung for their depredations, others to man the ships of the East

India trade. As Matar documents, 'in 1622 five "Turks" from Algiers who had been captured in a sea battle with the English ship "Exchange" were brought to Plymouth jail; soon after, nine more Turks were brought to Exeter "either to be arraigned according to the punishment of delinquents in that kind, or disposed of as the King and Council shall think meet"' (1999: 24–5). Examples multiply throughout the seventeenth century, with 'the Muslims ... being forgotten in jail' and 'totally ostracized by the populace'; those who did not die from the dire conditions in the prisons were executed if they were not released in one of the several exchanges for English captives that were negotiated throughout this period (1999: 26–32). By the beginning of the eighteenth century, a community of Indian sailors or lascars, for the most part from Muslim backgrounds, negotiated their precarious position as sailors in the East India trade through a variety of associations. As Fisher indicates, these Muslims languished at the literal margins of British society, vulnerable to economic exploitation and even slavery (2004: 32–42). However, particularly in the case of the lascars, their labour was indispensable for the eastward turn that led to the establishment of the second British Empire, based in India, over the next two centuries (2004: 65–71, 137–79). It will be only then, with prominent Victorian converts such as Abdullah (William Henry) Quilliam (Gilliat-Ray 2010: 39–41), that Muslims could openly practise their religion and claim their identity as Britons.

CHAPTER 32

SETTLERS IN NEW WORLDS

CHRISTOPHER HODGKINS

MIRANDA	How beauteous mankind is! O brave new world, that hath such people in it!
PROSPERO	'Tis new to thee.

(Shakespeare 1997b: The Tempest, V.i.183–4)

MIRANDA'S awestruck words capture the crucial appeal and the dangerous ambiguity of the 'new world' paradigm in religious and colonial discourse. She wonderingly sees beauty and 'bravery' (fortune and glory) in her first sight of unfamiliar faces, and we cannot miss the religiously Edenic possibilities of a 'new world'—some restoration of original goodness or a fresh start in the human endeavour, some place to recommence Adam's first empire without his first error. However, this newness is framed ironically by Prospero's reply: 'Tis new to thee'. The conceit of regarding the unfamiliar as a door to cultural or spiritual regeneration naively ignores the speaker's own ignorance, projecting 'newness' onto something already old, established, even corrupted, fallen, and criminal. Shakespeare uncannily anticipates both the quasi-religious hopes of regeneration, expansion, and settlement in a 'new world', and the dangerous and sometimes deadly results of ignoring the settled oldness of the worlds that must be unsettled to make way for the new.

This chapter will survey the varied shores where people from the Old World of Britain and Europe sought to 'settle' and 'plant' themselves—and usually their religious faiths and their churches—in worlds that were, indeed, new to them. The rigours of colonial survival meant that for much of the early modern period (roughly the Tudor–Stuart era of 1485–1714), imaginative writings *about* settlers in new worlds would significantly outnumber imaginative writings *by* those settlers. Nevertheless, from the beginning, new world settlers left literary artefacts of their interpretive communities, as well as their forts and towns and churches. Writing *about* new worlds and colonies tended to fire the fancy, either in fantastic exploration narratives, fabulous colonial prospecti, reflective essays, or in the more outright fictions of dramatic and utopian literature, and of lyric and epic poetry. Writing *in* and *from* new worlds was often, though not always, a more quotidian affair, with nonfiction prose genres like ships' logs, company reports, personal letters, spiritual diaries, and sermons predominating, though with a sprinkling of original poetry, proverb, and song. Old genres were modified, and new ones born, by necessity and invention: not only the traveller's tale and 'utopian' fiction, but also the conquest story, the atrocity exposé, the settlers' covenant, the captivity and conversion narrative, and the extended Eucharistic meditation and the puritan jeremiad—and ultimately, the novel.

Many of these genres are explicitly religious; but nearly all of them assume a spiritual and religious colouring from the pervasive influence of biblical and theological language on even the most supposedly secular communities beyond the seas. So in surveying the literature of colonial settlement—whether apologia for, reflections on, or dissents against—we will find that, in the midst of the most material and mercenary circumstances, we surprisingly confront spiritual matters. Correspondingly, we will see that even the most heavenly minded writers seem drawn to the earthly language of exploration, settlement, and conquest.

Ben Jonson claimed that 'The strength of empire is in religion' (Jonson 1998: 410), and generations of scholars have recognized that religion and colonial settlement are closely intertwined. Louis B. Wright, in *Religion and Empire* (1943), argued for the centrality of piety and commerce to the first wave of English overseas expansion between 1558 and 1625; and more recent historians and New Historicist literary scholars have re-examined the darker implications of Wright's rather celebratory thesis.[1] Most (though not all) of these studies assume the guilty complicity of Christian orthodoxy in imperial expansion, whilst focusing their interpretive attentions on the religious skeptics and rebels who questioned or opposed that project from the cultural margins.

However, if religion often provided Tudor–Stuart England with paradigms for settlement and dominion, it also gave the English their chief languages of anti-imperial dissent. From Thomas More's *Utopia* and Richard Hakluyt's *Principal Navigations* to Samuel Daniel's verse epistles and Milton's *Paradise Lost*, English literature about empire has turned with strange constancy to dissident religious themes of worship and idolatry, atrocity and deliverance, slavery and service, conversion, prophecy, apostasy, and coming doom (Hodgkins 2002: 4). As Debora Shuger has observed, 'the trouble with this [New Historicist] division of beliefs into orthodox and subversive is that so-called

---

[1] Among the most significant studies are Stephen Greenblatt's *Marvelous Possessions* (1991), Richard Helgerson's *Forms of Nationhood* (1992), Jeffrey Knapp's *An Empire Nowhere* (1992), Anthony Pagden's *Lords of All the World* (1995), David J. Baker's *Between Nations* (1997), and Joan Pong Linton's *The Romance of the New World* (1998), plus important articles and books by Andrew Fitzmaurice (2000), Frank Kelleter (2000), Carla Pestana (2003, 2009), Michael Winship (2006), David Boruchoff (2008), Stephanie Kirk and Sarah Rivett (2010), Linda Gregerson and Susan Juster (2011), Jessica Stern (2011), Kasey Evans (2012), Travis Glasson (2012), and A. D. Cousins (2013).

subversive ideas keep surfacing, however contained, within the confines of orthodoxy' (Shuger 1990: 1). When the supposedly 'hegemonic' religion often gives voice to such 'marginal' views on colonization, perhaps we need to reconsider terms like 'hegemonic' and 'marginal'.

Therefore, as we review early modern English literature about and by settlers in new worlds, we should attend carefully to historical contexts for the religious and colonial imaginations which often have been overlooked by both the old and the new historicisms. Firstly, we will treat religion as fully as possible on its own terms. The human impulse to worship—to organize life around invisible hopes, fears, and certainties—is so ancient, culturally persistent, and pervasive that it cannot be reduced to or adequately explained by materialist race-class-gender categories. Secondly, we will seek to illustrate how religion helped the English to imagine possession, but also how religion compelled many of the English, from the time of the British Empire's beginning, to denounce its abuses and even to desire its end.

LEYENDAS AMERICANAS: IBERIAN PRELUDE

Obviously, the English were relative latecomers in the competition for transatlantic settlement and colonization. Although Cristoforo Colombo (Christopher Colombus) had sought the sponsorship of England's new king Henry VII in 1485, the first Tudor monarch, engrossed in establishing his dynasty, declined to help. This decision returned to haunt his Protestant granddaughter Elizabeth I a century later, by which time Columbus's Spanish sponsors bestrode the oceans with a Catholic empire that included the rich mines of Mexico and Peru, and the Pacific outpost of the Philippines, and which claimed papal authority to exclude all other nations—especially (by then) Protestant England—from meddling in the Atlantic or Pacific worlds. Indeed by the 1580s the wealth of Spanish America was funding the Pope's cause in Europe, as Spanish armies sought to subjugate the Protestant Netherlands, whilst the Spanish Armada assembling in Cadiz planned an amphibious invasion to remove Elizabeth from England's throne and re-establish Roman sovereignty in church and state.

Nevertheless, the legacy of Columbus not only threatened England with obstruction and subjection; it also, ironically, motivated and enabled English expansion and settlement. England's peril inspired resistance to Spanish claims of hemispheric political and spiritual sovereignty, and also the purloining of Spain's cartographic knowledge and its wealth by bold Protestants like Richard Hakluyt and Francis Drake. Spain's first contacts with the Americas also established many of the imaginative paradigms that would define how English settlers saw American lands and native peoples, and often determined how the English would treat them. These paradigms, roughly speaking, fell into three categories: that of noble savages inhabiting a new Arcadia or Eden; of demonic heathens thirsting for human blood whilst hoarding untold treasure; and of innocent victims of Spanish rapacity and greed. All of these paradigms informed England's early dealings with the New World, and indeed still inform our thinking today.

The 'noble savage myth', as it is often called, dates back to classical antiquity, as in Virgil's portrayal of the unspoiled primitive Latins in the *Aeneid*, living in primeval forests after the manner of the Golden Age, or Tacitus's *Germania*, which renders the tribes beyond the Rhine as models of hardy, rugged, egalitarian virtue. The paradigm appears immediately in Columbus's earliest journals, which speak of the native Taino people whom he encountered on Hispaniola as gentle, open-handed, friendly, and eager to hear the Christian gospel—free of civilization's corrupting ways, naked as Adam and Eve, and behaving like natural Christians. Especially notable, in his view, is their lack of greed for the gold, which they innocently wear around their necks and about which Columbus eagerly enquires.

Columbus's quest for gold also leads him in his later voyages to originate the 'demonic heathen myth', as the natives whom he encounters increasingly fail to produce the riches which they have promised, pilfer his stores and ambush his men, persist in their idolatry and resist evangelization, and speak of other tribes who are very fierce and who eat their victims. But this 'demonic heathen' paradigm is even more firmly established in the European imagination by the sensational accounts of Hernán Cortés's conquest of Mexico, written by his chaplain Francisco López de Gómara, and especially by the writings of an eyewitness soldier named Bernal Díaz del Castillo. Bernal Díaz gives particularly vivid descriptions of Aztec religious practices involving frequent human sacrifice through the cutting out of beating human hearts with obsidian knives—images that would be even more vividly inscribed in European memories when Belgian Protestant engraver Theodor de Bry rendered them with exceptional skill in his multivolume work *America*, published between 1590 and 1634.

Significantly, both Gómara and Bernal Díaz wrote in an attempt to refute the originator of a third major imaginative paradigm describing the natives, Bartolomé de Las Casas, who described the American natives as innocent victims of unspeakable Iberian cruelty, a tradition still known as *la leyenda negra* or 'the Black Legend of Spain'. A former slaveholder who underwent a religious conversion, Las Casas gave up his human chattel with all his property, and eventually became a Dominican monk. He devoted his life to relieving the suffering of the natives and revealing the savage deeds of Christian conquest; in the process, he invented the genre of the atrocity exposé. A compelling and often accurate chronicler of abomination, he sometimes spikes his narrative with bitter humanist sarcasm. Telling of mutilation, mass rape, disembowelment, impaling of pregnant women, roasting, racking, tearing and trampling by horses, dismemberment by boar hounds, Las Casas's accounts of this 'hellish tyranny' expand over hundreds of dumbfounding pages (Las Casas 1992: 312–19 *passim*). Las Casas eventually convinced King Charles V of Spain to abolish Indian slavery in his realms (only to replace it with African slavery!) and his images also were rendered into shocking engravings by de Bry for consumption in the Low Countries and Protestant England. These three paradigms of noble savagery, vicious paganism, and innocent victimhood, taken together with stories of bloody Spanish violence, soon established America in the English mind as a paradoxical blend of paradise, purgatory, and hell, combining beauty, wealth, and welcome with pervasive danger and unspeakable brutality.

The first English writer to register these paradigmatic images of America did so in one of the most original, influential, and still controversial books of the Renaissance: Thomas More in his *Utopia* (1516). Famed for its often-repeated title and for its persistent irony and ambiguity, *Utopia* has entered our language as a word for an ideal society, and partakes heavily of the 'noble native' accounts by America's earliest discoverers: Utopians live on a far distant New World island in generous communal harmony, have few laws, no concept of private property, and are so contemptuous of gold that they use it to make chamber-pots, and chains for criminals. Though not yet evangelized, they show themselves to be naturally more 'Christian' in their behaviour and institutions than the corrupt nations of Europe and Britain, and eager to embrace Christ's gospel when they hear it, whilst remaining tolerant of others' varied beliefs. In short, they put Christendom to shame—a common humanist theme ever since.

Yet—and here *Utopia's* many ambiguities emerge—these natives' nobility is not actually native to them, but the result of conquest, colonization, and settlement long ago by a general named Utopus, who discovered a race of violent, backward savages whom he civilized through total (indeed one must say totalitarian) social engineering. Utopus's first act after his conquest put the natives to forced labour that cut off their peninsula from the mainland, removing outside contamination and giving him a free coercive hand on his own man-made egalitarian island. Compounding the irony, whilst *Utopia* is written in Latin, all Utopian place names are Greek, suggesting a common debt to reborn classical learning (the 'rebirth' from which the 'Renaissance' takes its name)— and, in fact, many of the book's situations and ideas allude clearly to Plato's great ancient Greek work of speculative statecraft, *The Republic*. Finally, the Utopians live very far from the stone-age simplicity of Columbus's Taino Indians; theirs is a complexly regimented urban life, with travel to and residence in the countryside illegal except for periods of conscripted service on collective farms. Thus, More is able to have his cake— criticizing the violent imperialism and the decadent institutions of Christian Europe— and eat it too, by suggesting that the right kinds of reform-minded men from the Old World might fruitfully conquer and settle the New, and settle it in ways that will teach needed lessons to the Old. Thus is born the idea of America as The Great Experiment, the land where Christian virtues can be rediscovered and reformed in a new soil.

Significantly, More published *Utopia* in 1516, only a year before the outbreak of the widespread movement of religious protest and reform that would far outstrip More's imagination and eventually undo More himself. At Wittenberg in 1517, the German Augustinian monk Martin Luther re-read the biblical Book of Romans and posted his Ninety-Five Theses exalting faith over works and the Bible over tradition; soon he set about translating into German the Greek New Testament compiled by More's friend Erasmus, thus setting off the vernacular biblical Reformation.[2] Among the many

---

[2] For further discussion of Erasmus, More, and their fellow humanists, see chapter 16; for the influence of biblical translations, see chapter 33.

consequences of Luther's religious revolution—some intended, many not—were: an explosion of printing and literacy, and a resulting popular hunger for printed literature; the division of Europe along 'Catholic' and 'Protestant' lines; the halting but eventual conversion of England to the cause of Reform, producing many Protestant martyrs, and some Catholic ones (More himself among the latter); the Protestant elevation of the Bible as the primary guide to life in this world as well as the next; a projection of 'popish' versus 'reformed' geopolitical rivalries across the Atlantic into the Americas; and the eventual flight of many persecuted religious minorities to seek freedom in the New World.

FIRST ENGLISH SETTLEMENTS: PROTESTANT POSSESSION AND DISSENT

England's first tentative forays across the Atlantic came before the Reformation under the early Tudor kings. Henry VII sought to redress his 1485 failure to sponsor Columbus by hiring his own Italian mariners, Giovanni and Sebastiano Caboto (John and Sebastian Cabot), to look for America. Although their 1497 landing in the present-day Canadian Maritime Provinces extended England's claims to North Atlantic cod fishing, no significant English settlement resulted until Sir Humphrey Gilbert claimed the region for England in 1583; and it took Britain more than another century to wrest full control of Acadia (1710) and Newfoundland (1713) from the natives and from the French. Thus, it was not until after the Reformation that England began settlement in earnest, and most of it much further down the Atlantic coast; and the Reformation provided other direct and indirect motives for English explorations, and actual English colonization.

Because the imperial Spain of Charles V and his son Philip II claimed all of the Americas (except for Portuguese Brazil) on papal authority, and because by the 1570s Mexican and Peruvian treasure was funding Spanish land and sea campaigns against the Protestant Low Countries and England, the establishment of a transatlantic Protestant presence took on increasingly existential urgency for the Elizabethans. John Hawkins and Francis Drake had attempted to open the Caribbean to English trade with a small fleet in 1567–8, only to be ambushed and decimated in a Mexican port by Spanish forces. So throughout the 1570s Drake waged a semi-private war of redress, raiding Caribbean ports from Panama to Hispaniola to Venezuela in 1572–3, and eventually, in his famous circumnavigation of 1577–80, passing through the Straits of Magellan to raid up the coasts of Chile, Peru, and western Mexico all the way to what is now Marin County in California. Although Drake's claim to 'Nova Albion' (now Drake's Bay north of San Francisco) never led to English settlement, he did manage to abscond with a hold full of Spanish gold, enough to challenge Spain's exclusive Western claims, and to help found the East India Company in 1600 (Drake 1854: 120–4; Sugden 1990: 120–31).

Mere incursions and raids would not be enough, however, argued the English preacher Richard Hakluyt; only settlement would establish a beachhead against Spain and make the Pope's 1494 Line of Tordesillas null and void. Hakluyt writes in *Divers Voyages* (1582) that, under God's providence, there yet remains 'unpossessed ... those blessed countries, from the point of Florida Northward', where strategic fortresses and settlements could be planted to hedge in King Philip's dominions, harrass them if necessary, and indeed roll them back (Hakluyt 1582: 1ʳ–1ᵛ). Informing Hakluyt's expansionist prophecy was the moral force of Spain's 'Black Legend', the sense that England's struggle was not merely against flesh and blood, but above all against profound spiritual evil, incarnate in the papal Antichrist and his Spanish legions.

Answering Hakluyt's call was the driving figure behind England's first attempted American colony, the Virgin Queen's dashing favourite Sir Walter Ralegh. Less devout than Drake, but no less anti-Catholic and anti-Spanish, Ralegh projected a 'Western Design' to settle in 'Virginia', and in 1584 fitted and dispatched a small fleet to the Outer Banks of what is now North Carolina. Landing on Roanoke, a forested island in Pamlico Sound, the settlers established a fort, and in 1585 were reinforced by a second fleet led by Sir Richard Grenville. The colony commenced sending home optimistic reports, along with splendid watercolours by the artist and eventual Governor John White, of a rich land sparsely inhabited by friendly and tractable natives. These reports were gathered together in 1588 into a Latin book by the expedition's 'natural philosopher', Thomas Hariot, and then in 1590 translated and published as *A briefe and true report of the new found land of Virginia*, with White's original drawings rendered into engravings, again by Theodor de Bry. These engravings support Hariot's text in portraying the native Algonkians as 'noble savages': not only does de Bry render the mostly naked natives as classically statuesque, but he also bookends these images between an opening picture of a naked Adam and Eve eating the forbidden fruit, and a closing series of ancient, naked British warriors covered in body paint, and one holding a severed head. These images remind the reader of the Edenic, though fallen, state of America and also that, as one caption says, 'the Inhabitants of the great Bretannie haue bin in times past as sauuage as those of Virginia' (Hariot 1590: 75).

Thus, even as this 'brief and true report' paints an inviting portrait of colonial life in an Arcadian land, it still registers some dangers of settling the wilderness. Other accounts of Roanoke, in Hakluyt's *Principal Navigations* (1598) for example, register something else: a bad conscience that haunts and dooms the Roanoke enterprise. In one account, Grenville torches a whole Algonkian town in 1585 for the theft of a silver cup (Hakluyt 1598: VIII, 315–16); and in a following account, the guilty colonists are shown in 1586 stampeding to board a relief ship captained by Drake in a frantic effort to escape, 'as if they had been chased from thence by a mighty army: and no doubt they were; for the hand of God came upon them for the cruelty and outrages committed by some of them against the native inhabitants of that countrey' (Hakluyt 1598: VIII, 346–7). The worst was yet to come: in 1587, Ralegh sent a fourth expedition of one hundred men and women to secure his foothold in 'this paradise of the world'; by the time that Governor White returned for them in 1590, they had disappeared quite famously from the face of the earth, becoming the notorious 'Lost Colony' (Hakluyt 1598: VIII, 386–8, 416–19). Expulsion from Eden seems complete for the would-be settlers of Virginia.

Thus, twin-born with England's project of Protestant colonial settlement were persistent English strains of remorseful, binding religious conscience and foreboding that dogged their empire from its post-Reformation beginnings to its modern end. Some strains were clearly anti-imperial: the Augustinian and Christian humanist critique decried empire-building as not only oppressing the colonized but as disastrously weakening the colonizer. To the degree that the Reformation was an Augustinian revival—and that degree is quite profound—Protestants would be influenced not only by Augustine's views on divine grace and saving faith, but also by his ideas on the limits of civil and imperial expansion.

In *The City of God*, written during Rome's decline in the early fifth century, Augustine writes not only against the neo-pagans who were blaming Rome's collapse on Christianization, but also against his own Christian pupil Orosius, whose *History against the Pagans* argued that Rome's Christian conversion was not its end as a great power, but a sanctification that would bring ever-wider conquests (Orosius 1936: 318–25, I.1–3). On the contrary, says Augustine, imperial megalomania brings the constant military mobilization which drains manpower, money, and resources, brutalizes both the conquered and the conquerors abroad, and eventually lowers moral and legal standards at home. He denounces the 'waging of constant and unremitting war', and laments the unsustainable bulk of empire. 'Why must an empire be unquiet in order to be great?' he asks (Augustine 1998: 103). Similarly, John Calvin writes in *The Institutes of the Christian Religion* (1536, 1559, 1560) exhorting the French King François I that an unjust monarch 'exercises not kingly rule but brigandage'. Calvin also roundly condemns expansionism, writing that 'a king or the lowest of the common folk who invades a foreign country … must, equally, be considered as robbers and punished accordingly' (Calvin 1960: Prefatory Address, 2; 4.20.11).

Another strain of Protestant imperial conscience might be called 'trusteeship', which did not flatly oppose empire, but saw it as inevitable, and sought to ameliorate its worst abuses, while imagining it as temporary. Of course, some Protestant expansionists also spoke in these terms, proposing to colonize on the grounds of delivering the oppressed Americas from the Catholic Spanish yoke. Ralegh, for instance, having failed at Roanoke, attempted a South American settlement in Guyana in the 1590s, and wrote *The Discoverie of Guiana* (1596) in an unsuccessful attempt to promote it. He stresses the paradisal, ore-bearing abundance of the feminized Guyanan landscape and the alluring prelapsarian nakedness of its female inhabitants; he also stresses, in contrast to the rapacious and lecherous Catholic Spaniards, the courteous and chaste restraint that distinguishes the servants of the Protestant Virgin Queen. '*Guiana* is a Countrey that yet hath her Maydenhead' (Ralegh 1898: 57, 82, 115). Thus, the English are cast, however fancifully (since Ralegh's settlement efforts again failed), as chaste protectors of a virgin America from Spanish ravishment.

IMAGINED AMERICAS: THE POETS
AND PREACHERS RESPOND

A decade later, the vision is equally favourable to colonization in Michael Drayton's 1606 celebration of England's next, and eventually successful, attempt at settling Virginia (1607). In 'Ode to the Virginian voyage', Edenic and Arcadian imagery are in full flower, as Britons brave the deep in the *Susan Constant* to arrive at 'Virginia, | Earth's only paradise' and enter its 'golden age', where Drayton calls the Jamestown settlers to conceive a brave new breed of men (Drayton 1953: I, 123–4, ll. 1, 7, 23–4, 37, 55–60). In 1610, the preacher William Crashaw adds a biblical warrant to this vision, exhorting the would-be settlers to evangelize the natives as 'our brethren' and make alliances with them as equals: 'for the time was when wee were sauage and vnciuill … then God sent some to make us ciuill, others to make vs christians' (Crashaw 1610: C3^r, C4^v).

Nonetheless, at this same moment of Jamestown's founding, others are cautioning the settlers against the very mixing and alliances with the 'savages' that Crashaw recommends. The preacher William Symonds had recently warned departing Virginia settlers to guard ceaselessly against intermarriage with pagan nations and to keep themselves entirely separate, like Abraham sojourning in Canaan (Symonds 1609: 35). Clearly, this Abrahamic model of separation imagines a kind of exclusive ethnic—and potentially racial—purity that Crashaw, with his more Apostolic model, rejects, both because for Crashaw, the Gospel belongs equally to all nations, and because old England would benefit from the admixture of new American blood.

However, other voices were warning against any sort of colonial expansion. The poet Samuel Daniel, writing in his 'Epistle to Prince Henry' in 1610, exhorts the ambitious young prince of Wales against empire-building and recapitulates in verse Augustine's ancient arguments against imperial over-reach. To heighten Henry's fear of effeminate decadence and economic ruin, Daniel points to the disastrous imperial logistics and finances of Spain's Charles V. Daniel notes that Charles's outlay of manpower and borrowed capital left Spain a debtor nation despite its mother lodes, vulnerable to the nearly successful invasions of French King François I in the 1520s (Daniel 1981: 131–7, ll. 31–3, 35–50).

Daniel also makes a barely veiled jab at Jamestown's viability only three years after its founding. The settlement's recent decimation by disease and famine in 1608–9, and its continued anxiety about Spanish attack, made colonization seem a suicide mission. And Daniel wonders (anticipating the American Revolution by 166 years), how long the American colonists can 'be kept ours, come once to be their owne' (l. 52)—that is, once they come to feel and perhaps declare their independence, and make alliance with England's enemies. Yet even amidst Daniel's warnings about imperial over-reach, he concedes the general concept of the *translatio imperii*, that 'When the vniversall wheele of things shall move | Vnto that point, … those rude lands throughout | Th'Europian arts and Customes shall approue' (ll. 76–8)—in other words, that inevitably Europe's empire will be transferred to the now 'rude' native Americans. Still, Daniel tells young Henry, let the inevitable happen without England expending its own blood and treasure.

Daniel's Augustinian critique of empire had no known effect on policy, for even if Henry Stuart had been disposed to listen, the prince was dead of typhoid fever within two years. Daniel was not alone, however, in foreseeing the westward transfer of empire. In George Herbert's better-known poem 'The Church Militant', this lyricist of the inner spiritual life shifts to the prophetic mode and presents a similar vision of events to come: one that denounces European greed and violence in the Americas, and yet nevertheless argues that, since the westward course of empire is inevitable, England must participate whilst avoiding the worst abuses. Written in 1618–19, though published posthumously in 1633, Herbert's prognosis is even more dire than Daniel's: 'Religion stands on tip-toe in our land, | Readie to passe to the *American* strand' (Herbert 1941: 196, ll. 235–6). Herbert predicts that England's doom is near, and that America's time for empire and dominance is coming.

Sacvan Bercovitch has shown that Herbert's words were taken in early New England to predict the success of the puritan colonies (Bercovitch 1975: 145–6). However, Herbert's 'they' refers not to English settlers, but to America's native inhabitants. As if Europe were a desecrated temple, the glory will depart from the Old World, and God will shed his grace on the New. For Herbert, as for Daniel, Christendom's spread will not remove the natives *from* the land but rather bless, and curse, them *in* the land. This cyclical vision is not one of displacement, but of inheritance, of the *translatio imperii*. Herbert portrays the American natives as no worse and no better than any other heathens—including British heathens—previously converted on the Gospel's way from Palestine. Where Daniel wants England to delay the inevitable evils of empire as long as possible, Herbert would instead manage those evils and, by God's grace, convert them to at least limited good. This concession to empire puts Herbert more in the meliorist line of the 'trusteeship' tradition, seeking to improve what cannot be prevented; as he writes elsewhere, colonization can be 'a noble', and even 'a religious imployment' if pursued with evangelistic and compassionate motives (Herbert 1941: 278). Indeed, Herbert's *Outlandish Proverbs* (1640) were to reappear among the many counsels to colonial employment in Benjamin Franklin's *Poor Richard's Almanac* (1732–58).

This debate between the more optimistic or pragmatic Protestant expansionists and the more pessimistic Christian humanist and Protestant critics and opponents of empire carries on among other leading English writers of the Tudor–Stuart era. John Donne, in both his 'profane' and sacred poetry, and later in his sermons, registers an intense awareness of exploration and settlement, not only as a basis for some famed metaphors, but also as a substantial topic in itself. He compares his and his lover's eyes to separate 'hemispheres' in 'The good morrow'; himself to an explorer and his mistress's body to seas and lands in 'The sun rising' and Elegies XVIII ('Love's progress') and XIX ('To his mistress, going to bed'); and his own diseased body to a chart and death to a voyage beyond the world's end in 'Hymn to God my God in my sickness'. Donne is alive to all that is exciting, sublime, exotic, and alluring in the discovery and claiming of new lands; he is perhaps England's chief poet of the erotics of conquest

(Donne 1971b: 60, 80, 122, 124, 347). Later in life, Donne the Anglican priest and dean is, like his friend Herbert, more of a 'meliorist' when it comes to settlement, exhorting the Virginia Company in 1622 to avoid violence against the natives, preaching to them both 'Doctrinally' and 'Practically', treating them with kindness and fairness, to the end that they should 'reverence' the name of King James, but 'adore' the name of King Jesus (Donne 1953–62: IV, 280).

On the other hand, Donne's friend Ben Jonson, writing with George Chapman and John Marston, gives would-be Jamestown colonists no quarter in their play *Eastward Hoe* (1605). Some characters gullibly echo Ralegh's and Donne's erotic colonial fantasies, whilst others repeat More's fancies about Utopian gold, but the characters who actually depart for Virginia make it no farther than the scabrous Isle of Dogs—an obvious metaphor for colonial disenchantment. Whilst the play's colonial satire may be more opportunistic than principled (for comedians love an easy target), it nevertheless strikes home in ways consistent with the Augustinian sense of expansionism as a fool's errand, spurred by the deadly sins of lust, greed, and pride.

If colonialist ideology is a species of enchantment, then Shakespeare's *The Tempest* would seem to be the sorcerer's own book. Many have noted the play's famed associations with Bermuda and Jamestown, despite its nominally Mediterranean setting, and over the past four decades influential interpreters have read the play as a kind of imperialist allegory.[3] As the Western embrace of Manifest Destiny has declined, so also has sympathy for Shakespeare's magus, Prospero. However, if *The Tempest* is 'about' anything, it is most likely about the glory, power, danger, and limits of dramatic art, about the joys and sorrows of living by and on the fantasies of others. Its pervasive allusions to colonization and magic, and its biblical and apocalyptic imagery, appear as extended metaphors.

Still, Shakespeare's metaphoric participation in the debate over settlement suggests a deep ambivalence about the settlers' project that is shot through with religious significance. Both Prospero's admirers and detractors can find plausible support for their views, because he is, by design, a complicated character in a contradictory setting. For instance, Shakespeare is alive to the fragility of initially friendly colonial relations. Though originally Prospero arrives on the island as the victim of injustice, and at first acts as friend and rescuer to the inhabitants Caliban and Ariel, in the wake of Caliban's attempted rape of Miranda, Prospero recoils from the prospect of an island 'peopled with Calibans', and discovers that the soft superior hand is not enough: if he is to rule this 'mooncalf' at all, he believes that he must rule by fear and coercion. In addition, Shakespeare complicates the paradigm of the innocent indigene oppressed by new settlers, for whilst Ariel fits the model, Caliban—so often the object of post-colonial sympathies—actually is not rightful king of the island as he claims, but rather the son of the imperialist witch Sycorax, whose god Setebos is no match for Prospero's books (Barton 1991: 54).

---

[3] See, for example, Greenblatt 1990.

Having stepped reluctantly into the place of a savage deity, Prospero warms to the office. We see him dismiss Ariel's just demands for 'liberty' as rank ingratitude, threaten to renew the tortures inflicted on Ariel by Sycorax, and, through the metaphysical technology of his magic, shackle and torment the erring Caliban. In so doing, the magus intertwines colonial and metaphysical power: he would, for a time, be master, so he must, for a while, be a god. Hence the wide variations in our emotional responses to Prospero: even from a Eurocentric viewpoint, he is a troubled and troubling ruler—alternately beneficent and vindictive, serene and capricious, a seemingly good man caught in a devil's bargain. His play with divine power is seducing him, binding him, corrupting his character. In the end, as we have seen, Prospero must give up his magic, and his master's and settler's claims, if he is to keep his humanity, and not become the monster that he has fought. Thus if *The Tempest* is to be read as contributing to a myth of Protestant possession, then that possession is imagined as temporary—and to be held with great danger to the possessor's soul.

POSSESSED BY POSSESSION: FRAGMENTATION, GROWTH, AND EXPERIMENT

Indeed, it is doubtful that we can speak of a single 'Protestant possession myth', because even as England's Protestant empire was being established, English Protestantism was nevertheless dividing increasingly along varied ecclesiastical fissures that projected across the sea. On the southerly coast of North America, Jamestown's founding Anglicanism made its church a more straightforward projection of English Crown authority into Virginia, and its mainland extensions into Carolina (1629, divided into North and South Carolina in 1712), and in its island extensions of Bermuda (1609), Barbados (1624), the Bahamas (1648), Anguilla (1650), and Cayman (1670). To the north, though the Puritans of Plymouth (1620) and Massachusetts Bay (1630) were nominally loyal to the early Stuart kings, they were actually in flight from their church policies and persecutions. So New England often honoured royal authority in the breach, especially during the English Civil Wars (1642–9), the puritan Commonwealth (1649–53), and Protectorate (1653–60).

Furthermore, New England Puritanism was itself notoriously fractile—with splinter groups from Massachusetts Bay settling the Connecticut Valley and Rhode Island (1636), and with an offshoot of Merry Mount apostates (1625)—whilst other religious minorities in flight from early Stuart Anglican Conformity were as unwelcome in Calvinist New England as in the Old: the English Catholics who settled Maryland (1633), and the Quakers who established Pennsylvania (1681). England's territorial expansions over the 'long seventeenth century' were also to absorb or displace settlements from other nations and churches: the Afro-Spanish Catholic island colonies of Montserrat

(1632), Jamaica (1655), and St. Kitts/Nevis (1713); the Swedish/German Lutheran colony of New Sweden (1655); the Dutch Reformed colonies of Delaware and New Jersey (1664), Nieuw Amsterdam rechristened New York (1665), and the Virgin Islands (1672); and the French Catholic settlements of Acadia/Maine (1652) and Vermont (1724).

As English settlements began to multiply, and to accumulate a record of failures and achievements, analytic public men such as Sir Francis Bacon took notice. In his own utopian fiction, *The New Atlantis* (1624), Bacon, like More, imagines an ideal island society on the far side of the world, protected from Europe's wars and errors. Yet unlike Utopia, Bacon's island has for 1,600 years been nurtured by a pure biblical wisdom augmented by the free operation of scientific enquiry, guided by the sages of 'Salomon's House'— a kind of research institute (and eventual prototype for the Royal Society). Bacon sees faith in the wisdom of the Creator as the surest foundation for exploring and exploiting the possibilities of the creation, thus renewing the ideal of the New World as a place of limitless religious reform and experimental enquiry.

A year later, Bacon published the final edition of his *Essays* (1625), including 'Of Plantations', in which he reflects on colonization, and gives practical advice to actual colonists. Bacon praises 'planting' as 'amongst ancient, primitive, and heroical works', but then turns to warning potential planters against a whole range of unheroic errors, clearly informed by the abuses and follies of New Spain, and also of England's still-struggling Jamestown. He warns against invasions that abuse and displace native peoples, as well as against settling in unhealthy marshland, relying on imported food, rushing to seek for gold or quick profits, and peopling the colony with convicts, slaves, and the urban poor. Instead, he recommends planting only previously unsettled land, building on higher ground, cultivating the native staple crops, specializing in useful products like timber, iron, salt, and pitch, and settling the colony with skilled and honest workmen— and eventually, with honest women. He advises settlers, 'above all', to 'make that profit, of being in the wilderness, as they have God always, and his service, before their eyes' (Bacon 1937: 58). Religion, for Bacon, was the tie that binds all to a common purpose, good order, and industry.

SETTLER SCRIPTURE:
NEW AND BLENDED GENRES

After decades of fitful advocacy and planning, and many failed settlement attempts, dispatches began to arrive *from* the English colonies. These writings took many forms, most of them workmanlike and pragmatic, but some of them more self-consciously artful. All of them, even the most mundane, were informed by one or more of the imaginative paradigms which we have been discussing—the noble savage, vicious heathen, or native victim myths of the indigene—or the settlement models of religious and imperial rivalry, Abrahamic sojourn, Mosaic exodus, holy conquest, apostolic evangelism; or of practical exploration, industry, and trade.

One of the first accounts from Jamestown combined the classical myth of the *trans-latio imperii* and the biblical paradigm of Apostolic mission: the news of John Rolfe's 1614 marriage to the Algonkian princess Pocahontas. Some reasons for the marriage are provided or suggested by Rolfe himself and by Ralph Hamor in the latter's 1615 *True Discourse of the Present State of Virginia*, and by Captain John Smith's 1624 *Historie of Virginia*: the bride's beauty, her diplomatic worth, and her Christian conversion. Remarkably, there is no mention of race: he writes before the importation of Virginia's first African slaves (1619), and the invention of the colonial colour line (1662).

Rolfe struggles to explain that his motives are not merely carnal, but evangelistic and civic-minded, for the salvation of a soul and the establishing of friendly relations with Pocahontas's father Powhatan. However, sexual attraction shows itself in his (and later John Smith's) comments about Pocahontas's 'nonpareil' looks, wit, and regal bearing. Like Virgil's Aeneas wedding Lavinia to make peace with the rustic King Latinus, Rolfe's explanation of his marriage foregrounds imperial and political motives, with Christian gospelling coming in a reasonably close second (Hamor 1615: 66–8). Indeed Rolfe displays a sensibility as profoundly Calvinist as William Bradford's or John Winthrop's, permeated with self-scrutiny, and saturated in Scripture.

Only a few years later on Cape Cod, William Bradford and his fellow colonists landed to found Plymouth Plantation in 1620. Bradford's eponymous memoir (1650) about the next three decades of settlement partakes both of the Mosaic and Abrahamic paradigms, with a flavouring of Jeremiah. Bradford sometimes speaks of the Puritans as 'pilgrims' through a strange wilderness, beset by the hostile heathen whilst on their way to freedom from Christendom's pharaohs; and sometimes he speaks of them as sojourners living on surprisingly friendly terms with the native peoples. As the new Israel, he and his brethren look not back to 'Egypt' for order, but to their God and themselves; they covenant together in a 'Civil Body Politic' to frame just and equal laws for the common good, laying the foundations of American self-government. His lean yet often moving prose spares no one, including himself, the close analysis of action and motive, as he traces the purposes of the Almighty in the blessings and calamities that befall the settlement. He concludes inconclusively, aware that as the colonists grow more prosperous and combine with the encroaching settlement at Boston, they risk gaining the world whilst losing the soul. Thus, the genre of the puritan jeremiad is born.

Ten years later, and a little further up the coast at Massachusetts Bay in 1630, John Winthrop landed with a better-prepared and more ambitious body of Puritans on 'an errand into the wilderness'. 'Errand' is the key word: though also leaving Anglican persecution behind, they were seeking not permanent asylum, but rather a staging ground on which to build their ideal Christian commonwealth, the 'city upon a Hill' that would occasion reform back in England and Europe—and eventually, they believed, their return to renew the Old World. The Abrahamic sojourner model prevails in Winthrop's *A modell of Christian charity*, his inaugural onboard sermon en route to America. Winthrop also is zealous for 'Christian liberty', yet as governor of the colony struggled with how much any polity founded on church membership could permit fundamental dissent and unorthodox behaviour. In the case of lay preacher Anne Hutchinson, who accused the colony's early leaders and ministers of abandoning God's grace for 'a coven-ant of works', Winthrop finally banished her to Rhode Island, a mild penalty by English standards but still, ironically, persecution by the persecuted. Yet Winthrop's insistence on government under covenant law, and on generally equitable justice, established Massachusetts on a firm footing, leading to greater security and prosperity.

Among the settlers of Boston was another woman, named Anne Bradstreet, who amid the rigours of colonial life and the rearing of eight children managed to write the first book of poems from the New World, *The Tenth Muse lately sprung up in America*, published in London in 1650 (ostensibly without her permission) to much acclaim. Bradstreet's collection makes witty and vivid poetry from everyday joys and sorrows: her surprisingly sensuous desire for her husband; the burning of their family home; the deaths of grandchildren; and the predicament of a woman writ-ing on the male-dominated frontier. Miraculously, she projects both modesty and confidence: disarmingly domestic in her imagery (she compares her book to a 'ram-bling brat' whom she cannot help loving), she nevertheless challenges the silly men who must have all the laurels to themselves, when she can be content with a wreath of kitchen herbs. Her matter-of-fact, sometimes psalmic piety looks back to George Herbert, but also ahead to the democratic glories of the American plain style.

Another early American poet, influenced by Bradstreet and even more by Herbert, was Edward Taylor, a Harvard graduate and Connecticut Valley pastor whose volu-minous poetry of private devotion was composed between 1680 and 1725, but not published until 1939. His metaphysical meditations, many of them preparatory for Holy Communion, are notable for their quirky, colloquial language and take their conceits from ordinary objects—stagecoaches, spinning wheels, flowerbeds, baker-ies—to figure heaven forth. Like Jonathan Edwards in the next generation, Taylor presents an exegesis of experience, discovering the infinite God nearby and reading his Word in common life, as also implied by Edwards's title, *Images of divine things* (1728).

Whilst Bradstreet and Taylor are developing a distinctly American poetry, other New Englanders are weighing their colonial project in the balance, and finding it want-ing. In *The Day of Doom* (1662), physician, pastor, and Harvard professor Michael Wigglesworth crafts his jeremiad into America's first best-selling book of poetry. Dismayed by the decline of spiritual life amid the settlers' increasing prosperity, Wigglesworth is also conceding that the puritan 'errand' has now become a perman-ent habitation. With the puritan Commonwealth having failed back in England, New England's city on a hill must shine all the brighter to counteract earth's growing dark-ness. Seeking to shock his countrymen out of their materialistic apathy, he writes scath-ingly of the vanities that distract the people from their true business of God's glory. And in her harrowing *Narrative of the captivity* (1682), Mary Rowlandson seems to confirm Wigglesworth, treating her terrible sufferings at the hands of her native Algonkian cap-tors as chastisement for 'Israel's' sins.

God's controversy with New England also animates Cotton Mather's *Magnalia Christi Americana* (1702), the work of a remarkable polymath: Harvard prodigy, preacher, historian, and scientist (the first American member of the Royal Society, and an inspiration to Benjamin Franklin), Mather sought not only to denounce American decline, but to rekindle her goodness and greatness. Beginning with Herbert's 'Church Militant' about religion's flight to the 'American Strand', Mather's seven-volume history provides biographies of New England's founding leaders and recounts the stirring trials and events of the past eighty years that refined the first generations. But the book is, above all, about the great works that *Christ* has done—and is still doing—in America. Mather points to the cloud of witnesses who call the present generation to renew those works, as America increasingly turns her eyes away from Britain and Europe, and inward and westward to the backcountry frontiers.

WRITING HOME: AMERICA RE-FORMS ENGLISH LITERATURE

Meanwhile, influences from the colonies continued to form, and re-form, literature back in England. After the Commonwealth's collapse in 1660, John Milton recuperated his political losses with the greatest literary and religious work of the age, *Paradise Lost* (1667, 1674), with strong New World echoes. Milton's Adam and Eve are portrayed both as innocent naked natives of a virgin land (Milton 1957: IV, 172, 288–99), and as settlers of an empire (IV, 144–5); and when Milton imagines the fallen angels debating ways to rise again, the proposal that carries the day is Beelzebub's colonial scheme: an attack on the 'happy isle' (II, 410) of Earth, this 'new world' (II, 403). Even Milton's paradise is informed by imperial geopolitics, whilst poems by both Edmund Waller and Andrew Marvell portray the Bermudas as an Edenic land of spices, with remarkable erotic and hedonic potential (Waller) and as a paradisal refuge from religious persecution (Marvell).

Most notably, many colonial genres contribute to the development of a major literary form, the novel. The earliest examples—Aphra Behn's *Oroonoko* (1688), Daniel Defoe's *Robinson Crusoe* (1719) and *Moll Flanders* (1722), and Jonathan Swift's *Gulliver's Travels* (1726)—take the paradises and perditions of colonial settlement among their main themes, and incorporate fictionalized voyages, ships logs, slave trading, shipwrecks, and encounters with terrible and wonderful natives. Behn's and Swift's portraits of overseas settlement are strikingly dystopian, with colonial Surinam being the site of the African 'royal slave' Oroonoko's hellish sufferings and death, and Gulliver's peregrinations building to a madly hilarious—and scalding—indictment of Eurocentric colonization. Defoe's treatments are somewhat more optimistic. Crusoe's famous island provides him, not unlike Prospero, with occasions for spiritual repentance, technological innovation, and cross-cultural friendship before returning home; Moll Flanders finds a permanent new home in Maryland and Virginia, and a sunnier America of second chances and fresh opportunities, as she turns away from the unlucky Old World.

Thus, our period ends with the original settlements well established as towns and cities, with emerging governments, institutions, infrastructure, and industry—and with the multiplying conflicts, crises, depredations, and disasters that such development can bring. The brave New World now has many people in it: people travelled to or born on a far shore, formed by different circumstances, confronting unprecedented problems, and defined by new alliances and allegiances—and their own interpretive communities. These settlers are rapidly displacing the indigenous peoples of the New World, and increasingly see themselves as somehow set apart from their cousins in the Old, as well. They have, in the psalmist's words, gone down to the sea in ships, done business on the great waters, and have seen the works of the LORD, and his wonders in the deep—and in that far country beyond the sea. As the children of wayfarers and pilgrims, and as pioneers themselves, they know better than most that 'here on earth have we no continuing place', and are perhaps more inclined to say to the LORD 'thou hast been our dwelling place in all generations'. So, as Caliban sang, they have a new master—their God, or themselves—and feel like new men.[4] 'Twas new to *them*', we may be inclined to say, with ironic hindsight. Yet since not even we know how their story ends—for it is being told still—perhaps irony is premature?

---

[4] Caliban's chant when he foolishly gives his allegiance to the drunken butler Stephano and the clown Trinculo at the end of act 2 scene 2 of *The Tempest*.

PART V

EARLY MODERN RELIGIOUS LIFE
Debates and Issues

CHAPTER 33

···

THE BIBLE

···

HANNIBAL HAMLIN

THE Bible was fundamental to Renaissance literature and culture. This statement is not likely to generate much controversy, but what exactly do we mean when we talk about the 'Bible'? This is a much more difficult question than it might appear. 'Bible' is an English word, cognate with German *Bibel* and French *Bible*, meaning, according to the *OED*, 'the Scriptures of the Old and New Testament'. The root is the Latin *biblia*, which, according to the *OED*, also meant 'the Scriptures'. Already there is some complexity, however, since *biblia*, while singular in late Latin ('the book'), was originally a plural, reflecting its origin in the Greek τὰ βιβλία (*ta biblia*), literally 'the books'. Whether the Bible is one book or many is a question that leads to the problem of the canon: which 'books' did the 'book' of the Bible actually include? While the canonical Christian Scriptures had been largely decided upon in the first centuries of the Church, some uncertainty remained about the so-called Apocrypha, writings contained in the Greek Septuagint but not in the Hebrew manuscript tradition. The Latin translation of Jerome known as the Vulgate included the Apocrypha: books like Judith, Ecclesiasticus, and 1 and 2 Maccabees, as well as 'additions' to the books of Esther and Daniel (Susanna and the Elders, for example). Martin Luther included most of these texts in his German Bible of 1534 (except 1 and 2 Esdras), but he placed them together between the Old and New Testaments with the separate title, 'Apocrypha' (literally 'hidden', or of unknown authorship). English Bible translators generally followed Luther's practice, but not entirely consistently. Miles Coverdale placed the Apocrypha between the testaments in his 1535 Bible, except for Baruch, which he put after Jeremiah (following the Lamentations). The Matthew Bible of 1537 added the Prayer of Manasses to the intertestamental section. Baruch was returned to the Apocrypha in subsequent English Bibles, and the Prayer of Manasses remained as well, though its position varied: in the Geneva Bible (1560), though labelled as 'apocrypha', it followed 2 Chronicles, while in the Great Bible (1539) and the King James Bible (1611) it came between Bel and the Dragon and 1 Maccabees in the Apocrypha (entitled 'Hagiographa', or 'sacred writings', in 1539). The Catholic Church further muddled things with the Clementine Vulgate of 1592, which moved the Prayer of Manasses and 3 and 4 Esdras (numbered 1 and 2 in the Geneva and King James Bibles, though not the 1568

Bishops', since they renamed 1 and 2 Esdras Ezra and Nehemiah) to a separate appendix. In the seventeenth century, some English Bibles began to be printed without the Apocrypha, and this became the modern standard (Greenslade 1963: 168–70). During the Renaissance, however, the Apocrypha were generally considered part of the Bible, but, since Protestants considered them less authoritative than the canonical Scriptures, which texts were included and where they were placed were matters of disagreement.

If the treatment of the Apocrypha varied, there was, of course, overwhelming consensus on the canon of the New Testament and on the remainder of the Old. Catholics and Protestants alike accepted the four gospels, Acts, twenty-one epistles, and Revelation, as they did the non-apocryphal Old Testament books, reordered from the Jewish canon to reflect the Christian understanding of prophecy (where the Prophets come last, since they were felt to foretell the Incarnation announced by the gospels). Scholars including Erasmus, Luther, and Sebastian Castellio raised doubts about the Song of Solomon, the Epistle of James, Hebrews, and Revelation, but none went so far as to omit them. Despite their rough, superficial similarity, however, Protestant and Catholic Bibles were notably different to any reader who moved beyond the table of contents. The vernacular Bible was at the heart of Protestant Reform, and following Luther's translations in German, William Tyndale and subsequent English Reformers produced a Bible in English. English Catholics remained opposed to the English Bible until the Rheims-Douai translation of 1582/1609–10; for them, the Bible was a book in Latin. Yet even this is an oversimplification.

Catholics were not universally opposed to translating the Bible, and vernacular Bibles existed in many European languages prior to the Reformation, including eighteen German editions, in several translations, between 1466 and Luther's New Testament of 1522. In England, the official attitude to the vernacular Bible was determined by the fourteenth- and fifteenth-century followers of John Wycliff, known as Lollards. There were two Lollard translations of the Bible, based on the Vulgate, which survive in dozens of manuscripts, testifying to their wide circulation. Because Lollards were also committed to radical reforms of church and state, translating the Bible into English was also seen as radical and was pronounced a heresy in 1408 by authorities made the more nervous by the Peasant's Revolt of 1381. The act *De haeretico comburendo* (1401) had made heresy a crime punishable by burning at the stake. Wycliff died of a stroke in 1384 while celebrating Mass, but in 1428 his bones were dug up, burned, and cast into the River Swift. No new English translation of the Bible was made for over a century.

Inspired by Luther, Tyndale took on the task of producing a new English Bible translated not from the Vulgate but from the original Hebrew and Greek. His tragic story is well known, but the fact that he first approached the bishop of London, Cuthbert Tunstall, to sponsor his project suggests that, at least in 1523, Tyndale himself thought a new vernacular Bible might be welcomed by the English Church. Tunstall rejected Tyndale, who ultimately did most of his translating on the continent. Tyndale completed all of the New Testament, the Pentateuch, the historical books from Joshua to 2 Chronicles, and Jonah, before he was executed for heresy in 1536. According to John Foxe, Tyndale's last words before being garrotted were 'Lord, open the King of

England's eyes'. Whether Henry VIII's eyes were divinely opened or not, he did authorize an English Bible, only a few years after Tyndale's death. Miles Coverdale had produced a complete English Bible, translated not from Hebrew and Greek but Latin and German, in 1535. He dedicated it optimistically to King Henry, but it was published in Antwerp and not officially accepted. In 1537, John Rogers, under the pseudonym Thomas Matthew, produced the 'Matthew' Bible, an edited compilation of Tyndale's surviving translations supplemented by parts of Coverdale's Bible. This too was printed on the continent, though later editions of both the Matthew and the Coverdale Bibles were printed in London into the 1550s. In 1539, King Henry finally authorized the Great Bible, Miles Coverdale's further revision of Rogers's Matthew Bible. From then on, the English Bible was an established fact. Even during the reign of Catholic Queen Mary, the Great Bible was not systematically suppressed, and Cardinal Reginald Pole, Archbishop of Canterbury from 1556 to 1558, may have been planning a new Catholic English translation (MacCulloch 2003: 283–4). (John Rogers, however, was the first heretic burned at the stake during Mary's reign.)

The vicissitudes of English Bible translation were tied to the power of kings and queens (as well as bishops). Only after Henry had assumed supreme control over the Church of England, and formally approved the Great Bible, could this English version be used in English churches. Bible translation also had political implications at the level of minute verbal detail, however. Thomas More famously challenged Tyndale's translation, arguing that his specific word choice was heretical and seditious. It mattered, he stressed, whether the Greek word πρεσβύτερος (*presbyteros*) was translated as 'bishop' or as 'senior'. The former translation suggested that the Presbyterian Church hierarchy was rooted in the language and practice of the early Church; the latter allowed the possibility that it was not. In response to More's criticism, Tyndale did modify his translation, but not in the direction More advocated: instead, he changed 'senior' to 'elder', noting simply that his first choice had been somewhat awkward English. Similarly, More objected to Tyndale's rendering of ἐκκλησία (*ekklesia*) as 'congregation' rather than 'church'. Again, the implications compromised the New Testament authority of the institutional Church, but then this was exactly what Tyndale had in mind. Even at the level of diction, Tyndale's translation shifted—his word would no doubt have been 'restored'—authority to the ordinary Christian at the expense of the Church.

Some of Tyndale's controversial translations cut more subtly against the established Church. His choice of 'love', for instance, in 1 Corinthians 13 seems at first sight unobjectionable as a translation of the Greek ἀγάπη (*agape*): 'Now abideth faith, hope, and love, even these three: but the greatest of these is love.' The Vulgate, however, translates the Greek as '*caritas*', which is reflected in the King James Bible's 'the greatest of these is charity' (1 Cor. 13:13). Is 'charity' simply a different word for 'love'? Or does it rather designate acts of charity, including the giving of alms, the sort of good works encouraged by the Catholic Church and rewarded (so the Church said) by God? Tyndale's choice of 'favour' over 'grace', 'repentance' over 'penance', and 'knowledge' over 'confession' similarly chipped away at the Church's teachings and authority. Whatever More's doctrinal allegiances, his point is valid and critical: translation does not, in the words of the King

James Bible translators, open a window but rather it replaces one window with another, perhaps with a different frame, different glass, a different tint—all of which changes what one sees beyond it (Cummings 2002: 187–206).

What kind of window could a translator make from sixteenth-century English? Tyndale claimed that the English language was naturally much closer to Hebrew than Latin was (Tyndale, *Obedience*, fol. 15ᵛ), but Latin had been working at it for over a thousand years, refining, for instance, its theological vocabulary. Indeed, it is fair to say that theology was itself refined and developed in Latin. Could theology even be expressed in another language? For instance, justification by faith alone is often cited as one of the fundamental theological principles of Protestantism, but what did 'justification' mean in the early sixteenth century? Was it perfectly synonymous with the Latin *justificare*, and also the Greek δικαιόω (*dikaioō*), which was the key word Paul had used in Romans 3? And was Paul's Greek word synonymous with the Hebrew צָדַק (tsadaq) from Psalm 51:4, which Paul was quoting, presumably from the Septuagint translation?

Indeed, the Christian Bible was a work of translation even before it existed, since, though the gospels were written in *koinē* Greek, the words of Jesus that they record were surely in Aramaic. Moreover, the gospel writers and Paul knew the Jewish Scriptures, what became known as the 'Old Testament', not in its original Hebrew (with some Aramaic) but in the Greek of the Septuagint. Jerome's Vulgate was, like the Septuagint, designed to make the Bible available to Christians in their native tongue. Only as Latin died out as a vernacular and became the specialized language of the Church did the Vulgate (literally 'common' or 'of the common people') become, ironically, the preserve of the priestly class. Tyndale and his followers were thus following the practice of Jerome, even as they were trying to supplant his translation with their own.

Translation continued to be a controversial problem throughout the English Renaissance. First, during the reign of Queen Mary, English Protestants in exile in Geneva worked to produce a new, improved English Bible, based on the best scholarship then available, and (for the first time) translating the entire Bible from the original languages. Published in Geneva in 1560, the 'Geneva' Bible was to become the most popular English translation for the next century, even though it was never authorized for use in English churches. Next, in response to the Geneva Bible, whose notes and other scholarly apparatus reflected a hotter Protestantism than was comfortable for the Elizabethan Church establishment, Archbishop Matthew Parker led a team of translators to produce the Bishops' Bible in 1568. This translation, though never widely popular, was approved for church use and was the English version heard in worship services until at least 1611. Then, in 1611 the King James Bible was first printed and, though it was never exactly 'authorized', it became the approved translation of the Church of England (Norton 2011: 17). The instructions of James I specified that the translators were to use the Bishops' Bible as their base text, but they consulted all previous English translations, including the Geneva. At the same time, the Geneva Bible itself continued to be popular. It was ultimately supplanted by the King James only after the Restoration of 1660, probably due more to the practice of printers than anything else.

Meanwhile, in 1582, a New Testament translated by and for English Catholics had been printed at Rheims, and the Old Testament followed, printed at Douai, in 1609–10. (The whole Bible had been translated earlier, but the publication of the Old Testament was delayed due to costs.) The 'Douai-Rheims' Bible was translated from the Vulgate, but it also reflected considerable linguistic and historical scholarship, having recourse to the Hebrew and Greek. In fact, the title of the Rheims New Testament made the same claims as the Protestant Bibles:

> *THE NEW TESTAMENT OF JESUS CHRIST, TRANSLATED FAITHFULLY INTO ENGLISH, out of the authentical Latin, according to the best corrected copies of the same, diligently conferred with the Greek and other editions in divers languages: With ARGUMENTS of books and chapters, ANNOTATIONS, and other necessary helps, for the better understanding of the text, and specially for the discovery of the CORRUPTIONS of divers late translations, and for clearing the CONTROVERSIES in religion, of these days.*

Only the phrase 'authentical Latin' differentiates the practice of these Bible translators from those of the Geneva, the Bishops', or the later King James. And the emphasis on arguments and annotations signals the intention to compete with the Geneva Bible, popular in large part because of its substantial apparatus of readers' aids. Both Bibles offered marginal notes interpreting difficult pages, though of course their interpretations differed widely. For example, where the Geneva editors glossed the Whore of Babylon (Rev. 17:3–6) as 'the Antichrist, that is, the Pope with the whole body of his filthy creatures', the Rheims editors retorted, 'whether Babylon or the great whore do here signify Rome or no, yet it cannot signify the Church of Rome' (King 2004: 31–5).

The Renaissance was a culture of translation (Rhodes, Kendal, and Wilson), and the translation of the Bible was at the centre of this culture, in both practice and theory. Renaissance Bible translators worked according to the principle of formal equivalence, the term introduced by Eugene Nida for following the original text word for word. John Selden remarked on the peculiarity of this approach:

> There is no Book so translated as the Bible for the purpose. If I translate a *French* Book into *English,* I turn it into *English* Phrase, not into *French English [Il fait froid]* I say 'tis cold, not, it makes cold; but the Bible is rather translated into *English* Words than into *English* Phrase. The *Hebraisms* are kept, and the Phrase of that Language is kept: As for Example, [He uncover'd her Shame] which is well enough, so long as Scholars have to do with it; but when it comes among the Common People, Lord, what Gear do they make of it! (1689: 3)

But Selden also praised the English Bible (by which he meant the Bishops' Bible as well as King James's) as the 'best Translation in the World', the one that 'renders the Sense of the Original best' (1689: 3). The English Bible may have contained some peculiar English, but this accurately reflected the original Hebrew. As a result, the English Bible had a profound shaping effect upon the English language, introducing Hebraicisms like 'the skin of his teeth' and 'the apple of his eye'. Also, when English Bibles (originating with the Wycliffite translation) stated that Adam 'knew' Eve in such a way as to make her pregnant with Cain, they introduce an entirely new sense to the verb. The point of this neologism was to capture a pun in the Hebrew, in which the words for the 'knowledge' of good and evil, Adam and Eve's 'knowledge' that they are naked, and Adam and Eve's sexual intercourse share a common root. When Mariana in Shakespeare's *Measure for Measure* says of Angelo, he 'thinks he knows that he ne'er knew my body, | But knows, he thinks, that he knows Isabel's', the brilliant punning would be incomprehensible without knowing the English translation of Genesis 4:1 (5.1.202–3).

Furthermore, English translations of the Bible introduced many new words and idioms into the language: 'busybody', 'the blind leading the blind', 'brokenhearted' (all Tyndale), 'salt of the earth' (Wycliffite), 'turn the world upside down' (King James), 'loving kindness' (Coverdale) (Malless and McQuain 2003; Crystal 2010). The English Bibles influenced the language more subtly as well. For instance, Paul's style in the Epistles shaped the style of English theological writing, and the language and style of prophecy in Isaiah, Daniel, and Revelation provided the vocabulary and style for the substantial apocalyptic literature of the sixteenth and seventeenth centuries (Patrides and Wittreich 1984). The impact of biblical style has been minimally explored, but at least one strong argument has been made for the influence of Paul's 'binary linkage of sentence (or verb phrases) in an antithetical, correlative, or comparative relation'. Tyndale translated Romans 7 as 'For we know that the law is spiritual: but I am carnal.... I delight in the law of God, concerning the inner man. But I see another law in my members rebelling against the law of my mind, and subduing me unto the law of sin, which is in my members' (Mueller 1984: 192–201). Here, Tyndale's syntax and sentence structures are derived from the Pauline model, and the same case has been made for Roger Ascham's 1579 *The Schoolmaster* (Mueller 1984: 339–43). The full extent of the influence of the prose of the English Bible on sixteenth- and seventeenth-century style remains to be discovered.

INTERPRETATION

Like any book, the Bible must not only be read but interpreted. Considerable interpretation was required already in the process of translation, which meant that some decisions about the meaning of words had been made before those words were even offered to general readers. But plenty of interpretive work was still required of the reader. Despite some popular claims, the meaning of the Bible is often difficult or even obscure, especially if one is trying to derive from it lessons for good living and eternal salvation. Tyndale, following Erasmus, expressed a longing to place the Bible in the hands of ploughboys and other ordinary working people. Rendering it in English, and a colloquial, non-academic English at that, was essential, but could they understand it even so? Obviously, Tyndale himself had doubts, since his Bible translations, like Luther's, added substantial interpretive prefaces to each book. Tyndale also provided copious marginal cross-references to other biblical verses. These too were intended as interpretive aids. Passages in one gospel were linked to similar passages in other gospels, so that one could compare the stories and teachings, interpreting one by means of others.

Cross-references ranged more widely across the Bible too, reflecting the idea of the Bible as perfectly consistent and homogeneous in its truth. Peter says in Acts 10, 'Of a truth I perceive, that God is not partial, but in all people he that feareth him and worketh righteousness, is accepted with him.' Tyndale's margin points readers to Deuteronomy 10, 2 Chronicles 19, Job 34, and Proverbs 6. The Geneva Bible, the first in English to include verse as well as chapter numbers, is more specific in referring to Deuteronomy 10:17, 2 Chronicles 19:17, and Job 34:19, and it adds references to Wisdom, Ecclesiasticus, Romans, Galatians, Ephesians, Colossians, and 1 Peter (though omitting Tyndale's to Proverbs). Even the translators of the King James Bible, instructed by James 'that no marginal notes should be added, having found in them which are added to the Geneva translation (which he saw in a Bible given him by an English lady) some notes very partial, untrue, seditious and savouring too much of dangerous and traitorous conceits' (Norton 2000: 84), nevertheless included copious marginal cross-references—in the case of Acts 10:34, the same references to Deuteronomy, Romans (2:11), and 1 Peter as in the Geneva. The verses cross-referenced at Acts 10 in the King James Bible all specifically refer to God as not respecting persons, which supports Peter's assertion in Acts. The same is true of the Geneva cross-references to 2 Chronicles (actually to 19:7 not 19:17), Job, and Romans. Ecclesiasticus 35:16 asserts, 'He that serveth the Lord, shalbe accepted with favour', which seems in the same universalist spirit as Peter's remarks. The story in Acts concerns the Roman Captain Cornelius, whose prayer is accepted by God, and in whose house Peter agrees to preach, again asserting the inclusiveness of his teaching. The Geneva's cross-reference to Wisdom 6:8, on the other hand, seems inappropriate: 'But for the mighty abideth the sorer trial.' The preceding verse in Wisdom reads, 'For he that is Lord over all, wil spare no person, nether shal he feare anie greatnes: for he hathe made the small and great, and careth for all alike.' This is indeed an expression of God's lack of respect for persons, but whereas Peter is emphasizing God's openness to all the faithful, even among the Romans, the point of Wisdom is that all the wicked will be punished, even the high and mighty. Were the Geneva translators thinking of Queen Mary? Or even the untested Queen Elizabeth? King James would likely have found the implications of this cross-reference rather unsavoury, though he might not have seen it, even if he had looked. Interestingly, the Wisdom reference is dropped from the later Tomson edition of the Geneva Bible New Testament (from 1576). Tyndale's cross-references are more ambiguous, especially since he did not include verse numbers (and, moreover, when Tyndale's New Testament was printed in 1534, no English version of these Old Testament passages was in print). In fact, the reference to Proverbs 6 presents a puzzle; there is no reference to respecting persons, and in fact the reference is not included in either Geneva or the King James.

Whatever their orthodox or seditious implications, the cross-references in English Bibles, not to mention the many interpretive notes in the Geneva, indicate that the translators believed their readers still needed assistance in understanding the text. The

Geneva Bible, the most copiously annotated, has been called the first English study Bible, or even a sort of 'Bible for Dummies' (Ferrell 2008: 132; Hamlin and Jones 2010: 5). Were the translators primarily interested in helping their readers, however, or were they rather concerned to keep them within proper interpretive limits? Both arguments have been made, and both are no doubt true. The Bible is a difficult book, and even Tyndale must have realized that his ploughboy would need some help to puzzle out the meaning of Paul's teachings on justification, say, or the appropriate application of Revelation. At the same time, the vast sixteenth-century proliferation of readers' aids to the Bible likely testifies to clerical anxiety about what might result if ordinary readers were given free reign not only to read but interpret the Scriptures. Henry VIII had authorized the publication and dissemination of the Great Bible, but his proclamation in 1541 specified that the Bible was 'to be fyxed and set up openlye in every of the sayd parishe churches' (Pollard 1911: 262). Parishioners could thus read the Bible, but only where their priests could keep an eye on them. Also, in 1542 the bishop of London issued an admonition to all those who might read the Bible, urging 'discretion, honest intent, charity, reverence, and quiet behaviour' and proclaiming that 'no number of people be especially congregate therefore to make a multitude, and that no exposition be made thereupon otherwise than is declared in the book itself; and that especial regard be had, no reading thereof be used, allowed, and with noise in the time of any divine service or sermon, or that in the same be used any disputation, contention, or any other misdemeanour' (Pollard 1911: 267–8). And in 1543 an Act was passed prohibiting women and the meaner sort from private or public reading of the Bible, and allowing it for the upper classes only under supervised conditions (34 and 35 Henry VIII ch. 1; Walsham 2003: 150).

The same concern to control lay readers, albeit it more subtly, may lie behind the publication of scores of Bible commentaries by Luther, Calvin, and Bullinger, as well as Englishmen like Anthony Gilby, John Udall, Robert F. Herrey, William Perkins, and others; Bible harmonies by Calvin, Hugh Broughton, and James Bentley; the biblical genealogies by John Speed (printed in many King James Bibles); concordances by Coverdale, Bullinger, Clement Cotton, and John Downame (or those appended to many Bibles); and other books like Robert Bruen's *A summary of the Bible wherein the generall heads of the severall bookes thereof are so methodically set downe, as may be a helpe to the unskilfull reader* (1623), John Rogers's *A table of the pryncypal matters conteyned in the Byble, in whyche the readers may find & practyse many commune places* (1549), and Arthur Jackson's *A help for the understanding of the Holy Scripture intended chiefly for the assistance and information of those that use constantly every day to reade some part of the Bible, and would gladly alwayes understand what they read if they had some man to help them* (1643). There were also vast numbers of sermons published throughout the sixteenth and seventeenth centuries, all of which were devoted to explicating biblical texts.

Whatever the motivations of the authors, printers would not have produced these books in such numbers if there had not been a market for them. Clearly, readers craved anything that might help them better understand their Bibles. To what extent, though, did the host of commentators shape the understanding of their readers? English people were now reading the Bible in vast numbers, and even more were hearing it read aloud in English in church. It has been suggested that the efforts by churchmen to control the laity were largely effective, and that most Bible readers were conditioned or programmed with doctrine and orthodox interpretation long before they opened the pages of their own copies (Narveson 2012: 19–50). At least after the first generation of Protestants, children would have grown up listening to sermons and learning the cathechism. Edward Dering's *A shorte catechisme for househoulders* (first printed in 1572 and many times reprinted), for instance, rehearsed the Ten Commandments as well as the meaning of each one. It even offered an interpretation of the Crucifixion narrative in its questions about the Creed, asking what it meant that Christ suffered under Pontius Pilate, or descended into Hell, or that Christ will come to judge the quick and the dead. But for any questions that remained, or that arose during reading, answers were readily available in one interpretive aid or another. For instance, the text of Genesis 4 offers no explanation as to why God accepts Abel's sacrifice and not Cain's, but the Geneva Bible note explained that Cain 'was an hypocrite and offred onely for an outward shew without sinceritie of heart'. A simple reader might be perplexed by James's statement that 'faith, if it have no works, is dead' (James 2:17), since Paul (Galatians 2:6) and all Protestant theologians affirmed that justification is by faith alone. The Geneva note explains that there is no contradiction: 'Paul sheweth the causes of our justification, and James the effects.'

On the other hand, lay readers were fully capable of interpreting the Bible for themselves, despite the careful guidance of church leaders. The most obvious evidence of this is in the proliferation of radical religious ideas during the Civil War period of the 1640s and 1650s, when Lodowicke Muggleton and John Reeve understood themselves to be the two witnesses written of in Revelation 11:3, the Digger Gerard Winstanley took the communism of the early Church (Acts 4–5) literally and put it into practice, and the Ranter Lawrence Clarkson took Paul's 'unto the pure all things are pure' (Titus 1:15) to condone even adultery among the elect (Hill 1975: 315). Critical readers could make their own interpretative decisions, once they had the Bible in their own hands, in their own language: when, during her trial for heresy, Anne Askew was asked by Sir William Paget how she could deny Christ's own statement that 'this is my body' (Matt. 26:26), she listed all the other metaphors Christ had used to describe himself: 'a very dore, a vyne, a lambe, and a stone' (Loewenstein 2013: 96). For thus interpreting the Communion bread metaphorically rather than literally, Askew was burned at the stake. Aemelia Lanyer, in her *Salve deus rex judaeorum*, published in the same year as the King James Bible, offered a radical reinterpretation of both the Fall and the Crucifixion, arguing that both catastrophes were more the fault of men than women. Eve's ignorance is not her own fault, and her motives in taking the forbidden fruit and sharing it with Adam were essentially good:

> Our Mother *Eve*, who tasted of the Tree,
> Giving to *Adam* what she held most deare,
> Was simply good, and had no powre to see,
> The after-comming harme did not appeare. (Lanyer 1993: 84, ll. 763–6)

Lanyer seems to have noticed that the Genesis account does not actually describe God (or Adam) informing Eve of the prohibition on the fruit of the knowledge of good and evil. She also points out that whereas Eve was tempted by the serpent, Adam simply eats the fruit when it is offered to him. As for the Crucifixion story, Pilate condemns Jesus but his wife tries to prevent him. Once again, it is the man who must take the blame. William Wilkinson condemned the allegorical reading of the story of Abraham by Hendrik Niclaes, founder of the Family of Love, which had many adherents in England in the 1570s and after (Wilkinson 1579: sig. Biii^r). Niclaes explained, for instance, that the name of Sara, Abraham's wife, signified 'a Ladie or Princesse which is free', while her servant Hagar signified 'the Service, the Lawe or Ordinaunce, and the serviceable Writing, or Letter of the Beleef of Abraham' (Niclaes 1575: fol. 21^v). Such allegorical interpretation had a powerful precedent, however, in the allegorical interpretation of Sara and Hagar as the spirit and the flesh in Paul's Epistle to the Galatians (Paul is explicit that these 'things are an allegory', Gal. 4:24). Indeed, the very word 'allegory' was introduced into the English language in the Wycliffite translation of Galatians. The English Bible thus encouraged the development of a popular, non-clerical culture of interpretation.

Paraphrase

When does translation become paraphrase? Since all translation involves a measure of interpretation, the distinction cannot be perfectly clear, especially in translations that attempt to create specific formal effects. Most modern readers would describe the metrical versions of the Psalms known as Sternhold and Hopkins as paraphrase. Yet the first complete edition of this psalter advertised that it had been 'conferred with the Hebrew'. Furthermore, in the sixteenth century the view that the original Hebrew Psalms were written in metre was widespread, so a metrical translation might well be considered more rather than less literal than one in prose. Nevertheless, when William Hunnis renders the nineteen verses of Psalm 51 into 160 four-line stanzas, we recognize that we are in the realm of paraphrase; something substantial has surely been added to the original Psalm. Bible readers have always engaged in paraphrase, however, in an effort to clarify and interpret difficult passages; the Jewish tradition of midrash often involves creative paraphrase. Hunnis, for instance, was largely trying to interpret rather than alter Psalm 51, especially by adding material from elsewhere in the Bible that he deemed relevant. Thus when he turns to the verse, 'wash me from my wickedness | and cleanse me from my sin', he inserts lines about the Israelites' attitudes to and practices concerning uncleanness (including swine and menstruation) and Naman being healed of leprosy in 2 Kings 5. These poetic insertions might be considered analogues of the kind of marginal cross-references found in most English Bibles.

Bible paraphrases of all sorts proliferated in the sixteenth and seventeenth centuries. Metrical paraphrases of the Psalms alone were legion: Anne Askew composed a version of Psalm 54, John Bale (who published Askew's) Psalms 130 and 13 (the latter passed off as the work of Elizabeth I), Sir Thomas Wyatt the seven Penitential Psalms (based on a prose paraphrase by Pietro Aretino), the earl of Surrey Psalms 8, 31, 55, and 88, Anne Vaughan Lock Psalm 51 (in sonnets, comprising the first sonnet sequence in English), and Sir Philip Sidney and Mary Sidney Herbert, countess of Pembroke, the entire Psalter. Dozens more poets, accomplished or incompetent, might be added to this list, including John Hall, Archbishop Matthew Parker, George Gascoigne, Richard Stanyhurst, Sir John Harington, Abraham Fraunce, Richard Verstegan, Francis Davison, Phineas Fletcher, Sir Francis Bacon, George Wither, Richard Crashaw, John Donne, George Herbert, Thomas Carew, George Sandys, Sir Thomas Fairfax, Henry Vaughan, and John Milton.

Some of these Psalm versions were written as devotional exercises. Bacon's, for instance, dedicated to George Herbert (1625), were written after a serious illness. Some others were written out of the exigencies of particular circumstances, such as the metrical Psalms written in the Tower of London by Surrey as well as other prisoners like Sir Thomas Smith, and John and Robert Dudley. Some were written to provide godly songs to compete with secular love songs. This seems to have been Thomas Sternhold's original motive, as it was John Hall's, whose Psalms in *The Court of Virtue* (1565) were designed to counter the anonymous and (for the godly) scandalous *Court of Venus* (1555). Some Psalms were written, at least in part, out of what might in retrospect be called literary motives, in order to render the Psalms as English poems matching the qualities understood to exist in the originals. The Sidney Psalms are the preeminent example, in which virtually every Psalm is cast in a different verse form, resulting in one of the most remarkable poetic achievements of the English Renaissance. Gascoigne's Psalm 130 was also self-consciously literary, as were Stanyhurst's four Psalms in Classical quantitative metres, part of his experiment to import the prosody of ancient Greece and Rome into Renaissance England. A number of Psalm poets after the Sidneys followed in their footsteps, including Fraunce, Davison, Donne, Carew, and Milton. Many others followed in the footsteps of Sternhold and Hopkins, trying to produce improved metrical Psalms for singing in English churches: Wither, Henry Dod, Henry Ainsworth, King James I (aided by William Alexander), and the authors of the Scottish Metrical Psalter. It may fairly be said that metrical Psalms were as dominant a component of English Renaissance lyric poetry as Petrarchan love poems, and just as important to the development of English poetry.

The Psalms were the most frequently paraphrased biblical literature, but much of the rest of the Bible was paraphrased as well. The earl of Surrey wrote a metrical version of Ecclesiastes as well as the Psalms, Hunnis a paraphrase of Genesis entitled *A Hive Full of Honey* (1578), and George Sandys paraphrased Job, Ecclesiastes, Lamentations, and the Song of Songs (1638, 1641). Other metrical versions of the Song of Solomon were written by William Baldwin (1549), Jud Smith (1575), Dudley Fenner (1587), Gervase Markham (1596, translated into 'eight Eclogues'), and Robert Aylett (1621). Aylett also wrote paraphrases of Susanna and the Elders (1622), the Joseph story (1623), and *David's troubles remembered* (1638). Ecclesiastes was also turned into verse by Henry Lok (Anne's son) and Francis Quarles (1645), Lamentations by John Donne, Quarles

(*Sion's Elegies*, 1625), and Quarles's son John (*Fons lachrymarum, or, A fountain of tears*, 1658). There were metrical paraphrases of Job by Quarles (1624) and Thomas Manley (1652). Even the book of Acts was paraphrased in verse by the composer Christopher Tye (1553), dedicated, like Sternhold's first Psalms, to Edward VI. Thomas Middleton's metrical paraphrase of the apocryphal Wisdom of Solomon was published in 1597, when he was seventeen. The apocryphal book of Judith was given a French metrical paraphrase by Guillaume de Salluste Du Bartas in 1574, and this epic retelling was translated into English by Thomas Hudson, on the orders of James VI of Scotland (later James I of England), in 1584.

If translation easily slips into paraphrase, paraphrase can broaden into what might be called adaptation, though as with the first pair of terms, the latter is perhaps impossible to distinguish neatly. The most famous English Renaissance biblical adaptation is Milton's *Paradise Lost*, which in part retells the story of Genesis 1–3, considerably expanded, with many additions, alterations, interpolations, and extrapolations, in order to interpret the original and, according to Milton, 'justify the ways of God to men'. Milton's other long poems, *Paradise Regained* and *Samson Agonistes*, are poetic adaptations of Matthew 4:1–11 (with Luke 4:1–13) and Judges 13–16, respectively. Milton had plenty of precedent for his biblical poems, however. The major work of Du Bartas, which influenced Milton as well as many other writers, was *La Sepmaine; ou, Creation du monde* (1578), translated into English by Joshua Sylvester as *Bartas his devine weekes and works* (1605). This was a hexameral epic, an expanded verse retelling of the story of God's six-day Creation in Genesis 1–2. Lady Anne Southwell included an imitation of Du Bartas, 'Gods first weekes worke', in her (unpublished) verse adaptation of and meditations on the Ten Commandments; this was an elaboration upon the fourth commandment, 'Remember the Sabbath day to keepe it holy' (Folger Shakespeare Library MS V.b.198; British Library MS Lansdowne 740; see Klene 1996). Lucy Hutchinson's *Order and disorder, or, The world made and undone, being meditations upon the creation and fall, as it is recorded in the beginning of Genesis* (1679) was another verse adaptation of Genesis in the line of Du Bartas. Like English Bibles (and unlike Sylvester's *Divine Weekes*), the margins of Hutchinson's biblical epic are packed with biblical cross-references. Another precedent for Milton was Abraham Cowley's epic retelling of the story of David from 1 and 2 Samuel in *Davideis*, published in four books (incomplete) in 1656. A different metrical version of the David story had been published by the composer John Merbecke in 1579, and George Peele's verse play *The Love of King David and Fair Bethsabe* was published in 1599. Other adaptations include Thomas Fuller's *David's Hainous Sinne. Heartie Repentance. Heavie Punishment* (1631), Michael Drayton's *David and Goliah* (published in 1630 along with *Noah's Floud* and *Moses, His Birth and Miracles*), Francis Sabie's *David and Bathsheba* (published in 1596 along with *Adam's Compaint*), and Aylett's *David's Troubles Remembered* (1638). John Dryden's thinly veiled satire of Charles II, *Absalom and Achitophel* (1681), is the greatest Restoration adaptation of the David story.

Turning to theatre, Peele's *David and Bethsabe* and Milton's closet drama of *Samson* were not the only plays to adapt biblical stories. Despite the closing down of the mystery cycles after 1579 (the last recorded performance at Chester), biblical plays continued to be popular throughout England. The Reformer John Bale wrote plays about *Johan the baptists preaching*, and *The temptation of Jesus Christ*, and *The chief promises of God*, consisting of dialogues between God and Adam, Noah, Abraham, Moses, David, Isaiah, and John the Baptist, in 1538. Biblical drama was a regular feature of school and university entertainment, such as the plays Thomas Ashton wrote for Shrewsbury School, including *The Passion of Christ* which attracted audiences of ten thousand to twenty thousand in 1569 (White 2004: 109). The English plays *Jacob and Esau* (printed 1568), *Godly queen Hester* (printed 1561), and Thomas Garter's *Susanna* (printed 1578) were performed for private household audiences. The only surviving public theatre plays are Greene's *David and Bethsabe* and Thomas Lodge and Greene's *A looking glass for London* (printed 1594), about Jonah and the fall of Nineveh. But there are records of many biblical plays that have not survived: Greene's *The history or tragedy of Job*, the anonymous *Abraham and Lot* (performed 1593), *Esther and Ahasuerus* (performed 1594), *Nebuchadnezzar* (performed 1596–7), and *Samson*. Philip Henslowe's diary also references payments to Thomas Dekker for work on *Pontius Pilate*, Dekker and Anthony Munday for *Tobias*, William Haughton and Samuel Rowley for *Judas*, and Rowley for *Joshua*. The Admiral's Men at the Rose seem to have specialized in biblical drama (Connolly 2007b). Biblical dramas performed in puppet plays are also on record, including *Jephtha's rash vow* performed at London's Bartholomew Fair, and *The Fall of Jerusalem*, performed in Coventry in 1584, 1605, and 1614. A 1628 puppet play in Oxford featured Adam and Eve in Eden, the Expulsion from Paradise, Cain and Abel, Abraham and Isaac, Nebuchadnezzar and the Fiery Furnace, the Nativity and the Adoration of the Three Kings, the Flight into Egypt and the Slaughter of the Innocents, and the parable of Dives and Lazarus (Rogerson 1998).

Biblical paraphrase was even more common than the huge number of literary adaptations might suggest. Among the volumes required to be purchased and made available in church to anyone who cared to read them were Erasmus's *Paraphrases on the New Testament*. An Injunction of Edward VI in 1546 ordered the *Paraphrases* to be placed conveniently in all parish churches, and Nicholas Udall, author of the play *Ralph Roister Doister*, produced an English translation of the first volume in 1548, assisted by Princess Mary (later Mary I; she translated part of John), Thomas Key, and perhaps others. This work was patronized by the widow of Henry VIII, Catherine Parr. Udall revised a later 1551–2 edition to more strongly reflect Protestant theology and biblical interpretation, changing, for instance, 'penaunce' to 'repentaunce' in Matthew 26:9 (Craig 2002: 318–22). A second volume of *Paraphrases*, translated by Miles Coverdale and John Old, was published in 1549. The leaders of the renewed Catholic Church during Mary's reign made no more attempt to suppress the Paraphrases than they did the Great Bible, and there were renewed efforts in the Elizabethan period to see that the volumes were available in churches. It is difficult to determine how extensively Erasmus's *Paraphrases* were read, but they may well have been read from even in worship services, and it is possible that this was a means by which parishioners came to know and understand the Gospels and Epistles.

Erasmus's New Testament *Paraphrases* were the only ones required to be available in parishes, but there were many other prose paraphrases available to English readers, and some were obviously extremely popular. Bale's *Image of Both Churches*, a paraphrase and commentary on Revelation, went through five editions from 1548, as did Theodore Beza's paraphrases of the Psalms (*The Psalmes of Dauid truely opened and explaned by paraphrasis*), translated into English by Anthony Gilby from 1580 (four editions). George Abbot published a prose paraphrase of Job, 'Made easie for any to understand', in 1640 (a single edition, though his earlier exposition of Jonah went through three), and Henry Hammond *A paraphrase, and annotations upon all the books of the New Testament briefly explaining all the difficult places thereof* in 1653 (twelve editions; Green 2000: appendix 1).

Given the numbers of biblical paraphrases produced, either in prose or verse, how did readers understand the relationship between these works and the original biblical texts? Despite John Dryden's attempt to define a taxonomy of translation, clarifying the distinctions between what he termed metaphrase, paraphrase, and adaptation, earlier writers were not so precise (Hamlin 2004: 8–12). When John Donne praised the Sidney Psalms, for instance, he described them as translations, and it is not clear just how he distinguished the 'Sidneyan Psalms' from David's, both of which were, in Donne's view, inspired by the Holy Spirit. In another case, Matthew Parker, in his preface to the Bishops' Bible, tells the reader that if he doesn't like a particular translation, he should substitute another, or one of his own, the 'truth' of Scripture seeming somehow to exist independently of any actual language (Norton 2000: 35–55). Given that John describes Jesus himself as the Word of God (John 1:1), and that Paul says he is a 'minister of the new testament, not of the letter, but of the spirit' (2 Cor. 3:6), as if the spirit is somehow independent of the letter, it is understandable that for its readers and translators the Bible had a peculiar textual status.

This may also explain the biblical writing which moves beyond even adaptation to what has been called writing 'in Scripture phrase' or in broader imitation of biblical language and style (Narveson 2012; Felch 2011). Given the popularity of writing metrical versions of the Psalms as a devotional exercise, it is no surprise that writers began to create their own 'Psalms' either by stringing together a pastiche of biblical quotations or by writing their own text using biblical words and idioms. *Petrarch's Seven Penitential Psalms* (1612), for instance, are not biblical at all, but an English translation by George Chapman of original Latin 'Psalms' written by Petrarch in a recognizably biblical style (with the actual seven Penitential Psalms the primary model):

> O me wretch, I have enrag'd
> My Redeemer; and engag'd
>   My life, on death's slow foot presuming:
> I have broke his blessed laws,
> Turning with accursed cause,
>   Saving love to wrath consuming.
>
> (Chapman 1612: 1)

Similarly, Ralph Buckland's *Seven Sparks of the Enkindled Soul* (1604–5) are entirely original compositions, though they mimic brilliantly the diction and parallelism of Coverdale's English translation of the Psalms. Many ordinary English men and women produced, sometimes for publication but more often for their own devotions, prayers and meditations in a biblical style.

The Book of Common Prayer itself provided a model for this practice, as in the General Confession, which would have been recited at least once a week by almost every man, woman, and child in England:

> Almighty and most merciful Father, we have erred and strayed from thy ways, like lost sheep. We have followed too much the devices and desires of our own hearts. We have offended against thy holy laws. We have left undone those things which we ought to have done, and we have done those things which we ought not to have done, and there is no health in us: but thou, O Lord, have mercy upon us miserable offenders. Spare thou them, O God, who confess their faults. Restore thou them that be penitent, according to thy promises declared unto mankind, in Christ Jesu our Lord. And grant, O most merciful Father, for his sake, that we may hereafter live a godly, righteous, and sober life, to the glory of thy holy Name. Amen. (*Book of Common Prayer*, 103–4, slightly modernized)

The kernel of this prayer is Romans 7:15, 'For that which I do, I allow not: for what I would, that do I not, but what I hate, that do I.' But it is freely adapted from and surrounded by other biblical and biblical-seeming language: from Psalm 119:176 ('I have gone astray like a lost sheep'), James 5:16 ('Confess your faults to one another'), and Titus 2:12 ('denying ungodliness and worldly lusts, we should live soberly, righteously, and godly, in this present world'). Also, the words 'erred', 'devices', 'desires', and 'miserable' are common in the English Bible, as are prayers and petitions for mercy and restoration. Biblical style can also be parodied, of course, as Ben Jonson does in the mouth of his hypocritical Puritan, Zeal-of-the-land Busy, who when asked if eating pork at Bartholomew Fair is lawful, responds:

> Surely, it may be otherwise, but it is subject to construction, subject, and hath a face of offence with the weak, a great face, a foul face, but that face may have a veil put over it, and be shadowed as it were; it may be eaten, and in the *Fair*, I take it, in a booth, the tents of the wicked. The place is not much, not very much; we may be religious in midst of the profane, so it be eaten with a reformed mouth, with sobriety, and humbleness; not gorged in with gluttony, or greediness; there's the fear; for, should she go there, as taking pride in the place, or delight in the unclean dressing, to feed the vanity of the eye, or the lust of the palate, it were not well, it were not fit, it were abominable, and not good. (Jonson 1977: *Bartholomew Fair*, 1.6.62–73)

Here, Jonson draws on several specific passages: 'lust of the eyes' (1 John 2:16) and 'Depart, I pray you, from the tents of these wicked men' (Numbers 16:26), as well as words like 'vanity', 'sobriety', and 'unclean' which are recognizably biblical. Given the name of his character, Jonson may even have in mind John 2:17, 'The zeal of thine house hath eaten me up.'

LITERATURE

The Bible shaped English literature, but was the Bible itself literature? In some ways, this is an anachronistic question, depending upon a distinctly post-Romantic definition of 'literature', in which the term implies standards of quality, aesthetic superiority, artistic intention, and a distinction from more mundane and uninspired sorts of writing. In the past several decades, there has been an attempt to redefine 'literature' to include kinds of writing excluded in the earlier twentieth century: sermons, for instance, devotional texts, essays, diaries, journals, and letters. If letters are included in the definition (as its etymology and most of the *OED* definitions would suggest), then surely Paul's letters are as literary as anybody else's. If the prophetic prose-poems of William Blake and Walt Whitman are literature, why not Isaiah, Daniel, and the Revelation of St John? The literariness of the so-called poetical books (Psalms, the Song of Solomon, Ecclesiastes, etc.) seems easiest to accept, because these most resemble literary forms and modes with which modern readers are familiar. Narratives like the stories of Saul and David, the Gospels, and Paul's adventures in Acts were analogous to any other stories of the rise and fall of kings (like those in *The Mirror for Magistrates*), biographies, saints' lives, or the journeys of Romance. Everyone in the Renaissance would have understood the Bible to be literature (though they would not have used this word), in the sense that the many biblical books demonstrate—in a preeminent style, it would have been argued—literary forms, genres, and modes. Milton was simply restating received wisdom dating back at least to Jerome when he praised biblical songs as greater even than the poems of Pindar and Callimachus, 'not in their divine argument alone, but in the very critical art of composition' (Hamlin 2004: 86).

C. S. Lewis, weighing in on the debates about the literary value of the King James Bible as compared to the New English Bible (in 1950), asserted that in a certain sense, ' "the Bible as literature" does not exist', that 'you can read it as literature only by a *tour de force*' (Lewis 1963: 4 and 33). Lewis's real objection, as a Christian, was to those would read the Bible *only* as literature, given that it was intended principally as Holy Scripture. Nevertheless, non-religious readers today do derive pleasure from reading or hearing at least certain portions of the Bible (perhaps not Leviticus or the Epistle to Philemon). Furthermore, Lewis creates a false dichotomy, since it is clear that for Renaissance Christians, reading the Bible as literature and appreciating its many aesthetic qualities did not impinge upon their belief in its sacred value and its importance as a guide to life. One might make a similar argument about the vast body of Renaissance religious writing that the Bible inspired. The poems of Robert Southwell, George Herbert, and

Thomas Traherne are primarily religious works, meditating upon biblical and theo-logical problems. That they are also beautiful, artful, aesthetically and emotionally powerful was of perhaps secondary importance to the poets and their first readers, but it was important nevertheless. So, for Herbert, the Bible was 'infinite sweetness' as well as absolute truth, and for Donne there was 'an infinite sweetness … in every Metaphor, in every elegancy of the Scripture' (Herbert 2007: 45–6; Donne 1955: 130).

CHAPTER 34

....

AUTHORITY, RELIGION, AND THE STATE

....

TIMOTHY ROSENDALE

THE first of Shakespeare's *Henry VI* plays begins at the funeral of Henry V, the monarch towards whom his history plays of the 1590s will drive. There, the uncles of the child-king Henry VI quarrel over the relative authorities of church and state. When the bishop of Winchester asserts that 'the Church's prayers made [Henry V] so prosperous', the duke of Gloucester (and Lord Protector) snorts derisively:

> The Church? Where is it? Had not churchmen prayed,
> His thread of life had not so soon decayed.
> None do you like but an effeminate prince,
> Whom like a schoolboy you may overawe. (1.1.32–6)

Having thus articulated a basically oppositional view of church–state relations, Gloucester a few scenes later threatens the bishop that 'In spite of Pope, or dignities of church, | Here by the cheeks I'll drag thee up and down' and Winchester responds that 'thou wilt answer this before the Pope' (1.3.50–2). The play presents us, in short, with a world of medieval contention between domestic secular authority on the one hand, and largely foreign religious authority on the other. These conflicts climax in *King John* (1595?), a play that airs the sixteenth-century rehabilitation of John into a heroic defier of corrupt Roman Catholic authority, and has him utter strikingly violent denunciations of it:

> no Italian priest
> Shall tithe or toll in our dominions;
> But as we, under [God], are supreme head,
> So under Him that great supremacy,
> Where we do reign, we will alone uphold,
> Without th' assistance of a mortal hand:
> So tell the pope, all reverence set apart
> To him and his usurp'd authority. (3.1.153–60)

These jurisdictional declarations, combined with more specifically doctrinal references to the 'slight, unworthy, and ridiculous' (150) Pope's 'corrupted pardon' (166) and 'juggling witchcraft' (169), have less to do with the thirteenth century than with the sixteenth in their contentiously wholesale rejection of Roman authority. And remarkably, in the Lancastrian plays that follow them, these conflicts evaporate: while Richard II, Henry IV, and Henry V face many challenges, none of those challenges issue from specifically Roman spiritual authority. Lancastrian-tetralogy clergymen are either aligned with (and subordinated to) their monarch, or they are defeated and discredited, but none of them so much as mentions the historically Roman and papal origins of their authority.[1] When we thus consider Shakespeare's 1590s history plays in their likely compositional order, we can see that the anachronistic proto-Reformation of *King John* enacts a dramatic reformation of its own by separating an essentially medieval world in the Yorkist plays from an essentially post-Reformation world in the Lancastrian plays, where church–state conflict has been domesticated and largely resolved in favour of the Crown.

This might be usefully regarded as a very compact rendition of the history and prehistory of early modern authority. The relation of secular and religious authority was directly addressed by Christ when he instructed his followers to 'render to Caesar the things that are Caesar's, and to God the things that are God's' (Mark 12:17, *KJV*). However, the apparent clarity of this dictum has historically proven difficult to implement, perhaps in part because Jesus did not clearly define his own terms. What exactly is Caesar's, and what God's? Does anything not ultimately belong to God? Conversely, if humans have both spiritual and temporal existence, is anything a social human body does not under the oversight of the secular ruler? What, if any, are that ruler's responsibilities to his subjects' spiritual selves? Does the temporal estate prevail over the spiritual estate in this world, or vice versa? Things are further complicated by Christ's potentially contradictory pronouncements that 'my kingdom is not of this world' (John 18:36) and 'the kingdom of God is within you' (Luke 17:21). So is the kingdom here, or not, and if it is, what is its relation to the secular? Augustine in his *Civitate Dei* saw the kingdom as both here and not quite. Between the Fall and the eschaton—that is, in history—the City of God is dispersed and intermixed with the City of Man, one characterized by its love of God, the other by its love of self and earthly things. The citizens of each are neighbours, not enemies, because as humans and social beings all they have shared interests. For this reason, the godly are to 'obey the laws of the earthly city, whereby the things necessary for the maintenance of this mortal life are administered; and thus, as this life is common to both cities, so there is a harmony between them in regard to what belongs to it' (XIX, 17). The two cities can coexist civilly, even though their ultimate natures and aims,

---

[1] In the Yorkist plays, the word *pope* is used six times, the word *Rome* three (and mostly contentious varieties of *priest* a remarkable fifteen times). In *King John*, where the claims of papal Rome come briefly but intensely under scrutiny, the word *pope* appears ten times (even more than in *Henry VIII*!), the word *Rome* ten times. But in all four Lancastrian plays, *Rome* appears only twice, and both references are to classical and not medieval papal Rome; *pope* appears not at all. This is much less likely to be a coincidence than a shift in Shakespeare's thinking.

distinguished not institutionally or jurisdictionally but by the orientation of their love, still differed radically.

In a hardened and politicized jurisdictional form, this relationship developed contentiously in the middle ages. By the eleventh century, the Church felt sufficiently confident to assert a very high view of its own authority. The Gregorian Reforms insisted on a hierarchy of spiritual over temporal authority, and specifically a papal supremacy to which secular rulers were required to bow. (The implicit assumption here, of course, is that the Pope is always the legitimate leader of the City of God, which secular rulers could thus either obey or oppose.) The scene at Canossa in 1077, with the Holy Roman Emperor prostrating himself in the snow while Gregory VII waited him out, is a famous tableau of this dynamic—though the fact that Henry IV may have been enabling a longer-term victory for himself and other secular rulers indicates just how fluid and tricky these relations really were.[2] Nevertheless, this hierarchical model is, in a characteristically moderated form, more or less the view of Aquinas, who wrote in *De regno* that 'to [the Pope] all the kings of the Christian people are to be subject as to our Lord Jesus Christ himself' (O'Donovan and O'Donovan 1999: 339). The theme was powerfully (if, again, contingently and for political ends) reiterated in the 1302 papal bull *Unam sanctam*, which flatly asserted that there was neither forgiveness nor salvation outside the Church, that submission to the Pope was absolutely necessary for every human creature, and that the temporal sword of secular authority was decisively subject to the spiritual authority of the Church.

These kinds of high-medieval pronouncements ring with the expansive swagger of an institution nearing the apex of its extraordinary power and authority. But they were not unanimously agreed upon. They were often made as tactical moves in highly fraught struggles with secular authorities for the upper hand, and these struggles included potent theological and philosophical arguments against the papal supremacy and the dominion of the church in worldly matters. The fourteenth century in particular generated multiple lines of argument from formidable figures, including William of Ockham, Marsilius of Padua, and John Wycliffe—all of whom were, unsurprisingly, condemned by the Church. Such writers, often under imperial protection, attacked the wealth and temporal power of the Church and the *plenitudo potestatis* claimed by the papacy, and variously argued that secular and ecclesiastical authority were largely distinct from one another; that the Church should exist, in Wycliffe's term, 'exproprietarily', without temporal wealth or power, so as to focus on its true duties of spiritual care; that since all power comes from God, Christian secular rulers are justly empowered to oversee all civil and temporal affairs, even the staffing and administration of churches within their realms; that the sword of coercive power belongs to the civil authority, not the spiritualty; that internally, the Church is not a monarchy, but more properly ruled by the aggregate judgement of general councils.[3] The Great Schism that began in 1378 further

---

[2] This was part of the protracted Investiture Controversy over whether episcopal appointments were the prerogative of secular rulers or the Church.

[3] For good, compact introductions to this history, see Skinner 1978: 20–64, 113–23; O'Donovan 2004: 11–42; Gregory 2012: 133–45; Evans 1992: 199–215 and 231–8; O'Donovan and O'Donovan 1999: *passim*.

exacerbated matters for the Church by visibly undermining its claims of unified truth and authority, and was only resolved by the Council of Constance, furthering intra-Church contention over whether ultimate authority resided with councils or popes. Secular rulers took advantage of the opportunity, and while they did not typically contest the doctrines or worship of the Church, they did assert considerable control over its administration within their realms. According to Brad Gregory, by the eve of the Reformation they had 'to a large extent regained the control over the church that had been wrested from their predecessors by the clerical authorities who devised and implemented the Gregorian reforms' since the eleventh century (Gregory 2012: 143). 'As it happened,' he observes, 'the pendulum would never swing back again.'

Thus, when Martin Luther's reformist critique of the Roman Catholic Church radicalized into outright rejection of it, he did not have to start from scratch. While he and his followers were undoubtedly indebted to their medieval precursors, however, Luther's own political views devolved more immediately from his radical rethinking of sin, grace, and the Church. His deep embrace of a thoroughly Augustinian notion of pervasive sin—and the correspondingly total need of each human for the arbitrary, undeserved, and radically transformative gift of saving grace—implied a direct one-on-one relationship with God, fundamentally mediated only by the Bible (as God's textual self-revelation) and the Holy Spirit. Consequently, Luther came to see the institutional practices of the Roman Catholic Church as not only beside the point, but deeply corrupt in ways that misled souls to eternal perdition. He argued that the true Church is not a specialized clerical estate, or the collective body of those who bow to the Pope and remain in his good graces; it is simply the *congregatio fidelium*, a 'priesthood of all believers' who understand that they cannot be saved by anything that they, or another sinner, or institution can do, but only by God's mysterious, sacrificial love. This has at least three important consequences: it asserts the competence and status of each individual believer, regardless of social or political rank, as a soul in direct relationship to God (this is why Luther promoted widespread vernacular Bible-reading); it demolishes the mediatory necessity and institutional authority of the Church; and it transfers the Church's usurped jurisdictional powers and temporal possessions back to the secular rulers to whom they rightly belong.[4] As Quentin Skinner puts it:

> For Luther, this means that the tremendous theoretical battle waged throughout the Middle Ages by the protagonists of the *regnum* and the *sacerdotium* is suddenly brought to an end. The idea of the Pope and Emperor as parallel and universal powers disappears, and the independent jurisdictions of the *sacerdotium* are handed over to the secular authorities. (II.15)

---

[4] The first of these caused some antinomian trouble early on, particularly in the catastrophic Peasants' Revolt of 1524–5. Luther's response was to emphasize even more strongly the necessity of civil power to maintain sociopolitical order and enable the growth of spiritual truth.

This colossal transfer of authority to secular states is generally seen as Luther's chief political legacy. Rulers like Henry VIII used the new possibility of defection to either justify their abandonment of the Church (and concomitant appropriation of its powers and possessions for themselves), or to leverage themselves into a more advantageous relationship with it, thus changing church–state relations permanently. This was visible in the progress of the English Reformation even before Henry was consciously on board.

William Tyndale's 1528 *Obedience of a Christian Man*—of which the otherwise unsympathetic Henry famously said 'this is a book for me and all kings to read'—unfolded these basic Lutheran principles into a polemically antipapal vision of Protestant society that is almost obsessive in its insistence on order and obedience, from household to state to one's encounters with the vernacular Scripture for which Tyndale would give his life. You must not obey the Pope, he argues, but you certainly must obey the king and everyone above you in the sociopolitical order. He outlines the proper 'obedience of children, servants, wives, and subjects' to the authority of parents, masters, husbands, and rulers, argues for their clear articulation in the revealed Word of God, and contends that 'all bodily service must be done to man in God's stead' (Tyndale 2000: 180–1). Those subjected bodies, crucially, include the clergy, which Tyndale insists are without exception under the authority of the king. 'Neither can the profession of monks or friars or anything that the Pope or bishops can lay for themselves, except them from the sword of the Emperor or kings, if they break the laws. For it is written, let every soul submit himself unto the authority of the higher powers' (40). Neither Peter, nor the other apostles, nor Christ himself were outside the jurisdiction of the temporal sword (49); the Church's only power and purpose is to proclaim God's law and gospel, and for Tyndale the exceeding of this mission is one of the visible marks of Antichrist.

The same proto-erastian logic of secular authority over churches is apparent, albeit in more measured legal terms, in the extraordinary Cromwellian legislative agenda of the 1530s, which asserted this new jurisdictional dispensation and dismantled papal authority in England piece by piece. In 1532 the English clergy submitted its canon-making authority to the approval of Henry VIII, and Parliament conditionally ended the payment of first fruits to the Pope (and made domestic provisions in case of retaliation). The 1533 Act in Restraint of Appeals famously declared that 'this realm of England is an empire … governed by one supreme head and king … with plenary, whole, and entire power, preeminence, authority, prerogative, and jurisdiction, to render and yield justice … without restraint, or provocation to any foreign princes or potentates of the world'; on the strength of these assertions, it forbade any legal appeals to foreign authority. The 1534 Ecclesiastical Appointments Act declared that episcopal nominations and appointments were the king's prerogative, and were not to be referred to Rome. In the same year, the Act of Succession did for Henry what the Pope would not: it invalidated his marriage to (and child with) Katherine of Aragon, and declared Anne Boleyn and her child the rightful queen and heir to the throne; those who resisted the act—like More and Fisher, who recognized its profound import—would suffer the penalties of high treason. The Convocation of Canterbury abjured the papal supremacy by a vote of 34–4. And in November, the Act of Supremacy epitomized what had been implicit in the previous legislation, declaring that the English monarch was 'the only supreme head in earth of the Church of England', absolutely authorized to reform and administer that church as he saw fit and without interference (all found in Gee and Hardy 1896).

These principles are anachronistically dear to the thirteenth-century protagonist of John Bale's 1538 play *King Johan*, a fascinating mix of religious and political polemic, allegory, history play, and morality play—and one of the earliest English manifestations of Protestant political theology in literary form. Here, the character of 'Usurped Power' is the Pope's alter ego, and Stephen Langton is not just a disputed archepiscopal nominee; he is, we learn, Sedition itself, the living emblem of upended order which Bale's heroic John must rectify. As he scolds his misbehaving clergy:

> Whan kynges correcte yow for yowr actes most vngodly,
> To [th]e pope, syttyng in the chayer of pestelens,
> Ye ronne, to remayne in yowr concupysens.
> Thus sett ye at nowght all princely prehemynens,
> Subdewying [th]e ordere of dew obedyens.
> But with in a whyle I shall so abate yowr pryde
> That to your popet ye shall noyther runne nor ryde;
> But ye shall be glad to seke to me, yowr prynce,
> For all such maters as shall be with in this provynce,
> Lyke as God wyllyth yow by his scripture evydente. (ll. 349–58)

This John is not a tyrant or craven schemer like Shakespeare's but a straightforwardly 'faythfull Moyses' standing up to Pharaoh, a prefiguration of the unmistakably Henrician character of 'Imperial Majesty' who sets all aright and reorders the kingdom after John's death in the second act. What John had abortively begun, Henry triumphantly completes three centuries later.

One piece of the evidence for the dating of *King Johan* is a document sent on 11 January 1539 (Cranmer 1846: 388) to Thomas Cromwell (chief minister to Henry VIII and the architect of the legislative Reformation in England) by Archbishop of Canterbury Thomas Cranmer (its theological and ecclesiastical supervisor), which describes a performance of a play that sounds very much like Bale's. The archbishop was himself an immensely influential writer, having composed, among many other things, the first Book of Common Prayer (1549; henceforth also referenced as BCP or Prayerbook). This text, the first full English liturgy, while put forth by the church, was authorized and enforced by the parliamentary Act of Uniformity, which under fairly stiff penalties banned other forms of worship and required all English subjects to use the BCP. Its status as a state-authorized, nationally uniform, coercively enforced text, woven into the fabric of an autonomous nation from sea to sea and from dawn to dark, radically amplified the inclination toward hierarchical order virtually always implicit in liturgy. As a prescriptive form for collective worship, liturgy tells people what to say, when to be quiet, when to stand, when to kneel, and so forth. To engage in such worship is to agree to the specific regimentation and ordering of that experience, and by implication to endorse the authority that does so. And in the case of the Prayerbook, this was a legal and sociopolitical as well as a religious obligation, both Protestant in theology and *English* in its language and politics. Much as the Bible was the master text of

Protestantism, this new liturgy was the textual emblem of what this theology would look and sound like in all English churches. The English Bible, as we shall see, was a text of revolutionary and indeed anarchic potential; the Prayerbook was a countervailing text of coercive community and sociopolitical order, a powerful assertion of the godly secular ruler's regimenting control over his subjects and his realm at worship.[5]

The relative speed and completeness with which the church–state jurisdictional question was resolved in England—it is telling that even the Marian resubmission to Rome hinged on royal and parliamentary action—might suggest that the authority problem had been largely put to bed. However, this is not so. When one looks closely at how that resolution was effected, it becomes apparent that it contained the seeds of its own eventual failure, and this may suggest that, as massive and important as the issue of church–state jurisdiction was, it may have been an epiphenomenon of even larger and deeper shifts in the structure of authority. The terms in which the de-authorization of Roman Catholicism was accomplished—not only a transfer of its jurisdictional authority to secular rulers, but also a rejection of institutional authority over the meaning of the biblical text, and a turn from tradition to individual reading as the mechanism by which that meaning would be determined—suggest in hindsight that the first could not stand alone, or for long.

It was recognized very early in the Reformation that the relatively new technology of print would be crucial to its success, and Luther's knack for exploiting it was crucial to this.[6] The mass-scale dissemination made possible by print exceeded the traditional forms of control, and made previously restricted critiques and debates—not to mention the vernacular Word of God, the effects of which can hardly be exaggerated—available to an increasingly wider and more literate public. Foxe, whose *Acts & Monuments* contains multiple gleeful accounts of the Protestant-friendly implications of print, saw the combination of divine providence, the emerging print market, and the Protestant will to read as the handwriting on the papal wall:

> hereby tongues are knowne, knowledge groweth, iudgemēt increaseth, books are dispersed, the Scripture is seene, the Doctours be read, stories be opened, times compared, truth decerned, falshod detected, and with finger poynted, and all (as I sayd) thorough the benefite of printing. Wherfore I suppose that eyther the pope must abolish printing, or he must seek a new world to raygne ouer: for els, as this world standeth, printing doubtles will abolish hym. But the pope, and all hys Colledge of

---

[5] For much more on this, see Rosendale 2007, especially ch. 1.

[6] While modern scholars disagree somewhat on the nature and extent of this correlation—see especially Gilmont's skeptical essay (in Cavallo and Chartier 1999), which seeks to question and qualify multiple axioms—there is wide agreement that there is something significantly true about it. See Pettegree 2010, chs 5, 6, 10; Eisenstein 2005, esp. ch. 6 and the feistily updating Afterword; Green 2000; Johns 1998; Febvre and Martin 1997: esp. 287–319; and the essays by Kastan, Mueller, and Collinson in CHEMEL. Cummings's magisterial book contends that 'not only the spread of protestantism, but its identity, is constituted by the exigencies of textual revolution' (6)—but also that Erasmus's Greek New Testament had already 'announced a new religion based on literature' (102).

Cardinals, must this vnderstãd, that through the light of printing, the worlde begin-
neth nowe to haue eyes to see, and heades to iudge.[7]

With the dissemination of texts and ideas came a wider distribution of the individual
authority to read, consider, judge, discuss. Robert Weimann perceptively contends that
'a new construction of the self emerged through the interiorization and privatization of
meaning' and that 'early modern uses of representation were unthinkable without the
growth in Protestant debate and interpretation; they went hand in hand with the gradual spread of literacy, nourished by the increased circulation of printed vernacular texts'.
A major consequence of this dynamic was that authority's relationship to discourse itself
changed: rather than being the authorizing precondition of discourse, authority became
discourse's consequence or product, and 'more and more people found themselves
involved in deliberations based on their responses to argumentative discourse … having to judge for themselves what was true and false, the 'correct' and 'incorrect' meaning
of Scripture' (Weimann 1996: 4, 11, 5, 56). Weimann's model compellingly suggests why
the jurisdictional triumph of kings over popes was only the beginning of profound early
modern shifts in the nature and location of authority.

If we return to Tyndale's *Obedience*, for example, it is quite clear that, while he certainly wanted the monarch to prevail over the Roman Antichrist, there is even more at
stake: the faultlines of authority do not simply run between crown and mitre. Tyndale is
best known as the seminal translator of the Bible into English, so it may be unsurprising that in addition to its interests in sociopolitical submission, a substantial amount of
the *Obedience* is dedicated to *textual* obedience to the Word of God, and this is crucially
a matter of interpretive method. He provokingly asserts that 'the greatest cause of this
captivity and the decay of the faith and this blindness wherein we now are, sprang first
of allegories' (160)—not their textual existence, but their hermeneutic overextension in
Catholic allegoresis. This began with Origen, and over time the scaffolding of allegorical
(and tropological and anagogical, or, as Tyndale lumps them all together, 'chopological')
readings of Scripture grew so thick that the Bible's core truths became entirely obscured.
The remedy to this problem, Tyndale argues, is for Christians to resubmit to the authority of the text itself, and this is the point of his famous pronouncement that 'the scripture
hath but one sense which is the literal sense' (156).

This claim has often been misunderstood as a statement of naively blinkered literalism, but Tyndale is much smarter and more complex than that. He readily admits that
the Bible 'useth proverbs, similitudes, riddles or allegories as all other speeches do' and
that these must be read accordingly for their instructive value to be realized. However,
these figural passages cannot prove anything; they can only illuminate and exemplify
what the Bible enunciates clearly elsewhere. Their validity requires internal corroboration, for 'the scripture giveth record to himself and ever expoundeth itself by another
text' (172), and 'thus doth the literal sense prove the allegory and bear it, as the foundation beareth the house' (159). Tyndale's 'literal sense' then, far from being a crudely

---

[7] http://www.johnfoxe.org/index.php?realm=text&edition=1583&pageid=731&gototype=modern.

mechanical hermeneutic, means something more like 'clear, consistent, and internally validated'. This enables him to embrace the multidimensional complexity of the Bible while anchoring it in its own textual facts and submitting all to the authority of God's linguistic self-revelation. This confidence in the authority and accessibility of Scripture is a central characteristic of Protestantism, which did away with the binding interpretive authorities of Catholic hierarchy and tradition that had historically defined the meaning of Scripture in relatively stable and unified ways. With those discarded, what can prevent interpretive chaos, and what kind of authority might restabilize truth? An intensified emphasis on the biblical text itself as, if not entirely literal or self-explicating, at least consistent and readily understood.

Of course, no complex text, and certainly not one as large and intricate as the Bible, is really self-explicating.[8] In the absence of externally authoritative interpretations, that work is inevitably done by individual readers, and this too plays an important role in Tyndale's schema of authority. 'If any man thirst for the truth,' he says, 'and read the scripture by himself desiring God to open the door of knowledge unto him, God for his truth's sake will and must teach him' (21–2). And this produces a vigorously critical, independent, even anti-authoritarian kind of reading that sets itself against manipulation by external authority:[9]

> Why shall I not see the scripture and the circumstances and what goeth before and after, that I may know whether thine interpretation be the right sense, or whether thou jugglest and drawest the scripture violently unto thy carnal and fleshly purpose? Or whether thou be about to teach me or to deceive me? (17)

Tyndale advocates obedience to the text, but not to other readers; this is the opposite of passive acceptance. While one might of course for whatever reason find another person's interpretation persuasive, the logic of Protestantism works against uncritical interpretive submission to tradition or institution or even a Luther or a Calvin (though whether this was consistently upheld in practice is another matter).[10] The final arbiter is

[8] See G. R. Evans's discussion (1992: ch. 1) of how the inquiries of humanist scholarship and the resulting decline in the authority of the Vulgate had raised acute questions about the text, translation, and interpretation of the Bible. She observes that 'it is a supreme irony that it was at the time when *Scriptura sola* became a reforming slogan that it became unprecedentedly difficult to point unequivocally to the Sacred Page and say, "That is Holy Scripture"' (56)—let alone know how to read it correctly. Nonetheless, as Pelikan (1984: IV, 9) observes, these textual questions 'acted as a catalyst in the reconsideration of the doctrine of authority during the age of the Reformation'. See also Cummings 2002: 190–206, for a fascinating discussion of translation, exegesis, and grammar issues in Tyndale and More.

[9] The Homily Against Disobedience and Wilful Rebellion (548–61), to give just one example, cites the cases of King John and Pope Gregory VII as instances of Roman usurpation made possible by keeping the Bible out of the hands of the common people, who surely would not have stood for such things if they had known better.

[10] Tyndale applies this principle even to himself. He closes his Prologue by encouraging his readers to 'when I allege any Scripture, look thou on the text, whether I interpret it right' (30). Gilmont notes (219–37 in Cavallo and Chartier 1999) the resistance of major reformers to utterly free reading, and their attempts to restrain and direct it, but concedes that Protestants 'were none the less invited to read'.

the Bible-reading, Spirit-guided individual. Thomas More found this utterly appalling, and argued in his 1529 *Dialogue Concerning Heresies* that it was absurd and dangerous to think that each person's interpretation could trump sixteen centuries of accumulated expertise and consensus. After his Protestant speaker declares himself wholly unobligated to accept the Church's reading of a biblical passage against his own, More's Catholic character responds indignantly that 'where as god wolde the chyrche sholde be your iudge | ye wolde nowe be iudge over the chyrche ... moche meruayle were it yf ye shold in holy scripture se better than the olde holy doctors and Crystes hole chyrche' (More 1981b: 169).[11] Despite More's humanist commitment to the value of reading good texts—to say nothing of the civil ecumenicism of his Utopia!—the radically authorized Protestant reader presented an unacceptable threat to the history and truth of Christianity, as well as to the institutional authority of the Church and in turn to the stability of Christian society.[12] For him, both reason and faith required aligning one's opinion with the historical and consensual truths of Catholicism, not the ahistorical solipsism of private reading.

Thus, very early in the English Reformation, and even as the church–state jurisdictional conflict was being worked out, we can see an even deeper and more fundamental fracture in the very grounds of authority itself. Catholics generally tended to conceive of authority in terms of submission, tradition, mediation, institution, history, hegemony, consensus, received truth; Protestants reconceived it in terms of dispersion, personal textual engagement with the primary source, interpretive assertion, private judgement, and individually determined truth in the present. The Reformation sought to radically de-authorize Catholicism, and while it relocated the jurisdictional aspects of that authority in the state, in some respects the more important moves were its decoupling of the biblical text from its institutional mediation and interpretive history, and its exposure of the text to self-authorizing individual readers. One might say generally that the Reformation trifurcated the authority of Roman Catholicism into three parcels: its jurisdictional claims were handed over to secular rulers, its institutional truth claims were recentred in the Bible, and its interpretive authority was distributed finally (if somewhat anxiously) among readers.[13]

---

[11] Pelikan notes (1984: IV, 125 and 263) Augustine's influential statement that 'I should not believe the gospel except as moved by the authority of the catholic church', but even this was subject to interpretive appropriation: Catholics tended to read it as a broad assertion of the Church's interpretive authority over the meaning of the biblical text, while Protestants limited Augustine's claim to canon formation.

[12] Henry himself recognized this near the end of his life, when he lamented to Parliament in 1545 that the English Bible he had made available was being 'disputed, rymed, song and jangeled in every Alehouse and Taverne, contrary to the true meaninge and doctrine of the same' (qtd. in Weimann 1987: 120; also reported in Foxe, Book 8, p. 1258 [http://www.johnfoxe.org/index.php?gotopage=1258&realm=text&edition=1583&gototype=modern&x=0&y=0]).

[13] The Bible also established the limits of other forms of authority. While its form and meaning were of course subject to dispute, the Thirty-Nine Articles take some care to assert that the Bible circumscribes the authority of the Church (20), general councils (21), and civil power (37).

We might usefully return to the Book of Common Prayer as a textual emblem, if an imperfect one, of a fleeting equipoise among these three elements.[14] It was authorized and nationally enforced by the monarchal state and its church, and served its interests in regulated order; it deferred constantly to Scripture, and was in large measure a vehicle for its structured reading and expounding in worship; and it recognized and affirmed in far-reaching ways the enhanced authority of the individuals that would engage in it. As I have argued elsewhere (Rosendale 2001 and 2007), the translation of worship into English made possible—indeed, demanded—new forms of individual involvement and comprehension that had been difficult or impossible in pre-vernacular Catholic worship. The Prayerbook's Protestant (if ambiguous and inconsistent) reconception of the Eucharistic elements as some kind of special signifiers, rather than Christ's actual body and blood, recast the sacrament as a complexly interpretive event, the effectiveness *and meaning* of which depended to a considerable degree on the understanding of each individual participant. Linguistically, scripturally, sacramentally, and interpretively, the BCP, for all the vertical power relations inscribed in its very existence and form, offered dehierarchizing access and authority to all who worshipped under its auspices.

Though the great majority conformed as church and state required, not many people were fully pleased with the 1549 Prayerbook. Religious conservatives found it dangerously progressive if not heretical, and resisted its use, even to the point of armed rebellion in the southwest; religious progressives found it redolent of papistry, and immediately pressured for a more thoroughly Reformed liturgy (which they got in 1552, to the pleasure of even fewer). And this points up a pressure in the tripartite system I have been describing: it works just fine if people feel their monarch to be governing in appropriately godly ways, but what if they do not? What is a self-authorized, Bible-reading subject to do if their ruler is a tyrant, or a heretic? Luther and Calvin, both deeply interested in minimizing the anarchic possibilities of Protestantism, both taught emphatically the biblical mandate (most clearly laid out in Romans 13) of submission to rulers, who are after all put in power by God to rule sinners. No, one should not follow ungodly directives, but neither should one resist divinely ordained authority; the Christian should follow God's law and suffer the consequences of the monarch's.[15] However, when Mary Tudor came to power, undid the Reformation, resubmitted England to Rome, married the king of Spain, and began burning Protestants, these questions became much more acute. Hundreds of exiles fled England for Protestant cities on the continent, and there they were more free to rethink

---

[14] Another such textual moment arrives eight decades later in George Herbert's *The Temple*, a poetic collection that celebrates the Bible, the liturgy, and the Church of England, and sees its own narrative as the submission of the individual will to God—but that is also at its most searching and powerful when the first-person lyric voice speaks directly to and with God.

[15] The classic Protestant statement of this tension is Luther's *Freedom of a Christian* (1520), with its paradoxical thesis that 'A Christian is a perfectly free lord of all, subject to none. A Christian is a perfectly dutiful servant of all, subject to all'. See also Calvin, *Institutes* 3.19 and 4.20, and Tyndale's *Obedience*.

things. An evangelical group in the Frankfurt congregation, for example, decided that the BCP was excessively prescriptive and had already outlived its usefulness, until they were outmanoeuvred by a group that insisted on its quintessential Englishness and demanded its continued use, thus saving it from early extinction. Even more consequentially, exiled thinkers like John Ponet, John Knox, and Christopher Goodman began to think their way around the obedience question, and to devise theoretical arguments for resisting and even overthrowing ungodly secular power. Drawing on constitutionalist arguments with medieval roots, they argued that secular authority is not absolute, but contingent on the justice and godliness of the ruler, and could be revoked in the case of, say, a tyrannous female Catholic idolater. In the absence of a supervening religious authority—like a pope, who rightly or wrongly could and did pronounce rulers illegitimate—this kind of judgement, crucially, is in the hands of the governed (the nobility or lesser magistrates, ideally), who have a consequent obligation to set things right. These obligations, to God and godliness and justice, are something distinct from rights, the notion and vocabulary of which were yet to be explicitly developed. In Skinner's influential account, this is what happened next, first among French Huguenots embroiled in the wars of religion, then among Scottish and English theorists. By the end of the century, arguments had been circulated for an astounding variety of principles: divine-right absolutism, nonresistance, contractual and constitutional models of political authority, popular sovereignty (if usually in alienated form), resistance to tyranny, deposition and overthrow, revolution, and even, in the truly radical case of George Buchanan, the advisability of individually undertaken tyrannicide—a position that vested lethal juridical and executive authority in anyone who cared to claim it.[16]

Queen Elizabeth managed to neutralize such deep radicalism, from both ends of the theological spectrum, by combining an absolute insistence on her authority as 'supreme governor' with a studied doctrinal ambiguity that allowed a wide range of acceptable views to her subjects. So long as one was not an actual Roman Catholic, or anarchically Protestant, or genuinely heretical, and did not challenge her authority to order the Church of England as she saw fit, one could peacefully find a place in it. While Catholic pressure continued, especially from outside England, the queen's wrath was just as easily provoked by Protestants at home who pushed too hard for furthering of the Reformation. The puritan authors of the 1572 *Admonition to Parliament* were imprisoned for their efforts, and Elizabeth suspended her own Archbishop of Canterbury, Edmund Grindal, from 1577 to 1582 for his refusal to clamp down on what she considered excessively puritan preaching and meeting practices. Grindal's resistance to royal command, and implicit assertion of the Church's ecclesiastical authority over strictly religious matters, earned him the admiration of at least two great writers.[17] The July eclogue of Spenser's 1579 *Shepheardes Calender* describes him as Algrind, 'a

---

[16] See his *The Powers of the Crown in Scotland* 1579: ch. 7, 29, 39, and esp. 47.

[17] The other is Milton, who in *Of Reformation* calls Grindal 'the best of' what he considered an otherwise drearily conservative and conformist Elizabethan episcopate.

shepheard great in gree, | but hath bene long ypent' (223–4), on whose head an eagle had dropped a shellfish that has 'bruzd his brayne, | So now astonied with the stroke, | he lyes in lingring payne' (235–7). That the author who celebrated his queen so fulsomely, both here and in the *Faerie Queene*, could sympathize so explicitly with one who resisted her, suggests that the church–state problem had not been wholly settled. And indeed, in the epic, the deferred wedding of Redcrosse and Una implies that the final union of England and Truth, of political and religious authority perfectly interfused, may not happen until the end of history. In the imperfect present, even a glorious monarch may err, and may on grounds of moral authority be disobeyed by an archbishop, and critiqued by a poet.

The most potent basis of such resistance was of course the Bible, which as we have seen provided a counterdiscourse of divine revelation by which earthly practice could be measured, even by those not atop the social/political/ecclesiastical hierarchy. Elizabethan Puritans, for example, pushed back against conservative residues in the Church—clerical vestments, set liturgy, the episcopal hierarchy—because in addition to smacking uncomfortably of Catholicism, they were not specifically commanded in the Bible, and thus prevented the realization of a fully godly kingdom on earth (and the fully authentic worship of individual subjects). Biblical authority would seem to be an unassailable high ground in early modern England, but when Richard Hooker wrote his massive *Laws of Ecclesiastical Polity* in the 1590s, he set out to demonstrate the limits of Biblicism, perfectionism, and the recalcitrant subjectivity they had engendered. The second book of the *Laws* takes on the bedrock puritan principle that '*Scripture is the only rule of all things which in this life may be done by men*'. This narrowly prescriptive conception of biblical authority, he argues, is unworkable: the Bible cannot possibly specify what is to be done in every situation, and God has also given us natural law and reason (indeed, Hooker argues devastatingly (I.14, II.4) that without the latter we could not even legitimately judge Scripture to be authoritative), which can guide us in matters where the Bible has not explicitly commanded or forbidden something. To rely too much on the Bible and too little on God's other gifts leads to error, arrogance (see his More-like indignation in II.7.6), paralysis, ignorance, solipsism, 'infinite perplexities, scrupulosities, doubts insoluble, and extreme despairs' (II.8.6). It also blinds us to the value of the good, the reasonable, the negotiable, the indifferent. Indeed, the notion of *adiaphora*, 'things indifferent' on which good Christians and citizens might disagree without harm, had been important to establishing whatever degree of religious concord could be found in early modern Europe; puritan scrupulosity threatened to undo that by requiring scriptural warrant for anything one might do.[18] So Hooker's great aim in the *Laws* is to make the case that while the English status quo is not perfect, it is reasonable, good, beneficial to the collective and its members, and not inconsistent with God's explicit directives. This extends to the law, the structure and teaching of the Church, the form and content of the liturgy, and the constitution and authority of the secular state

---

[18]   See Calvin's own statements on the matter in *Institutes* 3.19.7–8 and 4.1.9–12.

itself (which he importantly sees as accountable to God, the law, and the whole community).[19] The point is not to de-authorize the Bible, or the reader—on the contrary, it accords the rational reader with a kind of responsibility more nuanced than mechanical application—but rather to coordinate them appropriately and pragmatically in the real social world with optimistic models of reason and will derived from Aquinas and ultimately Aristotle. Authority in this polity depends on both God and the governed, and revelation is mediated by reason; better a flexibly pragmatic Christian society that works than a naively perfectionist one that cannot. In all this, Hooker's pragmatic Christian humanism, for all its devotion to order and authority, stands distinct from the various religious and political absolutisms of his time.

Two other writers contemporary to Hooker exemplify other kinds of the dispersed and individualized authority made more possible by the Reformation. John Donne's third satire, quite likely written while he was wrestling with the question of his own religious affiliation, confronts the necessity and difficulty of the still-new world of religious choice. He sourly surveys the options of Catholicism, Calvinism, erastian conformity, skepticism, and relativism, and gives the reader little reason to be attracted to any, while nonetheless maintaining that 'thou | Of force must one, and forc'd, but one allow; | And the right' (69–71). While Donne exhorts the reader, whose soul is at stake, to 'seek true religion', 'ask thy father', 'doubt wisely', 'inquir[e] right', 'strive', and 'do', he provides no positive guidance as to which option is 'right'. Instead he gives advice regarding what *not* to do, and this takes its clearest form in his insistence that one not rely on the authority of others:

> Fool and wretch, wilt thou let thy soul be tied
> To man's laws, by which she shall not be tried
> At the last day? Will it then boot thee
> To say a Philip, or a Gregory,
> A Harry, or a Martin taught thee this? (93–7)

Neither a monarch, nor a pope, nor a great reformer can get you into heaven by virtue of your blind adherence. Donne's even-handed rejection of authorities secular and spiritual, Protestant and Catholic (they can be neatly mapped on a 2x2 grid), underscores the central polemic of the poem: the intensely *individual* nature of the pursuit of truth. Only the individual's hard-won choice matters, since only they will receive its consequences for better or worse, and this is exactly why the poem cannot tell us what choice to make. No intermediating human party can substitute for the subject's authentic search for God's truth, let alone paper over a choice that turns out to be wrong.

---

[19] See, for example, *Laws* I.10. Ian Ward (2004: 17) emphasizes that while Hooker's 'sovereign is the essential link between church and people, the force that binds the community itself together', his insistence that authority fundamentally lay in the body of the commonwealth 'led John Locke to appraise the "judicious" Hooker as the founder of a distinct English liberal constitutionalism'.

If Donne's satire insists centrally on the authority and responsibility of the private subject independent of received authority, Aemelia Lanyer's feminist passion poem *Salve Deus Rex Judaeorum* (1611) extends this possibility in another direction. Here, the poet attempts to counter the entire history of patriarchal discourse by going straight to the Bible and radically rereading it against the grain of misogynist tradition. In her preamble to the Passion, Lanyer assures her readers that she 'humbly for [God's] Grace will pray, | That he will give me Power and Strength to Write ... | Yea in these Lines I may no further stray, | Than his most holy Spirit shall give me Light' (297–8, 301–2). Her prayer for divine inspiration, coupled with her assertion that she will not exceed it, stakes an implicit claim for direct authorization and illumination in the poem that follows. This is a shrewd move, because her revision of the biblical account of the Fall and Crucifixion is subversive of almost the entire interpretive tradition of orthodox Christianity. Indeed, this short-circuiting and revision is at the heart of her project to vindicate and liberate women from the history of misogyny so deeply founded on the feminine Fall. Lanyer collates these events and presents them as epochal instances of disastrously failed patriarchy whose authority gets endlessly recycled by its own interpretive tradition. In her account of Eden, a stronger, wiser Adam fails to prevent a loving and curious Eve from eating the forbidden fruit; at Calvary, an all-male conspiracy murders the son of God as his mostly female followers, historically debilitated by patriarchal misreadings of Genesis, weep faithfully but helplessly. In remarkably bold and contentious revisions of the biblical accounts, Lanyer seeks to rally women and persuade men that misogyny is a misreading, correctable by her own.

Although the destabilizing threat of Puritanism may have seemed substantially contained by the time of Hooker and Lanyer, it turned out to have an enormous impact on the coming century; by 1650, Calvinists and other progressive heirs of the Reformation had turned on the Church of England, and Parliament on the Crown, dismantling the two central hierarchical structures of religious and state authority in order to distribute those authorities more widely. The increasingly absolutist and autocratic tendencies of Charles I in the third and fourth decades of the century, and the corresponding high-church policies of his archbishop William Laud, dissuaded a young Cambridge student from pursuing a planned career in the Church of England. Instead, John Milton became a poet and polemicist, a public and passionate critic of what he saw as contemporary trends toward religious and political tyranny, and an advocate of liberty, republicanism, and regicide. In *Areopagitica*, his most enduringly famous tract, written in 1644 to protest a parliamentary ordinance for pre-publication licensing (an 'authentic Spanish policy', in his view (749)), Milton makes the extraordinary claim that 'a man may be a heretic in the truth; and if he believe things only because his pastor says so, or the Assembly so determines, without knowing other reason, though his belief be true, yet the very truth he holds becomes his heresy' (739). This is a radicalized version of the sentiment we have seen in Donne, who disapproved of the gamble of passively entrusting one's eternal fate to someone else; but for Milton, the entrusting is itself the heresy, and even the truth will not save one if it hasn't been authentically derived by an independent and vigorously critical religious subject. Hence the crucial importance of 'promiscuous' critical reading in the dialectical recovery of truth and the partial undoing of the Fall. Hence, too, Milton's contempt for the 'gross conforming stupidity' (747) that he considers the bane of a truly free and godly commonwealth. His striking description of the commonwealth as the 'mansion house of liberty'—

> there be pens and heads there, sitting by their studious lamps, musing, searching, revolving new notions and ideas wherewith to present, as with their homage and their fealty, the approaching reformation; others as fast reading, trying all things, assenting to the force of reason and convincement. What could a man require more from a nation so pliant and so prone to seek after knowledge? (743)

—sounds more like a library, or, more to the point, a university. While Milton differs, often profoundly, from Hooker on matters of politics and ecclesiology,[20] the two men share a commitment to reason, discourse, the primary status of the commonwealth, and limited toleration (though both draw a rather bright line at outright tyranny and popery)—in other words, a number of the elements we regard as constitutive of modern liberal society. Within this, Hooker's conservatism and pragmatism lead him to prioritize stable collective order over excessive individual authority, while Milton's radicalism and idealism lead him to do just the opposite: to support revolution and regicide in pursuit of a truly free and godly commonwealth, in which individual subjects would be free to pursue virtue and truth as they understood them and without coercion. There, a Christian citizen might find 'Happiness in his power left free to will' (*Paradise Lost* 5.235), in 'voluntary service' to God (5.529), and there citizens might aggregate in voluntary associations of 'rational libertie' (10.974) that combine agreement and tolerance. In Milton's ideal commonwealth, 'a wise man will make better use of an idle pamphlet than a fool will do of sacred scripture' (731); the reader matters more than the text, the reading more than its content, and thus all authority ultimately devolves upon the individual reading subject.

To Milton, the Restorations of 1660—which resurrected the monarchy, episcopate, and liturgy that he and his co-revolutionaries had destroyed in the 1640s—must have looked like Leviathan revenant, and the end of the dream of liberty. Hobbes, looking back during the Interregnum on the ruins of traditional authority, had made his powerfully conservative argument that authority, having been permanently surrendered by individuals as the price of civilization, could not be dispersed or divided without catastrophe. Where Milton had demanded continuity between the primary inner self and its outward expression, Hobbes saw little harm in thinking one thing as a private individual, and doing another as a public subject for the sake of stability and order.[21] Unitary

---

[20] Hooker, for example, devotes the longest book of the *Laws* to a defence of the existence, uniformity, and contents of the BCP; Milton denounces the liturgy as 'evill', both because of its residual popery and because authentic worship must be done by a unified subject for whom outward act and inner conviction coincide entirely.

[21] As I suggested in Rosendale 2004, and Christopher Warren argued at greater length in 2007, while Hobbes surely favours the public ordering of religious action, he is surprisingly protective of the private authority of individual belief.

sovereignty was all; in his *Behemoth*, Hobbes applauded Henry VIII's forcible unification of secular and religious authority, but lamented the fact that the English Bible had almost immediately reintroduced the problem in an even more intractable form by implicitly authorizing *everyone*, thus leading to the breakdowns and upheavals of the 1640s. How could the unified, authorized subject coexist with the sovereign beast?

In the quasi-Hobbesian story this chapter has outlined, after centuries of struggle between the powers of *imperium* and *sacerdotium*, the post-Reformation Church was domesticated and temporally subordinated to the monarchal state.[22] This shift, however, could not be uncomplicated, as Protestant biblicism and soteriology both implied a dispersal of authority away from hierarchical dictate and mediation, and toward the Bible and its individual readers; accordingly, and perhaps inevitably, Protestantism first reinforced and then undermined the Pauline doctrine of absolute obedience to state authority. These developments were initially deeply motivated by religion, and frequently dependent upon it, but would eventually declare themselves by setting it aside; this trajectory coincides with the evolution of modern notions of both individual rights and the extra-personal, constitutional, secular state of liberal democracy. Within a few decades of the apparent death of Milton's dream, limited religious toleration would be officially proclaimed in England; the commonwealth as represented in Parliament would demonstrate its supremacy by peacefully firing the monarch, and hiring a new one; and Locke would articulate a social contract theory that was thoroughly secularized (religion being categorically declared a fundamentally private affair) and, unlike those of Hooker or Hobbes, subject to revocation by the ruled and thus continually dependent on their present satisfaction. We can thus trace a multi-century migration of final authority from the ascendant high-medieval Church, to the early modern monarchic state (and its religious subjects), to those subjects themselves as the final ground of socio-political authority: in the Lockean order of modern liberal democracy, religious authority resides largely in the private judgement of the individual, and the secular state's political authority is conditionally constituted by the collective will of its citizens. In the context of these broad shifts in the conception, location, and nature of authority, the dynamics and subjectivities of early modern British literature can often be more deeply, sharply, and purposefully understood.

---

[22] I am speaking of Protestant kingdoms here, but as Gregory has observed (2012: 152–4 and elsewhere), this happened to a significant degree in Catholic ones as well.

CHAPTER 35

··

'FINDING THE GENUINE LIGHT OF NATURE'

Religion and Science

··

BRONWEN PRICE

...to the Rational and Religious there is a double Pleasure to carry them
on in this way of Philosophy: The one from the observation how far in
everything the Concatenation of Mechanical causes will reach; which
will wonderfully gratifie their Reason: the other from a distinct depre-
hension where they must needs break off, as not being able alone to reach
the Effect; which necessarily leads them to a more confirmed discovery
of the Principle we contend for, namely the Spirit of Nature, which is the
Vicarious power of God upon the Matter, and the first step to the abstrusest Mysteries in Natural Theologie; which must needs highly gratifie them
in point of Religion.

(More 1987: 20)[1]

HENRY More's statement from the Preface to his *The Immortality of the Soul* (1659)
addresses some of the fundamental concerns of seventeenth-century scientific writing: the extent to which the immediate causes of physical phenomena are separate from
those of metaphysical design and purpose; in what ways, if at all, matter is connected
to spirit; whether the soul and body are distinct entities; what the nature of spirit might
be and how it is linked to God; and the degree of God's continuing intervention in the
natural world. This knowledge, moreover, may be obtained through a combination of
observation, rational thought, and religious impulse.

---

[1] The quotation in the title of this chapter is from Bacon's *Great Instauration* (1965: 317).

This chapter will focus on four significant figures: Francis Bacon, Robert Boyle, Henry More, and Anne Conway, each of whom represents an important and distinct aspect of the relationship between sciences and religion. It will explore their responses to each other and negotiations with major contemporary debates, such as those identified by More, in order to exemplify not only competing modes of thought, but also the interconnections between different groups. In particular, my discussion will show how theories about the relationship between science and religion arose out of a self-conscious response to other voices and were informed by dialogue and exchange of ideas. In addition, it will demonstrate how such discussions were articulated in a wide range of genres and contexts and to a variety of audiences, from public manifestos, like Bacon's *The Great Instauration* (1620), to private letters, such as the correspondence between Conway and More of 1650–79.

What More's text demonstrates is how scientific and devotional considerations were often intertwined during the early modern period and how theological concerns frequently lie alongside scientific ones, whether to justify, defend, or question them. In the above quote, for example, More expresses an underlying anxiety about the religious implications of a mechanically driven view of the universe: his considerations about natural phenomena and their workings seem necessarily to include ones about God. Indeed, although there was a general trend towards a division between clerical and intellectual activity in the early modern period, numerous figures engaged in scientific enquiry were, like the Cambridge Platonist More, also ministers. Bishop Thomas Sprat defended the Royal Society from any suggestion of atheism on the grounds that it was supported by 'the Greatest and the most Reverend Churchmen' (1667: 132), while, as Richard G. Olson points out, being ordained as an Anglican Priest 'was ordinarily a condition for becoming a fellow of one of the colleges at Cambridge', where much scientific discussion took place (2004: 112).

Highlighting investigations into the natural world, this chapter sets out to explore the often complex relation between science and religion in this period when a significant reassessment of the connection between these areas began to emerge. Certainly 'science' in its modern sense was not a term used to classify the particular disciplines now associated with that field of enquiry. Although Michael Hunter notes that ' "Science" is occasionally used in something approaching its modern meaning in the seventeenth century' (1981: 8 n. 1), David Colclough considers that 'No one in the Renaissance would have recognized the term "scientific writing" ' (2000: 565). More commonly, early modern thinkers associated what we might now broadly class as 'science' with philosophical enquiry, as More does here, and still used the term 'natural philosophy' to describe the study of natural phenomena, a practice that could embrace Isaac Newton's interests in the medieval tradition of alchemy at one extreme and his ground-breaking theory of gravity at the other. Furthermore, natural philosophy was often directly associated with 'Natural Theologie', a concept to which More refers above: that is, the belief that, in addition to the Scriptures, the Book of Nature could be interpreted as a means to know God and discover his 'abstrusest Mysteries'.

The relationship between science and religion thus frequently centred on questions concerning the balance between the study of nature and the Scripture and considerations about what nature itself comprised and what caused it to act: was it simply matter operating only according to mechanistic principles or was it animated by spirit emanating from a divine source, as More's Platonic philosophy seems to suggest? Or did it even contain inherently self-moving properties of its own?—a view offered by Margaret Cavendish in the late seventeenth century. Was scientific knowledge thus connected to an understanding of divine considerations or, as Sprat's *History of the Royal Society* (1667) recommends, should the natural philosopher 'meddle no otherwise with Divine things, than onely as the Power, and Wisdom, and Goodness of the Creator is display'd in the admirable order, and workman-ship of the Creatures' (82)? Further, was it part of God's purpose for humanity to 'recover that right over nature which belongs to it by divine bequest', as Francis Bacon argues (1965: 374), and, if so, in what ways should natural philosophers interact with the natural world and what should be the extent of their knowledge? Could and should humans strive to obtain certain understanding about God's creation or should they aim instead to achieve a knowledge that was probable rather than sure? Moreover, who should be engaged in such activities and what was the purpose of acquiring such knowledge? Was it to draw 'us into a due meditation of the omnipotency of God' alone or should it also be gained for 'human utility and power' whereby nature could be transformed 'for the benefit and use of life' (Bacon 1965: 242, 310), and were these compatible objectives?

These issues signal the diverse approaches to scientific matters in the early modern period, which was partly a result of their connection with religious concerns. They also indicate the ways in which new knowledge about God's creation and its study might demand an engagement with or even a rethinking about religious concepts. In turn, Robert Boyle's coining of the term 'Christian virtuoso' highlights 'the degree to which' experimental scientists like himself 'were committed to the compatibility of Christianity and learning' (Shapiro 1991: 59), while the 'Boyle Lectures', established after his death in 1691 and designed to prove 'the Christian Religion, against notorious Infidels' (cited in Hunter 1981: 184) set a precedent for science being used to defend Christianity. Indeed, many of those involved in scientific activity regarded the new philosophy as complementing or even strengthening religion (Shapiro 1991: 57–61).

This chapter will examine some of the main areas of debate within this relationship. It is important to note how such discussions incorporated figures from a broad spectrum of religious backgrounds from moderate Anglicans, like More and Boyle, who operated during the crisis of the Civil War to well beyond the Restoration, to the converted Quaker, Anne Conway, whose ideas circulated in the latter part of the seventeenth century. As might be expected, those with similar religious interests often shared similar approaches to natural philosophy, such as the Latitudinarian Cambridge Platonists, among whom More was a prominent figure, or the scientific circle surrounding the puritan reformer, Samuel Hartlib, in the Civil War and Republican periods, many of whom were, like himself, Protestant exiles.[2] Examples such as these demonstrate how specific conditions of context frequently influenced the creation of scientific and religious communities.

However, particular scientific ideas were by no means dependent on religious persuasion. For example, Hartlib espoused the Baconian scientific methods of empiricism, experimentation, induction, and collaborative research that also formed the basis of the Royal Society, founded at the Restoration. Indeed, taking a non-sectarian line, Hartlib advocated religious unity together with a public-spirited notion of science, thus following 'Bacon's conception that true natural philosophy and the charitable use of its products would lead to religious enlightenment' (Sargent 1996: 165). Similarly, although Sprat's *History* conceals Republican Baconian activities, such as Hartlib's, highlighting instead the endeavours of the pre-Restoration Oxford Circle, who were 'well inclin'd to serve their Prince, and the Church' (1667: 54), it also argues for the harmonizing and inclusive effects of science. For Sprat and others, this counters the religious and political divisions of the Civil War period through its appeal 'to all reasonable men' (Hunter 1981: 29) 'to make all their Labours unite for the service of man-kind' (Sprat 1667: 57, 70), a concept also apparent in both the religious and scientific aspects of More's and Hartlib's works.[3] As John Hedley Brooke notes, there was a 'continuing dialogue between conservative and radical reformers, the form of which could change as social and political circumstances changed' (1991: 130–1).

On the surface, the anti-traditional bent of Reformist ideas might seem to lend themselves to new modes of enquiry that could be extended to the new philosophies whereby it was possible 'to think unthinkable thoughts' and 'to challenge those beliefs about the way the world was that previous generations had been incapable of questioning' (Loewenstein and Morrill 2002: 664–5).[4] However, as I have already indicated, the new philosophies sometimes incorporated older traditions, such as Platonism and Hermeticism, while earlier philosophical interests, such as Roger Bacon's mathematics and Paracelsus's empirical, anti-Galenic approach to medicine, sometimes anticipated later thought. Furthermore, there was of course a Catholic tradition of scientific enquiry on the Continent from Paracelsian medicine to Cartesian rationalism to Gassendian atomism to Marin Mersenne's mechanical philosophy that intersected with or was taken

---

[2] 'Puritan' incorporates a varied religious spectrum during this period. Hartlib's circle was itself fluid and diverse, including Boyle, John Milton, William Petty, and the evangelist John Dury. See Sargent 1996: 164–5.

[3] In his *History*, Sprat claims that the Society 'freely admitted Men of different Religions, Countries and Professions of Life', though the Anglican faith is still elevated 'above all others' in being 'equal ... to the general Reason of Mankind' in contrast to the 'spiritual frenzies' of Sectarianism (1667: 63). Notably Hartlib was not made a member. In addition, Hunter and Wood draw attention to the 'divergent intellectual positions' that characterized the early Royal Society, which 'reflect a tension in the Baconian corpus' (1986: 50, 65).

[4] Loewenstein and Morrill particularly refer to the puritan writing of 1640–60, but these ideas might be applied more broadly. However, Robert Merton's seminal work (1938) linking puritan values with the growth of scientific activity has long since been challenged. Shapiro, though, persuasively demonstrates the significant interrelations between the ideas informing the scientific revolution and the wider trajectory of Anglican and humanist thought (1991: 45–71).

up by and reworked in diverse ways by its Protestant counterparts in Britain and else-where.[5] Olson points out that the Jesuit community 'produced comprehensive text-books and reference works that were used by Protestant as well as Catholic scientists' (2004: 71). Indeed, even though Bacon locates 'a renovation … of all other knowledge' alongside the Protestant Reformation, he also acknowledges how 'the Jesuits … have much quickened and strengthened the state of learning' (1965: 241–2).

FRANCIS BACON (1561–1626)

While recognizing the significance of such religious contexts to the development of knowledge, Bacon was one of the first major figures who seems to signal a separation between religion and science that is often associated with the beginnings of modern thought. Although he did not make any significant discoveries or conduct major experi-ments himself, Bacon produced some of the most influential new philosophical theories of the period, setting out an extensive programme for advancing knowledge, offering a devastating critique of received ideas, especially those of Aristotle and the scholastic tradition, and promoting state funding for collaborative scientific research. Addressed to King James I, his *Advancement of Learning* (1605, expanded 1623) asserts that while one cannot 'be too well studied in the book of God's word or in the book of God's works, divinity or philosophy', we should 'not unwisely mingle or confound these learnings together' and warns that we must 'not presume by the contemplation of nature to attain to the mysteries of God' (1965: 204–5). Whereas the Scriptures reveal 'the will of God', God's creatures express 'his power', their study imparting 'the glory of the Creator', but not his purpose (242, 235).

While Bacon notes that some of the Scriptures 'will be found pregnant and swelling with natural philosophy', in *Novum Organum* (1620) he criticizes those who 'attempt to found a system of natural philosophy' from the Bible and 'mix their philosophy with theology' because it produces 'not only a fantastic philosophy but also an heretical reli-gion' (1965: 239, 345, 348). He connects such an approach to knowledge with supersti-tion, something which in his essay on that subject is viewed as being even worse than atheism as it results in 'contumely' towards God and 'deformity' of religion (347, 89–90). Therefore, we should 'give to faith that only which is faith's' (348).

However, while presenting theology and his new philosophy as separate disciplines, Bacon by no means excludes religious concepts from his 'reconstruction of the sciences'

---

[5] Neither Paracelsus nor Descartes represented Catholic orthodoxy, however. Even though Paracelsus considered himself to be 'a loyal Catholic', he was particularly popular with seventeenth-century radical Puritans because of his millenarian views. See Olson 2004: 49–50. Descartes was given the liberty to publish in Holland refused to him in his native France. See Brooke 1991: 82–116 for a critique of the view that 'Protestantism was more conducive than Catholicism to the expansion of science' even if 'Protestant cultures were more amenable to freedom of thought' (83, 115).

(1965: 319). Scriptural references pervade his work. For example, the wisdom of the first biblical king, Solomon, who himself compiled 'a natural history of all verdure', is repeatedly cited as a means of condoning his own enterprise, as well as being linked to the 'intellectual' King James, whose support he seeks (240, 198). Indeed, Bacon imitates Solomon's mode of writing in using aphorisms, a genre that his *Advancement* claims enables knowledge to be presented as provisional and 'in growth' rather than being reduced within a finite method (232) (see Vickers 1996: xxiv).

Throughout his work, Bacon makes a clear distinction between genuine, deep knowledge of the kind Solomon represents, whose purpose is 'the inquisition of truth' and that which is false, superficial and associated with 'error or vanity', such as alchemy, natural magic, and astrology, among others (1965: 240, 229). In his hugely ambitious, incomplete *The Great Instauration* (1620), which 'commence[s] a total reconstruction of sciences, arts, and all human knowledge', Bacon's rejection of 'All received or current falsehoods' takes on a hieratic quality (299, 321). Here he 'with a religious care' will 'eject, repress, and as it were exorcise every kind of phantasm' (321). This he will achieve by establishing 'a true and lawful marriage between the empirical and the rational faculty' (309). Moreover, through the use of experiments he will 'perform the office of a true priest' for 'finding the genuine light of nature' (317). While, as Brooke shows, Bacon's 'experimental philosopher should not be diverted by metaphysical considerations' that focus on Aristotelian concerns 'for final causes, for ends or purposes' (1991: 54), he must nonetheless follow the 'pattern' of 'divine wisdom and order' of the first day of creation when God 'created light only' and 'no material substance' (Bacon 1965: 350). Similarly, through his experiments of light, Bacon's philosopher will begin by investigating the underlying causes and axioms of natural phenomena, rather than simply producing material effects (350). Indeed, light adopts a religious resonance throughout Bacon's work, signalling the 'visible light' created by God in Genesis and the 'intellectual light' God bestowed on man that enables the 'new light' of knowledge for which Bacon now lays the foundations. It is by these means that Bacon hopes God will 'graciously grant to us to write an apocalypse or true vision of the footsteps of the Creator imprinted on his creatures' (323–4, 300).

Bacon continually acknowledges the defectiveness of human nature when left to its own devices both in terms of 'the uncertain light of the sense' and the 'Idols of the human mind', for the intellect is inclined to '[mix] up its own nature with the nature of things' (1965: 307, 334, 317). His method therefore sets out to 'correct' these 'errors' by providing 'safeguards to guide' their 'working' (316–19). Carefully distinguishing between 'uncorrupted natural knowledge' Adam possessed when he entered Eden and 'the ambitious and proud desire of moral knowledge' that led to the Fall, Bacon's new philosophy offers the 'termination of infinite error' (310–11). He thus provides it with both religious and scientific validation, for it will help to restore 'that commerce between the mind of man and the nature of things' 'to its perfect and original condition' by recovering man's 'dominion over creation' (298, 392).

Furthermore, Bacon's new philosopher embodies fundamental Christian virtues. Indeed, his own 'obedience to the everlasting love of truth' and reliance on 'divine assistance' demonstrates, Bacon claims, 'the true and legitimate humiliation of the human spirit' (1965: 308). The scientist who follows his rigorous programme must similarly demonstrate obedience to and humility before God by 'labour[ing] in thy works with the sweat of [his brow]' (324). In order to generate Bacon's 'seeds of a purer truth', he must undergo a sort of baptismal cleansing whereby the mind is 'purged and swept and levelled', ensuring that his course of inquiry is 'chaste' (367–8, 323). Thus, just as he should enter 'the kingdom of heaven' 'as a little child', so he may enter 'the kingdom of man, founded on the sciences' (348). Equally as important, though, the new philosopher should conduct his activities according to the 'theological virtue' that 'excels all the rest': good works, for he must 'cultivate truth in charity', undertaking his role 'for the common good' and 'the benefit of the human race' (414, 309, 311, 299). In this regard, while divinity and philosophy may be separate, they are intrinsically complementary in Bacon's work, for 'as in religion we are warned to show our faith by works, so in philosophy by the same rule the system should be judged by its fruits' (351).

ROBERT BOYLE (1627–91)

Brooke argues that what has often been characterized as a separation should be more accurately understood as a 'differentiation from and reintegration' between natural philosophy and religious belief in the early modern period, produced by 'successive shifts in the degree of subordination and the grounds of differentiation' between scientific and theological interests (1991: 58). If Bacon's writing signals such a process, so does the disparate work of the early Royal Society, whose diverse activities were connected by a general commitment to Baconian principles and the idea of religious toleration.

The corpuscular theories of Robert Boyle, one of its central founder members, represents a further shift in the relation between science and religion. In conducting and recording a range of experiments and creating instruments in order to do so, Boyle exemplifies Bacon's promotion of establishing reliable, comprehensive natural knowledge through cumulative, practically informed data. For example, Boyle's air-pump, which appears on the frontis-page of Sprat's *History*, created a vacuum-chamber so as to test 'the generally received axiom' that 'nature abhors a vacuum' (Boyle 1996: 119). His *New Experiments Physico–Mechanical, Touching the Spring of the Air and its Effects* (1660) not only demonstrated that it was possible to produce a vacuum mechanically, but also documents the properties of air and the effects of its withdrawal on living creatures and organisms. As in Bacon's work, such experimental practice and evidence is designed to 'intelligibly show the particular manner how that general cause produces the proposed effect', and is distinguished from 'superficial and narrow theories' that assign 'precarious or false' causes, such as those found in prevailing Aristotelian theories and much contemporary chemistry (Boyle 1996: 150; 1979: 140, 149).[6]

---

[6] Principe (1994) and Newman (1994) highlight the significance of alchemical studies to Boyle's work.

In addition, like other members of the Oxford Circle to which he was linked in the 1650s, Boyle fuses his Baconian approach with the influence of contemporary reworkings of ancient atomism, especially Cartesian mechanism. However, unlike Bacon and Descartes, Boyle combines his concern to investigate 'particular and immediate' physical causes with a teleological one so as to present a natural philosophy that is fundamentally informed by 'the first cause' of God's design and providence (1996: 15, 146).

It is through these principles that Boyle offers what he refers to in the title of one of his most important collection of works as being *A Free Enquiry into the Vulgarly Received Notion of Nature* (1686).[7] This notion of nature is attributed to 'the great ambiguity' of the word itself, which then generates 'imperfect and confused notions concerning nature' as a phenomenon. It is therefore unclear as to whether nature 'be a real existent being, or a notional entity' (17, 19, 32). Such ambivalence is especially associated with the Aristotelian school of philosophy, which education 'has imbued' in its students 'from their infancy', and which ascribes to nature wisdom, purpose, inherent principles, and productive agency, as if 'God has appointed an intelligent and powerful being called nature to be as his vicegerent' (16, 13). Nature is thereby treated as a 'semi-deity' that 'defrauds the true God of divers acts of veneration and gratitude that are due to him from men' (10, 62). Such a concept is both philosophically and theologically 'dark and odd' because it 'darken[s] the excellency of the divine management of things'. It is therefore 'both injurious to the glory of God and a great impediment to the solid and useful discovery of his works' (60, 10–11).

Boyle thus sets out to 'speak more distinctly and correctly about things' and to provide 'a more industrious scrutiny into the reasons of things' (6, 15). For Boyle, there is no 'sufficient proof' that nature has intelligence, nor is this notion necessary, for nature 'act[s] too blindly and impotently to discharge well the part she is said to be trusted with' (58–9, 14). Rather, it may be more accurately viewed as an 'admirably contrived automaton', operating through 'mechanical affections' (146, 148). Defined in terms of matter and motion, it is devoid of sense and purpose, comprising an 'almost infinite variety of coalitions and structures ... made of minute and insensible corpuscles' (141, 145). Nature therefore cannot abhor a vacuum because it has neither the intelligence nor agency 'to do irresistibly whatever is necessary to prevent it'. Nor does nature contain inherent laws, such as those of motion, for 'it is plain that nothing but an intellectual being can be properly capable of receiving and acting by a law' (15, 24).

However, Boyle is keen to distance himself both from the materialist atomism of his contemporary Thomas Hobbes (1588–1679), who argues not only for the corporeality of nature, but also the 'corporiety of God' (Boyle 1996: 159), leading Boyle and others to consider Hobbes to be an atheist (Davis and Hunter 1996: 159), and from the 'impious errors' of the 'atomists of old', who believed 'that atoms, meeting together by chance in an infinite vacuum, are able of themselves to produce the world and all its phenomena'

---

[7] Boyle's Preface indicates that he wrote this work over an extensive period, with some parts dating back to the 1660s (5). All references to Boyle come from this work unless indicated otherwise.

without reference to 'any divine Author of it' (Boyle 1979: 163, 155, 138). By contrast, for Boyle 'the wonderful construction and orderly operations of the world and its parts' are manifestations of the 'unsearchable wisdom' and design of the 'divine architect', who is 'both incorporeal and too excellent to be so united to matter as to animate it like the heathen's mundane soul' (1996: 103, 60, 158). It is God's 'almighty power' alone which 'did at first frame the corporeal world according to the divine ideas' and his 'divine wisdom that is so excellently displayed in the fabric and conduct of the universe'. Hence, God, who is 'the proprietor of the whole' of creation, is a completely distinct entity from his works in being 'infinitely perfect' and 'uncapable of being divided' (39, 147, 69, 158). He therefore has no need for a mediator, such as nature, to assist him, as he 'can immediately act upon human souls ... but they are not able so to act upon one another' (145). Following scriptural authority that 'ascribes the formation of [his creatures] to God's immediate fiat', Boyle's intention is thus 'to keep the glory of the divine author of things from being usurped or entrenched upon by his creatures' (28, 6).

In order to illustrate this radical distinction between God and his works, Boyle employs an analogy that pervades his writing: just as the intricate workings of a clock, like that of Strasbourg Cathedral, are the result of the 'designs of the artificer' rather than being inherent within the mechanisms of the clock itself, so one should 'admire and praise the most wise Author' of creation, rather than endowing reason and agency on the components of the 'exquisitely contrived system' that the world comprises (1979: 162; 1996: 72). It was God who 'gave motion to matter' and 'established those rules of motion, and that order amongst things corporeal, which we are wont to call the laws of nature'. Therefore nature is to be treated as a 'system of rules according to which those agents and the bodies they work on are, by the great author of things, determined to act and suffer' (1979: 139; 1996: 106). The laws of nature, then, are an expression of God's providence, agency, and will, to which his creation is subject. In this way, Boyle's corpuscular theory does not merely complement religion, but is 'an invincible ally' for it in being a means of illuminating God's omnipotence and sovereignty over his works (Davis and Hunter 1996: xiv). To this extent, as M. A. Stewart suggests, 'there is no clear line at which the science of nature ends and the theology of nature begins' (1979: xiii).

Furthermore, such a view opens up the boundaries of human knowledge, as 'the veneration wherewith men are imbued for what they call nature has been a discouraging impediment to the empire of man over the inferior creatures of God' (Boyle 1996: 15). Created in the image of God as a result of possessing a soul and reason, man is differentiated from a nature that is now divested of such qualities. Nature's subjection to human enquiry is thereby justified in Baconian terms, the study of God's works being distinguished, in turn, from the 'higher and more necessary truths' contained in the Scriptures (Boyle 1996: 30).

Not only is Boyle's natural philosophy underpinned by his argument for God's design and providence, but also, like many other seventeenth-century experimental philosophers, a voluntarist perspective whereby God is perceived as being 'a most free agent', having 'created the world not out of necessity but voluntarily', according to his inscrutable will (Boyle 1996: 160). This Boyle combines with insistently theistic principles, for he suggests that God can 'intermeddle' whenever he chooses to 'have an influence upon the operations of things corporeal' (173). Indeed, those moments 'when it pleases God to overrule or control the established course of things' can be understood as 'the extraordinary and supernatural interpositions of divine providence', which can 'overrule the physical laws of motion in matter' through 'prophecies, apparitions, true miracles and other ways' in order 'to execute his justice' (14, 69, 71). Therefore, although Boyle's corpuscular theory attempts to 'make [God's] works more thoroughly and solidly understood', it also acknowledges its own limitations because human understanding is recognized as being necessarily deficient in the face of God's 'unfathomable wisdom' and arbitrary will (6, 70). Hence, 'in some of God's works the ends or uses may be manifest ... in others the ends designed seem to be beyond our reach'. Through these means, 'the most wise author of them does both gratify our understandings and make us sensible of the imperfection of them' (162–3).

Where Bacon offers a set of methods for obtaining certain knowledge, therefore, Boyle only ever endeavours to provide one that is probable and sceptical, concluding his *Enquiry* by claiming to 'have written this discourse rather like a doubting seeker of truth than a man confident that he has found it' (165). Magnifying the position of humility before God's creation adopted by Bacon's scientist and complementing his own inclusive approach to religion, Boyle discounts any claim 'to have a right notion of nature', 'declining ... to say anything dogmatically about this matter', offering instead only 'a less degree of probability' than others and 'freely submit[ting]' his 'thoughts to better judgements' (6, 32, 142, 163). In his essay 'About the Excellency and Grounds of the Mechanical Hypothesis' (1674) he even suggests that his corpuscular philosophy can be made 'reconcilable' with other approaches rather than being in conflict with them (1979: 149).

This provisional, probabilistic approach to his philosophy is reflected in Boyle's mode of writing. The titles of the articles that comprise his immense corpus often include terms like 'hypothesis', 'digression', 'considerations', giving the impression of work in progress. Indeed, *Enquiry* is presented as being 'an apparatus' rather than a finished product, comprising a 'whole bundle of ... papers that I found and tacked together', 'written at very different times and in differing circumstances' (163–5). While Boyle's published work helped secure 'his reputation as the leading natural philosopher of his day' and was produced in Latin editions to ensure 'that his fame spread across Europe' (Davis and Hunter 1996: xiii), unlike Bacon's rhetorical public pronouncements, Boyle's writing is often addressed to an anonymous individual who is constructed as an ideal reader. *Enquiry*, for example, directs its discussion to 'dear Eleutherius', who is identified as being not only a 'considering person' and 'discerning' reader, who is not to be 'measure[d] by the prepossessed generality of men', but also 'a good Christian' (163, 19, 164, 10, 4). It is through this intermediary model figure, who combines both scientific curiosity and religious integrity and to whom Boyle 'intentionally addressed my thoughts' that the general reader gains access to the fundamental link between theology and natural philosophy that underscores Boyle's work as a whole (4).

HENRY MORE (1614–87) AND
THE CAMBRIDGE PLATONISTS

One group of philosophers who take a very different approach to the interconnection between science and religion from Boyle's, and to whom his 'vulgar notion of nature' seems implicitly to allude, is the Cambridge Platonists. Operating from the 1640s, this intellectual circle which, along with More, included Ralph Cudworth (1617–88) and Benjamin Whichcote (1609–83), shared Boyle's promotion of natural theology through their engagement in natural philosophy and, like Boyle, challenged Bacon's and Descartes's refusal to 'inquire of the final cause of anything', foregrounding instead the teleological notion that 'there is a superintendent principle over nature' designed by God (More 1968a: 181, 185).

But where Boyle and Bacon rejected scholasticism, the Cambridge Platonists drew heavily on classical metaphysics, integrating them into their mystical theology and natural philosophy so as to produce an epistemology that highlighted the immutability of moral concepts, hierarchical forms, the nature of the soul, and the role of reason. Where Boyle favoured an experimental method that downplayed 'the dim reason of man' (1979: 171), the Cambridge Platonists advocated a rationalist one, elevating reason as a supreme, albeit imperfect, faculty God has granted humanity and employing it both as a means of affirming faith and understanding the world God created. Thus, Whichcote asserts in his *Axioms* that 'He that useth his reason doth acknowledge God' (1968: 426), similarly, More declares 'certainty of faith presupposes certainty of reason' (1968b: 149). For the Cambridge Platonists, intellectual and religious concerns therefore converge.

In direct opposition to the Calvinist, deterministic notion of predestination and the voluntarism of Boyle and other empiricists, to whom God's will was paramount and might cause him to intervene in the world at any moment, the Cambridge Platonists followed an intellectualist view of divine justice and of God more generally. Cudworth suggests, for example, that 'there is an eternal and immutable wisdom in the mind of God', 'which is the archetypal intellect', so that 'the wisdom of God is as much God as the will of God' (1996: 77, 26–7). While the will is of itself 'blind' and 'indefinite', God's will is 'guided and determined by' the 'rule and measure' of 'an infinite wisdom' whose premise is 'infinite goodness' (26–7).[8] It thus follows that divine providence ensures 'that nothing shall come to pass but what is consistent with the good and welfare of honest and conscientious men' (More 1968a: 185).

In turn, it is human intellect, not simply blind faith, which, for the Cambridge Platonists, is linked to the soul and signals humanity's connection with God and potential to strive for perfection. Indeed, the very idea of God is, according to More, a

---

[8] In the context of his argument here, Cudworth particularly criticizes the precedence Descartes gives to divine will.

'necessary and natural emanation of the mind of man' (1968a: 177), while for Cudworth, 'all the knowledge and wisdom that is in creatures … is nothing else but a participation of that one eternal, immutable, and increated wisdom of God' (1996: 26). However, where God is 'essentially good and wise' and thus 'above' 'freewill', he has given human beings 'liberty of will' because it is 'a thing which of necessity belongs to the idea or nature of an imperfect rational being' (Cudworth 1996: 196). Therefore, arguing against the negative, necessitarian determinism Hobbes set out in *Of Liberty and Necessity* (1654), More asserts that it is this human faculty of the will, internally located in each soul, guided by a 'natural conscience' God has implanted in individuals, that enables humans 'to assert that Liberty which is most suitable to a creature made by God's image and a partaker of divine sense' (1968a: 184; 1968c: 301).[9] The Cambridge Platonists' concepts of divine providence and free will thus indicate the connection they make between religion and human understanding and the centrality of divine justice and intellect to their analysis of natural phenomenon.

Many of these features of Cambridge Platonism form the basis of More's *The Immortality of the Soul*, a major work within his prolific and diverse output, which included poems, essays, letters, and treatises on philosophy and theology. As with Cudworth's writing, this extensive, tripartite investigation into the nature of the soul, exemplifies More's thorough awareness of both ancient and contemporary philosophy through its dialogic quality and frequent use of counter argument. More certainly knew Boyle, Newton, Joseph Glanvill (1636–80), Anne Conway, Francis Mercury Van Helmont (1614–98), the Flemish physician through whom he came into contact with the German Cabbalist, Christian Knorr von Rosenroth (1636–89), and Hartlib, who introduced him as a correspondent to René Descartes (1596–1650) in 1648 (see Crocker 1990: 4). Indeed, More was largely responsible for first disseminating Cartesian philosophy in English intellectual circles, even though, like Cudworth, he later critiqued some fundamental aspects of Descartes's work.

The influence of Cartesian dualism is certainly apparent in the opening of *Immortality*. Here, More establishes a clear distinction between the properties of matter, which are 'Divisibility and Impenetrability', and those of spirit, which are 'Penetrability and Indiscerpibility', in order to establish his view that the notion of spirit is 'as intelligible and congruous to Reason, as in that of a Body' (1987: 30; all further references to More come from *Immortality*). In this, he directly attacks Hobbes's materialist assumption that spirits are 'not conceptible', that the notions of spirit and substance 'do flatly contradict one another' and that 'spirit … worketh not on the senses' (Hobbes 1994: 65–6). In answer to 'Mr Hobbs, that confident Exploder of Immaterial Substances out of the world', More asserts that 'there is an Incorporeal Substance distinct from the Matter' that 'is really and actually in Nature'. Indeed, to deny such a notion is, by implication, to deny 'that there should be any God, or Soul' (53, 62, 59, 49). Moreover, and departing

---

[9] Cudworth provides an even more extensive response to Hobbes and others on this subject in his *A Treatise of Freewill*.

from both Descartes and Hobbes, because spirit is a substance, it can be extended and, not only move itself, but 'also penetrate, move, and alter the Matter'. As a result, although matter and spirit are distinct, they nonetheless possess a 'Vital Congruity', for, unlike the 'superficiall' connection between one body and another, 'the very inward parts' of spirit and body 'are united point to point throughout' (34, 158, 44).

Having established the properties of spirit and their relation to matter, More goes on to explore how these apply to natural phenomena in the terrestrial world more specifically. Central to this are his notions of God's intellect, providence, and design. Unlike Hobbes, who perceives the 'ordinary Phaenomena of Nature' as being the result of 'the blind motions and jumblings of Matter', More draws on the design argument that 'there is discoverable' in them 'so profound Wisdome and Counsell ... that the Order of things in the world' must come 'from a higher Principle' (54). While More follows Descartes and other mechanists like Boyle in considering matter to be completely inert and passive, he views purely mechanical explanations of 'motion' and 'Modifications in Matter' as too limited. He thus suggests that 'when God created [matter], he superadded an impress of Motion upon it' (262, 64).

However, unlike Boyle, More does not believe that God continues to act immediately or contingently on ordinary nature, for there is no 'necessity that God should reiterate this impress of Motion on the Matter created'; rather, matter will retain 'the whole summe of Motion first communicated to it'. Instead, God enlists a 'Quartermaster-General of Divine providence' to continue this task (64, 268). Drawing on Platonic theories of the world's soul, More suggests that such a function is 'The Spirit of Nature', which 'is the Vicarious power of God ... upon the Universal Matter of the world' and 'goes through and assists all corporeal Beings' (267). This 'Inferiour Soul of the World' exercises a 'Plastick' faculty that enables it to 'intermeddle', animate, move, and modify matter beyond 'the pure laws of Mechanicks' through, for example, the sympathetic connection between 'different and distant Subjects' (160, 262–3, 137). Thus, in 'confutation of Mr Hobbs his Opinion', More's theory of gravity is explained by 'some Immaterial cause, such as we call The Spirit of Nature ... that must direct the motions of the Aethereal particles to act upon these grosser Bodies to drive them towards the Earth', for there is 'undeniable proof that heavy Bodies in the very Clime where we live will not descend perpendicularly to the Earth' (258, 260).

However, while More suggests that 'there is one Soul ready every where to pursue the advantages of prepared Matter', 'Men and Beasts', unlike nature, have 'particular Souls' that enable them to attain 'those enjoyments which the transcendent Wisdom of the Creatour has contrived' (263). It is, indeed, the existence and nature of 'an Immaterial Substance in Man', which forms the central part and is the 'main design' of More's *Immortality* (1987: 77).

Insistently arguing once more against Hobbes's materialistic view that, for example, humans 'have the perception of nothing but what is impressed from corporeal Objects' and 'resolves[s] Sense merely into Re-action of Matter', More asserts that 'there is Something in us Immaterial or Incorporeal' (92, 87–8). Like the Spirit of Nature in microcosm, this 'Substance', which 'is usually called the Soule', is 'distinct from the Body', yet also activates and guides it (144, 77). However, while the human soul 'may have a more than ordinary Union or Implication with the Spirit of Nature ... so far forth as it is Plastick', because each particular soul possesses reason, each should also 'be the Vital Architect of her own house' through 'that close connexion and sure possession she is to have of it, distinct and secure from the invasion of any other particular Soul' (177). Furthermore, the human soul comprises several faculties which 'rise by Degrees': 'those less pure' ones of 'Memory and 'Imagination' and 'those more Pure and Intellectual faculties of Will and Reason', but none 'are competible to mere Bodies' (136, 103).

More's dualistic concept of humans is once again reminiscent of Descartes's *Meditations*. However, it differs from Cartesian dualism in important ways. More challenges 'the mere Mechanical reasons' Descartes attaches to memory and imagination, for, while there exists a 'kind of Heterogeneity in the Soul', these are nonetheless faculties 'of the exquisite unity of the Soul with herself' (109, 144, 136). Furthermore, where Descartes locates the 'common Sensorium' in the conarion, More argues: 'that the chief Seat of the Soul ... from whence she commands all the parts of the Body, is those purer Animal Spirits in the fourth Ventricle of the Brain'. The reason for this specific anatomical situation is that 'betwixt the Head and the trunk of the Body is the most exactly convenient to receive the impresse of Objects from both' (125). However, and again unlike Descartes, More suggests that 'our Soul is not confined to any one part of the Head, but possesses the whole Body' because it is 'contractible and dilatable'. This is demonstrated by our experience of pain, which signals 'the Unity of Soul possessing the whole Body, and the Continuity of Spirits that is the cause thereof' as these are the 'immediate Instrument of the Soul' (137–8, 135, 176). Thus, where Descartes argues that 'our soul is of a nature entirely independent of the body, and that, consequently, it is not subject to die with it' (76), More suggests that the soul 'is vitally united with Matter' 'because it makes the Matter a congruous Subject for the Soul to reside in, and exercise the functions of life'. Indeed, even after death, the soul 'is not released from all vital union with all kind of Matter whatsoever', for 'it seems a very wilde leap in nature, that the Soul of Man, from being so deeply and muddlily immersed into Matter ... should so on a suddain be changed' (193, 158).

More's work makes evident how utterly dependent one part of his discussion is on another and how thoroughly interconnected his theology is with his natural philosophy and theory of human physiology because at the heart of his argument concerning the existence and nature of the soul, lies his proof for the existence of God (see Henry 1990: 64–5, who also highlights this feature of More's work). Moreover, his reliance on rational explanation and reasoned argument to support his case defends his concept of a wise and just divine creator, who has given human beings an intellect and free will to affirm such a philosophy. While Cambridge Platonism and the latitudinarian theology it promoted are usually associated with a probablilistic approach to natural philosophy, John Henry rightly observes the more dogmatic, less mainstream, line that More takes (57–9). Although More's Preface acknowledges that he offers a 'particular probable way', inviting those who are 'quicker-sighted ... to rectifie what is perverse, as to supply what is defectuous in the light of Nature' (1987: 13, 6), the whole tenor of the main text emphasizes 'the power of reason to arrive at certain truth' (Henry 1990: 57), offering, for example, 'a full and distinct Notion of a Spirit, with so unexceptionable accuracy, that no Reason can pretend to assert it impossible nor unintelligible' (More 1987: 42). Indeed, this assurance seems a necessary consequence of a natural philosophy that sets out not only to establish the efficacy of rationalism, but also to prove the moral certainty of intellectualist theology.

ANNE CONWAY (1631–79)

More's approach was not only questioned by empirical mechanists, like Boyle, but also by natural philosophers of quite different persuasions. The vitalist, Anne Conway, née Finch, who was a close friend of More, is one such figure. Conway was introduced to More by her brother John, who was taught by More at Cambridge (Hutton 1992: x). He subsequently became her mentor, conducting an intellectual correspondence with her from 1650 to her death, initially on Descartes, but later on a wide range of philosophical and theological issues. He dedicated his *Antidote* to her and his *Immortality* is addressed to her husband, Edward, Lord Viscount Conway.

Like other women of the period, Conway received no formal education, but was nonetheless widely read. Although she lived a relatively retired life at her husband's estate, Ragley Hall, like her contemporary, Margaret Cavendish, her family's social and intellectual connections gave her access to major contemporary philosophical discussions and brought her into contact with figures like Boyle and William Harvey, who was briefly her physician. She was indeed largely responsible for turning the Conway estate into an intellectual centre, her circle including, besides More, Cudworth, Whichcote, Glanvill, and, most significantly, van Helmont, who became her physician and lived at Ragley from 1670 (Hutton 1997: 220). As well as studying the mystical Lurianic Kabbalah under his auspices, it was through van Helmont that she was introduced to what was then treated as being the completely heretical sect of Quakerism, to which she, like him, eventually converted (see Hutton 1992: viii).[10] In addition, he introduced her work to Gottfried Wilhelm Leibniz (1646–1716), who was influenced by her concepts of harmony and the monad (see Frankel 1993: 197–216 and Coudert 1995: ch. 2). Conway published nothing in her lifetime, but van Helmont translated into Latin a compilation of her work, comprising 'writings abruptly and scatteredly … written in a Paper Book' (Conway 1982: 240), which was published in 1690 with a preface by More, along with two other treatises, including one by himself. This 'little Treatise' (Conway 1982: 147), which is far shorter than any of the works discussed so far, was retranslated into English

---

[10] In collaboration with his friend, Knorr von Rosenroth, van Helmont helped to compile and edit the texts that were published as the *Kabbala Denudata* (1677, 1684). Their Cabbalistic ideas were Lurianic, being drawn from the writings that circulated among the disciples of Isaac Luria (1534–72).

as *The Principles of the Most Ancient and Modern Philosophy Concerning God, Christ and the Creation* (1692).

Principles not only signals Conway's engagement with central philosophical ideas of the period and their relation to theology, but also her independence of thought from More and others, though she leaves directly naming her antagonists to her final chapter. Like More's philosophy, Conway's is 'diametrically opposite' to Hobbes's materialism and its attendant atheistic overtones (221). Where Hobbes 'affirms God himself to be Material ... and so confounds God and the Creatures in their Essences', her ideas are premised on the absolute distinction between God and his creatures (222). Contrary to Hobbes's view, God 'doth not nor cannot partake of the least Corporiety', but rather is 'the First and Supreme Spirit': he is 'a perpetual Creator', singularly 'Independent, Unchangeable, absolutely Infinite, and most Perfect' (192, 181, 196). His creatures, on the other hand, are 'changeable and successive', comprise 'Infinite' 'Multiplicity', are capable of 'Infinite Divisibility' and have 'no limits to [their] progression' (164–5, 210, 182). The only essence distinguished from these two is Christ, who is 'that true Medium, between God and the Creatures' and 'must needs exist within them, that so by his Operation he may stir them up to a Union with him' (170). Hence, Christ has an affinity with both God and his creatures that connects these two extremes.

As with More and the Cambridge Platonists, Conway adopts an intellectualist theology in which God 'cannot do that which is contrary to his Wisdom and Goodness' (163) (see Broad 2002: 85–8 on Conway's intellectualist theology). Conway's God is not 'a cruel Tyrant', but 'Just, and Merciful', the teleology underpinning divine wisdom being that 'Judgement is turned into Victory to the Salvation and Restoration of the Creature' (1982: 187). In complete contrast to Hobbesian determinism or the unpredictability of voluntarism, Conway's notions of divine providence and design are thus profoundly optimistic as well as rationalistic. In her view, God 'hath created every Creature good' and their essential changeability necessarily indicates that they can transform, so that 'by continual augmentations', they may perfect themselves '*ad infinitum*': it is only through their own 'voluntary Transgression' that humans can degenerate (180, 186). It is, indeed, God's 'Universal Law of Justice' that unites his creatures and, in spite of their diversity, draws them together into a 'Society of Fellowship' (209–10).

In keeping with her intellectualist stance, Conway's philosophical approach highlights reasoned argument, relying on notions of common sense and shared experience, supported primarily by scriptural reference and citations from the *Kabbala Denudata*. It is through these means that she identifies both the limits of mechanical philosophy and the fallaciousness of atomism, for, she argues, 'we cannot say of any Creature, that it is but one single Thing' because that would prevent it from being able to perfect itself. Indeed, mirroring the infinity of their creator, 'there is an Infiniteness of Spirits in every Spirit, and Infiniteness of Bodies in every Body' that cannot 'be measured by the knowledge of any Creature' (208).

Like More, Conway regards 'Nature, and her Operations' as surpassing the functions of 'a clock', they being 'far more than merely Mechanical' because nature is 'a living Body' (222). In viewing nature as such, she distinguishes between 'Local, or Mechanical

Motion' and 'Vital Action', the former being merely 'the Instrument' of the latter (225, 227). In this, More's intermediary Spirit of Nature to explain the movement of matter is treated as being entirely redundant because, for Conway, vital action indicates the God-given 'Divine Spirituality' which is 'intrinsically present' in every motion (227).

Conway's concept of vitalism is thus directly connected to her theology of transform-ation. It also signals her fundamentally different view of the body from both More's and mechanical philosophers', such as Descartes and Hobbes, as well as her complete antipathy for dualism. In accordance with her theological principles, she rejects the notion that bodies are 'uncapable of Life and Sense' and limited to the essences of 'Impenetrability', 'Discerpibility' and extension (196, 202). In treating body and matter in this way, Descartes and Hobbes specifically, but by implication More, too, have 'understood nothing of them', having 'never proceeded beyond the Husk or Shell' (225). The image of the husk, as Coudert and Corse highlight, derives from the Lurianic Kabbalah and refers to the shell of each individual which will fall away through 'positive redemptive acts' (1996: xix). Conway's allusion thus suggests not just superficiality, but also how their knowledge remains earthbound and fallen.[11] By contrast, for Conway, matter comprises 'Spirit, or Life, and Light', containing the potential for 'all kind of Power and Virtue', whereby even 'Dust and Sand, may be capable of ... Transmutations' towards 'greater Perfection' (1982: 225).

In effect, Conway treats body and spirit as 'one Substance', whose 'distinction is only modal and gradual, not essential or substantial' (222, 190). Where spirit 'is an Eye or Light beholding its own proper Image', body is a 'Darkness receiving that Image', so that 'to be a Body is not an Essential property of any Thing ... for nothing is so dark that it cannot be made Light' (189). Therefore, 'every Body is a Spirit', existing in a continuum 'from the lowest to the highest' and differing only by 'degrees' of 'Corporeity' (190, 223, 192). This means that everything has the potential to attain a greater state of spirituality.

Employing a strikingly Baconian architectural metaphor, Conway accuses those who insist on a dualistic philosophy as laying 'an ill Foundation ... whence the whole House and superstructure is so feeble ... that the whole Edifice and Building must in time decay'. In particular, she objects to the oppositional nature of dualism in which body and spirit are deemed 'to be contrary Things, and inconvertible one into another' because this inevitably results not only in an unsound philosophy, but also an unstable theology (221–2). Her monism, by contrast, is founded on a notion of 'that similitude they have one with another, or some Affinity in their Natures', for 'there is a certain Goodness in the Body, which moves the Spirit to love it' (200). Drawing on a conventional analogy in which the body is linked to a feminine principle of passivity and the spirit a mascu-line one of agency, Conway presents this relation as being one of 'Conjunction and Co-operation' rather than division (188). At one level, Conway thereby follows the one-sex model in which male and female were treated as being 'versions of the same unitary

[11] Coudert and Corse show how Conway's monism and vitalism are informed by the *Kabbala Denudata* (1996: xviii–xxii).

species' (Orgel 1996: 20). But where in this paradigm 'masculinity is a development out of and away from femininity' (Orgel 1996: 20), for Conway the 'Analogy of Nature' between them draws them together (1982: 201).

Moreover, although explicitly asserting that her monistic principles are 'Anti-Cartesian' (222), Conway also implicitly suggests the deficiencies of More's concept of 'vital congruity' between soul and body because, she says, not to explain what 'vital Agreement' comprises is to 'trifle with empty Words' (212) (see Broad 2002: 73–6 on Conway's implicit criticism of More's concept of 'vital congruity'). This is made particularly apparent in her analysis of the effects of pain. While both she and More agree that 'the Soul moves the Body, and suffers by it or with it' (214), for More this is a result of the close physiological connection between them, whereby spirits may penetrate the body. For Conway, however, it is more to do with a fundamental spiritual synergy between body and soul, whereby 'Pain and Torment excites or stirs up an operating Spirit and Life in every thing which suffers'. In promoting spiritual activity, pain therefore assists in restoring the soul to 'return unto Good' (193).

This affinity and cooperation between the corporeal and spiritual signals a more general unity linking all of God's creatures together. In harmony with his own love and beneficence, God 'implanted a certain Universal Sympathy and mutual Love in Creatures, as being all Members of one Body' because in 'their First Substance and Essence, they were all one and the same Thing' (179, 199). This means that each creature 'needs the assistance of its Fellow-Creatures' because they are all designed to work for the mutual benefit of helping to restore one another to their original, more perfect state (209).

Principles could not be clearer in illustrating how Conway's theology is inseparable from her natural philosophy. Like More, she is anxious to centralize the location and role of the spirit and soul within new philosophical discussions and to move what are regarded as being the narrow, reductive, and irreligious overtones of mechanical philosophy into a wider religious context, in which final causes remain paramount. Informed by both traditional Neoplatonic ideas and more unorthodox ones deriving from the Lurianic Kabbala, her monism and vitalism also anticipate Leibniz's ' "system of pre-established harmony" between body and mind' (Woolhouse and Francks 1997: 3). Furthermore, as Coudert and Corse suggest, the 'philosophical implications' of her work 'look forward to the more tolerant and ecumenical views of Enlightenment thinkers', despite their potentially heretical overtones in their own time (1996: xxx, xxi). In this way, Conway's work exemplifies the often diverse range of voices, intertextual conversations and complex interactions between old and new, orthodox and radical, that frequently underscore natural philosophical texts of the period.

More broadly, this chapter shows that, in spite of significant diversity within early modern discussions concerning the relationship between science and religion, the debates highlighted here all illustrate how the new philosophies demanded new ways of grappling with devotional issues and explaining and exploring religious ideas. In seeking to address anxieties about science's potential associations with atheism, science could indeed be put to the service of religion and used in various ways to support religious arguments and provide a proper definition of the relationship between God and humanity. However, there is not a steady line of progression from one mode of thought to another about the interactions between new philosophical and devotional ideas, but more of a continual renegotiation in the balance between them, whereby there could be disparate perspectives even within similar intellectual contexts. By the end of the seventeenth century, at one extreme Hobbes could argue that divinity should be completely excluded from philosophical debate, while, at the other, Conway viewed them as being intrinsically connected. And yet, through their fundamentally dialogic, intertextual quality, what all of the texts explored here hold in common and exemplify more generally is a sense of work in progress, open-ended discussion and continuing conversation from Bacon to Conway and beyond.

CHAPTER 36

·····································

BODY AND SOUL

·····································

MARGARET J. M. EZELL

SOUL O, who shall from this dungeon raise

A soul enslaved so many ways?

…

BODY O, who shall me deliver whole,

From bonds of this tyrannic soul?

Andrew Marvell, 'A Dialogue Between the Soul and Body'

THE diplomat and politician Andrew Marvell is believed to have written this poem in the 1670s and it simultaneously harkens back to a much earlier poetic genre while participating in the ongoing arguments about the nature of the soul and its relationship to the body that escalated over the course of the seventeenth century. Formatted as dialogues between the body and soul of a dying man facing eternal damnation, such intense debates were a staple of medieval literature, peaking in popularity the early fourteenth century, but as critics have observed, that genre became less common over the fifteenth and early sixteenth centuries (Osmond 1990: 55, 83). Throughout the late sixteenth and seventeenth centuries, however, the issues raised by considerations of the nature of the soul and its relationship to the body once again animated controversies in new scientific and political discourses as well as religious ones. Over the course of the late sixteenth and early seventeenth centuries, the soul, its nature, and its relationship with the body became focal points for religious, medical, political, and ethical debates, and the choice of vocabulary itself—soul, spirit, mind, flesh, body—had profound implications in how human and divine nature were represented in early modern literature.

The Grounds for Debate: Sources and Issues

The complexity of representing the nature of the soul and its relationship to the body can be seen in Edward Popham's (1619: A12^{r–v}) attempt to establish an appropriate vocabulary to describe the soul as it functions within the body:

> First, it [the soul] is an immatierall substance: While it doth revive the body, it is the Soule; when it willeth or chooseth any thing, it may (though improperly) be called the Minde: While it knoweth any thing, it may be called (though improperly againe) the Understanding: While it judgeth, some have tearmed it Reason: While it doth breathe or contemplate, a Spirit: While it calls any thing to minde, the Memorie: While it thinketh any thing (though more grosely) the Sense. But to speake of the Soule as it is, it is an immateriall substance, and Reason, Memory, Sence, &c. are the severall faculties and divers opperations Thereof.

To schematize in very general terms, early modern conceptualizations of body and soul are either monistic or dualistic. A monistic view of the body–soul relationship at its most extreme held that the material body is the only existence humans have (materialism) and that a 'person' simply is the material body, although some suggested that the material body could have experiences which were related to what had been described as the moving soul. Such views in the early modern period were in England frequently associated, rightly or wrongly, with atheism (Henry 1989: 88). The materialism developed by Thomas Hobbes in *De Corpore* (1655), for example, held that the soul was both material and mortal, a position that opened his writings to the frequent charge of atheism, although, as we shall see, such views were often being expressed by devout Christians in the 1640s and 1650s (Thomson 2008). Lady Anne Conway (1631–79), who enjoyed an extensive philosophical correspondence in the 1650s with the Cambridge Platonist Henry More, was in the 1670s increasingly influenced by the mysticism of the physician and kabbalist Francis Mercurius Van Helmont (1614–98/9). Conway also urged a monist understanding of body and soul. In contrast to the materialist view, however, she declared in writings published after her death that 'the Soul is of one Nature and Substance with the Body, although it is many degrees more excellent in regard of Life and Spirituality, as also in swiftness of Motion, and Penetrability, and divers other Perfections'; her argument was that such an understanding could counter the issues raised by dualism, and 'all the aforesaid difficulties will vanish, and it will be easily conceived, how the Body and Soul are united together', that 'the Spirit and Body differ not essentially, but gradually' (1692: 132, 126). Conway continued her investigations of the soul throughout her life, in the final years embracing the 'Inner Light' of Quakerism.

More commonly held views of the body–soul relationship involved forms of dualism, that the body did have something different in nature from the soul, and that a 'person' was the union of the body and soul. Dualism, as expressed in Platonism, for example, was central to the teachings of St Augustine and the Christian Church (Cross 2005). As we shall see, this conceptualization had a resurgence in popularity in England as seen in sixteenth- and seventeenth-century literary as well as philosophical texts: Neoplatonism, as expressed in Plotinus's writings that combined Plato's teachings with Aristotle's, experienced a revival of interest in Italy and was embraced in England in particular by an influential group, the Cambridge Platonists, among whose members were Ralph Cudworth, Henry More, Benjamin Whichcote, and Peter Sterry. Debates also emerged among believers of dualism, some arguing that the soul needs the body to perform its will, but others declaring it was not that the body possesses a soul, but instead that the human soul is encased or unhappily trapped in a fleshly body, wishing for nothing more than to be free of the body and to take flight to return to its source, as we shall see, both providing the imagery and discourse of the body–soul debates in texts ranging from commercially staged dramas to private devotional writings.

The specific elements of classical philosophy which were the source of the issues of the body and soul debates in English thought were found in the writings of Aristotle, Plato, and Epicurus and their followers. The soul (*psyche*) related to the body (*soma*) in two ways: first, as an animating spirit within the body responsible for the body's motions and cognitive actions and second, as an independent entity that could exist separately from the body and thus create a personal immortality (Michael 2000: 148). Aristotle's *De anima* and *Parva naturalia* were key texts shaping the discourse about the soul found in early modern natural philosophy and medical interrogations of the nature of the soul; Aristotelian sources, however, could be hotly contested in a theological context (Sutton 2003: 288). Early modern thinkers following Aristotle theorized that the soul had three types of faculties: a vegetative one governing reproduction and nurture shared with plants and animals; a sensitive faculty governing perception, memory, and movement shared with animals; and an intellective one, that exercises will and reason, permitting it to reflect on its own nature. Central to debates in the sixteenth and seventeenth centuries was this final concept of the soul as personal immortality: Pietro Pomponazzi in *De immortalitate animae* (1516) urged a theory of the rational soul as 'material', that is, that a soul has a substantial form of its own, but that it is dependent in all of its activities upon the body, and therefore like the body, the soul is mortal, a view which was strongly countered by the Catholic Church and seventeenth-century writers including Descartes (Michael 2000).

In his *Meditations*, Descartes asserts that 'as regards the soul, many people have considered that it is not easy to discover its nature, and some have even had the audacity to assert that, as far as human reasoning goes, there are persuasive grounds for holding that the soul dies along with the body and that the opposite view is based on faith alone' (1985: II, 4). This view he flatly rejected, arguing that while the body and soul could exist separately from each other, the body without the soul was merely a machine. Within the body, Descartes suggested, the soul resides within the pineal gland (Lokhorst 2014), a view which anatomists were quick to challenge. In England, Sir Kenelm Digby (1603–65), who had studied Descartes's writings and met with him in 1640, likewise took offence at Pomponazzi's work concerning the mortality of the soul, although not finding himself in agreement with Descartes, either. What Digby sought to establish in his writings was a type of Christian, Protestant Aristotelianism, where the soul has no parts, is not dependent on the body's life functions, and experiences no transformations or changes; for Digby there is no purgatory where the soul will wait with the body for redemption, nor any interval of sleep while awaiting the resurrection, but instead, based on one's actions during life, the soul at the body's death would instantaneously attain its future state, whether in heaven or hell (Sutton 2003).

In addition to Aristotle, another classical philosophy crucial to the shaping of early modern discussions of the soul and body was Platonism. Briefly, platonic dualism sees the mind and the soul as identical and that the soul pre-exists the body and survives it by transmigration; the soul unlike the body is indestructible and immortal. Cambridge Platonists such as Henry More, who had extensive correspondence with Lady Anne Conway, argued strongly for the incorporeality of the soul, taking as some of his principle targets writers who 'are so sunk into the dull sense of their Bodies' (1662: I.9.2) that they are incapable of appreciating this. Not only does the soul survive the body after death, More claims, it retains its memories of the individual lived life otherwise the soul 'could never tell | Why she were thus rewarded, wherefore ill | Or good she doth enjoy, whether ill or well | She lived here. Remembrance death doth spill' (1647: stanzas 2, 28–32). Joining together several strands of philosophical thought, Henry More argued that Platonism was 'the most noble and effectual Engine to fetch up a man's mind to true virtue and holinesse, next to the Bible, that is extant in the World', while the mechanical philosophy of Descartes was 'the best assistance to Religion that Reason and the Knowledge of Nature can afford' (1651: 36; 1662: 13).

The Neoplatonic belief that embodied beauty and human love are images of heavenly absolutes was embraced by English poets and dramatists throughout the early modern period. Scholars have declared that 'the influence of Platonism is everywhere to be felt in the writing of the English Renaissance', absorbed within the popular Petrarchan style of love poetry and embraced by aristocratic elite literary culture through the first part of the seventeenth century (Hutton 1994: 71–2). Writers such as Edmund Spenser, John Drayton, Sir Philip Sidney, Ben Jonson, John Donne, and the later court writers of Henrietta Maria celebrated as well as criticized the representation of human love as being between souls as opposed to between bodies. Important sources for poets such as Spenser include Marsilio Ficino's framing of the concept of 'platonic love' between two souls found in his commentary on Plato's *Symposium* in his work *De amore* (1484). The doctrine of platonic love dominated European courtly discourse in the sixteenth century in France as well as Italy; it became popular in England through translations, most notably the Latin translation of Baldasar Castiglione's *Il cortegiano* by Bartholomew Clerke (1571) and Sir Thomas Hoby's translation of it into English under the title of *The Courtyer* (1561). In France, the sixteenth-century group of poets who styled themselves *La Pléiade*, including Joachim de Bellay and Pierre de Ronsard, popularized Petrarchan sonnet cycles which also inspired English poets, where through an initial attraction to the physical body the lover would be led to discover the beauty of the soul.

During the same period, early modern readers encountered contrasting representations of both the body and the soul as mortal through the writings of Epicurus and his follower Lucretius, such as the mid-seventeenth-century translator and poet Lucy Hutchinson (1620–81). Hutchinson in the 1650s prepared a translation of *De rerum natura* of Lucretius; in Book III, she grapples with his representation of the relationship of the body and soul in death, 'while vitall sence thus flows through all | Bodie and soule make but one animall' and 'which if some violence should suddenly | Cleave in the midst, the force of soule would be | Parted to both, in neither piece entire | Soe would, disjointed in severd parts expire' (2011: 189). She concludes the passage 'Now immortalitie must be denied | To all things which have parts, or can devide' (191). When Hutchinson presented a fair copy of her manuscript to Arthur Annesley, earl of Anglesey in 1675, she records in the dedicatory epistle to him that she deeply regretted her time with such texts, and 'the Encomiums given to these Pagan Poets and Philosophers … is one greate means of debauchery of soule, which their first sin led them into, and of hindering their recovery, while they puddle all the streames of Truth,' that they 'are but the severall foolish and impious inventions of the old contemplative Heathen revivd, and brought forth in new dresses' (de Quehen 1996: 26). By making Latin into English, Hutchinson realizes, she may have unwittingly made Lucretius's ideas available to readers unsuited to withstand its seduction and be turned away from the truth; like these 'incautious travelers', she describes her own situation while engaged in the translation as being like a person who 'walking in the darke, had miraculously scapd a horrible precipice, by daylight coming back and discovering his late danger, startles and reviews it with affright' (de Quehen 1996: 26). By restricting her readership to this fair manuscript copy, unlike the royalist John Evelyn who published his translation of Book One in 1656, to be discussed later, and took authorial steps to protect himself from being accused of heresy, Hutchinson feels that Anglesey, her ideal reader, will be able to control access to her text, appreciate its poetic merit and her talents, and not be swayed into heresies such as mortalism (Parker 2013). A decade later, another translator of Lucretius, John Dryden (1631–1700) while applauding Lucretius's poetic genius nevertheless warned his unknown print readers that Lucretius's views on the mortality of the soul with the body 'are so absurd, that I cannot if I would believe them' and that a rejection of heaven and hell 'is only a pleasing prospect to a man who resolves beforehand not to live morally' (*Sylvae*; 1685: a2^r).

The controversies created by translations of Epicurean philosophy spilled over several decades and numerous texts. The physician and philosopher Walter (sometimes styled William) Charleton (1619–1707) translated *Physiologia Epicuro-Gassendo-Charltoniana* (1654), followed shortly by Epicurus's *Morals* in 1656 including his 'Apologie for Epicurus' in which he rejected the idea of the mortality of the soul and the denial of providence in human life. These texts profoundly influenced subsequent generations of natural philosophers and scientists including Robert Boyle, Isaac Newton, and John Locke (Kargon 1964). Charleton followed his translation with *The Immortality of the Human Soul, Demonstrated by the Light of Nature In Two Dialogues* (1657), in which the character 'Athanasius' (Charleton) debates with 'Lucretius' (John Evelyn) and

'Isodicastes' (Henry Pierrepoint, first marquess of Dorchester). In the advertisement to the reader, the publisher Henry Herringman explains that dialogue serves as a pleasing didactic tool and indeed these recreate conversations held in the Luxemburg Garden in Paris and that 'there is nothing of fiction, besides that of Names proper to each of the Speakers. And, as for those', Herringman concludes, 'the Parts they bear in the Discourse, sufficiently discover their Derivations.' John Evelyn (1620–1706) had published an English verse translation of the first book of Lucretius's *De rerum natura* in 1656; it came bolstered by an author portrait featuring Evelyn wearing a laurel wreath, with commendatory poems by the diplomat and translator Sir Richard Fanshawe as well as the Oxford classicist Christopher Wase to lend it authority. In contrast to the reaction to this carefully designed presentation of the controversial writer in scholarly academic garb, 'Athanasius' reveals to 'Lucretius' how the response to his translations produced not the admiration and applause he may have imagined, but instead, 'even to this very day, I have been embroil'd in as many troubles and distractions, as malice, persecution, and sharp adversity could accumulate upon me. I have been driven from my Country, House, Family, Books, Friends, and Acquaintances', he laments, for bringing Epicurean philosophy about the body and soul into English (Charlton: 11).

In terms of religious profession, however, the issues raised by body and soul were crucial in distinguishing one's beliefs during a period marked by change and instability. The language of the body–soul debates was often used as a means to separate Catholics from Protestants, and Anglicans from radical sectarians. It is not surprising that the 1590s produced a series of texts urgently exploring questions raised about the relationship between the body and soul. Because Protestants do not believe in purgatory, that time and place where a Christian soul goes to be cleansed of its sins before the Judgement Day, questions arising over what happens to the soul upon the death of the body are particularly pressing and central to debates distinguishing one's beliefs. Followers of Calvin believed that the souls of saints are predestined for salvation from the very moment of their creation and after the death of the body exist in an intermediate state awaiting the day of judgement; writing in the late 1590s, the influential Cambridge theologian William Perkins (1548–1602) explained this view, suggesting that although there was no such thing as purgatory, 'As there are two degrees of glorie, one incomplete and the other complete or perfect, (for the faithfull departed as in glorie but in part, and there remaineth fullness of glorie for them at the day of judgement, when the soule and bodie shall be both glorified together): so answerably there are two degrees of preparation of places in heaven' (*A Golden Chaine*; Perkins 1600: 400). On the other hand, Luther's argument that the soul either sleeps (psychosomnolence or soul sleep) or dies (thnetopsychism, where both body and soul die and are resurrected together) with the demise of the physical body rather than going to purgatory was used by William Tyndale against Sir Thomas More in their acrimonious polemical exchanges in the late 1520s and early 1530s. However, as with the controversy surrounding Thomas Hobbes's depiction of mortalism, by the mid-seventeenth century, the issue of the mortality of the soul became less a touchstone not to distinguish Protestant from Catholic, but an indication of radical political and religious sectarianism and atheism (McDowell 2003).

Mortalist debates over what happens to the body and soul at death and at resurrection, as well as the physical nature of hell, can be found across the spectrum of writing in the early modern period, from dramas and ballads to private meditations and public sermons. Christopher Marlowe's academic protagonist in *The Tragedie of Dr. Faustus*, after signing away his soul in his own blood, repeatedly questions Mephistopheles about the nature of hell, specifically wanting to know where it is. Faustus rejects Mephistopheles's explanation that 'Hell hath no limits ... for where we are is hell', defiantly declaring that 'Come, I think hell's a fable' (2.1.1.28). In the final scene Faustus is dragged offstage by devils as he describes the burning flames he now sees, agonizing that 'no end is limited to damned souls | ... | All beasts are happy, for when they die | Their souls are soon dissolv'd in elements | But mine must live still be to be plagu'd in hell' (5.2.96–104).

Forty years after the appearance of Marlowe's text, the prolific sectarian writer Richard Overton had printed a pamphlet that not only argued there was no physical heaven or hell, but also that souls die and are resurrected with their particular bodies. Published in 1643/4, the provocatively entitled *Mans mortallitie or a treatise wherein 'tis proved, both theologically and philosophically, that whole man (as a rationall creature) is a compound wholy mortall, contrary to the common distinction of soule and body: and that the present going of the soule into Heaven or Hell is a meer fiction: and that at the resurrection is the beginning of our immortallity, and then actuall condemnation, and salvation, and not before* was reprinted in 1655 with the title *Man Wholly Mortal* and reissued in 1675 with a new title page. Overton, a General Baptist, would become a significant voice in the Leveller movement and was imprisoned with John Lilliburne.

As McDowell has noted, the commendatory verses at the start of the pamphlet, which Overton may himself have written, owe a debt to Marlowe's *Dr. Faustus*. Whoever is the poet, he declares that the pamphlet will overturn 'The Hell hatch'd Doctrine of th'immortall Soule' and cause the 'Furies' to 'teare their snakey haire with griefe appal'd | To see their Errour-leading Doctrine quail'd'. In his text, Overton argued that before the fall, Adam was immortal, but after it, both body and soul died and are resurrected together at the Judgement Day, noting that God declared that 'Immortall *Adam* shall be made mortall, not a part of thee, but *Thou* shalt surely dye, even whole man, without the least exception of any, the worst or noblest part of him, unless God had a mental reservation' (1). Overton argues that 'the Soule (by his owne grounds) was chiefly, the body but instrumentally in the Transgression: And so, if the wages of sin be death, the Soule was under the divine Maledictions as well as the Body ... if the Souls Immortality may be pleaded, much more may the Bodies' (15). Declaring that both heaven and hell are fictions or metaphors to help man to comprehend salvation, Overton is adamant that neither is a physical place. Drawing on classical texts including Pliny and Ovid as well as scripture, the rhetorical style of the pamphlet suggests to some literary historians that Overton was no simple, semi-literate radical, but indeed a Cambridge-educated writer with experience of the parodic conventions of university humanist dramas (McDowell 2003: 51–7).

An anonymous reader published his response shortly after Overton's pamphlet first appeared, *The prerogative of man: or, The immortality of humane soules asserted against the vain cavils of a late worthlesse pamphlet, entituled, Mans mortality, &c.* (1645). Its thesis was that those who believe in the mortality of the soul are likely possessed of 'a depraved appetite or an unbridled and untamed sensuality that sollicites perpetually to be satisfied, and is desirous, without feare of future reckonings in the other world, to wallow and tumble like a swine in the mire of dirty pleasures' (A2ʳ). Similarly, an owner of Overton's book reissued in 1674, a John Fisher, kept up a running argument in the margin, declaring that Overton's logic was sophistical and with a pointing accusatory finger at one point noted that the argument was 'a dreadful reflection on ye Author' (Folger 151–435q, p. 74). In 1644, Overton's book, along with John Milton's controversial *Doctrine and Discipline of Divorce* was condemned by the Commons to be burned, but that did not prevent its repeated republication.

During the pamphlet wars of the late 1640s and 1650s, mortalism was frequently defined as heresy and often associated with radical sectarians and/or atheists. The title of the 1658 work by the two London tailors who declared themselves God's final prophets as foretold in Revelations, John Reeve and Lodowick Muggleton, leaves little doubt as to their views: *Joyful News from Heaven: Or, The Last Intelligence from our Glorified Jesus above the Stars: Wherein is infallibly record, How that the Soul dieth in the Body*. The Muggletonians, who also did not believe in the Trinity but instead that Jesus is God (and worked out his height as being between five and six feet), were viewed as scandalous even by the standards of the radical sectarian and Ranter Lawrence Clarkson (Lamont 2006). John Reeve received a vision commanding him to be God's spokesman on earth, and among the four things he was charged to deliver was the statement that 'look into they own body, there thou shalt see the Kingdom of Heaven, and the Kingdom of Hell' (Underwood 1999: 142–3). One of their early followers, Nathaniel Powell created a lengthy unprinted song in ballad form about Reeve's vision, in which he narrates the words of God to the prophet and sings the message:

> Then tell my flock their souls must dye
> That compounds all mortality
> They Silent Sleep untill the day
> I raise them to Immortall Ray.
>
> Last, tell the place where hell shall be
> Its Nature Torments fuelty
> This Earth where they their Sins commit
> The place they suffer must for it.
>
> Then shall their Bodys be their hell
> Their cursed Spirits the Devill
> Which burneth with such horrid flame
> They'll curse for to provoke their pain. (Underwood 1999: 217)

This belief in the inseparability of the body and soul is also found in Muggleton's messages to his followers. Writing to a dying young woman, Elizabeth Dickson, Muggleton comforts her that, 'in the Resurrection this Vile Distempered body of yours, which is now mortall shall rise an Immortall Spiritual body Capable of Eternal Joy and Glory, where no Diseases Pain nor Sorrow can come where body and Soul shall live in Joy and pleasure for Evermore' (Underwood 1999: 209).

Recently scholars have explored the heretical elements found in John Milton's writings, in the context of these debates and his seeming espousal of mortalism. Nigel Smith has observed of *Paradise Lost* that 'Milton believes that the entire universe is one substance, and is not divided into the material and the immaterial, any more than bodies are divisible from souls' (2009b: 515). In the manuscript of *De Doctrina Christiana*, usually believed to be composed during the 1650s, Milton makes it explicit that there are two deaths experienced, the first being the physical death of the body and the soul and the second a metaphorical one, being the punishment of the damned to exist for eternity in hell.

The title of a 1657 pamphlet by Thomas Hicks neatly encapsulates the opposition to the implications carried by such ways of thinking about the relation of the soul's life to that of the body's: *A discourse of the souls of men, women, and children; and of the holy and blessed angels in heaven, and of the evil and damned spirits in hell: shewing that they are immortal, spiritual substances, as well as the angels in heaven. Written because this author met with four willfull ignorant men at one time, which said, the souls of men, women, and children, were nothing but breath, and vanished into air, when as the body went to the grave. These unfaithful people ought to be answered and reproved.* We know nothing of Hicks, nor of the four ignorant men, but it is clear that by the mid-seventeenth century, passionate discussions over the body–soul are not confined to the realm of academic and theological discourse but infuse cheap print publications by authors from a variety of backgrounds.

At the opposite point of view of mortalism and the inseparability of body and soul is the perception that the soul is an unwilling captive within the body and desires passionately to be released from a prison of flesh and appetite so that it may fly upward and leave the earth behind. Popular printed broadside ballads such as 'A Farewell to the world' and its second part 'The Soules Petition at Heauen Gate' published as being the deathbed song of Thomas Byll have the repentant speaker declare, 'Nothing but one I in this world doe craue, | That is, to bring my Corpse dead to the grave', hoping that 'And Angells shall my Soule in safetie kéepe, | Whilst that my Bodie in the graue doth sleepe' (Byll 1630). The second part imagines the Soul knocking at the gates of heaven asking for admission, the 'key' to the entrance for the soul being Christ's promise that 'Vnto repentant Soules he promise gaue, | That they with him a place in Heauen should haue'.

The frequently reprinted broadside ballad 'Saint Bernards Vision' was first published in 1613 and based on the translation of the puritan minister and controversialist William Crashawe (1572–1625/6) of a medieval Latin manuscript 'Visio Philberti' (Osmond 1990: 84–90). In 'Saint Bernards Vision', the Soul and the Body take turns blaming each other for damnation. The Soul points to the vanity of the Body while it lived only now to be reduced in death, while 'I (poor Soule) was fram'd a noble creature, | In likeness to my God, of heavenly feature: | But by thy sinne whil at [*sic*] we on Earth aboade, | I am made fouler than a loathsome Toade' (Osmond 1990: 209).

The Body retorts that it was created by God to be the servant of the Soul and 'Twas in your power for to restraine my will, | And not to let me doe those things were ill. | The Bodies works be from the Soule derived, | And by the Soule the Body should be guided' (Osmond 1990: 210). The body's desire for physical pleasure can overwhelm the soul's voice, but equally, the tormenting soul can lead to a wracked and tortured body.

The popular and influential Protestant preacher Henry Smith (1569–91) explored this topic in his sermon *The Trumpet of the Soule, sounding to judgement* (London, 1593) on the text 'Rejoyce O young man in thy youth'. Smith muses that on reading this text:

> Me thinks I heare the Dialogue betweene the flesh and the Spirit, the flesh which is worst speaketh first, and saith: Soule, take thine ease, eate, drink, & goe braue, lyesoft, whatelse shouldest thou doe but take thy pleasure, thou knowst what a pleasant fellow I haue beene unto thee, thou knowest what delight thou hast had by my maeanes (sig. A6^v)

The soul 'burdened with that which hath beene spoken before', reminds the body to think about Judgement and 'unless thou repent thou shalt surely perrish'. The body is having none of that, however, retorting it wishes to hear only of 'fine matters, of soft beddes and pleasant things, and talke to me of braue pastimes, Apes, Beares, & Puppits: for I tell thee the forbidden fruite is the sweetest of all fruities, for I doe not like your telling me of Iudgement' (A7^r). Smith summarizes the exchange, characterizing the speakers as two 'counsellers', the spirit/soul weighted down with burdens while 'the fleshe goeth laughing and singing to hel'.

This antipathy between the body and soul in a forced union permeates much private meditations and devotional verse as well as sermons preached from the pulpit and printed. The voice of the fettered or imprisoned soul yearning for release was not confined to any particular religious group or medium of transmission. The manuscript devotional poetry of the London Presbyterian Julia Palmer includes poems with titles such as 'spirituall sloth the souls ruine' and in 'the soull reaching out after what it most desirs' the poet laments 'Fain I would dye | That I might lye | safe in Christs arms | ... | Fain would I fly | to heaven high' (2001: 182, 77). One of her lyrics, 'Longings to go hence', shows her, like many writers of religious poetry in the later seventeenth century, direct indebtedness to the Anglican George Herbert's *The Temple*, pleading that 'From earths dark den, fain would I fly | That in thy bosome, I might lye | Oh dearest Jesus, come away | My sweetest Lord, make no delay' (Palmer 2001:1; Wilcox 2000a: 455). The emblem writer Francis Quarles (1592–1644), one of the most frequently published poets in the seventeenth century, likewise compared his soul to being like a bird within a cage or one who has been maimed to control it: 'See how shee flutters with her idle wings; | Her wings are clipt, and eyes put out by Sense' (*Emblemes*; 1639: 62). In his mediation on Psalm VI.II, he formats it as a dialogue between a desperate soul and Christ as the physician (137–8). In Emblem XV he meditates upon Psalm XXXI.10, 'My life is spent with grief, and my years with sighing', exclaiming 'O that the pleased Heav'ns would once dissolve | | These fleshly fetters, that so fast involve | My hamper'd soul; then would my soul be blest | From all those ills, and wrap her thoughts in rest' (186).

Hester Pulter (*c*.1605–78) wrote primarily for her family, leaving behind a fair copy manuscript volume compilation of her poems and a prose romance. Her poems and emblems range widely, touching on contemporary political events of the civil war as well as domestic concerns and devotional meditations. Critics have noticed the shared imagery of the soul found in Pulter's verses with George Herbert and John Donne as well as suggesting she made have had access to unpublished manuscripts of Andrew Marvell (Pulter 2014: 25; Wilcox 2000a: 456n. 23). Pulter's verse, often written during illness or on the loss of her children, frequently wishes for death as a release for her tormented soul, while nevertheless acknowledging the body's fear of it and her perverse clinging to life. 'When little infants' new-created souls | Do easily fly about or star or poles', why should her soul, 'withered and worn with grief | Thinkst in this dunghill earth to find relief' she asks it (146). In a poem to her husband, she explains the competing struggle between her body and soul, asking him to, 'Pardon me, my dearest love, | That I place my thought above | What's susolary is yours | And so shall be while life endures': 'My soul remembers still her birth, | She being a sparkle of that light, | Which ne'er shall set in death or night' and she compares the separation of the soul from the body as the drawing and quartering of traitors permitting her 'enfranchised spirit' to be freed (142). In 'Must I thus ever interdicted be' Pulter concludes, 'Oh let thy spirit my sad soul sustain | Until those comforts I do reattain| ... | Until my captivated soul takes wing | Then will I hallelujahs ever sing' (163).

Pulter shared with the twin brothers Henry and Thomas Vaughan (1621–66) an interest in hermetic philosophy and alchemy (Linden 1996). Unlike her desire for her soul to escape the body through its death, its 'calcination', in his poetry Henry Vaughan seems able to have glimpses of his soul's former existence which foretell the soul's reunion with the divine: 'Happy those early days, when I | Shin'd in my angel-infancy! | Before I understood this place | Appointed for my second race, | Or taught my soul to fancy ought | But a white, celestial thought' ('The Retreat'). Thomas Vaughan declared in his medical writings that souls have 'an Explicite Methodicall knowledge ... before their Intrance into the body' (*Anthroposophia theomagica*; 1650: 2); for Henry, the soul, 'Who came (sure) from a sea of light' ('The Waterfall') even in adulthood mired in the senses, 'there's a restless, pure desire | And longing for thy bright and vital fire' ('The Star'). Thomas Traherne (*c*.1637–74) expressed a similar appreciation of the nature of childhood and access to the divine in his unpublished prose meditations, *Centuries of Mediation*, as well as his verse, declaring repeatedly, 'How wise was I | In infancy! | I then saw in the clearest light' ('Right Apprehension'). As Sharon Seelig has discussed, for Traherne, however, once right perception is restored, both the body and the soul can both delight in the splendours of divine creation on earth, 'In Pure, Transparent, Soft, Sweet, Melting Pleasures, | Like Precious and Diffusive Treasures, | A once my Body fed, and Soul did Crown' ('Speed'; 129).

MALE AND FEMALE, SOUL AND BODY?

In 1595, a brief treatise in Latin, *Disputatio nova contra mulieres, qua probatur eas homines non esse* created an immediate stir; it was republished throughout the seventeenth and eighteenth centuries, despite in 1651 being placed on the Vatican *Index Librorum Prohibitorum*. The title roughly translates as 'a new argument against women demonstrating they are not human' and is believed to have been written as a satire, perhaps by Valens Acidalius (Hart 1998). In 1647 it was published in Lyons in Italian with a slightly different title, asserting that 'women do not have a soul and do not belong to the human race'. John Donne's youthful paradox, problem seven, asks a similar question, 'Why hath the common opinion afforded women Soules?', which took as its starting point a popular point of misogyny, and which scholars point out is typically read as a type of academic joke, arguing an absurd premise to highlight one's debating skills. Nevertheless, the question was one that had apparently enjoyed some serious discussion and also continued to permeate through popular cultural representations (Johnson 2014). The notion that women might not have souls was derived from anti-Catholic writings, in which the medieval Council of Mâcon was falsely described as denying souls to women; nevertheless, it was in such common currency in early modern England that the mature Donne declared from the pulpit that 'no author of gravity, of piety, of conversation in the Scriptures could admit that doubt, whether a woman were created in the Image of God, that is, in possession of a reasonable and immortall soul' (Johnson 2014: 3). The notion, however, continued to be circulated and those writing in defence of the female sex frequently began by basing their arguments on the nature of the female soul, although there was conflicting opinion as to whether it was a soul within a female body or that the soul itself was female. Still others were making the argument that while bodies had sexes, souls did not.

'Here is neither Jew nor Greek, there is neither bond nor free, there is neither male nor female: for ye are all one in Christ Jesus' (Galatians 3:28). Many early modern radical sectarians found inspiration in this passage that all are one in Christ, and women prophets and visionaries from the sixteenth century onwards frequently asserted while women laboured under inferiority of the body, the souls of the sexes are equal. The doctrine of the priesthood of all believers combined with this understanding of the 'ungendered soul', as it was frequently invoked by women preaching and evangelizing, has been described by Hilary Hinds as being 'at the heart of women sectarians' reconfigurations of femininity' (1996: 56). The Quaker Margaret Fell, in *Women's speaking justified, proved and allowed of by the Scriptures* (1666), declared 'where Women are led by the Spirit of God, they are not under the Law, for Christ in the Male and in the Female is one' (Fell 1666: 2). Two other Quakers, Priscilla Cotton writing from jail in 1655 addressed the injunction that women must not speak in church in *To the priests and people of England, we discharge our consciences, and give them warning* retorting that 'we are all both male and female in Christ Jesus' and that men's mere academic education does not make them fit to preach (Cotton 1665: 6).

While some writers and preachers were thus inspired by the ungendered soul, the more traditional views of the relationship between flesh and spirit also involved tensions involving relationship between male and female, to the point of inquiring whether infants received their gendered souls from their parents or whether the soul was infused by God at conception. Such questions perplexed not only anatomists and theologians but also poets and dramatists pondering how the body–soul dualism was mirrored in the body as male–female. In general, we find the agreement that the relationship of the two was hierarchal, with the soul esteemed over the body, which lead to a natural metaphorical gendering of the two, with the soul being represented as male and the body female, often with the negative connotation of the fleshy temptation to sin that overrides reason (Johnson 2014). On the Jacobean stage, women who subvert the natural authority of their husbands, or whose beauty lures men into lasciviousness such as the character of Tamyra in George Chapman's *The Tragedy of Bussy d'Ambois* (1607) who, although a virtuous wife, admits that for women 'Our bodies are but thick clouds to our souls, | Through which they cannot shine when they desire' (III.i. 59–67). The body of Shakespeare's Desdemona, although she is chaste and innocent, will prove the undoing of Othello, as Iago notes 'His soul is so infetter'd to her love, | That she may make, unmake, do what she list, | Even as her appetite shall play the god | With his weak function' (II.ii. 336–9), the lures of the female body overcoming the male rational mind. Osmond has declared that in drama, which is structured around conflict, 'one sees best the dynamic implications of the body/soul dualism worked out in its various guises' and that women characters on stage, whether represented as virtuous or vicious 'are seen within the context of the analogy as body, not soul' (1990: xii, 166).

William Hill, a doctor of divinity, pondered the issue of how a soul got into the body, male or female, in *The infancie of the soule; or, The soule of an infant A subiect neuer yet treated of by any. Which sheweth the infusion there of whiles that the infant resteth in the wombe: the time when, with the manner how* (1605). Hill begins by looking at how poets, physicians, philosophers, lawyers, and the scriptures describe the nature of the soul and agreement among these diverse sources that that the soul is 'infused into the bodie [by God] … before the infant cometh out of his mothers wombe' (B2^r). Furthermore, Hill declares, 'it is the Soule that giueth power to be a Man, and not the Body: he is not a Man or Woman, before the soule be united unto the Body' and that 'the Body cannot be called after either sex, if it be once depriued of the Soule; but rather a Body or Carcasse' (C2^r). Although Hill may find agreement about the relationship between the body and the soul at their creation, Richard Overton's mortalist interpretation objects that 'then there must be He soules and She soules: for without Sexes is no generation' (33).

The poet and lawyer John Davies (1569–1626) the favourite of Queen Elizabeth also engaged these issues but in verse, in his frequently reprinted *Nosce teipsum this oracle expounded in two elegies, 1. Of humane knowledge, 2. Of the soule of man, and the immortalitie thereof* (1599). Dedicated to Elizabeth, whom he describes as 'A happie Angell to this happie Land', in the second elegy, Davies catalogues the diverse opinions of the soul and its sexes: 'For no craz'd braine could euer yet propound, | Touching the *Soule* so vaine and fond a thought, | But some among these Maisters haue bene found, | Which in their *Schooles* the selfe same thing haue taught', he observes. Only God truly sees the soul, 'Thou, that hast fashioned twise this *Soule* of ours, | So that she is by double title thine, | Thou onely knowest her nature and her powers, | Her subtile forme thou onely canst define' (Davies 1559: 11). Davies figures the soul as female, describing her as being much like a captive princess: 'These Actions in her Closet all alone, | (Retir'd within her selfe) she doth fulfill; | ... | Yet in the Bodies prison so she lyes, | As through the bodies windowes she must looke, | Her diuerse powers of *Sense* to exercise, | By gathering Notes out of the *VVorlds* great Booke (14).

William Austin (*c.*1587–1634) in the 1620s, perhaps writing in response the *Hic Mulier, or the Man-Woman* pamphlet controversy, penned the essay *Haec homo wherein the excellency of the creation of woman is described* which, like his meditations and poems celebrating the feast days of the Christian year, was circulated in manuscript prior to its posthumous publication in 1637. 'In the *sexe*, is all the *difference; which is but onely in the body*', Austin argues, 'for she hath the same *reasonable soule*; and, in that, there is neither *hees*, or *shees*' (5). However, Austin notes, '(in the *resurrection*) she shall, (without *exception of sexe*) obtaine *like body* with him; according to the *similitude of Angels*' (6). Likewise, several popular longer treatises tackled the preeminence of the soul within the female body. First translated into English in 1652 by Edward Fleetwood as *The Glory of Women*, Heinrich Cornelius Agrippa von Nettesheim's (1486?–1535) treatise *Declamatio de nobilitate et praecellentia foeminei sexus* (1529) was based on the premise that God 'gave one and the same in different soule to Male and Female, in which undoubtedly there in no distinction of Sex: The woman is endued with the same rationall power, and Speech with the man, and indeavoreth to the same end of blessednesse' (2). While there is no difference in the souls of men and those of women, souls within the bodies of women, Agrippa asserts, 'as for the exercise and operation of the soule, the illustrious Sex of women, infinitely almost excells the rough and unpolished generation of men'. A similar point is made in a manuscript essay dedicated to her young daughter, 'The Woman's Right' by the artist Mary More (1633–1716) arguing for the equality of the sexes before the Fall. More notes that 'most women ever since are of a finer mold and metal than most men are: nor do I see any Reason why we may not on good Grounds argue from thence; that the bodies of women being more fine; which body is the Organ that Acts and declares the soul, the souls of Women are acted more serene and agile than men's are' (Ezell 2015: 132).

The Cambridge Platonist Henry More consistently wrote about the soul as female. 'Of all the Speculations the *Soul* of man can entertain her self withall, there is none of greater moment, or of closer concernment to her, then this,' he opens his treatise, 'of her own Immortality, and Independence of this terrestriall body' (More 1659: 1). He tackles the question of whether the soul can remember existence prior to being in the body, deciding that the change from her initial state into the physical body would preclude this: 'without a miracle it is impossible the Soule should remember any particular circumstance of her former condition, though she did really *praeexist* ... her change being far greater by coming into the Body then can ever be made while she staies in it' (More 1659: 256).

In other mid-century devotional poets, the female soul can lead to a joyful union with her bridegroom, Christ. Helen Wilcox has observed, commenting on the poet known only as 'Eliza', 'the voice of the feminized soul and the speaker unite in a way that is impossible in equivalent male devotional poetry' (2000a: 460) 'Eliza' questions in her poem 'The Gift' why God, to whom the poet has given her heart, in turns gives her body to a man in marriage: 'My body here he may retain, | My heart in heaven, with thee must reigne'; her rejection of an earthly lover in 'The Dart' leads her to plead 'Shoot from above | Thou God of Love, | and with heaven's dart | Wound my blest heart', concluding 'And let be sed | Eliza's dead, | And of love dy'd, | That love defi'd' (460).

CONCLUSION

Although the issues raised by the body and soul permeate the literature as well as the philosophical and religious discourses of early modern readers and writers, not all felt the need to adhere to only one view of the body and soul debate. As Christia Mercer has noted about seventeenth-century texts incorporating platonic thought, many English and continental writers practiced what she terms 'conciliatory eclecticism' (2012: 107). Instead of debating the superiority of one classical model over the other, writers such as John Christoph Sturm, in *Eclectic Philosophy* (1686), urged readers to consider what was good and valuable from the competing systems of explanation. This became more attractive as medical and scientific discourse evolved over the seventeenth century, particularly medical discourse, the soul or spirit gradually began to be regarded as different from the physical brain itself. What would ultimately emerge from these debates in natural philosophy and epitomized in the work of the natural philosopher and physician Thomas Willis (1621–75) in his 1664 study of the neuroanatomies of the brain, *Cerebri anatome: cui accessit nervorum descriptio et usus*, intended as he announced in his dedication to 'unlock the secret places of Mans Mind', was a distinct separation of body, soul, and mind. While it is clear that John Locke believed in the afterlife, it is striking how in his *Essay on Human Understanding* (1690) the term 'mind' has replaced 'soul', in his rejection of the doctrine of innate ideas or principles and in his account of what creates personal identity. It has also been argued by some recent critics that this medical turn in the seventeenth century in terms of separating the brain from the soul and the eighteenth-century interest in mapping the physical brain as a complex cognitive neurosystem (Rousseau 2008; Zimmer 2004; Bulkeley 2005), has led to the modern cognitive neuroscience's obliteration of the soul as a topic for analysis (Churchland 2013). In the early modern period, however, English writers still found the complexities of the relationship between the body and the soul as laid out in the competing schools of classical philosophy to be fertile sources for analysing the human experience of life, death, and self.

CHAPTER 37

SACRED AND SECULAR LOVE

'I Will Lament, and Love'

HELEN WILCOX

IT can be said with some confidence that love is the over-riding theme of English Renaissance literature. The delights and frustrations of earthly love dominate the lyric poetry of the period, particularly the sonnet sequences so popular in the later sixteenth century; love is also the recurring topic of solo songs, sociable madrigals, and communal ballads. The power of love, in various guises, is the primary subject of pastoral writing and erotic epyllia, while the need to constrain love's effects is the concern of conduct books and the intellectual challenge of many a humanist dialogue. The folly of desire—whether for a fellow human being or for the power achieved through money or social status—drives the majority of the comedies from the period, and the complexities of love and jealousy set countless tragedies on their unhappy course. The great Renaissance project of translation, too, made classical lovers and their tales available to vernacular writers, with the influence of Ovid and his concept of love's metamorphosing impact being particularly widespread. In one of the first English novels, Aphra Behn's *Love Letters Between a Nobleman and His Sister* (1684–7), Philander writes to Sylvia, 'in my creation I was formed for love', and argues (somewhat opportunistically) that 'our souls were touched with the same shafts of love before they had a being in our bodies, and can we contradict divine decree?' (Behn 1997: 8). Even the English epic poem towering over the latter part of the early modern period, Milton's *Paradise Lost*, has at its centre the very human love story of Adam and Eve. Whatever the Renaissance genre, love has a way of becoming essential to its narrative as well as its appeal.

As the reference to Milton suggests, a similar claim could be made in relation to religious literature in English from the sixteenth and seventeenth centuries. Among the earliest English sonnets were those of sacred love by Anne Lok and her son Henry, and the turn of the sixteenth and into the seventeenth century witnessed the great flowering of the devotional lyric—the genre characterized by George Herbert as 'window-songs' with which to serenade God instead of a human beloved (Herbert 2007: 411). The secular lovers' dialogue found its spiritual equivalent as a genre in the dialogues between the soul and the body,[1] and the practice of sacred parody or 'contrafactum' converted many a worldly love song into collections such as the Scottish *Gude and Godlie Ballatis*.[2] Although the changes in theatrical practice after the Reformation prevented the treatment of sacred subjects in dramatic form for most of the period under discussion, plays such as Shakespeare's *Measure for Measure* and Carey's *Tragedy of Mariam* manage to explore the tensions between secular love, moral duty, and religious devotion in profound and challenging ways. The translation of pre- or non-Christian texts similarly gave rise to new works in English that were as much concerned with sacred as earthly love, 'moralizing'—or Christianizing—the wisdom of the classics.[3] Meanwhile, the enormous range of original religious prose produced during the period, extending from catechisms, prayer books, and commentaries to devotional treatises, sermons, and confessional autobiographies, has at its heart the two key questions of any anxious lover: how can I be sure that my beloved (in this case, God) will not reject me, and what (if anything) might I do to earn the love for which I yearn?

Many writers of the period, passionately asking themselves these questions in relation to a secular lover at first, moved in the course of their lives and writings towards a sense that the ultimate object of their devotion should be sacred. Probably the most famous of these transfers—or transformations—of affection is that expressed by Philip Sidney in his sonnet, 'Leave me ô Love', which is all the more striking for being written after his worldly sonnet sequence, *Astrophil and Stella*:

> Leave me ô Love, which reacheth but to dust,
> And thou, my mind, aspire to higher things:
> Grow rich in that which never taketh rust:
> What ever fades, but fading pleasure brings.
>
> Draw in thy beames, and humble all thy might,
> To that sweet yoke, where lasting freedomes be:
> Which breakes the clowdes and opens forth the light,
> That doth both shine and give us sight to see.
>
> O take fast hold; let that light be thy guide
> In this small course which birth drawes out to death,
> And think how evill becommeth him to slide,
> Who seeketh heav'n, and comes of heav'nly breath.
> Then farewell world, thy uttermost I see,
> Eternall love maintaine thy life in me. (Sidney 1962: 161–2)

---

[1] See chapter 36 of this volume.

[2] See MacDonald 1996; other notable examples of sacred parody from the period include Elizabeth Melville's contrafactum of Marlowe's 'Come live with me' (see Ross 2010), and George Herbert's 'A Parodie' based on a love lyric by William Herbert, third earl of Pembroke (Herbert 2007: 635–6).

[3] See, for example, the anonymous medieval French text offering a Christian version of Ovid's poetry, known as *Ovid Moralisé*; in the English Renaissance, see Chapman's verse translation of Homer (completed in 1611).

The opening of the poem encapsulates the futility of transient human love: the phrase 'reachest but to dust' concisely expresses both the lover's longing for that which is mortal, and the fact that this emotion leads inevitably to the grave. The characterization of the love of one human being for another as the source of merely 'fading pleasure', at best keeping lovers happy while life 'drawes out to death', is typical of such early modern poems of renunciation. Rather than urging the *carpe diem* argument—tearing at pleasures and giving time a run for his money, as in 'To his Coy Mistress' (Marvell 1971: I, 253)—the rhetoric of Sidney's sonnet pivots on the contrast between mortal and heavenly love. This 'Eternall Love' gives vision, light, and life, and Sidney echoes the language of the Bible in the speaker's choice of the treasure that will not 'rust', and the 'yoke' that is in fact freedom (Matthew 6:20, 11:30).[4] There is, it seems, an almost unbridgeable cleft between the two kinds of love posited in Sidney's impassioned poem of rejection and embrace.

The form of Sidney's poem, however, hints at other possible interpretations of the relationship between secular and sacred love. The choice of a sonnet is in itself a reminder of the earthly desires given expression so frequently in this genre; it is as though the dustbound love must always be a ghostly presence even when its absence is the poem's subject. Is it ever really possible to write about divine love in this period without a trace of its worldly shadow, or vice versa? Spenser had an analytical knowledge of the differences between the 'gentle furie' of earthly love and the eternally creative force of 'Heavenly Love', as his Hymns on the subjects indicate (Spenser 1999: 453, 472). In spite of this, his sonnet sequence *Amoretti* interprets the lover's devotion to his mistress not as opposition to God's love but as an imitation of it: 'loue is the lesson which the Lord vs taught' (Spenser 1999: 421). John Davies of Hereford mingled secular and divine sonnets into a hybrid sequence in his *Wittes Pilgrimage*, demonstrating the permeable boundary between the two kinds of love (Davies 1610). Donne's secular lyrics famously discover their most intense expressions of physical love in the metaphors of religion: 'miracle', 'relic', 'angels', 'saints' (Donne 1985: 112–13, 66, 58). Perhaps more surprisingly, the outspoken lyrics of the later seventeenth-century libertine poet, John Wilmot, earl of Rochester, also find many of their points of reference in the language of the fall, sin, and redemption.[5] Gaining inspiration in the opposite direction, the speaker in the anonymous collection of devotional lyrics, *Eliza's Babes: or The Virgins-Offering* (1652), models her relationship with Christ on that of a human couple—to such an extent that she brazenly compares her divine 'lover' to the inferior husbands of her friends and readers (Eliza 1652: 24). These and many other similar examples suggest that the conventions and discourses of the two loves are reciprocally enlightening (even, inseparable) in the early modern context; they appear to provide a beneficial and creative tension for those who sought to explore, in writing, the nature and experience of love.

---

[4]   *KJV*; this and all further references are to the 1997 Oxford World's Classics edition of the Authorized King James Version.

[5]   Poems such as 'The Fall' and 'All my past life' use remarkably spiritual language for a libertine poet; see Rochester 1968.

The question of *how* to write about love, particularly sacred love, is an issue of which the writers of the period were intensely aware. The poet George Herbert, for example, seems infuriated by the popularity of writing about secular love in his lifetime, growing up as he did in the heyday of the sonnet. In a pious youthful sonnet (the inescapably relevant form, once again), he asks frustratedly, 'Doth Poetry | Wear *Venus* Livery? Only serve her turn?' (Herbert 2007: 4). However, once he had dedicated himself to writing only about sacred love, one of Herbert's major concerns became the question of exactly how to do so. Like Sidney's Astrophel 'biting' his 'trewand pen' in the struggle to find words to express his love for Stella, the speaker in Herbert's 'Jordan' (II) wrestles with the problem of writing about 'heav'nly joyes': 'I often blotted what I had begunne; | This was not quick enough, and that was dead' (Sidney 1962: 165; Herbert 2007: 367). The conclusion of Herbert's poem offers a startlingly simple solution to the problem: '*There is in love a sweetnesse readie penn'd*: | *Copie out onely that, and save expense*' (Herbert 2007: 367). The challenge is not so much how to appreciate the 'sweetnesse' of God's love as how to 'copie' it in writing and in living. As Edmund Freake wrote in 1574, echoing countless other authors and preachers in the early modern period as they faced the impossibility of finding words for God's love, 'O how unspeakable therefore is this love and charitie? Or what tounge can express the sweetenes of thys affection?' (Freake 1574: I4^r).

There is no disputing the centrality of love—defined, longed-for, experienced, expressed, rejected, and celebrated—to early modern English texts. The literature of religious devotion reacts against, but also draws on, the literature of secular love; in a reversal of this cultural symbiosis, writings on divine love also give inspiration and vocabulary to literary depictions of earthly passions. The tensions between earthly and heavenly love as literary subjects, however, were particularly keenly felt in this era in relation to the perceived dangers of secular passion when enacted on the stage. As Lewis Bayly, bishop of Bangor, highlights in the preface to his immensely popular *Practise of Pietie* (*c*.1611), a threat of controversy always lurks even in the apparently docile territory of holy love. In attempting to reinstate the 'old Practice of true Pietie', he cannot resist an attack on those who 'pretend to love God' but 'seldome … come to prayers', hearing God's word 'irreverently' and being 'assiduous spectators … at Stage-plais' (Bayly 1620: A4^v, A3^r). Bayly was certainly not alone at this time in his anxious concern that 'most who now live, are become lovers of pleasures, more than lovers of God' (A3^r). But what did it mean to be a 'lover of God'? The following pages constitute an attempt to answer this question in relation to the devotional literature and spiritual practices of the early modern period.

BIBLICAL UNDERSTANDINGS OF LOVE

The concept of love, so present in early modern writing, is the founding principle of Christianity. In its primary meaning, the word denotes the essence of God: the New Testament of the Bible boldly declares that the divine nature itself 'is love' (1 John 4:8).

This Christian sense of God as the eternal source of love is rooted in the Jewish belief that God's relationship with his people can be defined as 'an everlasting love' (Jeremiah 31:3). According to the Christian faith, however, it is not only the 'creation' and 'preservation' of humankind that are seen as the outpouring of divine love; their 'redemption' in Christ is also crucially understood as the active fulfilment of it.[6] As St John sums it up, 'God so loved the world, that he gave his only-begotten Son, that whosoever believeth in him should not perish, but have everlasting life' (John 3:16). The incarnation, passion, and resurrection of Jesus are thus read as the narrative expression of God's essential quality, his redeeming love, seen dramatically intervening in history—an idea of huge significance to human literary endeavour.

The proper reaction of the creation to this all-encompassing divine love, a response expressed textually as well as in action, is also love; for 'love' is not only a noun, something to be identified and experienced, but it is also a very active verb. As the first epistle of John puts it with the utmost simplicity, 'We love him, because he first loved us' (1 John 4:19). The reciprocation of God's love by his creatures has a double aspect: it takes the form of both an individual's love for God and the love of human beings for each other. The first commandment in the Old Testament is to 'love the Lord thy God with all thine heart, and with all thy soul, and with all thy might' (Deuteronomy 6:5), and the second commandment set alongside it in the Gospels is that 'Thou shalt love thy neighbour as thyself' (Mark 12:31). According to the teachings of Jesus, this mutual love is limitless: his followers are exhorted to forgive their brethren and even 'love [their] enemies' (Matthew 5:44). The spiritual obligation to copy the comprehensively loving nature of God himself is made clear in John's epistle: 'Beloved, let us love one another: for love is of God' (1 John 4:7). These multiple aspects of love—observed in God's being and doing, and in humankind's responsive and mutual love—are therefore bound together inseparably: 'If we love one another, God dwelleth in us, and his love is perfected in us' (1 John 4:12). Without love, as Thomas Traherne lamented in his *Centuries of Meditations*, 'The Soul is shriveld up and Buried in a Grave' (Traherne 2005–14: V, 50).

The Bible, the most widely known text in early modern England, is thus shot through with love as both word and concept. In the Old Testament, the greatest concentration of references is found in the Song of Solomon, a deeply controversial biblical text that was familiarly known in the early modern period as the 'love book', and could cause consternation for its apparent overlapping of sensual and spiritual love: 'Let him kiss me with the kisses of his mouth: for thy love is better than wine' (Song of Solomon 1:2; Clarke 2011). Allegorized by the church fathers as a celebration of the love of Christ for his spouse the church, the Song speaks of mutual love—'my beloved is mine and I am his' (2:16)—and poetically claims love as the emblem of their relationship: 'his banner over me was love' (2:4). The sensual poetry of this scriptural text offered an archetype of love poetry that was vitally influential on early modern lyric expressions of love, both secular and religious. One of the most memorable assertions in the Song is also that 'love is

---

[6] These three terms come from the General Thanksgiving in the BCP 268.

strong as death', an idea echoed by St Paul in his confident celebration of the power of divine love: 'For I am persuaded, that neither death, nor life … nor things present, nor things to come, | Nor height, nor depth, nor any other creature, shall be able to separate us from the love of God, which is in Christ Jesus our Lord' (Romans 8:38–9).

As these statements make clear, divine love is perceived as a comfort, a reassurance, and a joy for the believer. However, such love also requires a response from the beloved, which is not always an easy task: the common phrase a 'labour of love' derives from the 1611 translation of St Paul's words as he congratulates the faithful Thessalonians on their 'work of faith, and labour of love, and patience of hope' (1 Thessalonians 1:3). The hard work of loving had been spelt out in Jesus's plain statement, 'If ye love me, keep my commandments' (John 14:15), words that also formed the opening text of the well-known mid-sixteenth-century anthem by Thomas Tallis.[7] A subsequent verse from the same chapter of St John's Gospel would have been especially familiar to early modern churchgoers as one of the post-Communion 'Sentences of holy Scripture' prescribed in the 1549 Book of Common Prayer for reading aloud during the liturgy: 'He that hath my commaundements, and kepeth them, the same is he that loveth me' (John 14:21; BCP 35). This apparently straightforward statement contains within it the seeds of human spiritual vocation but also struggle, failure, and yet renewal—the raw material of so much writing about spiritual love. As we saw in Herbert's poem 'Jordan' (II), the tension between the knowledge of God's love and the inability to match or reciprocate it drives some of the most powerful religious writing of the period.

Love and Charity, Sacrifice and Grace

Whereas the *verb* used for God's defining action, as well as for the human response to it, is consistently 'love' in early modern biblical translations, the English *noun* chosen to represent this vital phenomenon in the early modern period varies according to context, agent, and meaning. The concept of 'love', after all, encompasses *agape, eros*, and *caritas*—that is, the varieties of love variously defined as selfless, sexual, and caring—and the distinctions between them are upheld in some sixteenth- and seventeenth-century translations. In the King James Version of St Paul's hymn of praise to love, the trio of virtues is 'faith, hope, and charity', of which 'the greatest' is 'charity' (1 Corinthians 13:13). In some sixteenth-century translations, however, including Tyndale's 1526 New Testament, the 'cheyfe' of the virtues, which 'falleth never awaye', is rendered as 'love' (Tyndale 1526: 230ᵛ). On the other hand, Cranmer's collect for the Sunday before Lent, newly composed in 1549, begins: 'O Lord, who hast taught us, that all our doings without charity are nothing worth', and proceeds to ask for 'that most excellent gift of charity, the very

---

[7] Four-part anthem 'If ye love me', c.1565, one of the greatest examples of reformed word-setting from the period; see Tallis 1992.

bond of peace and of all virtues' (BCP: 293). Such modest differences in vocabulary can sometimes indicate deep-seated uncertainties about the interpretation of an idea, and that is undoubtedly true in the case of some early modern discussions of spiritual love. Theologians, writers, and translators tended to betray their particular interpretations of 'love' by the shift in terminology used in relation to it. For many pre-Reformation English writers, and for succeeding authors with more Catholic sympathies, the discourse of love is infused with the language of sacrifice. Crashaw's meditation 'Charitas Nimia, or The Dear Bargain', for example, uses the vocabulary of blood-sacrifice to contrast the 'shame' of the speaker's sin with the suffering endured by the innocent Christ in order to cancel out the power of sin:

> Why should his unstained brest make good
> My blushes with his own heart-blood?
>   O My Saviour, make me see
> How dearly thou hast payd for me
>   That lost again my Life may prove
> As then in Death, so now in love. (Crashaw 2013: 100)

Crashaw's focus here is on the intense physicality of the 'heart-blood', sweat, and tears epitomizing the sacrificial death of Christ on the cross, sacramentally re-enacted in the Eucharist and symbolically supplying the blood that ought to be blushing the sinful speaker's cheeks red. By contrast, writers in a more Calvinist tradition tend to colour their discourse of love with the vocabulary of 'grace', the freely given and totally unearned gift of God which overcomes the innate depravity of human nature. Anne Lok's penitential sonnets, for example, plead for a manifestation of divine love in the form of redemptive grace which will make the speaker 'pure in thy mercies sight' (Lok 1560: Aa6^r). These early sonnets, published anonymously in 1560 as *A Meditation of a Penitent Sinner*, an appendix to a translation of sermons by Calvin, 'crave' with desperate urgency some 'crummes of all sufficing grace' (X2^v) to counter a terrifying awareness of the sinfulness of human beings. The rhetoric of Crashaw and Lok, and their understandings of divine love as sacrifice and grace respectively, are worlds apart.

In practice, however, the passionate desire for the reassurance of God's forgiving love could blur simplistic categorizations, unexpectedly crossing boundaries of doctrine and sensibility. Two anonymous publications from across the spectrum of allegiance, for example, can be seen to come remarkably close to one another in their focus on heavenly love. In 1603, *A Breefe Collection concerning the Love of God towards mankinde* was published in Doway (Douai), the Belgian site of the exiled Catholics' English College. This manual of prayer and devotion entreats its readers to respond to God's love by matching it with their own, and serving him. In the mid-seventeenth century, another anonymous publication, *Divine Light manifesting the love of God unto the Whole World* (1646), was printed and circulated in London. The opening phrases of the title suggest the pamphlet's origins in reformed theology with Quaker sympathies, and the profuse rhetoric of the crammed title page exalts an 'all-saving Jesus' who has 'Redeemed us his Saints', employing the egalitarian language of Protestantism. However, despite their differences of origin and tone, the common ground between these works is that, in both, the love of God is the source of spiritual energy, galvanizing the lives of individual Christians. Within this shared focus on love, there is also the constant presence of a common fear—the dread of being what St Paul described as a 'sounding brass' or 'tinkling cymbal' (1 Corinthians 13:1) that speaks hollowly of faith because it fails to imbue either words or actions with genuine love. In his *Christian Dictionarie* (1612), the Calvinist divine Thomas Wilson defines true 'Christian Love' as 'an holy affection of the heart, causing us to delight in God for his goodnesse sake, and in our Neighbor for Gods sake' (Wilson 1612: 301). In this neat re-formulation of the two great commandments, the 'affection of the heart' betrays neither introversion nor hypocrisy; instead, the definition gives a strong impression of how earth and heaven may meet in the enacting of love. Nevertheless, Wilson ends his definition on a cautionary note: 'This is Christian Love, which is a fruite and signe of a justified person, but is not our Justice before God' (301). Good works inspired by love, in Wilson's explicitly Protestant clarification, are not the way to justify oneself—implying that an over-emphasis on charitable activities is a weakness of 'Papists' and one of the 'points of Controversie between us and them' (A8^r). Wilson's reformed view is clear: justification is by faith alone, but love in action, though not a route to salvation, is an unmistakeable sign of spiritual health.

Defining Holy Love

Wilson's *Dictionarie*, with its eight sub-sections on the topic of love, is an extreme example of how early modern writers were repeatedly drawn to attempt definitions of (or, as they would have put it, to 'anatomize') the love of God and the proper human response to it. At the very beginning of the sixteenth century, *Richard Rolle hermyte of Hampull in his contemplacyons of the drede and love of God* (1506) offers a systematic classification of four degrees of Christian love: 'ordeyned love', as in the command to 'love thyn enemie'; 'clene love', or the rejection of evil; 'stedfast love', the loyalty shown to God in worship and good works, and 'parfyte love', a spiritual passion given expression in prayer and devotion (Rolle 1506: aii^{r-v}). In contrast to Rolle's rising sequence of types of love, moving from that which is commanded to the love which aspires to perfection, Katherine Parr's *Prayers or Meditacions* (1545) establish a binary structure, defining 'fervent love' for God by its opposition to 'fleshly love' (Parr 1545: Biii^r). Echoing the words of Thomas à Kempis, Parr sets the love of 'worldly and fleshy deities' against the 'love of eternall thynges', and prays for 'wynges of perfect love, that I maye flye up from these worldly miseries, and reste in thee' (Bii^v, Avii^r). The hopeful intimacy of this prayer moves it away from the realm of 'drede and love' established by Rolle, and towards a relationship with God in which love is linked with mercy rather than awe-inspiring judgement.

In 1574, Edmund Freake urges 'the continuall meditation of Gods infinite love' as he dedicates his translation of Augustine's *Introduction to the love of God* to Parr's step-daughter, Elizabeth I (Freake 1574: A3^r). Freake commends Augustine's 'litle treatise' to Elizabeth for its evocation of 'the sensible seeing and taste of Gods love and mercy' (A3^v). The sensuality of this experience of divine love, recalling the scriptural invitation to 'taste, and see, how gracious the Lord is' (Psalm 34:8, BCP 494), suggests that discovering God's love will lead to transformation: 'to be altered into a new creature, to be altogether ravished in the love of God and heavenly desires' (Freake 1574: A3^v). This sense of the love of God as a passionate 'ravishment', a powerful force for personal renewal, is held in tension in early modern religious texts with a counter-balancing definition of religious love as an outward-facing, charitable duty. In his *Religio Medici* (1642), Sir Thomas Browne views the love of God as 'the Basis and Pillar' of charity: 'for this I thinke charity, to love God for himselfe, and our neighbour for God' (Browne 1977: 159). Towards the end of the seventeenth century, there is increasing emphasis on the second half of Browne's definition. In the posthumously published sermons of Isaac Barrow, *Of the Love of God and our Neighbour* (1680), the preacher analyses what it means to 'Walk in love' and to share 'that charity, which God himself in a wonderfull and incomprehensible manner doth exemplifie to us' (Barrow 1680: 153). In a summary of the meaning of charity, Barrow adds that it is 'the mother of friendship' (157), suggesting how far the understanding of holy love moves in the direction of a social concept during the two centuries under discussion here.

Keeping in mind these complex and shifting definitions of religious love in the sixteenth and seventeenth centuries, the remainder of this chapter will consider some of the period's most significant literary representations of divine love and its human impact. In almost every case, textual rhetoric and religious action are interrelated: when divine love is understood by a writer, this is an act of interpretation that has direct spiritual consequences; when the love of God is expressed in the detail of metaphor or literary form, this is a process of imaginative invention that has an immediate bearing on the devotional life of the author. A literary meditation on the love of God is a reflection and reconstruction of experience, yet it also instigates and renews that experience. This two-way partnership between religion and literature enables texts to share in the reciprocal relationship between God and humanity envisaged by so many writers from this period. Devotional texts express and inspire simultaneously, serving the needs of authors and their readers. Just as the love of God is defined variously as the basic divine principle, the human reciprocation of it and a mutual charity among men and women, so the texts address God, self, and other in an exploration of this complex and profound mystery. As Lewis Bayly pointedly commented in the early seventeenth century, 'Unlesse that a man doth truly *know* God, he neither can, nor wil *worship* him aright: for how can a man love him, whom hee knoweth not?' (Bayly 1629: B2^r).

INTERVENTIONS OF DIVINE LOVE

The first steps towards 'knowing' the love of God are often represented in the literature of this period, not as the initiative of the text's narrator, but as a divine intervention or revelation. In the dramatic opening of Robert Southwell's lyric, 'The Burning Babe', the speaker stands 'shivering in the snow' when he is 'surprised' by a 'sudden heat'. The contrast between the frozen landscape and the unexpected warmth immediately seizes the attention of narrator and reader:

> And lifting up a fearful eye to view what fire was near,
> A pretty babe all burning bright did in the sky appear,
> Who scorched with exceeding heat such floods of tears did shed,
> As though his tears should quench his flames with what his tears were fed.
>
> (Southwell 1967: 98)

The burning babe is not sought out but appears unbidden, accosting the speaker's senses with the impact of great heat and bright light. In a sacred parody of the extreme metaphors of Petrarchan love, the 'pretty babe' endures a paradoxical combination of flames and tears that is both destructive and redemptive:

> My faultless breast the furnace is, the fuel wounding thorns;
> Love is the fire and sighs the smoke, the ashes shame and scorns;
> The fuel Justice layeth on, and Mercy blows the coals;
> The metal in this furnace wrought are men's defiled souls. (98)

The poem reveals that the excruciating pain suffered by the innocent babe is caused by love itself; this is the fire which is burning, though never destroying, the babe. The nature of divine love in Southwell's vision is thus sacrificial, archetypal, and perpetual—and, as revealed by a subsequent image of the babe washing human souls with his 'blood', sacramental too. The conclusion of the poem is as remarkable as its beginning, for the babe disappears as suddenly as it first appeared:

> With this he vanish'd out of sight, and swiftly shrunk away,
> And straight I called unto mind that it was Christmas-day. (99)

Until the final line, the identity of the babe as the Christ-child has been implicit in the poem's imagery of the crucifixion and the Eucharist, but never explicitly stated. With these last words, the speaker realizes that the overwhelming love he has witnessed is that of the incarnate God: divine love takes human form. On the one hand, this babe, like all innocent newborn infants, is vulnerable and weak; on the other, it is made resilient through love, and is willing to suffer intense pain on behalf of sinful humanity in order to 'work them to their good' (99).

Southwell's poignant lyric of the incarnation highlights a number of aspects of divine love as expressed in early modern devotional poetry. At the poem's centre is an encounter between the speaker and God, typically unanticipated and in an unexpected form or place. The dynamic partner in this relationship is God: while the speaker shivers impotently in the cold, the holy babe is actively suffering the opposite extreme of heat as it burns with love for humankind. One of the most striking features of the poem is its profoundly metaphoric understanding of God's incarnate love, bringing to the fearful speaker's mind an allegorical vision which compresses into one moment the nativity ('but newly born') and the passion ('wounding thorns') of Christ. Metaphors of fire are frequently associated with this sacrificial interpretation of divine love, as well as with the appropriately loving response of the devout. In her *Prayers and Meditacions*, Katherine Parr asks God to 'Sende forthe the hotte flames of thy love, to burne and consume the cloudie fantasies of my mynde' (Parr 1545: Ciii^r). The paradoxical closeness of ecstasy and agony, burning and consuming, characterizes the sixteenth-century writers' meditations on Christ's passion; the 'hot flames' of his love will purge the sinful mind. This is also the principle of the many collections of sacred emblems in the 'Schola Cordis' [school of the heart] tradition in this period. Borrowed from continental Catholic sources, the emblem pictures themselves depict the heart variously wounded, burnt, and pummelled into purity. The conventional seat of love, the heart, becomes the locus for spiritual experience.[8]

Aemilia Lanyer's extended poem on the passion, *Salve Deus Rex Judaeorum* (1611), details more specifically the bodily horror of the crucifixion endured by Christ out of all-encompassing love:

> His joynts dis-joynted, and his legges hang downe,
> His alabaster breast, his bloody side,
> His members torne, and on his side a Crowne
> Of sharpest Thorns, to satisfie for pride:
> Anguish and Paine doe all his Sences drowne. (Lanyer 1993: 101)

Lanyer's narrative of the passion suggests the vital importance of the sensual in the spiritual appreciation of love, even in a poem such as this which focuses on the suffering of Christ rather than the internal agony of the believer. As the seventeenth century progresses, however, there is less emphasis on what Michael Schoenfeldt has described as 'the spectacularly gruesome suffering of the crucified Christ', with a shift of focus to 'the interior spaces of the believer' (Schoenfeldt 2006: 890) as the site where love is felt.

The seventeenth century is the first great period of confessional autobiography in the modern era, expressing both directly in prose and indirectly in verse the arresting moments when the love of God impinges on what Schoenfeldt calls the 'interior spaces' of a believer. In *God's Mighty Power Magnified* (1691), for example, the Quaker Joan Vokins writes of the 'tender dealing of the Lord with me ever since my Childhood', but particularly recalls the time when she was in a 'dejected condition' and 'the Spirit of Life and Light, which is the Spirit of Jesus, opened my Understanding' (Vokins 1691: 15, 17). 'Oh, how precious was the Heart-searching Light', she exclaims, adding later that the 'feeling' of this 'sweet refreshing Life' is 'a hundred-fold better than Husband or Children, or

---

[8] See Figure 37.1: Embleme 24, 'The Renewing of the Heart', from Christopher Harvey's *Schola Cordis: The School of the Heart* (Harvey 1647: 96–7).

FIGURE 37.1 Emblem 24, 'The Renewing of the Heart', from Christopher Harvey, *The School of the Heart* (London, 3rd edn, 1674); shelfmark (Vet.) 14770 f. 484, pp. 94 and 95. Reproduced by kind permission of The Bodleian Libraries, The University of Oxford.

The School of the Heart. 95

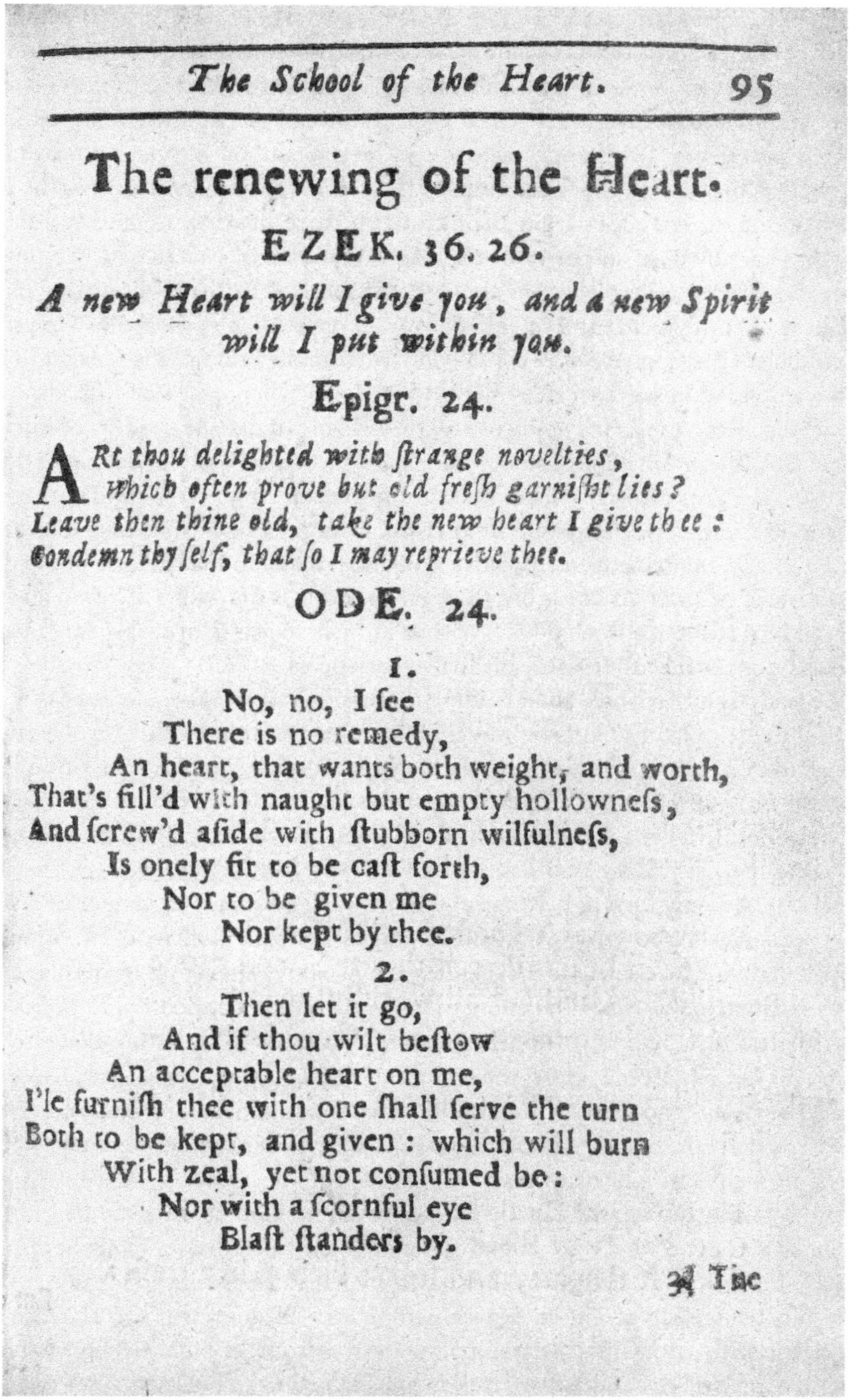

The renewing of the Heart.

EZEK. 36. 26.

A new Heart will I give you, and a new Spirit will I put within you.

Epigr. 24.

ART thou delighted with ſtrange novelties,
Which often prove but old freſh garniſht lies?
Leave then thine old, take the new heart I give thee:
Condemn thy ſelf, that ſo I may reprieve thee.

ODE. 24.

1.

No, no, I ſee
There is no remedy,
An heart, that wants both weight, and worth,
That's fill'd with naught but empty hollowneſs,
And ſcrew'd aſide with ſtubborn wilfulneſs,
Is onely fit to be caſt forth,
Nor to be given me
Nor kept by thee.

2.

Then let it go,
And if thou wilt beſtow
An acceptable heart on me,
I'le furniſh thee with one ſhall ſerve the turn
Both to be kept, and given: which will burn
With zeal, yet not conſumed be:
Nor with a ſcornful eye
Blaſt ſtanders by.

H The

FIGURE 37.1 Continued.

any other outward Mercies that he hath made me partaker of' (20, 66). Whether or not the love of God is perceived as rivalling (while always surpassing) earthly relationships, the divine intervention leading to conversion is frequently expressed in the language of courtship. Herbert's lyric 'The Glance' gives voice to the speaker's 'sugred strange delight', when God's 'sweet and gracious eye' first falls upon him and a heavenly joy works within his soul. In the final stanza of the poem, the speaker imagines the utterly overwhelming experience of seeing God's 'full-ey'd love', bearing in mind that the brief glance has already been so powerful. Heaven is that land of sweetness where love will 'look us out of pain' (Herbert 2007: 589–90). The sense of intimacy here, using physical metaphors of bodily touch and sight to convey an impression of divine love in practice, like so much of the language of devotion, derives from the Psalms. The speaker in Psalm 17, for example, addresses specific requests to the Lord in language rich with almost tangible details: 'Keep me as the apple of an eye: hide me under the shadow of thy wings' (Psalm 17: 8). The closing line of Henry Vaughan's devotional lyric, 'Quickness' (from his collection *Silex Scintillans*, 1655), defines true life in a startlingly tactile and sensual manner, as '*A quickness, which my God hath kissed*' (Vaughan 1976: 308). As Donne writes in 'The Ecstasy', referring to secular love though applying to it a rhetoric of the divine, 'Loves mysteries in soules doe grow, | But yet the body is his booke' (Donne 1985: 102). Early modern accounts of religious love thus ransack the store of corporeal metaphors in order to convey the full force of spiritual experience.

If the body is love's 'book', then reading and writing of the love of God (as we have seen in the case of Joan Vokins's comment on her husband) inevitably involves matters of the gendered body and its worldly relationships. Edmund Freake, translating from St Augustine in 1574, suggests that the loving soul is like 'an honest faithful wyfe' who will 'solace and comfort her selfe only in his love' (Freake 1574: A4^r–4^v). In the early seventeenth century, Lady Mary Wroth was firmly advised that, being a woman, she should write about heavenly love rather than the more dangerous subject matter of a secular sonnet sequence (Wroth 1983: 34). However, the evidence of early modern women who write about divine love suggests that gendered sensuality is never far from their expression of spiritual experience. The anonymous 1652 volume entitled *Eliza's Babes* is one of the clearest instances of this phenomenon. In addition to boasting that she is not 'asham'd' of her handsome 'lover', the 'Prince of Peace' (see above, p. 615), the speaker in the lyrics protests to God in 'The Gift' that she is not in need of a husband since she already has the 'blisse' of Christ's love. There is a sense of bewilderment and potential betrayal in the poem: since she has given her heart to her heavenly 'Lord', why would he want to give it away to the earthly partner to whom God has allowed her in turn to be given? Her only way of resolving the situation is to declare that, while her husband may have her body or 'earthly part', her heart (by which she seems to mean her soul or non-bodily being) will 'reigne' in heaven with Christ (Eliza 1652: 42–3). The idea of the soul's relationship with Christ as spousal love derives from the biblical Song of Solomon (see above, pp. 157–61) and is particularly applicable to the perspective of the female writer, as *Eliza's Babes* demonstrates, but its significance to all spiritual writers should not be underestimated. Francis Rous's *The mysticall marriage* (1635) draws heavily on the biblical image of the loving partnership between the soul and God, and suggests the deep sensuality on both sides of the relationship: speaking about God and addressing the reader, Rous writes that 'The bowels of love in him, melt at the sound of love in thee' (Rous 1635: 16). The soul, referred to throughout his work by the female pronoun, longs for a 'consummate marriage' with her heavenly lord, and is promised 'hony and sweet-nesse' which will come quickly to 'the soule that loveth her beloved' (Rous 1635: 350). The famous and rather more violent conclusion to Donne's Holy Sonnet XIV, where the speaker urges God to 'ravish' him as, paradoxically, the only way to render him 'chast[e]', constitutes one of the period's more radical appropriations of the metaphorically femi-nized soul in its passionate love of God (Donne 1985: 443). It highlights, too, the fun-damentally oppositional nature of human approaches to divine love, the writing about which is perpetually conscious of the tensions between body and soul, male and female, judgement and mercy, and—above all—love and rejection.

PERPLEXITY AND MYSTERY

The inimitable example of the love of God, coupled with a fearful awareness of the inad-equate human response to it, haunts early modern devotional writing. 'But how then shall I imitate thee, and | Copie thy fair, though bloodie hand?' asks Herbert in 'The Thanksgiving', desperate to know how to grieve for the crucified Christ who 'in all grief preventest me' (Herbert 2007: 112). Gertrude More, writing her *Spiritual Exercises* in Catholic exile in the Cambrai convent where she spent most of her short adult life, includes a series of confessions 'of a Loving & Pious Soul' in which she laments the weak-ness of her love for God:

> as for the *love* which only *thou* desirest, behold my soul is destitute of it. For if I have any towards *thee*, my *God* it is but a sensible, childish love, which is a love little beseeming the bestowing upon such a *God, who* is all Good, Beauty, Wisdom, yea even *Goodness* and *Love itself*; to *whom* is due a *love* which is able to suffer all things for this *love* is a strong *love*, more strong *than death* itself, the which kind of *love* is far from me, who am blown down with the least blast of temptation, and cannot endure any disgrace, desolation, or difficulty whatsoever, as it beseems a true *lover* of *his*. (More 1658: 232)

Even though More's focus is on her soul's destitution and the inappropriately 'childish love' with which she responds to God, the passage is so filled with the repeated word 'love' and its associated qualities that her confession becomes a celebration of the God who is '*Love itself*'. The paradox of divine comprehensiveness and mortal inadequacy contained in the same word lies at the heart of many early modern texts contemplating the mystery of love. However, for writers convinced of the doctrine of predestination, there was the additional paradox of a love that would condemn as well as redeem. The

Presbyterian Julia Palmer, in a poem from 1673 entitled 'Wonders & misterys of devine love', contemplates the 'strang[e]' and 'wonderfull' actions of God's love that is both an 'electing love' and a 'separating love', plunging some souls 'deep in misery' while others have their 'bonds' of sin removed (Palmer 2001: 263–4).

Whether influenced by Calvinist theology or merely driven by the daily ups and downs of spiritual life, the rich variety of devotional writing from the sixteenth and seventeenth centuries yields an overriding impression that divine love is experienced as perplexity. Herbert is particularly good at expressing this: his Lord is 'deare' and 'angrie' at the same time, divine love is a 'man of warre', and those trying to please God can simply do 'nothing' (Herbert 2007: 587, 621, 489). Herbert sums up the whole perplexing situation in the final couplet of 'Affliction' (I), after detailing both the joys and the frustrating miseries of being in God's 'service': 'Ah my deare God! though I am clean forgot, | Let me not love thee, if I love thee not' (163). Herbert's tantalizing conclusion hints that the love of the faithful for God, and their often patchy perception of his love for them, can prove puzzling, uncertain, fickle, or even a source of despair. As we have seen in texts from Rolle to Vokins, the love of God can be experienced as all-embracing, uplifting, and transforming, but it can also involve the extreme sorrow and self-doubt of a poet such as Anne Lok (see above, pp. 145–6). The Caroline preacher, Matthew Pinke, understood the challenges inherent in the call to love God: in *The Triall of a Christians Sincere Love unto Christ* (1636), Pinke confessed that even the strongest human love for the divine is 'subject to all variations or changes, ebbings and flowings' (Pinke 1636: 85). The essential Christian paradox is that love is triumphant in defeat, and serene through suffering, and therefore that this love leads to 'service' which is 'perfect freedom' (BCP 111). No wonder Donne wrote (in his Holy Sonnet XI) of his admiration for what he called, very simply, God's 'strange love' (Donne 1985: 441).

The *strangeness* of divine love is also one of the most powerful inspirations for devotional writing in this period: where there is surprise and mystery, there is scope for the imagination. Joseph Beaumont gave his epic allegorical poem, *Psyche* (1648), on the progress of the soul towards heaven, the very apt subtitle, 'Love's Mysteries', and Thomas Browne was certainly not the only early modern religious writer who 'love[d] to lose [him] selfe in a mystery' (Browne 1977: 69). Thomas Traherne's works repeatedly celebrate the mystery of God's presence as, and through, love: 'God is present by Lov alone. By Lov alone He is Great and Glorious. By Lov alone He liveth and feeleth in other Persons' (Traherne 2005–14: V, 50). While for Traherne love is the divine principle living (and *feeling*) within human beings, Julia Palmer celebrates the mysteries and 'wonders' of God's love as a book: as she tells God in a 1672 lyric, 'Love is the book, in which you always spell | Such wonders' (Palmer 2001: 157). Some of the most rhapsodic later seventeenth-century celebrations of the love of God are to be found in the prose works of the Independent minister Peter Sterry, a member of the Cromwell circle in the 1650s who turned to writing devotional prose in the Restoration period. *The Rise, Race and Royalty of the Kingdom of God* (1683), a collection of Sterry's sermons published eleven years after his death, includes a section entitled *The Loveliness & Love of Christ* in which he lays open 'the Book of Love' found in 'the Heart of God' (Sterry 1683: 353). For Sterry,

Love is 'the Divine Nature freely flowing', providing a 'Fountain ... to Eternity' (353, 375). In one of his most confident and ecstatic visions of God's love, he recounts St Paul's message that nothing 'shall be able to separate us from the love of God' (Romans 8:39) and then addresses his own soul:

> Dear Soul! dwell for ever in this good Land of Life, and Love, thy Saviour in the Spirit. Nothing here can separate thee from the Divine Love[.] Every thing then, that cometh to thee in life, or in death, must come in that Element of Love; it must come in a Love-dress; it must be Love itself in a Lovely form. Every thing, that toucheth thee here, must touch thee with the Heavenly kisses, and Embraces of Divine Love. Otherwise there would be a separation between Love, and thee. (Sterry 1683: 289)

The combination of logic and passion in this passage is remarkable. The basis of Sterry's argument is that, if there can be no 'separation', then everything we do must participate in divine love. His expansive embellishment of this statement of belief is awash with the language of heavenly intimacy: 'Love-dress', 'toucheth', 'kisses', 'Embraces'. For Sterry, divine love is, quite literally, everywhere. And as his sermon proceeds in neatly numbered paragraphs and sections, once more this painstaking anatomy of God's love releases a shower of superlatives:

> Grace is the name of Love in its Freedom, Sweetness, and Fulness. Every thing is in its Glory, in its Fountain. For there it is fairest, freshest, sweetest and fullest. Love is in its Fountain in the Person of the Father. For there Love is in its Glory. (365)

The rhetorical manner here is distinctively Sterry's, though the influence of the Cambridge Platonists, as well as Herbert and Milton, can be detected in his work. As is typical of the later seventeenth century, devotional writing moves across denominational and chronological limitations in its exploration of the mystery of divine love.

LOVE IN ACTION

It is likely that Sterry had links with the Quakers, and (as Catie Gill demonstrates in chapter 27) the rise of Quakerism and other sectarian groups in the mid-seventeenth century coincided with a democratizing of the presence of sacred love as the divine light within each person. However, these developments also reflect a move toward radical prophecy, missionary travels, and social reform—that is, love in action. This had always been an aspect of the general understanding of God's love throughout the early modern period: Katherine Parr, for instance, writing in the 1540s, understood that the love of God also entailed the love of 'Justice' and the hatred of 'wronge' (Parr 1545: Dvi^r), and Thomas Palfreyman, whose *Myrrour Conteinying the True Knowledge and Love of God* was published in 1560, asserted that showing the love of God meant applying ourselves 'with more pitifull and tender heartes, to see oure poore neyghbours and christen broth-erne better relieued and prouyded for' (Palfreyman 1560: Ciiii^r). By the later seventeenth century, however, this concern with what we would now refer to as charity becomes a predominant theme in the literature of love. Richard Baxter urged his readers and con-gregations to adopt a new trio of virtues for the post-Civil War era: not quite the Pauline 'faith, hope, and charity', but 'in necessary things, unity; in doubtful things, liberty; in all things, charity' (Baxter 1680: A7^r).[9] The consistent ingredient in these two trinities is 'charity', a concept much debated in the late seventeenth century. In 1680, a posthumous volume of sermons by Isaac Barrow, *Of the Love of God and our Neighbour*, defines love as 'an Affection or Inclination of the Soul toward an Object' and proposes not only God as the 'Object' of love but also our fellow human beings, since 'Charity is the mother of friendship' (Barrow 1680: 7, 157). This view is echoed in 1696 by Damaris Masham in her *Discourse Concerning the Love of God*, in which she goes out of her way to refute the arguments of her contemporary, John Norris. In his *Practical discourses upon several divine subjects* (1693), Norris emphasizes the importance of the contemplative life as an expression of the love of God, and plays down the role of charitable works. Incensed by this idea that 'God is the only proper Object of our Love', Masham makes the case for two kinds of love: in her view, Christians must love God with 'Love of Desire', and love their Neighbour with 'Love of Benevolence' (Masham 1696: 9, 12). Supporting Masham's moral and theological position the following year, Daniel Whitby's *Discourse of the Love of God* condemns those who would elevate the first part of the great commandment, to love God, above the second, to love one's neighbour. To do so, Whitby contends, is to destroy the very 'Foundation of these two great Virtues, Justice and Charity' (Whitby 1697: 47).

Whether emphasizing active benevolence or passionate spiritual desire, meditation, or praise, the common ground in all these early modern writings on love is the need to find an 'object' of love. The most frequently shared rhetorical feature, in consequence, is the tendency towards personification, not only of the beloved object but also of love itself. Where the secular authors have their Venus and Cupid, Christian writers turn to the incarnation as the supreme divine instance of personification. The opening of Crashaw's 'Hymn to the Name and Honor of the Admirable Sainte Teresa' puts it most succinctly: 'Love, thou art Absolute sole lord | Of LIFE & DEATH' (Crashaw 2015: 65), a formulation that leaves no doubt that Love is the word made flesh, the risen Christ. Nowhere is the personification of love as Christ himself—or perhaps, vice versa—more tellingly depicted in the early modern era than in the lyric which completes Herbert's sequence 'The Church', 'Love' (III):

> Love bade me welcome: yet my soul drew back,
>> Guiltie of dust and sinne.

---

[9] The phrase is a translation from the Latin, cited in Peter Meiderlin's *Paraenesis votiva pro pace ecclesiae ad theologos Augustanae* (1626).

> But quick-ey'd Love, observing me grow slack
> From my first entrance in,
> Drew nearer to me, sweetly questioning,
> If I lack'd any thing. (Herbert 2007: 661)

This is divine love in person: sociable and welcoming as the host of a tavern, concerned as a friend, 'sweet' as a lover, even when what he encounters in the lyric's narrator is profound uncertainty and reluctance. Here, again, the emphasis is on love defined by opposition, in the dialectics of engagement and withdrawal; here, too, the experience of love is expressed in terms of the senses, particularly sight, 'quick-eyed' and 'observing'. The speaker's reply in the second stanza reveals his recognizably human obsession with sin: he is not 'worthy to be here', being 'unkinde, ungratefull', nor is he able to look at the God who made his eyes. This generous host will brook no excuse, however, and the poem's final lines bring the catechistical yet courtly negotiations to a climax:

> And know you not, sayes Love, who bore the blame?
> My deare, then I will serve.
> You must sit down, sayes Love, and taste my meat:
> So I did sit and eat. (661)

In boldly monosyllabic lines, the essence of redeeming love is spelt out and, at the last possible moment, the uneasy speaker gives in and accepts it. Here the form that love takes is not only the person of God but the food of the Eucharistic elements; the board at which the guests eat in a tavern is also, in Herbert's poetic vision, the Lord's table in church and the site of the ultimate heavenly banquet. Love, he suggests, has the power to overwhelm even the basic dimensions of time and space.

CONCLUSION: THE UNIFYING POWER OF LOVE

What can we conclude from this array of early modern writing, biblical and non-biblical, secular and sacred, about the phenomenon of love? We may observe how fundamental it is to the literature of the period, and how intertwined are the subjects and metaphors of earthly and heavenly love. We may note that it takes us to the heart of the writers' concerns about themselves and what is 'speakable' in their writing, and leads to some of the finest works in poetry and prose across the two centuries. I would suggest that there are also several important trends to observe within the material presented in this chapter, including some chronological progressions to be noted, even if tentatively. There is clearly a move from the secular and largely Petrarchan love poetry of the sixteenth century to the emphasis on devotional love lyrics in the earlier seventeenth century, though it should be understood that this development is not neat or clear-cut, since the earliest sonnet sequences are in fact on religious subjects.[10] In devotional poetry, influenced by the patterns of the Reformation as it developed during the period under discussion, we can observe a shift in focus from external to internal manifestations of love, as suggested by the contrast between Robert Southwell's late-Elizabethan Christ-child 'burning' with love and Julia Palmer's 1671 cry to God to transform her into 'one, pure mase of love, | flaming up towards thee' (Palmer 2001: 69). On the other hand, it is also possible to discern a progression from texts that name and define love, both divine and human, in the sixteenth and early seventeenth century, to a greater emphasis in the later part of the seventeenth century on the vocabulary of benevolence, the tangible social evidence of love.

As we have seen throughout this chapter, there can be significant differences of emphasis in the definition of divine love, largely dependent upon denominational allegiance. These distinctions range from the view of love as sacrificially efficacious, as celebrated in the Catholic Mass, to the loving grace allotted to the elect in the predestinarian Calvinist vision. However, as we have seen, the writings on love in this period tend to reveal more similarities than differences, perhaps because the devotional response to love, praising divine generosity and lamenting the weakness of human love, tends to eschew overt polemic. Of course, the love of God could always be harnessed to a cause: in the mid-sixteenth century the Protestant poet William Samuel claimed that the death of Mary I demonstrated the love of God for the 'lytle Ile England' (Samuel 1559: A3[r]), while in 1611 Aemelia Lanyer depicted Christ's incarnation and passion in a strongly gendered context as a triumph of love brought about by God and virtuous women 'without the assistance of man' (Lanyer 1993: 49). However, for the most part the subject of love itself is a unifying force, giving rise to texts that deal with community, mystery, and a sense of the inexpressible. Cordelia's perplexity in *King Lear*—'love, and be silent' (Shakespeare 1998: 1.1.62)—is a sentiment frequently echoed in writings about divine love, the enormity of which taxes the imagination, perplexes the writer, and ultimately defeats the language. After all, as Traherne put it in his *Church's Year-Book*, God manages to converse with the human soul 'without the Noise of Words' (Traherne 2005–14: IV, 119). Where there are differences between the writers themselves in their use of 'noisy' words, I would suggest that these contrasts are at least as dependent on genre, gender, and audience as they are on theology or chronology. For example, the account of God's love for the individual soul as expressed in a manuscript of devotional lyric written by a woman and intended for a family readership, is significantly different from the expostulation of divine love in a sermon by a male cleric before a listening congregation. As the studies of communities elsewhere in this volume have also demonstrated, the audience for whom an author is writing—family, church, colony, the wider public, the self, or primarily God—is a fundamentally determining factor in the interplay of literature and religion.

---

[10] See Wilcox 2011.

Given the all-encompassing role of love in Christian theology and human experience, it is not surprising that the nature of divine and human love is a central fascination of early modern English literature. In contrast to the often fickle quality of secular love, the love of God is perceived as perpetual, recurrent, and—ideally—reciprocal, which lends an appropriateness to its recurring presence within and among the texts of the period. As Herbert wrote in the final stanza of his versification of Psalm 23:

> Surely thy sweet and wondrous love
>   Shall measure all my days;
> And as it never shall remove,
>   So neither shall my praise. (Herbert 2007: 594)

CHAPTER 38

....

THE ART
AND CRAFT OF DYING

....

PETER CARLSON

There died he without grudge, without anxiety, with good will and glad
hope, whereby he went into Abraham's bosom.

THOMAS More, referring in 1522 to the story of the beggar Lazarus in the Gospel of Luke,
described the ideal response of Christians whom God determined should die. However,
dying without anxiety or having no anxiety about death (which after all are not quite the
same things) is probably a superhuman quality, and even Jesus, according to the Gospel
accounts, agonized at his death. Thus, to speak of anxiety is to speak of the obvious.
How that anxiety is expressed, and the behaviours reflecting that anxiety, however, differ
according to time and circumstance—not least the circumstances of current theology,
liturgical practice, and popular understanding. This chapter seeks to provide both an
overview and explanation for various anxieties—and the religious and secular attempts
to relieve those anxieties—that accompanied death and dying in early modern England.
There is no lack of scholarship regarding death and the Protestant reformations over the
past few decades, but the intersections between religious authority, individual piety, and
the literature of the period can certainly benefit from further analysis, particularly as
those intersections suggest a more nuanced picture of the early modern person's understandings of death than have previously been offered.

Scholars have attempted to explain how (or whether) the theological changes of the
sixteenth century affected English women and men, common and noble, lay and religious. Whiggish interpretations portraying the Protestant reformations inexorably
replacing tired Roman Catholic authority have been sufficiently challenged for this theory no longer to be tenable. Eamon Duffy, in particular, has demonstrated vividly the
ongoing influence of Catholic belief and practice deep into reformation England, arguing

that royal edict and canon law had far less influence over individual piety and practice than scholars had previously assumed (Duffy 2005). Even so, the English churches *were* reformed, even if the process was 'slow, reluctant and untidy' (MacCulloch 2005). In recent decades, scholars have posited not only a more nuanced reformation influence, but have begun to look more closely at the various ways the reforms affected early modern behaviour and thinking. John Stachniewski (1981) sought to prove that the Calvinist doctrine of predestination and its attendant ambiguity regarding who would be counted among the Elect, created a deep uncertainty about death that was reflected in the literature of the period. Clare Gittings (1984), on the other hand, saw death and its rituals losing their religious influence and character, becoming increasingly secularized over the sixteenth and seventeenth centuries. Robert Watson (1999) took the idea of secularization a step further, suggesting that the real anxiety of death was annihilation: not who would be saved, or whether our rituals surrounding death were ultimately helpful, but whether people could look forward to anything at all at the end of their mortal span.

Every scholar who has written on death in the Protestant reformations has identified shifts in and anxieties regarding rituals and beliefs about death and the dead in early modern England. I hope to show in this chapter that all of those shifts were actually related to something other than a single doctrinal or political stand. It was not only the particular uncertainty of Calvin's doctrine of predestination with its anxiety about death and funerary rituals, nor the waverings of Henrician laws, nor even the significant trauma of swinging back and forth from Rome to Canterbury to Rome to Canterbury throughout the Tudor dynasty. The uncertainty surrounding death in the early modern period was something much deeper, more foundational, than the authority of a single soteriological doctrine or of a set of laws: it was the uncertainty of authority itself.

This chapter opens with the theological legacy of the high medieval period and a description of changes that took place under the reformers' influence, paying particular attention to the soteriological doctrines of grace (over and against the doctrine of works), of predestination, and of assurance, because these theological views re-set the stage, both positively and negatively, for the rituals and beliefs related to death and dying in early modern England. Those rituals were prescribed and proscribed by the authority of the English realm, both in its laws and in the ever-present authority of Church ritual, articulated in the Book of Common Prayer.

The next section examines the early modern recommendations for dying well, focusing on a corpus of literature exhorting Christians to a good death, reflecting the *ars moriendi* of the late medieval period but with a Protestant turn. A very important part of a good death was preparing a will, and this section includes a look at how wills changed under the reformations. I also examine the expectations regarding the disposal of the body, and how—or whether—a good Christian soul might be memorialized.

Sudden death, executions, and excommunications presented their own challenges and opportunities. In the final section, stories of sudden deaths, suicides, and theatrical scaffold speeches provide not only warnings but glimpses of last-minute grace and fears of damnation in the sixteenth and seventeenth centuries. Throughout this chapter, I hope to show that the anxieties expressed in the various types of literature all demonstrate the fundamental confusion of a world in which authority itself had lost much of its stability, affecting everything in life, including death.

DEATH THEOLOGICAL: CATHOLICS, LUTHERANS, CALVINISTS, AND OTHERS

Even if the changes of the sixteenth-century Protestant reforms were not achieved overnight, we must remember that they were sweeping in scope, lasting in influence, and they constituted the greatest shifts in the theologies and liturgies of death since the age of the martyrs ended. They also brought into question the previously unassailable authority of the Roman Church in Western Christianity. That authority included an elaborate theology of death supported by the sacraments with their soteriological efficacy, and by the doctrine of purgatory as a place to complete the penitential work begun in this life.

The medieval Church understood itself to be the instrument of mediation between humans and God, continuing the mediation that Jesus, as God's son, began with his life, death, and resurrection. This work was expressed most clearly in the Church's administration of the seven sacraments: particularly baptism, penance, and Eucharist. These three were perceived to be the primary spiritual tools that equipped Christians for salvation. Baptism was a ritual 'bath' that cleansed a person of the blot of original sin, inherited from Adam and Eve, who had disobeyed God in the Garden of Eden. It was therefore seen as essential to baptize newborn children as quickly as possible, to ensure removal of the stain of sin. The Eucharist, a ritual based on the biblical accounts of Jesus's last supper with his disciples, was proclaimed by the Church to be a re-enactment of Jesus's sacrificial death, interpreting literally the words of Jesus: 'This is my body,' and 'This is my blood.' The theology of transubstantiation assured the faithful at the Mass that the bread and wine on the altar became, when the priest repeated those words, the actual body and blood of Jesus,[1] once again sacrificed for them, once again paying the debt for their sins.

Jesus's payment did not, however, absolve Christians from personal responsibility; some form of restitution was required from the sinners as well, and they could not be absolved from sins they had not confessed. There were four steps in the sacrament of penance: demonstrating contrition; saying confession; receiving absolution; and performing (or showing intent to perform) payment. All four steps were theologically necessary to remove guilt, but the final one, payment, had the greatest effect on the rituals surrounding death. The Church taught that penance included some form of

---

[1] The distinction between the substance (the essence of a thing) and the accidents (the perceptible appearance of a thing) was an Aristotelian concept utilized in particular by Thomas Aquinas in the thirteenth century to explain how the bread and wine of the Eucharist could become in fact the body and blood of Christ, while still looking and tasting like bread and wine.

payment, much as we might be required to pay for a window we have broken, even if the neighbour has already expressed forgiveness—absolution—for our error. Some payment could be made in this life, of course: donating candles for the altar or vestments to a church, or making a pilgrimage. Most people, however, were sinners of such consequence that they made more of a mess than they could clean up in their earthly lives. For these people, who were neither such heroic saints whose entrance into heaven must be both guaranteed and immediate, nor such heinous villains as to be sent directly to hell, the intermediate location of purgatory provided an answer. This was where souls went to be purged: to pay off, through various helpful torments, any remaining guilt at the end of their lives. When a Christian's suffering in purgatory (described with fascinated detail in commonplace books, treatises, sermons, poetry, and handbooks on dying well) was completed,[2] she or he could finally enter heaven.

The doctrine of purgatory and the theology of the sacraments were directly related. Since the Eucharist, with its re-sacrifice of Christ, offered a salvific benefit for Christians at the altar, why not also for those Christian souls in purgatory? From the belief that Masses said on earth could assist those souls, speeding their passage through purgatory, an industry of prayers for the dead rose up, including chantries: Masses dedicated specifically to the remembrance and assistance of the dead.[3] Chantries were offered in chapels created in the transepts and apses of the churches, in monastic colleges founded by benefactors anticipating intercessory prayers from the brothers, and in chapels built and maintained expressly for that purpose. Galpern's oft-quoted description of medieval society as 'a cult of the living in service of the dead' is both dated and simplistic (Galpern in Trinkaus and Oberman 1974), but it makes a point. Death, and the ongoing awareness of the dead, were ever-present in the theologies and liturgies of the Church.

Martin Luther challenged all that. What began as an announcement of a scholastic debate became a powerful religious—and political—movement. The ninety-five theses posted by Luther at the University of Wittenberg in 1517 included disputations on the sacrament of penance, the pope's authority to remit guilt, purgatory, and the status of souls in purgatory. Luther did not, interestingly, directly deny the existence of purgatory (though he denied that we could assist Christians who were there). In 1535, however, he made clear his rejection of the doctrine of purgatory, declaring it to be 'nothing but dreams and human inventions' (Luther 1966, vol. 8: 316). All Luther's attacks, including those on purgatory, were rooted in the fundamental doctrine of Lutheranism: justification by faith alone. Luther understood Rome's basic heresy to be a doctrine of works, that what we do can assist our salvation, even if our works are the sacraments, or prayers for and to the dead. Luther rejected any kind of soteriological role for any human actions. His friend Philip Melanchthon (1537) wrote a defence of the Augsburg Confession

---

[2] In addition to the most familiar description of purgatory in Dante, see *The Arte or Crafte to Lyve Well and to Dye Well*, Wynkyn de Word, 1505, or the twelfth-century *Tractatus de Purgatorio Sancti Patricii*.

[3] Technically, chantries are the 'trust funds' set up to ensure that Masses will be said. The word is also used to describe the Masses themselves, and occasionally the chapels that were built for saying those Masses.

after the 1530 Diet of Augsburg, where Lutheranism stood trial before the Holy Roman Empire. In it Melanchthon declared, 'we do not prohibit [prayers for the dead], but we disapprove of the application *ex opere operato* of the Lord's Supper on behalf of the dead' (Melanchthon 1988: 417). Praying for the dead is fine, according to Melanchthon, but our prayers are of no benefit; only God's grace helps them.

This total rejection of our works helping us to heaven required re-casting the theology of the sacraments. Scrapping all but two, baptism and Eucharist, Luther denied that they save us. Baptism cannot erase our original sin: it is only a welcome into the Church. The Eucharist is only participation in the real (spiritual) presence of Christ, and need not become the actual body and blood of Christ. Even this real presence, though, does not save us, but is simply 'the assurance of the forgiveness of sins, to comfort' us (Schaff 1910). In rejecting the authority of priests to pronounce forgiveness for the dead, and in rejecting the authority of the Eucharist to do anything beyond reassure Christians of their forgiven state, Luther and his followers had fundamentally challenged the theologies and rituals of death.

The Swiss reforms caused more trouble for those theologies and rituals. This was due chiefly to the work of John Calvin, best known for his monumental *Institutes of the Christian Religion*. Calvin agreed that works are useless and purgatory is not real. However, he went further: the systematic theology of *Institutes* takes as its starting point a God in total control. Logically, it follows that God controls who will be saved (the Elect), and humans have no say in the matter. It follows that God, who is omniscient, has always known who would be Elected to salvation. Calvin articulates the doctrine of 'Eternal Election, by Which God has Predestined Some to Salvation, Others to Destruction'; he states, bluntly, 'We call predestination God's eternal decree [regarding] what he willed to become of each man. For ... eternal life is fore-ordained for some, eternal damnation for others' (Calvin 1960). This was perilous doctrine. Luther introduced the problem by arguing that salvation is received through faith alone. This could lead a Christian to question how much faith was needed. The concreteness of the penitential system in the Roman Church was attractive by comparison. Calvin complicated things further, though, by arguing that we cannot even have faith on our own: God preordains whether we will be faithful or reprobate, making our salvation even less assured. We might *think* we are faithful, but at the last moment, only God knows.

Calvin was aware of the danger of this uncertainty, and sought to reassure his readers: 'we have sufficiently clear and firm testimony that we have been inscribed in the book of life if we are in communion with Christ' (Calvin 1960). Other theologians attempted to provide more concrete evidence of election. William Perkins, a Cambridge theologian, wrote: 'For they whome God elected to ... eternall life, were also elected to those subordinate meanes [of doing good deeds], whereby, as by steppes, they might attaine this end, and without which, it were impossible to obtaine it' (Perkins 1597). God, Perkins assures his readers, not only elects the Christian to eternal life, but in so doing will clearly elect him to do those things that *lead* to eternal life. In 1571, the Thirty-Nine Articles of the Church of England found 'the godly consideration of Predestination [to be] full of sweet, pleasant, and unspeakable comfort', but only because those assured of election would be 'such as feel in themselves the working of the Spirit of Christ' (Church of England 1571). The doctrine of assurance was circular: your good deeds cannot save you, but you will do good deeds because you are saved; so do good deeds to prove that you have been saved.

Of course, the Protestant reformations would not have had the influence they did in England without the cooperation of the royal court. Henry's break from Rome over his Great Matter provided the initial impetus to those who were eager for reforms closer to home. While debates continue over how Protestant or Catholic Henry actually was,[4] there is no doubt that by replacing the pope's authority with his own in the 1534 Act of Supremacy, and by dismantling the monasteries in 1537 and 1539, he gave Protestant reformers a foothold in England.

With the ruler as head of the church, royal authority regarding death and the dead was found in Church law, such as the Henrician canons of 1535 forbidding churchyard burial to excommunicates, or the 1553 *Reformatio legum ecclesiasticarum*, which directed the making of wills and testaments (Bray 2000). The Book of Common Prayer was influential as well. Required by law to be in the churches (as were the people), it was therefore the single most readily available book in the sixteenth and seventeenth centuries, shaping not only worship, but popular understanding about death and dying. The liturgy for burial of the dead helps us understand how the Church expected the people both to think about death and to deal with the dead.

The Office of the Dead in the Sarum Missal[5] assumes performance in a monastic church; a rubric notes that it 'is said daily in the Chapter-house' (Pearson 1884). Traditional Catholic understandings of death and the dead are evident throughout this service: the collect that beseeches God to accept 'the oblation we offer unto Thee in behalf of the soul of Thy servant ... and grant that he may be restored and absolved from all the errors of this mortal state' assumes that prayers benefit the dead, and that we can be absolved from sin after death. Trental and Anniversary Masses include prayers 'that the soul of Thy servant ... may be cleansed by this Sacrifice, and alike obtain pardon and eternal rest' (Pearson 1884). The Mass is salvific for quick and dead alike.

The first Book of Common Prayer, published under Edward VI, offered a more reformed burial liturgy, though still with echoes of Sarum use: the minister was still called a priest; scriptural passages from Job, the Psalms, the Gospel of John, and the Epistle of I Timothy would have sounded familiar to the congregation; and the celebration of Holy Communion was still included. However, there were also significant changes: suggestions of continued cleansing in purgatory are gone, and the prayers on the whole shift their focus from the dead person toward the living: 'And his body we commit to the earth, besechyng thyne infinite goodnesse, to geve us grace to lyve in thy

---

[4] His will, for instance, contains distinctly Catholic leanings, such as requesting that 'the Blessed Virgin and holy company of Heaven ... pray for and with him ... that he may after this the sooner attain everlasting life' (*Letters and Papers* 1910).

[5] The Sarum Missal (named after the Latin name for Salisbury) was the liturgical text used in Catholic England.

feare and love, and to dye in thy favoure' (Church of England 1549). This startling shift from the dead to the living demonstrates what was really at stake here: not the soul of the dead, for which nothing more can be done, but the souls of the congregation. Similarly, Communion was offered for the living, praying that God will 'raise us from the death of sin, unto the life of righteousnes' (Church of England 1549).

The Book of Common Prayer was revised in 1552, reflecting an even more Protestant theology. The Order for the Burial of the Dead is less than half the length of the 1549 edition, eliminating a large number of prayers, and the Communion service. This excision is remarkable in its Protestant theology: Communion is simply a public confession of Christian faith; it has nothing to do with the dead. The burial service is almost entirely scriptural readings. After thanking God briefly for delivering 'our brother out of the myseryes of this sinneful world' (Church of England 1552), the mourners turn their attention back to themselves, praying that they will be found fit to be resurrected.

The 1552 prayer book was short-lived, as was Edward himself, who died in July 1553. Edward's Catholic sister Mary succeeded him and brought the country briefly back to the See of Rome. She, too, died without issue, however, and her sister Elizabeth once again established the Church of England, issuing an Act of Uniformity in 1559 requiring the people to use a common prayer book in English. This book was based on the 1552 edition, but was less Protestant. It restored a number of the ceremonies to all of the services, though the Burial of the Dead remained the same and remained essentially unchanged throughout the seventeenth century.

One stunning exception was *A Directory for the Publique Worship of God* issued during the Civil War by a parliament hostile to anything remotely royal or Catholic, and including in its front matter the Parliamentary ordinance banning the Book of Common Prayer. The *Directory* eliminates the Office of the Dead entirely, replacing it with a short rubric, 'Concerning Buriall of the Dead'. It is vehemently anti-Catholic:

> WHEN any person departeth this life, let the dead body, upon the day of Buriall, be decently attended from the house to the place appointed for publique Buriall, and there immediately interred, *without any Ceremony*.
>
> And because the customes of kneeling down, and praying by or towards the dead Corps, and other such usages, in the place where it lies, before it be carried to Buriall, *are Superstitious*: and for that, praying, reading, and singing, both in going to and at the Grave, *have been grosly abused, are no way beneficiall to the dead*, and have proved many wayes hurtfull to the living; therefore let all such things be laid aside.
>
> Howbeit, we judge it very convenient, that the Christian friends, which accompany the dead body to the place appointed for publique Buriall, do apply themselves to meditations and conferences suitable to the occasion: and that the Minister, as upon other occasions, so at this time, *if he be present*, may put them in remembrance of their duty.
>
> That this shall not extend to deny any civill respects or differences at the Buriall, suitable to the rank and condition of the party deceased, while he was living. (*Directory* 1644, emphases mine)

No churchyard—just 'the place appointed'. No ceremony—just an interment. No kneeling or praying—just 'meditations and conferences suitable to the occasion'. Not even a priest—just a minister, and then only 'if he be present'. Your friend is dead. Bury him, and get on with your Christian duty. Move on; nothing to see here, not even a minister.

It should be no surprise that the monarchy—as well as the Book of Common Prayer, with its Order for Burial—was reinstated before twelve years had passed. However much the *Directory of Publique Worship* denied the importance of the dead, it seems the English felt otherwise.

BRING US TO A GOODLY END: PREPARING FOR DEATH

Catholic or Protestant, the moments leading to death evoke dramatic import. They are, after all, the last opportunity we have this side of the veil for showing ourselves fit to enter heaven. A genre of literature dealing with these moments arose in the early fifteenth century, with the publication of a text called *Ars moriendi*, the Art of Dying. Immensely popular, it was translated into multiple languages, including English (Beatty 1970). A kind of self-help book, it listed the key elements of a good end in six broad points: death is not bad, if we have lived well; nevertheless, we will be tempted at our death by doubt, pride, and avarice; there are some important questions to consider when dying; dying does not end the need to imitate Christ; friends and family have particular responsibilities; and there are some helpful prayers that will assist a Christian at death. *Ars moriendi* was popular in England; an abridged version was printed in English by Philip Caxton in 1495, and continued through many editions and adaptations into the 1600s.[6] It is notable that every English adaptation of the *Ars* into the seventeenth century was small: the majority were duodecimos, designed to be portable and cheap, a cause or reflection of its popularity. Morgan has observed that, because clergymen play no role in the texts, they reflect 'the failings of the local church in not always providing a suitable support for the dying' (Morgan, in Jupp and Gittings 2000). Doebler associates the *Ars moriendi* with despair, but they are actually very hopeful texts. In the Caxton translation, the dying Christian is assured 'that thy place be in peas, And that thyn habytacyon be in clestyall Jherusalem' (Caxton 1495). Surely people felt that facing death would be easier if they knew 'their place will be in peace'.

---

[6] In fact, Doebler sees the *Ars* tradition continued, in the very broad definition of reminding people to prepare for death, in various types of literature beyond the actual handbooks. She argues that it can be read not only in the great allegorical works of Milton and Spenser, the plays of Shakespeare, and the sermons of John Donne, but also in cheaply printed broadsides in the *Dance of Death* tradition, making it accessible even to the poorer folk. Whether this warning constitutes a form of the *Ars moriendi* is moot, but it certainly demonstrates the ongoing importance attributed to remembering our mortality. For a review of *Ars moriendi* literature in the Tudor and Stuart monarchies, see Green 2000: 360–8.

This did not mean they would not suffer doubts. Indeed, the *Ars* warns Christians that doubting one's salvation is natural, 'For none is certain, if he be dynge or worthy to have deserved the love of god, or the hate of god. Nethelesse none ought to despayre, but ought always to adresse his herte to god' (Caxton 1495). The book provides reassurance in a variety of questions that should be put to a sick person, that serve as reminders that she or he is a sinner, but that he or she should be 'Ioyfull that thou deyest in the faith of our lorde Ihesu cryste', having denied 'all heresies, errours & superstycyons' (Caxton 1495).

Evidence for the continuing popularity of *Ars moriendi* literature is seen primarily in the fact that this very Catholic text survived the ruthlessly Protestant reformations. One of the most exquisitely Protestant variations was also one of the earliest, written in 1561 by Thomas Becon. *A Sick Mans Salve* contains the same recommendations as the *Ars*, but wrapped in Protestant theology. It is a conversation between a dying man and his three friends, reminiscent of Job. Unlike Job, however, Epaphroditus (the dying man) receives sage advice from his friends, and comes to a faithful end. The emphasis on the doctrine of assurance is made clear by the repetition of phrases like 'Doubt not', and 'Be ye sure'. Of course, Epaphroditus has doubts, but they are relieved when his friend Philemon confirms that 'this humbling of yourself in the sight Lord our God is a certain argument and sure token of your everlasting salvation' (Becon 1561). For Becon, in his Calvinist twist on dying well, doubt becomes tautologically, a sign of election.

Both Catholic and Protestant versions of *Ars moriendi* literature emphasize the importance of making a will: a Christian must see to the orderly disposal of his goods. Caxton's version advises against mind-blurring medicine, so a man can see to 'dysposinge lawfully his house other goodes and nedes' (Caxton 1495). Similarly, in the recusant English translation of *A Dialogue of Dying Wel*, Peter of Luca declares, 'The second principal rule of the arte to dy wel consisteth in the disposeing of a mannes last wil and testament.' There are specific things a good Catholic should attend to in his will. First, establish a trust to have Masses said for one's soul. Then, leave everything in good order, so that you 'leave thy heyres in peace without stryf, which is the best inheritance' (da Luca 1603). The primary reason for a will, after attending to one's soul, is to ensure that there will be no squabbling over your things once you are gone.

Protestant traditions, too, emphasize the importance of a will, though with some differences. The bequests Epaphroditus makes (or does not make) in his will are designed, not just to instruct dying people, but to refute Roman Catholic tradition. In some cases, the same bequests are made, but justified with Protestant theology. The Catholic tradition of bequeathing one's body and soul to God is continued, but the expectation is that 'Jesu, our alone Saviour and Redeemer, will receive my soul into his glory' (Becon 1561). No need of Virgin Mary or any other saints to help him on the journey, and certainly no purgatory. Epaphroditus's body is of no concern either. When asked if he wants to be interred in the churchyard, he states, 'All is one to me.... Wheresoever I lie, I doubt not but the Lord God at the last day shall raise me up again' (Becon 1561).

Epaphroditus gets testy when his friend suggest that he 'remember the poor', an act interpreted by many as assisting the soul to salvation:

I never forgot them ... For I have ever thought it better to send my works before me, while I live in this world, than to have them sent after me, I know not by whom, when I am gone. *These purgatory-rakers shall neither rake nor scrape for me with their masses and diriges, when I am departed; for I trust no such works* ... But, 'as touching the poor, I give unto them four hundred pounds'. (Becon 1561, emphasis added)

This was the Protestant challenge in wills: they needed to be clear that testamentary gifts were given *because* of salvation, not to ensure it. These apologetic details accompany all the good deeds financed in Epaphroditus's will.

Sick man's salve provides other examples of 'Protestantizing' the Catholic tradition. Epaphroditus funds no Masses for his soul, but he pays for sermons. He is still paying, technically, for services to be said, but with a critical difference: they are for the living, not him. He will not pay mourners with mourning gowns (reflecting the Protestant accusation that Catholics give 'fine black gowns' to the upper-class mourners, but give cheaper robes to the poor). Epaphroditus blasts this tradition, even as he wills 'that thirty poor men and women do accompany my body unto the burial, and that each of them have a gown of some convenient colour' (Becon 1561). These thirty, along with thirty poor children, should then come to his house for dinner after the burial. Once again, the Protestant Epaphroditus performs good Catholic deeds, but works hard to distance himself theologically from the tradition itself. Indeed, he suggests that people should not mourn at all, since he is going to 'a blessed and ioyfull state', in an argument that predates Feste's when he chides the grieving Olivia in *Twelfth Night*: 'The more fool, madonna, to mourn for your brother's soul being in heaven' (Shakespeare). Epaphroditus will not have the passing bell rung for him, though this practice was clearly established in Protestant tradition. Tessa Watt (1991) has observed the ongoing tradition of ringing the passing bell well into the reign of Queen Elizabeth, and we can also see it reflected in poetry and theological writings, including, famously, John Donne's *Devotions Upon Emergent Occasions*.[7]

Epaphroditus rejects as 'supersticions' the traditions of 'Solemn singing, devout ringing, holy censing, priests pattering, candles lightening, torches brenning, communions saying, and such like'. The service should only include those things that 'call to remembrance [of the living] the death of Christ' (Becon 1561). To make clear who is responsible for these superstitions, he declares, 'I have nothing to do with papists, nor with their doctrine.... For they are "enemies of the cross of Christ", depravers of the holy scriptures, and corrupters of Christian souls' (Becon 1561). Of course, Becon was not just writing a self-help book, but propaganda. The *Salve* was intended as an inspirational, (melo)dramatic work to help Protestants die well.

Real wills were rarely so clearly Protestant or Catholic, but they can provide us with some hints regarding the testator's religious sentiments. An example is the 1636 will of Richard Flatt:

---

[7] This is the famous passage: 'never send to know for whom the bells tolls; it tolls for thee.'

> Into the hands of God Almighty, my maker, my Saviour and Redeemer, trusting to be
> saved by the only sufficient merits of Jesus Christ my Saviour … when it shall please
> the lord in mercy to take me out of this world, being fully assured that this my mor-
> tal body shall one day put on immortality, and being raised again by the virtue of
> Christ's resurrection, I shall live forever with him. (Cited in Spufford, from Jupp and
> Gittings 2000)

This is variant on a scribe's traditional formula that expresses remarkably Protestant doctrine; the similarity to Epaphroditus's will is evident. Other indicators of Protestant testators can be seen in the desire to bequeath Bibles (reflecting the emphasis on scripture as sole religious authority) or Foxe's *Actes and Monuments*, an example of the 'Protestantization' of the very Catholic practice of hagiography.

Some Protestant wills specify the location of burial. Some separatists, as well as the more energetic Protestants in the Anglican Church followed Epaphroditus's example, and were emphatic that they should *not* be buried in a churchyard. Gerard Croese, in his *General History of the Quakers*, relates the case of Priscilla Moe. This Quaker widow died in prison:

> Next day her Friends the Quakers prepare to carry away the Corps, and to bury it in
> their own Burying-place, they had purchased for that purpose; but the Governour
> of the Town [had] her buryed in a Christian manner, to the great regret, and sore
> against the will of those Men…. [T]his they took very heinously … that their
> Enemies carried their Friends Corps with so many Ceremonies and Circumstances
> of their own, Prayers, and other Acts of such like Devotion, into hallowed and conse-
> crated Ground, which they then call a Christian Burial. (Croese 1696)

The irony that Quaker anti-ceremonial beliefs had become ceremonies themselves was not lost on Croese, but it demonstrates the repudiation by evangelical Protestants of anything that might seem Catholic.

Memorials were also a problem. Once again, Protestant theology came into conflict with the desire to commemorate the deceased. Becon implies that a sermon is more than adequate memorial. Gittings has observed that the funeral sermon was 'an increasingly popular addition [to funerals] in the seventeenth century' (Jupp and Gittings 2000). Another kind of word-as-memorial is evident in poetry, classically expressed in Shakespeare's sonnet 74: 'My life hath in this line some interest, | Which for memorial still with thee shall stay' (2002). It was not uncommon to try through sermon or sonnet to live forever in this world, however confidently Christians might expect to live forever in the next.

Physical monuments were more problematic than words, however: Protestant iconoclasm, along with the general Protestant belief that Catholics spent too much time worrying about the dead, suggest that monuments to the dead would be uncomplicatedly forbidden. In fact, at times under Edward and Elizabeth, and during the Interregnum, monument destruction was encouraged (Lindley 2007). Memorializing the dead did not stop, however; apparently the Psalmist's fear that 'I [will be] forgotten as a dead man out of mind' (*Geneva Bible* 1560) haunted even the most passionately iconoclastic Protestants. Llewellyn (2000) has identified thousands of monuments ranging from tablets to wooden and stone sculpture between 1560 and 1650. Panofsky suggests that funerary monuments at this time presented a fundamental shift in 'a rejection of Christian concern for the future in favor of pagan glorification of the past' (Panofsky 1992), reflected in Gittings's later suggestion that funerals became more secular in England in the sixteenth and seventeenth centuries. Peter Sherlock claimed by contrast, however, that monuments 'were more concerned with the sacred than most scholars have hitherto acknowledged' (Sherlock 2008). Whatever the 'religiosity' of the impulse, we can be assured that memorializing the dead, even in the face of a theology that says we can do nothing for them, was not a practice that the English were willing to abandon.

A kindly affection towards memorials was not limited to new monuments, either. At Ashridge, a Buckinghamshire monastic college suppressed under Henry VIII, we see examples of local families going to great lengths to preserve the monuments and the memories of dead family members. In the 1570s the monastic church was demolished. Presumably locals were notified, and took the opportunity to remove the tombs of their ancestors from the college to local parishes. Today in the tiny church of St John the Baptist, Aldbury, we can see the grand tomb of Lord and Lady Robert Whittingham, complete with surrounding tracery and fourteenth-century floor tiles from the monastic church. This monument, and others like it in nearby parish churches, demonstrates that families, however Protestant, sought to maintain the memory of their ancestors with material objects that bore their names and likenesses. Whatever the theology, memorials were not easily abandoned in reformation England.

Woe to the Unprepared: Executions, Excommunications, and Other Sudden Deaths

Tombs and memorials were marks of a good death, or a death that the family wanted to convince others was good. However, sudden death was problematic, theologically: did the deceased die in a state of grace? Should he or she be buried in consecrated ground? Did 'consecrated ground' even matter? What of prisoners, heretics, and excommunicants? What were the responsibilities of the living towards those particular bodies, if any? Thomas Tuke's *A Discourse of Death, Bodily, Ghostly, and Eternall* explicitly addresses itself to people for whom sudden death was a concern; its subtitle is '*nor unfit for Souldiers Warring, Seamen sayling, Strangers travelling, Women bearing*' (Tuke 1613). William Perkins, in his *Salve for a Sicke Man* likewise suggests that his work is especially for '1. Mariners when they goe to sea. 2. Souldiers when they goe to battel. 3. Women when they travaill of child' (Perkins 1595). Christopher Sutton's *Disce mori* reminds us that while everyone should Learn to Die, 'how much more ought those who enter into places of apparent peril, undertake attempts of greatest danger, to stand upon their guard, and be well provided for, to be ready for God!' (Sutton 1600). These writers all proclaim a two-sided message: preparing for death is a godly act, but death may not wait for you to prepare, particularly if you are in a dangerous profession.

Sometimes the most dangerous profession was a profession of faith, or a profession of anything against the monarch. Treason was broadly defined, and a capital crime. Morgan notes that 'Execution by one of several gruesome methods was … the price of political and religious opposition' (Jupp and Gittings 2000). Scholars have long noted the parallels between scaffold and stage, and the execution speeches of convicted criminals are some of the most dramatic soliloquies of early modern England. These dramas were written in John Foxe's *Actes and Monuments*, the Catholic hagiographies of Edmund Campion, printed scaffold speeches, and in popular broadsheets. Smith (1954) has noted a tendency of condemned prisoners to confess their guilt even when innocent, or at least to declare their loyalty and prayers for a long and fruitful life to the monarch.[8] While those occasions are remarkable, it is unhelpful to imagine them as normative; many accused protested their innocence to the end. Edmund Campion, the Jesuit executed for high treason against Queen Elizabeth in 1581, never confessed, but instead claimed that 'he was giltlesse & innocent of all treason and conspiracie', and even forgave the jury, assuming 'that touching this poynt [they had been] deceavid' (Alfield 1582). He acknowledged his fidelity to the Catholic faith, but denied it was treason, and he died, according to Alfield, praying for the long and prosperous reign of Queen Elizabeth.

What to do with executed bodies was a question, theologically, and the bodies of women were unique. They were usually executed 'off-stage', suggesting a reluctance to publicize the destruction of a woman's body that translates even to literature: the public execution of Anne Askew is skimmed over in Foxe's *Actes and Monuments*, a text generally more than willing to provide the reader with gruesome details (Dolan 1994; Foxe 1563). For men, hanging, drawing, and quartering was the most spectacular bodily desecration, applied to those convicted of treason.[9] If ever punishment was intended as deterrent, the spectacle of drawing the viscera from a (sometimes still living) body and dispersing the various parts around the city or country was certainly meant to act as such. John Donne claimed that 'our dead body … dries and molders into dust … and still, *still* God knows … in what part of the world every graine of every mans dust lies' (Donne 1962). What we do to dead bodies shouldn't matter, then; though the treatment of the executed dead demonstrates that Protestants still thought how bodies were disposed of was important. It may seem that theology had little to do with these mutilations; after all, these were the bodies of people who had fallen, not from God's grace, but

---

[8] The scaffold speeches of Anne Boleyn, declaring Henry to be both good and merciful, and of the earl of Essex's remarkable self-abnegation, are classic examples (Smith 1954).

[9] Though the idea of emasculating the corpse of the Jesuit (presumably celibate) priest Edmund Campion, in order to 'show his issue was disinherited with corruption of blood', as Sir Edmund Coke, Chief Justice of the King's Bench (presumably Protestant) suggested, is ironic at best (cited in Bellamy 1979).

the monarch's. Richard Hooker (or someone writing pseudo-epigraphically under his name) reminds his audience, however, that they are the same thing:

> In a word our estate is according to the pattern of God's own ancient elect people, which people was not part of them the *Commonwealth* and part of them the *Church of God*, but the selfsame people whole and entire. (Hooker 1989)

The state *was* the Church. The reformations in England had created a crisis of authority not just in what to do with a body, but even in trying to determine the distinction between a case of treason and a case of heresy.

The excommunicated body was treated less dramatically than the executed body in reformation England. Hooker equates excommunication with political exile, but does not explain what to do with the exiled/excommunicate dead. In the Henrician canons of 1535 we read that 'clergy shall [not] presume to bury anyone who has died excommunicate, or who has committed suicide, in their churches or churchyards; ... if they have in fact buried such people, they shall throw their remains out of the church or churchyard' (Bray 2000). Here, at least, Henry's Church was as Catholic as the pope's. The Elizabethan canons of 1571 provide a formula for excommunication, but make no legislation for the disposal of an excommunicate body, and the Jacobean canons of 1603 remark only in passing that a minister can refuse to bury a 'party ... denounced excommunicated *maiori excommunicatione*' (Bray 1998). The implication is that even under the authority of Protestant doctrine declaring the burial place to be unimportant, churchyard burial was still accorded spiritual importance.

The reference to suicide was problematic, too; it was certainly not limited to the climactic scene in *Romeo and Juliet*. Suicide was unique among crimes not only as *felonia de se*, a crime against the self, but as a crime to which a consideration of the age of discretion did not apply. Terence Murphy (1986) has determined that suicide rates for adolescents in early modern England were high, and John Sym in 1637 seems to confirm Murphy's assessment, noting that 'in these dayes ... so many doe most wretchedly, and unnaturally kill themselves'. Sym writes with some sympathy regarding the wretchedness to which a person must fall to commit such a crime, but he is still adamant (with a few very specific exceptions, such as self-sacrifice for others) that suicides are damned to hell, and cannot be given Christian burial, including 'ringing of Bells, or singing of Psalmes, or the like' (Sym 1637). (The reference to the Catholic tradition of ringing bells is the more surprising because Sym identifies himself as 'an expert calvist'.) While English Protestants might have claimed that churchyard burial had no salvific value, they were still unwilling to grant the privilege to those guilty of such a notorious sin as suicide.

Sudden death generally was often more problematic than suicide. Thomas Tuke differentiated between natural and violent death (Tuke 1631), but it was often difficult to know which category pertained. The notorious case of seventeenth-century society beauty Venetia Digby was one of the most remarkable and remarked-upon sudden deaths. She was reputed to have led a fairly tawdry life, at least until she married Sir

Kenelm Digby (it was probably a good match; neither one had a reputation for strict fidelity). There is no doubt that her death at age thirty-two caused great consternation. Later that century, John Aubrey wrote in *Brief Lives* that 'She dyed in her bed suddenly. Some suspected that she was poysoned' (Aubrey 1898). Sir Kenelm tried to prove not only his innocence, but that she had died a very good death indeed. He had a death mask and casts of her hands and feet made, as though to preserve her beauty, and summoned Van Dyck to paint her on her deathbed. She was praised in verse by Habington, Randolph, Feltham, Rutter, and even Ben Jonson. Digby 'wove an elaborate fiction to present her as having died well' (Jupp and Gittings 2000). Perhaps in an attempt to prove that he had not poisoned her, she even suffered the indignity of an autopsy. It is important to remember that Digby was Roman Catholic and a royalist, and that Aubrey's writings some fifty years later may reflect Protestant and parliamentarian varnishes, but the story still reveals the problems associated with sudden, unexplained death: it creates a need to construct a good life prior to that death. Kenelm Digby needed to appease both religious and social authorities that valorized a good death uncomplicatedly following a good life.

The sudden death of an infant was more common, though still problematic when trying to square it with divine providence. A young John Milton in 1628 questioned God's ways in his poem *On the Death of a Fair Infant*, but even in the midst of his questions, he admonishes the mother 'to curb thy sorrows wild' and accept God's mysterious will. Infant mortality was a common problem, and midwives had permission to baptize newborns 'in case of necessitie' (Garnet 1649), to ensure their burial in consecrated ground (which again demonstrates a Roman Catholic practice never fully reconciled with Protestant theology). Stillborn babies presented a different problem. According to the *Book of Oaths*, midwives swore that:

> If any childe bee dead borne, you your selfe shall see it buried in such secret place as neither Hogg nor Dogg, nor any other Beast may come unto it … And that you shall not suffer any such childe to be cast into the Jaques or any other inconvenient place. (Garnet 1649)

Enough care is given to the dead body to ensure it will not be tossed into the privy or eaten by animals, but it clearly should not be buried in a churchyard. Whether this is because of the belief that a stillborn child never achieved personhood and (presumably therefore) a soul, or because that an abortion was the result of God's vengeance is not clear; we can imagine, though, the emotional conflict that might arise between the ruthless guidelines for disposal of the body, and providing comfort to the grieving parents by treating the body with respect.

Sudden death in reformation England was complicated in new ways because the Church's authority, which in the past could determine if a person had received extreme unction, or was a regular communicant, or at the least had been baptized, would determine the appropriate rites and disposal of the body. Reformation theology also proclaimed that death ended the opportunity for redemption. In *Disce mori*, the reader is presented with an image of Christ in judgement and an angel just below, blowing a trumpet out of which a banner streams with the words 'As death leaveth thee, so shall iudgment find thee' (Sutton 1601). But as we have seen, reformed theology made it hard to determine a person's election even when there was time to prepare. How much harder in cases of sudden death? And though theologically it made no difference how or where the body was handled, it is clear that theological authority was no match for social authority and its demand for tradition. The basic concern remained: determining the state of the soul at the death of the body. But the tools available to respond to the concern had been dulled, and their lack of utility was most evident in cases of sudden death.

Conclusion—'I Kill You All'

Death, a skeleton holding a spear, has the bluntest and last line in the scene presented on a broadsheet depicting a bishop, a knight, a harlot, a lawyer, and a farmer all pursued by Death (Anon. 1569). The Dance of Death was a theme common enough through the late medieval and early modern periods, intended to remind everyone that they all came to the same end, whatever their stations in life. Protestant reformers thrilled to a new theology and a new authority that would end the perceived abuses of the Catholic Church. But more than papal authority crumbled in the process: political, ecclesiastical, and biblical authority all suffered, and in the process the rules about dealing with death were questioned too. Perhaps not surprisingly, though, many of the traditions that had grown up around dying well and the treatment of the dead proved resistant to change, and Protestant theology had to adapt to pre-existing behaviour rather than the other way around, because not even Protestant theology could make a believer die, like Lazarus, without grudge, without anxiety.

CHAPTER 39

··

SIN, JUDGEMENT,
AND ETERNITY

··

P. G. STANWOOD

HERE is a trinity of issues, or else a duality that leads to an endlessness, a place or a concept where time is of no matter. 'Sin is behovely', that is, of use, and that usefulness leads to its judgement. The nature of sin and the appropriateness of its remedy or punishment underlies the very purpose and consequence of human life. The complexion of that life has ever been a subject of concern, and in the early modern period a subject of special consequence for a wide and popular constituency.

WAYWARDNESS, RELIGIOUS DISSENT,
AND REFORMATION

··

Sin is endless, affecting both personal and public life. George Herbert writes powerfully of its compulsive and intertwining character in a way that gives fundamental shape to this present discussion. 'Sinnes round' is a poem that depicts impossibilities: sin and penitence, with judgement—its implied companion—dance forever in an unbroken eternal circle:

> Sorrie I am, my God, sorrie I am,
> That my offences course it in a ring.
> My thoughts are working like a busie flame,
> Untill their cockatrice they hatch and bring:
> And when they once have perfected their draughts,
> My words take fire from my inflamed thoughts.
>
> My words take fire from my inflamed thoughts,
> Which spit it forth like the Sicilian hill.
> They vent the wares, and passe them with their faults,
> And by their breathing ventilate the ill.

But words suffice not, where are lewd intentions:
My hands do joyn to finish the inventions.

My hands do joyn to finish the inventions:
And so my sinnes ascend three stories high,
As Babel grew, before there were dissentions.
Yet ill deeds loyter not: for they supplie
New thoughts of sinning: wherefore, to my shame,
Sorrie I am, my God, sorrie I am. (Herbert 2007: 430)

Our subject—sin, judgement, eternity—is difficult to begin, for the end is always in sight: 'There is no end of it | … No end to the withering of withered flowers' (Eliot 1963: 208). Yet let us begin by pointing to certain fundamental ways in which early modern England understood and attacked sin. We shall of course see that sin leads to penitence—the offspring of judgement—while everything hangs in eternity.

Sin—then as now—is commonly understood in Pauline terms: 'vile affections' define those whom God gave over 'to a reprobate mind, to do those things which are not convenient; being filled with all unrighteousness, fornication, wickedness, covetousness, maliciousness; full of envy, murder, debate, deceit, malignity; whisperers, backbiters, haters of God, despiteful, proud, boasters, inventors of evil things, disobedient to parents, without understanding, covenant breakers, without natural affection, implacable, unmerciful: who knowing the judgement of God, that they which commit such things are worthy of death, not only do the same, but have pleasure in them that do them' (Romans 2:26–32). And further, in his first letter to the Corinthians, Paul writes: 'I have written unto you not to keep company, if any man that is called a brother be a fornicator, or covetous, or an idolater, or a railer, or a drunkard, or an extortioner; with such an one no not to eat' (1 Cor. 5:11). In his manual dedicated to the right conduct of the country priest, or indeed to any priest charged with the care of souls, Herbert writes that the country parson is careful to avoid all covetousness, and 'because Luxury is a very visible sinne, the Parson is very carefull to avoid all the kinds thereof, but especially that of drinking, because it is the most popular vice' (Herbert 1959: 227).

Carnal sins, and sins of the spirit, then as now, receive condemnation; but in early modern times, wickedness is most often committed and registered through false belief or heresy, or of challenging authority. An individual's personal waywardness is less significant than his political or ecclesiastical life and denominational views. To invoke *The Thirty-Nine Articles of Religion* might, therefore, seem to set a distant and difficult step, but they have special importance in defining this kind of community malfeasance. Finally set forth by Convocation in 1563, they followed a number of earlier formularies: Ten Articles 1536; Bishops' Book 1537; Six Articles 1539; King's Book 1543; and Forty-Two Articles 1553. Subsequently, they were attached to the second Book of Common Prayer of 1559, where they have remained until modern times. The Articles aimed to provide summaries of Christian doctrine, while some addressed controversies of the time with Anglican views. Such an article is the ninth. This article is particularly intended to refute Pelagianism, the ancient heresy which claims that a person can deal with sin through individual effort and achieve salvation by one's own efforts, quite apart from

Divine grace: 'Of Original or Birth-Sin' reflects the general disfavour towards all kinds of dissenters, including the much despised Anabaptists, one of various Reformation sects thought to be especially dangerous, wildly heretical, and universally condemned by the established episcopacy. Article IX begins: 'Original Sin standeth not in the following of Adam, (as the Pelagians do vainly talk;) but it is the fault and corruption of the Nature of every man, that naturally is ingendered of the offspring of Adam.'

Humankind is generally afflicted by 'sin', what theologians understand as disobedience to God's will, a kind of disease or burden, or an evil enemy, with a heart turned away from God, and a will that is impaired and impoverished (see Bicknell [1919] 1955: 176). There is no dispute about the general sinfulness of human nature, but rather of its origin and its treatment. The huge wickedness rampant in the world is universally acknowledged and abhorred throughout the Christian centuries, but with renewed vigour in the early modern period: for new concerns about personal salvation became a general subject, and Pelagianism among other ancient heresies had renewed force. The danger of heresy is generally folded into threats to civil and ecclesiastical order. Richard Bancroft's famous sermon preached at Paul's Cross in 1588/9 on false prophets at large in the world is strident but on a familiar theme. Impudency, falsity—sinfulness—run rampant: In the Apostles' times, there were false prophets; such odious schismatics and heretics of former times are now again raised up among us: '*Arians, Donatists, Papists, Libertines, Anabaptists,* the *Familie of Love,* and sundrie other (I knowe not of what opinion)' (see Bancroft 1588–9: sigs B1^v–2^r, and C5^v).[1] When he needs to express 'the destruction and overthrow of all good rule and governement' (there could be few greater sins), Bancroft's commination is to call everything wicked as 'wholy Anabaptisticall'. Bancroft anticipates Justice Overdo, who discovers 'enormity' everywhere. Even so, much later in Bishop Sanderson's (anonymously written) preface to the Prayer Book of 1662, we are reminded of 'the growth of Anabaptism' and as well of 'the licentiousness of the late times crept in amongst us'. Sanderson is using the term in a highly charged way, referring not merely to adult baptism—an important principle of the Baptist belief that faith may be professed only by capably mature individuals—but also he uses 'Anabaptist' to connote all forms of presumed heresy that had risen up during the Reformation (Cummings 2011: 749).

Much of the popular literature of these years—to which sermons and theological treatises must surely belong and are most representative—is concerned with the danger of sedition and the failure of obedience to the state, or else to the challenge of authority and the overthrow of established authority. Bancroft suspected sedition in every corner, not only from such radical groups as the Anabaptists, but, along with Archbishop John Whitgift and many others, felt equally alarmed by such anti-episcopal figures as Dudley Fenner, author of 'The Counterpoison', or 'Martin Marprelate', all of whom urged that congregations or parishes should be governed by some kind of local, lay leadership, not by an episcopal hierarchy. One lively attack was mounted by Dr John Copcot in sermons and tracts in the 1580s. Copcot is eager to protect the queen against the

---

[1] Bancroft succeeded Archbishop John Whitgift to the See of Canterbury, in 1604.

dreadful phantasies of Fenner, 'chiefe elder of the English congregation of the church of Midleburroughe' and his like-minded friends who would mischieveously upset proper order, who would dismiss 'that forme of governement that is moost auncient', and in England well established and 'learned and godly'.[2]

'Martin Marprelate' deserves special consideration here, for Bancroft's sermon was only part of the official response to this pseudonymous author, who advocated puritan reform along Presbyterian lines in a series of satirical, often scurrilous pamphlets. There were seven works, widely and illegally disseminated, beginning with an attack against John Bridges, dean of Salisbury who had written an enormously prolix book entitled *A Defence of the Government Established in the Church of Englande for Ecclesiastical Matters* (1587). Martin Marprelate, whose identity has always remained a mystery (but perhaps a collaboration of at least two persons), wrote a tract called *The Epitome of the First Booke of this Worthye Volume written by My Brother Sarum, Deane John: Oh read over D. John Bridges, for it is a worthy worke*. This was the second of seven works (published between 1588 and 1589), all with similarly descriptive (and very long) titles, and all filled with ridicule and contempt for various episcopal figures, especially Bishop Thomas Cooper of Winchester; Archbishop Whitgift and his sometime mentor, Andrew Perne, Master of Peterhouse, Cambridge; Bishop John Aylmer of London, and many others. Bancroft was likely the genius behind the counterattack, not only for his famous sermon, but also for a barrage of Anti-Martin tracts he apparently encouraged or at least inspired. While he could not have been responsible for the extraordinary literary scene that soon flourished, he might well have been astonished by the number and variety of London 'wits' who joined in the vigorous Mar-Martin assault.

Among these vigorous contributors to a new literary scene must be included especially Robert Greene and his *Cony-Catching* pamphlets, and John Lyly, best known for *Euphues*, who also wrote *Pappe with an Hatchet, Alias, a Figge for my God Sonne. Or, Cracke me this Nut. Or, a Countrie Cuffe, that is, a Sound Boxe of the Eare for the Idiot Martin to Hold his Peace, etc.* This partial title typically conveys the fierce mockery and ribald humour of these writers. In *Pappe with an Hatchett*, Lyly tells of a Puritan who swore an oath not by his conscience but by his 'concupiscence' (Collinson 2013: 78–9). The most enduring of this lively but rather ephemeral tribe of critics is Thomas Nashe, remarkable amongst the Anti-Marprelate authors for his *An Almond for a Parrat, or Cuthbert Curry-knaves Almes*; but most memorable for his remarkable novel, *The Unfortunate Traveller* (1594). Nashe writes with excoriating vehemence of the Anabaptists in the terrible siege of Münster (1535):

> Very devout asses they were, for all they were so dunstically set forth, and such as thought they knew as much of God's mind as richer men. Why, inspiration was their

[2]   John Copcot (*d.* 1590), of Trinity College, Cambridge, was an outspoken defender of the Church of England, and, like Whitgift, a scourge of the Puritans, or of anyone deemed a false believer. The extract from the sermon quoted here is from the sole surviving copy, in the Lambeth Palace Library, MS 374, fols 155^v–156^r.

familiar, and buzzed in their ears like a bee in a box every hour what news from heaven, hell, and the land of whipperginnie.... When Christ said the kingdom of heaven must suffer violence, he meant not the violence of long babbling prayers to no purpose, nor the violence of tedious invective sermons without wit, but the violence of faith, the violence of good works, the violence of patient suffering. The ignorant arise and snatch the kingdom of heaven to themselves with greediness, when we with all our learning sink down into hell. (Nashe 1987: 230–1)

Nashe, writing long after the events he gives to his narrator to relate, does not rest from his condemnation of Anabaptists as the arch-perverters of natural order—the great purveyors of wickedness and sin.

Attacks against the established regime, both state and church, indeed are intertwined, and yet might seem some distance from any common view of 'sin'; but radical opposition to order and hierarchy was grievously perverse, and the rise of sects, with their frequent challenges to custom and tradition must be counted as expressive of the 'sin original'. Richard Hooker, in writing his *Laws of Ecclesiastical Polity* (1593, 1597) devoted the Sixth Book to a refutation of reformist views on Church government, against those who assert '*That our Laws are corrupt and repugnant to the Laws of God in matter belonging to the power of Ecclesiastical Jurisdiction, in that we have not throughout all Churches certain Lay-elders established for the exercise of that power*' (Hooker 2013: 3). The Sixth Book suddenly moves from analysis of these false claims to the 'discipline of repentance', which some scholars have regarded as a departure from the announced subject (Kirby 2008: 27–49). Hooker's argument may indeed be incomplete; but he does raise his argument for rightful governance above party claims, urging 'spiritual authority' and stating 'that the chiefest cause of spiritual jurisdiction is to provide for the health and safety of men's souls, by bringing them to see and repent their grievous offenses committed against God, as also to reform all injuries, offered with the breach of Christian love, and charity towards their brethren, in matters of Ecclesiastical cognizance; the use of this power shall by so much the plainlier appear, if first the nature of repentance itself be known' (Hooker 2013: 3.6). There follows a long discussion of penitence, the nature of penance and confession. The impropriety of misunderstanding right discipline, of setting it solely in terms of lay eldership leads, one may argue, to a consideration of sorrow with 'humble supplication'. Broadly speaking, Hooker is showing how one kind of 'sin' needs remediation.

The familiar words of the general confession first appear in the 1559 Prayer Book where they have ever remained; they follow the exhortation, and together respond to Reformation principles that regarded penitence as an important function of the laity: 'we ought at all tymes, humbly to knowlege our synnes before God ... We have left undone those thinges whiche we ought to have done, and we have done those thinges which we ought not to have done, and there is no health in us: but thou, O Lorde, have mercy upon us miserable offendours' (Cummings 2011: 103, 724), the whole section of course recalling Romans 7:15. This prayer was commonly repeated, phrase by phrase, after the minister, a custom condemned by some puritan reformers as an unseemly and noisy waste of time. Hooker answers this complaint in his Fifth Book of the *Laws* that systematically explains and celebrates the Book of Common Prayer. Of the General Confession, he writes:

> Could there be anything devised better than that we all at our first access to God by prayer should acknowledge meekly our sin and that not only in heart but with tongue, all which are present being made earwitnesses even of every man's distinct and deliberate assent to each particular branch of a common indictment drawn against ourselves? How were it possible that the Church should any way else with such ease and certainty provide, that none of her children may as Adam dissemble that wretchedness, the penitent confession whereof is so necessary a preamble, especially to common prayer? (Hooker 2013: 2.99)

Sin needs confession and the desire for reformation, for judgement awaits—one of the 'four last things', death, judgement, heaven, hell. There are many literary expressions of these final conditions, with different emphases, but all necessarily dwell upon the end of time by urging us to make ready for it. This is the theme of many sermons, much poetry, and literary documents of all sorts. The Gospel text of Luke 21:25–8 provides the dire warning of the return of Christ that inspired so many writers:

> And there shall be signs in the sun, and in the moon, and in the stars; and upon the earth distress of nations, with perplexity; the sea and the waves roaring; Men's hearts failing them for fear, and for looking after those things which are coming on the earth: for the powers of heaven shall be shaken. And then shall they see the Son of man coming in a cloud with power and great glory. And when these things begin to come to pass, then look up, and lift up your heads; for your redemption draweth nigh.

Readiness is all; and the terms of sin, dissolution, and punishment offered moments of supreme eloquence to such early Reformation preachers as Hugh Latimer (and other later ones, as we shall see, such as John Donne). Latimer's sermon on the Second Sunday of Advent in 1522—the day traditionally appointed for the text from Luke—is remarkable for its vivid pictures and horrendous warnings.

Inspired by the text, Latimer's concern for 'last things' touches on readiness, judgement, and redemption. Of the last day, he urges 'that it will be a heavy day unto them that be wicked; and again, a joyful, pleasant day unto them that have no delight in wickedness. He continues, reminding his auditory of Christ's promise that 'our redemption draweth near', and so 'his coming will be a glad and joyful coming unto the faithful, for they shall be the children of God; they shall be delivered and rid out of all calamities. But the unfaithful shall fall to desperation at that day: they that take their pleasures here, they that remember not this day, they shall be condemned with the irrevocable and unchangeable judgement of God' (Latimer 1845: 55–6). Latimer's emphasis on sin and judgement, the punishment of evildoers, and redemption of the godly obviously speaks to the text, and extends his concern for 'the last things'; but Latimer is also notably strenuous, and the lines between good and bad sharply drawn.

The time of judgement is always near, and always unpredictable; but other writers often manage gentler, or different modulations on the same theme. Such a one is George Herbert, whose poem 'Judgement' looks to salvation and life through redeeming love: 'Almightie Judge, how shall poore wretches brook | Thy dreadfull look … ?' The answer comes when God calls for his merits; he shall 'decline', but ask that 'a Testament' be thrust into God's hand: 'Let that be scann'd | There thou shalt finde my faults are thine' (Herbert 2007: 654). The poet's sins, or any person's sins, are atoned for through Christ's supreme sacrifice. In his Easter sermon of 1625, on John 5:28–9, John Donne deals also with judgement, seeing it as a means for celebrating two Resurrections: life, to all them that do good; and as well 'to all them, who having done evil, do yet repent the evill they have done'. Thus Donne urges in his conclusion. But he strongly condemns evil doers, yet ever with the promise:

> Let no man, that hath an holy anhelation and panting after the Resurrection, suspect that he shall sleepe in the dust, for ever.… Let no man, who because he hath made his course of life like a beast, would therefore be content his state in death might be like a beast too, hope that he shall sleepe in the dust, for ever. (Donne 1953–62: 6:279, 276–7; Stanwood 1986: 134–5).

Donne writes so often on the great themes of judgement, sin, and end times that this discussion might be concerned with him alone. Yet he is part of a greater literary and theological company that troubled ceaselessly over these overarching themes. Donne, however, is unusually passionate; he seems to speak to us from the depths of private experience, with a considered and uniquely personal voice. Of his nineteen 'Holy Sonnets', Donne agonizes over sin, its judgement, and his effort to shore up life against eventual dissolution: he is a poet of the *parousia*, of the Second Coming, the anticipation of which asks for readiness that is, alas, accompanied by the anxiety of inadequacy and unworthiness. Thus Donne writes, 'I am a little world made cunningly | Of Elements, and an Angelike spright, | But black sinne hath betraid to endlesse night | My worlds both parts, and (oh) both parts must die.' Would that I might be cleansed by floods and tears; but the fire of lust and envy require new fire: 'Let their flames retire, | And burne me o Lord, with a fiery zeale | Of thee and thy house, which doth in eating heale' (sonnet 5; Donne 1971: 295). Often a sonnet begins with a vigorous expostulation of dismay: 'O might those sighes and teares returne againe | Into my breast and eyes … ' 'Oh my blacke Soule! now thou art summoned | By sicknesse, deaths herald, and champion….' 'This is my playes last scene' … 'What if this present were the worlds last night?' And in one of the most anthologized of all his poems, 'Batter my heart, three person'd God', the poet offers no hope unless he sees God face-to-face, in a mystical ravishment.

In another remarkable sonnet, Donne looks to the end of time when the last trumpet sounds, for which he longs to be prepared. The poet imagines the general Resurrection in literal terms—characteristic of his time—when all bodies, no matter how dispersed, rise again, whole and intact:

At the round earths imagin'd corners, blow
Your trumpets, Angells, and arise, arise
From death, you numberlesse infinities
Of soules, and to your scattred bodies goe,
All whom the flood did, and fire shall o'erthrow,
All whom warre, dearth, age, agues, tyrannies,
Despaire, law, chance, hath slaine, and you whose eyes,
Shall behold God, and never tast deaths woe.
But let them sleepe, Lord, and mee mourne a space,
For, if above all these, my sinnes abound,
'Tis late to ask abundance of thy grace,
When wee are there; here on this lowly ground,
Teach mee how to repent; for that's as good
As if thou'hadst seal'd my pardon, with thy blood.

(Donne 1971: 293–302, esp. 296, Sonnet 7; Donne 2005: 106, 388 ff.)

The literature of last things naturally turns from judgement to Resurrection, pausing at times to celebrate this movement, in ways domestic and witty. Donne's older contemporary Lancelot Andrewes, for example, expatiates on the appearance of Mary Magdalene, the first to see the risen Christ, but mistakes him for the gardener. In his Easter sermon of 1620 (on John 20:11–17; see Andrewes 1651: 358 [sig. 2Y2^v]) he shows that Christ may well be a Gardener, and of the first and fairest garden—of Paradise—who makes all gardens green, bringing them to the fruitfulness of eternal life. 'He it is, that by the vertue of this mornings act, shall garden our bodies … turn all our graves into garden-plots: Yea, and shall one day turn land and sea, and all into a great Garden; and so husband them, as they shall in due time bring forth live bodies, even all our bodies alive again' (see McCullough 2005: 358).

Andrewes's sermons are characteristic of many preachers of his time. He is concerned with theological issues, which he reveals in many of his lectures and prose studies. In his preaching, he remains close to the text, expanding, expatiating, playing on its terms: this is homiletic preaching, where the text offers the basic plan of what follows. Many contemporary sermons are not especially homiletic, but vigorous animadversions on issues of the day—such is Bancroft's celebrated sermon that offered him an opportunity to condemn Puritans (and a wide and varied net of trespassers, those who challenge the established order of society). There was a ready audience for all kinds preaching—before the court or in the public sphere at St Paul's Cross—a principal form of communication in an age increasingly dominated by the printed word, yet before an auditory becoming well trained for hearing the spoken word. While sermons invariably begin by invoking a text, many—but not Andrewes—sometimes depart significantly from it. So much depends upon the occasion, and from which we are separated by having only the written word. Arnold Hunt has shown how important the sense of a sermon is determined not just from the written text, but also 'from an act of interpretative collaboration between preacher and audience'. This was indeed an age of 'sermon culture' and 'the art of hearing', when the generality of people sought knowledge of their lives here, and heard promises of the life to come (Hunt 2010: 292).

EPIC POETRY AND DEVOTIONAL PROSE

The great homiletic themes naturally embraced the discovery of sin, revealed modes of judgement, and looked for 'the sempiternal season'; just so, of course, did poetry speak, perhaps not to so various or large an audience as sermons, but nevertheless to a very fit one. Epic poetry especially, with its magnificent classical heritage, inspired the emulation of early modern writers. 'Genre theory' held epic poetry to be the highest form of imaginative composition, with dramatic writing next, followed by lyric poetry. Early modern writers—formerly and still commonly described as 'Renaissance' poets—at best aimed to write poetry of epic stature, commonly calling any very long poem an 'epic'. Only Milton would succeed in writing an epic that manages to embrace Homer and Vergil while establishing a distinctively English form.

Epic writing flourished in the decades before *Paradise Lost* (1667, 1674), and literary history is strewn with their dry bones that took on life only tentatively. Among the many once popular heroic poems must be counted Samuel Daniel's *Civil Wars* (1601, 1609), Thomas Heywood's *Troia Britannica* (1609), and Michael Drayton's vast work, *Poly-Olbion* (1612, 1622). Also popular were 'Ovidian' epics, of which Shakespeare's *Venus and Adonis* (1593, and numerous subsequent editions), Marlowe's (and Chapman's) *Hero and Leander* (1598), Shakerley Marmion's *Cupid and Psyche* (1637). Then there are the numerous secular romances, one notable verse example being *Pharonnida* (1659) by William Chamberlayne; and of enormous fame in its day, John Barclay's vast prose and poetic work *Argenis* (1621, 1625). These historical, heroic, classical, and romantic forms—in various blends and mixtures—were joined by the biblical epic, where we meet a frequent desire to Christianize classical themes.

Perhaps most popular of heroic poems in the earlier seventeenth-century is Joshua Sylvester's translation from Du Bartas of *The Divine Weeks and Works* (1605). *La Semaine, ou Création du Monde* (1578) is certainly the most substantial contribution to hexaemeral literature in the decades just before Milton, but with an outlook tiresomely moralistic and ploddingly Protestant. There are still other grand biblical epics before Milton, striking among them Abraham Cowley's *Davideis* (1656), but it is obviously much more concentrated and episodic than *Paradise Lost*. None of the several works mentioned do little to anticipate Milton's extraordinary theological and poetic brilliance, which moves us from sin to judgement, and to a tentative glimpse of a future that beholds eternity. But there is one further epic event that is especially useful to recall in this journey.

There are many condemnations of puritan zeal, of irregular and false worship that disregards authority: this is the hideous sin of blasphemy. In one of the longest of all contemporary epics is Joseph Beaumont's *Psyche, or, Loves Mysterie*,[3] which tells the long

---

[3] The first edition of 1648 was reprinted in 1651, and then much enlarged and emended in a second posthumous edition of 1702, the text edited by A. B. Grosart in 2 vols, 1880, for 'The Chertsey Worthies Library'. Beaumont (1616–99) was a Fellow and later Master of Peterhouse, Cambridge, who, with John Cosin and other notable High Churchmen, was ejected from the College at the beginning of the Civil War.

story of the Soul, accompanied by her guardian Phylax. Psyche is seduced by lust, briefly ailing from a 'delicious shipwreck' of the heart, and from wretched vanities. But she harbours the desire for redemption, which comes after much misery and mortification, and a deep and terrible dereliction of will; but at last Psyche reaches an ecstatic joy—the wonder of mystical revelation, and a view of eternity, a death in life. Throughout this history, Beaumont allegorizes the political and religious struggles of the time, sparing nothing, though obliquely commenting on 'Puritans and Presbyters' and manifold malefactors. Psyche runs the course, too, for she is sometimes guilty; but she is saved through contrition and right judgement, and is at last worthy of love's embrace. Beaumont sometimes loses sight of his subject, so engrossed he is with the enormities of his day, including, for example, a long and remarkable passage that lists heresies (in iambic pentameter) mostly ancient, but some modern; and elsewhere he describes reformist zeal in the guise of pagan prosecution. Such reformers destroy the Bible, for:

> ...they in a thousand peeces tor't:
> Then on Devotions Prop, the Liturgie,
> They made their equaly malitious sport,
> Crying, these are those leaves of Witcherie,
>   That Bulk of Conjurations and Charms,
>   Which have occasioned the whole Worlds Harms. (Canto xviii, stanza 152)

Psyche's progress is, aside from numerous pitfalls, steady and wholesome, and at the conclusion of the work, she dies in ecstasy:

> The double Fountain of her Tears was drie,
> Her Groans were weary, and her Languishment
> It selfe did languish: But her Exstasie
> Outrageous grew, and, like a Gyant, bent
>   The mighty Bow of her Desires, by which
>   The Mark of all her Hopes She was to reach.
>
> Then, having bid unto the Earth adieu,
> And firmly fix'd her loving longing Eye
> Upon the Heav'ns, to keep *her Aim* in view;
> Her Flames triumphant Tempest swell'd so high
>   That She, unable to contain its Tide,
>   With a deep Sigh, cri'd out, *O LOVE*, and di'd. (Canto xx, stanzas 218–19)

Beaumont ends his epic with a tentative vision of enlightenment, of an eternity that waits upon a mystical death. He has given his heroine a long and difficult path, one which, in a crude way, looks forward in some ways to Milton's great narrative:

> Of Man's First Disobedience, and the Fruit
> Of that Forbidden Tree, whose mortal tast
> Brought Death into the World, and all our woe,
> With loss of *Eden*. (I. 1–4)

As the representative of mankind, Adam opens the way of all discord, and God's judgement condemns him to a life of sorrow: 'In the sweat of thy Face shalt thou eat Bread, | Till thou return unto the ground, for thou | Out of the ground wast taken, know thy Birth, | For dust thou art, and shalt to dust return' (X, 205–8). But through penitence and contrition comes redemption; and Grace is offered through the defeat of Sin and Death by God's Son, who 'fresh as the dawning light' pays the ransom so that all may be saved. Confidence and joyful peace accompany Adam and Eve, and all of humankind, as they move into the common world, and at the last, into eternal life.

Milton sees eternity both in the glimpse of finite human time, but in the timelessness of life. The opening lines of his invocation to light best express this paradoxical vision:

> Hail holy Light, offspring of Heav'n first-born,
> Or of th'Eternal Coeternal beam
> May I express thee unblam'd? since God is Light,
> And never but in unapproached Light
> Dwelt from Eternity, dwelt then in thee,
> Bright effluence of bright essence increate. (III. 1–6)

For Milton, eternity resides in an invisible light, expressed through the drama of man's fall and redemption, and the promise of immortal life toward which this present is preparation. Finally, this age of epics, all of them asking—sometimes implying—questions of divine significance, reached its apogée in *Paradise Lost*.

Many prose works aim to describe sin and judgement, and offer advice toward living well and preparing for eternal life. There are at least two sorts: the one is liturgical, meditative, often formal; the other is the moral 'self-help' tract, or primer on how to live and make ready to die. Lancelot Andrewes's *Preces Privatae* is the supreme example of the first, posthumously published in 1630 as *Institutionis Piae: or Directions to Pray*, and in several subsequent editions, reaching a seventh edition in 1684. Andrewes evidently intended this small book of prayers, thanksgivings, and intercessions for his own private use and reflection, mostly adapted from medieval and patristic sources, arranged according to the days of the week. Although personal, their appeal is general; for their quiet intimacy and profound feeling touched many readers. A further work of this sort, but which aims for a general audience, is John Cosin's *A Collection of Private Devotions* (1627), a book based on the Divine Office, or the Canonical Hours. Cosin is said to have provided such a book for the court in the absence of any similar English work, a kind of antidote against the French influence of Queen Henrietta's entourage. Cosin's *Devotions*, at once well received, with three editions in less than a year, is a carefully structured book, with many prayers and supplications in addition to the usual readings and petitions of the canonical hours along with appropriate material for the feast days of the church year.

The second sort—the moral primer—and familiar to a wide readership were works of instruction and intense piety. Immensely popular was Thomas Becon (1512–67) who wrote *The Sicke mannes Salve, wherein the faithfull Christians may learne how to behave *themselves paciently and thankefully in the type of sickenes, and also vertuously to dispose their temporall goods, and finally to prepare themselves gladly and godly to dye* (1561), with at least fifteen editions by 1632. Lewis Bayly (1565–1631) was even more popular for his *The Practice of Pietie* (1613; 45th edn 1640). And of course the eminent theologian and preacher William Perkins (1558–1602), offered *A salve for a sicke man: or, a Treatise Containing the Nature of, Differences, and Kindes of Death; as Also the Right Manner of Dying Well* (1595; 5th edn 1632). Jeremy Taylor (1613–67) is a late contributor to this tradition, but surely the most eloquent. His *Holy Living* (1650) and *Holy Dying* (1651), in countless editions, have outlasted all other contemporary moral guides, from his own to the present time. Taylor writes boldly of this life, reflecting on its uncertainties, but with the need to make use of them for the sake of what is to come. He admonishes his readers in *Holy Living* to make good use of time, for 'He that is choice of his time will also be choice of his company, and choice of his actions, lest the first ingage him in vanity and losse, and the latter by being criminal be a throwing his time and himself away, and a going back in the accounts of eternity' (Taylor 1989: I, 19).

In *Holy Dying*, Taylor ruminates on the sadness of life and on the importance of preparing oneself for 'a blessed death' by means of prayer, contrition, and thoughtful confession:

> For we … need not be much troubled that we shall die, because we are not here in ease, nor do we dwell in a fair condition. But our dayes are full of sorrow and anguish, dishonoured and made unhappy with many sins, with a frail and a foolish spirit, intangled with difficult cases of conscience, insnared with passions, amazed with fears, full of cares, divided with curiosities and contradictory interests, made aery and impertinent with vanities, abused with ignorance and prodigious errours, made ridiculous with a thousand weaknesses, worne away with labours, loaden with diseases, daily vexed with dangers and temptations, and in love with misery; we are weakened with delights, afflicted with want, with the evils of my self, and of all my family, and with the sadnesses of all my friends, and of all good men, even of the whole Church; and therefore me thinks we need not be troubled that God is pleased to put an end to all these troubles, and to let them sit down in a natural period, which if we please, may be to us the beginning of a better life. (Taylor 1989: II, 46–7)

Eternity, indeed, lies beyond the miseries of this life. 'And yonder all before us lye | Desarts of vast Eternity.'

CIRCLES OF ETERNITY

And so, Marvell's conceit in 'To His Coy Mistress' sends us to poetry of eternity, and to literary inventions that attempt to capture a view of something known but impossible to fully understand or experience. Marvell comes near to expressing this ineffable nature of 'vast deserts' in his 'On a Drop of Dew'. A mere dew drop comes from the skies, rests on a flower, thus expressing in itself the world from above and now below, 'The greater Heaven in an Heaven less'. Like manna, it comes, but soon disappears. The drop of dew 'does, dissolving, run | Into the Glories of th'Almighty Sun' (Marvell 1971: I, 12–13; ll. 26, 39–40).

The contrast of Heaven and Earth is a familiar *topoi* that occurs frequently in Renaissance literature, usually with puzzled uncertainty about the perpetuity of life. How may its beginning be translated into an ending? Does every conclusion mark a recovery? Henry Vaughan records a vision of life in death, of a great ring of light into which everyone may enter, having once cast off grovelling mortality:

> I saw Eternity the other night
> Like a great *Ring* of pure and endlss light,
>   All calm, as it was bright,
> And round beneath it, Time in hours, days, years
>   Driv'n by the spheres
> Like a vast shadow mov'd, In which the world
>   And all her train were hurl'd. ('The World', ll. 1–7; Vaughan 1963: 299–301)

Eternity in Vaughan's view is obtainable through the true light of day 'Because it shews the way, | The way which from this dead and dark abode | Leads up to God, | A way where you might tread the Sun, and be | More bright than he' (ll. 52–6).

Vaughan often invokes light that is best discovered in darkness. His finest poems presume that eternity is within our reach now and always. In 'The Night', based on the visit of Nicodemus to Christ (John 3:2), Vaughan plays on the 'light' that shines through the 'night', for Heaven is at once available:

> There is in God (some say)
> A deep, but dazling darkness; As men here
> Say it is late and dusky, because they
>   See not all clear;
> O for that night! where I in him
> Might live invisible and dim. ('The Night', ll. 49–54; Vaughan 1963: 358–9)

Light makes darkness visible: the conceit is familiar in various contexts, from Milton's 'darkness visible' (I. 63), a dismal description of Satan's region; but light shines out of darkness and informs it, as the invocation to Book III, quoted above, reveals, or as, in mystical theology, knowledge bursts from 'The Cloud of Unknowing'. The aim in every context is to express endlessness, 'of eternity shut in a span'.

The fixation upon eternity as a sure state of being is variously comprehended in the literature of this time, and that certitude is mingled often with immortality. Sir Thomas Browne notably extends these ideas in his plangent prose; he depicts his world as 'divided and distinguished'. Speaking for us all, he lives in two worlds that 'inform each other'. 'Surely,' he writes in *Religio Medici* (1643), 'it is not a melancholy conceite to thinke we are all asleepe in this world, and that the conceits of this life are as meare

dreames to those of the next, as the Phantasmes of the night, to the conceits of the day'
(70). Browne's late work, *Hydriotaphia, [or] Urne-Buriall ... Together with The Garden
of Cyrus* (1658) expounds at large these mysteries. 'Life is a pure flame, and we live by an
invisible Sun within us' (123). His extraordinary 'discovery' of the 'quincunx'—that all of
nature, earthly and heavenly, is ordered inevitably by a mathematical perfection—might
seem consummate whimsy, yet Browne has a very serious plan. The letter X, he says,
'is the Emphaticall decussation, or fundamental figure' (Browne 1964: 131). This letter
has five points (like the wounds of Christ), and it expresses life, the principal theme of
The Garden of Cyrus, with its five chapters. But X (or chi), when turned around as in
solid geometry, reveals a theta, and that figure Φ reminds us of death (as in thanatop-
sis, or Thanatos), and should remind us of the study of death and burial customs, as
in *Hydriotaphia* (with its five chapters). These two complementary works depend upon
a further conceit of Browne: right lines and circles inform the structure of these profoundly fascinating books—mortality and immortality, earth and heaven, dark and
light—meet in these mysteriously complex books. The Quincunx of Heaven closes *The
Garden of Cyrus:* 'All things began in order, so shall they end, and so shall they begin
again; according to the ordainer of order and mystical Mathematicks of the City of
Heaven (Browne 1964: 174).

Eternity may be imagined as a straight line that stretches inside a circle—that is, its
diameter—a state and an image familiar not only in Browne, but also in many other
writers of his time. Imagery of circles is especially key to the development of many of
Donne's sermons, often with striking effect as in his Second Prebend Sermon (29
January 1625). Donne is preaching on Ps. 63:7, 'Because thou hast been my helpe, therefore in the shadow of thy wings will I rejoyce', a text that provides him with 'the whole
compasse of Time, Past, Present, and Future'. David's distress in the past, says Donne,
allowed him to consider the present, and so to look for future hope. Such remembrance
and assurance leads Donne to inform his auditors: 'Fixe upon God any where, and you
shall finde him a Circle; He is with you now, when you fix upon him; He was with you
before, for he brought you to this fixation; and he will be with you hereafter, for *He is
yesterday, and to day, and the same for ever*' (Donne, *Sermons*, 7:52). Donne is fascinated
by eternity, and the glorious light of Heaven that is already on earth: 'As my soule shall
not goe towards Heaven, but goe by Heaven to Heaven, to the Heaven of Heavens, So
the true joy of a good soule in this world is the very joy of Heaven' (Donne, *Sermons*,
7:71). Like Browne who declares that 'the sufficiency of Christian Immortality frustrates
all earthly glory' (Browne 1964: 123), Donne likewise sees the beginning in a seeming
end. And just as in one of his best known sonnets, 'Death be not proud', here also, in the
concluding lines of this sermon (composed as if in a great circle called eternity), Donne
cries out: 'In the face of Death, when he layes hold upon me, and in the face of the Devill,
when he attempts me, I shall see the face of God ... I shall have a joy, which shall no more
evaporate, then my soule shall evaporate, A joy, that shall passe up, and put on a more
glorious garment above, and be joy super-invested in glory' (Donne 1953–62: VII, 71).

We cannot leave such circles and such joy, even in glory, without calling on Spenser
who, in *The Faerie Queene*, embraces so many conditions of sorrow and majesty, from

sin to redemption to eternity. Probably there is no other work of these early modern years, not even *Paradise Lost,* that manifests so vividly and so variously the numberless conditions of life and death. The First Book tells of the Red Cross Knight, of his moral and spiritual growth. He meets on his travails, for example, the proud giant Orgoglio; but he is in fact confronting the embodiment of his own sin. Red Cross undergoes eventual regeneration in the House of Holiness, and he finally is able to triumph over the Dragon, whose death represents new life for Red Cross. Spenser's colourful portrayals and lively action in this first book of *The Faerie Queene* might seem sufficient for one epic; but of course there is much more to come. Sin—and Pride—never disappears; it is supremely embodied in the Blatant Beast, introduced in the Fifth Book, 'A monster ... A dreadfull feend of gods and men ydrad' (V.xii.37). The Blatant Beast is chiefly active in the Sixth Book in which Sir Calidore, the Knight of Courtesie, has the task of subduing the Beast, whose bite produces horrible sores—the outward signs of inward ugliness: 'Sorrow, and anguish, and impatient paine | In th'inner parts, and lastly scattering | Contagious poyson close through every vaine, | It never rests, till it have wrought his finall bane' (VI.vi.8). The Beast's principal consorts are Envy and Deceit, spread with venomous language that spews from an open mouth filled with iron teeth, speaking 'licentious words, and hateful things | Of good and bad alike, of low and hie; | Ne Kesars spared he a whit, nor Kings, | But either blotted them with infamie, | Or bit them with his banefull teeth of injury (VI.xii.26, 28).

Within these tales of deadly disaster occasioned through sin, harshly judged but tempered by active and regenerative forces, is the remarkable interlude in the Sixth Book that stands alone but overwhelms all surrounding darkness. Sir Calidore approaches Mount Acidale, a place that recalls an earthly paradise, perhaps Eden itself. There he has a splendid sight: 'An hundred naked maidens lily white, | All raunged in a ring, and dauncing in delight (VI.x.11):

> All they without were raunged in a ring,
>   And daunced round; but in the midst of them
>   Three other Ladies did both daunce and sing,
>   The whilest the rest them round about did hemme,
>
> And like a girlond did in compasse stemme:
>   And in the middest of those same three, was placed
>   Another Damzell, as a precious gemme,
>   Amidst a ring most richly well enchaced,
> That with her goodly presence all the rest much graced. (VI.x.12)

As the dancers move, a shepherd plays, that is, Spenser himself, figured as Colin Clout. But as soon as Sir Calidore approaches this ring, the dancers disappear, and Colin breaks his pipe. Sir Calidore has only a brief sight of this circle of harmony, as if he can touch eternity only when he need not inquire of its meaning.

Spenser ended his great poem with the two Cantos of Mutability, the rest of his work (some say) unfinished. Nevertheless, the final two stanzas do make a fit conclusion, both to the Mutability Cantos, to the whole of *The Faerie Queene* itself, and to this present discussion. Spenser recalls Mutability's speech of defence in the preceding Canto:

> When I bethinke me on that speech whyleare,
>   Of *Mutability*, and well it way:
>   Me seemes, that though she all unworthy were
>   Of the Heav'ns Rule; yet very sooth to say,
>   In all things else she beares the greatest sway.
>   Which makes me loath this state of life so tickle,
>   And love of things so vaine to cast away;
>   Whose flowring pride, so fading and so fickle,
> Short *Time* shall soon cut down with his consuming sickle.
>
> Then gin I thinke on that which Nature sayd,
>   Of that same time when no more *Change* shall be,
>   But stedfast rest of all things firmely stayd
>   Upon the pillours of Eternity,
>   That is contrayr to *Mutabiitie:*
>   For, all that moveth, doeth in *Change* delight:
>   But thence-forth all shall rest eternally
>   With Him that is the God of Sabbaoth hight:
> O that great Sabbaoth God, graunt me that Sabaoths sight. (VII.viii.1–2)

We come to the end and the beginning of time; for the lines of these two stanzas, in Spenser's unique form, anticipate a new key or even return us to an encircling eternity.

....

RESOURCES:
A BEGINNER'S GUIDE

....

JESSE DAVID SHARPE

This chapter discusses the information literacy skills needed to carry out research in early modern English literature and religion. Rather than giving information for performing specific searching techniques in individual databases, the following pages provide an overview of techniques, and attempt to balance print and digital resources. The chapter concludes with an annotated list of online resources, providing a representative view of scholarly resources available for free on the Internet.

The resources and techniques for research in the field of early modern religion and literature, as with other studies, have been made both more and less difficult with the advent of electronic databases. The easier access to greater quantities of data has aided an increase in scholarship as researchers are able to find information that would have been too obscure or costly to find physically; however, the vast quantities of information digitized and made available through the Internet and databases have also made it more difficult for scholars to determine when they have found 'enough' information for their projects. This is one of the great problems of modern research, and it is the focus of this chapter. While 'information overload' has become a cliché, the ability to navigate through very valuable troves of information quickly, yet efficiently, can help a researcher have the confidence to know when the books and articles retrieved are sufficient. With this in mind, this chapter will seek to provide a framework through which to perform research that gives results that are both of high scholarly value and relevant to the study undertaken by the researcher. Additionally, there will be a short list of titles that are considered core databases or Internet sites at the end of this chapter. It is hoped that the combination of instruction in search techniques and suggested readings will provide a beginning researcher with the tools and knowledge needed to find the excellent resources that have been made more readily available through digital formats.

Much of the difficulty and confusion regarding how to perform research with print and digital means is in knowing when to use which medium and how to locate the best resources. The following is a quick rule of thumb in current humanities research: if it is a book-length treatment, print is still the primary mode of delivery, but if it is reference or a journal article, then it is best to look to digital means. Much of this is reflected in how academic and research libraries build their collections. Very few add new print journals, dictionaries, or encyclopedias, and most are ceasing to have dedicated space for a reference collection; rather, the books are being interfiled with the regular circulating collection, having select titles put on permanent reserve, or sending them to remote storage or special collections, depending on the value of the titles. What this means is that physical browsing is still of vital importance when it comes to books or monographs in the study of early modern religion and literature. Likewise, it is best to start with the libraries' websites when trying to find anything that is a journal or a reference volume. Additionally, though most databases have different user interfaces, they are all built upon the same basic principles, so simply understanding the manner in which the databases' architecture functions means that one can move easily from one database to the next, without having to spend much time learning all of the functions. Academic research will often run on the same basic principles and techniques no matter what physical or digital source is needed. To know how and when strategically to browse the physical book stacks or to use advanced Boolean searches in databases will allow one to move through the world of modern research quickly without suffering from information overload.

In order to provide a strong base upon which to build research techniques for early modern studies, it is important to focus on some of the fundamental skills and core concepts required for a researcher. The basic concepts are fairly simple and widely applicable, so even as a university or institution changes the providers for its digital collections and moves its print collections around, you need not relearn how to perform research; instead, applying the basics to the ever-changing digital world will allow you to move easily through the changes. In this, there is also a book-length treatment of academic research that can be of great help. While this chapter's focus is on research in early modern religion and literature, there are two book-length treatments that can be helpful for library research. Jennifer Bowers and Peggy Keeran's *Literary Research and the British Renaissance and Early Modern Period* is a good resource for guidance in literary research in the time period, but strongly favours plays and does not specifically deal with religion (Bowers and Keeran 2010). Thomas Mann's *The Oxford Guide to Library Research* is a more general approach to library research, and it can act as an excellent reference guide for research of all types (Mann 2015).

This chapter will provide a short introduction to scholarly research before focusing specifically on the needs of the academic in religion and literature in the early modern period. Books will be discussed first, before moving on to databases, and then the open Internet.

Call Numbers and Subject Headings

While electronic resources have become one of the most visible aspects of current research methods, it must be noted that even our interaction with books often begins with the Internet, as catalogues exist almost exclusively in the online environment. Although even print research begins on a computer, it is important to realize that academic libraries are often structured in a way that should promote browsing the library's physical holdings. This is due to the fact that most academic libraries use the Library of Congress Classification System (LCCS). This uniformity of collection arrangement is of great benefit to the researcher, and it also means that familiarizing oneself with how the LCCS organizes books means that a researcher can go into any academic library and know exactly where to begin searching. The LCCS was created in such a way that books are arranged according to subject area. This was done not only to aid retrieval of materials, but to also make serendipitous finding of information an intentional aspect of research. A researcher using an academic library properly will browse the book stacks because she knows that this is one of the ways in which the system was designed. To use only a catalogue is to not use the collection and library to its fullest design. Browsing is not a sign of an inexperienced researcher, rather it is a sign that the researcher truly knows what she is doing. For this reason, I will provide a brief introduction to the LCCS and how and where browsing for early modern religion and literature books can be done in the best way possible.

If a researcher has a subject of focus, then that researcher need only know how the LCCS is arranged, because the classification system, especially in the study of literature, is made to allow a person to find as much information about an author or genre as easily as possible. This is because not only does the LCCS group authors according to nation and then time period and then alphabetically, but works by an author are followed by biographical works, and then critical works. In the LCCS all of this begins with the first two letters of the call number. As such, simply knowing which letters represent the subject of study is the easiest way to begin research in an academic library. For early modern literature and religion it is important to know that 'P' represents 'Languages and Literature', with 'PR' representing the subcategory of 'British Literature', so a scholar in British literature will find nearly all of her books in the 'PR' section of a library. Similarly, 'B' represents 'Religion and Philosophy', with the subheading of 'BR' representing 'Christianity'. This means that, for our purposes, a researcher should be spending most of her time in 'PR' and the 'B's. In specific, the 'PR' sections that one would want to focus on are: For general studies:

> PR421–(429) Elizabethan era (1550–1640)
> PR500–614 Poetry
> > PR521–614 By period
> PR621–744 Drama
> > PR641–744 By period
> PR750–890 Prose
> > PR767–818 By period

For specific author's works and criticism:

> PR2199–3195 English Renaissance (1500–1640)

Also worth considering is the 'PN' section, which is about literature in general. For example:

> PN715–749 Literary History—Renaissance (1500–1700)
> PN2171–2179 Drama—Renaissance

For the 'B' section, of special note is:

> BR280 Renaissance Renaissance and Reformation
> BR500–1510 By region or country
> BS1–2970 The Bible
> BT10–1480 Doctrinal Theology
> BV1–5099 Practical Theology

BX5001–5009	Anglican Communion (General)
BX5011–5207	Church of England
BX5011–5050	General
BX5051–5110	History. Local divisions

BX5115–5126	Special parties and movements
BX5127–5129.8	Church of England and other churches
BX5130–5132	General
BX5133	Sermons. Tracts. Addresses. Essays
BX5135–5136	Controversial works
BX5137–5139	Creeds and catechisms, etc.
BX5140.5–5147	Liturgy and ritual
BX5148–5149	Sacraments
BX5150–5182.5	Government. Organization. Discipline
BX5183–5187	Religious communities. Conventual life.
BX5194–5195	Cathedrals, churches, etc. in England and Wales
BX5197–5199	Biography
BX5200–5207	Dissent and nonconformity
BX5210–5395	Episcopal Church in Scotland
BX5410–5595	Church of Ireland
BX5596–5598	Church in Wales

The relevant areas in 'B' are not subdivided in such a way that they are as easily browsed as the 'PR' section; however, ease of browsing can still be achieved by finding one or two books in a subject area, writing down their call numbers, and then going to the stacks and seeing what is also shelved near the titles found in the catalogue. Since the LCCS arranges books by subject, the books will be about the same subject and may have chapters or essays that would have been missed through catalogue research alone. Also, as libraries are moving more of their collections to remote storage, it is extremely important to try to preserve as many of the books in the open stacks as possible. Luckily, this is very easily done. When deciding what books to move to remote storage, libraries look at the circulation statistics of a book, and that is really the only thing considered. By simply checking out books, even if it is just for a few hours or a day or two, the book will remain in the library rather than being moved to another location.

Subject Headings

In addition to the call number arrangement of the LCCS, the organizational system is also heavily supported by the Library of Congress Subject Headings (LCSH). While it has become common to use keyword searches in databases and catalogues, many have what is called 'controlled vocabulary' which can be used in research, and when used properly these can be amongst the most powerful searches in a scholar's retinue. While Thomas Mann provides an excellent discussion of LCSH (Mann 2015: 17–61), it is helpful to know the difference between keyword and controlled vocabulary searches and there follow here some specific examples that can be of assistance for early modern religion and literature research.

The default search in any online catalogue or database is a keyword search. This has some great advantages, in that it searches the bibliographic record or full text of a work to find where the terms may exist. This is an excellent way to get a lot of titles returned, but it can also result in a lot of false returns. A good example of this is searching for 'George Herbert'. While a keyword search will bring back books and articles on the poet 'George Herbert', you will also get results for 'George Herbert Palmer', 'George Herbert Walker Bush', 'Herbert George Wells', and any co-authored or multi-authored texts in which authors have a name 'George' or 'Herbert', as well as any full text result in which a 'George' or a 'Herbert' is mentioned at least once. However, there is a way around this problem—subject headings, with most catalogues using Library of Congress Subject Headings (LCSH).

A subject heading attempts to pull together all of the books and articles that are about a particular subject through using a set list of vocabulary, and a researcher can use this to her advantage by using a combination of keyword and subject searches to narrow and strengthen search queries. For example, an author's subject heading in LCSH is always 'Lastname, Firstname'. Therefore, a subject search for criticism on the writings of Richard Hooker would mean choosing the subject option from the drop-down search options and typing 'Hooker, Richard'. This would ensure that all titles returned would have to be about Richard Hooker. Combining this with a keyword, such as 'ceremony' would mean that the results from the search would have to be about Richard Hooker and also have the word ceremony somewhere in the bibliographic information or the full text of the work. Through beginning the search with Richard Hooker as a subject rather than a keyword, a researcher will have fewer titles brought back from the query, but the results that do appear will be more likely to contain information about the actual subject being studied, thereby cutting down on information overload and time lost to Internet searching. Finding subject headings that are not authors' names can be more difficult; however, in most online catalogues and databases subject terms are provided in the bibliographic information that appears with the record provided when clicking on an individual result. Furthermore, the subject terms are often hyperlinked so as to return all other titles that share that subject heading when the term is clicked on. By finding one book or article needed for a research project, a researcher can gain access very easily to all other works that share that subject heading and become familiar with the subject headings in her field of study.

When using subject headings, especially LCSH, it is wise to begin with a broad search and then narrow based upon the results. This will allow you a better perspective of what is being used as subject headings and will prevent you from narrowing your results too quickly, possibly missing out on some valuable titles. In using John Donne as an example, it is helpful to note that, in performing a LCSH search in the library catalogue at the University of Houston, my search returned fifty-nine different subject headings beginning with 'Donne, John'. Some examples of these returns are:

Donne John 1572 1631
Donne John 1572 1631 Aesthetics
Donne John 1572 1631 Appreciation France
Donne John 1572 1631 Bibliography
Donne John 1572 1631 Characters Women
Donne John 1572 1631 Concordances
Donne John 1572 1631 Correspondence
Donne John 1572 1631 Criticism And Interpretation
Donne John 1572 1631 Criticism And Interpretation Bibliography
Donne John 1572 1631 Criticism And Interpretation History
Donne John 1572 1631 Ethics
Donne John 1572 1631 Exhibitions
Donne John 1572 1631 Family
Donne John 1572 1631 Fiction
Donne John 1572 1631 Holy Sonnets
Donne John 1572 1631 In Literature
Donne John 1572 1631 Influence

Donne John 1572 1631 John Donne
Donne John 1572 1631 Knowledge And Learning
Donne John 1572 1631 Knowledge Art
Donne John 1572 1631 Knowledge Literature
Donne John 1572 1631 Knowledge Psychology
Donne John 1572 1631 Knowledge Theology
Donne John 1572 1631 Literary Style
Donne John 1572 1631 Manuscripts Facsimiles
Donne John 1572 1631 Marriage
Donne John 1572 1631 Musical Settings
Donne John 1572 1631 Philosophy
Donne John 1572 1631 Poems Selections
Donne John 1572 1631 Poetry Early Works To 1800
Donne John 1572 1631 Political And Social Views
Donne John 1572 1631 Prose
Donne John 1572 1631 Quotations
Donne John 1572 1631 Religion
Donne John 1572 1631 Style
Donne John 1572 1631 Symbolism
Donne John 1572 1631 Technique
Donne John 1572 1631 Translations Into French History And Criticism
Donne John 1572 1631 Travel Netherlands

This clearly shows that there can be both broad and narrow criteria used for what may fall under a given area of Donne studies. Moving out from an author LCSH search, it is helpful to note that the term 'Renaissance' is largely used for the visual art movement in continental Europe, whereas 'Early Modern' is primarily used as a way in which to subdivide a larger subject heading, and is used to denote aspects of literature and culture that are not the 'high' Renaissance of the popular usage. In this, subject heading strings will begin with entries such as:

English Literature Early Modern 1500 1700
English Drama Early Modern
English Poetry Early Modern

Similarly, the term 'Church of England' is distinguished from 'Episcopal' which represents the Church of England in the United States after its independence.

Journals

When it comes to journals for early modern literature and religion research, the majority of them will be searched through online databases, but it is important to remember that often a database will not carry all of the volumes and issues of a title. Usually databases will not go much further back than ten to fifteen years. It is expensive to digitize journals, and the older the issue the less demand there tends to be and the less likely that an electronic copy of it will exist. For this reason, it is often the case that only the most recent research can be fully searched in a database, though the database may allow for indexing back to earlier issues. The main exception to this is JSTOR, which always begins a journal with volume one and issue one. Due to these limitations of journal coverage, it is important to make sure that both electronic and print journals get searched.

Among the journals most often cited in bibliographies for early modern English literature and religion are titles such as *English Literary Renaissance, English Literary History*, and
Studies in English Literature, 1500–1900; however, there are many smaller journals that are especially important to the field of early modern literature and religion studies, and often these are
publications that can be put out by literary societies that celebrate an author. *Milton Studies,
The George Herbert Journal, Reformation*, and *The John Donne Journal* are examples of these,
with *The John Donne Journal* being an excellent title that does not appear to be available in full
text through any database. Additionally, titles such as *The John Donne Journal* and *The George
Herbert Journal* are known to do special issues dedicated to authors, critics, or themes that
make them invaluable not just for the articles they provide on the author the journal ostensibly
celebrates, but also for providing criticism on authors or subjects that may not have a society
devoted to them, such as the *John Donne Journal*'s special issue dedicated to Richard Crashaw
which begins with an excellent annotated bibliography by John R. Roberts (Roberts 2005) or
the *George Herbert Journal*'s special issues dedicated to Robert Herrick, and the possible writings of George's brother, Henry (1990–1, 1996–7, 2001–2). Some of these issues are either not
available electronically or are difficult to find, so searching both the print and electronic is
always recommended. While I will be discussing the databases and how to best approach them,
it is important to be reminded that in searching the physical journals, it is not only helpful to
find articles through citation searching (following articles that seem interesting in someone
else's work), but that very good annotated bibliographies are still available and should be consulted. Some of these are being created as online databases, such as the excellent Christopher
Marlowe bibliography, but there are also the print bibliographies, and in particular those by
John R. Roberts. Roberts has created some of the best annotated bibliographies available. There
is a single volume edition for George Herbert (Roberts 1988), a one volume edition for Richard
Crashaw (Roberts 1985) (to which he then added the previously mentioned bibliography in the
special issue of the *John Donne Journal*), and a four-volume edition on John Donne (Roberts
1973, 1982, 2004, 2013), all of which the John Donne Society has made available through their
website, *Digital Donne*. This allows for the Donne bibliographies to be consulted in print, or
downloaded for free from the Digital Donne website. The advantage of annotated bibliographies, such as the Marlowe bibliography or those created by Roberts, are that they provide very
powerful searches, in that they already provide a narrow focus, and the indexes and abstracts
actually allow a researcher to have a more informed search as she knows what the article is primarily about, and the search process actually tends to provide better results in less time. I still
consult annotated bibliographies (whether in print or electronically) first when beginning my
research, and then move on to the larger databases. This way of searching appears to provide
the best results in the shortest amount of time, and with the fewest frustrations.

Journals have probably been the area of research that has been best aided by the arrival of
online databases. Their shorter length and more varied content has been perfect for a technology that allows a researcher to search a broad area for information that is returned in a text that
is short enough that it can be printed or read with relative ease on a computer screen. The only
drawback is that journal databases are so good and so convenient that the print-only journals
are not consulted as often as they should be. There is a real concern that it is only the journals
that are able to be carried by large aggregators who help to populate the most frequently purchased or subscribed-to databases that will dictate much of the future research in any field. As
libraries are being asked to cut costs year after year, they are cutting print subscriptions and
allowing electronic databases that come with large and inflexible packages of journals (for what
are usually interdisciplinary coverage) to replace them. This can leave smaller titles behind.

Many of the print-only or smaller journals can still be found in the book stacks holding the print journals, and the more that they are used, the more likely it is that the library will keep the copies even when pressed for space. Also, through retaining use of journals that may not be covered by the big databases (which will be discussed below) this also allows for possibly more outside and dissenting opinions to flourish. It is therefore vital that, in the research of early modern literature and religion, both print and electronic journals are searched. This allows not only for greater research and scholarship, but also for more voices to contribute to the discussion of the field.

Databases

It is in the databases that most research is now conducted, and while this is not a surprise to any of us, it does indicate that there has been a great break from the past manner in which journal articles were found and read. Rather than researchers finding a few journals that they enjoy consulting for research, it appears that now scholars have a few databases that they enjoy using. Furthermore, when collections were primarily print, and research was done with physical resources, indexes and annotated bibliographies ruled the day. Although these resources are still of the utmost importance in research, the index has been, basically, entirely moved online, and the annotated bibliography has been nearly, and unfortunately, eliminated in the research process as the full text database has become the default search and retrieval method. This can have an interesting and normalizing effect on research. The databases that are subscribed to by academic libraries are making library collections largely generic in nature as every library has to subscribe to roughly the same databases, and the databases sell content in journal packages, meaning that libraries are now largely providing access to the same issues of the same journals. However, in doing this libraries are now provided with access to journals that they may not have purchased in the past, and searches in databases can return results from subject journals outside one's discipline. What this may be doing is both creating a common base from which most scholars will pull, and allowing deeper searches into the discipline's journals that may have never been consulted otherwise. This could potentially create a strong common core of articles consulted and discussed, or lead to a further narrowing of research as scholars keep plumbing the depths of 'new' journals and articles, creating a situation in which very few scholars practising outside of a narrowly defined area of study will ever be familiar with the scholarship being discussed.

While it will be of great interest to see how the current model of database subscriptions influences the scholarship of any given discipline, there are three databases that are advised to consult first when performing research for early modern literature and religion. WorldCat, MLA Bibliography, and ATLA are perhaps the most important starting points. The reasons for this is that WorldCat is the world's largest database of books and journals, MLA Bibliography is the official database of the Modern Language Association, and ATLA is the official database of the American Theological Library Association. Through beginning one's research with these three databases, one is likely to find most of the core and major supplementary writings on a given topic in the religion and literature field. One thing to keep in mind is that these three databases were initially created as indexes designed to provide bibliographic information about resources, not the full text of the resources themselves. This is especially true in the case of WorldCat which only consists of bibliographic data. Through the use of these three databases, much of the initial research can be performed fairly quickly, and any additional books or articles will most likely be found through the various texts being studied and following up on citations of interest in footnotes and bibliographies. Additionally, these databases use subject terms similar to those used by the Library of

Congress, so the combined use of keyword and subject heading searches is also of great value when searching these resources.

While WorldCat, MLA, and ATLA will catch much of the initial scholarship that a researcher will need, the use of databases such as Project Muse, JSTOR, and LION can give deeper results that can complement what has already been found. While these three databases do not seek to be as comprehensive as the others, they do provide full-text searching and results, and this can provide good articles that indexes may miss. Additionally, Project Muse and JSTOR often work together in filling holes in each other's collections, usually with JSTOR linking to Project Muse. This means that beginning one's search with JSTOR can allow for a search to be performed in both databases, thus saving time. Also, Early English Books Online (EEBO) provides access to primary texts, and can facilitate wide searches in texts published in the sixteenth and seventeenth century. However, EEBO does not have the best scans of the works, and the poor quality scans can make the texts illegible or unsearchable; therefore, results in this database can be of great value, but they are not comprehensive, and just because a search for a word or phrase yields no results does not mean that the word or phrase in question does not exist in English books from the time period.

In addition to the paid databases to which most academic libraries subscribe, there are many open web databases and websites that can greatly enhance the research of any early modern scholar. Though these databases are more prone to be poorly maintained or to disappear (due to the fact that they are often associated with one or two people at an institution, and can cease to exist when those people leave, or that the institution's small or non-existent budgets make it difficult to fund the infrastructure and work required), there are still many places that are well worth trying when gathering information for a project. It would be impossible for me to discuss all of them, due to the nature of the Internet, but it is very important to note that with the growth of the Open Access movement and Institutional Repositories, more money and resources are being put into building better and more permanent scholarly websites and free databases on the Internet. As these are in a constant state of growth and change, I will not spend much time discussing them directly; however, I have included several of the more established Internet resources available in the bibliography at the end of this chapter, with light annotation.

Resources to Consult

The goal of this final section is not to provide an exhaustive list of digital resources to consult, but to highlight some open Internet materials that will be of benefit to one studying early modern literature and religion. As the field is changing rapidly, and universities are creating new institutional repositories and digital humanities resources at speed, it would be foolish to try to provide an exhaustive or comprehensive list. For this reason, I have chosen to highlight a few resources as examples of websites that have survived for enough time to have become dependable. Furthermore, many of these websites maintain links to the ever-expanding world of online resources. Often these websites are tied to academic societies or institutions; therefore, it is highly recommended that one visit the website of a given author's association or a professional society for the time period (i.e. Renaissance Society of America) when beginning research. Often these websites either provide digital resources or links to them.

Luminarium (http://www.luminarium.org/)

This website was created in 1996 and has grown to be an excellent resource. It provides access to works, bibliographies, and criticism for a majority of the early modern writers studied in academia today. Luminarium also provides access to the University of Oregon's Renascence Editions.

English Short Title Catalogue (http://estc.bl.uk)

This database is maintained by the British Library and provides the Short Title Catalogue in a searchable format.

Voice of the Shuttle (http://vos.ucsb.edu/)

This website is a directory to resources for academic research created and maintained by Alan Liu at the University of California, Santa Barbara. Of particular interest are the sections for Renaissance and early modern literature (http://vos.ucsb.edu/browse.asp?id=2749) and religious studies (http://vos.ucsb.edu/browse.asp?id=2730#id474).

Centre for Reformation and Renaissance Studies (http://crrs.ca/)

Run by the University of Toronto, the website for the centre offers a particularly helpful collection of links to resources which can be found in the web resources section (http://crrs.ca/library-2/resources-2/web-resources/).

Digital Donne (http://digitaldonne.tamu.edu/)

This website is an excellent example of what academic associations are doing. Digital Donne is associated and maintained by the Donne Variorum project and the John Donne Society. It provides an expanding collection of digitized editions of Donne's works, as well as concordances, annotated bibliographies, and other resources of interest to Donne scholars.

Lexicons of Early Modern English (eme.library.utoronto.ca)

Maintained by the University of Toronto, the Lexicon is a searchable database of dictionaries and lexicons from 1480–1702.

HRI Online (http://hridigital.shef.ac.uk/hrionline)

This is the main directory for the many projects being supported or hosted by the Humanities Research Institute at the University of Sheffield. Of particular interest are 'The Hartlib Papers', 'Bess of Hardwick's Letters', 'Renaissance Cultural Crossroads', and 'The Acts and Monuments Online'—a fantastic digital resource comprising the four editions published during John Foxe's life and critical resources to assist scholars of any level in their studies of the work.

Project Canterbury (http://anglicanhistory.org/)

This database is devoted to Anglican history and provides editions of works from many major figures in Anglican history, including those by Lancelot Andrewes, Richard Hooker, and George Herbert. The website also provides some critical writings.

Early Modern Literary Studies (http://extra.shu.ac.uk/emls/emlshome.html)

This is a peer-reviewed journal that provides scholarly articles on all aspects of early modern literature. It also provides links to works by major authors of the time period. The website is published and supported by the Humanities Research Centre at Sheffield Hallam University.

Christian Classics Ethereal Library (http://www.ccel.org/)

Currently maintained by Calvin College, this database provides access to primary works from numerous Christian writers throughout the history of the Church.

Map of Early Modern London (http://mapoflondon.uvic.ca/index.htm)

This website provides an annotated edition of the so-called 'Agas map'. There are additional critical materials to assist in the study of London in the early modern period, and the resource is maintained by the University of Victoria.

Bibliography

Note: The Bible appears in many different versions and spellings in the period and references are given in the form used in the relevant chapter.

A. Early Modern Primary Texts (including Manuscripts, Later Editions, and Anthologies)

A declaration (1542) [Anon.]. *A declaration conteyning the iust causes and considerations of this present warre with the Scottis.* London: T. Berthelet.

A declaration (1646) [Anon.]. *A declaration of a strange and wonderful monster.* London: J. Coe.

A Directory for the Publique Worship of God, etc. (1644) [Anon.]. London: E. Tyler, A. Fifield, R. Smith, and J. Field.

A Discovery of 29. Sects here in London, all of which, except the first, are most Divelish and Damnable (1641) [Anon.]. London: n. pub.

A new Sect of Religion Descryed, called Adamites (1641) [Anon.]. London: n. pub.

A newe sermon of the newest fashion (n.d.) [Anon.]. Oxford Worcester College MS 38.

A parte of a register, contayninge sundrie memorable matters, written by divers godly and learned in our time (1593) [Anon.]. Middelburg: R. Schilders.

A short treatise (n.d.) [Anon.]. *A short treatise of the three principall vertues and vows of religious persons.* Archives Departementales du Nord, France. MS 20H-17: 'Virtues of a Religious Person'.

A. S. (1663). *Miracles not ceas'd to His Grace George Duke of Buckingham &c.* London: n. pub.

Abbott, W. C. (ed.) (1937). *The Writings and Speeches of Oliver Cromwell.* Volume III. Cambridge, MA: Harvard University Press.

Alexander, G. (ed.) (2004). *Sidney's 'The Defence of Poesy' and Selected Renaissance Literary Criticism.* London: Penguin.

Alfield, T. (1582). *A true reporte of the death & martyrdome of M. Campion Iesuite and preiste, & M. Sherwin, & M. Bryan preistes, at Tiborne the first of December 1581.* London: R. Rowlands or Verstegan. [*STC* 200:09.]

Alle, T. (1646). *A breif narration of the truth of some particulars in Mr Thomas Edwards his book called Gangraena.* London: R. Smith.

Alleine, T. (1671). *The Life and Death of ... Joseph Alleine.* London: n. pub.

Allen, H. (1683). *A Narrative of God's Gracious Dealings with that Choice Christian Mrs. Hannah Allen, afterwards married to Mr. Hatt.* London: J. Wallis. [Reprinted in A. Ingram (ed.) (1997), *Voices of Madness: Four Pamphlets, 1683–1796.* Stroud: Sutton Publishing.]

Allen, H. E. (ed.) (1931). *English Writings of Richard Rolle, hermit of Hampole.* Oxford: Clarendon Press.

Allen, P. S., H. M. Allen, and H. W. Garrod (eds) (1906–58). *Opus epistolarum Des. Erasmi Roterodami.* 12 vols. Oxford: Oxford University Press.

Allen, W. (1581). *An Apologie and True Declaration of the Institution and Endevours of the Two English Colleges*. Rheims: J. de Foigny.

Andrewes, L. (1648). *A manual of the private devotions and meditations of the Right Reverend Father in God, Lancelot Andrews, late Lord Bishop of Winchester*. London: H. Moseley.

Andrewes, L. (1661). *XCVI. Sermons*. 5th edn. London: G. Sawbridge.

Andrewes, L. (1903). *Preces Privatae*, translated by F. E. Brightman. London: Methuen.

Anon. (1556a). *The Catechisme or Manner to Teach Children the Christian Religion*, in *The Forme of Prayers ... Used in the Englishe Congregation at Geneva*. Geneva: J. Crespin.

Anon. (1556b). *The Forme of Prayers ... Used in the Englishe Congregation at Geneva: and Approved, by the famous and godly learned man, John Calvyn*. Geneva: J. Crespin.

Anon. (1556c). *One and Fiftie Psalmes of David in Englishe Metre*. In *The Forme of Prayers ... Used in the Englishe Congregation at Geneva*. Geneva: J. Crespin.

Anon. (1569). *The Daunce and Song of Death*. London: J. Awdely. [*STC* (2nd edn) 6222.]

Anon. (1603). *A Breefe Collection concerning the Love of God towards mankind*. Doway [Douai]: L. Kellam.

Anon. (1605). *An abridgment of that booke which the ministers of Lincoln diocess delivered to his Maiestie upon the first of December last*. London: W. Jones.

Anon. (1606a). *A survey of the Booke of common prayer*. Middelburg: R. Schilders.

Anon. (1606b). *The remooual of certaine imputations laid upon the ministers of Devon*. Middelburg: R. Schilders.

Anon. (1610a). *A briefe and plaine narration of proceedings at an assemsemblie [sic] in Glasco, 8. Iun. 1610. anent the innovation of the Kirk-governement*. Middelburg: R. Schilders.

Anon. (1610b). *The confession of faith of the Kirk of Scotland: Subscribed by the Kings Majestie and his housholde, in the yeare of God 1580*. [Leiden?: W. Christiaens?]

Anon. (1634). *Innocency Justified and Insolency Repressed; or a Round yet Modest Answere, to an Immodest and Slaunderous Libell Bearing this Title: A Briefe and Sincere Relation ... of the Late Controversy betwixt the Lady Mary Percy Abbesse and Her Religious*. BL Harley MS 4275.

Anon. (1640). *The Whole Booke of Psalmes Faithfully Translated into English Metre*. Cambridge, MA: S. Day. [The Bay Psalm Book.]

Anon. (1641a). *A Discovery of six women preachers, in Middlesex, Kent, Cambridge, and Salisbury*. London: n. pub.

Anon. (1641b). *The Arminian Nunnery or a Brief Description and Relation of the late erected monasticall Place, called the Arminian Nunnery at Little Gidding in Huntington-shire*. London: T. Underhill.

Anon. (1643). *An elegie upon the much lamented death of the Right Honourable, the Lord Brooke*. London: R. Austen and A. Coe.

Anon. (1646). *Divine Light manifesting the love of God unto the Whole World*. London: R. Overton.

Anon. (1647). *Tub-Preachers Overturned: Or, Independency to be Abandoned and Abhorred*. London: G. Lindsey.

Anon. (1649). *A Forme of Prayer Used in the King's Chappel upon Tuesdayes in These Times of Trouble & Distresse*. Paris: n. pub.

Anon. (1662). *The Third Part of the Cry of the Innocent*. London: n. pub.

Anon. (1663). *An Answer to Wild. Or, A Poem upon the Imprisonment of Robert Wild D.D. in Cripplegate. by a Brother of the same Congregation*. London: n. pub.

Anon. (1664). *The Cry of the Innocent and Oppressed for Justice*. London: n. pub.

Anon. (1665). *Another Out-Cry of the Innocent and Oppressed*. London: n. pub.

Anon. (1682a). *More Sad and Lamentable News from Bristol*. London: for J. Moderation.

Anon. ([1682]b). *The New and Strange Imprisonment of the People Called Quakers*. London: n. pub.

Anon. (1682c). *The Sad and Lamentable Cry of Oppression*. London: J. Alexander.

Anon. (1683). *A Narrative of the Cruelties and Abuses Acted by Isaac Dennis*. London: n. pub.

Anon. (1693). *Renewed Advice*. London: T. Sowle.

Anon. (1745–6). 'An Account of the Nunnery of St Monica in Louvain'. BL Additional MS 5813.

Aquinas, St Thomas (1983). *Quodlibetal Questions 1 & 2*, translation and introduction by S. Edwards. Toronto: Pontifical Institute of Mediaeval Studies.

Aristotle (1962). *The Nichomachean Ethics*. Loeb Classical Library, translated by H. Rackham. London/Cambridge, MA: William Heinemann/Harvard University Press.

Arnold, J. (ed.) (1988). *Queen Elizabeth's Wardrobe Unlock'd: The Inventories of the Wardrobe of Robes Prepared in July 1600 Edited from the Stowe MS 557 in the British Library, MS LR 2/121 in the Public Record Office, London, and MS V.b.72 in the Folger Shakespeare Library, Washington DC*. Leeds: W. S. Maney and Son.

Articles of Religion ([1563/71], 2009). 'The *Articles of Religion* of the Church of England (1563/71) commonly called the Thirty-Nine Articles', Latin and English versions together with an introduction and annotations by T. Kirby. In *Die Bekenntnisschriften der reformierten Kirchen*, vol. II, edited by K. H. Faulenbach, pp. 371–410. Neukirchen-Vluyn: Neukirchener Verlag.

Articles to be ministred, enquired of, and answered: in the fourth visitation of the Right Reverend father in God, Robert, by Gods divine providence, Lord Bishop of Bristol (1631). London: J. N. for W. Garrett.

Askew, A. (1996). *The Examinations of Anne Askew*, edited by E. V. Beilin. New York, NY: Oxford University Press.

Aubrey, J. (1898). *Brief Lives*, edited by A. Clark. Oxford: Clarendon Press.

Aubrey, J. (1960). *Brief Lives*, edited by O. L. Dick. London: Secker and Warburg.

Augustine, St. (1992). *Confessions*, translated by H. Chadwick. Oxford: Oxford University Press.

Augustine, St. (1998). *The City of God against the Pagans*, edited and translated by R. W. Dyson. Cambridge: Cambridge University Press.

Avale, L. (1969). *A Commemoration of Bastard Edmund Bonner*. London: J. Kingston. [*STC* 977.]

Ayre, J. (ed.) (1844). *The Catechism of Thomas Becon, S. T. P., Chaplain to Archbishop Cranmer, Prebendary of Canterbury &c*. Cambridge: Cambridge University Press, for the Parker Society.

Babington, G. (1588). *A profitable exposition of the Lord's prayer*. London: T. Orwin for T. Charde.

Babington, G. (1605). *Certaine considerations drawne from the canons of the last Sinod, and other the Kings ecclesiasticall and statue law*. Middelburg: R. Schilders.

Bacon, A. (1564). *An Apologie or answere in defence of the Church of England*. London: R. Wolfe.

Bacon, F. (1924). *The New Atlantis*, edited by A. B. Gough. Oxford: Clarendon Press.

Bacon, F. (1937). *Essays*, edited by R. F. Jones. New York, NY: Odyssey Press.

Bacon, F. (1965). *A Selection of His Works*, edited by S. Warhaft. Indianapolis: Bobbs-Merrill.

Bacon, F. (1996). *Francis Bacon: A Critical Edition of His Works*, edited by B. Vickers. Oxford: Oxford University Press.

Baillie, R. (1645). *A Dissuasive from the Errours of the Time wherein the tenets of the principall sects, especially of the Independents, are drawn together in one map*. London: S. Gellibrand.

Baker, A. (n.d.). 'Life and Death of Dame Margaret Gascoigne'. Stanbrook Baker MS 19, being a copy of Downside Abbey Baker MS 42. Available at: http://www.umilta.net/gascoign.html.

Baker, A. (1629). 'Letter to Robert Cotton'. BL Cotton MS Julius C III.

Baker, S. (1637). *The Arrivall and Intertainments of the Embassador, Alkaid Jaurar ben Abealla, with his Associate, Mr. Robert Blake*. London: I. Oakes.

Baldwin, W. (1552). *Wonderfull Newes of the Death of Paule the III*. London: T. Gaultier.

Bale, J. (1557–9). *Scriptorum illustrium maioris Brytanniae … Catalogus*. 2 vols. Basel: J. Oporinus.

Bale, J. (1969). *King Johan*, edited by B. Adams. San Marino: The Huntington Library.

Bancroft, R. (1588–9). *A sermon preached at Paules Crosse the 9. of Februarie, being the first Sunday in the Parleament, anno. 1588*. London: J. Jackson.

Bancroft, T. (1639). *Two bookes of epigrammes*. London: I. Okes for M. Walbancke.

Bancroft, T. (1658). *Time's out of tune, plaid upon however in XX satyres*. London: W. Godbid.

Banks, J. (1712). *A Journal of the Life*. London: J Sowle.

Banks, J. (ed.) (1800). 'A Breviate touching the Order and Governmente of a Nobleman's House, etc.' *Archaeologia* 12: 315–389.

Barbour, H., and A. O. Roberts (eds) (1973). *Early Quaker Writings 1650–1700*. Grand Rapids, MI: Eerdmans.

Barlowe, J., and W. Roy (1528). *Rede Me and Be Nott Wrothe*. Strasbourg: J. Schott.

Barlowe, J., and W. Roy (1992). *Rede Me and Be Nott Wrothe*, edited by D. H. Parker. Toronto: University of Toronto Press.

Barrow, H., and M. Mickle-bound (1611). *Mr Henry Barrowes Platform which may serve, as a preparative to purge away prelatisme: with some other parts of poperie*. London: n. pub.

Barrow, I. (1680). *Of the Love of God and our Neighbour*. London: M. Flesher for B. Aylmer.

Barthlett, J. (1566). *The Pedegrewe of Heretiques*. London: H. Denham for L. Harryson.

Basil (1557). *An Exhortation … to the study of humaine learnyne*, translated by W. Baker. London.

Bastard, T. (1598). *Chrestoleros*. London: R. Bradocke for I. Broome.

Baxter, R. (1670). *The Cure of Church-Divisions, or, Directions for weak Christians to keep them from being dividers or troublers of the church*. London: N. Symmons [sic].

Baxter, R. (1673). *A Christian Directory*. London: R. White for N. Simmons.

Baxter, R. (1680). *The True and Only Way of Concord of all the Christian Churches*. London: J. Hancock.

Baxter, R. (1681). *A Breviate of the Life of Margaret … Baxter*. London: B. Simmons.

Baxter, R. (1696). *Reliquiae Baxterianae, or, Mr. Richard Baxter's narrative of the most memorable passages of his life and times faithfully publish'd from his own original manuscript by Matthew Sylvester*. London: T. Parkhurst, J. Robinson, J. Lawrence, and J. Dunton.

Bayly, L. (1612). *The Practise of Pietie: directing a Christian how to walke that he may please God*. London: W. H. for J. Hodgets.

Bayly, L. (1620). *The Practise of Pietie*. 12th edn. London: J. Hodgetts [sic].

Beaumont, A. (1998). *The Narrative of the Persecution of Mrs. Agnes Beaumont*. In *John Bunyan: Grace Abounding, with other spiritual autobiographies*, edited by J. Stachniewski and A. Pacheco. Oxford: Oxford University Press.

Beaumont, J. (1648). *Psyche, or, Loves Mysterie in XX Canto's, Displaying the Intercourse Betwixt Christ and the Soule*. London: J. Dawson for G. Boddington.

Becon, T. (1542). *A newe pathwaye vnto praier*. London: J. Mayler for J. Gough.

Becon, T. (1550). *The Fortress of the Faithful against the Cruel Assaults of Poverty and Hunger.* London: J. Dale and W. Seres. [*STC* 1721.]

Bedford, T. (1624). *Luthers Predecessours.* London: F. Kingston for G. Winder.

Behn, A. (1987, 1997). *Love Letters Between a Nobleman and His Sister,* introduced by M. Duffy. London: Virago Press.

Behn, A. (2000). *Oroonoko, or the royal slave.* Boston: Bedford/St Martin's.

Beilin, E. V. (ed.) (1996). *The Examinations of Anne Askew.* Women Writers in English 1350–1850. New York, NY: Oxford University Press.

Bell, F. (trans.) (1624). *The Rule of the Religious of the Thirde Order of Sainte Francis.* Brussels: Pepermans.

Bell, F. (trans.) (1625). *The Historie, Life, and Miracles … of the Blessed Virgin, Sister Joane, of the Crosse.* St-Omer: for J. Heigham.

Bell, T. (1608). *The tryall of the new religion.* London: W. Jaggard.

Bellany, A., and A. McRae (eds) (2005). *Early Stuart Libels: an edition of poetry from manuscript sources.* Early Modern Literary Studies (Text Series I). Available at: http://www.earlystuartlibels.net.

Benet of Canfield (1609). *The Rule of Perfection.* Rouen: C. Hamillion.

Benet of Canfield (1646). *The Bright Starre, Leading to & Centring In Christ our Perfection.* London: H. Overton.

Bentley, T. (1582). *The monument of matrones.* London: H. Denham.

Bernard, R. (1623). *Looke beyond Luther.* London: F. Kyngston for E. Weaver.

Besse, J. (1753). *A Collection of the Sufferings of the People called Quakers, Taken from Original Records and Authentick Accounts.* 2 vols. London: L. Hindle.

Bestul, T. (ed.) (2000). *Walter Hilton: The Scale of Perfection.* Kalamazoo, MI: Medieval Institute Publications.

Bible (1535). *Biblia. The Bible, that is, the holy Scripture of the Olde and New Testament, faithfully and truly translated out of Douche and Latyn in to Englishe.* Cologne: E. Cervicornus & J. Soter? [The Coverdale Bible.]

Bible (1537). *The Bible, which is all the holy Scripture: in which are contained the Old and New Testament truly and purely translated into English by Thomas Matthew.* Antwerp: [M. Crom]. [The Matthew Bible.]

Bible (1539). *The Bible in Englyshe that is to saye the content of all the holy scrypture, both of ye olde and newe testament, truly translated after the veryte of the Hebrue and Greke texts, by ye dylygent studye of dyverse excellent learned men, expert in the forsayde tonges.* London: R. Grafton and E. Whitchurch. [The Great Bible.]

Biddle, H. (1662). *The Trumpet of the Lord.* London: n. pub.

Black, J. L. (ed.) (2008). *The Martin Marprelate Tracts: A Modernized and Annotated Edition.* Cambridge: Cambridge University Press.

Blackborrow, S. (1660). *The Just and Equall Balance.* London: M. W[estwood].

Blandford, S. (1698). *A Small Account given forth by one that hath been a Traveller for these 40 Years in the Good Old Way. And as an Incouragement to the Weary to go forward; I by Experience have found there is a Rest remains for all they that truly trusts in the Lord.* London: n. pub.

Blaugdone, B. (1691). *An Account of the Travels, Sufferings and Persecution of Barbara Blaugdone. Given forth as a Testimony to the Lord's Power, and for the Encouragement of Friends.* London: T. S.

Blom, J., and F. Blom (eds) (2006). *Catherine Greenbury and Mary Percy*. The Early Modern Englishwoman: A Facsimile Library of Essential Works, series I, part 2, vol. 2. Aldershot: Ashgate.

Bohun, E. (1853). *The Diary and Autobiography of Edmund Bohun Esq.*, edited by S. W. Rix. Beccles: R. Crisp.

Booty, J. E. (ed.) (1976). *The Book of Common Prayer 1559: The Elizabethan Prayer Book*. Washington, DC: Folger Shakespeare Library.

Booy, D. (ed.) (2002). *Personal Disclosures: An Anthology of Self-Writings from the Seventeenth Century*. Aldershot: Ashgate.

Booy, D. (ed.) (2004). *Autobiographical Writings by Early Quaker Women*. Aldershot: Ashgate.

Booy, D. (ed.) (2007). *The Notebooks of Nehemiah Wallington, 1618–1654: A Selection*. Aldershot: Ashgate.

Bose, M., and J. P. Hornbeck II (eds) (2011). *Wycliffite Controversies*. Turnhout: Brepols.

Bowden, C. (ed.) (2012a). *English Convents in Exile, 1600–1800: Volume I: History Writing*. London: Pickering & Chatto.

Bowden, C. et al. (eds) (2012–13). *English Convents in Exile, 1600–1800*, vols 1–6. London: Pickering & Chatto.

Boyle, R. (1979). *Selected Philosophical Papers*, edited by M. A. Stewart. Manchester: Manchester University Press.

Boyle, R. (1996). *A Free Enquiry into the Vulgarly Received Notion of Nature*, edited by E. B. Davis and M. Hunter. Cambridge: Cambridge University Press.

Bradford, W. (1952). *Of Plymouth Plantation*. New York, NY: Knopf.

Bradstreet, A. (1981). *The Complete Works of Anne Bradstreet*, edited by J. R. McElrath and A. P. Robb. Boston: Twayne.

Brathwaite, R. (1615). *Strappado for the Divell*. London: I. B. for R. Redmer.

Brathwaite, R. (1620). *Essaies upon the Five Senses*. London: E. G. for Richard Whittaker.

Bray, G. (ed.) (1994, 2004). *Documents of the English Reformation*. Cambridge: J. Clarke.

Bray, G. (ed.) (1998). *The Anglican Canons 1529–1947*. Church of England Record Society, no. 6. Woodbridge: Boydell Press.

Brice, T. (1559). *A Compendious Register in Metre*. London: J. Kingston for R. Adams. [*STC* 3726.]

Bridges, J. (1587). *A defence of the government established in the Church of Englande for ecclesiaticall matters*. London: J. Windet for T. Chard.

Brieff Discourse (1578) [Anon.]. *A Brieff Discourse off the Troubles Begonne at Franckford*. Heidelberg: M. Schirat.

Brinklow, H. ([1542a]). *The complaynt of Roderyck Mors, somtyme a gray fryre, unto the parliament howse of Ingland his natural cuntry for the redresse of certen wicked lawes, euel customes a[n]d cruell decreys*. [Strasbourg: W. Köpfel.]

Brinklow, H. (1542b). *The lamentacion of a Christian against the citie of London made by Roderigo Mors*. [Bonn: L. Mylius.]

Brinsley, J. (1606). *The True Watch. Or, A Direction for the Examination of our Spirituall Estate (according to the Word of God, whereby wee must be Judged at the last day) to helpe to preserve us from apostacie, or decaying in grace, and to further our daily growth in Christ*. London: G. Eld for S. Macham and M. Cooke.

Broke, T. (1569a). *An Epitaph Declaring the Life and End of Doctor Edmund Bonner*. London: J. Day. [*STC* 3817.4.]

Broke, T. (1569b). *A Slanderous Libel unto an Epitaph upon the Death of Doctor E. Bonner, with a Reply to the Same Lying Libel*. London: J. Day. [*STC* 3817.7.]

Brown, S. (ed.) (1999). *Women's Writing in Stuart England: The Mother's Legacies of Dorothy Leigh, Elizabeth Joscelin, and Elizabeth Richardson*. Stroud: Sutton.

Browne, T. (1964). *Religio Medici and Other Works*, edited by L. C. Martin. Oxford: Clarendon Press.

Browne, T. (1977). *The Major Works*, edited by C. A. Patrides. Harmondsworth: Penguin.

Bucer, M. (1535), *A treatise declaring and shewing ... that pictures and other ymages which were wont to be worshypped, ar in no wise to be suffred in the temples or churches of Christen men.* London: T. Godfray.

Buchanan, G. (1579). [De Jure Regni apud Scotos] *The Powers of the Crown in Scotland*. Edinburgh: John Ross.

Buchanan, G. (1983). *George Buchanan Tragedies*, edited by P. Sharratt and P. G. Walsh. Edinburgh: Scottish Academic Press.

Bull, H., and R. Day (1569). *Christian Prayers and Meditations*. London: J. Day.

Bunyan, J. (1678). *The Pilgrim's Progress*. London: N. Ponder.

Bunyan, J. (1998). *Grace Abounding to the Chief of Sinners, or, A Brief Relation Of the exceeding mercy of God in Christ, to his poor servant, John Bunyan* (1666). In *John Bunyan: Grace Abounding, with Other Spiritual Autobiographies*, edited by J. Stachniewski and A. Pacheco. Oxford: Oxford University Press.

Burges, C. (1641). *An humble examination of a printed abstract*. London: P. Stephens.

Burnet, G. (1897–1900). *Burnet's History of My Own Time*, edited by O. Airy. 2 vols. Oxford: Oxford University Press.

Burrough, E. (1657). *General Epistle ... to all the Saints*. London: T. Simmonds.

Burrough, E. (1659a). *A Declaration from the People Called Quakers*. London: T. Simmonds.

Burrough, E. (1659b). *A Message to the Present Rulers*. London: G. Calvert.

Burrough, E. (1659c). *To the Parliament of the Common-wealth of England, the Present Authority*. London: T. Simmonds.

Burrough, E. (1659d). *To the Parliament of the Common-wealth of England, who are in place of Authority*. London: n. pub.

Burrough, E. (1659e). *To the Rulers and to Such as are in Authority*. London: T. Simmonds.

Burrough, E. ([1659]f). *To the Whole English Army*. London: G. Calvert.

Burrough, E. (1672). *The Memorable Works of a Son of Thunder*. [London: n. pub.]

Burrough, E., and M. Dyar [and signed by 6 witnesses] (1661). *A Declaration of the Sad and Great Persecution and Martyrdom*. London: R. Wilson.

Burrow, C. (ed.) (2006). *Metaphysical Poetry*. London: Penguin.

Burton, R. (1621). *The anatomy of melancholy vvhat it is. VVith all the kindes, causes, symptomes, prognostickes, and seuerall cures of it*. Oxford: J. Lichfield and J. Short for H. Cripps.

Burton, W. (1594). *An exposition of the Lord's prayer*. London: the Widdow Orwin for T. Man.

Butler, J. A. (ed.) (2012). *Travels in Africa, Persia, and Asia the Great, by Thomas Herbert* (1677). Tempe, AZ: CMRS.

Byble (1540). *The Byble in Englyshe*. London: E. Whitchurch.

Byll, T. (1630). 'A Farewell to the world'. London: for H. Gossen.

C., R. (1665). *God's Holy Name*. London: n. pub.

Calderwood, D. (1619). *Perth Assembly*. [Leiden: W. Brewster].

Calderwood, D. (1620). *A defence of our arguments against kneeling in the act of receiving*. Amsterdam: G. Thorp.

[Calvin, J.] (1542). *La Forme des prières et chantz ecclésiastiques*. [Geneva.]

Calvin, J. (1550). *The forme of common praiers used in the churches of Geneva: the mynystracion of the sacraments, of baptisme and the Lordes supper*. London: E. Whitchurche.

Calvin, J. (1561). *The institution of Christian religion*. Translated by T. Norton. London: R. Wolfe and R. Harison.

Calvin, J. (1570). *Commentaries of that diuine Iohn Caluine, vpon the prophet Daniell*. Translated by A. Gilby. London: J. Daye.

Calvin, J. (1960). *Institutes of the Christian Religion*, translated by F. L. Battles and edited by J. T. McNeill. 2 vols. Louisville, KY: Westminster John Knox Press.

Calvin, J. (1975). *Institutes of the Christian Religion*, translated by H. Beveridge. 2 vols. Grand Rapids, MI: Eerdmans.

Calvin, J. (1995). *Calvin's New Testament Commentaries: 2 Corinthians and Timothy, Titus and Philemon*, translated by T. A. Smail. Grand Rapids, MI: Eerdmans.

Camden, W. (1630). *The History of Elizabeth, Queen of England*, translated by R. Norton. London: B. Fisher.

Campion, T. (1967). *The Works of Thomas Campion*, edited by W. R. Davis. Garden City, NY: Doubleday.

Carey, J. (ed.) (2000). *John Donne: A Critical Edition of the Major Works*. Oxford: Oxford University Press.

Carpenter, R. (1642). *Experience, Historie, and Divinitie. Divided into five Books. Written by Richard Carpenter, Vicar of Poling, a small and obscure Village by the Sea-side ...* London: R. C. for A. Crook.

Carte (1604). 'A Narrative of Proceedings by the Judges of England and Others Concerning Papists and Puritans'. Carte Manuscripts, Bodleian Library, Oxford University.

Cartwright, T. (1843). *The Diary of Dr Thomas Cartwright, bishop of Chester*, edited by J. Hunter. London: Camden Society, 22.

Caton, W. (1689). *A Journal of the Life*. London: T. Northcott.

Cavendish, G. (1959). *The Life and Death of Cardinal Wolsey*, edited by R. S. Sylvester. Early English Text Society 243.

Caxton, W. (1495). *Here begynneth a lityll treatyse*, etc. London: R. Pynson. *STC* 790.

Certain Sermons or Homilies (1852) [Anon.]. London: Prayerbook and Homily Society.

Chandos, J. (ed.) (1971). *In God's Name: Examples of Preaching in England from the Act of Supremacy to the Act of Uniformity, 1534–1662*. London: Hutchinson.

Chapman, G. (1611). *The Iliads of Homer, Prince of Poets*. London: N. Butter.

Chapman, G. (1612). *Petrarchs seuen penitentiall psalmes paraphrastically translated*. London: J. Brown.

Charleton, W. (1657). *The Immortality of the Human Soul, Demonstrated by the Light of Nature In Two Dialogues*. London: W. Wilson for H. Herringman.

Chidley, K. (1641). *Justification of the Independent Churches of Christ*. London: for W. Larnar.

Chidley, K. (1645). *Good Counsell, to the petitioners for Presbyterian government, that they may declare their faith before they build their church*. London: n. pub.

Church of England (1549). *The boke of common praier*, etc. Wigorniae: In officina Ioannis Oswaeni cum privilegio ad imprimendum solum, Anno Do. 1549. *STC* 16271.

Church of England (1552). *The boke of common praier*, etc. Londini: in officina Richardi Graftoni: Regij impressoris, Anno 1552. *STC* 16286.2.

Church of England (1581). *Articles whereupon it was agreed by the archbyshops and byshops of both prouinces and the whole cleargie, in the conuocation holden at London in the yeere of our Lord God 1562*. London: C. Barker.

Church of England (1979). *The Book of Common Prayer*. New York, NY: Oxford University Press.

Churchyard, T. (1938). 'How Thomas Wolsey did arise [etc.]'. In *A Mirror for Magistrates*, edited by L. B. Campbell, pp. 495–511. New York, NY: Barnes & Noble.

CL MS (n.d.). Congregational Library MS I.h.33 and MS I.i.25.

Clarendon, Edward, Earl of (1888). *The History of the Rebellion and Civil Wars in England*. Volume VI. Oxford: Clarendon Press.

Clarke, S. (1651). *A Generall Martyrologie, containing a collection of all the greatest persecutions which have befallen the church of Christ*. London: A. M. for T. Underhill and J. Rothwell.

Clarkson (alias Claxton), L. (1660). *The Lost Sheep Found*. London: 'printed for the author'.

Clifford, A. (1990). *The Diaries of Lady Anne Clifford*, edited by D. J. H. Clifford. Stroud: Sutton.

Colet, J. (1527). *Ioannis Coleti theologi, olim decani diui Pauli, aeditio. una cum quibusdam G. Lilij Grammatices rudimentis, G. Lilij epigramma*. Antwerp: C. Ruremond?

Colet, J. (1909). *A Life of John Colet ... With an Appendix of Some of His English Writings*, edited with introduction by J. H. Lupton. London: Bell & Sons.

Colet, J. (1965a). *Ioannis Coleti Enarratio in Epistolam S. Pauli ad Romanos. An Exposition of St. Paul's Epistle to the Romans*, edited and translated by J. H. Lupton. Ridgewood, NJ: Gregg Press; reprint of 1873 edn.

Colet, J. (1965b). *Ioannis Coleti Enarratio in Primam Epistolam S. Pauli ad Corinthios. An Exposition of St. Paul's First Epistle to the Corinthians*, edited and translated by J. H. Lupton. Ridgewood, NJ: Gregg Press; reprint of 1874 edn.

Collier, T. (1657). *A Looking Glasse for the Quakers*. London: T. Brewster.

Collop, J. (1962). *Poesis Rediviva* [1656], *The Poems of John Collop*, edited by C. Hilberry. Madison, WI: University of Wisconsin Press.

Columbus, C. (1989). *The Diary of Christopher Columbus' First Voyage to America*, translated and edited by O. Dunn and J. Kelly. Norman, OK: University of Oklahoma Press.

Constable, B. (1655). 'Considerations or Reflexions upon the Rule of the Most Glorious Father St Benedict'. Downside Abbey MS 82144/627.

Conway, A. (1692). *The principles of the most ancient and modern philosophy concerning God, Christ and the creatures*. [London]: printed in Latin at Amsterdam by M. Brown, 1690, and reprinted at London, 1692.

Conway, A. (1982). *The Principles of the Most Ancient and Modern Philosophy*, edited by P. Loptson. The Hague: M. Nijhoff.

Conway, A. (1996). *The Principles of the Most Ancient and Modern Philosophy*, edited by A. P. Coudert and T. Corse. Cambridge: Cambridge University Press.

Conway, A. et al. (1992). *The Conway Letters: The Correspondence of Anne, Viscountess Conway, Henry More, and their Friends 1642–1684*, edited by M. H. Nicolson. Rev. edn by S. Hutton. Oxford: Clarendon Press.

Cooper, T. (1589). *Admonition to the People of England*. London: [the deputies of] C. Barker.

Coryate, T. (1611). *Coryats Crudities*. London: W. Stansby.

Cosin, J. (1968). *A Collection of Private Devotions*, edited by P. G. Stanwood. Oxford: Clarendon Press.

Cosin, R. (1591). *An apologie: of, and for sundrie proceedings by Jurisdiction ecclesiasticall*. London: [the deputies of] C. Barker.

Cotton, P., and M. Cole (1655). *To the Priests*. London: G. Calvert.

Couper, S. (ed.) (1701a). *Life of the Lady Halket*. Edinburgh: for A. Symson and H. Knox.

Couper, S. (ed.) (1701b). *Instructions for Youth, written by the Lady Halkett*. Edinburgh: A. Symson.

Coward, B., and P. Gaunt (eds) (2010). *English Historical Documents: vol. 5B, 1603–1660*. Abingdon: Routledge.

Cranmer, T. (1833). *The Remains of Thomas Cranmer, D.D., Archbishop of Canterbury*, edited by H. Jenkyns. 2 vols. Oxford: Oxford University Press.

Cranmer, T. (1846). *Miscellaneous Writings and Letters of Thomas Cranmer*, edited by J. E. Cox. Cambridge: Parker Society.

Crashaw, R. (1646). *Steps to the Temple, Sacred Poems with Other Delights of the Muses*. London: T. W. for H. Moseley.

Crashaw, R. (1652). *Carmen Deo Nostro*. Paris: Peter Targa.

Crashaw, R. (1927). *The Poems, English, Latin and Greek of Richard Crashaw*, edited by L. C. Martin. Oxford: Clarendon Press.

Crashaw, R. (1957). *Crashaw's Poetical Works*, edited by L. C. Martin. 2nd edn. Oxford: Clarendon Press.

Crashaw, R. (2015). *Selected Poems, Secular and Sacred*, edited by R. Holloway. Manchester: Carcanet Press.

Crashaw, W. (1610). *[A newyeeres gift to Virginea] A sermon*. London: W. Welby.

Crashawe, W. (1613). 'Saint Bernards Vision', in *Querela … S. Bernardum*. London: N. O[kes] for L. Becket.

Croese, G. (1696). *The General History of the Quakers*. London: for J. Dunton.

Crook, J. (1662). *The Cry of the Innocent for Justice*. London?: n. pub.

Crook, J. (1706). *A short History of the Life of John Crook*. London: T. Sowle.

Crosignani, G., T. M. McCoog, and M. Questier (eds) (2010). *Recusancy and Conformity in Early Modern England: Manuscript and Printed Sources in Translation*. Rome: Monumenta Historica Societatis Iesu.

Crowley, R. (1550). *One and thyrtye epigramms wherein are bryefly touched so many abuses, that maye and ought to be put away*. London: R. Grafton.

Crowley, R. (1980). *Philargurie of greate Britayne*, edited by J. King. *ELR* 10: 46–75.

Cudworth, R. (1996). *A Treatise Concerning Eternal and Immutable Morality with A Treatise of Freewill*, edited by S. Hutton. Cambridge: Cambridge University Press.

Cummings, B. (ed.) (2011). *The Book of Common Prayer: The Texts of 1549, 1559, and 1662*. Oxford: Oxford University Press.

Curio, C. (1566). *Pasquin in a Traunce*. London: W. Seres.

Curwen, A. (1680). *A Relation of the Labour, Travail and Suffering of that faithful Servant of the Lord Alice Curwen. Who departed this life the 7th Day of the 6th Moneth, 1679. and resteth in Peace with the Lord*. London: n. pub.

da Lucca, P. (1603). *A Dialogue of Dying Wel*. Antwerp: A. Conincx.

Daemen-de Gelder, K. (ed.) (2013). 'Short Colections of the beginings of our English monastery of Teresians in Antwerp with some few perticulars of our dear deceased religious'. In *English Convents in Exile, 1600–1800*, vol. 4. London: Pickering & Chatto.

Dallam, T. (1893). 'The Diary of Master Thomas Dallam, 1599–1600'. In *Early Voyages and Travels in the Levant*, edited by J. T. Bent, pp. 1–98. London: Hakluyt Society.

Daniel, S. (1981). *Samuel Daniel, The Brotherton Manuscript: A Study in Authorship*, edited by J. Pitcher. Leeds: University of Leeds.

Daniell, D. (ed.) (1989). *Tyndale's New Testament: A Modern-spelling Edition of the 1534 Translation*. New Haven, CT: Yale University Press.

Davies, J. of Hereford (1610). *Wittes Pilgrimage*. London: J. Browne.

Davis, G. R. C. (trans.) (1989). *Magna Carta*. Rev. edn. London: British Library.

Day, A. (1607). *The English Secretary, or Methode of Writing of Epistles and Letters*. London: T. D. for C. Burby.

De Bry, T. (1976). *Discovering the New World*, edited by M. Alexander. New York, NY: Harper & Row.

De Quehen, H. (ed.) (1996). *Lucy Hutchinson's Translation of Lucretius De Rerum Natura*. London: Duckworth.

Dean, J. (ed.) (1996). *Medieval English Political Writings*. Kalamazoo, MI: Medieval Institute Publications. Available at: http://d.lib.rochester.edu/teams/publication/dean-medieval-english-political-writings.

Defoe, D. (1985). *Robinson Crusoe*, edited by A. Ross. London: Penguin.

Defoe, D. (2011). *Moll Flanders*, edited by G. A. Starr and L. Bree. Oxford: Oxford University Press.

Deios, L. (1590). *That the Pope is That Antichrist*. London: G. Bishop and R. Newberie.

Denison, S. (1620). *The Monument or Tombe-Stone: or, a Sermon Preached at Laurence Pountnies Church … at the Funerall of Mrs Elizabeth Iuxon*. London: R. Field.

Denison, S. (1621). *The doctrine of both the Sacraments: to witte, Baptisme, and the Supper of the Lord*. London: A. Mathewes.

Dennis, J. (1939). *The Critical Works of John Dennis*, edited by E. N. Hooker. 2 vols. Baltimore: Johns Hopkins University Press.

Dering, E. (1572). *A Briefe and Necessarie Instruction, Verye Needeful to bee knowen of all Housholders*. London: J. Awdely.

Descartes, R. (1968). *Discourse on Method and the Meditations*, edited and translated by F. E. Sutcliffe. Harmondsworth: Penguin.

Descartes, R. (1985). *The Philosophical Writings of Descartes*, edited and translated by J. Cottingham, R. Stoothoff, D. Murdoch, and A. Kenny. 3 vols. Cambridge: Cambridge University Press.

Descartes, R. (1993, repr. 2003). *Meditations and Other Metaphysical Writings*, translated by D. M. Clarke. London: Penguin.

Dewsbury, W. (1654a). *A True Prophecy of the Mighty Day of the Lord*. London: G. Calvert.

Dewsbury, W. (1654b). *The Discovery of Mans Returne to his First Estate*. London: G. Calvert.

Dewsbury, W. (1656a). *Christ Exalted*. London: G. Calvert.

Dewsbury, W. (1656b). *The Mighty Day of the Lord is Coming*. London: G. Calvert.

Dewsbury, W. ([1689]). *The Faithful Testimony of that Antient Servant of the Lord*. London: A. Sowle.

Díaz de Castillo, B. (1844). *The memoirs of the conquistador Bernal Díaz del Castillo*, translated by J. L. Lockhart. London: J. Hatchard.

DigitalDonne: The Online Variorum. http://donnevariorum.tamu.edu.

Donne, J. (1627). *A Sermon of Commemoration of the Lady Da[n]uers*. London: P. Stephens and C. Meredith.

Donne, J. (1651). *Letters to Severall Persons of Honour: Written by John Donne sometime Deane of St Pauls London. Published by John Donne, Dr. of the Civill Law*. London: J. Flesher for Richard Marriot.

Donne, J. (1933). *The Poems of John Donne*, edited by H. Grierson. Oxford: Clarendon Press.

Donne, J. (1953–62). *The Sermons of John Donne*, edited by G. R. Potter and E. Simpson. 10 vols. Berkeley, CA: University of California Press.

Donne, J. (1955). 'Sermon Preached at Lincolns Inn Second Sermon on Psal. 38:4'. In *The Sermons of John Donne*, edited by G. R. Potter and E. M. Simpson, Volume 2, pp. 119–30. Berkeley, CA: University of California Press.

Donne, J. (1962). 'A Sermon Preached At the Earl of Bridge-waters house in London at the marriage of his daughter, the Lady Mary, to the Eldest son of the Lord Herbert of Castle-iland,

November 19 1627'. In *The Sermons of John Donne*, vol. 8, edited by E. M. S. Simpson and G. R. Potter, pp. 94–109. Berkeley, CA: University of California Press.

Donne, J. (1971a). *Poetical Works*, edited by Herbert J. C. Grierson (1st edn 1929). Oxford: Oxford University Press.

Donne, J. (1971b). *The Complete English Poems*, edited by A. J. Smith. Harmondsworth: Penguin.

Donne, J. (1975). *Devotions upon Emergent Occasions*, edited by A. Raspa. Montreal: McGill-Queen's University Press.

Donne, J. (1985). *The Complete English Poems*, edited by C. A. Patrides. London: Dent.

Donne, J. (2001). *Complete Poetry*, edited by C. Coffin with an introduction by D. Donoghue. New York, NY: Modern Library Classics.

Donne, J. (2005). *The Variorum Edition of the Poetry of John Donne*, vol. 7, part 1: 'The Holy Sonnets'. Bloomington, IN: Indiana University Press.

Donne, J. (2007). *John Donne's Poetry*, edited by D. R. Dickson. New York: W. W. Norton and Company.

Donno, E. S. (ed.) (1963). *Elizabethan Minor Epics*. London: Routledge & Kegan Paul.

Downame, G. (1608). *A sermon defending the honourable function of bishops*. London: F. Kyngston.

Drake, F. (1854 [1624]). *The world encompassed by Sir Francis Drake*, edited by W. S. W. Vaux. London: The Hakluyt Society.

Drayton, M. (1953). *Poems*, edited by J. Buxton. 2 vols. Cambridge, MA: Harvard University Press.

Dryden, J. (1685). *Sylvae*. London: J. Tonson.

Dryden, J. (1987). *John Dryden (Oxford Authors)*, edited by K. Walker. Oxford: Oxford University Press.

Duplessis de Mornay, P. (1587). *De veritate religionis Christianae liber ... Gallice primum conscriptus, Latine versus, nunc autem ab eodem accuratissime correctus*. Lugduni Batavorum: Christopher Plantin.

Duplessis de Mornay, P. (1976). *A Woorke Concerning the Trewnesse of the Christian Religion*, trans. Sir Philip Sidney [?] and Arthur Golding. Delmar, NY: Scholars' Facsimiles & Reprints.

Duplessis de Mornay, P. (1979). *Vindiciae contra tyrannos. Traduction française de 1581*, by Etienne Junius Brutus, pseudonym, edited by A. Jouanna et al. Geneva: Droz.

Dyos, J. (1579). *A Sermon preached at Paules Crosse ... : setting forth the excellencye of Gods heavenlye worde*. London: J. Daye.

Earle, J. (1628). *Micro-cosmographie. Or, A peece of the world discouered in essayes and characters*. London: W. Stansby for R. Allot.

Edwards, J. (1957–2006). *The Works of Jonathan Edwards*, edited by P. Miller and H. Stout. New Haven, CT: Yale University Press.

Edwards, T. (1646a). *Gangraena: or a Catalogue and Discovery of many of the Errours, Heresies, Blasphemies and pernicious Practices of the Sectaries of this time, vented and acted in England in these last four years*. London: R. Smith.

Edwards, T. (1646b). *The first and second part of Gangraena, or, A catalogue and discovery of many of the errors, heresies, blasphemies and pernicious practices of the sectaries of this time, vented and acted in England in these four last years*. London: T. R. and E. M. for R. Smith.

Edwards, T. (1646c). *The third part of Gangraena. Or, A new and higher discovery of the errors, heresies, blasphemies, and insolent proceedings of the sectaries of these times; with some animadversions by way of confutation upon many of the errors and heresies named*. London: R. Smith.

Eliza (1652). *Eliza's Babes: or The Virgins-Offering*. London: M. S. for L. Blaiklock.

Elizabeth I (1580). *The Queenes Majestie Findeth the Continuance ... of Traiterous and Malitious Purposes*. London: C. Barker.

Elizabeth I (1581). *A Proclamation for Revocation of Sundrie Her Majesties Subjectes*. London: C. Barker.

Ellwood, T. (1885 [1714]). *The History of Thomas Ellwood*, edited by H. Morley. London: George Routledge and Sons.

English Benedictines (1911). *English Benedictines of the Convent of Our Blessed Lady of Good Hope in Paris, now St. Benedict's Priory, Colwich, Stafforshire, contributed by the Reverend Mother Prioress of Colwich*, edited by J. S. Hansom. Catholic Record Society, Misc. VII, Vol. 9.

Erasmus, D. (1533). *A booke called in latyn Enchiridion militis christiani*, translated by W. Tyndale. London: W. de Worde for I. Byddell.

Erasmus, D. (1534). *An exhortacyon to the dylygent study of scripture ... lately translated into Englysshe*. London: R. Wyer.

Erasmus, D. (1548). *The first tome or volume of the Paraphrase of Erasmus upon the newe testament*, translated by N. Udall. London: E. Whitchurche.

Erasmus, D. (1549). *The praise of folie*, translated by T. Chaloner. London: T. Berthelet.

Erasmus, D. (1974). *Collected Works of Erasmus, vol. 1: The Correspondence of Erasmus, Letters 1 to 141 (1484–1500)*, translated by R. A. B. Mynors and D. F. S. Thomson. Toronto: University of Toronto Press.

Erasmus, D. (1975). *Collected Works of Erasmus, vol. 2: The Correspondence of Erasmus, Letters 142 to 297 (1501–1514)*, translated by R. A. B. Mynors and D. F. S. Thomson. Toronto: University of Toronto Press.

Erasmus, D. (1986). *Collected Works of Erasmus: Literary and Educational Writings 6*, vol. 28, edited by A. H. T. Levi. Toronto: University of Toronto Press.

Erasmus, D. (1987a). *Collected Works of Erasmus, vol. 7: The Correspondence of Erasmus, Letters 993 to 1121 (1519–1520)*, translated by R. A. B. Mynors and D. F. S. Thomson. Toronto: University of Toronto Press.

Erasmus, D. (1987b). *Christian Humanism and the Reformation. Selected Writings*, edited by J. C. Olin. 3rd edn. New York, NY: Fordham University Press.

Erasmus, D. (1988a). *Collected Works of Erasmus, vol. 8: The Correspondence of Erasmus, Letters 1122 to 1251 (1520–1521)*, translated by R. A. B. Mynors and D. F. S. Thomson. Toronto: University of Toronto Press.

Erasmus, D. (1988b). *Collected Works of Erasmus, vol. 9: The Correspondence of Erasmus. Letters 1252 to 1355 (1522–1523)*, translated by R. A. B. Mynors, annotated by J. M. Estes. Toronto: University of Toronto Press.

Erasmus, D. (1997a). *Collected Works of Erasmus*, vol. 39, edited and translated by C. R. Thompson. Toronto: University of Toronto Press.

Erasmus, D. (1997b). *Collected Works of Erasmus*, vol. 40, edited and translated by C. R. Thompson. Toronto: University of Toronto Press.

Erasmus, D. (1998). *Collected Works of Erasmus*, vol. 70, edited by J. W. O'Malley. Toronto: University of Toronto Press.

Erasmus, D. (1999). *Collected Works of Erasmus*, vol. 69, edited by J. W. O'Malley and L. A. Perraud. Toronto: University of Toronto Press.

Erasmus, D. (2000). *Collected Works of Erasmus*, vol. 77, edited by C. Trinkaus. Toronto: University of Toronto Press.

Erasmus, D. (2003). *Collected Works of Erasmus, vol. 12: The Correspondence of Erasmus, Letters 1658 to 1801 (January 1526–March 1527)*, translated by A. Dalzell. Toronto: University of Toronto Press.

Erasmus, D. (2010). *Collected Works of Erasmus, vol. 13: The Correspondence of Erasmus, Letters 1802 to 1925 (March–December 1527)*, translated by C. Fantazzi. Toronto: University of Toronto Press.

Erasmus, D. (2011). *Collected Works of Erasmus, vol. 14: The Correspondence of Erasmus, Letters 1926 to 2081 (1528)*, translated by C. Fantazzi. Toronto: University of Toronto Press.

Evans, K., and S. Cheevers (1662). *This is a Short Relation*. London: R. Wilson.

Evelyn, J. (1669). *The History of the Three Late Famous Imposters, viz. Padre Ottomano, Mahomed Bei, and Sabatai Sevi*. [London]: H. Herringman.

Evelyn, J. (1906). *The Diary of John Evelyn*, 3 vols. London: Macmillan.

Farnworth, R. et al. (1665). *Truth Vindicated. Or, an Answer to … John Perrot*. London: n. pub.

Featley, D. (1626). *Ancilla pietatis: or, the hand-maid to priuate deuotion*. London: N. Bourne.

Feild [sic], J. (1711). *Piety Promoted: The Fourth Part*. London: J. Sowle.

Fell, M. (1664). *The Examination and Tryall of Margaret Fell and George Fox*. London: n. pub.

Fell, M. (1666). *Women's Speaking Justified, proved and allowed of by the Scriptures*. London: n. pub.

Fell, M. (1710). *A Brief Collection of Remarkable Passages*. London: J. Sowle.

Fell, M. (1992 [1690]). 'A Relation of Margaret Fell'. In *A Sincere and Constant Love: An Introduction to the Work of Margaret Fell*, edited by T. S. Wallace, pp. 105–14. Richmond, IN: Friends United Press.

Fenn, H. (1641). *The Last Will and Testament, with the Profession of Faith of Humfrey Fen*. London: n. pub.

Ferrar, J. (1996). *Materials for the Life of Nicholas Ferrar*, edited by L. R. Muir and J. A. White. Leeds: The Leeds Philosophical and Literary Society.

Firmin, G. (1656). *Stablishing Against Shaking; or, A Discovery of the Prince of Darkness*. London: N. Webb.

Firth, C. H., and R. S. Rait (eds) (1911). *Acts and Ordinances of the Interregnum*, 3 vols. London: HMSO.

Fisher, J. (1560). *A godlie treatisse*. London: J. Cawood.

Fitzherbert, D. (*c*.1608). Bodleian Library MS. e Mus. 169 (Dionys Fitzherbert her Booke); Lambeth Palace Library MS. Sion E47 ('An Anatomy for the poore in spirritt, or, the Case of an afflicted Conscience layd open by example'). [Reprinted in Hodgkin (2010).]

Fletcher, P. (1627). *Locustae*. Cambridge: T. and I. Bucke.

Ford, J. (1997). *'Tis Pity She's a Whore*, edited by D. Roper. Manchester: Manchester University Press.

Ford, J. (2000). *'Tis Pity She's a Whore*, edited by B. Morris. New Mermaids. London: A & C Black.

Forme (1649) [Anon.]. *A Forme of Prayer Used in the King's Chappel upon Tuesdayes in These Times of Trouble & Distresse*. Paris: n. pub.

Fox, G. (1656). *A Declaration of the Difference of the Ministers of the Word*. London: G. Calvert.

Fox, G. (1698). *A Collection of … Epistles*. London: T. Sowle.

Fox, G. ([1952] 1995). *Journal of George Fox* (*c*.1675), edited by J. Nickalls. Philadelphia: Religious Society of Friends.

Fox, G. (1998 [1694]). *The Journal*, edited by N. Smith. London: Penguin.

Fox, G., et al. (1661). *A Declaration from the Harmles & Innocent People of God, called Quakers, against all Plotters and Fighters in the World*. London: R. Wilson.

Foxe, J. (1563). *Acts and Monuments*. London: J. Day. Available at: http://www.johnfoxe.org (*The Unabridged Acts and Monuments Online*: HRI Online Publications, Sheffield, 2011).

Foxe, J. (1570). *Acts and Monuments*. Available at: http://www.johnfoxe.org.

Foxe, J. (1583). *Actes and Monumentes of matters most special and memorable*. 4th edn. London: J. Day.

Foxe, J. ([1583] 2011). *The Unabridged Acts and Monuments Online* or *TAMO* (1583 edition). Available at: http//www.johnfoxe.org.

Foxe, J. (1973a). 'Christus triumphans'. In *Two Latin Comedies by John Foxe the Martyrologist*, edited and translated by J. H. Smith. Ithaca, NY: Cornell University Press.

Foxe, J. (1973b). *Two Latin Comedies by John Foxe the Martyrologist*, edited and translated by J. H. Smith. Ithaca NY: Cornell University Press.

Franklin, B. (1940). *Poor Richard's Almanac*. Boston: Graphic Service Corp.

Fraunce, A. (1588). *The Lawiers Logike, exemplifying the præcepts of logike by the practise of the common lawe*. London: W. How for T. Newman and T. Gubbin.

Freake, E. (1574). *An Introduction to the Love of God*. London: T. Purfoote.

Freeman, T. (1614). *Rubbe, and A great Cast*. London: N. Okes.

Freis, C., R. Freis, and G. Miller (eds) (2012). *George Herbert: Memoriae matris sacrum = To the Memory of my Mother: A Consecrated Gift. A Critical Text, Translation, and Commentary*. George Herbert Journal special studies and monographs. Fairfield, CT: George Herbert Journal.

Fuller, N. (1607). *The argument of Nicholas Fuller of Grays Inne Esquire*. [n. pl.]: [William Jones' secret press].

Fytz, R. (*c.*1571). 'The trewe marks of Christes Church, &c', SP 15/20 f.256, CSP, *Domestic Series, of the Reign of Elizabeth*, Addenda, XX, 107.I.

Gallacher, P. J. (2005). *The Cloud of Unknowing*. Kalamazoo, MI: Medieval Institute Publications.

Gardiner, S. (1968). 'De vera obedientia (1535)'. In *Obedience in Church and State: Three Political Tracts*, edited by P. Janelle. New York, NY: Greenwood Press.

Gardiner, S. R. (ed.) (1889). *The Constitutional Documents of the Puritan Revolution, 1625–1660*. Oxford: Clarendon Press.

Gardner, H. (ed.) (1952, 1978). *John Donne: The Divine Poems*, 2nd edn. Oxford: Clarendon Press.

Garman, M., J. Applegate, M. Benefiel, and D. Meredith (eds) (1996). *Hidden in Plain Sight: Quaker Women's Writings 1650–1700*. Wallingford, PA: Pendle Hill Publications.

Garnet, R. (1649). *The Book of Oaths*. London: W. Lee, M. Walbancke, D. Pakeman, and G. Bedle. [Thomason 164:E.1129[1].]

Gascoigne, G. (2000). *A Hundreth Sundrie Flowres*, edited by G. W. Pigman III. Oxford: Clarendon Press.

Gataker, T. (1646). *Shadowes without substance, or, Pretended New Lights*. London: R. Bostock.

Gee, H., and W. H. Hardy (eds) (1896). *Documents Illustrative of the History of the English Church*. London: Macmillan.

Geneva Bible (1599). *The Bible, That Is, The Holy Scriptures*. London: C. Barker.

Geneva Bible (1969). Facsimile of 1560 edition. Madison, WI: University of Wisconsin Press.

Goodwin, J. (1646a). *Anapologesiates Antapologias, or the inexcusablenesse of that Grand Accusation of the Brethren, called Antapologia*. London: M. Simmons for H. Overton.

Goodwin, J. (1646b). *Cretensis: or A briefe answer to an ulcerous treatise, lately published by Mr Thomas Edvvards, intituled Gangraena*. London: M.S. for H. Overton.

Googe, B. (1989). *Eclogues, Epitaphs and Sonnets*, edited by J. M. Kennedy. Toronto: Toronto University Press.

Gordon, J. (1604). *Enōtikon, or a sermon of the union of Great Brittanie*. London: G. Bishop.

Gordon, J. (1612). *Eirenokoinonia. The peace of the communion of the Church of England. Or, The conformitie of the ceremonies of the communion of the Church of England*. London: N. Butter.

Gotherson, D. (1661). *To all that are Unregenerated: a call to Repentance from dead works, to Newness of life, By turning to the Light in the Conscience, which will give the knowledge of God in the face of Jesus Christ*. London: R. Wilson.

Gouge, W. (1622). *Of Domesticall Duties*. London: J. Haviland for W. Bladen.

Gouge, W. (1631). *The Extent of Gods Providence, set out in a sermon*. In *Gods Three Arrowes*. London: G. Miller for E. Brewster.

Graham, E., H. Hinds, E. Hobby, and H. Wilcox (eds) (1989). *Her Own Life: Autobiographical Writings by Seventeenth-Century Englishwomen*. London: Routledge.

Great king protect us (1628) [Anon.]. *Great king protect us with thy gratious hand, Or else Armenius will o're spred this land*. Amsterdam: H. Laurentz.

Greenbury, C. F. (trans.) (1628). *A Short Relation, of the Life, Virtues, and Miracles of S. Elizabeth*. Brussels: Pepermans.

Greene, R. (1588). *Perimedes the Blacksmith*. London: J. Wolfe for E. White.

Greville, R., Lord Brooke (1641). *A Discourse Opening the Nature of that Episcopacie which is exercised in England*. London: R. C. for S. Cartwright.

Grimald, N. (1925). 'Christus redivivus'. In *The Life and Poems of Nicholas Grimald*, edited by L. R. Merrill. Repr. 1969. New York, NY: Archon.

Grosart, A. B. (ed.) (1872–3). *The Complete Poems of John Donne*. 2 vols. Printed for private circulation. London: Robson and Sons.

Gude and Godlie Ballatis (2015) [Anon.]. *The Gude and Godlie Ballatis (1565)*, edited by A. A. MacDonald for the Scottish Text Society. Woodbridge: The Boydell Press.

Guild, W. (1627). *Popish Glorying in Antiquity*. London: R. Allot.

Guilpin, E. (1974). *Skialetheia or A Shadowe of Truth, in Certain Epigrams and Satyres*, edited by D. A. Carroll. Chapel Hill, NC: University of North Carolina Press.

Gwalther, R. (1546). *Antichristus*. Zurich: C. Froscher the elder. [VD16 W 1065]. Available at: http://www.e-rara.ch.

Gwalther, R. (1556). *Antichrist*. Translated by J. Old. Southwark: C. Truthall [i.e. Emden: Ae. van der Erwe].

Hakluyt, R. (1582). *Divers voyages touching the discoverie of America*. London: T. Woodcock.

Hakluyt, R. (1589). *The Principall Navigations, Voiages and Discoveries of the English nation*. London: G. Bishop and R. Newberie.

Hakluyt, R. (1598, 1903–5). *The principal navigations, voyages, traffiques and discoveries of the English nation*. 12 vols. Glasgow: J. MacLehose and Sons.

Hakluyt, R. (1599–1600). *The Principal Navigations, Voyages, Traffiques and Discoveries of the English Nation … Divided into three severall Volumes, according to the positions of the Regions, whereunto they were directed*. London: G. Bishop, R. Newberie, and R. Barker.

Halkett, A. (MS 6489). 'Expostulation about Prayer, including The Mothers Will to her vnborne child, beeing writ <at Pitfirrane> when I was with child of my deare Betty'. NLS. [*c.*1650–6].

Halkett, A. (MS 6490). 'Ocational Meditations'. NLS. [1658/9–60].

Halkett, A. (MS 6491). 'Ocational Meditations'. NLS. [1660–3].

Halkett, A. (MS 6492). 'Occationall Meditations and Select Contemplations. Instructions to my Son'. NLS. [1668–70/1].

Halkett, A. (MS 6493). 'The Widows Mite, & Occationall Meditations.' NLS.

Halkett, A. (MS 6498). 'Meditations on Exodus and 1 Samuel'. NLS. [1688–9].

Halkett, A. (MS 6500). 'Of Watchfullnese'. NLS. [1693/4–95].

Halkett, A. (MS 6501). 'Select & Occationall Obseruations'. NLS. [1696–7].

Halkett, A. (MS 6502). 'Select and Occationall Meditations'. [1697/8–9].

Hallett, N. (ed.) (2012a). *English Convents in Exile, 1600–1800: Volume 3: Life Writing I.* London: Pickering & Chatto.

Hall, J. (1660). 'Divine Light, and Reflexions. In a Sermon Preacht to his Majesty at White-Hall on Whitsunday 1640'. In *The Shaking of the Olive-Tree*, pp. 33–47. London: J. Cadwel for J. Crooke.

Hall, J. (1969). *The Collected Poems of Joseph Hall, Bishop of Exeter and Norwich*, edited by A. Davenport. Liverpool: Liverpool University Press.

Hamlin, H. (ed.) (2009). *The Sidney Psalter: The Psalms of Sir Philip and Mary Sidney.* Oxford: Oxford University Press.

Hamor, R. (1615). *A true discourse of the present state of Virginia.* London: W. Welby.

Hampton, C. (1611). *A sermon preached in the cittie of Glasco in Scotland, on the tenth day of Iune, 1610: At the holding of a generall assembly there.* London: T. S[nodham].

Harington, J. (2009). *The Epigrams of Sir John Harington*, edited by G. Kilroy. Farnham: Ashgate.

Hariot, T. (1590). *A briefe and true report of the new found land of Virginia.* Frankfurt: J. Wechel for T. de Bry.

Harris, B. (1679). *The Protestant Tutor.* London: for B. Harris.

Hart, C. (ed.) (1998). *Disputatio nova contra mulieres = A new argument against women: a critical translation from the Latin with commentary, together with the original Latin text of 1595.* Lewiston, NY: Edwin Mellon Press.

Harvey, C. (1647). *Schola Cordis [The School of the Heart].* London: H. Blunden.

Hastings, F. (1600). *An Apology and Defence of the Watchword.* London: F. Kingston for R. Jackson. [*STC* 12928.]

Hayes, A. (1723). *A Legacy, or Widow's Mite, left by Alice Hayes to Her Children and others. With an account of some of her dying sayings.* London: J. Sowle.

Healy, T. (ed.) (1969). *John Donne: Ignatius His Conclave.* Oxford: Clarendon Press.

Henderson, A., and A. Johnston (1638). *A Confession of Faith of the Kirk of Scotland.* Edinburgh: G. Anderson.

Henry VIII, King (1532). *A glasse of the truth.* London: T. Berthelet.

Henry VIII, King (1533). *Articles devised by the holle consent of the kynges moste honourable counsayl.* London: T. Berthelet.

Henry VIII, King (1536). *Articles devised by the kynges highnes maiestie, to stablyshe christen quietnes and unitie amonge us, and to auoyde contentious opinions.* London: T. Berthelet. [The Ten Articles.]

Henry VIII, King (1543). *A necessary doctrine and erudicion for any christen man set furth by the kynges maiestye of Englande. &c.* London: T. Berthelet. [Modern edition: *The King's Book; or, A Necessary Doctrine and Erudition for Any Christian Man*, edited by T. A. Lacey. Oxford: Clarendon Press.]

Henry VIII, King (1992). *Heinrich VIII: Assertio septem sacramentorum*, edited by P. Fraenkel. Corpus Catholicorum 43. Münster: Aschendorf.

Herbert, G. (1941). *The Works of George Herbert*, edited by F. E. Hutchinson. Oxford: Oxford University Press.

Herbert, G. (1959). *A Priest to the Temple, or The Country Parson*. In *Works of George Herbert*, edited by F. E. Hutchinson (1st edn 1941). Oxford: Clarendon Press.

Herbert, G. (2007). *The English Poems of George Herbert*, edited by H. Wilcox. Cambridge: Cambridge University Press.

Herbert, T. (1634). *A Relation of Some Yeares Travaile*. London: W. Stansy and J. Bloom.

Heylyn, P. (1636). *A coale from the Altar*. London: A. Mathewes.

Hicks, T. (1657). *A discourse of the souls of men, women, and children*. London: T. Newcomb.

Higginson, F. (1653). *A Brief Relation of the Irreligion of the Northern Quakers*. London: T. R.

Hinds, H. (ed.) (2000). *The Cry of a Stone, by Anna Trapnel*. Tempe, AZ: CMRS.

Hobbes, T. (1655, 1981). *De Corpore*, translated by A. P. Martinich. New York, NY: Abaris Books.

Hobbes, T. (1994). *Human Nature and De Corpore Politico*, edited by J. C. A. Gaskin. Oxford: Oxford University Press.

Hodgkin, K. (ed.) (2010). *Women, Madness and Sin in Early Modern England: The Autobiographical Writings of Dionys Fitzherbert*. Farnham: Ashgate.

Holland, C. (1664). 'Narration'. [Extracts in Booy (2002).]

Hooker, R. (1593). *Of the Lawes of Ecclesiasticall Politie*. London: J. Windet.

Hooker, R. (1989, 2013). *Of the Laws of Ecclesiastical Polity*, edited by A. S. McGrade. Cambridge: Cambridge University Press.

Hozjusz, S. (1565). *A Most Excellent Treatise of the begynnynge of heresyes in oure tyme*, translated by R. Shacklock. Antwerp: A. Diest.

Hudson, A. (ed.) (1997). *Selections from English Wycliffite Writings*. Toronto: University of Toronto Press.

Huggarde, M. (1556). *The displaying of the Protestantes*. London: R. Caly.

Huggarde, M. (1557). *A New A,B,C*. [London: R. Caley.]

Huit, E. (1643). *The whole Prophecie of Daniel explained, By a Paraphrase, Analysis and briefe Comment*. London: H. Overton.

Humphrey, L. (1588). *A View of the Romish Hydra and Monster*. Oxford: J. Barnes.

Hunter, T. (n.d.). 'The Life of Mary Xaveria of the Angels'. [Catherine Burton] in Douai Abbey, Reading.

Hutchinson, L. (n.d.). *Nottinghamshire Archives*. Literary commonplace book DD/HU1; Religious commonplace book, DD/HU3 (Microfilm Z 2244).

Hutchinson, L. (1817). *On the Principles of the Christian Religion, Addressed to her Daughter; and On Theology*. London: Longman, Hurst, Rees, Orme & Brown.

Hutchinson, L. (1906). *Memoirs of the Life of Colonel Hutchinson*, edited by C. H. Firth. London: G. Routledge.

Hutchinson, L. (1973). *Memoirs of the Life of Colonel Hutchinson*, edited by J. Sutherland. London: Oxford University Press.

Hutchinson, L. (1996). *Lucy Hutchinson's Translation of Lucretius: De rerum natura*, edited by H. de Quehen. London: Duckworth.

Hutchinson, L. (2000). *Memoirs of the Life of Colonel Hutchinson*, edited by N. H. Keeble. London: Phoenix Press [J. M. Dent, 1995]. [Contains 'The Life of Mrs Lucy Hutchinson, Written by Herself: A Fragment'; 'To My Children'; 'The Life of John Hutchinson of Owthorpe, in the County of Nottingham, Esquire'; 'Final Meditation', and 'Verses Written by Mrs Hutchinson'.]

Hutchinson, L. (2001). *Order and Disorder*, edited by D. Norbrook. Oxford: Blackwell.

Hutchinson, L. (2011). *The Works of Lucy Hutchinson: Volume I: The Translation of Lucretius*, edited by R. Barbour and D. Norbrook. Oxford: Oxford University Press.

Hutchinson, L. (2012). *The Works of Lucy Hutchinson Volume I, Parts 1 and 2*, edited by R. Barbour and D. Norbrook. Oxford: Oxford University Press.

Hutchinson, T. (1765). *The History of the Colony of Massachuset's Bay*. London: M. Richardson.

Hutton, H. (1619). *Follie's Anatomie*. London: M. Walbanke.

Ingram, A. (ed.) (1997). *Voices of Madness: Four Pamphlets, 1683–1796*. Stroud: Sutton Publishing.

Innocent VIII, Pope (1486). *Our holy fadre the Pope Innocent.viij*. London: W. de Machlinia.

Institution (1537). *The institution of a christen man, conteynynge the exposytion of the commune crede, of the seven sacramentes, of the .x. commandementes, and of the Pater noster, and the Aue Maria, iustyfication and purgatory*. London: T. Berthelet. [The Bishops' Book.]

Isham, E. (c.1639). *My Booke of Rememberance*. Princeton University Library, Robert Taylor Collection MS. RTC01, no. 62.

Isham, E. (2008). *My Booke of Rememberance*, edited by E. Longfellow and E. Clarke. Available at: http://web.warwick.ac.uk/english/perdita/Isham/index_bor.htm.

James VI. (1599). *Basilikon Doron*. Edinburgh: R. Walde-grave.

Jessey, H. (1647). *The Exceeding Riches of Grace advanced by the spirit of grace, in an empty nothing creature, viz. Mris. Sarah Wight*. London: M. Simmons for H. Overton and H. Allen.

Jewel, J. (1562). *Apologia ecclesiæ anglicanæ*. London: R. Wolfe.

Jewel, J. (1845). *The Works of John Jewel*, edited by Rev. J. Ayre for the Parker Society. Cambridge: Cambridge University Press.

John of the Cross, St. (1906, repr. 1928). *The Ascent Of Mount Carmel*, translated by D. Lewis. London and Aylesbury: T. Baker.

John of the Cross, St. (1943). *The Complete Works of Saint John of the Cross*, translated by P. S. de Santa Teresa, edited by E. A. Peers, vol. I. London: Burns Oates.

Johnson, S. (1925). *Lives of the English Poets*. 2 vols. London: J. M. Dent & Sons.

Jones, R. T., et al. (eds) (2006), *Protestant Nonconformist Texts*, vol. 1. Aldershot: Ashgate.

Jonson, B. (1977). *Bartholomew Fair*, edited by G. R. Hibbard. London: A & C Black; New York, NY: W. W. Norton.

Jonson, B. (1981). *The Complete Plays of Ben Jonson*, edited by G. A. Wilkes. Oxford: Clarendon Press.

Jonson, B. (1988). *The Complete Poems*, edited by G. Parfitt. Harmondsworth: Penguin.

Joye, G. (1545). *The exposicion of Daniel*. [Antwerp]: the successor of A. Gonius.

Julian of Norwich, Dame. (1670). *XVI Revelations of Divine Love Shewed to a Devout Servant of Ouyr Lord Called Mother Juliana, an Anchorete of Norwich Who Lived in the Dayes of King Edward the Third*. London: Cressy.

Kempis, Thomas à. (1952). *The Imitation of Christ*, edited and translated by L. Sherley-Price. Harmondsworth: Penguin.

Kendall, T. (1577). *Flowers of Epigrammes*. London: J. Kingston.

Kenyon, J. P. (ed.) (1986). *The Stuart Constitution: Documents and Commentary*. 2nd edn. Cambridge: Cambridge University Press.

Kerssenbrock, H. von (2007). *Narrative of the Anabaptist Madness*, edited and translated by C. S. Mackay. Leiden: Brill.

Kiffin, W., et al. (1644). *Confession of Faith of those Churches which are commonly (though falsly) called Anabaptists*. London: M. Simmons.

Kingdomes Monster (1643) [Anon.]. *The Kingdomes Monster Uncloaked*. London: n. pub.

Kirby, T. (ed.) (2009). 'The *Articles of Religion* of the Church of England (1563/71) commonly called the Thirty-Nine Articles', Latin and English versions together with an introduction and annotations. In *Die Bekenntnisschriften der reformierten Kirchen*, vol. II, edited by K. H. Faulenbach, pp. 371–410. Neukirchen-Vluyn: Neukirchener Verlag.

Klene, J. (ed.) (1996). *The Southwell-Sibthorpe Commonplace Book*. Tempe, AZ: MRTS.

Knatchbull, L. (1642). 'The relation of the holy and happy life and death of the Ladye Lucie Knatchbull'. MS of the Canonesses of the Holy Sepulchre, Colchester (box D1).

Lahey, S., F. Somerset, and P. J. Hornbeck II (eds and trans.) (2013). *Wycliffite Spirituality*. New York, NY: Paulist Press.

L., I. (1590). *A true and perfecte description of a straunge monstar*. London: J. Wolfe for W. Dight, to be sold by W. Wright.

L[inch]. S. (1660). *Three sermons viz. Davids tears for his rebellious son Absalom*. London: T. C. and L. P. for R. Crofts.

L'Estrange, R. (1681). *An Account of the Growth of Knavery, under the Pretended Fears of Arbitrary Government and Popery*. 2nd edn. London: T. B. for H. Brome.

Langbaine, G. (1641). *Episcopall inheritance. Or, a reply to the Humble Examination of a Printed Abstract*. Oxford: L. Lichfield.

Lanseter, J. (1646). *Lanseter's Lance for Edwards'es Gangrene: or, A ripping up, and laying open some rotten, putrified, corrupt, stinking matter*. London: n. pub.

Lanyer, A. (1993). *The Poems of Aemilia Lanyer: Salve Deus Rex Judaeorum*, edited by S. Woods. New York, NY: Oxford University Press.

Larkin, J. F., and P. L. Hughes (eds) (1973). *Stuart Royal Proclamations*. 2 vols. Oxford: Oxford University Press.

Larking, L. B. (ed.) (1862). *Proceedings, Principally in the County of Kent, in connection with the Parliaments called in 1640, and especially with the Committee of Religion appointed in that Year*. [Camden Society, vol. 80.] London: Camden Society.

Las Casas, B. de (1992). *A short account of the destruction of the Indies*, translated by A. Pagden. London: Penguin.

Latham, R., and W. Matthews (1970). *The Diary of Samuel Pepys*. 11 vols. London: G. Bell and Sons.

Latimer, H. (1845). *Works*, edited by G. E. Corrie for The Parker Society, 28 (2). Cambridge: Cambridge University Press.

Laud, W. (1625). *A sermon preached on Munday, the sixt of February, At Westminster, at the opening of parliament*. London: B. Norton.

Leibniz, G. W., et al. (1997). *Leibniz's 'New System' and Associated Contemporary Texts*, edited and translated by R. S. Woolhouse and R. Francks. Oxford: Clarendon Press.

Leslie, C. (1696). *The Snake in the Grass*. London: C. Brome.

Letters and Papers, Foreign and Domestic, Henry VIII, edited by J. Gairdner, vol. 12, part 2, no. 620, *British History Online*. Available at: http://www.history.ac.uk/projects/digital/british-history-online.

Lindsay, D. (1621). *A true narration of all the passages of the proceedings in the generall Assembly of the Church of Scotland, holden at Perth the 25. of August, anno Dom. 1618*. London: W. Stansby.

Limon, J., and D. J. Vitkus (eds) (2007). 'Sir Robert Sherley his Entertainment in Cracovia' (1609). In *Thomas Middleton: The Collected Works*, edited by G. Taylor and J. Lavagnino, pp. 670–8. Oxford: Clarendon Press.

Lithgow, W. (1614). *A Most Delectable and Trve Discourse, of an admired and painefull peregrination from* Scotland, *to the most famous Kingdomes in* Europe, *'Asia' and 'Affricke'.* London: N. Okes.

Locke, A. V. (1999). *The Collected Works,* edited by S. M. Felch. Tempe, AZ: RETS.

Locke, J. (1997). *Locke: Political Essays,* edited by M. Goldie. Cambridge: Cambridge University Press.

Loe, W. (1621). *Vox clamantis. Mark 1. 3 A stil voice, to the three thrice-honourable estates of Parliament.* London: T. S. for J. Teage.

Lok, A. (1560). *A Meditation of a Penitent Sinner,* appended to *Sermons of John Calvin, upon the Songe that Ezekias made.* London: J. Day.

London Gazette. 13–16 June 1670 (No. 478).

London: PRO (1910). *Letters and Papers, Foreign and Domestic,* Henry VIII, Volume 21, Part 2: September 1546–January 1547, edited by J. Gairdner and R. H. Brodie.

López de Gómara, F. (1964). *Cortés: the life of the conqueror, by his secretary,* translated by L. B. Simpson. Berkeley, CA: University of California Press.

Luther, M. (1966). *'Luther's Works, vol. 8: Lectures on Genesis Chapters 45–50,* edited by J. Pelikan. St Louis, MO: Concordia Publishing House.

Lux-Sterritt, L. (ed.) (2012). *English Convents in Exile, 1600–1800: Volume 2: Spirituality.* London: Pickering & Chatto.

Lyly, J. (1589). *Pappe with an Hatchet.* London: J. Anoke and J. Astile, for the Baylive of Withernam.

Lyly, J. (1902) *The Complete Works of John Lyly,* edited by R. W. Bond. Oxford: Clarendon Press.

Machiavelli, N. (1999). *The Prince,* translated by G. Bull. London: Penguin.

Machyn, H. (1848). *The Diary of Henry Machyn, Citizen and Merchant-taylor of London, from A.D. 1550 to A.D. 1563,* edited by J. G. Nichols. Camden Society 1st series, vol. 42. London: Camden Society.

Major, P. (ed.) (2010). *Literatures of Exile in the English Revolution and its Aftermath, 1640–1690.* Aldershot: Ashgate.

Mar (1589) [Anon.]. *Mar-Martine.* London: n. pub.

Marlowe, C. (1993). *Doctor Faustus, A and B Texts,* edited by D. Bevington and E. Rasmussen. The Revels Plays. Manchester: Manchester University Press.

Marlowe, C. (1995). *Doctor Faustus and Other Plays,* edited by D. Bevington and E. Rasmussen. Oxford: Oxford University Press.

Marlowe, C. (1999). *The Complete Plays,* edited by M. T. Burnett. London: J. M. Dent.

Marlowe, C. (2006). *The Collected Poems of Christopher Marlowe,* edited by P. Cheney and B. J. Striar. Oxford: Oxford University Press.

Marnix, P. (1636). *The Beehive of the Romish Church.* London: M. Dawson.

Marot, C., and T. de Bèze (1986). *Les Pseaumes en Vers Français avec leurs melodies,* introduced by P. Pidoux. Facsimile of the Genevan Psalter published by M. Blanchier, 1562. Geneva: Textes Littéraires Français.

Marotti, A. F. (ed.) (2009). *The Early Modern Englishwoman: A Facsimile Library of Essential Works, Series II: Printed Writings, 1641–1700: Part 4: Volume 3: Gertrude More.* Farnham: Ashgate.

Marre Mar (1589) [Anon.]. *Marre Mar-Martin, or Marre-Martins medling, in a manner misliked.* London: T. Orwin.

Marsiglio of Padua (1535). *The defence of peace: lately translated out of laten.* London: R. Wyer.

Marston, J. (1961). *The Poems of John Marston*, edited by A. Davenport. Liverpool: Liverpool University Press.

Martin, L. C. (ed.) (1957). *The Poems: English, Latin and Greek of Richard Crashaw.* Oxford: Clarendon Press.

Martyn, J. (1621). *New epigrams.* London: G. Eld.

Marvell, A. (1677 [1678]). *An Account of the Growth of Popery and Arbitrary Government.* Amsterdam: n. pub. [London: printed at Amsterdam.]

Marvell, A. (1971). *Poems and Letters*, edited by H. M. Margoliouth. 2 vols. 3rd edn. Oxford: Clarendon Press.

Marvell, A. (1978). *Andrew Marvell: The Complete Poems*, edited by E. S. Donno. Harmondsworth: Penguin.

Masham, D. (1696). *A Discourse Concerning the Love of God.* London: for A. and J. Churchil.

Massinger, P. (1976). *The Plays and Poems of Philip Massinger*, vol. III, edited by P. Edwards and C. Gibson. Oxford: Clarendon Press.

Massinger, P. (2010). *The Renegado*, edited by M. Neill. Arden Early Modern Drama. London: A & C Black.

Matar, N. (ed.) (2014). *Henry Stubbe and the Beginnings of Islam: The Originall & Progress of Mahometanism.* New York, NY: Columbia University Press.

Mather, C. (1967). *Magnalia Christi Americana; or, the ecclesiastical history of New England.* New York, NY: Russell and Russell.

Matthew, T. (trans.) (1620). *The Confessions of the incomparable doctour S. Augustine, translated into English.* St Omer: English College Press. [2nd edn. Paris, 1638.]

Matthew, T. (trans.) (1642). *The Flaming Hart or the Life of the Glorious S. Teresa.* Antwerp: I. Meursius.

May, E. (1633). *Epigrams Divine and Morall.* London: J. Grove.

May, S. W., and A. Bryson (eds) (2016). *Verse Libel in Renaissance England and Scotland.* Oxford: Oxford University Press.

Mayor, J. E. B. (ed.) (1855). *Nicholas Ferrar. Two Lives by his Brother John and by Doctor Jebb.* Cambridge: Cambridge University Press.

McCullough, P. E. (ed.) (2005). *Lancelot Andrewes: Selected Sermons and Lectures.* Oxford: Oxford University Press.

McGrade, A. S. (ed.) (1989). *Hooker: Of the Laws of Ecclesiastical Polity.* Cambridge: Cambridge University Press.

Meads, D. M. (ed.) (1930). *The Diary of Lady Margaret Hoby, 1599–1605.* London: Routledge.

Meiderlin, P. (1626). *Paraenesis votiva pro pace ecclesiae ad theologos Augustanae.* Rottenburg.

Melanchthon, P. (1537). *The Apology of the Augsburg Confession.* Available at: http://bookofconcord.org/augsburgdefense.php.

Melanchthon, P. (1579). *Of two vvoonderful popish monsters … Translated out of French into English by Iohn Brooke of Assh, next Sandwich.* London: T. East.

Melanchthon, P. (1988). *A Melanchthon Reader*, translated by R. Keen. New York: Lang.

Middleton, T. (1609). *Sir Robert Sherley, Sent Ambassadour in the Name of the King of Persia, … With His Pretended Comming into England.* London: J. Budge.

Middleton, T. (2007). *The Collected Works*, gen. eds G. Taylor and J. Lavagnino. Oxford: Oxford University Press.

Middleton, T., and W. Rowley (2006). *The Changeling*, edited by M. Neill. New Mermaids. London: Bloomsbury.

Miller, J. (1655). *Anti Christ in Man the Quakers Idol.* London: J. Macock.

Milton, J. (1644). *Areopagitica: a speech of Mr. John Milton for the liberty of vnlicens'd printing, to the Parlament of England*. London: n. pub.

Milton, J. (1645). *The Poems of Mr. John Milton, both English and Latin, compos'd at several times*. London: R. Raworth for H. Moseley.

Milton, J. (1953–82). *The Complete Prose Works of John Milton*, edited by D. M. Wolfe et al. 8 vols. New Haven, CT: Yale University Press.

Milton, J. (1957). *Complete Poems and Major Prose*, edited by M. Y. Hughes. Indianapolis, IN: Odyssey Press.

Milton, J. (1962a). *Complete Prose Works of John Milton*. Volume 3, edited by M. Y. Hughes. New Haven, CT: Yale University Press.

Milton, J. (1962b). *Paradise Lost*, edited by M. Y. Hughes. New York, NY: Odyssey Press.

Milton, J. (1980). *Complete Prose Works of John Milton*. Volume 7 (rev. edn), edited by R. W. Ayers. New Haven, CT: Yale University Press.

Milton, J. (2008). *John Milton: Complete Poetry and Essential Prose*, edited by W. Kerrigan, J. Rumrich, and S. M. Fallon. New York, NY: Random House.

Moore-Smith, G. C. (ed.) (1928). *The Letters of Dorothy Osborne to William Temple*. Oxford: Clarendon Press.

More, G. (1657). *The Holy Practises of a Devine Lover*. Paris: L. de la Fosse.

More, G. (1658). *The Spiritval Exercises of the Most Vertvovs and Religious D. Gertrude More of the holy order of S. Bennet*. Paris: L. de la Folle.

More, G. (2009). *The Early Modern Englishwoman: A Facsimile Library of Essential Works. Series II, Printed Writings, 1641–1700, Part 4, Volume 3: Gertrude More*, edited by A. F. Marotti. Farnham: Ashgate.

More, H. (1647, 1969). *Philosophical Poems*. Menston: Scholar Press.

More, H. (1651). *Alazonomastix Philalethes [i.e. Henry More], The Second Lash of Alazonomastix*. Cambridge: the printers to the university.

More, H. (1659). *The Immortality of the Soul*. London: J. Flesher for W. Morden [bookseller in Cambridge].

More, H. (1662, 1978). *A Collection of Several Philosophical Writings*. 2 vols. New York, NY: Garland.

More, H. (1968a). 'An Antidote against Atheism'. In *The Cambridge Platonists*, edited by G. R. Cragg, pp. 163–93. New York, NY: Oxford University Press.

More, H. (1968b). 'A Brief Discourse of the True Grounds of the Certainty of Faith in Points of Religion'. In *The Cambridge Platonists*, edited by G. R. Cragg, pp. 141–50. New York, NY: Oxford University Press.

More, H. (1968c). 'Of Free Will'. In *The Cambridge Platonists*, edited by G. R. Cragg, pp. 300–5. New York, NY: Oxford University Press.

More, H. (1987). *The Immortality of the Soul* [1659], edited by A. Jacob. Dordrecht: Martinus Nijhoff.

More, T. ('Rosseus, Gulielmus') (1523). *Opus elegans, quo refellit Lutheri calumnias quibus Angliae regem Henricium octavium insectatur*. London: R. Pynson.

More, T. (1529). *A Dialogue [Concerning Heresies]*. London: J. Rastell.

More, T. (1532). *The confutacyon of Tyndales answere*. London: W. Rastell.

More, T. (1903). *The Four Last Things*, edited by D. O'Connor. London: Art & Book Company.

More, T. (1963–85). *The Complete Works of St. Thomas More*, edited by R. Sylvester, et al. 15 vols. New Haven, CT: Yale University Press.

More, T. (1965a). *The Complete Works of St. Thomas More*. Volume IV, edited by E. Surtz, S. J. and J. H. Hexter. New Haven, CT: Yale University Press.

More, T. (1965b). *Utopia*, translated by P. Turner. Harmondsworth: Penguin.

More, T. (1969). *The Complete Works of St. Thomas More*. Volume V, pt 1, edited by J. M. Headley. New Haven, CT: Yale University Press.

More, T. (1973). *The Complete Works of St. Thomas More*. Volume VIII, pt 2, edited by L. A. Schuster, R. C. Marius, J. P. Lusardi, and R. J. Schoeck. New Haven, CT: Yale University Press.

More, T. (1976). *The Complete Works of St. Thomas More*. Volume XII, edited by L. L. Martz and F. Manley. New Haven, CT: Yale University Press.

More, T. (1981a). *The Complete Works of St. Thomas More*. Volume VI pt 1, edited by T. M. C. Lawler, G. Marc'hadour, and R. C. Marius. New Haven, CT: Yale University Press.

More, T. (1981b). *A Dialogue Concerning Heresies*, edited by T. M. C. Lawler, G. Marc'hadour, and R. C. Marius. New Haven, CT: Yale University Press.

More, T. (1990a). *The Complete Works of St. Thomas More*. Volume VII, edited by F. Manley, G. Marc'hadour, R. C. Marius, and C. H. Miller. New Haven, CT: Yale University Press.

More, T. (1990b). *The Complete Works of St. Thomas More*. Volume VIII pt 1, edited by L. A. Schuster, R. C. Marius, J. P. Lusardi, and R. J. Schoeck. New Haven, CT: Yale University Press.

More, T. (1997). *The Complete Works of St. Thomas More*. Volume I, edited by A. S. G. Edwards, K. G. Rodgers, and C. H. Miller. New Haven, CT: Yale University Press.

Morgan, E. D., and C. H. Coote (eds) (1886). *Early Voyages and Travels to Russia and Persia by Anthony Jenkinson and Other Englishmen*. 2 vols. London: Hakluyt Society.

Morrice, R. (2007–9). *The Entring Book of Roger Morrice*, gen. ed. Mark Goldie. 7 vols. Woodbridge: Boydell Press.

Mors, R. (1542a, 1542b). See Brinklow, H. (1542a, 1542b).

Nashe, T. (1592). *Pierce Penilesse: his supplication to the diuell. Barbaria grandis habere nihil*. London: A. Jeffes for J. Busbie.

Nashe, T. (1594). *The Unfortunate Traveller. Or, The life of Iacke Wilton Newly corrected and augmented*. London: T. Scarlet for C. Burby.

Nashe, T. (1904). *Works*. Volume 1, edited by R. B. McKerrow. London: Sidgwick and Jackson.

Nashe, T. (1987). 'The Unfortunate Traveller'. In *An Anthology of Elizabethan Prose Fiction*, edited by P. Salzman, pp. 205–310. The World's Classics. Oxford: Oxford University Press.

National Library of Scotland MS.Wod.Qu.XXVII.

Nayler, J. (1716). *A Collection of Sundry Books, Epistles and Papers Written by James Nayler*. London: J Sowle.

Nelson, T. (1590). *A memorable epitaph, made vpon the lamentable complaint of the people of England, for the death of the right honorable Sir Frauncis Walsingham Knight*. [London]: W. Wright.

Nelson, T. (1591). *The blessed state of England. Declaring the Sundrie Dangers which by Gods assistance, the Queenes most excellent Maiestie hath escaped in the whole course of her life*. [London]: W. Wright.

Nenna, G. B. (1595). *Nennio, or A Treatise of Nobility … Done into English by William Jones Gent*. London: P. Short.

Nichols, J. G. (ed.) (1859). *Narratives of the Days of the Reformation, Chiefly from the Manuscripts of John Foxe the Martyrologist*. Camden Society, o.s. 77. London: Camden Society.

Nicholson, H. W. (ed.) (1843). *The Remains of Edmund Grindal*. Cambridge: Parker Society.

Niclaes, H. (1575). *Evangelium regni*. Cologne: N. Bohmberg.

Norris, J. (1693). *Practical discourses upon several divine subjects*. London: S. Manship.

Norton, T. (1570). *A Disclosing of the great Bull*. London: J. Day.

Norwood, R. (*c*.1639, 1998). 'Confessions'. In *John Bunyan: Grace Abounding, with Other Spiritual Autobiographies*, edited by J. Stachniewski and A. Pacheco, pp. 123–56. Oxford: Oxford University Press.

Novum Testamentum Gracae (2013). 28th edn. Stuttgart: Deutsche Bibelgesellschaft.

O'Donovan, O., and J. L. O'Donovan (eds) (1999). *From Irenaeus to Grotius: A Sourcebook in Christian Political Thought*. Grand Rapids, MI: Eerdmans.

Obituary Notices (1917). *Obituary Notices of the Nuns of the English Benedictine Abbey of Ghent in Flanders 1627–1811, contributed by Lady Abbess and Community*. Catholic Record Society, Misc. XI, Vol. 19.

Of those Churches (1644) [Anon.]. *The Confession of faith of those Churches which are commonly (though falsely) called ANABAPTISTS*. London: M. Simmons.

Ogilvie-Thompson, S. J. (ed.) (1986). *Walter Hilton's Mixed Life, Edited from Lambeth Palace MS 472*. Salzburg: Salzburg Studies in English Literature: Elizabethan and Renaissance Studies.

Orosius, P. (1936). *Seven books of history against the pagans*, translated by I. W. Raymond. New York, NY: Columbia University Press.

Osborn, J. (ed.) (1961, 1962). *The Autobiography of Thomas Whythorne*. Oxford: Oxford University Press.

Osborne, D. (1928). *The Letters of Dorothy Osborne to William Temple*, edited by G. C. Moore-Smith. Oxford: Clarendon Press.

Overton, R. (1645). *Mans mortallitie or a treatise wherein 'tis proved, both theologically and philosophically, that whole man (as a rationall creature) is a compound wholy mortall, contrary to the common distinction of soule and body*. London: n. pub.

Ovid Moralisé (1915 [*c*.1316–28]) [Anon.]. *L'Ovide Moralisé: poème du commencement du quatorzième siècle*, edited by C. de Boer et al. Amsterdam: Müller.

Owen, J. (1619). *Epigrams of that most wittie and worthie epigrammatist Mr. Iohn Owen, Gentleman. Translated by Iohn Vicars*. London: W. S. for I. Smethwicke.

Owen, J. (1657). *Of communion with God the Father, Sonne, and Holy Ghost*. London: A. Lichfield for P. Stevens.

Oxford, University of (1603). *The Answere of the Vicechancelour, the Doctors, both the Proctors, and other Heads of Houses in the Vniversitie of Oxford*. Oxford: J. Barnes.

Paget, J. (1618). *An Arrow Against the Separation of the Brownists*. Amsterdam: G. Veseler.

Pagitt, E. (1645). *Heresiography: or, A description of the heretickes and sectaries of these latter times*. London: M. Okes for R. Trot.

Palfreyman, T. (1560). *A Myrrour Conteinying the True Knowledge and Love of God*. London: H. Sutton.

Palmer, J. (2001). *The 'Centuries' of Julia Palmer*, edited by V. Burke and E. Clarke. Nottingham: Nottingham Trent University Press.

Parkhurst, J. (1573). *Ludicra*. London: I. Dayum [i.e. J. Day].

Parr, A. (ed.) (1995). *The Travels of the Three English Brothers*, by J. Day, W. Rowley, and G. Wilkins (1607). In *Three Renaissance Travel Plays*, edited by A. Parr, pp. 55–134. Manchester: Manchester University Press.

Parr, C. (1545). *Prayers ... Meditacions*. London: T. Berthelet.

Parr, K. [or C.] (2011). *The Complete Works and Correspondence of Katherine Parr*, edited by J. Mueller. Chicago, IL: University of Chicago Press.

Parrot, H. (1626). *Cures for the Itch*. London: T. Jones.

Pasture, A. (ed.) (1930). 'Documents concernant quelques monastères anglais aux Pays-Bas au XVIIe siècle'. *Bulletin de l'institut historique Belge de Rome* 10: 155–223.

Patrides, C. A. (ed.) (1985). *The Complete English Poems of John Donne*. London: Everyman.

Paul of St Ubald (1654). *The Soul's Delight*. Antwerp: W. Lesteems.

Pearson, A. H. (trans.) (1884). *The Sarum Missal, done into English*. London: Church Printing.

Peel, A. (ed.) (1915). *The seconde part of a register*. 2 vols. Cambridge: Cambridge University Press.

Penington, I. (1661). *Concerning Persecution*. London: R. Wilson.

Penington, M. (*c.*1680, 1821). *Some Account of Circumstances in the life of Mary Penington, from her manuscript left for her family*. London: Harvey and Darton.

Penn, W. (1687). *Good Advice to the Church of England*. London: A. Sowle.

Penn, W. (1688). *The Great and Popular Objection against the Repeal of the Penal Laws*. London: A. Sowle.

Penn, W. (1993). 'The People's Ancient and Just Liberties Asserted'. In '*The Peace of Europe*', '*The Fruits of Solitude*' *and Other Writings*, edited by E. B. Bronner, pp. 135–52. London: J. M. Dent.

Penrose, B. (1938). *The Sherleian Odyssey: Being a Record of the Travels and Adventures of the Three Famous Brothers during the Reigns of Elizabeth, James I, and Charles I*. Taunton: The Wessex Press.

Pepys, S. (2000). *The Diary of Samuel Pepys*, edited by R. Latham and W. Matthews. 11 vols. London: HarperCollins.

Percy, W. (2006). *William Percy's 'Mahomet and His Heaven': A Critical Edition*, edited by M. Dimmock. Aldershot: Ashgate.

Perkins, W. (1591). *The foundation of Christian religion*. London: T. Orwin for J. Porter.

Perkins, W. (1595). *A Salve for a Sicke Man*. Cambridge: J. Legate.

Perkins, W. (1597). *A Golden Chaine, or The Description of Theologie, containing the order of the causes of Salvation and Damnation, according to Gods word*. London: J. Legate.

Perkins, W. (1600). *A Golden Chaine*. Cambridge: J. Legate.

Perkins, W. (1607). *The arte of prophecying*, translated by T. Tuke. London: F. Kyngston for E. E.

Perkins, W. (1608). *A godly and learned exposition of Christs sermon in the mount*. Cambridge: T. Brooke and C. Legge.

Perrin, J.-P. (1624). *Luthers Fore-runners: or a Cloud of Witnesses*. London: N. Newbery.

Pinke, M. (1636). *The Triall of a Christians Sincere Love unto Christ*. Oxford: L. Lichfield for E. Forrest.

Pisan, C. de (1489). *Here begynneth the table of the rubryshys of the boke of the fayt of arms and of chyualrye*. Westminster: W. Caxton.

Pitts, J. (1731). *A Faithful Account of the Religion and Manners of the Mahometans*. London: J. Osborn and T. Longman.

Pitts, J. (2012). *A Faithful Account* [1731], edited by P. Auchterlonie [re-titled *Encountering Islam*]. London: Arabian Publishing.

Pole, R. (1538). *Ad Henricum Octavum Britanniae Regem, pro ecclesiasticae unitatis defensione, libri quatuor*. Rome: A. Bladus, 1538. Engl. transl. in *Pole's Defense of the Unity of the Church*, edited by J. E. Dwyer. Westminster, MD: The Newman Press.

Pollard, A. W. (ed.) (1911). *Records of the English Bible: the documents relating to the translation and publication of the Bible in English, 1525–1611*. London: H. Frowde.

Popham, E. (1619). *A Looking-glasse for the Soule, and a Definition thereof*. London: T. S. for N. Newbery.

Powell, E. (1523). *Propugnaculum summi sacerdotii evangelici, ac septenarii sacramentorum … adversus Martinum Lutherum fratrem famosum et Wiclefistam insignem*. London: R. Pynson.

Powel, G. (1605). *Refutation of an epistle apologeticall written by a puritan-papist*. London: A. Hatfield for T. Man Junior.

Powell, V. (1653). *Spirituall Experiences, of Sundry Beleevers*. London: R. Ibbitson.

Preston, T. (1570). *Cambyses*. London: J. Allde. [*STC* 20287.]

Pricket, R. (1607). *The Jesuits Miracles or New Popish Wonders*. London: C. P. and R. J.

Prideaux, J. (1655). *Euchologia: or, The doctrine of practical praying*. London: for R. Marriot.

Proctor, J. (1549). *The Fall of the Late Arrian*. London: W. Powell. [*STC* 20406.]

Proctor, J. (1554). *History of Wyatt's Rebellion*. London: R. Caly. [*STC* 20407.]

Prynne, W. (1633). *Histrio-Mastix: The Players Scourge, or, Actors Tragaedie*. London: M. Sparke.

Prynne, W. (1637). *A Quench-Coale. Or A briefe disquisition and inquirie, in vvhat place of the church or chancell the Lords-table ought to be situated, especially vvhen the Sacrament is administered*. [Amsterdam]: [Richt Right press].

Prynne, W. (1645a). *A fresh discovery of some prodigious new wandring-blasing-stars, & fire-brands, stiling themselves nevv-lights, firing our church and state into new combustions*. London: J. Macock for M. Sparke senior.

Prynne, W. (1645b). *Truth Triumphing over Falsehood: antiquity over novelty. Or, The first part of a just and seasonable vindication*. London: J. Dawson for M. Sparke senior.

Prynne, W. (1656). *A Short Demurrer to the Jewes*. London: for E. Thomas.

Pulter, H. (2014). *Poems, Emblems, and The Unfortunate Florinda*, edited by A. Eardley. Toronto: Centre for Reformation and Renaissance Studies.

Puttenham, G. (1936). *The Arte of English Poesie* (London, 1589), edited by G. D. Willcock and A. Walker. Cambridge: Cambridge University Press.

Puttenham, G. (2007). *The Art of English Poesy*, edited by F. Whigham and W. A. Rebhorn. Ithaca, NY: Cornell University Press.

Quarles, F. (1639). *Emblemes*. London: I. D. for F. Eglesfeild [sic].

Rabelais, F. et al. (1594). *Satyre Ménippée*. Tours: J. Mettayer.

Ralegh, W. (1898). *The discoverie of the large, rich, and beautiful empire of Guiana*, edited by R. H. Schomburgk. London: The Hakluyt Society.

Ranters Monster (1652) [Anon.]. *The Ranters Monster*. London: G. Horton.

Raspa, A. (ed.) (1975). *John Donne, Devotions upon Emergent Occasions*. Montreal: McGill-Queen's University Press.

Raspa, A. (ed.) (1993). *John Donne, Pseudo-Martyr*. Montreal: McGill-Queen's University Press.

Raspa, A. (ed.) (2001). *John Donne, Essayes in Divinity*. Montreal: McGill-Queen's University Press.

Reeve, J., and L. Muggleton (1658). *Joyful News from Heaven: Or, The Last Intelligence from our Glorified Jesus above the Stars*. London: T. J. for F. Cosinet.

Reformatio legum ecclesiasticarum (1571) [Anon.]. London: J. Day.

Rhodes, N., G. Kendal, and L. Wilson (eds) (2013). *English Renaissance Translation Theory*. MHRA Tudor & Stuart Translations Volume 9. London: Modern Humanities Research Association.

Rich, M. (1672). 'Some Specialties in the Life of M. Warwicke'. BL Add. MS. 27357. Transcript by T. C. Croker (1848), *Autobiography of Mary Rich Countess of Warwick*. London: Percy Society Reprints 22.

Ringler, W. A., Jr, and M. Flachmann (eds) (1988). *Beware the Cat by William Baldwin: The First English Novel*. San Marino, CA: Huntington Library.

Robbins, R. (ed.) (2010). *The Complete Poems of John Donne*. Rev. edn. Harlow: Longman.

Roberts, J. A. (ed.) (1983). *The Poems of Lady Mary Wroth*. Baton Rouge, LA: Louisiana State University Press.

Robinson, H. (ed.) (1842–5), *Zurich Letters [Original letters relative to the English Reformation ... chiefly from the archives of Zurich]*. 1st series. Parker Society. Cambridge: Cambridge University Press.

Rochester, Earl of [Wilmot, J.] (1968). *Complete Poems*, edited by D. Veith. New Haven, CT: Yale University Press.

Rodriguez, A. (1627). *A Treatise of Mentall Prayer, With Another of the Presence of God*, translated by T. Matthew. St Omer: English College Press.

Rogers, J. (1650). *A Godly and Fruitful Exposition upon the First Epistle of Peter*. London: J. Field for P. Cole.

Rogers, J. (1653). *Ohel or Beth-Shemesh. A Tabernacle for the Sun*. London: R. I. and G. & H. Eversclen.

Rolle, R. (1506). *Rycharde Rolle hermyte of Hampull in his contemplacyons of the drede and love of God*. London: W. de Worde.

Romes ABC (1641) [Anon.]. London: n. pub.

Rosseus, G. (1523). See More, T. (1523).

Rouen Chronicles of the Poor Clare Sisters (n.d.). MS of the Poor Clares. Much Birch, Herefordshire.

Rous, F. (1635). *The mysticall marriage*. London: W. I. and T. P. for I. Emery.

Rowlandson, M. (1977). *A true history of the captivity and restoration of Mrs. Mary Rowlandson*. New York, NY: Garland.

Roy, W. (1589). *O Read me for I am of great Antiquitie*. London: n. pub. ['Printed either of this side, or of that side of some of the priestes'.]

Rycaut, P. (1680). *The History of the Turkish Empire*. London: J. Starkey.

Rythmes against Martin Marre-Prelate (1589) [Anon.]. London: T. Orwin. [See also *Whip* (1589).]

Sales, F. de (1616). *An Introduction to a Deuout Life, Leading to the Way of Eternitie*, translated by J. Yakesley. London: N. Okes.

Salgādo, G. (ed.) (1972). *Cony-Catchers and Bawdy Baskets: An Anthology of Elizabethan Low Life*. Harmondsworth: Penguin.

Samuel, W. (1559). *The Love of God*. London: n. pub.

Sargent, M. (ed.) (2005). *Nicholas Love, The Mirror of the Blessed Life of Jesus Christ: A Full Critical Edition*. Exeter: Exeter University Press.

Scot, P. (1622). *Calderwoods recantation: or, A tripartite discourse: Directed to such of the ministerie, and others in Scotland, that refuse conformitie to the ordinances of the church*. London: B. Alsop.

Scot, P. (1625). *Vox vera: or, Obseruations from Amsterdam: Examining the late insolencies of some pseudo-puritans, separatists from the Church of Great Brittaine*. London: B. Alsop.

Scotland, Army/Parliament (1640). *The intentions of the army of the kingdome of Scotland, declared to their brethren of England*. Edinburgh: R. Bryson.

Scudder, H. (1627). *The Christians daily walke in holy securitie and peace*. London: I. D. for W. Sheffard.

Second Treatise (n.d.). *Second Treatise, The Man of Prayer Or instructions for mental prayer according to the three states of a spiritual life*. MS of the Carmelite monastery, Towson, Maryland. [Available in microfilm from the Maryland State Archives (MSA SC 5366–B5–F9).]

Selden, J. (1689). *Table-talk*. London: E. Smith.

Semler, L. (ed.) (2001). *Eliza's Babes: or The Virgin's Offering (1652): A Critical Edition*. Madison, NJ: Fairleigh Dickinson University Press.

Seneca (1925). *Ad Lucilium Epistulae Morales*. Volume I, translated by R. M. Gunmere. 3 vols. London: Heinemann.

Shakespeare, W. (1965; repr. 1997). *Measure for Measure*, edited by J. W. Lever. Arden Shakespeare. Walton-on-Thames: Nelson.

Shakespeare, W. (1974). *The Riverside Shakespeare*, edited by G. B. Evans. Boston, MA: Houghton Mifflin.

Shakespeare, W. (1997a). *The Norton Shakespeare*, edited by S. Greenblatt et al. New York, NY: W. W. Norton.

Shakespeare, W. (1997b). *The Complete Works of Shakespeare*, edited by D. Bevington. New York, NY: Longman.

Shakespeare, W. (1998). *The Arden Shakespeare Complete Works*, edited by R. Proudfoot, A. Thompson, and D. S. Kastan. Walton-on-Thames: Nelson.

Shakespeare, W. (1999). *The Tempest*, edited by V. M. Vaughan and A. T. Vaughan. Walton-on-Thames: Nelson.

Shakespeare, W. (2002). *The Oxford Shakespeare: The Complete Sonnets and Poems*, edited by C. Burrow. Oxford: Oxford University Press.

Sharland, E. C. (ed.) (1899). *The Story Books of Little Gidding*. New York, NY: Dutton.

Shepherd, L. (2001). *Luke Shepherds Satires*, edited by J. Devereux. Tempe, AZ: MRTS.

Sheppard, S. (1651). *Epigrams theological, philosophical, and romantick*. London: T. Bucknell.

Shirley, E. (n.d.). 'The Life of our Reverent Ould Mother Margrit Clement'. From a transcript of MS at the convent of The Blessed Lady of Nazareth, Bruges, Belgium.

'Short Colections' (n.d.). 'Short Colections of the beginings of our English monastery of Teresians in Antwerp with some few perticulars of our dear deceased religious'. Antwerp city archives, MS KK 1018.

Shuger, D. K. (ed.) (2012). *Religion in Early Stuart England, 1603–38: An Anthology of Primary Sources*. Waco, TX: Baylor University Press.

Sidney Herbert, M. (1998). *The Collected Works of Mary Sidney Herbert, Countess of Pembroke*, edited by M. P. Hannay, N. Kinnamon, and M. Brennan. 2 vols. Oxford: Clarendon Press.

Sidney, P. (1962). *The Poems of Sir Philip Sidney*, edited by W. J. Ringler, Jr. Oxford: Clarendon Press.

Sidney, P. (1965). *An Apology for Poetry*, edited by G. Shepherd. Edinburgh: Nelson.

Sidney, P. (1987 [1973]). *The Countess of Pembroke's Arcadia* (The New Arcadia [The Old Arcadia]), edited by V. Skretkowicz. Oxford: Clarendon Press.

Sidney, P. (2012). *The Correspondence of Sir Philip Sidney*, 2 vols. edited by R. Kuin. Oxford: Clarendon Press.

Sidney, P. and M. (2009). *The Sidney Psalter*, edited by H. Hamlin, M. G. Brennan, M. P. Hannay, and N. Kinnamon. Oxford: Oxford World's Classics.

Sidney, P. et al. (2004). *Sidney's 'Defence of Poesy' and Selected Renaissance Literary Criticism*, edited by G. Alexander. London: Penguin.

Simpson, E. M. (ed.) (1930). *The Courtier's Library, or Catalogus librorum aulicorum in comparabilium et non vendibilium*. London: The Nonesuch Press.

Sixtus V, Pope (1588). *A Declaration of the Sentence and Deposition of Elizabeth, the Usurper and Pretensed Quene of Englande*. n.pl.: n.pub.

Smart, J. S. (ed.) (1966). *The Sonnets of Milton* [repr. 1921]. Oxford: Clarendon Press.

Smith, H. (1593). *The Trumpet of the Soule, sounding to judgement*. London: for the widdow Perrin.

Smith, J. (1986). *The Complete Works of Captain John Smith*, edited by P. L. Barbour. Chapel Hill, NC: University of North Carolina Press.

Smith, N. (ed.) (2014). *A Collection of Ranter Writings*. London: Pluto Press.

Southwell, R. (1591). *Marie Magdalens funeral teares*. London: G. Cawood. [*STC* 332:02.]

Southwell, R. (1597). *A shorte rule of good life*. London: V. Simmes.

Southwell, R. (1967). *The Poems of Robert Southwell*, edited by J. H. McDonald and N. Pollard. Oxford: Clarendon Press.

Sparke, T. (1607). *A brotherly persvvasion to vnitie, and vniformitie in iudgement, and practise touching the receiued, and present ecclesiasticall gouernment, and the authorised rites and ceremonies of the Church of England*. London: N. Okes.

Spencer, T. (1977). 'The genealogie, life and death of the Right Honorable Robert Lorde Brooke'. *Miscellany I*, edited by R. Bearman. Dugdale Society, 31.

Spenser, E. (1909). *The Faerie Queene*, edited by J. C. Smith. Repr. 1961. 2 vols. Oxford: Clarendon Press.

Spenser, E. (1977). *The Faerie Queene*, edited by A. C. Hamilton. London: Longman.

Spenser, E. (1981). *The Faerie Queene*, edited by T. P. Roche, Jr. New Haven, CT: Yale University Press.

Spenser, E. (1989). *The Yale Edition of the Shorter Poems of Edmund Spenser*, edited by W. A. Oram, E. Bjorvand, R. Bond, T. H. Cainn, A. Dunlop, and R. Schell. New Haven, CT: Yale University Press.

Spenser, E. (1999). *The Shorter Poems*, edited by R. McCabe. London: Penguin Books.

Sprat, T. (1667). *History of the Royal Society*. London.

Stachniewski, J., and A. Pacheco (eds) (1998). *John Bunyan: Grace Abounding, with Other Spiritual Autobiographies*. Oxford: Oxford University Press.

Standish, J. (1632). *All the French Psalm Tunes with English Words*. London: T. Harper, 'with permission of the Company of Stationers'.

Staphylus, F. (1565). *Apologie*, translated by T. Stapleton. Antwerp: J. Latius.

Sterry, P. (1683). *The Rise, Race, and Royalty of the Kingdom of God in the Soul of Man*. London: T. Cockerill.

Stirredge, E. (1711). *Strength in Weakness Manifest: in the Life, Various Trials, and Christian Testimony of that faithful Servant and Handmaid of the Lord ...* London: J. Sowle.

Storer, T. (1599). *The Life and Death of Thomas Wolsey*. London: V. Simms for T. Dawson. [*STC* 23294.]

Story, J. (1683). *The Memory of that Servant of God, John Story, Revived*. London: J. Gain.

Stringer, G. A., and P. A. Parrish (eds) (2005). *The Variorum Edition of the Poetry of John Donne, Volume 7, Part 1: The Holy Sonnets*. Bloomington, IN: Indiana University Press.

Strype, J. (1710). *The history of the life and acts of the most reverend father in God, Edmund Grindal*. London: J. Hartley.

Strype, J. (1721). *Ecclesiastical memorials; relating chiefly to religion, and the reformation of it, and the emergencies of the Church of England, under King Henry VIII. King Edward VI. and Queen Mary the First*. 3 vols. London: J. Wyat.

Sturm, J. (1574). *De imitatio oratoria libri tres*. Strasbourg.

Sullivan, E. W., II (ed.) (1984). *John Donne, Biathanatos*. Newark, DE: University of Delaware Press.

Sutcliffe, M. (1629). 'Will of Doctor Matthew Sutcliffe, Professor of Divinity and Doctor of Law, Dean of the Cathedral Church of Saint Peter Oxford, Oxfordshire'. Kew, Surrey: The National Archives, PRO, PROB 11/156, fols 270^v–272^r.

Sutton, C. (1600). *Disce Mori. Learn to Die*. London: I. Wolfe.

Swift, J. (1985). *Gulliver's Travels*, edited by P. Dixon and J. Chalker. London: Penguin.

Sym, J. (1637). *Lifes preservative against self-killing*. London: M. Flesher.

Symonds, W. (1609). *Virginea [Virginea Brittania]. A sermon preached at White-Chappel*. London: I. Windet for E. Edgar and W. Welby.

Tacitus (1894). *The Agricola and Germania*, translated by R. B. Townsend. Aberdeen: Aberdeen University Press.

Tallis, T. (1992). *A Tallis Anthology*, edited by J. Milsom. Oxford: Oxford University Press.

Taylor, E. (1939). *The Poetic Works of Edward Taylor*, edited by T. H. Johnson. New York, NY: Rockland Editions.

Taylor, J. (1641). *A Swarme of Sectaries, and Schismatiques*. London: n. pub. ['Printed luckily, and may be read unhappily, betwixt hawke and buzzard'.]

Taylor, J. (1651). *Epigrammes*. London: n. pub.

Taylor, J. (1989). *Holy Living* and *Holy Dying*, edited by P. G. Stanwood. 2 vols. Oxford: Clarendon Press.

Teresa of Avila (1944–6). *The Complete Works of St Teresa*, edited by E. A. Peers. London: Sheed & Ward. Volume I: *The Life; The Spiritual Relations* (1944); Volume II: *Book Called Way of Perfection; Interior Castle; Conceptions of the Love of God; Exclamations of the Soul to God* (1946); Volume III: *Book of the Foundations; Minor Prose Works; Poems* (1946).

The Bible (1576). *The Bible. That Is, The Holy Scriptures*. London: Christopher Barker.

The Bible (1599). *The Bible. That Is, The Holy Scriptures*. London: Christopher Barker.

The Bible in English (1996). Ann Arbor, MI: Chadwyck-Healey.

The Book of Common Prayer (2011). *The Book of Common Prayer: The Texts of 1549, 1559, and 1662*, edited by B. Cummings. Oxford: Oxford University Press.

The forme and maner of makyng and consecratyng of archebishoppes, bishoppes, priestes and deacons (1549) [Anon.]. [London]: R. Grafton.

The Geneva Bible: A Facsimile of the 1560 Edition (2007). Peabody, MA: Hendrickson.

The Holy Bible Quatercentenary Edition (2011). Oxford: Oxford University Press.

The humble petition of diverse wel-affected weomen of the cities of London and Westminster, the borrough of Southwark, hamblets, and places adjacent. Affecters and approvers of the petition of Sept. 11. 1648 (1649). London: n. pub.

The lineage of Locusts (1641) [Anon.]. London: n. pub.

The New Testament of Jesus Christ (1582). Rheims: J. Fogny.

The prerogative of man: or, The immortality of humane soules asserted against the vain cavils of a late worthlesse pamphlet, entituled, Mans mortality, &c. (1645) [Anon.]. Oxford: H. Hall.

The Restauration of the Jews: Or, A true Relation of Their Progress and Proceedings in order to the regaining of their Ancient Kingdom Being of the Substance of several LETTERS Viz. from ANT-WERP, LEGORN, FLORENCE, etc. (1665) [Anon.]. London: A. Maxwell.

Tichborne, J. (1609). *A triple antidote, against certaine very common scandals of this time*. London: N. Okes.

Timson, J. (1656). *The Quakers apostasie from the perfect rule of the scriptures*. London: T. Williams and W. Tomson.

Torshell, S. (1632). *The three questions of free justification. Christian liberty. The use of the Law Explicated in a briefe comment on St. Paul to the Galatians, from the 16. ver. of the second chapter, to the 26. of the third*. London: I. B. for H. Overton.

Traherne, T. (2005–14). *The Works of Thomas Traherne*, edited by J. Ross. 6 vols. Cambridge: D. S. Brewer.

Trapnel, A. (1654a). *Anna Trapnel's Report and Plea. Or, a narrative of her journey from London into Cornwal, etc.* London: Thomas Brewster.

Trapnel, A. (1654b). *The Cry of a Stone, or a vision of something spoken in Whitehall by Anna Trapnel, being in the visions of God.* London: n. pub.

Trapnel, A. (1654c). *A Legacy for Saints; Being Several Experiences of the dealings of God with Anna Trapnel.* London: T. Brewster.

Trapnel, A. (2000). *The Cry of a Stone*, edited by H. Hinds. Tempe, AZ: CMRS.

Trappes-Lomax, R. (ed.) (1922). *The English Franciscan Nuns 1619–1821 and the Friars Minor of the Same Province, 1618–1761.* London: Catholic Record Society.

Travers, R. ([1659?]). *Of that Eternal Breath.* London: n. pub.

Trill, S. (ed.) (2007). *Lady Anne Halkett: Selected Self-Writings.* Aldershot: Ashgate.

Trosse, G. (1714). *The Life of the Reverend Mr George Trosse.* Exon [Exeter]: J. Bliss for R. White. [A. W. Brink (ed.) (1974). Montreal: McGill-Queen's University Press.]

Tuke, T. (1613). *A Discourse of Death, Bodily, Ghostly, and Eternall, etc.* London: W. Stansbie.

Tunstall, C. (1539). *A sermon … made vpon Palme sondaye laste past, before the maiestie of our souerayne lorde kyng Henry the. VIII.* London: T. Berthelet.

Turner, J. (1653). *Choice Experiences of the kind dealings of God before, in, and after Conversion: Laid down in six general Heads.* London: H. Hils.

Tyndale, W. (trans.) (1526). *The newe Testament.* Worms: Schöffer.

Tyndale, W. (1528). *The Obedie[n]ce of A Christian Man.* Antwerp: J. Hoochstraten.

Tyndale, W. (1989). *Tyndale's New Testament*, edited by D. Daniell. New Haven, CT: Yale University Press.

Tyndale, W. (2000). *The Obedience of a Christian Man*, edited by D. Daniell. Harmondsworth: Penguin.

Tyrwhit, E. (2008). *Elizabeth Tyrwhit's Morning and Evening Prayers*, edited by S. M. Felch. Aldershot: Ashgate.

Underhill, E. B. (ed.) (1847). *The Records of a Church of Christ: Meeting in Broadmead, Bristol.* London: Hanserd Knollys Society.

Underhill, T. (1660). *Hell Broke Loose.* London: S. Miller.

Underwood, T. L. (ed.) (1999). *The Acts of the Witnesses: The Autobiography of Lodowick Muggleton and Other Early Muggletonian Writings.* Oxford: Oxford University Press.

Upchereinge or Pierce the ploughmans crede (1553) [Anon.]. London: R. Wolfe.

Vadianus (1534). See Watt, J. von (1534).

Valla, L. (1534). *A treatyse of the donation or gyfte and endowment of possessions, gyuen and graunted vnto Syluester pope of Rhome, by Constantyne.* London: T. Godfray.

Van Dixhoorn, C., M. A. Garcia, J. A. Halcomb, and I. Jones (eds) (2012). *The Minutes and Papers of the Westminster Assembly, 1643–1652.* 5 vols. Oxford: Oxford University Press.

Vaughan, H. (1650). *Silex Scintillans.* London: T. W. for H. Blunden.

Vaughan, H. (1957a). *Poetry and Selected Prose of Henry Vaughan*, edited by L. C. Martin. Oxford: Clarendon Press.

Vaughan, H. (1957b). *The Works of Henry Vaughan (Second Edition)*, edited by L. C. Martin. Oxford: Oxford Scholarly Editions Online. Available at: http://www.oxfordscholarlyeditions.com.

Vaughan, H. (1963). *Poetry and Selected Prose*, edited by L. C. Martin. Oxford Standard Authors. London: Oxford University Press.

Vaughan, H. (1976). *The Complete Poems*, edited by A. Rudrum. Harmondsworth: Penguin.

Vaughan, T. (1650). *Anthroposophia theomagica*. London: T. W. for H. Blunden.

Vicars, J. (1643). *Behold Romes monster on his monstrous beast!* London: W. Peake.

Villa Sancta, A. de (1523a). *De libero arbitrio adversus Melanchtonem*. London: R. Pynson.

Villa Sancta, A. de (1523b). *Problema indulgentiarum, quo Lutheri errata dissolvuntur, et theologorum de eisdem opinio hactenus apud eruditos vulgata astruitur*. London: R. Pynson.

Virgil (1983). *Aeneid*, translated by R. Fitzgerald. New York, NY: Random House.

Vitkus, D. (ed.) (2000). *Three Turk Plays from Early Modern England*. New York, NY: Columbia University Press.

Vives, J. L. (1913). *Vives: On Education. A Translation of 'De Tradendis Disciplinis' of Juan Luis Vives*, translation and introduction by F. Watson. Cambridge: Cambridge University Press.

Vives, J. L. (1987). *Selected Works of J. L. Vives, Volume I: Early Writings—De initiis Sectis et Laudibus Philosophiae, Veritas Fucata, Anima Senis, Pompeius Fugiens*, edited by C. Matheeussen, C. Fantazzi, and E. George. Leiden: E. J. Brill.

Vokins, J. (1691). *God's Mighty Power Magnified: as manifested and revealed in his faithful handmaid, Joan Vokins*. London: T. Northcott.

Wade, C. (1657). *Quakery Slain*. London: 'printed for the author'.

Wadsworth, J. (1630). *The English Spanish Pilgrime. Or, A New Discoverie of Spanish Popery, and Iesviticall Stratagems*. London: T. C. for M. Sparke.

Wager, L. (1968). *The Longer Thou Livest* and *Enough is as Good as a Feast*, edited by R. M. Benbow. London: Arnold.

Waller, E. (1893). *The Poems of Edmund Waller*, edited by G. Thorn-Drury. London: Routledge.

Walton, I. (1640). 'The Life and Death of Dr *Donne*, Late Deane of St Pauls London'. In *John Donne: LXXX Sermons*, sigs A5ʳ–C1ʳ. London: M. Fletcher for R. Royston and R. Marriot.

Walton, I. (1927). *The Lives of John Donne, Sir Henry Wotton, Richard Hooker, George Herbert and Robert Sanderson* (1670), edited by G. Saintsbury. London: Oxford University Press.

Watson, N. and J. Jenkins (eds) (2006). *The Writings of Julian of Norwich: A Vision Showed to a Devout Woman and a Revelation of Love*. University Park, PA: Pennsylvania State University Press.

Watson, S. (1695). *An Epistle by Way of Testimony … Mary Moss*. London: T. Northcott.

Watson, S. (1712). *A Short Account of the Convincement … Samuel Watson*. London: J. Sowle.

Watson, T. (1660). *The Beatitudes: or A Discourse upon part of Christs famous Sermon on the Mount*. London: R. Smith.

Watt, J. von (Vadianus) (1534). *A worke entytled of ye olde god and the newe*. London: J. Byddell.

Webbe, G. (1624). *Catalogus Protestantium: or, the Protestants kalender*. London: N. Butter.

Webster, J. (2008). *The White Devil*, edited by C. Luckyj. Methuen Drama. London: Bloomsbury.

Webster, J. (2009). *The Duchess of Malfi*, edited by L. Marcus. Arden Early Modern Drama. London: Bloomsbury.

Weld, T., R. Prideaux, S. Hammond, W. Cole, and W. Durant (1654). *The Perfect Pharise* [sic]. London: R. Tomlins.

Wentworth, A. (1677). *The Vindication of Anne Wentworth*. London: n. pub.

Whichcote, B. (1968). 'Moral and Religious Aphorisms'. In *The Cambridge Platonists*, edited by G. R. Cragg, pp. 421–60. New York, NY: Oxford University Press.

Whitby, D. (1697). *A Discourse of the Love of God*. London: A. and J. Churchill.

White, D. [D. W.] (1660). *A Lamentation unto this Nation*. London: R. Wilson.

White, D. [D. W.] (1661). *An Epistle of Love, and of Consolation*. London: R. Wilson.

White, D. [D. W.] (1662a). *A Trumpet of the Lord of Hosts*. [London?]: n. pub.

White, D. [D. W.] (1662b). *An Alarum Sounded forth … unto England's Rulers.* London: n. pub.

White, D. [D. W.] ([1662?]c). *Friends, you that are of the Parliament.* London: n. pub.

White, J. (1643). *The First Century of Scandalous, Malignant Priests.* London: G. Miller.

Whiteman, A. (ed.) (1986). *The Compton Census of 1676: A Critical Edition.* London: The British Academy.

Whitgift, J. (1589). *A most godly and learned sermon preached at Pauls crosse the 17 of November, in the yeare of our Lorde, 1583* [25th anniversary of Elizabeth's accession]. London: T. Orwin.

Whitgift, J. (1851–3). *The Works of John Whitgift,* edited by J. Ayre for the Parker Society series no. 48, 3 vols. Cambridge: Cambridge University Press.

Whiting, J. (1714/15). *Persecution Expos'd.* London: J. Sowle.

Whip (1589) [Anon.]. *A Whip for an Ape: or Martin displaied.* London: T. Orwin. [Also printed in the same year under the title *Rythmes against Martin Marre-Prelate.*]

Whythorne, T. (*c.*1576). *A book of songs and sonetts, with longe discoorses sett with them.* Bodleian MS Eng. Misc. C. 330.

Whythorne, T. (1961, 1962 modern spelling edition). *The Autobiography of Thomas Whythorne,* edited by J. Osborn. Oxford: Oxford University Press.

Wigglesworth, M. (1989). *The Poems of Michael Wigglesworth,* edited by R. A. Boscoe. Lanham, MD: University Press of America.

Wilcox, H. (ed.) (2007). *The English Poems of George Herbert.* Cambridge: Cambridge University Press.

Wildridge, T. (ed.) (1886). *The Hull Letters printed from a Collection of Original Documents found among the Borough Archives in the Town Hall, Hull, 1884.* Hull: Wildridge and Company.

Wilinsky, M. (1952). 'Four English Pamphlets on the Sabbatian Movement' [Hebrew]. *Zion* 17: 156–72.

Wilkinson, H. (1656/7). *The Hope of Glory or Christs Indwelling in True Believers … March 5. 1656. At the Funerall of That Eminently-Religious-Gentlewoman Mris Margaret Corbet.* Oxford: A. Lichfield.

Wilkinson, W. (1579). *A confutation of certaine articles delivered unto the Familye of Love.* London: J. Day.

Willet, A. (1592). *Synopsis Papismi.* London: T. Orwin for T. Man.

Wilson, T. (1612). *A Christian Dictionarie.* London: W. Jaggard.

Winstanley, G. (1652). *The Law of Freedom.* London: G. Calvert.

Winstanley, G. (2009). *The Complete Works of Gerrard Winstanley,* edited by T. N. Corns, A. Hughes, and D. Loewenstein. Volume 2. 2 vols. Oxford: Oxford University Press.

Winstanley, W. (1669). *The Protestant Almanack.* Cambridge: n. pub.

Winthrop, J. (1943). *The Winthrop Papers, 1623–1630,* edited by A. B. Forbes. Boston, MA: Massachusetts Historical Society.

Wright, R. (1631). *Articles to be ministred, enquired of, and answered: in the fourth visitation of the Right Reverend father in God, Robert, by Gods divine providence, Lord Bishop of Bristol.* London: J. M. for W. Garret.

Wright, T. ([1604], 1986). *The Passions of the Mind in General,* edited by T. A. Sloan. Urbana, IL: University of Illinois Press.

Wroth, M. (1983). *The Poems of Lady Mary Wroth,* edited by J. A. Roberts. Baton Rouge, LA: Louisiana State University Press.

XXXVI Several Religions Held And maintained by the Cavaliers (1645) [Anon.]. [Also known as *The Cavaliers Bible.*] London: J. Coe.

B. Secondary Texts (History, Literary Criticism, Theology)

Acheson, R. (1983). 'The Development of Religious Separatism in the Diocese of Canterbury, 1590–1660'. PhD thesis, University of Kent.

Achinstein, S. (2001). 'John Foxe and the Jews'. *Renaissance Quarterly* 54: 86–120.

Achinstein, S. (2002). 'Romance of the Spirit: Female Sexuality and Religious Desire in Early Modern England'. *ELH* 69: 413–38.

Achinstein, S., and E. Sauer (eds) (2007). *Milton and Toleration*. Oxford: Oxford University Press.

Adams, S. L. (1973). 'The Protestant Cause: Religious Alliance with the West European Calvinist Communities as a Political Issue in England, 1585–1630'. Unpublished DPhil. thesis, University of Oxford.

Adcock, R. (2011). 'Daughters of Zion and Mothers in Israel: The Writings of Separatists and Particular Baptist Women, 1632–1675'. Unpublished doctoral thesis, Loughborough University.

Adcock, R. (2015). *Baptist Women's Writings in Revolutionary Culture, 1640–1680*. Farnham: Ashgate.

Adelman, J. (2008). *Blood Relations: Christian and Jew in 'The Merchant of Venice'*. Chicago, IL: University of Chicago Press.

Adlington, H. (2003). 'Preaching the Holy Ghost: John Donne's Whitsunday Sermons'. *John Donne Journal* 22: 203–28.

Akbari, S. C. (2009). *Idols in the East: European Representations of Islam and the Orient, 1110–1450*. Ithaca, NY: Cornell University Press.

Alexander, G. (2006). *Writing after Sidney: The Literary Response to Sir Philip Sidney 1586–1640*. Oxford: Oxford University Press.

Allan, D. (2009). '"The Divine Fury of the Muses": Neo-Latin Poetry in Early Modern Scotland'. In *Literature and the Scottish Reformation*, edited by C. Gribben and D. G. Mullen, pp. 63–78. Aldershot: Ashgate.

Allen, R. C. (2013). 'Restoration Quakerism, 1660–1691'. In *The Oxford Handbook of Quaker Studies*, edited by S. W. Angell and P. Dandelion, pp. 29–46. Oxford: Oxford University Press.

Allinson, R. (2012). *A Monarchy of Letters: Royal Correspondence and English Diplomacy in the Reign of Elizabeth I*. New York, NY: Palgrave Macmillan.

Allison, A. F. (1955). 'Franciscan Books in English, 1559–1640'. *Biographical Studies, 1534–1829* 3 (1): 16–65.

Alonso, J. M. (1979). 'Erasmi Corpus Mariologicum (I)'. *Marian Library Studies* 11: 19–271.

Amussen, S. D. (1988). *An Ordered Society: Gender and Class in Early Modern England*. Oxford: Blackwell.

Anderson, B. (2006). *Imagined Communities: Reflections on the Origin and Spread of Nationalism*. Rev. edn. London: Verso.

Anderson, D. K. (2014). *Martyrs and Players in Early Modern England: Tragedy, Religion and Violence on Stage*. Aldershot: Ashgate.

Anderson, S. P. (1989). *An English Consul in Turkey: Paul Rycaut at Smyrna, 1667–1678*. Oxford: Oxford University Press.

Andrea, B. (2007). *Women and Islam in Early Modern English Literature*. Cambridge: Cambridge University Press.

Andrea, B. (2010). 'Persia, Tartaria, and Pamphilia: Ideas of Asia in Mary Wroth's *The Countess of Montgomery's Urania, Part II*'. In *The English Renaissance, Orientalism, and the Idea of Asia*, edited by D. Johanyak and Walter S. H. Lim, pp. 23–50. New York, NY: Palgrave Macmillan.

Andrea, B. (2011a). 'Elizabeth I and Persian Exchanges'. In *The Foreign Relations of Elizabeth I*, edited by Charles Beem, pp. 169–99. New York, NY: Palgrave Macmillan.

Andrea, B. (2011b). 'The Tartar King's Masque and Performances of Imperial Desire in Mary Wroth's *The Countess of Montgomery's Urania*'. In *Early Modern England and Islamic Worlds*, edited by B. Andrea and L. McJannet, pp. 73–95. New York, NY: Palgrave Macmillan.

Andrea, B. (2012). *English Women Staging Islam, 1696–1707: Delariver Manley and Mary Pix*. Toronto: ITER & Centre for Reformation and Renaissance Studies.

Andrea, B. (2015). 'The "Presences of Women" from the Islamic World in Sixteenth- to Early Seventeenth-Century British Literature and Culture'. In *Mapping Gendered Routes and Spaces in the Early Modern World*, edited by M. E. Wiesner-Hanks, pp. 291–306. Farnham: Ashgate.

Andrea, B. (2016a). 'Amazons, Turks, and Tartars in the *Gesta Grayorum* and *The Comedy of Errors*'. In *The Oxford Handbook of Shakespeare and Embodiment: Gender, Sexuality, Race*, edited by V. Traub, pp. 77–92. Oxford: Oxford University Press.

Andrea, B. (2016b). ' "Travelling Bodye": Native Women of the Northeast and Northwest Passage Ventures and English Dscourses of Empire'. In *Rethinking Feminism in Early Modern Studies*, edited by A. Loomba and M. E. Sanchez, pp. 135–48. Aldershot: Ashgate.

Andrea, B. (2017). *The Lives of Girls and Women from the Islamic World in Early Modern British Literature and Culture*. Toronto: University of Toronto Press.

Andrews, K. R. (1984). *Trade, Plunder and Settlement: Maritime Enterprise and the Genesis of the British Empire, 1480–1630*. Cambridge: Cambridge University Press.

Angell, S. W. (2012). 'William Penn's Debts to John Owen and Moses Amyraut on Questions of Truth, Grace, and Religious Toleration'. *Quaker Studies* 16 (2): 157–73.

Anglican Consultative Council (1988). *The Truth shall make you free*. London: Anglican Consultative Council.

Anselment, R. A. (1979). *'Betwixt Jest and Earnest': Marprelate, Milton, Marvell, Swift, and the Decorum of Religious Ridicule*. Toronto: Toronto University Press.

Appleby, D. A. (2007). *Black Bartholomew's Day: Preaching, Polemic and Restoration Nonconformity*. Manchester: Manchester University Press.

Aravamudan, S. (2012). *Enlightenment Orientalism: Resisting the Rise of the Novel*. Chicago, IL: University of Chicago Press.

Archer, I. W. (2011). 'Religious Identities'. In *Thomas Middleton in Context*, edited by S. Gossett, pp. 135–43. Cambridge: Cambridge University Press.

Archer, J. M. (2001). *Old Worlds: Egypt, Southwest Asia, India, and Russia in Early Modern English Writing*. Stanford, CA: Stanford University Press.

Ardolino, F. (1995). *Apocalypse and Armada in Kyd's Spanish Tragedy*. Kirksville, MO: Sixteenth Century Journal Publishers.

Arkell, T., N. Evans, and N. Goose (eds) (2000). *When Death Do Us Part: Understanding and Interpreting the Probate Records of Early Modern England*. Oxford: Leopard's Head Press.

Armstrong, C. A. J. (1983). 'The Piety of Cecily, Duchess of York: A Study in Late Medieval Culture'. In *England, France and Burgundy in the Fifteenth-Century*, pp. 135–56. London: Hambledon Press.

Armstrong, K. (2011). 'Sermons in Performance'. In *The Oxford Handbook of the Early Modern Sermon*, edited by P. McCullough, H. Adlington and E. Rhatigan, pp. 120–36. Oxford: Oxford University Press.

Arnold, J. (2005). *Belief and Unbelief in Medieval Europe*. London: Bloomsbury.

Arthur, K. (2011). '"You Will Say They Are Persian But Let Them Be Changed": Robert and Teresa Sherley's Embassy to the Court of James'. In *Britain and the Muslim World: Historical Perspectives*, edited by G. MacLean, pp. 37–51. Newcastle upon Tyne: Cambridge Scholars Publishing.

Asch, R. (2011). 'Sacred Kingship in France and England in the Age of the Wars of Religion: From Disenchantment to Re-enchantment?' In *England's Wars of Religion, Revisited*, edited by C. W. A. Prior and G. Burgess, pp. 27–48. Farnham: Ashgate.

Ashton, R. (1994). *Counter Revolution: The Second Civil War and its Origins, 1646–8*. London: Yale University Press.

Aston, M. (1996). 'Puritans and Iconoclasm, 1560–1660'. In *The Culture of English Puritanism, 1560–1700*, edited by C. Durston and J. Eales, pp. 92–121. London: Macmillan.

Aston, M. (2007). 'Moving Pictures: Foxe's Martyrs and Little Gidding'. In *Agent of Change: Print Culture Studies after Elizabeth L. Eisenstein*, edited by S. A. Baron, E. N. Lindquist, and E. F. Shevlin, pp. 82–104. Amherst, MA: University of Massachusetts Press.

Atherton, I. (1999). '"The Itch Grown a Disease": Manuscript Transmission of News in the Seventeenth Century'. In *News, Newspapers and Society in Early Modern Britain*, edited by J. Raymond, pp. 39–65. London: Cass.

Auchterlonie, P. (ed.) (2012). Introduction to *Encountering Islam: Joseph Pitts: An English Slave in 17th-Century Algiers and Mecca*, pp. 3–96. London: Arabian Publishing.

Aughterson, K. (ed.) (1995). *Renaissance Women: A Sourcebook*. London: Routledge.

Avis, P. D. L. (2002). *Anglicanism and the Christian Church: Theological Resources in Historical Perspective*. London: T&T Clark.

Avis, P. D. L. (2007). *The Identity of Anglicanism: Essentials of Anglican Ecclesiology*. London: T&T Clark.

Babbage, S. B. (1962). *Puritanism and Richard Bancroft*. London: SPCK.

Backus, I. (2003). *Historical Method and Confessional Identity in the Era of the Reformation, 1378–1615*. Leiden and Boston: Brill.

Backus, I. (2014). 'Patristics'. In *Brill's Encyclopaedia of the Neo-Latin World*, edited by P. Ford, J. Bloemendal, and C. Fantazzi, pp. 733–45. Leiden: Brill.

Bagchi, D. (1996). 'Diversity or Disunity? A Reformation Debate over Communion in Both Kinds'. In *Unity and Diversity in the Church*, edited by R. N. Swanson, pp. 207–19. Studies in Church History, 32. Oxford: Blackwell.

Bagchi, D. (2004). 'Luther and the Sacramentality of Penance'. In *Retribution, Repentance and Reconciliation*, edited by K. Cooper and J. Gregory, pp. 119–27. Studies in Church History, 40. Woodbridge: Boydell.

Bak, G. (2006). *Barbary Pirate: The Life and Crimes of John Ward, the Most Infamous Privateer of His Time*. Stroud: The History Press.

Baker, D. I. (1997). *Between Nations: Shakespeare, Spenser, Marvell, and the Question of Britain*. Stanford, CA: Standford University Press.

Baker, J. H. (2004). 'St German, Christopher (c.1460–1540/41)'. *ODNB*.

Bakhtin, M. M. (1981). *The Dialogic Imagination*, translated by C. Emerson and M. Holquist. Austin, TX: University of Texas Press.

Bald, R. C. (1970). *John Donne: A Life*. New York, NY: Oxford University Press.

Baldwin, R. C. D. (1987). 'Colonial Cartography under the Tudor and Early Stuart Monarchies, ca. 1480–ca. 1640'. In *The History of Cartography, Volume 3: Cartography in the European Renaissance*, edited by J. B. Harley and D. Woodward, pp. 1754–80. Chicago, IL: University of Chicago Press.

Ballaster, R. (2005). *Fabulous Orients: Fictions of the East in England, 1662–1785*. Oxford: Oxford University Press.

Balserak, J. (2014). 'Theological Discourse'. In *Brill's Encyclopaedia of the Neo-Latin World*, edited by P. Ford, J. Bloemendal, and C. Fantazzi, pp. 721–32. Leiden: Brill.

Barbour, R. (1997). 'Lucy Hutchinson, Atomism and the Atheist Dog'. In *Women, Science and Medicine 1500–1700*, edited by L. Hunter and S. Hutton, pp. 122–37. Stroud: Sutton Publishing.

Barbour, R. (2003). *Before Orientalism: London's Theatre of the East, 1576–1626*. Cambridge: Cambridge University Press.

Barbour, R. (2013). *Sir Thomas Browne: A Life*. Oxford: Oxford University Press.

Barbour, R., and D. Norbrook, et al. (eds) (2012). *The Works of Lucy Hutchinson, Volume 1: Translation of Lucretius*. Oxford: Oxford University Press.

Barish, J. (1981). *The Antitheatrical Prejudice*. Berkeley, CA: University of California Press.

Barker, S. (2007). *War and Nation in the Theatre of Shakespeare and his Contemporaries*. Edinburgh: Edinburgh University Press.

Barnard, J., and M. Bell (2002). 'Appendix 1: Statistical Tables'. In *The Cambridge History of the Book in Britain, Volume IV: 1557–1695*, edited by J. Barnard and D. F. McKenzie, with M. Bell. Cambridge: Cambridge University Press.

Barnett, S. J. (1999). 'Where Was your Church before Luther? Claims for the Antiquity of Protestantism Examined'. *Church History* 68 (1): 14–41.

Barton, A. (1991). 'Perils of Historicism'. *New York Review of Books*, 28 March.

Bauckham, R. (1978). *Tudor Apocalypse: Sixteenth Century Apocalypticism, Millenarianism, and the English Reformation from John Bale to John Foxe and Thomas Brightman*. Oxford: The Sutton Courtenay Press.

Bauman, R. (1998). *Let Your Words be Few: Symbolism of Speaking and Silence among Seventeenth-Century Quakers*. London: Quaker Home Service.

Bayer, M. (2009). 'The Red Bull Playhouse'. In *The Oxford Handbook of Early Modern Theatre*, edited by R. Dutton, pp. 225–39. Oxford: Oxford University Press.

Bearden, E. B. (2012). *The Emblematics of the Self: Ekphrasis and Identity in Renaissance Imitations of Greek Romance*. Toronto: University of Toronto Press.

Beaty, N. L. (1970). *The Craft of Dying: A Study in the Literary Tradition of the 'Ars Moriendi' in England*. New Haven, CT: Yale University Press.

Becker, L. M. (2003). *Death and the Early Modern Englishwoman*. Aldershot: Ashgate.

Beckwith, S. (2003). *Signifying God: Social Relation and Symbolic Act in the York Corpus Christi Plays*. Chicago, IL: University of Chicago Press.

Beckwith, S. (2011). *Shakespeare and the Grammar of Forgiveness*. Ithaca, NY: Cornell University Press.

Beddard, R. (1967). 'The Commission for Ecclesiastical Promotions, 1681–4: An Instrument of Tory Reaction'. *Historical Journal* 10: 11–40.

Bedford, R., L. Davis, and P. Kelly (eds) (2006). *Early Modern Autobiography: Theories, Practices, Genres*. Ann Arbor, MI: University of Michigan Press.

Bedford, R., L. Davis, and P. Kelly (2007). *Early Modern English Lives: Autobiography and Self-representation, 1500–1660*, Aldershot: Ashgate.

Beilin, E. V. (1987). *Redeeming Eve: Women Writers of the English Renaissance*. Princeton, NJ: Princeton University Press.

Bell, M. (1988). 'Mary Westwood: Quaker Publisher'. *Publishing History* 23: 5–66.

Bell, M., G. Parfitt, and S. Shepherd (1990). *A Bibliographical Dictionary of English Women Writers 1580–1720*. Brighton: Harvester Wheatsheaf.

Bellamy, J. (1979). *The Tudor Law of Treason: An Introduction*. London: Routledge & Kegan Paul.

Bellucci, D. (1998). *Science de la Nature et Réformation: la physique au service de la Réforme dans l'enseignement de Philippe Mélanchthon*. Rome: Edizioni Vivere.

Benedict, P. (2002). *Christ's Churches Purely Reformed: A Social History of Calvinism*. New Haven and London: Yale University Press.

Bennett, G. V. (1966). 'William III and the Episcopate'. In *Essays in Modern Church History in Memory of Norman Sykes*, edited by G. V. Bennett and J. D. Walsh, pp. 104–31. London: Adam and Charles Black.

Bennett, G. V. (1975). *The Tory Crisis in Church and State, 1688–1730: Career of Francis Atterbury, Bishop of Rochester*. Oxford: Oxford University Press.

Bennett, G. V. (1986). 'Against the Tide: Oxford under William III'. In *The History of the University of Oxford, Volume 5: The Eighteenth Century*, edited by L. S. Sutherland and L. G. Mitchell, pp. 31–60. Oxford: Oxford University Press.

Bennett, J. S. (2006). 'Mary Astell, Lucy Hutchinson, John Milton, and Feminist Liberation Theology'. In *Milton in the Age of Fish: Essays on Authorship, Text, and Terrorism*, edited by M. Lieb and A. C. Labriola, pp. 145–51. Pittsburgh, PA: Duquesne University Press.

Bennett, L. (2004). *Women Writing of Divinest Things: Rhetoric and the Poetry of Pembroke, Wroth and Lanyer*. Pittsburgh, PA: Duquesne University Press.

Benson, P. J. (2005). 'The Stigma of Italy Undone: Aemilia Lanyer's Canonization of Lady Mary Sidney'. In *Strong Voices, Weak History: Early Women Writers and Canons in England, France, and Italy*, edited by P. J. Benson and V. Kirkham, pp. 146–75. Ann Arbor, MI: University of Michigan Press.

Bercovitch, S. (1975). *The Puritan Origins of the American Self*. New Haven, CT: Yale University Press.

Berek, P. (1982). 'Tamburlaine's Weak Sons: Imitation as Interpretation before 1593'. *Renaissance Drama* 13: 55–82.

Berek, P. (1998). 'The Jew as Renaissance Man'. *Renaissance Quarterly* 51: 128–62.

Bergeron, D. M. (1971). *English Civic Pageantry, 1558–1642*. London: Edward Arnold.

Bergvall, A. (1989). *The "Enabling of Judgement": Sir Philip Sidney and the Education of the Reader*. Uppsala: Almquist & Wiksell.

Bergvall, A. (1994). 'Melanchthon and Tudor England'. In *Cultural Exchange between European Nations during the Renaissance*, edited by G. Sorelius and M. Srigley, pp. 85–96. Uppsala: Norstedts Tryckeri AB.

Bernard, G. W. (2005). *The King's Reformation: Henry VIII and the Remaking of the English Church*. New Haven, CT: Yale University Press.

Bernard, G. W. (2012). *The Late Medieval English Church: Vitality and Vulnerability before the Break with Rome*. New Haven, CT: Yale University Press.

Betteridge, T. (2004). *Literature and Politics in the English Reformation*. Manchester: Manchester University Press.

Betteridge, T. (2005). 'The Henrician Revolution and Mid-Tudor Culture'. *Journal of Medieval and Early Modern Studies* 35 (1): 91–109.

Betteridge, T. (2013). *Writing Faith and Telling Tales: Literature, Politics, and Religion in the Work of Thomas More*. Notre Dame, IN: University of Notre Dame Press.

Bhabha, H. (1994). *The Location of Culture*. New York, NY: Routledge; reprinted 2005.

Biberman, M. (2004). *Masculinity, Anti-Semitism and Early Modern English Literature: From the Satanic to the Effeminate Jew*. Aldershot: Ashgate.

Bicknell, E. J. ([1919], 1955). *A Theological Introduction to the Thirty-Nine Articles of the Church of England*. 3rd edn; with additional references by H. J. Carpenter. London: Longmans.

Bietenholz, P. G., and T. B. Deutscher (eds) (1985–7). *Contemporaries of Erasmus: A Biographical Register of the Renaissance and Reformation*. 3 vols. Toronto: University Press of Toronto.

Binns, J. W. (ed.) (1974). *The Latin Poetry of English Poets*. London: Routledge & Kegan Paul; repr. New York, NY: Routledge, 2014.

Birch, T. (1734). 'Donne (John)'. In *A General Dictionary, Historical and Critical*, edited by P. Bayle, vol. 4, pp. 631–7. 10 vols. London.

Birchwood, M. (2007). *Staging Islam in England: Drama and Culture, 1640–1685*. Cambridge: D. S. Brewer.

Bireley, R. (1999). *The Refashioning of Catholicism: 1450–1700*. Basingstoke: Palgrave Macmillan.

Blench, J. W. (1964). *Preaching in England in the Late Fifteenth and Sixteenth Centuries*. Oxford: Basil Blackwell.

Bloemendal. J., and H. B. Norland (2013). *Neo-Latin Drama and Theatre in Early Modern Europe*. Drama and Theatre in Early Modern Europe, 3. Leiden: Brill.

Boehrer, B. (2008). 'The Cardinal's Parrot: A Natural History of Reformation Polemic'. *Genre* 41: 1–37.

Bolam, R. (2003). 'Ford, Mary Wroth, and the Final Scene of *'Tis Pity She's a Whore*'. In *A Companion to English Renaissance Literature and Culture*, edited by M. Hattaway, pp. 276–86. Oxford: Blackwell.

Borris, K. (2010). 'Allegory, Emblem, and Symbol'. In *The Oxford Handbook of Edmund Spenser*, edited by R. A. McCabe, pp. 437–61. Oxford: Oxford University Press.

Boruchoff, D. A. (2008). 'New Spain, New England, and the New Jerusalem'. *Early American Literature* 43 (1): 5–34.

Bose, M. (2010). 'Writing, Heresy, and the Anticlerical Muse'. In *The Oxford Handbook of Medieval Literature in English*, edited by E. Treharne and G. Walker, pp. 276–96. Oxford: Oxford University Press.

Bossy, J. (1975). *The English Catholic Community, 1570–1850*. London: Dartman, Longman & Todd.

Bosworth, C. E. (2006). *An Intrepid Scot: William Lithgow's Travels in the Ottoman Lands, North Africa and Central Europe, 1690–21*. Aldershot: Ashgate.

Bouwsma, W. J. (1988). *John Calvin: A Sixteenth Century Portrait*. New York, NY: Oxford University Press.

Bowden, C. (2010). 'Collecting the Lives of Early Modern Women Religious: Obituary Writing and the Development of Collective Memory and Corporate Identity'. *Women's History Review* 19 (1): 7–20.

Bowden, C. (2012b). ' "A Distribution of Tyme": Reading and Writing Practices in the English Convents in Exile'. *Tulsa Studies in Women's Literature* 31 (1/2): 99–116.

Bowden, C., and J. E. Kelly (eds) (2013). *The English Convents in Exile, 1600–1800: Communities, Culture and Identity*. Farnham: Ashgate.

Bowers, J., and P. Keeran (2010). *Literary Research and the British Renaissance and Early Modern Period: Strategies and Sources*. Lanham, MD: Scarecrow Press.

Bowers, R. (1998). 'Tamburlaine in Ludlow'. *Notes and Queries* 243: 361–63.

Boyle, M. O. (1977). *Erasmus on Language and Method in Theology*. Toronto and London: University of Toronto Press.

Brachlow, S. (1989). *The Communion of Saints: Radical Puritan and Separatist Ecclesiology, 1570–1625*. Oxford: Oxford University Press.

Bradner, L. (1940). *Musae Anglicanae: A History of Anglo-Latin Poetry, 1500–1925*. The Modern Language Association of America, General Series, 10. New York, NY: The Modern Language Association of America.

Bradshaw, D. (2004). *Aristotle East and West: Metaphysics and the Division of Christendom*. Cambridge: Cambridge University Press.

Braithwaite, W. (1979 [1919]). *The Second Period of Quakerism*. York: W. Sessions.

Braithwaite, W. (1981 [1912]). *The Beginnings of Quakerism*. York: W. Sessions.

Bray, G. (2000). *Tudor Church Reform*. Woodbridge: Boydell Press.

Brayman Hackel, H. (2005). *Reading Material in Early Modern England: Print, Gender and Literacy*. Cambridge: Cambridge University Press.

Brennan, M. G. (1988). *Literary Patronage in the English Renaissance: The Pembroke Family*. London: Routledge.

Brennan, M. G. (2002). 'The Queen's Proposed Visit to Wilton House in 1599 and the "Sidney Psalms"'. *Sidney Journal* 20: 27–53.

Brennan, M. G. (2006), *The Sidneys of Penshurst and the Monarchy, 1500–1700*. Aldershot: Ashgate.

Brisman, L. (1973). *Milton's Poetry of Choice and its Romantic Heirs*. Ithaca, NY: Cornell University Press.

Britland, K. (2006). *Drama at the Courts of Queen Henrietta Maria*. Cambridge: Cambridge University Press.

Britton, D. (2014). *Becoming Christian: Race, Reformation, and Early Modern English Romance*. New York, NY: Fordham University Press.

Broad, J. (2002). *Women Philosophers of the Seventeenth Century*. Cambridge: Cambridge University Press.

Bromham, T., and Z. Bruzzi. (1990). *The Changeling and the Years of Crisis, 1619–1624: A Hieroglyph of Britain*. London: Pinter Publishers.

Brooke, J. H. (1991). *Science and Religion: Some Historical Perspectives*. Cambridge: Cambridge University Press.

Brooks, C. W. (2008). *Law, Politics and Society in Early Modern England*. Cambridge: Cambridge University Press.

Brooks, P. N. (1992). *Thomas Cranmer's Doctrine of the Eucharist: An Essay in Historical Development*. 2nd edn. Basingstoke: Macmillan.

Brown, S. (1998). ' "Over her Dead Body": Feminism, Poststructuralism, and the Mother's Legacy'. In *Discontinuities: New Essays on Renaissance Literature and Criticism*, edited by V. Comensoli, P. Stevens, and M. Straznicky, pp. 3–26. Toronto: University of Toronto Press.

Brown, S. (1999). *Women's Writing in Stuart England: The Mothers' Legacies of Dorothy Leigh, Elizabeth Joscelin, and Elizabeth Richardson*. Stroud: Sutton.

Brownlow, F. W. (1996). *Robert Southwell*. New York, NY: Twayne.

Bryan, J. (2008). *Looking Inward: Devotional Reading and the Private Self in Late Medieval England*. Philadelphia, PA: University of Pennsylvania Press.

Buchanan, C. O. (2006). *Historical Dictionary of Anglicanism*. Lanham, MD: Scarecrow Press.

Buck, L. P. (2014). *The Roman Monster: An Icon of the Papal Antichrist in Reformation Polemics*. Kirksville, MO: Truman State University Press.

Budiansky, S. (2005). *Her Majesty's Spymaster: Elizabeth I, Sir Francis Walsingham, and the Birth of Modern Espionage*. New York, NY: Penguin.

Bulkeley, K. (2005). *Soul, Psyche, Brain: New Directions in the Study of Religion and Brain-Mind Science*. New York, NY: Palgrave Macmillan.

Burden, M. (2013). 'Thomas Doolittle'. In *A Biographical Dictionary of Tutors at the Dissenters' Private Academies, 1660–1729*. London: Dr Williams's Centre for Dissenting Studies.

Burgess, G. (1992). *Absolute Monarchy and the Stuart Constitution*. New Haven, CT: Yale University Press.

Burgess, G. (2000). 'Was the English Civil War a War of Religion? The Evidence of Political Propaganda'. *The Huntington Library Quarterly* 61: 173–201.

Burgess, G. (2011). 'Wars of Religion and Royalist Political Thought'. In *England's Wars of Religion, Revisited*, edited by C. W. A. Prior and G. Burgess, pp. 169–92. Farnham: Ashgate.

Burke, M. E., et al. (eds) (2000). *Women, Writing, and the Reproduction of Culture in Tudor and Stuart Britain*. Syracuse, NY: Syracuse University Press.

Burke, V. (2002). 'Medium and Meaning in the Manuscripts of Anne, Lady Southwell'. In *Women's Writing and the Circulation of Ideas: Manuscript Publication in England, 1550–1800*, edited by G. Justice and N. Tinker, pp. 94–120. Cambridge: Cambridge University Press.

Burke, V., and J. Gibson (eds) (2004). *Early Modern Women's Manuscript Writing: Selected Papers of the Trinity-Trent Colloquium*. Aldershot: Ashgate.

Burrage, C. (1912). *The Early English Dissenters in the Light of Recent Research, 1550–1641*. Volume 2. Cambridge: Cambridge University Press.

Burton, J. (2005). *Traffic and Turning: Islam and English Drama, 1579–1624*. Newark, DE: University of Delaware Press.

Burton, J. (2009). 'The Shah's Two Ambassadors: *The Travels of the Three Sherley Brothers* and the Global Early Modern'. In *Emissaries in Early Modern Literature and Culture: Mediation, Transmission, Traffic, 1550–1700*, edited by B. Charry and G. Shahani, pp. 23–40. Farnham: Ashgate.

Bush, D. (1962). *English Literature in the Earlier Seventeenth Century: 1600–1660*. 2nd edn, revised. London: Oxford University Press.

Bushnell, R. W. (1990). *Tragedies of Tyrants: Political Thought and Theater in the English Renaissance*. Ithaca, NY: Cornell University Press.

Butler, M. (1984). *Theatre and Crisis, 1632–1642*. Cambridge: Cambridge University Press.

Butler, M. (2009). *The Stuart Court Masque and Political Culture*. Cambridge: Cambridge University Press.

Buxton, J. (1964). *Sir Philip Sidney and the English Renaissance*. New York, NY: St. Martin's Press.

Caldwell, M. M. (2007). 'Minds Indifferent: Milton, Lord Brooke, and the Value of Adiaphora on the Eve of the English Civil War'. *The Seventeenth Century* 22 (1): 97–123.

Caldwell, P. (1983). *The Puritan Conversion Narrative: The Beginnings of American Expression*. Cambridge: Cambridge University Press.

Cambers, A. (2007). 'Reading, the Godly, and Self-writing in England, circa 1580–1720'. *Journal of British Studies* 46 (4) (October): 796–825.

Cambers, A. (2011). *Godly Reading: Print, Manuscript and Puritanism in England, 1580–1720*. Cambridge: Cambridge University Press.

Cambers, A., and M. Wolfe (2004). 'Reading, Family Religion, and Evangelical Identity in Late Stuart England'. *The Historical Journal* 47 (4): 875–96.

Campbell, G. (2010). *Bible: The Story of the King James Version 1611–2011*. Oxford: Oxford University Press.

Campbell, G., and T. N. Corns (2008). *John Milton: Life, Work, and Thought*. Oxford: Oxford University Press.

Campbell, G., T. N. Corns, J. K. Hale, and F. J. Tweedie (2008). *Milton and the Manuscript of 'De Doctrina Christiana'*. Oxford: Oxford University Press.

Campbell, K. (2010). *The Call to Read: Reginald Pecock's Books and Textual Communities*. Notre Dame, IN: University of Notre Dame Press.

Campbell, L. B. (1959). *Divine Poetry and Drama in Sixteenth-Century England*. Cambridge: Cambridge University Press.

Canny, N. (ed.) (1998). *The Oxford History of the British Empire, Volume 1: The Origins of Empire: British Overseas Enterprise to the Close of the Seventeenth Century*. Oxford: Oxford University Press.

Capp, B. (1972). *The Fifth Monarchy Men: A Study in Seventeenth-Century English Millenarianism*. London: Faber and Faber.

Capp, B. (2013). 'The Religious Marketplace: Public Disputations in Civil War and Interregnum England'. *English Historical Review* 129 (536): 47–78.

Carey, D., and C. Jowitt (eds) (2012). *Richard Hakluyt and Travel Writing in Early Modern Europe*. Farnham: Ashgate.

Carey, J. (1981; rev. edn 1990). *John Donne: Life, Mind and Art*. London: Faber and Faber.

Carlson, E. (2003). 'The Boring of the Ear: Shaping the Pastoral Vision of Preaching in England, 1540–1640'. In *Preachers and People in the Reformations and Early Modern Period*, edited by L. Taylor, pp. 249–96. Boston, MA: Brill.

Carpenter, E. (1956). *The Protestant Bishop: Being the Life of Henry Compton, 1632–1713, Bishop of London*. London: Longmans, Green.

Carter, T. T. (ed.) (1893). *Nicholas Ferrar: His Household and his Friends*. London: Longman.

Catto, J. (1985). 'Religious Change under Henry V'. In *Henry V: The Practice of Kingship*, edited by G. L. Harriss, pp. 97–116. Oxford: Oxford University Press.

Catto, J. (1999). 'Fellows and Helpers: The Religious Identities of the Followers of Wyclif'. In *The Medieval Church: Universities, Heresy and the Religious Life, Essays in Honour of Gordon Leff*, edited by P. Biller and B. Dobson, pp. 141–61. Woodbridge: Boydell Press.

Catty, J. (1999). *Writing Rape, Writing Women in Early Modern England: Unbridled Speech*. London: Macmillan.

Cavallo, G., and R. Chartier (1999). *A History of Reading in the West*. Amherst, MA: University of Massachusetts Press.

Cavanagh, D. (2003). *Language and Politics in the Sixteenth-Century History Play*. Basingstoke: Palgrave Macmillan.

Cavanagh, S. T. (2001). *Cherished Torment: The Emotional Geography of Lady Mary Wroth's 'Urania'*. Pittsburgh, PA: Duquesne University Press.

Cefalu, P. (2003). 'Godly Fear, Sanctification, and Calvinist Theology in the Sermons and "Holy Sonnets" of John Donne'. *Studies in Philology* 100 (1) (Winter): 71–87.

Cefalu, P. (2004). *Moral Identity in Early Modern English Literature*. Cambridge: Cambridge University Press.

Chambers, E. K. (1965). *The Elizabethan Stage*. Volume IV. Oxford: Clarendon Press.

Champion, J. A. I. (1992). *The Pillars of Priestcraft Shaken: The Church of England and its Enemies, 1660–1730*. Cambridge: Cambridge University Press.

Chapman, M. D. (2006). *Anglicanism: A Very Short Introduction*. Oxford: Oxford University Press.

Chapman, M. D. (2007). *Bishops, Saints and Politics: Anglican Studies*. London: T&T Clark.

Charlton, K. (1999). *Women, Religion and Education in Early Modern England*. London: Routledge.

Chatterjee, K. K. (1974). *In Praise of Learning. John Colet and Literary Humanism in Education*. New Delhi: Affiliated East-West Press.

Chew, S. C. (1937). *The Crescent and the Rose: Islam and England during the Renaissance*. New York, NY: Oxford University Press.

Churchland, P. (2013). *Touching a Nerve: The Self as Brain*. New York, NY: W. W. Norton.

Clare, J. (1990). *Art Made Tongue-Tied by Authority: Elizabethan and Jacobean Dramatic Censorship*. Manchester: Manchester University Press.

Clare, J. (2002). *Drama of the English Republic, 1649–1660*. Manchester: Manchester University Press.

Clark, D. L. (1948). *John Milton at St Paul's School*. New York, NY: Columbia University Press.

Clark, J. C. D. (1986). *Revolution and Rebellion: State and Society in England in the Seventeenth and Eighteenth Centuries*. Cambridge: Cambridge University Press.

Clark, J. C. D. (2000). *English Society 1660–1832: Religion, Ideology and Politics during the Ancien Regime*. 2nd edn. Cambridge: Cambridge University Press.

Clarke, D. (1997). '"Lover's Songs Shall Turne to Holy Psalmes": Mary Sidney and the Transformation of Petrarch'. *Modern Language Review* 92: 282–94.

Clarke, D. (2001). *The Politics of Early Modern Women's Writing*. London: Longman.

Clarke, D. (2007). 'Mary Sidney Herbert and Women's Religious Verse'. In *Early Modern English Poetry: A Critical Companion*, edited by P. Cheney, A. Hadfield, and G. A. Sullivan, Jr., pp. 184–94. Oxford: Oxford University Press.

Clarke, D., and E. Clarke (eds) (2000). *'This Double Voice': Gendered Writing in Early Modern England*. Basingstoke: Macmillan.

Clarke, E. (1997). *Theory and Theology in George Herbert's Poetry: 'Divinitie, and Poesie, Met'*. Oxford: Oxford University Press.

Clarke, E. (2011). *Politics, Religion, and the Song of Songs in Seventeenth-Century England*. Basingstoke: Palgrave Macmillan.

Clarke, E., and E. Longfellow (2008). 'Examine My Life: Writing the Self in the Early Seventeenth Century'. Introduction to online edition of Elizabeth Isham's autobiography, 'Constructing Elizabeth Isham'. Warwick Centre for the Study of the Renaissance. Available at: http://www2.warwick.ac.uk/fac/arts/ren/projects/isham/.

Classen, C. J. (2000). *Rhetorical Criticism of the New Testament*. Tubingen: Mohr Siebeck.

Claydon, T. (1996). *William III and the Godly Revolution*. Cambridge: Cambridge University Press.

Claydon, T. (2000). 'The Sermon, the "Public Sphere" and the Political Culture of Late Seventeenth-Century England'. In *The English Sermon Revised: Religion, Literature, and History 1600–1750*, edited by L. A. Ferrell and P. McCullough, pp. 208–34. Manchester: Manchester University Press.

Claydon, T. (2011). 'The Sermon Culture of the Glorious Revolution: Williamite Preaching and the Jacobite Anti-Preaching, 1685–1702'. In *The Oxford Handbook of the Early Modern Sermon*, edited by P. McCullough, H. Adlington, and E. Rhatigan, pp. 480–94. Oxford: Oxford University Press.

Clegg, C. S. (1997). *Press Censorship in Elizabethan England*. Cambridge: Cambridge University Press.

Clement, C. (2013). 'Political and Religious Reactions in the Medway Towns of Rochester and Chatham during the English Revolution'. PhD thesis, Canterbury Christ Church University.

Cleugh, H. (2013). 'Teaching in Praying Words? Worship and Theology in the Early Modern English Parish'. In *Worship and the Parish Church in Early Modern Britain*, edited by N. Mears and A. Ryrie, pp. 11–30. Farnham: Ashgate.

Clifton, R. (1984). *The Last Popular Rebellion: The Western Rising of 1685*. London: Maurice Temple Smith.

Coffey, J. (2006a). *John Goodwin and the Puritan Revolution*. Woodbridge: Boydell Press.

Coffey, J. (2006b). 'A Ticklish Business: Defining Heresy and Orthodoxy in the Puritan Revolution'. In *Heresy, Literature and Politics in Early Modern English Culture*, edited by D. Loewenstein and J. Marshall, pp. 108–36. Cambridge: Cambridge University Press.

Coffey, J. (2006c). 'The Toleration Controversy during the English Revolution'. In *Religion in Revolutionary England*, edited by C. Durston and J. Maltby, pp. 42–68. Manchester: Manchester University Press.

Colclough, D. (2000). 'Scientific Writing'. *A Companion to English Renaissance Literature and Culture*, edited by M. Hattaway, pp. 565–75. Oxford: Blackwell.

Colclough, D. (ed.) (2013). *The Oxford Edition of the Sermons of John Donne, Volume III: Sermons at the Court of Charles I*, gen. ed. P. E. McCullough. Oxford: Oxford University Press.

Coldiron, A. E. B. (2010). 'Women in Early English Print Culture'. In *The History of British Women's Writing, 1500–1610*, edited by C. Bicks and J. Summit, pp. 60–83. New York, NY: Palgrave Macmillan.

Cole, A. (2007). 'Heresy and Humanism'. In *Middle English*, edited by P. Strohm, pp. 421–37. Oxford: Oxford University Press.

Cole, A. (2008). *Literature and Heresy in the Age of Chaucer*. Cambridge: Cambridge University Press.

Cole, A. (2011). 'Some Advice in Oxford, New College, MS 288: On Thomas Chaundler and Thomas Bekynton'. In *After Arundel: Religious Writing in Fifteenth-Century England*, edited by V. Gillespie and K. Ghosh, pp. 245–66. Turnhout: Brepols.

Coleman, D. (2007). *Drama and the Sacraments in Sixteenth-Century England: Indelible Characters*. Basingstoke: Palgrave Macmillan.

Coles, K. A. (2008). *Religion, Reform and Women's Writing in Early Modern England*. Cambridge: Cambridge University Press.

Collins, J. R. (2005). *The Allegiance of Thomas Hobbes*. Oxford: Oxford University Press.

Collinson, P. (1967). *The Elizabethan Puritan Movement*. London: Jonathan Cape.

Collinson, P. (1979). *Archbishop Grindal, 1519–1583: The Struggle for a Reformed Church*. London: Jonathan Cape.

Collinson, P. (1982). *The Religion of Protestants: The Church in English Society, 1559–1625*. Oxford: Oxford University Press.

Collinson, P. (1983). *Godly People: Essays on English Protestantism and Puritanism*. London: Hambledon Press.

Collinson, P. (1986). *From Iconcoclasm to Iconophobia: The Cultural Impact of the Second English Reformation*. Stenton Lecture 19. Reading: University of Reading.

Collinson, P. (1987). 'The Monarchical Republic of Queen Elizabeth I'. *Bulletin of the John Rylands University Library of Manchester University* 69 (2): 394–424 .

Collinson, P. (1988a). *The Birthpangs of Protestant England: Religious and Cultural Change in the Sixteenth and Seventeenth Centuries*. Basingstoke: Macmillan.

Collinson, P. (1988b). 'Puritans, Men of Business and Elizabethan Parliaments'. *Parliamentary History 7*, pt 2: 187–211.

Collinson, P. (1990a). *De Republica Anglorum: Or, History with the Politics Put Back*. Cambridge: Cambridge University Press.

Collinson, P. (1990b). *The Elizabethan Puritan Movement*. Oxford: Clarendon Press.

Collinson, P. (1997). 'Truth, Lies, and Fiction in Sixteenth-Century Protestant Historiography'. In *The Historical Imagination in Early Modern Britain: History, Rhetoric, and Fiction 1500–1800*, edited by D. R. Kelley and D. H. Sacks, pp. 37–68. Washington, DC: Cambridge University Press.

Collinson, P. (2004). 'Locke, Anne. *ODNB*.

Collinson, P. (2006). *From Cranmer to Sancroft*. London: Hambledon Press.

Collinson, P. (2013). *Richard Bancroft and Elizabethan Anti-Puritanism*. Cambridge: Cambridge University Press.

Collinson, P., D. McKitterick, and E. Leedham-Green (eds) (1991). *Andrew Perne: Quatercentenary Studies*. Cambridge Bibliographical Society Monograph 11. Cambridge: Cambridge University Library.

Como, D. (2000). 'Puritans, Predestination and the Construction of "Orthodoxy" in Early Seventeenth-Century England'. In *Conformity and Orthodoxy in the English Church, c.1560–1642*, edited by P. Lake and M. Questier, pp. 64–87. Woodbridge: Boydell and Brewer.

Como, D. (2004). *Blown by the Spirit: Puritanism and the Emergence of an Antinomian Underground in Pre-Civil War England*. Stanford, CA: Stanford University Press.

Como, D. (2008). 'Radical Puritanism'. In *The Cambridge Companion to Puritanism*, edited by J. Coffey and P. Lim, pp. 241–58. Cambridge: Cambridge: University Press.

Condee, R. W. (1974). 'The Latin Poetry of John Milton'. In *The Latin Poetry of English Poets*, edited by J. W. Binns, pp. 58–92. London: Routledge & Kegan Paul.

Connolly, A. (2007a). 'Evaluating Virginity: *A Midsummer Night's Dream* and the Iconography of Marriage'. In *Goddesses and Queens: The Iconography of Elizabeth I*, edited by A. Connolly and L. Hopkins, pp. 136–53. Manchester: Manchester University Press.

Connolly, A. (2007b). 'Peele's *David and Bethsabe*: Reconsidering Biblical Drama of the Long 1590s'. *Early Modern Literary Studies*. Special Issue no. 16, article 9. Available at: http://extra.shu.ac.uk/emls/si-16/connpeel.htm.

Cook, S. (1993). '"The Story I most particularly Intend": The Narrative Style of Lucy Hutchinson'. *Critical Survey* 5: 271–77.

Cooper, T. (2012). '"Wise as Serpents": The Form and Setting of Public Worship at Little Gidding in the 1630s'. In *Worship and the Parish Church in Early Modern Britain*, edited by N. Mears and A. Ryrie, pp. 197–219. Aldershot: Ashgate.

Corbellini, S. (ed.) (2013). *Cultures of Religious Reading in the Late Middle Ages: Instructing the Soul, Feeding the Spirit, and Awakening the Passion*. Turnhout: Brepols.

Corns, T. N. (2002). 'Milton before "Lycidas"'. In *Milton and the Terms of Liberty*, edited by G. Parry and J. Raymond, pp. 23–36. New York, NY: D. S. Brewer.

Corns, T. N. and D. Loewenstein (1994). Introduction, 'The Emergence of Quaker Writing'. *Prose Studies* 17 (3): 1–5.

Coudert, A. (1995). *Leibniz and the Kabbalah*. Dordrecht: Kluwer Academic Publishers.

Coudert, A. P., and T. Corse (1996). 'Introduction'. In *The Principles of the Most Ancient and Modern Philosophy*, by Anne Conway, pp. vii–xxxiii. Cambridge: Cambridge University Press.

Coudert, A. P., and J. S. Shoulson (eds) (2004). *Hebraica Veritas? Christian Hebraists and the Study of Judaism in Early Modern Europe*. Philadelphia, PA: University of Pennsylvania Press.

Cousins, A. D. (2013). 'Marvell's Devout Mythology of the New World: Homeland and Home in "Bermudas"'. *Parergon: Journal of the Australian and New Zealand Association for Medieval and Early Modern Studies* 30 (1): 203–19.

Cowan, I. B. (1982). *The Scottish Reformation: Church and Society in 16th Century Scotland.* London: Weidenfeld and Nicolson.

Craig, J. (2002). 'Forming a Protestant Consciousness? Erasmus' *Paraphrases* in English Parishes, 1547–1666'. In *Holy Scripture Speaks: The Production and Reception of Erasmus' Paraphrases on the New Testament*, edited by H. M. Pabel and M. Vessey, pp. 313–60. Toronto: University of Toronto Press.

Craig, J. (2011). 'Sermon Reception'. In *The Oxford Handbook of the Early Modern Sermon*, edited by P. McCullough, H. Adlington, and E. Rhatigan, pp. 178–97. Oxford: Oxford University Press.

Craig, J. (2013). 'Bodies at Prayer in Early Modern England'. In *Worship and the Parish Church in Early Modern Britain*, edited by N. Mears and A. Ryrie, pp. 173–96. Abingdon: Ashgate.

Craik, K. A. (2007). *Reading Sensations in Early Modern England.* Basingstoke: Palgrave Macmillan.

Craik, K., and T. Pollard (eds) (2013). *Shakespearean Sensations: Experiencing Literature in Early Modern England.* Cambridge: Cambridge University Press.

Cranfield, N. W. S. (2004). 'Sutcliffe, Matthew (1549/50–1629)'. *ODNB.*

Crawford, J. (2005). *Marvelous Protestantism: Monstrous Births in Post-Reformation England.* Baltimore, MD: Johns Hopkins University Press.

Crawford, J. (2014). *Mediatrix: Women, Politics, and Literary Production in Early Modern England.* Oxford: Oxford University Press.

Crawford, P. (1985). 'Women's Published Writings, 1600–1700'. In *Women in English Society, 1500–1880*, edited by M. Prior, pp. 211–82. London: Methuen.

Crawford, P. (1993). *Women and Religion in England 1500–1720.* London: Routledge.

Creasey, M. A. (1962). ' "Inward" and "Outward": A Study in Early Quaker Language'. *Journal of the Friends' Historical Society* 30: 1–24.

Cressy, D. (2002). 'The Protestation Protested, 1641 and 1642'. *The Historical Journal* 45: 251–79.

Cressey, D., and L. A. Ferrell (eds) (1996). *Religion and Society in Early Modern England: A Sourcebook.* London: Routledge.

Crocker, R. (1990) 'Henry More: a Biographical Essay'. In *Henry More (1614–1687) Tercentenary Studies*, edited by S. Hutton, pp. 1–17. Dordrecht: Kluwer Academic Publishers.

Crockett, B. (1995). *The Play of Paradox: Stage and Sermon in Renaissance England.* Philadelphia, PA: University of Pennsylvania Press.

Cromartie, A. (2006). *The Constitutionalist Revolution: An Essay on the History of England, 1450–1642.* Cambridge: Cambridge University Press.

Cromartie, A. (2011). 'The Mind of William Laud'. In *England's Wars of Religion, Revisited*, edited by C. W. A. Prior and G. Burgess, pp. 75–100. Farnham: Ashgate.

Cross, F. L., and E. A. Livingstone (eds) (2005). 'Platonism'. *The Oxford Dictionary of the Christian Church.* New York, NY: Oxford University Press.

Crowley, T. D. 'Sireno and Philisides: The Politics of Piety in Spanish Pastoral Romances and Sidney's *Old Arcadia'. Studies in Philology* 110 (1): 43–84.

Cruickshanks, E., S. Handley, and D. Hayton (eds) (2002). *The House of Commons 1690–1715.* 6 vols. Cambridge: Cambridge University Press.

Crystal, D. (2010). *Begat: The King James Bible and the English Language.* Oxford: Oxford University Press.

Cullen, P. (1970). *Spenser, Marvell, and Renaissance Pastoral.* Cambridge, MA: Harvard University Press.

Cummings, B. (1999). 'Reformed Literature and Literature Reformed'. In *The Cambridge Companion to Medieval English Literature*, edited by D. Wallace, pp. 821–51. Cambridge: Cambridge University Press.

Cummings, B. (2002). *The Literary Culture of the Reformation: Grammar and Grace*. Oxford: Oxford University Press.

Cummings, B., and F. Sierhuis (eds) (2013). *Passions and Subjectivity in Early Modern Culture*. Farnham: Ashgate.

Curtis, E. E. (2009). *Muslims in America: A Short History*. Oxford: Oxford University Press.

D'Addario, C. (2007). *Exile and Journey in Seventeenth-Century Literature*. Cambridge: Cambridge University Press.

Daiches, D. (1941). *The King James Version of the English Bible: An Account of the Development of the Sources of the English Bible of 1611 with Special Reference to the Hebrew Tradition*. Chicago, IL: University of Chicago Press.

Damrosch, L. (1996). *The Sorrows of the Quaker Jesus*. Cambridge, MA: Harvard University Press.

Daniell, D. (1994, 2001). *William Tyndale: A Biography*. New Haven, CT: Yale University Press.

Daniell, D. (2003). *The Bible in English: Its History and Influence*. New Haven, CT: Yale University Press.

Danielson, D. (1982). *Milton's Good God: A Study in Literary Theodicy*. Cambridge: Cambridge University Press.

Danielson, D. (2010). 'Astronomy'. In *Milton in Context*, edited by S. B. Dobranski, pp. 213–25. Cambridge: Cambridge University. Press.

Danner, D. G. (1999). *Pilgrimage to Puritanism: History and Theology of the Marian Exiles at Geneva, 1555 to 1560*. New York, NY: Peter Lang.

Darlow, T. H., M. F. Moule, and A. S. Herbert (1968). *Historical Catalogue of the Printed Editions of the English Bible, 1525–1961*. London: British and Foreign Bible Society.

Daussy, H. (2002). *Les Huguenots et Le Roi: Le combat politique de Philippe Duplessis-Mornay, 1572–1600*. Geneva: Droz.

Davidson, S. V. (2011). *Empire and Exile: Postcolonial Readings of the Book of Jeremiah*. New York, NY: T&T Clark.

Davies, H. (1970). *Worship and Theology in England: From Cranmer to Hooker, 1534–1603*. Princeton, NJ: Princeton University Press.

Davies, H. (1973 [1996]). *Worship and Theology in England: From Andrewes to Baxter and Fox, 1603–1690*. Princeton, NJ: Princeton University Press [repr. Grand Rapids, MI: Eerdmans, 1996].

Davies, H. (1986). *Like Angels from a Cloud: The English Metaphysical Preachers 1588–1645*. San Marino: Huntington Library.

Davis, E. B., and M. Hunter (1996). 'Introduction'. In *A Free Enquiry into the Vulgarly Received Notion of Nature*, edited by E. B. Davis and M. Hunter, pp. ix–xxvii. Cambridge: Cambridge University Press.

Davis, J. (1986). *Fear, Myth and History: The Ranters and the Historians*. Cambridge: Cambridge University Press.

Davis, J. B. (2004). 'Multiple Arcadias and the Literary Quarrel Between Fulke Greville and the Countess of Pembroke'. *Studies in Philology* 101: 401–30.

Davis, J. B. (2011). *The Countesse of Pembrokes Arcadia and the Invention of English Literature*. New York, NY: Palgrave Macmillan.

Davis, K. (2008). *Periodization and Sovereignty: How Ideas of Feudalism and Secularization Govern the Politics of Time*. Philadelphia, PA: University of Pennsylvania Press.

Dawson, J. E. A. (1994). 'The Apocalyptic Thinking of the Marian Exiles'. In *Prophecy and Eschatology*, edited by M. Wilks, pp. 75–91. Oxford: Ecclesiastical History Society.

Daybell, J. (2010). 'Gender, Obedience, and Authority in Sixteenth-Century Women's Letters'. *Sixteenth Century Journal* 41 (1): 49–67.

De Groot, J. (2008). 'John Denham and Lucy Hutchinson's Commonplace Book'. *Studies in English Literature 1500–1900* 48: 147–63.

De Krey, G. S. (2004–14). 'Stephen College'. *ODNB*.

De Krey, G. S. (2008). 'Between Revolutions: Re-Appraising the Restoration in Britain'. *History Compass* 6 (2): 738–73.

De Landtsheer, J. (2014). 'Letters'. In *Brill's Encyclopaedia of the Neo-Latin World*, edited by P. Ford, J. Bloemendal, and C. Fantazzi, 335–49. Leiden: Brill.

De Landtsheer, J., and H. Nellen (2011). *Between Scylla and Charybdis: Learned Letter Writers Navigating the Reefs of Religious and Political Controversy in Early Modern Europe*. Brill's Studies in Intellectual History, 192. Leiden: Brill.

De Madariaga, I. (2005). *Ivan the Terrible*. New Haven, CT: Yale University Press.

DeCook, T., and A. Galey (eds) (2012). *Shakespeare, the Bible, and the Form of the Book: Contested Scriptures*. New York, NY: Routledge.

Degenhardt, J. H. (2010). *Islamic Conversion and Christian Resistance on the Early Modern Stage*. Edinburgh: Edinburgh University Press.

Dekker, R. (ed.) (2002). *Egodocuments and History: Autobiographical Writing in its Social Contexts since the Middle Ages*. Hilversum: Verloren.

Delany, P. (1969). *British Autobiography in the Seventeenth Century*. London: Routledge & Kegan Paul.

Demers, P. (2006). ' "Warpe" and "Webb" in the Sidney Psalms: The "Coupled Worke" of the Countess of Pembroke and Sir Philip Sidney'. In *Literary Couplings: Writing Couples, Collaborators, and the Construction of Authorship*, edited by M. Stone and J. Thompson, pp. 41–58. Madison, WI: University of Wisconsin Press.

Dent, C. M. (1983). *Protestant Reformers in Elizabethan Oxford*. Oxford: Oxford University Press.

Devereux, E. J. (1983). *Renaissance English Translations of Erasmus: A Bibliography to 1700*. Erasmus Studies, 6. Toronto and London: University of Toronto Press.

Dickens, A. G., and D. Carr (eds) (1967), *The Reformation in England to the Accession of Elizabeth I*. London: E. Arnold.

Diehl, H. (1997). *Staging Reform, Reforming the Stage: Protestantism and Popular Theater in Early Modern England*. Ithaca, NY: Cornell University Press.

Dimmock, M. (2005a). ' "Captive to the Turke": Responses to the Anglo-Ottoman Capitulations of 1580'. In *Cultural Encounters between East and West, 1453–1699*, pp. 43–63. Newcastle upon Tyne: Cambridge Scholars Press.

Dimmock, M. (2005b). *New Turkes: Dramatizing Islam and the Ottomans in Early Modern England*. Aldershot: Ashgate.

Dimmock, M. (2006). Introduction to *William Percy's 'Mahomet and His Heaven': A Critical Edition*, pp. 1–58. Aldershot: Ashgate.

Dimmock, M. (2013a). 'Converting and Not Converting "Strangers" in Early Modern London'. *Journal of Early Modern History* 17: 457–78.

Dimmock, M. (2013b). *Mythologies of the Prophet Muhammad in Early Modern English Culture.* Cambridge: Cambridge University Press.

Distiller, N. (1998). ' "Philip's Phoenix"? Mary Sidney Herbert and the Identity of Author'. In *The Anatomy of Tudor Literature: Proceedings of the First International Conference of the Tudor Symposium*, edited by M. Pincombe, pp. 112–29. Aldershot: Ashgate.

Dixon, R. (2011). 'Sermons in Print, 1660–1700'. In *The Oxford Handbook of the Early Modern Sermon*, edited by P. McCullough, H. Adlington, and E. Rhatigan, pp. 460–77. Oxford: Oxford University Press.

Dobranksi, S. B., and J. P. Rumrich (1998). *Milton and Heresy.* Cambridge: Cambridge University Press.

Dodds, G. (2009). *Exploiting Erasmus: The Erasmian Legacy and Religious Change in Early Modern England.* Toronto: University of Toronto Press.

Doebler, B. A. (1994). *'Rooted Sorow': Dying in Early Modern England.* Rutherford, NJ: Associated University Presses.

Doelman, J. (1992). 'The Contexts of George Herbert's *Musae Responsoriae*'. *George Herbert Journal* 15: 42–54.

Doelman, J. (2000). *King James I and the Religious Culture of England.* Cambridge: D. S. Brewer.

Doersken, D. (1995). ' "Saint Paul's Puritan": John Donne's "Puritan" Imagination in the Sermons'. In *John Donne's Religious Imagination: Essays in Honor of John T. Shawcross*, edited by R.-J. Frontain and F. Malpezzi, pp. 350–65. Conway: University of Central Arkansas Press.

Dolan, F. E. (1993). 'Taking the Pencil out of God's Hand: Art, Nature, and the Face-Painting Debate in Early Modern England'. *PMLA* 108: 224–40.

Dolan, F. E. (1994). ' "Gentlemen, I Have One Thing More to Say": Women on Scaffolds in England, 1563–1680'. *Modern Philology* 92 (2) (November): 157–78.

Dolan, F. E. (2005). *Whores of Babylon: Catholicism, Gender, and Seventeenth-Century Print Culture.* 2nd edn. Notre Dame, IN: University of Notre Dame Press.

Donaldson, I. (2011). *Ben Jonson: A Life.* Oxford: Oxford University Press.

Donoghue, J. (2013). *Fire under the Ashes: An Atlantic History of the English Revolution.* Chicago, IL: University of Chicago Press.

Doran, S., and C. Durston (2002). *Princes, Pastors and People: The Church and Religion in England, 1500-1700.* 2nd edn. London: Routledge.

Dorsten, J. A. (1962). *Poets, Patrons, and Professors: Sir Philip Sidney, Daniel Rogers, and the Leiden Humanists.* Leiden: Leiden University Press.

Dove, M. (2007). *The First English Bible: The Text and Context of the Wycliffite Versions.* Cambridge: Cambridge University Press.

Dowd, M. M. (2007). 'Structures of Piety in Elizabeth Richardson's Legacie'. In *Genre and Women's Life Writing in Early Modern England*, edited by M. M. Dowd and J. A. Eckerle, pp. 115–30. Aldershot: Ashgate.

Dowd, M. M., and J. Eckerle (eds) (2007). *Genre and Women's Life Writing in Early Modern England.* Aldershot: Ashgate.

Dragstra, H., S. Otway, and H. Wilcox (eds) (2000). *Betraying Our Selves: Forms of Self-Representation in Early Modern Texts.* London: Macmillan.

Duffy, E. (1992). *The Stripping of the Altars: Traditional Religion in England, 1400–1580.* New Haven, CT: Yale University Press.

Duffy, E. (2005). *The Stripping of the Altars: Traditional Religion in England, 1400–1580.* 2nd edn. New Haven, CT: Yale University Press.

Duffy, E. (2006). *Marking the Hours: English People and their Prayers, 1240–1570*. New Haven, CT: Yale University Press.

Duncan-Jones, K. (1996). 'Sir Philip Sidney's Debt to Edmund Campion'. In *The Reckoned Expense: Edmund Campion and the Early English Jesuits*, edited by T. M. McCoog, pp. 85–102. Woodbridge: Boydell.

Dunlop, A. (1970). 'The Unity of Spenser's *Amoretti*'. In *Silent Poetry*, edited by A. Fowler, pp. 153–69. London: Routledge & Kegan Paul.

Dunn, L. C. (2008). 'Recent Studies in Poetry and Music of the English Renaissance (1986–2007)'. *ELR* 38: 172–92.

Durston, C., and J. Eales (1996a). *The Culture of English Puritanism, 1560–1700*. New York, NY: St Martin's Press.

Durston, C., and J. Eales (1996b). 'Introduction: The Puritan Ethos, 1560–1700'. In *The Culture of English Puritanism, 1560–1700*, edited by C. Durston and J. Eales, pp. 1–32. Basingstoke: Macmillan.

Dutton, R. (1991). *Mastering the Revels: The Regulation and Censorship of English Renaissance Drama*. London: Macmillan.

Dutton, R. (1997). 'Censorship'. In *A New History of Early English Drama*, edited by J. D. Cox and D. S. Kastan, pp. 287–304. New York, NY: Columbia University Press.

Dutton, R. (2000). *Licensing, Censorship and Authorship in Early Modern England: Buggeswords*. Basingstoke: Palgrave Macmillan.

Dutton, R. (2008). *Ben Jonson, Volpone and the Gunpowder Plot*. Cambridge: Cambridge University Press.

Dutton, R. (ed.) (2009). *The Oxford Handbook of Early Modern Theatre*. Oxford: Oxford University Press.

Dyson, J. (2013). *Staging Authority in Caroline England: Prerogative, Law and Order in Drama, 1625–1642*. Farnham: Ashgate.

Eales, J. (1990). *Puritans and Roundheads: The Harleys of Brampton Bryan and the Outbreak of the English Civil War*. Cambridge: Cambridge University Press.

Eales, J. (1996). 'A Road to Revolution: The Continuity of Puritanism, 1559–1642'. In *The Culture of English Puritanism, 1560–1700*, edited by C. Durston and J. Eales, pp. 184–209. Basingstoke: Macmillan.

Eales, J. (2002). 'Provincial Preaching and Allegiance in the First English Civil War (1640–1646)'. In *Politics, Religion and Popularity in Early Stuart Britain*, edited by T. Cogswell, R. Cust, and P. Lake, pp. 185–210. Cambridge: Cambridge University Press.

Earle, P. (1977). *Monmouth's Rebels: The Road to Sedgemoor, 1685*. London: Weidenfeld and Nicolson.

Eccles, M. (1935). 'Marlowe in Kentish Tradition'. *Notes and Queries* 169: 20–3, 39–41, 58–61, and 134–5.

Edwards, J. (1988). *The Jews in Christian Europe, 1400–1700*. London: Routledge.

Eire, C. (1986). *War against the Idols: The Reformation of Worship from Erasmus to Calvin*. Cambridge: Cambridge University Press.

Eisenstein, E. L. (1982). *The Printing Press as an Agent of Change*. 2 vols. Cambridge: Cambridge University Press.

Eisenstein, E. L. (2005). *The Printing Revolution in Early Modern Europe*. 2nd edn. Cambridge: Cambridge University Press.

Eliot, T. S. (1920). *The Sacred Wood: Essays on Poetry and Criticism*. London: Methuen.

Eliot, T. S. (1963). *Collected Poems 1909–1962*. London: Faber and Faber.

Elliot, D. (2004). *Proving Woman: Female Spirituality and Inquisitional Culture in the Later Middle Ages.* Princeton, NJ: Princeton University Press.

Ellrodt, R. (2000). *Seven Metaphysical Poets: A Structural Study of the Unchanging Self.* Oxford: Oxford University Press.

Elton, G. R. (1972). *Policy and Police: The Enforcement of the Reformation in the Age of Thomas Cromwell.* Cambridge: Cambridge University Press.

Elton, G. R. (1982). *The Tudor Constitution: Documents and Commentary.* Cambridge: Cambridge University Press.

Erler, M. C. (2002). *Women, Reading, and Piety in Late Medieval England.* Cambridge: Cambridge University Press.

Erler, M. C. (2012). 'The Effects of Exile on English Monastic Spirituality: William Peryn's *Spirituall Exercyses*'. *Journal of Medieval and Early Modern Studies* 42 (3): 519–37.

Erler, M. C. (2013). *Reading and Writing during the Dissolution: Monks, Friars, and Nuns 1530–1558.* Cambridge: Cambridge University Press.

Ettenhuber, K. (2011). 'The Preacher and Patristics'. In *The Oxford Handbook of the Early Modern Sermon*, edited by P. McCullough, H. Adlington, and E. Rhatigan, pp. 34–53. Oxford: Oxford University Press.

Evans, G. R. (1992). *Problems of Authority in the Reformation Debates.* Cambridge: Cambridge University Press.

Evans, K. (2012). 'Temperate Revenge: Religion, Profit, and Retaliation in 1622 Jamestown'. *Texas Studies in Literature and Language* 54 (1): 155–88.

Evans, R. J. W. (1975). *The Wechel Presses: Humanism and Calvinism in Central Europe, 1572–1627.* Oxford: Oxford University Press.

Evenden, E. (2008). *Patents, Pictures and Patronage: John Day and the Tudor Book Trade.* Aldershot: Ashgate.

Ezell, M. J. M. (1987). *The Patriarch's Wife: Literary Evidence and the History of the Family.* Chapel Hill, NC: The University of North Carolina Press.

Ezell, M. J. M. (2015). 'Handwriting and the Book'. In *The Cambridge Companion to the History of the Book*, edited by L. Howsam, pp. 92–106. Cambridge: Cambridge University Press.

Fabrizio, A. (2013). 'Women Writing their Faith: Doctrine, Genre, and Gender in *This is a Short Relation of the Cruel Sufferings (For the Truths Sake) of Katharine Evans and Sarah Cheevers*'. *Clio* 42 (3): 309–29.

Faldet, D. (1990). 'Of Readiness and Rhetoric in Bacon's *Advancement of Learning*'. In *A Humanist's Legacy: Essays in Honor of John Christian Bale*, edited by D. M. Jones, pp. 26–33. Decorah, IA: Luther College.

Fallon, S. M. (2007). *Milton's Peculiar Grace: Self-Representation and Authority.* Ithaca, NY: Cornell University Press.

Falls, D. J. (2013). 'The Carthusian Milieu of Love's *Mirror*'. In *The Pseudo-Bonaventuran Lives of Christ: Exploring the Middle English Tradition*, edited by I. Johnson and A. Westphall, pp. 311–40. Turnhout: Brepols.

Farnham, W. (1936). *The Medieval Heritage of Elizabethan Tragedy.* Repr. 1963. Oxford: Basil Blackwell.

Farr, D. (2005). 'Tamburlaine Wasn't Censored'. *The Guardian*, 25 November. Available at: http://www.guardian.co.uk/arts/comment/story/0,16472,1650659,00.html.

Febvre, L., and H.-J. Martin (1997). *The Coming of the Book*, translated by D. Gerard. London: Verso.

Felch, S. M. (2008). Introduction. In *Elizabeth Tyrwhit's Morning and Evening Prayers*, edited by S. M. Felch. Aldershot: Ashgate.

Felch, S. M. (2011). '"Halff a Scrypture Woman": Heteroglossia and Female Authorial Agency in Prayers by Lady Elizabeth Tyrwhit, Anne Lock, and Anne Wheathill'. In *English Women, Religion, and Textual Production 1500-1625*, edited by M. White, pp. 147-66. Abingdon: Ashgate.

Feldman, S. D. (1970). *The Morality-Patterned Comedy of the Renaissance*. Paris: Mouton.

Felsenstein, F. (1995). *Anti-Semitic Stereotypes: A Paradigm of Otherness in English Popular Culture, 1660-1830*. Baltimore, MD: Johns Hopkins University Press.

Ferguson, M. (2002). 'Sidney, Cary, Wroth'. In *A Companion to Renaissance Drama*, edited by A. F. Kinney, pp. 482-506. Malden, MA: Blackwell.

Ferradou, C., and R. P. H. Green (2009). 'Some Aspects and Examples of Biblical Inspiration in George Buchanan's Tragedies *Baptistes* and *Iephthes*'. In *George Buchanan: Poet and Dramatist*, edited by P. Ford and R. P. H. Green, pp. 197-213. Swansea: The Classical Press of Wales.

Ferrell, L. A. (1999). *Government by Polemic: James I, The King's Preachers, and the Rhetorics of Conformity, 1603-1625*. Stanford, CA: Stanford University Press.

Ferrell, L. A., and P. McCullough (eds) (2000). *The English Sermon Revised: Religion, Literature and History, 1600-1750*. Manchester: Manchester University Press.

Ferrell, L. A. (2008). *The Bible and the People*. New Haven, CT: Yale University Press.

Ferry, A. (1983). *The Inward Language: Sonnets of Wyatt, Sidney, Shakespeare and Donne*. Chicago, IL: University of Chicago Press.

Fesko, J. (2012). *After Calvin: Union with Christ in Early Modern Reformed Theology (1517-1700)*. Gottingen: Vanderhoeck.

Fetzer, M. (2010). *John Donne's Performances: Sermons, Poems, Letters and Devotions*. Manchester: Manchester University Press.

Fichtner, P. S. (2001). *Emperor Maximilian II*. New Haven, CT: Yale University Press.

Fincham, K., and N. Tyacke (2007). *Altars Restored: The Changing Face of English Religious Worship, 1547-c.1700*. Oxford: Oxford University Press.

Findlay, A. (2009). *Playing Spaces in Early Women's Drama*. Cambridge: Cambridge University Press.

Firth, K. (1979). *The Apocalyptic Tradition in Reformation Britain, 1530-1645*. Oxford: Oxford University Press.

Fisch, H. (1964). *Jerusalem and Albion: The Hebraic Factor in Seventeenth-Century Literature*. New York, NY: Schocken Books.

Fish, S. E. (1967). *Surprised by Sin: The Reader in 'Paradise Lost'* Berkeley, CA: University of California Press.

Fish, S. E. (1972). *Self-Consuming Artifacts: The Experience of Seventeenth-Century Literature*. Berkeley, CA: University of California Press.

Fisher, M. H. (2004). *Counterflows to Colonialism: Indian Travellers and Settlers in Britain, 1600-1857*. Delhi: Permanent Black.

Fisken, B. W. (1985). 'Mary Sidney's *Psalmes*: Education and Wisdom'. In *Silent But for the Word: Tudor Women as Patrons, Translators, and Writers of Religious Works*, edited by M. P. Hannay, pp. 166-83. Kent, OH: Kent State University Press.

Fisken, B. W. (1990). '"To the Angell Spirit … "': Mary Sidney's Entry into the "World of Words"'. In *The Renaissance Englishwoman in Print: Counterbalancing the Canon*, edited by A. M. Haselkorn and B. S. Travitsky, pp. 263-75. Amherst, MA: University of Massachusetts Press.

Fitzmaurice, A. (2000). '"Every Man, That Prints, Adventures": The Rhetoric of the Virginia Company Sermons'. In *The English Sermon Revised: Religion, Literature, and History 1600–1750*, edited by L. A. Ferrell and P. McCullough, pp. 24–42. Manchester: Manchester University Press.

Fixler, M. (1964). *Milton and the Kingdoms of God*. Evanston, IL: Northwestern University Press.

Flanagan, S. (2009). *Doubt in an Age of Faith: Uncertainty in the Long Twelfth Century*. Turnhout: Brepols.

Fletcher, A. (1981). *The Outbreak of the English Civil War*. London: Edward Arnold.

Fletcher, A. (1984). 'The Enforcement of the Conventicle Acts, 1664–1679'. *Studies in Church History* 21: 235–46.

Fletcher, A. (2006). 'The Protestant Idea of Marriage in Early Modern England'. In *Religion, Culture and Society in Early Modern Britain: Essays in Honour of Patrick Collinson*, edited by A. Fletcher and P. Roberts, pp. 161–81. Cambridge: Cambridge University Press.

Fletcher, A., and P. Roberts (eds) (1994). *Religion, Culture and Society in Early Modern Britain: Essays in Honour of Patrick Collinson*. Cambridge: Cambridge University Press.

Flynn, D. (1995). *John Donne and the Ancient Catholic Nobility*. Bloomington, IN: Indiana University Press.

Ford, A. (1995). 'The Structure of the Perth Articles Debate in Scotland, 1618–1638'. *Journal of Ecclesiastical History* 46: 256–77.

Ford, A. (1997). *The Protestant Reformation in Ireland, 1590–1641*. 2nd edn. Dublin: Four Courts Press.

Ford, D. F. (1999). *Theology: A Very Short Introduction*. Oxford: Oxford University Press.

Ford, P., and R. P. H. Green (eds) (2009). *George Buchanan: Poet and Dramatist*. Swansea: Classical Press of Wales.

Ford, P., J. Bloemendal, and C. Fantazzi (eds) (2014). *Brill's Encyclopaedia of the Neo-Latin World*. Leiden: Brill.

Forsyth, N. (2002). *The Satanic Epic*. Princeton, NJ: Princeton University Press.

Fox, A. (2001). *Oral and Literate Culture in England, 1500–1700*. Oxford: Clarendon Press.

Foxley, R. (2011). 'Oliver Cromwell on Religion and Resistance'. In *England's Wars of Religion, Revisited*, edited by C. W. A. Prior and G. Burgess, pp. 209–30. Farnham: Ashgate.

Foxton, R. (1994). 'Hear the Word of the Lord': A Critical and Bibliographical Study of Quaker Women's Writing 1650–1700*. Melbourne: The Bibliographical Society of Australia and New Zealand.

France, P. (ed.) (2000). *The Oxford Guide to Literature in English Translation*. Oxford: Oxford University Press.

Frankel, L. (1993). 'The Value of Harmony'. In *Causation in Early Modern Philosophy: Cartesianism, Occasionalism and Preestablished Harmony*, edited by S. Naylor, pp. 197–216. Pennsylvania, PA: Pennsylvania State University Press.

Freer, C. (1972). *Music for a King: George Herbert's Style and the Metrical Psalms*. Baltimore, MD: John Hopkins University Press.

Freinkel, L. (2002). *Reading Shakespeare's Will: The Theology of Figure from Augustine to the Sonnets*. New York, NY: Columbia University Press.

Friedeburg, R. von (2002). *Self-Defense and Religious Strife in Early Modern Europe: England and Germany 1530–1680*. Aldershot: Ashgate.

Frost, J. W. (1970). 'The Dry Bones of Quaker Theology'. *Church History* 39: 503–23.

Galpern, A. N. (1974). 'The Legacy of Late Medieval Religion in Sixteenth-Century Champagne'. In *The Pursuit of Holiness in Late Medieval and Renaissance Religion*, edited by C. Trinkaus and H. O. Oberman, pp. 141–76. Leiden: Brill.

Garcia, H. (2012). *Islam and the English Enlightenment, 1670–1840*. Baltimore, MD: Johns Hopkins University Press.

Garman, M. (1996). 'Introduction'. In *Hidden in Plain Sight: Quaker Women's Writings 1650–1700*, edited by M. Garman, J. Applegate, M. Benefiel, and D. Meredith, pp. 1–16. Wallingford, PA: Pendle Hill Publications.

Garret, C. H. (1938). *The Marian Exiles: A Study in the Origins of Elizabethan Protestantism*. Cambridge: Cambridge University Press.

Gasper, J. (1990). *The Dragon and the Dove: The Plays of Thomas Dekker*. Oxford: Clarendon Press.

Gehring, D. S. (2013). *Anglo-German Relations and the Protestant Cause*. London: Pickering & Chatto.

Gentles, I. (1978). 'London Levellers in the English Revolution: The Chidleys and their Circle'. *Journal of Ecclesiastical History* 29: 281–309.

Gertz, G. (2013). 'Barbara Constable's *Advice for Confessors* and the Tradition of Medieval Holy Women'. In *The English Convents in Exile, 1600–1800: Communities, Culture and Identity*, edited by C. Bowden and J. E. Kelly, pp. 123–38. Farnham: Ashgate.

Ghosh, K. (1991). *The Wycliffite Heresy: Authority and the Interpretation of Texts*. Cambridge: Cambridge University Press.

Gibbons, B. J. (1996). *Gender in Mystical and Occult Thought: Behemenism and its Development in England*. Cambridge: Cambridge University Press.

Gibbons, K. (2011). *English Catholic Exiles in Late Sixteenth-Century Paris*. Woodbridge: Boydell Press.

Gibson, K. (2010). 'Scudder, Henry (d. 1652)'. *ODNB*.

Gibson, W. (2009). *James II and the Trial of the Seven Bishops*. Basingstoke: Palgrave Macmillan.

Gill, C. (2005). *Women in the Seventeenth-Century Quaker Community*. Aldershot: Ashgate.

Gill, R. (ed.) (1990). *John Donne: Selected Poems*. Oxford: Oxford University Press.

Gillespie, K. (2004). *Domesticity and Dissent in the Seventeenth Century: English Women Writers and the Public Sphere*. Cambridge: Cambridge University Press.

Gillespie, K. (2012). 'Prophecy and Political Expression in Cromwellian England'. In *The Oxford Handbook of Literature and the English Revolution*, edited by L. L. Knoppers, pp. 462–80. Oxford: Oxford University Press.

Gillespie, R. (1997). *Devoted People: Belief and Religion in Early Modern Ireland*. Manchester: Manchester University Press.

Gillespie, V. (2011). 'Chicele's Church: Vernacular Theology in England after Thomas Arundel'. In *After Arundel: Religious Writing in Fifteenth-Century England*, edited by V. Gillespie and K. Ghosh, pp. 3–42. Turnhout: Brepols.

Gillespie, V. (2012). '1412–1534: Culture and History'. In *The Cambridge Companion to Medieval English Mysticism*, edited by S. Fanous and V. Gillespie, pp. 163–94. Cambridge: Cambridge University Press.

Gillespie, V., and K. Ghosh (eds) (2011). *After Arundel: Religious Writing in Fifteenth-Century England*. Turnhout: Brepols.

Gillespie, V., and S. Powell (eds) (2014). *A Companion to the Early Printed Book in Britain, 1476–1558*. Woodbridge: D. S. Brewer.

Gilliat-Ray, S. (2010). *Muslims in Britain: An Introduction*. Cambridge: Cambridge University Press.

Gilman, E. B. (1986). *Iconoclasm and Poetry in the English Reformation: Down Went Dagon*. Chicago, IL: Chicago University Press.

Gilman Richey, E. (1998). *The Politics of Revelation in the English Renaissance*. Columbia, MO: University of Missouri Press.

Gilmont, J.-F. (ed.) (1998). *The Reformation and the Book*. Aldershot: Ashgate.

Gittings, C. (1984). *Death, Burial and the Individual in Early Modern England*. London: Croom Helm.

Glaser, E. (2007). *Judaism without Jews: Philosemitism and Christian Polemic in Early Modern England*. Basingstoke: Palgrave Macmillan.

Glassman, B. (1975). *Anti-Semitic Stereotypes without Jews: Images of Jews in England, 1290–1700*. Detroit, MI: Wayne State University Press.

Glasson, T. (2012). *Mastering Christianity: Missionary Anglicanism and Slavery in the Atlantic World*. Oxford: Oxford University Press.

Gless, D. J. (1994). *Interpretation and Theology in Spenser*. Cambridge: Cambridge University Press.

Glickman, G. (2013). 'Christian Reunion, the Anglo-French Alliance and the English Catholic Imagination, 1660–72'. *English Historical Review* 128 (553): 263–91.

Goffart, W. (1988). *The Narrators of Barbarian History (A.D. 550–800): Jordanes, Gregory of Tours, Bede, and Paul the Deacon*. Notre Dame, IN: University of Notre Dame Press.

Goffman, D. (1998). *Britons in the Ottoman Empire, 1642–1660*. Seattle, WA: University of Washington Press.

Goldberg, J. (1989). *James I and the Politics of Literature: Jonson, Shakespeare, Donne, and their Contemporaries*. Stanford, CA: Stanford University Press.

Goldberg, J. (1997). *Desiring Women Writing: English Renaissance Examples*. Stanford, CA: Stanford University Press.

Goldberg, J. (2006). 'Lucy Hutchinson Writing Matter'. *ELH* 73: 275–301.

Goldie, M. (1977). 'Edmund Bohun and *jus gentium* in the Revolution Debate'. *Historical Journal* 20: 569–86.

Goldie, M. (1980). 'The Revolution of 1689 and the Structure of Political Argument: An Essay and an Annotated Bibliography of Pamphlets on the Allegiance Controversy'. *Bulletin of Research in the Humanities* 83: 473–564.

Goldie, M. (1990). 'Danby, the Bishops and the Whigs'. In *The Politics of Religion in Restoration England*, edited by T. Harris, P. Seaward, and M. Goldie, pp. 75–106. Oxford: Basil Blackwell.

Goldie, M. (1991). 'The Theory of Religious Intolerance in Restoration England'. In *From Persecution to Toleration: The Glorious Revolution and Religion in England*, edited by O. P. Grell, J. I. Israel, and N. Tyacke, pp. 331–68. Oxford: Oxford University Press.

Goldie, M. (2003). 'Voluntary Anglicans'. *The Historical Journal* 46 (4): 977–90.

Goldie, M. (2008). 'Roger L'Estrange's *Observator* and the Exorcism of the Plot'. In *Roger L'Estrange and the Making of Restoration Culture*, edited by A. Dunan-Page and B. Lynch, pp. 67–88. Aldershot: Ashgate.

Goodrich, J. (2011). ' "Ensigne-Bearers of Saint Clare": Elizabeth Evelinge's Translations and the Restoration of English Franciscanism'. In *English Women, Religion and Textual Production, 1500–1625*, edited by M. White, pp. 83–100. Aldershot: Ashgate.

Goodrich, J. (2013). 'Translating Mary Percy: Authorship and Authority among the Brussels Benedictine'. In *The English Convents in Exile, 1600–1800: Communities, Culture and Identity*, edited by C. Bowden and J. E. Kelly, pp. 109–22. Farnham: Ashgate.

Goodrich, J. (2014). *Faithful Translators: Authorship, Gender, and Religion in Early Modern England*. Evanston, IL: Northwestern University Press.

Gore, C. (1907). *The New Theology and the Old Religion: Being Eight Lectures, Together with Five Sermons*. London: John Murray.

Gosse, E. (1899). *The Life and Letters of John Donne*. 2 vols. London: William Heinemann.

Grabes, H. (ed.) (2001). *Writing the Early Modern English Nation: The Transformation of National Identity in Sixteenth- and Seventeenth-Century England*. Amsterdam: Rodopi.

Grafton, A., and J. Weinberg (2011). *'I have always loved the Holy Tongue': Isaac Casaubon, the Jews, and a Forgotten Chapter in Renaissance Scholarship*. Cambridge, MA: Harvard University Press.

Graham, K. J. E., and P. Codington (eds) (2009). *Shakespeare and Religious Change*. Basingstoke: Palgrave Macmillan.

Graham, E. (1996). 'Women's Writing and the Self'. In *Women and Literature 1500–1700*, edited by H. Wilcox, pp. 209–33. Cambridge: Cambridge University Press.

Graham, E. (2000). 'The Suffering of the Self'. In *Betraying Our Selves: Forms of Self-Representation in Early Modern Texts*, edited by H. Dragstra, S. Otway, and H. Wilcox, pp. 197–210. London/New York: Macmillan/St Martin's Press.

Graves, M. P. (2009). *Preaching the Inward Light: Early Quaker Rhetoric*. Waco, TX: Baylor University Press.

Greaves, R. L. (1986). *Deliver Us from Evil: The Radical Underground in Britain, 1660–1663*. Oxford: Oxford University Press.

Greaves, R. L. (1990). *Enemies under His Feet: Radicals and Nonconformists in Britain, 1664–1677*. Stanford, CA: Stanford University Press.

Greaves, R. L. (1992). *Secrets of the Kingdom: British Radicals from the Popish Plot to the Revolution of 1688–89*. Stanford, CA: Stanford University Press.

Greaves, R. L. (2002). *Glimpses of Glory: John Bunyan and English Dissent*. Stanford, CA: Stanford University Press.

Green, D. (2003). *The Double Life of Doctor Lopez: Spies, Shakespeare and the Plot to Poison Elizabeth I*. London: Century.

Green, I. M. (1978). *The Re-establishment of the Church of England 1660–1663*. Oxford: Oxford University Press.

Green, I. M. (1979). 'The Persecution of "Scandalous" and "Malignant" Parish Clergy during the English Civil War'. *English Historical Review* 94: 507–31.

Green, I. M. (1994). *'The Christian's ABC': Catechism and Catechizing in England c.1530–1740*. Oxford: Oxford University Press.

Green, I. M. (2000). *Print and Protestantism in Early Modern England*. Oxford: Oxford University Press.

Green, I. M. (2009a). *Humanism and Protestantism in Early Modern English Education*. St Andrews Studies in Reformation History. Farnham: Ashgate.

Green, I. M. (2009b). *Continuity and Change in Protestant Preaching in Early Modern England*. London: Dr Williams's Trust.

Green, I. M. (2011). 'Preaching in the Parishes'. In *The Oxford Handbook of the Early Modern Sermon*, edited by P. McCullough, H. Adlington, and E. Rhatigan, pp. 137–54. Oxford: Oxford University Press.

Green, I. M. (2012). 'Varieties of Domestic Devotion in Early Modern English Protestantism'. In *Private and Domestic Devotion in Early Modern Britain*, edited by J. Martin and A. Ryrie, pp. 9–31. Farnham: Ashgate.

Green, I. M. and K. Peters (2002). 'Religious Publishing in England 1640–1695'. In *The Cambridge History of the Book in Britain*, edited by J. Barnard and D. F. McKenzie, vol. 4, pp. 67–93. Cambridge: Cambridge University Press.

Green, R. P. H. (2014). 'Poetic Psalm Paraphrases'. In *Brill's Encyclopaedia of the Neo-Latin World*, edited by P. Ford, J. Bloemendal, and C. Fantazzi, pp. 461–9. Leiden: Brill.

Greenblatt, S. (1982). 'Filthy Rites'. *Daedalus* 111 (3): 1–16.

Greenblatt, S. (1984). *Renaissance Self-Fashioning: From More to Shakespeare*. Chicago, IL: Chicago University Press.

Greenblatt, S. (1990). *Learning to Curse: Essays in Early Modern Culture*. London: Routledge.

Greenblatt, S. (1991). *Marvelous Possessions: the Wonder of the New World*. Chicago, IL: University of Chicago Press.

Greenslade, S. L. (1963). 'English Versions of the Bible A.D. 1525–1611'. In *The Cambridge History of the Bible: The West from the Reformation to the Present Day*, edited by S. L. Greenslade, pp. 141–74. Cambridge: Cambridge University Press.

Gregerson, L. (1995). *The Reformation of the Subject: Spenser, Milton and the English Renaissance Protestant Epic*. Cambridge: Cambridge University Press.

Gregerson, L. and Juster, S. (2011). *Empires of God: Religious Encounters in the Early Modern Atlantic*. Pennsylvania, PA: University of Pennsylvania Press.

Gregory, B. S. (1999). *Salvation at Stake: Christian Martyrdom in Early Modern Europe*. Cambridge, MA: Harvard University Press.

Gregory, B. S. (2012). *The Unintended Reformation*. Cambridge, MA: Belknap/Harvard University Press.

Gregory, J. (1995). 'Canterbury and the *Ancien Régime*: The Dean and Chapter, 1660–1828'. In *A History of Canterbury Cathedral*, edited by P. Collinson, N. Ramsay, and M. Sparks, pp. 204–55. Oxford: Oxford University Press.

Greville, F. (1986). 'A Dedication to Sir Philip Sidney'. In *The Prose Works of Fulke Greville, Lord Brooke*, edited by J. Gouws, pp. 3–136. Oxford: Clarendon Press.

Griffin, B. (1997). 'Marring and Mending: Treacherous Likeness in Two Renaissance Controversies'. *Huntington Library Quarterly* 60 (4): 363–80.

Griffin, E. (2009). *English Renaissance Drama and the Specter of Spain: Ethnopoetics and Empire*. Philadelphia, PA: University of Pennsylvania Press.

Griffith, W. P. (1996). *Learning, Law and Religion: Higher Education and Welsh Society, 1540–1640*. Cardiff: University of Wales Press.

Griffiths, P., with A. Fox, and S. Hindle (eds) (1996). *The Experience of Authority in Early Modern England*. New York, NY: St Martin's Press.

Grogan, J. (2014). *The Persian Empire in English Renaissance Writing, 1649–1622*. New York, NY: Palgrave Macmillan.

Gross, J. (1992). *Shylock: Four Hundred Years in the Life of a Legend*. London: Chatto & Windus.

Gross, K. (1985). *Spenserian Poetics: Idolatry, Iconoclasm, and Magic*. Ithaca, NY: Cornell University Press.

Gross, K. (2006). *Shylock Is Shakespeare*. Chicago, IL: University of Chicago Press.

Groves, B. (2007). *Texts and Traditions: Religion in Shakespeare, 1592–1604*. Oxford: Clarendon Press.

Guibbory, A. (1998). *Ceremony and Community from Herbert to Milton: Literature, Religion and Cultural Conflict in Seventeenth-Century England*. Cambridge: Cambridge University Press.

Guibbory, A. (2001). 'Donne's Religion: Montagu, Arminianism and Donne's Sermons 1624–30'. *ELR* 31 (1): 412–39.

Guibbory, A. (2010). *Christian Identity, Jews, and Israel in Seventeenth-Century England*. Oxford: Oxford University Press.

Guibbory, A. (2011). 'Donne and Apostasy'. In *The Oxford Handbook of John Donne*, edited by J. Shami, D. Flynn, and M. T. Hester, pp. 664–77. Oxford: Oxford University Press.

Guilday, P. (1914). *The English Catholic Refugees on the Continent, 1558–1795*. London: Longmans, Green.

Gurnis-Farrell, M. (2005). 'Martyr Acts: Playing with Foxe's Martyrs on the Public Stage'. In *Religion and Drama in Early Modern England: Performances of the Sacred in Late Medieval and Early Modern England*, edited by J. H. Degenhardt and E. Williamson, pp. 175–93. Amsterdam: Rodopi.

Ha, P. (2011). *English Presbyterianism, 1590–1640*. Stanford, CA: Stanford University Press.

Habermas, J. (1989). *The Structural Transformation of the Public Sphere: An Inquiry into a Category of Bourgeois Society*, translated by T. Burger with F. Lawrence. Cambridge: Cambridge University Press.

Habib, I. (2008). *Black Lives in the English Archives, 1500–1677: Imprints of the Invisible*. Aldershot: Ashgate.

Habinek, L. (2012). 'Untying the "Subtle Knot": Anatomical Metaphor and the Case of the *rete irabile*'. *Configurations* 20 (3): 239–77.

Hackett, H. (2012). 'Women and Catholic Manuscript Networks in Seventeenth-Century England: New Research on Constance Aston Fowler's Miscellany of Sacred and Secular Verse'. *Renaissance Quarterly* 65: 1094–124.

Hadfield, A. (1994). *Literature, Politics and National Identity: Reformation to Renaissance*. Cambridge: Cambridge University Press.

Hadfield, A. (2012). *Edmund Spenser: A Life*. Oxford: Oxford University Press.

Hadfield, A. (ed.) (2013). *The Oxford Handbook of English Prose 1500–1640*. Oxford: Oxford University Press.

Hager, A. (1991). *Dazzling Images: The Masks of Sir Philip Sidney*. Newark, NJ: University of Delaware Press.

Haigh, C. (ed.) (1987). *The English Reformation Revised*. Cambridge: Cambridge University Press.

Haigh, C. (1993). *English Reformations: Religion, Politics, and Society under the Tudors*. Oxford: Clarendon Press.

Haigh, C. (1995). 'The Recent Historiography of the English Reformation'. In *Reformation to Revolution: Politics and Religion in Early Modern England*, edited by M. Todd, pp. 13–32. London: Routledge.

Hailey, R. C. (2011). 'The Publication Date of Marlowe's *Massacre at Paris*, with a Note on the Collier Leaf'. *Marlowe Studies* 1: 25–40.

Halasz, A. (1997). *The Marketplace of Print: Pamphlets and the Public Sphere in Early Modern England*. Cambridge: Cambridge University Press.

Hallett, N. (ed.) (2007). *Lives of Spirit: English Carmelite Self-Writing of the Early Modern Period*. Aldershot: Ashgate.

Hallett, N. (2012b). 'Philip Sidney in the Cloister: The Reading Habits of English Nuns in Seventeenth-Century Antwerp'. *Journal of Early Modern Cultural Studies* 12 (3): 88–116.

Hallett, N. (2013). *The Senses in Religious Communities, 1600–1800: Early Modern 'Convents of Pleasure'*. Farnham: Ashgate.

Hamilton, A. C. (1977) *Sir Philip Sidney: A Study of his Life and Works*. Cambridge: Cambridge University Press.

Hamilton, D. B. (1992). *Shakespeare and the Politics of Protestant England*. New York, NY: Harvester Wheatsheaf.

Hamilton, D. B. (2005). *Anthony Munday and the Catholics, 1560–1633*. Aldershot: Ashgate.

Hamlin, H. (2004). *Psalm Culture and Early Modern English Literature*. Cambridge: Cambridge University Press.

Hamlin, H. (2010). 'Strangers in Strange Lands: Biblical Models of Exile in Early Modern England'. *Reformation* 15: 63–81.

Hamlin, H. (2012). 'Sobs for Sorrowful Souls: Versions of the Penitential Psalms for Domestic Devotion'. In *Private and Domestic Devotion in Early Modern Britain*, edited by J. Martin and A. Ryrie, pp. 211–36. Farnham: Ashgate.

Hamlin, H., and N. W. Jones (eds) (2010). *The King James Bible after Four Hundred Years: Literary, Linguistic, and Cultural Influences*. Cambridge: Cambridge University Press.

Hamlin, W. (2005). *Tragedy and Scepticism in Shakespeare's England*. Basingstoke: Palgrave Macmillan.

Hamm, B. (2004). *The Reformation of Faith in the Context of Late Medieval Theology and Piety: Essays by Berndt Hamm*, edited and translated by Robert J. Bast. Leiden: Brill.

Hammond, G. (1982). *The Making of the English Bible*. Manchester: Carcanet.

Handley, S. (2012). 'From the Sacral to the Moral: Sleeping Practices, Household Worship and Confessional Cultures in Late Seventeenth-Century England'. *Cultural and Social History* 9 (1): 27–46.

Hanlon, Sister J. (1966). 'These Be but Women'. In *Renaissance to Counter-Reformation: Essays in Honour of Garrett Mattingley*, edited by C. H. Carter, pp. 371–400. London: Cape.

Hannaford, R. (ed.) (1996). *The Future of Anglicanism*. Leominster: Gracewing.

Hannay, M. P. (1990). *Philip's Phoenix: Mary Sidney, Countess of Pembroke*. New York, NY: Oxford University Press.

Hannay, M. P. (1991). '"Your Vertuous and Learned Aunt": The Countess of Pembroke as Mentor to Lady Wroth'. In *Reading Mary Wroth: Representing Alternatives in Early Modern England*, edited by N. Miller and G. Waller, pp. 15–34. Knoxville: University of Tennessee Press.

Hannay, M. P. (2001). '"So May I with the *Psalmist* Truly Say": Early Modern Englishwomen's Psalm Discourse'. In *Write or Be Written: Early Modern Women Poets and Cultural Constraints*, edited by B. Smith and U. Appelt, pp. 105–34. Aldershot: Ashgate.

Hannay, M. P. (2002). 'The Countess of Pembroke's Agency in Print and Scribal Culture'. In *Women's Writing and the Circulation of Ideas: Manuscript Publication in England, 1550–1800*, edited by G. Justice and N. Tinker, pp. 17–49. Cambridge: Cambridge University Press.

Hannay, M. P. (2006), 'Joining the Conversation: David, Astrophil, and the Countess of Pembroke'. In *Textual Conversations in the Renaissance: Ethics, Authors, and Technologies*, edited by Z. Lesser and B. S. Robinson, pp. 133–8. Aldershot: Ashgate.

Hannay, M. P. (2009). 'Introduction' to *Ashgate Critical Essays on Women Writers in England, 1550–1700: Volume 2*, edited by M. P. Hannay, pp. xv–xlvi. Farnham: Ashgate.

Hannay, M. P. (2010). *Mary Sidney, Lady Wroth*. Farnham: Ashgate.

Hannay, M. P. (ed.) (1985). *Silent But for the Word: Tudor Women as Patrons, Translators, and Writers of Religious Works*. Kent, OH: Kent State University Press.

Hardacre, P. H. (1956). *The Royalists during the Puritan Revolution*. The Hague: Martinus Nijhoff.

Harding, A. (1994). 'The Origins of the Concept of the State'. *History of Political Thought* 15: 57–72.

Hardy, D. W. (2001). *Finding the Church: The Dynamic Truth of Anglicanism*. London: SCM.

Harris, B. (2000). 'A Portrait of a Moor' (1958). In *Shakespeare and Race*, edited by C. M. S. Alexander and S. Wells, pp. 23–36. Cambridge: Cambridge University Press.

Harris, J. G. (1998). *Foreign Bodies and the Body Politic: Discourses of Social Pathology in Early Modern England*. Cambridge: Cambridge University Press.

Harris, T. (2004–14). 'James Scott, duke of Monmouth'. *ODNB*.

Harris, T. (2007). '"There is None That Loves Him but Drunk Whores and Whoremongers": Popular Criticisms of the Restoration Court'. In *Politics, Transgression, and Representation at the Court of Charles II*, edited by J. M. Alexander and C. MacLeod, pp. 35–58. New Haven, CT: Yale University Press.

Harris, T. (2009). '"A Sainct in Shewe, a Devill in Deede": Moral Panics and Anti-Puritanism in Seventeenth-Century England'. In *Moral Panics, the Media and the Law in Early Modern England*, edited by D. Lemmings and C. Walker. Basingstoke: Palgrave Macmillan.

Harris, T., P. Seaward, and M. Goldie (eds) (1990). *The Politics of Religion in Restoration England*. Oxford: Basil Blackwell.

Harriss, G. (2005). *Shaping the Nation: England 1360–1461*. Oxford: Oxford University Press.

Harth, P. (1993). *Pen for a Party: Dryden's Tory Propaganda in Its Contexts*. Princeton, NJ: Princeton University Press.

Hassett, M. K. (2007). *Anglican Communion in Crisis: How Episcopal Dissidents and Their African Allies Are Reshaping Anglicanism*. Princeton, NJ: Princeton University Press.

Hayton, D. (2004–14). 'Francis Atterbury'. *ODNB*.

Headley, J. M. (1998). 'The Habsburg World Empire and the Revival of Ghibellinism'. In *Theories of Empire, 1450–1800*, edited by D. Armitage, pp. 45–79. Aldershot: Ashgate.

Heal, F. (2003). *Reformation in Britain and Ireland*. Oxford: Clarendon Press.

Heal, F. (2005). 'What Can King Lucius Do for You? The Reformation and the Early British Church'. *The English Historical Review* 120: 593–614.

Heale, E. (2003). *Autobiography and Authorship in Renaissance Verse: Chronicles of the Self*. Basingstoke: Palgrave Macmillan.

Heale, E. (2010). 'Spenser and Sixteenth-Century Poetics'. In *The Oxford Handbook of Edmund Spenser*, edited by R. A. McCabe, pp. 586–601. Oxford: Oxford University Press.

Heinemann, M. (1980). *Puritanism and Theatre: Thomas Middleton and Opposition Drama under the Stuarts Early Modern Drama and the Bible: Contexts and Readings, 1570–1625*. Cambridge: Cambridge University Press.

Helgerson, R. (1983). *Self-Crowned Laureates: Spenser, Jonson, Milton, and the Literary System*. Berkeley, CA: University of California Press.

Helgerson, R. (1992). *Forms of Nationhood: The Elizabethan Writing of England*. Chicago, IL: University of Chicago Press.

Hellinga, L. (1997). 'Nicholas Love in Print'. In *Nicholas Love at Waseda*, edited by S. Oguro, R. Beadle, and M. G. Sargent, pp. 143–62. Woodbridge: D. S. Brewer.

Helmers, H. J. (2011). 'The Royalist Republic: Literature, Politics and Religion in the Anglo-Dutch Public Sphere (1639–1660)'. Doctoral thesis, University of Leiden.

Heninger, S. K. (1989). *Sidney and Spenser: The Poet as Maker*. University Park, PA: Pennsylvania State University Press.

Henry, J. (1986). 'A Cambridge Platonist's Materialism: Henry More and the Concept of Soul'. *Journal of the Warburg and Courtauld Institutes* 49: 172–95.

Henry, J. (1989). 'The Matter of Souls: Medical Theory and Theology in Seventeenth-Century England'. In *The Medical Revolution of the Seventeenth Century*, edited by R. K. French and A. Wear, pp. 87–113. Cambridge: Cambridge University Press.

Henry, J. (1990). 'Henry More versus Robert Boyle: The Spirit of Nature and the Nature of Providence'. In *Henry More (1614–1687) Tercentenary Studies*, edited by S. Hutton, pp. 55–76. Dordrecht: Kluwer Academic Publishers.

Herbert, A. (2011). 'Companions in Preaching and Suffering: Itinerant Female Quakers in the Seventeenth- and Eighteenth-Century British Atlantic World'. *Early American Studies* 9 (1): 73–113.

Herman, P. C. (1996). *Squitter-Wits and Muse-haters: Sidney, Spenser, Milton, and Renaissance Antipoetic Sentiment*. Detroit, MI: Wayne State University Press.

Herrick, M. T. (1955). *Tragicomedy: Its Origin and Development in Italy, France, and England*. Urbana, IL: University of Illinois Press.

Hessayon, A. (2007). '*Gold Tried in the Fire': The Prophet TheaurauJohn Tany and the English Revolution*. Aldershot: Ashgate.

Hessayon, A., and N. Keene (eds) (2006). *Scripture and Scholarship in Early Modern England*. Aldershot: Ashgate.

Heyd, M. (2004). 'The "Jewish Quaker": Christian Perceptions of Sabbatai Zevi as an Enthusiast'. In *Hebraica Veritas? Christian Hebraists and the Study of Judaism in Early Modern Europe*, edited by A. P. Coudert and J. S. Shoulson, pp. 234–65. Philadelphia, PA: University of Pennsylvania Press.

Hibbard, C. (1983). *Charles I and the Popish Plot*. Chapel Hill, NC: University of North Carolina Press.

Highley, C. (2008). *Catholics Writing the Nation in Early Modern Britain and Ireland*. Oxford: Oxford University Press.

Hildebrand, H. J. (ed.) (1996). *The Oxford Encyclopedia of the Reformation*. Oxford: Oxford University Press.

Hill, C. (1975). *The World Turned Upside Down*. Harmondsworth: Penguin.

Hill, C. (1977a). *Milton and the English Revolution*. London: Faber and Faber.

Hill, C. (1977b). 'Occasional Conformity'. In *Reformation Conformity and Dissent: Essays in Honour of Dr Geoffrey Nuttall*, edited by R. B. Knox, pp. 199–220. London: Epworth Press.

Hill, C. (1984). *The Experience of Defeat: Milton and Some Contemporaries*. London: Faber and Faber.

Hill, C. (1986). 'Till the Conversion of the Jews'. In *The Collected Essays of Christopher Hill: Religion and Politics in Seventeenth-Century England*, vol. 2, pp. 269–300. Amherst, MA: University of Massachusetts Press.

Hill, C. (1993). *The English Bible and the Seventeenth-Century Revolution*. London: Penguin.

Hill, J. S. (1979). *John Milton: Poet, Priest and Prophet*. London: Macmillan.

Hill, T. (2004). *Anthony Munday and Civic Culture: Theatre, History and Power in Early Modern London 1580–1633*. Manchester: Manchester University Press.

Hindmarsh, D. B. (2007). *The Evangelical Conversion Narrative: Spiritual Autobiography in Early Modern England*. Oxford: Oxford University Press.

Hinds, H. (1996). *God's Englishwomen: Seventeenth-Century Radical Sectarian Writing and Feminist Criticism*. Manchester: Manchester University Press.

Hinds, H. (2002). 'Anna Trapnel, Anna Trapnel's Report and Plea'. In *A Companion to Early Modern Women's Writing*, edited by A. Pacheco, pp. 177–88. Oxford: Blackwell.

Hinds, H. (2011). *George Fox and Early Quaker Culture*. Manchester: Manchester University Press.

Hirsch, B. D. (2009). 'Counterfeit Possessions: Jewish Daughters and the Drama of Failed Conversion in Marlowe's *The Jew of Malta* and Shakespeare's *The Merchant of Venice*'. *Early Modern Literary Studies* 19 (4): 1–37.

Hirschfeld, H. (2006). '"We All Expect a Gentle Answer, Jew": *The Merchant of Venice* and the Psychotheology of Conversion'. *ELH* 73: 61–81.

Hirschfeld, H. (2014). *The End of Satisfaction: Drama and Repentance in the Age of Shakespeare*. Ithaca, NY: Cornell University Press.

Hirst, D. (2004). 'Remembering a Hero: Lucy Hutchinson's *Memoirs* of her Husband'. *English Historical Review* 119: 682–91.

Hiscock, A. (2002). '"A Supernal, Lively Fayth": Katherine Parr and the Authoring of Devotion'. *Women's Writing* 9 (2): 177–98.

Hiscock, A. (2011). *Reading Memory in Early Modern Literature*. Cambridge: Cambridge University Press.

Hobby, E. (1991). '"O Oxford Thou Art Full of Filth": The Prophetical Writings of Hester Biddle, 1629[?]–1696'. In *Feminist Criticism: Theory and Practice*, edited by F. Sellers, pp. 157–69. Brighton: Harvester Wheatsheaf.

Hodgkin, K. (2007). *Madness in Seventeenth-Century Autobiography*. Basingstoke: Palgrave Macmillan.

Hodgkin, K. (2012). 'Elizabeth Isham's Everlasting Library: Memory and Self in Early Modern Autobiography'. In *History and Psyche: Culture, Psychoanalysis, and the Past*, edited by S. Alexander and B. Taylor, pp. 241–64. New York, NY: Palgrave Macmillan.

Hodgkins, C. (2002). *Reforming Empire: Protestant Colonialism and Conscience in British Literature*. Columbia, MO: University of Missouri Press.

Hof, W. J. op 't (1987). 'Engelse piëtistische geschriften in het Nederlands, 1598–1622'; 'English Pietistic Writings in Dutch (1598–1622)'; 'Englische pietistische Schriften im Niederländischen, 1598–1622'. Rotterdam: Lindenberg. Doctoral thesis, University of Utrecht.

Höfele, A. (2005). 'Stages of Martyrdom: John Foxe's Actes and Monuments'. In *Performances of the Sacred in Late Medieval and Early Modern England*, edited by S. Rupp and T. Döring, pp 81–93. Amsterdam: Rodopi.

Höfele, A. (2011). *Stake, Stage, and Scaffold*. Oxford: Oxford University Press.

Höfele, A. (2012). 'John Foxe: *Christus triumphans*'. In *The Oxford Handbook of Tudor Drama*, edited by T. Betteridge and G. Walker, pp. 123–43. Oxford University Press: Oxford.

Hoffmann, M. (1994). *Rhetoric and Theology: The Hermeneutics of Erasmus*. Toronto: University of Toronto Press.

Hollander, J. (1961). *The Untuning of the Sky: Ideas of Music in English Poetry, 1500–1700*. Princeton, NJ: Princeton University Press.

Hollander, J. (1972). 'Donne and the Limits of Lyric'. In *John Donne: Essays in Celebration*, edited by A. J. Smith, pp. 259–72. London: Methuen.

Holmes, G. (1973). *The Trial of Doctor Sacheverell*. London: Eyre Methuen.

Holmes, G. (1975). *Religion and Party in Late Stuart England*. London: Historical Association.

Holmes, G. (1987). *British Politics in the Age of Anne*. 2nd rev. edn. London: The Hambledon Press.

Holstun, J. (2000). *Ehud's Dagger: Class Struggle in the English Revolution*. London: Verso.

Hopkins, L. (1994). *John Ford's Political Theatre*. Manchester: Manchester University Press.

Hopkins, L. (2005). *A Christopher Marlowe Chronology*. Basingstoke: Palgrave.

Hopkins, L. (2011a). 'Antonios and Stewards'. In *Drama and the Succession to the Crown, 1561–1633*, pp. 97–114. Farnham: Ashgate.

Hopkins, L. (2011b). 'Playing with Matches: Christopher Marlowe's Incendiary Imagination'. *Marlowe Studies* 1: 125–40.

Horn, M. (2013). 'Texted Authorities: How Letters Helped Unify the Quakers in the Long Seventeenth Century'. *The Seventeenth Century* 23 (2): 290–314.

Horst, I. B. (1972). *The Radical Brethren: Anabaptism and the English Reformation to 1558*. Nieuwkoop: De Graaf.

Houghton, L. B. T., and G. Manuwald (eds) (2012). *Neo-Latin Poetry in the British Isles*. London: Bloomsbury Press.

Houlbrooke, R. (1998). *Death, Religion, and the Family in England 1480–1750*. Oxford: Oxford University Press.

House, S. B. (2008). 'More, Sir Thomas (1478–1535)'. *ODNB*.

Houston, A., and S. Pincus (eds) (2001). *A Nation Transformed: England after the Restoration*. Cambridge: Cambridge University Press.

Howard, D. (2008). 'Massinger's Political Tragedies'. In *Philip Massinger: A Critical Reassessment*, edited by D. Howard, pp. 117–37. Cambridge: Cambridge University Press.

Hoy, C. (1960). '"Ignorance in Knowledge": Marlowe's Faustus and Ford's Giovanni'. *Modern Philology* 57: 145–54.

Hsia, R. P. (1988). *The Myth of Ritual Murder: Jews and Magic in Reformation Germany*. New Haven, CT: Yale University Press.

Hsia, R. P. (1998). *The World of Catholic Renewal: 1540–1770*. Cambridge: Cambridge University Press.

Hudson, A. (1988). *The Premature Reformation: Wycliffite Texts and Lollard History*. Oxford: Oxford University Press.

Hughes, A. (1986). 'Thomas Dugard and his Circle in the 1630s—a 'Parliamentary-Puritan Connexion?' *Historical Journal* 29 (4): 771–93.

Hughes, A. (1987). *Politics, Society and Civil War in Warwickshire, 1620–1660*. Cambridge: Cambridge University Press.

Hughes, A. (1990). 'The Pulpit Guarded: Confrontations between Orthodox and Radicals in Revolutionary England'. In *John Bunyan and his England 1628–88*, edited by A. Laurence, W. R. Owens, and S. Sim, pp. 31–50. London: Hambledon Press.

Hughes, A. (1994). 'Early Quakerism: A Historian's Afterword'. In *The Emergence of Quaker Writing*, edited by T. N. Corns and D. Loewenstein. *Prose Studies* 17 (3): 142–8.

Hughes, A. (2004). *Gangraena and the Struggle for the English Revolution*. Oxford: Oxford University Press.

Hughes, A. (2006a). 'The Public Profession of these Nations: The National Church in Interregnum England'. In *Religion in Revolutionary England*, edited by C. Durston and J. Maltby, pp. 93–114. Manchester: Manchester University Press.

Hughes, A. (2006b). 'Thomas Edwards's *Gangraena* and heresiological traditions'. In *Heresy, Literature and Politics in Early Modern English Culture*, edited by D. Loewenstein and J. Marshall, pp. 137–59. Cambridge: Cambridge University Press.

Hume, A. (1984). *Edmund Spenser: Protestant Poet*. Cambridge: Cambridge University Press.

Hunt, A. (2010). *The Art of Hearing: English Preachers and Their Audiences, 1590–1640*. Cambridge: Cambridge University Press.

Hunt, A. (2011). 'Preaching the Elizabethan Settlement'. In *The Oxford Handbook of the Early Modern Sermon*, edited by P. McCullough, H. Adlington, and E. Rhatigan, pp. 366–86. Oxford: Oxford University Press.

Hunt, E. W. (1956). *Dean Colet and His Theology*. London: SPCK.

Hunter, L. (2014). 'Books for Daily Life: Household Husbandry, Behaviour'. In *The Cambridge History of the Book in Britain, Volume IV: 1557–1695*, edited by J. Barnard and D. F. McKenzie, with M. Bell, pp. 514–32. Cambridge: Cambridge University Press.

Hunter, M. (1981). *Science and Society in Restoration England*. Cambridge: Cambridge University Press.

Hunter, M., and P. B. Wood (1986). 'Towards Solomon's House: Rival Strategies for Reforming the Early Royal Society'. *History of Science* 24: 49–108.

Hunter, W. B. (1989). *The Descent of Urania: Studies in Milton 1949–1988*. Lewisburg, PA: Bucknell University Press.

Hunter, W. B. (1998). *Visitation Unimplor'd: Milton and the Authorship of De Doctrina Christiana*. Pittsburgh, PA: Duquesne University Press.

Hutchinson, A. (1995). 'What the Nuns Read: Literary Evidence from the English Bridgettine House, Syon Abbey'. *Mediaeval Studies* 57: 205–22.

Hutton, R. (1986). 'The Making of the Secret Treaty of Dover, 1668–70'. *Historical Journal* 29: 297–318.

Hutton, R. (1996). 'The Religion of Charles II'. In *The Stuart Court and Europe: Essays in Politics and Political Culture*, edited by R. M. Smuts, pp. 228–46. Cambridge: Cambridge University Press.

Hutton, S. (1992). 'Introduction'. In *The Conway Letters: The Correspondence of Anne, Viscountess Conway, Henry More, and their Friends 1642–1684*, edited by M. H. Nicolson. Rev. edn S. Hutton, pp. vii–xix. Oxford: Clarendon Press.

Hutton, S. (1994). 'Introduction: The Renaissance and the Seventeenth Century'. In *Platonism and the English Imagination*, edited by A. Baldwin, pp. 67–75. Cambridge: Cambridge University Press.

Hutton, S. (1997). 'Anne Conway, Margaret Cavendish and Seventeenth-Century Scientific Thought'. In *Women, Science and Medicine 1500–1700: Mothers and Sisters of the Royal Society*, edited by L. Hunter and S. Hutton, pp. 118–234. Stroud: Sutton Publishing.

Hymanson, A. (1951). *The Sephardim of England: A History of the Spanish and Portuguese Jewish Community, 1492–1951*. London: Methuen.

Imaekhai, F. J. (2003). *Understanding Anglicanism*. Ibadan [Nigeria]: Safmos Publishers.

Ingram, M. (1996). 'Puritans and the Church Courts, 1560–1640'. In *The Culture of English Puritanism, 1560–1700*, edited by C. Durston and J. Eales, pp. 58–91. Basingstoke: Macmillan.

Israel, J. (1991). 'William III and Toleration'. In *From Persecution to Toleration: The Glorious Revolution and Religion in England*, edited by O. P. Grell, J. I. Israel, and N. Tyacke, pp. 129–70. Oxford: Oxford University Press.

Jackson, K., and A. Marotti (2004). 'The Turn to Religion in Early Modern English Studies'. *Criticism* 46: 167–90.

Jackson, K., and A. Marotti (2011). *Shakespeare and Religion: Early Modern and Postmodern Perspectives*. Notre Dame, IN: University of Notre Dame Press.

Jackson, S. (2011). 'The Literary and Musical Activities of the Herbert Family'. Unpublished PhD dissertation, University of Cambridge.

Jacobsen, A.-C. (2009). 'Apologetics and Apologies—Some Definitions'. In *Continuity and Discontinuity in Early Christian Apologetics*, edited by J. Ulrich, A.-C. Jacobsen, and M. Kahlos, pp. 5–21. New York, NY: Peter Lang.

Jagodzinski, C. (1999). *Privacy and Print: Reading and Writing in Seventeenth-Century England*. Charlottesville, VA: University of Virginia Press.

James, A. (2014). 'Preaching the Good News: William Barlow Narrates the Fall of Essex and the Gunpowder Plot'. In *Paul's Cross and the Culture of Persuasion in England, 1520–1640*, edited by T. Kirby and P. G. Stanwood, pp. 345–60. Leiden: Brill.

James R. H. (1962). 'Inverted Rituals in Webster's *The White Devil*'. *The Journal of English and Germanic Philology* 61: 42–7.

Janacek, B. (2000). 'Catholic Natural Philosophy: Alchemy and the Revivification of Sir Kenelm Digby'. In *Rethinking the Scientific Revolution*, edited by M. Osler, pp. 89–118. Cambridge: Cambridge University Press.

Jardine, L., and J. Brotton (2000). *Global Interests: Renaissance Art between East and West*. Ithaca, NY: Cornell University Press.

Jayne, S. (1963). *John Colet and Marsilio Ficino*. Oxford: Oxford University Press.

Jed, S. H. (1989). *Chaste Thinking: The Rape of Lucrece and the Birth of Humanism*. Bloomington, IN: Indiana University Press.

Jenkinson, M. (2011). 'Preaching at the Court of Charles II: Court Sermons and the Restoration Chapel Royal'. In *The Oxford Handbook of the Early Modern Sermon*, edited by P. McCullough, H. Adlington, and E. Rhatigan, pp. 442–59. Oxford: Oxford University Press.

Jenner, M. S. R. (2002). 'The Roasting of the Rump'. *Past and Present* 177: 84–120.

Jessopp, A. (1888). 'Donne, John (1573–1631)'. In *DNB*, vol. 15, pp. 223–34. London: Smith, Elder.

Johns, A. (1998). *The Nature of the Book: Print and Knowledge in the Making*. Chicago, IL: University of Chicago Press.

Johnson, I., and A. Westphall (eds) (2013). *The Pseudo-Bonaventuran Lives of Christ: Exploring the Middle English Tradition*. Turnhout: Brepols.

Johnson, J. (1999). *The Theology of John Donne*. Woodbridge: Boydell & Brewer.

Johnson, S. E. (2014). *Staging Women and the Soul-Body Dynamic in Early Modern England*. Burlington, VT: Ashgate.

Johnston, W. M. (ed.) (2000). *Encyclopaedia of Monasticism*. Abingdon: Routledge.

Jones, H. (1989). *The Epicurean Tradition*. London: Routledge.

Jones, J. (1993). 'The Friends of the Constitution in Church and State'. In *Public and Private Doctrine: Essays in British History Presented to Maurice Cowling*, pp. 17–33. Cambridge: Cambridge University Press.

Jones, J. G., and V. Larminie (2008). 'Bayly, Lewis (c.1575–1631)'. *ODNB*.

Jones, J. R. (1979). 'Introduction: Main Trends in Restoration History'. In *The Restoration Monarchy 1660–1688*, edited by J. R. Jones, pp. 1–29. Basingstoke: Macmillan.

Jones, M. D. W. (1995). *The Counter Reformation: Religion and Society in Early Modern Europe*. Cambridge: Cambridge University Press.

Jones, M. K., and M. G. Underwood (1992). *The King's Mother: Lady Margaret Beaufort, Countess of Richmond and Derby*. Cambridge: Cambridge University Press.

Jones, M. R. (2011). *Radical Pastoral, 1381–1594*. Farnham: Ashgate. [Full details under Rodman Jones (2011).]

Jorgens, E. B. (1982). *The Well-Tun'd Word: Musical Interpretations of English Poetry 1597–1651*. Minneapolis, MN: University of Minnesota Press.

Jowitt, C. (2010). *The Culture of Piracy, 1580–1630: English Literature and Seaborne Crime*. Farnham: Ashgate.

Jupp, P. C., and C. Gittings (eds) (2000). *Death in England: An Illustrated History*. New Brunswick, NJ: Rutgers.

Jurkowski, M. (2011). 'Lollard Networks'. In *Wycliffite Controversies*, edited by M. Bose and J. P. Hornbeck II (eds), pp. 261–78. Turnhout: Brepols.

Justice, S. (2008). 'Did the Middle Ages Believe in their Miracles?' *Representations* 103 (1): 1–29.

Kamps, I. (1996). *Historiography and Ideology in Stuart Drama*. Cambridge: Cambridge University Press.

Kaplan, M. L. (2007). 'Jessica's Mother: Medieval Constructions of Jewish Race and Gender in *The Merchant of Venice*'. *Shakespeare Quarterly* 58: 1–30.

Kargon, R. (1964). 'Walter Charleton, Robert Boyle, and the Acceptance of Epicurean Atomism in England'. *Isis* 55: 184–92.

Kaske, C. V. (1999). *Spenser's Biblical Poetics*. Ithaca, NY: Cornell University Press.

Kaske, C. V. (2004). 'Spenser's *Amoretti and Epithalamion*: A Psalter of Love'. In *Centred on the Word: Literature, Scripture, and the Tudor-Stuart Middle Way*, edited by D. W. Doerksen and C. Hodgkins, pp. 28–49. Newark, DE: University of Delaware Press.

Katchen, A. (1984). *Christian Hebraists and Dutch Rabbis: Seventeenth Century Apologetics and the Study of Maimonides*. Cambridge, MA: Harvard University Press.

Katz, D. (1982). *Philo-Semitism and the Readmission of the Jews to England, 1603–1655*. Oxford: Clarendon Press/Oxford University Press.

Katz, D. (1994). *The Jews in the History of England, 1485–1850*. Oxford: Oxford University Press.

Kaufman, P. I. (2004). *Thinking of the Laity in Late Tudor England*. Notre Dame, IN: University of Notre Dame Press.

Keeble, N. H. (1987). *The Literary Culture of Nonconformity in Later Seventeenth-Century England*. Leicester: Leicester University Press.

Keeble, N. H. (1990). '"The Colonel's Shadow": Lucy Hutchinson, Women's Writing and the Civil War'. In *Literature and the English Civil War*, edited by T. Healy and J. Sawday, pp. 227–47. Cambridge: Cambridge University Press.

Keeble, N. H., and G. Nuttall (1991). *Calendar of the Correspondence of Richard Baxter*. 2 vols. Oxford: Clarendon Press.

Kelleter, F. (2000). 'Puritan Missionaries and the Colonization of the New World: A Reading of John Eliot's Indian Dialogues (1671)'. In *Early America Re-explored: New Readings in Colonial, Early National, and Antebellum Culture*, edited by K. Schmidt and F. Fleischmann, pp. 71–106. New York, NY: Peter Lang.

Kelliher, W. H. (1974). 'The Latin Poetry of George Herbert'. In *The Latin Poetry of English Poets*, edited by J. W. Binns, pp. 26–57. London: Routledge & Kegan Paul.

Kelly, S., and R. Perry (2011). 'Devotional Cosmopolitanism in Fifteenth-Century England'. In *After Arundel: Religious Writing in Fifteenth-Century England*, edited by V. Gillespie and K. Ghosh, pp. 362–80. Turnhout: Brepols.

Kelly, S., and R. Perry (2013). '"Citizens of Saints": Creating Christian Community in Oxford, Bodleian Library, MS Laud Misc. 23'. In *Middle English Writing in Practice: Texts, Readers and Transformations*, edited by N. Rice, pp. 215–38. Turnhout: Brepols.

Kelly, S., and R. Perry (eds) (2014). *Devotional Culture in Late Medieval England and Europe: Diverse Imaginations of Christ's Life*. Turnhout: Brepols.

Kemp, G. (2004–14). 'Stephen College'. *ODNB*.

Kemp, G. (2012). 'The "End of Censorship" and the Politics of Toleration, from Locke to Sacheverell'. In *Faction Displayed: Reconsidering the Impeachment of Dr Henry Sacheverell*, edited by M. Knights, pp. 47–68. Chichester: Wiley-Blackwell for The Parliamentary History Yearbook Trust.

Kemp, G., and J. McElligott (eds) (2009). *Censorship and the Press, 1580–1720*. 4 vols. London: Pickering & Chatto.

Kemperdick, S., and J. Sander (eds) (2009). *The Master of Flémalle and Rogier van der Weyden*. Berlin: Hatje Cantz Verlag.

Kendall, R. (2003). *Christopher Marlowe and Richard Baines: Journeys through the Elizabethan Underground*. London: Associated University Presses.

Kenyon, J. P. (1958). *Robert Spencer, Earl of Sunderland, 1641–1702*. London: Longmans, Green.

Kenyon, J. P. (1991). 'The Commission of Ecclesiastical Causes, 1686–1688: A Reconsideration'. *Historical Journal* 34 (3): 727–36.

Kerby-Fulton, K. (2006). *Books under Suspicion: Censorship and Tolerance of Revelatory Writing in Late Medieval England*. Notre Dame, IN: University of Notre Dame Press.

Kewes, P. (1998). *Authorship and Appropriation: Writing for the Stage in England, 1660–1710*. Oxford: Clarendon Press.

Kidd, C. (1999). *British Identities before Nationalism: Ethnicity and Nationhood in the Atlantic World, 1600–1800*. Cambridge: Cambridge University Press.

Killeen, K. (2011). 'Veiled Speech: Preaching, Politics, and Scriptural Typology'. In *The Oxford Handbook of the Early Modern Sermon*, edited by P. McCullough, H. Adlington, and E. Rhatigan, pp. 387–403. Oxford: Oxford University Press.

Killeen, K., and H. Smith (2015). ' "All Other Bookes … Are but Notes upon This": The Early Modern Bible'. In *The Oxford Handbook of the Bible in Early Modern England, c.1530–1700*, edited by K. Killeen, H. Smith, and R. Willie, pp. 1–15. Oxford: Oxford University Press.

Kim, M. (2013). ' "Atheism" in Late Medieval Travel Writings'. In *Bridging the Medieval–Modern Divide: Medieval Themes in the World of the Reformation*, edited by J. Muldoon, pp. 65–86. Farnham: Ashgate.

King, J. N. (1982). *English Reformation Literature: The Tudor Origins of the Protestant Tradition*. Princeton, NJ: Princeton University Press.

King, J. N. (1989). *Tudor Royal Iconography: Literature and Art in an Age of Religious Crisis*. Princeton, NJ: Princeton University Press.

King, J. N. (1990). *Spenser's Poetry and the Reformation Tradition*. Princeton, NJ: Princeton University Press.

King, J. N. (1997). 'Fiction and Fact in Foxe's *Book of Martyrs*'. In *John Foxe and the English Reformation*, edited by D. Loades, pp. 12–35. Aldershot: Scolar Press.

King, J. N. (1999). 'The Book Trade under Edward VI and Mary I'. In *The Cambridge History of the Book in Britain, Volume III: 1400–1557*, edited by J. B. Trapp and L. Hellinga, pp. 164–78. Cambridge: Cambridge University Press.

King, J. N. (2013). 'Paul's Cross and the Implementation of Protestant Reforms under Edward VI'. In *Paul's Cross and the Culture of Persuasion in England, 1520–1640*, edited by T. Kirby and P. G. Stanwood, pp. 141–59. Leiden: Brill.

King, J. N. (ed.) (2004). *Voices of the English Reformation: A Sourcebook*. Philadelphia, PA: University of Pennsylvania Press.

King, J. N. (2009). 'Religious Controversy during the Era of Sir Thomas More, and William Tyndale and His Associates'. In *The Oxford Handbook to Tudor Literature, 1485–1603*, edited by C. Shrank and M. Pincombe, pp. 106–20. Oxford: Oxford University Press.

King, P. (1968). 'The Episcopate during the Civil Wars, 1642–1649', *English Historical Review* 83: 523–37.

King, P. (2007). 'Why Isn't the Mind–Body Problem Medieval?' In *Forming the Mind: Essays on the Internal Senses and the Mind/Body Problem from Avicenna to the Enlightenment*, edited by H. Lagerlund, pp. 187–205. Berlin: Springer.

King, P. M. (2006). *The York Mystery Cycle and the Worship of the City*. Woodbridge: Boydell Press.

King, S. (2000). ' "Your Best and Maist Faithfull Subjects": Andrew and James Melville as James VI and I's "Loyal Opposition" '. *Renaissance and Reformation* 24: 17–30.

Kinney, C. R. (2003). ' "Love Which Hath Never Done": The Countess of Pembroke's Elegies and the Apology for Copia'. *Sidney Journal* 21: 31–40.

Kinney, C. R. (2010). 'The Shepheardes Calender (1579)'. In *The Oxford Handbook of Edmund Spenser*, edited by R. A. McCabe, pp. 160–77. Oxford: Oxford University Press.

Kintgen, E. R. (1996). *Reading in Tudor England*. Pittsburgh, PA: University of Pittsburgh Press.

Kirby, T. (1990). *Richard Hooker's Doctrine of the Royal Supremacy*. Leiden: Brill.

Kirby, T. (2005). *Richard Hooker, Reformer and Platonist*. Aldershot: Ashgate.

Kirby, T. (2007). 'Lay Supremacy: Reform of the Canon Law of England from Henry VIII to Elizabeth I (1529–1571)'. *Reformation and Renaissance Review: Journal of the Society for Reformation Studies* 8 (3): 351–72.

Kirby, T. (2010). 'Chiesa d'Inghilterra e Anglicanesimo'. In *Dizionario del sapere storico-religioso del Novecento*, edited by A. Melloni, pp. 309–20. Bologna: Il Mulino.

Kirby, T. (2013a). 'Religion and Propaganda: Thomas Cromwell's Use of Antoine de Marcourt's *Livre de Marchans*'. In *Persuasion and Conversion: Essays on Religion, Politics, and the Public Sphere*, pp. 9–35. Studies in the History of the Christian Tradition 166. Leiden: Brill.

Kirby, T. (2013b). 'Public Conversion: Richard Smyth's "Retraction" at Paul's Cross in 1547'. In *Paul's Cross and the Culture of Persuasion in England, 1520–1640*, edited by T. Kirby and P. G. Stanwood, pp. 161–74. Leiden: Brill.

Kirby, T. (ed.) (2008). *A Companion to Richard Hooker*, with a Foreword by Rowan Williams. Leiden: Brill.

Kirby, T., and P. G. Stanwood (eds) (2014). *Paul's Cross and the Culture of Persuasion in England, 1520–1640*. Leiden: Brill.

Kirby, T., P. G. Stanwood, M. Morrissey, and J. N. King (eds) (2017). *Sermons at Paul's Cross, 1521–1642*. Oxford: Oxford University Press.

Kirk, S., and S. Rivett (2010). 'Religious Transformations in the Early Modern Americas.' *Early American Literature* 45 (1): 61–91.

Klause, J. (1993). 'The Two Occasions of Donne's "Lamentations of Jeremy"'. *Modern Philology* 90 (3) (February): 337–59.

Klause, J. (2003). 'Catholic and Protestant, Jesuit and Jew: Historical Religion in *The Merchant of Venice*'. *Religion and the Arts* 7: 65–102.

Klein, L. M. (1998). *The Exemplary Sidney and the Elizabethan Sonneteer*. Newark, DE: University of Delaware Press.

Klibansky, R., E. Panofsky, and F. Saxl (1964). *Saturn and Melancholy: Studies in the History of Natural Philosophy, Art, and Religion*. New York, NY: Basic Books.

Knapp, J. (1992). *An Empire Nowhere: England, America, and Literature from* Utopia *to* The Tempest. Berkeley, CA: University of California Press.

Knapp, J. (2002). *Shakespeare's Tribe: Church, Nation, and Theater in Renaissance England*. Chicago, IL: University of Chicago Press.

Kneidel, G. (2011a). '*Ars Praedicandi*: Theory and Practice'. In *The Oxford Handbook of the Early Modern Sermon*, edited by P. McCullough, H. Adlington, and E. Rhatigan, pp. 72–86. Oxford: Oxford University Press.

Kneidel, G. (2011b). 'The Formal Verse Satire'. In *The Oxford Handbook of John Donne*, edited by J. Shami, D. Flynn, and M. T. Hester, pp. 122–33. Oxford: Oxford University Press.

Knights, M. (1994). *Politics and Opinion in Crisis, 1678–81*. Cambridge: Cambridge University Press.

Knights, M. (2001). ' "Meer Religion" and the "Church-State" of Restoration England: The Impact and Ideology of James II's Declarations of Indulgence'. In *A Nation Transformed: England after the Restoration*, edited by A. Houston and S. Pincus, pp. 41–70. Cambridge: Cambridge University Press.

Knights, M. (ed.) (2012). *Faction Displayed: Reconsidering the Impeachment of Dr Henry Sacheverell*. Chichester: Wiley-Blackwell for The Parliamentary History Yearbook Trust.

Knott, J. R. (1993). *Discourses of Martyrdom in English Literature, 1563–1694*. Cambridge: Cambridge University Press.

Koch, E. (1986). 'Der kursächsische Philippismus und seine Krise in den 1560er und 1570er Jahren'. In *Die reformierte Konfessionalisierung in Deutschland–Das Problem der 'Zweiten Reformation'*, edited by H. Schilling, pp. 60–78. Gütersloh: Gütersloher Verlagshaus Mohn.

Kolbrener, W. (2003). 'The Charge of Socinianism: Charles Leslie's High Church Defense of "True Religion"'. *Journal of the Historical Society* 111 (1): 1–23.

Krontiris, T. (1998). 'Mary Herbert: Englishing a Purified Cleopatra'. In *Readings in Renaissance Women's Drama: Criticism, History and Performance 1594–1998*, edited by S. P. Cerasano and M. Wynne-Davies, pp. 156–66. London: Routledge. Reprinted from *Oppositional Voices: Women as Writers and Translators of Literature in the English Renaissance* (1992), London: Routledge.

Kuchar, G. (2005). *Divine Subjection: The Rhetoric of Sacramental Devotion in Early Modern England*. Pittsburgh, PA: Duquesne University Press.

Kuchar, G. (2007). 'Gender and Recusant Melancholia in Robert Southwell's *Mary Magdalen's Funeral Tears*'. In *Catholic Culture in Early Modern England*, edited by R. Corthell, F. E. Dolan, C. Highley, and A. Marotti, pp. 135–57. Notre Dame, IN: University of Notre Dame Press.

Kuin, R. (1998a). *Chamber Music: Elizabethan Sonnet-Sequences and the Pleasure of Criticism*. Toronto: University of Toronto Press.

Kuin, R. (1998b). 'Querre-Muhau: Sir Philip Sidney and the New World'. *Renaissance Quarterly* 51 (2): 549–85.

Kuin, R. (1999). 'Sir Philip Sidney's Model of the Statesman'. *Reformation* 4: 93–117.

Kuin, R. (2015). 'The Sidneys and the Continent: The Tudor Period'. In *The Ashgate Research Companion to the Sidneys*, edited by M. P. Hannay, M. G. Brennan, and M. E. Lamb. Aldershot: Ashgate.

Kunze, B. Y. (1993, 1994). *Margaret Fell and the Rise of Quakerism*. Basingstoke: Macmillan.

Kupperman, K. (1989). 'Definitions of Liberty on the Eve of Civil War: Lord Saye and Sele, Lord Brooke, and the American Puritan Colonies'. *The Historical Journal* 32: 17–33.

Kupperman, K. O. (1993). *Providence Island, 1630–1641: The Other Puritan Colony*. Cambridge: Cambridge University Press.

Lacey, A. (2006). *The Cult of King Charles the Martyr*. Woodbridge: Boydell Press.

Lacey, D. R. (1969). *Dissent and Parliamentary Politics in England 1661–1689: A Study in the Perpetuation and Tempering of Parliamentarianism*. New Brunswick, NJ: Rutgers University Press.

Lake, P. (1982). *Moderate Puritans and the Elizabethan Church*. Cambridge: Cambridge University Press.

Lake, P. (1987). 'Calvinism and the English Church'. *Past and Present* 114: 32–76.

Lake, P. (1988). *Anglicans and Puritans? Presbyterianism and English Conformist Thought from Whitgift to Hooker*. London: Unwin Hyman.

Lake, P. (2006a). 'Introduction: Puritanism, Arminianism, and Nicholas Tyacke'. In *Religious Politics in Post-Reformation England: Essays in Honour of Nicholas Tyacke*, edited by K. Fincham and P. Lake, pp. 1–15. Woodbridge: Boydell and Brewer.

Lake, P. (2006b). 'Puritanism, Familism, and Heresy in Early Stuart England'. In *Heresy, Literature and Politics in Early Modern English Culture*, edited by D. Loewenstein and J. Marshall, pp. 82–107. Cambridge: Cambridge University Press.

Lake, P., and M. Questier (1998). 'Prisons, Priests and People'. In *England's Long Reformation 1500–1800*, edited by N. Tyacke, pp. 195–233. London: Routledge.

Lake, P., and M. Questier (eds) (2000a). *Conformity and Orthodoxy in the English Church, c.1560–1660*. Woodbridge: Boydell Press.

Lake, P., and M. Questier (2000b). 'Puritans, Papists, and the "Public Sphere" in Early Modern England: The Edmund Campion Affair in Context'. *Journal of Modern History* 72: 587–627.

Lake, P., with M. Questier (2002). *The Antichrist's Lewd Hat: Protestants, Papists, and Players in Post-Reformation England*. New Haven, CT: Yale University Press.

Lamb, M. E. (1982). 'The Countess of Pembroke's Patronage'. *English Literary Renaissance* 12: 162–79.

Lamb, M. E. (1986). 'The Countess of Pembroke and the Art of Dying'. In *Women in the Middle Ages and the Renaissance*, edited by M. B. Rose, pp. 207–26. Syracuse, NY: Syracuse University Press.

Lamb, M. E. (1990). *Gender and Authorship in the Sidney Circle*. Madison, WI: University of Wisconsin Press.

Lamont, W. M. (2006). *Last Witnesses: The Muggletonian History, 1652–1979*. Burlington, VT: Ashgate Press.

Lampert, L. (2004). *Gender and Jewish Difference from Paul to Shakespeare*. Philadelphia, PA: University of Pennsylvania Press.

Lander, J. M. (2006). *Inventing Polemic: Religion, Print and Literary Culture in Early Modern England*. Cambridge: Cambridge University Press.

Lares, J. (2001). *Milton and the Preaching Arts*. Pittsburgh, PA: Duquesne University Press.

Larsen, K. J. (1974). 'Richard Crashaw's *Epigrammata Sacra*'. *The Latin Poetry of English Poets*, edited by J. W. Binns, pp. 93–120. London: Routledge & Kegan Paul.

Larson, K. R. (2011). *Early Modern Women in Conversation*. New York, NY: Palgrave Macmillan.

Latz, D. L. (1990). 'The Mystical Poetry of Dame Gertrude More'. *Mystics Quarterly* 16 (2): 66–82.

Lay, J. (2011). 'An English Nun's Authority: Early Modern Spiritual Controversy and the Manuscripts of Barbara Constable'. In *Gender, Catholicism and Spirituality: Women and the Roman Catholic Church in Britain and Europe, 1200–1900*, edited by L. Lux-Sterritt and C. M. Mangion, pp. 99–114. Basingstoke: Palgrave Macmillan.

Leaver, R. A. (1991). *'Goostly Psalmes and Spirituall Songes': English and Dutch Metrical Psalms from Coverdale to Utenhove, 1535–1566*. Oxford: Clarendon Press.

Lee, M. (1974). 'James I and the Revival of Episcopacy in Scotland, 1596–1600'. *Church History* 43: 49–64.

Leff, G. (1968). *Paris and Oxford Universities in the Thirteenth and Fourteenth Centuries: An Institutional and Intellectual History*. London: Wiley.

Lein, C. D. (2011). 'The Final Period'. In *The Oxford Handbook of John Donne*, edited by J. Shami, D. Flynn, and M. T. Hester, pp. 600–15. Oxford: Oxford University Press.

Leo, R. (2015). 'Scripture and Tragedy in the Reformation'. In *The Oxford Handbook of the Bible in Early Modern England, c.1530–1700*, edited by K. Killeen, H. Smith, and R. Willie, pp. 498–517. Oxford: Oxford University Press.

Levao, R. (1985). *Renaissance Minds and their Fictions: Cusanus, Sidney, Shakespeare*. Berkeley, CA: University of California Press.

Levin, C. (2013). *'The Heart and Stomach of a King': Elizabeth I and the Politics of Sex and Power*. 2nd edn. Philadelphia, PA: University of Pennsylvania Press.

Levy, I. C. (ed.) (2006). *A Companion to John Wyclif, Late Medieval Theologian*. Brill's Companions to the Christian Tradition, 4. Leiden: Brill.

Levy, S. (2000). *The Bible as Theatre*. Brighton: Sussex Academic Press.

Lewalski, B. (1962). 'Biblical Allusion and Allegory in *The Merchant of Venice*'. *Shakespeare Quarterly* 13 (3): 327–43.

Lewalski, B. K. (1979). *Protestant Poetics and the Seventeenth-Century Religious Lyric*. Princeton, NJ: Princeton University Press.

Lewalski, B. K. (2003a). *The Life of John Milton*. Rev. edn. Malden, MA: Blackwell.

Lewalski, B. K. (2003b). 'Milton and the Millennium'. In *Milton and the Ends of Time*, edited by J. Cummins, pp. 13–23. Cambridge: Cambridge University Press.

Lewis, C. S. (1954). *English Literature in the Sixteenth Century excluding Drama*. Oxford: Oxford University Press.

Lewis, C. S. (1963). *The Literary Impact of the Authorized Version*. Philadelphia, PA: Fortress Press.

Limon, J. 1986. *Dangerous Matter: English Drama and Politics 1623–1624*. Cambridge: Cambridge University Press.

Lindberg, C. (ed.) (2000). *The European Reformations Sourcebook*. Oxford: Blackwell.

Linden, S. (1996). *Darke Hierogliphicks: Alchemy in English Literature from Chaucer to the Restoration*. Lexington, KY: University of Kentucky Press.

Lindley, D. (2006). *Shakespeare and Music*. London: Arden Shakespeare.

Lindley, P. (2007). *Tomb Destruction and Scholarship: Medieval Monuments in Early Modern England*. Donington: Shaun Tyas Publishing.

Linton, J. P. (1998). *The Romance of the New World: Gender and the Literary Formations of English Colonialism*. Cambridge: Cambridge University Press.

Llewellyn, N. (2000). *Funeral Monuments in Post-Reformation England*. Cambridge: Cambridge University Press.

Loach, J. (1986). 'The Marian Establishment and the Printing Press'. *English Historical Review* 101: 135–48.

Loades, D. (1979, repr. 2014). *The Reign of Mary Tudor: Politics Government, and Religion in England, 1553–58*. 2nd edn. London: Longman.

Lobo, G. I. (2012a). 'Lucy Hutchinson's Revisions of Conscience'. *ELR* 42: 317–41.

Lobo, G. I. (2012b). 'Early Quaker Writing, Oliver Cromwell, and the Nationalization of Conscience'. *Exemplaria* 24: 112–26.

Loewenstein, D. (2001). *Representing Revolution in Milton and His Contemporaries: Religion, Politics, and Polemics in Radical Puritanism*. Cambridge: Cambridge University Press.

Loewenstein, D., and J. Morrill (2002). 'Literature and Religion'. In *The Cambridge History of Early Modern English Literature*, edited by D. Loewenstein and J. Mueller, pp. 664–713. Cambridge: Cambridge University Press.

Loewenstein, D., and J. Mueller (eds) (2006). *The Cambridge History of Early Modern English Literature*. Cambridge: Cambridge University Press.

Loewenstein, D. (2013). *Treacherous Faith: The Specter of Heresy in Early Modern English Literature and Culture*. Oxford: Oxford University Press.

Lokhorst, G.-J. (2014). 'Descartes and the Pineal Gland'. *The Stanford Encyclopedia of Philosophy* (Spring Edition), edited by E. N. Zalta. Available at: http://plato.stanford.edu/archives/spr2014/entries/pineal-gland/.

Long, L. (2002). 'Spiritual Exile: Translating the Bible from Geneva and Rheims'. In *Displaced Persons: Conditions of Exile in European Culture*, edited by S. Ouditt, pp. 11–20. Aldershot: Ashgate.

Longfellow, E. (2004a). 'Lady Anne Southwell's Indictment of Adam'. In *Early Modern Women's Manuscript Writing: Selected Papers of the Trinity-Trent Colloquium*, edited by V. Burke and J. Gibson, 111–33. Aldershot: Ashgate.

Longfellow, E. (2004b). *Women and Religious Writing in Early Modern England*. Cambridge: Cambridge University Press.

Longfellow, E. (2006). 'Public, Private, and the Household in Early Seventeenth-Century England'. *Journal of British Studies* 45 (2): 313–34.

Longfellow, E. (2012). ' "My now Solitary Prayers": *Eikon basilike* and Changing Attitudes toward Religious Solitude'. In *Private and Domestic Devotion in Early Modern Britain*, edited by J. Martin and A. Ryrie, pp. 53–72. Farnham: Ashgate.

Looser, D. (2000). *British Women Writers and the Writing of History, 1670–1820*. Baltimore, MD: Johns Hopkins University Press.

Louthan, H. (1997). *The Quest for Compromise: Peace-Makers in Counter-Reformation Vienna*. Cambridge: Cambridge University Press.

Love, H. (2004–14). 'Roger L'Estrange'. *ODNB*.

Lucas, S. (2009). 'Hall's Chronicle and the *Mirror for Magistrates*: History and the Tragic Pattern'. In *The Oxford Handbook of Tudor Literature, 1485–1603*, edited by M. Pincombe and C. Shrank, pp. 356–71. Oxford: Oxford University Press.

Lund, M. A. (2010). 'Early Modern Sermon Paratexts and the Religious Politics of Reading'. In *Material Readings of Early Modern Culture: Texts and Social Practices, 1580–1730*, edited by J. Daybell and P. Hinds, pp. 143–62. Basingstoke: Palgrave Macmillan.

Lupton, J. R. (1996). *Afterlives of Saints: Hagiography, Typology, and Renaissance Literature*. Stanford, CA: Stanford University Press.

Lupton, J. R. (2005). *Citizen-Saints: Shakespeare and Political Theology*. Chicago, IL: University of Chicago Press.

Lutton, R. (2006). *Lollardy and Orthodox Religion in Pre-Reformation England: Reconstructing Piety*. Woodbridge: Boydell Press.

Luxon, T. H. (1995). *Literal Figures: Puritan Allegory and the Reformation Crisis in Representation*. Chicago, IL: University of Chicago Press.

Lyall, F. (1980). *Of Presbyters and Kings: Church and State in the Law of Scotland*. Aberdeen: Mercat Press.

Lynch, B. (2004). *John Bunyan and the Language of Conviction*. Cambridge: D. S. Brewer.

Lynch, K. (2012). *Protestant Autobiography in the Seventeenth-Century Anglophone World*. Oxford: Oxford University Press.

Maag, K. (ed.) (1999). *Melanchthon in Europe: His Work and its Influence beyond Wittenberg*. Cumbria: Baker Books.

MacConica, J. K. (1997). 'The English Reception of Erasmus'. In *Erasmianism: Idea and Reality*, edited by M. E. H. N. Mout, H. Smolinsky, and J. Trapman, pp. 37–46. Amsterdam: Royal Netherlands Academy of Arts and Sciences.

MacCulloch, D. (1996). *Thomas Cranmer: A Life*. New Haven, CT: Yale University Press.

MacCulloch, D. (1998). 'Henry VIII and the Reform of the Church'. In *The Reign of Henry VIII: Politics, Policy and Piety*, edited by D. MacCulloch, pp. 159–80. Basingstoke: Palgrave Macmillan.

MacCulloch, D. (2001). *The Later Reformation in England, 1547–1603*. Basingstoke: Palgrave.

MacCulloch, D. (2002). *The Boy King: Edward VI and the Protestant Reformation*. Berkeley, CA: University of California Press.

MacCulloch, D. (2003, 2005). *Reformation: Europe's House Divided, 1490–1700*. New York: Penguin Books.

MacCulloch, D. (2009). *Christianity: The First Three Thousand Years*. London: Allen Lane.

MacDonald, A. (1998). *The Jacobean Kirk, 1567–1625: Sovereignty, Polity and Liturgy*. Farnham: Ashgate.

MacDonald, A. A. (1996). 'Contrafacta and the *Gude and Godlie Ballatis*'. In *Sacred and Profane: Secular and Devotional Interplay in Early Modern British Literature*, edited by H. Wilcox, R. Todd, and A. A. MacDonald, pp. 33–44. Amsterdam: Free University Press.

MacDonald, M., and T. Murphy (1990). *Sleepless Souls: Suicide in Early Modern England*. Oxford: Clarendon Press.

McFarlane, I. D. (1981). *Buchanan*. London: Duckworth.

Mack, M. (2005) *Sidney's Poetics: Imitating Creation*. Washington, DC: Catholic University of America Press.

Mack, P. (1992). *Visionary Women: Ecstatic Prophecy in Seventeenth-Century England*. Oakland, CA: University of California Press.

Mack, P. (2004). *Elizabethan Rhetoric: Theory and Practice*. Cambridge: Cambridge University Press.

MacLane, P. E. (1961). *Spenser's Shepheardes Calender: A Study in Elizabethan Allegory*. Notre Dame, IN: University of Notre Dame Press.

MacLean, G. (2004). *The Rise of Oriental Travel: English Visitors to the Ottoman Empire, 1580–1720*. New York, NY: Palgrave Macmillan.

MacLean, G. (2011). '1660'. In *The Oxford History of Print Culture: Volume 1: Cheap Print in Britain and Ireland to 1660*, edited by J. Raymond, pp. 619–28. Oxford: Oxford University Press.

MacLean, G., and N. Matar (2011). *Britain and the Islamic World*. Oxford: Oxford University Press.

MacMillan, K. (2006). *Sovereignty and Possession in the English New World: The Legal Foundations of Empire, 1576–1640*. Cambridge: Cambridge University Press.

Maguire, N. K. (1992). *Regicide and Restoration: English Tragicomedy, 1660–1671*. Cambridge: Cambridge University Press.

Major, P. (2013). *Writings of Exile in the English Revolution and Restoration*. Farnham: Ashgate.

Malcolmson, C. (1994). 'George Herbert and Coterie Verse'. *George Herbert Journal* 18: 159–84.

Malcolmson, C. (2004). *George Herbert: A Literary Life*. New York, NY: Palgrave Macmillan.

Malless, S., and J. McQuain (2003). *Coined by God: Words and Phrases That First Appear in the English Translations of the Bible*. New York: W. W. Norton.

Maltby, J. (1998). *Prayer Book and People in Elizabethan and Early Stuart England*. Cambridge: Cambridge University Press.

Maltby, J. (2013). ' "Extravagancies and Impertinencies": Set Forms, Conceived and Extempore Prayer in Revolutionary England'. In *Worship and the Parish Church in Early Modern Britain*, edited by N. Mears and A. Ryrie, pp. 221–44. Abingdon: Ashgate.

Mann, T. (2015). *The Oxford Guide to Library Research*. 4th edn. Oxford: Oxford University Press.

Manning, A. (1852). *The Household of Sir Thomas More*. New York, NY: Charles Scribner.

Marcus, L. (1996). *Unediting the Renaissance: Shakespeare, Marlowe and Milton*. London: Routledge.

Marcus, L. (2009). 'Introduction' to John Webster, *The Duchess of Malfi*, edited L. Marcus. Arden Early Modern Drama. London: Bloomsbury.

Markley, R. (2006). *The Far East and the English Imagination, 1600–1730*. Cambridge: Cambridge University Press.

Marks, R. (2004). *Image and Devotion in Late Medieval England*. Stroud: Sutton Publishing.

Marlowe Bibliography Online, http://www.marlowebibliography.org/.

Marotti, A. F. (1986). *John Donne, Coterie Poet*. Madison, WI: University of Wisconsin Press.

Marotti, A. F. (1995). *Manuscript, Print and the English Renaissance Lyric*. Ithaca, NY: Cornell University Press,

Marsh, C. (1994). *The Family of Love in English Society, 1550–1630*. Cambridge: Cambridge University Press.

Marsh, C. (2010). *Music and Society in Early Modern England*. Cambridge: Cambridge University Press.

Marshall, P. (1994). *The Catholic Priesthood and the English Reformation*. Oxford: Oxford University Press.

Marshall P. (1995). 'The Rood of Boxley, the Blood of Hailes and the Defence of the Henrician Church'. *Journal of Ecclesiastical History* 46: 689–96.

Marshall, P. (2005). 'Is the Pope Catholic? Henry VIII and the Semantics of Schism'. In *Catholics and the 'Protestant Nation': Religious Politics and Identity in Early Modern England*, edited by E. H. Shagan, pp. 22–48. Manchester: Manchester University Press.

Marshall, P. (2006). *Religious Identities in Henry VIII's England*. Abingdon: Ashgate.

Marshall, P. (2011). 'Lollards and Protestants Revisited'. In *Wycliffite Controversies*, edited by M. Bose and J. P. Hornbeck II, pp. 295–318. Medieval Church Studies 23. Turnhout: Brepols.

Marshall, P. (2012). *Reformation England 1480–1642*. 2nd edn. London: Bloomsbury.

Marshall, P., and A. Ryrie (eds) (2002). *The Beginnings of English Protestantism*. Cambridge: Cambridge University Press.

Martin, C. G. (1998). *The Ruins of Allegory: 'Paradise Lost' and the Metamorphosis of Epic Convention*. Durham, NC: Duke University Press.

Martin, C. G. (2001). '"What If the Sun Be Centre to the World?": Milton's Epistemology, Cosmology, and Paradise of Fools Reconsidered'. *Modern Philology* 99, (2) (November): 231–65.

Martin, C. G. (2006). 'Unediting Milton: Historical Myth and Editorial Misconstruction in the Yale Prose Edition'. In *Milton, Rights and Liberties*, edited by C. Tournu, pp. 113–30. New York, NY: Peter Lang.

Martin, C. G. (2010). *Milton among the Puritans: The Case for Historical Revisionism*. Aldershot: Ashgate.

Martin, C. G. (ed.) (2004). *Milton and Gender*. Cambridge: Cambridge University Press.

Martin, J., and A. Ryrie (eds) (2012). *Private and Domestic Devotion in Early Modern Britain*. Farnham: Ashgate.

Martin, J. W. (1976). 'Elizabethan Protestant Separatism at its Beginnings: Henry Hart and the Free Will Men'. *Sixteenth Century Journal* 7: 55–74.

Martin, J. W. (1981). 'Miles Hogarde: Artisan and Aspiring Author in Sixteenth-Century England'. *Renaissance Quarterly* 34: 359–83.

Martz, L. L. (1954). *The Poetry of Meditation: A Study of English Religious Literature of the Seventeenth Century*. New Haven, CT: Yale University Press. [Rev. edn. London: Oxford University Press, 1962.]

Martz, L. L. (1969). *The Wit of Love: Donne, Crashaw, Carew, Marvell*. Notre Dame, IN: University of Notre Dame Press.

Marx, S. (2000). *Shakespeare and the Bible*. Oxford: Oxford University Press.

Mascuch, M. (1997). *Origins of the Individualist Self: Autobiography and Self-identity in England, 1591–1791*. Cambridge: Polity Press.

Matar, N. I. (1987). 'Milton and the Idea of the Restoration of the Jews'. *SEL: Studies in English Literature* 27: 109–124.

Matar, N. I. (1990). 'George Herbert, Henry Vaughan, and the Conversion of the Jews'. *Studies in English Literature* 30: 79–92.

Matar, N. I. (1998). *Islam in Britain, 1558–1685* Cambridge: Cambridge University Press.

Matar, N. I. (1999). *Turks, Moors, and Englishmen in the Age of Discovery*. New York, NY: Columbia University Press.

Matar, N. I. (2009). *Europe through Arab Eyes, 1578–1727*. New York, NY: Columbia University Press.

Matar, N. I. (2011). 'Elizabeth through Moroccan Eyes'. In *The Foreign Relations of Elizabeth I*, edited by C. Beem, pp. 145–67. New York, NY: Palgrave Macmillan.

Matar, N. I. (ed.) (2003). *In the Lands of the Christians: Arabic Travel Writing in the Seventeenth Century*. New York, NY: Routledge.

Matheson, P. (2001). *The Imaginative World of the Reformation*. Minneapolis, MN: Fortress Press.

Mayer, R. (2007). 'Lucy Hutchinson: A Life of Writing'. *The Seventeenth Century* 22: 305–35.

Mayer, T. F. (1989). *Thomas Starkey and the Commonweal: Humanist Politics and Religion in the Reign of Henry VIII*. Cambridge: Cambridge University Press.

Mayer, T. F. (2000). *Reginald Pole: Prince and Prophet*. Cambridge: Cambridge University Press.

Mayer, T. F. (2004), 'Pole, Reginald (1500–1558), cardinal and archbishop of Canterbury'. *ODNB*.

Mazzola, E. (2003). *Favorite Sons: The Politics and Poetics of the Sidney Family*. New York, NY: Palgrave Macmillan.

McAdoo, H. R. (1965). *The Spirit of Anglicanism: A Survey of Anglican Theological Method in the Seventeenth Century*. Hale memorial lectures of Seabury-Western Theological Seminary. London: A & C Black.

McAdoo, H. R. (1983). *The Unity of Anglicanism: Catholic and Reformed*. Wilton, CT: Morehouse-Barlow.

McCabe, I. B. (2008). *Orientalism in Early Modern France: Eurasian Trade, Exoticism, and the Ancien Regime*. Oxford: Berg Publishing.

McCabe, R. (2009). 'Spenser, Plato, and the Politics of State'. *Spenser Studies* 24: 433–52.

McCall, F. (2013). *Baal's Priests: The Loyalist Clergy and the English Revolution*. Cambridge: Cambridge University Press.

McColley, D. K. (1997). *Poetry and Music in Seventeenth-Century England*. Cambridge: Cambridge University Press.

McConica, J. K. (1965). *English Humanists and Reformation Politics under Henry VIII and Edward VI*. Oxford: Clarendon Press.

McCoog, T. M. (1993). ' "The Flower of Oxford": the Role of Edmund Campion in Early Recusant Polemics'. *Sixteenth Century Journal* 24: 899–913.

McCoog, T. M. (2012). *The Society of Jesus in Ireland, Scotland, and England, 1589–1597: Building the Faith of Saint Peter upon the King of Spain's Monarchy*. Farnham: Ashgate.

McCoog, T. M. (ed.) (1996). *The Reckoned Expense: Edmund Campion and the Early English Jesuits*. Woodbridge: Boydell.

McCullough, P. E. (1998a). *Sermons at Court: Politics and Religion in Elizabethan and Jacobean Preaching*. Cambridge: Cambridge University Press.

McCullough, P. E. (1998b). 'Making Dead Men Speak: Laudianism, Print, and the Works of Lancelot Andrewes, 1626–1642'. *The Historical Journal* 41 (2): 401–24.

McCullough, P. E. (2003). 'Donne as Preacher at Court: "Precarious Inthronization" '. In *John Donne's Professional Lives*, edited by D. Colclough, pp. 192–93. Cambridge: D. S. Brewer.

McCullough, P. E. (2006). 'Donne as Preacher'. In *The Cambridge Companion to John Donne*, edited by A. Guibbory, pp. 167–81. Cambridge: Cambridge University Press.

McCullough, P. E. (2008). 'Andrewes, Lancelot (1555–1626)'. *ODNB*.

McCullough, P. E. (2011). "Preaching and Context: John Donne's Sermon at the Funerals of Sir William Cokayne." In *The Oxford Handbook of the Early Modern Sermon*, edited by P. E. McCullough, H. Adlington, and E. Rhatigan, pp. 213–67. Oxford: Oxford University Press.

McCullough, P. E., H. Adlington, and E. Rhatigan (eds) (2011). *The Oxford Handbook of the Early Modern Sermon*. Oxford: Oxford University Press.

McDowell, N. (2003). *The English Radical Imagination: Culture, Religion, and Revolution, 1630–1660*. Oxford: Oxford University Press.

McDowell, N. (2010). 'Dead Souls and Modern Minds? Mortalism and the Early Modern Imagination, from Marlowe to Milton'. *Journal of Medieval and Early Modern Studies* 40: 559–92.

McDowell, P. (1998). *The Women of Grub Street: Press, Politics, and Gender in the London Literary Marketplace 1678–1730*. Oxford: Clarendon Press.

McEachern, C. (2010). 'Spenser and Religion'. In *The Oxford Handbook of Edmund Spenser*, edited by R. A. McCabe, pp. 30–47. Oxford: Oxford University Press.

McEachern, C., and D. Shuger (eds) (1997). *Religion and Culture in Renaissance England*. Cambridge: Cambridge University Press.

McGrath, A. E. (1993). *The Renewal of Anglicanism*. Harrisburg, PA: Morehouse.

McGrath, L. (2002). *Subjectivity and Woman's Poetry in Early Modern England: 'Why on the Ridge Should She Desire to Go?'*. Aldershot: Ashgate.

McJannet, L. (2006). *The Sultan Speaks: Dialogue in English Plays and Histories about the Ottoman Turks*. New York, NY: Palgrave Macmillan.

McKeon, M. (1977). 'Sabbatai Sevi in England'. *AJS Review* 2: 131–69.

McKeon, M. (2005). *The Secret History of Domesticity: Public, Private, and the Division of Knowledge*. Baltimore, MD: Johns Hopkins University Press.

McLane, P. E. (1961). *Spenser's Shepheardes Calender. A Study in Elizabethan Allegory*. Notre Dame, IN: University of Notre Dame Press.

McMillin, S., and S.-B. MacLean (1998). *The Queen's Men and Their Plays*. Cambridge: Cambridge University Press.

Meerhoff, K. (2001) *Entre logique et littérature: Autour de Philippe Melanchthon*. Orleans: Paradigme.

Meggitt, J. J. (2013). *Early Quakers and Islam: Slavery, Apocalyptic and Christian-Muslim Encounters in the Seventeenth Century*. Uppsala: Swedish Science Press.

Mercer, C. (2012). 'Knowledge and Suffering in Early Modern Philosophy: G. W. Leibniz and Anne Conway'. In *Emotional Minds: The Passions and the Limits of Enquiry in Early Modern Philosophy*, edited by S. Ebbersmeyer, pp. 179–206. Göttingen: de Gruyter.

Merritt, J. F. (2002). 'The Pastoral Tightrope: A Puritan Pedagogue in Jacobean London'. In *Politics, Religion and Popularity: Early Stuart Essays in Honour of Conrad Russell*, edited by T. Cogswell, R. Cust, and P. Lake, pp. 143–61. Cambridge: Cambridge University Press.

Merritt, J. F. (2005). *The Social World of Early Modern Westminster: Abbey, Court and Community, 1525–1640*. Manchester: Manchester University Press.

Merry, M., and P. Baker (2009). '"For the House her Self and One Servant": Family and Household in Late Seventeenth-Century London'. *The London Journal* 34 (3): 205–32.

Merton, R. (2002). *Science, Technology, and Society in Seventeenth-Century England*. Orig. pub. 1938. New York, NY: Howard Fertig.

Metzger, M. J. (1998). '"Now by My Hood, a Gentle and No Jew": Jessica, *The Merchant of Venice*, and the Discourse of Early Modern Identity'. *PMLA* 113: 52–63.

Michael, E. (2000). 'Renaissance Theories of Body, Soul, and Mind'. In *Psyche and Soma: Physicians and Metaphysicians on the Mind–Body Problem from Antiquity to the Enlightenment*, edited by J. P. Wright and P. Potter, pp. 148–72. Oxford: Clarendon Press.

Mignolo, W. D. (2003). *The Darker Side of the Renaissance: Literacy, Territoriality, and Colonization*. 2nd edn. Ann Arbor, MI: University of Michigan Press.

Miller, C. (2013). *Richard Hooker and the Vision of God: Exploring the Origins of Anglicanism.* Cambridge: James Clarke.

Miller, P. N. (2000). *Peiresc's Europe: Learning and Virtue in the Seventeenth Century.* New Haven, CT: Yale University Press.

Miller, S. (2001). 'Mary Sidney and Gendered Strategies for the Writing of Poetry'. In *Write or Be Written: Early Modern Women Poets and Cultural Constraints,* edited by B. Smith and U. Appelt, pp. 155–76. Aldershot: Ashgate.

Miller, S. (2008). 'Maternity, Marriage, and Contract: Lucy Hutchinson's Response to Patriarchal Theory in *Order and Disorder'.* In *Engendering the Fall: John Milton and Seventeenth-Century Women Writers.* Philadelphia, PA: University of Pennsylvania Press.

Milton, A. (1995, 2005). *Catholic and Reformed: The Roman and Protestant Churches in English Protestant Thought, 1600–1640.* Cambridge: Cambridge University Press.

Milton, A. (2009). 'Laud, William (1573–1645)'. *ODNB.*

Milton, A. (2011). 'New Horizons in the Early Jacobean Period'. In *The Oxford Handbook of John Donne,* edited by J. Shami, D. Flynn, and M. T. Hester, pp. 483–94. Oxford: Oxford University Press.

Milton, G. (2000). *Big Chief Elizabeth.* London: Hodder & Stoughton.

Milward, P. (1977). *Religious Controversies of the Elizabethan Age: A Survey of Printed Sources.* Lincoln: University of Nebraska Press.

Minton, G. (2010). ' "Suffer Me Not to Be Separated/And Let my Cry Come unto Thee": John Bale's Apocalypse and the Exilic Imagination'. *Reformation* 15: 83–97.

Miola, R. S. (2012). 'Publishing the Word: Robert Southwell's Sacred Poetry', *The Review of English Studies* n.s. 64 (265): 410–32.

Mitchell, W. F. (1962). *English Pulpit Oratory from Andrewes to Tillotson.* New York, NY: Russell & Russell.

Mohamed, F. G. (2008). *The Anteroom of Divinity: The Reformation of the Angels from Colet to Milton.* Toronto: University of Toronto Press.

Molekamp, F. (2010). 'Early Modern Women and Affective Devotional Reading'. *European Review of History* 17 (1): 53–74.

Monta, S. B. (2005). *Martyrdom and Literature in Early Modern England.* Cambridge: Cambridge University Press.

Moore, H. (2000). 'Ancient and Modern Romance'. *The Oxford History of Literary Translation in English, Volume 2: 1550–1600,* edited by G. Braden, R. Cummings, and S. Gillespie, pp. 333–46. Oxford: Oxford University Press.

Moore, M. (2000). *Desiring Voices: Women Sonneteers and Petrarchanism.* Carbondale, IL: Southern Illinois University Press.

Moore, R. (2000). *The Light in their Consciences: The Early Quakers in Britain 1646–1666.* University Park, PA: Pennsylvania State University Press.

Moore, R. (2004). 'Seventeenth Century Published Quaker Verse'. *Quaker Studies* 9 (11): 5–16.

More, E. (1982–3). 'John Goodwin and the Origins of the New Arminianism'. *Journal of British Studies* 22 (1): 50–70.

Morgan, J. (2009). 'Brinsley, John (*bap.* 1566, *d.* in or after 1624)'. *ODNB.*

Morgan, P. (1989). ' Frances Wolfreston and "Hor Boukes": A Seventeenth-Century Woman Book-Collector'. *Library,* 6th ser. 11 (3): 197–219.

Morison, S. (1945). *English Prayer Books: An Introduction to the Literature of Christian Public Worship.* Cambridge: Cambridge University Press.

Morrill, J. (1982). 'The Church in England, 1642–9'. In *Reactions to the English Civil War, 1642–1649*, edited by J. Morrill, pp. 89–114. Basingstoke: Macmillan.

Morrill, J. (1984). 'The Religious Context of the English Civil War'. *TRHS* (5th series) 34: 155–78.

Morrill, J. (1990). 'Rhetoric and Action: Charles I, Tyranny, and the English Revolution'. In *Religion, Resistance, and Civil War*, edited by G. Schochet, pp. 91–106. Washington, DC: Folger Library.

Morrill, J. (1993). *The Nature of the English Revolution: Essays*. London: Longman.

Morrill, J. (1994). 'A British Patriarchy? Ecclesiastical Imperialism under the Early Stuarts'. In *Religion, Culture and Society in Early Modern Britain: Essays in Honour of Patrick Collinson*, edited by A. Fletcher and P. Roberts, pp. 209–37. Cambridge: Cambridge University Press.

Morris, A. M. E. (2005). *Popular Measures: Poetry and Church Order in Seventeenth-Century Massachusetts*. Newark, DE: University of Delaware Press.

Morris, K. R. (2012). 'Theological Sources of William Penn's Concept of Religious Toleration'. *Quaker Studies* 16 (2): 190–212.

Morrissey, M. (2002). 'Scripture, Style and Persuasion in Seventeenth-Century English Theories of Preaching'. *Journal of Ecclesiastical History* 53 (4): 686–706.

Morrissey, M. (2011). *Politics and the Paul's Cross Sermons, 1558–1642*. Oxford: Oxford University Press.

Morse, R., H. Cooper, and P. Holland (2013). *Medieval Shakespeares: Pasts and Presents*. Cambridge: Cambridge University Press.

Mortimer, S. (2011). 'Natural Law and Holy War in the English Revolution'. In *England's Wars of Religion, Revisited*, edited by C. W. A. Prior and G. Burgess, pp. 194–208. Farnham: Ashgate.

Morton, A. L. (1970). *The World of the Ranters: Religious Radicalism in the English Revolution*. London: Lawrence and Wishart.

Moss, A. (1996). *Printed Commonplace-Books and the Structuring of Renaissance Thought*. Oxford: Oxford University Press.

Mueller, J. M. (1984). *The Native Tongue and the Word: Developments in English Prose Style 1380–1580*. Chicago, IL: University of Chicago Press.

Mullan, D. G. (1986). *Episcopacy in Scotland: The History of an Idea, 1560–1638*. Edinburgh: John Donald.

Muller, R. (2003). *After Calvin: Studies in the Development of a Theological Tradition*. Oxford: Oxford University Press.

Mullet, M. (1980). *Radical Religious Movements in Early Modern Europe*. London: George Allen and Unwin.

Munro, L. (2013). *Archaic Style in English Literature, 1590–1674*. Cambridge: Cambridge University Press.

Murphy, A. R. (2001). *Conscience and Community: Revisiting Toleration and Religious Dissent in Early Modern England and America*. University Park, PA: Pennsylvania State University Press.

Murphy, E. (2011). *Familial Forms: Politics and Genealogy in Seventeenth-Century English Literature*. Newark, DE: University of Delaware Press.

Murphy, E. K. M. (2014). '*Adoramus te Christe*: Music and Post-Reformation English Catholic Domestic Piety'. In *Religion and the Household*, edited by J. Doran, C. Methuen, and A. Walsham, pp. 240–53. Woodbridge: Boydell and Brewer.

Murphy, T. R. (1986). '"Woful Childe of Parents Rage": Suicide of Children and Adolescents in Early Modern England, 1507–1710'. *The Sixteenth Century Journal* 17 (3) (Autumn): 259–70.

Murray, M. (2009). 'Measured Sentences: Forming Literature in the Early Modern Period'. *Huntington Library Quarterly* 72 (2): 147–67.

Narveson, K. (2012). *Bible Readers and Lay Writers in Early Modern England: Gender and Self-Definition in an Emergent Writing Culture*. Farnham: Ashgate.

Nash, S. (2008). *Northern Renaissance Art*. Oxford: Oxford University Press.

Navitsky, J. (2008). 'Disputing Good Bishop's English: Martin Marprelate and the Voice of Menippean Opposition'. *Texas Studies in Literature and Language* 50 (2): 177–200.

Neill, M. (1997). *Issues of Death: Mortality and Identity in English Renaissance Tragedy*. Oxford: Oxford University Press.

Neill, M. (2010). 'Introduction' to Philip Massinger, *The Renegado*, edited by M. Neill. Arden Early Modern Drama. London: A & C Black.

Neill, S. (1958). *Anglicanism*. Harmondsworth: Penguin.

Nelson, E. (2010). *The Hebrew Republic: Jewish Sources and the Transformation of European Political Thought*. Cambridge, MA: Harvard University Press.

Neufeld, M. (2013). *The Civil Wars after 1660: Public Remembering in Late Stuart England*. Woodbridge: Boydell Press.

Neville-Sington, P. (1999). 'Press, Politics and Religion'. In *The Cambridge History of the Book in Britain*, vol. 3, edited by L. Hellinga and J. B. Trapp, pp. 576–607. Cambridge: Cambridge University Press.

Nevitt, M. (2006). *Women and the Pamphlet Culture of Revolutionary England, 1640–1660*. Aldershot: Ashgate.

Newman, B. (1985). 'Hildegard of Bingen: Visions and Validation'. *Church History* 54: 163–75.

Newman, B. (1998). *From Virile Woman to WomanChrist: Studies in Medieval Religion and Literature*. Philadelphia, PA: University of Pennsylvania Press.

Newman, W. R. (1994). 'Boyle's Debt to Corpuscular Alchemy'. In *Robert Boyle Reconsidered*, edited by M. Hunter, pp. 107–18. Cambridge: Cambridge University Press.

Nezam-Mafi, M. (1999). 'Persian Recreations: Theatricality in Anglo-Persian Diplomatic History, 1599–1828'. Unpublished PhD dissertation, Boston University.

Nicholson, G. (1988). 'The Act of Appeals and the English Reformation'. In *Law and Government under the Tudors*, edited by C. Cross, D. Loades, and J. J. Scarisbrick, pp. 19–30. Cambridge: Cambridge University Press.

Nicollier-de Weck, B. (1995). *Hubert Languet (1518–1581), un réseau politique international de Melanchthon à Guillaume d'Orange*. Geneva: Droz.

Nischan, B. (1999). *Lutherans and Calvinists in the Age of Confessionalism*. Aldershot: Ashgate.

Norbrook, D. (1984). *Poetry and Politics in the English Renaissance*. London: Routledge & Kegan Paul.

Norbrook, D. (1997). 'Lucy Hutchinson's "Elegies" and the Situation of the Republican Woman Writer (with Text)'. *ELR* 27: 468–521.

Norbrook, D. (2000). 'Lucy Hutchinson and *Order and Disorder*: The Manuscript Evidence'. *English Manuscript Studies 1100–1700* 9: 257–91.

Norbrook, D. (2003). 'John Milton, Lucy Hutchinson, and the Republican Biblical Epic'. In *Milton and the Grounds of Contention*, edited by M. R. Kelley, M. Lieb, and J. T. Shawcross, pp. 37–63. Pittsburgh, PA: Duquesne University Press

Norbrook, D. (2010). 'The Sublime Object: Milton, Lucy Hutchinson, and the Lucretian Sublime'. *Tate Papers* 13: 1–23. Available at: http://www.tate.org.uk/research/tateresearch/tatepapers/10spring/norbrook.shtm.

Norbrook, D. (2012). 'Memoirs and Oblivion: Lucy Hutchinson and the Restoration'. *Huntington Library Quarterly* 75: 233–82.

Norland, H. B. (2013a). 'John Foxe's Apocalyptic Comedy, *Christus Triumphans*'. In *The Early Modern Cultures of Neo-Latin Drama*, edited by P. J. Ford and A. Taylor, pp. 75–84. Supplementa Humanistica Lovaniensia, 32. Louvain: Universitaire Pers Leuven.

Norland, H. B. (2013b). 'Neo-Latin Drama in Britain'. In *Neo-Latin Drama and Theatre in Early Modern Europe*, edited by J. Bloemendal and H. B. Norland, pp. 471–544. Drama and Theatre in Early Modern Europe, 3. Leiden: Brill.

North, M. (2003). *The Anonymous Renaissance: Cultures of Discretion in Tudor-Stuart England*. Chicago, IL: Chicago University Press.

Norton, D. (2000). *A History of the English Bible as Literature*. Cambridge: Cambridge University Press.

Norton, D. (2011). *The King James Bible: A Short History from Tyndale to Today*. Cambridge: Cambridge University Press.

Norton, G. P. (1984). *The Ideology and Language of Translation in Renaissance France and Their Humanist Antecedents*. Geneva: Droz.

Null, A. (2011). 'Official Tudor Homilies'. In *The Oxford Handbook of the Early Modern Sermon*, edited by P. McCullough, H. Adlington, and E. Rhatigan, pp. 348–65. Oxford: Oxford University Press.

Nuttall, A. D. (1980). *Overheard by God: Fiction and Prayer in Herbert, Milton, Dante and St John*. London: Methuen.

Nuttall, G. F., intro. P. Lake (1992). *The Holy Spirit in Puritan Faith and Experience*. Chicago, IL: University of Chicago Press.

O'Connell, M. (2000). *The Idolatrous Eye: Iconoclasm and Theater in Early Modern England*. New York, NY: Oxford University Press.

O'Donovan, J. L. (2004). *Theology of Law and Authority in the English Reformation*. Grand Rapids, MI: Eerdmans.

O'Hara, L. (2006). '"Far beyond Her Nature and Her Sex:" The Creation of a Protestant Hagiography in England, 1590–1640'. Unpublished PhD dissertation, Fordham University.

O'Malley, J. (1993). *The First Jesuits*. Cambridge, MA: Harvard University Press.

O'Malley, T. (1982). '"Defying the Powers and Tempering the Spirit": A Review of Quaker Control of their Publications 1672–1689'. *Journal of Ecclesiastical History* 33 (1): 72–88.

O'Sullivan, O. (ed.) (2000). *The Bible as Book: The Reformation*. London: British Library.

Obermann, H. (1984). *The Roots of Anti-Semitism in the Age of the Renaissance and Reformation*. Philadelphia, PA: University of Pennsylvania Press.

Olson, R. G. (2004). *Science and Religion, 1450–1900: From Copernicus to Darwin*. Baltimore, MD: Johns Hopkins University Press.

Orgel, S. (1996). *Impersonations: The Performance of Gender in Shakespeare's England*. Cambridge: Cambridge University Press.

Orr, B. (2001). *Empire on the English Stage, 1600–1714*. Cambridge: Cambridge University Press.

Orr, D. A. (2002). 'Sovereignty, Supremacy and the Origins of the English Civil War'. *History* 87: 474–90.

Osborn, J. M. (1972). *The Young Sir Philip Sidney, 1572–77*. New Haven, CT: Yale University Press.

Osherow, M. (2009). *Biblical Women's Voices in Early Modern England*. Aldershot: Ashgate.

Osmond, R. (1990). *Mutual Accusation: Seventeenth-Century Body and Soul Dialogues in their Literary and Theological Context*. Toronto: University of Toronto Press.

Overell, A., and S. C. Lucas (2012). 'Whose Wonderful News? Italian Satire and William Baldwin's *Wonderfull Newes of the Death of Paule the III*'. *Renaissance Studies* 26 (2): 180–96.

Owen, S. J. (1996). *Restoration Theatre and Crisis*. Oxford: Oxford University Press.

Pacheco, A. (ed.) (2002). *A Companion to Early Modern Women's Writing*. Oxford: Blackwell.

Pagden, A. (1995). *Lords of All the World: Ideologies of Empire in Spain, Britain, and France c.1500–c.1800*. New Haven, CT: Yale University Press.

Panofsky, E. (1992). *Tomb Sculpture: Its Changing Aspects from Ancient Egypt to Bernini*. New York, NY: Harry N. Abrams.

Papazian, M. A. (ed.) (2003). *John Donne and the Protestant Reformation: New Perspectives*. Detroit, MI: Wayne State University Press.

Parker, B. L. (2011). '"Cursèd Necromancy": Marlowe's *Faustus* as Anti-Catholic Satire'. *Marlowe Studies* 1: 59–77.

Parker, J. (2013). 'Faustus, Confession, and the Sins of Omission'. *ELH* 80 (1): 29–59.

Parker, M. (2013). 'Writing Their Way in: The Dedicatory Epistles of Early Modern English Women Authors'. PhD thesis, Texas A&M University.

Partridge, A. C. (1978). *John Donne: Language and Style*. London: Andre Deutsch.

Paster, G. K., K. Rowe, and M. Floyd-Wilson (eds) (2004a). *Reading the Early Modern Passions: Essays in the Cultural History of Emotion*. Philadelphia, PA: University of Pennsylvania Press.

Paster, G. K., K. Rowe, and M. Floyd-Wilson (eds) (2004b). *Humouring the Body: Emotions and the Shakespearean Stage*. Chicago, IL: University of Chicago Press.

Patrides, C. A., and J. Wittreich (eds) (1984). *The Apocalypse in English Renaissance Thought and Literature*. Manchester: Manchester University Press.

Patterson, A. M. (1984). *Censorship and Interpretation: The Conditions of Writing and Reading in Early Modern England*. Madison, WI: University of Wisconsin Press.

Patterson, A. M. (1989). *Shakespeare and the Popular Voice*. Oxford: Blackwell.

Patterson, W. B. (1997). *King James VI and the Reunion of Christendom*. Cambridge: Cambridge University Press.

Patton, E. (2011). 'Dorothy Arundell's "Acts of Father John Cornelius": "We Should Hear from Her, Herself—She Who Left a record of It in These Words"'. *American Notes & Queries* 24 (1): 51–62.

Patton, E. (2013). 'From Community to Convent: The Collective Spiritual Life of Post-Reformation Englishwomen in Dorothy Arundell's Biography of John Cornelius'. In *The English Convents in Exile, 1600–1800: Communities, Culture and Identity*, edited by C. Bowden and J. E. Kelly, pp. 19–32. Farnham: Ashgate.

Peacey, J. (2004). *Politicians and Pamphleteers: Propaganda during the English Civil Wars and Interregnum*. Aldershot: Ashgate.

Peacey, J. (2013). *Print and Politics in the English Revolution*. Cambridge: Cambridge University Press.

Pearson, J. (1996). 'Women Reading, Reading Women'. In *Women and Literature in Britain 1500–1700*, edited by H. Wilcox, pp. 80–99. Cambridge: Cambridge University Press.

Peel, A. (1920). *The First Congregational Churches*. Cambridge: Cambridge University Press.

Pelikan, J. (1984). *The Christian Tradition: A History of the Development of Christian Doctrine*. 5 vols. Chicago, IL: University of Chicago Press.

Perry, N. (2006). '"Tis Heav'n She Speakes": Lady Religion, Saint Teresa, and the Politics of Ceremony in the Poetry of Richard Crashaw'. *Religion & Literature* 38 (2): 1–23.

Perry, N. (2014). *Imitatio Christi: The Poetics of Piety in Early Modern England*. Notre Dame, IN: University of Notre Dame Press.

Perry, R. (2013). '"Some Sprytuall Matter of gostly Edyfycacion": Readers and Readings of Nicholas Love's *Mirror of the Blessed Life of Jesus Christ*'. In *The Pseudo-Bonaventuran Lives of Christ: Exploring the Middle English Tradition*, edited by I. Johnson and A. Westphall, pp. 79–126. Turnhout: Brepols.

Pestana, C. G. (2003). 'Martyred by the Saints: Quaker Executions in Seventeenth-Century Massachusetts'. In *Colonial Saints: Discovering the Holy in the Americas 1500–1800*, edited by A. Greer and J. Bilinkoff. New York, NY: Routledge.

Pestana, C. G. (2009). *Protestant Empire: Religion and the Making of the British Atlantic World*. Pennsylvania, PA: University of Pennsylvania.

Peters, C. (2003). *Patterns of Piety: Women, Gender and Religion in Late Medieval and Reformation England*. Cambridge: Cambridge University Press.

Peters, K. (2005). *Print Culture and the Early Quakers*. Cambridge: Cambridge University Press.

Peterson, D. (1959). 'John Donne's *Holy Sonnets* and the Anglican Doctrine of Contrition'. *Studies in Philology* 56 (3): 504–18.

Pettegree, A. (1996). *Marian Protestantism: Six Studies*. Aldershot: Scolar Press.

Pettegree, A. (2000). 'The Law and the Gospel: The Evolution of an Evangelical Pictorial Theme in the Bibles of the Reformation'. In *The Bible as Book: The Reformation*, edited by O. O'Sullivan, pp. 123–36. London: British Library and Oak Knoll Press.

Pettegree, A. (2002). 'Printing and the Reformation: The English Exception'. In *The Beginnings of English Protestantism*, edited by P. Marshall and A. Ryrie, pp. 157–79. Cambridge: Cambridge University Press.

Pettegree, A. (2005). *Reformation and the Culture of Persuasion*. Cambridge: Cambridge University Press.

Pettegree, A. (2010). *The Book in the Renaissance*. New Haven, CT: Yale University Press.

Pettegree, A. (2014). *The Invention of News: How the World Came to Know about Itself*. New Haven, CT: Yale University Press.

Pfaff, R. W. (2009). *The Liturgy in Medieval England: A History*. Cambridge: Cambridge University Press.

Phillips, E. (1957). 'The Life of John Milton'. In *John Milton, The Complete Poetry and Major Prose*, edited by M. Y. Hughes, pp. 1025–37. New York, NY: Odyssey Press.

Pincombe, M. (2001). *Elizabethan Humanism: Literature and Learning in the Later Sixteenth Century*. Harlow: Longman.

Pincombe, M. (2010). 'Truth, Lies, and Fiction in William Baldwin's *Wonderful News of the Death of Paul III*'. *Reformation* 15: 3–22.

Pineas, R. (1968). *Thomas More and Tudor Polemics*. Bloomington, IN: Indiana University Press.

Pincus, S. (2007). 'The State and Civil Society in Early Modern England: Capitalism, Causation and Habermas's Bourgeois Public Sphere'. In *The Politics of the Public Sphere in Early Modern England*, edited by P. Lake and S. Pincus, pp. 213–31. Manchester: Manchester University Press.

Pincus, S. (2009). *1688: The First Modern Revolution*. New Haven, CT: Yale University Press.

Pincus, S. (2012). 'Addison's Empire: Whig Conceptions of Empire in the Early 18th Century'. In *Faction Displayed: Reconsidering the Impeachment of Dr Henry Sacheverell*, edited by M. Knights, pp. 99–117. Chichester: Wiley-Blackwell for The Parliamentary History Yearbook Trust.

Platten, S. (2003). *Anglicanism and the Western Christian Tradition: Continuity, Change and the Search for Communion.* Norwich: Canterbury Press.

Pocock, J. G. A. (1983). 'A Discourse of Sovereignty: Observations on the Work in Progress'. In *Political Discourse in Early Modern Britain*, edited by N. Phillipson and Q. Skinner, pp. 377–428. Cambridge: Cambridge University Press.

Pocock, J. G. A. (1985a). 'The History of British Political Thought: The Creation of a Center'. *Journal of British Studies* 24: 283–310.

Pocock, J. G. A. (1985b). *Virtue, Commerce, and History: Essays on Political Thought and History.* Cambridge: Cambridge University Press.

Pocock, J. G. A. (1987). *The Ancient Constitution and the Feudal Law: A Study of English Historical Thought in the Seventeenth Century. A Reissue with a Retrospect.* Cambridge: Cambridge University Press.

Pocock, J. G. A. (2005). *The Discovery of Islands: Essays in British History.* Cambridge: Cambridge University Press.

Polder, K. (2015). *Matrimony in the True Church: The Seventeenth-Century Quaker Marriage Approbation Discipline.* Abingdon: Routledge.

Poleg, E. (2013). 'Wycliffite Bibles as Orthodoxy'. In *Cultures of Religious Reading in the Late Middle Ages: Instructing the Soul, Feeding the Spirit, and Awakening the Passion*, edited by S. Corbellini, pp. 71–91. Turnhout: Brepols.

Pollock, L. A. (2010). 'Mildmay, Grace, Lady Mildmay (*c*.1552–1620)'. *ODNB*.

Pollock, L. A. (ed.) (1993). *With Faith and Physic: The Life of a Tudor Gentlewoman, Lady Grace Mildmay, 1552–1620.* London: Collins & Brown.

Poole, K. (1995). '"The Fittest Closet for All Goodness": Authorial Strategies of Jacobean Mothers' Manuals'. *Studies in English Literature* 35 (1): 69–88.

Poole, K. (2000). *Radical Religion from Shakespeare to Milton: Figures of Nonconformity in Early Modern England.* Cambridge: Cambridge University Press.

Popkin, R. H. (2004). 'Can One Be a True Christian and a Faithful Follower of the Law of Moses? The Answer of John Dury'. In *Secret Conversions to Judaism in Early Modern Europe*, edited by M. Muslow and R. H. Popkin, pp. 33–50. Leiden: Brill.

Potter, L. (1989). *Secret Rites and Secret Writing: Royalist Literature, 1641–1660.* Cambridge: Cambridge University Press.

Powell, S. (2011). 'After Arundel but before Luther: The First Half-Century of Print'. In *After Arundel: Religious Writing in Fifteenth-Century England*, edited by V. Gillespie and K. Ghosh, pp. 523–43. Turnhout: Brepols.

Powicke, F. J. (1901–4). 'The Early Separatists'. *Transactions of the Congregational Historical Society* 1: 141–58.

Powicke, M. (1941). *The Reformation in England.* Oxford: Oxford University Press.

Prescott, A. L. (1989). 'King David as a "Right Poet": Sidney and the Psalmist'. *English Literary Renaissance* 19 (2): 148–50.

Prescott, A. L. (1999). 'Rabelaisian (Non)Wonders and Renaissance Polemics'. In *Wonders, Marvels, and Monsters in Early Modern Culture*, edited by P. G. Platt, pp. 133–44. Newark, DE: University of Delaware Press.

Prescott, A. L. (2000). 'The Evolution of Tudor Satire'. In *The Cambridge Companion to English Literature, 1500–1600*, edited by A. Kinney, pp. 220–40. Cambridge: Cambridge University Press.

Prescott, A. L. (2003). 'The Ambivalent Heart: Thomas More's Merry Tales'. *Criticism* 45 (4): 417–33.

Prescott, A. L. (2005a). 'The Countess of Pembroke's *Ruins of Rome*'. *Sidney Journal* 23: 1–17.

Prescott, A. L. (2005b). 'Tracing Astrophil's "Coltish Gyres": Sidney and the Horses of Desire'. *Renaissance Papers*: 25–42.

Prescott, A. L. (2008). 'Mary Sidney's French Sophocles: The Countess of Pembroke Reads Robert Garnier'. In *Representing France and the French in Early Modern English Drama*, edited by Jean-Chrisophe Mayer, pp. 68–92. Newark, DE: University of Delaware Press.

Prestwich, M. (ed.) (1985). *International Calvinism 1548–1715*. Oxford: Oxford University Press.

Principe, L. M. (1994). 'Boyle's Alchemical Pursuits'. In *Robert Boyle Reconsidered*, edited by M. Hunter, pp. 91–105. Cambridge: Cambridge University Press.

Prior, C. W. A. (2005a). *Defining the Jacobean Church: The Politics of Religious Controversy, 1603–1625*. Cambridge: Cambridge University Press.

Prior, C. W. A. (2005b). 'Ecclesiology and Political Thought in England, 1580–c.1630'. *The Historical Journal* 48 (4): 855–84.

Prior, C. W. A. (2012). *A Confusion of Tongues: Britain's Wars of Reformation, 1625–1642*. Oxford: Oxford University Press.

Prior, C. W. A. (2013a). 'The Highest Powers': Grotius and the Internationalization of Church and State. *Grotiana* 34: 91–106.

Prior, C. W. A. (2013b). 'Religion, Political Thought and the English Civil War'. *History Compass* 11 (1): 24–42.

Prior, C. W. A. (2015). 'England's Wars of Religion: A Reassessment'. In *The European Wars of Religion: An Interdisciplinary Reassessment of Sources, Interpretations and Myths*, edited by W. Palaver, D. Regensberger, and H. Rudolf, pp. 119–38. Farnham: Ashgate.

Prior, C. W. A., and G. Burgess (eds) (2011). *England's Wars of Religion, Revisited*. Farnham: Ashgate.

Prior, R. (1990). 'A Second Jewish Community in Tudor London'. *Jewish Historical Studies: Transactions of the Jewish Historical Society of England* 31: 137–52.

Pugh, S. (2005). *Spenser and Ovid*. Aldershot: Ashgate.

Questier, M. (1996). *Conversion, Politics and Religion in England, 1580–1625*. Cambridge: Cambridge University Press.

Questier, M. (2006). *Catholicism and Community in Early Modern England: Politics, Aristocratic Patronage and Religion c.1550–1640*. Cambridge: Cambridge University Press.

Quilligan, M. (2005). *Incest and Agency in Elizabeth's England*. Philadelphia, PA: University of Pennsylvania Press.

Quitslund, B. (2008). *The Reformation in Rhyme: Sternhold, Hopkins and the English Metrical Psalter*. Aldershot: Ashgate.

Quitslund, B. (2012). 'Singing the Psalms for Fun and Profit'. In *Private and Domestic Devotion in Early Modern Britain*, edited by J. Martin and A. Ryrie, pp. 237–58. Farnham: Ashgate.

Raber, K. (2001). *Dramatic Difference: Gender, Class, and Genre in the Early Modern Closet Drama*. Newark, DE: University of Delaware Press.

Radzinowicz, M. A. (1978). *Toward 'Samson Agonistes': The Growth of Milton's Mind*. Princeton, NJ: Princeton University Press.

Raffe, A. (2012). *The Culture of Controversy: Religious Arguments in Scotland, 1660–1714*. Woodbridge: Boydell Press.

Ragussis, M. (1995). *Figures of Conversion: 'The Jewish Question' and English National Identity*. Durham, NC: Duke University Press.

Raiger, M. (1998). 'Sidney's Defense of Plato'. *Religion and Literature* 30 (2): 41–2.

Rambuss, R. (1998). *Closet Devotions*. Durham, NC: Duke University Press.

Ramsey, A. M. (1945). 'What Is Anglican Theology?' *Theology* 48: 2–6.

Randall, D. (1995). *Winter Fruit: English Drama, 1642–1660*. Lexington, KY: University Press of Kentucky.

Ransome, J. (2005). 'Monotessaron: The Harmonies of Little Gidding'. *The Seventeenth Century* 20 (1): 22–52.

Ransome, J. (2009). ' "Voluntary Anglicanism": The Contribution of Little Gidding'. *The Seventeenth Century* 24 (1): 52–73.

Rappaport, R. (1991). *Ritual and Religion in the Making of Humanity*. Cambridge: Cambridge University Press.

Raven, J. (2007). *The Business of Books: Bestsellers and the English Book Trade 1450–1850*. New Haven, CT: Yale University Press.

Ray, R. H. (1986). 'The Herbert Allusion Book: Allusions to George Herbert in the Seventeenth Century'. *Studies in Philology: Texts and Studies* 83 (4): i–ix, 1–182.

Raymond, J. (1999). 'The Newspaper, Public Opinion, and the Public Sphere in the Seventeenth Century'. In *News, Newspapers, and Society in Early Modern Britain*, edited by J. Raymond, pp. 109–40. London: Routledge.

Raymond, J. (2003). *Pamphlets and Pamphleteering in Early Modern Britain*. Cambridge: Cambridge University Press.

Read, S. (2013). *Eucharist and the Poetic Imagination in Early Modern England*. Cambridge: Cambridge University Press.

Reay, B. (1985). *The Quakers and the English Revolution*. Hounslow: Temple Smith.

Reisner, N. (2011). 'The Preacher and Prophane Learning'. In *The Oxford Handbook of the Early Modern Sermon*, edited by P. McCullough, H. Adlington, and E. Rhatigan, pp. 72–86. Oxford: Oxford University Press.

Remer, G. (1996). *Humanism and the Rhetoric of Toleration*. University Park, PA: Pennsylvania State University Press.

Rex, R. (1989). 'The English campaign against Luther in the 1520s', *TRHS* (5th series) 39: 85–106.

Rex, R. (2011). 'Thomas More and the Heretics: Statesman or Fanatic?' In *The Cambridge Companion to Thomas More*, edited by G. M. Logan, pp. 93–115. Cambridge: Cambridge University Press.

Reynolds, S. (1991). 'Social Mentalities and the Cases of Medieval Scepticism'. *TRHS* (6th series) 1: 21–41.

Rhatigan, E. (2011). 'Preaching Venues: Architecture and Auditories'. In *The Oxford Handbook of the Early Modern Sermon*, edited by P. McCullough, H. Adlington, and E. Rhatigan, pp. 87–119. Oxford: Oxford University Press.

Rhatigan, E. (2012). 'Reading the White Devil in Thomas Adams and John Webster'. In *Early Modern Drama and the Bible: Contexts and Readings, 1570–1625*, edited by A. Streete, pp. 176–94. Basingstoke: Palgrave Macmillan.

Richards, J. (1996). 'Philip Sidney, Mary Sidney, and Protestant Poetics'. *Sidney Journal* 14: 28–36.

Richardson, R. C. (2002). 'The Generation Gap: Parental Advice in Early Modern England'. *Clio* 32 (1): 1–25.

Richardson, R. C. (2004). 'Social Engineering in Early Modern England: Masters, Servants, and the Godly Discipline'. *Clio* 33 (2): 163–87.

Ricks, C. (1963). *Milton's Grand Style*. Oxford: Clarendon Press.

Rienstra, D. (2011–12). ' "Let Wits Contest": George Herbert and the English Sonnet Sequence'. *George Herbert Journal* 35: 23–44.

Rienstra, D., and N. Kinnamon (2002). 'Circulating the Sidney-Pembroke Psalter'. In *Women's Writing and the Circulation of Ideas: Manuscript Publication in England, 1550–1800*, edited by G. L. Justice and N. Tinker, pp. 50–72. Cambridge: Cambridge University Press.

Rigney, J. (2011). 'Sermons into Print'. In *The Oxford Handbook of the Early Modern Sermon*, edited by P. McCullough, H. Adlington, and E. Rhatigan, pp. 198–212. Oxford: Oxford University Press.

Riordan, M., and A. Ryrie (2003). 'Stephen Gardiner and the Making of a Protestant Villain'. *Sixteenth Century Journal* 34: 1039–63.

Rivard, D. (2009). *Blessing the World: Ritual and Lay Piety in Medieval Religion*. Washington, DC: Catholic University of America Press.

Rivers, I. (2009). 'Religious Publishing'. In *The Cambridge History of the Book in Britain, Volume V: 1695–1830*, edited by M. F. Suarez, S. J., and M. L. Turner. Cambridge: Cambridge University Press.

Roberts, J. R. (1973). *John Donne: An Annotated Bibliography of Modern Criticism, 1912–1967*. Columbia, MO: University of Missouri Press.

Roberts, J. R. (1982). *John Donne: An Annotated Bibliography of Modern Criticism, 1968–1978*. Columbia, MO: University of Missouri Press.

Roberts, J. R. (1985). *Richard Crashaw: An Annotated Bibliography of Criticism, 1632–1980*. Columbia, MO: University of Missouri Press.

Roberts, J. R. (1988). *George Herbert: An Annotated Bibliography of Modern Criticism, Revised Edition, 1905–1984*. Columbia, MO: University of Missouri Press.

Roberts, J. R. (2004). *John Donne: An Annotated Bibliography of Modern Criticism, 1979–1995*. Pittsburgh, PA: Duquesne University Press.

Roberts, J. R. (2005). 'Richard Crashaw: An Annotated Bibliography of Criticism, 1981–2002', *John Donne Journal* 24: 1–228.

Roberts, J. R. (2013). *John Donne: An Annotated Bibliography of Modern Criticism, 1996–2008*. DigitalDonne.

Roberts, J. R. (ed.) (1994). *New Perspectives on the Seventeenth-Century English Religious Lyric*. Columbia, MO: University of Missouri Press.

Robinson, B. (2007). *Islam and Early Modern English Literature: The Politics of Romance from Spenser to Milton*. New York, NY: Palgrave Macmillan.

Robinson, F. (1999). 'The British Empire and the Muslim World'. In *The Oxford History of the British Empire, Volume 4: The Twentieth Century*, edited by J. M. Brown and W. R. Louis, pp. 398–420. Oxford: Oxford University Press.

Robinson, M. (2010). *Absence of Mind: The Dispelling of Inwardness from the Modern Myth of the Self*. New Haven, CT: Yale University Press.

Robinson, M. S. (2002). *Writing the Reformation: 'Actes and Monuments' and the Jacobean History Play*. Aldershot: Ashgate.

Rodman Jones, M. (2011). *Radical Pastoral, 1381–1594: Appropriation and the Writing of Religious Controversy*. Farnham: Ashgate.

Rogerson, M. (1998). 'English Puppets and the Survival of Religious Theater'. *Theatre Notebook* 52 (2): 91–111.

Rose, C. (1999). *England in the 1690s: Revolution, Religion and War*. Oxford: Blackwell.

Rose, J. (2011). *Godly Kingship in Restoration England: The Politics of the Royal Supremacy, 1660–1688*. Cambridge: Cambridge University Press.

Rosenblatt, J. P. (1994). *Torah and Law in 'Paradise Lost'*. Princeton, NJ: Princeton University Press.

Rosenblatt, J. P. (2006). *Renaissance England's Chief Rabbi: John Selden*. Oxford: Oxford University Press.

Rosendale, T. (2001). ' "Fiery toungues": Language, Liturgy, and the Paradox of the English Reformation'. *Renaissance Quarterly* 54 (4): 1142–64.

Rosendale, T. (2004). 'Milton, Hobbes, and the Liturgical Subject'. *Studies in English Literature* 44 (1): 149–72.

Rosendale, T. (2007, 2015). *Liturgy and Literature in the Making of Protestant England*. Cambridge: Cambridge University Press.

Rosenthal, F. (1960/1). 'Al-Mubashshir ibn Fâtik: Prolegomena to an Abortive Edition'. *Oriens* 13/14: 132–58.

Ross, S. (2010). ' "Give Me thy Hairt and I Desire No More": The Song of Songs, Petrarchism and Elizabeth Melville's Puritan Poetics'. In *The Intellectual Culture of Puritan Women, 1558–1680*, edited by J. Harris and E. Scott-Baumann, pp. 96–107. Basingstoke: Palgrave Macmillan.

Roston, M. (1968). *Biblical Drama in England: From the Middle Ages to the Present Day*. London: Faber and Faber.

Roth, C. (1941). *A History of the Jews in England*. Oxford: Oxford University Press.

Roth, C. (1965). *The Jews in the Renaissance*. New York, NY: Harper & Row.

Rousseau, G. S. (2008). ' "Brainomania": Brain, Mind and Soul in the Long Eighteenth Century'. *British Journal for Eighteenth-Century Studies* 30: 161–91.

Rowell, G. (ed.), with a foreword by the Archbishop of Canterbury (1992). *The English Religious Tradition and the Genius of Anglicanism*. Nashville, TN: Abingdon Press.

Rozett, M. T. (1984). *The Doctrine of Election and the Emergence of Elizabethan Tragedy*. Princeton, NJ: Princeton University Press.

Rubin, M. (1991). *Corpus Christi: the Eucharist in Late Medieval Culture*. Cambridge: Cambridge University Press.

Rudenstine, N. (1967). *Sidney's Poetic Development*. Cambridge, MA: Harvard University Press.

Ruderman, D. (1995). *Jewish Thought and Scientific Discovery in Early Modern Europe*. New Haven, CT: Yale University Press.

Rummel, E. (1995). *The Humanist-Scholastic Debate in the Renaissance and Reformation*. Cambridge, MA: Harvard University Press.

Runyan, D. (1973). 'Appendix: Types of Quaker Writings by Year, 1650–1699'. In *Early Quaker Writing: 1650–1700*, edited by H. Barbour and A. O. Roberts, pp. 567–76. Grand Rapids, MI: Eerdmans.

Rupp, G. (1957). *Six Makers of English Religion, 1500–1700*. London: Hodder & Stoughton.

Russell, C. (1973). *Origins of the English Civil War*. New York, NY: Barnes & Noble.

Russell, C. (1990). *The Causes of the English Civil War*. Oxford: Oxford University Press.

Russell, C. (1991). *The Fall of the British Monarchies, 1637–1642*. Oxford: Oxford University Press.

Russell, C. (2000). 'Parliament, the Royal Supremacy and the Church'. *Parliamentary History* 19: 27–37.

Ryrie, A. (2002). 'The Strange Death of Lutheran England'. *Journal of Ecclesiastical History* 53: 64–92.

Ryrie, A. (2003). *The Gospel and Henry VIII: Evangelicals in the Early Church of England*. Cambridge: Cambridge University Press.

Ryrie, A. (2004). 'Marshall, William (*d.* 1540?)'. *ODNB*.

Ryrie, A. (2013, 2015). *Being Protestant in Reformation Britain*. Oxford: Oxford University Press.

Sachs, W. L. (1993). *The Transformation of Anglicanism: From State Church to Global Communion*. New York, NY: Cambridge University Press.

Şahin, K., and J. Schleck (2016). 'Courtly Connections: Anthony Sherley's *Relation of his Trauels* (1613) in a Global Context'. *Renaissance Quarterly* 69: 80–115.

Said, E. W. (1979). *Orientalism*. New York, NY: Vintage Books.

Salmon, J. H. M. (1959). *The French Religious Wars in English Political Thought*. Oxford: Clarendon Press.

Salter, E. (2009). 'What Kind of Horse Is It? Popular Devotional Reading during the Sixteenth Century'. In *Literature and Popular Culture in Early Modern England*, edited by A. Hadfield and M. Dimmock, pp. 105–20. Farnham: Ashgate.

Saltman, A. (1995). *The Jewish Question in 1655: Studies in Prynne's 'Demurrer'*. Ramat Gan: Bar-Ilan University Press.

Samuel, E. R. (1958). 'Portuguese Jews in Jacobean London'. *Transactions of the Jewish Historical Society of England* 18: 171–230.

Samuel, R. (1998). 'The Discovery of Puritanism, 1820–1914: A Preliminary Sketch'. In *Island Stories: Unravelling Britain*, edited by A. Light, pp. 276–322. London: Verso.

Sanchez, M. E. (2011). *Erotic Subjects: The Sexuality of Politics in Early Modern English Literature*. Oxford: Oxford University Press.

Sargent, M. (2011). 'Censorship or Cultural Change? Reformation and Renaissance in the Spirituality of Late Medieval England'. In *After Arundel: Religious Writing in Fifteenth-Century England*, edited by V. Gillespie and K. Ghosh, pp. 55–72. Turnhout: Brepols.

Sargent, R.-M. (1996). 'Bacon as an Advocate for Cooperative Scientific Research'. In *The Cambridge Companion to Bacon*, edited by M. Peltonen, pp. 146–71. Cambridge: Cambridge University Press.

Saurat, D. (1944). *Milton, Man and Thinker* [first publ. 1925]. London: J. M. Dent & Sons.

Scarisbrick, J. J. (1968). *Henry VIII*. London: Eyre & Spottiswoode.

Scase, W. (1995). 'Reginald Pecock'. In *Authors of the Middle Ages*, edited by M. C. Seymour, pp. 69–146. Aldershot: Variorum.

Schaff, P. (1910, 1998). *History of the Christian Church, Volume VII: Modern Christianity: The German Reformation*. New York, NY: Charles Scribner's Sons. Digitized by The Electronic Bible Society, Dallas, TX. Available at: http://www.ccel.org/s/schaff/history/About.htm#_edn1.

Schaffer, S. (1987). 'Godly Men and Mechanical Philosophers: Souls and Spirits in Restoration Natural Philosophy'. *Science in Context* 1: 55–85.

Scheible, H. (1997). *Melanchthon: Eine Biographie*. Munich: Verlag C. H. Beck.

Schildt, J. (2008). ' "Eying and Applying and Meditating on the Promises": Reading the Bible in Seventeenth-Century England'. Unpublished PhD thesis, Royal Holloway, University of London.

Schildt, J. (2012). ' "In my Private Reading of the Scriptures": Protestant Bible-reading in England, *c*.1580–1720'. In *Private and Domestic Devotion in Early Modern Britain*, edited by J. Martin and A. Ryrie, pp. 189–209. Farnham: Ashgate.

Schleck, J. (2011). *Telling True Tales of Islamic Lands: Forms of Mediation in English Travel Writing, 1575–1630*. Selinsgrove, PA: Susquehanna University Press.

Schleiner, L. (1984). *The Living Lyre in English Verse from Elizabeth through the Restoration*. Columbia, MO: University of Missouri Press.

Schleiner, L. (1986). 'Recent Studies in Poetry and Music of the English Renaissance'. *ELR* 16: 253–68.

Schmuck, S. (2006). 'From Sermon to Play: Literary Representations of "Turks" in Renaissance England 1550–1625'. *Literature Compass* 2: 1–29.

Schmuck, S. (2012). '"Familiar Strangers": Dissimulation, Tolerance and Faith in Early Anglo-Ottoman Travel'. In *Forgetting Faith? Negotiating Confessional Conflict in Early Modern Europe*, edited by I. Karremann, C. Zwierlein, and I. M. Groote, pp. 241–60. Berlin: De Gruyter.

Schochet, G. J. (1975). *Patriarchalism in Political Thought: The Authoritarian Family and Political Speculation and Attitudes, especially in Seventeenth-Century England*. Oxford: Blackwell.

Schoenfeldt, M. C. (1991). *Prayer and Power: George Herbert and Renaissance Courtship*. Chicago, IL: University of Chicago Press.

Schoenfeldt, M. C. (1999). *Bodies and Selves in Early Modern England: Physiology and Inwardness in Spenser, Shakespeare, Herbert, and Milton*. Cambridge: Cambridge University Press.

Schoenfeldt, M. C. (2006). '"That Spectacle of Too Much Weight": The Poetics of Sacrifice in Donne, Herbert, and Milton'. In *Seventeenth-Century British Poetry, 1603–1660*, edited by J. P Rumrich and G. Chaplin, pp. 890–907. New York, NY: Norton.

Schofield, J. (2006). *Philip Melanchthon and the English Reformation*. Aldershot: Ashgate.

Scholem, G. (1973). *Sabbatai Sevi: The Mystical Messiah*, translated by R. J. Zwi Werblowsky. Princeton, NJ: Princeton University Press.

Schwartz-Leeper, G. (2016). *From Princes to Pages: The Literary Lives of Cardinal Wolsey, Tudor England's 'Other King'*. Leiden: Brill.

Scodel, J. (1995). 'John Donne and the Religious Politics of the Mean'. In *John Donne's Religious Imagination: Essays in Honor of John T. Shawcross*, edited by R.-J. Frontain and F. M. Malpezzi, pp. 45–80. Conway, AR: University of Central Arkansas Press.

Scott, G. (2013). 'Cloistered Images: Representations of English Nuns, 1600–1800'. In *The English Convents in Exile, 1600–1800: Communities, Culture and Identity*, edited by C. Bowden and J. E. Kelly, pp. 191–210. Farnham: Ashgate.

Scott, J. (1991). *Algernon Sidney and the Restoration Crisis, 1677–1683*. Cambridge: Cambridge University Press.

Scott, J. (2000). *England's Troubles: Seventeenth-Century English Political Stability in European Context*. Cambridge: Cambridge University Press.

Scott-Baumann, E. (2011). 'Lucy Hutchinson, the Bible and *Order and Disorder*'. In *The Intellectual Culture of Puritan Women, 1558–1680*, edited by J. Harris and E. Scott-Baumann, pp. 176–89. Basingstoke: Palgrave Macmillan.

Scott-Baumann, E. (2013). *Forms of Engagement: Women, Poetry, and Culture 1640–1680*. Oxford: Oxford University Press.

Screech, M. A. (1988). *Erasmus: Ecstasy and the Praise of Folly*. London: Penguin.

Scult, M. (1978). *Millennial Expectations and Jewish Liberties: A Study of the Efforts to Convert the Jews in Britain, up to the Mid Nineteenth Century*. Leiden: Brill.

Seaver, P. S. (1970). *The Puritan Lectureships: The Politics of Religious Dissent, 1560–1662*. Stanford, CA: Stanford University Press.

Seaver, P. S. (1979). Review of Murray Tolmie's *The Triumph of the Saints*. *Journal of Modern History* 51 (1): 151–3.

Seaver, P. S. (1985). *Wallington's World: A Puritan Artisan in Seventeenth-Century London*. Stanford, CA: Stanford University Press.

Seelig, S. C. (1981). *The Shadow of Eternity: Belief and Structure in Herbert, Vaughan, and Traherne*. Lexington, KY: The University of Kentucky Press.

Shagan, E. H. (2002). 'Clement Armstrong and the Godly Commonwealth: Radical Religion in Early Tudor England'. In *The Beginnings of English Protestantism*, edited by P. Marshall and A. Ryrie, pp. 60–83. Cambridge: Cambridge University Press.

Shagan, E. H. (2003). *Popular Politics and the English Reformation*. Cambridge: Cambridge University Press.

Shagan, E. H. (2004). 'The English Inquisition: Constitutional Conflict and Ecclesiastical Law in the 1590s'. *The Historical Journal* 47: 541–65.

Shagan, E. H. (2011). *The Rule of Moderation: Violence, Religion and the Politics of Restraint in Early Modern England*. Cambridge: Cambridge University Press.

Shami, J. (1995). 'Thomas Middleton's *A Game at Chesse*: A Sermon Analogue'. *Notes and Queries* n.s. 42 (3): 366–9.

Shami, J. (2003). *John Donne and Conformity in Crisis in the Late Jacobean Pulpit*. Cambridge: D. S. Brewer.

Shami, J. (2011a). 'The Sermon'. In *The Oxford Handbook of John Donne*, edited by J. Shami, D. Flynn, and M. T. Hester, pp. 318–47. Oxford: Oxford University Press.

Shami, J. (2011b). 'Women and Sermons'. In *The Oxford Handbook of the Early Modern Sermon*, edited by P. McCullough, H. Adlington, and E. Rhatigan, pp. 155–77. Oxford: Oxford University Press.

Shami, J. (2013). 'Reading Funeral Sermons for Early Modern English Women: Some Literary and Historiographical Challenges'. In *Religious Diversity and Early Modern English Texts: Catholic, Judaic, Feminist, and Secular Dimensions*, edited by A. Marotti and C. Goodblatt, pp. 282–308. Detroit, MI: Wayne State University Press.

Shami, J. (2014). 'The Love-Sick Spouse: John Stoughton's 1624 Paul's Cross Sermon in Context'. In *Paul's Cross and the Culture of Persuasion in England, 1520–1640*, edited by T. Kirby and P. G. Stanwood, pp. 389–409. Leiden: Brill.

Shapiro, B. (1991). 'Early Modern Intellectual Life: Humanism, Religion and Science in Seventeenth-Century England'. *History of Science* 29: 45–71.

Shapiro, J. (1996). *Shakespeare and the Jews*. New York, NY: Columbia University Press.

Sharpe, K. (1992). *The Personal Rule of Charles I*. New Haven, CT: Yale University Press.

Sharpe, K. (2000). *Reading Revolutions: The Politics of Reading in Early Modern England*. New Haven, CT: Yale University Press.

Sharrock, R. (1959). 'The Origin of *A Relation of the Imprisonment of Mr John Bunyan*'. *Review of English Studies* n.s. 10: 250–6.

Shaw, W. A. (1894). 'Nelson, Thomas (fl. 1580)'. In *Dictionary of National Biography, Volume 40*, edited by S. Lee, pp. 213–14. New York, NY: Macmillan.

Sheils, W. (1994). 'Provincial Preaching on the Eve of the Civil War: Some West Riding Fast Sermons'. In *Religion, Culture and Society in Early Modern Britain: Essays in Honour of Patrick Collinson*, edited by A. Fletcher and P. Roberts, pp. 290–312. Cambridge: Cambridge University Press.

Sheils, W. (2006). 'John Shawe and Edward Bowles: Civic Preachers at Peace and War'. In *Religious Politics in Post-Reformation England: Essays in Honour of Nicholas Tyacke*, edited by K. Fincham and P. Lake, pp. 209–23. Woodbridge: Boydell.

Shell, A. (1999). *Catholicism, Controversy and the English Literary Imagination, 1558–1660*. Cambridge: Cambridge University Press.

Shell, A. (2010). *Shakespeare and Religion*. London: A & C Black.

Shell, A., and A. Hunt (2006). 'Donne's Religious World'. In *The Cambridge Companion to John Donne*, edited by A. Guibbory, pp. 65–82. Cambridge: Cambridge University Press.

Sherlock, P. (2008). *Monuments and Memory in Early Modern England*. Farnham: Ashgate.

Sherman, W. H. (1995). *John Dee: The Politics of Reading and Writing in the English Renaissance*. Amherst, MA: University of Massachusetts Press.

Shore, D. R. (1985). *Spenser and the Poetics of Pastoral: A Study of the World of Colin Clout.* Montreal: McGill-Queen's University Press.

Shoulson, J. S. (2001). *Milton and the Rabbis: Hebraism, Hellenism, and Christianity.* New York, NY: Columbia University Press.

Shoulson, J. S. (2013). *Fictions of Conversion: Jews, Christians, and Cultures of Change in Early Modern England.* Philadelphia, PA: University of Pennsylvania Press.

Shuger, D. K. (1986). *Sacred Rhetoric: The Christian Grand Style in the English Renaissance.* Princeton, NJ: Princeton University Press.

Shuger, D. K. (1990). *Habits of Thought in the English Renaissance: Religion, Politics, and the Dominant Culture.* Los Angeles, CA: University of California Press.

Shuger, D. K. (1994, 1998). *The Renaissance Bible: Scholarship, Sacrifice, and Subjectivity.* Berkeley, CA: University of California Press.

Shuger, D. K. (2000). 'Life-Writing in Seventeenth-Century England'. In *Representations of the Self from the Renaissance to Romanticism*, edited by P. Coleman, J. Lewis, and J. Kowalik, pp. 63–78. Cambridge: Cambridge University Press.

Simpson, J. (2002). *Reform and Cultural Revolution: The Oxford English Literary History.* Volume 2. Oxford: Oxford University Press.

Simpson, J. (2007). *Burning to Read: English Fundamentalism and its Reformation Opponents.* Cambridge, MA: Belknap Press.

Sinfield, A. (1992). 'Protestantism: Questions of Subjectivity and Control'. In *Faultlines: Cultural Materialism and the Politics of Dissident Reading*, pp. 143–80. Berkeley, CA: University of California Press.

Sinfield, A. (1979). 'Sidney, Du Plessis-Mornay and the Pagans'. *Philological Quarterly* 58 (1): 26–39.

Sirota, B. (2014a). *The Christian Monitors: The Church of England and the Age of Benevolence, 1680–1730.* New Haven, CT: Yale University Press.

Sirota, B. (2014b). 'The Occasional Conformity Controversy, Moderation, and the Anglican Critique of Modernity, 1700–1714'. *Historical Journal* 57 (1): 81–105.

Sisson, C. J. (1938). 'A Colony of Jews in Shakespeare's London'. *Essays and Studies by Members of the English Association* 23: 38–51.

Skilliter, S. A. (1965). 'Three Letters from the Ottoman "Sultana" Safiye to Queen Elizabeth I'. In *Documents from Islamic Chanceries*, edited by S. M. Stern, pp. 119–57. Cambridge, MA: Harvard University Press.

Skilliter, S. A. (1975). 'Catherine de' Medici's Turkish Ladies-in-Waiting: A Dilemma in Franco-Ottoman Diplomatic Relations'. *Turcica* 7: 188–204.

Skilliter, S. A. (1977). *William Harborne and the Trade with Turkey, 1578–1582: A Documentary Study of the First Anglo-Ottoman Relations.* Oxford: Oxford University Press.

Skinner, Q. (1978). *The Foundations of Modern Political Thought, Volume 2: The Age of Reformation.* Cambridge: Cambridge University Press.

Skretkowicz, V. (1986). 'Building Sidney's Reputation: Texts and Editors of the *Arcadia*'. In *Sir Philip Sidney: 1586 and the Creation of a Legend*, edited by J. Van Dorsten, D. Baker-Smith, and A. F. Kinney, pp. 111–24. Leiden: E. J. Brill and Leiden University Press.

Skretkowicz, V. (1996). 'Protestant *Men*, Protesting Women—A Sidney Family Discourse'. *Sidney Journal* 14: 3–13.

Skretkowicz, V. (1998). 'Sidney's *Defence of Poetry*, Henri Estienne, and Huguenot Nationalist Satire'. *Sidney Journal* 16: 3–24.

Skretkowicz, V. (1999). 'Mary Sidney Herbert's *Antonius*, English Philhellenism and the Protestant Cause'. *Women's Writing* 6: 7–26.

Slack, P. (2013). 'Hoby, Margaret, Lady Hoby *(bap.* 1571, *d.* 1633)'. *ODNB.*

Sleeper, S. (2000). 'Providence, Fortune, and Gender in Margaret Cavendish's *Life of William Cavendish* and Lucy Hutchinson's *Life of John Hutchinson*'. *The Early Modern Journal* 1: 1–11.

Sloane, T. O. (1985). *Donne, Milton, and the End of Humanist Rhetoric.* Berkeley, CA: University of California Press.

Smith, C. K. (1996). 'French Philosophy and English Politics in Interregnum Poetry'. In *The Stuart Court and Europe: Essays in Politics and Political Culture,* edited by R. M. Smuts, pp. 177–209. Cambridge: Cambridge University Press.

Smith, H. (1946). 'English Metrical Psalms in the Sixteenth Century and their Literary Significance'. *Huntington Library Quarterly* 9: 249–71.

Smith, H. (2010). '"More Swete vnto the Eare/than Holsome for ye Mynde": Embodying Early Modern Women's Reading'. *Huntington Library Quarterly* 73: 413–32.

Smith, L. B. (1954). 'English Treason Trials and Confessions in the Sixteenth Century'. *Journal of the History of Ideas* 15 (4) (October): 471–98.

Smith, N. (1989). *Perfection Proclaimed: Language and Literature in English Radical Religion 1640–1660.* Oxford: Clarendon Press.

Smith, N. (1998). 'Introduction'. In George Fox, *The Journal.* London: Penguin.

Smith, N. (2009a). 'The Anti-Episcopal Tracts: Republican Puritanism and the Truth in Poetry'. In *The Oxford Handbook of Milton,* edited by N. McDowell and N. Smith, pp. 155–73. Oxford: Oxford University Press.

Smith, N. (2009b). '*Paradise Lost* and Heresy'. In *The Oxford Handbook of Milton,* edited by N. McDowell and N. Smith, pp. 510–24. Oxford: Oxford University Press.

Smith, N. (2010). *Andrew Marvell: The Chameleon.* New Haven, CT: Yale University Press.

Smyth, A. (2010). *Autobiography in Early Modern England.* Cambridge: Cambridge University Press.

Sommerville, J. P. (1999). *Royalists and Patriots: Politics and Ideology in England, 1603–1642.* London: Routledge.

Southcombe, G. (2012). *English Nonconformist Poetry 1660–1700.* London: Pickering & Chatto.

Southcombe, G., and G. Tapsell (2010). *Restoration Politics, Religion and Culture: Britain and Ireland, 1660–1714.* Basingstoke: Palgrave Macmillan.

Southern, A. C. (1950). *Elizabethan Recusant Prose 1559–1582.* London: Sands.

Sowerby, S. (2013). *Making Toleration: The Repealers and the Glorious Revolution.* Cambridge, MA: Harvard University Press.

Sowerby, T. (2010). *Renaissance and Reform in Tudor England: The Careers of Sir Richard Morison, c.1513–1556.* Oxford: Oxford University Press.

Spargo, T. (1997). *The Writing of John Bunyan.* Aldershot: Ashgate.

Spedding, A. J. (2010). 'At the King's Pleasure: The Testament of Cecily Neville'. *Midland History* 35: 256–72.

Spijker, W. V., et al. (eds) (2001). *Het puritanisme: Geschiedenis, theologie en invloed.* Zoetermeer: Boekencentrum.

Spinks, B. D. (2013). 'The Elizabethan Primers: Symptoms of an Ambiguous Settlement or Devotional Weaning?' In *Worship and the Parish Church in Early Modern Britain,* edited by N. Mears and A. Ryrie, pp. 73–88. Abingdon: Ashgate.

Spinks, J. (2009). 'Monstrous Births and Counter-Reformation Visual Polemics: Johann Nas and the 1569 *Ecclesia Militans*'. *Sixteenth Century Journal* 40 (2): 335–63.

Spitz, L. W., and B. S. Tinsley (1995). *Johann Sturm on Education: The Reformation and Humanist Learning.* St. Louis, MO: Concordia Press.

Spitzer, L. (1963). *Classical and Christian Ideas of World Harmony*. Baltimore, MD: John Hopkins University Press.

Spohnholz, J., and G. K. Waite (eds) (2014). *Exile and Religious Identity, 1500–1800*. London: Pickering & Chatto.

Springer, C. P. H. (2014). 'Ch. 56: The Reformation'. In *Brill's Encyclopaedia of the Neo-Latin World*, edited by P. Ford, J. Bloemendal, and C. Fantazzi, pp. 747–58. Leiden: Brill.

Sprunger, K. L. (1982). *Dutch Puritanism: A History of English and Scottish Churches of the Netherlands in the Sixteenth and Seventeenth Centuries*. Leiden: Brill.

Sprunger, K. L. (1994). *Trumpets from the Tower: English Puritan Printing in the Netherlands, 1600–1640*. Leiden: Brill.

Spufford, M. (1979). 'First Steps in Literacy: The Reading and Writing Experiences of the Humblest Seventeenth-Century Spiritual Autobiographers'. *Social History* 4 (3): 407–33.

Spurr, J. (1989). 'The Church of England, Comprehension and the Toleration Act of 1689'. *English Historical Review* 104 (413): 927–46.

Spurr, J. (1990). ' "Virtue, Religion and Government": The Anglican Uses of Providence'. In *The Politics of Religion in Restoration England*, edited by T. Harris, P. Seaward, and M. Goldie, pp. 29–47. Oxford: Basil Blackwell.

Spurr, J. (1991). *The Restoration Church of England, 1646–1689*. New Haven, CT: Yale University Press.

Spurr, J. (1993). 'The Church, the Societies and the Moral Revolution of 1688'. In *The Church of England, c.1689–c.1833: From Toleration to Tractarianism*, edited by J. D. Walsh and S. Taylor, pp. 127–42. Cambridge: Cambridge University Press.

Spurr, J. (2000). *England in the 1670s: 'This Masquerading Age'*. Oxford: Blackwell.

Spurr, J. (2013). *The Laity and Preaching in Post-Reformation England*. London: Dr Williams's Trust.

Spurr, J. (2014). *The Post-Reformation: Religion, Politics and Society in Britain, 1603–1714*. London: Routledge.

Stacey, R. (1992). 'The Conversion of Jews to Christianity in Thirteenth-Century England'. *Speculum* 67: 263–83.

Stachniewski, J. (1981). 'John Donne: The Despair of the Holy Sonnets'. *ELH* 48 (4) (Winter): 677–705.

Stachniewski, J. (1991). *The Persecutory Imagination: English Puritanism and the Literature of Religious Despair*. Oxford: Clarendon Press.

Stallybrass, P. (2006). 'Marginal England: The View from Aleppo'. In *Center or Margin: Revisions of the English Renaissance in Honor of Leeds Barroll*, edited by L. C. Orlin, pp. 27–39. Danvers, MA: Rosemont Publishing.

Stanwood, P. G., and H. R. Asals (eds) (1986). *John Donne and the Theology of Language*. Columbia, MO: University of Missouri Press.

Stapleton, T. (1984). *The Life and Illustrious Martyrdom of Sir Thomas More*, edited by E. E. Reynolds, trans. P. Hallett. New York, NY: Fordham University Press.

Stark, R. J. (2008). 'Some Aspects of Christian Mystical Rhetoric, Philosophy and Poetry'. *Philosophy and Rhetoric* 41 (3): 260–77.

Stavreva, K. (2007). 'Prophetic Cries at Whitehall: The Gender Dynamics of Early Quaker Women's Injurious Speech'. In *Women, Gender, and Radical Religion in Early Modern Europe*, edited by S. Brown, pp. 17–38. Leiden: Brill.

Stein, A. (1942). 'Donne and the Couplet'. *PMLA* 57: 676–96.

Stein, A. (1944). 'Donne's Harshness and the Elizabethan Tradition'. *Studies in Philology* 41 (3): 390–409.

Stephens, I. (2011). 'Confessional Identity in Early Stuart England: the "Prayer Book Puritanism" of Elizabeth Isham'. *Journal of British Studies* 50 (1): 24–47.

Stern, J. (2011). 'A Key into *The Bloudy Tenent of Persecution*: Roger Williams, the Pequot War, and the Origins of Toleration in America'. *Early American Studies* 9 (2): 576–616.

Steuart, H. (1944). 'The Place of Allen, Campion and Parsons in the Development of English Prose'. *The Review of English Studies* 20 (80): 272–85.

Stewart, A. (2001). *Philip Sidney: A Double Life*. New York, NY: St. Martin's Press.

Stewart, M. A. (1979). 'Introduction'. In *Selected Philosophical Papers of Robert Boyle*, edited by M. A. Stewart, pp. xi–xxv. Manchester: Manchester University Press.

Stillman, R. E. (2002). ' "Deadly Stinging Adders": Sidney's Piety, Philippism, and *The Defence of Poesy*'. *Spenser Studies* 16: 231–69.

Stillman, R. E. (2008), *Philip Sidney and the Poetics of Renaissance Cosmopolitanism*. Aldershot: Ashgate.

Stillman, R. E. (2009), 'Fictionalizing Philippism in Sidney's *Arcadia*: Economy, Virtuous Pagans, and Early Modern Poetics'. *Sidney Journal* 27 (2): 13–39.

Stillman, R. E. (2012). ' "I Am Not I": Philip Sidney and the Energy of Fiction'. *Sidney Journal* 30 (1): 1–26.

Stone, C. (2012). 'An "Extremely Civile" Diplomacy'. *Saudi Aramco World: Arabic and Islamic Cultures and Connections* 63 (1): 16–23.

Streete, A. (2009a). *Protestantism and Drama in Early Modern England*. Cambridge: Cambridge University Press.

Streete, A. (2009b). ' "What Bloody Man Is That?" Questioning Biblical Typology in *Macbeth*'. *Shakespeare* 5 (1): 18–35.

Streete, A. (ed.) (2012). *Early Modern Drama and the Bible: Contexts and Readings, 1570–1625*. Basingstoke: Palgrave Macmillan.

Strider, R. E. L., II (1958). *Robert Greville, Lord Brooke*. Cambridge, MA: Harvard University Press.

Strier, R. (1989). 'John Donne Awry and Squint: the "Holy Sonnets," 1608–1610'. *Modern Philology* 86 (4) (May): 357–84.

Strier, R. (1996). 'Donne and the Politics of Devotion'. In *Religion, Literature, and Politics in Post-Reformation England, 1540–1688*, edited by D. B. Hamilton and R. Strier, pp. 93–114. Cambridge: Cambridge University Press.

Strohm, P. (1998). *England's Empty Throne: Usurpation and the Language of Legitimation, 1399–1422*. New Haven, CT: Yale University Press.

Subrahmanyam, S. (2011). *Three Ways to Be Alien: Travails and Encounters in the Early Modern World*. Waltham: Brandeis University Press.

Sugden, J. (1990). *Sir Francis Drake*. New York, NY: Holt.

Sullivan, E. W., II (2011). 'John Donne's Seventeenth-Century Readers'. In *The Oxford Handbook of John Donne*, edited by J. Shami, D. Flynn, and M. T. Hester, pp. 26–33. Oxford: Oxford University Press.

Summers, C. J., and T.-L. Pebworth (eds) (1987). *'Bright Shootes of Everlastingnesse': The Seventeenth-Century Religious Lyric*. Columbia, MO: University of Missouri Press.

Summers, C. J., and T.-L. Pebworth (eds) (1995). *The Wit of Seventeenth-Century Poetry*. Columbia, MO: University of Missouri Press.

Summers, C. J., and T.-L. Pebworth (eds) (1997). *Representing Women in Renaissance England.* Columbia, MO: University of Missouri Press.

Summit, J. (2000). *Lost Property: The Woman Writer and English Literary History, 1380–1589.* Chicago, IL: University of Chicago Press.

Summit, J. (2009). 'From Anchorhold to Closet: Julian of Norwich in 1670 and the Immanence of the Past'. In *Julian of Norwich's Legacy: Medieval Mysticism and Post-Medieval Reception,* edited by S. Salih and D. N. Baker, pp. 29–47. Basingstoke: Palgrave Macmillan.

Suranyi, A. (2008). *The Genius of the English Nation: Travel Writing and National Identity in Early Modern England.* Danvers, MA: Rosemont Publishing.

Sutton, J. (2003). 'Soul and Body in Seventeenth-Century British Philosophy'. In *The Oxford Handbook of British Philosophy in the Seventeenth Century,* edited by Peter Anstey, pp. 285–310. Oxford: Oxford University Press.

Swanson, R. N. (1999). 'Medieval English Liturgy: What's the Use?' *Studia Liturgica* 29 (2): 159–90.

Swatland, A. (1996). *The House of Lords in the Reign of Charles II.* Cambridge: Cambridge University Press.

Sykes, N. (1959). *From Sheldon to Secker: Aspects of English Church History, 1660–1768.* Cambridge: Cambridge University Press.

Sykes, S. W. (1978). *The Integrity of Anglicanism.* London: Mowbrays.

Sykes, S. W. (1995). *Unashamed Anglicanism.* London: Darton, Longman & Todd.

Sykes, S., J. E. Booty, and J. Knight (eds) (1998). *The Study of Anglicanism.* Minneapolis, MN: SPCK/Fortress Press.

Tadmor, N. (2010). *The Social Universe of the English Bible: Scripture, Society and Culture in Early Modern England.* Cambridge: Cambridge University Press.

Tapsell, G. (2007). *The Personal Rule of Charles II.* Woodbridge: Boydell Press.

Tapsell, G. (2010). 'Laurence Hyde and the Politics of Religion in Later Stuart England'. *English Historical Review* 125 (517): 1414–48.

Tapsell, G. (2015). 'Charles II's Commission for Ecclesiastical Promotions, 1681–1684: A Reconsideration'. *Journal of Ecclesiastical History* 66 (4): 735–54.

Tapsell, G. (ed.) (2012). 'Pastors, Preachers and Politicians: The Clergy of the Later Stuart Church'. In *The Later Stuart Church, 1660–1714,* edited by G. Tapsell, pp. 71–100. Manchester: Manchester University Press.

Targoff, R. (2001). *Common Prayer: The Language of Public Devotion in Early Modern England.* Chicago, IL: University of Chicago Press.

Targoff, R. (2008). *John Donne: Body and Soul.* Chicago, IL: University of Chicago Press.

Tarter, M. L. (1993). 'Nursing the New Wor(l)d: The Writings of Quaker Women in Early America'. *Women and Language* 16 (1): 22–6.

Tarter, M. L. (2015). ' "That You May Be Perfect in Love": The Prophecy of Dorothy White'. In *Early Quakers and their Theological Thought,* edited by S. W. Angell and B. P. Dandelion, pp. 155–72. Cambridge: Cambridge University Press.

Taunton, N. (2001). *1590s Drama and Militarism: Portrayals of War in Marlowe, Chapman and Shakespeare's Henry V.* Aldershot: Ashgate.

Thomas, K. (1997). *Religion and the Decline of Magic: Studies in Popular Beliefs in Sixteenth- and Seventeenth-Century England.* New York, NY: Oxford University Press.

Thomas, R. (1962). 'Comprehension and Indulgence'. In *From Uniformity to Unity 1662–1962,* edited by G. Nuttall and O. Chadwick, pp. 222–30. London: SPCK.

Thomson, A. (2008). *Bodies of Thought: Science, Religion, and the Soul in the Early Enlightenment*. Oxford: Oxford University Press.

Tierney, B. (1988). *The Crisis of Church and State, 1050–1300*. Toronto: University of Toronto Press.

Tilmouth, C. (2010). *Passion's Triumph over Reason: A History of the Moral Imagination from Spenser to Rochester*. Oxford: Oxford University Press.

Todd, M. (1980). 'Humanists, Puritans and the Spiritualized Household'. *Church History* 49 (1): 18–34.

Todd, M. (2002). *The Culture of Protestantism in Early Modern Scotland*. New Haven, CT: Yale University Press.

Tolan, J. V. (2002). *Saracens: Islam in the Medieval European Imagination*. New York, NY: Columbia University Press.

Tolmie, M. (1977). *The Triumph of the Saints: The Separate Churches of London 1616–49*. Cambridge: Cambridge University Press.

Tóth, P., and D. Falvay (2014). 'New Light on the Date and Authorship of the *Meditationes vitae Christi*'. In *Devotional Culture in Late Medieval England and Europe: Diverse Imaginations of Christ's Life*, edited by S. Kelly and R. Perry, pp. 11–62. Turnhout: Brepols.

Towers, S. M. (2003). *Control of Religious Printing in Early Stuart England*. Woodbridge: The Boydell Press.

Trill, S. (2002). 'A Feminist Critic in the Archives: Reading Anna Walker's *Sweete Savor for Woman* (*c.*1606)'. *Women's Writing* 9 (2): 199–214.

Trill, S. (2004). 'Early Modern Women's Writing in the Edinburgh Archive, *c.*1550–1740: A Preliminary Checklist'. In *Woman and the Feminine in Medieval and Early Modern Scottish Writing*, edited by S. Dunnigan, C. M. Harker, E. Newlyn, pp. 201–26. Basingstoke: Palgrave Macmillan.

Trill, S. (2010). ' "In Poesie the mirrois of our Age": The Countess of Pembroke's "Sydnean" Poetics'. In *A Companion to Tudor Literature*, edited by K. Cartwright, pp. 428–43. Oxford: Wiley-Blackwell.

Troeltsch, E. (1931). *The Social Teaching of the Christian Churches*. London: George Allen and Unwin.

Trubowitz, R. (1992). 'Female Preachers and Male Wives: Gender and Authority in Civil War England'. In *Pamphlet Wars: Prose in the England Revolution*, edited by J. Holston, pp. 112–33. London: Routledge.

Tudeau-Clayton, M. (1998). *Jonson, Shakespeare, and Early Modern Virgil*. Cambridge: Cambridge University Press.

Turner, C. (1928). *Anthony Munday: An Elizabethan Man of Letters*. Berkeley, CA: University of California Press.

Turner, J. G. (2007a). 'Libertinism and Toleration: Milton, Bruno, and Aretino'. In *Milton and Toleration*, edited by S. Achinstein and E. Sauer, pp. 107–25. Oxford: Oxford University Press.

Turner, J. G. (2007b). 'Milton among the Libertines'. In *Milton, Rights and Liberties*, edited by C. Tournu and N. Forsyth, pp. 447–60. Bern: Peter Lang.

Tutino, S. (2007). *Law and Conscience: Catholicism in Early Modern England, 1570–1625*. Farnham: Ashgate.

Tyacke, N. (1987a). *Anti-Calvinists: The Rise of English Arminianism, c.1590–1640*. Oxford: Oxford University Press.

Tyacke, N. (1987b). 'The Rise of Arminianism Reconsidered'. *Past and Present* 115: 201–16.

Tyacke, N. (1990a). *Anti-Calvinists: The Rise of English Arminianism c.1590–1640*. New York, NY: Oxford University Press.

Tyacke, N. (1990b). *The Fortunes of English Puritanism*. London: Dr Williams's Trust.

Tyacke, N. (2001). *Aspects of English Protestantism c.1530–1700*. Manchester: Manchester University Press.

Tyler, P. (2010). *St John of the Cross*. London: Continuum.

Underdown, D. (1971). *Pride's Purge*. Oxford: Oxford University Press.

Underwood, T. L. (2001). *Primitivism, Radicalism, and the Lamb's War: Baptist-Quaker Conflict in Seventeenth-Century England*. Oxford: Oxford University Press.

Underwood, W. (2004). 'Thomas Cromwell and William Marshall's Protestant books'. *Historical Journal* 47: 517–39.

Ungerer, G. (2003). 'Portia and the Prince of Morocco'. *Shakespeare Studies* 31: 89–126.

van der Wall, E. G. E. (1988). 'A Precursor of Christ or a Jewish Imposter? Petrus Serrarius and Jean de Labadie on the Jewish Messianic Movement around Sabbatai Sevi'. *Pietismus und Neuzeit* 14: 112–13.

Van Engen, J. (2008). 'Multiple Options: The World of the Fifteenth-Century Church'. *Church History* 77 (2): 257–84.

Van Hyning, V. (2013). 'Augustine Baker: Discerning the "Call" and Fashioning Dead Disciples'. In *Angels of Light? Sanctity and the Discernment of Spirits in the Early Modern Period*, edited by C. Copeland and J. Machielesen, pp. 143–68. Leiden: Brill.

Vander Molen, R. J. (1973). 'Anglican against Puritan: Ideological Origins during the Marian Exile'. *Church History* 42 (1): 45–57.

Vauchez, A. (1997). *Sainthood in the Later Middle Ages*, translated by J. Birrell. Cambridge: Cambridge University Press.

Vaughan, V. M. (2005). *Performing Blackness on English Stages, 1500–1800*. Cambridge: Cambridge University Press.

Vaughn, R. (2010). *Philip the Good: The Apogee of Burgundy*. Woodbridge: Boydell Press.

Vella, A. P. (1972). *An Elizabethan-Ottoman Conspiracy*. Malta: Royal University of Malta.

Vickers, B. (1996). 'Introduction'. In *Francis Bacon: A Critical Edition of the Major Works*, edited by B. Vickers, pp. xv–xliv. Oxford: Oxford University Press.

Vipont, E. (1975). *George Fox and the Valiant Sixty*. London: Hamish Hamilton.

Vitkus, D. (2003). *Turning Turk: English Theater and the Multicultural Mediterranean, 1570–1630*. Basingstoke: Palgrave Macmillan.

Vivier, E. D. (2014). 'John Bridges, Martin Marprelate, and the Rhetoric of Satire'. *ELR* 44 (1): 3–35.

Von Habsburg, M. (2011). *Catholic and Protestant Translations of the* Imitatio Christi, *1425–1650: From Late Medieval Classic to Early Modern Bestseller*. Farnham: Ashgate.

Wabuda, S. (2002). *Preaching during the English Reformation*. Cambridge: Cambridge University Press.

Wakelin, D. (2011). 'Religion, Humanism, and Humanity: Chaundler's *Dialogues* and the Winchester *Secretum*'. In *After Arundel: Religious Writing in Fifteenth Century England*, edited by V. Gillespie and K. Ghosh, pp. 225–44. Turnhout: Brepols.

Waldron, J. (2013). *Reformations of the Body: Idolatry, Sacrifice and Early Modern Theater*. Basingstoke: Palgrave Macmillan.

Walker, C. (2003). *Gender and Politics in Early Modern Europe: English Convents in France and the Low Countries*. Basingstoke: Palgrave Macmillan.

Walker, D. P. (1972). *The Ancient Theology: Studies in Christian Platonism from the Fifteenth to the Eighteenth Century*. Ithaca, NY: Cornell University Press.

Walker, G. (2005, 2007). *Writing under Tyranny: English Literature and Henrician Reformation*. Oxford: Oxford University Press.

Walker, K. (1996). *Women Writers of the English Renaissance*. London: Twayne.

Wall, C. (1998). *The Literary and Cultural Spaces of Restoration London*. Cambridge: Cambridge University Press.

Wall, W. (1993). *The Imprint of Gender: Authorship and Publication in the English Renaissance*. Ithaca, NY: Cornell University Press.

Waller, G. F. (1972). '"This Matching of Contraries", Bruno, Calvin, and the Sidney Circle'. *Neophilologus* 56: 331–43.

Waller, G. F. (1990). 'The Countess of Pembroke and Gendered Reading'. In *The Renaissance Englishwoman in Print: Counterbalancing the Canon*, edited by A. M. Haselkorn and B. S. Travitsky, pp. 327–45. Amherst, MA: University of Massachusetts Press.

Waller, G. F. (1993). *The Sidney Family Romance: Mary Wroth, William Herbert, and the Early Modern Construction of Gender*. Detroit, MI: Wayne State University Press.

Walsham, A. (1994). '"The Fatall Vesper": Providentialism and Anti-Popery in Late Jacobean London'. *Past and Present* 144: 36–87.

Walsham, A. (1998). '"Frantick Hacket": Prophecy, Sorcery, Insanity, and the Elizabethan Puritan Movement'. *The Historical Journal* 41 (1): 27–66.

Walsham, A. (1999, 2001). *Providence in Early Modern England*. Oxford: Oxford University Press.

Walsham, A. (2000). '"Domme Preachers"? Post-Reformation English Catholicism and the Culture of Print'. *Past and Present* 168: 72–123.

Walsham, A. (2003). 'Unclasping the Book? Post-Reformation English Catholicism and the Vernacular Bible'. *Journal of British Studies* 42 (2): 141–67.

Walsham, A. (2011). *The Reformation of the Landscape: Religion, Identity, and Memory in Early Modern Britain and Ireland*. Oxford: Oxford University Press.

Walsham, A. (2014). 'Migrations of the Holy: Explaining Religious Change in Medieval and Early Modern Europe'. *Journal of Medieval and Early Medieval Studies* 44 (1): 241–80.

Wanegffelen, T. (ed.) (2002). *De Michel de l'Hospital à l'Édit de Nantes: Politique et religion face aux Église*. Blaise-Pascal: Presses Universitaires.

Ward, I. (2004). *Introduction to Critical Legal Theory*. New York, NY: Routledge Cavendish.

Ward, K. (2006). *A History of Global Anglicanism*. Cambridge: Cambridge University Press.

Warner, J. C. (2013). *The Making and Marketing of Tottel's Miscellany, 1557: Songs and Sonnets in the Summer of the Martyrs' Fires*. Farnham: Ashgate.

Warren, C. (2007). 'When Self-Preservation Bids: Approaching Milton, Hobbes, and Dissent'. *ELR* 37 (1): 118–50.

Warren, N. B. (2007). 'Incarnational (Auto)biography'. In *Oxford Twenty-First Century Approaches to Literature*, edited by P. Strohm, pp. 369–85. Oxford: Oxford University Press.

Warren, N. B. (2010). *The Embodied Word: Female Spiritualities, Contested Orthodoxies and English Religious Cultures, 1350–1700*. Notre Dame, IN: University of Notre Dame Press.

Waswo, R. (1987). *Language and Meaning in the Renaissance*. Princeton, NJ: Princeton University Press.

Watkins, J. (2002). *Representing Elizabeth in Stuart England: Literature, History, and Sovereignty*. Cambridge: Cambridge University Press.

Watkins, O. (1972). *The Puritan Experience: Studies in Spiritual Autobiography.* London: Routledge & Kegan Paul.

Watson, J. R. (1997). *The English Hymn: A Critical and Historical Study.* Oxford: Clarendon Press.

Watson, N. (1995). 'Censorship and Cultural Change in Late-Medieval England: Vernacular Theology, the Oxford Translation Debate, and Arundel's Constitutions of 1409'. *Speculum* 70 (4): 822–64.

Watson, R. N. (1999). *The Rest Is Silence: Death as Annihilation in the English Renaissance.* Berkeley, CA: University of California Press.

Watt, D. (1997). 'Reconstructing the Word: The Political Prophecies of Elizabeth Barton (1506–1534)'. *Renaissance Quarterly* 50 (1): 136–63.

Watt, J. A. (1988). 'Spiritual and Temporal Powers'. In *The Cambridge History of Medieval Political Thought, c.350–1450,* edited by J. H. Burns, pp. 365–423. Cambridge: Cambridge University Press.

Watt, T. (1991). *Cheap Print and Popular Piety, 1550–1640.* Cambridge: Cambridge University Press.

Wauchope, P. (2006). 'Mackay, Hugh (*d.* 1692)'. *ODNB.*

Wayne, V. (1996). 'Advice for Women from Mothers and Patriarchs'. In *Women and Literature in Britain, 1500–1700,* edited by H. Wilcox, pp. 56–79. Cambridge: Cambridge University Press.

Weber, M. (1930). *The Protestant Ethic and the Spirit of Capitalism,* translated by T. Parsons. New York, NY: Scribner's.

Weber, M. (1946). 'Science as a Vocation'. In *From Max Weber: Essays in Sociology,* translated and edited by H. H. Gerth and C. Wright Mills. New York, NY: Oxford University Press.

Webster, C. (1970). *Samuel Hartlib and the Advancement of Learning.* Cambridge: Cambridge University Press.

Webster, T. (1997). *Godly Clergy in Early Stuart England: The Caroline Puritan Movement, c.1620–1643.* Cambridge: Cambridge University Press.

Weimann, R. (1987). 'Discourse, Ideology, and the Crisis of Authority'. *The Yearbook of Research in English and American Literature* 5: 109–40.

Weimann, R. (1996). *Authority and Representation in Early Modern Discourse.* Baltimore, MD: Johns Hopkins University Press.

Weimer, A. C. (2011). *Martyrs' Mirror: Persecution and Holiness in Early New England.* Oxford: Oxford University Press.

Werth, T. J. (2011). *The Fabulous Dark Cloister: Romance in England After the Reformation.* Baltimore, MD: Johns Hopkins University Press.

West, P. (2015). 'Little Gidding community (*act.* 1626–1657)'. *ODNB.*

Whalen, R. (2002). *The Poetry of Immanence.* Toronto: University of Toronto Press.

Whitaker, V. K. (1950). *The Religious Basis of Spenser's Thought.* Stanford, CA: Stanford University Press.

White, B. R. (1979). 'Henry Jessey: A Pastor in Politics'. *BQ* 25: 98–110.

White, H. C. (1931). *English Devotional Literature, 1600–1640.* Madison, WI: University of Wisconsin.

White, H. C. (1951). *The Tudor Books of Private Devotion.* Westport, CT: Greenwood Press.

White, H. C. (1956). *The Metaphysical Poets: A Study in Religious Experience.* New York, NY: Macmillan.

White, M. (2006). *Henrietta Maria and the English Civil Wars.* Aldershot: Ashgate.

White, P. W. (2004). 'The Bible as Play in Reformation England'. In *The Cambridge History of British Theater, Volume 1: Origins to 1660*, pp. 87–115. Cambridge: Cambridge University Press.

White, P. W. (2008). *Drama and Religion in English Provincial Society, 1485–1660*. Cambridge: Cambridge University Press.

White, S. R. (1996). *Authority and Anglicanism*. London: SCM Press.

Whitfield White, P. (1993). *Theatre and Reformation: Protestantism, Patronage and Playing in Tudor England*. Cambridge: Cambridge University Press.

Whitfield White, P. (2008). *Drama and Religion in English Provincial Society*. Cambridge: Cambridge University Press.

Whiting, G. W. (1936). 'Milton and Lord Brooke on the Church'. *Modern Language Notes* 51 (3): 161–6.

Wiesner-Hanks, M. E. (2000). *Christianity and Sexuality in the Early Modern World: Regulating Desire, Reforming Practice*. London: Routledge.

Wilcher, R. (2006). ' "Adventurous Song" or "Presumptuous Folly": The Problem of "Utterance" in John Milton's *Paradise Lost* and Lucy Hutchinson's *Order and Disorder*'. *The Seventeenth Century* 21: 304–14.

Wilcher, R. (2010). 'Lucy Hutchinson and *Genesis*: Paraphrase, Epic, Romance'. *English* 59: 25–42.

Wilcox, H. (1997). ' "My Soule in Silence"? Devotional Representations of Renaissance Englishwomen'. In *Representing Women in Renaissance England*, edited by C. J. Summers and T.-L. Pebworth, pp. 9–23. Columbia, MS: University of Missouri Press.

Wilcox, H. (2000a). ' "My Hart Is Full, My Soul Dos Ouer Flow": Women's Devotional Poetry in Seventeenth-Century England'. *Huntington Library Quarterly* 63: 447–66.

Wilcox, H. (2000b). ' "Whom the Lord with Love Affected": Gender and the Religious Poet, 1590–1633'. In *'This Double Voice': Gendered Writing in Early Modern England*, edited by D. Clarke and E. Clarke, pp. 185–207. London: Macmillan.

Wilcox, H. (2002). 'Literature and the Household'. In *The Cambridge History of Early Modern English Literature*, edited by D. Loewenstein and J. Mueller, pp. 737–62. Cambridge: Cambridge University Press.

Wilcox, H. (2004). 'Herbert, George (1593–1633)'. *ODNB*.

Wilcox, H. (2006a). 'Devotional Writing'. In *The Cambridge Companion to John Donne*, edited by A. Guibbory, pp. 149–66. Cambridge: Cambridge University Press.

Wilcox, H. (2006b). 'Selves in Strange Lands: Autobiography and Exile in the Mid-Seventeenth Century'. In *Early Modern Autobiography: Theories, Genres, Practices*, edited by R. Bedford, L. Davis, and P. Kelly, pp. 131–59. Ann Arbor, MI: University of Michigan.

Wilcox, H. (2009). 'In the Temple Precincts: George Herbert and Seventeenth-Century Community-Making'. In *Writing and Religion in England, 1558–1689: Studies in Community-Making and Cultural Memory*, edited by R. D. Sell and A. W. Johnson, pp. 253–71. Aldershot: Ashgate.

Wilcox, H. (2011). 'Sacred Desire, Forms of Belief: The Religious Sonnet in Early Modern Britain'. In *The Cambridge Companion to the Sonnet*, edited by A. D. Cousins and P. Howarth, pp. 145–65. Cambridge: Cambridge University Press.

Wilcox, H. (ed.) (1996). *Women and Literature 1500–1700*. Cambridge: Cambridge University Press.

Willen, D. (1992). 'Godly Women in Early Modern England: Puritanism and Gender'. *Journal of Ecclesiastical History* 43 (4): 561–80.

Willan, T. S. (1953). *The Muscovy Merchants of 1555*. Manchester: Manchester University Press.

Willan, T. S. (1956). *The Early History of the Russia Company, 1553–1603*. Manchester: Manchester University Press.

Willan, T. S. (1959). *Studies in Elizabethan Foreign Trade*. Manchester: Manchester University Press.

Williams, A. (2005). *Poetry and the Creation of a Whig Literary Culture 1681–1714*. Oxford: Oxford University Press.

Williams, E. N. (1960). *The Eighteenth-Century Constitution, 1688–1815: Documents and Commentary*. Cambridge: Cambridge University Press.

Williams, G. H. (1992). *The Radical Reformation*. 3rd edn. Kirksville, MO: Truman State University Press.

Williams, R. (1983). 'Literature'. In *Keywords: A Vocabulary of Culture and Society*, pp. 183–8. Rev. edn. New York, NY: Oxford University Press.

Williams, R. (2004). *Anglican Identities*. London: Darton, Longman & Todd.

Williamson, A. H. (1988). 'Latter Day Judah, Latter Day Israel: The Millennium, the Jews, and the British Future'. In *Chiliasmus in Deutschland und England im 17. Jahrhundert*, edited by M. Brecht, F. de Boor, K. Deppermann, and U. Gäbler, pp. 119–49. Göttingen: Vanderhoeck and Ruprecht.

Williamson, A. H. (2004). 'George Buchanan, Crypto-Judaism, and the Critique of European Empire'. In *Secret Conversions to Judaism in Early Modern Europe*, edited by M. Muslow and R. H. Popkin, pp. 19–32. Leiden: Brill.

Williamson, E. (2007). 'The Domestication of Religious Objects in *The White Devil*', *Studies in English Literature* 47: 473–90.

Williamson, E. (2009). *The Materiality of Religion in Early Modern English Drama*. Aldershot: Ashgate.

Willie, R. (2013). 'Viewing the Paper Stage: Civil War, Print, Theatre and the Public Sphere'. In *Making Space Public in Early Modern Europe: Performance, Geography, Privacy*, edited by A. Vanhaelen and J. Ward, pp. 54–75. New York, NY: Routledge.

Wills, G. (1995). *Witches and Jesuits: Shakespeare's Macbeth*. Oxford: Oxford University Press.

Wilson, L. (2011). 'Playful Paratexts: The Front Matter of Anthony Munday's Iberian Romance Translations'. In *Renaissance Paratexts*, edited by H. Smith and L. Wilson, pp. 121–32. Cambridge: Cambridge University Press.

Wilson, R. (2004). *Secret Shakespeare: Studies in Theatre, Religion and Resistance*. Manchester: Manchester University Press.

Wing, D. G. (1945). *Short-Title Catalogue of Books*. Volume 1. 3 vols. New York, NY: Columbia University Press.

Wingate, A. (ed.) (1998). *Anglicanism: A Global Communion*. New York, NY: Church Publications.

Winn, J. A. (1981). *Unsuspected Eloquence: A History of Relations between Poetry and Music*. New Haven, CT: Yale University Press.

Winship, M. P. (2006). 'Godly Republicanism and the Origins of the Massachusetts Policy'. *The William and Mary Quarterly* 63 (3): 427–62.

Winship, M. P. (2009). 'Freeborn (Puritan) Englishmen and Slavish Subjection: Popish Tyranny and Puritan Constitutionalism, c.1570–1606'. *The English Historical Review* 124: 1050–74.

Winship, M. P. (2012). *Godly Republicanism: Puritans, Pilgrims, and a City on a Hill*. Cambridge, MA: Harvard University Press.

Wiseman, S. (1998). *Drama and Politics in the English Civil War*. Cambridge: Cambridge University Press.

Wittreich, J. A. (1986). *Interpreting 'Samson Agonistes'*. Princeton, NJ: Princeton University Press.

Wittreich, J. A. (2002). *Shifting Context: Reinterpreting 'Samson Agonistes'*. Pittsburgh, PA: Duquesne University Press.

Wolf, L. (1928). 'Jews in Elizabethan England'. *Transactions of the Jewish Historical Society of England* 11: 1–91.

Wolf, L. (1934). 'Jews in Tudor England'. In *Essays in Jewish History*, edited by C. Roth, pp. 73–90. London: Jewish Historical Society of England.

Wolfe, H. (2004). 'Reading Bells and Loose Papers: Reading and Writing Practices of the English Benedictine Nuns of Cambrai and Paris'. In *Early Modern Women's Manuscript Writing: Selected Papers from the Trinity–Trent Colloquium*, edited by V. Burke and J. Gibson, pp. 135–56. Aldershot: Ashgate.

Wolfe, H. (2007). 'Dame Barbara Constable: Catholic Antiquarian, Advisor, and Closet Missionary'. In *Catholic Culture in Early Modern England*, edited by R. Corthell, F. E. Dolan, C. Highley, and A. Marotti, pp. 158–88. Notre Dame, IN: University of Notre Dame Press.

Womersley, D. (2010). *Divinity and State*. Oxford: Oxford University Press.

Wood, A. C. (1935). *A History of the Levant Company*. London: Oxford University Press.

Wooding, L. E. C. (2000). *Rethinking Catholicism in Reformation England*. Oxford: Oxford University Press.

Wooding, L. E. C. (2011). 'From Tudor Humanism to Reformation Preaching'. In *The Oxford Handbook of the Early Modern Sermon*, edited by P. McCullough, H. Adlington, and E. Rhatigan, pp. 329–47. Oxford: Oxford University Press.

Woods, G. (2013). *Shakespeare's Unreformed Fictions*. Oxford: Oxford University Press.

Woolhouse, R. S., and R. Francks (1997). 'Introduction'. In *Leibniz's 'New System' and Associated Contemporary Texts*, edited and translated by R. S. Woolhouse and R. Francks, pp. 1–6. Oxford: Clarendon Press.

Worden, B. (1985). 'Providence and Politics in Cromwellian England'. *Past and Present* 109: 55–99.

Woudhuysen, H. R. (1996). *Sir Philip Sidney and the Circulation of Manuscripts 1558–1640*. Oxford: Clarendon Press.

Wright, L. B. (1943). *Religion and Empire: The Alliance between Piety and Commerce in English Expansion 1558–1625*. Chapel Hill, NC: University of North Carolina Press.

Wright, L. M. (1932). *The Literary Life of Early Friends*. New York, NY: Columbia University Press.

Wright, L. M. (1937). 'John Bunyan and Stephen Crisp'. *Journal of Religion* 19 (2): 95–109.

Wright, R. J. (ed.) (1988). *Quadrilateral at One Hundred: Essays on the Centenary of the Chicago-Lambeth Quadrilateral, 1886/88–1986/88*. London: Mowbray.

Wright, S. (2006). *The Early English Baptists, 1603–1649*. Woodbridge: Boydell and Brewer.

Yaffe, M. (1997). *Shylock and the Jewish Question*. Baltimore, MD: Johns Hopkins University Press.

Yamamoto-Wilson, J. R. (2002). *Catholic Literature and the Rise of Anglicanism*. Tokyo: The Renaissance Institute, Sophia University.

Young, R. V. (2000). *Doctrine and Devotion in Seventeenth-Century Poetry: Studies in Donne, Herbert, Crashaw, and Vaughan*. Woodbridge: D. S. Brewer.

Young, R. V. (2011). 'The Religious Sonnet'. In *The Oxford Handbook of John Donne*, edited by J. Shami, D. Flynn, and M. T. Hester, pp. 218–32. Oxford: Oxford University Press.

Yovel, Y. (2009). *The Other Within: The Marranos: Split Identity and Emerging Modernity.* Princeton, NJ: Princeton University Press.

Zagorin, P. (1992). *Milton: Aristocrat and Rebel: The Poet and His Politics.* New York, NY: D. S. Brewer.

Zahl, P. F. M. (1998). *The Protestant Face of Anglicanism.* Grand Rapids, MI: W. B. Eerdmans.

Zim, R. (1987). *English Metrical Psalms: Poetry as Praise and Prayer, 1535–1601.* Cambridge: Cambridge University Press.

Zimmer, C. (2004). *Soul Made Flesh: The Discovery of the Brain.* New York, NY: Free Press.

Zucker, A., and A. B. Farmer (eds) (2006). *Localizing Caroline Drama: Politics and Economics of the Early Modern Stage, 1625–1642.* Basingstoke: Palgrave Macmillan.

INDEX